37th ANNUAL EDITION

GUNS
ILLUSTRATED®
2005

Edited by
Ken Ramage

© 2004
by Krause Publications

Published by

700 East State Street • Iola, WI 54990-0001
715-445-2214 • 888-457-2873
www.krause.com

Our toll-free number to place an order or obtain a free catalog is 800-258-0929.

Manuscripts, contributions and inquiries, including first class return postage, should be sent to the GUNS ILLUSTRATED Editorial Offices, Krause Publications, 700 E. State Street, Iola, WI 54990-0001. All materials received will receive reasonable care, but we will not be responsible for their safe return. Material accepted is subject to our requirements for editing and revisions. Author payment covers all rights and title to the accepted material, including photos, drawings and other illustrations. Payment is at our current rates.

CAUTION: Technical data presented here, particularly technical data on the handloading and on firearms adjustment and alteration, inevitably reflects individual experience with particular equipment and components under specific circumstances the reader cannot duplicate exactly. Such data presentations therefore should be used for guidance only and with caution. Krause Publications, Inc., accepts no responsibility for results obtained using this data.

Library of Congress Catalog Number: 0072-9078

ISBN: 0-87349-881-X

Designed by Patsy Howell and Tom Nelsen
Edited by Ken Ramage

Printed in the United States of America

—GUNS ILLUSTRATED STAFF—

EDITOR
Ken Ramage

CONTRIBUTING EDITORS

Holt Bodinson   John Haviland   Layne Simpson

Doc Carlson   John Malloy   John Taffin

Editorial Comments and Suggestions

We're always looking for feedback on our books. Please let us know what you like about this edition. If you have suggestions for articles you'd like to see in future editions, please contact.

Ken Ramage/GUNS ILLUSTRATED
700 East State St.
Iola, WI 54990
email: ramagek@krause.com

About Our Covers...

Today there is a tremendous interest in smaller handguns for personal defense. Only a handful of states do not have some kind of concealed carry law on the books, and citizens are buying this type of handgun in growing numbers.

Logically, there has been a surge in new model offerings from manufacturers. We have several of them on the covers of this edition of GUNS ILLUSTRATED.

The Front Cover

S&W M642

INTRODUCED THIS YEAR by **Smith & Wesson** for the concealed carry/personal defense trade is the J-frame **Model 642** hammerless 5-shot revolver *(above)* chambered for the

38 Special +P cartridge. The aluminum alloy frame and stainless steel barrel & cylinder help keep the weight to only 15 ounces. Sighting options include a set of Crimson Trace laser grips, which are supplemented by the rugged and reliable notch rear sight and ramp front sight.

Billed as the world's smallest hi-cap 45 ACP autoloader, the new **Para-Ordnance Warthog** *(right)* incorporates a new extractor design, plus other advanced

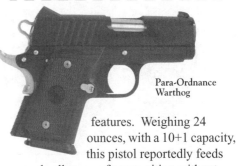

Para-Ordnance Warthog

features. Weighing 24 ounces, with a 10+1 capacity, this pistol reportedly feeds nearly all types of ammunition without missing a beat.

The Back Cover

Walther's P99QA *(below)* is a DAO autoloader available in both 9mm and 40 S&W *(shown)*. Capacity in either is 10+1 *(law enforcement gets hi-cap mags.)* and the weight is listed as 25 ounces. The polymer frame is mated with a Tenifer-finished steel slide, and the grip is designed to accept interchangeable backstraps

Walther P99QA

(three furnished) to better fit the individual. The sighting system consists of a two-dot adjustable rear and a white-dot interchangeable front blade *(four blades furnished)*.

Heckler & Koch's P2000 series of subcompact pistols *(right)* are a bit smaller and lighter than the USP series, and have different trigger mechanisms. Presently available in 9mm or 40 S&W, either weighs around 1-1/2 pounds. Advanced features found on this new series include two sets of changeable grip

H&K P2000

panels to allow better fit to individual hands, a new trigger system, handy operating controls and molded-in accessory mounting rails beneath the frame ahead of the trigger guard.

Guns Illustrated 2005

~ The Standard Reference for Today's Firearms ~

Page 15

Page 23

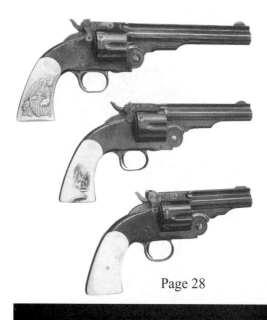

Page 28

CONTENTS

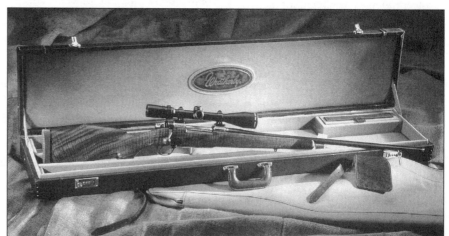

Page 42

CATALOG OF TODAY'S FIREARMS

Page 96

Page 88

Page 146

Page 196

Page 229

HANDGUN NEWS

AUTOLOADERS

by John Malloy

*I*T IS SOMETIMES *difficult to understand some of the factors that influence the world of autoloading handguns.*

Certainly, the purchase of sidearms by various governmental bodies is a factor. Companies who make service-type pistols would naturally like to get a contract for a large number of guns of the same type. A number of companies have supplied semiautomatic pistols to various police and military organizations, and then make similar models for commercial sale.

Sometimes, things are not so straightforward. In November 2002, President George Bush approved arming of the pilots of commercial passenger aircraft. The Transportation Security Administration (TSA) apparently opposed the program and set up requirements that tended to discourage participation. A year later, in November 2003, only some 200 pilots had reportedly been armed. Yet, in July 2003, the TSA contracted for up to 9600 40-caliber pistols to arm pilots who completed the program.

The economy appears to be improving, and according to one report, handgun sales are up, and about three-quarters of all new handguns sold now are semiautomatics. Most autoloading handguns can be used for personal protection, and many–perhaps most–are bought with this factor in mind. Personal protection is a valid reason for handgun use, and most states now recognize this fact.

"License to carry" or "carry of concealed weapons" (CCW) legislation continues to grow across the country. Forty-seven states are reported to allow some sort of concealed carry. Only Vermont and Alaska have true "right-to-carry" provisions, under which citizens do not need the government's permission to be armed. (New Hampshire, at the time of this writing, is considering a similar program). In the other states, those with "shall issue," license provisions avoid the bias and favoritism that characterizes states with "may issue" provisions.

How many "shall issue" states are there? Probably about 37 at the time of this writing. Hard to tell at any given moment, though, as anti-gun forces are constantly trying to undermine such laws, and things keep changing.

In Missouri, the legislature passed a CCW law, then the Governor vetoed it, then the legislature overrode the veto, then a judge struck down the law, then the Missouri Supreme Court upheld the law…except in four counties! In addition, the court decided the law imposed an unfounded mandate, and at the time of this writing, no permits have been issued.

In Wisconsin, the legislature passed a CCW law, then the Governor vetoed it, then the state Senate overrode the veto, but then one of the Representatives who had originally cosponsored the legislation changed his mind and the state House failed to override the veto by one vote.

In Ohio, after ten years of effort, a "shall issue" law was passed by the legislature and signed by the Governor, but it contained some ludicrous provisions. Motorists who carry must wear the handgun visible to law enforcement (and everyone else) while in a vehicle, then must immediately put on a concealing outer garment when exiting the vehicle.

Texas has had a "shall issue" law for some time, but anti-gun municipal leaders, with disregard for the law,

have held that any public property—including municipal transit and parking areas—is off-limits for concealed carry. Such municipalities have had to be taken to court, one by one, and forced to obey the law. In Houston, the mayor conceded that licensed people could carry concealed on city property, but required that armed citizens wear a special red identification badge.

Georgia also has had CCW for some years, the Metropolitan Atlanta Rapid Transit Authority (MARTA) has required that legally-carried handguns must be separate from their ammunition (illegally-carried handguns are apparently not restricted). I guess, in a way, such a ridiculous provision actually favors autoloading handguns for honest people. In an emergency, it is generally easier to charge a semiauto with a loaded magazine than to draw, open and load a revolver.

In spite of these occasional setbacks and absurdities, we should take heart. Public acceptance of individual carry is growing, as people realize that Wild West shootouts do not occur, and that crime rates go down.

Autoloading handguns are used for many purposes other than for military and police use, or for personal protection. Competitive target shooting of many kinds, small game and / or big game hunting, informal target shooting and plinking, collecting, or just for pride of ownership—all these are reasons for semiautomatic pistols. At times, decorated pistols have been used as a way of raising money for worthy causes.

So, what are the trends in autoloading handguns today?

The Colt / Browning 1911 design seems to be going stronger than ever. Most new pistols introduced are variations on the 1911 theme. However, long-time manufacturers of other types of autoloading pistols now also offer their own 1911 models.

The 22 Long Rifle cartridge remains immensely popular, and new 22 pistols—and conversion kits for centerfire pistols—continue to be introduced.

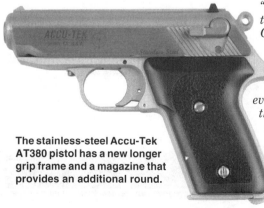

The stainless-steel Accu-Tek AT380 pistol has a new longer grip frame and a magazine that provides an additional round.

In a sense, cartridge choices remain the same. The 45 Automatic Colt Pistol (45 ACP) cartridge celebrates its 100th birthday in 2005, and still seems to be king of the hill. 9mm and 40 S&W are very popular. Pocket pistols are still mostly 32 and 380.

In another sense, however, cartridge innovation has seldom offered a wider range of calibers than this year's new offerings. New cartridges ranging from 17- to 50-caliber were introduced, with new 25-, 32- and 45-caliber options in between.

The 38 Super cartridge, never a first choice for military or police use, has maintained a certain popularity since its introduction in 1929. It seems to be undergoing a small rejuvenation now, as several companies are bringing out new 38 Super pistols.

The resurrection of good things from the past continues to the guns themselves. Two names too long absent from the pistol scene are now back. Look for them in the report below.

Collectable and commemorative pistols seem to find a following, and a number have appeared this year. An interesting new twist consists of pistols with grips made of the wood of historic trees. Some special pistols offer a way of contributing to worthy causes.

Pistol-carbines are popular. Lacking a better definition, let's include pistols that can be made into carbines, and carbines based on pistols. Not really the proper subjects

ADCO is importing the TT 45, a new 45 ACP polymer-frame pistol made in the Czech Republic. This is a peek at one of the first to be displayed.

The new nickel-plated Beretta Cheetah has wood grips and comes in 380 ACP.

for this report, perhaps, but related and certainly interesting.

Much is going on. Let's take a look at what the companies are doing:

ADCO

ADCO, a Massachusetts firm, is now offering a 45-caliber pistol. The new TT 45 is being imported from the Czech Republic. The original CZ firearms factory, established in 1919, began making firearms again after the end of the Soviet Union. That Czech company is now producing the TT 45, and ADCO describes the new pistols as "original CZ."

The mechanism is basically that of the CZ-75, in a polymer-frame package. The design allows carrying the pistol hammer down *(for a double-action first shot)* or cocked-and-locked with the frame-mounted thumb safety. The pistol has a 3.77-inch barrel and measures 7.6 x 5.9 inches. Unloaded weight is about 26 ounces.

The new 45 will probably be followed by other variants in other calibers, and various accessories are available.

Advantage Arms

Advantage Arms has offered, for several years, 22 Long Rifle (22 LR) conversion kits for most models of Glock pistols. Now, the company has introduced a new 22 LR conversion kit for 1911-type pistols. The conversion features Millett adjustable Sights, and has last-round hold-open. Availability was scheduled for summer 2004.

Beretta

Beretta has introduced a number of new models, primarily modifications of the company's basic pistol line.

The Model 92/96 STEEL 1 is designed for the competitive shooter. It has a heavier steel frame, vertex grip, a heavier "Brigadier" slide, and a nickel-alloy finish. With a frame-mounted safety, the STEEL 1 can be carried cocked-and-locked. Recall that Model 92 pistols are 9mm, and Model 96 pistols are 40 Smith & Wesson (40 S&W).

The Model 92 / 96 FS Olive Drab pistols are similar to the United States' M9 military pistol, with an OD finish.

The 92 INOX Lasergrips model is a 9mm in stainless-steel finish with a laser-aiming device contained in the grip panels.

New Cougar INOX pistols are stainless steel with checkered wood grips, a nice-looking combination. The new pistols feature the Cougar's rotating-barrel locking system and are available in 9mm and 40 S&W.

A kit is now available to convert the Beretta NEOS 22 pistol into a light carbine. A carbine barrel and grip/buttstock component are furnished, and extra stock combs and extensions are available.

Ever wonder if Ken Ramage, the editor of this publication, can shoot a handgun well? He proves that he can at a windswept range in Nevada. The pistol is Beretta's new stainless-steel Cougar in 40 S&W.

Bersa has brought out a version of its Thunder 45 polymer-frame pistol with a stainless-steel slide. A similar 9mm is also available.

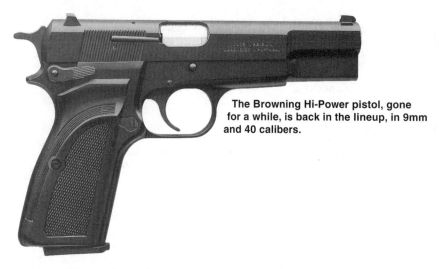
The Browning Hi-Power pistol, gone for a while, is back in the lineup, in 9mm and 40 calibers.

The 84 / 85 FS Cheetah Nickel variant has wood grips and comes in 380 ACP. The Model 84 has a 10-shot magazine. The lighter Model 85 has an 8-shot magazine.

The U22 NEOS carbine kit is now available to convert the NEOS 22-caliber pistol into a light semiautomatic carbine for plinking or small-game hunting. Simply removing the pistol's grip frame and barrel allows installation of the carbine stock and barrel.

Bernardelli

The Bernardelli polymer-frame pistol, based on the CZ-75 mechanism, is now in full production, and a new variant has been introduced. Resurrecting the company's former "Baby" terminology, the new compact version is called the Bernardelli 2000 Baby.

Bersa

New versions of the Thunder 45 and Thunder 9 Ultra Compact pistols are now available with stainless-steel slides. The new Bersa pistols have alloy frames with polymer grips, and are of the tilting-barrel locking system. Barrel length is 3.6 inches, and the pistols measure 4.9 x 6.7 inches. Weight is about 27 ounces. Bersa pistols are made in Argentina and are imported by Eagle Imports.

Browning

The standby Browning Hi-Power pistol was absent for a while, but is now back in the Browning lineup. It is available in 9mm and 40 S&W, in several options.

The PRO-9 and PRO-40 double-action-only (DAO) polymer-frame pistols were introduced last year. The 9mm version, the PRO-9, is now in production. The 40-caliber variant may arrive soon.

At the 2004 SHOT Show, Browning also displayed a "Liberty Tree" Hi-Power pistol. The grips of the pistol are made from the wood of the last surviving Liberty Tree. The Liberty Tree story is an interesting part of American history. In the 1770s, Great Britain sought to prevent rebellion by forbidding private meetings in the colonies. Each colony selected a tree, a "Liberty Tree," as a meeting place, in order to get around the British order. The last tree, a tulip poplar in Maryland, came down during a hurricane in 1999. The wood was harvested and preserved by the American Forests organization, and the wood has been used for the grips. For each of the 228 pistols sold (numbered 1776 to 2004) trees will be planted in environmental restoration projects.

Bushmaster

Late in 2003, Bushmaster Firearms, Inc. acquired the Professional Ordnance firm. Professional Ordnance's 223-caliber Carbon 15 pistols (and rifles) now are part of Bushmaster's product line. The former Professional Ordnance facility in Arizona has become Bushmaster's western division. The Carbon 15 arms are made on the AR-15 pattern, but are built from a carbon composition material instead of aluminum. The weight reduction allows pistols that weigh about 46 ounces.

The new Bushmaster Carbon 15 pistols are designated Type 97 (fluted barrel) or Type 21 (unfluted barrel). Two variants of the Type 21, mechanically the same, are offered. The commercial version has a bright stainless-steel barrel and comes with a 10-round magazine. The law-enforcement pistol has a black-coated stainless-steel barrel, and can be had with a 30-round magazine.

Century

New additions to Century's line of Philippine-made 45-caliber 1911-type pistols are twofold. The first type has most of the features modern shooters seem to like—beavertail grip safety, low profile rear sight and

◄ The Korean Daewoo pistol, absent for some time, is now being imported by Century International Arms. This is the compact DP51C in 9mm. Full-size variants in 9mm and 40 S&W are also available.

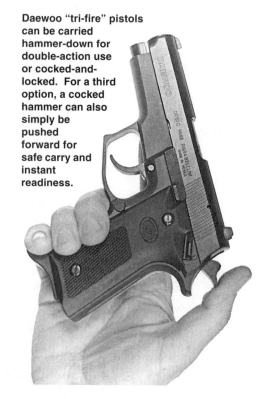
Daewoo "tri-fire" pistols can be carried hammer-down for double-action use or cocked-and-locked. For a third option, a cocked hammer can also simply be pushed forward for safe carry and instant readiness.

The new polymer-frame Browning PRO 9 pistol, announced last year, is in full production.

The smallest of Charles Daly's 1911 pistols, the Ultra X, hopes to join the line soon, as modifications to permit its importation are planned.

▲ Colt has brought back the 38 Super, and a blued version with enhancements is standard.

▲ A brand-new Colt Model 1911, in the pattern of the WWI pistols, is now a catalog item.

round spur hammer. Another variant has these features, but in addition, the top of the slide is flat and the front of the frame is squared. This treatment adds weight, mostly forward, to help control recoil and muzzle rise. The new 45s were scheduled for mid-2004 availability.

Century is importing the Korean Daewoo pistols, which have been absent for a while. Recall that these pistols use the "tri-fire" system that allows the pistol to be carried hammer-down for a double-action (DA) first shot, or cocked-and-locked for a single-action (SA) first shot. In addition, a third method may be used. A cocked hammer can simply be pushed forward for safe carry, after which a light pull on the trigger will cock the hammer again.

Century also offers newly-manufactured Egyptian 9mm Helwan pistols, and also Arcus 9mm pistols in several variations.

Charles Daly

Brand new in the Charles Daly lineup is the ZDA pistol, which bears something of a resemblance to the SIG P 226, both in looks and function. The new ZDA has a 4-inch barrel and will be available in 9mm and 40 S&W.

A new variant added to the HP (Hi-Power) line has a chrome finish and express sights. This pistol will probably be cataloged as an Empire Grade entry.

The M-5 line of 1911-type polymer-frame pistols has a new addition. A 5-inch bull-barrel version is now available, made on the 10-round high-capacity frame. The Ultra X version of the Daly M-5, the little 3-inch barrel variant, was announced last year but will probably not make an appearance until late in 2004. It ran afoul of the BATF's absurd point system and could not be imported. The company hopes that by adding features such as a loaded-chamber indicator, the Ultra X will gain approval.

Colt

The 38 Super is back in the Colt lineup! Introduced in 1929, Colt's 38 Super pistol for a time held the position of being the most powerful handgun made, in terms of energy and penetration. The pistol and cartridge developed a following among lawmen and outdoorsmen. More recently, the 38 Super has become a favorite for action- and practical-style shooting competition.

Colt offers the 38 Super in three different models, all full-size with 5-inch barrels. The blued version has a Commander hammer, aluminum trigger and rubber composite grips. The stainless variant has these same features in a stainless-steel pistol. The top of the line Super is made of stainless steel, polished bright to resemble the early nickel finishes. It features a traditional spur hammer and checkered "big diamond" wood grips.

The World War I-style 1911 pistol, displayed in prototype last year at the 2003 SHOT Show, is now a standard catalog item. A WWI-type screwdriver and copy of an original manual are included with each pistol.

CZ USA

The new CZ Model 2075 "RAMI" is a compact little pistol based on the CZ 75 mechanism. This version is the smallest yet made, with a 3-inch barrel and weight of less than 25 ounces. At 4.7 x 6.5 inches, it falls just between our arbitrary categories of compact (5 x 7) and subcompact (4 x 6). The pistol is offered in 9mm and 40 S&W. The staggered-column magazine gives 10+1 capacity in 9mm and 8+1 in 40.

Detonics

Detonics is back! The original Detonics company was formed in

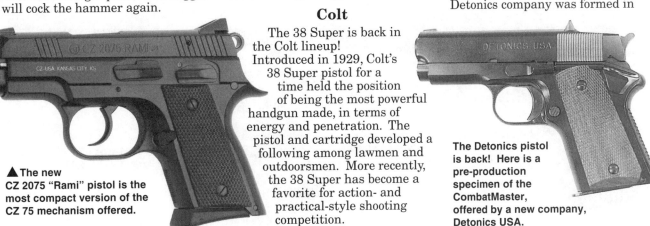

▲ The new CZ 2075 "Rami" pistol is the most compact version of the CZ 75 mechanism offered.

The Detonics pistol is back! Here is a pre-production specimen of the CombatMaster, offered by a new company, Detonics USA.

Principals of the original Detonics company are involved with Detonics USA. Sid Woodcock *(left)* the original designer, and Peter Dunn, gunsmith, hold variants that will be offered by the new company.

New offerings by Excel Arms: Richard Gilliam holds the 17 HRM carbine, Kathy Gilliam shows the Accu-Tek AT 380 II pistol, and Excel President Larry Gilliam displays the 17 HRM pistol.

Washington state about 1976 and stayed in business until 1988. It was sold to another group in Phoenix, AZ who did business as New Detonics Manufacturing Co. Within a few years, however, at least by 1992, that company had ceased to do business.

Now a new company, Detonics USA, has been formed in Atlanta, GA by some of the principals of the original firm. Designer Sid Woodcock and gunsmith Peter Dunn are back making Detonics pistols. Author Jerry Ahern, an early proponent of the Detonics design, is also involved with the company.

Woodcock, with his background in explosives, named the first pistol "Detonics," a word related to the science of explosives. That early pistol, the first compact 45-caliber pistol, introduced a number of concepts that are widely used today. The cone-shaped bushingless barrel, captive counter-wound recoil spring and enlarged ejection port were all introduced with the early Detonics pistols. The company was also one of the early users of stainless steel as a suitable material for autoloading pistols.

▲ As companions to their new 17 HRM and 22 WMR pistols, Excel Arms offers carbines in the same calibers.

Detonics USA will offer the small version—the 3 1/2-inch barrel CombatMaster—as its first product, because "that is the Detonics that people remember." The mid-size ServiceMaster and full-size ScoreMaster—also produced by the original company—will be offered later. Initial production was scheduled for October 2004.

EAA

European American Armory (EAA) has added a few new variants to its popular Witness line of Tanfoglio-made pistols.

A Witness P variant with a polymer frame and stainless-steel slide is now available in 10mm chambering with the short 3.6-inch barrel. A Witness PS can be had in 9mm with an accessory rail on the forward part of the frame.

The Witness Limited target pistol, a big single-action pistol in chrome finish and with adjustable Sights, is now available in 38 Super chambering.

Ed Brown

Ed Brown Products of Perry, MO, offers the Executive Elite (5-inch barrel) and Executive Carry (4 1/4-inch barrel) lines. These 1911-type pistols are offered in three finishes—blue, stainless steel, and blue slide on a stainless-steel frame. Front straps and mainspring housings are checkered at 25 lines per inch (lpi), and grips are checkered Cocobolo wood.

The larger Elite pistols have straight mainspring housings. The smaller Carry guns feature the Ed Brown "Bobtail" treatment, in which the end of the mainspring housing and grip frame angles forward. The Bobtail shape makes concealment easier, and many like the feel of the modified grip.

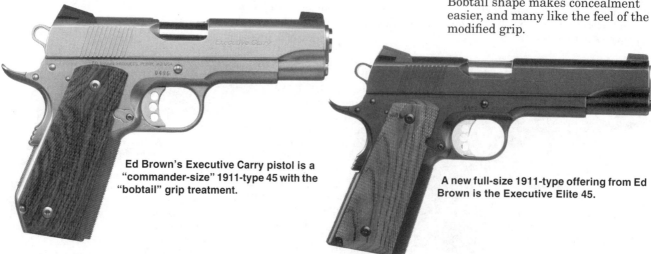

Ed Brown's Executive Carry pistol is a "commander-size" 1911-type 45 with the "bobtail" grip treatment.

A new full-size 1911-type offering from Ed Brown is the Executive Elite 45.

▶ The Excel Arms MP 17 is a new semiauto pistol for the 17 HRM cartridge. A similar pistol is also made for the 22WMR.

The 45 GAP (45 Glock Automatic Pistol) cartridge, introduced last year, already has a number of different loads offered for it.

Excel

Excel Industries makes the Accu-Tek AT-380 pistol, and for 2004, the Accu-Tek was designed with a slightly longer grip and a magazine holding an extra round. Measuring just over 4 x 6 inches, the little stainless-steel 380 is still in the subcompact class, and has 6+1 capacity. Each new AT-380 pistol comes with two 6-round magazines, a hard case and a lock.

A totally new pistol, the Accelerator, is now offered, chambered for either the 17 Hornady Magnum Rimfire (17 HMR) or 22 Winchester Magnum Rimfire (22 WMR). Model numbers are MP-17 and MP-22, respectively. Either pistol has an 8 1/2-inch barrel and weight of about 54 ounces. The big pistols are constructed from stainless steel, with a polymer grip. An aluminum top rib contains fully adjustable sights and allows mounting of optical or other types of Sighting devices. The Excel Accelerator is the second semiautomatic pistol to be offered for the 17 HMR cartridge.

A carbine with a related mechanism is also offered in the same calibers. This will not convert to a pistol, or vice versa, but it uses the same ammunition and same 9-shot magazine, and would make a neat companion piece with the pistol.

Excel also makes a conversion kit that will adapt a 1911 pistol to use either the 17 HMR or the 22 WMR cartridges, in 8-round magazines. This is a serious conversion, with an 8 1/2-inch barrel and fully adjustable Sights.

FNH

FNH USA is the American arm of FN Herstal, offering some firearms similar to those sold under the Browning name.

The 9mm FNP-9 was introduced last year, and it has now been joined by the FNP-40, in 40 S&W caliber. The pistol is a conventional double action with a high-capacity polymer frame and an ambidextrous decocker. With a 4-inch barrel, the FNP-40 is only 7 inches long, and weighs about 25 ounces.

Glock

The Glock Model 37—chambered for the new 45 Glock Automatic Pistol (45 GAP) cartridge—was introduced last year and is now in production. The 45 GAP uses a shorter case (about 0.750") and shorter overall length (about 1.10") than the standard 45 Automatic Colt Pistol (45 ACP) cartridge. Some changes have been made since the introduction of the Model 37, noticeably the use of a heavier slide—a modified Model 21 slide. However, the Model 37 is still about the same general size as the original Model 17 9mm pistol. The shorter 45 GAP cartridge allows the use of a smaller frame, but limits the loadings to the shorter-length 45-caliber bullets. Chamber pressure of the 45 GAP is somewhat higher than that of the 45 ACP, but several companies have begun to produce it, and at least one other manufacturer plans to offer a 45 GAP chambering in its pistol line.

Olive-drab (OD) frames are now available on some Glock pistols. Available only through Acusport, Models 17, 19, 21, 22, 23 and 27 can be had in OD after June 2004.

Guncrafter Industries

Displayed for the first time at the February 2004 SHOT Show, the GI Model No. 1 from Guncrafter Industries attracted considerable attention. At first glance, the new pistol appears to be another modernized

▲ Glock or 1911 pistols can be converted into carbines with Mech-Tech's Carbine Conversion Unit. This is a Glock conversion.

▲ Here is a pre-production version of the Glock Model 37. The production model has a heavier slide, and the cartridge is now called the 45 GAP (45 Glock Automatic Pistol).

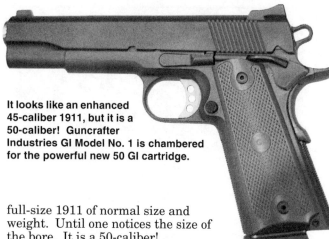

It looks like an enhanced 45-caliber 1911, but it is a 50-caliber! Guncrafter Industries GI Model No. 1 is chambered for the powerful new 50 GI cartridge.

Three different loadings of 50 GI cartridges are offered. The rebated rims are the same diameter as that of the 45 ACP, and the overall length is about the same. A 45 ACP is on the right for comparison.

full-size 1911 of normal size and weight. Until one notices the size of the bore. It is a 50-caliber!

The new GI pistol is chambered for the new 50 GI cartridge. The cartridge is a new one, with a case slightly shorter in length than a 45 ACP, and with a rebated rim the same diameter as the 45 ACP. The loaded 50-caliber round is about the same overall length as the 45 ACP. Ammunition, brass, bullets and reloading dies *(dies made by Hornady and Lee Precision)* are available from the company. The 50 GI ammunition, as loaded, features a light load (300-grain bullet at 725 fps) and a heavier load (300-grain bullet at 900 fps). At the introduction, three bullet types—jacketed flat point, soft point and hollow point—were displayed.

Although the pistol is externally the same as a 45-caliber 1911, there are internal dimensional differences. The pistol uses a cone barrel that is fitted directly into the front of the slide. The magazine well in the frame is machined larger to accept the fatter 50-caliber magazine. These changes preclude using those standard 1911 parts, but GI offers a conversion kit of their special parts to convert their Model No. 1 to 45 ACP.

Heckler & Koch

In July 2003, the Transportation Security Administration (TSA) made plans to acquire up to 9600 40-caliber pistols. The pistols were to be used to arm U. S. commercial airline pilots who passed the Federal Flight Deck Officer (FFDO) program administered by the TSA. The contract was awarded to Heckler & Koch (HK) for their USP 40 pistol. In August 2003, HK announced its first U. S. factory, which would be at a site at Columbus, GA. The official groundbreaking for the plant was on October 14, 2003. Reportedly, the contract USP pistols will be made at this location. The USP 40 is a conventional double-action pistol *(although it can be converted to DAO)*, with a 4 1/4-inch barrel. The pistol measures 5.3 x 7.6 inches. The USP is a polymer-frame pistol with a blued slide.

Newly introduced at the February 2004 SHOT Show were two variants of the P 2000 K subcompact pistol, in 9mm and 40 S&W. Smaller and lighter than the USP series, the P 2000 series pistols have different trigger mechanisms. With 3.6-inch barrels, the pistols measure 5 x 7 inches.

High Standard

High Standard and Aguila worked together, and last year introduced the 17 Hi-Standard cartridge, basically a 22 Long Rifle case necked down to 17-caliber, and loaded with a 20-grain bullet. The new round worked perfectly in rebarreled Hi-Standard semiautomatic pistols. However, High Standard has held off marketing the 17-caliber pistols.

In February 2004, a new 17-caliber cartridge based on the 22 LR case was announced. Hornady and CCI worked together to develop a similar—but not quite the same—short 17 round, the 17 Mach 2, with a 17-grain bullet. Eley also plans to make the ammunition. There seems to be a substantial amount of interest in a Long Rifle-length 17, and it will be interesting to see how this situation plays out.

High Standard continues its line of 22 LR target pistols, 45-caliber

The 17-caliber rimfire scene has seen a surprising amount of activity. From left, a 17 Hi-Standard, made by Aguila; a 17 Mach 2, made by CCI and the 17 Mach 2 as made by Eley. The earlier 17 Hornady Magnum Rimfire is at the right for comparison.

The 40 and 45-caliber polymer-frame Hi-Point pistols are in full production. Here, Malloy shoots the new 45.

The new Hi-Point polymer-frame 40 and 45-caliber pistols have undergone some refinements and are now in full production. Adjustable Sights and accessory rails are standard.

Best-known for replicas of 1800s firearms, IAR also offers a small number of 45 ACP Chinese copies of the Mauser "broomhandle" pistol. IAR president Will Hanson holds a specimen.

1911-type pistols and conversion kits to adapt the 1911 to 22 LR.

Among the new items is the Shea Custom 10X pistol, a 22 target pistol to be hand-built in small quantities by High Standard gunsmith Bob Shea. Shea worked for High Standard from 1943 to 1984, then as an independent gunsmith specializing in Hi-Standard pistols after that. He apparently knows what he is doing.

Another new item is the Marine Corps Trial Pistol, a 45-caliber 1911-type pistol that has the features of the pistol that High Standard submitted for the United States Marine Corps (USMC) sidearm trials.

Hi-Point

Last year, Hi-Point introduced new polymer-frame 40- and 45-caliber pistols. Some minor refinements have been made, and the pistols are now in full production. These are the least expensive new handguns made in these calibers, but seem to work fine and shoot well. Recall that these are blowback pistols, yet are rated for +P ammunition, and have a lifetime warranty.

New for 2004 is the Hi-Point carbine in 40 S&W. The carbine, of course, belongs in another report, but is mentioned here because the 10-shot magazine is identical to, and interchangeable with, that of the new 40-caliber pistol. In the Old West, it was an advantage to have a carbine and a handgun that used the same ammunition. Hi-Point offers that advantage with the added factor that extra magazines will work in either carbine or pistol.

IAR

One thinks of the IAR (International Antique Reproductions) firm as a source of shooting replicas of 19th century historical firearms. However, they have a small quantity of the original big 45 ACP Chinese "broom-handle Mauser" copies made in the 20th century. It may be of interest to collectors to know that a small stock of these interesting and historical autoloading pistols still exists.

Kahr

Kahr has introduced a number of new models, all variations of the company's patented DAO mechanism. As the number of models has grown, so have the designations for these models. Here is a breakdown that may help in understanding the Kahr offerings: "K" alone before a number indicates the original stainless-steel Kahr offering, a mid-size pistol with a 3.5-inch barrel. The numbers 9 or 40 following always indicate the caliber. A "P" prefix indicates a polymer-frame pistol. "M" indicates a Micro Compact, with a 3-inch barrel. "T" represents target or tactical pistols, which have 4-inch barrels.

With this in mind, the new PM 40 pistol is a small 40-caliber, polymer-frame pistol with a 3-inch barrel. The slide is matte stainless steel, and the pistol comes with two magazines—one flush, one elongated for extended grip and an extra round.

The TP 9 is a new 4-inch barrel, polymer-frame 9mm pistol. The polymer frame is black and the slide is matte stainless steel. Either 3-dot sights or tritium night sights are available. Delivery was scheduled for mid-2004.

The T 40 is a 29-ounce 40-caliber stainless-steel frame pistol with a 4-inch barrel. Checkered wood Hogue grips offset the matte-finish stainless steel, and make a sharp-looking pistol. This variant began shipping in February 2004.

Recall that Kahr also offers the Auto-Ordnance line of Thompson 45-caliber pistols. The Custom 1911 pistol, announced last year, is now a catalog item. It is all stainless steel, a full-size pistol with a 5-inch barrel. It features a beavertail grip safety, lightened hammer, adjustable trigger and other niceties. Grips are laminate with big-diamond checkering and have the Thompson bullet logo inlaid.

Kel-Tec

Kel-Tec's little 380 pistol, the P-3AT, which was introduced last year, is now in full production. Like its predecessor, the P-32, it uses a tilting-barrel locked-breech system.

The 7-ounce Kel-Tec 380-caliber pistol, the Model P3AT, is now in full production.

Impress your friends by being able to tell the difference between the P-3AT *(above)* and the earlier P-32. The P-32 *(right)* has narrower grasping grooves and a lightening cut at the front of the slide.

The 380 is very slightly longer than the 32, and weight has gone up a bit over 1/2-ounce to 7.3 ounces. Visually, about all that distinguishes the new 380 are the wider spacing of the grasping grooves and the absence of some lightening cuts on the slide.

Mechanically, the P-3AT does not have the internal slide lock of the P-32. This apparently was omitted to make space for the larger-diameter 380 cartridge and still keep the width to 3/4-inch. The greater diameter of the cartridge also decreases the magazine to six rounds (6+1 total) capacity. However, a magazine extension is available as an accessory to increase the capacity by an extra round.

Other accessories avail for the P-3AT are a belt clip *(very useful in some carry situations)* and a lanyard kit. The lanyard kit includes an attachment unit for the rear of the pistol, and an elastic lanyard with a latching hook. Handgun guru Jeff Cooper pointed out the benefits of using a lanyard over 40 years ago, and it is interesting that Kel-Tec is offering the option.

Kimber

In 2004, Kimber celebrated its 25th anniversary. To commemorate this special event, the company decided that a number of special 1911 pistols would be made. A total of 1,911 *(a logical number)* 25th Anniversary "Custom" pistols would be made. In addition, 500 25th Anniversary "Gold Match" pistols would be produced. 250 pairs of one each of the Custom

and Gold Match pistols, with matching serial numbers, would also be put up in wood presentation cases.

In their regular line, the company offers the Stainless TLE II pistol, a 45 ACP version of the Kimber selected for duty carry by the LAPD's SWAT team. The gun is a full-size 1911-type pistol with a 5-inch barrel. It has tritium night sights.

From the Kimber Custom Shop, the 22 LR pistol introduced last year now is available in a "Rimfire Super" version, with two-tone finish, adjustable Sights, ambidextrous thumb safety, big diamond wood grips and other niceties. Performance has not taken a back seat to looks, though—the 22 pistol has turned in 1 1/2-inch groups at 25 yards.

As of February 2004, Kimber had donated $200,000 to the USA Shooting team. Kimber is thus the largest firearms corporate donor in USA Shooting Team history. The money comes from the sales of special guns, and goes straight to benefit the team. Way to go, Kimber!

Korth

Willi Korth began business by making blank revolvers in 1954, so 2004 became the 50th anniversary of the German Korth company. The firm now has a reputation for making very fine *(and very expensive)* handguns. To commemorate this 50-year milestone, a few specially–embellished Korth pistols and revolvers were scheduled. Five semiautomatic pistols, in 9mm, and five 357 Magnum revolvers will be available, Korth USA reports.

Les Baer

New from Les Baer Custom are two 1911-type 45-caliber pistols in the Thunder Ranch series, which was introduced last year. The Comanche is a serious self-defense pistol with a 4 1/4-inch barrel. It is chrome-plated.

The Home Defense pistol is designed for use in dark environments. It has an M3 tactical illuminator mounted to the front of the "Monolith" frame. The light can be selected to be on for constant or momentary time periods. Night Sights are also provided.

Lone Star

In February 2003, Lone Star Armament introduced a new series of 1911-type pistols. In November 2003, it was announced that Lone Star had been acquired by STI. *(see STI)*

Mech-Tech

Mech-Tech offers a Carbine Conversion Unit (CCU) that uses the frame of a 1911 or Glock pistol to form a pistol-caliber carbine. Pistol-carbines seem to be of interest now, and this is an interesting device.

Mitchell

The new 1911-type pistols shown in prototype last year are now in production. The first display of production models was at the February 2004 SHOT Show in Las Vegas, NV. The guns are called "Mitchell Gold Series" 1911s, and combine the original 1911 mechanism with 21st century enhancements.

Chamberings have been expanded from the original 45 ACP to also include 40 S&W, 9mm and 38 Super. Standard features include beavertail grip safety, lowered ejection port, skeletonized hammer and trigger, extended thumb safety, walnut big-diamond grips and other niceties.

North American

North American Arms (NAA) has introduced a new pistol in its Guardian series, chambered for the new 25

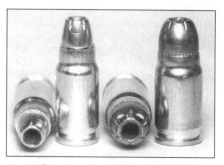

North American Arms has provided two new cartridges for pocket pistols. The 32NAA has been joined this year by the new 25NAA round.

NAA cartridge. The pistol is the same size as their 13-ounce 32 ACP Guardian, and has been in development for several years. The first concept was to neck down the semi-rimmed 32 ACP to 25-caliber. That approach was tried, but did not give the 100-percent reliability desired. Working with Cor-Bon, NAA developed a new rimless case with a longer body, and the body diameter of the 32 Harrington & Richardson Magnum (32 H&R Magnum). Although this newer case is longer than that of the 32 ACP, the overall length of the loaded cartridge is about the same.

The performance of the 25 NAA is of some interest. A 35-grain Hornady XTP bullet screams out of its 2.2-inch barrel at about 1200 feet per second (fps). Considering that the case is about three-quarters of an inch long, the bullet only has about 1-1/2 inches to get up to speed. Pretty impressive.

North American has also introduced an optional 10-shot extended magazine adapter for its 32 ACP and 380 ACP Guardians. Made by Hogue, the adaptor uses the original magazine and floorplate. It increases capacity, while providing additional grip surface.

Olympic Arms

The Whitney is back! At the February 2004 SHOT Show, Olympic Arms announced the return of the Whitney Wolverine. As many old-timers may remember, the original Whitney pistol appeared about 1955 or 1956. Its streamlined, futuristic styling and light aluminum-alloy frame made it stand out from other postwar pistols. The company, however, ran into financial problems, and production stopped

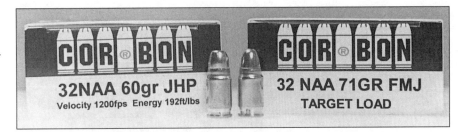

Ammunition for the potent 32NAA is in production. Cor-Bon now produces two loads—a zippy 60-grain jacketed hollow-point, and a 71-grain full-metal-jacket "target load."

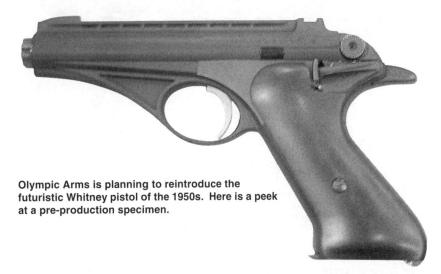

Olympic Arms is planning to reintroduce the futuristic Whitney pistol of the 1950s. Here is a peek at a pre-production specimen.

after fewer than 14,000 pistols had been produced.

Olympic Arms has improved the Whitney design, and displayed a pre-production specimen at the show. Handguns with aluminum-alloy frames were a novel idea in the 1950s. Now, half a century later, polymer plastics have gained acceptance, and Olympic has updated the Whitney with a new polymer frame. Other additions will be a ventilated rib, a dovetailed rear Sight, and better distinction of the manual safety positions.

The Whitney name was on the pre-production specimen, and is planned to appear on the final production model.

The original designer, Bob Hillberg, reportedly requested that the name be retained. Production was scheduled to begin in mid-2004.

Many older shooters liked the original Whitney pistol and hoped for its return to production. Olympic's new version should please them, and introduce younger generations to the Whitney.

The 25 NAA cartridge was developed for a small 32-size pistol. From left, a 32 ACP; an experimental 25 formed by necking down the 32 ACP; and the final 25 NAA with a longer rimless case, but of about the same overall length as the 32.

After several years of development, the hot new 25 NAA version of North American Arms' Guardian series has been introduced.

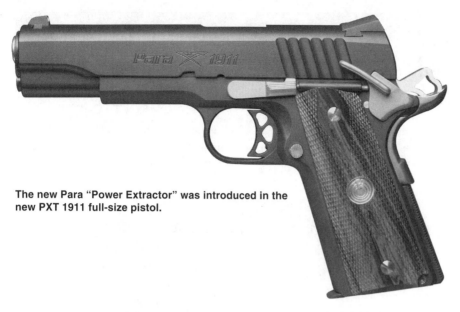

The new Para "Power Extractor" was introduced in the new PXT 1911 full-size pistol.

Pacific Armament

Pacific Armament has introduced a line of Argentine-made FM Hi-Power 9mm pistols. These have the original-style round hammer spurs of the early Belgian-made Hi-Powers, and come with 10-round magazines. The standard "Military" model has a 4.65-inch barrel. A more compact version, the "Detective" model, has a 3.65-inch barrel. Kits to convert existing pistols to Detective configuration are offered. Also, a conversion kit to adapt the Hi-Power pistols to 22 LR is available.

The company also imports a line of Philippine-made 45-caliber 1911-style pistols in full-size (5-inch barrel), mid-size (4-inch barrel) and compact (3 1/2-inch barrel) variants. These pistols are offered in the United States under the Rock Island Armory name.

Para-Ordnance

Para-Ordnance's big news is the introduction of its new "Power Extractor." In the past several years, many makers of 1911-type pistols have begun using coil-spring-loaded external extractors instead of the tempered-steel internal extractor of the original 1911 design.

Para's answer was a new internal extractor, spring-loaded, that reportedly maintains constant pressure against the rim of the cartridge case and has twice the surface area of the original 1911 design. The rear of the Power Extractor is the same size as that of the original, and thus maintains the classic 1911 appearance.

The first two Para pistols with the new extractor are the 5-inch barrel PXT 1911, and the 4 1/4-inch barrel PXT LTC. The Power Extractor will soon become standard on all Para models. Both new PXT pistols also have ramped barrels and supported chambers, features that have been made standard on all Para pistols. As with all Para-Ordnance pistols, they are shipped with two magazines.

The company has a number of new introductions. Of interest to those who favor small, big-bore pistols with as many shots as possible is the new Warthog. It is a 3-inch barrel 10-shot 45 that weighs only 24 ounces. Para is coming up with so many new options that the company plans to publish two catalogs a year to keep shooters current on their offerings.

Para-Ordnance is proud that the Para CCW pistol was chosen as the winner of the *Guns & Ammo* "Gun of the Year" award for 2003. This makes the fourth time one of the company's products has won the award. The Para CCW introduced "Griptor" grasping grooves on the frame front strap and sides of the slide.

World Champion shooter Todd Jarrett has used different Para pistols to win all four United States Practical Shooting Association (USPSA) national championships—Open, Limited, Limited 10 and Production. This seems to speak well for Para's accuracy and functioning.

Phoenix

Phoenix Arms, maker of affordable 22- and 25-caliber pistols for personal protection and informal target shooting, is working on a larger-caliber 380 pistol. No prototype was available for observation at the February 2004 SHOT Show. However, a representative said the pistol would probably be similar in design to the present pistols in the Phoenix line. The new 380 was expected to be announced during Summer 2004.

Professional Ordnance

Late in 2003, Professional Ordnance was acquired by

▲ This cutaway slide shows the enlarged gripping surfaces of the new Para Power Extractor.

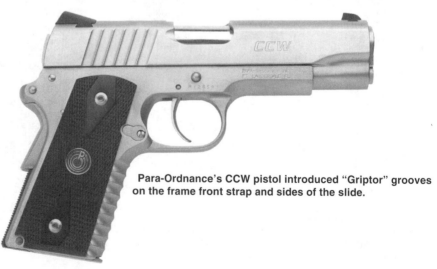

Para-Ordnance's CCW pistol introduced "Griptor" grooves on the frame front strap and sides of the slide.

A "commander-size" Para pistol, the PXT LTC, comes with the new Power Extractor.

Bushmaster Firearms, Inc. Professional Ordnance's Carbon 15 pistols (and rifles) will be manufactured under the Bushmaster name. *(see Bushmaster)*

Rock River Arms

Rock River has added a new "basic carry" pistol to its offerings of 1911-type pistols. This is a lower-priced model in Parkerized finish, but still includes a beavertail grip safety, and ventilated trigger and hammer.

A 9mm long-slide version with a 6-inch barrel is also new. This configuration is aimed toward PPC shooters, and has a supported chamber.

For those who want to build their own pistols, a frame and slide kit is available. Most of the fitting is done, and a shooter can build a 1911 to his own specifications.

Rohrbaugh

The little DAO Rohrbaugh R9 pistol, introduced as a prototype two years ago, and as a pre-production specimen one year ago, is now in production. Several hundred guns had been made by early 2004.

Recall that the pistol uses standard 9mm ammunition, and has a tilting-barrel locked breech action. It is all metal, with 7075 aluminum frame and 17-4 stainless-steel slide and barrel. With a 2.9-inch barrel, the pistol measures only 3.7 x 5.2 inches, putting it in the smallest part of the subcompact class. Weight is 12.8 ounces, and capacity is 6 +1. The R9 is available with or without Sights.

Ruger

All Ruger adjustable-sight 22-caliber pistols will now be drilled and tapped for a Weaver-type base, and the base itself will be included with each drilled pistol. The base fits in front of the rear sight, and does not interfere with the pistol's metallic sights, but allows easy mounting of optical or electronic sights.

Two special model 22 pistols were scheduled for production during 2004. The first, the William B. Ruger Endowment Special NRA Edition pistol, is a blued Mark II with simulated ivory grips, with red eagle Ruger grip medallions. William B. Ruger's signature is rollmarked on the top of the receiver, along with the Ruger and NRA crests. For every pistol sold, a donation is made to the National Rifle Association's basic marksmanship training program.

The U. S. A. Shooting commemorative is a Mark II with gold plating on the bolt, and black laminate grip panels. For every pistol sold, a donation is made to the United States Shooting Team, which is preparing for the Olympic contests in Athens, Greece. As of February 2004, Ruger had contributed $30,000 to the U.S.A. Shooting Team. Bravo!

SIGARMS

Will the popularity of the 1911 design ever level out? Last year, Smith & Wesson added a 1911 to that company's offerings. In February 2004, SIGARMS unveiled their own 1911.

SIGARMS realized that American practical shooting is dominated by the 1911, and in order to be competitive, the company needed to add a 1911 to their line. The result was the GSR pistol. "GSR" stands for "Granite Series Rail," and denotes the accessory rail on the front portion of the slide. The rail is one thing that makes the SIG 1911 GSR visually distinctive from some other 1911s. Another factor is the shape of the slide's top and side cuts, which make the GSR look a little bit more "SIGgy." The GSR is a high-end pistol, and has an external extractor and many of the enhancements that are now in favor. It comes as a stainless-steel, or a blued stainless-steel finish.

Other SIGARMS models now have variants that incorporate an accessory rail. Among them are the P 220, P 226 and P 229. The single-action P 210 is now available with a U. S.-style magazine release on the left side of the frame.

An interesting new development is the "K trigger" option for some of the company's pistols. The K trigger is a new DAO with a pull similar to the best double-action revolver triggers. The frame of the pistol has to be changed to accommodate the new trigger mechanism, which involves new parts, spring rates and cam angles.

Smith & Wesson

The SW1911, introduced last year, has been out long enough to warrant a minor recall. Some specimens

The Ruger NRA pistol has special markings and simulated ivory grips. For each pistol sold, a donation is made to NRA's training programs.

might need to have the firing pin safety plunger repaired. If you have an SW1911 between the numbers JRD 0000 and JRD 4750, call 1-800-331-0852 for information on the free repair program.

Two variants of the SW1911 are new. The SW1911 adjustable-sight target pistol is a full-size 5-inch model, with ambidextrous manual safety controls. A 1911 Sc, a scandium Commander-size arm, is available as a lighter (28-ounce) variant with a 4 1/4-inch barrel.

The Model 952 is now available in stainless steel. Recall that the 952 is a 9mm target pistol based on the earlier Model 52.

The Model 22A, the full-size 22 LR autoloader, is now available as the 22A Camo. The entire gun is covered with a Mossy Oak camouflage finish.

Springfield

It is back to basics for part of Springfield Armory's new 1911A1 offerings. The "GI" series guns are made with low-profile military-type sights and standard hammer, trigger and grip safety. The ejection port is standard, not lowered, and a lanyard loop again appears at the rear of the butt. Slide serrations are the older narrow vertical type. Some concessions have been made to the modern era, as the barrels have ramped barrels with fully supported chambers. Except for the big-diamond walnut grips, the 5-inch Parkerized version is a dead ringer for the World War II 1911A1 configuration. There are also other versions in the GI line—a 5-inch OD green Armory Kote, a 5-inch stainless steel variant, and 3-inch and 4-inch

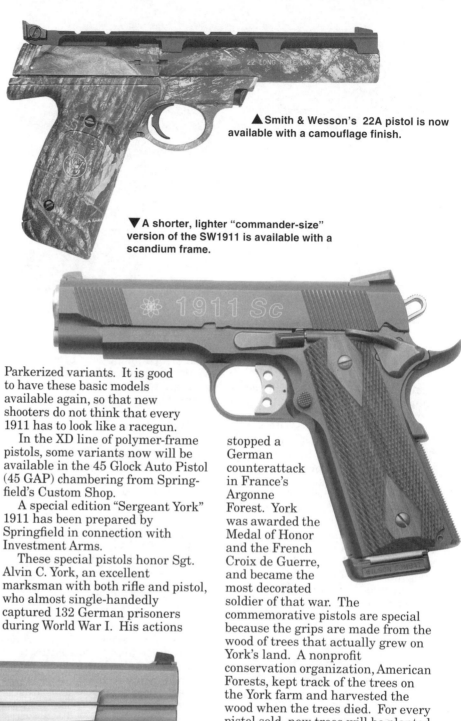

▲ Smith & Wesson's 22A pistol is now available with a camouflage finish.

▼ A shorter, lighter "commander-size" version of the SW1911 is available with a scandium frame.

Parkerized variants. It is good to have these basic models available again, so that new shooters do not think that every 1911 has to look like a racegun.

In the XD line of polymer-frame pistols, some variants now will be available in the 45 Glock Auto Pistol (45 GAP) chambering from Springfield's Custom Shop.

A special edition "Sergeant York" 1911 has been prepared by Springfield in connection with Investment Arms.

These special pistols honor Sgt. Alvin C. York, an excellent marksman with both rifle and pistol, who almost single-handedly captured 132 German prisoners during World War I. His actions stopped a German counterattack in France's Argonne Forest. York was awarded the Medal of Honor and the French Croix de Guerre, and became the most decorated soldier of that war. The commemorative pistols are special because the grips are made from the wood of trees that actually grew on York's land. A nonprofit conservation organization, American Forests, kept track of the trees on the York farm and harvested the wood when the trees died. For every pistol sold, new trees will be planted in special Liberty Forests. 132 Peerless Grade pistols, plated and engraved, and with grips made of cherry wood from York's farm will be made. 5000 additional Issue Grade pistols, with grips made from the black walnut tree that actually shaded the cabin in which York was born, will also be made.

STI

STI, of Georgetown, TX, in November 2003 acquired Lone Star Armament of Stephenville, TX. The

▲ A stainless-steel version of the S&W Model 952 9mm target pistol is now available.

▶ A target version of the SW1911 pistol is now offered, with adjustable sights.

▼ Springfield's new "GI" series includes a stainless-steel version.

▲ A 4-inch barrel Parkerized version of Springfield's new "GI" series is available.

▲ A full-size Parkerized 45 with a 5-inch barrel, Springfield's new "GI" pistol resembles previous military pistols.

▲ Springfield has introduced "GI" series pistols. This is a Parkerized version with a 3-inch barrel.

▲ Springfield's two special Sgt. York commemorative pistols, the Peerless Grade and the Issue Grade, rest on a piece of cherry wood from the York farm, from which the grips of the Peerless pistols are made.

acquisition essentially doubled STI's capacity for producing 1911-type pistols and parts. Beside the increase in pistol production, STI planned to begin providing a full line of parts to other manufacturers.

The Lone Star name has been phased out. Recall, however, that Lone Star offered two basic single-column 1911 pistols—the 5-inch Lawman and the 4-inch Ranger. The Ranger has been dropped, but the full-size pistol continues on as the STI Lawman. The Lawman is suitable for IDPA competition as well as IPSC and USPSA.

Taurus

In mid-2003, Taurus announced its new polymer-frame DAO service pistol, the 24/7. It was introduced in 9mm and 40 S&W, and those options are now available. In the meantime, Taurus developed a larger-bore version, and the 24/7 in 45 ACP was introduced at the February 2004 SHOT Show. The new 45 has a bushingless flared barrel and a captive flat-coil recoil spring. An accessory rail is present at the front of the frame. The 45-caliber was scheduled for production in late 2004.

The nice PT 922 22-caliber pistol has undergone some revisions in the

◀ The Taurus 24/7 service pistol, introduced last year in 9mm and 40, is now offered in 45 ACP.

▼ A Taurus pistol in 38 Super, the Model PT38S, is now available.

past two years, and is now in final form. It has a 6-inch barrel, 10+1 capacity and weighs 29 ounces. The polymer frame has a slanty "Woodsman" look and feel, and the pistol has an adjustable rear sight and fiber-optic front sight.

The 38 Super cartridge came on the scene in 1929, and although it has never been a standard military or police service round, it has remained popular. Taurus has introduced its first 38 Super pistol, the PT 38S. The pistol is conventional double-action, and comes in either blue or stainless steel finishes. With a 4 1/4-inch barrel, it weighs 30 ounces. Availability was scheduled for late 2004.

Uselton

A new line of 1911-style pistols was presented for the first time at the February 2004 SHOT Show, under the name Uselton Arms. Made on Caspian steel frames, the pistols have Uselton stainless-steel slides, barrels and triggers. The Uselton trigger is very distinctive, and has a flat vertical front surface. Other features now in vogue, such as beavertail grip safeties and extended manual safety levers, are also present.

Variants with 5-inch, 4 1/4-inch, 3 1/2-inch and 3-inch barrels are offered. Special features such as titanium frames and Damascus slides are also offered on select models. Calibers are 45 ACP, 40 S&W

and 357 SIG. In some versions, interchangeable barrels are provided to make the pistol both a 40 S&W and a 357 SIG, at the choice of the shooter.

Uselton considers their pistols "totally customized" out of the box.

Volquartsen

Known for their Ruger-style 22-caliber pistols, Volquartsen plans to introduce a new lightweight version. The pistol will have a steel receiver and a barrel of 12mm diameter sleeved in titanium. They will offer it in 22 LR, and tentatively plan to offer the 17 Aguila (17 Hi-Standard) when the ammunition becomes available.

Walther

Walther didn't really offer anything new in the autoloading pistol line this year. However, they introduced a 22 LR carbine. It is not really a pistol-carbine, but it is related, so let's give it a quick look. The new G22 carbine is of the bullpup design, so the action is under the stock's cheekpiece. With a 20-inch barrel, the overall length is only 28 inches. The grip of the polymer stock is similar to that of Walther's P22 rimfire pistol, and the carbine can use the same magazines.

Wildey

Wildey is working with the government of Jordan on the Jordanian Armament Weapons Systems (JAWS) pistol project, and the new pistol, introduced last year, is well into development. Recall that the pistol is service-type, with a conventional double-action trigger system.

Uselton Arms president Rick Uselton holds one of his company's 1911 variants, built with a titanium frame and a Damascus slide.

After several years of development, the 22-caliber Taurus PT922 is now in final form.

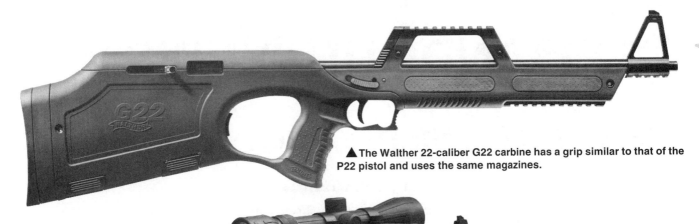

▲ The Walther 22-caliber G22 carbine has a grip similar to that of the P22 pistol and uses the same magazines.

► Optical sights can be added to the Walther G22 carbine.

One of its distinctive features is the ability to convert from 9mm to 40 S&W to 45 ACP with the change of a few parts. The replaceable bolt face can be changed by removing the extractor. The rotating barrel and the magazine can both be readily replaced when the pistol is stripped for cleaning. Internal parts can be reached by removing a frame sideplate, which is retained by the slide.

The pistol has a name now. It will be called the JAWS "Viper." A standard model will have a stainless-steel frame, either natural or blackened, and a lightweight version will have an aluminum-alloy frame and shorter barrel. The design has a true ambidextrous magazine catch, which can be pressed from either side.

Wilson

Wilson Combat has added the Professional Model to its line of 1911-based pistols. It has a full-size frame with a compact slide and matching 4.1-inch barrel. Features such as beavertail grip safety, lightened hammer and extended thumb safety are standard. It is available in all-black, gray-and-black, and green-and-black. Available in 45 ACP, it weighs 35 ounces. The match barrel is hand-fitted, and the accuracy guarantee is an impressive one inch at 25 yards.

POSTSCRIPT

As this is written in 2004, a number of things lie ahead in the remainder of this year and into 2005 that hold great importance for the industry and for the shooters involved with autoloading handguns. Things unknown to me now—such as the fate of the 1994 "Assault Weapon" and magazine ban (due to sunset in September 2004), and the results of the November 2004 elections—may be history when you read this. Regardless of the outcomes, we know we will face continuing battles over license-to-carry legislation and reciprocity, and the enemies of freedom continue to call for greater restrictions on firearms. Please resolve to know where your legislators stand, and to let your legislators know where you stand. ●

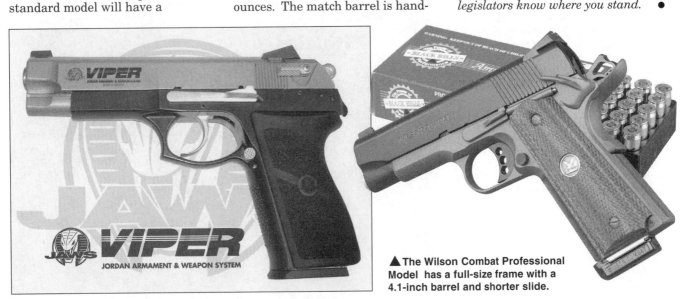

The pistol developed by Wildey and the country of Jordan has been given a name, and will appear as the Jaws Viper.

▲ The Wilson Combat Professional Model has a full-size frame with a 4.1-inch barrel and shorter slide.

HANDGUN NEWS

REVOLVERS, SINGLE-SHOTS & OTHERS

by John Taffin

*I*T WAS *50 years ago, in 1955, when Smith & Wesson produced the first 44 Magnum. Everyone knew we had reached the top; there was simply no way six-guns could ever be made more powerful. Then, in 1983 Freedom Arms produced their first 454 Casull. John Linebaugh arrived on the scene giving us the 475 and 500 Linebaughs and then stretching both to approximately 1.60 inches for "Maximum" versions of the same two cartridges. Custom revolver-builders offered heavy-duty, five-shot 45 Colt six-guns to allow heavy loading of this grand old cartridge, and Hornady and Ruger collaborated on the 480. Had we reached the end of powerful six-gun cartridge development?*

Not quite. The big news last year was the 500 S&W Magnum cartridge and the new Smith & Wesson X-frame revolver. We have now had a year to test this largest of all double-action six-guns, as well as the 500 cartridge. Other manufacturers have joined with Smith & Wesson in supplying 500-chambered revolvers–with Magnum Research offering a single action BFR revolver while Taurus has countered with their Raging Bull version in 500 S&W Magnum. Two custom makers, Gary Reeder Custom Guns and SSK Industries, have offered their 500 Magnums in revolver and single-shot form, respectively. It has been my good (?) fortune to have test-fired the 500 Magnum extensively over the past year, chambered in the original 8 3/8-inch Smith & Wesson Model 500, a 10 1/2-inch BFR, an SSK Custom Encore, and a Gary Reeder single action. The cartridge has proven to be extremely accurate, as well as speaking with authority and finality when used on game.

One might think this would be the end of cartridge development; however, I have been shown three new cartridges that will be arriving on the scene this year. As this is written they must remain as "mystery cartridges", however I can share the fact that two of them will be standard length 50-caliber cartridges for use in single-action revolvers,

while the other will be a "Maximum"-length 45-caliber cartridge. We are still looking and hoping for a five-shot Ruger single action in 480 Ruger or 50-caliber, however none of these will be in handguns marked with the Ruger label. Once again it is time for our annual alphabetical trip down the path labeled "Six-guns, Single Shots, and Others."

American Western Arms: AWA has been offering both the Longhorn and Peacekeeper traditionally-styled SAAs for several years. Available in most of the standard frontier calibers, these six-guns were offered in the blue and case-colored finish, as well as in hard chrome. Normally, I would say chrome belongs on the bumpers of a '49 Ford Club Coupe. However, I must admit AWA's hard chrome is very attractive, much like brushed stainless steel. The combination of hard chrome and 45 Colt make an excellent outdoorsman's revolver.

Last year AWA made a major change in their Peacekeeper and Longhorn revolvers. As one takes a close look at the back to the hammer, one notices something quite strange for a traditionally-styled single action. The area of the hammer between the two ears of the back strap is slotted to accept a strut. AWA began fitting their revolvers–on special order–with a coil mainspring system, as well as offering a kit consisting of a new hammer with an attached strut, a coil spring, and a shelf that attaches to the back strap to accept the strut. Changing from a flat mainspring to a coil spring is not quite a drop-in, as the inside of the back of the front strap must be milled out to accept the coil spring. With a coil spring-operated hand and hammer mated up with a Wolff trigger and bolt spring, the action of a single action comes very close to being indestructible. Now AWA has made another significant change. The Longhorn and Peacekeeper have been dropped and replaced by The

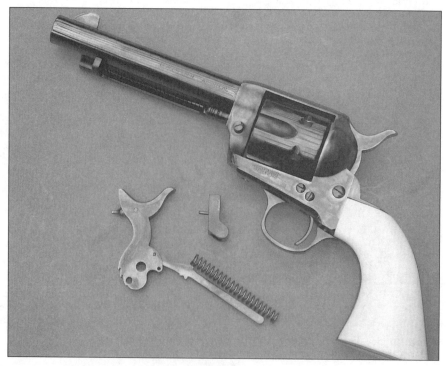

The Ultimate by AWA features a coil mainspring.

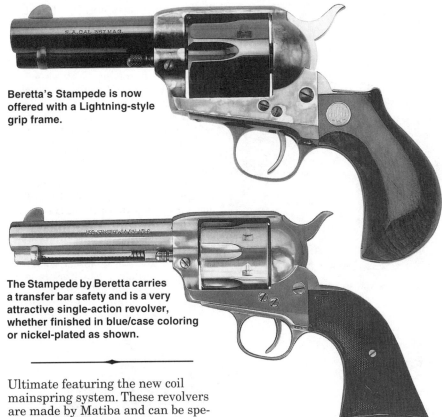

Beretta's Stampede is now offered with a Lightning-style grip frame.

The Stampede by Beretta carries a transfer bar safety and is a very attractive single-action revolver, whether finished in blue/case coloring or nickel-plated as shown.

Ultimate featuring the new coil mainspring system. These revolvers are made by Matiba and can be specially ordered with one-piece *faux* ivory grips by Tru-Art. Those six-guns I have seen have been very well finished and timed.

Beretta: This is not only the oldest firearms manufacturer in existence, it is the oldest company of any kind–dating back nearly 500 years. In the early 1990s it was my pleasure to be escorted through the Beretta factory, which included a personally conducted tour of their private museum housing several centuries of firearms development. We've all known Beretta as a manufacturer of high quality semi-automatic pistols and shotguns. Then the unexpected happened. Beretta, of semi-automatic fame, purchased Uberti, known for producing replicas of 19th-century firearms. Suddenly, Beretta was in the business of producing single-action six-guns.

In addition to now owning Uberti, Beretta is also offering a revolver under the Beretta name. That single-action six-gun is known as the Stampede. Although traditionally sized and styled, it contains a transfer bar safety, making it safe to carry with six rounds. Available in both the standard grip frame style as well as the Lightning grip frame, the well-built and smoothly operating Stampede has been warmly accepted by single-action shooters. Currently it is available in both 45 Colt and 357 Magnum, in either the standard blue and case-coloring, or nickel finishes.

Bond Arms: Most of us six-gunners will probably admit a fascina-

tion with derringers. When I was the kid growing up, one could still find original Remington 41RF derringers at very reasonable prices. They were, of course, chambered for hard-to-get rimfire ammunition. Then Great Western came along and, in addition to bringing out the first true replica single action army, also duplicated the Remington double-barreled derringer in 38 Special. Great Western Arms is long gone now and in the

intervening years several companies have offered derringers that run the gamut from excellent quality all the way down to extremely poor. Unfortunately the latter is what too many folks have purchased to use for self-defense.

Bond Arms offers extremely high quality double-barreled derringers in both the spur trigger and trigger guard style. All Bond Arms derringers are made of stainless steel with a spring-loaded extractor, rebounding firing pin, cross-bolt safety, and a nearly endless list of available chamberings. Barrels are interchangeable, allowing the use of 26 different cartridges—all the way from 22 Long Rifle up to the 45 Colt––as well as a special rendition that not only accepts the 45 Colt but .410 shotshells as well. The standard offering, looking much like the traditional Remington Derringer, is known as the Cowboy Defender. Add a trigger guard and it becomes the Texas Defender. For those desirous of the ultimate in snake protection, there is the Century 2000, which handles 3-inch .410 shells. I have been in some places, while hunting, where I would have felt a lot more comfortable packing a Century 2000.

Cimarron Firearms (CFA): Cimarron recently celebrated its 20th year as a leader in supplying authentic replica revolvers, leverguns, and single-shot rifles to cowboy action shooters and those who appreciate the firearms of the Old West. Cimarron's Model P, a traditionally styled SAA, is now offered in stainless steel as well as blue/case-coloring and nickel. Barrel lengths are 4 3/4- and 5 1/2- with 7 1/2-inch versions now arriving.

The Bond Arms Cowboy Defender is offered in 26 chamberings, including the easy-handling 32 H&R Magnum.

This Texas rattler met up with a .410-chambered Bond Arms Cowboy Defender.

Cimarron's Model P Jr. is an easy-to-handle, lightweight single action chambered in 38 Special/38LC and 32-20.

perfect single action in this latest Model P including easy-to-see square-shaped sights. All of the special guns feature Evil Roy's signature on the barrel. Cimarron says of this revolver: "Featuring internal parts produced exclusively for Cimarron, and springs from U.S. manufacturers. The rear sight notch is large and square while the front sight is wide—with no taper—giving the shooter the finest sight picture.... Grips are hand-checkered or smooth walnut; very slim and trim for fast and safe handling. The actions are set up in the U.S.A. to function safely with lighter hammer action, no creep, and safe but crisp trigger pull. Each revolver is regulated to shoot dead-center left and right windage." Shooters have a choice of the standard finish or a special U.S.A. premium finish with case-coloring by Doug Turnbull.

Thus far, chamberings offered are 45 Colt and 357 Magnum.

For those desiring a specially tuned and smoothed single action for cowboy action shooting, Cimarron offers the Evil Roy Model P. Evil Roy is one of the top shooters in CAS and has incorporated his ideas of the

▲ Colt's 44 Magnum offering is the stainless steel Anaconda.

▲ The Colt Single Action Army is once again offered with a 7 1/2-inch barrel in 45 Colt, 44-40, 38-40, 38 Special, 357 Magnum, and 32-20.

Normally I am known for shooting the biggest six-guns available; however, I have a kinder, gentler side that has been indulged by shooting Cimarron's Model P Jr. These little six-guns have the standard single-action grip frame of the Model P with a smaller frame and cylinder. Chambered in 38 Special/38 Long Colt, or 32-20, they are not only fun guns for experienced six-gunners, they are also just the ticket for younger shooters—or anyone who cannot handle the recoil of larger six-guns.

There are several classes of shooters under the banner of cowboy action shooting. One group looks to authenticity in their costumes and firearms, especially their six-guns. For these folks, Cimarron offers their Model P with what they call an Original Finish, which is actually no finish at all, or perhaps we should say a specially-induced finish to make a six-gun look like it has been in use since the 1870s—although literally brand-new and in perfect mechanical shape. Original Finish six-guns may be used with either smokeless or blackpowder loads; however, they are an excellent choice for those who shoot blackpowder as they not only sound like the Old West, they also look like a six-gun with a definite story to tell.

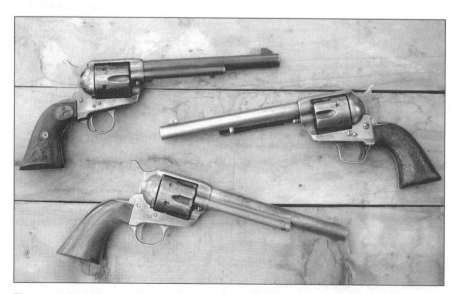

The top and middle 44-40s are original Colt Single Actions; the bottom six-gun is Cimarron's Model P with the antique-looking Original Finish.

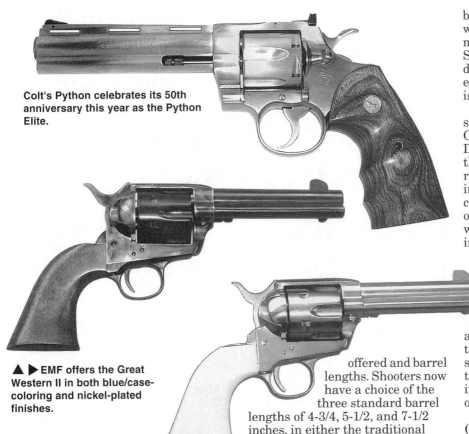

Colt's Python celebrates its 50th anniversary this year as the Python Elite.

▲ ► EMF offers the Great Western II in both blue/case-coloring and nickel-plated finishes.

Colt: Colt has made a lot of drastic, and very welcome, changes over the past few years. Three years ago Colt Single Actions were offered only in 45 Colt and 44-40, only in barrel lengths of 4-3/4 and 5-1/2 inches, and with a price tag coming very close to $2000! The last two years the price was reduced to make it more competitive with replica single actions, while still remaining a genuine Colt Single Action. Now, for this year, the Single Action part of the catalog has been greatly expanded as to calibers offered and barrel lengths. Shooters now have a choice of the three standard barrel lengths of 4-3/4, 5-1/2, and 7-1/2 inches, in either the traditional blue/case-colored finish or full nickel finish; chambered for the 45 Colt, 44-40, 38-40, 38 Special, 357 Magnum, and—for the first time in nearly three-quarters of a century—32-20. Just to prove shooters can never be satisfied, I have to ask, "Where is the 44 Special?"

Every day, in nearly every way and every location, single-action shooters argue the merits of replica single actions and the original Colt Single Action Army. When all the arguing and debating is through—there is only one genuine Single Action Army that says COLT on the barrel. No replica, no matter how well it is finished and tuned, can make that statement. While the Colt Single Action Army remains in 36 different versions when one considers calibers, barrel lengths, and finish, the Colt Cowboy is no more.

At one time Colt had a whole stable full of snakes. The Viper, Cobra, King Cobra, and Diamondback are all gone; however, the Anaconda and the Python remain. Although originally offered in both 45 Colt and 44 Magnum, currently the Anaconda is offered only in a stainless steel 44 Magnum with barrel lengths of 4, 6, and 8 inches, complete with fully adjustable sights and finger-groove rubber grips. It has proven to be a sturdy, reliable, accurate hunting handgun. Many shooters would argue that the Python is the finest double-action revolver ever offered at any time. I don't argue; I just enjoy shooting the Python. It continues in the Colt lineup as the Python Elite, in either blue or stainless with a 4- or 6-inch barrel.

Early And Modern Firearms (EMF): Last year EMF introduced the Great Western II. The Great Western originally appeared in 1954 as a totally American-made replica of the Colt Single Action Army. EMF was one of the early distributors of the Great Western, which disappeared in the early 1960s. The Great Western II line has been greatly expanded this year. The Custom Great Western is offered in nickel, satin nickel, blue/case colored, and all-blue finish, in the three standard barrel lengths of 4-3/4, 5-1/2, and 7-1/2 inches; in 45 Colt, 44-40, and 357 Magnum with other calibers–as well as engraving–available on special

50 years separates these two Great Westerns. The top six-gun is an original Great Western, while the bottom revolver is EMF's Pietta-manufactured Great Western II.

The two greatest 44 Specials of all times? The S&W 1907 Triple-Lock and the Freedom Arms Model 97.

Freedom Arms offers the small game/varmint hunter the Model 97 chambered in 357 Magnum, 22 Long Rifle/22 Magnum, and 32 Magnum/32-20.

order. All Custom Series Great Westerns are fitted with one-piece ivory-style grips.

In addition to the Great Western, which is made by Pietta, EMF also offers the Hartford Premiere in the three standard barrel lengths and chambered in 45 Colt, 44-40, 44 Special, 38-40, and 32-20. Special versions offered include the Bisley Model in all three barrel lengths, a 3-inch ejectorless Sheriff's Model, the round-butted 4-inch Pinkerton Model, and the 3 1/2-inch Deputy Model—all chambered in 45 Colt. Both the 1875 and 1890 Remingtons are offered and the Remington and the SAA models are also offered with the Antique Finish, making them appear to have experienced more than a century of service. Finally, EMF also offers a Buntline Special version of their 1873 six-guns.

Freedom Arms: Last year Freedom Arms introduced their Model 97 five-shot 44 Special, which I have now had a pleasurable year shooting. In addition, two more six-shot Model 97s have arrived on the scene. One is a 32 Magnum *(with an extra 32-20 cylinder available)*, while the other is chambered in the hot new 17 HMR. Since its inception in 1907, the 44 Special has been chambered in some of the finest revolvers ever produced. From Smith & Wesson we have the Triple-Lock, the Model 1926, the 1950 Target and, in more recent times, the Model 24 and Model 624—as well as a five-shot 296 and 696. Colt waited a while to chamber the 44 Special; however, when they finally moved in that direction they gave us the New Service, the Single Action Army, and the New Frontier. All great six-guns; however, the 44

Special Triple-Lock is most often considered the finest 44 Special—if not the finest revolver-period—ever manufactured. It now has a rival. The 44 Special Model 97 from Freedom Arms is surely the finest single-action 44 Special ever offered, and may just be every bit as good as that first Special 44.

Freedom Arms spent a long time studying barrel twists and different loads in both the 32 Magnum and the 32-20 before deciding to offer this combination in their Model 97. I personally supplied some loads for testing, and spent time with Bob Baker of Freedom Arms shooting the prototype model—both on paper for accuracy and over Oehler's Model 35P chronograph for muzzle velocity. Shooting 32s is always educational and this was no exception as some loads that were expected to do well performed poorly, while others gave surprisingly better results than expected.

The Freedom Arms Model 97 32 is superbly accurate. All testing was done with a 2x Leupold in place to remove as much human sighting error as possible. Five-shot groups, with either the 32 Magnum or 32-20 cylinder in place, were exceptionally

small with groups of well under one inch at 25 yards being commonplace. When it comes to varmints and small game one can cover all the bases with three 7 1/2-inch Model 97s chambered in 357 Magnum, 32 Magnum/32-20, and 22 Long Rifle/22 Magnum. While excellent ammunition abounds in both the 357 Magnum and both 22s, the 32 Magnum and 32-20 require handloading for the best results. The most accurate load in 32 Magnum has proven to be Sierra's 90-grain JHC over 10 grains of H110 for five shots in 1/2-inch and a muzzle velocity of 1260 fps, while the 32-20 shoots best *(thus far)* with Speer's 100-grain JHP over 10.0 grains of #2400 for slightly under 1200 fps and five shots in 5/8-inch. This year the Model 97 chambered in 17 HMR has joined the three small game/varmint-gathering Model 97 six-guns.

As expected, this has also proven to be an exceptionally accurate revolver; my 10-inch test gun from Freedom Arms is capable of groups well under 1/2-inch at 25 yards, and probably even better in the hands of the younger, steadier shooter.

Hartford Armory: A new six-gun manufacturer has arrived on the scene. Hartford Armory is now offering the Remington 1890 and 1875 Single Actions. Go back 125 years. Colt, Remington, and Smith & Wesson all made beautiful single-action revolvers. The Colt handled black-powder extremely well, while the Remington and Smith & Wesson had such tight tolerances they were actually smokeless-powder guns in a blackpowder age. In other words, they were so tightly fitted and closely machined they fouled easily when used with blackpowder. Fast-forward to today and we have the return of the Remington at a time when most shooters use them with smokeless powder. At last we will find out what excellent six-guns the Remingtons actually

The newest offering from Freedom Arms is the Model 97 chambered in 17 HMR.

The BFR from Magnum Research has proven to be an exceptionally accurate revolver.

versions: the Short Cylinder chambered in 454 Casull and 480 Ruger/475 Linebaugh, and 22 Hornet; the Long Cylinder is offered in 444 Marlin, 450 Marlin, 45-70, a special 45 Colt that also accepts 3-inch .410 shotgun shells, and–new for this year–500 S&W Magnum.

All BFR revolvers are American-made with cut-rifled, hand-lapped, recessed-muzzle-crowned barrels; tight tolerances; soft brushed stainless steel finish; and are normally equipped with an adjustable rear sight mated with a front sight with interchangeable blades of differing heights. They can be ordered from the factory set up with a scope and an SSK base. The SSK mounting system is the strongest available anywhere for scoping hard-kicking handguns. For the past year I have been extensively testing two BFR six-guns in 480/475 Linebaugh and 500 S&W Magnum. They have proven to be exceptionally accurate and have performed flawlessly.

Navy Arms: When it comes to replica firearms, Val Forgett of Navy Arms started it all. With the passing of Val Forgett this past year, Navy Arms is now headed up by his son, Val Forgett III. The leadership may have changed, but Navy Arms continues to offer some of the finest replicas available. These include The Gunfighter, a specially-tuned single-action army offered in the three standard barrel lengths, chambered in 357 Magnum, 44-40, and 45 Colt. Finish is blue with a case-colored frame and the German silver-plated back strap and trigger guard. Springs are all U.S.-made Wolff springs, and the standard grips are black-checkered gunfighter style.

were. Hartford Armory is building truly authentic versions of the originals that have, at least in my hand, a different feel from the Italian replicas. Both the 1875 and 1890 will be offered in a full blue finish, classified as Hartford Armory Dark Blue, or with a Turnbull case-colored frame; and also in stainless steel. Stocks are two-piece walnut.

Now comes the real surprise: this new version of the old Remington Single Action is chambered in 45 Colt and rated for +P loads; and is also offered in 44 Magnum. Other calibers will be 357 Magnum and 44-40. Although sights are the traditionally fixed single-action style; the front sight, which screws into the barrel, will be offered in different heights for sighting-in heavy-duty hunting loads. I am definitely looking forward to fully testing of this new/old revolver.

Magnum Research: Magnum Research offers the all-stainless steel BFR *(Biggest Finest Revolver)*. The BFR looks much like a Ruger Super Blackhawk; the grip frames will accept the same grips—however, unlike Ruger six-guns, the BFR has a freewheeling cylinder that rotates either clockwise or counter-clockwise when the loading gate is opened. It is offered in two

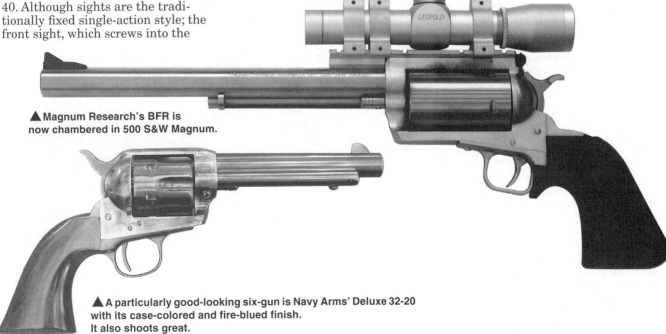

▲ Magnum Research's BFR is now chambered in 500 S&W Magnum.

▲ A particularly good-looking six-gun is Navy Arms' Deluxe 32-20 with its case-colored and fire-blued finish. It also shoots great.

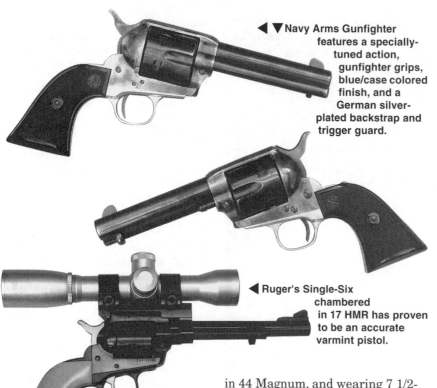

Navy Arms Gunfighter features a specially-tuned action, gunfighter grips, blue/case colored finish, and a German silver-plated backstrap and trigger guard.

Ruger's Ken Jorgensen with the new Ruger Hunter Model 22 Long Rifle/22 Magnum version.

◄ Ruger's Single-Six chambered in 17 HMR has proven to be an accurate varmint pistol.

Navy Arms has also added the stainless steel Gunfighter with the same barrel lengths and chamberings. Stainless steel may not be authentic Old West, however it sure makes a lot of sense for shooting blackpowder loads. Navy Arms also continues to offer the standard 1873 Cavalry six-gun, the 1895 Artillery Model, the Bisley Model, and the two great Smith & Wesson single actions: the 1875 Schofield and the New Model Russian. The latter is offered only in 44 Russian with a 6 1/2-inch barrel, while the Schofield comes in the original 7-inch version, the 5-inch Wells Fargo Model, and a 3 1/2-inch Hideout Model. Navy Arm's Schofields are available in both 45 Colt and 38 Special.

Ruger: In 1953 Ruger resurrected the SAA six-gun with their 22 Single-Six. Over the years it has been offered with both fixed and adjustable sights, and barrel lengths of 4-5/8, 5-1/2, 6-1/2, and 9-1/2 inches. For whatever reason, my preferred barrel length for a hunting handgun — 7-1/2 inches — has never been offered during the first 50 years of the 22 Single-Six. However, Ruger starts off their second half-century with the most popular 22 single-action revolver ever offered by correcting this mistake.

Ruger single actions have always been favorites of handgun hunters—especially their Hunter Models which continue to be offered in both the Super Blackhawk and Bisley models, in stainless steel, chambered

in 44 Magnum, and wearing 7 1/2-inch heavy-ribbed barrels set up to accept Ruger scope rings. These are exceptionally popular hunting handguns and it is proper and fitting that they are now joining by a 22 RF model. The newest Hunter Model is a 7 1/2-inch 22 Long Rifle/22 Magnum version with a heavy-ribbed barrel set up to accept Ruger scope rings.

▲ The 1875 Schofield from Navy Arms is offered as the Cavalry, Wells Fargo, and Hideout Models. Custom grips are by Buffalo Brothers and Eagle Grips.

A half-century of Ruger 44 Magnums. *From top right*: original Flattop, Super Blackhawk, Bisley Model, Super Blackhawk Hunter, and the Bisley Hunter.

▶ The Savage Striker is a stainless steel, synthetic-stocked, bolt-action pistol chambered for such cartridges as the 7-08 Remington and 308 Winchester.

For those of us who have been shooting the original 22 Single-Six since the 1950s, a longer-barrel scope-sighted version has arrived none too soon. I don't know what goes on in the gun safe but something causes those sights to become a little fuzzier every year.

The scope-sighted 22 Hunter Model can take care of this problem. This new Hunter Model is also being offered in 17 HMR. There is still no word from Ruger on a five-shot, large-bore single-action six-gun. *Maybe next year….*

Ruger continues to offer their excellent lineup of six-guns: the Blackhawk, the Bisley Model, the Vaquero, the Bisley Vaquero, the Redhawk, the Super Redhawk, the GP-100, and the Single-Six. This year marks the Golden Anniversary of the immensely popular Ruger 357 Blackhawk. Also new this year from Ruger is the Ruger Studio Of Art and Decoration for providing engraved versions of Ruger firearms. There will be no set patterns; rather, each firearm will be individually embellished to fit the desires of the owner. The work will be performed only on new Ruger firearms. In the past this service has only been available for special presentations or occasions, and for Bill Ruger's personal collection.

Savage: Savage continues to offer their excellent Striker series of bolt-action pistols. The Sport Striker, designed for small game and varmints is chambered in 17 HMR, 22 LR, and 22 Magnum. The stainless steel Striker comes with a black synthetic stock, muzzle brake, left-hand bolt, and chambered in 223 Remington, 270 WSM, 7-08 Remington, 7mm WSM, 308 Winchester, and 300 WSM

Smith & Wesson: Thousands of the Model 500 X-Frame 500 S&W Magnum were sold in its first year of production and now a new, easier-packing version is offered. The new-est Model 500 has a 4-inch barrel–actually 3 inches of barrel, plus a compensator. This could be just the ticket for those who regularly travel areas where four-legged beasts can be mean and nasty. This new version also wears the finger-grooved rubber grips of the original 8 3/8-inch Model 500. As far as grips go, I have found a better way—I should say the bet-ter way has been shown to me by Rod Herrett of Herrett's Stocks.

Some shooters experience a phenomenon when shooting the 500 Magnum in that the cylinder

Recoil is heavy with Cor-Bon's 440-grain 500 Magnum load; however accuracy is excellent.

Two of the greatest bargains offered to handgun hunters are Ruger's Hunter Model 44 Magnum in the Bisley and Super Blackhawk versions.

◄ Taffin shooting the 500 Smith & Wesson X-Frame revolver.

Herrett's Jordan stocks improve the handling of Smith & Wesson's Model 500.

◄ Eight shots and a 2-inch barrel—Smith & Wesson's latest 357 Magnum.

▲ Senior citizens rejoice! At last we have a J-framed Smith & Wesson chambered in 22 Magnum.

unlocks and rotates backwards. One of the reasons for this—and it does not happen with every shooter—is the rubber grips cause the Model 500 to bounce off the web of the hand, resulting in the trigger hitting the trigger finger—which naturally causes the trigger to start backwards and the cylinder to unlock. The solution from Rod Herrett was a pair of smooth-finished walnut Jordan stocks. These grips fill in the backstrap and do not bounce off the hand, as the rubber grips have a tendency to do with some shooters.

Other new offerings from Smith & Wesson this year include the Model 325PD, a lightweight, 21 1/2-ounce scandium and titanium 45 ACP revolver with a 2 1/2-inch barrel and Hi-Viz front sight. Used with full-moon clips, this lightweight but powerful revolver should become very popular for those with concealed weapons permits. When it comes to concealed firearms, one of the most neglected groups has been senior citizens. The AARP, which should be doing everything they can to protect their vulnerable members, instead is rabidly anti-gun. Quite often, senior citizens have a hard time finding a firearm they can easily handle. Smith & Wesson has greatly solved this problem by offering their Air-Lite PD in a seven-shot 22 Magnum version. Bill Jordan often asked for a J-Frame 22 Magnum, and it is now reality.

Smith & Wesson also offers two other special CCW packages with

▲ The Smith & Wesson Mountain Gun is offered this year in 45 Colt.

Smith & Wesson now offers an Airweight 38 Special, paired with a Kydex holster.

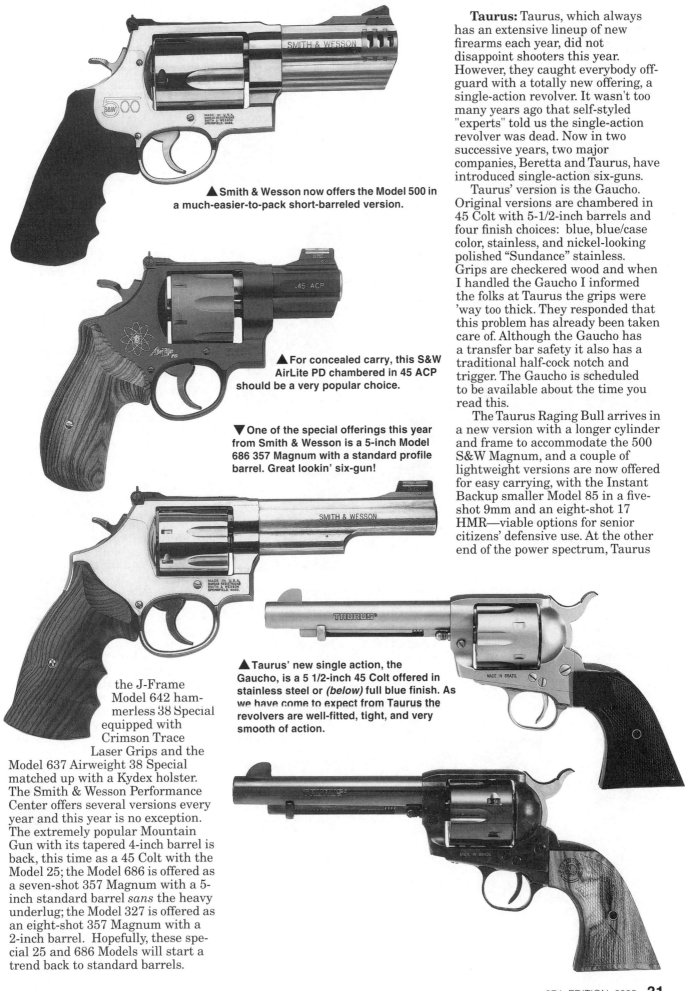

▲ Smith & Wesson now offers the Model 500 in a much-easier-to-pack short-barreled version.

▲ For concealed carry, this S&W AirLite PD chambered in 45 ACP should be a very popular choice.

▼ One of the special offerings this year from Smith & Wesson is a 5-inch Model 686 357 Magnum with a standard profile barrel. Great lookin' six-gun!

Taurus: Taurus, which always has an extensive lineup of new firearms each year, did not disappoint shooters this year. However, they caught everybody off-guard with a totally new offering, a single-action revolver. It wasn't too many years ago that self-styled "experts" told us the single-action revolver was dead. Now in two successive years, two major companies, Beretta and Taurus, have introduced single-action six-guns.

Taurus' version is the Gaucho. Original versions are chambered in 45 Colt with 5-1/2-inch barrels and four finish choices: blue, blue/case color, stainless, and nickel-looking polished "Sundance" stainless. Grips are checkered wood and when I handled the Gaucho I informed the folks at Taurus the grips were 'way too thick. They responded that this problem has already been taken care of. Although the Gaucho has a transfer bar safety it also has a traditional half-cock notch and trigger. The Gaucho is scheduled to be available about the time you read this.

The Taurus Raging Bull arrives in a new version with a longer cylinder and frame to accommodate the 500 S&W Magnum, and a couple of lightweight versions are now offered for easy carrying, with the Instant Backup smaller Model 85 in a five-shot 9mm and an eight-shot 17 HMR—viable options for senior citizens' defensive use. At the other end of the power spectrum, Taurus

the J-Frame Model 642 hammerless 38 Special equipped with Crimson Trace Laser Grips and the Model 637 Airweight 38 Special matched up with a Kydex holster. The Smith & Wesson Performance Center offers several versions every year and this year is no exception. The extremely popular Mountain Gun with its tapered 4-inch barrel is back, this time as a 45 Colt with the Model 25; the Model 686 is offered as a seven-shot 357 Magnum with a 5-inch standard barrel *sans* the heavy underlug; the Model 327 is offered as an eight-shot 357 Magnum with a 2-inch barrel. Hopefully, these special 25 and 686 Models will start a trend back to standard barrels.

▲ Taurus' new single action, the Gaucho, is a 5 1/2-inch 45 Colt offered in stainless steel or *(below)* full blue finish. As we have come to expect from Taurus the revolvers are well-fitted, tight, and very smooth of action.

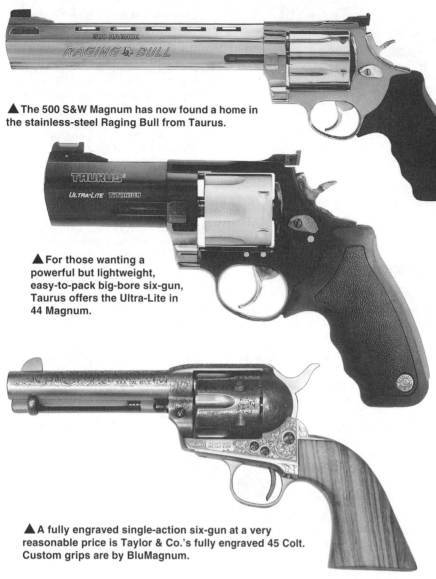

▲ The 500 S&W Magnum has now found a home in the stainless-steel Raging Bull from Taurus.

▲ For those wanting a powerful but lightweight, easy-to-pack big-bore six-gun, Taurus offers the Ultra-Lite in 44 Magnum.

▲ A fully engraved single-action six-gun at a very reasonable price is Taylor & Co.'s fully engraved 45 Colt. Custom grips are by BluMagnum.

offers the Hip Carry, a 28-ounce, 4-inch barreled Raging Bull chambered in 44 Magnum. Grips are the recoil-reducing cushioned insert grips found on the standard Raging Bull.

Taylor's & Co.: Last year we mentioned that Taylor's & Co. was offering R&D Conversion Cylinders for both the Remington 1858 and the Ruger Old Army. I have now had plenty of time to use these conversion cylinders in a pair of Ruger Old Armies. My particular 5 1/2-inch Rugers shoot right to point of aim with the conversion cylinders and 255-grain 45 Colt bullets. Not only do they shoot to the right spot, they also do it with excellent accuracy.

This year Taylor's has expanded

Thompson/Center's Encore is now offered in 375 JDJ.

their line of conversion cylinders with the 32 S&W Short for the 1849 Wells Fargo, 45 Colt cylinders for the Colt Dragoon and 1860 Army, 38 Long Colt cylinders for the 1851 and 1861 Navy, and 38 Special cylinders for the 36-caliber 1858 Remington. The cylinders, of course, are for cowboy action shooting-level loads only.

Taylor's is also offering the "Outfitter", a stainless steel Model 1873 in all three barrel lengths chambered in 357 Magnum or 45 Colt. The Model 1873 is also offered in the standard blue/case color finish in all standard barrel lengths and the same chamberings, as well as 44-40, 44 Special, 38-40, 32-20, and 45 ACP. A very special 1873 Model is the photo-engraved version in 45 Colt. This is an exceptionally attractive revolver with full engraving at a most reasonable price. It comes in the white; however, I have had mine blued. Taylor's & Co. will also be the exclusive distributor for the Hartford Armory line of 1875 and 1890 Remington revolvers.

Thompson/Center: Thompson/Center single-shot pistols have long been favorites both at long-range silhouette matches and in the hunting field. They have been chambered for dozens of factory and wildcat cartridges for those looking for long-range accuracy and adequate power for either target shooting or taking big game. T/C offers two versions of their break-open, single-shot pistols: the standard Contender now in its second phase with the easier-opening G2, and the Encore. The G2 will handle cartridges in the 30-30 and 44 Magnum range, while the larger, heavier Encore feels quite at home with the higher-pressure cartridges such as the 308 and 30-06. Some cartridges, such as the 45-70, are offered in both versions.

Two new cartridges have been added this year, both chambered in the Contender and the Encore. The first cartridge is the new 20-caliber varmint cartridge, the 204 Ruger; while the second is capable of taking any big-game animal found anywhere in the world. The latter cartridge is the 375 JDJ, designed by J.D. Jones of SSK Industries. J.D. is a longtime friend and the absolute authority when it comes to many things concerned with firearms, especially with single-shot pistol cartridges. The 375 JDJ is to single-shot pistols what the 375 H&H is to bolt-action rifles. It may be larger than necessary for some critters and a little light for others, but in capable hands it will always do the job with authority. If I could have only one–and wouldn't that be terrible–single-shot pistol for hunting big game, it

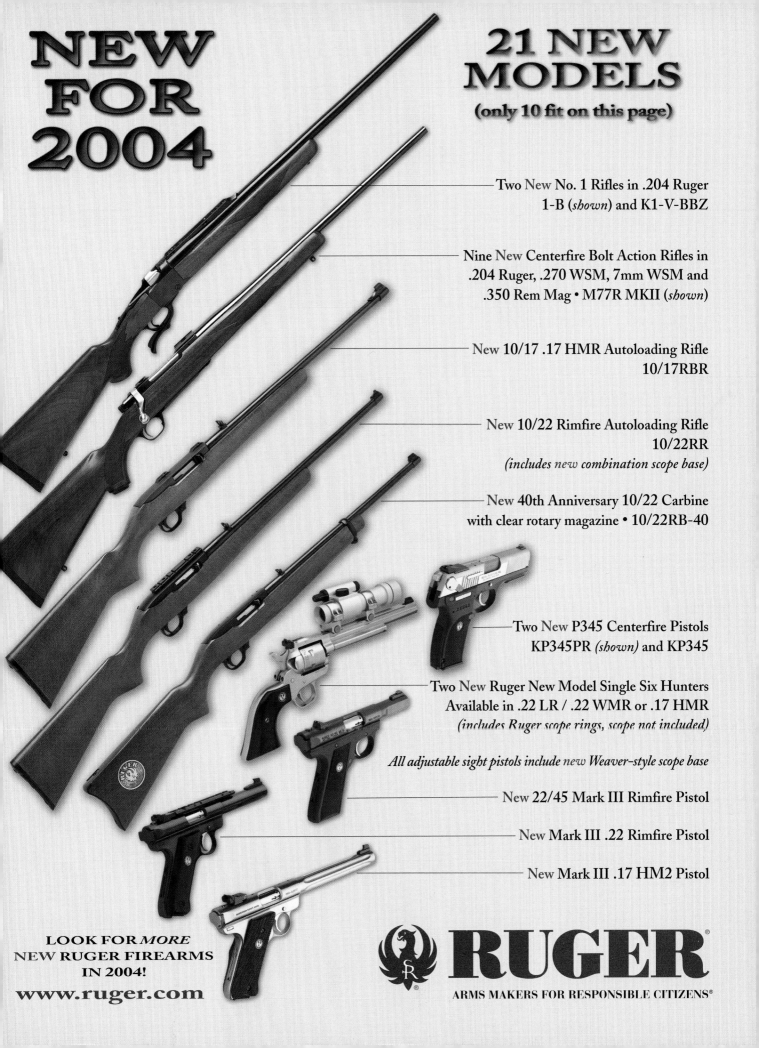

THE MOST ACCLAIMED REVOLVER IN THE WORLD

Day or Night... Dark or Light... Or Anything In-Between.

Trijicon's self-luminous sights and optics guarantee a bright aiming point in any light.

Bright & Tough Night Sights

Our three-dot Night Sights are the most popular illuminated iron sights in the world. The tritium-illuminated sights are the first choice of police, many leading firearms manufacturers, and defense-minded civilians.

ACOG® (Advanced Combat Optical Gunsight)

A combat-proven telescopic sight with a battery-free, tritium-illuminated ranging reticle. The most versatile sighting system in the world and standard equipment for most of the United States military's special forces. Choose from 4 X 32, 3.5 X 35 or 5.5 X 50 magnification.

Compact ACOG®

Precision, any light aiming in a small, lightweight package. Dual illuminated with fiber optics and tritium and totally battery-free. A superior choice for quick response units. Available in 1.5 X 16, 1.5 X 24, 2. X 20 and 3 X 24.

AccuPoint® Riflescope

A dual illuminated sporting scope specifically designed to help hunters take a trophy in any light. The patented triangle-shaped reticle is illuminated by tritium and fiber optics for optimum brightness and contrast in bright light or low light.

Reflex Sight

The fastest, most user-friendly red dot-style sights in the business use a bright amber-colored tritium-illuminated reticle for dark or low-light sighting and a fiber optic system for reducing contrast in bright light. Perfect for some law enforcement applications and competition venues as well as hunting at close or medium ranges. Dot, triangle or chevron-shaped reticle available.

TriPower™ Tactical Sight

The industry's first triple-illuminated sight featuring a tritium-illuminated reticle for a vivid, distinct aiming point...an integrated fiber optic system that adjusts the brightness level of ambient light conditions...and a dependable, on-call battery backup system for crisis-level situations.

Want to improve your shooting in any lighting condition?
We're The Any Light Shooting Specialists.

Trijicon, Inc.
49385 Shafer Ave. P.O. Box 930059
Wixom, MI 48393-0059
Phone: (800) 338-0563   (248) 960-7700
Fax: (248) 960-7725
www.trijicon.com

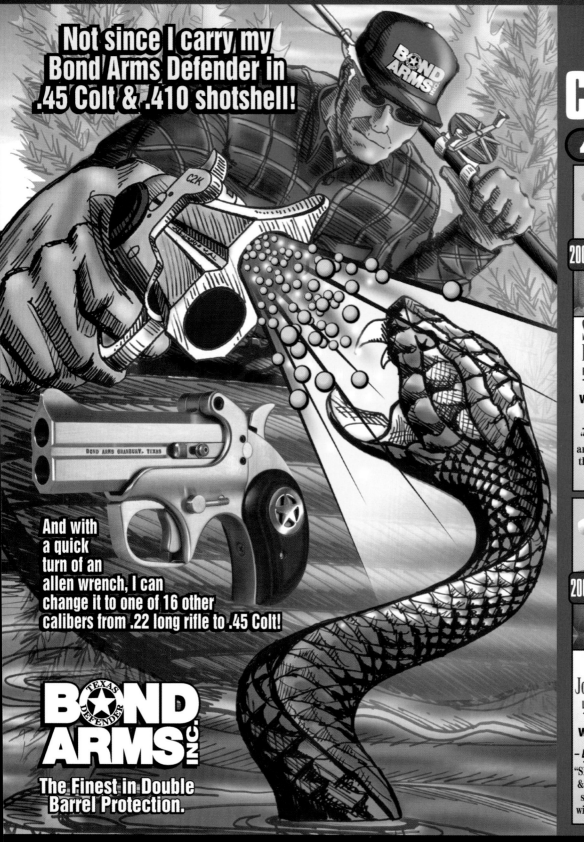

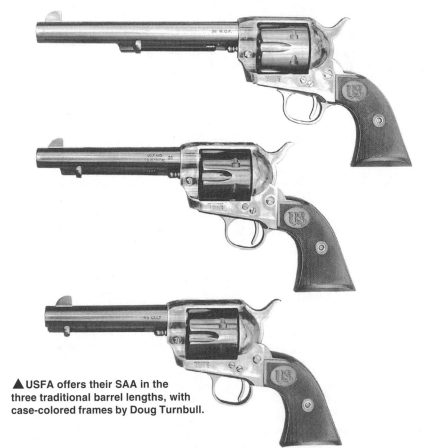

▲USFA offers their SAA in the three traditional barrel lengths, with case-colored frames by Doug Turnbull.

These three "Mystery Cartridges" should be revealed by the time you read this. The first two are 50-caliber for standard-sized single actions, while the Maximum length 45 is for use in stretch-framed, long-cylindered revolvers.

would be chambered in 375 JDJ. I have been using my custom SSK 375 JDJ with great satisfaction for nearly two decades now. The introduction of this cartridge in a standard factory handgun should increase its popularity even more.

United States Firearms (USFA): The first thing most notice about the USFA Single Action Army is the absolutely beautiful finish with the main frame and the hammer beautifully case-colored by Doug Turnbull. Standard grips, of checkered hard rubber with a "US" molded into the top part of the grip, are perfectly fitted to the frame and feel exceptionally good to my hand. Custom grips are available in smooth or checkered walnut, as well as ivory and pearl.

For the past year I have been shooting two USFA SAAs, a 4 3/4-inch 45 Colt and a 7 1/2-inch 38-40. All six chambers on the 45 Colt from USFA measure a uniform and perfect 0.452-inch, and the 38-40 is also uniform and correct at 0.400-inch. Trigger pulls on both six-guns are set at three pounds. Cylinders lock up tight when the hammer is down on an empty chamber, as well as when the hammer is in the cocked position.

All USFA six-guns are available with a V- or square-notch rear sight and a choice of a cross pin or screw-in blackpowder-style cylinder pin latch.

Standard chamberings for USFA single actions are 45 Colt as well as 32-20, 41 Long Colt, 38 Special, 38-40, 44-40, 45 ACP, and 44 Special/44 Russian. The latter can be marked "RUSSIAN AND S&W SPECIAL 44" as early Colt Single Actions were marked. USFA also offers the Rodeo in 45 Colt, 44-40, and 38 Special in 4 3/4-, 5 1/2-, and 7 1/2-inch lengths. This less expensive six-gun is the same basic revolver as the single action army; however, it comes with bead-blasted satin blue finish instead of the beautiful finish of the standard revolver.

Last year, as the switch to all American-made parts was completed, the USFA catalog line was drastically reduced to only traditional single action army six-guns with the three standard barrel lengths. However, this year the Bisley, the Flat-Top Target, and the Omnipotent have all returned with all the parts, finishing, and fitting being totally American.

It has been another most interesting handgun year with many new models and cartridges being offered. It is easy, at least at my age, to wax nostalgic and long for the good old days with hand-fitted double-action revolvers with beautiful bright blue finishes. *(Remember S&W Bright Blue and Colt Royal Blue?)* I still look for such guns at gun shows–especially if offered at bargain prices. We will never see guns like this again. The upside is that with today's machinery and manufacturing processes, guns are better than ever and, relatively speaking, much less expensive. They are stronger, built to tighter tolerances, and in every case in which I have run one of the new production revolvers against one of its counterparts from back in the "good old days", the new gun always wins in the accuracy department. Today's shooters have a wide and varied choice of the best guns ever offered. Yep, it looks like another great six-gunnin' year! ●

Gary Germaine of United States Firearms with a pair of USFA's SAAs.

RIFLE REPORT

by Layne Simpson

Anschutz

LIKE A NUMBER of other companies who build 22 rimfire rifles, Anschutz is, as I write this, feverishly working toward the day when it will begin the delivery of rifles in 17 Mach 2, a co-development of CCI and Hornady. Announced in February of 2004, it is basically the CCI 22 Long Rifle Stinger case necked down. Rated at a muzzle velocity of 2100 fps with a 17-grain bullet, the 17 Mach 2 is said to shoot three inches flatter and deliver 50 percent more energy at 100 yards than the standard-velocity loading of the 22 Long Rifle. How it will fare in the field when pitted against hyper-velocity loadings of the 22 Long Rifle *(such as the CCI Stinger)* remains to be seen. Can the 17 Mach 1 on the 22 Short case or perhaps even the 17 Mach 1/2 on the 22 CB case be far behind?

New sporters from Anschutz for 2004 are the Model 1717DKL with Model 54 action and 23-inch, standard-weight barrel and Model 1517D with a left-hand Model 64 action and heavy 23-inch barrel, both in 17 HMR. Their triggers are set at the factory to pull 34 ounces. The Model 1712 Silhouette Sporter wears no sights, weighs 7.3 pounds and has a relatively light barrel in 22 Long Rifle only.

Armalite

The new AR-10T Ultra Mag from Armalite is chambered for Remington's 300 Short Action Ultra Mag cartridge. It is available as a complete rifle or as a top assembly designed to convert the AR-10 you already own to that powerful cartridge.

Benelli

Last year, the sleek R1 autoloading rifle from Benelli was available in 30-06 and 300 Winchester Magnum. This year, the 308 Winchester chambering has been added to the list but, unfortunately, the 7mm-08 Remington has not.

Ed Brown

I recently examined the new lightweight Damara from Ed Brown and found it to be a very nice rifle. Built on Brown's short action, it has a McMillan fiberglass stock and 22-inch barrel and it weighs just over six pounds. Available chamberings include about anything you can squeeze into a short-action rifle, from the 243 Winchester to the short magnums from Remington and Winchester. You can buy this one with a right- or left-hand action.

Browning

With their racy European styling, the new ShortTrac and LongTrac versions of the BAR autoloader were obviously spooked from the bushes by last year's introduction of the R1 rifle by Benelli. As you might have guessed, one is chambered for short cartridges such as the 243 Winchester, 308 Winchester and the three WSM cartridges in 270, 7mm and 300 calibers while the other is offered in 270 Winchester, 30-06, 7mm Remington Magnum and 300 Winchester Magnum. Both variations have lightweight aluminum receivers and their trigger guards and floorplates are synthetic. Depending on caliber and barrel length, nominal weights range from 6-3/4 to 7-1/2 pounds. Weights for the standard BAR run from 7-1/4 to 8-1/2 pounds.

With its titanium receiver, lightweight 23-inch stainless steel barrel and synthetic stock, the new Mountain Ti version of the A-Bolt rifle is rated at only 5-1/2 pounds. Add a sensible-size scope, a magazine full of cartridges and a lightweight nylon carrying sling and the one you decide to carry up the tallest sheep mount should not weigh much over 7-1/4 pounds. For now, it is available in the three WSM chamberings of 270, 7mm and 300. As other Browning A-Bolts go, the 223 Remington, 223 WSSM and the 25 WSSM are now available in the Hunter, the Varmint

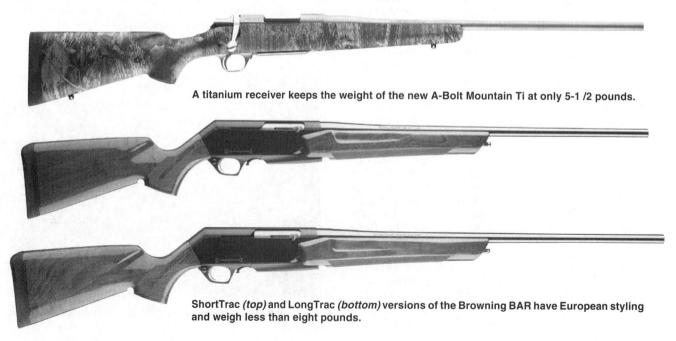

A titanium receiver keeps the weight of the new A-Bolt Mountain Ti at only 5-1 /2 pounds.

ShortTrac *(top)* and LongTrac *(bottom)* versions of the Browning BAR have European styling and weigh less than eight pounds.

Stalker, the Composite Stalker and the Medallion. Why Browning chose to chamber the new 25 WSSM in 22-inch barrels rather than something longer is a question to which I do not have the answer.

Browning's lever-action 22, the BL-22 is now available with a nitride finish on its engraved receiver and octagon barrel. Called the Classic Series, Grade II Octagon, its tubular magazine holds 15 Long Rifles, 17 Longs or 22 Shorts. Its receiver is grooved for scope mounting.

Chipmunk vs. Crickett

A big question on the minds of world-traveled hunters and shooters these past few years has been which is the cutest 22 rimfire rifle—the Chipmunk from Rogue Rifles or the Crickett from Keystone Arms. The Crickett began to pull away in the race when none other than Davey Crickett became its official spokesbug *(quite devastating since this happened not long after Chipmunk spokesrodent, Chipper Chipmunk, hung up his guns and retired)*. Then came a candy-pink laminate stock built especially for girl kids and the Chipmunk started eating even more dust kicked up by the four *(or is it six?)* heels of Davey Crickett. While the spunky Chipmunk may be down, it most certainly is not out of the race and the new .410 shotgun is sure to get plenty of attention from toddling bunny hunters. On top of that, the Chipmunk is also available in 17 HMR and 22 WMR while the Crickett is not. As you may have guessed by now, both of those tiny little rifles are made for tiny little people who consider a length of pull of 11-1/2 inches plenty long. Single-shots both, they weigh 2-1/2 pounds. Barrel length is just over 16 inches and they measure around 30 inches overall. Regardless of what we grownups have to say, only kids and their tremendous buying power will determine in the end which is cutest, the Chipmunk or Crickett.

CZ-USA

New chamberings you will soon see added to the CZ rifle lineup are 17 Remington, 221 Remington Fire Ball, 458 Lott and three WSMs in 270, 7mm and 300 calibers. I particularly like the idea of the 17 Remington in the 527 Varmint with its heavy, 24-inch barrel and Turkish walnut stock. And if that's not enough, "American-pattern" wood stocks are now available on sporter- and varmint-weight rifles in both centerfire and rimfire persuasions. Same goes for the 550 Safari Magnum in two grades of American walnut as well as a tri-color laminate. Another rifle I saw had a Winchester Model 70-style bolt action *(complete with three-position safety)* and from five yards away it even looked a lot like a Winchester Model 70–but it was not a Winchester Model 70. They say it was designed specifically for the families of short magnums introduced during the past few years by Remington and Winchester.

Daisy

Like many who grew up during the very best of times in America, my first rifle was a Daisy, the Red Ryder version to be exact. The Red Ryder offered by Daisy today differs a bit from the one I once used to terrorize the sparrows in our neighborhood but it is close enough to make me yearn for those innocent days of yesteryear. The one I recently shot weighs 2.2 pounds, measures 29 inches overall, holds 650 BBs, has a maximum range of 195 yards *(honest)* and is fully capable of minute-of-tomato soup-can accuracy if you can hold that close. The genuine wood stock of the Model 1938 has Red Ryder galloping across the prairie; put there, no doubt, by a red-hot branding iron. Just like on my old Daisy, the ever-familiar saddle ring with leather thong makes this one easy to tie onto the saddle of your favorite broomstick steed. The Model 1938 has something my old Red Ryder did not have—a crossbolt safety. It also comes in an attractive cardboard box decorated with Old West scenes that would make Red Ryder and his sidekick, Little Beaver, feel right at home on the range. The same rifle is also available in a bubble-pack kit replete with carrying case, shooting glasses, ShatterBlast reactive targets, a supply of PrecisionMax BBs for shooting and a smaller quantity in a tin for collecting. Add one youngster to those ingredients, stir gently, and you will become an instant hero. There was a time when every kid in America wanted a Red Ryder. I'm betting a lot still do. After all—It's a Daisy.

Harrington & Richardson/NEF

The break-action H&R single-shot Handi-Rifle is now available in a varmint version chambered in 22-250. Equally new are both adult and youth rifles in 7mm-08 and stainless steel rifles in 30-06 and 270 Winchester. Then we have the Huntsman Combos. The Pardner and Handi-Rifle sets come with interchangeable shotgun and muzzleloader barrels in 12-gauge and 50-caliber, while the Handi-Rifle set has barrels in 243 Winchester and 50-caliber. Regardless of which you choose, all represent excellent buys and are surprisingly accurate considering their cost. In my report on new rifles from Marlin I tell about taking a nice caribou bull in the Northwest Territories of Canada with a Model 1895 lever action in the 444 chambering. My license allowed me to take two bulls on that hunt so I decided to go after the second one with an H&R Ultra Rifle in 308 Winchester. Like the Marlin lever action, it wore a Burris 3-9x Fullfield II scope. One shot at just under 200 yards was all it took.

Henry Repeating Arms

A knockabout lever-action rifle in 22 rimfire, the Henry is now available with an oversized finger lever, similar to those worn by Winchester rifles used in the past by John Wayne and Chuck Connors to settle the accounts of untold numbers of bad guys. The Model H001L has an 18 1/4-inch barrel, holds 15 Long Rifle cartridges and weighs 5-1/4 pounds. Same goes for the Golden Boy with its "Brasslite" receiver. Other chamberings include 17 HMR and 22 WMR. Henry also offers an economy-grade slide-action 22 with an 18 1/4-inch barrel; it weighs 5-1/2 pounds.

H-S Precision

Long known for its super-accurate *(but relatively heavy)* big-game rifles, H-S Precision now brings us one that no sheep hunter would mind toting up the steepest mountain. Called the ProHunter Lightweight, it weighs 5–1/2 pounds and comes with a right- or left-hand action. Barrel lengths are 20 or 22 inches, depending on caliber and that includes the entire family of Remington and Winchester short magnums. All metal is Teflon-coated for rust resistance.

The 6-1/2 pound Howa Model 1500 Mountain Rifle has a 20-inch barrel in 243 Winchester, 7mm-08 Remington or 308 Winchester.

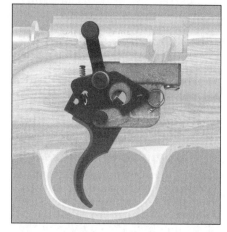

Marlin Model 60DL

Kimber

New from Kimber for 2004 is the Pro Varmint on the Kimber 22 action in 22 Long Rifle and on the Model 84M action in 22-250. Both have stainless steel barrels and laminated wood stocks. The rimfire version has a 20-inch barrel and weighs 6-3/4 pounds while its centerfire mate has a 24-inch barrel and weighs 7-1/4 pounds. The new Rimfire Super from the custom shop comes with a test-target proving it is capable of shooting a 0.400-inch group at 50 yards on an indoor range. Commemorating Kimber's 25th anniversary is the Custom Match Limited Edition in 22 rimfire with 22-inch barrel and a weight of 6-1/2 pounds. Among other very nice things, it has a stock of triple-A grade French walnut, 24-line cut checkering and ebony forend tip.

Legacy Sports International

The 6-1/2 pound Howa Model 1500 Mountain Rifle is available

holds six 480s or five 475s. Nominal weight is seven pounds, same as for rifles in the other three calibers.

The new T-900 fire control system, now on all 900-series Marlin bolt-action single-shots and repeaters in 22 Long Rifle, 22 WMR and 17 HMR, features a wide fingerpiece with serrated surface and a two-position safety lever with positive stops in its *"Safe"* and *"Fire"* positions. The trigger is noticeably smoother than the old design. A red dot at the top of the bolt shroud is exposed when the striker is cocked. Beginning in 2004, the receivers of all Marlin bolt guns will be drilled and tapped for scope mounting. Bases that take Weaver-style rings are available from Marlin, as well as Burris and Warne.

I hunted barren ground caribou in the Northwest Territories of Canada in September of 2003 and, since I was allowed to take two bulls, I decided to double my fun by using a different rifle when hunting each of them. I took the first bull with a Marlin

All Marlin bolt-action 22s now have the new T-900 fire control system.

Model 444 and a handload that pushed the 280-grain Swift A-Frame along at 2200 fps. Realizing I might have no choice but to shoot at relatively long range, I equipped the rifle with a Burris 3-9X Signature scope with the Ballistic Plex reticle. And since my handload averaged around five inches at 300 yards, I decided to chart the trajectory of the Swift bullet in 50-yard increments

with a 20-inch barrel in 243 Winchester, 7mm-08 Remington and 308 Winchester. The action has a hollowed bolt handle knob and lightening cuts along the receiver and bolt shroud for weight reduction. All metal has a dark, non-glare finish and the stock is hardwood with a black, rough-textured finish. With the exception of its 12-5/8 inch length of pull the new Youth Rifle is quite similar to that one. As for new chamberings, the Hunter and Lightning rifles are now available in 25-06 Remington.

Marlin

The New Model Marlin 1895 is now available in five chamberings. Joining the 444 Marlin, 45-70 Government and 450 Marlin are the 480 Ruger and 475 Linebaugh. Called the Model 1895RL, it has an 18 1/2-inch barrel with six-groove rifling with a 1:20 twist and its magazine

The New Model 1895 from Marlin is now available in 480 Ruger and 475 Linebaugh.

Not many people hunt caribou with lever-action rifles these days but the Marlin 1895 in 444 did a great job on this Northwest Territories bull.

Biggest news from Remington is the new Model 502 in 22 rimfire.

out to that range. With the rifle zeroed to place its bullets three inches above the intersection of the crosshairs at 100 yards it was only slightly low at 200. Then by using the first and second tick marks of the special reticle, I could hold dead on at 250 and 300 yards. Knowing the range precisely was important so I took along a Bushnell Yardage Pro Scout laser rangefinder. As it turned out, all that range time prior to the hunt was time well spent. When the Bushnell rangefinder read 248 yards I was as close as I could possibly get–but it was close enough, and I got my bull.

Remington

Biggest news from Remington for 2004 is the introduction of a new bolt-action 22-rimfire sporter called the Model 504. It gets its name from the old 500 series of Remington rifles, along with the year of its introduction. Since I have filed a "Testfire" report elsewhere I will say no more on the 504 here and now.

For several years now I have urged Remington decision-makers to offer the 8x57mm Mauser chambering in the limited edition Model 700 Classic. After all, what could be more classic than an old cartridge that continues to be more popular among American hunters than a whole slew of American-designed cartridges. I finally get my wish in 2004. Number 24 in a series that started back in 1981 with the 7x57mm Mauser, the Model 700 Classic in 8x57mm has a 24-inch barrel and weighs just over seven pounds.

Remington describes the new short-action Model 700 LVSF (Light Varmint, Stainless-Fluted) as the ideal walking varmint rifle. With a weight of less than seven pounds, along with 17 Remington, 221 Fire-Ball, 223 Remington and 22–250 chambering options, few would argue. The 22-inch medium-heavy stainless steel barrel measures a nominal 0.657-inch at the muzzle and has six lightening flutes for

weight reduction. Other features include a stainless-steel action with blind magazine, pillar-bedded receiver, semi-beavertail forearm and R3 recoil pad.

They call it the Model 700 CDL (Classic Deluxe) but to me it looks like a reintroduction of the original Model 700 Mountain Rifle. Which is okay by me because the Model 700 MR is one of the best-looking, best-handling and best-feeling big-game rifles I have ever carried in the field. The new version does have a longer barrel: 24 inches in 243 Winchester, 7mm-08, 270 Winchester and 30-06, and 26 inches in 7mm Remington Magnum, 7mm Remington Ultra Mag, 300 Winchester Magnum and 300 Remington Ultra Mag. Weights run around 7-1/2 pounds in standard chamberings and 7-3/4 pounds for the magnums. All metal has a satin blued finish and the classically styled stock has cut checkering, black forearm tip and gripcap and Remington's own R3 recoil pad.

The Model 700 Titanium, which is America's first affordable rifle with a titanium receiver, is now available in a short-action magnum version with 24-inch barrel in 7mm and 300 Remington Short Action Ultra Mag. Nominal weight is 6-3/8 pounds which means that its field-ready weight with scope, lightweight carrying sling and loaded magazine should not greatly exceed eight pounds. That's darned light for a rifle capable of squeezing maximum performance from Remington's two ultra-short magnum cartridges.

For the fourth consecutive year, a portion of the proceeds from the sale of a special edition of the Model 700 rifle will go to the Rocky Mountain Elk Foundation. Called the Model 700 BDL/SS Camo, it is offered only with a 26-inch barrel in 300 Winchester Magnum. The barreled action is stainless steel while the synthetic stock wears the Hardwoods Gray HD camo pattern from Real-tree. Other features include a laser engraving on the hinged floorplate, and the highly efficient R3 recoil pad. Nominal weight is 7-1/2 pounds.

The original Model 600 Magnum was available in 350 and 6.5 Remington Magnum so it stands to reason that the latest version of that old classic called the Model 673 be chambered for the same cartridges.

A super-light rifle like the Remington Model 700 Titanium in 243 Winchester is just the thing to have when hunting chamois at 10,000 feet in the Southern Alps of New Zealand.

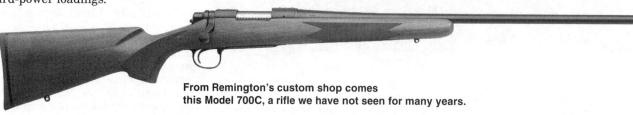

Bolt-action *(top)* and single-shot *(bottom)* rifles from Ruger are now chambered for a new cartridge called 204 Ruger.

Remington did the 350 last year and this year the 6.5 Magnum has been added, along with a resurrection of the old factory load with a 120-grain bullet at 3200 fps. I once owned a Model 660 in 6.5 Magnum and believe me when I say when it comes to hunting game the size of deer and pronghorn antelope, the 6.5 will do anything the 270 Winchester can do– and it will do it from a short-action rifle. And just as I predicted last year, you can now buy a Model 673 in 308 Winchester as well. Who knows, we may eventually see the 7mm-08 added to its list of options.

Considered by many who own it to offer the most performance for the least amount of money, the Model 710 is now available in a magnum version with a 24-inch barrel in 7mm Remington Magnum or 300 Winchester Magnum. Its detachable magazine holds three rounds and the rifle comes with a Bushnell 3-9X Sharpshooter scope riding up top. Nominal weight is 7-1/4 pounds.

As its name implies, the Model Seven YS (Youth Synthetic) has a synthetic stock and a 12 3/8-inch length of pull for short arms. Surface texturing on the grip and forearm are just the thing for slippery hands and the R3 recoil pads tames what little recoil is generated by the 223 Remington, 243 Winchester, and 7mm-08 cartridges. The satin-blued barrel is 20 inches long and nominal weight is 6-1/4 pounds. A long-action version with a 22-inch barrel in 270 Winchester and 30-06 might represent the best of all deals. The young hunter can start out with Remington's new Managed Recoil loadings of those two cartridges and then after a few deer seasons have come and gone he or she can graduate to standard-power loadings.

I enjoy hunting with vintage firearms so you can bet the smile on my face reached from ear to ear when I was recently invited on a mule deer hunt in Colorado and told I could use any Remington firearm so long as I teamed it up with Remington ammo loaded with the relatively new Core-Lokt Ultra bullet. So I opted for a Model 700 BDL I bought in 1963, about a year after the Model 700 was introduced. It is chambered for the 7mm Remington Magnum *(which was also introduced in 1962)* and if I told you about all the times, good and bad, that old rifle and I have shared in the field, there would be room left for nothing else in this issue of GUN DIGEST. My old Model 700 averaged close to an inch for three-shot groups at 100 yards with the 140-grain CLU load, not too shabby for a 40-year-old rifle with hundreds of rounds of wear on its barrel. It still works nicely on mule deer too, or I should say it does when it is fed ammo with the Core-Lokt Ultra bullet. One shot at about 150 yards did it. I still like that rifle a lot and I am beginning to like the new Remington bullet equally well.

Another old Model 700 I hunted with during 2003 was one of the first built by Remington in 416 Magnum several months before that cartridge was officially introduced. Remington took us and our new 416 Magnum rifles to Alaska where we each shot a gigantic moose. All were one-shot kills. Sixteen years later, in 2003, I took that same rifle to Australia where it accounted for one very large Asiatic buffalo, again with a single shot. One of the things I like about a rifle in 416 Remington Magnum is that it does not use up a lot of ammo.

Rifles, Incorporated

Among my proudest possessions is a trio of Lightweight Strata rifles built by Lex Webernick on Remington Model 700 actions in 257 STW, 6.5 STW and 7mm STW. Those rifles weigh around five pounds each. Even lighter at 4-1/2 pounds is the Titanium Strata built on the Model 700 titanium action in most chamberings up to and including the 300 Weatherby Magnum. One of those rifles on the short action in 243 Winchester, 6mm Remington or 257 Roberts would be especially nice for rough-country deer hunting and, in 7mm-08 Remington, would tough to beat for sheep hunting. Moving on up in weight to 5-3/4 pounds we have the Lightweight 70 on the Winchester Model 70 action. You can order this one in most any commercial chambering up to 375 H&H Magnum. With its slightly heavier barrel and synthetic stock, the Classic weighs 6-1/2 pounds and is available in the same calibers. When I start planning my next trip to Africa my plans might just include the Safari on the Model 70 action in 416 Remington Magnum. It weighs 8-1/2 pounds, has express-style open sights and is also available in 375 H&H Magnum, 458 Winchester Magnum and 458 Lott. Last but not least is the Master Series in most calibers up to the 300 Remington Ultra Mag. This rifle weighs 7-3/4 pounds and is guaranteed to shoot half-minute-of-angle with loads developed for it by Webernick.

Rossi

Last year, Rossi introduced its "Matched Pairs" combo set version of its single-shot gun with both centerfire rifle and shotgun barrels. This year, you can buy a three-barrel set with those–plus a muzzleloader barrel. One combination is made up of barrels in 17 HMR, 270 Winchester and 50-caliber. In case you are not familiar with the Rossi, it is an economy-grade,

From Remington's custom shop comes this Model 700C, a rifle we have not seen for many years.

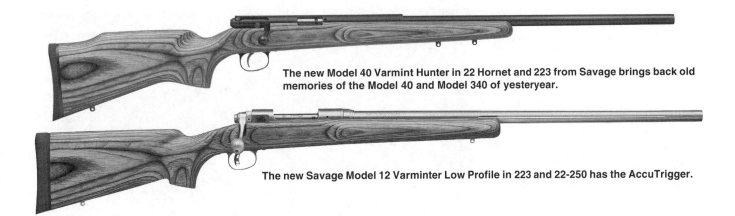

The new Model 40 Varmint Hunter in 22 Hornet and 223 from Savage brings back old memories of the Model 40 and Model 340 of yesteryear.

The new Savage Model 12 Varminter Low Profile in 223 and 22-250 has the AccuTrigger.

break-action, knockabout gun with exposed hammer (replete with hammer-block safety). To break down its barrel for loading and unloading you simply press down on a lever located at the side of its receiver.

Ruger

Biggest news from Ruger is the 204 Ruger chambering. Developed by–and presently loaded only by–Hornady, the 204 Ruger pretty much duplicates the performance of the 223 Remington when that cartridge is loaded with a 40-grain bullet. The new chambering is slated for availability in three Model 77 Mark II variations and two versions of the No. 1 single-shot. Also new from Ruger is a 40th Anniversary edition of the 10/22 carbine and a "rifle" version of the 10/22 carbine. The former will be manufactured only during 2004 and comes with a special transparent rotary magazine replete with red rotor. The latter has a 20-inch barrel and is available in 22 Long Rifle and 17 HMR.

Sako

New Model 75 variants from Sako for 2004 include the Hunter and Stainless Synthetic in 270 WSM and 300 WSM. Three additional chambering options for the Model 75 Deluxe are 416 Remington Magnum and the two just-mentioned Winchester shorty magnums. Also new is the Custom Single-Shot in 308 Winchester with heavy, fluted, stainless-steel barrel, laminated wood stock replete with beavertail forearm. Why it is not also available in 22-250 and 243 Winchester is a question Sako and Beretta officials do not–at the moment–have an answer for. What is the most handsome of all Sako rifles is a question I have the answer for. It is the Anniversary Limited Edition in 375 H&H Magnum. But then, at a price of $16,500 it cannot be anything but handsome.

Savage

The Model 40 and Model 340 rifles once offered by Savage were economy-grade rifles, a description that fits the new Model 40 Varmint Hunter equally well. It has a tubular receiver and is available in 223 and 22 Hornet. The 24-inch, heavy barrel is button-rifled and it free-floats in a laminated wood stock replete with Monte Carlo at the rear and beavertail forearm up front. A third sling swivel stud on the forearm is correctly positioned for use with a Harris folding bipod. The fact that this rifle does not wear Savage's relatively new AccuTrigger is to be expected, considering its low price.

I am no great fan of muzzle brakes but if ever I become one the adjustable brake from Savage is the one my rifles will wear. Twist the brake one way to open its gas ports and your rifle is ready for a shooting session at the benchrest or practice range. Twist it in the opposite direction and you are ready to head for the field. The AMB is presently available on the Model 116SAK and the Safari Express. The relatively new AccuTrigger is something Savage bolt guns have needed for a very long time and I am glad to see it standard issue on practically every model variation, including the in-line muzzleloader. Weight of pull on most rifles is owner-adjustable from 2-1/2 to 6 pounds, although the triggers on the varmint and law enforcement series can be adjusted down to 24 ounces. Latest rifle to wear the new trigger is the Model 12 Varminter Low Profile with its 26-inch heavy fluted stainless-steel barrel, in 223 and 22-250.

Schuerman Arms, Ltd.

For the second year in a row, the Model SA40 from Schuerman Arms has received my vote as the bolt-action rifle with the smoothest action. Somewhat like the Colt Sauer rifle of yesteryear, it has

three pivoting locking lugs–but in this case they are located quite close to the front of the bolt. The bolt glides to and fro in the receiver like hot grease on glass. It is available in about any chambering you can think of, from 22-250 to 416 Remington Magnum.

Taurus

The new pump-action Thunderbolt from Taurus is a Brazilian-made knockoff of the old Colt Lightning in 45 Colt only. It is available in two styles: Model C45BR in blued steel and Model C45SSR in polished stainless. Both have 26-inch barrels, 14-round magazines, adjustable open sights and hardwood stocks with curved steel buttplates. Weight is just over eight pounds.

SIGARMS

Several custom options are now available on Blaser rifles. The R93 Lexus Plus, as an example, comes with a black receiver and a choice of sideplate finishes, including color casehardening by Doug Turnbull. The R93 Synthetic wears a Mossy Oak camo finish and the R93/SRHS (Steel Receiver Heavy Safari) has an "American-style" stock and heavy barrel in 375 H&H and 416 Remington Magnum.

Springfield, Inc.

The SOCOM 16 is the latest version of Springfield's M1A rifle, with a 16-inch barrel in 308 Winchester. Other features include a muzzle brake, hooded front sight, synthetic stock and forward-positioned scope mount.

Thompson/Center

The Classic in 22 Long Rifle from T/C has quickly earned a reputation for excellent accuracy. As autoloaders go, the one I have been shooting for about a year is second in accuracy only to custom 10/22s built by Volquartsen, Clark, Briley and a few others. On top of that, with its blued steel and real walnut, it looks the way many of us like to see a rifle look. Those who march to a different drummer will like the looks of a new variation called the Silver Lynx. Even I will have to admit its stainless steel barreled action and synthetic stock make a lot of sense for rough-weather hunting. The 17 Hornady Mach 2 is a new chambering for this rifle.

The G2 Contender rifle will be offered in 375 JDJ and 204 Ruger and the Encore rifle is now available in 280 Remington, 375 JDJ, and 405 Winchester. Also available from Thompson/Center is 375 JDJ ammo loaded with a 220-grain flatnose bullet at about 2200 fps in Encore and Contender pistols, and 2300 to 2400 fps in rifle versions of those guns. The new carbine variation of the Encore 209x50 muzzleloader has a 20-inch barrel.

I had never hunted with the Encore in anything except its handgun form until the performance I was getting out of a 26-inch custom shop barrel in 6mm-06 and the new 90-grain Swift Scirocco bullet indicated it was time I did. My handload consisted of cases formed by simply necking down Remington 25-06 brass, the Remington 9-1/2M primer and 58.0 grains of H4831SC for a velocity of 3450 fps. So I took the rig antelope hunting. I had been chasing that particular New Mexico pronghorn on foot all morning long of the last day and when it suddenly paused momentarily from chasing a doe, I dropped to the prone position and rested the rifle atop my daypack. I was zeroed three inches high at 100 yards and when the trusty Bushnell laser rangefinder indicated 365 yards away, I held about four inches high and about as much into the light breeze I felt against the side of my face and squeezed the trigger. The bullet struck, caught the buck in the shoulder, dropping it where it stood. After seeing how much damage that tiny 90-grain bullet did to all that shoulder bone I decided then and there that I would be using Scirocco bullets on more hunts in the future. I later used that same Encore receiver and stock along with a 205x50 muzzleloader barrel to take a 140s-class whitetail while hunting with Judd Cooney in Iowa.

A 26-inch barrel in 6mm-06 for my Encore rifle from the T/C custom shop and the new 90-grain Scirocco from Swift Bullets were the perfect combination for this New Mexico pronghorn.

Tikka

The T3 Lite Stainless is my favorite Tikka big-game rifle. It has a stainless-steel barreled action, a black synthetic stock and weighs a mere 6-1/4 pounds in standard chamberings, and 6-1/2 pounds in the magnums. Barrel lengths are 22-1/2 and 24-1/2 inches. Chambering options range from the 223 Remington to the 338 Winchester Magnum. My pick for this rifle is the 7mm-08 Remington. Latest in the lineup is the T3 Laminated Stainless with those same barrel lengths and calibers. Just as new is the T3 Varmint with synthetic stock and heavy 23-1/2 inch blued or stainless steel barrel in 223 Remington, 22-250 and 308. The shape of the stock on this one makes it just about ideal for shooting over sandbags. According to the catalog, no T3 rifle is allowed to depart Finland and head our way until it has fired a one-inch, 3-shot group at 100 yards.

U.S. Firearms

One of the more interesting firearms I have seen lately is the slide-action Lightning Rifle in 45 Colt, 44-40 Winchester and 38-40 Winchester from United States Firearms. Similar in appearance to the Colt Lightning of yesteryear, it is available with a 20- or 26-inch barrel and wears a walnut stock with curved steel buttplate. The 15-round magazine of the rifle will surely make this one a winner among cowboy action shooters. A fancy-grade version with half-octagon barrel, figured wood and pistol grip-style stock is also available. If what they say about it being made in America is true, every would-be cowpoke in America owes it to himself to sell his foreign-made replica to some unsuspecting greenhorn and buy one of these.

USRAC

U.S. Repeating Arms has announced the availability of

Thompson/Center's new Silver Lynx version of its Classic 22 autoloader is now available in 17 Hornady Mach 2.

Tom Volquartsen's new super-accurate centerfire autoloader is initially chambered to 204 Ruger and 223 Remington.

grain TNT. I have not tried Tom's new switch-barrel gun in 17 HMR and 22 WMR but I plan to this summer and expect it to be superbly accurate. Its two barrels are quickly switched in mere seconds by loosening a collar just in front of the receiver. Volquartsen will be chambering his rifles for the new 17 Mach 2 and will also offer a switch-barrel rifle with one barrel in that caliber and the other barrel in 22 Long Rifle. He has also moved into the centerfire field with a new super-accurate, semiautomatic rifle chambered for the 223 Remington and 204 Ruger.

Weatherby

Who'd ever have thought we'd see a Weatherby big-game rifle with a fully adjustable trigger priced at $476? That's retail for the Vanguard Synthetic and I've seen them go for a bit less. The one in 22-250 I took on a deer hunt in Texas proved to be better than accurate enough with Federal Premium ammo loaded with the 55-grain Bear Claw bullet. The latest Vanguard synthetic stock is the Monte Carlo style and it is injection-molded of lightweight composite materials for maximum durability and stability. Also new for 2004 is the Vanguard Sporter with walnut stock replete with rosewood forend tip, 18 lines-per-inch cut checkering and a nice rubber recoil pad. It has a 24-inch barrel and is chambered for a variety of cartridges. Both new variations have Monte Carlo-style stocks simply because a Weatherby doesn't look or feel like a Weatherby unless it has a Monte Carlo stock. Others have attempted to copy the design but nobody has managed to capture the true essence of the Monte Carlo stock like Weatherby.

Up until now the Vanguard has been available in 223 Remington, 22-250, 243 Winchester, 270 Winchester, 308 Winchester, 30-06, 7mm Remington Magnum, 300 Winchester Magnum, 300 Winchester Short Magnum, 300 Weatherby Magnum and 338 Winchester Magnum. A new chambering this year is the 257 Magnum—which just happens to be one of the most popular Weatherby cartridges. Loaded to respective

Winchester's new 25 WSSM cartridge in three Model 70 Ultimate Shadow variations, blued, stainless and camo. Oddly enough, all have 22-inch barrels. The new chambering is also available in the Classic Featherweight and it too has a too-short barrel. In case you are not familiar with the 25 WSSM, it is a super-short magnum capable of duplicating the 25-06 Remington in a short-action rifle. Like the old 25-06, the new 25 WSSM will be seen at its best when used in barrels no shorter than 24 inches.

Those who shoot from the left shoulder will surely be pleased to learn that the Featherweight and Sporter versions of the Model 70 now come with the bolt handle over on their side. The left-hand Featherweight is available in three WSM chamberings: 270, 7mm and 300, while Sporter options include those three, plus 270 Winchester, 30-06, 7mm Remington Magnum and 300 Winchester Magnum. Believe it

or not, USRAC now offers seven variations of the Model 9410 with the Semi-Fancy Traditional being the latest. It gets its name from—you guessed it—its stock of semi-fancy walnut. The latest version of the Model 94 lever action is called the Timber *(who comes up with these names?)*. It has an 18-inch ported barrel in 450 Marlin and, even more interesting, it comes from the factory wearing an aperture sight.

Volquartsen Custom

I have shot Tom Volquartsen's rifles enough to become thoroughly convinced that they have no peer when it comes to squeezing maximum accuracy from autoloaders. The one in 22 Long Rifle I own shoots five-shot groups at 50 yards averaging just over 1/4-inch with Remington/Eley ammunition. The other rifle in 22 WMR will consistently shoot five bullets inside 3/4-inch at 100 yards with Federal ammo loaded with the Speer 30-

The Weatherby Vanguard wears a new Monte Carlo style stock and is now available in 257 Weatherby Magnum.

This Vanguard, with its pillar-bedded Outfitter stock, is available from Weatherby's custom shop.

velocities of 3825, 3600 and 3400 fps with 87-, 100- and 117-grain bullets, it also just happens to be the fastest 25-caliber factory cartridge available. I simply cannot imagine a better long-range antelope/deer/caribou/sheep/goat rifle for the money than the Weatherby Vanguard in 257 Weatherby Magnum.

For those who simply cannot be satisfied by an off-the-shelf rifle, the Weatherby custom shop offers a number of modifications to the Vanguard. They include hand-bedded synthetic stocks in various camo patterns, replete with pillar bedding. Special metal finishes such as black Teflon and titanium nitride are also available.

One of my very best hunts ever took place in August of 2003 when I hunted Dall sheep in the Wrangell mountain range of Alaska with outfitter Terry Overly of Pioneer Outfitters (907-734-0007). I took a very nice ram on the seventh day with a Weatherby Super Big GameMaster in 280 Remington. Wearing a Zeiss 3-9X scope, a

I took this Dall sheep with a Weatherby Super Big GameMaster in 280 Remington while hunting in the Wrangell mountain range of Alaska with outfitter Terry Overly.

This rifle, along with another just like it, raised $40,000 for the National High School Rodeo Association.

The Winchester Model 70 Ultimate Shadow comes in three variations: blued *(top)*, stainless *(middle)*, and camouflage *(bottom)*.

lightweight Weatherby nylon sling and a magazine full of cartridges, the entire outfit weighed just 7-1/2 pounds. It was a tough hunt but I loved every minute of it and I would go back tomorrow if given the opportunity. I especially appreciated the lightweight of the Weatherby rifle on that hunt. It proved to be tough as nails, too. Mine lost a lot of its finish on rocks during many steep climbs but it and its scope managed to hold zero perfectly. My hunting partner also took his ram with a Super Big GameMaster, but in 240 Weatherby Magnum. When his horse fell and rolled over the rifle three times we both thought it was a goner, but it held its zero perfectly. That's the kind of rifle you most definitely want to be carrying in

country where the nearest gunsmith is hundreds of miles away.

Before leaving the subject of things Weatherby I must mention that I survived another cold winter hunting season in large part due to the warmth of excellent wool clothing sold by this company. Its most severe test of 2003 came during a muzzleloader hunt for deer in Iowa. Sitting on a deer stand all day long in temperatures that drop below zero is not very high up on my list of fun things to do and had I not been wearing extremely warm wool clothing I could not have done it. I managed to survive by wearing the Double Yoke Shirt, the Heavyweight Parka and the Late Season Cargo Pant over several layers of long underwear. Anytime it snowed or

the wind blew I wore a Browning rain jacket and pant on the outside. I also wore the Weatherby Heavyweight Gloves with chemical warmers placed inside. Like Ralphie's little brother in "The Christmas Story", I had on so much clothing I could hardly lower my arms but I stayed warm and just as important, I got my buck. ●

NOTE: Autographed copies of Layne's full-color, hardback books, "Shotguns and Shotgunning" and "Rifles and Cartridges For Large Game", are available for $39.95 plus $6 for shipping and handling each from High Country Press, 306 Holly Park Lane, Dept. GD, Simpsonville, SC 29681. Also available is a softcover edition of his "The Custom 1911 Pistol" for $30.95 plus $4 s&h.

Winchester Model 94 Timber.

Winchester Model 9410 Semi-Fancy Traditional.

SHOTGUN UPDATE

by John Haviland

IN 2004 SHOTGUN companies have added refinements and camouflage patterns to their existing lines of guns, with Browning leading the way with its new Cynergy over/under that incorporates a new locking and trigger system—all wrapped up in futuristic styling. Meanwhile, the 16-gauge is continuing its comeback with four new guns this year.

Beretta

The Silver Pigeon III has more extensive floral and scroll decorations and hunting scenes on its frame than the Silver Pigeon S and II. The Pigeon III features ducks and pheasants in flight on the 12-gauge and quail and woodcock on the 20- and 28-gauge guns. A TRU-GLO fiber-optic front sight is standard. For about $800 more, the Silver Pigeon V showcases the embellishments of a color case-hardened frame and gold inlays of ducks in flight and flushing pheasants on the 12-gauge gun, or quail and grouse on the 20 and 28. High-grade wood finishes the guns.

The AL391 Urika and A391 Xtrema 3.5 go discrete with MAX-4 HD camo on their synthetic stocks. The A391 Xtrema 3.5 autoloader Turkey Package comes in several camo patterns, with a Weaver base for optical sights, TRU-GLO

fiber-optic sights, sling and a ported extended turkey choke tube.

DT10 Trident line has added the L Sporting 12-gauge. The gun features floral engraving and fancy walnut. Like all Trident guns, it can be ordered with a palm swell on the left side of the grip for left-hand shooters.

The White Onyx Sporting 12-gauge joins the 686 line of sporting over/unders, distinguishing itself with a nickel-alloy finish on the receiver with a jeweled surface. An oiled finish and schnabel forearm finish the gun.

Benelli

The light weight and recoil-operating system of Benelli's Super Black Eagle and M1 shotguns have always kicked more than gas-operated guns. Benelli has addressed that concern with its new ComforTech system that it claims reduces recoil by 30 percent. The ComforTech system reduces recoil three ways: with a gel

recoil butt pad, gel pad on the comb and 11 gel inserts placed diagonally in the buttstock that absorb recoil and also allow the buttstock to flex.

To determine how well the Comfo-Tech system worked, I first shot the old M1 and then the new M2 with the ComforTech system at clay targets with Federal's Gold Medal Target shells firing 1-1/8 ounces of shot. The M1's recoil built to a sharp snap against my cheek and shoulder, then trailed off. The ComforTech system incorporated in the M2 removed that jolt, and recoil was more of a long push. Switching my concentration to the clay targets, I noticed the M2's muzzle jump was also somewhat less than that of the old M1.

Shooting the Benelli M2 12-gauge in the Arkansas swamps.

▲The new Benelli M4 shotgun is available with MAX4 camouflage covering the entire gun.

The new Benelli Super Black Eagle II features the ComforTech recoil reduction system; the synthetic stock comes plain or covered in HD Timber camouflage.

The ComforTech system is available on the new Benelli M4 Field with synthetic stock. Other features include a wide loop trigger guard, dimpled surface on the grip; a set of shims between the receiver and buttstock adjusts comb height.

The new Benelli M2 shotgun is available with Timber camouflage covering the entire gun.

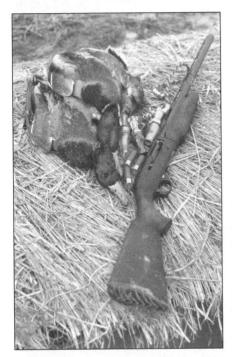

Benelli M2 took these Arkansas mallards.

The ComforTech system is available on the Benelli new Super Black Eagle II, M2 and the SuperSport. These three new guns have additional features:

* A wider loop trigger guard allows easier access for a gloved finger.
* AirTouch is a dimpled surface molded on the grip that provides a sure hold even in the wettest day in the duck marsh.
* A set of shims between the receiver and buttstock adjusts comb height. Adjusting the steel recoil rod in the buttstock tailors buttstock cast.
* A new design adds more flats and flowing lines to the receiver. The new forearm has a pear-shape to its belly to fill the palm of your hand and a full-length scallop along the top for fingers to grip, allowing a sure grip anywhere along the forend.

* A stainless steel recoil tube in the buttstock is corrosion-resistant and is easily removed for cleaning by detaching the gel recoil pad and removing the lock nut.

Bill Hanus Birdguns

Hanus is selling a limited run of Browning Citori Lightning Feather over/unders in 16-gauge. The gun features a round knob, half-pistol grip and aluminum receiver with a steel breech face. The guns weigh about six pounds. Barrels are 26 or 28 inches, and back-bored with chromed chambers. Browning furnishes Improved Cylinder, Modified and Full screw-in choke tubes. Hanus adds two Skeet chokes and a bottle of Colonial Arms Choke Tube Lube.

The 28-gauge Bill Hanus Birdgun model over/under is built on B. Rizzini's new small frame and weighs only five pounds, 12 ounces. It's stocked in two configurations: 28-inch barrels choked Skeet 1/Skeet 2, or with 26-inch barrels and screw-in chokes. Cylinder, Skeet, Improved Cylinder, Modified and Full choke tubes are included. A custom .410 is also available. These guns feature a schnabel forend and a half- or semi-pistol grip, with an initial plate in the butt stock. All the guns come with snap caps, a bottle of Clenzoil and cloth protective sheaths in a lockable case.

Boss & Company

Boss & Company's roots in shotgun-making date back to 1773 when William Boss began his gun-making apprenticeship in Birmingham, England. In 1891 John Robertson took over the business and added to the reputation of Boss by inventing the famous Boss single trigger in 1894, the Boss ejector in 1898 and an over-and-under gun in 1909. Boss still makes guns today and one of their side-by-sides will set you back at least $55,000 and an over/under $75,000. Gary Clark manned the Boss booth at the 2004 SHOT Show in Las Vegas to show a few of Boss's best guns. But mainly, Clark was there to determine what features Americans want and like in a shotgun in hopes of entering the American market. "We have started making designs of these guns so they can be produced on CNC machines and that has enabled us to reduce the price to around $10,000," Clark said.

Send Clark your ideas of what Americans want in a shotgun to: mail@Bossguns.com.

Boss over/under.

Boss side-by-side.

Browning over/under Cynergy.

has a HiViz TriComp sight mounted on a 26-, 28- or 30-inch barrel.

Franchi

The new Model 712 (12-gauge) and 720 (20-gauge) autoloaders have a more rounded receiver top than the established 612 and 620s. The 712 and 720 wood stock models also wear the Franchi WeatherCoat, which provides a water-resistant finish with matching blued metal. A synthetic stock in black or several camo patterns is also available with a matte metal finish. The 712 has a 24-, 26- or 28-inch barrel and three screw-in choke tubes. The 712 weighs a light seven pounds. The 720 has all the same features as the 712, but weighs six pounds. The 720 Short Stock has length of pull shortened 1-1/2 inches.

The Alcione over/under Field Classic has a blued receiver. The SX Classic has a blued frame with gold inlays of pheasants and quail.

Legacy Sports

The Escort line of Field Hunter pump and semi-auto guns will be covered in Mossy Oak Shadow Grass and Obsession camo. In a few months, all models in the Escort line will add a lightweight 20-gauge. The Escort semi-auto Aim-Guard 12 gauge has a 20-inch Cylinder-bore barrel with a five-shot magazine and studs for a sling. A dovetail milled in the top of the receiver accepts various sights.

Ithaca

Ithaca is celebrating its 125th anniversary with a 125-gun edition of the Model 37 pump shotgun. The guns feature a walnut stock and forearm with 22 lines per inch checkering, engraving on the blued receiver that depicts Ithaca's history and products and a 26-inch ventilated rib barrel with a set of interchangeable choke tubes. To further customize the gun, length of pull can be chosen, a medallion

Browning

I knew Browning's Cynergy shotgun was something special when the Perazzi people showed up to study the shotgun at the Browning booth during the SHOT Show last February. Browning states the Cynergy has the lowest profile of any over/under shotgun. That was partially accomplished by a trigger system similar to a rifle. The firing pin springs lay forward of the trigger and a "Reverse Striker," as Browning calls it, reverses the springs' energy to power the firing pins. Doing away with hammers to hit the firing pins meant the Cynergy's profile could be lowered. The gun's MonoLock Hinge also makes the receiver more compact. The Cynergy's barrels pivot on a pair of C-shaped humps in the receiver that lock into matching cuts in the monoblock. "The MonoLock Hinge pivots on significantly more surface area... resulting in less wear over time," according to Browning.

The Cynergy's butt pad is odd-looking, to say the least. But the Inflex Recoil Pad soaks up recoil like a shock absorber. Browning states the pad and the ported barrels reduce felt recoil by 25 percent. Three pad lengths are available in 1/2-inch increments to adjust length of pull. A 1/4-inch spacer further regulates length of pull.

The Cynergy's styling is based on straight lines. The front of the trigger guard, back and front of the forearm, receiver outline, checkering pattern and lines cut here and there in the stocks are all straight lines. Its appearance grows on you, after awhile.

The Cynergy is available with wood or synthetic stock, in Field and Sporting models. The synthetic stock also has an adjustable comb.

The Cynergy will not replace Browning's Citori. The Citori Lightning, White Lightning and Gran Lightning have new engraving patterns on their receivers. The Citori XS Special target gun features a light contour and ported barrels with ventilated side rib. An adjustable comb and Triple Trigger System, which slightly adjusts length of pull, fits the gun to you.

The BT-99 Micro joins the two other BT-99 single-barrel target guns. The Micro has a 13 3/4-inch length of pull and six ounces shaved off the weight of the regular BT-99 to better fit smaller shooters. Barrels are 30 or 32 inches.

The Gold Evolve autoloader differs from the standard Gold with a slightly altered receiver, magazine cap and full checkering pattern and sculpting to the forearm that provide a sure grip. The Evolve also

The Escort Turkey pump gun wears a 24-inch barrel with FH TriViz sights and a polymer stock covered with Mossy Oak Break-up camo.

The Escort pump Hunter wears a 28-inch barrel threaded for choke tubes, and a black polymer stock.

The Aimguard pump is designed for personal defense, and is fitted with a 20-inch Cylinder-bore barrel, 5-shot magazine, and a dovetail rib on the receiver for mounting accessory sights.

The 12-gauge Field Hunter weighs seven pounds, and is fitted with a 28-inch barrel threaded for choke tubes, and a synthetic stock.

inlaid in the stock and your name or initials engraved upon the receiver.

For slug shooters, Ithaca has a rifled 24-inch barrel with a 1:34 twist that fits Remington, Browning and Benelli shotguns. The barrels have either a steel cantilever scope mount or TRUGLO fiber-optic sights. Ithaca states two-inch groups at 100 yards should not be uncommon.

Last year's introduction of the Storm series of 12-gauge guns was so well received that a 20-gauge "lite" version is now available. The Deerslayer has a 24-inch rifled barrel with open sights. All metal parts have a Parkerized finish to go along with a black synthetic stock and forearm. A Sims Limb Saver recoil pad takes the sting out of recoil. The Turkeyslayer wears a 24-inch ported barrel with TRUGLO fiber-optic sights and a screw-in Full choke tube designed for Remington's Hevi-Shot loads. The camo pattern is HD Hardwoods Green. The Upland wears a 26-inch ventilated rib barrel with a Raybar front sight. The Parkerized metal and synthetic stock and forearm will withstand any foul weather. The gun can also be cloaked in Realtree Advantage MAX-4 HD camo.

Mossberg

The 935 Magnum is Mossberg's new gas-operated autoloader, which handles the 12-gauge 3 1/2-inch shell. The 935's synthetic stocks come in basic black or dressed in various camo patterns. The gun includes a ventilated rib on a 22-, 24-, 26-, or 28-inch barrel with three screw-in Accu-Mag choke tubes. Nice touches include stock spacers, a button to quickly empty the magazine and a fiber-optic front bead.

The Grand Slam series includes the 935 and the 835 Ultra-Mag and 500 pumps. The 935 Grand Slam has a 22-inch barrel; 20-inch barrels are on the 835s and 500s. All the guns are covered in a variety of camouflage patterns and come with

a camo-colored sling. Adjustable fiber-optic sights are standard, along with an Extra Full extended choke tube for turkey hunting.

The 835 pump 12-gauge comes in several additional models. The Field wears hardwood stocks and a 26-inch ventilated rib barrel. The Synthetic is the same gun with a matte metal finish and synthetic stocks. The Turkey/Waterfowl Combo is dressed in camo with 24- and 28-inch barrels. Adjustable fiber-optic sights are attached to the shorter barrel. The longer barrel wears a fiber-optic front bead. The Turkey/Deer Combo comes with a 24-inch barrel with an Ulti-Full choke tube screwed in. The deer barrel is 24 inches long, rifled for slugs and has a cantilever scope ring base.

The 500 pump Waterfowl wears Mossy Oak Obsession camo with a 20-gauge 28-inch barrel and Advantage Max 4 camo with the 12-gauge's 28-inch barrel. The Bantam Slug 20-gauge has a rifled barrel 24 inches long. The stock has a 13-inch length of pull, grip closer to the trigger and forearm set closer to the receiver. The Bantam Field/Slug Combo has a 20-gauge 22-inch barrel for birds, and a 24-inch rifled slug barrel. The regular size Field/Slug Combo 12-gauge has a 24-inch rifled barrel with adjustable sights and a 28-inch smoothbore barrel that accepts choke tubes. The Muzzleloader/Slug Combo has a 50-caliber muzzleloader barrel and a 24-inch rifled slug barrel.

New England Arms Corporation

F.A.I.R.- I. Rizzini guns are imported by New England. The Model 400 and 400 Gold over/unders are new and include a boxlock action, chrome-lined bores with a ventilated top rib and screw in choke tubes. The 12-, 16-, 20- and 28-gauge guns are fit to proportionally sized frames. The .410 shares the 28's frame. Stocks of Turkish walnut

are finished with a wood buttplate, straight or curved grip and a schnabel forend. The Gold model features gold inlays of pheasants and quail. Meltas Marangos, of New England, said the 16 is by far the most popular gauge–across the board–in New England's shotguns.

New England Firearms

A pump-action shotgun is always the right choice. NEF thinks so and has introduced the 12-gauge Pardner Pump. The Pardner includes an American walnut forearm and stock with a cushioned recoil pad. The steel receiver has a matte finish, double action bars and a cross-bolt safety at the rear of the trigger guard. The 28-inch ventilated rib barrel slips out of the receiver by removing the magazine cap for easy takedown. The barrel muzzle is threaded for choke tubes and comes with a Modified tube.

Remington

The Model 332 over/under, introduced last year, is now offered in an enhanced version with a high-gloss American walnut stock.

The 20-gauge has been added to the Model 1100 Classic Field, which features white-line spacers on the grip cap and butt plate, and the Model 1100 Tournament Skeet with a 26-inch barrel and twin sight beads. The 28-gauge and .410 bore have also been added to the Model 1100 Sporting with a 27-inch barrel.

The 20-gauge is also the choice for the Dale Earnhardt Limited Edition 11-87 Premier autoloader for 2004. This is the second gun in a four-year series. The gun wears a 28-inch light contoured barrel, blued receiver engraved with Earnhardt's likeness and signature and "Seven Time Winston Cup Champion" in 24-karat gold.

A Model 11-87 decked out in Mossy Oak Shadow Grass camo is called the Waterfowl Camo. The gun comes with a fiber optic front

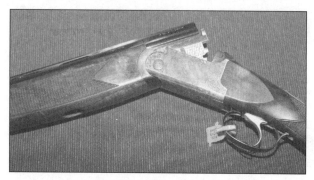

F.A.I.R.- I. Rizzini guns are imported by New England Arms. The Model 400 Gold over/under features a boxlock action, chromed bores, plus a ventilated top rib and screw-in choke tubes. The 12-, 16-, 20- and 28-gauge guns are built on proportionally sized frames.

sight with interchangeable light pipes. The loading carrier has also been lengthened to speed loading.

The Model 870 pump has been around in one version or another since ducks were invented. This year an 870 Special Purpose Shotgun in 20-gauge has a fully rifled 18 1/2-inch barrel, black synthetic stocks, R3 recoil pad and a cantilever scope base that is attached to the barrel and reaches back over the receiver to allow using a scope, or other optic sight with normal eye relief.

Rizzini USA

The Aurum Classic over/under is now chambered in 16-gauge. Jack Dudley, the national sales manager for Rizzini USA, said the gun's frame is scaled to fit the 16-gauge. The gun has a single trigger, walnut wood and 28-inch barrels with fixed chokes. Rizzini now offers five models in 16-gauge.

The Aurum Small Action is available in 28-gauge or .410. It weighs about half a pound less than other steel-frame Rizzini over/unders.

Rossi

Rossi has added a fully rifled 12-gauge barrel to its hinge action. To take the sting out of shooting slugs, the barrel is ported back of

the front sight. Adjustable rear and front dot TRU-GLO fiber-optic sights are standard, as is a scope ring base.

Stoeger

The three models of Coach Gun Supreme double barrels will help you guard the strongbox in the stagecoach coming from the gold mine during cowboy action shoots. The Coach Gun offers the choice of blued barrels and receiver, blued barrels and stainless receiver or nickel-plated barrels and receiver. The Coach Gun is chambered in 12, 20 or .410, with 20- or 24-inch barrels. The .410 has fixed Improved Cylinder and Modified chokes. The 12 and 20 have screw-in chokes and come with Improved Cylinder and Modified choke tubes. The Supreme name comes from the nice American walnut stock and soft rubber recoil pad.

The Combo joins the Condor over/under line. It has a 12-gauge 28-inch barrel set and a 26-inch 20-gauge barrel set to fit one forearm and receiver. Both sets have a bead sight and screw-in Improved Cylinder and Modified chokes.

The Special joins the Single Barrel line with a matte stainless steel receiver.

Traditions

Traditions imports over/under shotguns made by Fausti Stefano in Brescia, Italy. The rising popularity of the 16-gauge has prompted Traditions to introduce the Real 16 and Real 16 Gold over/unders. These guns are built on a receiver proportioned to the 16-gauge shells and weigh 6 3/4-pounds; the same weight as the Fausti 20-gauge Field guns. The 16-gauge guns have

chrome-lined bores, ventilated ribs and three screw-in choke tubes. The barrels lock with a cross bolt. Refinements include a barrel selector inside the trigger guard, engraved game scenes on the receiver flats and point pattern checkering on the grip and forearm. The Gold comes in a hard case.

Like its name implies, the Field II 20/.410 Combo is a two-barrel set with 20-gauge and .410 barrels. Weight is six pounds with 26-inch barrels.

Tristar

Tristar imports a variety of shotguns from Europe as follows:

Breda Shotguns from Italy include the Grizzly Mag inertia-operated autoloading shotguns chambered for the 3 1/2-inch 12-gauge. The Grizzly has a synthetic stock and forend, either in black or covered with Advantage Timber HD camo. The gun wears a 28-inch barrel and comes in a hard case.

The Pegaso Sporting over/under has 30-inch barrels chambered in 3-inch 12-gauge and ventilated top and side ribs. The trigger is adjustable and the whole trigger assembly is easily removed. The blued receiver sports the Breda logo inlaid in gold to match the walnut stocks. The Pegaso Hunter is similar, except it has a silver receiver and is also chambered in 20-gauge.

The HP and HP Marine join the TR-Diana line of semi-autos. Both models have synthetic black handles and a 19-inch barrel with three extended 12-gauge choke tubes. An adjustable rear sight and front blade are for shooting slugs and buckshot. Metal of the standard HP model is finished in black chrome. The Marine is finished in white chrome.

The four models of the TR-Diana pumps are all new. The Synthetic is chambered in 12-gauge three-inch and the Synthetic Mag in 3 1/2-inch 12-gauge. Both guns have a 20-inch barrel with a fixed Cylinder choke, and barrel and receiver

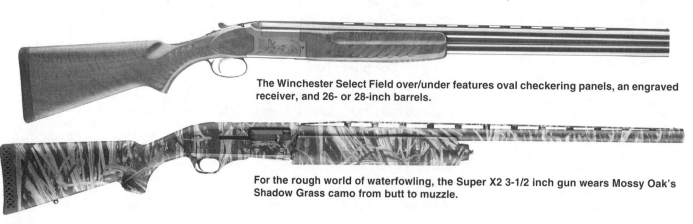

The Winchester Select Field over/under features oval checkering panels, an engraved receiver, and 26- or 28-inch barrels.

For the rough world of waterfowling, the Super X2 3-1/2 inch gun wears Mossy Oak's Shadow Grass camo from butt to muzzle.

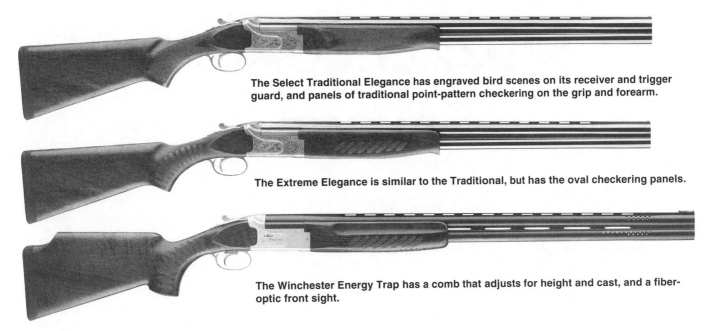

The Select Traditional Elegance has engraved bird scenes on its receiver and trigger guard, and panels of traditional point-pattern checkering on the grip and forearm.

The Extreme Elegance is similar to the Traditional, but has the oval checkering panels.

The Winchester Energy Trap has a comb that adjusts for height and cast, and a fiber-optic front sight.

finished in black chrome. The Synthetic VR and Mag VR are similar to the standard Synthetic and Mag, except have a 28-inch barrel with a ventilated top rib and a front bead. The barrel is threaded for choke tubes and comes with a Modified tube. The Field is similar to the VR, but with a walnut stock and forearm handle. A 20-gauge has a scaled-down stock for smaller shooters. The Camo Mag is masked in Mossy Oak Breakup camo and its 24-inch barrel is chambered in 3 1/2-inch 12-gauge. Sights include an adjustable rear and front blade. A Full choke tube is supplied.

The Silver II series of over/unders has added a youth/ladies model in 20-gauge, at six pounds, ten ounces. The gun's grip is one inch closer to the trigger and its stock has slightly more drop on the comb and a 7/8-inch shorter length of pull.

Winchester

The Winchester Model 9410 is too much fun. It's a grouse and rabbit-potting machine. The Packer Compact lets the kids in on the fun with its shorter 12 1/2-inch length of pull and 20-inch barrel. At six pounds, the Compact weighs 3/4-pound less than the regular 9410. A semi-fancy Traditional model sports a figured walnut stock.

The Select over/unders are a big makeover of Winchester's previous Supreme Select guns. The Select Energy models all have ported barrels, vented top- and side- ribs and adjustable trigger shoes. The Energy Trap's comb adjusts for height and cast and also has a fiber-optic front sight. The Energy Sporting comes with a regular buttstock, or one with an adjustable comb. Barrel lengths are 28, 30 or 32 inches. The checkering is a pattern of small ovals. The Monte Carlo comb on the Energy Trap keeps your head up.

The Select Field features the same checkering ovals and an engraved receiver. The 26- or 28-inch barrels are not ported. The Select Traditional Elegance has engraved bird scenes on the receiver and trigger guard. More traditional panels of point pattern checkering adorn the grip and forearm. The Extreme Elegance is similar to the Traditional, but has the oval checkering.

For the rough world of waterfowl, the Super X2 wears Mossy Oak's Shadow Grass camo from butt to muzzle. So does the Model 1300 pump. For those who like to look at their gun, not look for it, the 1300 Walnut Field has a gloss-finished walnut stock. The 1300 Upland Special Field wears the same stock finish, but with a straight grip and 24-inch barrel, in 12- or 20-gauge, and weighs 1/2-pound less than the standard 1300. Just right to carry after mountain grouse. ●

The Winchester 1300 Upland Special Field wears a gloss-finish, straight-grip walnut stock, has a 24-inch barrel in either 12- or 20-gauge, and weighs a half-pound less than the standard 1300—just right to carry after mountain grouse.

The Winchester Model 9410 Semi-Fancy Traditional sports a figured walnut stock and is a grouse- and rabbit-potting machine. The related Packer Compact lets the kids in on the fun with it's shorter 12-1/2 inch length of pull and 20-inch barrel. At six pounds, the Compact weighs 3/4-pound less than the full-size 9410.

MUZZLELOADER NEWS

by Doc Carlson

A COUPLE OF hundred years ago, a couple of captains headed up the Missouri River to its source, hoping to find the Northwest Passage to the Pacific Ocean. The captains were, of course, Lewis and Clark. The bicentennial of the expedition has fostered a renewed interest in the history of the era, and the guns involved. After several years of the blackpowder market being driven primarily by the requirements of hunters, it appears traditional guns are making a comeback. The same phenomenon occurred back in the 1960s when the centennial of the Civil War was celebrated. There was a great deal of interest in Civil War guns which, in turn, sparked interest in other firearms of the era—and muzzleloaders in general. I'm sure we'll see the same pattern over the next few years.

Interest in the guns of the Lewis and Clark Expedition is hampered, to some extent, by a lack of information as to exactly what the guns were. There is very sketchy information contained in the Lewis and Clark journals, but details of the firearms are lacking. We know that Lewis took delivery of 15 rifles from the Harpers Ferry Armory, along with powder horns, knives, tomahawks and other accoutrements. He also had shooting bags made for the expedition. Exactly what they all looked like remains elusive. Unfortunately all the equipment belonging to the government that remained when the expedition returned to St. Louis, was sold at auction and the money returned to the U.S. Treasury—so there are no known Lewis and Clark guns in existence.

However, a great deal of research has been done on the guns of the Corps of Discovery and some pretty solid conclusions can be drawn. The 1803 Harpers Ferry rifle has often been promoted as the rifle carried by the Corps. Unfortunately for the promoters of the 1803, the design for the rifle was not finalized until May of 1803, after Lewis had received his

rifles. The likely rifle carried by the expedition was probably made up from 1792-1794 Contract Rifles that were in storage at Harpers Ferry at the time. These were full-stocked rifles of 49-caliber that had been made up to government specifications by private gunsmiths in the late 1700s. Lewis had the rifles fitted with new Harpers Ferry locks and sling swivels for carrying straps, a very practical addition for the trip. The locks were of a common pattern, and interchangeable. Also furnished were replacement locks and parts. The lock was probably the same as was used on the Harpers Ferry 1803 Rifle.

Village Restorations & Consulting, Inc., of Claysburg, PA is reproducing a rifle that is likely correct for the rifle that the expedition carried. The full-stocked rifle is 49-caliber, with a typical 1803-type Harpers Ferry flintlock. The brass patchbox is what is found on the 1803 also; the few surviving 1792-94 contract rifles have this type of patchbox. The patchbox release button is in the top of the typical Harpers Ferry brass buttplate and the brass trigger guard is reminiscent of the 1803, again typical of the 1792-94 series of rifle. The ramrod pipes are brass with the entry pipe having a rounded tail, typical of the 1803 but unusual on full-stock Kentucky-type rifles. The ramrod is wood, whereas the 1803 utilized a steel ramrod. The stock is of seasoned maple. These guns are hand-built from standardized parts by some of the more notable contemporary custom gunsmiths in the United States. The rifles are supplied with a hand-made

horn with a spring-loaded brass cutoff. The horn is copied from an infantry horn, which appears in a painting of Lewis done shortly after the expedition returned home. The horn holds 1/2-pound of powder and is made by well-known contemporary horn makers. Also supplied with the rifle is a reproduction shot pouch, patterned after a military rifleman's pouch of the correct period in the Smithsonian collection. The shot pouch is also handmade by custom leather workers. All in all, this is probably as close to duplicating the guns and accoutrements Lewis acquired for the trip as is possible, without original artifacts to examine.

The rifles are offered in two grades: The Presentation Grade features a highly-figured curly maple stock; the powder horn

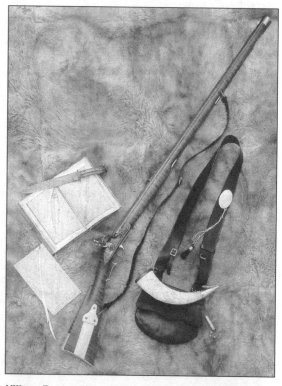

Village Restorations & Consulting reproduction of the likely rifle that the Corps of Discovery requisitioned from the Harpers Ferry Arsenal for the trip up the Missouri.

having a federal eagle, panoply of arms, and personalized cartouche engraved. The shot pouch has a silver cross belt-plate, with federal eagle, fitted to it. The Standard Issue has a plain maple stock, non-engraved horn, and shot pouch with a brass plate installed. The Standard Issue rifle would be pretty much what the Corps carried up the Missouri. For the Lewis and Clark *aficionado* or re-enactor, these rifles would be the ultimate.

Another gun of interest to the Lewis and Clark re-enactor is a reproduction of the 1795 U.S. Musket. This firearm would have undoubtedly made up the rest of the guns the expedition carried. The 1795 was the first standardized "official" military musket the new nation produced. Various contractors made parts and the guns were assembled at the Springfield Armory, the first military arms to be made there. They were, basically, an updated copy of the French Charleville musket that was issued in quantity during the Revolutionary War. France supplied a large quantity of these muskets to the colonies, and it was logical that the first U.S. musket would follow the lines of this gun.

A few details were changed to reflect American thinking. The major change was to give the buttstock more drop so the gun could be properly aimed. The Charleville stock was very straight; it was difficult to get one's head down on the comb enough to sight along the barrel. The Charleville was intended for heads-up volley fire, not aimed shots. *As an aside, the 1795 musket used metric screws, as did the Charleville, setting a trend for military arms that continued through most of the 19th century—through the 1873 trap-door. The French gun utilized both a gooseneck and a double-throated hammer. The Americans went with the double-throated hammer for its greater strength.* The basic design

and shape of this musket remained little changed through U.S. military musket models for the next 50 years.

Dixie Gun Works is importing the 1795 repro, made in Italy by Pedersoli. The gun is a faithful copy and shows good quality. The tapered barrel is 69-caliber, smoothbore, and 44-3/4 inches long, finished "bright" (polished, with no blue or browned finish). The steel butt-plate, trigger guard, sideplate and barrel bands are also finished "bright". The walnut oil-finished stock is 60 inches overall. There is a bayonet stud on top of the muzzle, and a front sight is incorporated into the front barrel band. The ramrod is steel. The "bright"-finished lock features a thinner pan than the Charleville and is marked with the federal eagle, and "US" is script in front of the hammer, with "Springfield" and a date on the tail of the lock. There is no rear sight, in keeping with the thinking of the time.

A number of these muskets, along with spare parts, would have undoubtedly been a major part of the expedition's armament. The Corps went through drills and marching to impress the various Indian tribes along the way, and this military musket would have played a part in those demonstrations, I'm sure. Lewis and Clark *aficionados* would do well to give this well-made musket a look.

There is a relatively new company making some very nice semi-custom traditional guns. **Caywood Gunmakers** is offering a line of fusils that include a Wilson chiefs-grade trade gun, a typical English Northwest trade gun, two

Lock of the Dixie 1795 U.S. Musket reproduction; a very well done copy.

French-type trade guns (types C and D), an English sporting fowler and a French-type pistol. The guns are available with 20-gauge (62-cal), 24-gauge (58-cal) and 28-gauge (55-cal.) smoothbore, and 50-, 54- and 58-caliber rifled barrels. All the guns are available with interchangeable barrels, so a great variety of calibers–in both smoothbore and rifled–can be installed on the same gun for versatility. The furniture on the fusils: buttplates, trigger guards etc. carry tasteful engraving patterns correct for the particular gun and its time period.

The flintlocks used on the guns are of very high quality, a fundamental requirement for a flintlock firearm. The lock is the heart of the firing system and a good lock is necessary for fast, sure ignition. All the internal parts of the locks are made of low carbon steel that is case-hardened. This gives a relatively soft, tough interior and a wear-resistant hard skin, ideal for protecting critical parts from wear and breakage. The frizzens of the locks are made of a high-carbon steel hardened all the way through, so they will never wear out and quit throwing good, hot sparks–essential for reliable ignition. The locks feature a single-position sear bar, meaning the sear bar is in the same place whether the lock is in full cock, half cock or fired position. This allows a trigger position that never changes, and never has excessive slack and "rattle".

One can order these traditional firearms as kits, which include all parts and an inletted stock, with whatever amount of work remaining the craftsman feels comfortable doing. Parts must be fitted to the wood, although the inlets require very little work. Some shaping of the stock, such as lock panels etc. remains to be done. The next step up

The Dixie Gun Works copy of the 1795 U.S. Musket produced at the Springfield Armory.

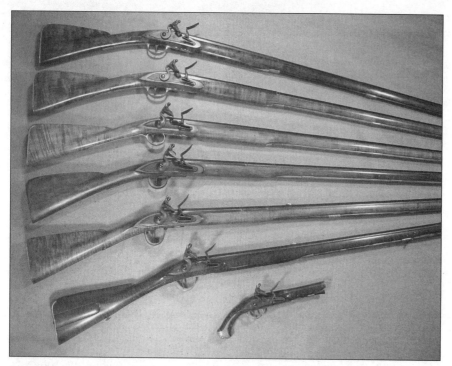

Caywood Gunmakers line of semi-custom flintlock fusils are available in kit form or as finished guns.

is the semi-finished kit that has the stock smoothed more, and lock and tang panels shaped. Also available is the assembled-in-the-white kit, which consists of a basically completed rifle left unfinished. Or the guns can be ordered completed and finished with a full warranty. Prices are very reasonable, considering quality. These fusils, both as kits and completed guns, are done on a semi-custom basis. Machine-inlet stocks, etc. are used but there is much hand-fitting involved, depending upon the percent of finish done on the kit. For this reason, there is a waiting period of two to four months after ordering.

Want something different? Caywood Gunmakers is doing a run of David Crockett rifles. This run of rifles, limited to 100 units, is a reproduction of Davy Crockett's first rifle. This is a high-dollar gun with a beautiful curly maple stock featuring extensive relief carving. It has all brass furniture and an engraved four-piece patchbox. Each rifle is personalized with a sterling silver plate inside the patchbox engraved "David Crockett-Freedom Fighter" and the number of the gun out of the

100. An additional sterling patchbox plate is engraved with the customer's name, and a framed signed & numbered certificate of authenticity is included with each firearm.

These are top-drawer custom rifles. Each gun comes with a hard case, fire-blued bag-type mould, screwdriver, David Crockett's autobiography, Crockett and Boone videos by Native Sun Productions and a document of ownership history. The 49-caliber guns weigh in at 9 lbs. and have an overall length of 62-1/2 inches. This is a rifle that can be shot, hunted with and handed down as a family heirloom.

For those more interested in the modern-type muzzleloader, there are several new guns coming into the market that will be well-received, I believe. The greatly increasing deer herds in many states have resulted in expanded hunting opportunities, many of which are available to the muzzleloading hunter. The ranks of hunters using muzzle-loading guns is increasing and, while many of these hunters are using traditional arms, the majority seem to be inter-

ested in the high-performance, non-traditional guns.

Prairie River Arms is marketing a modern-type muzzleloader that is about as far from the traditional long rifle as one can get. They have incorporated the inline principal into a bullpup design that is truly innovative. The bullpup design, where the action is moved back into the buttstock under the shooter's cheek, surfaced in the mid-1900s in custom centerfire varmint rifles. It is most recently seen in the current British military assault rifle. The advantage is a standard length barrel in a very short rifle.

The Prairie River rifle features a 28-inch barrel, and an overall length of 31-1/2 inches. This is accomplished by moving the action back into the buttstock, and moving the trigger forward. The stock design is a thumbhole type: very straight, putting the shoulder directly in line with the barrel. This makes recoil very manageable with little or no muzzle raise on firing. Balance is very good, putting the weight of the gun between the hands. The short length makes it a very handy gun in brush or tree stands. The rifle is available with a hardwood stock in either a natural or an "all weather" black epoxy finish. It can be had in either 50- or 54-caliber. The 1:28 rifling twist is correct for conical bullets or sabotted projectiles.

The rifle uses standard #11 caps. The nipple is reached by pushing up a door in the offside of the buttstock. After capping, this door is pushed back down, effectively sealing the ignition system from moisture, dirt, etc.— as well as containing any cap fragmentation or blowback. The nipple sets in a drum that protrudes from the bottom of the barrel, which assures the drum will fill with powder via gravity when the gun is loaded. The cocking handle is just to the rear of the trigger and has two safety positions. There is an additional safety inside the trigger guard that blocks trigger movement. An anodized hard aluminum ramrod fits into the stock under the barrel. The mechanism is very simple, just two moving parts, and takedown is by the removal of one screw.

The guns are available with Williams Guide-type sights, front and rear, or an optional M-16-type carrying handle that contains a M-16 national match sight, matched with a Williams front. The carrying handle will also accept standard M-16/AR-15 scope mounts, if you are so inclined. With the carrying handle installed

The Prairie River Arms "Bull Pup" inline; note the nipple access door in the buttstock.

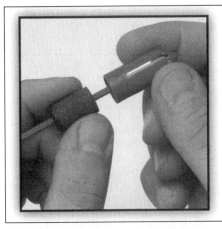 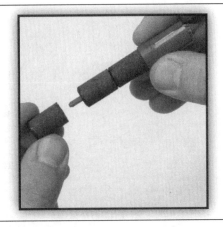 

Hornady's new Lock and Load Speed Sabot.

and the tall front sight–*ala* assault rifles–this one is certainly not your grandfather's muzzleloader!

Knight Rifles has a couple of things for the in-line shooter also. First, they have added something to their Disc Extreme rifles. The new offering is a 52-caliber with a totally redesigned breech plug called the Power Stem. The breech plug is made with a thin, hollow extension on the front that channels the fire from the 209 primer to the front of the powder charge. By igniting the front of the powder charge first, the bullet gains more uniform acceleration, yielding higher velocities, increased energy and less punishing recoil, according to Knight. To further add to shooter comfort, the gun comes with an Xcoil recoil pad by HiViz shooting systems. This pad is said to dampen felt recoil by 33 percent more than conventional recoil pads. The recommended charge of 150 grains of FFg loose blackpowder, or its equivalent, gives velocities approaching 2000 fps with a 375-grain bullet. Pellets or charges less than 90 grains are not recommended. The 52-caliber outperforms the 54-caliber due to the bullet/sabot fit. The thinner petals on the 52-cal. sabot allow it to

release from the bullet quicker, enhancing accuracy. The rifle uses the Full Plastic Jacket ignition system, with 209 primers, found on the other Disc Supreme rifles.

The other new offering from Knight is a revolutionary in-line that looks, at first glance, like a Winchester High Wall without a hammer. This rotating-block action is activated by pulling the trigger guard down and forward to expose the breech plug. A full plastic jacket is inserted into the breechblock and raising the trigger guard closes the action. The gun, assuming a loaded barrel, is ready to fire. The hammer is enclosed in the swinging-action block.

For cleaning, the trigger guard is rotated forward and the entire action block — trigger, hammer, springs, etc.—can be removed from the rifle without tools. Called the Knight Revolution, the new rifle features a 27-inch barrel in either blued or stainless finish, a two-piece synthetic stock and fully adjustable metallic fiber optic sights. Caliber is .50. The trigger is fully adjustable for both creep and pull weight. With an overall length of 43-1/2 inches and a weight of just under 8 lbs., this is a handy rifle that will find favor with hunters everywhere, I predict.

Hornady Manufacturing Co., a Nebraska-based outfit that has been one of the leaders in developing projectiles for the muzzle-loading hunter, is out with a new sabot that should simplify things in the hunting field. Called the Lock and Load Speed Sabot, this is a typical plastic sabot–but with a "tail." A plastic stem, cast in the center of the bottom of the sabot, is designed to fit into the hole in the center of the Pyrodex or new Triple 7 pellets from Hodgdon. The stem will hold three of the 50-grain pellets or it can be cut off if two pellets are required for the favorite load. This is the closest anyone has come to bringing the convenience of cartridge loading to muzzleloading since the days of combustible paper cartridges. The sabots are combined with Hornady's SST-ML bullet. This bullet, developed specifically for muzzleloading, features a polymer tip that increases ballistic efficiency and initiates expansion of the jacketed bullet to twice its diameter upon impact. Hornady claims true 200-yard performance from this bullet, properly loaded. The Lock and Load Speed Sabot is available in 50-caliber with two 45-caliber bullet weights, 250- and 300-grain. It is packaged in 5-load pocket field

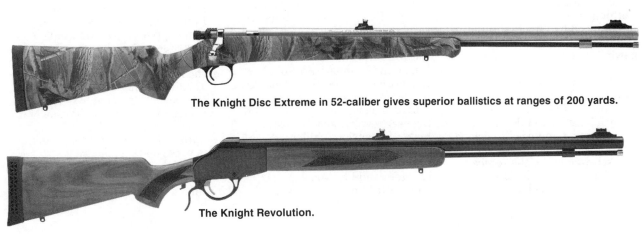

The Knight Disc Extreme in 52-caliber gives superior ballistics at ranges of 200 yards.

The Knight Revolution.

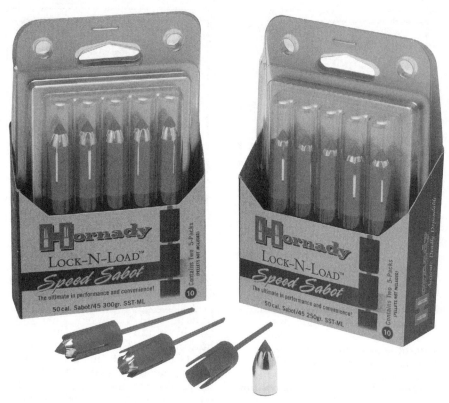

Hornady packages their Speed Sabot in handy 5-shot packages.

packs that will hold the sabots, with pellets attached; keeping them clean and moisture-free until needed. A real handy system for the hunter.

Every year at the Shooting, Hunting and Outdoor Trade Show, I always look forward to stopping by the **Taylor's & Company** display. Over the years they have imported reproductions of many muzzleloading and cartridge guns of a bygone era. The quality and authenticity of their entire line is top-drawer, and they usually have something new and interesting to see. This year was no exception. They had a few things that will be of interest to cowboy action shooters— or anyone interested in replica or antique firearms.

While several companies are importing very nice copies of the venerable Winchester '92, Taylor's is doing a takedown version. Something over a million '92s were produced by Winchester but the takedown version was somewhat rare.

The Taylor's reproduction of this classic firearm is of top quality, as are all their offerings. It is available with an octagon barrel in either 20- or 24-inch length. To take the gun down, a folding handle is lifted at the muzzle end of the magazine tube, the tube is screwed out of the receiver and the barrel, magazine and forearm unit is turned out of the

receiver unit, exactly as with the original Winchester. This allows the gun to be packed into either a 20- or 24-inch space, depending upon barrel length. The little rifle is offered in 32/20, 32 H&R Magnum, 357 Magnum, 38 Special, 38/40, 44/40, 44 S&W and 45 Colt chamberings, which pretty well covers things. This one should be popular with the cowboy action shooters, as well as anyone who likes a light, handy rifle that can be packed into a small space while traveling.

Another new "must have" from Taylor's is a Uberti-made, steel frame copy of the 31-caliber Colt Pocket Model 1849 cap-and-ball revolver, with an interchangeable cylinder to allow it to fire 32 S&W Short. The conversion cylinder is available separately, if you already have the gun. This conversion cylinder joins the others offered in 45 Colt for Remington and Ruger 44/45 revolvers, in 38 Special for the Remington 36 Navy, and 38 LC for the 1851/1861 Navies. Other than Ruger, the cylinders are sold to convert either Uberti or Pietta steel-frame revolvers only. They also offer conversion cylinders for Rogers & Spencer revolvers by the same makers in various calibers.

Something else new this year that will delight both cowboy action shooters and blackpowder cartridge silhouette shooters who are

interested in the new scope class, is a scope and mounts of correct timeframe for Sharps and other single-shot blackpowder cartridge rifles. The 6X scope will be made with either a brass or steel tube and is 32-1/2 inches long. There will also be a shorter version in 4X, 26 inches long for shorter barreled guns. Both scopes should meet NRA Silhouette rules and can be used in BRCS competition.

Taylor's can supply arms for anyone interested in reenacting from the 1700s period through the Civil War era to the cowboy action shooters. Their fine line of guns and equipment is worth a serious look.

A remake of a famous old rifle that should "trip the trigger" of cowboy action shooters is the reproduction Colt Lightning pump rifle from **American Western Arms.** This faithful copy of the centerfire Lightning is nicely reproduced with round or octagon barrel in 32/20, 38 Special, 38/40, 44/40 and 45 Colt. Both rifle and carbine versions are available, with 24- and 20-inch barrels, respectively. Stocks are American walnut, as were the originals. Sights are a standard blade front, paired with an elevation-adjustable semi-buckhorn rear. A firing pin block safety has been added as a concession to modern life. The guns all sport the engraved logo of American Western Arms, so there is little chance of these guns being passed off as originals. As Colt brought out these guns in the early 1880s, they will fit the time period covered by the cowboy action game.

One can't help but be amazed by the wide selection of both traditional and modern-type blackpowder guns being made. It seems that every year we see major improvements in the modern hunting muzzleloading firearms and the ammunition available for them. Manufacturers and suppliers are continually improving and upgrading. We have taken the muzzleloading firearm to levels never dreamed of by our forefathers. The muzzleloading hunter has a vast selection of guns and supplies to choose from – a larger selection than at any time in our history, including the era when the muzzleloader reigned supreme. Traditional firearm reproductions also cover darn near everything that was made during the heyday of this type firearm. Quality and authenticity of these reproductions is very good. If you are a muzzleloading hunter, re-enactor, or lover of these old guns, it's a great time to be alive. Life is good. •

AMMO UPDATE

HODGDON BUYS THE IMR Powder Company. Imagine what Bruce Hodgdon would have thought. Here was an entrepreneur at the end of WWII, shoveling surplus 4831 out of a boxcar and selling it in paper bags, whose company has gone on to acquire one of Dupont's former crown jewels, IMR. It's a great American business story.

The varmint cartridge rage just keeps raging with the announcement of yet another 17-caliber rimfire, the wee Hornady 17 Mach2, plus the legitimization of the 20-caliber in the form of the 204 Ruger, said to be the fastest commercial cartridge ever offered.

Winchester surprised us once again with the roll out of their 25 WSSM (Winchester Super Short Magnum), following so closely on the heels of the 223 WSSM and the 243 WSSM. Making another rather dramatic, surprise appearance was the short 45 Glock Automatic Pistol (G.A.P.) cartridge that permits Glock to pack the punch of the 45 ACP into a smaller framed pistol.

"Low-recoil," " Managed-recoil," whatever the name, Remington and Federal are actively promoting reduced-power centerfire rifle loads that are aimed at those under 18, over 50, and the female sector of the shooting and hunting public.

In the "Why didn't I think of it" category is Hodgdon's "Xperimental Pack." The same innovative marketing and packaging concept is apparent in Ballistic Products' "Hull Integrated Technology System" packs. There may be a trend developing here—small samples of various reloading components that allow handloaders to develop the best load at the least cost for each firearm.

The commercial bullet makers are doing well as more and more Barnes, Hornady, Nosler, Sierra, Swift and Woodleigh bullets are integrated into the major ammunition lines.

Did you know that Norma–along with RWS, Geco, SM and Hirtenberg–is owned by RUAG of Thun, Switzerland? It's a fascinating story covered in Norma's first real reloading manual released this year.

It's been a busy year in ammunition, ballistics and components.

Aguila

The race is on at Aguila to get their little 17-caliber rimfire, the 17 Aguila, into production and into the marketplace after the surprise introduction by Hornady of its 17-caliber Mach 2 cartridge that is also based on the 22 Long Rifle case. www.aguilaammo.com

Alliant

No new formulations this year in a line that now includes ten shotgun powders, three pistol powders and six rifle powders; however, there is a new, free reloading manual this year chock-full of recipes for the E3 shotgun powder, as well as international shotgun, cowboy action and silhouette competition loadings. www.alliantpowder.com

American Pioneer Powder

Offering a sulfurless, volume-for-volume, replacement for blackpowder that cleans up with water, American Pioneer is supplying its FFG and FFFG formulas as granular powder, as 100- and 150-grain pre-measured loads, and as 45- and 50-caliber compressed stick charges. Ballistics and accuracy data for muzzle-stuffers and cowboy action cartridges look very good. www.americanpioneerpowder.com

Ballistic Products

Here is the most specialized shotshell component headquarters in the field. If Ballistic Products doesn't stock it or hasn't invented it, it probably doesn't exist. Having access to their own in-house ballistics laboratory, the company has issued a series of "Master Load" recommendations over the years. These loads were the best that could be assembled for a specific purpose such as sporting clays or pheasant hunting, but, of course, you had to have exactly the right components on hand to duplicate them. Well, why not box up the specific components and

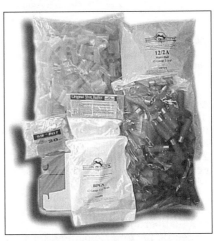

Ballistic Products Prepackaged: Just add powder and shot to Ballistic Products' prepackaged components and you'll produce a true Master load.

market them as a package? They've done it. Called HITS—Hull Integrated Technology System—you can now buy the pre-packaged components with instructions for assembling "Master" steel duck/goose, pheasant, sporting clays, and 20-gauge field loads. All you need to add is the shot and powder. If you reload shotshells, don't miss their fascinating catalog. www.ballisticproducts.com

Barnes

Building on the phenomenal success they have had with the performance, accuracy and shooter

Ballistic Products Guide: Ballistic Products is now issuing a simple to follow recipe guide for assembling Master loads.

Barnes streamlined 50-caliber spitzer boattail is the latest addition to its successful Expander line of muzzleloading bullets.

acceptance of the "Triple-Shock" X-bullet, Barnes is adding six new bullets to the line: a 53-grain 224; 85-grain 6mm; 130-grain 6.5mm; 200-grain 308; and a 185- and 225-grain 338. *(Note: Lazzeroni is also offering a proprietary plated version of the Triple-Shock bullet under the trade name, "LazerHead.")* Imagine a 50-caliber spitzer boattail projectile for muzzleloaders. Barnes just made it. Called the Spit-Fire MZ and offered in both 245- and 285-grain weights with matching sabots, these streamlined bullets are part of the successful Expander MZ line that features solid copper HP projectiles, delivering 100 percent

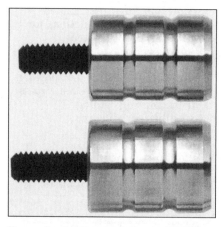

If you shoot Barnes sabot muzzleloading bullets, you'll want to add their Aligner tip to your ramrod.

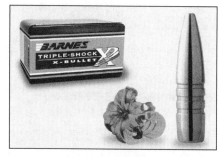

Barnes accurate and deadly "Triple Shock" X bullet line is being expanded this year with new 224, 6mm, 6.5mm, 308, and 338-caliber offerings.

weight retention. If you do try the Expander line, be sure to buy Barnes "Aligner" jags that conform to the ogive of the bullets and insure concentric seating. Speaking of spitzers, over in their XPB pistol bullet line, which is also based on a solid copper HP design, there are two new 500 S&W spitzers in 325- and 375-grain weights. In their more conventional XPB pistol designs, new offerings include a 115-grain 9mm; 155-grain 40 S&W; 185-grain 45 ACP; and 275-grain 500 S&W. Finally, for the big, booming 577 Nitro Express, there is a 750-grain XLC coated X-Bullet. *Kudos* has to go to Barnes this year for their imaginative advertising campaign based on the gasoline pump grades: "Leaded," "Unleaded," and "Premium." Refreshing! www.barnesbullets.com

Berger Bullets

Focused on filling all the niches in the 17- and 20-caliber classes, Berger now offers seven 17-caliber bullets in weights ranging from 15 to 30 grains and five 20-caliber pills weighing from 30 to 50 grains. And that pretty well covers the waterfront. www.bergerbullets.com

Berry's Manufacturing

This is the home of the copper plated, swaged lead core bullet readily available in all popular handgun and rifle calibers. They're inexpensive, too. New in the line this year is a 350-grain 500 S&W bullet and a 150-grain 30-30 Win. bullet. The latter is sized after plating to insure absolute concentricity. www.berrysmfg.com

Black Hills Ammunition

Can the 22-250 be an effective deer and antelope cartridge? With care, yes it can, with Black Hills

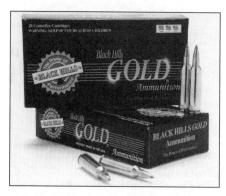

In their premium Gold line, Black Hills is introducing a 60-grain Nosler Partition in the 22-250 Rem. for those who wish to use this high performance 224-caliber for light big game.

newest 60-grain Nosler Partition loading. The 77-grain Sierra MatchKing has proved to be the most accurate and effective bullet that can be loaded in the 223 Rem./5.56mm. Black Hills currently provides all the 5.56mm match ammunition for the military branches, and you can buy it, too. The Black Hills are famous for gold, and the Black Hills Gold line is famous for being one of the greatest premium hunting ammunition lines ever assembled. It's the product of a careful selection of bullets and methodical loading practices. See it at www.black-hills.com

Buffalo Arms Co.

Some great new bullets for the blackpowder silhouette competitor. From a 20:1 alloy, Buffalo Arms is swaging a variety of grease-groove bullets in .410" and .459" diameter.

The grease grooves are actually machined into the bearing surface of the swaged slug, and the bullets are being held to a tolerance of plus-or-minus 2-1/2 tenths of a grain. In 40-caliber, there are 400- and 427-grain

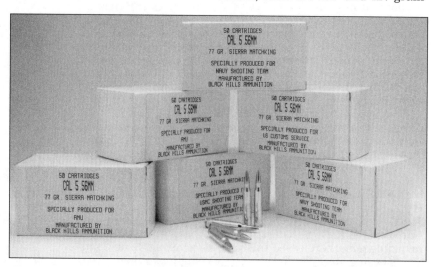

The highly accurate and effective 77-grain bullet loaded in the 223 Rem/5.56mm by Black Hills has proven to be their most popular match, varmint and military loading.

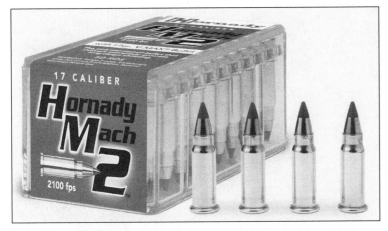

Hornady and CCI teamed up to build the Hornady Mach2—an exciting 17-caliber rimfire based on a necked-down 22 LR case.

Cor-Bon now offers the 325-grain Barnes XPB spitzer in their extensive 500 S&W ammunition line.

Creedmoor designs. In 45-caliber, there are 510-, 545- and 575-grain Creedmoor designs and a 545-grain Postell. Nice company to do business with as well. www.buffaloarms.com

Calhoon

Prolific varmint bullet maker, James Calhoon, is entering the 20-caliber race with two new .204" bullets featuring his proprietary double hollowpoint and electro-chemically applied "Slick Silver" plating. Look for 33- and 39-grain pills this year in his famous 250-count boxes. www.jamescalhoon.com

CCI

Combine CCI's mastery in the rimfire world with a Hornady 17-caliber V-Max bullet and what do you get? The Hornady 17 Mach2, that's what. Based on a CCI 22 LR case, this new little varmint cartridge pushes a 17-grain V-Max along at 2100 fps. Accuracy is reported to be exceptional, and the target price for the ammo affordable. Gun makers are lining up to chamber this little mosquito. What happened to last year's 17 HMR? Well, CCI just made it more lethal with the addition of a 17-grain TNT hollowpoint. Look for reloadable brass cases in CCI's inexpensive Blazer line. The throwaway aluminum cases will still be with

us while the reloadable brass cases will prove a boon to reloaders. www.cci-ammunition.com

Cor-Bon

When Smith & Wesson went looking for a new magnum handgun cartridge, Cor-Bon designed the 500 S&W Magnum cartridge. This year Cor-Bon has focused on hunting loads for the big fifty that include a 325-grain Barnes XPB spitzer at 1800 fps; a 350-grain JHP at 1600 fps; and a heavy bonded-core 385-grain spitzer at 1725 fps, just right for those African safaris. For those of us who like to carry *(and shoot!)* the new titanium lightweights, Cor-Bon has added three new loadings based on their light-kicking 100-grain "Pow'Rball" bullet—a 38 Special+P at 1400 fps; a 9x23 at 1600 fps; and a 357 Mag. at 1600 fps. Teaming up with Barnes, Cor-Bon has created

an entirely new DPX (Deep Penetrating X) line. The DPX bullets are a proprietary design and are currently available as a 115-grain 9mm+P at 1275 fps, a 140-grain 40 S&W at 1300 fps and a 185-grain 45ACP+P at 1075 fps. It really has happened. Cor-Bon, in concert with North American Arms, has released the 25NAA—a 25-caliber cartridge based on the 32 ACP case and chambered in NAA's little Guardian automatic. Ballistics of the wee round are pretty hot—a 35-grain JHP at 1200 fps. Cor-Bon also loads

Built on the 32 ACP case by Cor-Bon, the 25 NAA propels a 35-grain JHP at 1200 fps from NAA's little Guardian automatic.

Cor-Bon has developed an entirely new Deep Penetrating X line of bullets for its high-velocity handgun cartridge line.

The 45 G.A.P. cartridge in the Federal line this year gets a 150-grain Hydra-Shok JHP and a 150-grain FMG at 1090 fps.

rifle cartridges—lots of them. Two new loadings this year are long range tactical loads for the 223 Rem. featuring a 69-grain BTHP match bullet at 3000 fps and for the 308 Win, a 175-grain BTHP match bullet at 2600 fps. In the pipeline are a variety of new Cor-Bon recipes for the 45 G.A.P. www.corbon.com

Federal

Federal's rifle ammunition lines have expanded exponentially with the addition of numerous new loadings using Nosler's Partition, Solid Base, Accubond and Ballistic Tip bullets. Just as an example, in their Premium Vital-Shok line, Federal has introduced the following loadings for the 270 Win. Short Magnum: 130-grain Nosler Solid Base; 130-grain Nosler Ballistic Tip; 140-grain Nosler Accubond; and 150-grain Nosler Partition. Plus, the company is filling in other niches with the Barnes Triple-Shock X bullet and Federal's own Trophy Bonded Bear Claw. At last count, there were 80 new rifle loads this year, so be sure to send for the latest catalog. While everything seems to be getting faster in the cartridge

field, Federal decided to slow things down with the introduction of a "Low Recoil" deer load featuring a 170-grain softpoint at 2000 fps for the 308 Win. and 30-06. The load is designed to reduce recoil of a standard load by 50 percent while still providing excellent performance on medium-size game out to 200 yards. It's a great idea for new shooters, recoil-sensitive shooters, and youngsters. The 45 Glock Automatic Pistol (G.A.P.) cartridge is a hot new item this year, and Federal is fielding a 150-grain Hydra-Shok JHP and 150-grain FMJ at 1090 fps. In the Premium line, there are two V-Shok loadings for the 17 HMR—a 17-grain Speer TNT and a 17-grain Hornady V-Max bullet. Velocity of both loads is a sizzling 2550 fps. And who would have thought the 20-gauge slug gun would have come back in vogue? It has, and Federal has brought out a 5/8-oz. Barnes Sabot round at 1900 fps. It appears that the marriage between Federal and ATK is working very well!
www.federalcartridge.com

Fiocchi

Loaded with nickel-plated shot, Fiocchi's Golden Pheasant line of shotshells has always been considered premium upland game ammunition. It just got better with a new 12-gauge load consisting of 1-3/8 oz. of #s 4, 5, or 6 at 1485 fps! Fiocchi has also added a 28-gauge loading to the Golden Pheasant line consisting of 7/8-oz. of #s 6, 7-1/2 or 8 at 1300 fps. Pheasants beware. There's a new 20-gauge steel, low-recoil load of 7/8-oz. of #7s at 1225. Finally, there's an interesting 9mm Luger leadless loading featuring a 100-grain, truncated cone, encapsulated base bullet at 1400 fps. Delivering less recoil, the new cartridge is also said to be more accurate than standard 9mm ammunition. www.fiocchiusa.com

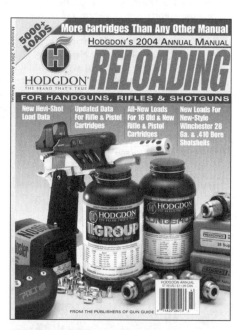

Hodgdon's latest and best "Handloading Annual" is packed with 5000+ loads for even the most recent factory cartridges.

Designed to lower the cost of load development, Hodgdon's Xperimental Pack of four quarter-pound samples of powder is sure to prove popular with reloaders.

Hodgdon's popular Triple Seven powder is now available in easy loading pellet form for muzzleloaders and metallic cartridges.

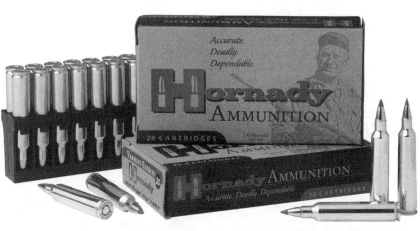

The Ruger 204 loaded by Hornady delivers 4225 fps from a 32-grain V-Max bullet and is the fastest factory cartridge currently offered.

Graf & Sons

For everyone who enjoys shooting the military warhorses, Graf has done an outstanding job of supplying obsolete cases and bullets being produced under contract by Hornady. You can now buy loaded ammunition or components for the 6.5x52 Carcano, 7.5x55 Swiss and 7.65x53 Argentine. Brass only is available for the 7.5x54 MAS, 455 Webley and 9mm Steyr. Awaiting production are the 6.5x50 Jap, 7.7x58 Jap, and 8x56R Mannlicher. Available component bullets include a unique 123-grain V-Max bullet for the 7.62x39, a 160-grain round nose (.268") bullet for the 6.5 Carcano, a 123-grain SP (.300") for the 7.35mm Carcano, and a 205-grain SP (.330") for the 8x56R. Buy them while you can. www.grafs.com

Lightfield is entering the less lethal shotgun ammunition market with rubber buckshot, rubber slugs, and their unique, rubber spider-looking projectiles called Tri-Star and Super Star.

Hodgdon Powder

The BIG news this year is Hodgdon's acquisition of the IMR Powder Company. It's too soon to know what the future holds, but it's certainly an exciting development for both companies. In a brilliant marketing move, Hodgdon has developed the "Xperimental Pack." For approximately the price of one pound of powder, the handloader can now buy a pack of four 4-oz. canisters of Hodgdon powders organized by burning rate. For example, the Magnum Rifle pack contains H4350, H4831, H1000 and Retumbo. The Light Varmint pack-- H322, Benchmark, H335, and Varget. The Xperimental Packs enable the handloader to test a variety of powders without having to buy, and possibly never use again, full pounds of powder. Building on the success of their Triple Seven blackpowder substitute, there are two new Triple Seven pellet loads this year–a 45-caliber 50-grain and a 50-caliber 30-grain. Hodgdon's latest and best *Handloading Annual* is packed with 5000+ loads for even the most recent factory cartridges and contains some great, old stories by Elmer Keith and Bill Jordan. www.hodgdon.com

Hornady

The creative cartridge designers at Hornady seem to generate a new cartridge each year. This year there are two surprises. The 20-caliber, 204 Ruger varmint cartridge has emerged as the fastest factory cartridge currently loaded with a 32-grain V-Max bullet at 4225 fps and a 40-grain V-Max at 3900 fps. Then there's the 17 Hornady Mach2 rimfire that is a petite bottleneck cartridge based on the 22 Long Rifle case. The Mach2 was developed cooperatively with CCI. It zips a 17-grain V-Max bullet down range at 2100 fps and tests indicate that its accuracy exceeds that of its 22 LR parent. Wheel out your Model 1895 Winchesters in 405 Win. Hornady now offers a factory load with a 300-grain SP at 2200 fps. And while we're discussing big bores, Hornady has introduced a new loading for the 500 S&W—a 350-grain XTP Mag. bullet at 1900 fps. And for the muzzle-stuffers, Hornady has come up with a neat idea–the Lock-N-Load Speed Sabot. Take the SST-ML bullet, place it in a sabot that has a soda straw-looking projecting tail, and slide three Pyrodex or Triple Seven pellets onto that tail. It's a complete round–bullet, sabot, and attached powder charge. Look for it initially in 50-caliber with a choice of either 250- or 300-grain SST-ML's. www.hornady.com

Huntington

If you need brass, bullets, or RCBS products, Huntington is the first stop. They are particularly strong in the rare and obsolete caliber department. For example, this year they're adding brass for the 6.5x68mm, 8x68mm, 6.5 Rem SPC,

7.62 Nagant Revolver, 7.92x33 Kurtz, 8x50R Lebel, 50 Alaskan and 50-110 Win. New custom jacketed bullets include 200-grain SPs for the 9x57mm (.352" and .356"), and a 200-grain SP for the 9.3x72R (.364"). Huntington has them plus they offer a unique service for cartridge collectors and handloaders. They will sell you a single case in every conceivable caliber for a very reasonable price. See their extensive catalog at www.huntington.com

Igman

Just beginning to appear on dealers' shelves are sporting rifle and pistol cartridges produced by Igman, a Bosnian company. Igman International USA is the importer. Phone number (203) 375-8544.

International Cartridge Corp.

International is a 100-percent "green" cartridge maker using copper/tin composites and sintered, powder metal technology to create bullets, slugs and shot. They offer a full range of tactical, duty, and special application handgun, rifle and shotgun ammunition for the law enforcement community. www.internationalcartridge.com

Jada Enterprise

Here's an interesting development. Daun Suarez of Jada Enterprise is marketing a homogeneous bullet with a hole through it. He claims it delivers superior velocity, accuracy and penetration from muzzleloading or cartridge rifles. Available in .429", .452", .454", and .458" diameters, the bullet with a hole in it is loaded in a ML with a sabot or seated in a cartridge case with a lexan insert under the base. www.jadaenterprise.com

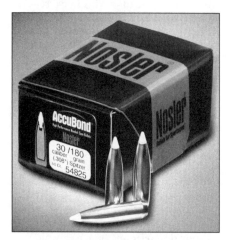

Nosler has added a 180-grain, 30-caliber bonded core bullet to its successful AccuBond line.

Lightfield

Well known for their shotgun slugs, Lightfield is making a major push into the non-lethal shotgun ammunition market with the introduction of rubber buckshot, rubber slugs and some unique, rubber spider-looking projectiles called the Tri-Star and Super Star. The primary applications for their new ammunition lines are law enforcement and wildlife control. www.lightfieldslugs.com

Magtech

"First Defense" is the label for Magtech's latest line of 100% copper hollowpoint ammunition for law enforcement and personal defense. It's available in 9mm, 40 S&W and 45 ACP. There's a new 400-grain semi-jacketed softpoint loading for the 500 S&W, a selection of solid brass shotshells for the cowboy action crowd, and a completely new line of rimfire ammunition. www.magtechammunition.com

Meister Bullets

This well-known brand of hard cast bullets is expanding this year to include 167-grain 30-30 Win.; 170-grain 32-40 Win.; and 330-grain 500 S&W bullets. www.meisterbullets.com

Natec

It's an idea whose time has come again—polymer cased rifle ammunition. Combining a solid brass head and a special, engineered polymer from Dupont, Natec is currently producing 223 and 308 ammunition. The claimed benefits for the polymer-cased ammo are reduced weight and, because of its insulating qualities, improved propellant combustion and reduced heat transference to the firearm. www.natec-us.com

Norma

Finally, Norma has produced a complete and thoroughly fascinating reloading manual. The history of the Norma Company and the technical manufacturing and ballistics data contained in the first 150 pages are worth the price of the book alone.

Excellent text and illustrations, and very clearly written. The loading data is right up-to-date to include the Winchester short magnums as well as less covered cartridges like the 9.3x74mm, 404 Jeffery and 505 Gibbs. Of course, the powders are all Norma, but the bullets span the spectrum of makers including Hornady, Nosler, Sierra, Swift and Woodleigh. There's a new Norma

"First Defense" is Magtech's latest line of 100-percent copper hollowpoint ammunition in 9mm, 40 S&W, and 45 ACP.

component bullet this year, a 7mm 175-grain Oryx, featuring a bonded core and long bearing surface to promote improved alignment and stability. Don't miss this new manual. www.norma.cc

Oregon Trail has expanded its silver alloy True Shot cast bullet line to include new gas check designs in 308-, 41-, 44-, 45-, 480-, and 500-caliber.

Nosler

Building on the success and industry acceptance of their Accubond bullets, Nosler has added two new bonded-core bullets to the line—a 7mm 140-grain and a 30-caliber 180-grain. www.nosler.com

Oregon Trail Bullet Co.

Home of those beautiful, accurate "True Shot" silver alloy bullets, Oregon Trail has developed eight new gas-checked designs: 30-caliber 170-grain RNFP and 200-grain RN; 41-caliber 265-grain WNFP; 44-caliber 310-grain WNFP; 45 Colt (.452) 360-grain WNFP; 45-70 (.459) 430-grain FP; 480-caliber 355-grain WNFP; and a 500 S&W 370-grain WNFP. Top quality. Great folks. www.trueshotbullets.com

Powerbelt

This popular copper-clad muzzleloading bullet line that features an attached plastic gas seal has expanded to include a 45-caliber 175-grain and a 50-caliber 223-grain. Both bullets feature a poly tip named the "Aerotip." www.powerbeltbullets.com

Precision Reloading, Inc.

Here's a great source for a variety of common and hard-to-find reloading components. The company has just released their first shotshell reloading manual, entitled "Blanks to Supersonics." There are articles and loading data on environmentally friendly loads; sub-sonic loads; international target loads; as well as 42 tables covering every subject from

Precision Reloading's first shotshell manual covers environmentally friendly loads, subsonic loads, international target loads as well as 42 invaluable reference tables.

Sierra has designed a true light big game bullet for the high velocity 22 centerfires— a 65-grain SBT GameKing.

Ed Lowry's shotshell ballistics charts to Italian proof marks. www.precisionreloading.com

Remington

"Managed recoil" has become an industry trend, and Remington has it covered. There are three new reduced centerfire loads designed to be lethal on big game out to 200 yards, as well as reduced-recoil 12-ga. slug and buckshot loads. The rifle loads consist of a 115-grain bullet at 2710 fps in the 270 Win; a 125-grain bullet at 2660 fps in the 30-06; and a 140-grain bullet at 2710 fps in the 7mm Rem. Mag. Over in the shotshell area, the managed recoil loadings in the 2-3/4"/ 12-gauge case are a 1-oz. slug and 9 pellets of OO buck at 1200 fps. At the beefier end of the new shotshell lineup are a 1-3/8 oz. "BuckHammer" slug at 1500 fps from the 3-inch 12-gauge case and a 1-oz. 20-gauge slug at 1550 fps in the 2-3/4" hull. Tactical has become practical overnight with the public release of Remington's special operational cartridge, the 6.8mm Rem. SPC (Special Purpose Cartridge). This is a 270-caliber cartridge based on the old 30 Remington case. It fits a M-15/16 magazine box and modified bolt face and was designed to provide increased incapacitation at ranges out to 500 meters. The BTHP or FMJ 115-grain bullets have a muzzle velocity of 2800 fps. Old Remington cases? Here's another one. The 6.5 Rem. Mag. cartridge has been revived. It's good and hot featuring a 120-grain Core-Lokt bullet at 3210 fps. Remington's highly successful bonded bullet, the Core-Lokt Ultra, and the varmint weight AccuTip

bullet are being loaded in a number of new cartridges this year. The Premier Match ammunition line is being expanded to include Sierra MatchKings in the 6.8 Rem. SPC, 300 Win. Mag. and 300 Rem. SA Ultra Mag. There's even a new shotgun wad design this year in which the petals of the Fig8 and TGT12 wads are connected by a thin tab of plastic at the mouth of the wad. The "stitching" prevents wads from sticking together in bags and eliminates folded petals during the loading process. The stitched petals separate the moment the wad leaves of the muzzle. www.remington.com

Sellier & Bellot

S&B is loading Barnes XLC bullets across most of its big game centerfire line this year. There's a hot, new 30-30 loading consisting of a 140-grain SP bullet at 2388 fps.

The 32 S&W Long loaded with a 100-grain bullet at 886 fps has been added to the pistol line, and a 22 WMR with a 45-grain bullet at 1562 fps to the rimfire offerings. www.sb-usa.com

Sierra Bullets

There has always been a market for a stout deer bullet for the 22 centerfires. For years, Sierra's 63-grain semi-pointed Varminter bullet served that purpose well. Sierra has taken the challenge one step further with the release of a true GameKing spitzer BT bullet weighing 65 grains. It will take a 1:10" or faster twist to stabilize the new bullet, but for game up to the size of deer, it should be a dilly. www.sierrabullets.com

Speer

Finally, a carefully crafted cartridge is available for 38-caliber snubbies. Speer is offering a 38 Special +P loading featuring a 135-

Winchester selected the classic 230-grain bullet for their line of 45 G.A.P. cartridges that includes four commercial and two law enforcement loads.

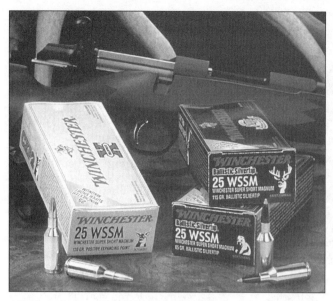

After introducing the 223 and 243 WSSMs last year, Winchester surprised everyone with their new 25 WSSM designed for varmints and medium size game.

Designed to appeal to the high-volume, cost conscious shooter, Winchester's new Super Target loads in 12- and 20-gauge are available in competitively priced case lots.

grain Gold Dot HP bullet at 975 fps. The load is designed to provide optimal ballistics from a 2" barrel. New to the Gold Dot Hunting ammunition line is the 41 Mag. loaded with a 210-grain Gold Dot HP at 1280 fps. The 45 Glock Automatic Pistol round gets four new loadings—a 185-grain Gold Dot HP at 1050 fps, a 200-grain GDHP at 950 fps and two similar weight FMJ loadings for training purposes. New component bullets this year in the Gold Dot HP handgun line include 110-, 135- and 145-grain bullets for the 38 Spl.; the 210-grain 41 Mag.;

and in the Trophy Bonded Bear Claw rifle line, a 250-grain 375-caliber; and a 500-grain 470 NE (.474") bullet. www.speer-bullets.com

Starline

At the request of S&W and Cor-Bon, Starline has re-designed the 500 S&W case to accept a large magnum rifle primer to eliminate pierced primer problems that have occurred with the big boomer. The new cases are clearly marked with an "R" after the word "MAG" on the head stamp, so be forewarned. www.starlinebrass.com

Swift

Swift has announced that they intend on adding 224-, 257- and 6.5mm caliber bullets to their Scirocco line. Stay tuned. www.swiftbullets.com

Vihtavuori and Lapua

Vihtavuori and Lapua have created a new website this year. See their products at www.vihtavuori-lapua.com.

Winchester Ammunition

Winchester did it again. They caught all of us by surprise when they announced the creation of the 25 WSSM (Winchester Super Short Magnum). Designed for varmints and medium-size game, the 25 WSSM will be loaded with an 85-grain Ballistic Silvertip at 3470 fps; a 115-grain Ballistic Silvertip at 3060 fps; and a 120-grain Positive Expanding Point at 2990 fps. Teamed together with super short action Winchester Model 70s and Browning A Bolts, the 25 WSSM is sure to generate a lot of excitement in the hunting field. Should be an ideal combination for women and beginning shooters. Nosler's successful bonded core, AccuBond bullet has been given a Lubalox coating by Winchester and will be loaded in eight Supreme rifle calibers: 270 Win., 270 WSM, 7mm WSM, 7mm Rem. Mag., 30-06, 300 WSM, 300 Win. Mag. and the 338 Win. Mag. The 45 G.A.P. is getting quite a play this year. In their economically priced "USA" line, Winchester is fielding a 230-grain FMJ round at 850 fps and a 230 JHP loading at an impressive 880 fps. For

Winchester is adding bonded core Accubond CT bullets to its popular Supreme rifle line in 270 Win., 270 WSM, 7mm WSM, 30-06 Spfld, 300 WSM, 300 Win. Mag., and 338 Win. Mag.

Loaded with five OOO buckshot, Winchester's new .410 round is designed for hunting and home defense.

Own a classic English double with 2 1/2-inch chambers? Zanders carries a complete line of 2 1/2-inch shotshell loads.

target ranges, there is a lead-free Winclean loading featuring a 230-grain FMJ at 875 fps. Then for personal protection purposes, there is a hot 185-grain Silvertip HP loading at 1000 fps on your dealer's shelf. For the high volume, cost-conscious target shooter who doesn't reload, Winchester is introducing a new "Super-Target line of 12- and 20-gauge loads with a suggested retail price of $57 a case. The 12-gauge line includes both 2-3/4 and 3-dram level loadings plus a 1-1/8 oz. #7 steel shot load retailing for $84 a case. The smaller bores, and particularly the 28-gauge, are growing in popularity for target shooting and upland game. To maximize the effectiveness of the 28-gauge on larger species of upland game, Winchester is adding a 1-oz. loading of hard #5s to its Super-X High Brass Game line. There is a new 3-inch .410 load carrying five

OOO buck pellets at a velocity of 1135 fps. The HS hull based AA Super Sport line is being expanded with a 12-gauge, 1-1/8 oz. load of #9s at 1300 fps and a .410-bore 2-1/2" load carrying 1/2-oz. of #8s at 1300 fps. There are several new screaming 1550 fps steel shot shells for the 3-1/2", 3", and 2-3/4" 12-gauge in #s BB, 2, 3, 4 appearing in time for the next waterfowling season in the affordable Xpert line. And finally, for those tough, old, fall roosters, Winchester is introducing two Super-X Super Pheasant loadings—a 2-3/4" 12-gauge load consisting of 1-3/8 oz. of copper-plated hard lead shot in #s 4, 5, 6 at 1300 fps and a 20-gauge 2-3/4" load of 1 oz. of #s 5, 6 at the same, sizzling 1300 fps. The folks at Winchester Ammunition have been very busy this year! www.winchester.com

Woodleigh Bullets

Long respected for their bonded core, big caliber, big game bullets, Woodleigh is applying its experience and technology to a number of new smaller caliber bullets including a 140-grain 6.5mm; a 250-grain 8mm (.323"); a 200-grain 8x57 (.318"); 286- and 320-grain 9.3mm; as well as some heavies, a 400-grain 416-caliber; 500-grain 458-caliber; 600-grain 505 Gibbs; 600-grain 500 Jeffery; and 650-grain 577 Nitro. See them at www.woodleighbullets.com.

Wolf Ammunition

Expect to see FMJ loads for the 308 Win., 30-06, and 30 Carbine added to this popular and inexpensive line sometime during the year. www.wolfammo.com

Zanders Sporting Goods

Zanders is importing a new line of 2-1/2" English Classic 12-gauge shells with 1-1/16 or 1 oz. of #s 6, 7-1/2 and 8 manufactured by Nobel Sport Martignoni. Zanders is also stocking a new line of Eley Tenex and Eley Match 22 LR loads engineered specifically for semi-auto pistols and rifles. The new Eley ammunition features a special round nose bullet profile and lubricant that facilitate feeding while reducing fouling build-up. www.gzanders.com

With the increasing popularly of the 28-gauge for upland game, Winchester has added #5 shot to its 28-gauge Super-X line.

Zanders is importing Eley's new semi-auto 22 LR cartridges featuring a special round-nose bullet and lubricant to facilitate feeding and reduce fouling in semi-auto 22s.

SHOOTER'S MARKETPLACE

INTERESTING PRODUCT NEWS
FOR THE ACTIVE SHOOTING SPORTSMAN

The companies represented on the following pages will be happy to provide additional information – feel free to contact them.

Doug Turnbull Restoration
Big Bore Classics

Turnbull Restoration Big Bore Classics Rifles are constructed using original and new manufactured Model 1886 Winchester & Browning Rifles. Available in calibers: 45-70, 45-90 & 50-110 (50 Express). For more information contact us at:
6680 Route 5 & 20, P.O. Box 471 Bloomfield, NY 14469
Phone: 585-657-6338 Email: turnbullrest@mindspring.com Website:www.turnbullrestoration.com

HIGH QUALITY OPTICS

One of the best indicators of quality is a scope's resolution number. The smaller the number, the better. Our scope has a resolution number of 2.8 seconds of angle. This number is about 20% smaller (better) than other well-known scopes costing much more. It means that two .22 caliber bullets can be a hair's breadth apart and edges of each still be clearly seen. With a Shepherd at 800 yards, you will be able to tell a four inch antler from a four inch ear and a burrowing owl from a prairie dog. Bird watchers will be able to distinguish a Tufted Titmouse from a Ticked-Off Field Mouse. Send for free catalog.

SHEPHERD ENTERPRISES, INC.
Box 189, Waterloo, NE 68069
Phone: 402-779-2424 • Fax: 402-779-4010
E-mail: shepherd@shepherdscopes.com • Web: www.shepherdscopes.com

BEAR TRACK CASES

Designed by an Alaskan bush pilot! Polyurethane coated, zinc plated corners and feet, zinc plated— spring loaded steel handles, stainless steel hinges, high density urethane foam inside with a neoprene seal. Aluminum walls are standard at .070 with riveted ends. Committed to quality that will protect your valuables regardless of the transportation method you use. Exterior coating also protects other items from acquiring "aluminum black."

Many styles, colors and sizes available. Wheels come on large cases and special orders can be accommodated. Call for a brochure or visit online.

Bear Track Cases when top quality protection is a must.

BEAR TRACK CASES
314 Highway 239, Freedom, WY 83120
Phone: 307-883-2468 • Fax: 307-883-2005
Web: www.beartrackcases.com

Rare, Original Weapons From the British Empire

Atlanta Cutlery Corporation and International Military Antiques of New Jersey are pleased to announce the procurement of these **rare Antique British Victorian Weapons** from the Royal Nepalese Armoury.

These weapons were supplied to Nepal when it was allied with the British Crown after the signing of the Treaty of Sagauli in 1815. Stored in the 16th century ancestral palace of the Thapa family (whose most famous member, Bhimsen Thapa, was Nepal's first Prime Minister). These weapons have laid undisturbed for **over 100 years**.

This find is a time capsule. These weapons were put away after they were used and basically forgotten. They were truly filthy when we acquired them from Nepal. Each has undergone a rudimentary cleaning, but still displays the blemishes of old age.

These old, genuine firearms are marvelous historic artifacts with an impeccable provenance and make for impressive display pieces.

Removing antique guns from Lagan Silekhana Palace

(A) British P-1841 Smooth-bored Brunswick Rifle–conceivably made for comparison testing against the rifled-barrel version that had already been in use since 1837. This experimental model was soon abandoned. Distinctive for the omission of the traditional brass patchbox. Bayonet bar on right side of barrel. Gurkha regimental markings enhance the mystery of how this unique rifle ended up in Nepal. #600454...$695

(B) P-1864 .577 Calibre Snider Breech Loading Rifle–utilized the breech loading system originally developed for the P-1853 Enfield (which was the most prolific imported percussion rifle used in the Civil War) by New Yorker Jacob Snider. Condition fair to good. #600424...$495

(C) British P-1871 Short Lever Rifle–probably the most famous military rifle of the Victorian era. The first manufactured breech loader issued by the British Army. Known for its role in the movies "Zulu" and "Zulu Dawn".

Dates 1870's–#600410...$795

Dates 1880's–#600428...$595

(D) British P-1885 Long Lever Rifle–developed to provide better leverage for case extraction than the P-1871 Short Lever, which occasionally had trouble ejecting spent cartridges because of powder residue clogging the chamber. #600406...$595

The Gurkha Warrior

Brave, loyal and cheerful even under the most adverse circumstances, this wiry and tough little warrior from the Himalayan Mountains knows no peer when the battle starts. The Gurkha warrior has long been recognized as one of the finest mercenaries in the history of warfare, and also one of the most ferocious. The kukri has been his hand weapon of choice for hundreds of years. The combination of Gurkha and kukri has thrown fear into the toughest soldiers.

Traditional Bhojpure Kukri

Approx. 17" long, 2½" wide, ⅜" thick. Made prior to 1890. Some were made much earlier, but it's difficult to determine the exact date. This large kukri's blade was made for war. As spears and the Kora sword were being replaced by firearms, this was the weapon of choice for hand-to-hand combat. In the skilled hands of the Gurkha, it was a frightening weapon indeed. These have all seen service with both the Nepali military and the British Army. Many of the blades are marked in Devangari script with the date of manufacture. *Limited quantity available.*

With original scabbard and 2 small kukri knives.
Original scabbard not sold separately. #401166...$189

Without scabbard–#401126...$129

New Scabbard–#800882...$35

(A)   (B)   (C)   (D)

Companion Volumes to **Gun Digest 2005**

Handguns 2005
17th Edition
edited by Ken Ramage

Find information on all of today's commercially available handguns and accessories, gathered directly from manufacturers and assembled in the latest edition of this wide-ranging, well-illustrated guide. Each listing contains detailed technical information, including caliber, weight, barrel length, sights, features, retail price and more. All the latest semi-custom handguns and commercials centerfire, rimfire and blackpowder pistols, as well as airguns are covered. The accessories section covers handgun grips, sights, scopes, metallic reloading presses and spotting scopes. You'll also enjoy the new feature articles, with information about cowboy action shooting, long-range marksmanship, and much more.

Softcover • 8-1/2 x 11 • 320 pages
450 b&w photos
Item# H2005 • $24.99

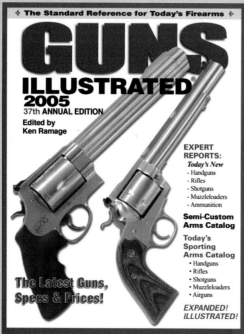

Guns Illustrated® 2005
37th Annual Edition
edited by Ken Ramage

Every firearm enthusiast, collector and buyer needs this all-encompassing reference with the most current information on today's latest and greatest guns. This expanded 37th edition includes updated retail prices and gun specifications for revolvers, rifles, airguns, shotguns, muzzleloaders, and many more. New feature articles examine the latest trends in the industry and other related topics. The easy-to-use "Gundex" indexing system allows you to easily locate a specific gun and the Directory of Arms Trade includes updated listings of firearms manufacturers and importers.

Softcover • 8-1/2 x 11 • 320 pages
450 b&w photos
Item# GI2005 • $19.99

SHOOTER'S MARKETPLACE

NYLON COATED GUN CLEANING RODS

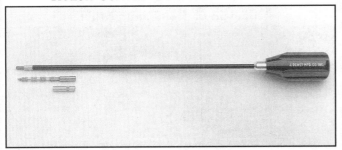

J. Dewey cleaning rods have been used by the U.S. Olympic shooting team and the benchrest community for over 20 years. These one-piece, spring-tempered, steel-base rods will not gall delicate rifling or damage the muzzle area of front-cleaned firearms. The nylon coating elminiates the problem of abrasives adhering to the rod during the cleaning operation. Each rod comes with a hard non-breakable plastic handle supported by ball-bearings, top and bottom, for ease of cleaning.

The brass cleaning jags are designed to pierce the center of the cleaning patch or wrap around the knurled end to keep the patch centered in the bore.

Coated rods are available from 17-caliber to shotgun bore size in several lengths to meet the needs of any shooter. Write for more information.

J. DEWEY MFG. CO., INC.
P.O. Box 2014, Southbury, CT 06488
Phone: 203-264-3064 • Fax: 203-262-6907
Web: www.deweyrods.com

ULTIMATE 500

Gary Reeder Custom Guns, builder of full custom guns for over 25 years, and with over 50 different series of custom hunting handguns, cowboy guns, custom Encores and large caliber hunting rifles, has a free brochure for you. Or visit their website. One of the most popular is their Ultimate 500, chambered in the 500 S&W Magnum. This beefy 5-shot revolver is for the serious handgun hunter and is one of several series of large caliber handguns, such as 475 Linebaugh and 475 Maximum, 500 Linebaugh and 500 Maximum. For more information, contact:

GARY REEDER CUSTOM GUNS
2601 E. 7th Avenue, Flagstaff, AZ 86004
Phone: 928-527-4100 or 928-526-3313
Website: www.reedercustomguns.com

FINE GUN STOCKS

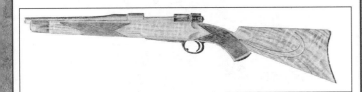

Manufacturing custom and production gunstocks for hundreds of models of rifles and shotguns—made from the finest stock woods and available in all stages of completion.

Visit www.gunstocks.com to view their bargain list of fine custom gunstocks. Each displayed in full color.

GREAT AMERICAN GUNSTOCK COMPANY
3420 Industrial Drive
Yuba City, CA 95993
Phone: 530-671-4570
Fax: 530-671-3906
Gunstock Hotline: 800-784-GUNS (4867)
Web: www.gunstocks.com
E-mail: gunstox@syix.com

COMBINATION RIFLE AND OPTICS REST

The Magna-Pod weighs less than two pounds, yet firmly supports more than most expensive tripods. It will hold 50 pounds at its low 9-inch height and over 10 pounds extended to 17 inches. It sets up in seconds where there is neither time nor space for a tripod and keeps your expensive equipment safe from knock-overs by kids, pets, pedestrians, or even high winds. It makes a great mono-pod for camcorders, etc., and its carrying box is less than 13" x 13" x 3 1/4" high for easy storage and access.

Attached to its triangle base it becomes an extremely stable table pod or rifle bench rest. The rifle yoke pictured in photo is included.

It's 5 pods in 1: Magna-Pod, Mono-Pod, Table-Pod, Shoulder-Pod and Rifle Rest. Send for free catalog.

SHEPHERD ENTERPRISES, INC.
Box 189, Waterloo, NE 68069
Phone: 402-779-2424 • Fax: 402-779-4010
E-mail: shepherd@shepherdscopes.com • Web: www.shepherdscopes.com

SHOOTER'S MARKETPLACE

BORDER CLASSIC

Gary Reeder Custom Guns, builder of full custom guns including hunting handguns, custom Encores, large caliber hunting rifles and over 20 different series of cowboy guns, including our Border Classic, shown. This beauty is the first ever snubbie Schofield, and can be built on any current Schofield. Fully engraved, round butted, with their Black Chromex finish and a solid silver Mexican coin for the front sight, this one is truly a masterpiece. See them all at their website, or call for a brochure.

GARY REEDER CUSTOM GUNS
2601 E. 7th Avenue, Flagstaff, AZ 86004
Phone: 928-527-4100 or 928-526-3313
Website: www.reedercustomguns.com

GARY LEVINE FINE KNIVES
A DEALER OF HANDMADE KNIVES

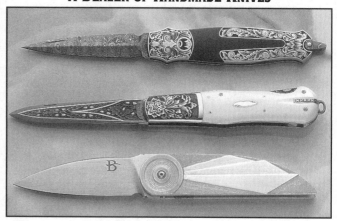

Gary's goal is to offer the collector the best custom knives available, in stock and ready for delivery. He has the best makers as well as the rising stars at fair prices. Gary enjoys working with collectors who want to enhance their collections, as well as someone who just wants a great knife to carry. Gary is also always on the lookout for collections, as well as single custom knives to purchase. Please stop by his website.

GARY LEVINE FINE KNIVES
P.O. Box 382, Chappaqua, NY 10514
Phone: 914-238-5748 • Fax: 914-238-6524
Web: http://www.levineknives.com
Email: gary@levineknives.com

QUALITY GUNSTOCK BLANKS

Cali'co Hardwoods has been cutting superior-quality shotgun and rifle blanks for more than 31 years. Cali'co supplies blanks to many of the major manufacturers—Browning, Weatherby, Ruger, Holland & Holland, to name a few—as well as custom gunsmiths the world over.

Profiled rifle blanks are available, ready for inletting and sanding. Cali'co sells superior California hardwoods in Claro walnut, French walnut, Bastogne, maple and myrtle.

Cali'co offers good, serviceable blanks and some of the finest exhibition blanks available. Satisfaction guaranteed.

Color catalog, retail and dealer price list (FFL required) free upon request.

CALI'CO HARDWOODS, INC.
3580 Westwind Blvd., Santa Rosa, CA 95403
Phone: 707-546-4045 • Fax: 707-546-4027

BLACK HILLS GOLD AMMUNITION

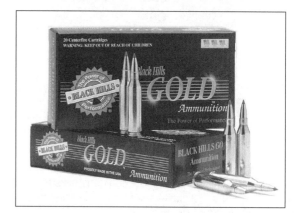

Black Hills Ammunition has introduced a new line of premium performance rifle ammunition. Calibers available in the Black Hills Gold Line are .243, .270, .308, .30-06, and .300 Win Mag. This line is designed for top performance in a wide range of hunting situations. Bullets used in this ammunition are the Barnes X-Bullet with XLC coating and the highly accurate Nosler Ballistic-Tip™.

Black Hills Ammunition is sold dealer direct. The Gold line is packaged in 20 rounds per box, 10 boxes per case. Black Hills pays all freight to dealers in the continental United States. Minimum dealer order is only one case.

BLACK HILLS AMMUNITION
P.O. Box 3090, Rapid City, SD 57709
Phone: 1-605-348-5150 • Fax: 1-605-348-9827
Web: www.black-hills.com

SHOOTER'S MARKETPLACE

FOLDING BIPODS

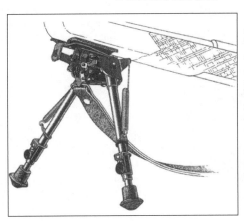

Harris Bipods clamp securely to most stud-equipped bolt-action rifles and are quick-detachable. With adapters, they will fit some other guns. On all models except the Model LM, folding legs have completely adjustable spring-return extensions. The sling swivel attaches to the clamp. This time-proven design is manufactured with heat-treated steel and hard alloys and has a black anodized finish.

Series S Bipods rotate 35° for instant leveling on uneven ground. Hinged base has tension adjustment and buffer springs to eliminate tremor or looseness in crotch area of bipod. They are otherwise similar to non-rotating Series 1A2.

Thirteen models are available from Harris Engineering; literature is free.

HARRIS ENGINEERING INC.
Dept: GD54, Barlow, KY 42024
Phone: 270-334-3633 • Fax: 270-334-3000

PRECISION RIFLE REST

Bald Eagle Precision Machine Co. offers a rifle rest perfect for the serious benchrester or dedicated varminter.

"The Slingshot" or Next Generation has 60° front legs. The rest is constructed of aircraft-quality aluminum or fine grain cast iron and weighs 12 to 20 lbs. The finish is 3 coats of Imron clear. Primary height adjustments are made with a rack and pinion gear. Secondary adjustment uses a mariner wheel with thrust bearings for smooth operation. A hidden fourth leg allows for lateral movement on the bench.

Bald Eagle offers approximately 150 rest combinations to choose from, including windage adjustable, right or left hand, cast aluminum or cast iron.

Prices: $175.00 to $345.00

BALD EAGLE PRECISION MACHINE CO.
101-K Allison Street, Lock Haven, PA 17745
Phone: 570-748-6772 — Fax: 570-748-4443
Web: www.baldeaglemachine.com

SHOOTER'S MARKETPLACE

RUGER 10-22® COMPETITION MATCHED HAMMER AND SEAR KIT

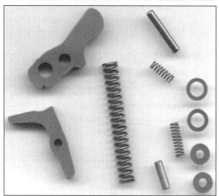

Precision EDM/CNC machined custom hammer and sear for your Ruger 10-22®. Both parts are machined from a solid billet of steel. Case hardened to RC-58-60. These are the highest quality drop in parts available on the market. They will produce a crisp 2-1/2 lbs. trigger pull. They are precision ground with Vapor hand honed engagement surfaces. Includes an Extra Power hammer spring, Extra Power disconnector spring, replacement trigger return spring, 2 hammer shims, and 2 trigger shims.

Price $55.95 plus $3.85 Priority Mail

POWER CUSTOM, INC.

29739 Hwy. J, Dept. KP, Gravois Mills, MO 65037
Phone: 1-573-372-5684 • Fax: 1-573-372-5799
Web: www.powercustom.com • E-mail: rwpowers@laurie.net

GATCO 5-STONE SHARPENING SYSTEM

The GATCO 5-Stone Sharpening System is the only fixed-angle sharpening kit needed to restore a factory perfect edge on even the most well-used knives.

Instructions are permanently mounted inside the storage case to make the job easy.

Just secure the blade in the polymer vise, select the proper angle guide, insert one of the five hone-stone angle guide bars into the guide slot, then put a few drops of mineral oil on the stone and start sharpening.

The GATCO 5-Stone Sharpening System includes extra coarse, coarse, medium and fine honing stones that are made from high-density aluminum oxide for long wear. The fifth, triangular-shaped hone is used for serrated blades.

All stones are mounted in color-coded grips.

To locate a GATCO dealer, call 1-800-LIV-SHARP.

GATCO SHARPENERS

P.O. Box 600, Getzville, NY 14068-0600
Phone: 716-877-2200 • Fax: 716-877-2591
E-mail: gatco@buffnet.net • www.gatcosharpeners.com

SHOOTER'S MARKETPLACE

10-22® HAMMER AND SEAR PAC

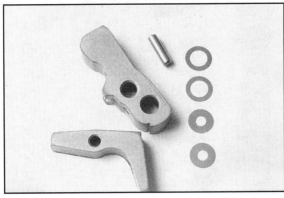

Power Custom introduces a new Ruger 10-22® Matched Hammer & Sear to reduce the trigger pull weight for your 10-22® & 10-22 Magnum. This allows for a 2 1/2lb. trigger pull. Manufactured by the E.D.M. process out of carbon steel and heat treated to a 56-58 Rc and precision ground with honed engagement surfaces. Kit includes extra power hammer & sear disconnector spring, 2 precision trigger shims, 2 precision hammer shims, and a replacement trigger return spring. Price $55.95.

10-22® is a registered trademark of Sturm, Ruger & Co. Inc.

POWER CUSTOM, INC.
29739 Hwy J, Dept GD,
Gravois Mills, MO 65037
Phone: 573-372-5684 • Fax: 573-372-5799
Website: www.powercustom.com

FOR THE SERIOUS RELOADER...

Rooster Labs' line of professional-quality high-performance lubricants and polishes for the shooting industry now includes:
- **ZAMBINI** 220° Pistol Bullet Lubricant (1x4 & 2x6)
- **HVR** 220° High Velocity Rifle Bullet Lube (1x4)
- **ROOSTER JACKET** Waterproof Liquid Bullet Film Lube
- **BP-7 BLACK POWDER** Bullet Lube 210° melt (1x4)
- **PL-16 BLACK POWDER** Patch Lube 265° melt (2 oz tin)
- **ROOSTER BRIGHT** Brass Case Polish Media Additive ...Brilliant!
- **CFL-56** Radical Case Forming Lube...for the Wildcatter
- **PDQ-21** Spray Case Sizing Lube...quick, no contamination
- **DF-7303 DEEP DRAWING FLUID** (commercial concentrate)

 Rooster LABORATORIES®
P.O. Box 414605, Kansas City, MO 64141
Phone: 816-474-1622 • Fax: 816-474-7622
E-mail: roosterlabs@aol.com

The oldest mail order knife company, celebrating over 40 years in the knife industry, has a tradition of offering the finest quality knives and accessories worldwide. Lines include Randall, Dozier, William Henry, Leatherman, Case, Gerber, SOG, Ka-Bar, Kershaw, CRKT, Al Mar, Klotzli, Boker, Marbles, Schatt & Morgan, A. G. Russell and more. Call for a free catalog or shop online to see the entire inventory.

A. G. RUSSELL KNIVES
1920 North 26th Street, Dept. KA04, Lowell, AR 72745-8489
Phone: 479-571-6161 • Fax: 479-631-8493
E-mail: ag@agrussell.com • Web: www.agrussell.com

NEW CATALOG!

Catalog #26 is Numrich's latest edition! This 1,216 page catalog features more than 500 schematics for use in identifying obsolete and current commercial, military, antique and foreign guns. Edition #26 contains 180,000 items from their inventory of over 550 million parts and accessories and is a necessity for any true gunsmith or hobbyist. It has been the industry's leading reference book for firearm parts and identification for over 50 years!

Order Item #YP-26 $12.95
U.S. Orders: Bulk mail, shipping charges included.
Foreign Orders: Air mail, 30-day delivery; or surface 90-day delivery. Shipping charges additional.

NUMRICH GUN PARTS CORPORATION
226 Williams Lane, P.O. Box 299, West Hurley, NY 12491
Orders Toll-Free: 866-NUMRICH (866-686-7424)
Customer Service: (845) 679-4867
Toll-Free Fax: (877) GUNPART
Web: e-GunParts.com • E-mail: info@gunpartscorp.com

SHOOTER'S MARKETPLACE

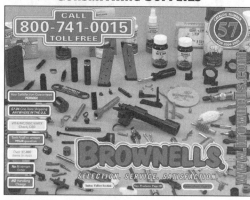
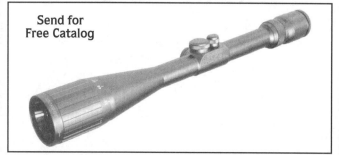

2005
GUNS ILLUSTRATED
Complete Compact
CATALOG

GUNDEX

SEMI-CUSTOM

HANDGUNS

RIFLES

SHOTGUNS

BLACKPOWDER

AIRGUNS

MANUFACTURERS DIRECTORY

GUNDEX

GUNDEX

Browning Luxus
Grade B2

Browning Luxus
Renaissance Argent

Browning Luxus
Renaissance OR

Ed Brown Classic Class A

Ed Brown Kobra Carry

Kimber Ultra CDP

Kimber Ultra Royal II

BRILEY 1911-STYLE AUTO PISTOLS

Caliber: 9mm Para., 38 Super, 40 S&W, 10-shot magazine; 45 ACP, 8-shot magazine. **Barrel:** 3.6" or 5". **Weight:** NA. **Length:** NA. **Grips:** Rosewood or rubber. **Sights:** Bo-Mar adjustable rear, Briley dovetail blade front. **Features:** Modular or Caspian alloy, carbon steel or stainless steel frame; match barrel and trigger group; lowered and flared ejection port; front and rear serrations on slide; beavertail grip safety; hot blue, hard chrome or stainless steel finish. Introduced 2000. Made in U.S. From Briley Manufacturing Inc.

Price: Fantom (3.6" bbl., fixed low-mount rear sight, armor coated lower receiver) . . . . from **$1,900.00**
Price: Fantom with two-port compensator . . . . from **$2,245.00**
Price: Advantage (5" bbl., adj. low-mount rear sight, checkered mainspring housing) . . . . from **$1,650.00**
Price: Versatility Plus (5" bbl., adj. low-mount rear sight, modular or Caspian frame) . . . . from **$1,850.00**
Price: Signature Series (5" bbl., adj. low-mount rear sight, 40 S&W only) . . . . from **$2,250.00**
Price: Plate Master (5" bbl. with compensator, lightened slide, Briley scope mount) . . . . from **$1,895.00**
Price: El Presidente (5" bbl. with Briley quad compensator, Briley scope mount) . . . . from **$2,550.00**

BROWNING HI-POWER LUXUS

The legendary Browning Hi-Power pistol still produced in Belgium is available in four grades in the Luxus series: Grade II, Renaissance Argent, Grade B2 and the gold-finished Renaissance OR. Other specifications NA.
Price: . . . . **NA**

ED BROWN CLASSIC CUSTOM AND CLASS A LIMITED 1911-STYLE AUTO PISTOLS

Caliber: 45 ACP; 7-shot magazine; 40 S&W, 400 Cor-Bon, 38 Super, 9x23, 9mm Para. **Barrel:** 4.25", 5", 6". **Weight:** NA. **Length:** NA. **Grips:** Hogue exotic checkered wood. **Sights:** Bo-Mar or Novak rear, blade front. **Features:** Blued or stainless steel frame; ambidextrous safety; beavertail grip safety; checkered forestrap and mainspring housing; match-grade barrel; slotted hammer; long lightweight or Videki short steel trigger. Many options offered. Made in U.S. by Ed Brown Products.

Price: Classic Custom (45 ACP, 5" barrel) . . . . from **$2,895.00**
Price: Class A Limited (all calibers; several bbl. lengths in competition and carry forms) . . . . from **$2,250.00**

Price: Commander Bobtail (most calibers, 4.25" bbl., has "bobtail" modification to reduce overall length) . . . . from **$2,300.00**
Price: Kobra (45 ACP only, 5" bbl., completely hand-fitted with heavy dehorning) . . . . from **$1,795.00**
Price: Kobra Carry (45 ACP only, 4.25" bbl., has exclusive snakeskin pattern on frame, top portion of mainspring housing and slide) . . . . from **$1,995.00**

KIMBER CUSTOM II 1911-STYLE AUTO PISTOLS

Caliber: 9mm Para., 38 Super, 9-shot magazines; 40 S&W, 8-shot magazine; 45 ACP, 7-shot magazine. **Barrel:** 5". **Weight:** 38 oz. **Length:** 8.7" overall. **Grips:** Black synthetic, smooth or double-diamond checkered rosewood, or double-diamond checkered walnut. **Sights:** McCormick low profile or Kimber adjustable rear, blade front. **Features:** Machined steel slide, frame and barrel; front and rear beveled slide serrations; cut and button-rifled, match-grade barrel; adjustable aluminum trigger; full-length guide rod; Commander-style hammer; high-ride beavertail safety; beveled magazine well. Other models available. Made in U.S. by Kimber Mfg. Inc.

Price: Custom II (black matte finish) $730.00
Price: Custom Royal II (polished blue finish, checkered rosewood grips) $886.00
Price: Custom Stainless II (satin-finished stainless steel frame and slide) $832.00
Price: Custom Target II (matte black or stainless finish, Kimber adj. sight) $945.00
Price: Custom Compact CDP II (4" bbl., alum. frame, tritium three-dot sights, 28 oz.) $1,141.00
Price: Custom Pro CDP II (4" bbl., alum. frame, tritium sights, full-length grip, 28 oz.) $1,141.00
Price: Ultra CDP II (3" bbl., aluminum frame, tritium sights, 25 oz.) $1,141.00
Price: Gold Match II (polished blue finish, hand-fitted barrel, ambid. safety) . . . . from $1,168.00
Price: Stainless Gold Match II (stainless steel frame and slide, hand-fitted bbl., amb. safety) . . . . $1,315.00 to $1,345.00

Les Baer Thunder Ranch Special

Rock River Arms Limited Match

Volquartsen Stingray

LES BAER CUSTOM 1911-STYLE AUTO PISTOLS

Caliber: 9mm Para., 38 Super, 40 S&W, 45 ACP, 400 Cor-Bon; 7- or 8-shot magazine. **Barrel:** 4-1/4", 5", 6". **Weight:** 28 to 40 oz. **Length:** NA. **Grips:** Checkered cocobolo. **Sights:** Low-mount combat fixed, combat fixed with tritium inserts or low-mount adjustable rear, dovetail front. **Features:** Forged steel or aluminum frame; slide serrated front and rear; lowered and flared ejection port; beveled magazine well; speed trigger with 4-pound pull; beavertail grip safety; ambidextrous safety. Other models available. Made in U.S. by Les Baer Custom.

Price: Baer 1911 Premier II 5" Model (5" bbl., optional stainless steel frame and slide) . . . . from **$1,498.00**
Price: Premier II 6" Model (6" barrel) . . . . from **$1,675.00**
Price: Premier II LW1 (forged aluminum frame, steel slide and barrel)
. . . . from **$1,835.00**
Price: Custom Carry (4" or 5" barrel, steel frame) . . . . from **$1,728.00**
Price: Custom Carry (4" barrel, aluminum frame) . . . . from **$2,039.00**
Price: Swift Response Pistol (fixed tritium sights, Bear Coat finish)
. . . . from **$2,339.00**
Price: Monolith (5" barrel and slide with extra-long dust cover)
. . . . from **$1,660.00**
Price: Stinger (4-1/4" barrel, steel or aluminum frame). . . . from **$1,552.00**
Price: Thunder Ranch Special (tritium fixed combat sight, Thunder Ranch logo) . . . . from **$1,685.00**
Price: National Match Hardball (low-mount adj. sight; meets DCM rules)
. . . . from **$1,425.00**
Price: Bullseye Wadcutter Pistol (Bo-Mar rib w/ adj. sight, guar. 2-1/2" groups) . . . . from **$1,560.00**
Price: Ultimate Master Combat (5" or 6" bbl., adj. sights, checkered front strap) . . . . from **$2,530.00**
Price: Ultimate Master Combat Compensated (four-port compensator, adj. sights) . . . . from **$2,558.00**

ROCK RIVER ARMS 1911-STYLE AUTO PISTOLS

Caliber: 9mm Para., 38 Super, 40 S&W, 45 ACP. **Barrel:** 4" or 5". **Weight:** NA. **Length:** NA. **Grips:** Double-diamond, checkered cocobolo or black synthetic. **Sights:** Bo-Mar low-mount adjustable, Novak fixed with tritium inserts, Heine fixed or Rock River scope mount; dovetail front blade. **Features:** Chrome-moly, machined steel frame and slide; slide serrated front and rear; aluminum speed trigger with 3.5-4 lb. pull; national match KART barrel; lowered and flared ejection port; tuned and polished

extractor; beavertail grip safety; beveled mag. well. Other frames offered. Made in U.S. by Rock River Arms Inc.

Price: Elite Commando (4" barrel, Novak tritium sights) **$1,395.00**
Price: Standard Match (5" barrel, Heine fixed sights) **$1,150.00**
Price: National Match Hardball (5" barrel, Bo-Mar adj. sights)
. . . . from **$1,275.00**
Price: Bullseye Wadcutter (5" barrel, Rock River slide scope mount)
. . . . from **$1,380.00**
Price: Basic Limited Match (5" barrel, Bo-Mar adj. sights) . from **$1,395.00**
Price: Limited Match (5" barrel, guaranteed 1-1/2" groups at 50 yards)
. . . . from **$1,795.00**
Price: Hi-Cap Basic Limited (5" barrel, four frame choices) from **$1,895.00**
Price: Ultimate Match Achiever (5" bbl. with compensator, mount and Aimpoint) . . . . from **$2,255.00**
Price: Match Master Steel (5" bbl. with compensator, mount and Aimpoint)
. . . . **$5,000.00**

STI COMPACT AUTO PISTOLS

Caliber: 9mm, 40 S&W. **Barrel:** 3.4". **Weight:** 28 oz. **Length:** 7" overall. **Grips:** Checkered double-diamond rosewood. **Sights:** Heine Low Mount fixed rear, slide integral front. **Features:** Similar to STI 2011 models except has compact frame, 7-shot magazine in 9mm (6-shot in 40 cal.), single-sided thumb safety, linkless barrel lockup system, matte blue finish. From STI International.

Price: (9mm or 40 S&W). . . . . from **$746.50**

VOLQUARTSEN CUSTOM 22 CALIBER AUTO PISTOLS

Caliber: 22 LR; 10-shot magazine. **Barrel:** 3.5" to 10"; stainless steel air gauge. **Weight:** 2-1/2 to 3 lbs. 10 oz. **Length:** NA. **Grips:** Finger-grooved plastic or walnut. **Sights:** Adjustable rear and blade front or Weaver-style scope mount. **Features:** Conversions of Ruger Mk. II Auto pistol. Variety of configurations featuring compensators, underlug barrels, etc. Stainless steel finish; black Teflon finish available for additional $85; target hammer, trigger. Made in U.S. by Volquartsen Custom.

Price: 3.5 Compact (3.5" barrel, T/L adjustable rear sight, scope base optional) **$640.00**
Price: Deluxe (barrel to 10", T/L adjustable rear sight) **$675.00**
Price: Deluxe with compensator **$745.00**
Price: Masters (6.5" barrel, finned underlug, T/L adjustable rear sight, compensator) **$950.00**
Price: Olympic (7" barrel, recoil-reducing gas chamber, T/L adjustable rear sight) **$870.00**
Price: Stingray (7.5" ribbed, ported barrel; red-dot sight) **$995.00**
Price: Terminator (7.5" ported barrel, grooved receiver, scope rings)
. . . . **$730.00**
Price: Ultra-Light Match (6" tensioned barrel, Weaver mount, weighs 2-1/2 lbs.) **$885.00**
Price: V-6 (6", triangular, ventilated barrel with underlug, T/L adj. sight)
. . . . **$1,030.00**
Price: V-2000 (6" barrel with finned underlug, T/L adj. sight) . . . **$1,095.00**
Price: V-Magic II (7.5" barrel, red-dot sight) **$1,055.00**

Gary Reeder
Doc Holiday Classic

Gary Reeder
Ultimate 41

Gary Reeder
Black Widow

Gary Reeder
Professional Hunter

Gary Reeder
Ultimate 500

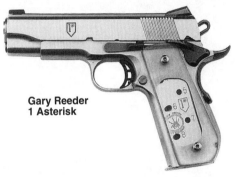

Gary Reeder
1 Asterisk

GARY REEDER CUSTOM GUNS REVOLVERS

Caliber: 22 WMR, 22 Hornet, 218 Bee, 356 GMR, 41 GNR, 410 GNR, 510 GNR, 357 Magnum, 45 Colt, 44-40, 41 Magnum, 44 Magnum, 454 Casull, 475 Linebaugh, 500 Linebaugh. **Barrel:** 2-1/2" to 12". **Weight:** Varies by model. **Length:** Varies by model. **Grips:** Black Cape buffalo horn, laminated walnut, simulated pearl, black and ivory micarta, others. **Sights:** Notch fixed or adjustable rear, blade or ramp front. **Features:** Custom conversions of Ruger Vaquero, Blackhawk Bisley and Super Blackhawk frames. Jeweled hammer and trigger, tuned action, model name engraved on barrel, additional engraving on frame and cylinder, integral muzzle brake, finish available in high-polish or satin stainless steel or black Chromex finish. Also available on customer's gun at reduced cost. Other models available. Made in U.S. by Gary Reeder Custom Guns.

Price: Gamblers Classic (2-1/2" bbl., engraved cards and dice, no ejector rod housing). . . . . from **$995.00**
Price: Tombstone Classic (3-1/2" bbl. with gold bands, notch sight, birdshead grips). . . . . from **$995.00**
Price: Doc Holliday Classic (3-1/2" bbl., engraved cards and dice, white pearl grips). . . . . from **$995.00**
Price: Border Classic (Built on customer furnished Schofield; 3" bbl., full scroll engraving, solid silver Mexican coin front sight, custom grips) . . . . from **$1,095.00**
Price: Cowboy Classic (stainless finish, cattle brand engraved, limited to 100 guns). . . . . from **$995.00**
Price: Lawman Classic (Full custom Vaquero, two-tone finish, Lawman-style engraving, special Lawman gripframe with lanyard ring. . . . . from **$1,295.00**
Price: Classic 45 (shoots 45 Colt, 45 ACP or 45 Schofield without moon clips, built to customer specs on customer furnished Ruger frame) . . . . from **$1,295.00**
Price: Classic 475 (Built on customer furnished base gun. 475 Linebaugh, 5 shot; satin black finish, gunfighter grip, set-back trigger. from **$1,295.00**
Price: Coyote Classic (chambered in 22 Hornet, 22 K-Hornet, 218 Bee, 218 Mashburn Bee, 17 Ackley Bee, 17 Ackley Hornet, 256 Winchester, 25-20, 6-shot unfluted cylinder, heavy 8" barrel, Super Blackhawk gripframe, finish of satin stainless, satin Black Chromex or high polished, comes with laminated cherry grips and Gunfighter grip). . . . from **$995.00**
Price: Black Widow (4-5/8" bbl., black Chromex finish, black widow spider engraving). . . . . from **$1,095.00**
Price: Alaskan Survivalist (3" bbl., Redhawk frame, engraved bear, 45 Colt or 44 Magnum). . . . . from **$1,095.00**
Price: Ultimate Backup (3-1/2" bbl., fixed sights, choice of animal engraving, 475 Linebaugh, 500 Linebaugh built on customer's gun.) . . . . from **$1,295.00**

Price: Ultimate Vaquero (engraved barrel, frame and cylinder, made to customer specs) . . . . from **$995.00**
Price: Ultimate 41 (410 GNR 5-shot, built on customer furnished Ruger frame) . . . . from **$1,295.00**
Price: Ultimate 44 (ported, special recoil-taming grip frame, sling swivels, 44 Mag. 5-shot, built on customer furnished Ruger Hunter) . . . . from **$1,295.00**
Price: Ultimate 480 (choice of barrel lengths in any caliber, full vapor honed stainless steel, satin finish Black Chromex or two-toned finish, 5 shot cylinder, heavy barrel, Gunfightor grip, full action job, custom laminated grips, freewheeling cylinder, Belt Mountain base pin) . . . . from **$995.00**
Price: Ultimate Long Colt (Built on customer-furnished 45 Long Colt Vaquero. 5 shot. Satin black finish, gunfighter grip. . . . . . . from **$1,295.00**
Price: Ultimate 50 (choice of barrel lengths in any centerfire caliber, 5 shot stainless steel 50 Action Express, freewheeling cylinder) from **$1,195.00**
Price: Ultimate 500 (built on stretch frame in 500 S&W. Five shot. Choice of bbl. lengths, gunfigher grip, set-back trigger. . . . . from **$2,495.00**
Price: Ultimate Black Widow (475 Linebaugh or 500 Linebaugh, heavy duty 5 shot cylinder, heavy high grade barrel, Gunfighter Grip with black Micarta grips, Belt Mountain base pin) . . . . from **$1,295.00**
Price: 1 Asterisk (Full custom M1911. Stainless or blued finish. Full combat features including see-thru Lexan grip panel. . . . . . . from **$1,095.00**
Price: Double Deuce (8" heavy bbl., adjustable sights, laminated grips, 22 WMR 8-shot). . . . . from **$1,195.00**
Price: 510 Hunter (octagonal bbl., set back trigger, adjustable sights, 510 GNR 5-shot, built on customer furnished Ruger frame) . . from **$1,495.00**
Price: American Hunter (475 Linebaugh or 500 Linebaugh, built to customers specs on furnished Ruger frame). . . . . from **$1,295.00**
Price: African Hunter (6" bbl., with or without muzzle brake, 475 or 500 Linebaugh. Built on customer's gun. . . . . from **$1,295.00**

SEMI-CUSTOM HANDGUNS — REVOLVERS

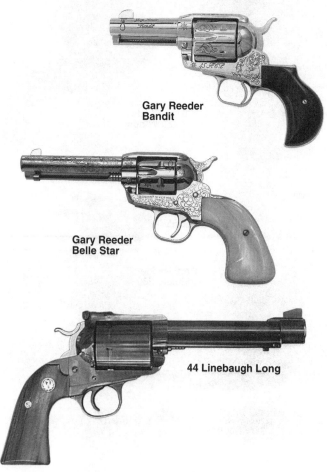

Gary Reeder Bandit

Gary Reeder Belle Star

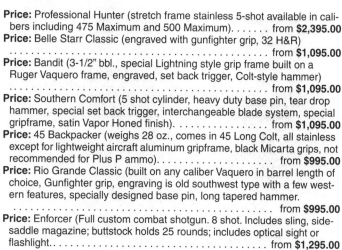

44 Linebaugh Long

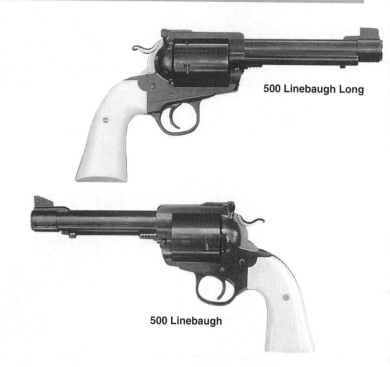

500 Linebaugh Long

500 Linebaugh

Price: Professional Hunter (stretch frame stainless 5-shot available in calibers including 475 Maximum and 500 Maximum). . . . . . . from **$2,395.00**
Price: Belle Starr Classic (engraved with gunfighter grip, 32 H&R)
. . . . from **$1,095.00**
Price: Bandit (3-1/2" bbl., special Lightning style grip frame built on a Ruger Vaquero frame, engraved, set back trigger, Colt-style hammer)
. . . . from **$1,095.00**
Price: Southern Comfort (5 shot cylinder, heavy duty base pin, tear drop hammer, special set back trigger, interchangeable blade system, special gripframe, satin Vapor Honed finish). . . . . from **$1,095.00**
Price: 45 Backpacker (weighs 28 oz., comes in 45 Long Colt, all stainless except for lightweight aircraft aluminum gripframe, black Micarta grips, not recommended for Plus P ammo). . . . . from **$995.00**
Price: Rio Grande Classic (built on any caliber Vaquero in barrel length of choice, Gunfighter grip, engraving is old southwest type with a few western features, specially designed base pin, long tapered hammer.
. . . . from **$995.00**
Price: Enforcer (Full custom combat shotgun. 8 shot. Includes sling, side-saddle magazine; buttstock holds 25 rounds; includes optical sight or flashlight. . . . . from **$1,295.00**

LINEBAUGH CUSTOM SIXGUNS REVOLVERS
Caliber: 45 Colt, 44 Linebaugh Long, 458 Linebaugh, 475 Linebaugh, 500 Linebaugh, 500 Linebaugh Long, 445 Super Mag. **Barrel:** 4-3/4", 5-1/2", 6", 7- 1/2"; other lengths available. **Weight:** NA. **Length:** NA. **Grips:** Dustin Linebaugh Custom made to customer's specs. **Sights:** Bowen steel rear or factory Ruger; blade front. **Features:** Conversions using customer's Ruger Blackhawk Bisley and Vaquero Bisley frames. Made in U.S. by Linebaugh Custom Sixguns.
Price: Small 45 Colt conversion (rechambered cyl., new barrel)
. . . . from **$1,200.00**
Price: Large 45 Colt conversion (oversized cyl., new barrel, 5- or 6- shot) . . . . from **$1,800.00**
Price: 475 Linebaugh, 500 Linebaugh conversions . . . . . . from **$1,800.00**
Price: Linebaugh and 445 Super Mag calibers on 357 Maximum frame
. . . . from **$3,000.00**

Gary Reeder Ultimate Encore

Gary Reeder Kodiak
Hunter Dall Sheep

SEMI-CUSTOM

GARY REEDER CUSTOM GUNS CONTENDER AND ENCORE PISTOLS

Caliber: 22 Cheetah, 218 Bee, 22 K-Hornet, 22 Hornet, 218 Mashburn Bee, 22-250 Improved, 6mm/284, 7mm STW, 7mm GNR, 30 GNR, 338 GNR, 300 Win. Magnum, 338 Win. Magnum, 350 Rem. Magnum, 358 STA, 375 H&H, 378 GNR, 416 Remington, 416 GNR, 450 GNR, 475 Linebaugh, 500 Linebaugh, 50 Alaskan, 50 AE, 454 Casull; others available. **Barrel:** 8" to 15" (others available). **Weight:** NA. **Length:** Varies with barrel length. **Grips:** Walnut fingergroove. **Sights:** Express-style adjustable rear and barrel band front (Kodiak Hunter); none furnished most models. **Features:** Offers complete guns and barrels in the T/C Contender and Encore. Integral muzzle brake, engraved animals and model name, tuned action, high-polish or satin stainless steel or black Chromex finish. Made in U.S. by Gary Reeder Custom Guns.
Price: Kodiak Hunter (50 AE, 475 Linebaugh, 500 Linebaugh, 510 GNR, or 454 Casull, Kodiak bear and Dall sheep engravings) .... from **$1,195.00**
Price: Ultimate Encore (15" bbl. with muzzle brake, custom engraving) .... from **$1,095.00**

SSK Industries Contender

SSK INDUSTRIES CONTENDER AND ENCORE PISTOLS

Caliber: More than 200, including most standard pistol and rifle calibers, as well as 226 JDJ, 6mm JDJ, 257 JDJ, 6.5mm JDJ, 7mm JDJ, 6.5mm Mini-Dreadnaught, 30-06 JDJ, 280 JDJ, 375 JDJ, 6mm Whisper, 300 Whisper and 338 Whisper. **Barrel:** 10" to 26"; blued or stainless; variety of configurations. **Weight:** Varies with barrel length and features. **Length:** Varies with barrel length. **Grips:** Pachmayr, wood models available. **Features:** Offers frames, barrels and complete guns in the T/C Contender and Encore. Fluted, diamond, octagon and round barrels; flatside Contender frames; chrome-plating; muzzle brakes; trigger jobs; variety of stocks and forends; sights and optics. Made in U.S. by SSK Industries.
Price: Blued Contender frame .... from **$390.00**
Price: Stainless Contender frame .... from **$390.00**
Price: Blued Encore frame .... from **$290.00**
Price: Stainless Encore frame .... from **$318.00**
Price: Contender barrels .... from **$315.00**
Price: Encore barrels .... from **$340.00**

SEMI-CUSTOM

Ed Brown 702 Varmint

Ed Brown 702 Bushveld

ED BROWN CUSTOM BOLT-ACTION RIFLES

Caliber: 222, 223, 22-250, 220 Swift, 243, 243 Ackley Imp., 25-06, 270 Win., 280 Rem., 280 Ackley Imp., 6mm, 6.5/284, 7mm/08, 7mm Rem. Mag., 7STW, 30/06, 308, 300 Win. Mag., 338 Win. Mag., 375 H&H, 404 Jeffery, 416 Rem. Mag., 416 Rigby, 458 Win. Mag. **Barrel:** 21", 24", 26". **Weight:** NA. **Length:** NA. **Stock:** Fiberglass synthetic; swivel studs; recoil pad. **Sights:** Optional; Talley scope rings and base furnished; scope mounting included in price (scope extra). **Features:** Machined receiver; hand-fitted bolt with welded handle; M16-type extractor; three-position safety; trigger adjustable for pull and overtravel; match-quality, hand-lapped barrel with deep countersunk crowning. Made in U.S. by Ed Brown Custom, Inc.

Price: Model 702 Savanna short- or long-action repeater (lightweight 24" or medium-weight 26" barrel) . . from **$2,800.00**
Price: Model 702 Tactical long-action repeater (heavy contour 26" barrel) . . . . from **$2,900.00**
Price: Model 702 Ozark short-action repeater (lightweight 21" barrel) . . . . from **$2,800.00**
Price: Model 702 Varmint short-action single shot (med. 26" or hvy. 24") . . . . from **$2,800.00**
Price: Model 702 Light Tactical short-action repeater (med. 21" barrel) . . . . from **$2,800.00**
Price: Model 702 Bushveld dangerous game rifle (24" med. or heavy barrel) . . . . from **$2,900.00**
Price: Model 702 Denali mountain hunting rifle (22" super light weight bbl. or 23" light weight bbl.) . . . . . . from **$2,800.00**
Price: Model 702 Tactical sniper rifle (26" heavy bbl.) . . . . from **$2,900.00**
Price: Model 702 Marine Sniper (24" heavy bbl.) . . . . from **$2,900.00**

Dakota 76 Classic

Dakota 97 Hunter

DAKOTA 76 RIFLE

Caliber: All calibers from 22-250 through 458 Win. Mag. **Barrel:** 23". **Weight:** 6-1/2 lbs. **Length:** NA. **Stock:** Choice of X-grade oil-finished English, Bastogne or Claro walnut. **Features:** Short, standard short magnum or long magnum actions, hand checkered stock with 1" black recoil pad, steel grip cap and single screw stud sling swivels. Many options and upgrades available.

Price: Dakota 76 Classic . . . . from **$4,995.00**
Price: Dakota 76 Safari (23" bbl., calibers from 257 Roberts through 458 Win. Mag. drop belly magazine with straddle floorplate)
. . . . from **$5,995.00**
Price: Dakota 76 African (24" bbl., 450 Dakota, 416 Dakota, 416 Rigby, 404 Jeffrey,
four-round magazine) . . . . from **$6,795.00**
Price: Dakota 97 Hunter (24" bbl., calibers from 25-06 to 375 Dakota, synthetic stock) . . . . from **$2,195.00**
Price: Longbow Tactical Engagement Rifle (28" bbl., 338 Lapua Mag., 330 Dakota, 300 Dakota, McMillan fiberglass stock with
full-length action bedding) . . . . from **$4,500.00**

SEMI-CUSTOM RIFLES — BOLT-ACTION

Remington Model ABG

REMINGTON MODEL 700 CUSTOM SHOP RIFLES

Caliber: 270 Win., 280 Rem., 30-06, 7mm Rem. Mag., 7mm STW, 300 Win. Mag., 300 Wea. Mag., 338 Win. Mag., 8mm Rem. Mag., 35 Whelen, 375 H&H Mag., 416 Rem. Mag., 458 Win. Mag., 7mm RUM, 300 RUM, 338 RUM, 375 RUM. **Barrel:** 22", 24", 26". **Weight:** 6 lbs. 6 oz. to 9 lbs. **Length:** 44-1/4" to 46-1/2" overall. **Stock:** Laminated hardwood, walnut or Kevlar-reinforced fiberglass. **Sights:** Adjustable rear (Safari models); all receivers drilled and tapped for scope mounts. **Features:** Black matte, satin blue or uncolored stainless steel finish; hand-fitted action is epoxy-bedded to stock; tuned trigger; bolt-supported extractor for sure extraction; fancy wood and other options available. Made in U.S. by Remington Arms Co.

Price: Custom KS Mountain Rifle (24" barrel, synthetic stock, 6-3/4 lbs. in mag. cals.) . . . . from **$1,314.00**
Price: Custom KS Safari Stainless (22" barrel, synthetic stock, 9 lbs.) . . . . from **$1,697.00**
Price: Model ABG (African Big Game - 26" bbl., laminated stock, satin blue finish) . . . . from **$1,726.00**
Price: APR (African Plains Rifle - 26" barrel, laminated stock, satin blue finish) . . . . from **$1,716.00**
Price: AWR (Alaskan Wilderness Rifle - 24" barrel, syn. stock, black matte finish) . . . . from **$1,593.00**
Price: Model 700 Custom C Grade - from **$1,733.00**; Custom High Grade . . . . from **$3,297.00**

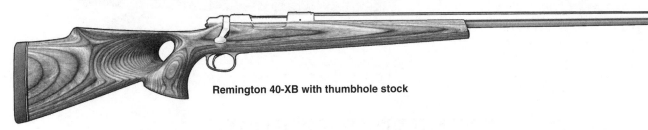

Remington 40-XB with thumbhole stock

REMINGTON MODEL 40-X CUSTOM SHOP TARGET RIFLES

Caliber: 22 LR, 22 WMR, 22 BR Rem., 222 Rem., 223 Rem., 22-250, 220 Swift, 6mm BR Rem., 6mm Rem., 243 Win., 25-06, 260 Rem., 7.62mm NATO, 7mm BR Rem., 7mm Rem. Mag., 7mm STW, 308 Win., 30-06, 300 Win. Mag. **Barrel:** 24", 27-1/4"; various twist rates offered. **Weight:** 9-3/4 to 11 lbs. **Length:** 40" to 47" overall. **Stock:** Walnut, laminated wood or Kevlar-reinforced fiberglass. **Sights:** None; receiver drilled and tapped for scope mounts. **Features:** Single shot or 5-shot repeater; carbon steel or stainless steel receiver; externally adjustable trigger (1-1/2 to 3-1/2 lbs.); rubber butt pad. From Remington Arms Co.

Price: 40-XB Rangemaster (27-1/4" bbl., walnut stock, forend rail with hand stop) . . . . from **$1,636.00**
Price: 40-XB (with thumbhole stock) . . . . from **$1,848.00**
Price: 40-XB KS (27-1/4" bbl., black synthetic stock) . . . . from **$1,876.00**
Price: 40-XRBR KS (24" bbl., Remington green synthetic stock with straight comb) . . . . from **$1,894.00**
Price: 40-XC KS (24" bbl., gray synthetic stock with adj. comb) . . . . from **$1,821.00**
Price: 40-XB Tactical (27-1/4" bbl., synthetic stock, matte finish) . . . . from **$2,108.00**

Remington Model Seven Custom MS

REMINGTON MODEL SEVEN CUSTOM SHOP RIFLES

Caliber: 222 Rem., 223 Rem., 22-250 Rem., 243 Win., 6mm Rem., 250 Savage, 257 Roberts, 260 Rem., 308 Win., 7mm-08 Rem., 35 Rem., 350 Rem. Mag. **Barrel:** 20". **Weight:** 5-3/4 to 6-1/2 lbs. **Length:** 39-1/2" overall. **Stock:** Laminated hardwood or Kevlar-reinforced fiberglass. **Sights:** Adjustable ramp rear, hooded blade front. **Features:** Hand-fitted action; epoxy bedded; deep blue or non-reflective black matte finish; drilled and tapped for scope mounts. From Remington Arms Co.

Price: Model Seven Custom MS (20" bbl., Mannlicher stock, deep blue finish) . . . . from **$1,332.00**
Price: Model Seven Custom KS (20" bbl., synthetic stock, matte finish) . . . . from **$1,314.00**
Price: Model Seven AWR Alaskan Wilderness Rifle (22" bbl., synthetic stock, 7mm Rem. SAUM,
300 Rem. SAUM) . . . . from **$1,546.00**

SEMI-CUSTOM

John Rigby African Express Rifle

JOHN RIGBY CUSTOM AFRICAN EXPRESS RIFLE

Caliber: 375 H&H Magnum, 416 Rigby, 450 Rigby, 458 Winchester, 505 Gibbs. **Barrel:** To customer specs. **Weight:** NA. **Length:** To customer specs. **Stock:** Customer's choice. **Sights:** Express-type rear, hooded ramp front; scope mounts offered. **Features:** Handcrafted bolt-action rifle built to customer specifications. Variety of engraving and stock wood options available. Imported from England by John Rigby & Co.

    Price: African Express Rifle
. . . . from **$18,600.00**

John Rigby African Express Rifle engraving

JOHN RIGBY BOLT-ACTION RIFLES

Caliber: 300 H&H, 375 H&H, 416 Rigby, 458 Win., 500 Jeffrey (other calibers upon request) **Barrel:** NA. **Weight:** NA. **Length:** NA. **Stock:** Exhibition grade English walnut. **Sights:** Quarter rib with Express sights containing flip up night sight. **Features:** Stock custom-fitted to buyer specifications, detachable scope mounts included, Pac Nor Match grade barrel.
    Price: John Rigby Bolt Action Rifle . . . . from **$14,500.00**

TIME PRECISION BOLT-ACTION RIFLES

Caliber: 22 LR, 222, 223, 308, 378, 300 Win. Mag., 416 Rigby, others. **Barrel:** NA. **Weight:** 10 lbs. and up. **Length:** NA. **Stock:** Fiberglass. **Sights:** None; receiver drilled and tapped for scope mount. **Features:** Thirty different action types offered, including single shots and repeaters for bench rest, varmint and big-game hunting. Machined chrome-moly action; three-position safety; Shilen match trigger (other triggers available); twin cocking cams; dual firing pin. Built to customer specifications. From Time Precision.
    Price: 22 LR Bench Rest Rifle (Shilen match-grade stainless steel bbl., fiberglass stock) . . . . from **$2,202.00**
    Price: 22 LR Target Rifle . . . . from **$2,220.00**
    Price: 22 LR Sporter . . . . from **$1,980.00**
    Price: 22 LR Benchrest Rifle . . . . from **$2,202.00**
    Price: Hunting Rifle (calibers to 30-06) . . . . from **$2,202.00**
    Price: Benchrest Rifle (most calibers) . . . . from **$2,202.00**
    Price: Hunting Rifle (7mm Rem. Mag., 300 Win. Mag., 338 Win. Mag.) . . . . from **$2,322.00**

CONSULT
SHOOTER'S MARKETPLACE
Page 64, This Issue

Weatherby Safari Grade

Weatherby Crown Custom

Weatherby Custom close-up

WEATHERBY CUSTOM SHOP BOLT-ACTION RIFLES

Caliber: 257 Wby. Mag., 270 Wby. Mag., 7mm Wby. Mag., 300 Wby. Mag., 340 Wby. Mag., 375 H&H Mag., 378 Wby. Mag., 416 Wby. Mag., 460 Wby. Mag. **Barrel:** 24", 26", 28". **Weight:** NA. **Length:** NA. **Stock:** Monte Carlo, modified Monte Carlo or Classic design in Exhibition- or Exhibition Special Select grades of claro or French walnut; injection-molded synthetic in Snow Camo, Alpine Camo or Dark Timber colors. **Sights:** Quarter-rib rear with one standing and one folding leaf, hooded ramp front (Safari Grade); drilled and tapped for scope mount. Features: Rosewood or ebony pistol-grip caps with inlaid diamonds in rosewood, walnut or maple; three grades of engraving patterns for receiver, bolt and handle; gold inlays; wooden inlaid buttstock, forearm and magazine box; three grades of engraved and gold inlaid rings and bases; canvas/leather, solid leather or leather with oak trim case. From the Weatherby Custom Shop.

Price: Safari Grade (engr. floorplate, oil-finished French wal. stock w/fleur-de-lis checkering.)	**$6.050.00**
Price: Crown (engr., inlaid floorplate, engr. bbl. and receiver, hand-carved walnut stock)	**$7,757.00**
Price: Crown Custom (engraved barrel, receiver and triggerguard, hand-carved walnut stock, damascened bolt and follower with checkered knob)	from **$7,757.00**
Price: Outfitter Krieger (Krieger stainless steel bbl.)	**$3,639.00**
Price: Outfitter Custom (standard barrel, Bell and Carlson syn. camo stock)	from **$2,583.00**
Price: Dangerous Game Rifle (chrome moly Criterion barrel by Krieger Monte Carlo-style composite stock, Mark V action)	from **$3,095.00**

Winchester African Express

WINCHESTER MODEL 70 CLASSIC CUSTOM RIFLES

Caliber: 375 H&H Mag., 416 Rem. Mag., 458 Win. Mag., 458 Lott, 470 Capstick, 257 Roberts, 260 Rem., 7mm-08 Rem., 300 WSM, 270 WSM, 7mm WSM, 308 Win., 358 Win., 450 Marlin, 270 Win., 7mm Win., 30-06 Spfld., 25-06 Rem., 6.5x55 Swe., 264 Win. Mag., 280 Rem., 35 Whelen, 7mm Rem. Mag., 7mm Ultra Mag., 7mm STW, 300 Win. Mag., 300 Wea. Mag., 300 Ultra. Mag., 338 Ultra Mag., 375 H&H (Lwt). **Barrel:** 22", 24", 26". **Weight:** 6.5 to 9.5 lbs. **Length:** NA. **Stock:** Various grades of walnut and synthetic stocks available. **Sights:** Three-leaf express rear, adjustable front, (Express models); none furnished on other models. **Features:** Match-grade cut rifled barrels with squared, hand-honed actions. Most are available in stainless or blued, and right- or left-handed, hand-fitted actions. All utilize the pre-'64 type action with controlled round feed, receiver-mounted blade ejector and specially-tuned trigger systems. All are shipped in a hard case. Made in U.S.A. by Winchester/U.S. Repeating Arms Co.

Price: Model 70 Classic Custom African Express (22" or 24" barrel, 9.25 to 9.5 lbs)	from **$4,572.00**
Price: Safari Express (24" barrel, 9 to 9.25 lbs.)	from **$3,043.00**
Price: Short Action (24" barrel, 7.5 to 8.25 lbs.)	from **$2,708.00**
Price: Featherweight (22" barrel, 7.25 lbs., 270 Win., 7mm Win., 30-06 Spfld.)	from **$2,708.00**
Price: Carbon (24" or 26" barrel, 6.5 to 7 lbs.)	from **$3,233.00**
Price: Ultimate Classic (24" or 26" barrel, 7.5 to 7.75 lbs.)	from **$2,941.00**
Price: Extreme Weather (22", 24" or 26" barrel, 7.25 to 7.5 lbs.)	from **$2,525.00**

SEMI-CUSTOM RIFLES — AUTOLOADERS

Bushmaster DCM Competition Rifle

Volquartsen Grey Ghost

BROWNING SEMI-AUTO 22 LUXE

Caliber: 22 LR. **Barrel:** 19-1/4". **Weight:** 5 lbs. 3 oz. **Length:** 37". **Stock:** Polished walnut. **Sights:** Adjustable folding leaf rear, gold bead front. **Features:** The traditional John Browning-designed .22 takedown autoloader with bottom eject. Grooved receiver will accept most groove or tip-off type mounts or receiver sights. Custom shop versions are available in two grades of: SA 22 Grade II, and SA 22 Grade III.
    Price: . . . . **NA**

BROWNING BAR MARK I

The original Browning BAR Mark I from the Browning Custom Shop in Belgium available in two grades: Grade IV and Grade D.
    Price: . . . . **NA**

BUSHMASTER SEMI-AUTO RIFLES

Caliber: 223. **Barrel:** 16" regular or fluted, 20" regular, heavy or fluted, 24" heavy or fluted. **Weight:** 6.9 to 8.37 lbs. **Length:** 34.5" to 38.25" overall. **Stock:** Polymer. **Sights:** Fully adjustable dual flip-up aperture rear, blade front or Picatinny rail for scope mount. **Features:** Versions of the AR-15 style rifle. Aircraft-quality aluminum receiver; chrome-lined barrel and chamber; chrome-moly-vanadium steel barrel with 1:9" twist; manganese phosphate matte finish; forged front sight; receiver takes down without tools; serrated, finger groove pistol grip. Made in U.S.A. by Bushmaster Firearms/Quality Parts Co.
    Price: DCM Competition Rifle **$1,495.00**

LES BAER AR 223 AUTO RIFLES

Caliber: 223. **Barrel:** 16-1/4", 20", 22" or 24"; cryo-treated, stainless steel bench-rest grade. **Weight:** NA. **Length:** NA. **Stock:** Polymer. **Sights:** None; Picatinny rail for scope mount. **Features:** Forged and machined upper and lower receiver; single- or double-stage adjustable trigger; free-float handguard; Bear Coat protective finish. Made in U.S.A. by Les Baer Custom.
    Price: Ultimate Super Varmint (Jewell two-stage trigger, guar. to shoot 1/2 MOA groups) . . . . from **$1,989.00**
    Price: Ultimate M4 Flattop (16-1/4" bbl., Ultra single-stage trigger) . . . . from **$2,195.00**
    Price: Ultimate IPSC Action (20" bbl., Jewell two-stage trigger) . . . . from **$2,230.00**

SSK INDUSTRIES AR-15 RIFLES

Caliber: 223, 6mm PPC, 6.5mm PPC, Whisper and other wildcats. **Barrel:** 16-1/2" and longer (to order). **Weight:** NA. **Length:** NA. **Stock:** Black plastic. **Sights:** Blade front, adjustable rear (scopes and red-dot sights available). **Features:** Variety of designs to full match-grade guns offered. Customer's gun can be rebarreled or accurized. From SSK Industries.
    Price: Complete AR-15 . . . . from **$1,800.00**
    Price: A2 upper unit (front sight, short handguard **$1,100.00**
    Price: Match Grade upper unit (bull barrel, tubular handguard, scope mount) **$1,100.00**

VOLQUARTSEN CUSTOM 22 CALIBER AUTO RIFLES

Caliber: 22 LR, 22 Magnum. **Barrel:** 16-1/2" to 20"; stainless steel air gauge. **Weight:** 4-3/4 to 5-3/4 lbs. **Length:** NA. **Stock:** Synthetic or laminated. **Sights:** Not furnished; Weaver base provided. **Features:** Conversions of the Ruger 10/22 rifle. Tuned trigger with 2-1/2 to 3-1/2 lb. pull. Variety of configurations and features. From Volquartsen Custom.
    Price: Ultra-Light (22 LR, 16-1/2" tensioned barrel, synthetic stock) . . . . from **$670.00**
    Price: Grey Ghost (22 LR, 18-1/2" barrel, laminated wood stock) . . . . from **$690.00**
    Price: Deluxe (22 LR, 20" barrel, laminated wood or fiberglass stock) . . . . from **$850.00**
    Price: Mossad (22 LR, 20" fluted and ported barrel, fiberglass thumbhole stock) . . . . from **$970.00**
    Price: VX-2500 (22 LR, 20" fluted and ported barrel, aluminum/fiberglass stock) . . . . from **$1,044.00**
    Price: Volquartsen 22 LR (stainless steel receiver) . . . . from **$920.00**
    Price: Volquartsen 22 Mag (22 WMR, stainless steel receiver) . . . . from **$950.00**

SEMI-CUSTOM RIFLES — DOUBLE RIFLES

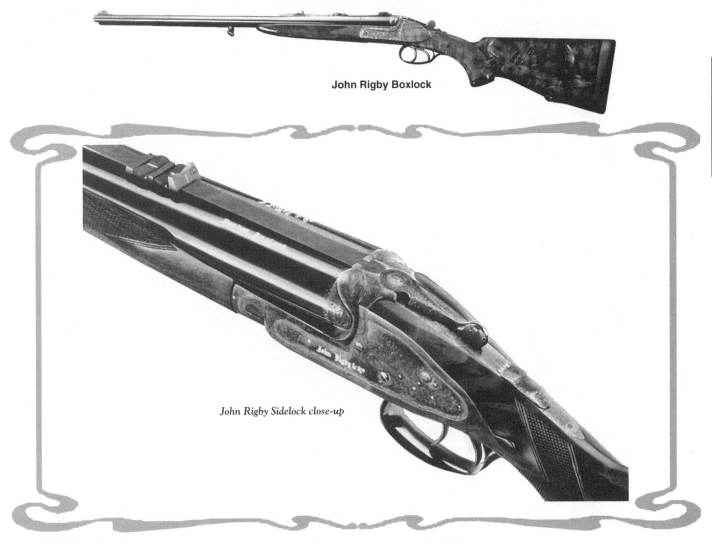

John Rigby Boxlock

John Rigby Sidelock close-up

BERETTA EXPRESS DOUBLE RIFLES

Caliber: 9.3x74R, 375 H&H Mag., 416 Rigby, 458 Win. Mag., 470 Nitro Express, 500 Nitro Express. **Barrel:** 23" to 25". **Weight:** 11 lbs. **Length:** NA. **Stock:** Hand-finished, hand-checkered walnut with cheek rest. **Sights:** Folding-leaf, Express-type rear, blade front. **Features:** High-strength steel action with reinforced receiver sides; top tang extends to stock comb for strength; double triggers (articulated front trigger and automatic blocking device eliminate chance of simultaneous discharge); hand-cut, stepped rib; engraved roooivor; trapdoor compartment in stock for extra cartridges; spare front sights stored in pistol-grip cap. Imported from Italy by Beretta USA.

    Price: SSO6 o/u (optional claw mounts for scope) . . . . from **$21,000.00**
    Price: SSO6 EELL o/u (engraved game scenes or color case-hardened with gold inlays) . . . . from **$23,500.00**
    Price: 455 s/s (color case-hardened action) . . . . from **$36,000.00**
    Price: 455 EELL s/s (receiver engraved with big-game animals) . . . . from **$47,000.00**

BROWNING EXPRESS RIFLES

Still made in Belgium in the traditional manner, two models are available, Herstal and CCS 375. Produced in five different grades of embellishment. Other specifications NA.
    Price: . . . . **NA**

JOHN RIGBY DOUBLE RIFLES

Caliber: 375 H&H, 500/416, 450 Nitro Express, 470 Nitro Express, 500 Nitro Express, 577 Nitro Express. **Barrel:** To customer specs. **Weight:** NA. **Length:** To customer specs. **Stock:** To customer specs. **Sights:** Dovetail, express-type sights; claw-foot scope mount available. **Features:** Handcrafted to customer specifications. Boxlock or sidelock action, hand-fitted; variety of engraving and other options offered. Imported from England by John Rigby & Co.
    Price: Rigby Boxlock . . . . from **$23,500.00**
    Price: Rigby Sidelock . . . . from **$41,700.00**

Ballard No. 1-3/4 Far West

SEMI-CUSTOM

Ballard No. 3 Gallery

Ballard No. 6 Off Hand

Ballard No. 8 Union Hill

BALLARD RIFLE, LLC

Caliber: 22 LR, 32-40, 38-55, 40-65 Win., 40-70 SS, 40-90, 45-70 Gov't., 45-90, 45-110, 50-70 Gov't., 50-90 **Barrel:** 24", 26", 30", 32", 34". **Weight:** 7-1/2 to 11-1/2 lbs. **Stock:** American black walnut. **Sights:** Blade front, Rocky Mountain rear, others. **Features:** Authentic reproductions faithful to the original patent. Receivers and internal parts machined from solid 8620 steel stock, not castings. Hand finished. Many options. **Price:** No. 1-1/2 Hunter's Rifle (30" round bbl., single trigger, S lever) . . . . from **$2,050.00**
Price: No. 1-3/4 Far West (30" round regular or heavyweight bbl., S lever) . . . . from **$2,250.00**
Price: No. 3 Gallery Rifle (24", 26" or 30" lightweight octagon bbl., rifle bottsrock with steel crescent buttplate, S lever) . . . . . . from **$2,050.00**
Price: No. 3F Fine Gallery Rifle (26", 28" or 30" octagon bbl., pistol grip, single or double set triggers) . . . . from **$2,500.00**
Price: No. 4 Perfection (30" or 32" octagon bbl. single or double set trigger) . . . . from **$2,250.00**
Price: No. 4-1/2 Mid Range (30" or 32" standard or heavyweight half octagon bbl., single or double set triggers, pistol grip shotgun buttstock) . . . . from **$2,250.00**
Price: No. 5 Pacific (30" or 32" standard or heavyweight octagon bbl., standard stocks in rifle or shotgun configuration) . . . . from **$2,575.00**
Price: No. 5-1/2 Montana Model (30" or 32" heavyweight octagon bbl., under-barrel wiping rod, set triggers, ring lever) . . . . from **$2,725.00**
Price: No. 6 Off Hand Rifle (30", 32" or 34" half octagon bbl., blade front sight, pistol grip receiver, double set triggers) . . . . from **$2,550.00**
Price: No. 7 Long Range (32" or 34" standard or heavyweight half octagon bbl., pistol grip shotgun buttstock, single or double set trigger) . . . . from **$2,250.00**
Price: No. 8 Union Hill Model (30" half octagon standard or heavyweight bbl., double set triggers, pistol grip stock with cheekpiece, full loop lever) from **$2,500.00**
Price: Standard Sporting Model 1885 High Wall (30" or 32" octagonal bbl., single trigger, small S lever). . . . . from **$2,050.00**
Price: Special Sporting Model 1885 High Wall (32" bbl., shotgun buttstock with cheekpiece, shotgun buttplate, double set triggers) . . . . . . from **$2,200.00**

Ballard No. 5 Pacific

Ballard No. 5-1/2 Montana

Ballard Standard Sporting Model

Ballard No. 7 Long Range

Ballard Special Sporting Model

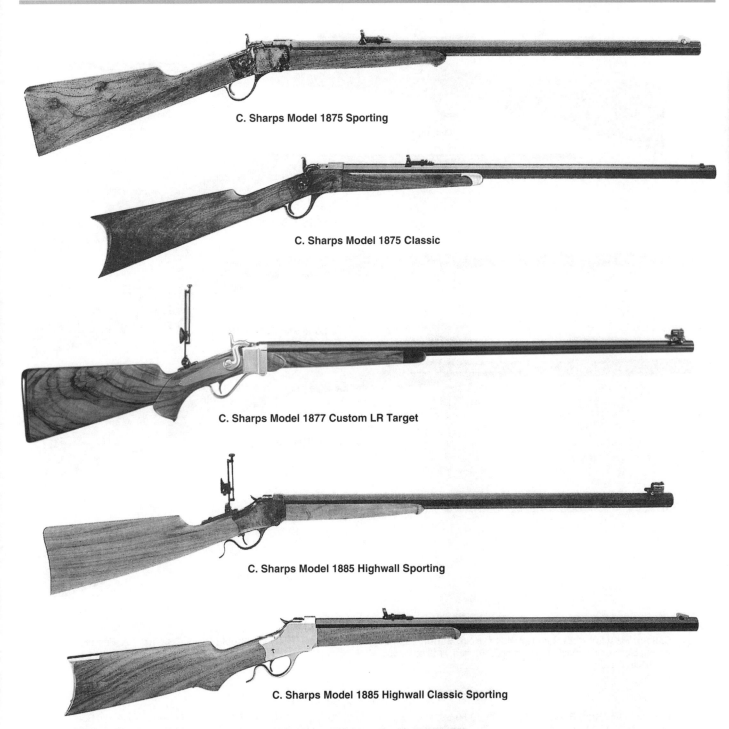

C. Sharps Model 1875 Sporting

C. Sharps Model 1875 Classic

C. Sharps Model 1877 Custom LR Target

C. Sharps Model 1885 Highwall Sporting

C. Sharps Model 1885 Highwall Classic Sporting

C. SHARPS ARMS RIFLES

Caliber: 22 RF to 50-140-3 1/4 Sharps. **Barrel:** Octagon 18" to 34". **Weight:** 9-18 lbs. **Stock:** American English walnut (premium straight grain to presentation). **Sights:** Short range to long range target. **Features:** Authentic replicas of Sharps rifles. Models 1874, 1877 & 1885 machined from solid steel. Made in U.S. by C. Sharps Arms Co. Inc.

Price: Model 1874 Hartford	from **$1,775.00**
Price: Model 1874 Bridgeport	from **$1,495.00**
Price: Model 1875 Sporting	from **$1,095.00**
Price: Model 1875 Classic	from **$1,385.00**
Price: Model 1875 Target	from **$1,136.63**
Price: Model 1877 Custom LR Target	from **$5,500.00**
Price: Model 1885 Highwall Sporting	from **$1,350.00**
Price: Model 1885 Highwall Classic Sporting	from **$1,550.00**

Dakota Model 10

Lone Star No. 5 Sporting

Lone Star Silhouette

Lone Star Sporting

Lone Star Buffalo

DAKOTA MODEL 10

Caliber: Most from 22 LR through 404 Dakota. **Barrel:** 23". **Length:** NA. **Weight:** 5-1/2 lbs. **Stock:** Walnut. **Sights:** NA. **Features:** Falling block action machined from prehardened 4140 bar stock. Many options.
    Price: Dakota Model 10 . . . . from **$3,795.00**

LONE STAR ROLLING BLOCK RIFLES

Caliber: 30-40 Krag, 30-30, 32-40, 38-55, 40-50 SS, 40-50 BN, 40-65, 40-70 SS, 40-70 BN, 40-82, 40-90 SBN, 40-90 SS, 44-90 Rem. Sp., 45 Colt, 45-110 (3-1/4"), 45-110 (2-7/8"), 45-100, 45-90, 45- 70, 50-70, 50-90. **Barrel:** 26" to 34". **Weight:** 6 to 11 lbs. **Length:** NA. **Stock:** American walnut. **Sights:** Buckhorn rear, blade or Beech front. **Features:** Authentic replicas of Remington rolling block rifles. Octagon barrel (except Creedmore model); bone-pack, color case-hardened action; drilled and tapped for Vernier sight; single, single-set or double-set trigger; variety of sight, finish and engraving options. Fires blackpowder or factory ammo. Made in U.S. by Lone Star Rifle Co. Inc.
    Price: No. 5 Sporting Rifle (30-30 or 30-40 Krag, 26" barrel, buckhorn rear sight) **$1,595.00**
    Price: Cowboy Action Rifle (28" octagonal barrel, buckhorn rear sight) **$1,595.00**
    Price: Silhouette Rifle (32" or 34" octagonal barrel, drilled and tapped for Vernier sight) **$1,595.00**
    Price: Sporting Rifle (straight grip, semi-crescent butt, octagonal bbl.) . . . . from **$1,995.00**
    Price: Creedmoor (34" bbl. identical to original rifle) **$2,195.00**
    Price: Buffalo Rifle (12 or 16 lbs., octagonal bbl.) **$2,900.00**
    Price: Custer Commemorative (50-70 only, octagonal bbl.) exact replica of General George Armstrong Custer's
    Remington Sporting Rifle **$2,900.00**

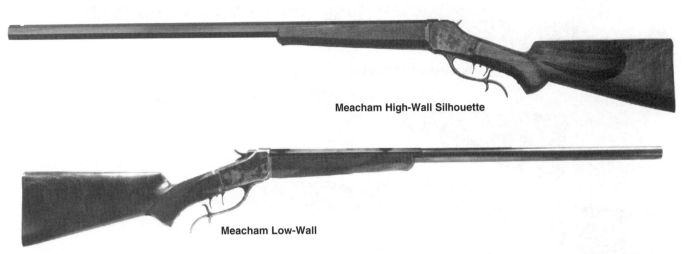

Meacham High-Wall Silhouette

Meacham Low-Wall

MEACHAM HIGH-WALL SILHOUETTE RIFLE

Caliber: Any rimmed cartridge. **Barrel:** 30", 34" octagon. **Weight:** 11-1/2 to 11.9 lbs. **Length:** NA. **Stock:** Fancy eastern black walnut with cheekpiece and shadow line. **Sights:** Tang drilled for Win. base, 3/8" front dovetail. **Features:** Parts interchangeable copy of '85 Winchester. Numerous options include single trigger, single set trigger, or Schuetzen double set triggers, thick side or thin side bone charcoal color case-hardened action.
    Price: Meacham High-Wall Silhouette . . . . from **$3,299.00**
    Price: Meacham Low-Wall Rifle (Calibers: 22 RF Match or 17 HMR, rimfire and centerfire pistol cartridges,
    .22 Hornet or Bee) . . . . from **$3,299.00**

Remington No. 1 Mid-Range Sporter

Remington No. 1 Silhouette

REMINGTON CUSTOM SHOP ROLLING BLOCK RIFLES

Caliber: 45-70. **Barrel:** 30". **Weight:** NA. **Length:** NA. **Stock:** American walnut. **Sights:** Buckhorn rear and blade front (optional tang-mounted Vernier rear, globe with spirit level front). **Features:** Satin blue finish with case-colored receiver; single set trigger; steel Schnabel fore end tip; steel buttplate. From Remington Arms Co. Custom Gun Shop.
    Price: No. 1 Mid-Range Sporter (round or half-octagon barrel) **$1,450.00**
    Price: No. 1 Silhouette (heavy barrel with 1:18" twist; no sights) **$1,560.00**

SEMI-CUSTOM SHOTGUNS

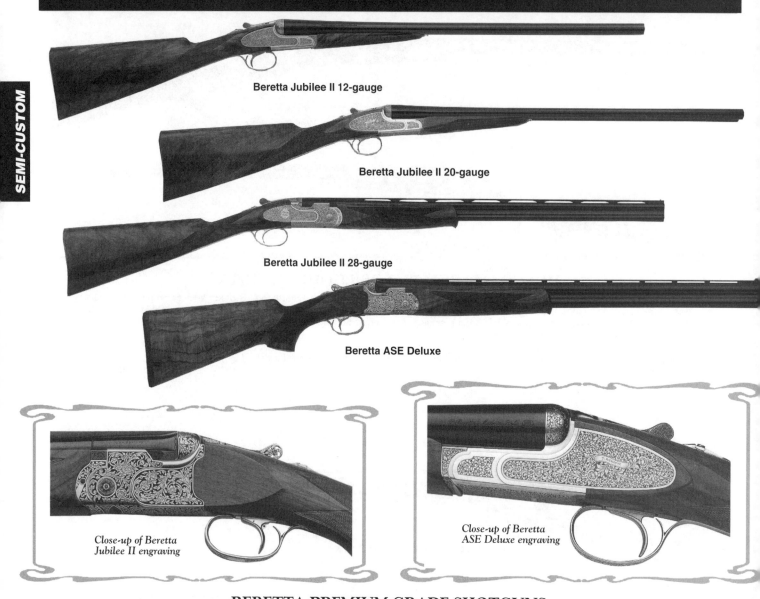

Beretta Jubilee II 12-gauge

Beretta Jubilee II 20-gauge

Beretta Jubilee II 28-gauge

Beretta ASE Deluxe

Close-up of Beretta
Jubilee II engraving

Close-up of Beretta
ASE Deluxe engraving

BERETTA PREMIUM GRADE SHOTGUNS

Gauge: 12, 20, 410, 3" chamber; 28, 2-3/4" chamber. **Barrel:** 26", 28", 30", 32". **Weight:** 5 to 7-1/2 lbs. **Length:** NA. **Stock:** Highly figured English or American walnut; straight or pistol grip; hand-checkered. **Features:** Machined nickel-chrome-moly action, hand-fitted; cross-bolt breech lock; Boehler Antinit steel barrels with fixed chokes or Mobilchoke tubes; single selective or non-selective or double trigger; numerous stock and engraving options. From Beretta USA.

Price: Giubileo (Jubilee) o/u (engraved sideplates, trigger guard, safety and top lever) . . . . from **$12,900.00**
Price: Giubileo II (Jubilee II) s/s (English-style stock, engraved sideplates and fixtures) . . . . from **$12,900.00**
Price: ASE Deluxe o/u (engraved receiver and forend cap) . . . . from **$24,000.00**
Price: SO5 Trap (single, non-selective trigger, heavy beavertail forend, fixed chokes) . . . . from **$17,490.00**
Price: SO5 Skeet (26" or 28" bbl., heavy beavertail forend, fixed chokes) . . . . from **$17,490.00**
Price: SO5 Sporting (single, selective trigger, Mobilchoke tubes) . . . . from **$17,490.00**
Price: SO6 EELL o/u (engraved receiver with gold inlays, custom-fit stock) . . . . from **$34,900.00**
Price: SO6 EL o/u (light English scroll engravings on receiver) . . . . from **$23,900.00**
Price: SO6 EESS o/u (enamel-colored receiver in green, red or blue, arabesque engravings) . . . . from **$34,900.00**
Price: SO9 o/u (single, non-selective trigger, engraved receiver and fixtures) . . . . from **$44,500.00**

Beretta SO5 Skeet 12-gauge

SEMI-CUSTOM SHOTGUNS

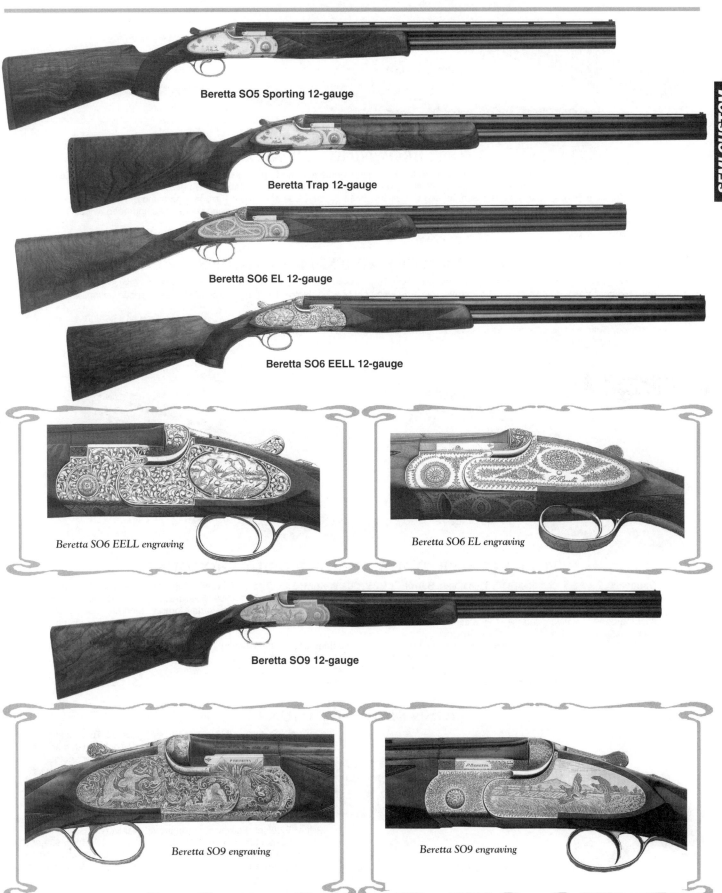

Beretta SO5 Sporting 12-gauge

Beretta Trap 12-gauge

Beretta SO6 EL 12-gauge

Beretta SO6 EELL 12-gauge

Beretta SO6 EELL engraving

Beretta SO6 EL engraving

Beretta SO9 12-gauge

Beretta SO9 engraving

Beretta SO9 engraving

SEMI-CUSTOM SHOTGUNS

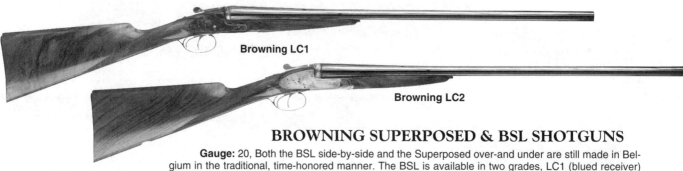

Browning LC1

Browning LC2

BROWNING SUPERPOSED & BSL SHOTGUNS

Gauge: 20, Both the BSL side-by-side and the Superposed over-and-under are still made in Belgium in the traditional, time-honored manner. The BSL is available in two grades, LC1 (blued receiver) and LC2 (silver-colored receiver). The Superposed is available in 18 grades. Custom options include: engraving of name or initials, second set of barrels, special finish or checkering, special stock dimensions, personalized engraving scenes and upgraded wood. Other specifications NA.

    Price: . . . . **NA**

DAKOTA LEGEND/PREMIER SHOTGUNS

Available in all standard gauges, features include exhibition English walnut stock, French grey finish, 50% coverage engraving, straight grip, splinter forend, double trigger, 27" barrels, game rib with gold bead, selective ejectors, choice of chokes. Various options available.

    Price: Dakota Premier Grade . . . . from **$13,950.00**
    Price: Dakota Legend Shotgun (27" bbls., special selection English walnut stock,
      straight grip, splinter forend) . . . . from **$18,000**

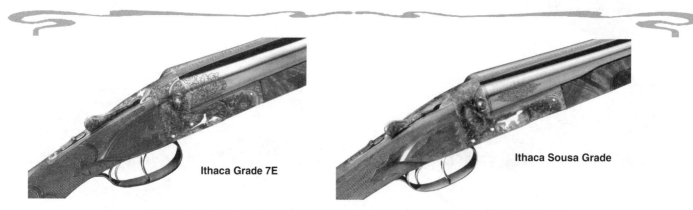

Ithaca Grade 7E

Ithaca Sousa Grade

ITHACA CLASSIC DOUBLES SIDE-BY-SIDE SHOTGUNS

Gauge: 20, 28, 2-3/4" chamber; 410, 3" chamber. **Barrel:** 26", 28", 30". **Weight:** 5 lbs. 5 oz. (410 bore) to 5 lbs. 14 oz. (20 ga.). **Length:** NA. **Stock:** Exhibition-grade American black walnut, hand-checkered with hand-rubbed oil finish. **Features:** Updated duplicates of original New Ithaca Double double-barrel shotguns. Hand-fitted box-lock action; splinter or beavertail forend; bone-charcoal color case-hardened receiver; chrome-moly steel rust-blued barrels; ejectors; gold double triggers; fixed chokes; hand-engraved game scenes. Made in U.S. by Ithaca Classic Doubles.

    Price: Special Skeet Grade (plain color case-hardened receiver, feather crotch walnut stock) **$3,465.00**
    Price: Grade 4E (gold-plated triggers, jeweled barrel flats, engraved game-bird scene) **$4,625.00**
    Price: Grade 7E (gold-inlaid ducks, pheasants and bald eagle on scroll engraving) **$9,200.00**
    Price: Sousa Grade (gold-inlaid setter, pointer, flying ducks and Sousa mermaid) **$11,550.00**

JOHN RIGBY SHOTGUNS

John Rigby Side-by-Side 12-gauge engraving

Gauge: 12, 16, 20, 28 and 410 bore. **Barrel:** To customer specs. **Weight:** NA. **Length:** To customer specs. **Stock:** Customer's choice. **Features:** True sidelock side-by-side and over-under shotguns made to customer's specifications. Hand-fitted actions and stocks; engraved receivers embellished with game scenes; over-under includes removable choke tubes. Imported from England by John Rigby & Co.

    Price: Sidelock over-under (single selective, non-selective
      or double triggers) . . . . from **$36,500.00**
    Price: Sidelock side-by-side (engraved receiver,
      choice of stock wood) . . . . from **$39,950.00**
    Price: Hammer shotguns (manual-cocking hammers, rebounding
      firing pins and hammers; extractors only) . . . . . from **$18,000.00**

SEMI-CUSTOM SHOTGUNS

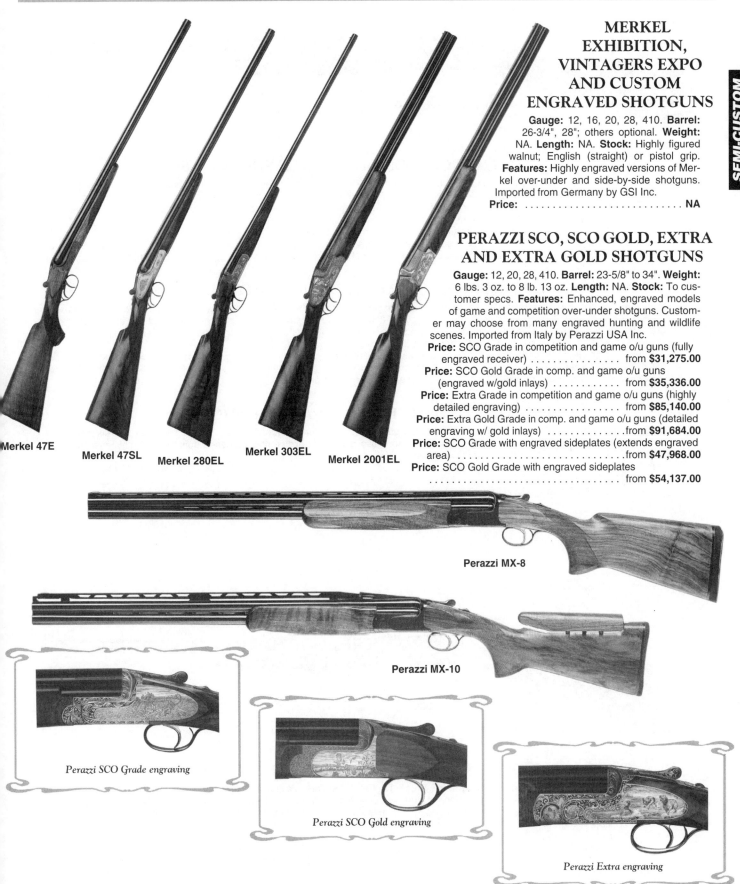

Merkel 47E

Merkel 47SL

Merkel 280EL

Merkel 303EL

Merkel 2001EL

MERKEL EXHIBITION, VINTAGERS EXPO AND CUSTOM ENGRAVED SHOTGUNS

Gauge: 12, 16, 20, 28, 410. **Barrel:** 26-3/4", 28"; others optional. **Weight:** NA. **Length:** NA. **Stock:** Highly figured walnut; English (straight) or pistol grip. **Features:** Highly engraved versions of Merkel over-under and side-by-side shotguns. Imported from Germany by GSI Inc.
Price: . . . . **NA**

PERAZZI SCO, SCO GOLD, EXTRA AND EXTRA GOLD SHOTGUNS

Gauge: 12, 20, 28, 410. **Barrel:** 23-5/8" to 34". **Weight:** 6 lbs. 3 oz. to 8 lb. 13 oz. **Length:** NA. **Stock:** To customer specs. **Features:** Enhanced, engraved models of game and competition over-under shotguns. Customer may choose from many engraved hunting and wildlife scenes. Imported from Italy by Perazzi USA Inc.
Price: SCO Grade in competition and game o/u guns (fully engraved receiver) . . . . from **$31,275.00**
Price: SCO Gold Grade in comp. and game o/u guns (engraved w/gold inlays) . . . . from **$35,336.00**
Price: Extra Grade in competition and game o/u guns (highly detailed engraving) . . . . from **$85,140.00**
Price: Extra Gold Grade in comp. and game o/u guns (detailed engraving w/ gold inlays) . . . . from **$91,684.00**
Price: SCO Grade with engraved sideplates (extends engraved area) . . . . from **$47,968.00**
Price: SCO Gold Grade with engraved sideplates . . . . from **$54,137.00**

Perazzi MX-8

Perazzi MX-10

Perazzi SCO Grade engraving

Perazzi SCO Gold engraving

Perazzi Extra engraving

SEMI-CUSTOM SHOTGUNS

Remington 11-87 "F" Grade

REMINGTON CUSTOM SHOP AUTO SHOTGUNS

Gauge: 10, 12, 20, 28. **Barrel:** 21" to 30". **Weight:** NA. **Length:** NA. **Stock:** Two grades of American walnut. **Features:** Engraved versions of the Model 11-87 and Model 1100 shotgun. "D" or "F" grade fancy walnut, hand-checkered stock; choice of ebony, rosewood, skeleton steel or solid steel grip cap; choice of solid steel, standard, Old English or ventilated recoil pad; optional inletted gold oval with three initials on bottom of stock. From Remington Arms. Co. Custom Gun Shop.
  Price: 11-87 and 1100 "D" Grade (English scroll engraving on receiver, breech and trig. guard) **$3,723.00**
  Price: 11-87 and 1100 "F" Grade (engraved game scene, "F" Grade walnut stock) **$7,245.00**
  Price: 11-87 and 1100 "F" Grade with gold inlay (inlaid three-panel engraved game scene) **$10,663.00**

REMINGTON CUSTOM SHOP PUMP SHOTGUNS

Gauge: 10, 12, 20, 28, 410. **Barrel:** 20" to 30". **Weight:** NA. **Length:** NA. **Stock:** Two grades of American walnut. **Features:** Engraved versions of the Model 870 shotgun. "D" or "F" grade fancy walnut hand-checkered stock; choice of ebony, rosewood, skeleton steel or solid steel grip cap; choice of solid steel, standard, Old English or ventilated recoil pad; optional inletted gold oval with three initials on bottom of stock. From Remington Arms Co. Custom Gun Shop.
  Price: 870 "D" Grade (English scroll engraving on receiver, breech and trig. guard) **$3,723.00**
  Price: 870 "F" Grade (engraved game scene, "F" grade walnut stock) **$7,245.00**
  Price: 870 "F" Grade with gold inlay (inlaid three-panel engraved game scene) **$10,663.00**

REMINGTON CUSTOM SHOP OVER/UNDER SHOTGUNS

Gauge: 12. **Barrel:** 26", 28", 30". **Weight:** 7-1/2 to 8 lbs. **Length:** 42-1/2" to 47-1/4". **Stock:** American walnut. **Features:** Barrels made of chrome-moly steel with 3" chambers, finger grooved forend, fully brazed barrel side ribs, hardened trunions, automatic ejectors. Made in U.S. by Remington Arms Co. Custom Gun Shop.
  Price: Remington Model 332 D Grade . . . . from **$4,184.00**
  Price: Model 332 F Grade . . . . from **$7,706.00**
  Price: Model 332 F Grade w/gold inlay . . . . from **$11,122.00**

Tar-Hunt DSG

TAR-HUNT DSG (DESIGNATED SLUG GUN)

Gauge: 12, 16. **Barrel:** 23". **Weight:** NA. **Length:** NA. **Stock:** NA **Features:** Tar-Hunt converts the basic Remington 870 shotgun into a configuration for shooting slugs only by installation of a non-removable custom fit Shaw rifled slug barrel with muzzle brake. The 870 Wingmaster is fitted with a barrel with 2-3/4" chamber, the 870 Express Mag. and Wingmaster Mag. have a 3-inch chamber and the 870 Express Super Mag. will have a 3-1/2" chamber. Included are Leupold two-piece windage bases which will accept any standard type turn in rings.
  Price: Tar-Hunt DSG . . . . $450.00 (with customer furnished Remington 870)
  Price: Tar-Hunt Express . . . . $695.00 (complete gun with black synthetic stock)
  Price: Tar-Hunt Wingmaster **$950.00**

Includes models suitable for several forms of competition and other sporting purposes.

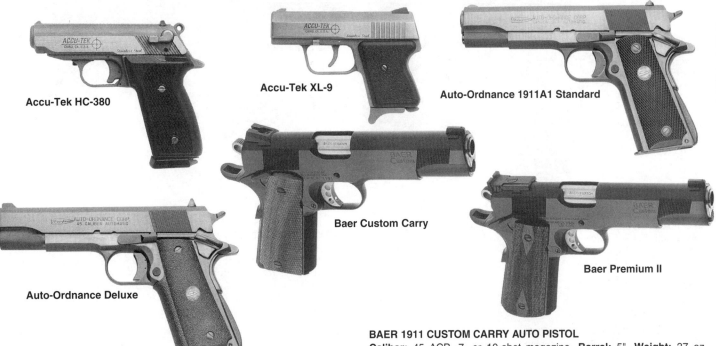

Accu-Tek HC-380

Accu-Tek XL-9

Auto-Ordnance 1911A1 Standard

Baer Custom Carry

Baer Premium II

Auto-Ordnance Deluxe

ACCU-TEK MODEL HC-380 AUTO PISTOL

Caliber: 380 ACP, 10-shot magazine. **Barrel:** 2.75". **Weight:** 26 oz. **Length:** 6" overall. **Grips:** Checkered black composition. **Sights:** Blade front, rear adjustable for windage. **Features:** External hammer; manual thumb safety with firing pin and trigger disconnect; bottom magazine release. Stainless steel construction. Introduced 1993. Price includes cleaning kit and gun lock. Made in U.S.A. by Accu-Tek.
Price: Satin stainless $249.00

ACCU-TEK XL-9 AUTO PISTOL

Caliber: 9mm Para., 5-shot magazine. **Barrel:** 3". **Weight:** 24 oz. **Length:** 5.6" overall. **Grips:** Black pebble composition. **Sights:** Three-dot system; rear adjustable for windage. **Features:** Stainless steel construction; double-action-only mechanism. Introduced 1999. Price includes cleaning kit and gun lock, two magazines. Made in U.S.A. by Accu-Tek.
Price: $267.00

AMERICAN DERRINGER LM-5 AUTOMATIC PISTOL

Caliber: 25 ACP, 5-shot magazine. **Barrel:** 2-1/4". **Weight:** 15 oz. **Length:** NA. **Grips:** Wood. **Sights:** Fixed. **Features:** Compact, stainless, semi-auto, single-action hammerless design. Hand assembled and fitted.
Price: $425.00

AUTO-ORDNANCE 1911A1 AUTOMATIC PISTOL

Caliber: 45 ACP, 7-shot magazine. **Barrel:** 5". **Weight:** 39 oz. **Length:** 8-1/2" overall. **Grips:** Checkered plastic with medallion. **Sights:** Blade front, rear adjustable for windage. **Features:** Same specs as 1911A1 military guns-parts interchangeable. Frame and slide blued; each radius has non-glare finish. Made in U.S.A. by Auto-Ordnance Corp.
Price: 45 ACP, blue $511.00
Price: 45 ACP, Parkerized $515.00
Price: 45 ACP Deluxe (three-dot sights, textured rubber wraparound grips) $525.00

AUTAUGA 32 AUTO PISTOL

Caliber: 32 ACP, 6-shot magazine. **Barrel:** 2". **Weight:** 11.3 oz. **Length:** 4.3" overall. **Grips:** Black polymer. **Sights:** Fixed. **Features:** Double-action-only mechanism. Stainless steel construction. Uses Winchester Silver Tip ammunition.
Price: .... NA

BAER 1911 CUSTOM CARRY AUTO PISTOL

Caliber: 45 ACP, 7- or 10-shot magazine. **Barrel:** 5". **Weight:** 37 oz. **Length:** 8.5" overall. **Grips:** Checkered walnut. **Sights:** Baer improved ramp-style dovetailed front, Novak low-mount rear. **Features:** Baer forged NM frame, slide and barrel with stainless bushing; fitted slide to frame; double serrated slide (full-size only); Baer speed trigger with 4-lb. pull; Baer deluxe hammer and sear, tactical-style extended ambidextrous safety, beveled magazine well; polished feed ramp and throated barrel; tuned extractor; Baer extended ejector, checkered slide stop; lowered and flared ejection port, full-length recoil guide rod; recoil buff. Partial listing shown. Made in U.S.A. by Les Baer Custom, Inc.
Price: Standard size, blued $1,640.00
Price: Standard size, stainless $1,690.00
Price: Comanche size, blued $1,640.00
Price: Comanche size, stainless $1,690.00
Price: Comanche size, aluminum frame, blued slide $1,923.00
Price: Comanche size, aluminum frame, stainless slide $1,995.00

BAER 1911 PREMIER II AUTO PISTOL

Caliber: 9x23, 38 Super, 400 Cor-Bon, 45 ACP, 7- or 10-shot magazine. **Barrel:** 5". **Weight:** 37 oz. **Length:** 8.5" overall. **Grips:** Checkered rosewood, double diamond pattern. **Sights:** Baer dovetailed front, low-mount Bo-Mar rear with hidden leaf. **Features:** Baer NM forged steel frame and barrel with stainless bushing; slide fitted to frame; double serrated slide; lowered, flared ejection port; tuned, polished extractor; Baer extended ejector, checkered slide stop, aluminum speed trigger with 4-lb. pull, deluxe Commander hammer and sear, beavertail grip safety with pad, beveled magazine well, extended ambidextrous safety; flat mainspring housing; polished feed ramp and throated barrel; 30 lpi checkered front strap. Made in U.S.A. by Les Baer Custom, Inc.
Price: Blued $1,428.00
Price: Stainless $1,558.00
Price: 6" model, blued, from $1,595.00

BAER 1911 S.R.P. PISTOL

Caliber: 45 ACP. **Barrel:** 5". **Weight:** 37 oz. **Length:** 8.5" overall. **Grips:** Checkered walnut. **Sights:** Trijicon night sights. **Features:** Similar to the F.B.I. contract gun except uses Baer forged steel frame. Has Baer match barrel with supported chamber, Wolff springs, complete tactical action job. All parts Mag-na-fluxed; deburred for tactical carry. Has Baer Ultra Coat finish. Tuned for reliability. Contact Baer for complete details. Introduced 1996. Made in U.S.A. by Les Baer Custom, Inc.
Price: Government or Comanche length $2,240.00

Beretta M8000/8040 Cougar

Beretta 96

Beretta U22 Neos

Bersa Thunder 380

BERETTA MODEL 92FS PISTOL

Caliber: 9mm Para., 10-shot magazine. **Barrel:** 4.9". **Weight:** 34 oz. **Length:** 8.5" overall. **Grips:** Checkered black plastic. **Sights:** Blade front, rear adjustable for windage. Tritium night sights available. **Features:** Double action. Extractor acts as chamber loaded indicator, squared trigger guard, grooved front and backstraps, inertia firing pin. Matte or blued finish. Introduced 1977. Made in U.S.A. and imported from Italy by Beretta U.S.A.
Price: With plastic grips **$712.00**
Price: Vertec with access rail **$751.00**
Price: Vertec Inox **$801.00**

Beretta Model 92FS/96 Brigadier Pistols

Similar to the Model 92FS/96 except with a heavier slide to reduce felt recoil and allow mounting removable front sight. Wrap-around rubber grips. Three-dot sights dovetailed to the slide, adjustable for windage. Weighs 35.3 oz. Introduced 1999.
Price: 9mm or 40 S&W, 10-shot **$772.00**
Price: Inox models (stainless steel) **$822.00**

Beretta Model 96 Pistol

Same as the Model 92FS except chambered for 40 S&W. Ambidextrous safety mechanism with passive firing pin catch, slide safety/decocking lever, trigger bar disconnect. Has 10-shot magazine. Available with three-dot sights. Introduced 1992.
Price: Model 96, plastic grips **$712.00**
Price: Stainless, rubber grips **$772.00**
Price: Vertec with access rail **$751.00**
Price: Vertec Inox **$801.00**

BERETTA MODEL 80 CHEETAH SERIES DA PISTOLS

Caliber: 380 ACP, 10-shot magazine (M84); 8-shot (M85); 22 LR, 7-shot (M87). **Barrel:** 3.82". **Weight:** About 23 oz. (M84/85); 20.8 oz. (M87). **Length:** 6.8" overall. **Grips:** Glossy black plastic (wood optional at extra cost). **Sights:** Fixed front, drift-adjustable rear. **Features:** Double action, quick takedown, convenient magazine release. Introduced 1977. Imported from Italy by Beretta U.S.A.
Price: Model 84 Cheetah, plastic grips **$615.00**
Price: Model 85 Cheetah, plastic grips, 8-shot **$579.00**
Price: Model 87 Cheetah, wood, 22 LR, 7-shot **$615.00**
Price: Model 87 Target, plastic grips **$708.00**

Beretta Model 86 Cheetah

Similar to the 380-caliber Model 85 except has tip-up barrel for first-round loading. Barrel length is 4.4", overall length of 7.33". Has 8-shot magazine, walnut grips. Introduced 1989.
Price: **$615.00**

Beretta Model 21 Bobcat Pistol

Similar to the Model 950 BS. Chambered for 22 LR or 25 ACP. Both double action. Has 2.4" barrel, 4.9" overall length; 7-round magazine on 22 cal.; 8 rounds in 25 ACP, 9.9 oz., available in nickel, matte, engraved or blue finish. Plastic grips. Introduced in 1985.
Price: Bobcat, 22 or 25, blue **$300.00**
Price: Bobcat, 22, stainless **$329.00**
Price: Bobcat, 22 or 25, matte **$265.00**

BERETTA MODEL 3032 TOMCAT PISTOL

Caliber: 32 ACP, 7-shot magazine. **Barrel:** 2.45". **Weight:** 14.5 oz. **Length:** 5" overall. **Grips:** Checkered black plastic. **Sights:** Blade front, drift-adjustable rear. **Features:** Double action with exposed hammer; tip-up barrel for direct loading/unloading; thumb safety; polished or matte blue finish. Imported from Italy by Beretta U.S.A. Introduced 1996.
Price: Blue **$393.00**
Price: Matte **$358.00**
Price: Stainless **$443.00**
Price: With Tritium sights **$436.00**

BERETTA MODEL 8000/8040/8045 COUGAR PISTOL

Caliber: 9mm Para., 10-shot, 40 S&W, 10-shot magazine; 45 ACP, 8-shot. **Barrel:** 3.6". **Weight:** 33.5 oz. **Length:** 7" overall. **Grips:** Checkered plastic. **Sights:** Blade front, rear drift adjustable for windage. **Features:** Slide-mounted safety; rotating barrel; exposed hammer. Matte black Bruniton finish. Announced 1994. Imported from Italy by Beretta U.S.A.
Price: 8000 and 8000L **$729.00**
Price: D model, 9mm, 40 S&W **$729.00**
Price: D model, 45 ACP **$779.00**
Price: Inox **$794.00**

BERETTA MODEL 9000S COMPACT PISTOL

Caliber: 9mm Para., 40 S&W; 10-shot magazine. **Barrel:** 3.4". **Weight:** 26.8 oz. **Length:** 6.6". **Grips:** Soft polymer. **Sights:** Windage-adjustable white-dot rear, white-dot blade front. **Features:** Glass-reinforced polymer frame; patented tilt-barrel, open-slide locking system; chrome-lined barrel; external serrated hammer; automatic firing pin and manual safeties. Introduced 2000. Imported from Italy by Beretta USA.
Price: 9000S Type F (single and double action, external
hammer) **$472.00**

BERETTA MODEL U22 NEOS

Caliber: 22 LR, 10-shot magazine. **Barrel:** 4.2"; 6". **Weight:** 32 oz.; 36 oz. **Length:** 8.8"; 10.3". **Sights:** Target. **Features:** Integral rail for standard scope mounts, light, perfectly weighted, 100% American made by Beretta.
Price: **$265.00**
Price: Inox **$315.00**
Price: DLX **$336.00**
Price: Inox **$386.00**

BERSA THUNDER LITE 380 AUTO PISTOLS

Caliber: 380 ACP, 7-shot (Thunder 380 Lite), 9-shot magazine (Thunder 380 DLX). **Barrel:** 3.5". **Weight:** 23 oz. **Length:** 6.6" overall. **Grips:** Black polymer. **Sights:** Blade front, notch rear adjustable for windage; three-dot system. **Features:** Double action; firing pin and magazine safeties. Available in blue, nickel, or duo tone. Introduced 1995. Distributed by Eagle Imports, Inc.
Price: Thunder 380, 7-shot, deep blue finish **$266.95**
Price: Thunder 380 Deluxe, 9-shot, satin nickel **$299.95**
Price: Thunder 380 Gold, 7-shot **$299.95**

Browning
Buck Mark Standard

Browning Buck
Mark Challenge

HANDGUNS

Bersa Thunder 45 Ultra Compact Pistol

Similar to the Bersa Thunder 380 except in 45 ACP. Available in three finishes. Introduced 2003. Imported from Argentina by Eagle Imports, Inc.
Price: Thunder 45, matte blue **$400.95**
Price: Thunder 45, Duotone **$424.95**
Price: Thunder 45, Satin nickel **$441.95**

BLUE THUNDER/COMMODORE 1911-STYLE AUTO PISTOLS

Caliber: 45 ACP, 7-shot magazine. **Barrel:** 4-1/4", 5". **Weight:** NA. **Length:** NA. **Grips:** Checkered hardwood. **Sights:** Blade front, drift-adjustable rear. **Features:** Extended slide release and safety, spring guide rod, skeletonized hammer and trigger, magazine bumper, beavertail grip safety. Imported from the Philippines by Century International Arms Inc.
Price: . . . . **$464.80 to $484.80**

AUTOBOND 450

Caliber: 450 Autobond (also 45 ACP). Model 1911-style. **Barrel:** 5 inches.
Price: **$1150.00**

BROWNING HI-POWER 9mm AUTOMATIC PISTOL

Caliber: 9mm Para.,10-shot magazine. **Barrel:** 4-21/32". **Weight:** 32 oz. **Length:** 7-3/4" overall. **Grips:** Walnut, hand checkered, or black Polyamide. **Sights:** 1/8" blade front; rear screw-adjustable for windage and elevation. Also available with fixed rear (drift-adjustable for windage). **Features:** External hammer with half-cock and thumb safeties. A blow on the hammer cannot discharge a cartridge; cannot be fired with magazine removed. Fixed rear sight model available. Includes gun lock. Imported from Belgium by Browning.
Price: Fixed sight model, walnut grips **$680.00**
Price: Fully adjustable rear sight, walnut grips **$730.00**
Price: Mark III, standard matte black finish, fixed sight, moulded grips, ambidextrous safety **$662.00**

Browning Hi-Power Practical Pistol

Similar to the standard Hi-Power except has silver-chromed frame with blued slide, wrap-around Pachmayr rubber grips, round-style serrated hammer and removable front sight, fixed rear (drift-adjustable for windage). Available in 9mm Para. Includes gun lock. Introduced 1991.
Price: **$717.00**

BROWNING BUCK MARK STANDARD 22 PISTOL

Caliber: 22 LR, 10-shot magazine. **Barrel:** 5-1/2". **Weight:** 32 oz. **Length:** 9-1/2" overall. **Grips:** Black moulded composite with checkering. **Sights:** Ramp front, Browning Pro Target rear adjustable for windage and elevation. **Features:** All steel, matte blue finish or nickel, gold-colored trigger. Buck Mark Plus has laminated wood grips. Includes gun lock. Made in U.S.A. Introduced 1985. From Browning.
Price: Buck Mark Standard, blue **$310.00**
Price: Buck Mark Nickel, nickel finish with contoured rubber grips **$366.00**
Price: Buck Mark Plus, matte blue with laminated wood grips . . . **$379.00**
Price: Buck Mark Plus Nickel, nickel finish, laminated wood grips **$415.00**

Browning Buck Mark Camper

Similar to the Buck Mark except 5-1/2" bull barrel. Weight is 34 oz. Matte blue finish, molded composite grips. Introduced 1999. From Browning.
Price: **$279.00**
Price: Camper Nickel, nickel finish, molded composite grips **$311.00**

Browning Buck Mark Challenge

Similar to the Buck Mark except has a lightweight barrel and smaller grip diameter. Barrel length is 5-1/2", weight is 25 oz. Introduced 1999. From Browning.
Price: **$346.00**

Browning Buck Mark Micro

Same as the Buck Mark Standard and Buck Mark Plus except has 4" barrel. Available in blue or nickel. Has 16-click Pro Target rear sight. Introduced 1992.
Price: Micro Standard, matte blue finish. **$310.00**
Price: Micro Nickel, nickel finish **$366.00**
Price: Buck Mark Micro Plus Nickel **$415.00**

Browning Buck Mark Bullseye

Same as the Buck Mark Standard except has 7-1/4" fluted barrel, matte blue finish. Weighs 36 oz.
Price: Bullseye Standard, molded composite grips **$420.00**
Price: Bullseye Target, contoured rosewood grips **$541.00**

Browning Buck Mark 5.5

Same as the Buck Mark Standard except has a 5-1/2" bull barrel with integral scope mount, matte blue finish.
Price: 5.5 Field, Pro-Target adj. rear sight, contoured walnut grips. **$459.00**
Price: 5.5 Target, hooded adj. target sights, contoured walnut grips **$459.00**

BROWNING PRO-9

Caliber: 9mm Luger, 10-round magazine. **Barrel:** 4". **Weight:** 30 oz. **Overall length:** 7 1/4". **Features:** Double-action, ambidextrous decocker and safety. Fixed, three-dot-style sights, 6" sight radius. Molded composite grips with interchangeable backstrap inserts.
Price: **$628.00**

BROWNING HI-POWER

Caliber: 9mm, 40 S&W. **Barrel:** 4 3/4". **Weight:** 32 to 35 oz. **Overall length:** 7 3/4". **Features:** Blued, matte, polymer or silver-chromed frame; molded, wraparound Pachmayr or walnut grips; Commander-style or spur-type hammer.
Price: Practical model, fixed sights. **$791.00**
Price: Mark II model, epoxy finish. **$730.00**
Price: HP Standard, blued, fixed sights, walnut grips **$751.00**
Price: HP Standard, blued, adj. sights **$805.00**

CHARLES DALY M-1911-A1P AUTOLOADING PISTOL

Caliber: 45 ACP, 7- or 10-shot magazine. **Barrel:** 5". **Weight:** 38 oz. **Length:** 8-3/4" overall. **Grips:** Checkered. **Sights:** Blade front, rear drift adjustable for windage; three-dot system. **Features:** Skeletonized combat hammer and trigger; beavertail grip safety; extended slide release; oversize thumb safety; Parkerized finish. Introduced 1996. Imported from the Philippines by K.B.I., Inc.
Price: **$469.95**

Charles Daly M-1911-A1P

Cobra FS380

Cobra CA32

Colt 1991 Model O

Colt 1991 Model O Commander

Colt XSE Model O Commander

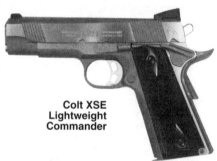

Colt XSE Lightweight Commander

COBRA ENTERPRISES FS380 AUTO PISTOL

Caliber: 380 ACP, 7-shot magazine. **Barrel:** 3.5". **Weight:** 2.1 lbs. **Length:** 6-3/8" overall. **Grips:** Black composition. **Sights:** Fixed. **Features:** Choice of bright chrome, satin nickel or black finish. Introduced 2002. Made in U.S.A. by Cobra Enterprises.
Price: **$130.00**

COBRA ENTERPRISES FS32 AUTO PISTOL

Caliber: 32 ACP, 8-shot magazine. **Barrel:** 3.5". **Weight:** 2.1 lbs. **Length:** 6-3/8" overall. **Grips:** Black composition. **Sights:** Fixed. **Features:** Choice of black, satin nickel or bright chrome finish. Introduced 2002. Made in U.S.A. by Cobra Enterprises.
Price: **$130.00**

COBRA INDUSTRIES PATRIOT PISTOL

Caliber: 380ACP, 9mm Luger, 10-shot magazine. **Barrel:** 3.3". **Weight:** 20 oz. **Length:** 6" overall. **Grips:** Checkered polymer. **Sights:** Fixed. **Features:** Stainless steel slide with load indicator; double-action-only trigger system. Introduced 2002. Made in U.S.A. by Cobra Enterprises, Inc.
Price: **$279.00**

COBRA INDUSTRIES CA32, CA380

Caliber: 32ACP, 380 ACP. **Barrel:** 2.8" **Weight:** 22 oz. **Length:** 5.4". **Grips:** Laminated wood (CA32); Black molded synthetic (CA380). **Sights:** Fixed. **Features:** True pocket pistol size and styling without bulk. Made in U.S.A. by Cobra Enterprises.
Price: . . . . **NA**

COLT MODEL 1991 MODEL O AUTO PISTOL

Caliber: 45 ACP, 7-shot magazine. **Barrel:** 5". **Weight:** 38 oz. **Length:** 8.5" overall. **Grips:** Checkered black composition. **Sights:** Ramped blade front, fixed square notch rear, high profile. **Features:** Matte finish. Continuation of serial number range used on original G.I. 1911 A1 guns. Comes with one magazine and moulded carrying case. Introduced 1991.
Price: **$645.00**
Price: Stainless **$800.00**

Colt Model 1991 Model O Commander Auto Pistol

Similar to the Model 1991 A1 except has 4-1/4" barrel. Overall length is 7-3/4". Comes with one 7-shot magazine, molded case.
Price: Blue **$645.00**
Price: Stainless steel **$800.00**

COLT XSE SERIES MODEL O AUTO PISTOLS

Caliber: 45 ACP, 8-shot magazine. **Barrel:** 4.25", 5". **Grips:** Checkered, double diamond rosewood. **Sights:** Drift-adjustable three-dot combat. **Features:** Brushed stainless finish; adjustable, two-cut aluminum trigger; extended ambidextrous thumb safety; upswept beavertail with palm swell; elongated slot hammer; beveled magazine well. Introduced 1999. From Colt's Manufacturing Co., Inc.
Price: XSE Government (5" barrel) **$950.00**
Price: XSE Commander (4.25" barrel) **$950.00**

COLT XSE LIGHTWEIGHT COMMANDER AUTO PISTOL

Caliber: 45 ACP, 8-shot. **Barrel:** 4-1/4". **Weight:** 26 oz. **Length:** 7-3/4" overall. **Grips:** Double diamond checkered rosewood. **Sights:** Fixed, glare-proofed blade front, square notch rear; three-dot system. **Features:** Brushed stainless slide, nickeled aluminum frame; McCormick elongated-slot enhanced hammer, McCormick two-cut adjustable aluminum hammer. Made in U.S.A. by Colt's Mfg. Co., Inc.
Price: 45, stainless **$950.00**

COLT DEFENDER

Caliber: 40 S&W, 45 ACP, 7-shot magazine. **Barrel:** 3". **Weight:** 22-1/2 oz. **Length:** 6-3/4" overall. **Grips:** Pebble-finish rubber wraparound with finger grooves. **Sights:** White dot front, snag-free Colt competition rear. **Features:** Stainless finish; aluminum frame; combat-style hammer; Hi Ride grip safety, extended manual safety, disconnect safety. Introduced 1998. Made in U.S.A. by Colt's Mfg. Co.
Price: **$773.00**
Price: 41 Magnum Model, from **$825.00**

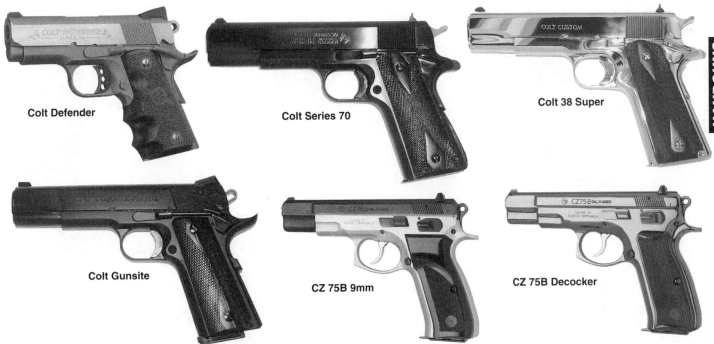

Colt Defender

Colt Series 70

Colt 38 Super

Colt Gunsite

CZ 75B 9mm

CZ 75B Decocker

CZ 85

COLT SERIES 70

Caliber: 45 ACP. **Barrel:** 5". **Weight:** NA **Length:** NA **Grips:** Rosewood with double diamond checkering pattern. **Sights:** Fixed. **Features:** A custom replica of the Original Series 70 pistol with a Series 70 firing system, original rollmarks. Introduced 2002. Made in U.S.A. by Colt's Manufacturing.
Price: . . . . **NA**

COLT 38 SUPER

Caliber: 38 Super **Barrel:** 5" **Weight:** NA. **Length:** 8-1/2" **Grips:** Checkered rubber (Stainless and blue models); Wood with double diamond checkering pattern (Bright stainless model). **Sights:** 3-dot. **Features:** Beveled magazine well, standard thumb safety and service-style grip safety. Introduced 2003. Made in U.S.A. by Colt's Mfg. Co.
Price: . . . . (Blue) **$864.00** (Stainless steel) **$943.00**
Price: . . . . (Bright stainless steel) **$1,152.00**

COLT GUNSITE PISTOL

Caliber: 45 ACP **Barrel:** 5". **Weight:** NA. **Length:** NA. **Grips:** Rosewood. **Sights:** Heinie, front; Novak, rear. **Features:** Contains most all of the Gunsite school recommended features such as Series 70 firing system, Smith & Alexander metal grip safety w/palm swell, serrated flat mainspring housing, dehorned all around. Available in blue or stainless steel. Introduced 2003. Made in U.S.A. by Colt's Mfg. Co.
Price: . . . . **NA**

CZ 75B AUTO PISTOL

Caliber: 9mm Para., 40 S&W, 10-shot magazine. **Barrel:** 4.7". **Weight:** 34.3 oz. **Length:** 8.1" overall. **Grips:** High impact checkered plastic. **Sights:** Square post front, rear adjustable for windage; three-dot system. **Features:** Single action/double action design; firing pin block safety; choice of black polymer, matte or high-polish blue finishes. All-steel frame. Imported from the Czech Republic by CZ-USA.
Price: Black polymer. **$529.00**
Price: Glossy blue. **$559.00**
Price: Dual tone or satin nickel **$559.00**
Price: 22 LR conversion unit. **$399.00**

CZ 75B Decocker

Similar to the CZ 75B except has a decocking lever in place of the safety lever. All other specifications are the same. Introduced 1999. Imported from the Czech Republic by CZ-USA.
Price: 9mm, black polymer **$559.00**
Price: 40 S&W **$569.00**

CZ 75B Compact Auto Pistol

Similar to the CZ 75 except has 10-shot magazine, 3.9" barrel and weighs 32 oz. Has removable front sight, non-glare ribbed slide top. Trigger guard is squared and serrated; combat hammer. Introduced 1993. Imported from the Czech Republic by CZ-USA.
Price: 9mm, black polymer **$559.00**
Price: Dual tone or satin nickel **$569.00**
Price: D Compact, black polymer **$569.00**
Price: CZ2075 Sub-compact RAMI **$559.00**

CZ 75M IPSC Auto Pistol

Similar to the CZ 75B except has a longer frame and slide, slightly larger grip to accommodate new heavy-duty magazine. Ambidextrous thumb safety, safety notch on hammer; two-port in-frame compensator; slide racker; frame-mounted Firepoint red dot sight. Introduced 2001. Imported from the Czech Republic by CZ USA.
Price: 40 S&W, 10-shot mag. **$1,551.00**
Price: CZ 75 Standard IPSC (40 S&W, adj. sights) **$1,038.00**

CZ 85B Auto Pistol

Same gun as the CZ 75 except has ambidextrous slide release and safety-levers; non-glare, ribbed slide top; squared, serrated trigger guard; trigger stop to prevent overtravel. Introduced 1986. Imported from the Czech Republic by CZ-USA.
Price: Black polymer **$483.00**
Price: Combat, black polymer **$540.00**
Price: Combat, dual tone **$487.00**
Price: Combat, glossy blue. **$499.00**

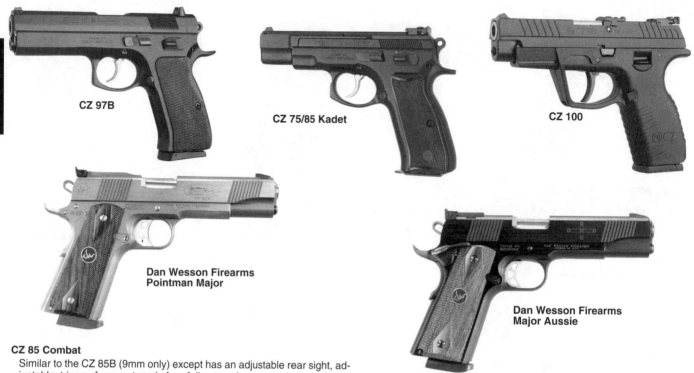

CZ 97B

CZ 75/85 Kadet

CZ 100

Dan Wesson Firearms
Pointman Major

Dan Wesson Firearms
Major Aussie

CZ 85 Combat

Similar to the CZ 85B (9mm only) except has an adjustable rear sight, adjustable trigger for overtravel, free-fall magazine, extended magazine catch. Does not have the firing pin block safety. Introduced 1999. Imported from the Czech Republic by CZ-USA.

Price: 9mm, black polymer **$540.00**
Price: 9mm, glossy blue **$566.00**
Price: 9mm, dual tone or satin nickel **$586.00**

CZ 83B DOUBLE-ACTION PISTOL

Caliber: 9mm Makarov, 32 ACP, 380 ACP, 10-shot magazine. **Barrel:** 3.8". **Weight:** 26.2 oz. **Length:** 6.8" overall. **Grips:** High impact checkered plastic. **Sights:** Removable square post front, rear adjustable for windage; three-dot system. **Features:** Single action/double action; ambidextrous magazine release and safety. Blue finish; non-glare ribbed slide top. Imported from the Czech Republic by CZ-USA.

Price: Blue **$378.00**
Price: Nickel **$397.00**

CZ 97B AUTO PISTOL

Caliber: 45 ACP, 10-shot magazine. **Barrel:** 4.85". **Weight:** 40 oz. **Length:** 8.34" overall. **Grips:** Checkered walnut. **Sights:** Fixed. **Features:** Single action/double action; full-length slide rails; screw-in barrel bushing; linkless barrel; all-steel construction; chamber loaded indicator; dual transfer bars. Introduced 1999. Imported from the Czech Republic by CZ-USA.

Price: Black polymer.................................. **$625.00**
Price: Glossy blue................................... **$641.00**

CZ 75/85 KADET AUTO PISTOL

Caliber: 22 LR, 10-shot magazine. **Barrel:** 4.88". **Weight:** 36 oz. **Grips:** High impact checkered plastic. **Sights:** Blade front, fully adjustable rear. **Features:** Single action/double action mechanism; all-steel construction. Duplicates weight, balance and function of the CZ 75 pistol. Introduced 1999. Imported from the Czech Republic by CZ-USA.

Price: Black polymer.................................. **$486.00**

CZ 100 AUTO PISTOL

Caliber: 9mm Para., 40 S&W, 10-shot magazine. **Barrel:** 3.7". **Weight:** 24 oz. **Length:** 6.9" overall. **Grips:** Grooved polymer. **Sights:** Blade front with dot, white outline rear drift adjustable for windage. **Features:** Double action only with firing pin block; polymer frame, steel slide; has laser sight mount. Introduced 1996. Imported from the Czech Republic by CZ-USA.

Price: 9mm Para...................................... **$405.00**
Price: 40 S&W **$424.00**

DAN WESSON FIREARMS POINTMAN MAJOR AUTO PISTOL

Caliber: 45 ACP. **Barrel:** 5". **Grips:** Rosewood checkered. **Features:** Blued or stainless steel frame and serrated slide; Chip McCormick match-grade trigger group, sear and disconnect; match-grade barrel; high-ride beavertail safety; checkered slide release; **Sights:** High rib; interchangeable sight system; laser engraved. Introduced 2000. Made in U.S.A. by Dan Wesson Firearms.

Price: Model PM1-B (blued) **$799.00**
Price: Model PM1-S (stainless) **$699.00**

Dan Wesson Firearms Pointman Seven Auto Pistols

Similar to Pointman Major, dovetail adjustable target rear sight and dovetail target front sight. Available in blued or stainless finish. Introduced 2000. Made in U.S.A. by Dan Wesson Firearms.

Price: PM7 (blued frame and slide) **$999.00**
Price: PM7S (stainless finish)........................... **$799.00**

Dan Wesson Firearms Pointman Guardian Auto Pistols

Similar to Pointman Major, more compact frame with 4.25" barrel. Avaiable in blued or stainless finish with fixed or adjustable sights. Introduced 2000. Made in U.S.A. by Dan Wesson Firearms.

Price: PMG-FS, all new frame (fixed sights)............... **$769.00**
Price: PMG-AS (blued frame and slide, adjustable sights)...... **$799.00**
Price: PMGD-FS Guardian Duce, all new frame (stainless frame and blued slide, fixed sights) **$829.00**
Price: PMGD-AS Guardian Duce (stainless frame and blued slide, adj. sights)... **$799.00**

Dan Wesson Firearms Major Tri-Ops Packs

Similar to Pointman Major. Complete frame assembly fitted to 3 match grade complete slide assemblied (9mm, 10mm, 40 S&W). Includes recoil springs and magazines that come in hard cases fashioned after high-grade European rifle case. Constructed of navy blue cordura stretched over hardwood with black leather trim and comfortable black leather wrapped handle. Brass corner protectors, dual combination locks, engraved presentation plate on the lid. Inside, the Tri-Ops Pack components are nested in precision die-cut closed cell foam and held sercurely in place by convoluted foam in the inside of the lid. Introduced 2002. Made in U.S.A. by Dan Wesson Firearms.

Price: TOP1B (blued), TOP1-S (stainless) **$2,459.00**

Dan Wesson Firearms
Patriot Marksman

Desert Eagle Mark XIX

Desert Baby Eagle

EAA Witness

Dan Wesson Firearms Major Aussie

Similar to Pointman Major. Available in 45 ACP. Features Bomar-style adjustable rear target sight, unique slide top configuration exclusive to this model (features radius from the flat side surfaces of the slide to a narrow flat on top and then a small redius and reveal ending in a flat, low (1/16" high) sight rib 3/8" wide with lengthwise serrations). Clearly identified by the Southern Cross flag emblem laser engraved on the sides of the slide (available in 45 ACP only). Introduced 2002. Made in U.S.A. by Dan Wesson Firearms.

Price: PMA-B (blued) **$799.00**
Price: PMA-S (stainless). **$799.00**

Dan Wesson Firearms Pointman Minor Auto Pistol

Similar to Pointman Major. Full size (5") entry level IDPA or action pistol model with blued carbon alloy frame and round top slide, bead blast matte finish on frame and slide top and radius, satin-brushed polished finish on sides of slide, chromed barrel, dovetail mount fixed rear target sight and tactical/target ramp front sight, match trigger, skeletonized target hammer, high ride beavertail, fitted extractor, serrations on thumb safety, slide release and mag release, lowered and relieved ejection port, beveled mag well, exotic hardwood grips, serrated mainspring housing, laser engraved. Introduced 2000. Made in U.S.A. by Dan Wesson Firearms.

Price: Model PM2-P **$599.00**

Dan Wesson Firearms Pointman Hi-Cap Auto Pistol

Similar to Pointman Minor, full-size high-capacity (10-shot) magazine with 5" chromed barrel, blued finish and dovetail fixed rear sight. Match adjustable trigger, ambidextrous extended thumb safety, beavertail safety. Introduced 2001. From Dan Wesson Firearms.

Price: PMHC (Pointman High-Cap) **$689.00**

Dan Wesson Firearms Pointman Dave Pruitt Signature Series

Similar to other full-sized Pointman models, customized by Master Pistolsmith and IDPA Grand Master Dave Pruitt. Alloy carbon-steel with black oxide bluing and bead-blast matte finish. Front and rear chevron cocking serrations, dovetail mount fixed rear target sight and tactical/target ramp front sight, ramped match barrel with fitted match bushing and link, Chip McCormick (or equivalent) match grade trigger group, serrated ambidextrous tactical/carry thumb safety, high ride beavertail, serrated slide release and checkered mag release, match grade sear and hammer, fitted extractor, lowered and relieved ejection port, beveled mag well, full length 2-piece recoil spring guide rod, cocobolo double diamond checkered grips, serrated steel mainspring housing, special laser engraving. Introduced 2001. From Dan Wesson Firearms.

Price: PMDP (Pointman Dave Pruitt) **$899.00**

DAN WESSON FIREARMS PATRIOT 1911 PISTOL

Caliber: 45 ACP. **Grips:** Exotic exhibition grade cocobolo, double diamond hand cut checkering. **Sights:** New innovative combat/carry rear sight that completely encloses the dovetail. **Features:** The new Patriot Expert and Patriot Marksman are full size match grade series 70 1911s machined from steel forgings. Available in blued chome moly steel or stainless steel. Beveled mag well, lowered and flared ejection port, high sweep beavertail safety. Introduced June 2002.

Price: Model PTM-B (blued) **$797.00**
Price: Model PTM-S (stainless) **$898.00**
Price: Model PTE-B (blued) **$864.00**
Price: Model PTE-S (stainless). **$971.00**

DESERT EAGLE MARK XIX PISTOL

Caliber: 357 Mag., 9-shot; 44 Mag., 8-shot; 50 AE, 7-shot. **Barrel:** 6", 10", interchangeable. **Weight:** 357 Mag.-62 oz.; 44 Mag.-69 oz.; 50 AE - 72 oz. **Length:** 10-1/4" overall (6" bbl.). **Grips:** Polymer; rubber available. **Sights:** Blade on ramp front, combat-style rear. Adjustable available. **Features:** Interchangeable barrels; rotating three-lug bolt; am-bidextrous safety; adjustable trigger. Military epoxy finish. Satin, bright nickel, chrome, brushed, matte or black finishes available. 10" barrel extra. Imported from Israel by Magnum Research, Inc.

Price: 357, 6" bbl., standard pistol **$1,249.00**
Price: 44 Mag., 6", standard pistol **$1,249.00**
Price: 50 Magnum, 6" bbl., standard pistol **$1,249.00**

DESERT BABY EAGLE PISTOLS

Caliber: 9mm Para., 40 S&W, 45 ACP, 10-round magazine. **Barrel:** 3.5", 3.7", 4.72". **Weight:** 26.8 - 39.8 oz. **Length:** 7.25" to 8.25" overall. **Grips:** Polymer. **Sights:** Drift-adjustable rear, blade front. **Features:** Steel frame and slide; polygonal rifling to reduce barrel wear; slide safety; decocker. Reintroduced in 1999. Imported from Israel by Magnum Research Inc.

Price: Standard (9mm or 40 cal.; 4.72" barrel, 8.25" overall) **$499.00**
Price: Semi-Compact (9mm, 40 or 45 cal.; 3.7" barrel,
7.75" overall) **$499.00**
Price: Compact (9mm or 40 cal.; 3.5" barrel, 7.25" overall) **$499.00**
Price: Polymer (9mm or 40 cal; polymer frame; 3.25" barrel,
7.25" overall) **$499.00**

Ed Brown Commander Bobtail

Ed Brown Kobra Carry

Entréprise Elite P500

Entréprise Boxer P500

Entréprise Tactical 500

EAA WITNESS DA AUTO PISTOL

Caliber: 9mm Para., 10-shot magazine; 38 Super, 40 S&W, 10-shot magazine; 45 ACP, 10-shot magazine. **Barrel:** 4.50". **Weight:** 35.33 oz. **Length:** 8.10" overall. **Grips:** Checkered rubber. **Sights:** Undercut blade front, open rear adjustable for windage. **Features:** Double-action trigger system; round trigger guard; frame-mounted safety. Introduced 1991. Imported from Italy by European American Armory.

Price: 9mm, blue	$449.00
Price: 9mm, Wonder finish	$459.00
Price: 9mm Compact, blue, 10-shot	$449.00
Price: As above, Wonder finish	$459.00
Price: 38 Super, blue	$449.00
Price: 38 Super, Wonder finish	$459.00
Price: 40 S&W, blue	$449.00
Price: As above, Wonder finish	$459.00
Price: 40 S&W Compact, 9-shot, blue	$449.00
Price: As above, Wonder finish	$459.00
Price: 45 ACP, blue	$449.00
Price: As above, Wonder finish	$459.00
Price: 45 ACP Compact, 8-shot, blue	$449.00
Price: As above, Wonder finish	$459.00

ED BROWN CLASSIC CUSTOM

Caliber: 45 ACP, 7 shots. **Barrel:** 5 inches. **Weight:** 39 oz. **Stocks:** Cocobolo wood. **Sights:** Bo-Mar adjustable rear, dovetail front. **Features:** Single-action, M1911 style, custom made to order, stainless frame and slide available.

Price: **$2,895.00**

ED BROWN COMMANDER BOBTAIL

Caliber: 45 ACP, 400 Cor-Bon, 40 S&W, 357 SIG, 38 Super, 9mm Luger, 7-shot magazine. **Barrel:** 4.25". **Weight:** 34 oz. **Grips:** Hogue exotic wood. **Sights:** Customer preference front; fixed Novak low-mount, rear. Optional night inserts available. **Features:** Checkered forestrap and bobtailed mainspring housing. Other options available.

Price: Executive Carry **$2,295.00**
Price: Executive Elite **$2,195.00**

ED BROWN KOBRA

Caliber: 45 ACP, 7-shot magazine. **Barrel:** 5" (Kobra); 4.25" (Kobra Carry). **Weight:** 39 oz. (Kobra); 34 oz. (Kobra Carry). **Grips:** Hogue exotic wood. **Sights:** Ramp, front; fixed Novak low-mount night sights, rear. **Features:** Has snakeskin pattern serrations on forestrap and mainspring housing, denorned edges, beavertail grip safety.

Price: Kobra **$1,895.00**
Price: Kobra Carry **$1,995.00**

ENTRÉPRISE ELITE P500 AUTO PISTOL

Caliber: 45 ACP, 10-shot magazine. **Barrel:** 5". **Weight:** 40 oz. **Length:** 8.5" overall. **Grips:** Black ultra-slim, double diamond, checkered synthetic. **Sights:** Dovetailed blade front, rear adjustable for windage; three-dot system. **Features:** Reinforced dust cover; lowered and flared ejection port; squared trigger guard; adjustable match trigger; bolstered front strap; high grip cut; high ride beavertail grip safety; steel flat mainspring housing; extended thumb lock; skeletonized hammer, match grade sear, disconnector; Wolff springs. Introduced 1998. Made in U.S.A. by Entréprise Arms.

Price: **$739.90**

Entréprise Boxer P500 Auto Pistol

Similar to the Medalist model except has adjustable Competizione "melded" rear sight with dovetailed Patridge front; high mass chiseled slide with sweep cut; machined slide parallel rails; polished breech face and barrel channel. Introduced 1998. Made in U.S.A. by Entréprise Arms.

Price: **$1,399.00**

Entréprise Medalist P500 Auto Pistol

Similar to the Elite model except has adjustable Competizione "melded" rear sight with dovetailed Patridge front; machined slide parallel rails with polished breech face and barrel channel; front and rear slide serrations; lowered and flared ejection port; full-length one-piece guide rod with plug; National Match barrel and bushing; stainless firing pin; tuned match extractor; oversize firing pin stop; throated barrel and polished ramp; slide lapped to frame. Introduced 1998. Made in U.S.A. by Entréprise Arms.

Price: 45 ACP **$979.00**
Price: 40 S&W **$1,099.00**

Entréprise Tactical P500 Auto Pistol

Similar to the Elite model except has Tactical2 Ghost Ring sight or Novak lo-mount sight; ambidextrous thumb safety; front and rear slide serrations; full-length guide rod; throated barrel, polished ramp; tuned match extractor; fitted barrel and bushing; stainless firing pin; slide lapped to frame; dehorned. Introduced 1998. Made in U.S.A. by Entréprise Arms.

Price: **$979.90**
Price: Tactical Plus (full-size frame, Officer's slide) **$1,049.00**

ERMA KGP68 AUTO PISTOL

Caliber: 32 ACP, 6-shot, 380 ACP, 5-shot. **Barrel:** 4". **Weight:** 22-1/2 oz. **Length:** 7-3/8" overall. **Grips:** Checkered plastic. **Sights:** Fixed. **Features:** Toggle action similar to original "Luger" pistol. Action stays open after last shot. Has magazine and sear disconnect safety systems.

Price: **$499.95**

FEG PJK-9HP

Felk MTF 450

Firestorm Mini

Firestorm 45 Gov't

Glock 17C

Glock 22

FEG PJK-9HP AUTO PISTOL

Caliber: 9mm Para., 10-shot magazine. **Barrel:** 4.75". **Weight:** 32 oz. **Length:** 8" overall. **Grips:** Hand-checkered walnut. **Sights:** Blade front, rear adjustable for windage; three dot system. **Features:** Single action; polished blue or hard chrome finish; rounded combat-style serrated hammer. Comes with two magazines and cleaning rod. Imported from Hungary by K.B.I., Inc.

Price: Blue **$259.95**
Price: Hard chrome. **$259.95**

FEG SMC-380 AUTO PISTOL

Caliber: 380 ACP, 6-shot magazine. **Barrel:** 3.5". **Weight:** 18.5 oz. **Length:** 6.1" overall. **Grips:** Checkered composition with thumbrest. **Sights:** Blade front, rear adjustable for windage. **Features:** Patterned after the PPK pistol. Alloy frame, steel slide; double action. Blue finish. Comes with two magazines, cleaning rod. Imported from Hungary by K.B.I., Inc.

Price: **$224.95**

FELK MTF 450 AUTO PISTOL

Caliber: 9mm Para. (10-shot); 40 S&W (8-shot); . 357 Mag, 45 ACP (9-shot magazine). **Barrel:** 3.5". **Weight:** 19.9 oz. **Length:** 6.4" overall. **Grips:** Checkered. **Sights:** Blade front; adjustable rear. **Features:** Double-action only trigger, striker fired; polymer frame; trigger safety, firing pin safety, trigger bar safety; adjustable trigger weight; fully interchangeable slide/barrel to change calibers. Introduced 1998. Imported by Felk Inc.

Price: **$395.00**
Price: 45 ACP pistol with 9mm and 40 S&W slide/barrel assemblies **$999.00**

FIRESTORM AUTO PISTOL

Features: 7 or 10 rd. double action pistols with matte, duotone or nickel finish. Distributed by SGS Importers International.

Price: 22 LR 10 rd, 380 7 rd. matte. **$264.95**
Price: Duotone **$274.95**
Price: Mini 9mm, 40 S&W, 10 rd. matte **$383.95**
Price: Duotone **$391.95**
Price: Nickel **$408.95**
Price: Mini 45, 7 rd. matte **$383.95**
Price: Duotone 45. . . . . **$399.95**
Price: Nickel 45. . . . . **$416.95**
Price: 45 Government, Compact, 7 rd. matte **$324.95**
Price: Duotone **$333.95**
Price: Extra magazines. **$29.95-49.95**

GLOCK 17 AUTO PISTOL

Caliber: 9mm Para., 10-shot magazine. **Barrel:** 4.49". **Weight:** 22.04 oz. (without magazine). **Length:** 7.32" overall. **Grips:** Black polymer. **Sights:** Dot on front blade, white outline rear adjustable for windage. **Features:** Polymer frame, steel slide; double-action trigger with "Safe Action" system; mechanical firing pin safety, drop safety; simple takedown without tools; locked breech, recoil operated action. Adopted by Austrian armed forces 1983. NATO approved 1984. Imported from Austria by Glock, Inc.

Price: Fixed sight, extra magazine, magazine loader, cleaning kit. . **$641.00**
Price: Adjustable sight **$671.00**
Price: Model 17L (6" barrel) **$800.00**
Price: Model 17C, ported barrel (compensated) **$646.00**

Glock 19 Auto Pistol

Similar to the Glock 17 except has a 4" barrel, giving an overall length of 6.85" and weight of 20.99 oz. Magazine capacity is 10 rounds. Fixed or adjustable rear sight. Introduced 1988.

Price: Fixed sight **$641.00**
Price: Adjustable sight **$671.00**
Price: Model 19C, ported barrel **$646.00**

Glock 20 10mm Auto Pistol

Similar to the Glock Model 17 except chambered for 10mm Automatic cartridge. Barrel length is 4.60", overall length is 7.59", and weight is 20.9 oz. (without magazine). Magazine capacity is 10 rounds. Fixed or adjustable rear sight. Comes with an extra magazine, magazine loader, cleaning rod and brush. Introduced 1990. Imported from Austria by Glock, Inc.

Price: Fixed sight **$700.00**
Price: Adjustable sight **$730.00**

Glock 21 Auto Pistol

Similar to the Glock 17 except chambered for 45 ACP, 10-shot magazine. Overall length is 7.59", weight is 25.2 oz. (without magazine). Fixed or adjustable rear sight. Introduced 1991.

Price: Fixed sight **$700.00**
Price: Adjustable sight **$730.00**

Glock 22 Auto Pistol

Similar to the Glock 17 except chambered for 40 S&W, 10-shot magazine. Overall length is 7.28", weight is 22.3 oz. (without magazine). Fixed or adjustable rear sight. Introduced 1990.

Price: Fixed sight **$641.00**
Price: Adjustable sight **$671.00**
Price: Model 22C, ported barrel **$646.00**

Glock 26

Glock 30

Glock 31

Glock 35

Hammerli Trailside

Glock 23 Auto Pistol

Similar to the Glock 19 except chambered for 40 S&W, 10-shot magazine. Overall length is 6.85", weight is 20.6 oz. (without magazine). Fixed or adjustable rear sight. Introduced 1990.
Price: Fixed sight **$641.00**
Price: Model 23C, ported barrel **$646.00**
Price: Adjustable sight **$671.00**

GLOCK 26, 27 AUTO PISTOLS

Caliber: 9mm Para. (M26), 10-shot magazine; 40 S&W (M27), 9-shot magazine. **Barrel:** 3.46". **Weight:** 21.75 oz. **Length:** 6.29" overall. **Grips:** Integral. Stippled polymer. **Sights:** Dot on front blade, fixed or fully adjustable white outline rear. **Features:** Subcompact size. Polymer frame, steel slide; double-action trigger with "Safe Action" system, three safeties. Matte black Tenifer finish. Hammer-forged barrel. Imported from Austria by Glock, Inc. Introduced 1996.
Price: Fixed sight **$641.00**
Price: Adjustable sight **$671.00**

GLOCK 29, 30 AUTO PISTOLS

Caliber: 10mm (M29), 45 ACP (M30), 10-shot magazine. **Barrel:** 3.78". **Weight:** 24 oz. **Length:** 6.7" overall. **Grips:** Integral. Stippled polymer. **Sights:** Dot on front, fixed or fully adjustable white outline rear. **Features:** Compact size. Polymer frame steel slide; double-recoil spring reduces recoil; Safe Action system with three safeties; Tenifer finish. Two magazines supplied. Introduced 1997. Imported from Austria by Glock, Inc.
Price: Fixed sight **$700.00**
Price: Adjustable sight **$730.00**

Glock 31/31C Auto Pistols

Similar to the Glock 17 except chambered for 357 Auto cartridge; 10-shot magazine. Overall length is 7.32", weight is 23.28 oz. (without magazine). Fixed or adjustable sight. Imported from Austria by Glock, Inc.
Price: Fixed sight **$641.00**
Price: Adjustable sight **$671.00**
Price: Model 31C, ported barrel **$646.00**

Glock 32/32C Auto Pistols

Similar to the Glock 19 except chambered for the 357 Auto cartridge; 10-shot magazine. Overall length is 6.85", weight is 21.52 oz. (without magazine). Fixed or adjustable sight. Imported from Austria by Glock, Inc.
Price: Fixed sight **$616.00**
Price: Adjustable sight **$644.00**
Price: Model 32C, ported barrel **$646.00**

Glock 33 Auto Pistol

Similar to the Glock 26 except chambered for the 357 Auto cartridge; 9-shot magazine. Overall length is 6.29", weight is 19.75 oz. (without magazine). Fixed or adjustable sight. Imported from Austria by Glock, Inc.
Price: Fixed sight **$641.00**
Price: Adjustable sight **$671.00**

GLOCK 34, 35 AUTO PISTOLS

Caliber: 9mm Para. (M34), 40 S&W (M35), 10-shot magazine. **Barrel:** 5.32". **Weight:** 22.9 oz. **Length:** 8.15" overall. **Grips:** Integral. Stippled polymer. **Sights:** Dot on front, fully adjustable white outline rear. **Features:** Polymer frame, steel slide; double-action trigger with "Safe Action" system; three safeties; Tenifer finish. Imported from Austria by Glock, Inc.
Price: Model 34, 9mm. **$770.00**
Price: Model 35, 40 S&W **$770.00**

GLOCK 36 AUTO PISTOL

Caliber: 45 ACP, 6-shot magazine. **Barrel:** 3.78". **Weight:** 20.11 oz. **Length:** 6.77" overall. **Grips:** Integral. Stippled polymer. **Sights:** Dot on front, fully adjustable white outline rear. **Features:** Polymer frame, steel slide; double-action trigger with "Safe Action" system; three safeties; Tenifer finish. Imported from Austria by Glock, Inc.
Price: Fixed sight **$700.00**
Price: Adj. sight **$730.00**

HAMMERLI "TRAILSIDE" TARGET PISTOL

Caliber: 22 LR. **Barrel:** 4.5", 6". **Weight:** 28 oz. **Grips:** Synthetic. **Sights:** Fixed. **Features:** 10-shot magazine. Imported from Switzerland by Sigarms. Distributed by Hammerli U.S.A.
Price: **$579.00**

HECKLER & KOCH USP AUTO PISTOL

Caliber: 9mm Para., 10-shot magazine, 40 S&W, 10-shot magazine, 357 Mag. **Barrel:** 4.25". **Weight:** 28 oz. (USP40). **Length:** 6.9" overall. **Grips:** Non-slip stippled black polymer. **Sights:** Blade front, rear adjustable for windage. **Features:** New HK design with polymer frame, modified Browning action with recoil reduction system, single control lever. Special "hostile environment" finish on all metal parts. Available in SA/DA, DAO, left- and right-hand versions. Introduced 1993. Imported from Germany by Heckler & Koch, Inc.
Price: Right-hand **$769.00**
Price: Left-hand **$794.00**

Heckler & Koch USP Compact Auto Pistol

Similar to the USP except has 3.58" barrel, measures 6.81" overall, and weighs 1.60 lbs. (9mm). Available in 9mm Para. 357 SIG or 40 S&W with 10-shot magazine. Introduced 1996. Imported from Germany by Heckler & Koch, Inc.
Price: Blue **$799.00**
Price: Blue with control lever on right **$824.00**
Price: Same as USP Compact DAO, enhanced trigger
performance **$799.00**

Heckler & Koch
USP Compact

Heckler & Koch USP45

Heckler & Koch
USP45 Compact

Heckler & Koch
USP45 Tactical

Heckler & Koch
Elite

Heckler & Koch
Mark 23 Special Operations

Heckler & Koch P7M8

Heckler & Koch USP45 Auto Pistol

Similar to the 9mm and 40 S&W USP except chambered for 45 ACP, 10-shot magazine. Has 4.13" barrel, overall length of 7.87" and weighs 30.4 oz. Has adjustable three-dot sight system. Available in SA/DA, DAO, left- and right-hand versions. Introduced 1995. Imported from Germany by Heckler & Koch, Inc.

Price: Right-hand **$839.00**
Price: Left-hand **$864.00**

Heckler & Koch USP45 Compact

Similar to the USP45 except has stainless slide; 8-shot magazine; modified and contoured slide and frame; extended slide release; 3.80" barrel, 7.09" overall length, weighs 1.75 lbs.; adjustable three-dot sights. Introduced 1998. Imported from Germany by Heckler & Koch, Inc.

Price: With control lever on left, stainless **$909.00**
Price: As above, blue **$857.00**
Price: With control lever on right, stainless **$944.00**
Price: As above, blue **$892.00**

HECKLER & KOCH USP45 TACTICAL PISTOL

Caliber: 45 ACP, 10-shot magazine. **Barrel:** 4.92". **Weight:** 2.24 lbs. **Length:** 8.64" overall. **Grips:** Non-slip stippled polymer. **Sights:** Blade front, fully adjustable target rear. **Features:** Has extended threaded barrel with rubber O-ring; adjustable trigger; extended magazine floorplate; adjustable trigger stop; polymer frame. Introduced 1998. Imported from Germany by Heckler & Koch, Inc.

Price: **$1,115.00**

HECKLER & KOCH MARK 23 SPECIAL OPERATIONS PISTOL

Caliber: 45 ACP, 10-shot magazine. **Barrel:** 5.87". **Weight:** 43 oz. **Length:** 9.65" overall. **Grips:** Integral with frame; black polymer. **Sights:** Blade front, rear drift adjustable for windage; three-dot. **Features:** Polymer frame; double action; exposed hammer; short recoil, modified Browning action. Civilian version of the SOCOM pistol. Introduced 1996. Imported from Germany by Heckler & Koch, Inc.

Price: **$2,112.00**

Heckler & Koch USP Expert Pistol

Combines features of the USP Tactical and HK Mark 23 pistols with a new slide design. Chambered for 45 ACP, .40 S&W & 9mm; 10-shot magazine. Has adjustable target sights, 5.20" barrel, 8.74" overall length, weighs 1.87 lbs. Match-grade single- and double-action trigger pull with adjustable stop; ambidextrous control levers; elongated target slide; barrel O-ring that seals and centers barrel. Suited to IPSC competition. Introduced 1999. Imported from Germany by Heckler & Koch, Inc.

Price: **$1,869.00**

Heckler & Koch Elite

A long slide version of the USP combining features found on standard-sized and specialized models of the USP. Most noteworthy is the 6.2-inch-barrel, making it the most accurate of the USP series. In 9mm and .45 ACP. Imported from Germany by Heckler & Koch, Inc. Introduced 2003.

Price: **$1,569.00**

HECKLER & KOCH P7M8 AUTO PISTOL

Caliber: 9mm Para., 8-shot magazine. **Barrel:** 4.13". **Weight:** 29 oz. **Length:** 6.73" overall. **Grips:** Stippled black plastic. **Sights:** Blade front, adjustable rear; three dot system. **Features:** Unique "squeeze cocker" in frontstrap cocks the action. Gas-retarded action. Squared combat-type trigger guard. Blue finish. Compact size. Imported from Germany by Heckler & Koch, Inc.

Price: P7M8, blued **$1,515.00**

HECKLER & KOCH P2000 GPM PISTOL

Caliber: 9mmx19; 10-shot magazine. 13- or 16-round law enforcment/military magazines. **Barrel:** 3.62". **Weight:** 21.87 ozs. **Length:** 7". **Grips:** Interchangeable panels. **Sights:** Fixed Patridge style, drift adjustable for windage, standard 3-dot. **Features:** German Pistol Model incorporating features of the HK USP Compact such as the pre-cocked hammer system which combines the advantages of a cocked striker with the double action hammer system. Introduced 2003. Imported from Germany by Heckler & Koch, Inc.

Price: **$887.00**

HECKLER & KOCK P2000SK SUBCOMPACT

Caliber: 9mm and 40 S&W. **Barrel:** 2.48". **Weight:** 1.49 lbs. (9mm) or 1.61 lbs. (40 S&W). **Sights:** Fixed Patridge style, drift adjustable. **Features:** Standard accessory rails, ambidextrous slide release, polymer frame, polygonal bore profile.

Price: **$887.00**

Hi-Point 9MM Comp

Kahr K9

Kahr MK40

Kel-Tec P-11

HI-POINT FIREARMS 9MM COMP PISTOL

Caliber: 9mm, Para., 10-shot magazine. **Barrel:** 4". **Weight:** 39 oz. **Length:** 7.72" overall. **Grips:** Textured acetal plastic. **Sights:** Adjustable; low profile. **Features:** Single-action design. Scratch-resistant, non-glare blue finish, alloy frame. Muzzle brake/compensator. Compensator is slotted for laser or flashlight mounting. Introduced 1998. From MKS Supply, Inc.
Price: Matte black $159.00

HI-POINT FIREARMS MODEL 9MM COMPACT PISTOL

Caliber: 9mm Para., 8-shot magazine. **Barrel:** 3.5". **Weight:** 29 oz. **Length:** 6.7" overall. **Grips:** Textured acetal plastic. **Sights:** Combat-style adjust-able three-dot system; low profile. **Features:** Single-action design; frame-mounted magazine release; polymer or alloy frame. Scratch-resistant matte finish. Introduced 1993. Made in U.S.A. by MKS Supply, Inc.
Price: Black, alloy frame $149.00
Price: With polymer frame (29 oz.), non-slip grips $149.00
Price: Aluminum with polymer frame $149.00

Hi-Point Firearms Model 380 Polymer Pistol

Similar to the 9mm Compact model except chambered for 380 ACP, 8-shot magazine, adjustable three-dot sights. Weighs 29 oz. Polymer frame. Introduced 1998. Made in U.S.A. by MKS Supply.
Price: $114.00

Hi-Point Firearms 380 Comp Pistol

Similar to the 380 Polymer Pistol except has a 4" barrel with muzzle compensator; action locks open after last shot. Includes a 10-shot and an 8-shot magazine; trigger lock. Introduced 2001. Made in U.S.A. by MKS Supply Inc.
Price: $135.00
Price: With laser sight $229.00

HI-POINT FIREARMS 45 POLYMER FRAME

Caliber: 45 ACP, 9-shot, 40 S&W . **Barrel:** 4.5". **Weight:** 35 oz. **Sights:** Adjustable 3-dot. **Features:** Last round lock-open, grip mounted magazine release, magazine disconnect safety, integrated accessory rail. Introduced 2002. Made in U.S.A. by MKS Supply Inc.
Price: $179.00

IAI M-2000 PISTOL

Caliber: 45 ACP, 8-shot. **Barrel:** 5", (Compact 4.25"). **Weight:** 36 oz. **Length:** 8.5", (6" Compact). **Grips:** Plastic or wood. **Sights:** Fixed. **Features:** 1911 Government U.S. Army-style. Steel frame and slide parkerized. GI grip safety. Beveled feed ramp barrel. By IAI, Inc.
Price: $465.00

KAHR K9, K40 DA AUTO PISTOLS

Caliber: 9mm Para., 7-shot, 40 S&W, 6-shot magazine. **Barrel:** 3.5". **Weight:** 25 oz. **Length:** 6" overall. **Grips:** Wrap-around textured soft polymer. **Sights:** Blade front, rear drift adjustable for windage; bar-dot combat style. **Features:** Trigger-cocking double-action mechanism with passive firing pin block. Made of 4140 ordnance steel with matte black finish. Contact maker for complete price list. Introduced 1994. Made in U.S.A. by Kahr Arms.

Price: E9, black matte finish $425.00
Price: Matte black, night sights 9mm $668.00
Price: Matte stainless steel, 9mm. . . $638.00
Price: 40 S&W, matte black $580.00
Price: 40 S&W, matte black,
night sights $668.00
Price: 40 S&W, matte stainless $638.00
Price: K9 Elite 98 (high-polish stainless slide flats, Kahr combat
trigger), from $694.00
Price: As above, MK9 Elite 98, from $694.00
Price: As above, K40 Elite 98, from $694.00
Price: Covert, black, stainless slide, short grip $599.00
Price: Covert, black, tritium nite sights $689.00

Kahr K9 9mm Compact Polymer Pistol

Similar to K9 steel frame pistol except has polymer frame, matte stainless steel slide. Barrel length 3.5"; overall length 6"; weighs 17.9 oz. Includes two 7-shot magazines, hard polymer case, trigger lock. Introduced 2000. Made in U.S.A. by Kahr Arms.
Price: $599.00

Kahr MK9/MK40 Micro Pistol

Similar to the K9/K40 except is 5.5" overall, 4" high, has a 3" barrel. Weighs 22 oz. Has snag-free bar-dot sights, polished feed ramp, dual recoil spring system, DA-only trigger. Comes with 6- and 7-shot magazines. Introduced 1998. Made in U.S.A. by Kahr Arms.
Price: Matte stainless $638.00
Price: Elite 98, polished stainless, tritium night sights $791.00

KAHR PM9 PISTOL

Caliber: 9x19. **Barrel:** 3", 1:10 twist. **Weight:** 15.9 oz. **Length:** 5.3" overall. **Features:** Lightweight black polymer frame, polygonal rifling, stainless steel slide, DAO with passive striker block, trigger lock, hard case, 6 and 7 rd. mags.
Price: Matte stainless slide $622.00
Price: Tritium night sights $719.00

KEL-TEC P-11 AUTO PISTOL

Caliber: 9mm Para., 10-shot magazine. **Barrel:** 3.1". **Weight:** 14 oz. **Length:** 5.6" overall. **Grips:** Checkered black polymer. **Sights:** Blade front, rear adjustable for windage. **Features:** Ordnance steel slide, aluminum frame. Double-action-only trigger mechanism. Introduced 1995. Made in U.S.A. by Kel-Tec CNC Industries, Inc.
Price: Blue $314.00
Price: Hard chrome. $368.00
Price: Parkerized $355.00

KEL-TEC P-32 AUTO PISTOL

Caliber: 32 ACP, 7-shot magazine. **Barrel:** 2.68". **Weight:** 6.6 oz. **Length:** 5.07" overall. **Grips:** Checkered composite. **Sights:** Fixed. **Features:** Double-action-only mechanism with 6-lb. pull; internal slide stop. Textured composite grip/frame. Now available in 380 ACP. Made in U.S.A. by Kel-Tec CNC Industries, Inc.
Price: Blue $300.00
Price: Hard chrome. $340.00
Price: Parkerized $355.00

Kel-Tec P-32

Kimber Custom II

Kimber Pro Carry II

Kimber Ultra Carry II

Kimber Ten II High Capacity Polymer

Kimber Gold Match II

KIMBER CUSTOM II AUTO PISTOL

Caliber: 45 ACP, 40 S&W, .38 Super, 9 mm. **Barrel:** 5", match grade; 9 mm, .40 S&W, .38 Super barrels ramped. **Weight:** 38 oz. **Length:** 8.7" overall. **Grips:** Checkered black rubber, walnut, rosewood. **Sights:** Dovetail front and rear, Kimber low profile adj. or fixed three dot (green) Meptrolight night sights. **Features:** Slide, frame and barrel machined from steel or stainless steel. Match grade barrel, chamber and trigger group. Extended thumb safety, beveled magazine well, beveled front and rear slide serrations, high ride beavertail grip safety, checkered flat mainspring housing, kidney cut under trigger guard, high cut grip, match grade stainless steel barrel bushing, polished breech face, Commander-style hammer, lowered and flared ejection port, Wolff springs, bead blasted black oxide finish. Intro-duced in 1996. Made in U.S.A. by Kimber Mfg., Inc.

Price: Custom	**$745.00**
Price: Custom Walnut (double-diamond walnut grips)	**$767.00**
Price: Custom Stainless	**$848.00**
Price: Custom Stainless 40 S&W	**$799.00**
Price: Custom Stainless Target 45 ACP (stainless, adj. sight)	**$989.00**
Price: Custom Stainless Target 38 Super	**$994.00**

Kimber Stainless II Auto Pistol

Similar to Custom II except has stainless steel frame, 4-inch bbl., grip is .400" shorter than standard, no front serrations. Weighs 34 oz. 45 ACP only. Introduced in 1998. Made in U.S.A. by Kimber Mfg., Inc.

Price: ... **$964.00**

Kimber Pro Carry II Auto Pistol

Similar to Custom II, has aluminum frame, 4" bull barrel fitted directly to the slide without bushing. HD with stainless steel frame. Introduced 1998. Made in U.S.A. by Kimber Mfg., Inc.

Price: Pro Carry	**$789.00**
Price: Pro Carry w/night sights	**$893.00**
Price: Pro Carry Stainless w/night sights	**$862.00**
Price: Pro Carry HD II 38 Super	**$936.00**

Kimber Ultra Carry II Auto Pistol

Similar to Compact Stainless II, lightweight aluminum frame, 3" match grade bull barrel fitted to slide without bushing. Grips .400" shorter. Special slide stop. Low effort recoil. Weighs 25 oz. Introduced in 1999. Made in U.S.A. by Kimber Mfg., Inc.

Price:	**$783.00**
Price: Stainless	**$858.00**
Price: Stainless 40 S&W	**$903.00**

Kimber Ten II High Capacity Polymer Pistol

Similar to Custom II, Pro Carry II and Ultra Carry II depending on barrel length. Ten-round magazine capacity (double stack and flush fitting). Polymer grip frame molded over stainless steel or aluminum (BP Ten pistols only) frame insert. Checkered front strap and belly of trigger guard. All models have fixed sights except Gold Match Ten II, which has adjustable sight. Frame grip dimensions approximate that of the standard 1911 for natural aiming and better recoil control. **Weight:** 24 to 34 oz. Improved version of the Kimber Polymer series. Made in U.S.A. by Kimber Mfg., Inc.

Price: Pro Carry Ten II	**$828.00**
Price: Stainless Ten II	**$812.00**

Kimber Gold Match II Auto Pistol

Similar to Custom II models. Includes stainless steel barrel with match grade chamber and barrel bushing, ambidextrous thumb safety, adjustable sight, premium aluminum trigger, hand-checkered double diamond rosewood grips. Barrel hand-fitted to bushing and slide for target accuracy. Made in U.S.A. by Kimber Mfg., Inc.

Price: Gold Match II	**$1,192.00**
Price: Gold Match Stainless II 45 ACP	**$1,342.00**
Price: Gold Match Stainless II 40 S&W	**$1,373.00**

Kimber Gold Match Ten II Polymer Auto Pistol

Similar to Stainless Gold Match II. High capacity polymer frame with ten-round magazine. No ambi thumb safety. Polished flats add elegant look. Introduced 1999. Made in U.S.A. by Kimber Mfg., Inc.

Price: ... **$1,373.00**

Kimber Gold Combat II Auto Pistol

Similar to Gold Match I! except designed for concealed carry. Extended and beveled magazine well, Meprolight tritium night sights; premium aluminum trigger; 30 lpi front strap checkering; special Custom Shop markings; KimPro premium finish. Introduced 1999. Made in U.S.A. by Kimber Mfg., Inc.

Price: 45 ACP	**$1,716.00**
Price: Stainless (stainless frame and slide, special markings)	**$1,657.00**

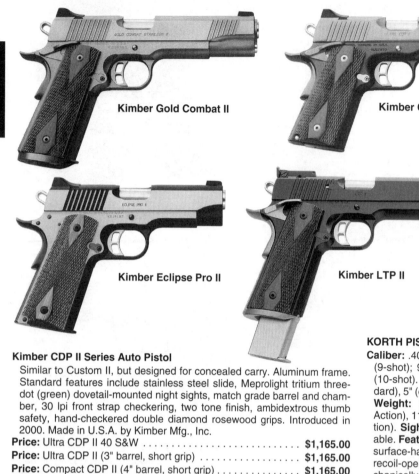

Kimber Gold Combat II

Kimber CDP II

Kimber Eclipse II

Kimber Eclipse Pro II

Kimber LTP II

Llama Micromax 380

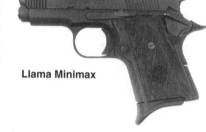

Llama Minimax

Kimber CDP II Series Auto Pistol

Similar to Custom II, but designed for concealed carry. Aluminum frame. Standard features include stainless steel slide, Meprolight tritium three-dot (green) dovetail-mounted night sights, match grade barrel and chamber, 30 lpi front strap checkering, two tone finish, ambidextrous thumb safety, hand-checkered double diamond rosewood grips. Introduced in 2000. Made in U.S.A. by Kimber Mfg., Inc.

Price: Ultra CDP II 40 S&W **$1,165.00**
Price: Ultra CDP II (3" barrel, short grip) **$1,165.00**
Price: Compact CDP II (4" barrel, short grip) **$1,165.00**
Price: Pro CDP II (4" barrel, full length grip) **$1,165.00**
Price: Custom CDP II (5" barrel, full length grip) **$1,203.00**

Kimber Eclipse II Series Auto Pistol

Similar to Custom II and other stainless Kimber pistols. Stainless slide and frame, black anodized, two tone finish. Gray/black laminated grips. 30 lpi front strap checkering. All have night sights, with Target versions having Meprolight adjustable Bar/Dot version. Made in U.S.A. by Kimber Mfg., Inc.

Price: Eclipse Ultra II (3" barrel, short grip) **$1,074.00**
Price: Eclipse Pro II (4" barrel, full length grip) **$1,074.00**
Price: Eclipse Pro Target II (4" barrel, full length grip,
adjustable sight) **$1,177.00**
Price: Eclipse Custom II (5" barrel, full length grip) **$1,077.00**
Price: Eclipse Target II (5" barrel, full length grip,
adjustable sight) **$1,177.00**

Kimber LTP II Auto Pistol

Similar to Gold Match II. Built for Limited Ten competition. First Kimber pistol with new, innovative Kimber external extractor. KimPro premium finish. Stainless steel match grade barrel. Extended and beveled magazine well. Checkered front strap and trigger guard belly. Tungsten full length guide rod. Premium aluminum trigger. Ten-round single stack magazine. Wide ambidextrous thumb safety. Made in U.S.A. by Kimber Mfg., Inc.

Price: **$2,078.00**

Kimber Super Match II Auto Pistol

Similar to Gold Match II. Built for target and action shotting competition. Tested for accuracy. Target included. Stainless steel barrel and chamber. KimPro finish on stainless steel slide. Stainless steel frame. 30 lpi checkered front strap, premium aluminum trigger, Kimber adjustable sight. Introduced in 1999.

Price: **$1,966.00**

KORTH PISTOL

Caliber: .40 S&W, .357 SIG (9-shot); 9mm Para, 9x21 (10-shot). **Barrel:** 4" (standard), 5" (optional). Trigger **Weight:** 3.3 lbs. (single Action), 11 lbs. (double action). **Sights:** Fully adjustable. **Features:** All parts of surface-hardened steel; recoil-operated action, mechanically-locked via large pivoting bolt block maintaining parallel positioning of barrel during the complete cycle. Accessories include sound suppressor for qualified buyers. A masterpiece of German precision. Imported by Korth USA.

Price: **$5,602.00**

LLAMA MICROMAX 380 AUTO PISTOL

Caliber: 32 ACP, 8-shot, 380 ACP, 7-shot magazine. **Barrel:** 3-11/16". **Weight:** 23 oz. **Length:** 6-1/2" overall. **Grips:** Checkered high impact polymer. **Sights:** 3-dot combat. **Features:** Single-action design. Mini custom extended slide release; mini custom extended beavertail grip safety; combat-style hammer. Introduced 1997. Distributed by Import Sports, Inc.

Price: Matte blue. **$291.95**
Price: Satin chrome (380 only) **$308.95**

LLAMA MINIMAX SERIES

Caliber: 40 S&W, 7-shot; 45 ACP, 6-shot magazine. **Barrel:** 3-1/2". **Weight:** 35 oz. **Length:** 7-1/3" overall. **Grips:** Checkered rubber. **Sights:** Three-dot combat. **Features:** Single action, skeletonized combat-style hammer, extended slide release, cone-style barrel, flared ejection port. Introduced 1996. Distributed by Import Sports, Inc.

Price: Blue **$341.95**
Price: Duo-Tone finish (45 only) **$349.95**
Price: Satin chrome **$358.95**

Llama Minimax Sub-Compact Auto Pistol

Similar to the Minimax except has 3.14" barrel, weighs 31 oz.; 6.8" overall length; has 10-shot magazine with finger extension; beavertail grip safety. Introduced 1999. Distributed by Import Sports, Inc.

Price: 45 ACP, matte blue. **$358.95**
Price: As above, satin chrome **$374.95**
Price: Duo-Tone finish (45 only) **$366.95**

Llama Max-1 Government Deluxe

North American Arms Guardian

Para-Ordnance P12.45

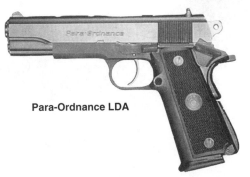

Para-Ordnance LDA

Para-Ordnance C5 45 LDA Para Carry

Para-Ordnance C7 45 LDA Para Companion

LLAMA MAX-I AUTO PISTOLS

Caliber: 45 ACP, 7-shot. **Barrel:** 5-1/8". **Weight:** 36 oz. **Length:** 8-1/2" overall. **Grips:** Polymer. **Sights:** Blade front; three-dot system. **Features:** Single-action trigger; skeletonized combat-style hammer; steel frame; extended manual and grip safeties, matte finish. Introduced 1995. Distributed by Import Sports, Inc.
Price: 45 ACP, 7-shot, Government model **$358.95**

NORTH AMERICAN ARMS GUARDIAN PISTOL

Caliber: 32 ACP, 380 ACP, 32NAA, 6-shot magazine. **Barrel:** 2.1". **Weight:** 13.5 oz. **Length:** 4.36" overall. **Grips:** Black polymer. **Sights:** Fixed. **Features:** Double-action-only mechanism. All stainless steel construction; snag-free. Introduced 1998. Made in U.S.A. by North American Arms.
Price: . . . . **$402.00 to $479.00**

OLYMPIC ARMS OA-96 AR PISTOL

Caliber: 223. **Barrel:** 6", 8", 4140 chrome-moly steel. **Weight:** 5 lbs. **Length:** 15-3/4" overall. **Grips:** A2 stowaway pistol grip; no buttstock or receiver tube. **Sights:** Flat-top upper receiver, cut-down front sight base. **Features:** AR-15-type receivers with special bolt carrier; short aluminum hand guard; Vortex flash hider. Introduced 1996. Made in U.S.A. by Olympic Arms, Inc.
Price: **$858.00**

Olympic Arms OA-98 AR Pistol

Similar to the OA-93 except has removable 7-shot magazine, weighs 3 lbs. Introduced 1999. Made in U.S.A. by Olympic Arms, Inc.
Price: **$990.00**

PARA-ORDNANCE P-SERIES AUTO PISTOLS

Caliber: 9mm Para., 40 S&W, 45 ACP, 10-shot magazine. **Barrel:** 3", 3-1/2", 4-1/4", 5". **Weight:** From 24 oz. (alloy frame). **Length:** 8.5" overall. **Grips:** Textured composition. **Sights:** Blade front, rear adjustable for windage. High visibility three-dot system. **Features:** Available with alloy, steel or stainless steel frame with black finish (silver or stainless gun). Steel and stainless steel frame guns weigh 40 oz. (P14.45), 36 oz. (P13.45), 34 oz. (P12.45). Grooved match trigger, rounded combat-style hammer. Beveled magazine well. Manual thumb, grip and firing pin lock safeties. Solid barrel bushing. Contact maker for full details. Introduced 1990. Made in Canada by Para-Ordnance.
Price: Steel frame **$795.00**
Price: Alloy frame **$765.00**
Price: Stainless steel **$865.00**

Para-Ordnance Limited Pistols

Similar to the P-Series pistols except with full-length recoil guide system; fully adjustable rear sight; tuned trigger with overtravel stop; beavertail grip safety; competition hammer; front and rear slide serrations; ambidextrous safety; lowered ejection port; ramped match-grade barrel; dovetailed front sight. Introduced 1998. Made in Canada by Para-Ordnance.
Price: 9mm, 40 S&W, 45 ACP . . . . **$945.00 to $999.00**

Para-Ordnance LDA Auto Pistols

Similar to P-series except has double-action trigger mechanism. Steel frame with matte black finish, checkered composition grips. Available in 9mm Para., 40 S&W, 45 ACP. Introduced 1999. Made in Canada by Para-Ordnance.
Price: **$775.00**

Para-Ordnance LDA Limited Pistols

Similar to LDA, has ambidextrous safety, adjustable rear sight, front slide serrations and full-length recoil guide system. Made in Canada by Para-Ordnance.
Price: Black finish **$975.00**
Price: Stainless **$1,049.00**

PARA-ORDNANCE C5 45 LDA PARA CARRY

Caliber: 45 ACP. **Barrel:** 3", 6+1 shot. **Weight:** 30 oz. **Length:** 6.5". **Grips:** Double diamond checkered Cocobolo. **Features:** Stainless finish and receiver, "world's smallest DAO 45 auto." Para LDA trigger system and safeties.
Price: **$899.00**

PARA-ORDNANCE C7 45 LDA PARA COMPANION

Caliber: 45 ACP. **Barrel:** 3.5", 7+1 shot. **Weight:** 32 oz. **Length:** 7". **Grips:** Double diamond checkered Cocobolo. **Features:** Para LDA trigger system with Para LDA 3 safeties (slide lock, firing pin block and grip safety). Lightning speed, full size capacity.
Price: **$899.00**

PETERS STAHL AUTOLOADING PISTOLS

Caliber: 9mm Para., 45 ACP. **Barrel:** 5" or 6". **Grips:** Walnut or walnut with rubber wrap. **Sights:** Fully adjustable rear, blade front. **Features:** Stainless steel extended slide stop, safety and extended magazine release button; speed trigger with stop and approx. 3-lb. pull; polished ramp. Introduced 2000. Imported from Germany by Phillips & Rogers.
Price: High Capacity (accepts 15-shot magazines in 45 cal.; includes 10-shot magazine) **$1,695.00**
Price: Trophy Master (blued or stainless, 7-shot in 45, 8-shot in 9mm) **$1,995.00**
Price: Millennium Model (titanium coating on receiver and slide) **$2,195.00**

HANDGUNS

Peters Stahl High Capacity

Peters Stahl Trophy Master

Peters Stahl Millennium

Phoenix Arms HP22

Ruger P89

Ruger P90

Rock River Standard Match

PHOENIX ARMS HP22, HP25 AUTO PISTOLS
Caliber: 22 LR, 10-shot (HP22), 25 ACP, 10-shot (HP25). **Barrel:** 3". **Weight:** 20 oz. **Length:** 5-1/2" overall. **Grips:** Checkered composition. **Sights:** Blade front, adjustable rear. **Features:** Single action, exposed hammer; manual hold-open; button magazine release. Available in satin nickel, polished blue finish. Introduced 1993. Made in U.S.A. by Phoenix Arms.
Price: With gun lock and cable lanyard.................... **$130.00**
Price: HP Rangemaster kit with 5" bbl., locking case
and assessories **$171.00**
Price: HP Deluxe Rangemaster kit with 3" and 5" bbls.,
2 mags., case **$210.00**

ROCK RIVER ARMS STANDARD MATCH AUTO PISTOL
Caliber: 45 ACP. **Barrel:** NA. **Weight:** NA. **Length:** NA. **Grips:** Cocobolo, checkered. **Sights:** Heine fixed rear, blade front. **Features:** Chrome-moly steel frame and slide; beavertail grip safety with raised pad; checkered slide stop; ambidextrous safety; polished feed ramp and extractor; aluminum speed trigger with 3.5 lb. pull. Made in U.S.A. From Rock River Arms.
Price: **$1,025.00**

ROCKY MOUNTAIN ARMS PATRIOT PISTOL
Caliber: 223, 10-shot magazine. **Barrel:** 7", with muzzle brake. **Weight:** 5 lbs. **Length:** 20.5" overall. **Grips:** Black composition. **Sights:** None furnished. **Features:** Milled upper receiver with enhanced Weaver base; milled lower receiver from billet plate; machined aluminum National Match handguard. Finished in DuPont Teflon-S matte black or NATO green. Comes with black nylon case, one magazine. Introduced 1993. From Rocky Mountain Arms, Inc.
Price: With A-2 handle top .... **$2,500.00 to $2,800.00**
Price: Flat top model.................... **$3,000.00 to $3,500.00**

RUGER P89 AUTOLOADING PISTOL
Caliber: 9mm Para., 10-shot magazine. **Barrel:** 4.50". **Weight:** 32 oz. **Length:** 7.84" overall. **Grips:** Grooved black synthetic composition. **Sights:** Square post front, square notch rear adjustable for windage, both with white dot inserts. **Features:** Double action, ambidextrous slide-mounted safety-levers. Slide 4140 chrome-moly steel or 400-series stainless steel, frame lightweight aluminum alloy. Ambidextrous magazine release. Blue, stainless steel. Introduced 1986; stainless 1990.
Price: P89, blue, extra mag and mag loader, plastic case locks . **$475.00**
Price: KP89, stainless, extra mag and mag loader,
plastic case locks **$525.00**

Ruger P89D Decocker Autoloading Pistol
Similar to standard P89 except has ambidextrous decocking levers in place of regular slide-mounted safety. Decocking levers move firing pin inside slide where hammer can not reach, while simultaneously blocking firing pin from forward movement-allows shooter to decock cocked pis-tol without manipulating trigger. Conventional thumb decocking proce-dures are therefore unnecessary. Blue, stainless steel. Introduced 1990.
Price: P89D, blue, extra mag and mag loader, plastic case locks **$475.00**
Price: KP89D, stainless, extra mag and mag loader,
plastic case locks **$525.00**

Ruger P89 Double-Action-Only Autoloading Pistol
Same as KP89 except operates only in double-action mode. Has spurless hammer, gripping grooves on each side of rear slide; no external safety or decocking lever. Internal safety prevents forward movement of firing pin unless trigger is pulled. Available 9mm Para., stainless steel only. In-troduced 1991.
Price: Lockable case, extra mag and mag loader............ **$525.00**

RUGER P90 MANUAL SAFETY MODEL AUTOLOADING PISTOL
Caliber: 45 ACP, 8-shot magazine. **Barrel:** 4.50". **Weight:** 33.5 oz. **Length:** 7.75" overall. **Grips:** Grooved black synthetic composition. **Sights:** Square post front, square notch rear adjustable for windage, both with white dot. **Features:** Double action ambidextrous slide-mounted safety-levers move firing pin inside slide where hammer can not reach, simultaneously blocking firing pin from forward movement. Stainless steel only. Introduced 1991.
Price: KP90 with extra mag, loader, case and gunlock......... **$565.00**
Price: P90 (blue).. **$525.00**

Ruger P93D   Ruger KP94D   Ruger KP95DAO

Ruger KMK 4

Ruger 22/45-P4

Ruger KP90 Decocker Autoloading Pistol

Similar to the P90 except has a manual decocking system. The ambidextrous decocking levers move the firing pin inside the slide where the hammer can not reach it, while simultaneously blocking the firing pin from forward movement-allows shooter to decock a cocked pistol without manipulating the trigger. Available only in stainless steel. Overall length 7.75", weighs 33.5 oz. Introduced 1991.

Price: KP90D with case, extra mag and mag loading tool **$565.00**

RUGER P93 COMPACT AUTOLOADING PISTOL

Caliber: 9mm Para., 10-shot magazine. **Barrel:** 3.9". **Weight:** 31 oz. **Length:** 7.25" overall. **Grips:** Grooved black synthetic composition. **Sights:** Square post front, square notch rear adjustable for windage. **Features:** Front of slide crowned with convex curve; slide has seven finger grooves; trigger guard bow higher for better grip; 400-series stainless slide, lightweight alloy frame; also blue. Decocker-only or DAO-only. Includes hard case and lock. Introduced 1993. Made in U.S.A. by Sturm, Ruger & Co.

Price: KP93DAO, double-action-only **$575.00**
Price: KP93D ambidextrous decocker, stainless **$575.00**
Price: P93D, ambidextrous decocker, blue.................. **$495.00**

Ruger KP94 Autoloading Pistol

Sized midway between full-size P-Series and compact P93. 4.25" barrel, 7.5" overall length, weighs about 33 oz. KP94 manual safety model; KP94DAO double-action-only (both 9mm Para., 10-shot magazine); KP94D is decocker-only in 40-caliber with 10-shot magazine. Slide gripping grooves roll over top of slide. KP94 has ambidextrous safety-levers; KP94DAO has no external safety, full-cock hammer position or decocking lever; KP94D has ambidextrous decocking levers. Matte finish stainless slide, barrel, alloy frame. Also blue. Includes hard case and lock. Introduced 1994. Made in U.S.A. by Sturm, Ruger & Co.

Price: P94, P944, blue (manual safety) **$495.00**
Price: KP94 (9mm), KP944 (40-caliber) (manual
safety-stainless) **$575.00**
Price: KP94DAO (9mm), KP944DAO (40-caliber) **$575.00**
Price: KP94D (9mm), KP944D (40-caliber)-decock only **$575.00**

RUGER P95 AUTOLOADING PISTOL

Caliber: 9mm Para., 10-shot magazine. **Barrel:** 3.9". **Weight:** 27 oz. **Length:** 7.25" overall. **Grips:** Grooved; integral with frame. **Sights:** Blade front, rear drift adjustable for windage; three-dot system. **Features:** Moulded polymer grip frame, stainless steel or chrome-moly slide. Suitable for +P+ ammunition. Safety model, decocker or DAO. Introduced 1996. Made in U.S.A. by Sturm, Ruger & Co. Comes with lockable plastic case, spare magazine, loader and lock.

Price: P95 DAO double-action-only **$425.00**
Price: P95D decocker only **$425.00**
Price: KP95D stainless steel decocker only **$475.00**
Price: KP95DAO double-action only, stainless steel.......... **$475.00**
Price: KP95 safety model, stainless steel.................. **$475.00**
Price: P95 safety model, blued finish **$425.00**

RUGER P97 AUTOLOADING PISTOL

Caliber: 45 ACP 8-shot magazine. **Barrel:** 4-1/8". **Weight:** 30-1/2 oz. **Length:** 7-1/4" overall. Grooved: Integral with frame. **Sights:** Blade front, rear drift adjustable for windage; three dot system. **Features:** Moulded polymer grip frame, stainless steel slide. Decocker or DAO. Introduced 1997. Made in U.S.A. by Sturm, Ruger & Co. Comes with lockable plastic case, spare magazine, loading tool.

Price: KP97D decocker only........................... **$495.00**
Price: KP97DAO double-action only **$495.00**
Price: P97D decocker only, blued **$460.00**

RUGER MARK II STANDARD AUTOLOADING PISTOL

Caliber: 22 LR, 10-shot magazine. **Barrel:** 4-3/4" or 6". **Weight:** 35 oz. (4-3/4" bbl.). **Length:** 8-5/16" (4-3/4" bbl.). **Grips:** Checkered composition grip panels. **Sights:** Fixed, wide blade front, fixed rear. **Features:** Updated design of original Standard Auto. New bolt hold-open latch. 10-shot magazine, magazine catch, safety, trigger and new receiver contours. Introduced 1982.

Price: Blued (MK 4, MK 6) **$289.00**
Price: In stainless steel (KMK 4, KMK 6) **$379.00**

Ruger 22/45 Mark II Pistol

Similar to other 22 Mark II autos except has grip frame of Zytel that matches angle and magazine latch of Model 1911 45 ACP pistol. Available in 4" bull, 4-3/4" standard and 5-1/2" bull barrels. Comes with extra magazine, plastic case, lock. Introduced 1992.

Price: P4, 4" bull barrel, adjustable sights **$290.00**
Price: KP 4 (4-3/4" barrel), stainless steel, fixed sights **$315.00**
Price: KP512 (5-1/2" bull barrel), stainless steel, adj. sights **$380.00**
Price: P512 (5-1/2" bull barrel, all blue), adj. sights **$290.00**

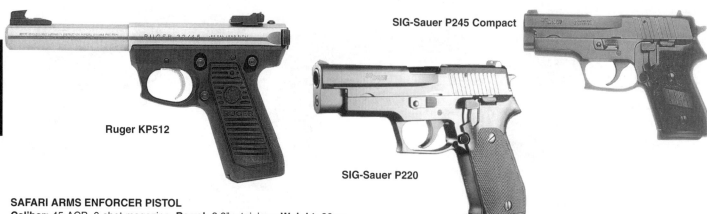

SIG-Sauer P245 Compact

Ruger KP512

SIG-Sauer P220

SAFARI ARMS ENFORCER PISTOL

Caliber: 45 ACP, 6-shot magazine. **Barrel:** 3.8", stainless. **Weight:** 36 oz. **Length:** 7.3" overall. **Grips:** Smooth walnut with etched black widow spider logo. **Sights:** Ramped blade front, LPA adjustable rear. **Features:** Extended safety, extended slide release; Commander-style hammer; beavertail grip safety; throated, polished, tuned. Parkerized matte black or satin stainless steel finishes. Made in U.S.A. by Safari Arms.
Price: $630.00

SAFARI ARMS GI SAFARI PISTOL

Caliber: 45 ACP, 7-shot magazine. **Barrel:** 5", 416 stainless. **Weight:** 39.9 oz. **Length:** 8.5" overall. **Grips:** Checkered walnut. **Sights:** G.I.-style blade front, drift-adjustable rear. **Features:** Beavertail grip safety; extended thumb safety and slide release; Commander-style hammer. Parkerized finish. Reintroduced 1996.
Price: $439.00

SAFARI ARMS CARRIER PISTOL

Caliber: 45 ACP, 7-shot magazine. **Barrel:** 6", 416 stainless steel. **Weight:** 30 oz. **Length:** 9.5" overall. **Grips:** Wood. **Sights:** Ramped blade front, LPA adjustable rear. **Features:** Beavertail grip safety; extended controls; full-length recoil spring guide; Commander-style hammer. Throated, polished and tuned. Satin stainless steel finish. Introduced 1999. Made in U.S.A. by Safari Arms, Inc.
Price: $714.00

SAFARI ARMS COHORT PISTOL

Caliber: 45 ACP, 7-shot magazine. **Barrel:** 3.8", 416 stainless. **Weight:** 37 oz. **Length:** 8.5" overall. **Grips:** Smooth walnut with laser-etched black widow logo. **Sights:** Ramped blade front, LPA adjustable rear. **Features:** Combines the Enforcer model, slide and MatchMaster frame. Beavertail grip safety; extended thumb safety and slide release; Commander-style hammer. Throated, polished and tuned. Satin stainless finish. Introduced 1996. Made in U.S.A. by Safari Arms, Inc.
Price: $654.00

SAFARI ARMS MATCHMASTER PISTOL

Caliber: 45 ACP, 7-shot. **Barrel:** 5" or 6", 416 stainless steel. **Weight:** 38 oz. (5" barrel). **Length:** 8.5" overall. **Grips:** Smooth walnut. **Sights:** Ramped blade, LPA adjustable rear. **Features:** Beavertail grip safety; extended controls; Commander-style hammer; throated, polished, tuned. Parkerized matte-black or satin stainless steel. Made in U.S.A. by Olympic Arms, Inc.
Price: 5" barrel $594.00
Price: 6" barrel $654.00

Safari Arms Carry Comp Pistol

Similar to the Matchmaster except has Wil Schueman-designed hybrid compensator system. Made in U.S.A. by Olympic Arms, Inc.
Price: $1,067.00

SEECAMP LWS 32 STAINLESS DA AUTO

Caliber: 32 ACP Win. Silvertip, 6-shot magazine. **Barrel:** 2", integral with frame. **Weight:** 10.5 oz. **Length:** 4-1/8" overall. **Grips:** Glass-filled nylon. **Sights:** Smooth, no-snag, contoured slide and barrel top. **Features:** Aircraft quality 17-4 PH stainless steel. Inertia-operated firing pin. Hammer fired double-action-only. Hammer automatically follows slide down to safety rest position after each shot-no manual safety needed. Magazine safety disconnector. Polished stainless. Introduced 1985. From L.W. Seecamp.
Price: $425.00

SEMMERLING LM-4 SLIDE-ACTION PISTOL

Caliber: 45 ACP, 4-shot magazine. **Barrel:** 2". **Weight:** 24 oz. **Length:** NA. **Grips:** NA. **Sights:** NA. **Features:** While outwardly appearing to be a semi-automatic, the Semmerling LM-4 is a unique and super compact pistol employing a thumb activated slide mechanism (the slide is manually retracted between shots). Hand-built and super reliable, it is intended for professionals in law enforcement and for concealed carry by licensed and firearms knowledgeable private citizens. From American Derringer Corp.
Price: $2,635.00

SIG-SAUER P220 SERVICE AUTO PISTOL

Caliber: 45 ACP, (7- or 8-shot magazine). **Barrel:** 4-3/8". **Weight:** 27.8 oz. **Length:** 7.8" overall. **Grips:** Checkered black plastic. **Sights:** Blade front, drift adjustable rear for windage. Optional Siglite nightsights. **Features:** Double action. Decocking lever permits lowering hammer onto locked firing pin. Squared combat-type trigger guard. Slide stays open after last shot. Imported from Germany by SIGARMS, Inc.
Price: Blue SA/DA or DAO $790.00
Price: Blue, Siglite night sights $880.00
Price: K-Kote or nickel slide $830.00
Price: K-Kote or nickel slide with Siglite night sights $930.00

SIG-Sauer P220 Sport Auto Pistol

Similar to the P220 except has 4.9" barrel, ported compensator, all-stainless steel frame and slide, factory-tuned trigger, adjustable sights, extended competition controls. Overall length is 9.9", weighs 43.5 oz. Introduced 1999. From SIGARMS, Inc.
Price: $1,320.00

SIG-Sauer P245 Compact Auto Pistol

Similar to the P220 except has 3.9" barrel, shorter grip, 6-shot magazine, 7.28" overall length, and weighs 27.5 oz. Introduced 1999. From SIGARMS, Inc.
Price: Blue $780.00
Price: Blue, with Siglite sights $850.00
Price: Two-tone $830.00
Price: Two-tone with Siglite sights $930.00
Price: With K-Kote finish $830.00
Price: K-Kote with Siglite sights $930.00

SIG-Sauer P229 DA Auto Pistol

Similar to the P228 except chambered for 9mm Para., 40 S&W, 357 SIG. Has 3.86" barrel, 7.08" overall length and 3.35" height. Weight is 30.5 oz. Introduced 1991. Frame made in Germany, stainless steel slide assembly made in U.S.; pistol assembled in U.S. From SIGARMS, Inc.
Price: $795.00
Price: With nickel slide $890.00
Price: Nickel slide Siglite night sights $935.00

SIG-Sauer Pro 2009

SIG-Sauer P229 Sport

SIG-Sauer P232

Smith & Wesson 457 TDA

Smith & Wesson 908

Smith & Wesson 4013 TSW

SIG PRO AUTO PISTOL

Caliber: 9mm Para., 40 S&W, 10-shot magazine. **Barrel:** 3.86". **Weight:** 27.2 oz. **Length:** 7.36" overall. **Grips:** Composite and rubberized one-piece. **Sights:** Blade front, rear adjustable for windage. Optional Siglite night sights. **Features:** Polymer frame, stainless steel slide; integral frame accessory rail; replaceable steel frame rails; left- or right-handed magazine release. Introduced 1999. From SIGARMS, Inc.

Price: SP2340 (40 S&W) $596.00
Price: SP2009 (9mm Para.) $596.00
Price: As above with Siglite night sights $655.00

SIG-Sauer P226 Service Pistol

Similar to the P220 pistol except has 4.4" barrel, and weighs 28.3 oz. 357 SIG or 40 S&W. Imported from Germany by SIGARMS, Inc.

Price: Blue SA/DA or DAO $830.00
Price: With Siglite night sights $930.00
Price: Blue, SA/DA or DAO 357 SIG $830.00
Price: With Siglite night sights $930.00
Price: K-Kote finish, 40 S&W only or nickel slide $830.00
Price: K-Kote or nickel slide Siglite night sights $930.00
Price: Nickel slide 357 SIG $875.00
Price: Nickel slide, Siglite night sights $930.00

SIG-Sauer P229 Sport Auto Pistol

Similar to the P229 except available in 357 SIG only; 4.8" heavy barrel; 8.6" overall length; weighs 40.6 oz.; vented compensator; adjustable target sights; rubber grips; extended slide latch and magazine release. Made of stainless steel. Introduced 1998. From SIGARMS, Inc.

Price: $1,320.00

SIG-SAUER P232 PERSONAL SIZE PISTOL

Caliber: 380 ACP, 7-shot. **Barrel:** 3-3/4". **Weight:** 16 oz. **Length:** 6-1/2" overall. **Grips:** Checkered black composite. **Sights:** Blade front, rear adjustable for windage. **Features:** Double action/single action or DAO. Blow-back operation, stationary barrel. Introduced 1997. Imported from Germany by SIGARMS, Inc.

Price: Blue SA/DA or DAO $505.00
Price: In stainless steel $545.00
Price: With stainless steel slide, blue frame $525.00
Price: Stainless steel, Siglite night sights, Hogue grips $585.00

SIG-SAUER P239 PISTOL

Caliber: 9mm Para., 8-shot, 357 SIG 40 S&W, 7-shot magazine. **Barrel:** 3.6". **Weight:** 25.2 oz. **Length:** 6.6" overall. **Grips:** Checkered black composite. **Sights:** Blade front, rear adjustable for windage. Optional Siglite night sights. **Features:** SA/DA or DAO; blackened stainless steel slide, aluminum alloy frame. Introduced 1996. Made in U.S.A. by SIGARMS, Inc.

Price: SA/DA or DAO $620.00
Price: SA/DA or DAO with Siglite night sights $720.00
Price: Two-tone finish $665.00
Price: Two-tone finish, Siglite sights $765.00

SMITH & WESSON MODEL 22A SPORT PISTOL

Caliber: 22 LR, 10-shot magazine. **Barrel:** 4", 5-1/2", 7". **Weight:** 29 oz. **Length:** 8" overall. **Grips:** Two-piece polymer. **Sights:** Patridge front, fully adjustable rear. **Features:** Comes with a sight bridge with Weaver-style integral optics mount; alloy frame; .312" serrated trigger; stainless steel slide and barrel with matte blue finish. Introduced 1997. Made in U.S.A. by Smith & Wesson.

Price: 4" $264.00
Price: 5-1/2" $292.00
Price: 7" $331.00

SMITH & WESSON MODEL 457 TDA AUTO PISTOL

Caliber: 45 ACP, 7-shot magazine. **Barrel:** 3-3/4". **Weight:** 29 oz. **Length:** 7-1/4" overall. **Grips:** One-piece Xenoy, wrap-around with straight backstrap. **Sights:** Post front, fixed rear, three-dot system. **Features:** Aluminum alloy frame, matte blue carbon steel slide; bobbed hammer; smooth trigger. Introduced 1996. Made in U.S.A. by Smith & Wesson.

Price: $591.00

SMITH & WESSON MODEL 908 AUTO PISTOL

Caliber: 9mm Para., 8-shot magazine. **Barrel:** 3-1/2". **Weight:** 26 oz. **Length:** 6-13/16". **Grips:** One-piece Xenoy, wrap-around with straight backstrap. **Sights:** Post front, fixed rear, three-dot system. **Features:** Aluminum alloy frame, matte blue carbon steel slide; bobbed hammer; smooth trigger. Introduced 1996. Made in U.S.A. by Smith & Wesson.

Price: $535.00

SMITH & WESSON MODEL 4013, 4053 TSW AUTOS

Caliber: 40 S&W, 9-shot magazine. **Barrel:** 3-1/2". **Weight:** 26.4 oz. **Length:** 6-7/8" overall. **Grips:** Xenoy one-piece wrap-around. **Sights:** Novak three-dot system. **Features:** Traditional double-action system; stainless slide, alloy frame; fixed barrel bushing; ambidextrous decocker; reversible magazine catch, equipment rail. Introduced 1997. Made in U.S.A. by Smith & Wesson.

Price: Model 4013 TSW $886.00
Price: Model 4053 TSW, double-action-only $886.00

Smith & Wesson
410 DA

Smith & Wesson
910 DA

Smith & Wesson
3913 LadySmith

Smith & Wesson 4006

Smith & Wesson
4566 TSW

SMITH & WESSON MODEL 22S SPORT PISTOLS

Similar to the Model 22A Sport except with stainless steel frame. Available only with 5-1/2" or 7" barrel. Introduced 1997. Made in U.S.A. by Smith & Wesson.

Price: 5-1/2" standard barrel **$358.00**
Price: 5-1/2" bull barrel, wood target stocks with thumbrest **$434.00**
Price: 7" standard barrel **$395.00**
Price: 5-1/2" bull barrel, two-piece target stocks with thumbrest . **$353.00**

SMITH & WESSON MODEL 410 DA AUTO PISTOL

Caliber: 40 S&W, 10-shot magazine. **Barrel:** 4". **Weight:** 28.5 oz. **Length:** 7.5 oz. **Grips:** One-piece Xenoy, wrap-around with straight backstrap. **Sights:** Post front, fixed rear; three-dot system. **Features:** Aluminum alloy frame; blued carbon steel slide; traditional double action with left-side slide-mounted decocking lever. Introduced 1996. Made in U.S.A. by Smith & Wesson.

Price: Model 410 . . . . **$591.00**
Price: Model 410, HiViz front sight **$612.00**

SMITH & WESSON MODEL 910 DA AUTO PISTOL

Caliber: 9mm Para., 10-shot magazine. **Barrel:** 4". **Weight:** 28 oz. **Length:** 7-3/8" overall. **Grips:** One-piece Xenoy, wrap-around with straight backstrap. **Sights:** Post front with white dot, fixed two-dot rear. **Features:** Alloy frame, blue carbon steel slide. Slide-mounted decocking lever. Introduced 1995.

Price: Model 910 . . . . **$535.00**
Price: Model 410, HiViz front sight **$535.00**

SMITH & WESSON MODEL 3913 TRADITIONAL DOUBLE ACTION

Caliber: 9mm Para., 8-shot magazine. **Barrel:** 3-1/2". **Weight:** 26 oz. **Length:** 6-13/16" overall. **Grips:** One-piece Delrin wrap-around, textured surface. **Sights:** Post front with white dot, Novak LoMount Carry with two dots. **Features:** Aluminum alloy frame, stainless slide (M3913) or blue steel slide (M3914). Bobbed hammer with no half-cock notch; smooth .304" trigger with rounded edges. Straight backstrap. Equipment rail. Extra magazine included. Introduced 1989.

Price: **$760.00**

Smith & Wesson Model 3913-LS Ladysmith Auto

Similar to the standard Model 3913 except has frame that is upswept at the front, rounded trigger guard. Comes in frosted stainless steel with matching gray grips. Grips are ergonomically correct for a woman's hand. Novak LoMount Carry rear sight adjustable for windage, smooth edges for snag resistance. Extra magazine included. Introduced 1990.

Price: **$782.00**

Smith & Wesson Model 3953 DAO Pistol

Same as the Model 3913 except double-action-only. Model 3953 has stainless slide with alloy frame. Overall length 7"; weighs 25.5 oz. Extra magazine included. Equipment rail. Introduced 1990.

Price: **$760.00**

Smith & Wesson Model 3913TSW/3953TSW Auto Pistols

Similar to the Model 3913 and 3953 except TSW guns have tighter tolerances, ambidextrous manual safety/decocking lever, flush-fit magazine, delayed-unlock firing system; magazine disconnector. Compact alloy frame, stainless steel slide. Straight backstrap. Introduced 1998. Made in U.S.A. by Smith & Wesson.

Price: Single action/double action **$760.00**
Price: Double action only **$760.00**

SMITH & WESSON MODEL 4006 TDA AUTO

Caliber: 40 S&W, 10-shot magazine. **Barrel:** 4". **Weight:** 38.5 oz. **Length:** 7-7/8" overall. **Grips:** Xenoy wrap-around with checkered panels. **Sights:** Replaceable post front with white dot, Novak LoMount Carry fixed rear with two white dots, or micro. click adjustable rear with two white dots. **Features:** Stainless steel construction with non-reflective finish. Straight backstrap, quipment rail. Extra magazine included. Introduced 1990.

Price: With adjustable sights. **$944.00**
Price: With fixed sight **$907.00**
Price: With fixed night sights. **$1,040.00**
Price: With Saf-T-Trigger, fixed sights **$927.00**

SMITH & WESSON MODEL 4006 TSW

Caliber: 40, 10-shot. **Barrel:** 4". **Grips:** Straight back strap grip. **Sights:** Fixed Novak LoMount Carry. **Features:** Traditional double action, ambidextrous safety, Saf-T-Trigger, equipment rail, satin stainless.

Price: **$927.00**

Smith & Wesson Model 4043, 4046 DA Pistols

Similar to the Model 4006 except is double-action-only. Has a semi-bobbed hammer, smooth trigger, 4" barrel; Novak LoMount Carry rear sight, post front with white dot. Overall length is 7-1/2", weighs 28 oz. Model 4043 has alloy frame, equipment rail. Extra magazine included. Introduced 1991.

Price: Model 4043 (alloy frame) **$886.00**
Price: Model 4046 (stainless frame) **$907.00**
Price: Model 4046 with fixed night sights **$1,040.00**

Smith & Wesson
Sigma SW40V

Smith & Wesson 99

SMITH & WESSON MODEL 4500 SERIES AUTOS

Caliber: 45 ACP, 8-shot magazine. **Barrel:** 5" (M4506). **Weight:** 41 oz. (4506). **Length:** 8-1/2" overall. **Grips:** Xenoy one-piece wrap-around, arched or straight backstrap. **Sights:** Post front with white dot, adjustable or fixed Novak LoMount Carry on M4506. **Features:** M4506 has serrated hammer spur, equipment rail. All have two magazines. Contact Smith & Wesson for complete data. Introduced 1989.
Price: Model 4566 (stainless, 4-1/4", traditional DA, ambidextrous
safety, fixed sight) **$942.00**
Price: Model 4586 (stainless, 4-1/4", DA only) **$942.00**
Price: Model 4566 (stainless, 4-1/4" with Saf-T-Trigger,
fixed sight) **$961.00**

SMITH & WESSON MODEL 4513TSW/4553TSW PISTOLS

Caliber: 45 ACP, 7-shot magazine. **Barrel:** 3-3/4". **Weight:** 28 oz. (M4513TSW). **Length:** 6-7/8 overall. **Grips:** Checkered Xenoy; straight backstrap. **Sights:** White dot front, Novak LoMount Carry 2-Dot rear. **Features:** Model 4513TSW is traditional double action, Model 4553TSW is double action only. TSW series has tighter tolerances, ambidextrous manual safety/decocking lever, flush-fit magazine, delayed-unlock firing system; magazine disconnector. Compact alloy frame, stainless steel slide, equipment rail. Introduced 1998. Made in U.S.A. by Smith & Wesson.
Price: Model 4513TSW. **$924.00**
Price: Model 4553TSW. **$924.00**

SMITH & WESSON MODEL 4566 TSW

Caliber: 45 ACP. **Barrel:** 4-1/4", 8-shot . **Grips:** Straight back strap grip. **Sights:** Fixed Novak LoMount Carry. **Features:** Ambidextrous safety, equipment rail, Saf-T-Trigger, satin stainless finish. Traditional double action.
Price: **$961.00**

SMITH & WESSON MODEL 5900 SERIES AUTO PISTOLS

Caliber: 9mm Para., 10-shot magazine. **Barrel:** 4". **Weight:** 28-1/2 to 37-1/2 oz. (fixed sight); 38 oz. (adjustable sight). **Length:** 7-1/2" overall. **Grips:** Xenoy wrap-around with curved backstrap. **Sights:** Post front with white dot, fixed or fully adjustable with two white dots. **Features:** All stainless, stainless and alloy or carbon steel and alloy construction. Smooth .304" trigger, .260" serrated hammer. Equipment rail. Introduced 1989.
Price: Model 5906 (stainless, traditional DA, adjustable sight,
ambidextrous safety). **$904.00**
Price: As above, fixed sight. **$841.00**
Price: With fixed night sights. **$995.00**
Price: With Saf-T-Trigger. **$882.00**
Price: Model 5946 DAO (as above, stainless frame and slide). . . **$863.00**

SMITH & WESSON ENHANCED SIGMA SERIES DAO PISTOLS

Caliber: 9mm Para., 40 S&W, 10-shot magazine. **Barrel:** 4". **Weight:** 26 oz. **Length:** 7.4" overall. **Grips:** Integral. **Sights:** White dot front, fixed rear; three-dot system. Tritium night sights available. **Features:** Ergonomic polymer frame; low barrel centerline; internal striker firing system; corrosion-resistant slide; Teflon-filled, electroless-nickel coated magazine, equipment rail. Introduced 1994. Made in U.S.A. by Smith & Wesson.
Price: SW9E, 9mm, 4" barrel, black finish, fixed sights **$447.00**
Price: SW9V, 9mm, 4" barrel, satin stainless, fixed night sights . . **$447.00**
Price: SW9VE, 4" barrel, satin stainless, Saf-T-Trigger,
fixed sights **$466.00**
Price: SW40E, 40 S&W, 4" barrel, black finish, fixed sights **$657.00**
Price: SW40V, 40 S&W, 4" barrel, black polymer, fixed sights . . . **$447.00**
Price: SW40VE, 4" barrel, satin stainless, Saf-T-Trigger,
fixed sights **$466.00**

SMITH & WESSON MODEL CS9 CHIEF'S SPECIAL AUTO

Caliber: 9mm Para., 7-shot magazine. **Barrel:** 3". **Weight:** 20.8 oz. **Length:** 6-1/4" overall. **Grips:** Hogue wrap-around rubber. **Sights:** White dot front, fixed two-dot rear. **Features:** Traditional double-action trigger mechanism. Alloy frame, stainless or blued slide. Ambidextrous safety. Introduced 1999. Made in U.S.A. by Smith & Wesson.
Price: Blue or stainless **$680.00**

Smith & Wesson Model CS40 Chief's Special Auto

Similar to CS9, chambered for 40 S&W (7-shot magazine), 3-1/4" barrel, weighs 24.2 oz., measures 6-1/2" overall. Introduced 1999. Made in U.S.A. by Smith & Wesson.
Price: Blue or stainless. **$717.00**

Smith & Wesson Model CS45 Chief's Special Auto

Similar to CS40, chambered for 45 ACP, 6-shot magazine, weighs 23.9 oz. Introduced 1999. Made in U.S.A. by Smith & Wesson.
Price: Blue or stainless. **$717.00**

SMITH & WESSON MODEL 99

Caliber: 9mm Para. 4" barrel; 40 S&W 4-1/8" barrel; 10-shot, adj. sights. **Features:** Traditional double action satin stainless, black polymer frame, equipment rail, Saf-T-Trigger.
Price: 4" barrel **$648.00**
Price: 4-1/8" barrel **$648.00**

SPRINGFIELD, INC. FULL-SIZE 1911A1 AUTO PISTOL

Caliber: 9mm Para., 9-shot; 38 Super, 9-shot; 40 S&W, 9-shot; 45 ACP, 7-shot. **Barrel:** 5". **Weight:** 35.6 oz. **Length:** 8-5/8" overall. **Grips:** Cocobolo. **Sights:** Fixed three-dot system. **Features:** Beveled magazine well; lowered and flared ejection port. All forged parts, including frame, barrel, slide. All new production. Introduced 1990. From Springfield, Inc.
Price: Mil-Spec 45 ACP, Parkerized **$559.00**
Price: Standard, 45 ACP, blued, Novak sights **$824.00**
Price: Standard, 45 ACP, stainless, Novak sights. **$828.00**
Price: Lightweight 45 ACP (28.6 oz., matte finish, night sights) . . **$877.00**
Price: 40 S&W, stainless **$860.00**
Price: 9mm, stainless **$837.00**

Springfield, Inc. TRP Pistols

Similar to 1911A1 except 45 ACP only, checkered front strap and mainspring housing, Novak Night Sight combat rear sight and matching dovetailed front sight, tuned, polished extractor, oversize barrel link; lightweight speed trigger and combat action job, match barrel and bushing, extended ambidextrous thumb safety and fitted beavertail grip safety. Carry bevel on entire pistol; checkered cocobolo wood grips, comes with two Wilson 7-shot magazines. Frame is engraved "Tactical," both sides of frame with "TRP." Introduced 1998. From Springfield, Inc.
Price: Standard with Armory Kote finish. **$1,395.00**
Price: Standard, stainless steel **$1,370.00**
Price: Standard with Operator Light Rail Armory Kote **$1,473.00**

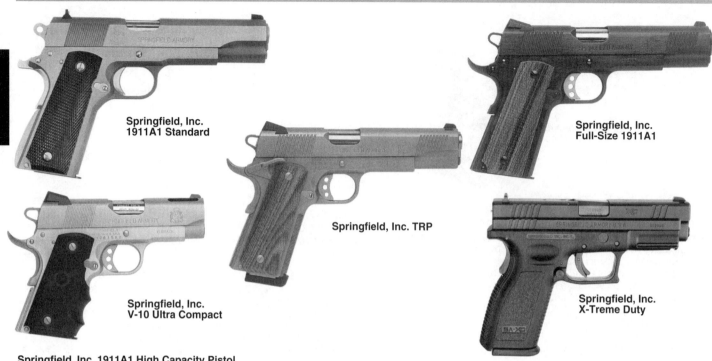

Springfield, Inc.
1911A1 Standard

Springfield, Inc.
Full-Size 1911A1

Springfield, Inc. TRP

Springfield, Inc.
V-10 Ultra Compact

Springfield, Inc.
X-Treme Duty

Springfield, Inc. 1911A1 High Capacity Pistol

Similar to Standard 1911A1, available in 45 ACP with 10-shot magazine. Commander-style hammer, walnut grips, beveled magazine well, plastic carrying case. Can accept higher-capacity Para-Ordnance magazines. Introduced 1993. From Springfield, Inc.
Price: Mil-Spec 45 ACP **$756.00**
Price: 45 ACP Ultra Compact (3-1/2" bbl.) **$909.00**

Springfield, Inc. 1911A1 V-Series Ported Pistols

Similar to standard 1911A1, scalloped slides with 10, 12 or 16 matching barrel ports to redirect powder gasses and reduce recoil and muzzle flip. Adjustable rear sight, ambi thumb safety, Videki speed trigger, and beveled magazine well. Checkered walnut grips standard. Available in 45 ACP, stainless or bi-tone. Introduced 1992.
Price: V-16 Long Slide, stainless **$1,121.00**
Price: Target V-12, stainless **$878.00**
Price: V-10 (Ultra-Compact, bi-tone) **$853.00**
Price: V-10 stainless **$863.00**

Springfield, Inc. 1911A1 Champion Pistol

Similar to standard 1911A1, slide is 4". Novak Night Sights. Delta hammer and cocobolo grips. Available in 45 ACP only; Parkerized or stainless. Introduced 1989.
Price: Stainless. **$849.00**

Springfield, Inc. Ultra Compact Pistol

Similar to 1911A1 Compact, shorter slide, 3.5" barrel, beavertail grip safety, beveled magazine well, Novak Low Mount or Novak Night Sights, Videki speed trigger, flared ejection port, stainless steel frame, blued slide, match grade barrel, rubber grips. Introduced 1996. From Springfield, Inc.
Price: Parkerized 45 ACP, Night Sights **$589.00**
Price: Stainless 45 ACP, Night Sights. **$849.00**
Price: Lightweight, 9mm, stainless **$837.00**

Springfield, Inc. Compact Lightweight

Mates a Springfield Inc. Champion length slide with the shorter Ultra-Compact forged alloy frame for concealability. In 45 ACP.
Price: **$733.00**

Springfield, Inc. Long Slide 1911 A1 Pistol

Similar to Full Size model, 6" barrel and slide for increased sight radius and higher velocity, fully adjustable sights, muzzle-forward weight distribution for reduced recoil and quicker shot-to-shot recovery. From Springfield Inc.

Price: Target, 45 ACP, stainless with Night Sights **$1,049.00**
Price: Trophy Match, stainless with adj. sights **$1,452.00**
Price: V-16 stainless steel **$1,121.00**

SPRINGFIELD, INC. MICRO-COMPACT 1911A1 PISTOL

Caliber: 45 ACP, 40 S&W 6+1 capacity. **Barrel:** 3" 1:16 LH. **Weight:** 24 oz. **Length:** 5.7". **Sights:** Novak LoMount tritium. Dovetail front. **Features:** Forged frame and slide, ambi thumb safety, extreme carry bevel treatment, lockable plastic case, 2 magazines.
Price: . . . . **$993.00 to $1,021.00**

SPRINGFIELD, INC. X-TREME DUTY

Caliber: 9mm, 40 S&W, 357 Sig. **Barrel:** 4.08". **Weight:** 22.88 oz. **Length:** 7.2". **Sights:** Dovetail front and rear. **Features:** Lightweight, ultra high-impact polymer frame. Trigger, firing pin and grip safety. Two 10-rod steel easy glide magazines. Imported from Croatia.
Price: . . . . **$489.00 to $1,099.00**

STEYR M & S SERIES AUTO PISTOLS

Caliber: 9mm Para., 40 S&W, 357 SIG; 10-shot magazine. **Barrel:** 4" (3.58" for Model S). **Weight:** 28 oz. (22.5 oz. for Model S). **Length:** 7.05" overall (6.53" for Model S). **Grips:** Ultra-rigid polymer. **Sights:** Drift-adjustable, white-outline rear; white-triangle blade front. **Features:** Polymer frame; trigger-drop firing pin, manual and key-lock safeties; loaded chamber indicator; 5.5-lb. trigger pull; 111-degree grip angle enhances natural pointing. Introduced 2000. Imported from Austria by GSI Inc.
Price: Model M (full-sized frame with 4" barrel) **$609.95**
Price: Model S (compact frame with 3.58" barrel) **$609.95**
Price: Extra 10-shot magazines (Model M or S) **$39.00**

TAURUS MODEL PT 22/PT 25 AUTO PISTOLS

Caliber: 22 LR, 8-shot (PT 22); 25 ACP, 9-shot (PT 25). **Barrel:** 2.75". **Weight:** 12.3 oz. **Length:** 5.25" overall. **Grips:** Smooth rosewood or mother-of-pearl. **Sights:** Fixed. **Features:** Double action. Tip-up barrel for loading, cleaning. Blue, nickel, duotone or blue with gold accents. Introduced 1992. Made in U.S.A. by Taurus International.
Price: 22 LR, 25 ACP, blue, nickel or with duo-tone finish
with rosewood grips **$219.00**
Price: 22 LR, 25 ACP, blue with gold trim, rosewood grips. **$234.00**
Price: 22 LR, 25 ACP, blue, nickel or duotone finish with checkered
wood grips. **$219.00**
Price: 22 LR, 25 ACP, blue with gold trim, mother of pearl grips . **$250.00**

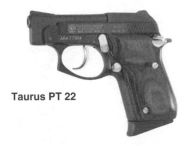

Taurus PT 22

Taurus PT-911

Taurus PT-938

Taurus PT-940

TAURUS MODEL PT24/7

Caliber: 9mm, 10+1 shot; .40 Cal., 10+1 shot. **Barrel:** 4". **Weight:** 27.2 oz. **Length:** 7-18". **Grips:** RIBBER rubber-finned overlay on polymer. **Sights:** Adjustable. **Features:** Accessory rail, four safeties, blue or stainless finish, consistent trigger pull weight and travel. Introduced 2003. Imported from Brazil by Taurus International.
Price: 9mm $578.00
Price: .40 Cal. $594.00

TAURUS MODEL PT92 AUTO PISTOL

Caliber: 9mm Para., 10-shot mag. **Barrel:** 5". **Weight:** 34 oz. **Length:** 8.5" overall. **Grips:** Checkered rubber, rosewood, mother-of-pearl. **Sights:** Fixed notch rear. Three-dot sight system. Also offered with micrometer-click adjustable night sights. **Features:** Double action, ambidextrous 3-way hammer drop safety, allows cocked & locked carry. Blue, stainless steel, blue with gold highlights, stainless steel with gold highlights, forged aluminum frame, integral key-lock. .22 LR conversion kit available. Imported from Brazil by Taurus International.
Price: Blue .... $578.00 to $672.00

Taurus Model PT99 Auto Pistol

Similar to PT92, fully adjustable rear sight.
Price: Blue .... $575.00 to $670.00
Price: 22 Conversion kit for PT 92 and PT99 (includes barrel and slide)
.... $266.00

TAURUS MODEL PT-100/101 AUTO PISTOL

Caliber: 40 S&W, 10-shot mag. **Barrel:** 5". **Weight:** 34 oz. **Length:** 8-1/2". **Grips:** Checkered rubber, rosewood, mother-of-pearl. **Sights:** 3-dot fixed or adjustable; night sights available. **Features:** Single/double action with three-position safety/decocker. Re-introduced in 2001. Imported by Taurus International.
Price: PT100.............................. $578.00 to $672.00
Price: PT101.............................. $594.00 to $617.00

TAURUS MODEL PT-111 MILLENNIUM PRO AUTO PISTOL

Caliber: 9mm Para., 10-shot mag. **Barrel:** 3.25". **Weight:** 18.7 oz. **Length:** 6-1/8" overall. **Grips:** Polymer. **Sights:** 3-dot fixed; night sights available. Low profile, three-dot combat. **Features:** Double action only, polymer frame, matte stainless or blue steel slide, manual safety, integral key-lock. Deluxe models with wood grip inserts. Now issued in a third generation series with many cosmetic and internal improvements.
Price: .... $445.00 to $539.00

Taurus Model PT-111 Millennium Titanium Pistol

Similar to PT-111, titanium slide, night sights.
Price: $586.00

TAURUS PT-132 MILLENIUM PRO AUTO PISTOL

Caliber: 32 ACP, 10-shot mag. **Barrel:** 3.25". **Weight:** 18.7 oz. **Grips:** Polymer. **Sights:** 3-dot fixed; night sights available. **Features:** Double action only, polymer frame, matte stainless or blue steel slide, manual safety, integral key-lock action. Introduced 2001.
Price: .... $445.00 to $461.00

TAURUS PT-138 MILLENIUM PRO SERIES

Caliber: 380 ACP, 10-shot mag. **Barrel:** 3.25". **Weight:** 18.7 oz. **Grips:** Polymer. **Sights:** Fixed 3-dot fixed. **Features:** Double action only, polymer frame, matte stainless or blue steel slide, manual safety, integral key-lock.
Price: .... $445.00 to $461.00

TAURUS PT-140 MILLENIUM PRO AUTO PISTOL

Caliber: 40 S&W, 10-shot mag. **Barrel:** 3.25". **Weight:** 18.7 oz. **Grips:** Checkered polymer. **Sights:** 3-dot fixed; night sights available. **Features:** Double-action only; matte stainless or blue steel slide, black polymer frame, manual safety, integral key-lock action. From Taurus International.
Price: .... $484.00 to $578.00

TAURUS PT-145 MILLENIUM AUTO PISTOL

Caliber: 45 ACP, 10-shot mag. **Barrel:** 3.27". **Weight:** 23 oz. **Stock:** Checkered polymer. **Sights:** 3-dot fixed; night sights available. **Features:** Double-action only, matte stainless or blue steel slide, black polymer frame, manual safety, integral key-lock. From Taurus International.
Price: .... $484.00 to $578.00

TAURUS MODEL PT-911 AUTO PISTOL

Caliber: 9mm Para., 10-shot mag. **Barrel:** 4". **Weight:** 28.2 oz. **Length:** 7" overall. **Grips:** Checkered rubber, rosewood, mother-of-pearl. **Sights:** Fixed, three-dot blue or stainless; night sights optional. **Features:** Double action, semi-auto ambidextrous 3-way hammer drop safety, allows cocked and locked carry. Blue, stainless steel, blue with gold highlights, or stainless steel with gold highlights, forged aluminum frame, integral key-lock.
Price: .... $523.00 to $617.00

TAURUS MODEL PT-938 AUTO PISTOL

Caliber: 380 ACP, 10-shot mag. **Barrel:** 3.72". **Weight:** 27 oz. **Length:** 6.5" overall. **Grips:** Checkered rubber. **Sights:** Fixed, three-dot. **Features:** Double action, ambidextrous 3-way hammer drop allows cocked & locked carry. Forged aluminum frame. Integral key-lock. Imported by Taurus International.
Price: Blue $516.00
Price: Stainless... $531.00

TAURUS MODEL PT-940 AUTO PISTOL

Caliber: 40 S&W, 10-shot mag. **Barrel:** 3-5/8". **Weight:** 28.2 oz. **Length:** 7" overall. **Grips:** Checkered rubber, rosewood or mother-of-pearl. **Sights:** Fixed, three-dot blue or stainless; night sights optional. **Features:** Double action, semi-auto ambidextrous 3-way hammer drop safety, allows cocked & locked carry. Blue, stainless steel, blue with gold highlights, or stainless steel with gold hightlights, forged aluminum frame, integral key-lock.
Price: .... $523.00 to $617.00

Taurus PT-945

Taurus PT-957

Walther PPK/S

Walther PPK

Walther P99

Walther P22

Wilkinson Sherry

TAURUS MODEL PT-945 SERIES
Caliber: 45 ACP, 8-shot mag. **Barrel:** 4.25". **Weight:** 28.2/29.5 oz. **Length:** 7.48" overall. **Grips:** Checkered rubber, rosewood or mother-of-pearl. **Sights:** Fixed, three-dot; night sights optional. **Features:** Double-action with ambidextrous 3-way hammer drop safety allows cocked & locked carry. Forged aluminum frame, PT-945C has ported barrel/slide. Blue, stainless, blue with gold highlights, stainless with gold highlights, integral key-lock. Introduced 1995. Imported by Taurus International.
Price: .... **$563.00 to $641.00**

TAURUS MODEL PT-957 AUTO PISTOL
Caliber: 357 SIG, 10-shot mag. **Barrel:** 4". **Weight:** 28 oz. **Length:** 7" overall. **Grips:** Checkered rubber, rosewood or mother-of-pearl. **Sights:** Fixed, three-dot blue or stainless; night sights optional. **Features:** Double-action, blue, stainless steel, blue with gold accents or stainless with gold accents, ported barrel/slide, three-position safety with decocking lever and ambidextrous safety. Forged aluminum frame, integral key-lock. Introduced 1999. Imported by Taurus International.
Price: .... **$525.00 to $620.00**
Price: Non-ported .... **$525.00 to $535.00**

TAURUS MODEL 922 SPORT PISTOL
Caliber: .22 LR, 10-shot magazine. **Barrel:** 6". **Weight:** 24.8 oz. **Length:** 9-1/8". **Grips:** Polymer. **Sights:** Adjustable. **Features:** Matte blue steel finish, machined target crown, polymer frame, single and double action, easy disassembly for cleaning.
Price: .... (blue) **$310.00**
Price: .... (stainless) **$328.00**

WALTHER PPK/S AMERICAN AUTO PISTOL
Caliber: 380 ACP, 7-shot magazine. **Barrel:** 3.27". **Weight:** 23-1/2 oz. **Length:** 6.1" overall. **Stocks:** Checkered plastic. **Sights:** Fixed, white markings. **Features:** Double action; manual safety blocks firing pin and drops hammer; chamber loaded indicator on 32 and 380; extra finger rest magazine provided. Made entirely in the United States. Introduced 1980.
Price: 380 ACP only, blue **$540.00**
Price: As above, 32 ACP or 380 ACP, stainless **$540.00**

Walther PPK American Auto Pistol
Similar to Walther PPK/S except weighs 21 oz., has 6-shot capacity. Made in the U.S. Introduced 1986.
Price: Stainless, 32 ACP or 380 ACP **$540.00**
Price: Blue, 380 ACP only **$540.00**

WALTHER P99 AUTO PISTOL
Caliber: 9mm Para., 9x21, 40 S&W,10-shot magazine. **Barrel:** 4". **Weight:** 25 oz. **Length:** 7" overall. **Grips:** Textured polymer. **Sights:** Blade front (comes with three interchangeable blades for elevation adjustment), micrometer rear adjustable for windage. **Features:** Double-action mechanism with trigger safety, decock safety, internal striker safety; chamber loaded indicator; ambidextrous magazine release levers; polymer frame with interchangeable backstrap inserts. Comes with two magazines. Introduced 1997. Imported from Germany by Carl Walther USA.
Price: **$799.00**

Walther P990 Auto Pistol
Similar to the P99 except is double action only. Available in blue or silver tenifer finish. Introduced 1999. Imported from Germany by Carl Walther USA.
Price: **$749.00**

WALTHER P22 PISTOL
Caliber: 22 LR. **Barrel:** 3.4", 5". **Weight:** 19.6 oz. (3.4"), 20.3 oz. (5"). **Length:** 6.26", 7.83". **Grips:** NA. **Sights:** Interchangeable white dot, front, 2-dot adjustable, rear. **Features:** A rimfire version of the Walther P99 pistol, available in nickel slide with black frame, or green frame with black slide versions. Made in Germany and distributed in the U.S. by Smith & Wesson.
Price: .... **NA**

WILKINSON SHERRY AUTO PISTOL
Caliber: 22 LR, 8-shot magazine. **Barrel:** 2-1/8". **Weight:** 9-1/4 oz. **Length:** 4-3/8" overall. **Grips:** Checkered black plastic. **Sights:** Fixed, groove. **Features:** Cross-bolt safety locks the sear into the hammer. Available in all blue finish or blue slide and trigger with gold frame. Introduced 1985.
Price: **$280.00**

WILKINSON LINDA AUTO PISTOL
Caliber: 9mm Para. **Barrel:** 8-5/16". **Weight:** 4 lbs., 13 oz. **Length:** 12-1/4" overall. **Grips:** Checkered black plastic pistol grip, walnut forend. **Sights:** Protected blade front, aperture rear. **Features:** Fires from closed bolt. Semi-auto only. Straight blowback action. Cross-bolt safety. Removable barrel. From Wilkinson Arms.
Price: **$675.00**

Includes models suitable for several forms of competition and other sporting purposes.

Baer 1911 Ultimate Master

Baer 1911 Bullseye Wadcutter

BF Ultimate

Browning Buck Mark Target 5.5

BAER 1911 ULTIMATE MASTER COMBAT PISTOL
Caliber: 9x23, 38 Super, 400 Cor-Bon 45 ACP (others available), 10-shot magazine. **Barrel:** 5", 6"; Baer NM. **Weight:** 37 oz. **Length:** 8.5" overall. **Grips:** Checkered rosewood. **Sights:** Baer dovetail front, low-mount Bo-Mar rear with hidden leaf. **Features:** Full-house competition gun. Baer forged NM blued steel frame and double serrated slide; Baer triple port, tapered cone compensator; fitted slide to frame; lowered, flared ejection port; Baer reverse recoil plug; full-length guide rod; recoil buff; beveled magazine well; Baer Commander hammer, sear; Baer extended ambidextrous safety, extended ejector, checkered slide stop, beavertail grip safety with pad, extended magazine release button; Baer speed trigger. Made in U.S.A. by Les Baer Custom, Inc.
Price: Compensated, open sights. **$2,476.00**
Price: 6" Model 400 Cor-Bon **$2,541.00**

BAER 1911 NATIONAL MATCH HARDBALL PISTOL
Caliber: 45 ACP, 7-shot magazine. **Barrel:** 5". **Weight:** 37 oz. **Length:** 8.5" overall. **Grips:** Checkered walnut. **Sights:** Baer dovetail front with undercut post, low-mount Bo-Mar rear with hidden leaf. **Features:** Baer NM forged steel frame, double serrated slide and barrel with stainless bushing; slide fitted to frame; Baer match trigger with 4-lb. pull; polished feed ramp, throated barrel; checkered front strap, arched mainspring housing; Baer beveled magazine well; lowered, flared ejection port; tuned extractor; Baer extended ejector, checkered slide stop; recoil buff. Made in U.S.A. by Les Baer Custom, Inc.
Price: **$1,335.00**

Baer 1911 Bullseye Wadcutter Pistol
Similar to National Match Hardball except designed for wadcutter loads only. Polished feed ramp and barrel throat; Bo-Mar rib on slide; full-length recoil rod; Baer speed trigger with 3-1/2-lb. pull; Baer deluxe hammer and sear; Baer beavertail grip safety with pad; flat mainspring housing checkered 20 lpi. Blue finish; checkered walnut grips. Made in U.S.A. by Les Baer Custom, Inc.
Price: From **$1,495.00**
Price: With 6" barrel, from. **$1,690.00**

BF ULTIMATE SILHOUETTE HB SINGLE SHOT PISTOL
Caliber: 7mm U.S., 22 LR Match and 100 other chamberings. **Barrel:** 10.75" Heavy Match Grade with 11-degree target crown. **Weight:** 3 lbs., 15 oz. **Length:** 16" overall. **Grips:** Thumbrest target style. **Sights:** Bo-

Mar/Bond ScopeRib I Combo with hooded post front adjustable for height and width, rear notch available in .032", .062", .080" and .100" widths; 1/2-MOA clicks. **Features:** Designed to meet maximum rules for IHMSA Production Gun. Falling block action gives rigid barrel-receiver mating. Hand fitted and headspaced. Etched receiver; gold-colored trigger. Introduced 1988. Made in U.S.A. by E. Arthur Brown Co. Inc.
Price: **$669.00**

BF Classic Hunting Pistol
Similar to BF Ultimate Silhouette HB Single Shot Pistol, except no sights; drilled and tapped for scope mount. Barrels from 8" to 15". Variety of options offered. Made in U.S.A. by E. Arthur Brown Co. Inc.
Price: **$599.00**

BROWNING BUCK MARK TARGET 5.5
Caliber: 22 LR, 10-shot magazine. **Barrel:** 5-1/2" barrel with .900" diameter. **Weight:** 35-1/2 oz. **Length:** 9-5/8" overall. **Grips:** Contoured walnut grips with thumbrest, or finger-groove walnut. **Sights:** Hooded sights mounted on scope base that accepts optical or reflex sight. Rear sight is Browning fully adjustable Pro Target, front sight is adjustable post that customizes to different widths, can be adjusted for height. **Features:** Matte blue finish. Introduced 1990. From Browning.
Price: **$496.00**

BROWNING BUCK MARK FIELD 5.5
Same as Target 5.5, hoodless ramp-style front sight and low profile rear sight. Matte blue finish, contoured or finger-groove walnut stocks. Introduced 1991.
Price: **$496.00**

BROWNING BUCK MARK BULLSEYE
Similar to Buck Mark Silhouette, 7-1/4" heavy barrel with three flutes per side; trigger adjusts from 2-1/2 to 5 lbs.; specially designed rosewood target or three-finger-groove stocks with competition-style heel rest, or with contoured rubber grip. Overall length 11-5/16", weighs 36 oz. Introduced 1996. Made in U.S.A. From Browning.
Price: With ambidextrous moulded composite stocks. **$454.00**
Price: With rosewood stocks, or wrap-around finger groove **$586.00**

Browning Buck Mark Bullseye

Colt Special Combat

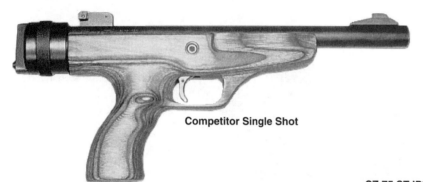

Competitor Single Shot

EAA Witness Gold Team

COLT GOLD CUP MODEL O PISTOL

Caliber: 45 ACP, 8-shot magazine. **Barrel:** 5", with new design bushing. **Weight:** 39 oz. **Length:** 8-1/2". **Grips:** Checkered rubber composite with silver-plated medallion. **Sights:** Patridge-style front, Bomar-style rear adjustable for windage and elevation, sight radius 6-3/4". **Features:** Arched or flat housing; wide, grooved trigger with adjustable stop; ribbed-top slide, hand fitted, with improved ejection port.
Price: Blue **$1,050.00**
Price: Stainless. **$1,116.00**

COLT SPECIAL COMBAT GOVERNMENT

Caliber: 45 ACP. **Barrel:** 5" **Weight:** NA. **Length:** 8-1/2" **Grips:** Rosewood w/double diamond checkering pattern. **Sights:** Clark dovetail, front; Bomar adjustable, rear. **Features:** A competition ready pistol with enhancements such as skeletonized trigger, upswept grip safety, custom tuned action, polished feed ramp. Blue or satin nickel finish. Introduced 2003. Made in U.S.A. by Colt's Mfg. Co.
Price: **$1,640.00**

COMPETITOR SINGLE SHOT PISTOL

Caliber: 22 LR through 50 Action Express, including belted magnums. **Barrel:** 14" standard; 10.5" silhouette; 16" optional. **Weight:** About 59 oz. (14" bbl.). **Length:** 15.12" overall. **Grips:** Ambidextrous; synthetic (standard) or laminated or natural wood. **Sights:** Ramp front, adjustable rear. **Features:** Rotary canon-type action cocks on opening; cammed ejector; interchangeable barrels, ejectors. Adjustable single stage trigger, sliding thumb safety and trigger safety. Matte blue finish. Introduced 1988. From Competitor Corp., Inc.
Price: 14", standard calibers, synthetic grip **$414.95**
Price: Extra barrels, from **$159.95**

CZ 75 CHAMPION COMPETITION PISTOL

Caliber: 9mm Para., 9x21, 40 S&W, 10-shot mag. **Barrel:** 4.49". **Weight:** 35 oz. **Length:** 9.44" overall. **Grips:** Black rubber. **Sights:** Blade front, fully adjustable rear. **Features:** Single-action trigger mechanism; three-port compensator (40 S&W, 9mm have two port) full-length guide rod; extended magazine release; ambidextrous safety; flared magazine well; fully adjustable match trigger. Introduced 1999. Imported from the Czech Republic by CZ USA.
Price: 9mm Para., 9x21, 40 S&W, dual-tone finish **$1,551.00**

CZ 75 ST IPSC AUTO PISTOL

Caliber: 40 S&W, 10-shot magazine. **Barrel:** 5.12". **Weight:** 2.9 lbs. **Length:** 8.86" overall. **Grips:** Checkered walnut. **Sights:** Fully adjustable rear. **Features:** Single-action mechanism; extended slide release and ambidextrous safety; full-length slide rail; double slide serrations. Introduced 1999. Imported from the Czech Republic by CZ-USA.
Price: Dual-tone finish **$1,038.00**

EAA/BAIKAL IZH35 AUTO PISTOL

Caliber: 22 LR, 5-shot mag. **Barrel:** 6". **Grips:** Walnut; fully adjustable right-hand target-style. **Sights:** Fully adjustable rear, blade front; detachable scope mount. **Features:** Hammer-forged target barrel; machined steel receiver; adjustable trigger; manual slide hold back, grip and manual trigger-bar disconnect safeties; cocking indicator. Introduced 2000. Imported from Russia by European American Armory.
Price: Blued finish. **$489.00**

EAA WITNESS GOLD TEAM AUTO

Caliber: 9mm Para., 9x21, 38 Super, 40 S&W, 45 ACP. **Barrel:** 5.1". **Weight:** 44 oz. **Length:** 10.5" overall. **Grips:** Checkered walnut, competition style. **Sights:** Square post front, fully adjustable rear. **Features:** Triple-chamber cone compensator; competition SA trigger; extended safety and magazine release; competition hammer; beveled magazine well; beavertail grip. Hand-fitted major components. Hard chrome finish. Match-grade barrel. From E.A.A. Custom Shop. Introduced 1992. From European American Armory.
Price: **$1,699.00**

EAA Witness Silver Team Auto

Similar to Witness Gold Team, double-chamber compensator, oval magazine release, black rubber grips, double-dip blue finish. Super Sight and drilled and tapped for scope mount. Built for the intermediate competition shooter. Introduced 1992. From European American Armory Custom Shop.
Price: 9mm Para., 9x21, 38 Super, 40 S&W, 45 ACP. **$968.00**

ED BROWN CLASSIC CUSTOM PISTOL

Caliber: 45 ACP. **Barrel:** 5". **Weight:** 39 oz. **Grips:** Hogue exotic wood. **Sights:** Modified ramp or post, front; fully-adjustable Bo-Mar, rear. **Features:** Highly-polished slide, two-piece guide rod, oversize mag release, ambidextrous safety.
Price: **$2,895.00**

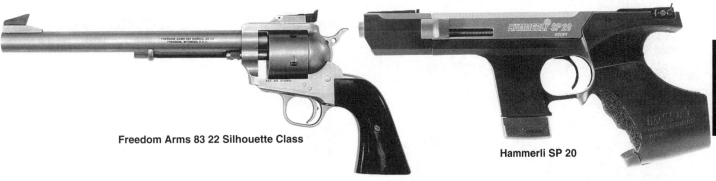

Freedom Arms 83 22 Silhouette Class

Hammerli SP 20

High Standard Trophy

ED BROWN CLASS A LIMITED
Caliber: 45 ACP, 400 Cor-Bon, 10mm, 40 S&W, 357 SIG, 38 Super, 9x23, 9mm Luger, 7-shot magazine. **Barrel:** 4.25", 5". **Weight:** 34 to 39 oz. **Grips:** Hogue exotic wood. **Sights:** Customer preference, front; fixed Novak low-mount or fully-adjustable Bo-Mar, rear. **Features:** Checkered forestrap and mainspring housing, matte finished top sighting surface. Many options available.
Price: **$2,250.00**

ENTRÉPRISE TOURNAMENT SHOOTER MODEL I
Caliber: 45 ACP, 10-shot mag. **Barrel:** 6". **Weight:** 40 oz. **Length:** 8.5" overall. **Grips:** Black ultra-slim double diamond checkered synthetic. **Sights:** Dovetailed Patridge front, adjustable Competizione "melded" rear. **Features:** Oversized magazine release button; flared magazine well; fully machined parallel slide rails; front and rear slide serrations; serrated top of slide; stainless ramped bull barrel with fully supported chamber; full-length guide rod with plug; stainless firing pin; match extractor; polished ramp; tuned match extractor; black oxide. Introduced 1998. Made in U.S.A. by Entréprise Arms.
Price: **$2,300.00**
Price: TSMIII (Satin chrome finish, two-piece guide rod) **$2,700.00**

EXCEL INDUSTRIES CP-45, XP-45 AUTO PISTOL
Caliber: 45 ACP, 6-shot & 10-shot mags. **Barrel:** 3-1/4". **Weight:** 31 oz. & 25 oz. **Length:** 6-3/8" overall. **Grips:** Checkered black nylon. **Sights:** Fully adjustable rear. **Features:** Stainless steel frame and slide; single action with external hammer and firing pin block, manual thumb safety; last-shot hold open. Includes gun lock and cleaning kit. Introduced 2001. Made in U.S.A. by Excel Industries Inc.
Price: CP-45 .... **$425.00**
Price: XP-45 .... **$465.00**

FEINWERKEBAU AW93 TARGET PISTOL
Caliber: 22. **Barrel:** 6". **Grips:** Fully adjustable orthopaedic. **Sights:** Fully adjustable micrometer. **Features:** Advanced Russian design with German craftmanship. Imported from Germany by Nygord Precision Products.
Price: **$1,495.00**

FREEDOM ARMS MODEL 83 22 FIELD GRADE SILHOUETTE CLASS
Caliber: 22 LR, 5-shot cylinder. **Barrel:** 10". **Weight:** 63 oz. **Length:** 15.5" overall. **Grips:** Black Micarta. **Sights:** Removable patridge front blade; Iron Sight Gun Works silhouette rear, click adjustable for windage and elevation (optional adj. front sight and hood). **Features:** Stainless steel, matte finish, manual sliding-bar safety system; dual firing pins, lightened hammer for fast lock time, pre-set trigger stop. Introduced 1991. Made in U.S.A. by Freedom Arms.
Price: Silhouette Class **$1,901.75**
Price: Extra fitted 22 WMR cylinder **$264.00**

FREEDOM ARMS MODEL 83 CENTERFIRE SILHOUETTE MODELS
Caliber: 357 Mag., 41 Mag., 44 Mag.; 5-shot cylinder. **Barrel:** 10", 9" (357 Mag. only). **Weight:** 63 oz. (41 Mag.). **Length:** 15.5", 14-1/2" (357 only). **Grips:** Pachmayr Presentation. **Sights:** Iron Sight Gun Works silhouette rear sight, replaceable adjustable front sight blade with hood. **Features:** Stainless steel, matte finish, manual sliding-bar safety system. Made in U.S.A. by Freedom Arms.
Price: Silhouette Models........................... **$1,634.85**

GAUCHER GP SILHOUETTE PISTOL
Caliber: 22 LR, single shot. **Barrel:** 10". **Weight:** 42.3 oz. **Length:** 15.5" overall. **Grips:** Stained hardwood. **Sights:** Hooded post on ramp front, open rear adjustable for windage and elevation. **Features:** Matte chrome barrel, blued bolt and sights. Other barrel lengths available on special order. Introduced 1991. Imported by Mandall Shooting Supplies.
Price: **$425.00**

HAMMERLI SP 20 TARGET PISTOL
Caliber: 22 LR, 32 S&W. **Barrel:** 4.6". **Weight:** 34.6-41.8 oz. **Length:** 11.8" overall. **Grips:** Anatomically shaped synthetic Hi-Grip available in five sizes. **Sights:** Integral front in three widths, adjustable rear with changeable notch widths. **Features:** Extremely low-level sight line; anatomically shaped trigger; adjustable JPS buffer system for different recoil characteristics. Receiver available in red, blue, gold, violet or black. Introduced 1998. Imported from Switzerland by SIGARMS, Inc and Hammerli Pistols USA.
Price: Hammerli 22 LR **$1,668.00**
Price: Hammerli 32 S&W **$1,743.00**

HAMMERLI X-ESSE SPORT PISTOL
An all-steel .22 LR target pistol with a Hi-Grip in a new anatomical shape and an adjustable hand rest. Made in Switzerland. Introduced 2003.
Price: **$710.00**

HARRIS GUNWORKS SIGNATURE JR. LONG RANGE PISTOL
Caliber: Any suitable caliber. **Barrel:** To customer specs. **Weight:** 5 lbs. **Stock:** Gunworks fiberglass. **Sights:** None furnished; comes with scope rings. **Features:** Right- or left-hand benchrest action of titanium or stainless steel; single shot or repeater. Comes with bipod. Introduced 1992. Made in U.S.A. by Harris Gunworks, Inc.
Price: **$2,700.00**

HIGH STANDARD TROPHY TARGET PISTOL
Caliber: 22 LR, 10-shot mag. **Barrel:** 5-1/2" bull or 7-1/4" fluted. **Weight:** 44 oz. **Length:** 9.5" overall. **Stock:** Checkered hardwood with thumbrest. **Sights:** Undercut ramp front, frame-mounted micro-click rear adjustable for windage and elevation; drilled and tapped for scope mounting. **Features:** Gold-plated trigger, slide lock, safety-lever and magazine release; stippled front grip and backstrap; adjustable trigger and sear. Barrel weights optional. From High Standard Manufacturing Co., Inc.
Price: 5-1/2", scope base **$540.00**
Price: 7.25" **$689.00**
Price: 7.25", scope base **$625.00**

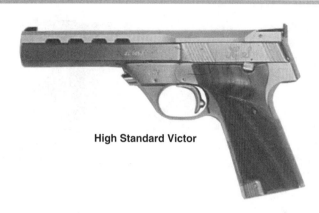

High Standard Victor

Ruger Mark II Target

Ruger Mark II Government Target

HIGH STANDARD VICTOR TARGET PISTOL

Caliber: 22 LR, 10-shot magazine. **Barrel:** 4-1/2" or 5-1/2"; push-button takedown. **Weight:** 46 oz. **Length:** 9.5" overall. **Stock:** Checkered hardwood with thumbrest. **Sights:** Undercut ramp front, micro-click rear adjustable for windage and elevation. Also available with scope mount, rings, no sights. **Features:** Stainless steel construction. Full-length vent rib. Gold-plated trigger, slide lock, safety-lever and magazine release; stippled front grip and backstrap; polished slide; adjustable trigger and sear. Comes with barrel weight. From High Standard Manufacturing Co., Inc.
Price: 4-1/2" scope base $564.00
Price: 5-1/2", sights $625.00
Price: 5-1/2" scope base $564.00

KIMBER SUPER MATCH II

Caliber: 45 ACP, 7-shot magazine. **Barrel:** 5". **Weight:** 38 oz. **Length:** 18.7" overall. **Sights:** Blade front, Kimber fully adjustable rear. **Features:** Guaranteed to have shot 3" group at 50 yards. Stainless steel frame, black KimPro slide; two-piece magazine well; premium aluminum match-grade trigger; 30 lpi front strap checkering; stainless match-grade barrel; ambidextrous safety; special Custom Shop markings. Introduced 1999. Made in U.S.A. by Kimber Mfg., Inc.
Price: $1,927.00

KORTH MATCH REVOLVER

Caliber: 357 Mag., 38 Special, 32 S&W Long, 9mm Para., 22 WMR, 22 LR. **Barrel:** 5-1/4", 6". **Grips:** Adjustable match of oiled walnut with matte finish. **Sights:** Fully adjustable with rear sight leaves (wide th of sight notch: 3.4 mm, 3.5 mm, 3.6 mm), rear; undercut partridge, front. Trigger: Equipped with completely machined trigger shoe. Interchangeable caliber cylinders available as well as a variety of finishes. Made in Germany.
Price: . . . . From $5,632.00

MORINI MODEL 84E FREE PISTOL

Caliber: 22 LR, single shot. **Barrel:** 11.4". **Weight:** 43.7 oz. **Length:** 19.4" overall. **Grips:** Adjustable match type with stippled surfaces. **Sights:** Interchangeable blade front, match-type fully adjustable rear. **Features:** Fully adjustable electronic trigger. Introduced 1995. Imported from Switzerland by Nygord Precision Products.
Price: $1,450.00

PARDINI MODEL SP, HP TARGET PISTOLS

Caliber: 22 LR, 32 S&W, 5-shot magazine. **Barrel:** 4.7". **Weight:** 38.9 oz. **Length:** 11.6" overall. **Grips:** Adjustable; stippled walnut; match type. **Sights:** Interchangeable blade front, interchangeable, fully adjustable rear. **Features:** Fully adjustable match trigger. Introduced 1995. Imported from Italy by Nygord Precision Products.
Price: Model SP (22 LR) $995.00
Price: Model HP (32 S&W) $1,095.00

PARDINI GP RAPID FIRE MATCH PISTOL

Caliber: 22 Short, 5-shot magazine. **Barrel:** 4.6". **Weight:** 43.3 oz. **Length:** 11.6" overall. **Grips:** Wrap-around stippled walnut. **Sights:** Interchangeable post front, fully adjustable match rear. Introduced 1995. Imported from Italy by Nygord Precision Products.
Price: Model GP $1,095.00
Price: Model GP-E Electronic, has special parts $1,595.00

PARDINI K22 FREE PISTOL

Caliber: 22 LR, single shot. **Barrel:** 9.8". **Weight:** 34.6 oz. **Length:** 18.7" overall. **Grips:** Wrap-around walnut; adjustable match type. **Sights:** Interchangeable post front, fully adjustable match open rear. **Features:** Removable, adjustable match trigger. Toggle bolt pushes cartridge into chamber. Barrel weights mount above the barrel. New upgraded model introduced in 2002. Imported from Italy by Nygord Precision Products.
Price: $1,295.00

PARDINI GT45 TARGET PISTOL

Caliber: 45, 9mm, 40 S&W. **Barrel:** 5", 6". **Grips:** Checkered fore strap. **Sights:** Interchangeable post front, fully adjustable match open rear. **Features:** Ambi-safeties, trigger pull adjustable. Fits Helweg Glock holsters for defense shooters. Imported from Italy by Nygord Precision Products.
Price: 5" $1,050.00
Price: 6" $1,125.00
Price: Frame mount available . . . . $75.00 extra
Price: Slide mount available . . . . $35.00 extra

PARDINI/NYGORD "MASTER" TARGET PISTOL

Caliber: 22 cal. **Barrel:** 5-1/2". **Grips:** Semi-wrap-around. **Sights:** Micrometer rear and red dot. **Features:** Elegant NRA "Bullseye" pistol. Superior balance of Pardini pistols. Revolutionary recirpcating internal weight barrel shroud. Imported from Italy by Nygord Precision Products.
Price: $1,145.00

RUGER MARK II TARGET MODEL AUTOLOADING PISTOL

Caliber: 22 LR, 10-shot magazine. **Barrel:** 6-7/8". **Weight:** 42 oz. **Length:** 11-1/8" overall. **Grips:** Checkered composition grip panels. **Sights:** .125" blade front, micro-click rear, adjustable for windage and elevation. Sight radius 9-3/8". Plastic case with lock included.
Features: Introduced 1982.
Price: Blued (MK-678) $349.00
Price: Stainless (KMK-678) $439.00

Ruger Mark II Government Target Model

Same gun as Mark II Target Model except has 6-7/8" barrel, higher sights and is roll marked "Government Target Model" on right side of receiver below rear sight. Identical in all aspects to military model used for training U.S. Armed Forces except for markings. Comes with factory test target, also lockable plastic case. Introduced 1987.
Price: Blued (MK-678G) $425.00
Price: Stainless (KMK-678G) $509.00

Ruger Mark II Bull Barrel - MK10

Safari Arms Big Deuce

Smith & Wesson Model 41

Springfield, Inc. 1911A1
Bullseye Wadcutter

Ruger Stainless Competition Model Pistol

Similar to Mark II Government Target Model stainless pistol, 6-7/8" slab-sided barrel; receiver top is fitted with Ruger scope base of blued, chrome moly steel; has Ruger 1" stainless scope rings for mounting variety of optical sights; checkered laminated grip panels with right-hand thumbrest. Blued open sights with 9-1/4" radius. Overall length 11-1/8", weight 45 oz. Case and lock included. Introduced 1991.
Price: KMK-678GC **$529.00**

Ruger Mark II Bull Barrel

Same gun as Target Model except has 5-1/2" or 10" heavy barrel (10" meets all IHMSA regulations). Weight with 5-1/2" barrel is 42 oz., with 10" barrel, 51 oz. Case with lock included.
Price: Blued (MK-512) **$349.00**
Price: Blued (MK-10) **$357.00**
Price: Stainless (KMK-10) **$445.00**
Price: Stainless (KMK-512) **$439.00**

SAFARI ARMS BIG DEUCE PISTOL

Caliber: 45 ACP, 7-shot magazine. **Barrel:** 6", 416 stainless steel. **Weight:** 40.3 oz. **Length:** 9.5" overall. **Grips:** Smooth walnut. **Sights:** Ramped blade front, LPA adjustable rear. **Features:** Beavertail grip safety; extended thumb safety and slide release; Commander-style hammer. Throated, polished and tuned. Parkerized matte black slide with satin stainless steel frame. Introduced 1995. Made in U.S.A. by Safari Arms, Inc.
Price: **$714.00**

SMITH & WESSON MODEL 41 TARGET

Caliber: 22 LR, 10-shot clip. **Barrel:** 5-1/2", 7". **Weight:** 44 oz. (5-1/2" barrel). **Length:** 9" overall (5-1/2" barrel). **Grips:** Checkered walnut with modified thumbrest, usable with either hand. **Sights:** 1/8" Patridge on ramp base; micro-click rear adjustable for windage and elevation. **Features:** 3/8" wide, grooved trigger; adjustable trigger stop drilled and tapped.
Price: S&W Bright Blue, either barrel **$958.00**

SMITH & WESSON MODEL 22A TARGET PISTOL

Caliber: 22 LR, 10-shot magazine. **Barrel:** 5-1/2" bull. **Weight:** 38.5 oz. **Length:** 9-1/2" overall. **Grips:** Dymondwood with ambidextrous thumbrests and flared bottom or rubber soft touch with thumbrest. **Sights:** Patridge front, fully adjustable rear. **Features:** Sight bridge with Weaver-style integral optics mount; alloy frame, stainless barrel and slide; blue finish. Introduced 1997. Made in U.S.A. by Smith & Wesson.
Price: **$367.00**
Price: HiViz front sight **$387.00**
Price: Camo model **$355.00**

Smith & Wesson Model 22S Target Pistol

Similar to the Model 22A except has stainless steel frame. Introduced 1997. Made in U.S.A. by Smith & Wesson.
Price: **$434.00**
Price: HiViz front sight **$453.00**

SPRINGFIELD, INC. 1911A1 BULLSEYE WADCUTTER PISTOL

Caliber: 38 Super, 45 ACP. **Barrel:** 5". **Weight:** 45 oz. **Length:** 8.59" overall (5" barrel). **Grips:** Checkered walnut. **Sights:** Bo-Mar rib with undercut blade front, fully adjustable rear. **Features:** Built for wadcutter loads only. Has full-length recoil spring guide rod, fitted Videki speed trigger with 3.5-lb. pull; match Commander hammer and sear; beavertail grip safety; lowered and flared ejection port; tuned extractor; fitted slide to frame; recoil buffer system; beveled and polished magazine well; checkered front strap and steel mainspring housing (flat housing standard); polished and throated National Match barrel and bushing. Comes with two magazines with slam pads, plastic carrying case, test target. Introduced 1992. From Springfield, Inc.
Price: **$1,499.00**
Price: Adj. Target. **$1,049.00**
Price: M1911SC, Commander style **$1,029.00**

Springfield, Inc. Basic Competition Pistol

Has low-mounted Bo-Mar adjustable rear sight, undercut blade front; match throated barrel and bushing; polished feed ramp; lowered and flared ejection port; fitted Videki speed trigger with tuned 3.5-lb. pull; fitted slide to frame; recoil buffer system; checkered walnut grips; serrated, arched mainspring housing. Comes with two magazines with slam pads, plastic carrying case. Introduced 1992. From Springfield, Inc.
Price: 45 ACP, blue, 5" only **$1,295.00**

Springfield, Inc. Expert

Springfield, Inc. Distinguished

Springfield, Inc. N.M. Hardball

Springfield, Inc. 1911A1 Trophy Match

Springfield, Inc. Expert Pistol

Similar to the Competition Pistol except has triple-chamber tapered cone compensator on match barrel with dovetailed front sight; lowered and flared ejection port; fully tuned for reliability; fitted slide to frame; extended ambidextrous thumb safety, extended magazine release button; beavertail grip safety; Pachmayr wrap-around grips. Comes with two magazines, plastic carrying case. Introduced 1992. From Springfield, Inc.

Price: 45 ACP, Duotone finish. **$1,724.00**
Price: Expert Ltd. (non-compensated) **$1,624.00**

Springfield, Inc. Distinguished Pistol

Has all the features of the 1911A1 Expert except is full-house pistol with deluxe Bo-Mar low-mounted adjustable rear sight; full-length recoil spring guide rod and recoil spring retainer; checkered frontstrap; S&A magazine well; walnut grips. Hard chrome finish. Comes with two magazines with slam pads, plastic carrying case. From Springfield, Inc.

Price: 45 ACP **$2,445.00**
Price: Distinguished Limited (non-compensated) **$2,345.00**

Springfield, Inc. 1911A1 N.M. Hardball Pistol

Has Bo-Mar adjustable rear sight with undercut front blade; fitted match Videki trigger with 4-lb. pull; fitted slide to frame; throated National Match barrel and bushing, polished feed ramp; recoil buffer system; tuned extractor; Herrett walnut grips. Comes with two magazines, plastic carrying case, test target. Introduced 1992. From Springfield, Inc.

Price: 45 ACP, blue **$1,336.00**

Springfield, Inc. Leatham Legend TGO Series Pistols

Three models of 5" barrel, 45 ACP 1911 pistols built for serious competition. TGO 1 has deluxe low mount BoMar rear sight, Dawson fiber optics front sight, 3.5 lb. trigger pull. TGO 2 has BoMar low mount adjustable rear sight, Dawson fiber optic front sight, 4.5 to 5 lb. trigger pull. TGO 3 has Springfield Armory fully adjustable rear sight with low mount BoMar cut Dawson fiber optic front sight, 4.5 to 5 lb. trigger.

Price: TGO 1 . . . . **$2,999.00**
Price: TGO 2 . . . . **$1,899.00**
Price: TGO 3 . . . . **$1,295.00**

Springfield, Inc. Trophy Match Pistol

Similar to Springfield, Inc.'s Full Size model, but designed for bullseye and action shooting competition. Available with a Service Model 5" frame with matching slide and barrel in 5" and 6" lengths. Fully adjustable sights, checkered frame front strap, match barrel and bushing. In 45 ACP only. From Springfield Inc.

Price: **$1,248.00**

STI EAGLE 5.0, 6.0 PISTOL

Caliber: 9mm, 9x21, 38 & 40 Super, 40 S&W, 10mm, 45 ACP, 10-shot magazine. **Barrel:** 5", 6" bull. **Weight:** 34.5 oz. **Length:** 8.62" overall. **Grips:** Checkered polymer. **Sights:** STI front, Novak or Heine rear. **Features:** Standard frames plus 7 others; adjustable match trigger; skeletonized hammer; extended grip safety with locator pad; match-grade fit of all parts. Many options available. Introduced 1994. Made in U.S.A. by STI International.

Price: . . . . (5.0 Eagle) **$1,794.00**, (6.0 Eagle) **$1,894.00**

STI EXECUTIVE PISTOL

Caliber: 40 S&W. **Barrel:** 5" bull. **Weight:** 39 oz. **Length:** 8-5/8". **Grips:** Gray polymer. **Sights:** Dawson fiber optic, front; STI adjustable rear. **Features:** Stainless mag. well, front and rear serrations on slide. Made in U.S.A. by STI.

Price: **$2,389.00**

STI TROJAN

Caliber: 9mm, 38 Super, 40S&W, 45 ACP. **Barrel:** 5", 6". **Weight:** 36 oz. **Length:** 8.5". **Grips:** Rosewood. **Sights:** STI front with STI adjustable rear. **Features:** Stippled front strap, flat top slide, one-piece steel guide rod.

Price: (Trojan 5") **$1,024.00**
Price: (Trojan 6", not available in 38 Super) **$1,232.50**

WALTHER GSP MATCH PISTOL

Caliber: 22 LR, 32 S&W Long (GSP-C), 5-shot magazine. **Barrel:** 4.22". **Weight:** 44.8 oz. (22 LR), 49.4 oz. (32). **Length:** 11.8" overall. **Grips:** Walnut. **Sights:** Post front, match rear adjustable for windage and elevation. **Features:** Available with either 2.2-lb. (1000 gm) or 3-lb. (1360 gm) trigger. Spare magazine, barrel weight, tools supplied. Imported from Germany by Nygord Precision Products.

Price: GSP, with case **$1,495.00**
Price: GSP-C, with case **$1,595.00**

Includes models suitable for hunting and competitive courses of fire, both police and international.

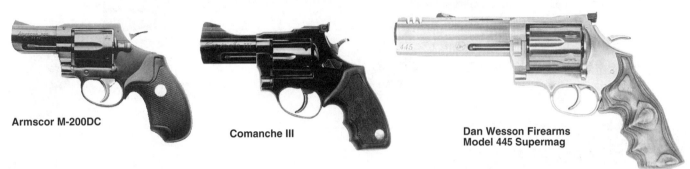

Armscor M-200DC

Comanche III

Dan Wesson Firearms Model 445 Supermag

ARMSCOR M-200DC REVOLVER
Caliber: 38 Spec., 6-shot cylinder. **Barrel:** 2-1/2", 4". **Weight:** 22 oz. (2-1/2" barrel). **Length:** 7-3/8" overall (2-1/2" barrel). **Grips:** Checkered rubber. **Sights:** Blade front, fixed notch rear. **Features:** All-steel construction; floating firing pin, transfer bar ignition; shrouded ejector rod; blue finish. Reintroduced 1996. Imported from the Philippines by K.B.I., Inc.
Price: 2-1/2" **$199.99**
Price: 4" **$205.00**

ARMSPORT MODEL 4540 REVOLVER
Caliber: 38 Special. **Barrel:** 4". **Weight:** 32 oz **Length:** 9" overall. **Sights:** Fixed rear, blade front. **Features:** Ventilated rib; blued finish. Imported from Argentina by Armsport Inc.
Price: **$140.00**

COMANCHE I, II, III DA REVOLVERS
Features: Adjustable sights. Blue or stainless finish. Distributed by SGS Importers.
Price: I 22 LR, 6" bbl, 9-shot, blue **$236.95**
Price: I 22LR, 6" bbl, 9-shot, stainless **$258.95**
Price: II 38 Special, 3", 4" bbl, 6-shot, blue. **$219.95**
Price: II 38 Special, 4" bbl, 6-shot, stainless. **$236.95**
Price: III 357 Mag, 3", 4", 6" bbl, 6-shot, blue **$253.95**
Price: III 357 Mag, 3", 4", 6" bbl, 6-shot, stainless **$274.95**
Price: II 38 Special, 3" bbl, 6-shot, stainless steel **$236.95**

DAN WESSON FIREARMS MODEL 722 SILHOUETTE REVOLVER
Caliber: 22 LR, 6-shot. **Barrel:** 10", vent heavy. **Weight:** 53 oz. **Grips:** Combat style. **Sights:** Patridge-style front, .080" narrow notch rear. **Features:** Single action only. Satin brushed stainless finish. Reintroduced 1997. Made in U.S.A. by Dan Wesson Firearms.
Price: 722 VH10 (vent heavy 10" bbl.) **$888.00**
Price: 722 VH10 SRS1 (Super Ram Silhouette, Bo-Mar sights, front hood, trigger job). **$1,164.00**

DAN WESSON FIREARMS MODEL 3220/73220 TARGET REVOLVER
Caliber: 32-20, 6-shot. **Barrel:** 2.5", 4", 6", 8", 10" standard vent, vent heavy. **Weight:** 47 oz. (6" VH). **Length:** 11.25" overall. **Grips:** Hogue Gripper rubber (walnut, exotic hardwoods optional). **Sights:** Red ramp interchangeable front, fully adjustable rear. **Features:** Bright blue (3220) or stainless (73220). Reintroduced 1997. Made in U.S.A. by Dan Wesson Firearms.
Price: 3220 VH2.5 (blued, 2.5" vent heavy bbl.) **$643.00**
Price: 73220 VH10 (stainless 10" vent heavy bbl.) **$873.00**

DAN WESSON FIREARMS MODEL 40/740 REVOLVERS
Caliber: 357 Maximum, 6-shot. **Barrel:** 4", 6", 8", 10". **Weight:** 72 oz. (8" bbl.). **Length:** 14.3" overall (8" bbl.). **Grips:** Hogue Gripper rubber (walnut or exotic hardwood optional). **Sights:** 1/8" serrated front, fully adjustable rear. **Features:** Blue or stainless steel. Made in U.S.A. by Dan Wesson Firearms.
Price: Blue, 4" **$702.00**
Price: Blue, 6" **$749.00**

Price: Blue, 8" **$795.00**
Price: Blue, 10" **$858.00**
Price: Stainless, 4" **$834.00**
Price: Stainless, 6" **$892.00**
Price: Stainless, 8" slotted **$1,024.00**
Price: Stainless, 10" **$998.00**
Price: 4", 6", 8" Compensated, blue . . . . **$749.00 to $885.00**
Price: As above, stainless. . . . . **$893.00 to $1,061.00**

Dan Wesson Firearms Model 414/7414 and 445/7445 SuperMag Revolvers
Similar size and weight as Model 40 revolvers. Chambered for 414 SuperMag or 445 SuperMag cartridge. Barrel lengths of 4", 6", 8", 10". Contact maker for complete price list. Reintroduced 1997. Made in the U.S. by Dan Wesson Firearms.
Price: 4", vent heavy, blue or stainless **$904.00**
Price: 8", vent heavy, blue or stainless **$1,026.00**
Price: 10", vent heavy, blue or stainless **$1,103.00**
Price: Compensated models . . . . **$965.00 to $1,149.00**

DAN WESSON FIREARMS MODEL 22/722 REVOLVERS
Caliber: 22 LR, 22 WMR, 6-shot. **Barrel:** 2-1/2", 4", 6", 8" or 10"; interchangeable. **Weight:** 36 oz. (2-1/2"), 44 oz. (6"). **Length:** 9-1/4" overall (4" barrel). **Grips:** Hogue Gripper rubber (walnut, exotic woods optional). **Sights:** 1/8" serrated, interchangeable front, white outline rear adjustable for windage and elevation. **Features:** Built on the same frame as the Wesson 357; smooth, wide trigger with over-travel adjustment, wide spur hammer, with short double-action travel. Available in blue or stainless steel. Reintroduced 1997. Contact Dan Wesson Firearms for complete price list.
Price: 22 VH2.5/722 VH2.5 (blued or stainless 2-1/2" bbl.) **$551.00**
Price: 22VH10/722 VH10 (blued or stainless 10" bbl.) **$750.00**

Dan Wesson 722M Small Frame Revolver
Similar to Model 22/722 except chambered for 22 WMR. Blued or stainless finish, 2-1/2", 4", 6", 8" or 10" barrels.
Price: Blued or stainless finish . . . . **$643.00 to $873.00**

DAN WESSON FIREARMS MODEL 15/715 and 32/732 REVOLVERS
Caliber: 32-20, 32 H&R Mag. (Model 32), 357 Mag. (Model 15). **Barrel:** 2-1/2", 4", 6", 8" (M32), 2-1/2", 4", 6", 8", 10" (M15); vent heavy. **Weight:** 36 oz. (2-1/2" barrel). **Length:** 9-1/4" overall (4" barrel). **Grips:** Checkered, interchangeable. **Sights:** 1/8" serrated front, fully adjustable rear. **Features:** New Generation Series. Interchangeable barrels; wide, smooth trigger, wide hammer spur; short double-action travel. Available in blue or stainless. Reintroduced 1997. Made in U.S.A. by Dan Wesson Firearms. Contact maker for full list of models.
Price: Model 15/715, 2-1/2" (blue or stainless). **$551.00**
Price: Model 15/715, 8" (blue or stainless) **$612.00**
Price: Model 15/715, compensated . . . . **$704.00 to $827.00**
Price: Model 32/732, 4" (blue or stainless) **$674.00**
Price: Model 32/732, 8" (blue or stainless) **$766.00**

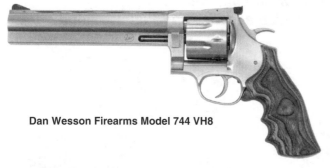

Dan Wesson Firearms Model 744 VH8

Dan Wesson Firearms
Alaskan Guide Special

Dan Wesson Firearms
Super Ram Silhouette

DAN WESSON FIREARMS MODEL 41/741, 44/744 and 45/745 REVOLVERS

Caliber: 41 Mag., 44 Mag., 45 Colt, 6-shot. **Barrel:** 4", 6", 8", 10"; interchangeable; 4", 6", 8" Compensated. **Weight:** 48 oz. (4"). **Length:** 12" overall (6" bbl.) **Grips:** Smooth. **Sights:** 1/8" serrated front, white outline rear adjustable for windage and elevation. **Features:** Available in blue or stainless steel. Smooth, wide trigger with adjustable over-travel, wide hammer spur. Available in Pistol Pac set also. Reintroduced 1997. Contact Dan Wesson Firearms for complete price list.

Price: 41 Mag., 4", vent heavy (blue or stainless). **$643.00**
Price: 44 Mag., 6", vent heavy (blue or stainless). **$689.00**
Price: 45 Colt, 8", vent heavy (blue or stainless) **$766.00**
Price: Compensated models (all calibers) . . . . **$812.00 to $934.00**

DAN WESSON FIREARMS LARGE FRAME SERIES REVOLVERS

Caliber: 41, 741/41 Magnum; 44, 744/44 Magnum; 45, 745/45 Long Colt; 360, 7360/357; 460, 7460/45. **Barrel:** 2"-10". **Weight:** 49 oz.-69 oz. **Grips:** Standard, Hogue rubber Gripper Grips. **Sights:** Standard front, serrated ramp with color insert. Standard rear, adustable wide notch. Other sight options available. **Features:** Available in blue or stainless steel. Smooth, wide trigger with overtravel, wide hammer spur. Double and single action.

Price: . . . . **$769.00 to $889.00**

DAN WESSON FIREARMS MODEL 360/7360 REVOLVERS

Caliber: 357 Mag. **Barrel:** 4", 6", 8", 10"; vent heavy. **Weight:** 64 oz. (8" barrel). **Grips:** Hogue rubber finger groove. **Sights:** Interchangeable ramp or Patridge front, fully adjustable rear. **Features:** New Generation Large Frame Series. Interchangeable barrels and grips; smooth trigger, wide hammer spur. Blue (360) or stainless (7360). Introduced 1999. Made in U.S.A. by Dan Wesson Firearms.

Price: 4" bbl., blue or stainless **$735.00**
Price: 10" bbl., blue or stainless **$873.00**
Price: Compensated models . . . . **$858.00 to $980.00**

DAN WESSON FIREARMS MODEL 460/7460 REVOLVERS

Caliber: 45 ACP, 45 Auto Rim, 45 Super, 45 Winchester Magnum and 460 Rowland. **Barrel:** 4", 6", 8", 10"; vent heavy. **Weight:** 49 oz. (4" barrel). **Grips:** Hogue rubber finger groove; interchangeable. **Sights:** Interchangeable ramp or Patridge front, fully adjustable rear. **Features:** New Generation Large Frame Series. Shoots five cartridges (45 ACP, 45 Auto Rim, 45 Super, 45 Winchester Magnum and 460 Rowland; six half-moon

clips for auto cartridges included). Interchangeable barrels and grips. Available with non-fluted cylinder and Slotted Lightweight barrel shroud. Introduced 1999. Made in U.S.A. by Dan Wesson Firearms.

Price: 4" bbl., blue or stainless **$735.00**
Price: 10" bbl., blue or stainless **$888.00**
Price: Compensated models . . . . **$919.00 to $1,042.00**

DAN WESSON FIREARMS STANDARD SILHOUETTE REVOLVERS

Caliber: 357 SuperMag/Maxi, 41 Mag., 414 SuperMag, 445 SuperMag. **Barrel:** 8", 10". **Weight:** 64 oz. (8" barrel). **Length:** 14.3" overall (8" barrel). **Grips:** Hogue rubber finger groove; interchangeable. **Sights:** Patridge front, fully adjustable rear. **Features:** Interchangeable barrels and grips, fluted or non-fluted cylinder, satin brushed stainless finish. Introduced 1999. Made in U.S.A. by Dan Wesson Firearms.

Price: 357 SuperMag/Maxi, 8" **$1,057.00**
Price: 41 Mag., 10" **$888.00**
Price: 414 SuperMag., 8" **$1,057.00**
Price: 445 SuperMag., 8" **$1,057.00**

Dan Wesson Firearms Super Ram Silhouette Revolver

Similar to Standard Silhouette except has 10 land and groove Laser Coat barrel, Bo-Mar target sights with hooded front, special laser engraving. Fluted or non-fluted cylinder. Introduced 1999. Made in U.S.A. by Dan Wesson Firearms.

Price: 357 SuperMag/Maxi, 414 SuperMag., 445 SuperMag., 8", blue or stainless **$1,364.00**
Price: 41 Magnum, 44 Magnum, 8", blue or stainless **$1,241.00**
Price: 41 Magnum, 44 Magnum, 10", blue or stainless **$1,333.00**

DAN WESSON FIREARMS ALASKAN GUIDE SPECIAL

Caliber: 445 SuperMag, 44 Magnum. **Barrel:** Compensated 4" vent heavy barrel assembly. **Features:** Stainless steel with baked on, non-glare, matte black coating, special laser engraving.

Price: Model 7445 VH4C AGS **$995.00**
Price: Model 744 VH4C AGS **$855.00**

EAA WINDICATOR REVOLVERS

Caliber: 38 Spec., 6-shot; 357 magnum, 6-shot. **Barrel:** 2", 4". **Weight:** 38 oz. (22 rimfire, 4"). **Length:** 8.5" overall (4" bbl.). **Grips:** Rubber with finger grooves. **Sights:** Blade front, fixed or adjustable on rimfires; fixed only on 32, 38. **Features:** Swing-out cylinder; hammer block safety; blue finish. Introduced 1991. Imported from Germany by European American Armory.

Price: 38 Special 2" **$249.00**
Price: 38 Special, 4" **$259.00**
Price: 357 Magnum, 2" **$259.00**
Price: 357 Magnum, 4" **$279.00**

KORTH COMBAT REVOLVER

Caliber: .357 Mag., .32 S&W Long, 9mm Para., .22 WMR, .22 LR. **Barrel:** 3", 4", 5-1/4", 6", 8". **Sights:** Fully-adjustable, rear; Baughman ramp, front. **Grips:** Walnut (checkered or smooth). Also available as a Target model in .22 LR, .38 Spl., .32 S&W Long, .357 Mag. with undercut partridge front sight; fully-adjustable rear. Made in Germany. Imported by Korth USA.

Price: . . . . From **$5,442.00**

Medusa Model 47 **Ruger GP-161** **Ruger KGP-141**

Ruger KSP-331X

KORTH TROJA REVOLVER
Caliber: .357 Mag. **Barrel:** 6". **Finish:** Matte blue. **Grips:** Smooth, oversized finger contoured walnut. **Features:** Maintaining all of the precision German craftsmanship that has made this line famous, the final surface finish is not as finely polished as the firm's other products - thus the lower price. Introduced 2003. Imported from Germany by Korth USA.
Price: . . . . From **$3,995.00**

MEDUSA MODEL 47 REVOLVER
Caliber: Most 9mm, 38 and 357 caliber cartridges; 6-shot cylinder. **Barrel:** 2-1/2", 3", 4", 5", 6"; fluted. **Weight:** 39 oz. **Length:** 10" overall (4" barrel). **Grips:** Gripper-style rubber. **Sights:** Changeable front blades, fully adjustable rear. **Features:** Patented extractor allows gun to chamber, fire and extract over 25 different cartridges in the .355 to .357 range, without half-moon clips. Steel frame and cylinder; match quality barrel. Matte blue finish. Introduced 1996. Made in U.S.A. by Phillips & Rogers, Inc.
Price: **$899.00**

ROSSI MODEL 351/352 REVOLVERS
Caliber: 38 Special +P, 5-shot. **Barrel:** 2". **Weight:** 24 oz. **Length:** 6-1/2" overall. **Grips:** Rubber. **Sights:** Blade front, fixed rear. **Features:** Patented key-lock Taurus Security System; forged steel frame handles +P ammunition. Introduced 2001. Imported by BrazTech/Taurus.
Price: Model 351 (blued finish) **$298.00**
Price: Model 352 (stainless finish) **$345.00**

ROSSI MODEL 461/462 REVOLVERS
Caliber: 357 Magnum +P, 6-shot. **Barrel:** 2". **Weight:** 26 oz. **Length:** 6-1/2" overall. **Grips:** Rubber. **Sights:** Fixed. **Features:** Single/double action. Patented key-lock Taurus Security System; forged steel frame handles +P ammunition. Introduced 2001. Imported by BrazTech/Taurus.
Price: Model 461 (blued finish) **$298.00**
Price: Model 462 (stainless finish) **$345.00**

ROSSI MODEL 971/972 REVOLVERS
Caliber: 357 Magnum +P, 6-shot. **Barrel:** 4", 6". **Weight:** 40-44 oz. **Length:** 8-1/2" or 10-1/2" overall. **Grips:** Rubber. **Sights:** Fully adjustable. **Features:** Single/double action. Patented key-lock Taurus Security System; forged steel frame handles +P ammunition. Introduced 2001. Imported by BrazTech/Taurus.
Price: Model 971 (blued finish, 4" barrel) **$345.00**
Price: Model 972 (stainless steel finish, 6" barrel) **$391.00**

Rossi Model 851
Similar to Model 971/972, chambered for 38 Special +P. Blued finish, 4" barrel. Introduced 2001. From BrazTech/Taurus.
Price: **$298.00**

RUGER GP-100 REVOLVERS
Caliber: 38 Spec., 357 Mag., 6-shot. **Barrel:** 3", 3" full shroud, 4", 4" full shroud, 6", 6" full shroud. **Weight:** 3" barrel-35 oz., 3" full shroud-36 oz., 4" barrel-37 oz., 4" full shroud-38 oz. **Sights:** Fixed; adjustable on 4" full shroud, all 6" barrels. **Grips:** Ruger Santoprene Cushioned Grip with Goncalo Alves inserts. **Features:** Uses action, frame incorporating improvements and features of both the Security-Six and Redhawk revolvers. Full length, short ejector shroud. Satin blue and stainless steel.
Price: GP-141 (357, 4" full shroud, adj. sights, blue) **$499.00**
Price: GP-160 (357, 6", adj. sights, blue) **$499.00**
Price: GP-161 (357, 6" full shroud, adj. sights, blue), 46 oz. **$499.00**
Price: GPF-331 (357, 3" full shroud) **$495.00**

Price: GPF-340 (357, 4") **$495.00**
Price: GPF-341 (357, 4" full shroud) **$495.00**
Price: KGP-141 (357, 4" full shroud, adj. sights, stainless) **$555.00**
Price: KGP-160 (357, 6", adj. sights, stainless), 43 oz. **$555.00**
Price: KGP-161 (357, 6" full shroud, adj. sights, stainless) 46 oz. . **$555.00**
Price: KGPF-330 (357, 3", stainless) **$555.00**
Price: KGPF-331 (357, 3" full shroud, stainless) **$555.00**
Price: KGPF-340 (357, 4", stainless), KGPF-840 (38 Special). . . **$555.00**
Price: KGPF-341 (357, 4" full shroud, stainless) **$555.00**
Price: KGPF-840 (38 Special, 4", stainless) **$555.00**

Ruger SP101 Double-Action-Only Revolver
Similar to standard SP101 except double-action-only with no single-action sear notch. Spurless hammer for snag-free handling, floating firing pin and Ruger's patented transfer bar safety system. Available with 2-1/4" barrel in 357 Magnum. Weighs 25 oz., overall length 7.06". Natural brushed satin, high-polish stainless steel. Introduced 1993.
Price: KSP321XL (357 Mag.) **$495.00**

RUGER SP101 REVOLVERS
Caliber: 22 LR, 32 H&R Mag., 6-shot; 38 Spec. +P, 357 Mag., 5-shot. **Barrel:** 2-1/4", 3-1/16", 4". **Weight:** (38 & 357 mag models) 2-1/4"-25 oz.; 3-1/16"-27 oz. **Sights:** Adjustable on 22, 32, fixed on others. **Grips:** Ruger Cushioned Grip with inserts. **Features:** Incorporates improvements and features found in the GP-100 revolvers into a compact, small frame, double-action revolver. Full-length ejector shroud. Stainless steel only. Introduced 1988.
Price: KSP-821X (2-1/4", 38 Spec.) **$495.00**
Price: KSP-831X (3-1/16", 38 Spec.) **$495.00**
Price: KSP-241X (4" heavy bbl., 22 LR), 34 oz. **$495.00**
Price: KSP-3231X (3-1/16", 32 H&R), 30 oz. **$495.00**
Price: KSP-321X (2-1/4", 357 Mag.). **$495.00**
Price: KSP-331X (3-1/16", 357 Mag.). **$495.00**
Price: KSP-3241X (32 Mag., 4" bbl) **$495.00**

CONSULT

SHOOTER'S MARKETPLACE

Page 231, This Issue

Ruger Redhawk

Ruger Super Redhawk

Smith & Wesson Model 10

Smith & Wesson Model 629 Classic DX

Smith & Wesson Model 36LS

RUGER REDHAWK

Caliber: 44 Rem. Mag., 45 Colt, 6-shot. **Barrel:** 5-1/2", 7-1/2". **Weight:** About 54 oz. (7-1/2" bbl.). **Length:** 13" overall (7-1/2" barrel). **Grips:** Square butt cushioned grip panels. **Sights:** Interchangeable Patridge-type front, rear adjustable for windage and elevation. **Features:** Stainless steel, brushed satin finish, blued ordnance steel. 9-1/2" sight radius. Introduced 1979.
Price: Blued, 44 Mag., 5-1/2" RH-445, 7-1/2" RH-44 . . . . **$585.00**
Price: Blued, 44 Mag., 7-1/2" RH44R, with scope mount, rings . . **$625.00**
Price: Stainless, 44 Mag., KRH445, 5-1/2", 7-1/2" KRH-44 . . . . . **$645.00**
Price: Stainless, 44 Mag., 7-1/2", with scope mount, rings
KRH-44R. **$685.00**
Price: Stainless, 45 Colt, KRH455, 5-1/2", 7-1/2" KRH-45 . . . . . . **$645.00**
Price: Stainless, 45 Colt, 7-1/2", with scope mount and rings
KRH-45R. **$685.00**

Ruger Super Redhawk Revolver

Similar to standard Redhawk except has heavy extended frame with Ruger Integral Scope Mounting System on wide topstrap. Also available 454 Casull and 480 Ruger. Wide hammer spur lowered for better scope clearance. Incorporates mechanical design features and improvements of GP-100. Choice of 7-1/2" or 9-1/2" barrel, both ramp front sight base with Redhawk-style Interchangeable Insert sight blades, adjustable rear sight. Comes with Ruger "Cushioned Grip" panels with wood panels. Target gray stainless steel. Introduced 1987.
Price: KSRH-7 (7-1/2"), KSRH-9 (9-1/2"), 44 Mag **$685.00**
Price: KSRH-7454 (7-1/2") 454 Casull, 9-1/2 KSRH-9454 . . . . . . **$775.00**
Price: KSRH-7480 (7-1/2") 480 Ruger **$775.00**
Price: KSRH-9480 (9-1/2") 480 Ruger **$775.00**

SMITH & WESSON MODEL 10 M&P HB REVOLVER

Caliber: 38 Spec., 6-shot. **Barrel:** 4". **Weight:** 33.5 oz. **Length:** 9-5/16" overall. **Grips:** Uncle Mike's Combat soft rubber; square butt. **Sights:** Fixed; ramp front, square notch rear.
Price: Blue **$496.00**

SMITH & WESSON COMMEMORATIVE MODEL 29

Features: Reflects original Model 29: 6-1/2" barrel, four-screw side plate, over-sized target grips, red vamp front and black blade rear sights, 150th Anniversary logo, engraved, gold-plated, blue, in wood presentation case. Limited.
Price: . . . . **NA**

SMITH & WESSON MODEL 629 REVOLVERS

Caliber: 44 Magnum, 44 S&W Special, 6-shot. **Barrel:** 5", 6", 8-3/8". **Weight:** 47 oz. (6" bbl.). **Length:** 11-3/8" overall (6" bbl.). **Grips:** Soft rubber; wood optional. **Sights:** 1/8" red ramp front, white outline rear, internal lock, adjustable for windage and elevation.
Price: Model 629, 4" **$717.00**
Price: Model 629, 6" **$739.00**
Price: Model 629, 8-3/8" barrel **$756.00**

Smith & Wesson Model 629 Classic Revolver

Similar to standard Model 629, full-lug 5", 6-1/2" or 8-3/8" barrel, chamfered front of cylinder, interchangeable red ramp front sight with adjustable white outline rear, Hogue grips with S&W monogram, frame is drilled and tapped for scope mounting. Factory accurizing and endurance packages. Overall length with 5" barrel is 10-1/2"; weighs 51 oz. Introduced 1990.
Price: Model 629 Classic (stainless), 5", 6-1/2" **$768.00**
Price: As above, 8-3/8" **$793.00**
Price: Model 629 with HiViz front sight **$814.00**

Smith & Wesson Model 629 Classic DX Revolver

Similar to Model 629 Classic, offered only with 6-1/2" or 8-3/8" full-lug barrel, five front sights: red ramp, black Patridge, black Patridge with gold bead, black ramp, black Patridge with white dot, white outline rear sight, adjustable sight, internal lock. Hogue combat-style and wood round butt grip. Introduced 1991.
Price: Model 629 Classic DX, 6-1/2". **$986.00**
Price: As above, 8-3/8". **$1,018.00**

SMITH & WESSON MODEL 37 CHIEF'S SPECIAL & AIRWEIGHT

Caliber: 38 Spec. +P, 5-shot. **Barrel:** 1-7/8". **Weight:** 19-1/2 oz. (2" bbl.); 13-1/2 oz. (Airweight). **Length:** 6-1/2" (round butt). **Grips:** Round butt soft rubber. **Sights:** Fixed, serrated ramp front, square notch rear. Glass beaded finish.
Price: Model 37. . . . . **$523.00**

Smith & Wesson Model 637 Airweight Revolver

Similar to the Model 37 Airweight except has alloy frame, stainless steel barrel, cylinder and yoke; rated for 38 Spec. +P; Uncle Mike's Boot Grip. Weighs 15 oz. Introduced 1996. Made in U.S.A. by Smith & Wesson.
Price: **$548.00**

SMITH & WESSON MODEL 36LS, 60LS LADYSMITH

Caliber: .38 S&W Special +P, 5-shot. **Barrel:** 1-7/8". **Weight:** 20 oz. **Length:** 6-5/16 overall (1-7/8" barrel). **Grips:** Combat Dymondwood® grips with S&W monogram. **Sights:** Serrated ramp front, fixed notch rear. **Features:** Speedloader cutout. Comes in a fitted carry/storage case. Introduced 1989.
Price: Model 36LS **$518.00**
Price: Model 60LS, 2-1/8" barrel stainless, 357 Magnum. **$566.00**

Smith & Wesson Model 65LS

Smith & Wesson
Model 317 AirLite

Smith & Wesson Model 625

Smith & Wesson
Model 340 PD Airlite Sc

SMITH & WESSON MODEL 60 CHIEF'S SPECIAL
Caliber: 357 Magnum, 5-shot. **Barrel:** 2-1/8" or 3". **Weight:** 24 oz. **Length:** 7-1/2 overall (3" barrel). **Grips:** Rounded butt synthetic grips. **Sights:** Fixed, serrated ramp front, square notch rear. **Features:** Stainless steel construction. 3" full lug barrel, adjustable sights, internal lock. Made in U.S.A. by Smith & Wesson.
Price: 2-1/8" barrel $541.00
Price: 3" barrel $574.00

SMITH & WESSON MODEL 65
Caliber: 357 Mag. and 38 Spec., 6-shot. **Barrel:** 4". **Weight:** 34 oz. **Length:** 9-5/16" overall (4" bbl.). **Grips:** Uncle Mike's Combat. **Sights:** 1/8" serrated ramp front, fixed square notch rear. **Features:** Heavy barrel. Stainless steel construction. Internal lock.
Price: $531.00

SMITH & WESSON MODEL 317 AIRLITE, 317 LADYSMITH REVOLVERS
Caliber: 22 LR, 8-shot. **Barrel:** 1-7/8" 3". **Weight:** 9.9 oz. **Length:** 6-3/16" overall. **Grips:** Dymondwood Boot or Uncle Mike's Boot. **Sights:** Serrated ramp front, fixed notch rear. **Features:** Aluminum alloy, carbon and stainless steels, and titanium construction. Short spur hammer, smooth combat trigger. Clear Cote finish. Introduced 1997. Made in U.S.A. by Smith & Wesson.
Price: With Uncle Mike's Boot grip $550.00
Price: With DymondWood Boot grip, 3" barrel, HiViz front sight, internal lock. $600.00
Price: Model 317 LadySmith (DymondWood only, comes with display case) $596.00

SMITH & WESSON MODEL 351PD
Caliber: 22 Mag. **Barrel:** 2". **Features:** Seven-shot, Scandium alloy.
Price: $625.00

SMITH & WESSON MODEL 64 STAINLESS M&P
Caliber: 38 Spec. +P, 6-shot. **Barrel:** 2", 3", 4". **Weight:** 34 oz. **Length:** 9-5/16" overall. **Grips:** Soft rubber. **Sights:** Fixed, 1/8" serrated ramp front, square notch rear. **Features:** Satin finished stainless steel, square butt.
Price: 2" $522.00
Price: 3", 4" $532.00

SMITH & WESSON MODEL 65LS LADYSMITH
Caliber: 357 Magnum, 38 Spec. +P, 6-shot. **Barrel:** 3". **Weight:** 31 oz. **Length:** 7.94" overall. **Grips:** Rosewood, round butt. **Sights:** Serrated ramp front, fixed notch rear. **Features:** Stainless steel with frosted finish. Smooth combat trigger, service hammer, shrouded ejector rod. Comes with case. Introduced 1992.
Price: $584.00

SMITH & WESSON MODEL 66 STAINLESS COMBAT MAGNUM
Caliber: 357 Mag. and 38 Spec. +P, 6-shot. **Barrel:** 2-1/2", 4", 6". **Weight:** 36 oz. (4" barrel). **Length:** 9-9/16" overall. **Grips:** Soft rubber. **Sights:** Red ramp front, micro-click rear adjustable for windage and elevation. **Features:** Satin finish stainless steel. Internal lock.
Price: 2-1/2" $590.00
Price: 4" $579.00
Price: 6" $608.00

SMITH & WESSON MODEL 67 COMBAT MASTERPIECE
Caliber: 38 Special, 6-shot. **Barrel:** 4". **Weight:** 32 oz. **Length:** 9-5/16" overall. **Grips:** Soft rubber. **Sights:** Red ramp front, micro-click rear ad-justable for windage and elevation. **Features:** Stainless steel with satin finish. Smooth combat trigger, semi-target hammer. Introduced 1994.
Price: $585.00

Smith & Wesson Model 686 Magnum PLUS Revolver
Similar to the Model 686 except has 7-shot cylinder, 2-1/2", 4" or 6" barrel. Weighs 34-1/2 oz., overall length 7-1/2" (2-1/2" barrel). Hogue rubber grips. Internal lock. Introduced 1996. Made in U.S.A. by Smith & Wesson.
Price: 2-1/2" barrel $631.00
Price: 4" barrel $653.00
Price: 6" barrel $663.00

SMITH & WESSON MODEL 625 REVOLVER
Caliber: 45 ACP, 6-shot. **Barrel:** 5". **Weight:** 46 oz. **Length:** 11.375" overall. **Grips:** Soft rubber; wood optional. **Sights:** Patridge front on ramp, S&W micrometer click rear adjustable for windage and elevation. **Features:** Stainless steel construction with .400" semi-target hammer, .312" smooth combat trigger; full lug barrel. Glass beaded finish. Introduced 1989.
Price: 5" $745.00
Price: 4" with internal lock. $745.00

SMITH & WESSON MODEL 640 CENTENNIAL DA ONLY
Caliber: 357 Mag., 38 Spec. +P, 5-shot. **Barrel:** 2-1/8". **Weight:** 25 oz. **Length:** 6-3/4" overall. **Grips:** Uncle Mike's Boot Grip. **Sights:** Serrated ramp front, fixed notch rear. **Features:** Stainless steel. Fully concealed hammer, snag-proof smooth edges. Internal lock. Introduced 1995 in 357 Magnum.
Price: $599.00

SMITH & WESSON MODEL 617 K-22 MASTERPIECE
Caliber: 22 LR, 6- or 10-shot. **Barrel:** 4", 6", 8-3/8". **Weight:** 42 oz. (4" barrel). **Length:** NA. **Grips:** Soft rubber. **Sights:** Patridge front, adjustable rear. Drilled and tapped for scope mount. **Features:** Stainless steel with satin finish; 4" has .312" smooth trigger, .375" semi-target hammer; 6" has either .312" combat or .400" serrated trigger, .375" semi-target or .500" target hammer; 8-3/8" with .400" serrated trigger, .500" target hammer. Introduced 1990.
Price: 4" $644.00
Price: 6", target hammer, target trigger $625.00
Price: 6", 10-shot $669.00
Price: 8-3/8", 10 shot $679.00

SMITH & WESSON MODEL 610 CLASSIC HUNTER REVOLVER
Caliber: 10mm, 40 S&W, 6-shot cylinder. **Barrel:** 6-1/2" full lug. **Weight:** 52 oz. **Length:** 12" overall. **Grips:** Hogue rubber combat. **Sights:** Interchangeable blade front, micro-click rear adjustable for windage and elevation. **Features:** Stainless steel construction; target hammer, target trigger; unfluted cylinder; drilled and tapped for scope mounting. Introduced 1998.
Price: $785.00

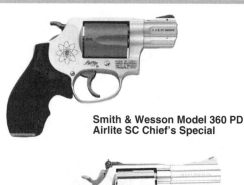

Smith & Wesson Model 360 PD Airlite SC Chief's Special

Smith & Wesson Model 386 PD Airlite SC

Smith & Wesson Model 442

Smith & Wesson Model 696

Smith & Wesson Model 500

SMITH & WESSON MODEL 340 PD AIRLITE Sc CENTENNIAL

Caliber: 357 Magnum, 38 Spec. +P, 5-shot. **Barrel:** 1-7/8". **Grips:** Rounded butt grip. **Sights:** HiViz front. **Features:** Synthetic grip, internal lock. Blue.
Price: **$799.00**

SMITH & WESSON MODEL 360 PD AIRLITE Sc CHIEF'S SPECIAL

Caliber: 357 Magnum, 38 Spec. +P, 5-shot. **Barrel:** 1-7/8". **Grips:** Rounded butt grip. **Sights:** Fixed. **Features:** Synthetic grip, internal lock. Stainless.
Price: Red ramp front **$767.00**
Price: HiViz front **$781.00**

SMITH & WESSON MODEL 386 PD AIRLITE Sc

Caliber: 357 Magnum, 38 Spec. +P, 7-shot. **Barrel:** 2-1/2". **Grips:** Rounded butt grip. **Sights:** Adjustable, HiViz front. **Features:** Synthetic grip, internal lock.
Price: Blue **$815.00**

SMITH & WESSON MODEL 331, 332 AIRLITE Ti REVOLVERS

Caliber: 32 H&R Mag., 6-shot. **Barrel:** 1-7/8". **Weight:** 11.2 oz. (with wood grip). **Length:** 6-15/16" overall. **Grips:** Uncle Mike's Boot or Dymondwood Boot. **Sights:** Black serrated ramp front, fixed notch rear. **Features:** Aluminum alloy frame, barrel shroud and yoke; titanium cylinder; stainless steel barrel liner. Matte finish. Introduced 1999. Made in U.S.A. by Smith & Wesson.
Price: Model 331 Chiefs **$716.00**
Price: Model 332, internal lock **$734.00**

SMITH & WESSON MODEL 337 CHIEF'S SPECIAL AIRLITE Ti

Caliber: 38 Spec. +P, 5-shot. **Barrel:** 1-7/8". **Weight:** 11.2 oz. (Dymondwood grips). **Length:** 6-5/16" overall. **Grips:** Uncle Mike's Boot or Dymondwood Boot. **Sights:** Black serrated front, fixed notch rear. **Features:** Aluminum alloy frame, barrel shroud and yoke; titanium cylinder; stainless steel barrel liner. Matte finish. Introduced 1999. Made in U.S.A. by Smith & Wesson.
Price: **$716.00**

SMITH & WESSON MODEL 342 CENTENNIAL AIRLITE Ti

Caliber: 38 Spec. +P, 5-shot. **Barrel:** 1-7/8". **Weight:** 11.3 oz. (Dymondwood stocks). **Length:** 6-15/16" overall. **Grips:** Uncle Mike's Boot or Dymondwood Boot. **Sights:** Black serrated ramp front, fixed notch rear. **Features:** Aluminum alloy frame, barrel shroud and yoke; titanium cylinder; stainless steel barrel liner. Shrouded hammer. Matte finish. Internal lock. Introduced 1999. Made in U.S.A. by Smith & Wesson.
Price: **$734.00**

Smith & Wesson Model 442 Centennial Airweight

Similar to Model 640 Centennial, alloy frame giving weighs 15.8 oz. Chambered for 38 Special +P, 1-7/8" carbon steel barrel; carbon steel cylinder; concealed hammer; Uncle Mike's Boot grip. Fixed square notch rear sight, serrated ramp front. DA only, glass beaded finish. Introduced 1993.
Price: Blue **$547.00**

SMITH & WESSON MODEL 638 AIRWEIGHT BODYGUARD

Caliber: 38 Spec. +P, 5-shot. **Barrel:** 1-7/8". **Weight:** 15 oz. **Length:** 6-15/16" overall. **Grips:** Uncle Mike's Boot grip. **Sights:** Serrated ramp front, fixed notch rear. **Features:** Alloy frame, stainless cylinder and barrel; shrouded hammer. Glass beaded finish. Introduced 1997. Made in U.S.A. by Smith & Wesson.
Price: With Uncle Mike's Boot grip **$564.00**

Smith & Wesson Model 642 Airweight Revolver

Similar to Model 442 Centennial Airweight, stainless steel barrel, cylinder and yoke with matte finish; Uncle Mike's Boot Grip; DA only; weighs 15.8 oz. Introduced 1996. Made in U.S.A. by Smith & Wesson.
Price: **$571.00**

Smith & Wesson Model 642LS Ladysmith Revolver

Same as Model 642 except has smooth combat wood grips, comes with deluxe soft case; Dymondwood grip; aluminum alloy frame, stainless cylinder, barrel and yoke; frosted matte finish. Weighs 15.8 oz. Introduced 1996. Made in U.S.A. by Smith & Wesson.
Price: 1-7/8" **$597.00**

SMITH & WESSON MODEL 649 BODYGUARD REVOLVER

Caliber: 357 Mag., 38 Spec. +P, 5-shot. **Barrel:** 2-1/8". **Weight:** 20 oz. **Length:** 6-5/16" overall. **Grips:** Uncle Mike's Combat. **Sights:** Black pinned ramp front, fixed notch rear. **Features:** Stainless steel construction; shrouded hammer; smooth combat trigger. Internal lock. Made in U.S.A. by Smith & Wesson.
Price: **$594.00**

SMITH & WESSON MODEL 657 REVOLVER

Caliber: 41 Mag., 6-shot. **Barrel:** 7-1/2" full lug. **Weight:** 48 oz. **Grips:** Soft rubber. **Sights:** Pinned 1/8" red ramp front, micro-click rear adjustable for windage and elevation. Target hammer, drilled and tapped, unfluted cylinder. **Features:** Stainless steel construction.
Price: **$706.00**

SMITH & WESSON MODEL 696 REVOLVER

Caliber: 44 Spec., 5-shot. **Barrel:** 3". **Weight:** 35.5 oz. **Length:** 8-1/4" overall. **Grips:** Uncle Mike's Combat. **Sights:** Red ramp front, click adjustable white outline rear. **Features:** Stainless steel construction; round butt frame; satin finish. Introduced 1997. Made in U.S.A. by Smith & Wesson.
Price: **$620.00**

Taurus Model 82

Taurus Model 85

Taurus Model 94 UL

Taurus Model 22H Raging Hornet

Taurus Model 44

SMITH & WESSON MODEL 500

Caliber: 50. **Barrel:** 4 and 8-3/8". **Weight:** 72.5 oz. **Length:** NA. **Grips:** Rubber. **Sights:** Interchangeable blade, front, adjustable rear. **Features:** Built on the massive, new X-Frame, recoil compensator, ball detent cylinder latch. Made in U.S.A. by Smith & Wesson.
Price: **$1,150.00**

Taurus Silhouette Revolvers

Available in calibers from 22 LR through 454 Casull, the common trait is a 12" vent rib barrel. An optional arm support that wraps around the forearm is available.
Price: . . . . **$414.00 to $859.00**

TAURUS MODEL 17 "TRACKER"

Caliber: 17 HMR, 7-shot. **Barrel:** 6-1/2". **Weight:** 45.8 oz. **Grips:** Rubber. **Sights:** Adjustable. **Features:** Double action, matte stainless, integral key-lock.
Price: . . . . **$430.00 to $438.00**

TAURUS MODEL 17-12 TARGET "SILHOUETTE"

Caliber: 17 HMR, 7-shot. **Barrel:** 12". **Weight:** 57.8 oz. **Grips:** Rubber. **Sights:** Adjustable. **Features:** Vent rib, double action, adjustable main spring and trigger stop. Matte stainless, integral key-lock.
Price: **$430.00**

Taurus Model 17-C Series

Similar to the Models 17 Tracker and Silhouette series but 8-shot cylinder, 2", 4" or 5" barrel, blue or stainless finish and regular (24 oz.) or UltraLite (18.5 oz.) versions available. All models have target crown for enhanced accuracy.
Price: . . . . **$359.00 to $391.00**

TAURUS MODEL 63

Caliber: 22 LR, 10 + 1 shot. **Barrel:** 23". **Weight:** 97.9 oz. **Grips:** Premium hardwood. **Sights:** Adjustable. **Features:** Auto loading action, round barrel, manual firing pin block, integral security system lock, trigger guard mounted safety, blue or stainless finish.
Price: . . . . **$295.00 to $310.00**

TAURUS MODEL 65 REVOLVER

Caliber: 357 Mag., 6-shot. **Barrel:** 4". **Weight:** 38 oz. **Length:** 10-1/2" overall. **Grips:** Soft rubber. **Sights:** Fixed. **Features:** Double action, integral key-lock. Imported by Taurus International.
Price: Blue or matte stainless . . . . **$375.00 to $422.00**

Taurus Model 66 Revolver

Similar to Model 65, 4" or 6" barrel, 7-shot cylinder, adjustable rear sight. Integral key-lock action. Imported by Taurus International.
Price: Blue or matte stainless . . . . **$422.00 to $469.00**

TAURUS MODEL 66 Silhouette Revolver

Similar to Model 6, 12" barrel, 7-shot cylinder, adjustable sight. Integral key-lock action, blue or matte stainless steel finish, rubber grips. Introduced 2001. Imported by Taurus International.
Price: . . . . **$414.00 to $461.00**

TAURUS MODEL 82 HEAVY BARREL REVOLVER

Caliber: 38 Spec., 6-shot. **Barrel:** 4", heavy. **Weight:** 36.5 oz. **Length:** 9-1/4" overall (4" bbl.). **Grips:** Soft black rubber. **Sights:** Serrated ramp front, square notch rear. **Features:** Double action, solid rib, integral key-lock. Imported by Taurus International.
Price: Blue or matte stainless . . . . **$352.00 to $398.00**

TAURUS MODEL 85 REVOLVER

Caliber: 38 Spec., 5-shot. **Barrel:** 2". **Weight:** 17-24.5 oz., titanium 13.5-15.4 oz. **Grips:** Rubber, rosewood or mother-of-pearl. **Sights:** Ramp front, square notch rear. **Features:** Blue, matte stainless, blue with gold accents, stainless with gold accents; rated for +P ammo. Integral key-lock. Introduced 1980. Imported by Taurus International.
Price: . . . . **$375.00 to $547.00**
Price: Total Titanium **$531.00**

TAURUS MODEL 94 REVOLVER

Caliber: 22 LR, 9-shot cylinder. **Barrel:** 2", 4", 5". **Weight:** 18.5-27.5 oz. **Grips:** Soft black rubber. **Sights:** Serrated ramp front, click-adjustable rear. **Features:** Double action, integral key-lock. Introduced 1989. Imported by Taurus International.
Price: Blue **$325.00**
Price: Matte stainless **$375.00**
Price: Model 94 UL, forged aluminum alloy, 18-18.5 oz. **$365.00**
Price: As above, stainless. **$410.00**

TAURUS MODEL 22H RAGING HORNET REVOLVER

Caliber: 22 Hornet, 8-shot. **Barrel:** 10". **Weight:** 50 oz. **Length:** 6.5" overall. **Grips:** Soft black rubber. **Sights:** Fully adjustable, scope mount base included. **Features:** Ventilated rib, stainless steel construction with matte finish. Double action, integral key-lock. Introduced 1999. Imported by Taurus International.
Price: **$898.00**

TAURUS MODEL 30C RAGING THIRTY

Caliber: 30 Carbine, 8-shot. **Barrel:** 10". **Weight:** 72.3 oz. **Grips:** Soft black rubber. **Sights:** Adjustable. **Features:** Double action, ventilated rib, matte stainless, comes with five "Stellar" full-moon clips, integral key-lock.
Price: **$898.00**

TAURUS MODEL 44 REVOLVER

Caliber: 44 Mag., 6-shot. **Barrel:** 4", 6-1/2", 8-3/8". **Weight:** 44-3/4 oz. **Grips:** Rubber. **Sights:** Adjustable. **Features:** Double action. Integral key-lock. Introduced 1994. New Model 44S12 has 12" vent rib barrel. Imported from Brazil by Taurus International Manufacturing, Inc.
Price: Blue or stainless steel . . . . **$445.00 to $602.00**

HANDGUNS — DOUBLE ACTION REVOLVERS, SERVICE & SPORT

Taurus Model 415

Taurus Model 608

Taurus Model 450

Taurus Model 454 Raging Bull

TAURUS MODEL 217 TARGET "SILHOUETTE"
Caliber: 218 Bee, 8-shot. Barrel: 12". Weight: 52.3 oz. Grips: Rubber. Sights: Adjustable. Features: Double action, ventilated rib, adjustable mainspring and trigger stop, matte stainless, integral key-lock.
Price: $461.00

TAURUS MODEL 218 RAGING BEE
Caliber: 218 Bee, 7-shot. Barrel: 10". Weight: 74.9 oz. Grips: Rubber. Sights: Adjustable rear. Features: Ventilated rib, adjustable action, matte stainless, integral key-lock. Also Available as Model 218SS6 Tracker with 6-1/2" vent rib barrel.
Price: . . . . (Raging Bee) $898.00
Price: . . . . (Tracker) $406.00

TAURUS MODEL 415 REVOLVER
Caliber: 41 Mag., 5-shot. Barrel: 2-1/2". Weight: 30 oz. Length: 7-1/8" overall. Grips: Rubber. Sights: Fixed. Features: Stainless steel construction; matte finish; ported barrel. Double action. Integral key-lock. Introduced 1999. Imported by Taurus International.
Price: $508.00
Price: Total Titanium $602.00

TAURUS MODEL 425/627 TRACKER REVOLVERS
Caliber: 357 Mag., 7-shot; 41 Mag., 5-shot. Barrel: 4" and 6". Weight: 28.8-40 oz. (titanium) 24.3-28. (6"). Grips: Rubber. Sights: Fixed front, adjustable rear. Features: Double action stainless steel, Shadow Gray or Total Titanium; vent rib (steel models only); integral key-lock action. Imported by Taurus International.
Price: . . . . $508.00 to $516.00
Price: Total Titanium $688.00

TAURUS MODEL 445
Caliber: 44 Special, 5-shot. Barrel: 2". Weight: 20.3-28.25 oz. Length: 6-3/4" overall. Grips: Rubber. Sights: Ramp front, notch rear. Features: Blue or stainless steel. Standard or DAO concealed hammer, optional porting. Introduced 1997. Imported by Taurus International.
Price: . . . . $345.00 to $500.00
Price: Total Titanium 19.8 oz. $600.00

TAURUS MODEL 455 "STELLAR TRACKER"
Caliber: 45 ACP, 5-shot. Barrel: 2", 4", 6". Weight: 28/33/38.4 oz. Grips: Rubber. Sights: Adjustable. Features: Double action, matte stainless, includes five "Stellar" full-moon clips, integral key-lock.
Price: $523.00

TAURUS MODEL 460 "TRACKER"
Caliber: 45 Colt, 5-shot. Barrel: 4" or 6". Weight: 33/38.4 oz. Grips: Rubber. Sights: Adjustable. Features: Double action, ventilated rib, matte stainless steel, comes with five "Stellar" full-moon clips.
Price: $516.00
Price: . . . . (Shadow gray, Total Titanium) $688.00

TAURUS MODEL 605 REVOLVER
Caliber: 357 Mag., 5-shot. Barrel: 2". Weight: 24 oz. Grips: Rubber. Sights: Fixed. Features: Double action, blue or stainless, concealed hammer models DAO, porting optional, integral key-lock. Introduced 1995. Imported by Taurus International.
Price: . . . . $375.00 to $438.00

Taurus Model 731 Revolver
Similar to the Taurus Model 605, except in .32 Magnum.
Price: . . . . $438.00 to $531.00

TAURUS MODEL 608 REVOLVER
Caliber: 357 Mag. 38 Spec., 8-shot. Barrel: 4", 6-1/2", 8-3/8". Weight: 44-57 oz. Length: 9-3/8" overall. Grips: Soft black rubber. Sights: Adjustable. Features: Double action, integral key-lock action. Available in blue or stainless. Introduced 1995. Imported by Taurus International.
Price: . . . . $469.00 to $547.00

Taurus Model 44 Series Revolver
Similar to Taurus Model 60 series, but in .44 Rem. Mag. With six-shot cylin-der, blue and matte stainless finishes.
Price: . . . . $500.00 to $578.00

TAURUS MODEL 650CIA REVOLVER
Caliber: 357 Magnum, 5-shot. Barrel: 2". Weight: 24.5 oz. Grips: Rubber. Sights: Ramp front, square notch rear. Features: Double-action only, blue or matte stainless steel, integral key-lock, internal hammer. Introduced 2001. From Taurus International.
Price: . . . . $406.00 to $453.00

TAURUS MODEL 651 CIA REVOLVER
Caliber: 357 Magnum, 5-shot. Barrel: 2". Weight: 17-24.5 oz. Grips: Rubber. Sights: Fixed. Features: Concealed single action/double action design. Shrouded cockable hammer, blue, matte stainless, Shadow Gray, Total Titanium, integral key-lock. Made in Brazil. Imported by Taurus International Manufacturing, Inc.
Price: . . . . $406.00 to $578.00

TAURUS MODEL 450 REVOLVER
Caliber: 45 Colt, 5-shot. Barrel: 2". Weight: 21.2-22.3 oz. Length: 6-5/8" overall. Grips: Rubber. Sights: Ramp front, notch rear. Features: Double action, blue or stainless, ported, integral key-lock. Introduced 1999. Imported from Brazil by Taurus International.
Price: $492.00
Price: Ultra-Lite (alloy frame) $523.00
Price: Total Titanium, 19.2 oz. $600.00

TAURUS MODEL 444/454/480 RAGING BULL REVOLVERS
Caliber: 44 Mag., 45 LC, 454 Casull, 480 Ruger, 5-shot. Barrel: 5", 6-1/2", 8-3/8". Weight: 53-63 oz. Length: 12" overall (6-1/2" barrel). Grips: Soft black rubber. Sights: Patridge front, adjustable rear. Features: Double action, ventilated rib, ported, integral key-lock. Introduced 1997. Imported by Taurus International.
Price: Blue . . . . $578.00 to $797.00
Price: Matte stainless . . . . $641.00 to $859.00

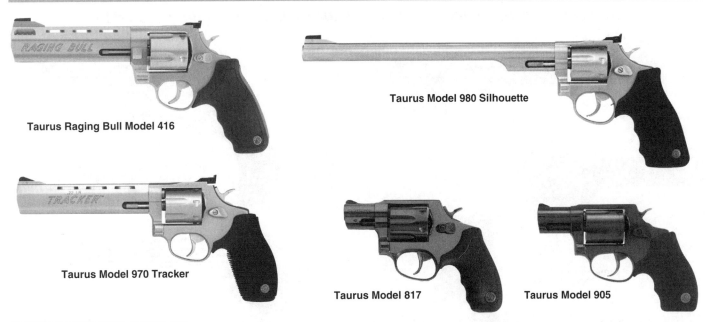

Taurus Raging Bull Model 416

Taurus Model 980 Silhouette

Taurus Model 970 Tracker

Taurus Model 817

Taurus Model 905

TAURUS RAGING BULL MODEL 416
Caliber: 41 Magnum, 6-shot. **Barrel:** 6-1/2". **Weight:** 61.9 oz. **Grips:** Rubber. **Sights:** Adjustable. **Features:** Double action, ported, ventilated rib, matte stainless, integral key-lock.
Price: **$641.00**

TAURUS MODEL 617 REVOLVER
Caliber: 357 Magnum, 7-shot. **Barrel:** 2". **Weight:** 28.3 oz. **Length:** 6-3/4" overall. **Grips:** Soft black rubber. **Sights:** Fixed. **Features:** Double action, blue, shadow gray, bright spectrum blue or matte stainless steel, integral key-lock. Available with porting, concealed hammer. Introduced 1998. Imported by Taurus International.
Price: . . . . **$391.00 to $453.00**
Price: Total Titanium, 19.9 oz. **$602.00**

Taurus Model 445 Series Revolver
Similar to Taurus Model 617 series except in .44 Spl. with 5-shot cylinder.
Price: . . . . **$389.00 to $422.00**

Taurus Model 617ULT Revolver
Similar to Model 617 except aluminum alloy and titanium components, matte stainless finish, integral key-lock action. Weighs 18.5 oz. Available ported or non-ported. Introduced 2001. Imported by Taurus International.
Price: (5-shot cylinder) . . . . **$530.00 to $545.00**

TAURUS MODEL 817 ULTRA-LITE REVOLVER
Caliber: 38 Spec., 7-shot. **Barrel:** 2". **Weight:** 21 oz. **Length:** 6 1/2" overall. **Grips:** Soft rubber. **Sights:** Fixed. **Features:** Double action, integral key-lock. Rated for +P ammo. Introduced 1999. Imported from Brazil by Taurus International.
Price: Blue **$375.00**
Price: Blue, ported **$395.00**
Price: Matte, stainless. **$420.00**
Price: Matte, stainless, ported **$440.00**

TAURUS MODEL 850CIA REVOLVER
Caliber: 38 Special, 5-shot. **Barrel:** 2". **Weight:** 17-24.5 oz. **Grips:** Rubber. **Sights:** Ramp front, square notch rear. **Features:** Double action only, blue or matte stainless steel, rated for +P ammo, integral key-lock, internal hammer. Introduced 2001. From Taurus International.
Price: . . . . **$406.00 to $453.00**
Price: Total Titanium **$578.00**

TAURUS MODEL 851CIA REVOLVER
Caliber: 38 Spec., 5-shot. **Barrel:** 2". **Weight:** 17-24.5 oz. **Grips:** Rubber. **Sights:** Fixed-UL/ULT adjustable. **Features:** Concealed single action/double action design. Shrouded cockable hammer, blue, matte stainless, Total Titanium, blue or stainless UL and ULT, integral key-lock. Rated for +P ammo.
Price: . . . . **$406.00 to $578.00**

TAURUS MODEL 94, 941 REVOLVER
Caliber: 22 LR (Mod. 94), 22 WMR (Mod. 941), 8-shot. **Barrel:** 2", 4", 5". **Weight:** 27.5 oz. (4" barrel). **Grips:** Soft black rubber. **Sights:** Serrated ramp front, rear adjustable. **Features:** Double action, integral key-lock. Introduced 1992. Imported by Taurus International.
Price: Blue . . . . **$328.00 to $344.00**
Price: Stainless (matte) . . . . **$375.00 to $391.00**
Price: Model 941 Ultra Lite,
forged aluminum alloy, 2" . . . . **$359.00 to $375.00**
Price: As above, stainless. **$406.00 to $422.00**

TAURUS MODEL 970/971 TRACKER REVOLVERS
Caliber: 22 LR (Model 970), 22 Magnum (Model 971); 7-shot. **Barrel:** 6". **Weight:** 53.6 oz. **Grips:** Rubber. **Sights:** Adjustable. **Features:** Double barrel, heavy barrel with ventilated rib; matte stainless finish, integral key-lock. Introduced 2001. From Taurus International.
Price: . . . . **$391.00 to $406.00**

TAURUS MODEL 980/981 SILHOUETTE REVOLVERS
Caliber: 22 LR (Model 980), 22 Magnum (Model 981); 7-shot. **Barrel:** 12". **Weight:** 68 oz. **Grips:** Rubber. **Sights:** Adjustable. **Features:** Double action, heavy barrel with ventilated rib and scope mount, matte stainless finish, integral key-lock. Introduced 2001. From Taurus International.
Price: (Model 980) **$398.00**
Price: (Model 981) **$414.00**

TAURUS MODEL 905, 405, 455 PISTOL CALIBER REVOLVERS
Caliber: 9mm, .40, .45 ACP, 5-shot. **Barrel:** 2", 4", 6-1/2". **Weight:** 21 oz. to 40.8 oz. **Grips:** Rubber. **Sights:** Fixed, adjustable on Model 455SS6 in .45 ACP. **Features:** Produced as a backup gun for law enforcement officers who desire to carry the same caliber ammunition in their back-up revolver as they do in their service sidearm. Introduced 2003. Imported from Brazil by Taurus International Manufacturing, Inc.
Price: . . . . **$383.00 to $523.00**

Both classic six-shooters and modern adaptations for hunting and sport.

Century Model 100

Cimarron Lightning

Cimarron Model P
New Sheriff

Cimarron Bisley

Cimarron Roughrider

Cimarron Open Top

CABELA'S MILLENNIUM REVOLVER
Caliber: 45 Colt. **Barrel:** 4-3/4". **Weight:** NA. **Length:** 10" overall. **Grips:** Hardwood. **Sights:** Blade front, hammer notch rear. **Features:** Matte black finish; unpolished brass accents. Introduced 2001. From Cabela's.
Price: **$279.99**

CENTURY GUN DIST. MODEL 100 SINGLE-ACTION
Caliber: 30-30, 375 Win., 444 Marlin, 45-70, 50-70. **Barrel:** 6-1/2" (stan-dard), 8", 10". **Weight:** 6 lbs. (loaded). **Length:** 15" overall (8" bbl.). **Grips:** Smooth walnut. **Sights:** Ramp front, Millett adjustable square notch rear. **Features:** Highly polished high tensile strength manganese bronze frame, blue cylinder and barrel; coil spring trigger mechanism. Contact maker for full price information. Introduced 1975. Made in U.S.A. From Century Gun Dist., Inc.
Price: 6-1/2" barrel, 45-70. . . . . **$2,000.00**

CIMARRON LIGHTNING SA
Caliber: 38 Colt, 38 Special. **Barrel:** 3-1/2", 4-3/4", 5-1/2". **Grips:** Smooth or checkered walnut. **Sights:** Blade front. **Features:** Replica of the Colt 1877 Lightning DA. Similar to Cimarron Thunderer™, except smaller grip frame to fit smaller hands. Standard blue, charcoal blue or nickel finish with forged, old model, or color case hardened frame. Introduced 2001. From Cimarron F.A. Co.
Price: . . . . **$499.00 to $559.00**

CIMARRON MODEL P
Caliber: 32 WCF, 38 WCF, 357 Mag., 44 WCF, 44 Spec., 45 Colt. **Barrel:** 4-3/4", 5-1/2", 7-1/2". **Weight:** 39 oz. **Length:** 10" overall (4" barrel). **Grips:** Walnut. **Sights:** Blade front, fixed or adjustable rear. **Features:** Uses "old model" blackpowder frame with "Bullseye" ejector or New Model frame. Imported by Cimarron F.A. Co.
Price: . . . . **$489.00 to $549.00**
Price: New Sheriff . . . . **$489.00 to $564.00**

Cimarron Bisley Model Single-Action Revolvers
Similar to 1873 Model P, special grip frame and trigger guard, knurled wide-spur hammer, curved trigger. Available in 357 Mag., 44 WCF, 44 Spl., 45 Colt. Introduced 1999. Imported by Cimarron F.A. Co.
Price: **$525.00**

Cimarron Flat-Top Single-Action Revolvers
Similar to 1873 Model P, flat top strap with windage-adjustable rear sight, elevation-adjustable front sight. Available in 44 WCF, 45 Colt; 7-1/2" barrel. Introduced 1999. Imported by Cimarron F.A. Co.
Price: **$525.00**

CIMARRON MODEL "P" JR.
Caliber: 38 Special. **Barrel:** 3-1/2", 4-3/4", 5-1/2". **Grips:** Checkered walnut. **Sights:** Blade front. **Features:** Styled after 1873 Colt Peacemaker, except 20 percent smaller. Blue finish with color-case hardened frame; Cowboy Comp® action. Introduced 2001. From Cimarron F.A. Co.
Price: . . . . **$419.00 to $479.00**

CIMARRON ROUGHRIDER ARTILLERY MODEL SINGLE-ACTION
Caliber: 45 Colt. **Barrel:** 5-1/2". **Weight:** 39 oz. **Length:** 11-1/2" overall. **Grips:** Walnut. **Sights:** Fixed. **Features:** U.S. markings and cartouche, case-hardened frame and hammer; 45 Colt only. Imported by Cimarron F.A. Co.
Price: . . . . **$549.00 to $599.00**

HANDGUNS — SINGLE ACTION REVOLVERS

Cimarron Thunderer

Colt Single-Action Army

EAA Bounty Hunter

EMF Hartford

EMF 1894 Bisley

CIMARRON 1872 OPEN TOP REVOLVER
Caliber: 38, 44 Special, 45 S&W Schofield. **Barrel:** 5-1/2" and 7-1/2". **Grips:** Walnut. **Sights:** Blade front, fixed rear. **Features:** Replica of first cartridge-firing revolver. Blue, charcoal blue, nickel or Original® finish; Navy-style brass or steel Army-style frame. Introduced 2001 by Cimarron F.A. Co.
Price: . . . . $529.00 to $599.00

CIMARRON THUNDERER REVOLVER
Caliber: 357 Mag., 44 WCF, 44 Spl, 45 Colt, 6-shot. **Barrel:** 3-1/2", 4-3/4", 5-1/2", 7-1/2", with ejector. **Weight:** 38 oz. (3-1/2" barrel). **Grips:** Smooth walnut. **Sights:** Blade front, notch rear. **Features:** Thunderer grip; color case-hardened frame with balance blued. Introduced 1993. Imported by Cimarron F.A. Co.
Price: 3-1/2", 4-3/4", smooth grips . . . . $519.00 to $549.00
Price: As above, checkered grips . . . . $564.00 to $584.00
Price: 5-1/2", 7-1/2", smooth grips . . . . $519.00 to $549.00
Price: As above, checkered grips . . . . $564.00 to $584.00

COLT SINGLE-ACTION ARMY REVOLVER
Caliber: 357 Mag., 38 Special, .32/20, 44-40, 45 Colt, 6-shot. **Barrel:** 4-3/4", 5-1/2", 7-1/2". **Weight:** 40 oz. (4-3/4" barrel). **Length:** 10-1/4" overall (4-3/4" barrel). **Grips:** Black Eagle composite. **Sights:** Blade front, notch rear. **Features:** Available in full nickel finish with nickel grip medallions, or Royal Blue with color case-hardened frame. Reintroduced 1992.
Price: $1,380.00

EAA BOUNTY HUNTER SA REVOLVERS
Caliber: 22 LR/22 WMR, 357 Mag., 44 Mag., 45 Colt, 6-shot. **Barrel:** 4-1/2", 7-1/2". **Weight:** 2.5 lbs. **Length:** 11" overall (4-5/8" barrel). **Grips:** Smooth walnut. **Sights:** Blade front, grooved topstrap rear. **Features:** Transfer bar safety; three position hammer; hammer forged barrel. Introduced 1992. Imported by European American Armory.
Price: Blue or case-hardened $369.00
Price: Nickel $399.00
Price: 22LR/22WMR, blue $269.00
Price: As above, nickel $299.00

EMF HARTFORD SINGLE-ACTION REVOLVERS
Caliber: 357 Mag., 32-20, 38-40, 44-40, 44 Spec., 45 Colt. **Barrel:** 4-3/4", 5-1/2", 7-1/2". **Weight:** 45 oz. **Length:** 13" overall (7-1/2" barrel). **Grips:** Smooth walnut. **Sights:** Blade front, fixed rear. **Features:** Identical to the original Colts with inspector cartouche on left grip, original patent dates and U.S. markings. All major parts serial numbered using original Colt-style lettering, numbering. Bullseye ejector head and color case-hardening on frame and hammer. Introduced 1990. From E.M.F.
Price: $500.00
Price: Cavalry or Artillery $390.00
Price: Nickel plated, add. $125.00
Price: Casehardened New Model frame. $365.00

EMF 1894 Bisley Revolver
Similar to the Hartford single-action revolver except has special grip frame and trigger guard, wide spur hammer; available in 38-40 or 45 Colt, 4-3/4", 5-1/2" or 7-1/2" barrel. Introduced 1995. Imported by E.M.F.
Price: Casehardened/blue $400.00
Price: Nickel $525.00

EMF Hartford Pinkerton Single-Action Revolver
Same as the regular Hartford except has 4" barrel with ejector tube and birds head grip. Calibers: 357 Mag., 45 Colt. Introduced 1997. Imported by E.M.F.
Price: $375.00

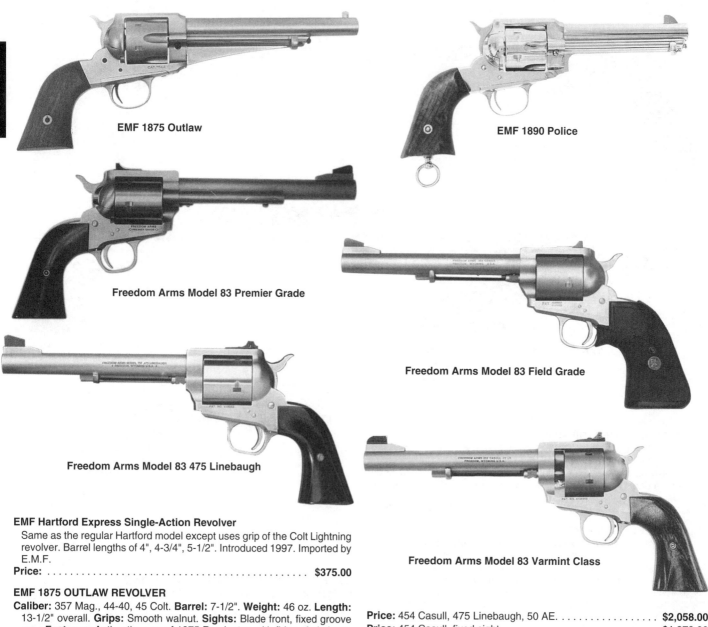

EMF 1875 Outlaw

EMF 1890 Police

Freedom Arms Model 83 Premier Grade

Freedom Arms Model 83 Field Grade

Freedom Arms Model 83 475 Linebaugh

Freedom Arms Model 83 Varmint Class

EMF Hartford Express Single-Action Revolver

Same as the regular Hartford model except uses grip of the Colt Lightning revolver. Barrel lengths of 4", 4-3/4", 5-1/2". Introduced 1997. Imported by E.M.F.

Price: **$375.00**

EMF 1875 OUTLAW REVOLVER

Caliber: 357 Mag., 44-40, 45 Colt. **Barrel:** 7-1/2". **Weight:** 46 oz. **Length:** 13-1/2" overall. **Grips:** Smooth walnut. **Sights:** Blade front, fixed groove rear. **Features:** Authentic copy of 1875 Remington with firing pin in hammer; color case-hardened frame, blue cylinder, barrel, steel backstrap and brass trigger guard. Also available in nickel, factory engraved. Imported by E.M.F.

Price: All calibers **$575.00**
Price: Nickel **$735.00**

EMF 1890 Police Revolver

Similar to the 1875 Outlaw except has 5-1/2" barrel, weighs 40 oz., with 12-1/2" overall length. Has lanyard ring in butt. No web under barrel. Calibers 357, 44-40, 45 Colt. Imported by E.M.F.

Price: All calibers **$590.00**
Price: Nickel **$750.00**

FREEDOM ARMS MODEL 83 PREMIER GRADE REVOLVER

Caliber: 357 Mag., 41 Mag., 44 Mag., 454 Casull, 475 Linebaugh, 50 AE, 5-shot. **Barrel:** 4-3/4", 6", 7-1/2", 9" (357 Mag. only), 10". **Weight:** 52.8 oz. **Length:** 13" (7-1/2" bbl.). **Grips:** Impregnated hardwood. **Sights:** Blade front, notch or adjustable rear. **Features:** All stainless steel construction; sliding bar safety system. Lifetime warranty. Made in U.S.A. by Freedom Arms, Inc.

Price: 454 Casull, 475 Linebaugh, 50 AE. **$2,058.00**
Price: 454 Casull, fixed sight **$1,979.00**
Price: 357 Mag., 41 Mag., 44 Mag. **$1,976.00**
Price: 44 Mag., fixed sight **$1,911.00**

Freedom Arms Model 83 Field Grade Revolver

Model 83 frame. Weighs 52-56 oz. Adjustable rear sight, replaceable front blade, matte finish, Pachmayr grips. All stainless steel. Introduced 1988. Made in U.S.A. by Freedom Arms Inc.

Price: 454 Casull, 475 Linebaugh, 50 AE, adj. sights. **$1,591.00**
Price: 454 Casull, fixed sights. **$1,553.00**
Price: 357 Mag., 41 Mag., 44 Mag. **$1,527.00**

FREEDOM ARMS MODEL 83 VARMINT CLASS REVOLVERS

Caliber: 22 LR, 5-shot. **Barrel:** 5-1/8, 7-1/2". **Weight:** 58 oz. (7-1/2" bbl.). **Length:** 11-1/2" (7-1/2" bbl.). **Grips:** Impregnated hardwood. **Sights:** Steel base adjustable "V" notch rear sight and replaceable brass bead front sight. **Features:** Stainless steel, matte finish, manual sliding-bar system, dual firing pins, pre-set trigger stop. One year limited waraanty to original owner. Made in U.S.A. by Freedom Arms, Inc.

Price: Varmint Class **$1,828.00**
Price: Extra fitted 22 WMR cylinder **$264.00**

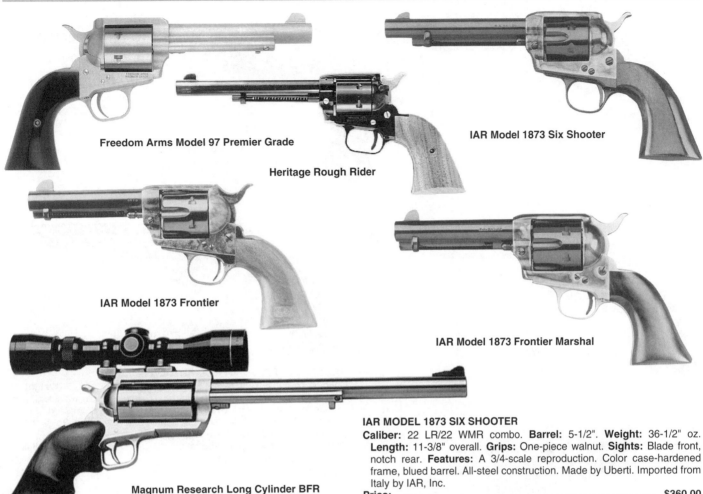

Freedom Arms Model 97 Premier Grade

Heritage Rough Rider

IAR Model 1873 Six Shooter

IAR Model 1873 Frontier

IAR Model 1873 Frontier Marshal

Magnum Research Long Cylinder BFR

FREEDOM ARMS MODEL 97 PREMIER GRADE REVOLVER

Caliber: 22 LR, 357 Mag., 41 Mag., 44 Special, 45 Colt, 5-shot. **Barrel:** 4-1/2", 5-1/2", 7-1/2", 10". **Weight:** 37 oz. (45 Colt 5-1/2"). **Length:** 10-3/4" (5-1/2" bbl.). **Grips:** Impregnated hardwood. **Sights:** Adjustable rear, replaceable blade front. **Features:** Stainless steel, brushed finish, automatic transfer bar safety system. Introduced in 1997. Made in U.S.A. by Freedom Arms.

Price: 357 Mag., 41 Mag., 45 Colt $1,668.00
Price: 357 Mag., 45 Colt, fixed sight $1,576.00
Price: Extra fitted cylinders 38 Special, 45 ACP $264.00
Price: 22 LR with sporting chambers $1,732.00
Price: Extra fitted 22 WMR cylinder $264.00
Price: Extra fitted 22 LR match grade cylinder $476.00
Price: 22 match grade chamber instead of 22 LR sport chamber
. . . . $214.00

HERITAGE ROUGH RIDER REVOLVER

Caliber: 22 LR, 22 LR/22 WMR combo, 6-shot. **Barrel:** 2-3/4", 3-1/2", 4-3/4", 6-1/2", 9". **Weight:** 31 to 38 oz. **Length:** NA. **Grips:** Exotic hardwood, laminated wood or mother of pearl; bird's head models offered. **Sights:** Blade front, fixed rear. Adjustable sight on 6-1/2" only. **Features:** Hammer block safety. High polish blue or nickel finish. Introduced 1993. Made in U.S.A. by Heritage Mfg., Inc.
Price: . . . . $184.95 to $239.95

IAR MODEL 1873 SIX SHOOTER

Caliber: 22 LR/22 WMR combo. **Barrel:** 5-1/2". **Weight:** 36-1/2" oz. **Length:** 11-3/8" overall. **Grips:** One-piece walnut. **Sights:** Blade front, notch rear. **Features:** A 3/4-scale reproduction. Color case-hardened frame, blued barrel. All-steel construction. Made by Uberti. Imported from Italy by IAR, Inc.
Price: $360.00

IAR MODEL 1873 FRONTIER REVOLVER

Caliber: 22 RL, 22 LR/22 WMR. **Barrel:** 4-3/4". **Weight:** 45 oz. **Length:** 10-1/2" overall. **Grips:** One-piece walnut with inspector's cartouche. **Sights:** Blade front, notch rear. **Features:** Color case-hardened frame, blued barrel, black nickel-plated brass trigger guard and backstrap. Bright nickel and engraved versions available. Introduced 1997. Imported from Italy by IAR, Inc.
Price: $380.00
Price: Nickel-plated $425.00
Price: 22 LR/22WMR combo $420.00

IAR MODEL 1873 FRONTIER MARSHAL

Caliber: 357 Mag., 45 Colt. **Barrel:** 4-3/4", 5-1/2, 7-1/2". **Weight:** 39 oz. **Length:** 10-1/2" overall. **Grips:** One-piece walnut. **Sights:** Blade front, notch rear. **Features:** Bright brass trigger guard and backstrap, color case-hardened frame, blued barrel and cylinder. Introduced 1998. Imported from Italy by IAR, Inc.
Price: $395.00

MAGNUM RESEARCH BFR SINGLE-ACTION REVOLVER

(Long cylinder) Caliber: 30/30, 45/70 Government, 444 Marlin, 45 LC/410, 450 Marlin, 50 AE, .500 S&W. **Barrel:** 7.5", 10". **Weight:** 4 lbs., 4.36 lbs. **Length:** 15", 17.5".
(Short cylinder) Caliber: 454 Casull, 22 Hornet, BFR 480/475. **Barrel:** 6.5", 7.5", 10". **Weight:** 3.2 lbs., 3.5 lbs., 4.36 lbs. (10"). **Length:** 12.75 (6"), 13.75", 16.25"
Sights: All have fully adjustable rear, black blade ramp front. **Features:** Stainless steel construction, rubber grips, all 5-shot capacity. Barrels are stress-relieved and cut rifled. Made in U.S.A. From Magnum Research, Inc.
Price: $999.00

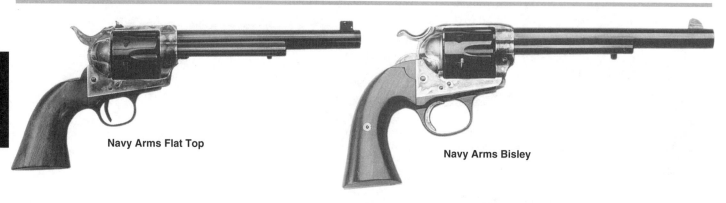

Navy Arms Flat Top

Navy Arms Bisley

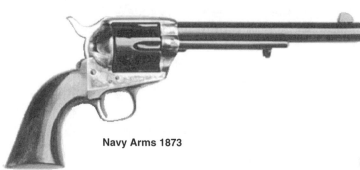

Navy Arms 1873

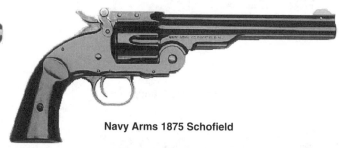

Navy Arms 1875 Schofield

Navy Arms New Model Russian

NAVY ARMS FLAT TOP TARGET MODEL REVOLVER

Caliber: 45 Colt, 6-shot cylinder. **Barrel:** 7-1/2". **Weight:** 40 oz. **Length:** 13-1/4" overall. **Grips:** Smooth walnut. **Sights:** Spring-loaded German silver front, rear adjustable for windage. **Features:** Replica of Colt's Flat Top Frontier target revolver made from 1888 to 1896. Blue with color case-hardened frame. Introduced 1997. Imported by Navy Arms.
Price: **$450.00**

NAVY ARMS BISLEY MODEL SINGLE-ACTION REVOLVER

Caliber: 44-40 or 45 Colt, 6-shot cylinder. **Barrel:** 4-3/4", 5-1/2", 7-1/2". **Weight:** 40 oz. **Length:** 12-1/2" overall (7-1/2" barrel). **Grips:** Smooth walnut. **Sights:** Blade front, notch rear. **Features:** Replica of Colt's Bisley Model. Polished blue finish, color case-hardened frame. Introduced 1997. Imported by Navy Arms.
Price: .... **$425.00 to $460.00**

NAVY ARMS 1873 SINGLE-ACTION REVOLVER

Caliber: 357 Mag., 44-40, 45 Colt, 6-shot cylinder. **Barrel:** 4-3/4", 5-1/2", 7-1/2". **Weight:** 36 oz. **Length:** 10-3/4" overall (5-1/2" barrel). **Grips:** Smooth walnut. **Sights:** Blade front, notch rear. **Features:** Blue with color case-hardened frame. Introduced 1991. Imported by Navy Arms.
Price: **$405.00**

NAVY ARMS 1875 SCHOFIELD REVOLVER

Caliber: 44-40, 45 Colt, 6-shot cylinder. **Barrel:** 3-1/2", 5", 7". **Weight:** 39 oz. **Length:** 10-3/4" overall (5" barrel). **Grips:** Smooth walnut. **Sights:** Blade front, notch rear. **Features:** Replica of Smith & Wesson Model 3 Schofield. Single-action, top-break with automatic ejection. Polished blue finish. Introduced 1994. Imported by Navy Arms.
Price: Hideout Model, 3-1/2" barrel. **$695.00**
Price: Wells Fargo, 5" barrel **$695.00**
Price: U.S. Cavalry model, 7" barrel, military markings **$695.00**

NAVY ARMS NEW MODEL RUSSIAN REVOLVER

Caliber: 44 Russian, 6-shot cylinder. **Barrel:** 6-1/2". **Weight:** 40 oz. **Length:** 12" overall. **Grips:** Smooth walnut. **Sights:** Blade front, notch rear. **Features:** Replica of the S&W Model 3 Russian Third Model revolver. Spur trigger guard, polished blue finish. Introduced 1999. Imported by Navy Arms.
Price: **$769.00**

NAVY ARMS 1851 NAVY CONVERSION REVOLVER

Caliber: 38 Spec., 38 Long Colt. **Barrel:** 5-1/2", 7-1/2". **Weight:** 44 oz. **Length:** 14" overall (7-1/2" barrel). **Grips:** Smooth walnut. **Sights:** Bead front, notch rear. **Features:** Replica of Colt's cartridge conversion revolver. Polished blue finish with color case-hardened frame, silver plated trigger guard and backstrap. Introduced 1999. Imported by Navy Arms.
Price: **$165.00**

NAVY ARMS 1860 ARMY CONVERSION REVOLVER

Caliber: 38 Spec., 38 Long Colt. **Barrel:** 5-1/2", 7-1/2". **Weight:** 44 oz. **Length:** 13-1/2" overall (7-1/2" barrel). **Grips:** Smooth walnut. **Sights:** Blade front, notch rear. **Features:** Replica of Colt's conversion revolver. Polished blue finish with color case-hardened frame, full-size 1860 Army grip with blued steel backstrap. Introduced 1999. Imported by Navy Arms.
Price: **$190.00**

NORTH AMERICAN MINI REVOLVERS

Caliber: 22 Short, 22 LR, 22 WMR, 5-shot. **Barrel:** 1-1/8", 1-5/8". **Weight:** 4 to 6.6 oz. **Length:** 3-5/8" to 6-1/8" overall. **Grips:** Laminated wood. **Sights:** Blade front, notch fixed rear. **Features:** All stainless steel construction. Polished satin and matte finish. Engraved models available. From North American Arms.
Price: 22 Short, 22 LR **$193.00**
Price: 22 WMR, 1-1/8" or 1-5/8" bbl. **$193.00**
Price: 22 WMR, 1-1/8" or 1-5/8" bbl. with extra 22 LR cylinder. ... **$193.00**

North American Mini

Ruger "Bird's Head" Single Six

North American Mini-Master

North American Black Widow

Ruger Blackhawk

Ruger SSMBH-4F

Ruger Bisley Single-Action

NORTH AMERICAN MINI-MASTER
Caliber: 22 LR, 22 WMR, 17 HMR, 5-shot cylinder. **Barrel:** 4". **Weight:** 10.7 oz. **Length:** 7.75" overall. **Grips:** Checkered hard black rubber. **Sights:** Blade front, white outline rear adjustable for elevation, or fixed. **Features:** Heavy vent barrel; full-size grips. Non-fluted cylinder. Introduced 1989.
Price: Adjustable sight, 22 WMR, 17 HMR or 22 LR $301.00
Price: As above with extra WMR/LR cylinder $330.00
Price: Fixed sight, 22 WMR, 17 HMR or 22 LR $272.00
Price: As above with extra WMR/LR cylinder $330.00

North American Black Widow Revolver
Similar to Mini-Master, 2" heavy vent barrel. Built on 22 WMR frame. Non-fluted cylinder, black rubber grips. Available with Millett Low Profile fixed sights or Millett sight adjustable for elevation only. Overall length 5-7/8", weighs 8.8 oz. From North American Arms.
Price: Adjustable sight, 22 LR, 17 HMR or 22 WMR $287.00
Price: As above with extra WMR/LR cylinder $316.00
Price: Fixed sight, 22 LR, 17 HMR or 22 WMR $287.00
Price: As above with extra WMR/LR cylinder $287.00

RUGER NEW MODEL SINGLE SIX REVOLVER
Caliber: 32 H&R. **Barrel:** 4-5/8", 6-shot. **Grips:** Black Micarta "birds head", rosewood with color case. **Sights:** Fixed. **Features:** Instruction manual, high impact case, gun lock standard.
Price: Stainless, KSSMBH-4F, birds head $576.00
Price: Color case, SSMBH-4F, birds head $576.00
Price: Color case, SSM-4F-S, rosewood $576.00

RUGER NEW MODEL BLACKHAWK AND BLACKHAWK CONVERTIBLE
Caliber: 30 Carbine, 357 Mag./38 Spec., 41 Mag., 45 Colt, 6-shot. **Barrel:** 4-5/8" or 5-1/2", either caliber; 7-1/2" (30 Carbine and 45 Colt). **Weight:**

42 oz. (6-1/2" bbl.). **Length:** 12-1/4" overall (5-1/2" bbl.). **Grips:** American walnut. **Sights:** 1/8" ramp front, micro-click rear adjustable for windage and elevation. **Features:** Ruger transfer bar safety system, independent firing pin, hardened chrome-moly steel frame, music wire springs throughout. Case and lock included.
Price: Blue 30 Carbine, 7 1/2" (BN31) $435.00
Price: Blue, 357 Mag., 4-5/8", 6-1/2" (BN34, BN36) $435.00
Price: As above, stainless (KBN34, KBN36) $530.00
Price: Blue, 357 Mag./9mm Convertible, 4-5/8", 6-1/2" (BN34X, BN36X) includes extra cylinder $489.00
Price: Blue, 41 Mag., 4-5/8", 6-1/2" (BN41, BN42) $435.00
Price: Blue, 45 Colt, 4-5/8", 5-1/2", 7-1/2" (BN44, BN455, BN45) $435.00
Price: Stainless, 45 Colt, 4-5/8", 7-1/2" (KBN44, KBN45) $530.00
Price: Blue, 45 Colt/45 ACP Convertible, 4-5/8", 5-1/2" (BN44X, BN455X) includes extra cylinder $489.00

Ruger Bisley Single-Action Revolver
Similar to standard Blackhawk, hammer is lower with smoothly curved, deeply checkered wide spur. The trigger is strongly curved with wide smooth surface. Longer grip frame has hand-filling shape. Adjustable rear sight, ramp-style front. Unfluted cylinder and roll engraving, adjustable sights. Chambered for 357, 44 Mags. and 45 Colt; 7-1/2" barrel; overall length of 13"; weighs 48 oz. Plastic lockable case. Introduced 1985.
Price: RB-35W, 357Mag, RBD-44W, 44Mag, RB-45W, 45 Colt . . $535.00

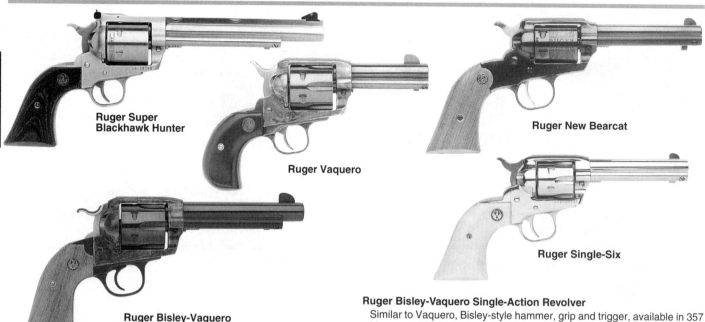

Ruger Super Blackhawk Hunter

Ruger Vaquero

Ruger New Bearcat

Ruger Single-Six

Ruger Bisley-Vaquero

RUGER NEW MODEL SUPER BLACKHAWK

Caliber: 44 Mag., 6-shot. Also fires 44 Spec. **Barrel:** 4-5/8", 5-1/2", 7-1/2", 10-1/2" bull. **Weight:** 48 oz. (7-1/2" bbl.), 51 oz. (10-1/2" bbl.). **Length:** 13-3/8" overall (7-1/2" bbl.). **Grips:** American walnut. **Sights:** 1/8" ramp front, micro-click rear adjustable for windage and elevation. **Features:** Ruger transfer bar safety system, fluted or un-fluted cylinder, steel grip and cylinder frame, round or square back trigger guard, wide serrated trigger, wide spur hammer. With case and lock.

Price: Blue, 4-5/8", 5-1/2", 7-1/2" (S458N, S45N, S47N) **$519.00**
Price: Blue, 10-1/2" bull barrel (S411N) **$529.00**
Price: Stainless, 4-5/8", 5-1/2", 7-1/2" (KS458N, KS45N, KS47N) **$535.00**
Price: Stainless, 10-1/2" bull barrel (KS411N) **$545.00**

RUGER NEW MODEL SUPER BLACKHAWK HUNTER

Caliber: 44 Mag., 6-shot. **Barrel:** 7-1/2", full-length solid rib, unfluted cylinder. **Weight:** 52 oz. **Length:** 13-5/8". **Grips:** Black laminated wood. **Sights:** Adjustable rear, replaceable front blade. **Features:** Reintroduced Ultimate SA revolver. Includes instruction manual, high-impact case, set 1" medium scope rings, gun lock, ejector rod as standard.
Price: **$639.00**

RUGER VAQUERO SINGLE-ACTION REVOLVER

Caliber: 357 Mag., 44-40, 44 Mag., 45 LC, 6-shot. **Barrel:** 4-5/8", 5-1/2", 7-1/2". **Weight:** 38-41 oz. **Length:** 13-1/8" overall (7-1/2" barrel). **Grips:** Smooth rosewood with Ruger medallion. **Sights:** Blade front, fixed notch rear. **Features:** Uses Ruger's patented transfer bar safety system and loading gate interlock with classic styling. Blued model color case-hardened finish on frame, rest polished and blued. Stainless has high-gloss. Introduced 1993. From Sturm, Ruger & Co.
Price: 357 Mag. BNV34, KBNV34 (4-5/8"), BNV35, KBNV35 (5-1/2") **$535.00**
Price: 44-40 BNV40, KBNV40 (4-5/8"). BNV405, KBNV405 (5-1/2"). BNV407, KBNV407 (7-1/2") **$535.00**
Price: 44 Mag., BNV474, KBNV474 (4-5/8"). BNV475, KBNV475 (5-1/2"). BNV477, KBNV477 (7-1/2") **$535.00**
Price: 45 LC, BN444, KBNV44 (4-5/8"). BNV455, KBNV455 (5-1/2"). BNV45, KBNV45 (7-1/2") **$535.00**
Price: 45 LC, BNVBH453, KBNVBH453 3-3/4" with "birds head" grip **$576.00**
Price: 357 Mag., RBNV35 (5-1/2") **$535.00**; KRBNV35 (5-1/2") . **$555.00**
Price: 45 LC, RBNV44 (4-5/8"), RBNV455 (5-1/2") **$535.00**
Price: 45 LC, KRBNV44 (4-5/8"), KRBNV455 (5-1/2") **$555.00**

RUGER BISLEY-VAQUERO SINGLE-ACTION REVOLVER

Similar to Vaquero, Bisley-style hammer, grip and trigger, available in 357 Magnum, 44 Magnum and 45 LC only, 4-5/8" or 5-1/2" barrel. Smooth rosewood grips with Ruger medallion. Roll-engraved, unfluted cylinder. Introduced 1997. From Sturm, Ruger & Co.
Price: Color case-hardened frame, blue grip frame, barrel and cylinder, RBNV-475, RBNV-474, 44 Mag. **$535.00**
Price: High-gloss stainless steel, KRBNV-475, KRBNV-474 . . . . **$555.00**
Price: For simulated ivory grips add . . . . **$41.00 to $44.00**

RUGER NEW BEARCAT SINGLE-ACTION

Caliber: 22 LR, 6-shot. **Barrel:** 4". **Weight:** 24 oz. **Length:** 8-7/8" overall. **Grips:** Smooth rosewood with Ruger medallion. **Sights:** Blade front, fixed notch rear. **Features:** Reintroduction of the Ruger Bearcat with slightly lengthened frame, Ruger patented transfer bar safety system. Available in blue only. Introduced 1993. With case and lock. From Sturm, Ruger & Co.
Price: SBC4, blue **$379.00**
Price: KSBC-4, ss **$429.00**

RUGER MODEL SINGLE-SIX REVOLVER

Caliber: 32 H&R Magnum. **Barrel:** 4-5/8", 6-shot. **Weight:** 33 oz. **Length:** 10-1/8". **Grips:** Blue, rosewood, stainless, simulated ivory. **Sights:** Blade front, notch rear fixed. **Features:** Transfer bar and loading gate interlock safety, instruction manual, high impact case and gun lock.
Price: **$576.00**
Price: Blue, SSM4FS **$576.00**
Price: SS, KSSM4FSI **$576.00**

RUGER SINGLE-SIX AND SUPER SINGLE-SIX CONVERTIBLE

Caliber: 22 LR, 6-shot; 22 WMR in extra cylinder; 17 HMR. **Barrel:** 4-5/8", 5-1/2", 6-1/2", 9-1/2" (6-groove). **Weight:** 35 oz. (6-1/2" bbl.). **Length:** 11-13/16" overall (6-1/2" bbl.). **Grips:** Smooth American walnut. **Sights:** Improved Patridge front on ramp, fully adjustable rear protected by integral frame ribs (super single-six); or fixed sight (single six). **Features:** Ruger transfer bar safety system, loading gate interlock, hardened chrome-moly steel frame, wide trigger, music wire springs throughout, independent firing pin.
Price: 4-5/8", 5-1/2", 6-1/2", 9-1/2" barrel, blue, adjustable sight NR4, NR5, NR6, NR9 . . . . **$399.00**
Price: 5-1/2", 6-1/2" bbl. only, stainless steel, adjustable sight KNR5, KNR6 . . . . **$485.00**
Price: 5-1/2", 6-1/2" barrel, blue fixed sights **$399.00**
Price: 6-1/2" barrel, NR 617, 17 HMR **$399.00**
Price: Ruger 50th Anniversary Single Six with 4-5/8" barrel and a gold-colored rollmark "50 years of Single Six 1953 to 2003," blued steel finish, Cocobolo wood grips with red Ruger medallions and both .22 LR and .22 WMR cylinders **$599.00**
Price: Stainless Hunter **$650.00**

Ruger Super Single-Six

Ruger Bisley

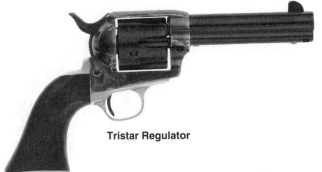

Tristar Regulator

Uberti 1873 Cattleman

Uberti 1875 Army Outlaw

Ruger Bisley Small Frame Revolver

Similar to Single-Six, frame is styled after classic Bisley "flat-top." Most mechanical parts are unchanged. Hammer is lower and smoothly curved with deeply checkered spur. Trigger is strongly curved with wide smooth surface. Longer grip frame designed with hand-filling shape, and trigger guard is a large oval. Adjustable dovetail rear sight; front sight base accepts interchangeable square blades of various heights and styles. Unfluted cylinder and roll engraving. Weighs 41 oz. Chambered for 22 LR, 6-1/2" barrel only. Plastic lockable case. Introduced 1985.
Price: RB-22AW **$422.00**

SMITH & WESSON COMMEMORATIVE MODEL 2000

Caliber: 45 S&W Schofield. **Barrel:** 7". **Features:** 150th Anniversary logo, engraved, gold-plated, walnut grips, blue, original style hammer, trigger, and barrel latch. Wood presentation case. Limited.
Price: . . . . **NA**

TRISTAR/UBERTI REGULATOR REVOLVER

Caliber: 45 Colt. **Barrel:** 4-3/4", 5-1/2". **Weight:** 32-38 oz. **Length:** 8-1/4" overall (4-3/4" bbl.) **Grips:** One-piece walnut. **Sights:** Blade front, notch rear. **Features:** Uberti replica of 1873 Colt Model "P" revolver. Color-case hardened steel frame, brass backstrap and trigger guard, hammer block safety. Imported from Italy by Tristar Sporting Arms.
Price: Regulator **$335.00**
Price: Regulator Deluxe (blued backstrap, trigger guard) **$367.00**

UBERTI 1873 CATTLEMAN SINGLE-ACTION

Caliber: 22 LR/22 WMR, 38 Spec., 357 Mag., 44 Spec., 44-40, 45 Colt/45 ACP, 6-shot. **Barrel:** 4-3/4", 5-1/2", 7-1/2"; 44-40, 45 Colt also with 3", 3-1/2", 4". **Weight:** 38 oz. (5-1/2" bbl.). **Length:** 10-3/4" overall (5-1/2" bbl.). **Grips:** One-piece smooth walnut. **Sights:** Blade front, groove rear; fully adjustable rear available. **Features:** Steel or brass backstrap, trigger guard; color case-hardened frame, blued barrel, cylinder. Imported from Italy by Uberti U.S.A.
Price: Steel backstrap, trigger guard, fixed sights. **$410.00**
Price: Brass backstrap, trigger guard, fixed sights **$359.00**
Price: Bisley model **$435.00**

Uberti 1873 Buckhorn Single-Action

A slightly larger version of the Cattleman revolver. Available in 44 Magnum or 44 Magnum/44-40 convertible, otherwise has same specs.
Price: Steel backstrap, trigger guard, fixed sights. **$410.00**

UBERTI 1875 SA ARMY OUTLAW REVOLVER

Caliber: 357 Mag., 44-40, 45 Colt, 45 Colt/45 ACP convertible, 6-shot. **Barrel:** 5-1/2", 7-1/2". **Weight:** 44 oz. **Length:** 13-3/4" overall. **Grips:** Smooth walnut. **Sights:** Blade front, notch rear. **Features:** Replica of the 1875 Remington S.A. Army revolver. Brass trigger guard, color case-hardened frame, rest blued. Imported by Uberti U.S.A.
Price: **$483.00**
Price: 45 Colt/45 ACP convertible **$525.00**

UBERTI 1890 ARMY OUTLAW REVOLVER

Caliber: 357 Mag., 44-40, 45 Colt, 45 Colt/45 ACP convertible, 6-shot. **Barrel:** 5-1/2", 7-1/2". **Weight:** 37 oz. **Length:** 12-1/2" overall. **Grips:** American walnut. **Sights:** Blade front, groove rear. **Features:** Replica of the 1890 Remington single-action. Brass trigger guard, rest is blued. Imported by Uberti U.S.A.
Price: **$483.00**

UBERTI NEW MODEL RUSSIAN REVOLVER

Caliber: 44 Russian, 6-shot cylinder. **Barrel:** 6-1/2". **Weight:** 40 oz. **Length:** 12" overall. **Grips:** Smooth walnut. **Sights:** Blade front, notch rear. **Features:** Repica of the S&W Model 3 Russian Third Model revolver. Spur trigger guard, polished blue finish. Introduced 1999. Imported by Uberti USA.
Price: **$800.00**

UBERTI 1875 SCHOFIELD-STYLE BREAK-TOP REVOLVER

Caliber: 44-40, 45 Colt, 6-shot cylinder. **Barrel:** 5", 7". **Weight:** 39 oz. **Length:** 10-3/4" overall (5" barrel). **Grips:** Smooth walnut. **Sights:** Blade front, notch rear. **Features:** Replica of Smith & Wesson Model 3 Schofield. Single-action, top-break with automatic ejection. Polished blue finish. Introduced 1994. Imported by Uberti USA.
Price: **$750.00**

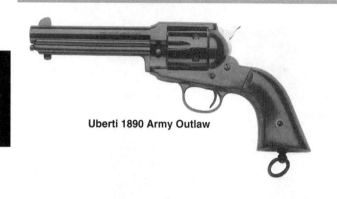

Uberti 1890 Army Outlaw

Uberti Russian

Uberti 1875 Schofield

Uberti Bisley

Uberti Bisley Flat Top

UBERTI BISLEY MODEL SINGLE-ACTION REVOLVER
Caliber: 38-40, 357 Mag., 44 Spec., 44-40 or 45 Colt, 6-shot cylinder. **Barrel:** 4-3/4", 5-1/2", 7-1/2". **Weight:** 40 oz. **Length:** 12-1/2" overall (7-1/2" barrel). **Grips:** Smooth walnut. **Sights:** Blade front, notch rear. **Features:** Replica of Colt's Bisley Model. Polished blue finish, color case-hardened frame. Introduced 1997. Imported by Uberti USA.
Price: **$435.00**

Uberti Bisley Model Flat Top Target Revolver
Similar to standard Bisley model, flat top strap, 7-1/2" barrel only, spring-loaded German silver front sight blade, standing leaf rear sight adjustable for windage. Polished blue finish, color case-hardened frame. Introduced 1998. Imported by Uberti USA.
Price: **$435.00**

U.S. FIRE ARMS SINGLE ACTION ARMY REVOLVER
Caliber: 45 Colt (standard); 32 WCF, 38 WCF, 38 S&W, 41 Colt, 44WCF, 44 S&W (optional, additional charge), 6-shot cylinder. **Barrel:** 4- 3/4", 5-1/2", 7-1/2". **Weight:** 37 oz. **Length:** NA. **Grips:** Hard rubber. **Sights:** Blade front, notch rear. **Features:** Recreation of original guns; 3" and 4" have no ejector. Available with all-blue, blue with color case-hard-ening, or full nickel-plate finish. Made in U.S.A. by United States Fire Arms Mfg. Co.
Price: Blue/cased-colors............................... **$949.00**
Price: Nickel **$1220.00**

U. S. FIRE ARMS NETTLETON CAVALRY
Caliber: 45 Colt, 6-shot cylinder. **Barrel:** 5 1/2 (Artillery model), 7 1/2 inch-es. **Grips:** One-piece walnut. **Features:** Military armory blue and bone case finish. Made in U. S. by Fire Arms Mfg. Co.
Price: Blued finish.................................... **$1,265.00**
Price: Nickel finish **$1,380.00**

U.S. FIRE ARMS RODEO COWBOY ACTION REVOLVER
Caliber: 45 Colt. **Barrel:** 4-3/4", 5-1/2". **Grips:** Rubber. **Features:** Histori-cally correct armory bone case hammer, blue satin finish, transfer bar safety system, correct solid firing pin. Entry level basic cowboy SASS gun for beginner or expert.
Price: **$649.00**

U.S. FIRE ARMS UNITED STATES PRE-WAR
Caliber: 45 Colt, other caliber available. **Barrel:** 4-3/4", 5-1/2", 7-1/2". **Grips:** Hard rubber. **Features:** Armory bone case/Armory blue finish stan-dard, cross-pin or black powder frame. Introduced 2002. Made in U.S.A. by United States Firearms Manufacturing Co.
Price: **$1,195.00**

Specially adapted single-shot and multi-barrel arms.

American Derringer Model 1

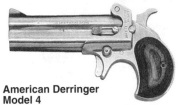

American Derringer Model 4

American Derringer Model 6

American Derringer Model 7

American Derringer Lady Derringer

American Derringer DA 38

AMERICAN DERRINGER MODEL 1

Caliber: 22 LR, 22 WMR, 30 Carbine, 30 Luger, 30-30 Win., 32 H&R Mag., 32-20, 380 ACP, 38 Super, 38 Spec., 38 Spec. shotshell, 38 Spec. +P, 9mm Para., 357 Mag., 357 Mag./45/410, 357 Maximum, 10mm, 40 S&W, 41 Mag., 38-40, 44-40 Win., 44 Spec., 44 Mag., 45 Colt, 45 Win. Mag., 45 ACP, 45 Colt/410, 45-70 single shot. **Barrel:** 3". **Weight:** 15-1/2 oz. (38 Spec.). **Length:** 4.82" overall. **Grips:** Rosewood, Zebra wood. **Sights:** Blade front. **Features:** Made of stainless steel with high-polish or satin finish. Two-shot capacity. Manual hammer block safety. Introduced 1980. Available in almost any pistol caliber. Contact the factory for complete list of available calibers and prices. From American Derringer Corp.

Price: 22 LR	**POR**
Price: 38 Spec.	**POR**
Price: 357 Maximum	**POR**
Price: 357 Mag.	**POR**
Price: 9mm, 380	**POR**
Price: 40 S&W	**POR**
Price: 44 Spec.	**POR**
Price: 44-40 Win.	**POR**
Price: 45 Colt	**POR**
Price: 30-30, 45 Win. Mag.	**POR**
Price: 41, 44 Mags.	**POR**
Price: 45-70, single shot	**POR**
Price: 45 Colt, 410, 2-1/2"	**POR**
Price: 45 ACP, 10mm Auto	**POR**

American Derringer Model 4

Similar to the Model 1 except has 4.1" barrel, overall length of 6", and weighs 16-1/2 oz.; chambered for 357 Mag., 357 Maximum, 45-70, 3" 410-bore shotshells or 45 Colt or 44 Mag. Made of stainless steel. Manual hammer block safety. Introduced 1980.

Price: 3" 410/45 Colt	$425.00
Price: 45-70	$560.00
Price: 44 Mag. with oversize grips	$515.00
Price: Alaskan Survival model (45-70 upper barrel, 410 or 45 Colt lower)	$475.00

American Derringer Model 6

Similar to the Model 1 except has 6" barrel chambered for 3" 410 shotshells or 22 WMR, 357 Mag., 45 ACP, 45 Colt; rosewood stocks; 8.2" o.a.l. and weighs 21 oz. Shoots either round for each barrel. Manual hammer block safety. Introduced 1980.

Price: 22 WMR	$440.00
Price: 357 Mag.	$440.00
Price: 45 Colt/410	$450.00
Price: 45 ACP	$440.00

American Derringer Model 7 Ultra Lightweight

Similar to Model 1 except made of high strength aircraft aluminum. Weighs 7-1/2 oz., 4.82" o.a.l., rosewood stocks. Available in 22 LR, 22 WMR, 32 H&R Mag., 380 ACP, 38 Spec., 44 Spec. Introduced 1980.

Price: 22 LR, WMR	$325.00
Price: 38 Spec.	$325.00
Price: 380 ACP	$325.00
Price: 32 H&R Mag/32 S&W Long	$325.00
Price: 44 Spec.	$565.00

American Derringer Model 10 Ultra Lightweight

Similar to the Model 1 except frame is of aluminum, giving weight of 10 oz. Stainless barrels. Available in 38 Spec., 45 Colt or 45 ACP only. Matte gray finish. Introduced 1980.

Price: 45 Colt	$385.00
Price: 45 ACP	$330.00
Price: 38 Spec.	$305.00

American Derringer Lady Derringer

Same as the Model 1 except has tuned action, is fitted with scrimshawed synthetic ivory grips; chambered for 32 H&R Mag. and 38 Spec.; 357 Mag., 45 Colt, 45/410. Deluxe Grade is highly polished; Deluxe Engraved is engraved in a pattern similar to that used on 1880s derringers. All come in a French-fitted jewelry box. Introduced 1989.

Price: 32 H&R Mag.	$375.00
Price: 357 Mag.	$405.00
Price: 38 Spec.	$360.00
Price: 45 Colt, 45/410	$435.00

American Derringer Texas Commemorative

A Model 1 Derringer with solid brass frame, stainless steel barrel and rosewood grips. Available in 38 Spec., 44-40 Win., or 45 Colt. Introduced 1980.

Price: 38 Spec.	$365.00
Price: 44-40	$420.00
Price: Brass frame, 45 Colt	$450.00

AMERICAN DERRINGER DA 38 MODEL

Caliber: 22 LR, 9mm Para., 38 Spec., 357 Mag., 40 S&W. **Barrel:** 3". **Weight:** 14.5 oz. **Length:** 4.8" overall. **Grips:** Rosewood, walnut or other hardwoods. **Sights:** Fixed. **Features:** Double-action only; two-shots. Manual safety. Made of satin-finished stainless steel and aluminum. Introduced 1989. From American Derringer Corp.

Price: 22 LR	$435.00
Price: 38 Spec.	$460.00
Price: 9mm Para.	$445.00
Price: 357 Mag.	$450.00
Price: 40 S&W	$475.00

ANSCHUTZ MODEL 64P SPORT/TARGET PISTOL

Caliber: 22 LR, 22 WMR, 5-shot magazine. **Barrel:** 10". **Weight:** 3 lbs., 8 oz. **Length:** 18-1/2" overall. **Stock:** Choate Rynite. **Sights:** None furnished; grooved for scope mounting. **Features:** Right-hand bolt; polished blue finish. Introduced 1998. Imported from Germany by AcuSport.

Price: 22 LR	$455.95
Price: 22 WMR	$479.95

HANDGUNS

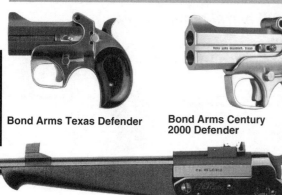

Bond Arms Texas Defender

Bond Arms Century 2000 Defender

Cobra Big Bore

Cobra D-Series

Comanche Super Single Shot

Downsizer WSP Single Shot

IAR Model 1872 Derringer

Gaucher GN1 Silhouette

BOND ARMS DEFENDER DERRINGER

Caliber: 410 Buckshot or slug, 45 Colt/45 Schofield (2.5" chamber), 45 Colt (only), 450 Bond Super/45 ACP/45 Super, 44 Mag./44 Special/44 Russian, 10mm, 40 S&W, 357 SIG, 357 Maxi-mum/357 Mag./38 Special, 357 Mag/38 Special & 38 Long Colt, 38 Short Colt, 9mm Luger (9x19), 32 H&R Mag./38 S&W Long/32 Colt New Police, 22 Mag., 22 LR., 38-40, 44-40. **Barrel:** 3", 3-1/2". **Weight:** 20-21 oz. **Length:** 5"-5-1/2". **Grips:** Exotic woods or animal horn. **Sights:** Blade front, fixed rear. **Features:** Interchangeable barrels, retracting and rebounding firing pins, cross-bolt safety, automatic extractor for rimmed calibers. Stainless steel construction. Right or left hand.
Price: Texas (with TG) 3" bbl. **$379.00**
Price: Super (with TG) 3" bbl., 450 Bond Super and 45 ACP . . . **$379.00**
Price: Cowboy (no TG) **$379.00**
Price: Century 2000 (with TG), Cowboy Century 2000 (no TG), 3-1/2" bbls., 410/45 Colt **$394.00**
Price: Additional calibers - available separately

BROWN CLASSIC SINGLE SHOT PISTOL

Caliber: 17 Ackley Hornet through 375x444. **Barrel:** 15" airgauged match grade. **Weight:** About 3 lbs., 7 oz. **Grips:** Walnut; thumbrest target style. **Sights:** None furnished; drilled and tapped for scope mounting. **Features:** Falling block action gives rigid barrel-receiver mating; hand-fit-ted and headspaced. Introduced 1998. Made in U.S.A. by E.A. Brown Mfg.
Price: **$589.00**

COBRA BIG BORE DERRINGERS

Caliber: 22 WMR, 32 H&R Mag, 38 Spec., 9mm Para. **Barrel:** 2.75". **Weight:** 11.5 oz. **Length:** 4.65" overall. **Grips:** Textured black synthetic. **Sights:** Blade front, fixed notch rear. **Features:** Alloy frame, steel-lined barrels, steel breech block. Plunger-type safety with integral hammer block. Chrome or black Teflon finish. Introduced 2002. Made in U.S.A. by Cobra Enterprises.
Price: **$98.00**
Price: 9mm Para. **$136.00**

COBRA LONG-BORE DERRINGERS

Caliber: 22 WMR, 38 Spec., 9mm Para. **Barrel:** 3.5". **Weight:** 13 oz. **Length:** 5.65" overall. **Grips:** Textured black synthetic. **Sights:** Fixed. **Features:** Chrome or black Teflon finish. Larger than Davis D-Series models. Introduced 2002. Made in U.S.A. by Cobra Enterprises.
Price: **$136.00**
Price: 9mm Para. **$136.00**
Price: Big-Bore models (same calibers, 3/4" shorter barrels) **$136.00**

COBRA STARBIRD-SERIES DERRINGERS

Caliber: 22 LR, 22 WMR, 25 ACP, 32 ACP. **Barrel:** 2.4". **Weight:** 9.5 oz. **Length:** 4" overall. **Grips:** Laminated wood or pearl. **Sights:** Blade front, fixed notch rear. **Features:** Choice of black powder coat, satin nickel or chrome finish; spur trigger. Introduced 2002. Made in U.S.A. by Cobra Enterprises.
Price: **$112.00**

COMANCHE SUPER SINGLE SHOT PISTOL

Caliber: 45 LC, 410 ga. **Barrel:** 10." **Sights:** Adjustable. **Features:** Blue finish, not available for sale in CA, MA. Distributed by SGS Importers International, Inc.
Price: **$174.95**
Price: Satin nickel **$191.95**
Price: Duo tone **$185.95**

DOWNSIZER WSP SINGLE SHOT PISTOL

Caliber: 357 Magnum, 45 ACP, 38 Special. **Barrel:** 2.10." **Weight:** 11 oz. **Length:** 3.25" overall. **Grips:** Black polymer. **Sights:** None. **Features:** Single shot, tip-up barrel. Double action only. Stainless steel construction. Measures .900" thick. Introduced 1997. From Downsizer Corp.
Price: **$499.00**

GAUCHER GN1 SILHOUETTE PISTOL

Caliber: 22 LR, single shot. **Barrel:** 10". **Weight:** 2.4 lbs. **Length:** 15.5" overall. **Grips:** European hardwood. **Sights:** Blade front, open adjustable rear. **Features:** Bolt action, adjustable trigger. Introduced 1990. Imported from France by Mandall Shooting Supplies.
Price: About **$525.00**
Price: Model GP Silhouette **$425.00**

IAR MODEL 1872 DERRINGER

Caliber: 22 Short. **Barrel:** 2-3/8". **Weight:** 7 oz. **Length:** 5-1/8" overall. **Grips:** Smooth walnut. **Sights:** Blade front, notch rear. **Features:** Gold or nickel frame with blue barrel. Reintroduced 1996 using original Colt designs and tooling for the Colt Model 4 Derringer. Made in U.S.A. by IAR, Inc.
Price: **$109.00**
Price: Single cased gun **$125.00**
Price: Double cased set **$215.00**

IAR MODEL 1866 DOUBLE DERRINGER

Caliber: 38 Special. **Barrel:** 2-3/4". **Weight:** 16 oz. **Grips:** Smooth walnut. **Sights:** Blade front, notch rear. **Features:** All steel construction. Blue barrel, color case-hardened frame. Uses original designs and tooling for the Uberti New Maverick Derringer. Introduced 1999. Made in U.S.A. by IAR, Inc.
Price: **$395.00**

HANDGUNS — MISCELLANEOUS

Maximum Single Shot

RPM XL Pistol

Thompson/Center G2 Contender

MAXIMUM SINGLE SHOT PISTOL

Caliber: 22 LR, 22 Hornet, 22 BR, 22 PPC, 223 Rem., 22-250, 6mm BR, 6mm PPC, 243, 250 Savage, 6.5mm-35M, 270 MAX, 270 Win., 7mm TCU, 7mm BR, 7mm-35, 7mm INT-R, 7mm-08, 7mm Rocket, 7mm Super-Mag., 30 Herrett, 30 Carbine, 30-30, 308 Win., 30x39, 32-20, 350 Rem. Mag., 357 Mag., 357 Maximum, 358 Win., 375 H&H, 44 Mag., 454 Casull. **Barrel:** 8-3/4", 10-1/2", 14". **Weight:** 61 oz. (10-1/2" bbl.); 78 oz. (14" bbl.). **Length:** 15", 18-1/2" overall (with 10-1/2" and 14" bbl., respectively). **Grips:** Smooth walnut stocks and forend. Also available with 17" finger groove grip. **Sights:** Ramp front, fully adjustable open rear. **Features:** Falling block action; drilled and tapped for M.O.A. scope mounts; integral grip frame/receiver; adjustable trigger; Douglas barrel (interchangeable). Introduced 1983. Made in U.S.A. by M.O.A. Corp.

Price: Stainless receiver, blue barrel	$799.00
Price: Stainless receiver, stainless barrel	$883.00
Price: Extra blued barrel	$254.00
Price: Extra stainless barrel	$317.00
Price: Scope mount	$60.00

RPM XL SINGLE SHOT PISTOL

Caliber: 22 LR through 45-70. **Barrel:** 8", 10-3/4", 12", 14". **Weight:** About 60 oz. **Grips:** Smooth Goncalo Alves with thumb and heel rests. **Sights:** Hooded front with interchangeable post, or Patridge; ISGW rear adjustable for windage and elevation. **Features:** Barrel drilled and tapped for scope mount. Visible cocking indicator. Spring-loaded barrel lock, positive hammer-block safety. Trigger adjustable for weight of pull and over-travel. Contact maker for complete price list. Made in U.S.A. by RPM.

Price: XL Hunter model (action only)	$1,045.00
Price: Extra barrel, 8" through 10-3/4"	$407.50
Price: Extra barrel, 12" through 14"	$547.50
Price: Muzzle brake	$160.00
Price: Left hand action, add	$50.00

SAVAGE STRIKER BOLT-ACTION HUNTING HANDGUN

Caliber: 223, 243, 7mm-08, 308, 300 WSM 2-shot mag. **Barrel:** 14". **Weight:** About 5 lbs. **Length:** 22-1/2" overall. **Stock:** Black composite ambidextrous mid-grip; grooved forend; "Dual Pillar" bedding. **Sights:** None furnished; drilled and tapped for scope mounting. **Features:** Short left-hand bolt with right-hand ejection; free-floated barrel; uses Savage Model 110 rifle scope rings/bases. Introduced 1998. Made in U.S.A. by Savage Arms, Inc.

Price: Model 503 (blued barrel and action)	$285.00
Price: Model 503 R17FSS (stainless barrel and action)	$281.00
Price: Model 516FSAK black stock (SS, AMB, 300WSM)	$260.00

SAVAGE SPORT STRIKER BOLT-ACTION HUNTING HANDGUN

Similar to Striker, but chambered in 22 LR and 22 WMR. Detachable, 10-shot magazine (5-shot magazine for 22 WMR). Overall length 19", weighs 4 lbs. Ambidextrous fiberglass/graphite composite rear grip. Drilled and tapped, scope mount installed. Introduced 2000. Made in U.S.A. by Savage Arms Inc.

Price: Model 501F (blue finish, 22LR)	$236.00
Price: Model 501FXP with soft case, 1.25-4x28 scope	$258.00
Price: Model 502F (blue finish, 22 WMR)	$238.00

SPRINGFIELD M6 SCOUT PISTOL

Caliber: 22 LR/45 LC/.410, 22 Hornet, 45 LC/.410. **Barrel:** 10". **Weight:** NA. **Length:** NA. **Grips:** NA. **Sights:** NA. **Features:** Adapted from the U.S. Air Force M6 Survival Rifle, it is also available as a carbine with 16" barrel.

Price:	$169.00 to $197.00
Price: Pistol/Carbine	$183.00 to $209.00

THOMPSON/CENTER ENCORE PISTOL

Caliber: 22-250, 223, 260 Rem., 7mm-08, 243, 308, 270, 30-06, 375 JDJ, 204 Ruger, 44 Mag., 454 Casull, 480 Ruger, 444 Marlin single shot, 450 Marlin with muzzle tamer, no sights. **Barrel:** 12", 15", tapered round. **Weight:** NA. **Length:** 21" overall with 12" barrel. **Grips:** American walnut with finger grooves, walnut forend. **Sights:** Blade on ramp front, adjustable rear, or none. **Features:** Interchangeable barrels; action opens by squeezing the trigger guard; drilled and tapped for scope mounting; blue finish. Announced 1996. Made in U.S.A. by Thompson/Center Arms.

Price:	$578.00 to $641.00
Price: Extra 12" barrels	$260.00
Price: Extra 15" barrels	$267.00
Price: 45 Colt/410 barrel, 12"	$289.00
Price: 45 Colt/410 barrel, 15"	$297.00

Thompson/Center Stainless Encore Pistol

Similar to blued Encore, made of stainless steel, available with 15" barrel in 223, 22-250, 243 Win., 7mm-08, 308, 30/06 Sprgfld., 45/70 Gov't., 45/410 VR. With black rubber grip and forend. Made in U.S.A. by Thompson/Center Arms.

Price:	$633.00 to $670.00

Thompson/Center G2 Contender Pistol

A second generation Contender pistol maintaining the same barrel interchangeability with older Contender barrels and their corresponding forends (except Herrett forend). The G2 frame will not accept old-style grips due to the change in grip angle. Incorporates an automatic hammer block safety with built-in interlock. Features include trigger adjustable for overtravel, adjustable rear sight; ramp front sight blade, blued steel finish.

Price:	$566.75

UBERTI ROLLING BLOCK TARGET PISTOL

Caliber: 22 LR, 22 WMR, 22 Hornet, 357 Mag., 45 Colt, single shot. **Barrel:** 9-7/8", half-round, half-octagon. **Weight:** 44 oz. **Length:** 14" overall. **Stock:** Walnut grip and forend. **Sights:** Blade front, fully adjustable rear. **Features:** Replica of the 1871 rolling block target pistol. Brass trigger guard, color case-hardened frame, blue barrel. Imported by Uberti U.S.A.

Price:	$410.00

Both classic arms and recent designs in American-style repeaters for sport and field shooting.

Armalite M15A2

Armalite AR-10A4

Armalite AR-180B

Auto-Ordnance 1927 A-1 Thompson

ARMALITE M15A2 CARBINE

Caliber: 223, 7-shot magazine. **Barrel:** 16" heavy chrome lined; 1:9" twist. **Weight:** 7 lbs. **Length:** 35-11/16" overall. **Stock:** Green or black composition. **Sights:** Standard A2. **Features:** Upper and lower receivers have push-type pivot pin; hard coat anodized; A2-style forward assist; M16A2-type raised fence around magazine release button. Made in U.S.A. by ArmaLite, Inc.

Price: Green **$930.00**
Price: Black **$945.00**

ARMALITE AR-10A4 SPECIAL PURPOSE RIFLE

Caliber: 308 Win., 10-shot magazine. **Barrel:** 20" chrome-lined, 1:12" twist. **Weight:** 9.6 lbs. **Length:** 41" overall **Stock:** Green or black composition. **Sights:** Detachable handle, front sight, or scope mount available; comes with international style flattop receiver with Picatinny rail. **Features:** Proprietary recoil check. Forged upper receiver with case deflector. Receivers are hard-coat anodized. Introduced 1995. Made in U.S.A. by ArmaLite, Inc.

Price: Green **$1,383.00**
Price: Black **$1,383.00**
Price: Green or black with match trigger **$1,483.00**
Price: Green or Black with match trigger and stainless barrel . . **$1,583.00**

Armalite AR-10(T)

Similar to the Armalite AR-10A4 but with stainless steel, barrel, machined tool steel, two-stage National Match trigger group and other features.
Price: AR-10(T) Rifle **$2,080.00**
Price: AR-10(T) Carbine **$2,080.00**

Armalite AR-10A2

Utilizing the same 20" double-lapped, heavy barrel as the Armalite AR-10A4 Special Purpose Rifle, the AR-10A2 has a clamping front sight base allowing the removeable front sight to be rotated to zero the front sight. This assures the rear sight is centered and full left and right windage movement is available when shooting in strong winds. Offered in 308 caliber only. Made in U.S.A. by Armalite, Inc.

Price: AR-10A2 Rifle or Carbine **$1,435.00**
Price: AR-10A2 Rifle or Carbine with match trigger **$1,535.00**
Price: AR-10A2 Rifle with stainless steel barrel **$1,535.00**

ARMALITE AR-180B RIFLE

Caliber: 223, 10-shot magazine. **Barrel:** 19.8" **Weight:** 6 lbs. **Length:** 38". **Stock:** Synthetic. **Sights:** Rear sight adjustable for windage, small and large apertures. **Features:** Lower receiver made of polymer, upper formed of sheet metal. Uses standard AR-15 magazines. Made in U.S.A. by Armalite. **Price:** **$650.00**
Price: With match trigger **$750.00**

ARSENAL USA SSR-56

Caliber: 7.62x39mm **Barrel:** 16.25" **Weight:** 7.4 lbs. **Length:** 35.5" **Stock:** Black polymer. **Sights:** Adjustable rear. **Features:** An AK-47 style rifle built on a hardened Hungarian FEG receiver with the required six U.S. made parts to make it legal for use with all extra-capacity magazines. From Arsenal I, LLC.
Price: **$565.00**

CENTERFIRE RIFLES — AUTOLOADERS

Barrett Model 82A-1

Browning Mark II Safari

ARSENAL USA SSR-74-2
Caliber: 5.45x39mm **Barrel:** 16.25" **Weight:** 7 lbs. **Length:** 36.75" **Stock:** Polymer or wood. **Sights:** Adjustable. **Features:** Built with parts from an unissued Bulgarian AK-74 rifle, it has a Buffer Technologies recoil buffer, and enough U.S.-made parts to allow pistol grip stock, and use with all extra-capacity magazines. Assembled in U.S.A. From Arsenal I, LLC.
Price: **$499.00**

ARSENAL USA SSR-85C-2
Caliber: 7.62x39mm **Barrel:** 16.25" **Weight:** 7.1 lbs. **Length:** 35.5" **Stock:** Polymer or wood. **Sights:** Adjustable rear calibrated to 800 meters. **Features:** Built from parts obtained from unissued Polish AK-47 rifles, the gas tube is vented and the receiver cover is plain. Rifle contains enough U.S.-sourced parts to allow pistol grip stock and use with all extra-capacity magazines. Assembled in U.S.A. by Arsenal USA I, LLC.
Price: **$499.00**

AUTO-ORDNANCE 1927 A-1 THOMPSON
Caliber: 45 ACP. **Barrel:** 16-1/2". **Weight:** 13 lbs. **Length:** About 41" overall (Deluxe). **Stock:** Walnut stock and vertical forend. **Sights:** Blade front, open rear adjustable for windage. **Features:** Recreation of Thompson Model 1927. Semi-auto only. Deluxe model has finned barrel, adjustable rear sight and compensator; Standard model has plain barrel and military sight. From Auto-Ordnance Corp.
Price: Deluxe **$950.00**
Price: 1927A1C Lightweight model (9-1/2 lbs.) **$950.00**

Auto-Ordnance Thompson M1/M1-C
Similar to the 1927 A-1 except is in the M-1 configuration with side cocking knob, horizontal forend, smooth unfinned barrel, sling swivels on butt and forend. Matte black finish. Introduced 1985.
Price: M1 semi-auto carbine............................ **$950.00**
Price: M1-C lightweight semi-auto **$925.00**

Auto-Ordnance 1927A1 Commando
Similar to the 1927A1 except has Parkerized finish, black-finish wood butt, pistol grip, horizontal forend. Comes with black nylon sling. Introduced 1998. Made in U.S.A. by Auto-Ordnance Corp.
Price: **$950.00**

BARRETT MODEL 82A-1 SEMI-AUTOMATIC RIFLE
Caliber: 50 BMG, 10-shot detachable box magazine. **Barrel:** 29". **Weight:** 28.5 lbs. **Length:** 57" overall. **Stock:** Composition with energy-absorbing

recoil pad. **Sights:** Scope optional. **Features:** Semi-automatic, recoil operated with recoiling barrel. Three-lug locking bolt; muzzle brake. Adjustable bipod. Introduced 1985. Made in U.S.A. by Barrett Firearms.
Price: From **$7,200.00**

BENELLI RI RIFLE
Caliber: 300 Win. Mag., 30-06 Springfield. **Barrel:** 20", 22", 24". **Weight:** 7.1 lbs. **Length:** 43.75" **Stock:** Select satin walnut. **Sights:** None. **Features:** Auto-regulating gas-operated system, three-lugged rotary bolt, interchangeable barrels. Introduced 2003. Imported from Italy by Benelli USA.
Price: .... **$1065.00 to $1,080.00**

BROWNING BAR MARK II SAFARI SEMI-AUTO RIFLE
Caliber: 243, 25-06, 270, 30-06, 308, 270 WSM, 7mm WSM. **Barrel:** 22" round tapered. **Weight:** 7-3/8 lbs. **Length:** 43" overall. **Stock:** French walnut pistol grip stock and forend, hand checkered. **Sights:** Gold bead on hooded ramp front, click adjustable rear, or no sights. **Features:** Has new bolt release lever; removable trigger assembly with larger trigger guard; redesigned gas and buffer systems. Detachable 4-round box magazine. Scroll-engraved receiver is tapped for scope mounting. BOSS barrel vibration modulator and muzzle brake system available only on models without sights. Mark II Safari introduced 1993. Imported from Belgium by Browning.
Price: Safari, with sights **$833.00**
Price: Safari, no sights **$815.00**
Price: Safari, 270 and 30-06, no sights, BOSS............. **$891.00**

Browning BAR Mark II Safari Rifle (Magnum)
Same as the standard caliber model, except weighs 8-3/8 lbs., 45" overall, 24" bbl., 3-round mag. Cals. 7mm Mag., 300 Win. Mag., 338 Win. Mag. BOSS barrel vibration modulator and muzzle brake system available only on models without sights. Introduced 1993.
Price: Safari, no sights **$908.00**
Price: Safari, no sights, BOSS **$1,007.00**

BROWNING BAR SHORT TRAC/LONG TRAC AUTO RIFLES
Caliber: (Short Trac models): 270 WSM, 7mm WSM, 300 WSM, 243 Win., 308 Win.; (Long Trac models) 270 Win., 30-06 Sprfld., 7mm Rem. Mag., 300 Win. Mag. **Barrel:** 23". **Weight:** 6 lbs., 10 oz. to 7 lbs., 4 oz. **Length:** 41 1/2" to 44". **Stock:** Satin-finish walnut, pistol-grip, fluted forend. **Sights:** Adj. rear, bead front standard, no sights on BOSS models (optional). **Features:** Designed to handle new WSM chamberings. Gas-operated, blued finish, rotary bolt design (Long Trac models)
Price: Short Trac, WSM calibers **$902.00**
Price: Short Trac, 243, 308 .... **$827.00**
Price: Long Trac calibers .... **$827.00 to 902.00**

NEW!

Bushmaster M17S Bullpup

Bushmaster XM15 E2S Carbine

Bushmaster Varminter

Colt Match Target Lightweight

BROWNING BAR STALKER AUTO RIFLES

Caliber: 243, 308, 270, 30-06, 7mm Rem. Mag., 300 Win. Mag., 338 Win. Mag., 270 WSM, 7mm WSM. **Barrel:** 20", 22" and 24". **Weight:** 6 lbs., 12 oz. (243) to 8 lbs., 2 oz. (magnum cals.) **Length:** 41" to 45" overall. **Stock:** Black composite stock and forearm. **Sights:** Hooded front and adjustable rear or none. **Features:** Optional BOSS (no sights); gas-operated action with seven-lug rotary bolt; dual action bars; 3- or 4-shot magazine (depending on caliber). Introduced 2001. Imported by Browning.
Price: BAR Stalker, open sights (243, 308, 270, 30-06) **$825.00**
Price: BAR Stalker, open sights (7mm, 300 Win. Mag.,
338 Win. Mag.) **$901.00**

BUSHMASTER M17S BULLPUP RIFLE

Caliber: 223, 10-shot magazine. **Barrel:** 21.5", chrome lined;1:9" twist. **Weight:** 8.2 lbs. **Length:** 30" overall. **Stock:** Fiberglass-filled nylon. **Sights:** Designed for optics-carrying handle incorporates scope mount rail for Weaver-type rings; also includes 25-meter open iron sights. **Features:** Gas-operated, short-stroke piston system; ambidextrous magazine release. Introduced 1993. Made in U.S.A. by Bushmaster Firearms, Inc./Quality Parts Co.
Price: **$765.00**

BUSHMASTER SHORTY XM15 E2S CARBINE

Caliber: 223,10-shot magazine. **Barrel:** 16", heavy; 1:9" twist. **Weight:** 7.2 lbs. **Length:** 34.75" overall. **Stock:** A2 type; fixed black composition. **Sights:** Fully adjustable M16A2 sight system. **Features:** Patterned after Colt M-16A2. Chrome-lined barrel with manganese phosphate finish. "Shorty" handguards. Has forged aluminum receivers with push-pin. Made in U.S.A. by Bushmaster Firearms Inc.
Price: (A2) **$985.00**
Price: (A3) **$1,085.00**

Bushmaster XM15 E2S Dissipator Carbine

Similar to the XM15 E2S Shorty carbine except has full-length "Dissipator" handguards. Weighs 7.6 lbs.; 34.75" overall; forged aluminum receivers with push-pin style takedown. Made in U.S.A. by Bushmaster Firearms, Inc.
Price: (A2 type) **$995.00**
Price: (A3 type) **$1,095.00**

Bushmaster XM15 E25 AK Shorty Carbine

Similar to the XM15 E2S Shorty except has 14.5" barrel with an AK muzzle brake permanently attached giving 16" barrel length. Weighs 7.3 lbs. Introduced 1999. Made in U.S.A. by Bushmaster Firearms, Inc.
Price: (A2 type) **$1,005.00**
Price: (A3 type) **$1,105.00**

Bushmaster M4/M4A3 Post-Ban Carbine

Similar to the XM15 E2S except has 14.5" barrel with Mini Y compensator, and fixed tele-stock. MR configuration has fixed carry handle; M4A3 has removeable carry handle.
Price: (M4) **$1,065.00**
Price: (M4A3) **$1,165.00**

BUSHMASTER VARMINTER RIFLE

Caliber: 223 Rem., 5-shot. **Barrel:** 24", 1:9" twist, fluted, heavy, stainless. **Weight:** 8/3/4 lbs. **Length:** 42-1/4". **Stock:** Rubberized pistol grip. **Sights:** 1/2" scope risers. **Features:** Gas-operated, semi-auto, 2 stage trigger, slotted free floater forend, lockable hard case.
Price: **$1,245.00**

COLT MATCH TARGET RIFLE

Caliber: 223 Rem., 5-shot magazine. **Barrel:** 16.1" or 20". **Weight:** 7.1 to 8-1/2 lbs. **Length:** 34-1/2" to 39" overall. **Stock:** Composition stock, grip, forend. **Sights:** Post front, rear adjustable for windage and elevation. **Features:** 5-round detachable box magazine, flash suppressor, sling swivels. Forward bolt assist included. Introduced 1991. Made in U.S.A. by Colt's Manufacturing Co. Inc.
Price: Colt Light Rifle **$779.00**
Price: Match Target HBAR, from **$1,194.00**

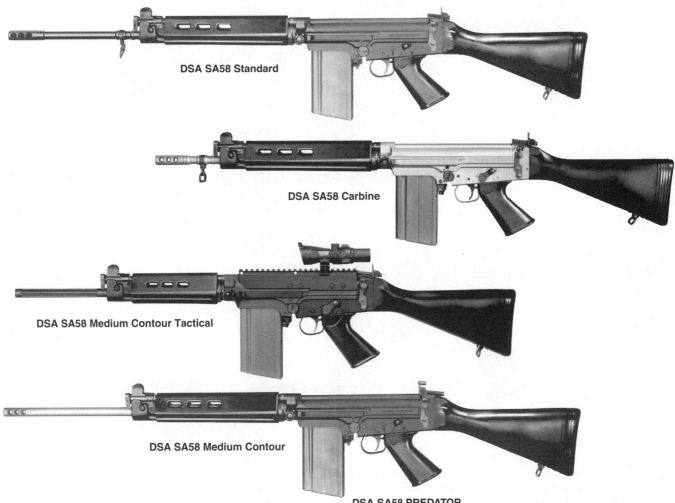

DSA SA58 Standard

DSA SA58 Carbine

DSA SA58 Medium Contour Tactical

DSA SA58 Medium Contour

DPMS PANTHER ARMS A-15 RIFLES

Caliber: 223 Rem., 7.62x39. **Barrel:** 16" to 24". **Weight:** 7-3/4 to 11-3/4 lbs. **Length:** 34-1/2 to 42-1/4" overall. **Stock:** Black Zytel® composite. **Sights:** Square front post, adjustable A2 rear. **Features:** Steel or stainless steel heavy or bull barrel; hard-coat anodized receiver; aluminum free-float tube handguard; many options. From DPMS Panther Arms.
Price: Panther Bull A-15 (20" stainless bull barrel) **$915.00**
Price: Panther Bull Twenty-Four (24" stainless bull barrel) **$945.00**
Price: Bulldog (20" stainless fluted barrel, flat top receiver) **$1,219.00**
Price: Panther Bull Sweet Sixteen (16" stainless bull barrel) **$885.00**
Price: DCM Panther (20" stainless heavy bbl., n.m. sights) **$1,099.00**
Price: Panther 7.62x39 (20" steel heavy barrel) **$849.00**

DSA SA58 CONGO, PARA CONGO

Caliber: 308 Win. **Barrel:** 18" w/short muzzle brake. **Weight:** 8.6 lbs. (Congo); 9.85 lbs. (Para Congo). **Length:** 39.75" **Stock:** Synthetic w/military grade furniture (Congo); Synthetic with non-folding steel para stock (Para Congo). **Sights:** Post, front, windage adjustable peep, rear (Congo); Belgian style para flip peep, rear (Para Congo). **Features:** Fully-adjustable gas system, high-grade steel upper receiver with carry handle. Made in U.S.A. by DSA, Inc.
Price: . . . . **$1,695.00** (Congo); **$1,995.00** (Para Congo)

DSA SA58 GRAY WOLF

Caliber: 308 Win., 300 WSM. **Barrel:** 21" match-grade bull w/target crown. **Weight:** 13 lbs. **Length:** 41.75" **Stock:** Synthetic. **Sights:** Elevation adjustable post, front; windage adjustable match peep, rear. **Features:** Fully-adjustable gas system, high-grade steel upper receiver, Picatinny scope mount, DuraCoat finish. Made in U.S.A. by DSA, Inc.
Price: **$2,120.00**

DSA SA58 PREDATOR

Caliber: 260 Rem., 243 Win., 308 Win. **Barrel:** 16" and 19" w/target crown. **Weight:** 9 to 9.3 lbs. **Length:** 36.25" to 39.25". **Stock:** Synthetic. **Sights:** Elevation adjustable post, front; windage adjustable match peep, rear. **Features:** Fully-adjustable gas system, high-grade steel upper receiver, Picatinny scope mount, DuraCoat solid and camo finishes.
Price: . . . . **$1,595.00** (308 win.); **$1,695.00** (243 Win., 260 Rem.)

DSA SA58 T48

Caliber: 308 Win. **Barrel:** 16.25" with Browning replica flash hider. **Weight:** 9.3 lbs. **Length:** 44.5". **Stock:** European walnut. **Sights:** Adjustable post front, adjustable rear peep. **Features:** Gas-operated semi-auto with fully adjustable gas system, high grade steel upper receiver. DuraCoat finishes. Made in U.S.A. by DSA, Inc.
Price: **$1,795.00**

DSA SA58 GI

Similar to the SA58 T48, except has steel bipod cut handguard with hardwood stock and synthetic pistol grip, original GI steel lower receiver with GI bipod. Made in U.S.A. by DSA, Inc.
Price: **$1,695.00**

DSA SA58 TACTICAL CARBINE, CARBINE

Caliber: 308 Win., limited 243 and 260. **Barrel:** 16.25" with integrally machined muzzle brake. **Weight:** 8.75 lbs. **Length:** 38.25". **Stock:** Fiberglass reinforced synthetic handguard. **Sights:** Adjustable post front, adjustable rear peep. **Features:** Gas-operated semi-auto with fully adjustable gas system, high grade steel or 416 stainless upper receiver. In variety of camo finishes. Made in U.S.A. by DSA, Inc.
Price: Tactical Fluted bbl. **$1,475.00**
Price: Carbine stainless steel bbl. **$1,645.00**
Price: Carbine high-grade steel bbl. **$1,395.00**

DSA SA58 Bull

DSA SA58 T48

DSA SA58 OSW

Heckler & Koch USC

DSA SA58 MEDIUM CONTOUR

Caliber: 308 Win., limited 243 and 260. **Barrel:** 21" with integrally machined muzzle brake. **Weight:** 9.75 lbs. **Length:** 43". **Stock:** Fiberglass reinforced synthetic handguard. **Sights:** Adjustable post front with match rear peep. **Features:** Gas-operated semi-auto with fully adjustable gas system, high grade steel or 416 stainless upper receiver. In variety of camo finishes. Made in U.S.A. by DSA, Inc.

Price: chrome moly	**$1,475.00**
Price: stainless steel	**$1,725.00**

DSA SA58 21" OR 24" BULL BARREL RIFLE

Caliber: 308 Win., 300 WSM. **Barrel:** 21" or 24". **Weight:** 11.1 and 11.5 lbs. **Length:** 41.5" and 44.5". **Stock:** Synthetic, free floating handguard. **Sights:** Elevation adjustable protected post front, match rear peep. **Features:** Gas-operated semi-auto with fully adjustable gas system, high grade steel or stainless upper receiver. Made in U.S.A. by DSA, Inc.

Price: 21", 24"	**$1,745.00**
Price: 24" fluted bbl.	**$1,795.00**

DSA SA58 MINI OSW

Caliber: 7.62 NATO. **Barrel:** 11" or 13" with muzzle brake. **Weight:** 9 to 9.35 lbs. **Length:** 33". **Stock:** Synthetic. **Features:** Gas-operated semi-auto or select fire with fully adjustable short gas system, optional FAL Rail Interface Handguard, SureFire Vertical Foregrip System, EOTech HOLOgraphic Sight and ITC Cheekrest. Made in U.S.A. by DSA, Inc.

Price:	**$1,525.00**

EAA/SAIGA SEMI-AUTO RIFLE

Caliber: 7.62x39, 308, 223. **Barrel:** 20.5", 22", 16.3". **Weight:** 7 to 8-1/2 lbs. **Length:** 43". **Stock:** Synthetic or wood. **Sights:** Adjustable, sight base. **Features:** Based on AK Combat rifle by Kalashnikov. Imported from Russia by EAA Corp.

Price: 7.62x39 (syn.)	**$239.00**
Price: 308 (syn. or wood)	**$429.00**
Price: 223 (syn.)	**$389.00**

EAGLE ARMS AR-10 RIFLE

Caliber: 308. **Barrel:** 20", 24". **Weight:** NA **Length:** NA **Stock:** Synthetic. **Sights:** Adjustable A2, front, Std. A2, rear; Flat top and Match Rifle have no sights but adjustable Picatinny rail furnished. **Features:** A product of the latest in manufacturing technology to provide a quality rifle at a reasonable price. Introduced 2003. Made in U.S.A. by Eagle Arms.

Price: AR-10 Service Rifle	**$1,055.00**
Price: AR-10 Flat Top Rifle	**$999.95**
Price: AR-10 Match Rifle	**$1,480.00**

EAGLE ARMS M15 RIFLE

Caliber: 223. **Barrel:** 16", 20". **Weight:** NA **Length:** NA **Stock:** Synthetic. **Sights:** Adjustable A2, front; Std. A2, rear; Flat Top Rifle & Carbine versions, no sights furnished. **Features:** Available in 4 different configurations, the latest manufacturing technology has been employed to keep the price reasonable. Introduced 2003. Made in U.S.A. by Eagle Arms.

Price: A2 Rifle	**$795.00**
Price: A2 Carbine	**$795.00**
Price: Flat Top Rifle	**$835.00**
Price: Flat Top Carbine	**$835.00**

HECKLER & KOCH USC CARBINE

Caliber: 45 ACP, 10-shot magazine. **Barrel:** 16". **Weight:** 8.6 lb. **Length:** 35.4" overall. **Stock:** Skeletonized polymer thumbhole. **Sights:** Blade front with integral hood, fully adjustable diopter. **Features:** Based on German UMP submachine gun. Blowback operation; almost entirely constructed of carbon fiber-reinforced polymer. Free-floating heavy target barrel. Introduced 2000. From H&K.

Price:	**$1,249.00**

Hi-Point Carbine

Remington Model 7400

RIFLES

HI-POINT 9MM CARBINE

Caliber: 9mm Para., 40 S&W, 10-shot magazine. **Barrel:** 16-1/2" (17-1/2" for 40 S&W). **Weight:** 4-1/2 lbs. **Length:** 31-1/2" overall. **Stock:** Black polymer, camouflage. **Sights:** Protected post front, aperture rear. Integral scope mount. **Features:** Grip-mounted magazine release. Black or chrome finish. Sling swivels. Available with laser or red dot sights. Introduced 1996. Made in U.S.A. by MKS Supply, Inc.

Price: Black or chrome, 9mm $199.00
Price: 40 S&W $225.00
Price: Camo stock. $210.00

IAI M-333 M1 GARAND

Caliber: 30-06, 8-shot clip. **Barrel:** 24". **Weight:** 9-1/2 lbs. **Length:** 43.6" overall. **Stock:** Hardwood. **Sights:** Blade front, aperture adjustable rear. **Features:** Parkerized finish; gas-operated semi-automatic; remanufactured to military specifications. From IAI.

Price: $971.75

IAI M-888 M1 CARBINE SEMI-AUTOMATIC RIFLE

Caliber: 22, 30 Carbine. **Barrel:** 18"-20". **Weight:** 5-1/2 lbs. **Length:** 35"-37" overall. **Stock:** Laminate, walnut or birch. **Sights:** Blade front, adjustable rear. **Features:** Gas-operated, air cooled, manufactured to military specifications. 10/15/30 rnd. mag. scope available. From IAI.

Price: 30 cal. . . . . $556.00 to $604.00
Price: 22 cal. . . . . $567.00 to $654.00

Intrac Arms IAI-65 Rifle

A civilian-legal version of the original HKM rifle manufactured in Hungary. Manufactured by Gordon Technologies using an original AMD-65 matching parts kit built on an AKM receiver. The original wire stock is present, but it is welded in the open position as per BATF regulations. Furnished with a 12.6" barrel with large weld-in-place muzzle brake to bring its length over the 16" federal minimum. This rifle accepts all 7.62x39mm magazines and drums. Introduced 2002. From Intrac Arms International, Inc.

Price: $799.00

LES BAER CUSTOM ULTIMATE AR 223 RIFLES

Caliber: 223. **Barrel:** 18", 20", 22", 24". **Weight:** 7-3/4 to 9-3/4 lb. **Length:** NA. **Stock:** Black synthetic. **Sights:** None furnished; Picatinny-style flat top rail for scope mounting. **Features:** Forged receiver; Ultra single-stage trigger (Jewell two-stage trigger optional); titanium firing pin; Versa-Pod bipod; chromed National Match carrier; stainless steel, hand-lapped and cryo-treated barrel; guaranteed to shoot 1/2 or 3/4 MOA, depending on model. Made in U.S.A. by Les Baer Custom Inc.

Price: Super Varmint Model $1,989.00
Price: M4 Flattop Model $2,195.00
Price: IPSC Action Model $2,195.00

LR 300 SR LIGHT SPORT RIFLE

Caliber: 223. **Barrel:** 16-1/4"; 1:9" twist. **Weight:** 7.2 lbs. **Length:** 36" overall (extended stock), 26-1/4" (stock folded). **Stock:** Folding, tubular steel, with thumbhold-type grip. **Sights:** Trijicon post front, Trijicon rear. **Features:** Uses AR-15 type upper and lower receivers; flattop receiver with weaver base. Accepts all AR-15/M-16 magazines. Introduced 1996. Made in U.S.A. from Z-M Weapons.

Price: $2,550.00

OLYMPIC ARMS CAR-97 RIFLES

Caliber: 223, 7-shot; 9mm Para., 45 ACP, 40 S&W, 10mm, 10-shot. **Barrel:** 16". **Weight:** 7 lbs. **Length:** 34.75" overall. **Stock:** A2 stowaway grip, telescoping-look butt. **Sights:** Post front, fully adjustable aperature rear. **Features:** Based on AR-15 rifle. Post-ban version of the CAR-15. Made in U.S.A. by Olympic Arms, Inc.

Price: 223 . . . . $780.00
Price: 9mm Para., 45 ACP, 40 S&W, 10mm $840.00
Price: PCR Eliminator (223, full-length handguards) $803.00

OLYMPIC ARMS PCR-4 RIFLE

Caliber: 223, 10-shot magazine. **Barrel:** 20". **Weight:** 8 lbs., 5 oz. **Length:** 38.25" overall. **Stock:** A2 stowaway grip, trapdoor buttstock. **Sights:** Post front, A1 rear adjustable for windage. **Features:** Based on the AR-15 rifle. Barrel is button rifled with 1:9" twist. No bayonet lug. Introduced 1994. Made in U.S.A. by Olympic Arms, Inc.

Price: $792.00

OLYMPIC ARMS PCR-6 RIFLE

Caliber: 7.62x39mm (PCR-6), 10-shot magazine. **Barrel:** 16". **Weight:** 7 lbs. **Length:** 34" overall. **Stock:** A2 stowaway grip, trapdoor buttstock. **Sights:** Post front, A1 rear adjustable for windage. **Features:** Based on the CAR-15. No bayonet lug. Button-cut rifling. Introduced 1994. Made in U.S.A. by Olympic Arms, Inc.

Price: $845.00

REMINGTON MODEL 7400 AUTO RIFLE

Caliber: 243 Win., 270 Win., 308 Win., 30-06, 4-shot magazine. **Barrel:** 22" round tapered. **Weight:** 7-1/2 lbs. **Length:** 42-5/8" overall. **Stock:** Walnut, deluxe cut checkered pistol grip and forend. Satin or high-gloss finish. **Sights:** Gold bead front sight on ramp; step rear sight with windage adjustable. **Features:** Redesigned and improved version of the Model 742. Positive cross-bolt safety. Receiver tapped for scope mount. Introduced 1981.

Price: $624.00
Price: Carbine (18-1/2" bbl., 30-06 only) $624.00
Price: With black synthetic stock, matte black metal,
rifle or carbine $520.00
Price: Weathermaster, nickel-plated w/synthetic stock and forend,
270, 30-06. . . . . $624.00

ROCK RIVER ARMS STANDARD A2 RIFLE

Caliber: 45 ACP. **Barrel:** NA. **Weight:** 8.2 lbs. **Length:** NA. **Stock:** Thermoplastic. **Sights:** Standard AR-15 style sights. **Features:** Two-stage, national match trigger; optional muzzle brake. Made in U.S.A. From River Rock Arms.

Price: $925.00

Ruger Deerfield 99/44 Carbine

Ruger PC4 Carbine

Ruger Ranch Mini 14/5R

Springfield M1A

RUGER DEERFIELD 99/44 CARBINE

Caliber: 44 Mag., 4-shot rotary magazine. **Barrel:** 18-1/2". **Weight:** 6-1/4 lbs. **Length:** 36-7/8" overall. **Stock:** Hardwood. **Sights:** Gold bead front, folding adjustable aperture rear. **Features:** Semi-automatic action; dual front-locking lugs lock directly into receiver; integral scope mount; push-button safety; includes 1" rings and gun lock. Introduced 2000. Made in U.S.A. by Sturm, Ruger & Co.
Price: $675.00

RUGER PC4, PC9 CARBINES

Caliber: 9mm Para., 40 cal., 10-shot magazine. **Barrel:** 16.25". **Weight:** 6 lbs., 4 oz. **Length:** 34.75" overall. **Stock:** Black high impact synthetic checkered grip and forend. **Sights:** Blade front, open adjustable rear; integral Ruger scope mounts. **Features:** Delayed blowback action; manual push-button cross bolt safety and internal firing pin block safety automatic slide lock. Introduced 1997. Made in U.S.A. by Sturm, Ruger & Co.
Price: PC9, PC4, (9mm, 40 cal.) $605.00
Price: PC4GR, PC9GR, (40 auto, 9mm, post sights, ghost ring) $628.00

RUGER MINI-14/5 AUTOLOADING RIFLE

Caliber: 223 Rem., 5-shot detachable box magazine. **Barrel:** 18-1/2". Rifling twist 1:9". **Weight:** 6.4 lbs. **Length:** 37-1/4" overall. **Stock:** American hardwood, steel reinforced. **Sights:** Ramp front, fully adjustable rear. **Features:** Fixed piston gas-operated, positive primary extraction. New buffer system, redesigned ejector system. Ruger S100RM scope rings included on Ranch Rifle.
Price: Mini-14/5R, Ranch Rifle, blued, scope rings. $695.00
Price: K-Mini-14/5R, Ranch Rifle, stainless, scope rings.. . . . . . $770.00
Price: Mini-14/5, blued.. . . . . $655.00
Price: K-Mini-14/5, stainless. $715.00
Price: K-Mini-14/5P, stainless, synthetic stock.. . . . . $715.00
Price: K-Mini-14/5RP, Ranch Rifle, stainless, synthetic stock. . . . $770.00

RUGER MINI THIRTY RIFLE

Similar to the Mini-14 Ranch Rifle except modified to chamber the 7.62x39 Russian service round. Weight is about 6-7/8 lbs. Has 6-groove barrel with 1:10" twist, Ruger Integral Scope Mount bases and folding peep rear sight. Detachable 5-shot staggered box magazine. Blued finish. Introduced 1987.
Price: Blue, scope rings $695.00
Price: Stainless, scope rings $770.00

SPRINGFIELD, INC. M1A RIFLE

Caliber: 7.62mm NATO (308), 5- or 10-shot box magazine. **Barrel:** 25-1/16" with flash suppressor, 22" without suppressor. **Weight:** 9-3/4 lbs. **Length:** 44-1/4" overall. **Stock:** American walnut with walnut-colored heat-resistant fiberglass handguard. Matching walnut handguard available. Also available with fiberglass stock. **Sights:** Military, square blade front, full click-adjustable aperture rear. **Features:** Commercial equivalent of the U.S. M-14 service rifle with no provision for automatic firing. From Springfield, Inc.
Price: Standard M1A, black fiberglass stock $1,319.00
Price: Standard M1A, black fiberglass stock, stainless $1,629.00
Price: Standard M1A, black stock, carbon barrel $1,379.00
Price: Standard M1A, Mossy Oak stock, carbon barrel $1,443.00
Price: Scout Squad M1A . . . . $1,529 to $1,639.00
Price: National Match . . . . $1,995.00 to $2,040.00
Price: Super Match (heavy premium barrel), about $2,449.00
Price: M21 Tactical Rifle (adj. cheekpiece), about $2,975.00
Price: M25 White Feather Tactical Rifle $4,195.00

SPRINGFIELD M1 GARAND RIFLE

Caliber: 308, 30-06. **Barrel:** 24". **Weight:** 9.5 lbs. **Length:** 43-3/5". **Stock:** Walnut. **Sights:** Military aperture with MOA adjustments for both windage and elevation, rear; military square post, front. **Features:** Original U.S. government-issue parts on a new walnut stock.
Price: . . . . $1,099 to $1,129.00

Springfield National Match M1A

Springfield Super Match with Camo M1A

STONER SR-15 M-5 RIFLE

Caliber: 223. **Barrel:** 20". **Weight:** 7.6 lbs. **Length:** 38" overall. **Stock:** Black synthetic. **Sights:** Post front, fully adjustable rear (300-meter sight). **Features:** Modular weapon system; two-stage trigger. Black finish. Introduced 1998. Made in U.S.A. by Knight's Mfg.
Price: $1,650.00
Price: M-4 Carbine (16" barrel, 6.8 lbs) $1,555.00

STONER SR-25 CARBINE

Caliber: 7.62 NATO, 10-shot steel magazine. **Barrel:** 16" free-floating **Weight:** 7-3/4 lbs. **Length:** 35.75" overall. **Stock:** Black synthetic. **Sights:** Integral Weaver-style rail. Scope rings, iron sights optional. **Features:** Shortened, non-slip handguard; removable carrying handle. Matte black finish. Introduced 1995. Made in U.S.A. by Knight's Mfg. Co.
Price: $3,345.00

WILKINSON LINDA CARBINE

Caliber: 9mm Para. **Barrel:** 16-3/16". **Weight:** 7 lbs. **Stocks:** Fixed tubular with wood pad. **Sights:** Aperture rear sight. **Features:** Aluminum receiver, pre-ban configuration (limited supplies), vent. barrel shroud, small wooden forearm, 18 or 31 shot mag. Many accessories.
Price: $1,800.00

Wilkinson Linda L2 Limited Edition

Manufactured from the last 600 of the original 2,200 pre-ban Linda Carbines, includes many upgrades and accessories. New 2002.
Price: $4,800.00

WILKINSON TERRY CARBINE

Caliber: 9mm Para. **Barrel:** 16-3/16". **Weight:** 7 lbs. **Stocks:** Black or maple. **Sights:** Adjustable. **Features:** Blowback semi-auto action, 31 shot mag., closed breech.
Price: . . . . NA

CONSULT

SHOOTER'S MARKETPLACE

Page 64, This Issue

Both classic arms and recent designs in American-style repeaters for sport and field shooting.

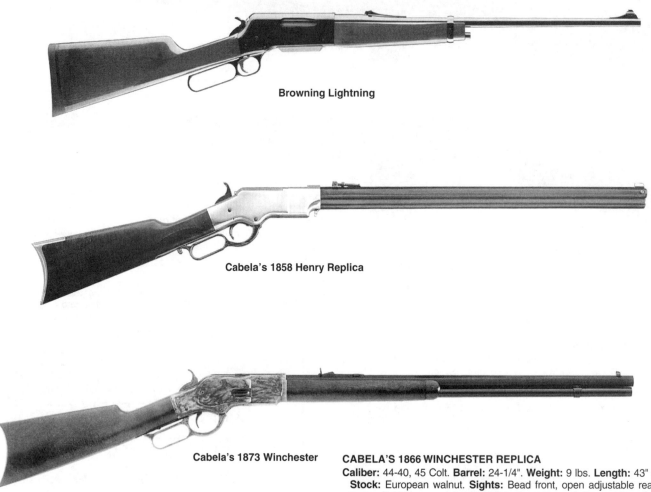

Browning Lightning

Cabela's 1858 Henry Replica

Cabela's 1873 Winchester

RIFLES

BROWNING MODEL '81 LIGHTNING LEVER-ACTION RIFLE
Caliber: 22-250, 243, 7mm-08, 308 Win., 270 WSM, 7mm WSM, 300 WSM, 358 Win., 450 Marlin, 270 Win., 30-06 Sprg., 7mm Rem. Mag., 300 Win. Mag. 4-shot detachable magazine. **Barrel:** 20" round tapered. **Weight:** 6 lbs., 8 oz. **Length:** 39-1/2" overall. **Stock:** Walnut. Checkered grip and forend, high-gloss finish. **Sights:** Gold bead on ramp front; low profile square notch adjustable rear. **Features:** Wide, grooved trigger; half-cock hammer safety; fold-down hammer. Receiver tapped for scope mount. Recoil pad installed. Introduced 1996. Imported from Japan by Browning.
Price: **$710.00**

BROWNING MODEL '81 LIGHTNING LONG ACTION
Similar to the standard Lightning BLR except has long action to accept 30-06, 270, 7mm Rem. Mag. and 300 Win. Mag. Barrel lengths are 22" for 30-06 and 270, 24" for 7mm Rem. Mag. and 300 Win. Mag. Has six-lug rotary bolt; bolt and receiver are full-length fluted. Fold-down hammer at half-cock. Weighs about 7 lbs., overall length 42-7/8" (22" barrel). Introduced 1996.
Price: **$686.00**

CABELA'S 1858 HENRY REPLICA
Caliber: 44-40, 45 Colt. **Barrel:** 24-1/4". **Weight:** 9.3 lbs. **Length:** 43.75" overall. **Stock:** American walnut. **Sights:** Bead front, open adjustable rear. **Features:** Brass receiver and buttplate. Uses original Henry loading system. Faithful to the original rifle. Introduced 1994. Imported by Cabela's.
Price: **$999.99**

CABELA'S 1866 WINCHESTER REPLICA
Caliber: 44-40, 45 Colt. **Barrel:** 24-1/4". **Weight:** 9 lbs. **Length:** 43" overall. **Stock:** European walnut. **Sights:** Bead front, open adjustable rear. **Features:** Solid brass receiver, buttplate, forend cap. Octagonal barrel. Faithful to the original Winchester '66 rifle. Introduced 1994. Imported by Cabela's.
Price: **$799.99**

CABELA'S 1873 WINCHESTER REPLICA
Caliber: 44-40, 45 Colt. **Barrel:** 24-1/4", 30". **Weight:** 8.5 lbs. **Length:** 43-1/4", 50" overall. **Stock:** European walnut. **Sights:** Bead front, open adjustable rear; globe front, tang rear. **Features:** Color case-hardened steel receiver. Faithful to the original Model 1873 rifle. Introduced 1994. Imported by Cabela's.
Price: Sporting model, 30" barrel, 44-40, 45 Colt **$999.99**
Price: Sporting model, 24" or 25" barrel **$899.99**

CIMARRON 1860 HENRY REPLICA
Caliber: 44 WCF, 13-shot magazine. **Barrel:** 24-1/4" (rifle), 22" (carbine). **Weight:** 9-1/2 lbs. **Length:** 43" overall (rifle). **Stock:** European walnut. **Sights:** Bead front, open adjustable rear. **Features:** Brass receiver and buttplate. Uses original Henry loading system. Faithful to the original rifle. Introduced 1991. Imported by Cimarron F.A. Co.
Price: **$1,029.00**

CIMARRON 1866 WINCHESTER REPLICAS
Caliber: 22 LR, 22 WMR, 38 Spec., 44 WCF. **Barrel:** 24-1/4" (rifle), 19" (carbine). **Weight:** 9 lbs. **Length:** 43" overall (rifle). **Stock:** European walnut. **Sights:** Bead front, open adjustable rear. **Features:** Solid brass receiver, buttplate, forend cap. Octagonal barrel. Faithful to the original Winchester '66 rifle. Introduced 1991. Imported by Cimarron F.A. Co.
Price: Rifle **$839.00**
Price: Carbine **$829.00**

CENTERFIRE RIFLES — LEVER AND SLIDE

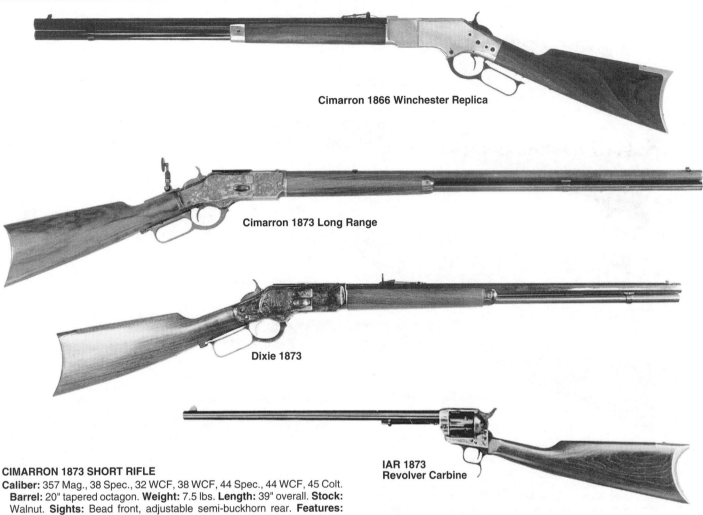

Cimarron 1866 Winchester Replica

Cimarron 1873 Long Range

Dixie 1873

IAR 1873
Revolver Carbine

CIMARRON 1873 SHORT RIFLE
Caliber: 357 Mag., 38 Spec., 32 WCF, 38 WCF, 44 Spec., 44 WCF, 45 Colt. **Barrel:** 20" tapered octagon. **Weight:** 7.5 lbs. **Length:** 39" overall. **Stock:** Walnut. **Sights:** Bead front, adjustable semi-buckhorn rear. **Features:** Has half "button" magazine. Original-type markings, including caliber, on barrel and elevator and "Kings" patent. From Cimarron F.A. Co.
Price: . . . . **$949.00 to $999.00**

CIMARRON 1873 LONG RANGE RIFLE
Caliber: 44 WCF, 45 Colt. **Barrel:** 30", octagonal. **Weight:** 8-1/2 lbs. **Length:** 48" overall. **Stock:** Walnut. **Sights:** Blade front, semi-buckhorn ramp rear. Tang sight optional. **Features:** Color case-hardened frame; choice of modern blue-black or charcoal blue for other parts. Barrel marked "Kings Improvement." From Cimarron F.A. Co.
Price: . . . . **$999.00 to $1,199.00**

Cimarron 1873 Sporting Rifle
Similar to the 1873 Short Rifle except has 24" barrel with half-magazine.
Price: . . . . **$949.00 to $999.00**

DIXIE ENGRAVED 1873 RIFLE
Caliber: 44-40, 11-shot magazine. **Barrel:** 20", round. **Weight:** 7-3/4 lbs. **Length:** 39" overall. **Stock:** Walnut. **Sights:** Blade front, adjustable rear. **Features:** Engraved and case-hardened frame. Duplicate of Winchester 1873. Made in Italy. From 21 Gun Works.
Price: **$1,350.00**
Price: Plain, blued carbine **$850.00**

E.M.F. 1860 HENRY RIFLE
Caliber: 44-40 or 45 Colt. **Barrel:** 24.25". **Weight:** About 9 lbs. **Length:** About 43.75" overall. **Stock:** Oil-stained American walnut. **Sights:** Blade front, rear adjustable for elevation. **Features:** Reproduction of the original Henry rifle with brass frame and buttplate, rest blued. From E.M.F.
Price: Brass frame **$850.00**
Price: Steel frame **$950.00**

E.M.F. 1866 YELLOWBOY LEVER ACTIONS
Caliber: 38 Spec., 44-40. **Barrel:** 19" (carbine), 24" (rifle). **Weight:** 9 lbs. **Length:** 43" overall (rifle). **Stock:** European walnut. **Sights:** Bead front, open adjustable rear. **Features:** Solid brass frame, blued barrel, lever, hammer, buttplate. Imported from Italy by E.M.F.
Price: Rifle **$690.00**
Price: Carbine **$675.00**

E.M.F. HARTFORD MODEL 1892 LEVER-ACTION RIFLE
Caliber: 45 Colt. **Barrel:** 24", octagonal. **Weight:** 7-1/2 lbs. **Length:** 43" overall. **Stock:** European walnut. **Sights:** Blade front, open adjustable rear. **Features:** Color case-hardened frame, lever, trigger and hammer with blued barrel, or overall blue finish. Introduced 1998. Imported by E.M.F.
Price: Standard **$590.00**

E.M.F. MODEL 1873 LEVER-ACTION RIFLE
Caliber: 32/20, 357 Mag., 38/40, 44-40, 44 Spec., 45 Colt. **Barrel:** 24". **Weight:** 8 lbs. **Length:** 43-1/4" overall. **Stock:** European walnut. **Sights:** Bead front, rear adjustable for windage and elevation. **Features:** Color case-hardened frame (blue on carbine). Imported by E.M.F.
Price: Rifle **$865.00**
Price: Carbine, 19" barrel **$865.00**

IAR MODEL 1873 REVOLVER CARBINE
Caliber: 357 Mag., 45 Colt. **Barrel:** 18". **Weight:** 4 lbs., 8 oz. **Length:** 34" overall. **Stock:** One-piece walnut. **Sights:** Blade front, notch rear. **Features:** Color case-hardened frame, blue barrel, backstrap and trigger-guard. Introduced 1998. Imported from Italy by IAR, Inc.
Price: Standard **$490.00**

Marlin 336C

Marlin 336 Cowboy

Marlin 336Y Spikehorn

Marlin 444P Outfitter

MARLIN MODEL 336C LEVER-ACTION CARBINE

Caliber: 30-30 or 35 Rem., 6-shot tubular magazine. **Barrel:** 20" Micro-Groove®. **Weight:** 7 lbs. **Length:** 38-1/2" overall. **Stock:** Checkered American black walnut, capped pistol grip. Mar-Shield® finish; rubber butt pad; swivel studs. **Sights:** Ramp front with Wide-Scan hood, semi-buck-horn folding rear adjustable for windage and elevation. **Features:** Hammer-block safety. Receiver tapped for scope mount, offset hammer spur; top of receiver sandblasted to prevent glare. Includes safety lock.
Price: **$529.00**

Marlin Model 336 Cowboy

Similar to the Model 336C except chambered for 38-55 Win., 24" tapered octagon barrel with deep-cut Ballard-type rifling; straight-grip walnut stock with hard rubber buttplate; blued steel forend cap; weighs 7-1/2 lbs.; 42-1/2" overall. Introduced 1999. Includes safety lock. Made in U.S.A. by Marlin.
Price: **$735.00**

Marlin Model 336A Lever-Action Carbine

Same as the Marlin 336C except has cut-checkered, walnut-finished hardwood pistol grip stock with swivel studs, 30-30 only, 6-shot. Hammer-block safety. Adjustable rear sight, brass bead front. Includes safety lock.
Price: **$451.00**
Price: With 4x scope and mount **$501.00**

Marlin Model 336CC Lever-Action Carbine

Same as the Marlin 336A except has Mossy Oak® Break-Up camouflage stock and forearm. 30-30 only, 6-shot; receiver tapped for scope mount or receiver sight. Introduced 2001. Includes safety lock. Made in U.S.A. by Marlin.
Price: **$503.00**

Marlin Model 336SS Lever-Action Carbine

Same as the 336C except receiver, barrel and other major parts are machined from stainless steel. 30-30 only, 6-shot; receiver tapped for scope. Includes safety lock.
Price: **$640.00**

Marlin Model 336W Lever-Action Rifle

Similar to the Model 336CS except has walnut-finished, cut-checkered Maine birch stock; blued steel barrel band has integral sling swivel; no front sight hood; comes with padded nylon sling; hard rubber butt plate. Introduced 1998. Includes safety lock. Made in U.S.A. by Marlin.
Price: **$457.00**
Price: With 4x scope and mount **$506.00**

Marlin Model 336 Y "Spikehorn"

Similar to the Models in the 336 series except in a compact format with 16-1/2" barrel measuring only 34" in overall length. Weight is 6-1/2 lbs., length of pull 12-1/2". Blued steel barrel and receiver. Chambered for 30/30 cartridge. Introduced 2003.
Price: **$536.00**

MARLIN MODEL 444 LEVER-ACTION SPORTER

Caliber: 444 Marlin, 5-shot tubular magazine. **Barrel:** 22" deep cut Ballard rifling. **Weight:** 7-1/2 lbs. **Length:** 40-1/2" overall. **Stock:** Checkered American black walnut, capped pistol grip, rubber rifle butt pad. Mar-Shield® finish; swivel studs. **Sights:** Hooded ramp front, folding semi-buckhorn rear adjustable for windage and elevation. **Features:** Hammer-block safety. Receiver tapped for scope mount; offset hammer spur. Includes safety lock.
Price: **$618.00**

Marlin Model 444P Outfitter Lever-Action

Similar to the 444SS with deep-cut Ballard-type rifling; weighs 6-3/4 lbs.; overall length 37". Available only in 444 Marlin. Introduced 1999. Includes safety lock. Made in U.S.A. by Marlin.
Price: **$631.00**

MARLIN MODEL 1894 LEVER-ACTION CARBINE

Caliber: 44 Spec./44 Mag., 10-shot tubular magazine. **Barrel:** 20" Ballard-type rifling. **Weight:** 6 lbs. **Length:** 37-1/2" overall. **Stock:** Checkered American black walnut, straight grip and forend. Mar-Shield® finish. Rubber rifle butt pad; swivel studs. **Sights:** Wide-Scan hooded ramp front, semi-buckhorn folding rear adjustable for windage and elevation. **Features:** Hammer-block safety. Receiver tapped for scope mount, offset hammer spur, solid top receiver sand blasted to prevent glare. Includes safety lock.
Price: **$544.00**

Marlin 1894PG

Marlin 1894 Cowboy

Marlin 1894SS

Marlin 1895

Marlin 1895GS

Marlin Model 1894PG/1894FG

Pistol-gripped versions of the Model 1894. Model 1894PG is chambered for .44 Magnum; Model 1894FG is chambered for .41 Magnum.
Price: (Model 1894PG) **$610.00**
Price: (Model 1894FG) **$610.00**

Marlin Model 1894C Carbine

Similar to the standard Model 1894S except chambered for 38 Spec./357 Mag. with full-length 9-shot magazine, 18-1/2" barrel, hammer-block safety, hooded front sight. Introduced 1983. Includes safety lock.
Price: **$556.00**

MARLIN MODEL 1894 COWBOY

Caliber: 357 Mag., 44 Mag., 45 Colt, 10-shot magazine. **Barrel:** 20" except .45 Colt which has a 24" tapered octagon, deep cut rifling. **Weight:** 7-1/2 lbs. **Length:** 41-1/2" overall. **Stock:** Straight grip American black walnut, hard rubber buttplate, Mar-Shield® finish. **Sights:** Marble carbine front, adjustable Marble semi-buckhorn rear. **Features:** Squared finger lever; straight grip stock; blued steel forend tip. Designed for Cowboy Shooting events. Introduced 1996. Includes safety lock. Made in U.S.A. by Marlin.
Price: **$820.00**

Marlin Model 1894 Cowboy Competition Rifle

Similar to Model 1894 except 20" barrel, 37-1/2" long, weighs only 6 lbs., antique finish on receiver, lever and bolt. Factory-tuned for competitive cowboy action shooting. Available in .38 Spl. And .45 Colt.
Price: **$986.00**

Marlin Model 1894SS

Similar to Model 1894 except has stainless steel barrel, receiver, lever, guard plate, magazine tube and loading plate. Nickel-plated swivel studs.
Price: **$680.00**

MARLIN MODEL 1895 LEVER-ACTION RIFLE

Caliber: 45-70, 4-shot tubular magazine. **Barrel:** 22" round. **Weight:** 7-1/2 lbs. **Length:** 40-1/2" overall. **Stock:** Checkered American black walnut, full pistol grip. Mar-Shield® finish; rubber butt pad; quick detachable swivel studs. **Sights:** Bead front with Wide-Scan hood, semi-buckhorn folding rear adjustable for windage and elevation. **Features:** Hammer- block safety. Solid receiver tapped for scope mounts or receiver sights; offset hammer spur. Includes safety lock.
Price: **$631.00**

Marlin Model 1895G Guide Gun Lever-Action Rifle

Similar to Model 1895 with deep-cut Ballard-type rifling; straight-grip walnut stock. Overall length is 37", weighs 7 lbs. Introduced 1998. Includes safety lock. Made in U.S.A. by Marlin.
Price: **$646.00**

Marlin Model 1895GS Guide Gun

Similar to Model 1895G except receiver, barrel and most metal parts are machined from stainless steel. Chambered for 45-70, 4-shot, 18-1/2" barrel. Overall length is 37", weighs 7 lbs. Introduced 2001. Includes safety lock. Made in U.S.A. by Marlin.
Price: **$760.00**

Marlin Model 1895 Cowboy Lever-Action Rifle

Similar to Model 1895 except has 26" tapered octagon barrel with Ballard-type rifling, Marble carbine front sight and Marble adjustable semi-buckhorn rear sight. Receiver tapped for scope or receiver sight. Overall length is 44-1/2", weighs about 8 lbs. Introduced 2001. Includes safety lock. Made in U.S.A. by Marlin.
Price: **$802.00**

Marlin Model 1895M Lever-Action Rifle

Similar to Model 1895 except has an 18-1/2" barrel with Ballard-type cut rifling. New Model 1895MR variant has 22" barrel, pistol grip. Chambered for 450 Marlin. Includes safety lock.
Price: (Model 1895M) **$695.00**
Price: (Model 1895MR) **$761.00**

RIFLES

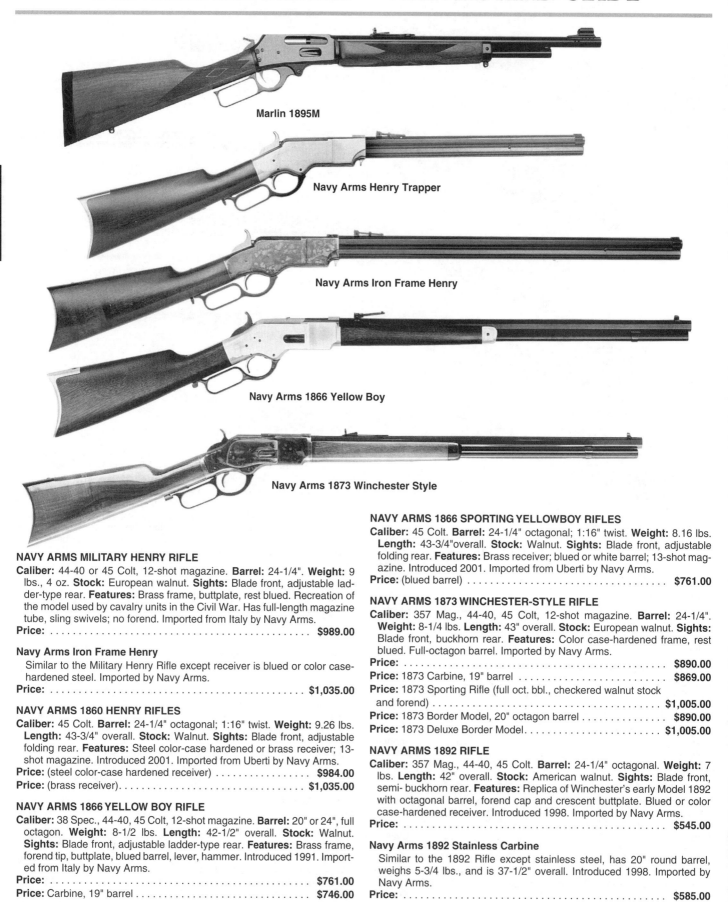

Marlin 1895M

Navy Arms Henry Trapper

Navy Arms Iron Frame Henry

Navy Arms 1866 Yellow Boy

Navy Arms 1873 Winchester Style

NAVY ARMS MILITARY HENRY RIFLE
Caliber: 44-40 or 45 Colt, 12-shot magazine. **Barrel:** 24-1/4". **Weight:** 9 lbs., 4 oz. **Stock:** European walnut. **Sights:** Blade front, adjustable ladder-type rear. **Features:** Brass frame, buttplate, rest blued. Recreation of the model used by cavalry units in the Civil War. Has full-length magazine tube, sling swivels; no forend. Imported from Italy by Navy Arms.
Price: **$989.00**

Navy Arms Iron Frame Henry
Similar to the Military Henry Rifle except receiver is blued or color case-hardened steel. Imported by Navy Arms.
Price: **$1,035.00**

NAVY ARMS 1860 HENRY RIFLES
Caliber: 45 Colt. **Barrel:** 24-1/4" octagonal; 1:16" twist. **Weight:** 9.26 lbs. **Length:** 43-3/4" overall. **Stock:** Walnut. **Sights:** Blade front, adjustable folding rear. **Features:** Steel color-case hardened or brass receiver; 13-shot magazine. Introduced 2001. Imported from Uberti by Navy Arms.
Price: (steel color-case hardened receiver) **$984.00**
Price: (brass receiver). **$1,035.00**

NAVY ARMS 1866 YELLOW BOY RIFLE
Caliber: 38 Spec., 44-40, 45 Colt, 12-shot magazine. **Barrel:** 20" or 24", full octagon. **Weight:** 8-1/2 lbs. **Length:** 42-1/2" overall. **Stock:** Walnut. **Sights:** Blade front, adjustable ladder-type rear. **Features:** Brass frame, forend tip, buttplate, blued barrel, lever, hammer. Introduced 1991. Imported from Italy by Navy Arms.
Price: **$761.00**
Price: Carbine, 19" barrel **$746.00**

NAVY ARMS 1866 SPORTING YELLOWBOY RIFLES
Caliber: 45 Colt. **Barrel:** 24-1/4" octagonal; 1:16" twist. **Weight:** 8.16 lbs. **Length:** 43-3/4" overall. **Stock:** Walnut. **Sights:** Blade front, adjustable folding rear. **Features:** Brass receiver; blued or white barrel; 13-shot magazine. Introduced 2001. Imported from Uberti by Navy Arms.
Price: (blued barrel) **$761.00**

NAVY ARMS 1873 WINCHESTER-STYLE RIFLE
Caliber: 357 Mag., 44-40, 45 Colt, 12-shot magazine. **Barrel:** 24-1/4". **Weight:** 8-1/4 lbs. **Length:** 43" overall. **Stock:** European walnut. **Sights:** Blade front, buckhorn rear. **Features:** Color case-hardened frame, rest blued. Full-octagon barrel. Imported by Navy Arms.
Price: **$890.00**
Price: 1873 Carbine, 19" barrel **$869.00**
Price: 1873 Sporting Rifle (full oct. bbl., checkered walnut stock
  and forend) **$1,005.00**
Price: 1873 Border Model, 20" octagon barrel **$890.00**
Price: 1873 Deluxe Border Model. **$1,005.00**

NAVY ARMS 1892 RIFLE
Caliber: 357 Mag., 44-40, 45 Colt. **Barrel:** 24-1/4" octagonal. **Weight:** 7 lbs. **Length:** 42" overall. **Stock:** American walnut. **Sights:** Blade front, semi- buckhorn rear. **Features:** Replica of Winchester's early Model 1892 with octagonal barrel, forend cap and crescent buttplate. Blued or color case-hardened receiver. Introduced 1998. Imported by Navy Arms.
Price: **$545.00**

Navy Arms 1892 Stainless Carbine
Similar to the 1892 Rifle except stainless steel, has 20" round barrel, weighs 5-3/4 lbs., and is 37-1/2" overall. Introduced 1998. Imported by Navy Arms.
Price: **$585.00**

Navy Arms 1892 Rifle

Navy Arms 1892 Short Rifle

Puma Model 92

Remington 7600 Rifle

Ruger Model 96/44

Navy Arms 1892 Short Rifle

Similar to the 1892 Rifle except has 20" octagonal barrel, weighs 6-1/4 lbs., and is 37-3/4" overall. Replica of the rare, special order 1892 Winchester nicknamed the "Texas Special." Blued or color case-hardened receiver and furniture. Introduced 1998. Imported by Navy Arms.
Price: **$545.00**
Price: (stainless steel, 20" octagon barrel) **$585.00**

NAVY ARMS 1892 STAINLESS RIFLE

Caliber: 357 Mag., 44-40, 45 Colt. **Barrel:** 24-1/4" octagonal. **Weight:** 7 lbs. **Length:** 42". **Stock:** American walnut. **Sights:** Brass bead front, semi- buckhorn rear. **Features:** Designed for the Cowboy Action Shooter. Stain-less steel barrel, receiver and furniture. Introduced 2000. Imported by Navy Arms.
Price: **$585.00**

PUMA MODEL 92 RIFLES & CARBINES

Caliber: 38 Spec./357 Mag., 44 Mag., 45 Colt, 454 Casull (20" carbine only), 480 Ruger. **Barrel:** 20" round, 24"octagonal. **Weight:** 6.1-7.7 lbs. **Stock:** Walnut-stained hardwood. **Sights:** Open, buckhorn front & rear available. **Features:** Blue, case-hardened, stainless steel and brass receivers, matching buttplates. Blued, stainless steel barrels, full-length magazines. Thumb safety on top of both. 454 Casull carbine loads through magazine tube, has rubber recoil pad. 45 Colt brass-framed, saddle-ring rifle and 454 Casull carbine introduced 2002. The 480 Ruger version was introduced in 2003. Imported from Brazil by Legacy Sports International.
Price: Octagonal barrel. . . . . **$500.00 to $561.00**
Price: Round barrel. . . . . **$407.00 to $549.00**

REMINGTON MODEL 7600 PUMP ACTION

Caliber: 243, 270, 30-06, 308. **Barrel:** 22" round tapered. **Weight:** 7--1/2 lbs. **Length:** 42-5/8" overall. **Stock:** Cut-checkered walnut pistol grip and forend, Monte Carlo with full cheekpiece. Satin or high-gloss finish. **Sights:** Gold bead front sight on matted ramp, open step adjustable sporting rear. **Features:** Redesigned and improved version of the Model 760. Detachable 4-shot clip. Cross-bolt safety. Receiver tapped for scope mount. Introduced 1981.
Price: **$588.00**
Price: Carbine (18-1/2" bbl., 30-06 only) **$588.00**
Price: With black synthetic stock, matte black metal, rifle or carbine **$484.00**

RUGER MODEL 96/44 LEVER-ACTION RIFLE

Caliber: 44 Mag., 4-shot rotary magazine. **Barrel:** 18-1/2". **Weight:** 5-7/8 lbs. **Length:** 37-5/16" overall. **Stock:** American hardwood. **Sights:** Gold bead front, folding leaf rear. **Features:** Solid chrome-moly steel receiver. Manual cross-bolt safety, visible cocking indicator; short-throw lever action; integral scope mount; blued finish; color case-hardened lever. Introduced 1996. Made In U.S. by Sturm, Ruger & Co.
Price: 96/44M, 44 Mag **$525.00**

TRISTAR/UBERTI 1873 SPORTING RIFLE

Caliber: 44-40, 45 Colt. **Barrel:** 24-1/4", 30", octagonal. **Weight:** 8.1 lbs. **Length:** 43-1/4" overall. **Stock:** Walnut. **Sights:** Blade front adjustable for windage, open rear adjustable for elevation. **Features:** Color case-hardened frame, blued barrel, hammer, lever, buttplate, brass elevator. Imported from Italy by Tristar Sporting Arms Ltd.
Price: 24-1/4" barrel **$925.00**
Price: 30" barrel **$969.00**

Tristar 1873 Sporting Rifle

Tristar 1866 Yellowboy Carbine

Tristar 1860 Henry

Winchester 94 Traditional

TRISTAR/UBERTI 1866 SPORTING RIFLE, CARBINE
Caliber: 22 LR, 22 WMR, 38 Spec., 44-40, 45 Colt. **Barrel:** 24-1/4", octagonal. **Weight:** 8.1 lbs. **Length:** 43-1/4" overall. **Stock:** Walnut. **Sights:** Blade front adjustable for windage, rear adjustable for elevation. **Features:** Frame, buttplate, forend cap of polished brass, balance charcoal blued. Imported by Tristar Sporting Arms Ltd.
Price: **$779.00**
Price: Yellowboy Carbine (19" round bbl.). **$739.00**

TRISTAR/UBERTI 1860 HENRY RIFLE
Caliber: 44-40, 45 Colt. **Barrel:** 24-1/4", half-octagon. **Weight:** 9.2 lbs. **Length:** 43-3/4" overall. **Stock:** American walnut. **Sights:** Blade front, rear adjustable for elevation. **Features:** Frame, elevator, magazine follower, buttplate are brass, balance blue. Imported by Tristar Sporting Arms Ltd. Arms, Inc.
Price: **$989.00**

Tristar/Uberti 1860 Henry Trapper Carbine
Similar to the 1860 Henry Rifle except has 18-1/2" barrel, measures 37-3/4" overall, and weighs 8 lbs. Introduced 1999. Imported from Italy by Tristar Sporting Arms Ltd.
Price: Brass frame, blued barrel **$989.00**

U.S. FIRE-ARMS LIGHTNING MAGAZINE RIFLE
Caliber: 45 Colt, 44 WCF, 44 Spl., 38 WCF, 32 WCF, 15-shot. **Barrel:** 26" (rifle); 20" carbine, round or octagonal. **Stock:** Oiled walnut. **Finish:** Dome blue. Introduced 2002. Made in U.S.A. by United States Fire Arms Manufacturing Co.
Price: **$995.00**

VEKTOR H5 SLIDE-ACTION RIFLE
Caliber: 223 Rem., 5-shot magazine. **Barrel:** 18", 22". **Weight:** 9 lbs., 15 oz. **Length:** 42-1/2" overall (22" barrel). **Stock:** Walnut thumbhole. **Sights:** Comes with 1" 4x32 scope with low-light reticle. **Features:** Rotating bolt mechanism. Matte black finish. Introduced 1999. Imported from South Africa by Vektor USA.
Price: **$849.95**

WINCHESTER TIMBER CARBINE
Caliber: Chambered for 450 Marlin. **Barrel:** 18" barrel, ported. **Weight:** 6 lbs. **Length:** 36-1/4" overall. **Stock:** Half-pistol grip stock with butt pad; checkered grip and forend. **Sights:** XS ghost-ring sight. **Features:** Introduced 1999. Made in U.S.A. by U.S. Repeating Arms Co., Inc.
Price: **$610.00**

WINCHESTER MODEL 94 TRADITIONAL-CW
Caliber: 30-30 Win., 6-shot; 44 Mag., 11-shot tubular magazine. **Barrel:** 20". **Weight:** 6-1/2 lbs. **Length:** 37-3/4" overall. **Stock:** Straight grip checkered walnut stock and forend. **Sights:** Hooded blade front, semi-buckhorn rear. Drilled and tapped for scope mount. Post front sight on Trapper model. **Features:** Solid frame, forged steel receiver; side ejection, exposed rebounding hammer with automatic trigger-activated transfer bar. Introduced 1984.
Price: 30-30 . . . . **$469.00**
Price: 44 Mag. **$492.00**
Price: Traditional (no checkering, 30-30 only). **$435.00**

Winchester Model 94 Trapper
Similar to Model 94 Traditional except has 16" barrel, 5-shot magazine in 30-30, 9-shot in 357 Mag., 44 Magnum/44 Special, 45 Colt. Has stainless steel claw extractor, saddle ring, hammer spur extension, smooth walnut wood.
Price: 30-30 . . . . **$459.00**
Price: 44 Mag., 357 Mag., 45 Colt **$459.00**

Winchester Model 94 Trapper

Winchester Model 94 Trails End

Winchester Model 94 Legacy

Winchester Model 94 Ranger

Winchester Model 94 Ranger Compact

Winchester Model 94 Trails End
Similar to the Model 94 Walnut except octagon-barrel version available, chambered only for 357 Mag., 44-40, 44 Mag., 45 Colt; 11-shot magazine. Available with standard lever loop. Introduced 1997. From U.S. Repeating Arms Co., Inc.
Price: With standard lever loop $474.00

Winchester Model 94 Legacy
Similar to the Model 94 Traditional-CW except has half-pistol grip walnut stock, checkered grip and forend. Chambered for 30-30, 357 Mag., 44

CONSULT

SHOOTER'S

MARKETPLACE

Page 64, This Issue

Mag., 45 Colt; 24" barrel. Introduced 1995. Made in U.S.A. by U.S. Repeating Arms Co., Inc.
Price: With 24" barrel $487.00

Winchester Model 94 Ranger
Similar to the Model 94 Traditional except has a hardwood stock, post-style front sight and hammer-spur extension.
Price: (20" barrel) $379.00
Price: Trail's End octagon $757.00
Price: Trail's End octagon, case color $815.00

Winchester Model 94 Ranger Compact
Similar to the Model 94 Ranger except 357, 30-30 calibers, has 16" barrel and 12-1/2" length of pull, rubber recoil pad, post front sight. Introduced 1998. Made in U.S.A. by U.S. Repeating Arms Co., Inc.
Price: $402.00

WINCHESTER MODEL 1895 LEVER-ACTION RIFLE
Caliber: 405 Win, 4-shot magazine. **Barrel:** 24", round. **Weight:** 8 lbs. **Length:** 42" overall. **Stock:** American walnut. **Sights:** Gold bead front, buckhorn rear adjustable for elevation. **Features:** Recreation of the original Model 1895. Polished blue finish. Two-piece cocking lever, schnabel forend, straight-grip stock. Introduced 1995. From U.S. Repeating Arms Co., Inc.
Price: Grade I $1,116.00

CENTERFIRE RIFLES — BOLT ACTION

Includes models for a wide variety of sporting and competitive purposes and uses.

Anschutz 1733D

Barrett Model 95

Blaser R93 Classic

ANSCHUTZ 1743D BOLT-ACTION RIFLE

Caliber: 222 Rem., 3-shot magazine. **Barrel:** 19.7". **Weight:** 6.4 lbs. **Length:** 39" overall. **Stock:** European walnut. **Sights:** Hooded blade front, folding leaf rear. **Features:** Receiver grooved for scope mounting; single stage trigger; claw extractor; sling safety; sling swivels. Imported from Germany by AcuSport Corp.

Price: **$1,588.95**

ANSCHUTZ 1740 MONTE CARLO RIFLE

Caliber: 22 Hornet, 5-shot clip; 222 Rem., 3-shot clip. **Barrel:** 24". **Weight:** 6-1/2 lbs. **Length:** 43.25" overall. **Stock:** Select European walnut. **Sights:** Hooded ramp front, folding leaf rear; drilled and tapped for scope mounting. **Features:** Uses match 54 action. Adjustable single stage trigger. Stock has roll-over Monte Carlo cheekpiece, slim forend with Schnabel tip, Wundhammer palm swell on grip, rosewood gripcap with white diamond insert. Skip-line checkering on grip and forend. Introduced 1997. Imported from Germany by AcuSport Corp.

Price: From **$1,439.00**
Price: Model 1730 Monte Carlo, as above except in
22 Hornet **$1,439.00**

Anschutz 1733D Rifle

Similar to the 1740 Monte Carlo except has full-length, walnut, Mannlicher-style stock with skip-line checkering, rosewood Schnabel tip, and is chambered for 22 Hornet. Weighs 6.4 lbs., overall length 39", barrel length 19.7". Imported from Germany by AcuSport Corp.

Price: **$1,588.95**

BARRETT MODEL 95 BOLT-ACTION RIFLE

Caliber: 50 BMG, 5-shot magazine. **Barrel:** 29". **Weight:** 22 lbs. **Length:** 45" overall. **Stock:** Energy-absorbing recoil pad. **Sights:** Scope optional. **Features:** Bolt-action, bullpup design. Disassembles without tools; extendable bipod legs; match-grade barrel; high efficiency muzzle brake. Introduced 1995. Made in U.S.A. by Barrett Firearms Mfg., Inc.

Price: From **$4,950.00**

BLASER R93 BOLT-ACTION RIFLE

Caliber: 22-250, 243, 6.5x55, 270, 7x57, 7mm-08, 308, 30-06, 257 Wea. Mag., 7mm Rem. Mag., 300 Win. Mag., 300 Wea. Mag., 338 Win Mag.,

375 H&H, 416 Rem. Mag. **Barrel:** 22" (standard calibers), 26" (magnum). **Weight:** 7 lbs. **Length:** 40" overall (22" barrel). **Stock:** Two-piece European walnut. **Sights:** None furnished; drilled and tapped for scope mounting. **Features:** Straight pull-back bolt action with thumb-activated safety slide/cocking mechanism; interchangeable barrels and bolt heads. Introduced 1994. Imported from Germany by SIGARMS.

Price: R93 Classic **$3,680.00**
Price: R93 LX **$1,895.00**
Price: R93 Synthetic (black synthetic stock). **$1,595.00**
Price: R93 Safari Synthetic (416 Rem. Mag. only) **$1,855.00**
Price: R93 Grand Lux **$4,915.00**
Price: R93 Attaché **$5,390.00**

BRNO 98 BOLT-ACTION RIFLE

Caliber: 7x64, 243, 270, 308, 30-06, 300 Win. Mag., 9.3x62. **Barrel:** 23.6". **Weight:** 7.2 lbs. **Length:** 40.9" overall. **Stock:** European walnut. **Sights:** Blade on ramp front, open adjustable rear. **Features:** Uses Mauser 98-type action; polished blue. Announced 1998. Imported from the Czech Republic by Euro-Imports.

Price: Standard calibers **$507.00**
Price: Magnum calibers **$547.00**
Price: With set trigger, standard calibers **$615.00**
Price: As above, magnum calibers **$655.00**
Price: With full stock, set trigger, standard calibers **$703.00**
Price: As above, magnum calibers **$743.00**
Price: 300 Win. Mag., with BOSS **$933.00**

BROWNING A-BOLT RIFLES

Caliber: 223, 22-250, 243, 7mm-08, 308, 25-06, 260, 270, 30-06, 260 Rem., 7mm Rem. Mag., 300 Win. Short Mag., 300 Win. Mag., 338 Win. Mag., 375 H&H Mag, 223 WSSM, 243 WSSM, 270 WSM, 7mm WSM, 300 WSM. **Barrel:** 22" medium sporter weight with recessed muzzle; 26" on mag. cals. **Weight:** 6-1/2 to 7-1/2 lbs. **Length:** 44-3/4" overall (magnum and standard); 41-3/4" (short action). **Stock:** Classic style American walnut; recoil pad standard on magnum calibers. **Features:** Short-throw (60") fluted bolt, three locking lugs, plunger-type ejector; adjustable trigger is grooved and gold-plated. Hinged floorplate, detachable box magazine (4 rounds std. cals., 3 for magnums). Slide tang safety. BOSS barrel vibration modulator and muzzle brake system not available in 375 H&H. Introduced 1985. Imported from Japan by Browning.

Price: Hunter, no sights **$672.00**
Price: Hunter, no sights, magnum calibers **$698.00**
Price: For BOSS add **$80.00**

Browning A-Bolt Hunter

Browning A-Bolt Medallion

Browning A-Bolt White Gold Medallion

Browning A-Bolt Eclipse M-1000

Browning A-Bolt Medallion
Similar to standard A-Bolt except has glossy stock finish, rosewood grip and forend caps, engraved receiver, high-polish blue, no sights. New calibers include 223 WSSM, 243 WSSM< 270 WSM, 7mm WSM.
Price: Short-action calibers. **$782.00**
Price: Long-action calibers **$782.00**
Price: Medallion, 375 H&H Mag., open sights **$811.00**
Price: 300 Win. Short Magnum. **$811.00**
Price: For BOSS, add **$80.00**

Browning A-Bolt Medallion Left-Hand
Same as the Medallion model A-Bolt except has left-hand action and is available in 270, 30-06, 7mm Rem. Mag., 300 Win. Mag. Introduced 1987.
Price: 270, 30-06 (no sights) **$813.00**
Price: 7mm Mag., 300 Win. Mag. (no sights) **$840.00**
Price: For BOSS, add **$80.00**

Browning A-Bolt White Gold Medallion
Similar to the standard A-Bolt except has select walnut stock with brass spacers between rubber recoil pad and between the rosewood gripcap and forend tip; gold-filled barrel inscription; palm-swell pistol grip, Monte Carlo comb, 22 lpi checkering with double borders; engraved receiver flats. In 270, 30-06, 7mm Rem. Mag. and 300 Win. Mag. Introduced 1988.
Price: 270, 30-06 . . . . **$1,121.00**
Price: 7mm Rem. Mag, 300 Win. Mag. **$1,149.00**
Price: For BOSS, add **$80.00**

BROWNING A-BOLT WHITE GOLD RMEF
Caliber: 7mm Rem. Mag. Similar to the A-Bolt Medallion except has select walnut stock with rosewood forend cap, RMEF-engraved grip cap:

continental cheekpiece; gold engraved, stainless receiver and bbl. Introduced 2004. Imported from Japan by Browning.
Price: **$1,224.00**

Browning A-Bolt Eclipse Hunter
Similar to the A-Bolt II except has gray/black laminated, thumbhole stock, BOSS barrel vibration modulator and muzzle brake. Available in long and short action with heavy barrel. In 270 Win., 30-06, 7mm Rem. Mag. Introduced 1996. Imported from Japan by Browning.
Price: 270, 30-06, with BOSS. **$1,101.00**
Price: 7mm Rem. Mag, with BOSS. **$1,128.00**

Browning A-Bolt Eclipse M-1000
Similar to the A-Bolt II Eclipse except has long action and heavy target barrel. Chambered only for 300 Win. Mag. Adjustable trigger, bench-style forend, 3-shot magazine; laminated thumbhole stock; BOSS system standard. Introduced 1997. Imported for Japan by Browning.
Price: **$1,134.00**

Browning A-Bolt Micro Hunter
Similar to the A-Bolt II Hunter except has 13-5/16" length of pull, 20" barrel, and comes in 260 Rem., 243, 308, 7mm-08, 223, 22-250, 22 Hornet, 270 WSM, 7mm WSM, 300 WSM. Weighs 6 lbs., 1 oz. Introduced 1999. Imported by Browning. Also available in left-hand version.
Price: (no sights). **$664.00**

Browning A-Bolt Classic Hunter
Similar to the A-Bolt Hunter except has low-luster bluing and walnut stock with Monte Carlo comb, pistol grip palm swell, double-border checkering. Available in 223 WSSM, 243 WSSM. Introduced 1999. Imported by Browning.
Price: WSM. **$784.00**
Price: WSSM **$805.00**

CENTERFIRE RIFLES — BOLT ACTION

Browning A-Bolt Stalker

Charles Daly Superior

CZ 527 Lux

CZ 550 Lux

Browning A-Bolt Stainless Stalker

Similar to the Hunter model A-Bolt except receiver and barrel are made of stainless steel; the rest of the exposed metal surfaces are finished with a durable matte silver-gray. Graphite-fiberglass composite textured stock. No sights are furnished. Available in 260, 243, 308, 7mm-08, 270, 280,30-06, 7mm Rem. Mag., 300 WSM, 300 Rem. Ultra Mag., 338 Win. Mag., 338 Rem. Ultra Mag., 375 H&H, 223 WSSM, 243 WSSM, 270 WSM, 7mm WSM. Introduced 1987.

Price: Short-action calibers. $871.00
Price: Magnum calibers $899.00
Price: 300 Win. Short Magnum. $899.00
Price: For BOSS, add $80.00
Price: Left-hand, 270, 30-06 . . . . $898.00
Price: Left-hand, 7mm, 300 Win. Mag., 338 Win. Mag.. . . . . . . $926.00
Price: Left-hand, 375 H&H, with sights $926.00
Price: Left-hand, for BOSS, add $80.00

Browning A-Bolt Composite Stalker

Similar to the A-Bolt Hunter except has black graphite-fiberglass stock with textured finish. Matte blue finish on all exposed metal surfaces. Available in 223, 22-250, 243, 7mm-08, 308, 30-06, 270, 280, 25-06, 7mm Rem. Mag., 300 WSM, 300 Win. Mag., 338 Win. Mag, 223 WSSM, 243 WSSM, 270 WSM, 7mm WSM. BOSS barrel vibration modulator and muzzle brake system offered in all calibers. Introduced 1994.

Price: Standard calibers, no sights $684.00
Price: Magnum calibers, no sights $713.00
Price: For BOSS, add $80.00

CARBON ONE BOLT-ACTION RIFLE

Caliber: 22-250 to 375 H&H. **Barrel:** Up to 28". **Weight:** 5-1/2 to 7-1/4 lbs. **Length:** Varies. **Stock:** Synthetic or wood. **Sights:** None furnished. **Features:** Choice of Remington, Browning or Winchester action with free-floated Christensen graphite/epoxy/steel barrel, trigger pull tuned to 3 to 3-1/2 lbs. Made in U.S.A. by Christensen Arms.

Price: Carbon One Hunter Rifle, 6-1/2 to 7 lbs. $1,499.00
Price: Carbon One Custom, 5-1/2 to 6-1/2 lbs., Shilen trigger . . $2,750.00

Price: Carbon Ranger, 50 BMG, 5-shot repeater $4,750.00
Price: Carbon Ranger, 50 BMG, single shot. $3,950.00

CHARLES DALY SUPERIOR BOLT-ACTION RIFLE

Caliber: 22 Hornet, 5-shot magazine. **Barrel:** 22.6". **Weight:** 6.6 lbs. **Length:** 41.25" overall. **Stock:** Walnut-finished hardwood with Monte Carlo comb and cheekpiece. **Sights:** Ramped blade front, fully adjustable open rear. **Features:** Receiver dovetailed for tip-off scope mount. Introduced 1996. Imported by K.B.I., Inc.

Price: $364.95

Charles Daly Empire Grade Rifle

Similar to the Superior except has oil-finished American walnut stock with 18 lpi hand checkering; black hardwood gripcap and forend tip; highly polished barreled action; jewelled bolt; recoil pad; swivel studs. Imported by K.B.I., Inc.

Price: $469.95

CZ 527 LUX BOLT-ACTION RIFLE

Caliber: 22 Hornet, 222 Rem., 223 Rem., detachable 5-shot magazine. **Barrel:** 23-1/2"; standard or heavy barrel. **Weight:** 6 lbs., 1 oz. **Length:** 42-1/2" overall. **Stock:** European walnut with Monte Carlo. **Sights:** Hooded front, open adjustable rear. **Features:** Improved mini-Mauser action with non-rotating claw extractor; single set trigger; grooved receiver. Imported from the Czech Republic by CZ-USA.

Price: $566.00
Price: Model FS, full-length stock, cheekpiece $658.00

CZ 527 American Classic Bolt-Action Rifle

Similar to the CZ 527 Lux except has classic-style stock with 18 l.p.i. checkering; free-floating barrel; recessed target crown on barrel. No sights furnished. Introduced 1999. Imported from the Czech Republic by CZ-USA.

Price: 22 Hornet, 222 Rem., 223 Rem. . . . . $586.00 to $609.00

CZ 550 LUX BOLT-ACTION RIFLE

Caliber: 22-250, 243, 6.5x55, 7x57, 7x64, 308 Win., 9.3x62, 270 Win., 30-06. **Barrel:** 20.47". **Weight:** 7.5 lbs. **Length:** 44.68" overall. **Stock:** Turkish walnut in Bavarian style or FS (Mannlicher). **Sights:** Hooded front, adjustable rear. **Features:** Improved Mauser-style action with claw extractor, fixed ejector, square bridge dovetailed receiver; single set trigger. Imported from the Czech Republic by CZ-USA.

Price: Lux . . . . $566.00 to $609.00
Price: FS (full stock) $706.00

CZ 550 American Classic

CZ 550 Magnum

Dakota 76 Classic

Dakota 76 Safari

CZ 550 American Classic Bolt-Action Rifle

Similar to CZ 550 Lux except has American classic-style stock with 18 l.p.i. checkering; free-floating barrel; recessed target crown. Has 25.6" barrel; weighs 7.48 lbs. No sights furnished. Introduced 1999. Imported from the Czech Republic by CZ-USA.
Price: . . . . **$586.00 to $609.00**

CZ 550 Medium Magnum Bolt-Action Rifle

Similar to the CZ 550 Lux except chambered for the 300 Win. Mag. and 7mm Rem. Mag.; 5-shot magazine. Adjustable iron sights, hammer-forged barrel, single-set trigger, Turkish walnut stock. Weighs 7.5 lbs. Introduced 2001. Imported from the Czech Republic by CZ USA.
Price: **$621.00**

CZ 550 Magnum Bolt-Action Rifle

Similar to CZ 550 Lux except has long action for 300 Win. Mag., 375 H&H, 416 Rigby, 458 Win. Mag. Overall length is 46.45"; barrel length 25"; weighs 9.24 lbs. Hooded front sight, express rear with one standing, two folding leaves. Imported from the Czech Republic by CZ-USA.
Price: 300 Win. Mag. **$717.00**
Price: 375 H&H **$756.00**
Price: 416 Rigby **$809.00**
Price: 458 Win. Mag.. . . . . **$744.00**

CZ 700 M1 SNIPER RIFLE

Caliber: 308 Winchester, 10-shot magazine. **Barrel:** 25.6". **Weight:** 11.9 lbs. **Length:** 45" overall. **Stock:** Laminated wood thumbhole with adjustable buttplate and cheekpiece. **Sights:** None furnished; permanently attached Weaver rail for scope mounting. **Features:** 60-degree bolt throw; oversized trigger guard and bolt handle for use with gloves; full-length equipment rail on forend; fully adjustable trigger. Introduced 2001. Imported from the Czech Republic by CZ USA.
Price: **$2,097.00**

DAKOTA 76 TRAVELER TAKEDOWN RIFLE

Caliber: 257 Roberts, 25-06, 7x57, 270, 280, 30-06, 338-06, 35 Whelen (standard length); 7mm Rem. Mag., 300 Win. Mag., 338 Win. Mag., 416 Taylor, 458 Win. Mag. (short magnums); 7mm, 300, 330, 375 Dakota Magnums. **Barrel:** 23". **Weight:** 7-1/2 lbs. **Length:** 43-1/2" overall. **Stock:** Medium fancy-grade walnut in classic style. Checkered grip and forend; solid butt pad. **Sights:** None furnished; drilled and tapped for scope mounts. **Features:** Threadless disassembly-no threads to wear or stretch, no interrupted cuts, and headspace remains constant. Uses mod-ified Model 76 design with many features of the Model 70 Winchester. Left-hand model also available. Introduced 1989. Made in U.S.A. by Dakota Arms, Inc.
Price: Classic **$4,495.00**
Price: Safari **$5,495.00**
Price: Extra barrels . . . . **$1,650.00 to $1,950.00**

DAKOTA 76 CLASSIC BOLT-ACTION RIFLE

Caliber: 257 Roberts, 270, 280, 30-06, 7mm Rem. Mag., 338 Win. Mag., 300 Win. Mag., 375 H&H, 458 Win. Mag. **Barrel:** 23". **Weight:** 7-1/2 lbs. **Length:** 43-1/2" overall. **Stock:** Medium fancy grade walnut in classic style. Checkered pistol grip and forend; solid butt pad. **Sights:** None furnished; drilled and tapped for scope mounts. **Features:** Has many features of the original Model 70 Winchester. One-piece rail trigger guard assembly; steel gripcap. Model 70-style trigger. Many options available. Left-hand rifle available at same price. Introduced 1988. From Dakota Arms, Inc.
Price: **$3,595.00**

DAKOTA 76 SAFARI BOLT-ACTION RIFLE

Caliber: 270 Win., 7x57, 280, 30-06, 7mm Dakota, 7mm Rem. Mag., 300 Dakota, 300 Win. Mag., 330 Dakota, 338 Win. Mag., 375 Dakota, 458 Win. Mag., 300 H&H, 375 H&H, 416 Rem. **Barrel:** 23". **Weight:** 8-1/2 lbs. **Length:** 43-1/2" overall. **Stock:** XXX fancy walnut with ebony forend tip; point-pattern with wrap-around forend checkering. **Sights:** Ramp front, standing leaf rear. **Features:** Has many features of the original Model 70 Winchester. Barrel band front swivel, inletted rear. Cheekpiece with shadow line. Steel gripcap. Introduced 1988. From Dakota Arms, Inc.
Price: Wood stock. **$4,595.00**

CENTERFIRE RIFLES — BOLT ACTION

Dakota Longbow

Dakota 97 Lightweight Hunter

Dakota Hunter

Ed Brown 702 Savanna

Dakota African Grade

Similar to 76 Safari except chambered for 338 Lapua Mag., 404 Jeffery, 416 Rigby, 416 Dakota, 450 Dakota, 4-round magazine, select wood, two stock cross-bolts. 24" barrel, weighs 9-10 lbs. Ramp front sight, standing leaf rear. Introduced 1989.

Price: **$4,995.00**

DAKOTA LONGBOW TACTICAL E.R. RIFLE

Caliber: 300 Dakota Magnum, 330 Dakota Magnum, 338 Lapua Magnum. **Barrel:** 28", .950" at muzzle **Weight:** 13.7 lbs. **Length:** 50" to 52" overall. **Stock:** Ambidextrous McMillan A-2 fiberglass, black or olive green color; adjustable cheekpiece and buttplate. **Sights:** None furnished. Comes with Picatinny one-piece optical rail. **Features:** Uses the Dakota 76 action with controlled-round feed; three-position firing pin block safety, claw extractor; Model 70-style trigger. Comes with bipod, case tool kit. Introduced 1997. Made in U.S.A. by Dakota Arms, Inc.

Price: **$4,250.00**

DAKOTA 97 LIGHTWEIGHT HUNTER

Caliber: 22-250 to 330. **Barrel:** 22"-24". **Weight:** 6.1-6.5 lbs. **Length:** 43" overall. **Stock:** Fiberglass. **Sights:** Optional. **Features:** Matte blue finish, black stock. Right-hand action only. Introduced 1998. Made in U.S.A. by Dakota Arms, Inc.

Price: **$1,995.00**

DAKOTA LONG RANGE HUNTER RIFLE

Caliber: 25-06, 257 Roberts, 270 Win., 280 Rem., 7mm Rem. Mag., 7mm Dakota Mag., 30-06, 300 Win. Mag., 300 Dakota Mag., 338 Win. Mag., 330 Dakota Mag., 375 H&H Mag., 375 Dakota Mag. **Barrel:** 24", 26", match-quality; free-floating. **Weight:** 7.7 lbs. **Length:** 45" to 47" overall. **Stock:** H-S Precision black synthetic, with one-piece bedding block system. **Sights:** None furnished. Drilled and tapped for scope mounting. **Features:** Cylindrical machined receiver controlled round feed; Mauser-style extractor; three-position striker blocking safety; fully adjustable match trigger. Right-hand action only. Introduced 1997. Made in U.S.A. by Dakota Arms, Inc.

Price: **$1,995.00**

ED BROWN MODEL 702, SAVANNA

Caliber: (long action) 25-06, 270 Win., 280 Rem., 7mm Rem. Mag., 7STW, 30-06, 300 Win. Mag., 300 Weatherby, 338 Win. Mag. (Short action) 223, 22-250, 243, 6mm, 260 Rem. 7mm-08, 308, 300 WSM, 270 WSM, 7mm WSM. **Barrel:** 23" (standard calibers) light weight #3 contour; medium weight 24", 26" with #4 contour on medium calibers. **Weight:** 8 to 8.5-lbs. **Stock:** Fully glass-bedded McMillan fiberglass sporter. **Sights:** None furnished. Talley scope mounts utlizing heavy duty 8-40 screws. **Features:** Custom action with machined steel trigger guard and hinged floor plate. Available in left-hand version.

Price: From **$2,800.00**

Ed Brown 702 Ozark

Ed Brown 702 Bushveld

Ed Brown 702 Varmint

Harris Gunworks Alaskan

Ed Brown Model 702 Denali, Ozark

Similar to the Ed Brown Model 702 Savanna but the Denali is a lighter weight rifle designed specifically for mountain hunting, especially suited to the 270 and 280 calibers. Right hand only. Weighs about 7.75 lbs. The Model 702 Ozark is another lighter weight rifle made on a short action with a very light weight stock. Ozark calibers are 223, 243, 6mm, 260 Rem., 7mm-08, 308. Weight 6.5 lbs.
Price: From (either model) $2,800.00

ED BROWN MODEL 702 BUSHVELD

Caliber: 338 Win. Mag., 375 H&H, 416 Rem. Mag., 458 Win. Mag. And all Ed Brown Savanna long action calibers. **Barrel:** 24" medium or heavy weight. **Weight:** 8.25 lbs. **Stock:** Fully bedded McMillan fiberglass with Monte Carlo style cheekpiece, Pachmayr Decelerator recoil pad. **Sights:** None furnish. Talley scope mounts utilizing heavy duty 8-40 screws. **Features:** A dangerous game rifle with options including left-hand action, stainless steel barrel, additional calibers, iron sights.
Price: From $2,900.00

ED BROWN MODEL 702 VARMINT

Caliber: 223, 22-250, 220 Swift, 243, 6mm, 308. **Barrel:** Medium weight #5 contour 24"; heavy weight #17 contour 24"; 26" optional. **Weight:** 9 lbs. **Stock:** Fully glass-bedded McMillan fiberglass with recoil pad. **Sights:** None furnished. Talley scope mounts with heavy duty 8-40 screws. **Features:** Fully-adjustable trigger, steel trigger guard and floor plate, many options available.
Price: From $2,500.00

HARRIS GUNWORKS SIGNATURE CLASSIC SPORTER

Caliber: 22-250, 243, 6mm Rem., 7mm-08, 284, 308 (short action); 25-06, 270, 280 Rem., 30-06, 7mm Rem. Mag., 300 Win. Mag., 300 Wea. (long action); 338 Win. Mag., 340 Wea., 375 H&H (magnum action). **Barrel:** 22", 24", 26". **Weight:** 7 lbs. (short action). **Stock:** Fiberglass in green, beige, brown or black. Recoil pad and 1" swivels installed. Length of pull up to 14-1/4". **Sights:** None furnished. Comes with 1" rings and bases. **Features:** Uses right- or left-hand action with matte black finish. Trigger pull set at 3 lbs. Four-round magazine for standard calibers; three for magnums. Aluminum floorplate. Wood stock optional. Introduced 1987. From Harris Gunworks, Inc.
Price: $2,700.00

Harris Gunworks Signature Classic Stainless Sporter

Similar to Signature Classic Sporter except action is made of stainless steel. Same calibers, in addition to 416 Rem. Mag. Fiberglass stock, right- or left-hand action in natural stainless, glass bead or black chrome sulfide finishes. Introduced 1990. From Harris Gunworks, Inc.
Price: $2,900.00

Harris Gunworks Signature Alaskan

Similar to Classic Sporter except match-grade barrel with single leaf rear sight, barrel band front, 1" detachable rings and mounts, steel floorplate, electroless nickel finish. Wood Monte Carlo stock with cheekpiece, palm-swell grip, solid butt pad. Chambered for 270, 280 Rem., 30-06, 7mm Rem. Mag., 300 Win. Mag., 300 Wea., 358 Win., 340 Wea., 375 H&H. Introduced 1989.
Price: $3,800.00

Harris Gunworks Signature Titanium Mountain

Harris Gunworks Signature Super Varminter

Harris Gunworks Talon Safari

Howa Lightning

Harris Gunworks Signature Titanium Mountain Rifle

Similar to Classic Sporter except action made of titanium alloy, barrel of chrome-moly steel. Stock is graphite reinforced fiberglass. Weight is 5-1/2 lbs. Chambered for 270, 280 Rem., 30-06, 7mm Rem. Mag., 300 Win. Mag. Fiberglass stock optional. Introduced 1989.

Price: **$3,300.00**
Price: With graphite-steel composite light weight barrel **$3,700.00**

Harris Gunworks Signature Varminter

Similar to Signature Classic Sporter except has heavy contoured barrel, adjustable trigger, field bipod and special hand-bedded fiberglass stock. Chambered for 223, 22-250, 220 Swift, 243, 6mm Rem., 25-06, 7mm-08, 7mm BR, 308, 350 Rem. Mag. Comes with 1" rings and bases. Introduced 1989.

Price: **$2,700.00**

HARRIS GUNWORKS TALON SAFARI RIFLE

Caliber: 300 Win. Mag., 300 Wea. Mag., 300 Phoenix, 338 Win. Mag., 30/378, 338 Lapua, 300 H&H, 340 Wea. Mag., 375 H&H, 404 Jeffery, 416 Rem. Mag., 458 Win. Mag. (Safari Magnum); 378 Wea. Mag., 416 Rigby, 416 Wea. Mag., 460 Wea. Mag. (Safari Super Magnum). **Barrel:** 24". **Weight:** About 9-10 lbs. **Length:** 43" overall. **Stock:** Gunworks fiberglass Safari. **Sights:** Barrel band front ramp, multi-leaf express rear. **Features:** Uses Harris Gunworks Safari action. Has quick detachable 1" scope mounts, positive locking steel floorplate, barrel band sling swivel. Match-grade barrel. Matte black finish standard. Introduced 1989. From Harris Gunworks, Inc.

Price: Talon Safari Magnum **$3,900.00**
Price: Talon Safari Super Magnum **$4,200.00**

HARRIS GUNWORKS TALON SPORTER RIFLE

Caliber: 22-250, 243, 6mm Rem., 6mm BR, 7mm BR, 7mm-08, 25-06, 270, 280 Rem., 284, 308, 30-06, 350 Rem. Mag. (long action); 7mm Rem. Mag., 7mm STW, 300 Win. Mag., 300 Wea. Mag., 300 H&H, 338 Win. Mag., 340 Wea. Mag., 375 H&H, 416 Rem. Mag. **Barrel:** 24" (standard). **Weight:** About 7-1/2 lbs. **Length:** NA. **Stock:** Choice of walnut or fiberglass. **Sights:** None furnished; comes with rings and bases. Open sights optional. **Features:** Uses pre-'64 Model 70-type action with cone breech, controlled feed, claw extractor and three-position safety. Barrel and action are of stainless steel; chrome-moly optional. Introduced 1991. From Harris Gunworks, Inc.

Price: **$2,900.00**

HOWA LIGHTNING BOLT-ACTION RIFLE

Caliber: 223, 22-250, 243, 6.5x55, 270, 308, 30-06, 7mm Rem. Mag., 300 Win. Mag., 338 Win. Mag, 300 WSM, 7mm WSM, 270 WSM. **Barrel:** 22", 24" magnum calibers. **Weight:** 7-1/2 lbs. **Length:** 42" overall (22" barrel). **Stock:** Black Bell & Carlson Carbelite composite with Monte Carlo comb; checkered grip and forend. **Sights:** None furnished. Drilled and tapped for scope mounting. **Features:** Sliding thumb safety; hinged floorplate; polished blue/black finish. Introduced 1993. From Legacy Sports International.

Price: Blue, standard calibers. **$479.00**
Price: Blue, magnum calibers. **$502.00**
Price: Stainless, standard calibers **$585.00**
Price: Stainless, magnum calibers **$612.00**

Howa M-1500 Hunter Bolt-Action Rifle

Similar to Lightning Model except has walnut-finished hardwood stock. Polished blue finish or stainless steel. Introduced 1999. From Legacy Sports International.

Price: Blue, standard calibers. **$539.00**
Price: Stainless, standard calibers **$638.00**
Price: Blue, magnum calibers. **$560.00**
Price: Stainless, magnum calibers **$662.00**

CENTERFIRE RIFLES — BOLT ACTION

Howa M-1500 Hunter

Howa M-1500 Ultralight

Howa M-1500 Varmint Supreme

Kimber 84M Classic

Kimber 84M Varmint

Howa M-1500 Supreme Rifles

Similar to Howa M-1500 Lightning except stocked with JRS Classic or Thumbhole Sporter laminated wood stocks in Nutmeg (brown/black) or Pepper (gray/black) colors. Barrel 22"; 24" magnum calibers. Weights are JRS stock 8 lbs., THS stock 8.3 lbs. Introduced 2001. Imported from Japan by Legacy Sports International.

Price: Blue, standard calibers, JRS stock. $616.00
Price: Blue, standard calibers, THS stock. $668.00
Price: Blue, magnum calibers, JRS stock. $638.00
Price: Blue, magnum calibers, THS stock. $638.00
Price: Stainless, standard calibers, JRS stock $720.00
Price: Stainless, standard calibers, THS stock $771.00
Price: Stainless, magnum calibers, JRS stock $720.00
Price: Stainless, magnum calibers, THS stock $742.00

Howa M-1500 Ultralight

Similar to Howa M-1500 Lightning except receiver milled to reduce weight, tapered 22" barrel; 1-10" twist. Chambered for 243 Win. Stocks are black texture-finished hardwood. Weighs 6.4 lbs. Length 40"overall.
Price: Blued $511.00

Howa M-1500 Varmint and Varmint Supreme Rifles

Similar to M-1500 Lightning except has heavy 24" hammer-forged barrel. Chambered for 223, 22-250, 308. Weighs 9.3 lbs.; overall length 44.5". Introduced 1999. Imported from Japan by Interarms/Howa. Varminter Supreme has heavy barrel, target crown muzzle. Heavy 24" barrel, laminated wood with raised comb stocks, rollover cheekpiece, vented beavertail forearm; available in 223 Rem., 22-250 Rem., 308 Win. Weighs 9.9 lbs. Introduced 2001. Imported from Japan by Legacy Sports International.
Price: Varminter, blue, polymer stock $517.00
Price: Varminter, stainless, polymer stock $626.00
Price: Varminter, blue, wood stock $575.00
Price: Varminter, stainless, wood stock. $677.00
Price: Varminter Supreme, blued . . . . $612.00 to $641.00
Price: Varminter Supreme, stainless. . . . . $714.00 to $743.00

KIMBER MODEL 84M BOLT-ACTION RIFLE

Caliber: 22-250, 243, 260 Rem., 7mm-08, 308, 5-shot. **Barrel:** 22", 24", 26". **Weight:** 5 lbs., 10 oz. to 10 lbs. **Length:** 41"-45". **Stock:** Claro walnut, checkered with steel grip cap or gray laminate. **Sights:** None; drilled and tapped for bases. **Features:** Mauser claw extractor, two-position wing safety, action bedded on aluminum pillars, free-floated barrel, match-grade trigger set at 4 lbs., matte blue finish. Includes cable lock. Introduced 2001. Made in U.S.A. by Kimber Mfg. Inc.
Price: Classic (243, 260, 7mm-08, 308) $917.00
Price: Varmint (22-250). $1,001.00

CENTERFIRE RIFLES — BOLT ACTION

L.A.R. Grizzly

Magnum Research Tactical

Raptor Bolt-Action

Remington 673 Guide

L.A.R. GRIZZLY 50 BIG BOAR RIFLE
Caliber: 50 BMG, single shot. **Barrel:** 36". **Weight:** 30.4 lbs. **Length:** 45.5" overall. **Stock:** Integral. Ventilated rubber recoil pad. **Sights:** None furnished; scope mount. **Features:** Bolt-action bullpup design, thumb and bolt stop safety. All-steel construction. Unsurpassed accuracy and impact. Introduced 1994. Made in U.S.A. by L.A.R. Mfg., Inc.
Price: **$2,195.00**

MAGNUM RESEARCH MAGNUM LITE TACTICAL RIFLE
Caliber: 223 Rem., 22-250, 308 Win., 300 Win. Mag., 300 WSM. **Barrel:** 26" Magnum Lite™ graphite. **Weight:** 8.3 lbs. **Length:** NA. **Stock:** H-S Precision™ tactical black synthetic. **Sights:** None furnished; drilled and tapped for scope mount. **Features:** Accurized Remington 700 action; adjustable trigger; adjustable comb height. Tuned to shoot 1/2" MOA or better. Introduced 2001. From Magnum Research Inc.
Price: **$2,400.00**

MOUNTAIN EAGLE MAGNUM LITE RIFLE
Caliber: 22-250, 223 Rem. (Varmint); 280, 30-06 (long action); 7mm Rem. Mag., 300 Win. Mag., (magnum action). **Barrel:** 24", 26", free floating. **Weight:** 7 lbs., 13 oz. **Length:** 44" overall (24" barrel). **Stock:** Kevlar-graphite with aluminum bedding block, high comb, recoil pad, swivel studs; made by H-S Precision. **Sights:** None furnished; accepts any Remington 700-type base. **Features:** Special Sako action with one-piece forged bolt, hinged steel floorplate, lengthened receiver ring; adjustable trigger. Krieger cut-rifled benchrest barrel. Introduced 1996. From Magnum Research, Inc.
Price: Magnum Lite (graphite barrel) **$2,295.00**

NEW ULTRA LIGHT ARMS BOLT-ACTION RIFLES
Caliber: 17 Rem. to 416 Rigby (numerous calibers available). **Barrel:** Douglas, length to order. **Weight:** 4-3/4 to 7-1/2 lbs. **Length:** Varies. **Stock:** Kevlar®/ graphite composite, variety of finishes. **Sights:** None furnished; drilled and tapped for scope mount. **Features:** Timney trigger, hand-lapped action, button-rifled barrel, hand-bedded action, recoil pad, sling-swivel studs, optional Jewell Trigger. Made in U.S.A. by New Ultra Light Arms.
Price: Model 20 (short action). **$2,500.00**
Price: Model 24 (long action) **$2,600.00**
Price: Model 28 (magnum action). **$2,900.00**
Price: Model 40 (300 Wea. Mag., 416 Rigby) **$2,900.00**
Price: Left-hand models, add **$100.00**

RAPTOR BOLT-ACTION RIFLE
Caliber: 270, 30-06, 243, 25-06, 308; 4-shot magazine. **Barrel:** 22". **Weight:** 7 lbs., 6 oz. **Length:** 42.5" overall. **Stock:** Black synthetic, fiberglass reinforced; checkered grip and forend; vented recoil pad; Monte Carlo cheekpiece. **Sights:** None furnished; drilled and tapped for scope mounts. **Features:** Rust-resistant "Taloncote" treated barreled action; pillar bedded; stainless bolt with three locking lugs; adjustable trigger. Announced 1997. Made in U.S.A. by Raptor Arms Co., Inc.
Price: **$249.00**

Remington Model 673 Guide Rifle
Available in 350 Rem. Mag., 300 Rem. SAUM with 22" magnum contour barrel with machined steel ventilated rib, iron sights, wide laminate stock.
Price: **$825.00**

CENTERFIRE RIFLES — BOLT ACTION

Remington 700 Classic

Remington 700 ADL Synthetic

Remington 700 BDL

Remington 700 BDL Left Hand

REMINGTON MODEL 700 CLASSIC RIFLE
Caliber: 300 Savage. **Barrel:** 24". **Weight:** About 7-1/4 lbs. **Length:** 44-1/2" overall. **Stock:** American walnut, 20 lpi checkering on pistol grip and forend. Classic styling. Satin finish. **Sights:** None furnished. Receiver drilled and tapped for scope mounting. **Features:** A "classic" version of the BDL with straight comb stock. Fitted with rubber recoil pad. Sling swivel studs installed. Hinged floorplate. Limited production in 2003 only.
Price: **$683.00**

REMINGTON MODEL 700 ADL DELUXE RIFLE
Caliber: 270, 30-06. **Barrel:** 22" round tapered. **Weight:** 7-1/4 lbs. **Length:** 41-5/8" overall. **Stock:** Walnut. Satin-finished pistol grip stock with fine-line cut checkering, Monte Carlo. **Sights:** Gold bead ramp front; removable, step-adjustable rear with windage screw. **Features:** Side safety, receiver tapped for scope mounts.
Price: **$580.00**

Remington Model 700 ADL Synthetic
Similar to the 700 ADL except has a fiberglass-reinforced synthetic stock with straight comb, raised cheekpiece, positive checkering, and black rubber butt pad. Metal has matte finish. Available in 22-250, 223, 243, 270, 308, 30-06 with 22" barrel, 300 Win. Mag., 7mm Rem. Mag. with 24" barrel. Introduced 1996.
Price: From . . . . **$500.00 to $527.00**

Remington Model 700 ADL Synthetic Youth
Similar to the Model 700 ADL Synthetic except has 1" shorter stock, 20" barrel. Chambered for 243, 308. Introduced 1998.
Price: **$500.00**

Remington Model 700 BDL Custom Deluxe Rifle
Same as 700 ADL except chambered for 222, 223 (short action, 24" barrel), 7mm-08, 280, 22-250, 25-06, (short action, 22" barrel), 243, 270, 30-06, skip-line checkering, black forend tip and gripcap with white line spacers. Matted receiver top, quick-release floorplate. Hooded ramp front sight, quick detachable swivels.
Price: **$683.00**
Also available in 17 Rem., 7mm Rem. Mag., 7mm Rem. Ultra Mag., 300 Win. Mag. (long action, 24" barrel); 300 Rem. Ultra Mag. (26" barrel). Overall length 44-1/2", weight about 7-1/2 lbs.
Price: . . . . **$709.00 to $723.00**

Remington Model 700 BDL Left-Hand Custom Deluxe
Same as 700 BDL except mirror-image left-hand action, stock. Available in 270, 30-06, 7mm Rem. Mag., 300 Rem. Ultra Mag, 338 Rem. Ultra Mag., 7mm Rem. Ultra Mag.
Price: . . . . **$709.00 to $749.00**

Remington Model 700 BDL DM Rifle
Same as 700 BDL except detachable box magazine (4-shot, standard calibers, 3-shot for magnums). Glossy stock finish, open sights, recoil pad, sling swivels. Available in 270, 30-06, 7mm Rem. Mag., 300 Win. Mag. Introduced 1995.
Price: From . . . . **$749.00 to $776.00**

Remington Model 700 BDL SS Rifle
Similar to 700 BDL rifle except hinged floorplate, 24" standard weight barrel in all calibers; magnum calibers have magnum-contour barrel. No sights supplied, but comes drilled and tapped. Corrosion-resistant follower and fire control, stainless BDL-style barreled action with fine matte finish. Synthetic stock has straight comb and cheekpiece, textured finish, positive checkering, plated swivel studs. Calibers-270, 30-06; mag-nums-7mm Rem. Mag., 7mm Rem. UltraMag., 300 Rem. Ultra Mag. (26" barrel) 300 Win. Mag., 338 Rem. Ultra Mag., 7mm Rem. SAUM, 300 Rem. SAUM. Weighs 7-3/8 to 7-1/2 lbs. Introduced 1993.
Price: From . . . . **$735.00 to $775.00**

Remington 700 BDL SS

Remington 700 BDL SS DM

Remington 700 LSS Mountain

Remington 700 Safari KS

Remington Model 700 BDL SS DM Rifle

Same as 700 BDL SS except detachable box magazine. Barrel, receiver and bolt made of #416 stainless steel; black synthetic stock, fine-line engraving. Available in 270, 30-06, 7mm Rem. Mag., 300 Win. Mag. Introduced 1995.

Price: From . . . . **$801.00 to $828.00**

Remington Model 700 Custom KS Mountain Rifle

Similar to 700 BDL except custom finished with aramid fiber reinforced resin synthetic stock. Available in left- and right-hand versions. Chambered 270 Win., 280 Rem., 30-06, 7mm Rem. Mag., 7mm STW, 300 Rem. Ultra Mag., 338 Rem. Ultra Mag., 300 Win. Mag., 300 Wea. Mag., 35 Whelen, 338 Win. Mag., 8mm Rem. Mag., 375 H&H, with 24" barrel (except 300 Rem. Ultra Mag., 26"), 7mm RUM, 375 RUM. Weighs 6 lbs., 6 oz. Introduced 1986.

Price: Right-hand **$1,314.00**
Price: Left-hand **$1,393.00**
Price: Stainless . . . . **$1,500 to $1,580.00**

Remington Model 700 LSS Mountain Rifle

Similar to Model 700 Custom KS Mountain Rifle except stainless steel 22" barrel and two-tone laminated stock. Chambered in 260 Rem., 7mm-08, 270 Winchester and 30-06. Overall length 42-1/2", weighs 6-5/8 oz. Introduced 1999.

Price: **$800.00**

Remington Model 700 Safari Grade

Similar to 700 BDL aramid fiber reinforced fiberglass stock, blued carbon steel bbl. and action, or stainless, w/cheekpiece, custom finished and tuned. In 8mm Rem. Mag., 375 H&H, 416 Rem. Mag. or 458 Win. Mag. calibers only with heavy barrel. Right- and left-hand versions.

Price: Safari KS . . . . **$1,520.00 to $1,601.00**
Price: Safari KS (stainless right-hand only) **$1,697.00**

Remington Model 700 AWR Alaskan Wilderness Rifle

Similar to the 700 BDL except has stainless barreled action finishBlack Teflon 24" bbl. 26" Ultra Mag raised cheekpiece, magnum-grade black rubber recoil pad. Chambered for 7mm RUM., 375 RUM, 7mm STW, 300 Rem. Ultra Mag., 300 Win. Mag., 300 Wea. Mag., 338 Rem. Ultra Mag., 338 Win. Mag., 375 H&H. Aramid fiber reinforced fiberglass stock. Introduced 1994.

Price: . . . . **$1,593.00** (right-hand); **$1,673.00** (left-hand)

Remington Model 700 APR African Plains Rifle

Similar to Model 700 BDL except magnum receiver and specially contoured 26" Custom Shop barrel with satin blued finish, laminated wood stock with raised cheekpiece, satin finish, black butt pad, 20 lpi cut checkering. Chambered for 7mm Rem. Mag., 7mm RUM, 375 RUM, 300 Rem. Ultra Mag., 300 Win. Mag., 300 Wea. Mag., 338 Win. Mag., 338 Rem. Ultra Mag., 375 H&H. Introduced 1994.

Price: **$1,716.00**

Remington Model 700 LSS Rifle

Similar to 700 BDL except stainless steel barreled action, gray laminated wood stock with Monte Carlo comb and cheekpiece. No sights furnished. Available in (RH) 7mm Rem. Mag., 300 Win. Mag., 300 RUM, 338 RUM, 7mm Rem. Ultra Mag., 375 Rem. Ultra Mag., (LH) 7mm Rem. Ultra Mag., 300 Rem. Ultra Mag., and 338 Rem. RUM. Introduced 1996.

Price: From . . . . (Right-hand) **$820.00 to $840.00**; (LH) **$867.00**

Remington Model 700 MTN DM Rifle

Similar to 700 BDL except weighs 6-1/2 to 6-5/8 lbs., 22" tapered barrel. Redesigned pistol grip, straight comb, contoured cheekpiece, hand-rubbed oil stock finish, deep cut checkering, hinged floorplate and magazine follower, two-position thumb safety. Chambered for 260 Rem., 270 Win., 7mm-08, 25-06, 280 Rem., 30-06, 4-shot detachable box magazine. Overall length is 41-5/8"-42-1/2". Introduced 1995.

Price: **$728.00**

Remington 700 APR African Plains

Remington 700 Titanium

Remington 700 VLS

Remington 700 VS

Remington 700 VS SF

Remington 700 Sendero SF

Remington Model 700 Titanium
Similar to 700 BDL except has titanium receiver, spiral-cut fluted bolt, skeletonized bolt handle and carbon-fiber and aramid fiber reinforced stock with sling swivel studs. Barrel 22"; weighs 5-1/4 lbs. (short action) or 5-1/2 lbs. (long action). Satin stainless finish. 260 Rem., 270 Win., 7mm-08, 30-06, 308 Win. Introduced 2001.
Price: **$1,239.00**

Remington Model 700 VLS Varmint Laminated Stock
Similar to 700 BDL except 26" heavy barrel without sights, brown laminated stock with beavertail forend, gripcap, rubber butt pad. Available in 223 Rem., 22-250, 6mm, 243, 308. Polished blue finish. Introduced 1995.
Price: From **$705.00**

Remington Model 700 VS SF Rifle
Similar to Model 700 Varmint Synthetic except satin-finish stainless barreled action with 26" fluted barrel, spherical concave muzzle crown. Chambered for 223, 220 Swift, 22-250. Introduced 1994.
Price: **$976.00**

Remington Model 700 VS Varmint Synthetic Rifles
Similar to 700 BDL Varmint Laminated except composite stock reinforced with aramid fiber reinforced, fiberglass and graphite. Aluminum bedding block that runs full length of receiver. Free-floating 26" barrel. Metal has black matte finish; stock has textured black and gray finish and swivel studs. Available in 223, 22-250, 308. Right- and left-hand. Introduced 1992.
Price: . . . . **$811.00 to $837.00**

Remington Model 700 EtronX VSSF Rifle
Similar to Model 700 VS SF except features battery-powered ignition system for near-zero lock time and electronic trigger mechanism. Requires ammunition with EtronX electrically fired primers. Aluminum-bedded 26" heavy, stainless steel, fluted barrel; overall length 45-7/8"; weight 8 lbs., 14 oz. Black, Kevlar-reinforced composite stock. Light-emitting diode display on grip top indicates fire or safe mode, loaded or unloaded chamber, battery condition. Introduced 2000.
Price: 220 Swift, 22-250 or 243 Win. **$1,332.00**

Remington Model 700 Sendero SF Rifle
Similar to 700 Sendero except stainless steel action and 26" fluted stainless barrel. Weighs 8-1/2 lbs. Chambered for 7mm Rem. SAUM, 300 Rem. SAUM, 7mm Rem. Mag., 7mm STW, 300 Rem. Ultra Mag., 338 Rem. Ultra Mag., 300 Win. Mag., 7mm Rem. Ultra Mag. Introduced 1996.
Price: . . . . **$1,003.00 to $1,016.00**

REMINGTON MODEL 700 RMEF
Caliber: 300 Rem. SAUM. **Barrel:** 26". **Weight:** 7-5/8 lbs. **Length:** 46.5". **Stock:** Synthetic, Realtree Hardwoods HD finish. **Sights:** None; drilled and tapped. **Features:** Special Edition (sold one year only), Rocky Mountain Elk Foundation rifle, 416 stainless bolt, varrel, receiver. Portion of proceeds to RMEF.
Price: **$835.00**

Remington Seven LS

Remington Model Seven LS Mag

Remington Model Seven SS Mag

Remington Model Seven Custom MS

Remington Seven Custom KS

REMINGTON MODEL 710 BOLT-ACTION RIFLE
Caliber: 270 Win., 30-06. **Barrel:** 22". **Weight:** 7-1/8 lbs. **Length:** 42-1/2" overall. **Stock:** Gray synthetic. **Sights:** Bushnell Sharpshooter 3-9x scope mounted and bore-sighted. **Features:** Unique action locks bolt directly into barrel; 60-degree bolt throw; 4-shot dual-stack magazine; key-operated Integrated Security System locks bolt open. Introduced 2001. Made in U.S.A. by Remington Arms Co.
Price: **$425.00**

REMINGTON MODEL SEVEN LS
Caliber: 223 Rem., 243 Win., 7mm-08 Rem., 308 Win. **Barrel:** 20". **Weight:** 6-1/2 lbs. **Length:** 39-1/4" overall. **Stock:** Brown laminated, satin finished. **Features:** Satin finished carbon steel barrel and action, 4-round magazine, hinged magazine floorplate. Furnished with iron sights and sling swivel studs, drilled and tapped for scope mounts.
Price: **$701.00**
Price: 7mmRSAUM, 300RSAUM, LS Magnum, 22" bbl. **$741.00**

Remington Model Seven SS
Similar to Model Seven LS except stainless steel barreled action and black synthetic stock, 20" barrel. Chambered for 243, 260 Rem., 7mm-08, 308. Introduced 1994.
Price: **$729.00**
Price: 7mmRSAUM, 300RSAUM, Model Seven SS
Magnum, 22" bbl. **$769.00**

Remington Model Seven Custom MS Rifle
Similar to Model Seven LS except full-length Mannlicher-style stock of laminated wood with straight comb, solid black recoil pad, black steel forend tip, cut checkering, gloss finish. Barrel length 20", weighs 6-3/4 lbs. Available in 222 Rem., 223, 22-250, 243, 6mm Rem., 260 Rem., 7mm-08 Rem., 308, 350 Rem. Mag. Calibers 250 Savage, 257 Roberts, 35 Rem. Polished blue finish. Introduced 1993. From Remington Custom Shop.
Price: From **$1,332.00**

Remington Model Seven Youth Rifle
Similar to Model Seven LS except hardwood stock, 1" shorter length of pull, chambered for 223, 243, 260 Rem., 7mm-08. Introduced 1993.
Price: **$547.00**

Remington Model Seven Custom KS
Similar to Model Seven LS except gray aramid fiber reinforced stock with 1" black rubber recoil pad and swivel studs. Blued satin carbon steel barreled action. No sights on 223, 260 Rem., 7mm-08, 308; 35 Rem. and 350 Rem. have iron sights.
Price: **$1,314.00**

RUGER MAGNUM RIFLE
Caliber: 375 H&H, 416 Rigby, 458 Lott. **Barrel:** 23". **Weight:** 9-1/2 to 10-1/4 lbs. **Length:** 44". **Stock:** AAA Premium Grade Circassian walnut with live-rubber recoil pad, metal grip cap, and studs for mounting sling swivels. **Sights:** Blade, front; V-notch rear express sights (one stationary, two folding) drift-adjustable for windage. **Features:** Patented floorplate latch secures the hinged floorplate against accidental dumping of cartridges; one-piece bolt has a non-rotating Mauser-type controlled-feed extractor; fixed-blade ejector.
Price: M77RSMMKII **$1,695.00**

Ruger Magnum

Ruger 77/22 Hornet Varmint

Ruger M77 Mark II

Ruger KM77RLFP MKII

Ruger KM77RSFP MKII

RUGER 77/22 HORNET BOLT-ACTION RIFLE

Caliber: 22 Hornet, 6-shot rotary magazine. **Barrel:** 20". **Weight:** About 6 lbs. **Length:** 39-3/4" overall. **Stock:** Checkered American walnut, black rubber butt pad. **Sights:** Brass bead front, open adjustable rear; also available without sights. **Features:** Same basic features as rimfire model except slightly lengthened receiver. Uses Ruger rotary magazine. Three-position safety. Comes with 1" Ruger scope rings. Introduced 1994.

Price: 77/22RH (rings only) **$589.00**
Price: 77/22RSH (with sights) **$609.00**
Price: K77/22VHZ Varmint, laminated stock, no sights **$625.00**

RUGER M77 MARK II RIFLE

Caliber: 223, 220 Swift, 22-250, 243, 6mm Rem., 257 Roberts, 25-06, 6.5x55 Swedish, 270, 7x57mm, 260 Rem., 280 Rem., 308, 30-06, 7mm Rem. Mag., 7mm Rem. Short Ultra Mag., 300 Rem. Short Ultra Mag., 300 WSM, 300 Win. Mag., 338 Win. Mag., 4-shot magazine. **Barrel:** 20", 22"; 24" (magnums). **Weight:** About 7 lbs. **Length:** 39-3/4" overall. **Stock:** Synthetic American walnut; swivel studs, rubber butt pad. **Sights:** None furnished. Receiver has Ruger integral scope mount base, Ruger 1" rings. Some with iron sights. **Features:** Short action with new trigger, 3-position safety. Steel trigger guard. Left-hand available. Introduced 1989.

Price: M77RMKII (no sights) **$675.00**
Price: M77RSMKII (open sights) **$759.00**
Price: M77LRMKII (left-hand, 270, 30-06, 7mm Rem.
  Mag.,300 Win. Mag.) **$675.00**
Price: KM77REPMKII (Shorts) **$675.00**

Ruger M77RSI International Carbine

Same as standard Model 77 except 18" barrel, full-length International-style stock, steel forend cap, loop-type steel sling swivels. Integral-base receiver, open sights, Ruger 1" steel rings. Improved front sight. Available in 243, 270, 308, 30-06. Weighs 7 lbs. Length overall is 38-3/8".

Price: M77RSIMKII **$769.00**

Ruger M77 Mark II All-Weather and Sporter Model Stainless Rifle

Similar to wood-stock M77 Mark II except all metal parts are stainless steel, has an injection-moulded, glass-fiber-reinforced polymer stock. Laminated wood stock. Chambered for 223, 243, 270, 308, 30-06, 7mm Rem. Mag., 300 Win. Mag., 338 Win. Mag. Fixed-blade-type ejector, 3-position safety, new trigger guard with patented floorplate latch. Integral Scope Base Receiver, 1" Ruger scope rings, built-in sling swivel loops. Introduced 1990.

Price: K77RFPMKII **$675.00**
Price: K77RLFPMKII Ultra-Light, synthetic stock, rings, no sights **$675.00**
Price: K77LRBBZMKII, left-hand bolt, rings, no sights, laminated
  stock **$729.00**
Price: K77RSFPMKII, synthetic stock, open sights **$759.00**
Price: K77RBZMKII, no sights, laminated wood stock, 223,
  22/250, 243, 270, 280 Rem., 7mm Rem. Mag., 30-06,
  308, 300 Win. Mag., 338 Win. Mag. **$729.00**
Price: K77RSBZMKII, open sights, laminated wood stock, 243,
  270, 7mm Rem. Mag., 30-06, 300 Win. Mag., 338 Win. Mag. . . . **$799.00**
Price: KM77RFPMKII (Shorts), M77RMKII. **$675.00**

Ruger M77RL Ultra Light

Similar to standard M77 except weighs 6 lbs., chambered for 223, 243, 308, 270, 30-06, 257 Roberts, barrel tapped for target scope blocks, 20" Ultra Light barrel. Overall length 40". Ruger's steel 1" scope rings supplied. Introduced 1983.

Price: M77RLMKII **$729.00**

Ruger M77 Mark II Compact Rifles

Similar to standard M77 except reduced 16-1/2" barrel, weighs 5-3/4 lbs. Chambered for 223, 243, 260 Rem., 308, and 7mm-08.

Price: M77CR MKII (blued finish, walnut stock) **$675.00**
Price: KM77CRBBZ MkII (stainless finish, black laminated stock) **$729.00**

Ruger KM77RFP MKII

Ruger 77/44

Ruger M77VT Target

Sako TRG-S

Sako 75 Hunter

RUGER 77/44 BOLT-ACTION RIFLE

Caliber: 44 Magnum, 4-shot magazine. **Barrel:** 18-1/2". **Weight:** 6 lbs. **Length:** 38-1/4" overall. **Stock:** American walnut with rubber butt pad and swivel studs or black polymer (stainless only). **Sights:** Gold bead front, folding leaf rear. Comes with Ruger 1" scope rings. **Features:** Uses same action as the Ruger 77/22. Short bolt stroke; rotary magazine; three-position safety. Introduced 1997. Made in U.S.A. by Sturm, Ruger & Co.
Price: Blue, walnut, 77/44RS **$605.00**
Price: Stainless, polymer, stock, K77/44RS **$605.00**

RUGER M77VT TARGET RIFLE

Caliber: 22-250, 220 Swift, 223, 243, 25-06, 308. **Barrel:** 26" heavy stainless steel with target gray finish. **Weight:** 9-3/4 lbs. **Length:** Approx. 44" overall. **Stock:** Laminated American hardwood with beavertail forend, steel swivel studs; no checkering or gripcap. **Sights:** Integral scope mount bases in receiver. **Features:** Ruger diagonal bedding system. Ruger steel 1" scope rings supplied. Fully adjustable trigger. Steel floorplate and trigger guard. New version introduced 1992.
Price: K77VTMKII **$819.00**

SAKO TRG-S BOLT-ACTION RIFLE

Caliber: 338 Lapua Mag., 30-378 Weatherby, 3-shot magazine. **Barrel:** 26". **Weight:** 7.75 lbs. **Length:** 45.5" overall. **Stock:** Reinforced polyurethane with Monte Carlo comb. **Sights:** None furnished. **Features:** Resistance-free bolt with 60-degree lift. Recoil pad adjustable for length. Free-floating barrel, detachable magazine, fully adjustable trigger. Matte blue metal. Introduced 1993. Imported from Finland by Beretta USA.
Price: **$896.00**

Sako TRG-42 Bolt-Action Rifle

Similar to TRG-S except 5-shot magazine, fully adjustable stock and competition trigger. Offered in 338 Lapua Mag. and 300 Win. Mag. Imported from Finland by Beretta USA.
Price: **$2,829.00**

SAKO 75 HUNTER BOLT-ACTION RIFLE

Caliber: 17 Rem., 222, 223, 22-250, 243, 7mm-08, 308 Win., 25-06, 270, 280, 30-06; 270 Wea. Mag., 7mm Rem. Mag., 7mm STW, 7mm Wea. Mag., 300 Win. Mag., 300 Wea. Mag., 338 Win. Mag., 340 Wea. Mag., 375 H&H, 416 Rem. Mag. **Barrel:** 22", standard calibers; 24", 26" magnum calibers. **Weight:** About 6 lbs. **Length:** NA. **Stock:** European walnut with matte lacquer finish. **Sights:** None furnished; dovetail scope mount rails. **Features:** New design with three locking lugs and a mechanical ejector, key locks firing pin and bolt, cold hammer-forged barrel is free-floating, 2-position safety, hinged floorplate or detachable magazine that can be loaded from the top, short 70 degree bolt lift. Five action lengths. Introduced 1997. Imported from Finland by Beretta USA.
Price: Standard calibers $1,129.00
Price: Magnum Calibers $1,163.00

Sako 75 Stainless Synthetic Rifle

Similar to 75 Hunter except all metal is stainless steel, synthetic stock has soft composite panels moulded into forend and pistol grip. Available in 22-250, 243, 308 Win., 25-06, 270, 30-06 with 22" barrel, 7mm Rem. Mag., 7mm STW, 300 Win. Mag., 338 Win. Mag. and 375 H&H Mag. with 24" barrel and 300 Wea. Mag., 300 Rem.Ultra Mag. with 26" barrel. Introduced 1997. Imported from Finland by Beretta USA.
Price: Standard calibers $1,212.00
Price: Magnum calibers $1,246.00

Sako 75 Stainless Hunter

Sako 75 Deluxe

Sako 75 Varmint

Savage 110GXP3

Price: Standard calibers, right-hand $1,035.00
Price: Magnum calibers, right-hand $1,106.00
Price: Standard calibers, synthetic stock $985.00
Price: Magnum calibers, synthetic stock. $1,056.00

Sako 75 Deluxe Rifle

Similar to 75 Hunter except select wood rosewood gripcap and forend tip. Available in 17 Rem., 222, 223, 25-06, 243, 7mm-08, 308, 25-06, 270, 280, 30-06; 270 Wea. Mag., 7mm Rem. Mag., 7mm STW, 7mm Wea. Mag., 300 Win. Mag., 300 Wea. Mag., 338 Win. Mag., 340 Wea. Mag., 375 H&H, 416 Rem. Mag. Introduced 1997. Imported from Finland by Beretta USA.
Price: Standard calibers $1,653.00
Price: Magnum calibers $1,688.00

Sako 75 Varmint Stainless Laminated Rifle

Similar to Sako 75 Hunter except chambered only for 222, 223, 22-250, 22 PPC USA, 6mm PPC, heavy 24" barrel with recessed crown, all metal is stainless steel, laminated wood stock with beavertail forend. Introduced 1999. Imported from Finland by Beretta USA.
Price: $1,448.00

Sako 75 Varmint Rifle

Similar to Model 75 Hunter except chambered only for 17 Rem., 222 Rem., 223 Rem., 22-250 Rem., 22 PPC and 6mm PPC, 24" heavy barrel with recessed crown, beavertail forend. Introduced 1998. Imported from Finland by Beretta USA.
Price: $1,337.00

SAUER 202 BOLT-ACTION RIFLE

Caliber: Standard-243, 6.5x55, 270 Win., 308 Win., 30-06; magnum-7mm Rem. Mag., 300 Win. Mag., 300 Wea. Mag., 375 H&H. **Barrel:** 23.6" (standard), 26" (magnum). **Weight:** 7.7 lbs. (standard). **Length:** 44.3" overall (23.6" barrel). **Stock:** Select American Claro walnut with high-gloss epoxy finish, rosewood grip and forend caps; 22 lpi checkering. Synthetic also available. **Sights:** None furnished; drilled and tapped for scope mounting. **Features:** Short 60° bolt throw; detachable box magazine; six-lug bolt; quick-change barrel; tapered bore; adjustable two-stage trigger; firing pin cocking indicator. Introduced 1994. Imported from Germany by SIGARMS, Inc.

SAVAGE MODEL 10GXP3, 110GXP3 PACKAGE GUNS

Caliber: 223 Rem., 22-250 Rem., 243 Win., 7mm-08 Rem., 308 Win., 300 WSM (10GXP3). 25-06 Rem., 270 Win., 30-06 Spfld., 7mm Rem. Mag., 300 Win. Mag., 300 Rem. Ultra Mag. (110GXP3). **Barrel:** 22" 24", 26". **Weight:** 7.5 lbs. average. **Length:** 43"-47". **Stock:** Walnut Monte Carlo with checkering. **Sights:** 3-9X40mm scope, mounted & bore sighted. **Features:** Blued, free floating and button rifled, internal box magazines, swivel studs, leather sling. Left-hand available.
Price: $495.00

SAVAGE MODEL 11FXP3, 111FXP3, 111FCXP3, 11FYXP3 (Youth) PACKAGE GUNS

Caliber: 223 Rem., 22-250 Rem., 243 Win., 308 Win., 300 WSM (11FXP3). 270 Win., 30-06 Spfld., 25-06 Rem., 7mm Rem. Mag., 300 Win. Mag., 338 Win. Mag., 300 Rem. Ultra Mag. (11FCXPE & 111FXP3). **Barrel:** 22"-26". **Weight:** 6.5 lbs. **Length:** 41"-47". **Stock:** Synthetic checkering, dual pillar bed. **Sights:** 3-9X40mm scope, mounted & bore sighted. **Features:** Blued, free floating and button rifled, Top loading internal box mag (except 111FXCP3 has detachable box mag.). Nylon sling and swivel studs. Some left-hand available.
Price: Model 11FXP3 . . . . $505.00
Price: Model 111FCXP3 . . . . $425.00
Price: Model 11FYXP3, 243 Win., 12.5" pull (youth) $471.00

SAVAGE MODEL 16FXP3, 116FXP3 SS ACTION PACKAGE GUNS

Caliber: 223 Rem., 243 Win., 308 Win., 300 WSM, 270 Win., 30-06 Spfld., 7mm Rem. Mag., 300 Win. Mag., 338 Win. Mag., 375 H&H, 7mm S&W, 7mm Rem. Ultra Mag., 300 Rem. Ultra Mag. **Barrel:** 22", 24", 26". **Weight:** 6.75 lbs. average. **Length:** 41"-46". **Stock:** Synthetic checkering, dual pillar bed. **Sights:** 3-9X40mm scope, mounted & bore sighted. **Features:** Free floating and button rifled. Internal box mag., nylon sling and swivel studs.
Price: $556.00

RIFLES

CENTERFIRE RIFLES — BOLT ACTION

Savage 11FXP3

Savage 111FCXP3

Savage 10FCM Scout Ultra Light

Savage Model 10FP

Savage Model 10FPLE1

SAVAGE MODEL 10FM SIERRA ULTRA LIGHT RIFLE

Caliber: 223, 243, 308. **Barrel:** 20". **Weight:** 6 lbs. **Length:** 41-1/2". **Stock:** "Dual Pillar" bedding in black synthetic stock with silver medallion in grip-cap. **Sights:** None furnished; drilled and tapped for scope mounting. **Features:** True short action. Comes with sling and quick-detachable swivels. Introduced 1998. Made in U.S.A. by Savage Arms, Inc.
Price: $495.00

SAVAGE MODEL 10FCM SCOUT ULTRA LIGHT RIFLE

Caliber: 7mm-08 Rem., 308 Win. **Barrel:** 20", 4-shot. **Weight:** 6.25 lbs. **Length:** 39.75" overall. **Stock:** Synthetic checkering, dual pillar bed. **Sights:** Ghost ring rear, gold bead front. **Features:** Blued, detachable box magazine, Savage shooting sling/carry strap. Quick detach swivels.
Price: $581.00

SAVAGE MODEL 10/110FP LONG RANGE RIFLE

Caliber: 223, 25-06, 308, 30-06, 300 Win. Mag., 7mm Rem. Mag., 4-shot magazine. **Barrel:** 24", heavy; recessed target muzzle. **Weight:** 8-1/2 lbs. **Length:** 45.5" overall. **Stock:** Black graphite/fiberglass composition; positive checkering. **Sights:** None furnished. Receiver drilled and tapped for scope mounting. **Features:** Pillar-bedded stock. Black matte finish on all metal parts. Double swivel studs on the forend for sling and/or bipod mount. Right or left-hand. Introduced 1990. From Savage Arms, Inc.
Price: Right- or left-hand. $558.00

Savage Model 10FP Tactical Rifle

Similar to the Model 110FP except has true short action, chambered for 223, 308; black synthetic stock with "Dual Pillar" bedding. Introduced 1998. Made in U.S.A. by Savage Arms, Inc.
Price: $558.00
Price: Model 10FLP (left-hand). $558.00
Price: Model 10FP-LE1 (20"), 10FPLE2 (26") $566.00
Price: Model 10FPXP-LE w/Burris 3.5-10X50 scope,
Harris bipod package $1,632.00

Savage Model 10FP-LE1A Tactical Rifle

Similar to the Model 110FP except weighs 10.75 lbs. and has overall length of 39.75". Chambered for 223 Rem., 308 Win. Black synthetic Choate™ adjustable stock with accessory rail and swivel studs.
Price: $684.00

184 • GUNS ILLUSTRATED

Savage Model 10FPXP-LE

Savage Model 111F

Savage Model 11FNS

Savage Model 11G

Savage Model 10GY

SAVAGE MODEL 111 CLASSIC HUNTER RIFLES

Caliber: 25-06 Rem., 270 Win., 30-06 Spfld., 7mm Rem. Mag, 300 Win. Mag., 7mm RUM, 300 RUM. **Barrel:** 22", 24", 26" (magnum calibers). **Weight:** 6.5 to 7.5 lbs. **Length:** 42.75" to 47.25". **Stock:** Walnut-finished hardwood (M111G, GC); graphite/fiberglass filled composite. **Sights:** Ramp front, open fully adjustable rear; drilled and tapped for scope mounting. **Features:** Three-position top tang safety, double front locking lugs, free-floated button-rifled barrel. Comes with trigger lock, target, ear puffs. Introduced 1994. Made in U.S.A. by Savage Arms, Inc.
Price: Model 111F (270 Win., 30-06 Spfld., 7mm Rem. Mag., 300 win. Mag.). **$411.00**
Price: Model 111F (25-06 Rem., 338 Win. Mag., 7mm Rem. Ultra Mag, 300 Rem. Ultra Mag.) **$461.00**
Price: Model 111G
  (wood stock, top-loading magazine, right- or left-hand) **$436.00**
Price: Model 111GNS (wood stock,
  top-loading magazine, no sights, right-hand only) **$428.00**

Savage Model 11 Classic Hunter Rifles, Short Action

Similar to the Model 111F except has true short action, chambered for 22-250, Rem., 243 Win., 7mm-08 Rem., 308 Win.; black synthetic stock with "Dual Pillar" bedding, positive checkering. Introduced 1998. Made in U.S.A. by Savage Arms, Inc.
Price: Model 11F **$461.00**
Price: Model 11FL (left-hand) **$461.00**
Price: Model 11FNS (right-hand, no sights) **$453.00**
Price: Model 11G (wood stock). **$436.00**
Price: Model 11GL (as above, left-hand) **$436.00**
Price: Model 11FC (right hand, open sights) **$487.00**

Savage Model 10GY

Similar to the Model 111G except weighs 6.3 lbs., is 42-1/2" overall, and the stock is scaled for ladies, small-framed adults and youths. Chambered for 223, 243, 308. Ramp front sight, open adjustable rear; drilled and tapped for scope mounts. Made in U.S.A. by Savage Arms, Inc.
Price: Model 10GY (short action, calibers 223, 243, 308) **$436.00**

CENTERFIRE RIFLES — BOLT ACTION

Savage Model 114U

Savage Model 12FV

Savage Model 12VSS

Savage Model 116SE Safari Express

SAVAGE MODEL 114U ULTRA RIFLE

Caliber: 270 Win., 30-06 Spfld., 7mm Rem. Mag., 7mm STW, 300 Win. Mag. **Barrel:** 22"-24". **Weight:** 7-7.5 lbs. **Length:** 43.25"-45.25" overall. **Stock:** Ultra high gloss American walnut with black tip and custom cut checkering. **Sights:** None furnished; drilled and tapped for scope mounting. **Features:** High-luster blued barrel action, internal box magazine.
Price: $552.00

SAVAGE MODEL 112 LONG RANGE RIFLES

Caliber: 22-250, 223, 5-shot magazine. **Barrel:** 26" heavy. **Weight:** 8.8 lbs. **Length:** 47.5" overall. **Stock:** Black graphite/fiberglass filled composite with positive checkering. **Sights:** None furnished; drilled and tapped for scope mounting. **Features:** Pillar-bedded stock. Blued barrel with recessed target-style muzzle. Double front swivel studs for attaching bipod. Introduced 1991. Made in U.S.A. by Savage Arms, Inc.
Price: Model 112FVSS (cals. 223, 22-250, 25-06, 7mm Rem. Mag., 300 Win. Mag., stainless barrel, bolt handle, trigger guard),
right- or left-hand. $626.00
Price: Model 112FVSS-S (as above, single shot) $675.00
Price: Model 112BVSS (heavy-prone laminated stock with high comb, Wundhammer swell, fluted stainless barrel, bolt handle,
trigger guard) $675.00
Price: Model 112BVSS-S (as above, single shot) $675.00

Savage Model 12 Long Range Rifles

Similar to the Model 112 Long Range except with true short action, chambered for 223, 22-250, 308. Models 12FV, 12FVSS have black synthetic stocks with "Dual Pillar" bedding, positive checkering, swivel studs; model 12BVSS has brown laminated stock with beavertail forend, fluted stainless barrel. Introduced 1998. Made in U.S.A. by Savage Arms, Inc.
Price: Model 12FV (223, 22-250, 243 Win., 308 Win., blue)..... $515.00
Price: Model 12FVSS (blue action, fluted stainless barrel)...... $626.00
Price: Model 12FLVSS (as above, left-hand) $626.00
Price: Model 12FVSS-S
(blue action, fluted stainless barrel, single shot) $934.00

Price: Model 12BVSS (laminated stock)................... $675.00
Price: Model 12BVSS-S (as above, single shot) $675.00
Price: Model 12BVSS-XP (hard case, Burris 6-18X37) $1,100.00

Savage Model 12VSS Varminter Rifle

Similar to other Model 12s except blue/stainless steel action, fluted stainless barrel, Choate full pistol-grip, adjustable synthetic stock, Sharp Shooter trigger. Overall length 47-1/2 inches, weighs appx. 15 lbs. No sights; drilled and tapped for scope mounts. Chambered in 223, 22-250, 308 Win. Made in U.S.A. by Savage Arms Inc.
Price: $934.00

SAVAGE MODEL 116SE SAFARI EXPRESS RIFLE

Caliber: 458 Win. Mag. **Barrel:** 24". **Weight:** 8.5 lbs. **Length:** 45.5" overall. **Stock:** Classic-style select walnut with ebony forend tip, deluxe cut checkering. Two cross bolts; internally vented recoil pad. **Sights:** Bead on ramp front, three-leaf express rear. **Features:** Controlled-round feed design; adjustable muzzle brake; one-piece barrel band stud. Satin-finished stainless steel barreled action. Introduced 1994. Made in U.S.A. by Savage Arms, Inc.
Price: $1,013.00

SAVAGE MODEL 116 WEATHER WARRIORS

Caliber: 375 H&H, 300 Rem. Ultra Mag., 308 Win., 300 Rem. Ultra Mag., 300 WSM, 7mm Rem. Ultra Mag., 7mm Rem. Short Ultra Mag., 7mm S&W, 7mm-08 Rem. **Barrel:** 22", 24" for 7mm Rem. Mag., 300 Win. Mag., 338 Win. Mag. (M116FSS only). **Weight:** 6.25 to 6.5 lbs. **Length:** 41"-47". **Stock:** Graphite/fiberglass filled composite. **Sights:** None furnished; drilled and tapped for scope mounting. **Features:** Stainless steel with matte finish; free-floated barrel; quick-detachable swivel studs; laser-etched bolt; scope bases and rings. Left-hand models available in all models, calibers at same price. Model 116FSS introduced 1991; 116FSAK introduced 1994. Made in U.S.A. by Savage Arms, Inc.
Price: Model 116FSS (top-loading magazine) $520.00
Price: Model 116FSAK (top-loading magazine, Savage Adjustable Muzzle
Brake system)...................................... $601.00
Price: Model 16BSS (brown laminate, 24") $668.00
Price: Model 116BSS (brown laminate, 26") $668.00

RIFLES

Savage Model 16FSS

Savage Model 116FSAK

Sigarms SHR 970

Steyr Mannlicher SBS

Steyr SBS Forester

Steyr SBS Prohunter

Savage Model 16FSS Rifle

Similar to Model 116FSS except true short action, chambered for 223, 243, 22" free-floated barrel; black graphite/fiberglass stock with "Dual Pillar" bedding. Also left-hand. Introduced 1998. Made in U.S.A. by Savage Arms, Inc.

Price: **$520.00**

SIGARMS SHR 970 SYNTHETIC RIFLE

Caliber: 270, 30-06. **Barrel:** 22". **Weight:** 7.2 lbs. **Length:** 41.9" overall. **Stock:** Textured black fiberglass or walnut. **Sights:** None furnished; drilled and tapped for scope mounting. **Features:** Quick takedown; interchangeable barrels; removable box magazine; cocking indicator; three-position safety. Introduced 1998. Imported by Sigarms, Inc.

Price: Synthetic stock **$499.00**
Price: Walnut stock **$550.00**

STEYR CLASSIC MANNLICHER SBS RIFLE

Caliber: 243, 25-06, 308, 6.5x55, 6.5x57, 270, 7x64 Brenneke, 7mm-08, 7.5x55, 30-06, 9.3x62, 6.5x68, 7mm Rem. Mag., 300 Win. Mag., 8x68S, 4-shot magazine. **Barrel:** 23.6" standard; 26" magnum; 20" full stock standard calibers. **Weight:** 7 lbs. **Length:** 40.1" overall. **Stock:** Hand-checkered fancy European oiled walnut with standard forend. **Sights:** Ramp

front adjustable for elevation, V-notch rear adjustable for windage. **Features:** Single adjustable trigger; 3-position roller safety with "safe-bolt" setting; drilled and tapped for Steyr factory scope mounts. Introduced 1997. Imported from Austria by GSI, Inc.

Price: Full-stock, standard calibers...................... **$1,749.00**

STEYR SBS FORESTER RIFLE

Caliber: 243, 25-06, 270, 7mm-08, 308 Win., 30-06, 7mm Rem. Mag., 300 Win. Mag. Detachable 4-shot magazine. **Barrel:** 23.6", standard calibers; 25.6", magnum calibers. **Weight:** 7.5 lbs. **Length:** 44.5" overall (23.6" barrel). **Stock:** Oil-finished American walnut with Monte Carlo cheekpiece. Pachmayr 1" swivels. **Sights:** None furnished. Drilled and tapped for Browning A-Bolt mounts. **Features:** Steyr Safe Bolt systems, three-position ambidextrous roller tang safety, for Safe, Loading Fire. Matte finish on barrel and receiver; adjustable trigger. Rotary cold-hammer forged barrel. Introduced 1997. Imported by GSI, Inc.

Price: Standard calibers **$799.00**
Price: Magnum calibers **$829.00**

STEYR SBS PROHUNTER RIFLE

Similar to the SBS Forester except has ABS synthetic stock with adjustable butt spacers, straight comb without cheekpiece, palm swell, Pachmayr 1" swivels. Special 10-round magazine conversion kit available. Introduced 1997. Imported by GSI.

Price: Standard calibers **$769.00**
Price: Magnum calibers **$799.00**

RIFLES

CENTERFIRE RIFLES — BOLT ACTION

Steyr Scout Rifle

Tikka T-3 Hunter

STEYR SCOUT BOLT-ACTION RIFLE
Caliber: 308 Win., 5-shot magazine. **Barrel:** 19", fluted. **Weight:** NA. **Length:** NA. **Stock:** Gray Zytel. **Sights:** Pop-up front & rear, Leupold M8 2.5x28 IER scope on Picatinny optic rail with Steyr mounts. **Features:** luggage case, scout sling, two stock spacers, two magazines. Introduced 1998. From GSI.
Price: From **$1,969.00**

STEYR SSG BOLT-ACTION RIFLE
Caliber: 308 Win., detachable 5-shot rotary magazine. **Barrel:** 26" **Weight:** 8.5 lbs. **Length:** 44.5" overall. **Stock:** Black ABS Cycolac with spacers for length of pull adjustment. **Sights:** Hooded ramp front adjustable for elevation, V-notch rear adjustable for windage. **Features:** Sliding safety; NATO rail for bipod; 1" swivels; Parkerized finish; single or double-set triggers. Imported from Austria by GSI, Inc.
Price: SSG-PI, iron sights. **$1,699.00**
Price: SSG-PII, heavy barrel, no sights **$1,699.00**
Price: SSG-PIIK, 20" heavy barrel, no sights **$1,699.00**
Price: SSG-PIV, 16.75" threaded heavy barrel with flash hider . **$2,659.00**

TIKKA WHITETAIL HUNTER LEFT-HAND BOLT-ACTION RIFLE
Caliber: 22-250, 223, 243, 7mm-08, 25-06, 270, 308, 30-06, 7mm Rem. Mag., 300 Win. Mag., 338 Win. Mag. **Barrel:** 22-1/2" (std. cals.), 24-1/2" (magnum cals.). **Weight:** 7-1/8 lbs. **Length:** 43" overall (std. cals.). **Stock:** European walnut with Monte Carlo comb, rubber butt pad, checkered grip and forend. **Sights:** None furnished. **Features:** Detachable four-shot magazine (standard calibers), three-shot in magnums. Receiver dovetailed for scope mounting. Reintroduced 1996. Imported from Finland by Beretta USA.
Price: Left-hand **$710.00**

Tikka Continental Varmint Rifle
Similar to the standard Tikka rifle except has 26" heavy barrel, extra-wide forend. Chambered for 17 Rem., 22-250, 223, 308. Reintroduced 1996. Made in Finland by Sako. Imported by Beretta USA.
Price: **$720.00**

Tikka Continental Long Range Hunting Rifle
Similar to the Whitetail Hunter except has 26" heavy barrel. Available in 25-06, 270 Win., 7mm Rem. Mag., 300 Win. Mag. Introduced 1996. Imported from Finland by Beretta USA.
Price: 25-06, 270 Win. **$720.00**
Price: 7mm Rem. Mag., 300 Win. Mag. **$750.00**

Tikka Whitetail Hunter Stainless Synthetic
Similar to the Whitetail Hunter except all metal is of stainless steel, and it has a black synthetic stock. Available in 22-250, 223, 243, 7mm-08,

25-06, 270, 308, 30-06, 7mm Rem. Mag., 300 Win. Mag., 338 Win. Mag. Introduced 1997. Imported from Finland by Beretta USA.
Price: Standard calibers **$775.00**
Price: Magnum calibers **$745.00**

VEKTOR BUSHVELD BOLT-ACTION RIFLE
Caliber: 243, 308, 7x57, 7x64 Brenneke, 270 Win., 30-06, 300 Win. Mag., 300 H&H, 9.3x62. **Barrel:** 22"-26". **Weight:** NA. **Length:** NA. **Stock:** Turkish walnut with wrap-around hand checkering. **Sights:** Blade on ramp front, fixed standing leaf rear. **Features:** Combines the best features of the Mauser 98 and Winchester 70 actions. Controlled-round feed; Mauser-type extractor; no cut-away through the bolt locking lug; M70-type three-position safety; Timney-type adjustable trigger. Introduced 1999. Imported from South Africa by Vektor USA.
Price: . . . . **$1,595.00 to $1,695.00**

VEKTOR MODEL 98 BOLT-ACTION RIFLE
Caliber: 243, 308, 7x57, 7x64 Brenneke, 270 Win., 30-06, 300 Win. Mag., 300 H&H, 375 H&H, 9.3x62. **Barrel:** 22"-26". **Weight:** NA. **Length:** NA. **Stock:** Turkish walnut with hand-checkered grip and forend. **Sights:** None furnished; drilled and tapped for scope mounting. **Features:** Bolt has guide rib; non-rotating, long extractor enhances positive feeding; polished blue finish. Updated Mauser 98 action. Introduced 1999. Imported from South Africa by Vektor USA.
Price: . . . . **$1,149.00 to $1,249.00**

WEATHERBY MARK V DELUXE BOLT-ACTION RIFLE
Caliber: All Weatherby calibers plus 22-250, 243, 25-06, 270 Win., 280 Rem., 7mm-08, 30-06, 308 Win. **Barrel:** 24" barrel on standard calibers. **Weight:** 8-1/2 to 10-1/2 lbs. **Length:** 46-5/8" to 46-3/4" overall. **Stock:** Walnut, Monte Carlo with cheekpiece; high luster finish; checkered pistol grip and forend; recoil pad. **Sights:** None furnished. **Features:** Cocking indicator; adjustable trigger; hinged floorplate, thumb safety; quick detachable sling swivels. Made in U.S.A. From Weatherby.
Price: 257, 270, 7mm. 300, 340 Wea. Mags., 26" barrel. **$1,767.00**
Price: 416 Wea. Mag. with Accubrake, 28" barrel **$2,079.00**
Price: 460 Wea. Mag. with Accubrake, 28" barrel **$2,443.00**
Price: 24" barrel **$1,715.00**

Weatherby Mark V Lazermark Rifle
Same as Mark V Deluxe except stock has extensive oak leaf pattern laser carving on pistol grip and forend. Introduced 1981.
Price: 257, 270, 7mm Wea. Mag., 300, 340, 26" **$1,923.00**
Price: 378 Wea. Mag., 28" **$2,266.00**
Price: 416 Wea. Mag. 28", Accubrake **$2,266.00**
Price: 460 Wea. Mag. 28", Accubrake **$2,661.00**

RIFLES

CENTERFIRE RIFLES — BOLT ACTION

Weatherby Mark V Lazermark

Weatherby Mark V Sporter

Weatherby Mark V Stainless

Weatherby Mark V Synthetic

Weatherby Mark V Accumark

Weatherby Mark V Sporter Rifle
Same as the Mark V Deluxe without the embellishments. Metal has low-luster blue, stock is Claro walnut with matte finish, Monte Carlo comb, recoil pad. Introduced 1993. From Weatherby.
Price: 22-250, 243, 240 Wea. Mag., 25-06, 7mm-08, 270 WCF, 280, 30-06, 308; 24"... **$1,091.00**
Price: 257 Wea., 270, 7 mm Wea., 7mm Rem., 300 Wea., 300 Win., 340 Wea., 338 Win. Mag., 26" barrel for Wea. Calibers;
24" for non-Wea. Calibers. **$1,143.00**

Weatherby Mark V Stainless Rifle
Similar to the Mark V Deluxe except made of 410-series stainless steel. Also available in 30-378 Wea. Mag. Has lightweight injection-moulded synthetic stock with raised Monte Carlo comb, checkered grip and forend, custom floorplate release. Right-hand only. Introduced 1995. Made in U.S.A. From Weatherby.
Price: 22-250 Rem., 243 Win., 240 Wby. Mag., 25-06 Rem., 270 Win., 280 Rem., 7mm-08 Rem., 30-06 Spfld., 308 Win., 24" barrel. . **$1,018.00**
Price: 257, 270, 7mm, 300, 340 Wby. Mag., 26" barrel....... **$1,070.00**
Price: 7mm Rem. Mag., 300 Win. Mag., 338 Win. Mag.,
375 H&H Mag., 24" barrel........................... **$1,070.00**

Weatherby Mark V Synthetic
Similar to the Mark V Stainless except made of matte finished blued steel. Injection moulded synthetic stock. Weighs 6-1/2 lbs., 24" barrel. Available in 22-250, 240 Wea. Mag., 243, 25-06, 270, 7mm-08, 280, 30-06, 308. Introduced 1997. Made in U.S.A. From Weatherby.
Price: **$923.00**
Price: 257, 270, 7mm, 300, 340 Wea. Mags., 26" barrel **$975.00**
Price: 7mm STW, 7mm Rem. Mag., 300, 338 Win. Mags....... **$975.00**
Price: 375 H&H, 24" barrel............................. **$975.00**
Price: 30-378 Wea. Mag., 338-378 Wea 28" barrel.......... **$1,151.00**

WEATHERBY MARK V ACCUMARK RIFLE
Caliber: 257, 270, 7mm, 300, 340 Wea. Mags., 338-378 Wea. Mag., 30-378 Wea. Mag., 7mm STW, 7mm Rem. Mag., 300 Win. Mag. **Barrel:** 26", 28". **Weight:** 8-1/2 lbs. **Length:** 46-5/8" overall. **Stock:** Bell & Carlson with full length aluminum bedding block. **Sights:** None furnished. Drilled and tapped for scope mounting. **Features:** Uses Mark V action with heavy-contour stainless barrel with black oxidized flutes, muzzle diameter of .705". Introduced 1996. Made in U.S.A. From Weatherby.
Price: 26" **$1,507.00**
Price: 30-378 Wea. Mag., 338-378 Wea. Mag., 28",
Accubrake....................................... **$1,724.00**
Price: 223, 22-250, 243, 240 Wea. Mag., 25-06, 270,
280 Rem., 7mm-08, 30-06, 308; 24".................... **$1,455.00**
Price: Accumark Left-Hand 257, 270, 7mm, 300, 340 Wea.
Mag., 7mm Rem. Mag., 7mm STW, 300 Win. Mag. **$1,559.00**
Price: Accumark Left-Hand 30-378, 333-378 Wea. Mags...... **$1,788.00**

RIFLES

Weatherby Mark V SVR

Weatherby Mark V Fibermark

Weatherby Mark V Dangerous Game Rifle

Weatherby Mark V Accumark Ultra Lightweight Rifles

Similar to the Mark V Accumark except weighs 5-3/4 lbs, 6-3/4 lbs. in Mag. calibers.; 24", 26" fluted barrel with recessed target crown; hand- laminated stock with CNC-machined aluminum bedding plate and faint gray "spider web" finish. Available in 257, 270, 7mm, 300 Wea. Mags., (26"); 243, 240 Wea. Mag., 25-06, 270 Win., 280 Rem., 7mm-08, 7mm Rem. Mag., 30-06, 338-06 A-Square, 308, 300 Win. Mag. (24"). Intro-duced 1998. Made in U.S.A. by Weatherby.

Price: . . . . **$1,459.00 to $1,517.00**
Price: Left-hand models **$1,559.00**

Weatherby Mark V Special Varmint Rifle (SVR)

A new entrant in the Mark V series similar to the Super VarmintMaster and Accumark with 22", #3 contour chrome moly 4140 steel Krieger Cri-terion botton-rifled barrel with 1-degree target crown and hand-laminated composite stock. Available in .223 Rem. (5+1 magazine capacity) and .22-250 Rem. (4+1 magazine capacity) in right-hand models only.

Price: **$999.00**

Weatherby Mark V SVM/SPM Rifles

Similar to the Mark V Accumark except has 26" fluted (SVM) or 24" fluted Krieger barrel, spiderweb-pattern tan laminated synthetic stock. SVM has a fully adjustable trigger. Chambered for 223, 22-250, 220 Swift (SVM only), 243, 7mm-08 and 308. Made in U.S.A. by Weatherby.

Price: SVM (Super VarmintMaster), repeater or single-shot. . . . **$1,517.00**
New! **Price:** SPM (Super PredatorMaster) **$1,459.00**

Weatherby Mark V Fibermark Rifles

Similar to other Mark V models except has black Kevlar® and fiberglass composite stock and bead-blast blue or stainless finish. Chambered for 19 standard and magnum calibers. Introduced 1983; reintroduced 2001. Made in U.S.A. by Weatherby.

Price: Fibermark . . . . **$1,070.00 to $1,347.00**
Price: Fibermark Stainless . . . . **$1,165.00 to $1,390.00**

WEATHERBY MARK V DANGEROUS GAME RIFLE

Caliber: 375 H&H, 375 Wea. Mag., 378 Wea. Mag., 416 Rem. Mag., 416 Wea. Mag., 458 Win. Mag., .458 Lott, 460 Wea. Mag. 300 Win. Mag., 300 Wby., Mag., 338 Win. Mag., 340 Wby. Mag., 24" only **Barrel:** 24" or 26". **Weight:** 8-3/4 to 9-1/2 lbs. **Length:** 44-5/8" to 46-5/8" overall. **Stock:** Kevlar® and fiberglass composite. **Sights:** Barrel-band hooded front with large gold bead, adjustable ramp/shallow "V" rear. **Features:** Designed for dangerous-game hunting. Black oxide matte finish on all metalwork; Pachmayr Decelerator™ recoil pad, short-throw Mark V action. Introduced 2001. Made in U.S.A. by Weatherby.

Price: . . . . **$2,703.00 to $2,935.00**

WEATHERBY MARK V SUPER BIG GAMEMASTER DEER RIFLE

Caliber: 240 Wby. Mag., 25-06 Rem., 270 Win., 280 Rem., 30-06 Spfld., 257 Wby. Mag., 270 Wby. Mag., 7mm Rem., Mag., 7mm Wby. Mag., 338-06 A-Square, 300 Win. Mag., 300 Wby. Mag. **Barrel:** 26", target crown. **Weight:** 5-3/4 lbs., (6-3/4 lbs. Magnum). **Stock:** Raised comb Monte Carlo composite. **Features:** Fluted barrel, aluminum bedding block, Pachmayr decelerator, 54-degree bolt lift, adj. trigger.

Price: **$1,459.00**
Price: Magnum **$1,517.00**

WEATHERBY MARK V ROYAL CUSTOM RIFLE

Caliber: 257, 270, 7mm, 300, 340 all Wby. Mags. Other calibers available upon request. **Barrel:** 26". **Stock:** Monte Carlo hand-checkered claro walnut with high gloss finish. **Features:** Bolt and follower are damascened with checkered knob. Engraved receiver, bolt sleeve and floorplate sport scroll pattern. Animal images on floorplate optional. High gloss blue, 24-karat gold and nickel-plating. Made in U.S.A. From Weatherby.

Price: **$5,831.00**

WEATHERBY THREAT RESPONSE RIFLES (TRR) SERIES

Caliber: TRR 223 Rem., 300 Win. TRR Magnum and Magnum Custom 300 Win. Mag., 300 Wby. Mag., 30-378 Wby. Mag., 328-378 Wby. Mag. **Barrel:** 22", 26", target crown. **Stock:** Hand-laminated composite. TTR & TRR Magnum have raised comb Monte Carlo style. TRR Magnum Custom adjustable ergonomic stock. **Features:** Adjustable trigger, aluminum bedding block, beavertail forearms dual tapered, flat-bottomed. "Rocker Arm" lockdown scope mounting. 54 degree bolt. Pachmayr decelerator pad. Made in U.S.A.

Price: TRR Magnum Custom 300 . . . . **$2,699.00**
Price: 30-378, 338-378 with accubrake **$2,861.00**

WILDERNESS EXPLORER MULTI-CALIBER CARBINE

Caliber: 22 Hornet, 218 Bee, 44 Magnum, 50 A.E. (interchangeable). **Barrel:** 18", match grade. **Weight:** 5.5 lbs **Length:** 38-1/2" overall. **Stock:** Synthetic or wood. **Sights:** None furnished; comes with Weaver-style mount on barrel. **Features:** Quick-change barrel and bolt face for caliber switch. Removable box magazine; adjustable trigger with side safety; detachable swivel studs. Introduced 1997. Made in U.S.A. by Phillips & Rogers, Inc.

Price: **$995.00**

Wilderness Explorer

Winchester Model 70 Classic

Winchester Model 70 Classic Stainless

Winchester Model 70 Classic Featherweight

Winchester Model 70 Classic Compact

RIFLES

WINCHESTER MODEL 70 CLASSIC SPORTER LT

Caliber: 25-06, 270 Win., 30-06, 7mm STW, 7mm Rem. Mag., 300 Win. Mag., 338 Win. Mag., 3-shot magazine; 5-shot for 25-06, 270 Win., 30-06. **Barrel:** 24", 26" for magnums. **Weight:** 7-3/4 to 8 lbs. **Length:** 46-3/4" overall (26" bbl.). **Stock:** American walnut with cut checkering and satin finish. Classic style with straight comb. **Sights:** None furnished. Drilled and tapped for scope mounting. **Features:** Uses pre-64-type action with controlled round feeding. Three-position safety, stainless steel magazine follower; rubber butt pad; epoxy bedded receiver recoil lug. From U.S. Repeating Arms Co.

Price: 25-06, 270, 30-06 . . . . **$727.00**
Price: Other calibers **$756.00**
Price: Left-hand, 270 or 30-06 . . . . **$762.00**
Price: Left-hand, 7mm Rem. Mag or 300 Win. Mag. **$793.00**

Winchester Model 70 Classic Stainless Rifle

Same as Model 70 Classic Sporter except stainless steel barrel and pre-64-style action with controlled round feeding and matte gray finish, black composite stock impregnated with fiberglass and graphite, contoured rubber recoil pad. No sights (except 375 H&H). Available in 270 Win., 30-06, 7mm STW, 7mm Rem. Mag., 300 Win. Mag., 300 Ultra Mag., 338 Win. Mag., 375 H&H Mag. (24" barrel), 3- or 5-shot magazine. Weighs 7-1/2 lbs. Introduced 1994.

Price: 270, 30-06 . . . . **$800.00**
Price: 375 H&H Mag., with sights **$924.00**
Price: Other calibers **$829.00**

Winchester Model 70 Classic Featherweight

Same as Model 70 Classic except action bedded in standard-grade walnut stock. Available in 22-250, 243, 6.5x55, 308, 7mm-08, 270 Win., 30-06. Drilled and tapped for scope mounts. Weighs 7 lbs. Introduced 1992.

Price: **$726.00**

Winchester Model 70 Classic Compact

Similar to Classic Featherweight except scaled down for smaller shooters. 20" barrel, 12-1/2" length of pull. Pre-'64-type action. Available in 243, 308 or 7mm-08. Introduced 1998. Made in U.S.A. by U. S. Repeating Arms Co.

Price: **$740.00**

Winchester Model 70 Coyote

Winchester Model 70 Stealth

Winchester Model 70 Classic Super Grade

Winchester Model 70 Safari Express

Winchester Model 70 WSM

Winchester Model 70 Coyote

Similar to Model 4 Ranger except laminated wood stock, 24" medium-heavy stainless steel barrel Available in223 Rem., 22-250 Rem., 243 Win., or 308 Win.

Price: **$705.00**

WINCHESTER MODEL 70 STEALTH RIFLE

Caliber: 223, 22-250, 308 Win. **Barrel:** 26". **Weight:** 10-3/4 lbs. **Length:** 46" overall. **Stock:** Kevlar/fiberglass/graphite Pillar Plus Accu-Block with full-length aluminum bedding block. **Sights:** None furnished. **Features:** Push-feed bolt design; matte finish. Introduced 1999. Made in U.S.A. by U.S. Repeating Arms Co.

Price: **$785.00**

WINCHESTER MODEL 70 CLASSIC SUPER GRADE

Caliber: 25-06, 270, 30-06, 5-shot magazine; 7mm Rem. Mag., 300 Win. Mag., 338 Win. Mag., 3-shot magazine. **Barrel:** 24", 26" for magnums. **Weight:** 7-3/4 lbs. to 8 lbs. **Length:** 44-1/2" overall (24" bbl.) **Stock:** Walnut with straight comb, sculptured cheekpiece, wrap-around cut checkering, tapered forend, solid rubber butt pad. **Sights:** None furnished; comes with scope bases and rings. **Features:** Controlled round feeding with stainless steel claw extractor, bolt guide rail, three-position safety; all steel bottom metal, hinged floorplate, stainless magazine follower. Introduced 1994. From U.S. Repeating Arms Co.

Price: 25-06, 270, 30-06 .... **$995.00**
Price: Other calibers **$1,024.00**

WINCHESTER MODEL 70 CLASSIC SAFARI EXPRESS

Caliber: 375 H&H Mag., 416 Rem. Mag., 458 Win. Mag., 3-shot magazine. **Barrel:** 24". **Weight:** 8-1/4 to 8-1/2 lbs. **Stock:** American walnut with Monte Carlo cheekpiece. Wrap-around checkering and finish. **Sights:** Hooded ramp front, open rear. **Features:** Controlled round feeding. Two steel cross bolts in stock for added strength. Front sling swivel stud mounted on barrel. Contoured rubber butt pad. From U.S. Repeating Arms Co.

Price: **$1,124.00**
Price: Left-hand, 375 H&H only **$1,163.00**

WINCHESTER MODEL 70 WSM RIFLES

Caliber: 300 WSM, 3-shot magazine. **Barrel:** 24". **Weight:** 7-1/4 to 7-3/4 lbs. **Length:** 44" overall. **Stock:** Checkered walnut, black synthetic or laminated wood. **Sights:** None. **Features:** Model 70 designed for the new 300 Winchester Short Magnum cartridge. Short-action receiver, three-position safety, knurled bolt handle. Introduced 2001. From U.S. Repeating Arms Co.

Price: Classic Featherweight WSM (checkered walnut stock and forearm) **$769.00**
Price: Classic Stainless WSM (black syn. stock, stainless steel bbl.) **$829.00**
Price: Classic Laminated WSM (laminated wood stock) **$793.00**

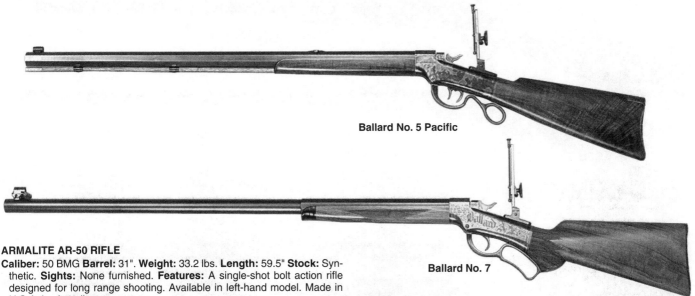

Ballard No. 5 Pacific

Ballard No. 7

ARMALITE AR-50 RIFLE

Caliber: 50 BMG **Barrel:** 31". **Weight:** 33.2 lbs. **Length:** 59.5" **Stock:** Synthetic. **Sights:** None furnished. **Features:** A single-shot bolt action rifle designed for long range shooting. Available in left-hand model. Made in U.S.A. by Armalite.
Price: **$2,745.00**

ARMSPORT 1866 SHARPS RIFLE, CARBINE

Caliber: 45-70. **Barrel:** 28", round or octagonal. **Weight:** 8.10 lbs. **Length:** 46" overall. **Stock:** Walnut. **Sights:** Blade front, folding adjustable rear. Tang sight set optionally available. **Features:** Replica of the 1866 Sharps. Color case-hardened frame, rest blued. Imported by Armsport.
Price: **$865.00**
Price: With octagonal barrel **$900.00**
Price: Carbine, 22" round barrel **$850.00**

BALLARD NO. 1 3/4 FAR WEST RIFLE

Caliber: 22 LR, 32-40, 38-55, 40-65, 40-70, 45-70, 45-110, 50-70, 50-90. **Barrel:** 30" std. or heavyweight. **Weight:** 10-1/2 lbs. (std.) or 11-3/4 lbs. (heavyweight bbl.) **Length:** NA. **Stock:** Walnut. **Sights:** Blade front, Rocky Mountain rear. **Features:** Single or double-set triggers, S-lever or ring-style lever; color case-hardened finish; hand polished and lapped Badger barrel. Made in U.S.A. by Ballard Rifle & Cartridge Co.
Price: **$2,250.00**

BALLARD NO. 4 PERFECTION RIFLE

Caliber: 22 LR, 32-40, 38-55, 40-65, 40-70, 45-70, 45-90, 45-110, 50-70, 50-90. **Barrel:** 30" or 32" octagon, standard or heavyweight. **Weight:** 10-1/2 lbs. (standard) or 11-3/4 lbs. (heavyweight bbl.). **Length:** NA. **Stock:** Smooth walnut. **Sights:** Blade front, Rocky Mountain rear. **Features:** Rifle or shotgun-style buttstock, straight grip action, single or double-set trigger, "S" or right lever, hand polished and lapped Badger barrel. Made in U.S.A. by Ballard Rifle & Cartridge Co.
Price: **$2,250.00**

BALLARD NO. 5 PACIFIC SINGLE-SHOT RIFLE

Caliber: 32-40, 38-55, 40-65, 40-90, 40-70 SS, 45-70 Govt., 45-110 SS, 50-70 Govt., 50-90 SS. **Barrel:** 30", or 32" octagonal. **Weight:** 10-1/2 lbs. **Length:** NA. **Stock:** High-grade walnut; rifle or shotgun style. **Sights:** Blade front, Rocky Mountain rear. **Features:** Standard or heavy barrel; double-set triggers; under-barrel wiping rod; ring lever. Introduced 1999. Made in U.S.A. by Ballard Rifle & Cartridge Co.
Price: **$2,575.00**

BALLARD NO. 7 LONG RANGE RIFLE

Caliber: 32-40, 38-55, 40-65, 40-70 SS, 45-70 Govt., 45-90, 45-110. **Barrel:** 32", 34" half-octagon. **Weight:** 11-3/4 lbs. **Length:** NA. **Stock:** Walnut; checkered pistol grip shotgun butt, ebony forend cap. **Sights:** Globe front. **Features:** Designed for shooting up to 1000 yards. Standard or heavy barrel; single or double-set trigger; hard rubber or steel buttplate. Introduced 1999. Made in U.S.A. by Ballard Rifle & Cartridge Co.
Price: From **$2,475.00**

BALLARD NO. 8 UNION HILL RIFLE

Caliber: 22 LR, 32-40, 38-55, 40-65 Win., 40-70 SS. **Barrel:** 30" half-octagon. **Weight:** About 10-1/2 lbs. **Length:** NA. **Stock:** Walnut; pistol grip butt with cheekpiece. **Sights:** Globe front. **Features:** Designed for 200-yard offhand shooting. Standard or heavy barrel; double-set triggers; full loop lever; hook Schuetzen buttplate. Introduced 1999. Made in U.S.A. by Bal-lard Rifle & Cartridge Co.
Price: From **$2,500.00**

BALLARD MODEL 1885 HIGH WALL SINGLE SHOT RIFLE

Caliber: 17 Bee, 22 Hornet, 218 Bee, 219 Don Wasp, 219 Zipper, 22 Hi-Power, 225 Win., 25-20 WCF, 25-35 WCF, 25 Krag, 7mmx57R, 30-30, 30-40 Krag, 303 British, 33 WCF, 348 WCF, 35 WCF, 35-30/30, 9.3x74R, 405 WCF, 50-110 WCF, 500 Express, 577 Express. **Barrel:** Lengths to 34". **Weight:** NA. **Length:** NA. **Stock:** Straight-grain American walnut. **Sights:** buckhorn or flat top rear, blade front. **Features:** Faithful copy of original Model 1885 High Wall; parts interchange with original rifles; variety of options available. Introduced 2000. Made in U.S.A. by Ballard Rifle & Cartridge LLC.
Price: From **$2,255.00**
Price: With single set trigger from **$2,355.00**

BARRETT MODEL 99 SINGLE SHOT RIFLE

Caliber: 50 BMG. **Barrel:** 33". **Weight:** 25 lbs. **Length:** 50.4" overall. **Stock:** Anodized aluminum with energy-absorbing recoil pad. **Sights:** None furnished; integral M1913 scope rail. **Features:** Bolt action; detachable bipod; match-grade barrel with high-efficiency muzzle brake. Introduced 1999. Made in U.S.A. by Barrett Firearms.
Price: From **$3,000.00**

BROWN MODEL 97D SINGLE SHOT RIFLE

Caliber: 17 Ackley Hornet through 45-70 Govt. **Barrel:** Up to 26", air gauged match grade. **Weight:** About 5 lbs., 11 oz. **Stock:** Sporter style with pistol grip, cheekpiece and Schnabel forend. **Sights:** None furnished; drilled and tapped for scope mounting. **Features:** Falling block action gives rigid barrel-receiver matting; polished blue/black finish. Hand-fitted action. Many options. Made in U.S.A. by E. Arthur Brown Co. Inc.
Price: From **$699.00**

BROWNING MODEL 1885 HIGH WALL SINGLE SHOT RIFLE

Caliber: 22-250, 30-06, 270, 7mm Rem. Mag., 454 Casull, 45-70. **Barrel:** 28". **Weight:** 8 lbs, 12 oz. **Length:** 43-1/2" overall. **Stock:** Walnut with straight grip, Schnabel forend. **Sights:** None furnished; drilled and tapped for scope mounting. **Features:** Replica of J.M. Browning's high-wall falling block rifle. Octagon barrel with recessed muzzle. Imported from Japan by Browning. Introduced 1985.
Price: **$1,027.00**

RIFLES

CENTERFIRE RIFLES — SINGLE SHOT

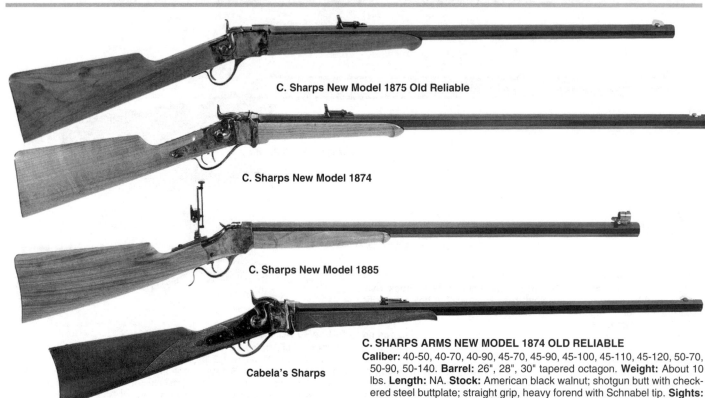

C. Sharps New Model 1875 Old Reliable

C. Sharps New Model 1874

C. Sharps New Model 1885

Cabela's Sharps

BRNO ZBK 110 SINGLE SHOT RIFLE

Caliber: 222 Rem., 5.6x52R, 22 Hornet, 5.6x50 Mag., 6.5x57R, 7x57R, 8x57JRS. **Barrel:** 23.6". **Weight:** 5.9 lbs. **Length:** 40.1" overall. **Stock:** European walnut. **Sights:** None furnished; drilled and tapped for scope mounting. **Features:** Top tang opening lever; cross-bolt safety; polished blue finish. Announced 1998. Imported from The Czech Republic by Euro-Imports.

Price: Standard calibers **$223.00**
Price: 7x57R, 8x57JRS **$245.00**
Price: Lux model, standard calibers **$311.00**
Price: Lux model, 7x57R, 8x57JRS **$333.00**

C. SHARPS ARMS NEW MODEL 1875 OLD RELIABLE RIFLE

Caliber: 22LR, 32-40 & 38-55 Ballard, 38-56 WCF, 40-65 WCF, 40-90 3-1/4", 40-90 2-5/8", 40-70 2-1/10", 40-70 2-1/4", 40-70 2-1/2", 40-50 1-11/16", 40- 50 1-7/8", 45-90, 45-70, 45-100, 45-110, 45-120. Also available on special order only in 50-70, 50-90, 50-140. **Barrel:** 24", 26", 30" (standard), 32", 34" optional. **Weight:** 8-12 lbs. **Stock:** Walnut, straight grip, shotgun butt with checkered steel buttplate. **Sights:** Silver blade front, Rocky Mountain buck-horn rear. **Features:** Recreation of the 1875 Sharps rifle. Production guns will have case colored receiver. Available in Custom Sporting and Target versions upon request. Announced 1986. From C. Sharps Arms Co.
Price: 1875 Sporting Rifle (30" tapered oct. bbl.) **$1,185.00**

C. Sharps Arms 1875 Classic Sharps

Similar to New Model 1875 Sporting Rifle except 26", 28" or 30" full octagon barrel, crescent buttplate with toe plate, Hartford-style forend with cast German silver nose cap. Blade front sight, Rocky Mountain buckhorn rear. Weighs 10 lbs. Introduced 1987. From C. Sharps Arms Co.
Price: **$1,470.00**

C. Sharps Arms New Model 1875 Target & Long Range

Similar to New Model 1875 in all listed calibers except 22 LR; 34" tapered octagon barrel; globe with post front sight, Long Range Vernier tang sight with windage adjustments. Pistol grip stock with cheek rest; checkered steel buttplate. Introduced 1991. From C. Sharps Arms Co.
Price: **$1,549.50**

C. SHARPS ARMS NEW MODEL 1874 OLD RELIABLE

Caliber: 40-50, 40-70, 40-90, 45-70, 45-90, 45-100, 45-110, 45-120, 50-70, 50-90, 50-140. **Barrel:** 26", 28", 30" tapered octagon. **Weight:** About 10 lbs. **Length:** NA. **Stock:** American black walnut; shotgun butt with checkered steel buttplate; straight grip, heavy forend with Schnabel tip. **Sights:** Blade front, buckhorn rear. Drilled and tapped for tang sight. **Features:** Recreation of the Model 1874 Old Reliable Sharps Sporting Rifle. Double set triggers. Reintroduced 1991. Made in U.S.A. by C. Sharps Arms.
Price: **$1,584.00**

C. SHARPS ARMS NEW MODEL 1885 HIGHWALL RIFLE

Caliber: 22 LR, 22 Hornet, 219 Zipper, 25-35 WCF, 32-40 WCF, 38-55 WCF, 40-65, 30-40-Krag, 40-50 ST or BN, 40-70 ST or BN, 40-90 ST or BN, 45-70 2-1/10" ST, 45-90 2-4/10" ST, 45-100 2-6/10" ST, 45-110 2-7/8" ST, 45-120 3-1/4" ST. **Barrel:** 26", 28", 30", tapered full octagon. **Weight:** About 9 lbs., 4 oz. **Length:** 47" overall. **Stock:** Oil-finished American walnut; Schnabel-style forend. **Sights:** Blade front, buckhorn rear. Drilled and tapped for optional tang sight. **Features:** Single trigger; octagonal receiver top; checkered steel buttplate; color case-hardened receiver and buttplate; blued barrel. Many options available. Made in U.S.A. by C. Sharps Arms Co
Price: From **$1,439.00**

C. SHARPS ARMS CUSTOM NEW MODEL 1877 LONG RANGE TARGET RIFLE

Caliber: 44-90 Sharps/Rem., 45-70, 45-90, 45-100 Sharps. **Barrel:** 32", 34" tapered round with Rigby flat. **Weight:** Appx. 10 lbs. **Stock:** Walnut checkered. Pistol grip/forend. **Sights:** Classic long range with windage. **Features:** Elegant single shot, limited to custom production only.
Price: .... **$5,550.00 and up**

CABELA'S SHARPS BASIC RIFLE

Caliber: .45-70. **Barrel:** 28" tapered round. **Weight:** 8.7 lbs. **Length:** 44" overall. **Stock:** European walnut. **Sights:** Buckhorn rear, blade front. **Features:** Utilitarian look of the original with single trigger and 1-in-18 twist rate. Imported by Cabela's.
Price: **$799.99**

CABELA'S SHARPS SPORTING RIFLE

Caliber: 45-70, 45-120, .45-110, .50-70. **Barrel:** 32", tapered octagon. **Weight:** 9 lbs. **Length:** 47-1/4" overall. **Stock:** Checkered walnut. **Sights:** Blade front, open adjustable rear. **Features:** Color case-hardened receiver and hammer, rest blued. Introduced 1995. Imported by Cabela's.
Price: **$949.99**
Price: (Deluxe engraved Sharps, .45-70) **$1,599.99**
Price: (Heavy target Sharps, 45-70, 45-120, .50-70) **$1,099.99**
Price: (Quigley Sharps, 45-70, 45-120, 45-110) **$1,399.99**

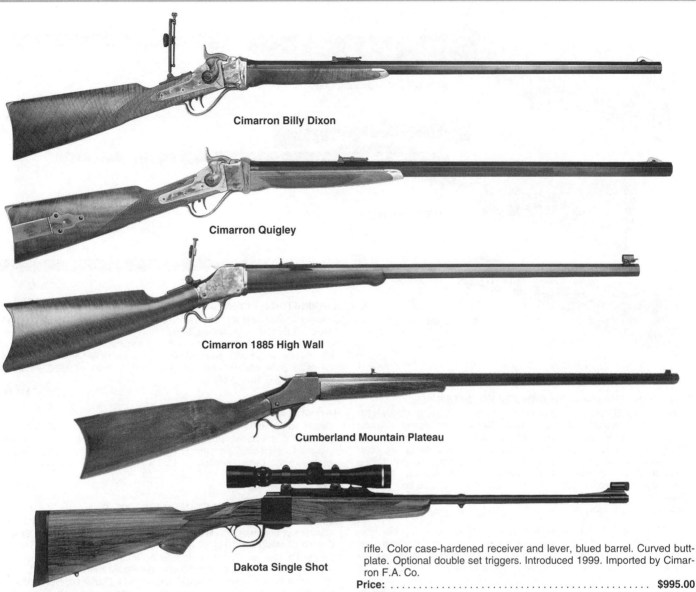

Cimarron Billy Dixon

Cimarron Quigley

Cimarron 1885 High Wall

Cumberland Mountain Plateau

Dakota Single Shot

CIMARRON BILLY DIXON 1874 SHARPS SPORTING RIFLE
Caliber: 40-90, 45-70. **Barrel:** 32" tapered octagonal. **Weight:** NA. **Length:** NA. **Stock:** European walnut. **Sights:** Blade front, Creedmoor rear. **Features:** Color case-hardened frame, blued barrel. Hand-checkered grip and forend; hand-rubbed oil finish. Introduced 1999. Imported by Cimarron F.A. Co.
Price: $1,525.00

CIMARRON QUIGLEY MODEL 1874 SHARPS SPORTING RIFLE
Caliber: 45-70, 45-90, 45-120. **Barrel:** 34" octagonal. **Weight:** NA. **Length:** NA. **Stock:** Checkered walnut. **Sights:** Blade front, adjustable rear. **Features:** Blued finish; double set triggers. From Cimarron F.A. Co.
Price: $1,625.00

CIMARRON SILHOUETTE MODEL 1874 SHARPS SPORTING RIFLE
Caliber: 45-70. **Barrel:** 32" octagonal. **Weight:** NA. **Length:** NA. **Stock:** Walnut. **Sights:** Blade front, adjustable rear. **Features:** Pistol-grip stock with shotgun-style butt plate; cut-rifled barrel. From Cimarron F.A. Co.
Price: $1,299.00

CIMARRON MODEL 1885 HIGH WALL RIFLE
Caliber: 38-55, 40-65, 45-70, 45-90, 45-120. **Barrel:** 30" octagonal. **Weight:** NA. **Length:** NA. **Stock:** European walnut. **Sights:** Bead front, semi-buckhorn rear. **Features:** Replica of the Winchester 1885 High Wall rifle. Color case-hardened receiver and lever, blued barrel. Curved buttplate. Optional double set triggers. Introduced 1999. Imported by Cimarron F.A. Co.
Price: $995.00
Price: With pistol grip $1,175.00

CUMBERLAND MOUNTAIN PLATEAU RIFLE
Caliber: 40-65, 45-70. **Barrel:** Up to 32"; round. **Weight:** About 10-1/2 lbs. (32" barrel). **Length:** 48" overall (32" barrel). **Stock:** American walnut. **Sights:** Marble's bead front, Marble's open rear. **Features:** Falling block action with underlever. Blued barrel and receiver. Stock has lacquer finish, crescent buttplate. Introduced 1995. Made in U.S.A. by Cumberland Mountain Arms, Inc.
Price: $1,085.00

DAKOTA MODEL 10 SINGLE SHOT RIFLE
Caliber: Most rimmed and rimless commercial calibers. **Barrel:** 23". **Weight:** 6 lbs. **Length:** 39-1/2" overall. **Stock:** Medium fancy grade walnut in classic style. Checkered grip and forend. **Sights:** None furnished. Drilled and tapped for scope mounting. **Features:** Falling block action with under-lever. Top tang safety. Removable trigger plate for conversion to single set trigger. Introduced 1990. Made in U.S.A. by Dakota Arms.
Price: $3,595.00
Price: Barreled action $2,095.00
Price: Action only $1,850.00
Price: Magnum calibers $3,595.00
Price: Magnum barreled action $2,050.00
Price: Magnum action only $1,675.00

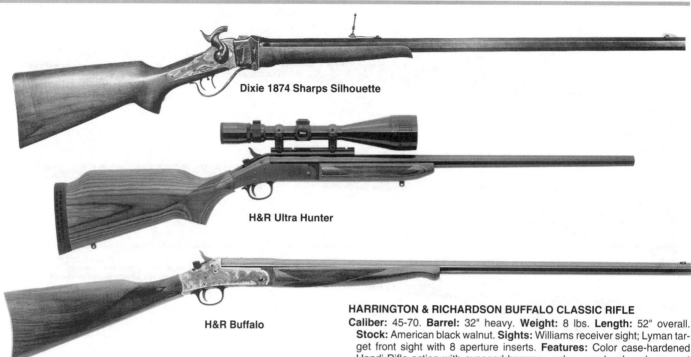

Dixie 1874 Sharps Silhouette

H&R Ultra Hunter

H&R Buffalo

DIXIE 1874 SHARPS BLACKPOWDER SILHOUETTE RIFLE
Caliber: 45-70. **Barrel:** 30"; tapered octagon; blued; 1:18" twist. **Weight:** 10 lbs., 3 oz. **Length:** 47-1/2" overall. **Stock:** Oiled walnut. **Sights:** Blade front, ladder-type hunting rear. **Features:** Replica of the Sharps #1 Sporter. Shotgun-style butt with checkered metal buttplate; color case-hardened receiver, hammer, lever and buttplate. Tang is drilled and tapped for tang sight. Double-set triggers. Meets standards for NRA blackpowder cartridge matches. Introduced 1995. Imported from Italy by Dixie Gun Works.
Price: **$1,025.00**

Dixie 1874 Sharps Lightweight Hunter/Target Rifle
Same as the Dixie 1874 Sharps Blackpowder Silhouette model except has a straight-grip buttstock with military-style buttplate. Based on the 1874 military model. Introduced 1995. Imported from Italy by Dixie Gun Works.
Price: **$995.00**

E.M.F. 1874 METALLIC CARTRIDGE SHARPS RIFLE
Caliber: 45-70, 45/120. **Barrel:** 28", octagon. **Weight:** 10-3/4 lbs. **Length:** NA. **Stock:** Oiled walnut. **Sights:** Blade front, flip-up open rear. **Features:** Replica of the 1874 Sharps Sporting rifle. Color case-hardened lock; double-set trigger; blue finish. Imported by E.M.F.
Price: From **$700.00**
Price: With browned finish **$1,000.00**
Price: Military Carbine **$650.00**

HARRINGTON & RICHARDSON ULTRA VARMINT RIFLE
Caliber: 223, 243. **Barrel:** 24", heavy. **Weight:** About 7.5 lbs. **Stock:** Hand-checkered laminated birch with Monte Carlo comb. **Sights:** None furnished. Drilled and tapped for scope mounting. **Features:** Break-open action with side-lever release, positive ejection. Scope mount. Blued receiver and barrel. Swivel studs. Introduced 1993. From H&R 1871, Inc.
Price: **$332.00**

Harrington & Richardson Ultra Hunter Rifle
Similar to Ultra Varmint rifle except chambered for 25-06 with 26" barrel, or 308 Win., 450 Marlin with 22" barrel. Stock and forend are of cinnamon-colored laminate; hand-checkered grip and forend. Introduced 1995. Made in U.S.A. by H&R 1871, LLC.
Price: **$332.00**

HARRINGTON & RICHARDSON BUFFALO CLASSIC RIFLE
Caliber: 45-70. **Barrel:** 32" heavy. **Weight:** 8 lbs. **Length:** 52" overall. **Stock:** American black walnut. **Sights:** Williams receiver sight; Lyman target front sight with 8 aperture inserts. **Features:** Color case-hardened Handi-Rifle action with exposed hammer; color case-hardened crescent buttplate; 19th century checkering pattern. Introduced 1995. Made in U.S.A. by H&R 1871, LLC.
Price: About **$418.00**

Harrington & Richardson 38-55 Target Rifle
Similar to the Buffalo Classic rifle except chambered for 38-55 Win., has 28" barrel. The barrel, steel trigger guard and forend spacer, are highly polished and blued. Color case-hardened receiver and buttplate. Williams receiver sight; Lyman target front sight with 8 aperture inserts. Introduced 1998. Made in U.S.A. by H&R 1871, LLC.
Price: **$418.00**

HARRIS GUNWORKS ANTIETAM SHARPS RIFLE
Caliber: 40-65, 45-75. **Barrel:** 30", 32", octagon or round, hand-lapped stainless or chrome-moly. **Weight:** 11.25 lbs. **Length:** 47" overall. **Stock:** Choice of straight grip, pistol grip or Creedmoor with Schnabel forend; pewter tip optional. Standard wood is A Fancy; higher grades available. **Sights:** Montana Vintage Arms #111 Low Profile Spirit Level front, #108 mid-range tang rear with windage adjustments. **Features:** Recreation of the 1874 Sharps sidehammer. Action is color case-hardened, barrel satin black. Chrome-moly barrel optionally blued. Optional sights include #112 Spirit Level Globe front with windage, #107 Long Range rear with windage. Introduced 1994. Made in U.S.A. by Harris Gunworks.
Price: **$2,400.00**

KRIEGHOFF HUBERTUS SINGLE-SHOT RIFLE
Caliber: 222, 243, 270, 308, 30-06, 5.6x50R Mag., 5.6x52R, 6x62R Freres, 6.5x57R, 6.5x65R, 7x57R, 7x65R, 8x57JRS, 8x75RS, 7mm Rem. Mag., 300 Win. Mag. **Barrel:** 23-1/2". **Weight:** 6-1/2 lbs. **Length:** NA. **Stock:** High-grade walnut. **Sights:** Blade front, open rear. **Features:** Break-loading with manual cocking lever on top tang; take-down; extractor; schnabel forearm; many options. Imported from Germany by Krieghoff International Inc.
Price: Hubertus single shot, from **$5,850.00**
Price: Hubertus, magnum calibers **$6,850.00**

LONE STAR NO. 5 REMINGTON PATTERN ROLLING BLOCK RIFLE
Caliber: 25-35, 30-30, 30-40 Krag. **Barrel:** 26" to 34". **Weight:** NA. **Length:** NA. **Stock:** American walnut. **Sights:** Beech style, Marble bead, Rocky Mountain-style, front; Buckhorn, early or late combination, rear. **Features:** Round, tapered round, octagon, tapered octagon, half octagon-half round barrels; bone-pack color case-hardened actions; single, single set, or double set triggers. Made in U.S.A. by Lone Star Rifle Co., Inc.
Price: **$1,595.00**

Lonestar Silhouette

Model 1885 High Wall

Mossberg SSi-One Sporter

Mossberg SSi-One Varminter

Lone Star Cowboy Action Rifle

Similar to the Lone Star No. 5 rifle, but designed for Cowboy Action Shooting with 28-33" barrel, buckhorn rear sight.

Price: **$1,595.00**

Lone Star Standard Silhouette Rifle

Similar to the Lone Star No. 5 rifle but designed for silhouette shooting with 30-34" barrel.

Price: **$1,595.00**

MERKEL K-1 MODEL LIGHTWEIGHT STALKING RIFLE

Caliber: 243 Win., 270 Win., 7x57R, 308 Win., 30-06, 7mm Rem. Mag., 300 Win. Mag., 9.3x74R. **Barrel:** 23.6". **Weight:** 5.6 lbs. unscoped. **Stock:** Satin-finished walnut, fluted and checkered; sling-swivel studs. **Sights:** None (scope base furnished). **Features:** Franz Jager single-shot break-open action, cocking/uncocking slide-type safety, matte silver receiver, selectable trigger pull weights, integrated, quick detach 1" or 30mm optic mounts (optic not included). Imported from Germany by GSI.

Price: Standard, simple border engraving **$3,795.00**
Price: Premium, light arabesque scroll **$3,795.00**
Price: Jagd, fine engraved hunting scenes................. **$4,395.00**

MODEL 1885 HIGH WALL RIFLE

Caliber: 30-40 Krag, 32-40, 38-55, 40-65 WCF, 45-70. **Barrel:** 26" (30-40), 28"-30" all others. Douglas Premium #3 tapered octagon. **Weight:** 9 lbs, 4 oz. **Length:** 47" overall. **Stock:** Premium American black walnut. **Sights:** Marble's standard ivory bead front, #66 long blade top rear with reversible notch and elevator. **Features:** Receiver with octagon top, thick-

wall High Wall with coil spring action. Tang drilled, tapped for High Wall tang sight. Receiver, lever, hammer and breechblock color case-hardened. Available from Montana Armory, Inc.

Price: **$1,350.00**

MOSSBERG SSi-ONE SINGLE SHOT RIFLE

Caliber: 223 Rem., 22-250 Rem., 243 Win., 270 Win., 308 Rem., 30-06. **Barrel:** 24". **Weight:** 8 lbs. **Length:** 40". **Stock:** Satin-finished walnut, fluted and checkered; sling-swivel studs. **Sights:** None (scope base furnished). **Features:** Frame accepts interchangeable barrels, including 12-gauge, fully rifled slug barrel and 12 ga., 3-1/2" chambered barrel with Ulti-Full Turkey choke tube. Lever-opening, break-action design; single-stage trigger; ambidextrous, top-tang safety; internal eject/extract selector. Introduced 2000. From Mossberg.

Price: SSi-One Sporter (standard barrel) or 12 ga.,
3-1/2" chamber **$459.00**
Price: SSi-One Varmint (bull barrel, 22-250 Rem. only;
weighs 10 lbs.) **$480.00**
Price: SSi-One 12-gauge Slug (fully rifled barrel, no sights,
scope base) **$480.00**

NAVY ARMS 1873 SHARPS "QUIGLEY"

Caliber: 45/70. **Barrel:** 34" heavy octagonal. **Stock:** Walnut. **Features:** Case-hardened receiver and military patchbox. Exact reproduction from "Quigley Down Under."

Price: **$1,390.00**

NAVY ARMS 1873 SHARPS NO. 2 CREEDMOOR RIFLE

Caliber: 45/70. **Barrel:** 30" tapered round. **Stock:** Walnut. **Sights:** Front globe, "soule" tang rear. **Features:** Nickel receiver and action. Lightweight sporting rifle.

Price: **$1,300.00**

RIFLES

Navy Arms #2 Creedmoor

Navy Arms 1874 Sharps Cavalry Carbine

Navy Arms 1874 Sharps Plains

Navy Arms 1874 Sharps Sporting

Navy Arms 1873 Springfield

Navy Arms Rolling Block Buffalo

NAVY ARMS 1874 SHARPS CAVALRY CARBINE

Caliber: 45-70. **Barrel:** 22". **Weight:** 7 lbs., 12 oz. **Length:** 39" overall. **Stock:** Walnut. **Sights:** Blade front, military ladder-type rear. **Features:** Replica of the 1874 Sharps miltary carbine. Color case-hardened receiver and furniture. Imported by Navy Arms.
Price: **$1,000.00**

NAVY ARMS 1874 SHARPS BUFFALO RIFLE

Caliber: 45-70, 45-90. **Barrel:** 28" heavy octagon. **Weight:** 10 lbs., 10 oz. **Length:** 46" overall. **Stock:** Walnut; checkered grip and forend. **Sights:** Blade front, ladder rear; tang sight optional. **Features:** Color case-hardened receiver, blued barrel; double-set triggers. Imported by Navy Arms.
Price: **$1,160.00**

Navy Arms Sharps Plains Rifle

Similar to Sharps Buffalo rifle except 45-70 only, 32" medium-weight barrel, weighs 9 lbs., 8 oz., and is 49" overall. Imported by Navy Arms.
Price: **$1,125.00**

Navy Arms Sharps Sporting Rifle

Same as the Navy Arms Sharps Plains Rifle except has pistol grip stock. Introduced 1997. Imported by Navy Arms.
Price: 45-70 only **$1,160.00**

NAVY ARMS 1885 HIGH WALL RIFLE

Caliber: 45-70; others available on special order. **Barrel:** 28" round, 30" octagonal. **Weight:** 9.5 lbs. **Length:** 45-1/2" overall (30" barrel). **Stock:** Walnut. **Sights:** Blade front, vernier tang-mounted peep rear. **Features:** Replica of Winchester's High Wall designed by Browning. Color case-hardened receiver, blued barrel. Introduced 1998. Imported by Navy Arms.
Price: 28", round barrel, target sights **$920.00**
Price: 30" octagonal barrel, target sights **$995.00**

NAVY ARMS 1873 SPRINGFIELD CAVALRY CARBINE

Caliber: 45-70. **Barrel:** 22". **Weight:** 7 lbs. **Length:** 40-1/2" overall. **Stock:** Walnut. **Sights:** Blade front, military ladder rear. **Features:** Blued lockplate and barrel; color case-hardened breechblock; saddle ring with bar. Replica of 7th Cavalry gun. Imported by Navy Arms.
Price: **$930.00**

NAVY ARMS ROLLING BLOCK RIFLE

Caliber: 45-70. **Barrel:** 26", 30". **Stock:** Walnut. **Sights:** Blade front, adjustable rear. **Features:** Reproduction of classic rolling block action. Available with full-octagon or half-octagon-half-round barrel. Color case-hardened action, steel fittings. From Navy Arms.
Price: Buffalo **$825.00**
Price: Special Sporting, 26" half round bbl. **$730.00**

NAVY ARMS "JOHN BODINE" ROLLING BLOCK RIFLE

Caliber: 45-70. **Barrel:** 30" heavy octagonal. **Stock:** Walnut. **Sights:** Globe front, "soule" tang rear. **Features:** Double set triggers.
Price: **$1,385.00**

CENTERFIRE RIFLES — SINGLE SHOT

New England
Firearms Handi-Rifle

New England Firearms Super Light

New England Firearms Survivor

Remington No. 1 Mid-Range

NAVY ARMS SHARPS NO. 3 LONG RANGE RIFLE

Caliber: 45-70, 45-90. **Barrel:** 34" octagon. **Weight:** 10 lbs., 12 oz. **Length:** 51-1/2". **Stock:** Deluxe walnut. **Sights:** Globe target front and match grade rear tang. **Features:** Shotgun buttplate, German silver forend cap, color case hardenend receiver. Imported by Navy Arms.

Price: **$1,885.00**

NEW ENGLAND FIREARMS HANDI-RIFLE

Caliber: 22 Hornet, 223, 243, 30-30, 270, 280 Rem., 300, 30-06, 357 Mag., 44 Mag., 45-70. **Barrel:** 22", 24"; 26" for 280 Rem. **Weight:** 7 lbs. **Stock:** Walnut-finished hardwood; black rubber recoil pad. **Sights:** Ramp front, folding rear (22 Hornet, 30-30, 45-70). Drilled and tapped for scope mount; 223, 243, 270, 280, 30-06 have no open sights, come with scope mounts. **Features:** Break-open action with side-lever release. The 223, 243, 270 and 30-06 have recoil pad and Monte Carlo stock for shooting with scope. Swivel studs on all models. Blue finish. Introduced 1989. From New England Firearms.

Price: **$270.00**
Price: 280 Rem., 26" barrel **$270.00**
Price: Synthetic Handi-Rifle (black polymer stock and forend, swivels, recoil pad) **$281.00**
Price: Handi-Rifle Youth (223, 243). **$270.00**
Price: Stainless Handi-Rifle (223 Rem., 243 Rem.) **$337.00**

New England Firearms Super Light Rifle

Similar to Handi-Rifle except new barrel taper, shorter 20" barrel with recessed muzzle, special lightweight synthetic stock and forend. No sights furnished on 223 and 243 versions, but have factory-mounted scope base and offset hammer spur; Monte Carlo stock; 22 Hornet has ramp front, fully adjustable open rear. Overall length 36", weight is 5.5 lbs. Introduced 1997. Made in U.S.A. by New England Firearms.

Price: 22 Hornet, 223 Rem. or 243 Win. **$281.00**

NEW ENGLAND FIREARMS SURVIVOR RIFLE

Caliber: 223, 308 Win., single shot. **Barrel:** 22". **Weight:** 6 lbs. **Length:** 36" overall. **Stock:** Black polymer, thumbhole design. **Sights:** None furnished; scope mount provided. **Features:** Receiver drilled and tapped for scope mounting. Stock and forend have storage compartments for ammo, etc.; comes with integral swivels and black nylon sling. Introduced 1996. Made in U.S.A. by New England Firearms.

Price: Blue finish. **$284.00**

REMINGTON NO. 1 ROLLING BLOCK MID-RANGE SPORTER

Caliber: 45-70. **Barrel:** 30" round. **Weight:** 8-3/4 lbs. **Length:** 46-1/2" overall. **Stock:** American walnut with checkered pistol grip and forend. **Sights:** Beaded blade front, adjustable center-notch buckhorn rear. **Features:** Recreation of the original. Polished blue metal finish. Many options available. Introduced 1998. Made in U.S.A. by Remington.

Price: **$1,450.00**
Price: Silhouette model with single-set trigger, heavy barrel . . . **$1,560.00**

ROSSI SINGLE SHOT CENTERFIRE RIFLE

Caliber: 308 Win., 270 Win., 30-06 Spfld., 223 Rem., 243 Win. **Barrel:** 23". **Weight:** 6-6.5 lbs. **Stock:** Monte carlo, exotic woods, walnut finish & swivels with white line space and recoil pad. **Sights:** None, scope rails and hammer extension included. **Features:** Break Open, positive ejection, internal transfer bar mechanism and manual external safety. Trigger block system included.

Price: **$179.95**

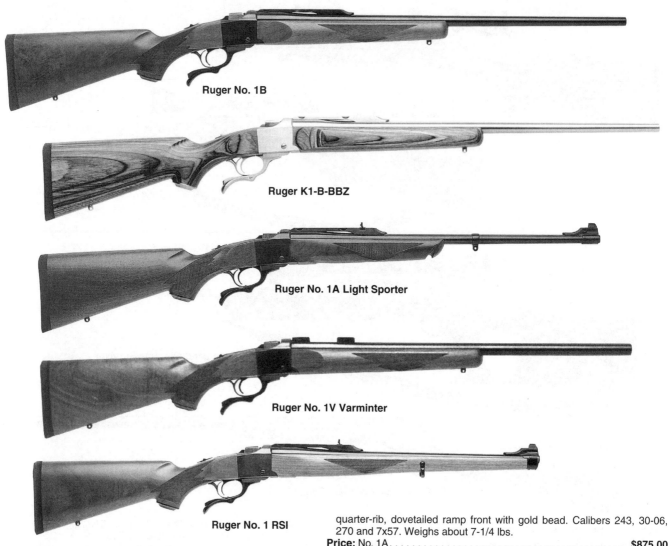

Ruger No. 1B

Ruger K1-B-BBZ

Ruger No. 1A Light Sporter

Ruger No. 1V Varminter

Ruger No. 1 RSI

ROSSI CENTERFIRE/SHOTGUN "MATCHED PAIRS"

Caliber: 12 ga./223 Rem., full size, 20 ga./223 Rem. full & youth, 12 ga./342 Win. full, 20 ga./243 Win., full & youth, 12 ga./308 Win. full, 20 ga./308 Win. full & youth, 12 ga./30-06 Spfld. full, 20 ga./30-06 Spfld. full, 12 ga./270 Win. full, 20 ga./270 Win. full. **Barrel:** 28"/23" full, 22"/22" youth. **Weight:** 5-7 lbs. **Stock:** Straight, exotic woods, walnut finish and swivels with white line space and recoil pad. **Sights:** Bead front shotgun, fully adjustable rifle, drilled and tapped. **Features:** Break Open, positive ejection, internal transfer bar mechanism and manual external safety. Trigger block system included.
Price: **350.00**

RUGER NO. 1B SINGLE SHOT

Caliber: 218 Bee, 22 Hornet, 220 Swift, 22-250, 223, 243, 6mm Rem., 25-06, 257 Roberts, 270, 280, 30-06, 7mm Rem. Mag., 300 Win. Mag., 308 Win., 338 Win. Mag., 270 Wea., 300 Wea. **Barrel:** 26" round tapered with quarter-rib; with Ruger 1" rings. **Weight:** 8 lbs. **Length:** 42-1/4" overall. **Stock:** Walnut, two-piece, checkered pistol grip and semi-beavertail forend. **Sights:** None, 1" scope rings supplied for integral mounts. **Features:** Under-lever, hammerless falling block design has auto ejector, top tang safety.
Price: 1B. **$875.00**
Price: Barreled action **$600.00**
Price: K1-B-BBZ Stainless steel, laminated stock 25-06, 7MM mag,
7MM STW, 300 Win Mag., 243 Win., 30-06, 308 Win. **$910.00**

Ruger No. 1A Light Sporter

Similar to the No. 1B Standard Rifle except has lightweight 22" barrel, Alexander Henry-style forend, adjustable folding leaf rear sight on quarter-rib, dovetailed ramp front with gold bead. Calibers 243, 30-06, 270 and 7x57. Weighs about 7-1/4 lbs.
Price: No. 1A. **$875.00**
Price: Barreled action **$600.00**

Ruger No. 1V Varminter

Similar to the No. 1B Standard Rifle except has 24" heavy barrel. Semi-beavertail forend, barrel ribbed for target scope block, with 1" Ruger scope rings. Calibers 22-250, 220 Swift, 223, 25-06, 6mm Rem. Weight about 9 lbs.
Price: No. 1V. **$875.00**
Price: Barreled action **$600.00**
Price: K1-V-BBZ stainless steel, laminated stock 22-250. . . . . . . **$910.00**

Ruger No. 1 RSI International

Similar to the No. 1B Standard Rifle except has lightweight 20" barrel, full-length International-style forend with loop sling swivel, adjustable folding leaf rear sight on quarter-rib, ramp front with gold bead. Calibers 243, 30-06, 270 and 7x57. Weight is about 7-1/4 lbs.
Price: No. 1 RSI **$890.00**
Price: Barreled action **$600.00**

Ruger No. 1H Tropical Rifle

Similar to the No. 1B Standard Rifle except has Alexander Henry forend, adjustable folding leaf rear sight on quarter-rib, ramp front with dovetail gold bead, 24" heavy barrel. Calibers 375 H&H, 416 Rem. Mag., 416 Rigby, and 458 Win. Mag. (weighs about 9 lbs.).
Price: No. 1H. **$875.00**
Price: Barreled action **$600.00**
Price: K1-H-BBZ, S/S, 375 H&H, 416 Rigby. **$910.00**

RIFLES

Ruger No. 1H Tropical

Ruger No. 1S Medium Sporter

Shiloh 1874 Long Range Express

Shiloh 1874 Quigley

Shiloh 1874 Saddle

Ruger No. 1S Medium Sporter
Similar to the No. 1B Standard Rifle except has Alexander Henry-style forend, adjustable folding leaf rear sight on quarter-rib, ramp front sight base and dovetail-type gold bead front sight. Calibers 218 Bee, 7mm Rem. Mag., 338 Win. Mag., 300 Win. Mag. with 26" barrel, 45-70 with 22" barrel. Weighs about 7-1/2 lbs. In 45-70.
Price: No. 1S **$875.00**
Price: Barreled action **$600.00**
Price: K1-S-BBZ, S/S, 45-70 . . . . **$910.00**

SHILOH RIFLE CO. SHARPS 1874 LONG RANGE EXPRESS
Caliber: 40-50 BN, 40-70 BN, 40-90 BN, 45-70 ST, 45-90 ST, 45-110 ST, 50-70 ST, 50-90 ST, 38-55, 40-70 ST, 40-90 ST. **Barrel:** 34" tapered octagon. **Weight:** 10-1/2 lbs. **Length:** 51" overall. **Stock:** Oil-finished semi-fancy walnut with pistol grip, shotgun-style butt, traditional cheek rest, Schnabel forend. **Sights:** Globe front, sporting tang rear. **Features:** Recreation of the Model 1874 Sharps rifle. Double set triggers. Made in U.S.A. by Shiloh Rifle Mfg. Co.
Price: **$1,796.00**
Price: Sporting Rifle No. 1 (similar to above except with 30" bbl., blade front, buckhorn rear sight). **$1,706.00**
Price: Sporting Rifle No. 3 (similar to No. 1 except straight-grip stock, standard wood) **$1,504.00**

Price: 1874 Hartford (Hartford collar, pewter tip) **$1,702.00**
Price: 1874 Sporter #1 (30" bbl, blade, buckhorn sights) **$1,706.00**
Price: 1874 Sporter #3 (walnut, shotgun or military stock) **$1,504.00**

SHILOH RIFLE CO. SHARPS 1874 QUIGLEY
Caliber: 45-70, 45-110. **Barrel:** 34" heavy octagon. **Stock:** Military-style with patch box, standard grade American walnut. **Sights:** Semi buckhorn, interchangeable front and midrange vernier tang wight with windage. **Features:** Gold inlay initials, pewter tip, hartford collar, case color or antique finish. Double set triggers.
Price: **$2,860.00**

SHILOH RIFLE CO. SHARPS 1874 SADDLE RIFLE
Caliber: 38-55, 40-50 BN, 40-65 Win., 40-70 BN, 40-70 ST, 40-90 BN, 40-90 ST, 44-77 BN, 44-90 BN, 45-70 ST, 45-90 ST, 45-100 ST, 45-110 ST, 45-120 ST, 50-70 ST, 50-90 ST. **Barrel:** 26" full or half octagon. **Stock:** Semi fancy American walnut. Shotgun style with cheekrest. **Sights:** Buckhorn and blade. **Features:** Double set trigger, numerous custom features can be added.
Price: **$1,504.00**

SHILOH RIFLE CO. SHARPS 1874 MONTANA ROUGHRIDER
Caliber: 38-55, 40-50 BN, 40-65 Win., 40-70 BN, 40-70 ST, 40-90 BN, 40-90 ST, 44-77 BN, 44-90 BN, 45-70 ST, 45-90 ST, 45-100 ST, 45-110 ST, 45-120 ST, 50-70 ST, 50-90 ST. **Barrel:** 30" full or half octagon. **Stock:** American walnut in shotgun or military style. **Sights:** Buckhorn and blade. **Features:** Double set triggers, numerous custom features can be added.
Price: **$1,504.00**

Shiloh 1874 Montana Roughrider

Shiloh 1874 Creedmoor

Thompson/Center Encore

Thompson/Center Encore "Katahdin"

Thompson/Center Contender

SHILOH RIFLE CO. SHARPS CREEDMOOR TARGET
Caliber: 38-55, 40-50 BN, 40-65 Win., 40-70 BN, 40-70 ST, 40-90 BN, 40-90 ST, 44-77 BN, 44-90 BN, 45-70 ST, 45-90 ST, 45-100 ST, 45-110 ST, 45-120 ST, 50-70 ST, 50-90 ST. **Barrel:** 32", half round-half octagon. **Stock:** Extra fancy American walnut. Shotgun style with pistol grip. **Sights:** Customer's choice. **Features:** Single trigger, AA finish on stock, polished barrel and screws, pewter tip.
Price: **$2,442.00**

THOMPSON/CENTER ENCORE RIFLE
Caliber: 22-250, 223, 243, 25-06, 270, 7mm-08, 308, 30-06, 7mm Rem. Mag., 300 Win. Mag. **Barrel:** 24", 26". **Weight:** 6 lbs., 12 oz. (24" barrel). **Length:** 38-1/2" (24" barrel). **Stock:** American walnut. Monte Carlo style; Schnabel forend or black composite. **Sights:** Ramp-style white bead front, fully adjustable leaf-type rear. **Features:** Interchangeable barrels; action opens by squeezing trigger guard; drilled and tapped for T/C scope mounts; polished blue finish. Introduced 1996. Made in U.S.A. by Thompson/Center Arms.
Price: . . . . **$599 to $632.00**
Price: Extra barrels **$270.00**

Thompson/Center Stainless Encore Rifle
Similar to blued Encore except stainless steel with blued sights, black composite stock and forend. Available in 22-250, 223, 7mm-08, 30-06, 308. Introduced 1999. Made in U.S.A. by Thompson/Center Arms.
Price: . . . . **$670.00 to $676.00**

THOMPSON/CENTER ENCORE "KATAHDIN" CARBINE
Caliber: 45-70 Gov't., 444 Marlin, 450 Marlin. **Barrel:** 18" with muzzle tamer. **Stock:** Composite.
Price: **$619.00**

Thompson/Center G2 Contender Rifle
Similar to the G2 Contender pistol, but in a compact rifle format. **Features:** interchangeable 23" barrels, chambered for 17 HMR, 22LR, 223 Rem., 30/30 Win. and 45/70 Gov't; plus a 45 Cal. Muzzleloading barrel. All of the 16-1/4" and 21" barrels made for the old style Contender will fit. **Weight:** 5-1/2 lbs. Introduced 2003. Made in U.S.A. by Thompson/Center Arms.
Price: . . . . **$592.40 to $607.00**

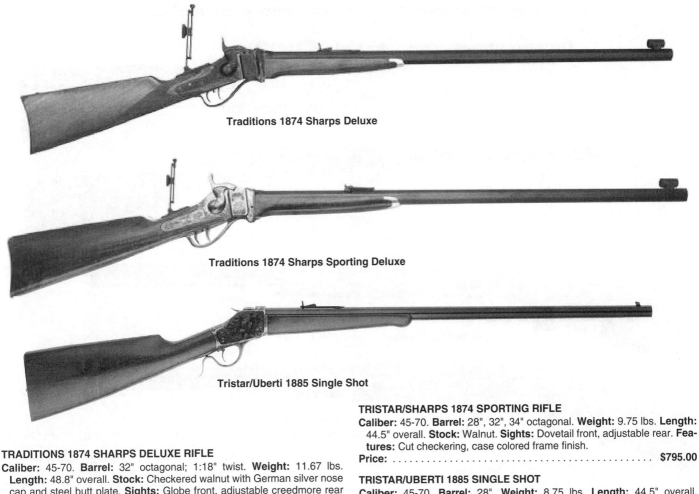

Traditions 1874 Sharps Deluxe

Traditions 1874 Sharps Sporting Deluxe

Tristar/Uberti 1885 Single Shot

TRADITIONS 1874 SHARPS DELUXE RIFLE
Caliber: 45-70. **Barrel:** 32" octagonal; 1:18" twist. **Weight:** 11.67 lbs. **Length:** 48.8" overall. **Stock:** Checkered walnut with German silver nose cap and steel butt plate. **Sights:** Globe front, adjustable creedmore rear with 12 inserts. **Features:** Color-case hardened receiver; double-set triggers. Introduced 2001. Imported from Pedersoli by Traditions.
Price: **$999.00**

Traditions 1874 Sharps Sporting Deluxe Rifle
Similar to Sharps Deluxe but custom silver engraved receiver, European walnut stock and forend, satin finish, set trigger, fully adjustable.
Price: **$1,999.00**

Traditions 1874 Sharps Standard Rifle
Similar to 1874 Sharps Deluxe Rifle, except has blade front and adjustable buckhorn-style rear sight. Weighs 10.67 pounds. Introduced 2001. Imported from Pedersoli by Traditions.
Price: **$769.00**

TRADITIONS ROLLING BLOCK SPORTING RIFLE
Caliber: 45-70. **Barrel:** 30" octagonal; 1:18" twist. **Weight:** 11.67 lbs. **Length:** 46.7" overall. **Stock:** Walnut. **Sights:** Blade front, adjustable rear. **Features:** Antique silver, color-case hardened receiver, drilled and tapped for tang/globe sights; brass butt plate and trigger guard. Introduced 2001. Imported from Pedersoli by Traditions.
Price: **$769.00**

TRADITIONS
ROLLING BLOCK SPORTING RIFLE IN 30-30 WINCHESTER
Caliber: 30-30. **Barrel:** 28" round, blued. **Weight:** 8.25 lbs. **Stock:** Walnut. **Sights:** Fixed front, adjustable rear. **Features:** Steel butt plate, trigger guard, barrel band.
Price: **$769.00**

TRISTAR/SHARPS 1874 SPORTING RIFLE
Caliber: 45-70. **Barrel:** 28", 32", 34" octagonal. **Weight:** 9.75 lbs. **Length:** 44.5" overall. **Stock:** Walnut. **Sights:** Dovetail front, adjustable rear. **Features:** Cut checkering, case colored frame finish.
Price: **$795.00**

TRISTAR/UBERTI 1885 SINGLE SHOT
Caliber: 45-70. **Barrel:** 28". **Weight:** 8.75 lbs. **Length:** 44.5" overall. **Stock:** European walnut. **Sights:** Bead on blade front, open step-adjustable rear. **Features:** Recreation of the 1885 Winchester. Color case-hardened receiver and lever, blued barrel. Introduced 1998. Imported from Italy by Tristar Sporting Arms Ltd.
Price: **$765.00**

UBERTI BABY ROLLING BLOCK CARBINE
Caliber: 22 LR, 22 WMR, 22 Hornet, 357 Mag., single shot. **Barrel:** 22". **Weight:** 4.8 lbs. **Length:** 35-1/2" overall. **Stock:** Walnut stock and forend. **Sights:** Blade front, fully adjustable open rear. **Features:** Resembles Remington New Model No. 4 carbine. Brass trigger guard and buttplate; color case-hardened frame, blued barrel. Imported by Uberti USA Inc.
Price: **$490.00**
Price: Baby Rolling Block Rifle, 26" bbl. **$590.00**

DRILLINGS, COMBINATION GUNS, DOUBLE GUNS

Designs for sporting and utility purposes worldwide.

Beretta Express SSO

Beretta Model 455 SxS

Charles Daly Superior

Charles Daly Empire Combo

BERETTA EXPRESS SSO O/U DOUBLE RIFLES
Caliber: 375 H&H, 458 Win. Mag., 9.3x74R. **Barrel:** 25.5". **Weight:** 11 lbs. **Stock:** European walnut with hand-checkered grip and forend. **Sights:** Blade front on ramp, open V-notch rear. **Features:** Sidelock action with color case-hardened receiver (gold inlays on SSO6 Gold). Ejectors, double triggers, recoil pad. Introduced 1990. Imported from Italy by Beretta U.S.A.
Price: SSO6 .... $21,000.00
Price: SSO6 Gold................................. $23,500.00

BERETTA MODEL 455 SxS EXPRESS RIFLE
Caliber: 375 H&H, 458 Win. Mag., 470 NE, 500 NE 3", 416 Rigby. **Barrel:** 23-1/2" or 25-1/2". **Weight:** 11 lbs. **Stock:** European walnut with hand-checkered grip and forend. **Sights:** Blade front, folding leaf V-notch rear. **Features:** Sidelock action with easily removable sideplates; color case-hardened finish (455), custom big game or floral motif engraving (455EELL). Double triggers, recoil pad. Introduced 1990. Imported from Italy by Beretta U.S.A.
Price: Model 455.................................. $36,000.00
Price: Model 455EELL $47,000.00

BRNO 500 COMBINATION GUNS
Caliber/Gauge: 12 (2-3/4" chamber) over 5.6x52R, 5.6x50R, 222 Rem., 243, 6.x55, 308, 7x57R, 7x65R, 30-06. **Barrel:** 23.6". **Weight:** 7.6 lbs. **Length:** 40.5" overall. **Sights:** Bead front, V-notch rear; grooved for scope mounting. **Features:** Boxlock action; double set trigger; blue finish with etched engraving. Announced 1998. Imported from The Czech Republic by Euro-Imports.
Price: $1,023.00
Price: O/U double rifle, 7x57R, 7x65R, 8x57JRS $1,125.00

BRNO ZH 300 COMBINATION GUN
Caliber/Gauge: 22 Hornet, 5.6x50R Mag., 5.6x52R, 7x57R, 7x65R, 8x57JRS over 12, 16 (2-3/4" chamber). **Barrel:** 23.6". **Weight:** 7.9 lbs. **Length:** 40.5" overall. **Stock:** European walnut. **Sights:** Blade front, open adjustable rear. **Features:** Boxlock action; double triggers; automatic safety. Announced 1998. Imported from The Czech Republic by Euro-Imports.
Price: $724.00

BRNO ZH Double Rifles
Similar to ZH 300 combination guns except double rifle barrels. Available in 7x65R, 7x57R and 8x57JRS. Announced 1998. Imported from The Czech Republic by Euro-Imports.
Price: $1,125.00

CHARLES DALY SUPERIOR COMBINATION GUN
Caliber/Gauge: 12 ga. over 22 Hornet, 223 Rem., 22-250, 243 Win., 270 Win., 308 Win., 30-06. **Barrel:** 23.5", shotgun choked Imp. Cyl. **Weight:** About 7.5 lbs. **Stock:** Checkered walnut pistol grip buttstock and semi-beavertail forend. **Features:** Silvered, engraved receiver; chrome-moly steel barrels; double triggers; extractors; sling swivels; gold bead front sight. Introduced 1997. Imported from Italy by K.B.I. Inc.
Price: $1,249.95

Charles Daly Empire Combination Gun
Same as the Superior grade except has deluxe wood with European-style comb and cheekpiece; slim forend. Introduced 1997. Imported from Italy by K.B.I., Inc.
Price: $1,789.95

CZ 584 SOLO COMBINATION GUN
Caliber/Gauge: 7x57R; 12, 2-3/4" chamber. **Barrel:** 24.4". **Weight:** 7.37 lbs. **Length:** 45.25" overall. **Stock:** Circassian walnut. **Sights:** Blade front, open rear adjustable for windage. **Features:** Kersten-style double lump locking system; double-trigger Blitz-type mechanism with drop safety and adjustable set trigger for the rifle barrel; auto safety, dual extractors; receiver dovetailed for scope mounting. Imported from the Czech Republic by CZ-USA.
Price: $851.00

DRILLINGS, COMBINATION GUNS, DOUBLE GUNS

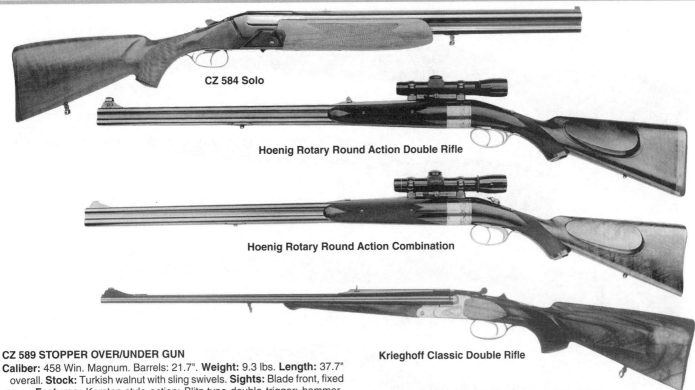

CZ 584 Solo

Hoenig Rotary Round Action Double Rifle

Hoenig Rotary Round Action Combination

Krieghoff Classic Double Rifle

CZ 589 STOPPER OVER/UNDER GUN

Caliber: 458 Win. Magnum. **Barrels:** 21.7". **Weight:** 9.3 lbs. **Length:** 37.7" overall. **Stock:** Turkish walnut with sling swivels. **Sights:** Blade front, fixed rear. **Features:** Kersten-style action; Blitz-type double trigger; hammer-forged, blued barrels; satin-nickel, engraved receiver. Introduced 2001. Imported from the Czech Republic by CZ USA.
Price: **$2,999.00**
Price: Fully engraved model **$3,999.00**

DAKOTA DOUBLE RIFLE

Caliber: 470 Nitro Express, 500 Nitro Express. **Barrel:** 25". **Stock:** Exhibition-grade walnut. **Sights:** Express. **Features:** Round action; selective ejectors; recoil pad; Americase. From Dakota Arms Inc.
Price: **$25,000.00**

EAA/BAIKAL IZH-94 COMBINATION GUN

Caliber/Gauge: 12, 3" chamber; 222 Rem., 223, 5.6x50R, 5.6x55E, 7x57R, 7x65R, 7.62x39, 7.62x51, 308, 7.62x53R, 7.62x54R, 30-06. **Barrel:** 24", 26"; imp., mod. and full choke tubes. **Weight:** 7.28 lbs. **Stock:** Walnut; rubber butt pad. **Sights:** Express style. **Features:** Hammer-forged barrels with chrome-lined bores; machined receiver; single-selective or double triggers. Imported by European American Armory.
Price: Blued finish. **$549.00**
Price: 20 ga./22 LR, 20/22 Mag, 3" **$629.00**

GARBI EXPRESS DOUBLE RIFLE

Caliber: 7x65R, 9.3x74R, 375 H&H. **Barrel:** 24-3/4". **Weight:** 7-3/4 to 8-1/2 lbs. **Length:** 41-1/2" overall. **Stock:** Turkish walnut. **Sights:** Quarter-rib with express sight. **Features:** Side-by-side double; H&H-pattern sidelock ejector with reinforced action, chopper lump barrels of Boehler steel; double triggers; fine scroll and rosette engraving, or full coverage ornamental; coin-finished action. Introduced 1997. Imported from Spain by Wm. Larkin Moore.
Price: **$19,900.00**

HOENIG ROTARY ROUND ACTION DOUBLE RIFLE

Caliber: Most popular calibers from 225 Win. to 9.3x74R. **Barrel:** 22"-26". **Stock:** English Walnut; to customer specs. **Sights:** Swivel hood front with button release (extra bead stored in trap door gripcap), express-style rear on quarter-rib adjustable for windage and elevation; scope mount. **Features:** Round action opens by rotating barrels, pulling forward. Inertia extractor system, rotary safety blocks strikers. single lever quick-detachable scope mount. Simple takedown without removing forend. Introduced 1997. Made in U.S.A. by George Hoenig.
Price: **$24,975.00**

HOENIG ROTARY ROUND ACTION COMBINATION

Caliber: 28 ga. **Barrel:** 26". **Weight:** 7 lbs. **Stock:** English Walnut to customer specs. **Sights:** Front ramp with button release blades. Foldable aperture tang sight windage and elevation adjustable. Quarter rib with scope mount. **Features:** Round action opens by rotating barrels, pulling forward. Inertia extractor; rotary safety blocks strikers. Simple takedown without removing forend. Made in U.S.A. by George Hoenig.
Price: **$24,975.00**

KRIEGHOFF CLASSIC DOUBLE RIFLE

Caliber: 7x65R, 308 Win., 30-06, 8x57 JRS, 8x75RS, 9.3x74R. **Barrel:** 23.5". **Weight:** 7.3 to 8 lbs. **Stock:** High grade European walnut. Standard has conventional rounded cheekpiece, Bavaria has Bavarian-style cheekpiece. **Sights:** Bead front with removable, adjustable wedge (375 H&H and below), standing leaf rear on quarter-rib. **Features:** Boxlock action; double triggers; short opening angle for fast loading; quiet extractors; sliding, self-adjusting wedge for secure bolting; Purdey-style barrel extension; horizontal firing pin placement. Many options available. Introduced 1997. Imported from Germany by Krieghoff International.
Price: With small Arabesque engraving **$7,850.00**
Price: With engraved sideplates **$9,800.00**
Price: For extra barrels **$4,500.00**
Price: Extra 20-ga., 28" shotshell barrels **$3,200.00**

Krieghoff Classic Big Five Double Rifle

Similar to the standard Classic excpet available in 375 Flanged Mag. N.E., 500/416 N.E., 470 N.E., 500 N.E. 3". Has hinged front trigger, non-removable muzzle wedge (larger than 375-caliber), Universal Trigger System, Combi Cocking Device, steel trigger guard, specially weighted stock bolt for weight and balance. Many options available. Introduced 1997. Imported from Germany by Krieghoff International.
Price: **$9,450.00**
Price: With engraved sideplates **$11,400.00**

LEBEAU - COURALLY EXPRESS RIFLE SxS

Caliber: 7x65R, 8x57JRS, 9.3x74R, 375 H&H, 470 N.E. **Barrel:** 24" to 26". **Weight:** 7-3/4 to 10-1/2 lbs. **Stock:** Fancy French walnut with cheekpiece. **Sights:** Bead on ramp front, standing left express rear on quarter-rib. **Features:** Holland & Holland-type sidelock with automatic ejectors; double triggers. Built to order only. Imported from Belgium by Wm. Larkin Moore.
Price: **$41,000.00**

DRILLINGS, COMBINATION GUNS, DOUBLE GUNS

Merkel 96K Engraved

Merkel 140-1

Rizzini Express

Savage 24F Combination

Springfield M6 Scout

MERKEL DRILLINGS
Caliber/Gauge: 12, 20, 3" chambers, 16, 2-3/4" chambers; 22 Hornet, 5.6x50R Mag., 5.6x52R, 222 Rem., 243 Win., 6.5x55, 6.5x57R, 7x57R, 7x65R, 308, 30-06, 8x57JRS, 9.3x74R, 375 H&H. **Barrel:** 25.6". **Weight:** 7.9 to 8.4 lbs. depending upon caliber. **Stock:** Oil-finished walnut with pistol grip; cheekpiece on 12-, 16-gauge. **Sights:** Blade front, fixed rear. **Features:** Double barrel locking lug with Greener cross-bolt; scroll-engraved, case-hardened receiver; automatic trigger safety; Blitz action; double triggers. Imported from Germany by GSI.
Price: Model 96K (manually cocked rifle system), from **$7,495.00**
Price: Model 96K Engraved (hunting series on receiver) **$8,595.00**

Merkel Boxlock Double Rifles
Similar to the Model 160 double rifle except with Anson & Deely boxlock action with cocking indicators, double triggers, engraved color case-hardened receiver. Introduced 1995. Imported from Germany by GSI.
Price: Model 140-1, from **$6,695.00**
Price: Model 140-1.1 (engraved silver-gray receiver), from **$7,795.00**

RIZZINI EXPRESS 90L DOUBLE RIFLE
Caliber: 30-06, 7x65R, 9.3x74R. **Barrel:** 24". **Weight:** 7-1/2 lbs. **Length:** 40" overall. **Stock:** Select European walnut with satin oil finish; English-style cheekpiece. **Sights:** Ramp front, quarter-rib with express sight. **Features:** Color case-hardened boxlock action; automatic ejectors; single selective trigger; polished blue barrels. Extra 20-gauge shotshell barrels available. Imported for Italy by Wm. Larkin Moore.
Price: With case **$3,850.00**

SAVAGE 24F PREDATOR O/U COMBINATION GUN
Caliber/Gauge: 22 Hornet, 223, 30-30 over 12 (24F-12) or 22 LR, 22 Hornet, 223, 30-30 over 20-ga. (24F-20); 3" chambers. **Action:** Takedown, low re-bounding visible hammer. Single trigger, barrel selector spur on hammer. **Barrel:** 24" separated barrels; 12-ga. has mod. choke tubes, 20-ga. has fixed Mod. choke. **Weight:** 8 lbs. **Length:** 40-1/2" overall. **Stock:** Black Rynite composition. **Sights:** Blade front, rear open adjustable for elevation. **Features:** Introduced 1989.
Price: 24F-12 . . . . **$586.00**
Price: 24F-20 . . . . **$556.00**

SPRINGFIELD, INC. M6 SCOUT RIFLE/SHOTGUN
Caliber/Gauge: 22 LR or 22 Hornet over 410-bore. **Barrel:** 18.25". **Weight:** 4 lbs. **Length:** 32" overall. **Stock:** Folding detachable with storage for 15 22 LR, four 410 shells. **Sights:** Blade front, military aperture for 22; V-notch for 410. **Features:** All-metal construction. Designed for quick disas-sembly and minimum maintenance. Folds for compact storage. Intro-duced 1982; reintroduced 1996. Imported from the Czech Republic by Springfield, Inc.
Price: Parkerized **$185.00**
Price: Stainless steel **$219.00**

Designs for hunting, utility and sporting purposes, including training for competition

Armscor M-20C Carbine

Browning Buck Mark Target

Browning Semi-Auto 22

CZ 511 Auto

AR-7 EXPLORER CARBINE
Caliber: 22 LR, 8-shot magazine. **Barrel:** 16". **Weight:** 2-1/2 lbs. **Length:** 34-1/2" / 16-1/2" stowed. **Stock:** Moulded Cycolac; snap-on rubber butt pad. **Sights:** Square blade front, aperture rear. **Features:** Takedown design stores barrel and action in hollow stock. Light enough to float. Reintroduced 1999. From AR-7 Industries, LLC.
Price: Black matte finish **$150.00**
Price: AR-20 Sporter (tubular stock, barrel shroud) **$200.00**
New! **Price:** AR-7 camo- or walnut-finish stock.............. **$164.95**

ARMSCOR MODEL AK22 AUTO RIFLE
Caliber: 22 LR, 10-shot magazine. **Barrel:** 18.5". **Weight:** 7.5 lbs. **Length:** 38" overall. **Stock:** Plain mahogany. **Sights:** Adjustable post front, leaf rear adjustable for elevation. **Features:** Resembles the AK-47. Matte black finish. Introduced 1987. Imported from the Philippines by K.B.I., Inc.
Price: About **$219.95**

ARMSCOR M-1600 AUTO RIFLE
Caliber: 22 LR, 10-shot magazine. **Barrel:** 18.25". **Weight:** 6.2 lbs. **Length:** 38.5" overall. **Stock:** Black finished mahogany. **Sights:** Post front, aper-ture rear. **Features:** Resembles Colt AR-15. Matte black finish. Introduced 1987. Imported from the Philippines by K.B.I., Inc.
Price: About **$199.95**

ARMSCOR M-20C AUTO CARBINE
Caliber: 22 LR, 10-shot magazine. **Barrel:** 18.25". **Weight:** 6.5 lbs. **Length:** 38" overall. **Stock:** Walnut-finished mahogany. **Sights:** Hooded front, rear adjustable for elevation. **Features:** Receiver grooved for scope mounting. Blued finish. Introduced 1990. Imported from the Philippines by K.B.I., Inc.
Price: **$154.95**

BROWNING BUCK MARK SEMI-AUTO RIFLES
Caliber: 22 LR, 10-shot magazine. **Barrel:** 18" tapered (Sporter), heavy bull (Target), or carbon composite barrel (Classic Carbon). **Weight:** 4 lbs., 2 oz. (Sporter) or 5 lbs., 4 oz. (Target). **Length:** 34" overall. **Stock:** Walnut stock and forearm with full pistol grip. **Sights:** Hi-Viz adjustable (Sporter). **Features:** A rifle version of the Buck Mark Pistol; straight blowback action; machined aluminum receiver with integral rail scope mount; recessed muzzle crown; manual thumb safety. Introduced 2001. From Browning.
Price: Sporter (adj. sights) **$518.00**
Price: Target (heavy bbl., no sights) **$518.00**

BROWNING SEMI-AUTO 22 RIFLE
Caliber: 22 LR, 11-shot. **Barrel:** 19-1/4". **Weight:** 5 lbs., 3 oz. **Length:** 37" overall. **Stock:** Checkered select walnut with pistol grip and semi-beavertail forend. **Sights:** Gold bead front, folding leaf rear. **Features:** Engraved receiver with polished blue finish; cross-bolt safety; tubular magazine in buttstock; easy takedown for carrying or storage. Imported from Japan by Browning.
Price: Grade I **$479.00**

Browning Semi-Auto 22, Grade VI
Same as the Grade I Auto-22 except available with either grayed or blued receiver with extensive engraving with gold-plated animals: right side pictures a fox and squirrel in a woodland scene; left side shows a beagle chasing a rabbit. On top is a portrait of the beagle. Stock and forend are of high-grade walnut with a double-bordered cut checkering design. Introduced 1987.
Price: Grade VI, blue or gray receiver.................... **$1,028.00**

BRNO ZKM 611 AUTO RIFLE
Caliber: 22 WMR, 6- or 10-shot magazine. **Barrel:** 20.4". **Weight:** 5.9 lbs. **Length:** 38.9" overall. **Stock:** European walnut. **Sights:** Hooded blade front, open adjustable rear. **Features:** Removable box magazine; polished blue finish; cross-bolt safety; grooved receiver for scope mounting; easy takedown for storage. Imported from The Czech Republic by Euro-Imports.
Price: **$475.00**

CZ 511 AUTO RIFLE
Caliber: 22 LR, 8-shot magazine. **Barrel:** 22.2". **Weight:** 5.39 lbs. **Length:** 38.6" overall. **Stock:** Walnut with checkered pistol grip. **Sights:** Hooded front, adjustable rear. **Features:** Polished blue finish; detachable magazine; sling swivel studs. Imported from the Czech Republic by CZ-USA.
Price: **$351.00**

CZ 511 Auto

Henry U.S. Survival

Marlin Model 60

Marlin Model 60SSK

Marlin Model 70PSS

Marlin 7000

Price: **$297.00**
Price: Model 60SSK (black fiberglass-filled stock) **$257.00**
Price: Model 60SB (walnut-finished birch stock) **$235.00**
Price: Model 60SB with 4x scope **$251.00**

HENRY U.S. SURVIVAL RIFLE .22

Caliber: 22 LR, 8-shot magazine. **Barrel:** 16" steel lined. **Weight:** 2.5 lbs. **Stock:** ABS plastic. **Sights:** Blade front on ramp, aperture rear. **Features:** Takedown design stores barrel and action in hollow stock. Light enough to float. Silver, black or camo finish. Comes with two magazines. Introduced 1998. From Henry Repeating Arms Co.
Price: **$165.00**

MARLIN MODEL 60 AUTO RIFLE

Caliber: 22 LR, 14-shot tubular magazine. **Barrel:** 19" round tapered. **Weight:** About 5-1/2 lbs. **Length:** 37-1/2" overall. **Stock:** Press-checkered, walnut-finished Maine birch with Monte Carlo, full pistol grip; Mar-Shield® finish. **Sights:** Ramp front, open adjustable rear. **Features:** Matted receiver is grooved for scope mount. Manual bolt hold-open; automatic last-shot bolt hold-open. Model 60C is similar except has hardwood Monte Carlo stock with Mossy Oak Break-Up camouflage pattern. From Marlin.
Price: **$185.00**
Price: With 4x scope **$193.00**
Price: (Model 60C) $220.00

Marlin Model 60SS Self-Loading Rifle

Same as the Model 60 except breech bolt, barrel and outer magazine tube are made of stainless steel; most other parts are either nickel-plated or coated to match the stainless finish. Monte Carlo stock is of black/gray Maine birch laminate, and has nickel-plated swivel studs, rubber butt pad. Introduced 1993. From Marlin.

MARLIN 70PSS PAPOOSE STAINLESS RIFLE

Caliber: 22 LR, 7-shot magazine. **Barrel:** 16-1/4" stainless steel, Micro-Groove® rifling. **Weight:** 3-1/4 lbs. **Length:** 35-1/4" overall. **Stock:** Black fiberglass-filled synthetic with abbreviated forend, nickel-plated swivel studs, moulded-in checkering. **Sights:** Ramp front with orange post, cut-away Wide Scan® hood; adjustable open rear. Receiver grooved for scope mounting. **Features:** Takedown barrel; cross-bolt safety; manual bolt hold-open; last shot bolt hold-open; comes with padded carrying case. Introduced 1986. Made in U.S.A. by Marlin.
Price: **$304.00**

MARLIN MODEL 7000 AUTO RIFLE

Caliber: 22 LR, 10-shot magazine **Barrel:** 18" heavy target with 12-groove Micro-Groove® rifling, recessed muzzle. **Weight:** 5-1/2 lbs. **Length:** 37" overall. **Stock:** Black fiberglass-filled synthetic with Monte Carlo combo, swivel studs, moulded-in checkering. **Sights:** None furnished; comes with ring mounts. **Features:** Automatic last-shot bolt hold-open, manual bolt hold-open; cross-bolt safety; steel charging handle; blue finish, nickel-plated magazine. Introduced 1997. Made in U.S.A. by Marlin Firearms Co.
Price: **$249.00**

Marlin Model 795 Auto Rifle

Similar to Model 7000 except standard-weight 18" barrel with 16-groove Micro-Groove rifling. Ramp front sight with brass bead, screw adjustable open rear. Receiver grooved for scope mount. Introduced 1997. Made in U.S.A. by Marlin Firearms Co.
Price: **$176.00**

Marlin 795

Marlin 552 BDL Speedmaster

Remington 597

Ruger 10/22 Deluxe Sporter

Marlin Model 795SS Auto Rifle
Similar to Model 795 excapt stainless steel barrel. Most other parts nickel-plated. Adjustable folding semi-buckhorn rear sights, ramp front high-visibility post and removeable cutaway wide scan hood.
Price: **$235.00**

REMINGTON MODEL 552 BDL DELUXE SPEEDMASTER RIFLE
Caliber: 22 S (20), L (17) or LR (15) tubular mag. **Barrel:** 21" round tapered. **Weight:** 5-3/4 lbs. **Length:** 40" overall. **Stock:** Walnut. Checkered grip and forend. **Sights:** Big game. **Features:** Positive cross-bolt safety, receiver grooved for tip-off mount.
Price: **$393.00**

REMINGTON 597 AUTO RIFLE
Caliber: 22 LR, 10-shot clip. **Barrel:** 20". **Weight:** 5-1/2 lbs. **Length:** 40" overall. **Stock:** Black synthetic. **Sights:** Big game. **Features:** Matte black finish, nickel-plated bolt. Receiver is grooved and drilled and tapped for scope mounts. Introduced 1997. Made in U.S.A. by Remington.
Price: **$169.00**
Price: Model 597 Magnum, 22 WMR, 8-shot clip **$335.00**
Price: Model 597 LSS (laminated stock, stainless). **$279.00**
Price: Model 597 SS
(22 LR, stainless steel, black synthetic stock). **$224.00**
Price: Model 597 LS Heavy Barrel (22 LR, laminated stock) **$265.00**
Price: Model 597 Magnum LS Heavy Barrel
(22 WMR, lam. stock) **$399.00**
Price: Model 597 Magnum 17 HMR, 8-shot clip **$361.00**

RUGER 10/22 AUTOLOADING CARBINE
Caliber: 22 LR, 10-shot rotary magazine. **Barrel:** 18-1/2" round tapered. **Weight:** 5 lbs. **Length:** 37-1/4" overall. **Stock:** American hardwood with pistol grip and barrel band or synthetic. **Sights:** Brass bead front, folding leaf rear adjustable for elevation. **Features:** Detachable rotary magazine fits flush into stock, cross-bolt safety, receiver tapped and grooved for scope blocks or tip-off mount. Scope base adaptor furnished with each rifle.
Price: Model 10/22 RB (blue) **$239.00**
Price: Model K10/22RB (bright finish stainless barrel) **$279.00**
Price: Model 10/22RPF (blue, synthetic stock). **$239.00**

Ruger 10/22 International Carbine
Similar to the Ruger 10/22 Carbine except has full-length International stock of American hardwood, checkered grip and forend; comes with rubber butt pad, sling swivels. Reintroduced 1994.
Price: Blue (10/22RBI) **$279.00**
Price: Stainless (K10/22RBI) **$299.00**

Ruger 10/22 Deluxe Sporter
Same as 10/22 Carbine except walnut stock with hand checkered pistol grip and forend; straight buttplate, no barrel band, has sling swivels.
Price: Model 10/22 DSP **$299.00**

Ruger 10/22T Target Rifle
Similar to the 10/22 except has 20" heavy, hammer-forged barrel with tight chamber dimensions, improved trigger pull, laminated hardwood stock dimensioned for optical sights. No iron sights supplied. Introduced 1996. Made in U.S.A. by Sturm, Ruger & Co.
Price: 10/22T **$425.00**
Price: K10/22T, stainless steel **$485.00**

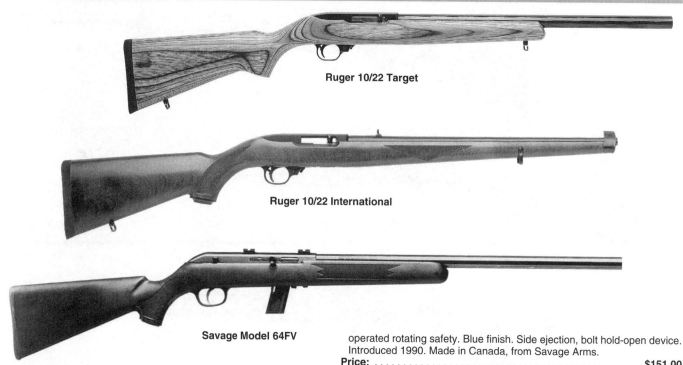

Ruger 10/22 Target

Ruger 10/22 International

Savage Model 64FV

Ruger K10/22RPF All-Weather Rifle

Similar to the stainless K10/22/RB except has black composite stock of thermoplastic polyester resin reinforced with fiberglass; checkered grip and forend. Brushed satin, natural metal finish with clear hardcoat finish. Weighs 5 lbs., measures 36-3/4" overall. Introduced 1997. From Sturm, Ruger & Co.

Price: **$279.00**

RUGER 10/22 MAGNUM AUTOLOADING CARBINE

Caliber: 22 WMR, 9-shot rotary magazine. **Barrel:** 18-1/2". **Weight:** 6 lbs. **Length:** 37-1/4" overall. **Stock:** Birch. **Sights:** Gold bead front, folding rear. **Features:** All-steel receiver has integral Ruger scope bases for the included 1" rings. Introduced 1999. Made in U.S.A. by Sturm, Ruger & Co.

Price: 10/22RBM **$499.00**

SAVAGE MODEL 64G AUTO RIFLE

Caliber: 22 LR, 10-shot magazine. **Barrel:** 20", 21". **Weight:** 5-1/2 lbs. **Length:** 40", 41". **Stock:** Walnut-finished hardwood with Monte Carlo-type comb, checkered grip and forend. **Sights:** Bead front, open adjustable rear. Receiver grooved for scope mounting. **Features:** Thumb-

CONSULT

SHOOTER'S MARKETPLACE

Page 64, This Issue

operated rotating safety. Blue finish. Side ejection, bolt hold-open device. Introduced 1990. Made in Canada, from Savage Arms.

Price: **$151.00**
Price: Model 64FSS, stainless **$196.00**
Price: Model 64F, black synthetic stock **$135.00**
Price: Model 64GXP Package Gun includes
4x15 scope and mounts **$156.00**
Price: Model 64FXP (black stock, 4x15 scope) **$144.00**
Price: Model 64F Camo **$166.00**

Savage Model 64FV Auto Rifle

Similar to the Model 64F except has heavy 21" barrel with recessed crown; no sights provided-comes with Weaver-style bases. Introduced 1998. Imported from Canada by Savage Arms, Inc.

Price: **$182.00**
Price: Model 64FVSS, stainless **$235.00**

TAURUS MODEL 63 RIFLE

Caliber: 22 LR, 10-shot tube-fed magazine. **Barrel:** 23". **Weight:** 72 oz. **Length:** 32-1/2". **Stock:** Hand-fitted walnut-finished hardwood. **Sights:** Adjustable rear, fixed front. **Features:** Manual safety, metal buttplate, can accept Taurus tang sight. Charged and cocked with operating plunger at front of forend. Available in blue or polished stainless steel.

Price: 63 . . . . **$295.00**
Price: 63SS **$311.00**

THOMPSON/CENTER 22 LR CLASSIC RIFLE

Caliber: 22 LR, 8-shot magazine. **Barrel:** 22" match-grade. **Weight:** 5-1/2 pounds. **Length:** 39-1/2" overall. **Stock:** Satin-finished American walnut with Monte Carlo-type comb and pistol grip cap, swivel studs. **Sights:** Ramp-style front and fully adjustable rear, both with fiber optics. **Features:** All-steel receiver drilled and tapped for scope mounting; barrel threaded to receiver; thumb-operated safety; trigger guard safety lock included. New .22 Classic Benchmark TGT target rifle variant has 18" heavy barrel, brown laminated target stock, blued with matte finish, 10-shot magazine and no sights; drilled and tapped.

Price: T/C 22 LR Classic (blue). **$370.00**
Price: T/C 22 LR Classic Benchmark **$472.00**

Classic and modern models for sport and utility, including training.

Browning BL-22

Henry Lever-Action 22

Henry Golden Boy 22

Henry Pump-Action 22

Marlin Model 39AS

BROWNING BL-22 LEVER-ACTION RIFLE

Caliber: 22 S (22), L (17) or LR (15), tubular magazine. **Barrel:** 20" round tapered. **Weight:** 5 lbs. **Length:** 36-3/4" overall. **Stock:** Walnut, two-piece straight grip Western style. **Sights:** Bead post front, folding-leaf rear. **Features:** Short throw lever, half-cock safety, receiver grooved for tip-off scope mounts, gold-colored trigger. Imported from Japan by Browning.

Price: Grade I **$415.00**
Price: Grade II (engraved receiver, checkered grip and forend) . . **$471.00**
Price: Classic, Grade I (blued trigger, no checkering) **$415.00**
Price: Classic, Grade II (cut checkering, satin wood finish,
      polished blueing) **$471.00**

HENRY LEVER-ACTION 22

Caliber: 22 Long Rifle (15-shot). **Barrel:** 18-1/4" round. **Weight:** 5-1/2 lbs. **Length:** 34" overall. **Stock:** Walnut. **Sights:** Hooded blade front, open adjustable rear. **Features:** Polished blue finish; full-length tubular magazine; side ejection; receiver grooved for scope mounting. Introduced 1997. Made in U.S.A. by Henry Repeating Arms Co.

Price: **$239.95**
Price: Youth model (33" overall, 11-rounds 22 LR) **$229.95**

HENRY GOLDEN BOY 22 LEVER-ACTION RIFLE

Caliber: 22 LR, 22 Magnum, 16-shot. **Barrel:** 20" octagonal. **Weight:** 6.25 lbs. **Length:** 38" overall. **Stock:** American walnut. **Sights:** Blade front, open rear. **Features:** Brasslite receiver, brass buttplate, blued barrel and lever. Introduced 1998. Made in U.S.A. from Henry Repeating Arms Co.

Price: **$379.95**
Price: Magnum **$449.95**

HENRY PUMP-ACTION 22 PUMP RIFLE

Caliber: 22 LR, 15-shot. **Barrel:** 18.25". **Weight:** 5.5 lbs. **Length:** NA. **Stock:** American walnut. **Sights:** Bead on ramp front, open adjustable rear. **Features:** Polished blue finish; receiver groved for scope mount; grooved slide handle; two barrel bands. Introduced 1998. Made in U.S.A. from Henry Repeating Arms Co.

Price: **$249.95**

MARLIN MODEL 39A GOLDEN LEVER-ACTION RIFLE

Caliber: 22, S (26), L (21), LR (19), tubular mag. **Barrel:** 24" Micro-Groove®. **Weight:** 6-1/2 lbs. **Length:** 40" overall. **Stock:** Checkered American black walnut; Mar-Shield® finish. Swivel studs; rubber butt pad. **Sights:** Bead ramp front with detachable Wide-Scan™ hood, folding rear semi-buckhorn adjustable for windage and elevation. **Features:** Hammer block safety; rebounding hammer. Takedown action, receiver tapped for scope mount (supplied), offset hammer spur, gold-plated steel trigger. From Marlin Firearms.

Price: **$552.00**

RIMFIRE RIFLES — LEVER & SLIDE ACTION

Remington Model 572 BDL Deluxe Fieldmaster

Ruger Model 96/22

Ruger Model 96/17

Taurus 62R

Taurus 72C-SS

Winchester 9422 Legacy

REMINGTON 572 BDL DELUXE FIELDMASTER PUMP RIFLE
Caliber: 22 S (20), L (17) or LR (15), tubular mag. **Barrel:** 21" round tapered. **Weight:** 5-1/2 lbs. **Length:** 40" overall. **Stock:** Walnut with checkered pistol grip and slide handle. **Sights:** Big game. **Features:** Cross-bolt safety; removing inner magazine tube converts rifle to single shot; receiver grooved for tip-off scope mount.
Price: $407.00

RUGER MODEL 96 LEVER-ACTION RIFLE
Caliber: 22 LR, 10 rounds; 22 WMR, 9 rounds; 44 Magnum, 4 rounds; 17 HMR 9 rounds. **Barrel:** 18-1/2". **Weight:** 5-1/4 lbs. **Length:** 37-1/4" overall. **Stock:** Hardwood. **Sights:** Gold bead front, folding leaf rear. **Features:** Sliding cross button safety, visible cocking indicator; short-throw lever action. Introduced 1996. Made in U.S.A. by Sturm, Ruger & Co.
Price: 96/22 (22 LR) $349.00
Price: 96/22M (22 WMR) $375.00
Price: 96/22M (44 Mag.) $525.00
New! **Price:** 96/17M (17 HMR) $375.00

TAURUS MODEL 62 PUMP RIFLE
Caliber: 22 LR, 12- or 13-shot. **Barrel:** 16-1/2" or 23" round. **Weight:** 72 oz-80 oz. **Length:** 39" overall. **Stock:** Premium hardwood. **Sights:** Adjustable rear, bead blade front, optional tang. **Features:** Blue, case hardened or stainless, bolt-mounted safety, pump action, manual firing pin block, integral security lock system. Imported from Brazil by Taurus International.
Price: M62C (blue) $280.00
Price: M62C-CH (case hardened-blue) $280.00
Price: M62CCH-T (case hardened-blue) $358.00
Price: M62C-SS (stainless steel) $295.00
Price: M62CSS-T (stainless steel) $373.00
Price: M62C-SS-Y (stainless steel) $327.00

Price: M62C-T (blue) $358.00
Price: M62C-Y (blue) $311.00
Price: M62R (blue) $280.00
Price: M62R-CH (case hardened-blue) $280.00
Price: M62RCH-T (case hardened-blue) $358.00
Price: M62R-SS (stainless steel) $295.00
Price: M62RSS-T (stainless steel) $373.00
Price: M62R-T (blue) $358.00

Taurus Model 72 Pump Rifle
Same as Model 62 except chambered in 22 Magnum or .17 HMR; 16-1/2" bbl. holds 10-12 shots, 23" bbl. holds 11-13 shots. Weighs 72 oz.-80 oz. Introduced 2001. Imported from Brazil by Taurus International.
Price: M72C (blue) $295.00
Price: M72C-CH (case hardened-blue) $295.00
Price: M72CCH-T (case hardened-blue) $373.00
Price: M72C-SS (stainless steel) $311.00
Price: M72CSS-T (stainless steel) $389.00
Price: M72C-T (blue) $373.00
Price: M72R (blue) $295.00
Price: M72R-CH (case hardened-blue) $295.00
Price: M72RCH-T (case hardened-blue) $373.00
Price: M72R-SS (stainless steel) $311.00
Price: M72RSS-T (stainless steel) $389.00
Price: M72R-T (blue) $373.00

WINCHESTER MODEL 9422 LEVER-ACTION RIFLES
Caliber: 22 LR, 22 WMR, tubular magazine. **Barrel:** 20-1/2". **Weight:** 6-1/4 lbs. **Length:** 37-1/8" overall. **Stock:** American walnut, two-piece, straight grip (Traditional) or semi-pistol grip (Legacy). **Sights:** Hooded ramp front, adjustable semi-buckhorn rear. **Features:** Side ejection, receiver grooved for scope mounting, takedown action. From U.S. Repeating Arms Co.
Price: Traditional, 22 LR 15-shot. $465.00
Price: Traditional, 22WMR, 11-shot $487.00
Price: Legacy, 22 LR 15-shot $498.00
Price: Legacy 22 WMR, 11-shot. $521.00

RIFLES

Includes models for a variety of sports, utility and competitive shooting.

Anschutz 1518D Luxus

Anschutz 1710D

Chipmunk Deluxe

CZ 452 Lux

ANSCHUTZ 1416D/1516D CLASSIC RIFLES

Caliber: 22 LR (1416D), 5-shot clip; 22 WMR (1516D), 4-shot clip. **Barrel:** 22-1/2". **Weight:** 6 lbs. **Length:** 41" overall. **Stock:** European hardwood with walnut finish; classic style with straight comb, checkered pistol grip and forend. **Sights:** Hooded ramp front, folding leaf rear. **Features:** Uses Match 64 action. Adjustable single stage trigger. Receiver grooved for scope mounting. Imported from Germany by AcuSport Corp.

Price: 1416D, 22 LR **$755.95**
Price: 1516D, 22 WMR **$779.95**
Price: 1416D Classic left-hand **$679.95**

Anschutz 1416D/1516D Walnut Luxus Rifles

Similar to the Classic models except have European walnut stocks with Monte Carlo cheekpiece, slim forend with Schnabel tip, cut checkering on grip and forend. Introduced 1997. Imported from Germany by AcuSport Corp.

Price: 1416D (22 LR) **$755.95**
Price: 1516D (22 WMR) **$779.95**

ANSCHUTZ 1518D LUXUS BOLT-ACTION RIFLE

Caliber: 22 WMR, 4-shot magazine. **Barrel:** 19-3/4". **Weight:** 5-1/2 lbs. **Length:** 37-1/2" overall. **Stock:** European walnut. **Sights:** Blade on ramp front, folding leaf rear. **Features:** Receiver grooved for scope mounting; single stage trigger; skip-line checkering; rosewood forend tip; sling swivels. Imported from Germany by AcuSport Corp.

Price: **$1,186.95**

ANSCHUTZ 1710D CUSTOM RIFLE

Caliber: 22 LR, 5-shot clip. **Barrel:** 24-1/4". **Weight:** 7-3/8 lbs. **Length:** 42-1/2" overall. **Stock:** Select European walnut. **Sights:** Hooded ramp front, folding leaf rear; drilled and tapped for scope mounting. **Features:** Match 54 action with adjustable single-stage trigger; roll-over Monte Carlo cheekpiece, slim forend with Schnabel tip, Wundhammer palm swell on pistol grip, rosewood gripcap with white diamond insert; skip-line checker-ing on grip and forend. Introduced 1988. Imported from Germany by AcuSport Corp.

Price: **$1,289.95**

CHIPMUNK SINGLE SHOT RIFLE

Caliber: 22 LR, 22 WMR, single shot. **Barrel:** 16-1/8". **Weight:** About 2-1/2 lbs. **Length:** 30" overall. **Stocks:** American walnut. **Sights:** Post on ramp front, peep rear adjustable for windage and elevation. **Features:** Drilled and tapped for scope mounting using special Chipmunk base ($13.95). Engraved model also available. Made in U.S.A. Introduced 1982. From Rogue Rifle Co., Inc.

Price: Standard **$194.25**
Price: Standard 22 WMR **$209.95**
Price: Deluxe (better wood, checkering) **$246.95**
Price: Deluxe 22 WMR **$262.95**
Price: Laminated stock **$209.95**
Price: Laminated stock, 22 WMR **$225.95**
Price: Bull barrel models of above, add **$16.00**

CHIPMUNK TM (TARGET MODEL)

Caliber: 22 S, L, or LR. **Barrel:** 18" blue. **Weight:** 5 lbs. **Length:** 33". Stocks: Walnut with accessory rail. **Sights:** 1/4 minute micrometer adjustable. **Features:** Manually cocking single shot bolt action, blue receiver, adjustable butt plate and butt pad.

Price: **$329.95**

COOPER MODEL 57-M BOLT-ACTION RIFLE

Caliber: 22 LR, 22 WMR, 17 HMR. **Barrel:** 23-3/4" stainless steel or 41-40 match grade. **Weight:** 6.6 lbs. **Stock:** Claro walnut, 22 lpi hand checkering. **Sights:** None furnished. **Features:** Three rear locking lug, repeating bolt-action with 5-shot mag. Fully adjustable trigger. Many options. Made 100% in the U.S.A. by Cooper Firearms of Montana, Inc.

Price: Classic **$1,100.00**
Price: LVT **$1,295.00**
Price: Custom Classic **$1,895.00**
Price: Western Classic **$2,495.00**

CZ 452 LUX BOLT-ACTION RIFLE

Caliber: 22 LR, 22 WMR, 5-shot detachable magazine. **Barrel:** 24.8". **Weight:** 6.6 lbs. **Length:** 42.63" overall. **Stock:** Walnut with checkered pistol grip. **Sights:** Hooded front, fully adjustable tangent rear. **Features:** All-steel construction, adjustable trigger, polished blue finish. Imported from the Czech Republic by CZ-USA.

Price: 22 LR, 22 WMR **$378.00**

CZ 452 Varmint

CZ 452 American Classic

Henry "Mini" Bolt 22

Kimber 22 Classic

Kimber 22 SuperAmerica

CZ 452 Varmint Rifle
Similar to the Lux model except has heavy 20.8" barrel; stock has beavertail forend; weighs 7 lbs.; no sights furnished. Available only in 22 LR. Imported from the Czech Republic by CZ-USA.
Price: **$407.00**

CZ 452 American Classic Bolt-Action Rifle
Similar to the CZ 452 M 2E Lux except has classic-style stock of Circassian walnut; 22.5" free-floating barrel with recessed target crown; receiver dovetail for scope mounting. No open sights furnished. Introduced 1999. Imported from the Czech Republic by CZ-USA.
Price: 22 LR, 22 WMR **$420.00**

HARRINGTON & RICHARDSON
ULTRA HEAVY BARREL 22 MAG RIFLE
Caliber: 22 WMR, single shot. **Barrel:** 22" bull. **Stock:** Cinnamon laminated wood with Monte Carlo cheekpiece. **Sights:** None furnished; scope mount rail included. **Features:** Hand-checkered stock and forend; deep-crown rifling; tuned trigger; trigger locking system; hammer extension. Introduced 2001. From H&R 1871 LLC.
Price: **$193.00**

HENRY "MINI" BOLT 22 RIFLE
Caliber: 22 LR, single shot. **Barrel:** 16" stainless, 8-groove rifling. **Weight:** 3.25 lbs. **Length:** 30", LOP 11-1/2". **Stock:** Synthetic, pistol grip, wrap-

around checkering and beavertail forearm. **Sights:** William Fire sights. **Features:** One piece bolt configuration manually operated safety. Ideal for beginners or ladies.
Price: **$169.95**

KIMBER 22 CLASSIC BOLT-ACTION RIFLE
Caliber: 22 LR, 5-shot magazine. **Barrel:** 18", 22", 24" match grade; 11-degree target crown. **Weight:** 5-8 lbs. **Length:** 35"-43". **Stock:** Classic Claro walnut, hand-cut checkering, steel gripcap, swivel studs. **Sights:** None, drilled and tapped. **Features:** All-new action with Mauser-style full-length claw extractor, two-position wing safety, match trigger, pillar-bedded action with recoil lug. Introduced 1999. Made in U.S.A. by Kimber Mfg., Inc.
Price: New Classic **$1,085.00**
Price: Classic **$949.00**
Price: Hunter **$678.00**
Price: Youth **$746.00**

Kimber 22 SuperAmerica Bolt-Action Rifle
Similar to 22 Classic except has AAA Claro walnut stock with wraparound 22 l.p.i. hand-cut checkering, ebony forened tip, beaded cheekpiece. Introduced 1999. Made in U.S.A. by Kimber Mfg., Inc.
Price: **$1,764.00**

Kimber 22 SVT Bolt-Action Rilfe
Similar to 22 Classic except has 18" stainless steel, fluted bull barrel, gray laminated, high-comb target-style stock with deep pistol grip, high comb, beavertail forend with bipod stud. Weighs 7.5 lbs., overall length 36.5". Matte finish on action. Introduced 1999. Made in U.S.A. by Kimber Mfg., Inc.
Price: **$949.00**

Kimber 22 SVT

Kimber 22 HS

Marlin 17V

Marlin Model 15YN "Little Buckaroo"

Marlin Model 880SS

Kimber 22 HS (Hunter Silhouette) Bolt-Action Rifle

Similar to 22 Classic except 24" medium sporter match-grade barrel with half-fluting; high comb, walnut, Monte Carlo target stock with 18 l.p.i. checkering; matte blue metal finish. Introduced 1999. Made in U.S.A. by Kimber Mfg., Inc.

Price: **$814.00**

MARLIN MODEL 17V HORNADY MAGNUM

Caliber: 17 Magnum, 7-shot. **Barrel:** 22. **Weight:** 6 lbs., stainless 7 lbs. **Length:** 41". **Stock:** Checkered walnut Monte Carlo SS, laminated black/grey. **Sights:** No sights but receiver grooved. **Features:** Swivel studs, positive thumb safety, red cocking indicator, safety lock, SS 1" brushed aluminum scope rings.

Price: **$269.00**
Price: Bead blasted SS barrel & receiver **$402.00**

MARLIN MODEL 15YN "LITTLE BUCKAROO"

Caliber: 22 S, L, LR, single shot. **Barrel:** 16-1/4" Micro-Groove®. **Weight:** 4-1/4 lbs. **Length:** 33-1/4" overall. **Stock:** One-piece walnut-finished, press-checkered Maine birch with Monte Carlo; Mar-Shield® finish. **Sights:** Ramp front, adjustable open rear. **Features:** Beginner's rifle with thumb safety, easy-load feed throat, red cocking indicator. Receiver grooved for scope mounting. Introduced 1989.

Price: **$209.00**
Price: Stainless steel with fire sights. **$233.00**

MARLIN MODEL 880SS BOLT-ACTION RIFLE

Caliber: 22 LR, 7-shot clip magazine. **Barrel:** 22" Micro-Groove®. **Weight:** 6 lbs. **Length:** 41" overall. **Stock:** Black fiberglass-filled synthetic with nickel-plated swivel studs and moulded-in checkering. **Sights:** Ramp front with orange post and cutaway Wide-Scan™ hood, adjustable semi-buckhorn folding rear. **Features:** Stainless steel barrel, receiver, front breech bolt and striker; receiver grooved for scope mounting. Introduced 1994. Model 880SQ (Squirrel Rifle) is similar but has heavy 22" barrel. Made in U.S.A. by Marlin.

Price: (Model 880SS) **$316.00**
Price: (Model 880SQ) **$330.00**

Marlin Model 81TS Bolt-Action Rifle

Same as Marlin 880SS except blued steel, tubular magazine, holds 17 Long Rifle cartridges. Weighs 6 lbs.

Price: **$213.00**

Marlin Model 880SQ Squirrel Rifle

Similar to Model 880SS except uses heavy target barrel. Black synthetic stock with moulded-in checkering, double bedding screws, matte blue finish. Without sights, no dovetail or filler screws; receiver grooved for scope mount. Weighs 7 lbs. Introduced 1996. Made in U.S.A. by Marlin.

Price: **$322.00**

Marlin Model 25N Bolt-Action Repeater

Similar to Marlin 880, except walnut-finished hardwood stock, adjustable open rear sight, ramp front.

Price: **$212.00**
Price: With 4x scope and mount. **$220.00**

Marlin 880SQ Squirrel

Marlin 25N

Marlin 25MNC

Marlin 883SS

Marlin 83TS

Marlin Model 25NC Bolt-Action Repeater

Same as Model 25N except Mossy Oak® Break-Up camouflage stock. Made in U.S.A. by Marlin.
Price: **$248.00**

Marlin Model 25MN/25MNC Bolt-Action Rifles

Similar to the Model 25N except chambered for 22 WMR. Has 7-shot clip magazine, 22" Micro-Groove® barrel, checkered walnut-finished Maine birch stock. Introduced 1989.
Price: 25MN **$241.00**
New! **Price:** 25MNC (Mossy Oak® Break-Up camouflage stock) . **$278.00**

Marlin Model 882 Bolt-Action Rifle

Same as the Marlin 880 except 22 WMR cal. only with 7-shot clip magazine; weight about 6 lbs. Comes with swivel studs.
Price: **$324.00**
Price: Model 882L (laminated hardwood stock; weighs 6-1/4 lbs.) **$342.00**

Marlin Model 882SS Bolt-Action Rifle

Same as the Marlin Model 882 except has stainless steel front breech bolt, barrel, receiver and bolt knob. All other parts are either stainless steel or nickel-plated. Has black Monte Carlo stock of fiberglass-filled polycarbonate with moulded-in checkering, nickel-plated swivel studs. Introduced 1995. Made in U.S.A. by Marlin Firearms Co.
Price: **$345.00**

Marlin Model 882SSV Bolt-Action Rifle

Similar to the Model 882SS except has selected heavy 22" stainless steel barrel with recessed muzzle, and comes without sights; receiver is grooved for scope mount and 1" ring mounts are included. Weighs 7 lbs. Introduced 1997. Made in U.S.A. by Marlin Firearms Co.
Price: **$338.00**

MARLIN MODEL 883 BOLT-ACTION RIFLE

Caliber: 22 WMR. **Barrel:** 22"; 1:16" twist. **Weight:** 6 lbs. **Length:** 41" overall. **Stock:** Walnut Monte Carlo with sling swivel studs, rubber butt pad. **Sights:** Ramp front with brass bead, removable hood; adjustable semi-buckhorn folding rear. **Features:** Thumb safety, red cocking indicator, receiver grooved for scope mount. Made in U.S.A. by Marlin Firearms Co.
Price: **$337.00**

Marlin Model 883SS Bolt-Action Rifle

Same as the Model 883 except front breech bolt, striker knob, trigger stud, cartridge lifter stud and outer magazine tube are of stainless steel; other parts are nickel-plated. Has two-tone brown laminated Monte Carlo stock with swivel studs, rubber butt pad. Introduced 1993.
Price: **$358.00**

Marlin Model 83TS Bolt-Action Rifle

Same as the Model 883 except has a black Monte Carlo fiberglass-filled synthetic stock with sling swivel studs. Weighs 6 lbs., length 41" overall. Introduced 2001. Made in U.S.A. by Marlin Firearms Co.
Price: **$259.00**

MEACHAM LOW WALL RIFLE

Caliber: 22 RF Match, 17 HMR. **Barrel:** 28". **Weight:** 10 lbs. **Sights:** None. Tang drilled for Win. base, 3/8" dovetail slot, front. **Stock:** Fancy eastern black walnut with cheekpiece; ebony insert in forend. **Features:** Available with single trigger, single set trigger, or Schuetzen-style double set triggers. Introduced 2002. From Meacham T&H, Inc.
Price: **$2,999.00**

NEW ENGLAND FIREARMS SPORTSTER™ SINGLE-SHOT RIFLES

Caliber: 22 LR, 22 WMR, 17 HMR, single-shot. **Barrel:** 20". **Weight:** 5-1/2 lbs. **Length:** 36-1/4" overall. **Stock:** Black polymer. **Sights:** None furnished; scope mount included. **Features:** Break open, side-lever release; automatic ejection; recoil pad; sling swivel studs; trigger locking system. Introduced 2001. Made in U.S.A. by New England Firearms.
Price: **$149.00**
Price: Youth model (20" bbl., 33" overall, weighs 5-1/3 lbs.) **$149.00**
Price: Sportster 17 HMR **$180.00**

Ruger K77/22 Varmint

Ruger 77/22R

Sako Finnfire

Savage Mark I-G

RIFLES

NEW ULTRA LIGHT ARMS 20RF BOLT-ACTION RIFLE

Caliber: 22 LR, single shot or repeater. **Barrel:** Douglas, length to order. **Weight:** 5-1/4 lbs. **Length:** Varies. **Stock:** Kevlar®/graphite composite, variety of finishes. **Sights:** None furnished; drilled and tapped for scope mount. **Features:** Timney trigger, hand-lapped action, button-rifled barrel, hand-bedded action, recoil pad, sling-swivel studs, optional Jewell Trigger. Made in U.S.A. by New Ultra Light Arms.

Price: 20 RF single shot **$800.00**
Price: 20 RF repeater **$850.00**

ROSSI MATCHED PAIR SINGLE-SHOT RIFLE/SHOTGUN

Caliber: 22 LR or 22 Mag. **Barrel:** 18-1/2" or 23". **Weight:** 6 lbs. **Stock:** Hardwood (brown or black finish). **Sights:** Fully adjustable front and rear. **Features:** Break-open breech, transfer-bar manual safety, includes matched 410-, 20- or 12-gauge shotgun barrel with bead front sight. Introduced 2001. Imported by BrazTech/Taurus.

Price: blue **$139.95**
Price: stainless steel **$169.95**

RUGER K77/22 VARMINT RIFLE

Caliber: 22 LR, 10-shot, 22 WMR, 9-shot detachable rotary magazine. **Barrel:** 24", heavy. **Weight:** 6-7/8 lbs. **Length:** 43.25" overall. **Stock:** Laminated hardwood with rubber butt pad, quick-detachable swivel studs. **Sights:** None furnished. Comes with Ruger 1" scope rings. **Features:** Stainless steel or blued finish. Three-position safety, dual extractors. Stock has wide, flat forend. Introduced 1993.

Price: K77/22VBZ, 22 LR **$645.00**
Price: K77/22VMBZ, 22 WMR **$645.00**

RUGER 77/22 RIMFIRE BOLT-ACTION RIFLE

Caliber: 22 LR, 10-shot rotary magazine; 22 WMR, 9-shot rotary magazine. **Barrel:** 20". **Weight:** About 5-3/4 lbs. **Length:** 39-3/4" overall. **Stock:**

Checkered American walnut, laminated hardwood, or synthetic stocks, stainless sling swivels. **Sights:** Brass bead front, adjustable folding leaf rear or plain barrel with 1" Ruger rings. **Features:** Mauser-type action uses Ruger's rotary magazine. Three-position safety, simplified bolt stop, patented bolt locking system. Uses the dual-screw barrel attachment system of the 10/22 rifle. Integral scope mounting system with 1" Ruger rings. Blued model introduced 1983. Stainless steel and blued with synthetic stock introduced 1989.

Price: 77/22R (no sights, rings, walnut stock) **$580.00**
Price: 77/22RS (open sights, rings, walnut stock) **$605.00**
Price: K77/22RP (stainless, no sights, rings, synthetic stock) . . . **$580.00**
Price: K77/22RSP (stainless, open sights, rings, synthetic stock) **$605.00**
Price: 77/22RM (22 WMR, blue, walnut stock) **$580.00**
Price: K77/22RSMP (22 WMR, stainless, open sights, rings, synthetic stock) **$605.00**
Price: K77/22RMP (22 WMR, stainless, synthetic stock) **$580.00**
Price: 77/22RSM
  (22 WMR, blue, open sights, rings, walnut stock) **$585.00**
New!! **Price:** K77/17RM, 17RMP, 17VMBBZ (17 HMR, walnut, synthetic or laminate stocks, no sights, rings, blued or stainless) **$580.00 to $645.00**

SAKO FINNFIRE HUNTER BOLT-ACTION RIFLE

Caliber: 22 LR, 5-shot magazine. **Barrel:** 22". **Weight:** 5.75 lbs. **Length:** 39-1/2" overall. **Stock:** European walnut with checkered grip and forend. **Sights:** Hooded blade front, open adjustable rear. **Features:** Adjustable single-stage trigger; has 50-degree bolt lift. Introduced 1994. Imported from Finland by Beretta USA.

Price: **$854.00**
Price: Varmint (heavy barrel) **$896.00**

SAKO FINNFIRE TARGET RIFLE

Caliber: 22 LR. **Barrel:** 22"; heavy, free-floating. **Stock:** Match style of European walnut; adjustable cheekpiece and buttplate; stippled pistol grip and forend. **Sights:** None furnished; has 11mm integral dovetail scope mount. **Features:** Based on the Sako P94S action with two bolt locking lugs, 50-degree bolt lift and 30mm throw; adjustable trigger. Introduced 1999. Imported from Finland by Beretta USA.

Price: **$951.00**

RIFLES

Savage Mark I-Y

Savage Mark II-BV

Savage Mark II-FXP

Savage Mark II-FSS

Savage Model 93G

Price: Mark II-GXP Package Gun (comes with 4x15 scope),
right- or left-handed. **$164.00**
Price: Mark II-FXP (as above with black synthetic stock) **$151.00**
Price: Mark II-F (as above, no scope). **$144.00**
Price: Mark II-FVXP (as above, with scope and rings) **$252.00**

Savage Mark II-FSS Stainless Rifle
Similar to the Mark II-G except has stainless steel barreled action and
graphite/polymer filled stock; free-floated barrel. Weighs 5 lbs. Introduced
1997. Imported from Canada by Savage Arms, Inc.
Price: **$205.00**

SAVAGE MODEL 93G MAGNUM BOLT-ACTION RIFLE
Caliber: 22 WMR, 5-shot magazine. **Barrel:** 20-3/4". **Weight:** 5-3/4 lbs.
Length: 39-1/2" overall. **Stock:** Walnut-finished hardwood with Monte
Carlo-type comb, checkered grip and forend. **Sights:** Bead front, adjust-
able open rear. Receiver grooved for scope mount. **Features:** Thumb-op-
erated rotary safety. Blue finish. Introduced 1994. Made in Canada, from
Savage Arms.
Price: **$182.00**
Price: Model 93F (as above with black graphite/fiberglass stock) **$175.00**

Savage Model 93FSS Magnum Rifle
Similar to Model 93G except stainless steel barreled action and black syn-
thetic stock with positive checkering. Weighs 5-1/2 lbs. Introduced 1997.
Imported from Canada by Savage Arms, Inc.
Price: **$236.00**

Savage Model 93FVSS Magnum Rifle
Similar to Model 93FSS Magnum except 21" heavy barrel with recessed
target-style crown, satin-finished stainless barreled action, black graph-
ite/fiberglass stock. Drilled and tapped for scope mounting; comes with
Weaver-style bases. Introduced 1998. Imported from Canada by Savage
Arms, Inc.
Price: . . . . **$252.00**, With scope **$287.00**

SAVAGE MARK I-G BOLT-ACTION RIFLE
Caliber: 22 LR, single shot. **Barrel:** 20-3/4". **Weight:** 5-1/2 lbs. **Length:** 39-
1/2" overall. **Stock:** Walnut-finished hardwood with Monte Carlo-type
comb, checkered grip and forend. **Sights:** Bead front, open adjustable
rear. Receiver grooved for scope mounting. **Features:** Thumb-operated
rotating safety. Blue finish. Rifled or smooth bore. Introduced 1990. Made
in Canada, from Savage Arms Inc.
Price: Mark IG, rifled or smooth bore, right- or left-handed **$144.00**
Price: Mark I-GY (Youth), 19" bbl., 37" overall, 5 lbs. **$144.00**
Price: Mark I-LY (Youth), 19" bbl., color laminate **$175.00**
Price: Mark I-Y (Youth), 19" bbl., camo. **$174.00**
Price: Mark I-GYXP (Youth), with scope **$162.00**
Price: Mark I-GSB (22 LR shot cartridge). **$144.00**

SAVAGE MARK II BOLT-ACTION RIFLE
Caliber: 22 LR, 10-shot magazine. **Barrel:** 20-1/2". **Weight:** 5-1/2 lbs.
Length: 39-1/2" overall. **Stock:** Walnut-finished hardwood with Monte
Carlo-type comb, checkered grip and forend. **Sights:** Bead front, open ad-
justable rear. Receiver grooved for scope mounting. **Features:** Thumb-
operated rotating safety. Blue finish. Introduced 1990. Made in Canada,
from Savage Arms, Inc.
Price: Mark II-BV **$248.00**
Price: Mark II Camo **$174.00**
Price: Mark II-GY (youth), 19" barrel, 37" overall, 5 lbs. **$156.00**
Price: Mark II-GL, left-hand **$156.00**
Price: Mark II-GLY (youth) left-hand $156.00

Savage Model 93FSS

Savage Model 93FVSS

Savage Model 30G Stevens "Favorite"

Savage Cub G Youth

Winchester Model 52B

Winchester Model 1885 Low Wall

SAVAGE MARK 30G STEVENS "FAVORITE"

Caliber: 22 LR, 22WMR - Model 30GM, 17 HMR - Model 30R17. **Barrel:** 21". **Weight:** 4.25 lbs. **Length:** 36.75". **Stock:** Walnut, straight grip, Schnabel forend. **Sights:** Adjustable rear, bead post front. **Features:** Lever action falling block, inertia firing pin system, Model 30G half octagonal bbl. Model 30GM full octagonal bbl.

Price: Model 30G	$221.00
Price: Model 30GM	$258.00
Price: Model 30R17	$284.00

SAVAGE CUB G YOUTH

Caliber: 22 S, L, LR. **Barrel:** 16.125" **Weight:** 3.3 lbs. **Length:** 33" **Stock:** Walnut finished hardwood. **Sights:** Bead post, front; peep, rear. **Features:** Mini single shot bolt action, free-floating button-rifled barrel, blued finish. From Savage Arms.

Price:	$149.00

WINCHESTER MODEL 52B BOLT-ACTION RIFLE

Caliber: 22 Long Rifle, 5-shot magazine. **Barrel:** 24". **Weight:** 7 lbs. **Length:** 41-3/4" overall. **Stock:** Walnut with checkered grip and forend. **Sights:** None furnished; grooved receiver and drilled and tapped for scope mounting. **Features:** Has Micro Motion trigger adjustable for pull and over-travel; match chamber; detachable magazine. Reintroduced 1997. From U.S. Repeating Arms Co.

Price:	$662.00

WINCHESTER MODEL 1885 LOW WALL RIMFIRE

Caliber: 17 HMR, single-shot. **Barrel:** 24-1/2"; half-octagon. **Weight:** 8 lbs. **Length:** 41" overall. **Stock:** Walnut. **Sights:** Blade front, semi-buckhorn rear. **Features:** Drilled and tapped for scope mount or tang sight; target chamber. From U.S. Repeating Arms Co.

Price: Grade I	$965.00

*Includes models for classic American and ISU target competition
and other sporting and competitive shooting.*

Anschutz 1451 Target

Anschutz 2013

ANSCHUTZ 1451R SPORTER TARGET RIFLE

Caliber: 22 LR, 5-shot magazine. **Barrel:** 22" heavy match. **Weight:** 6.4 lbs. **Length:** 39.75" overall. **Stock:** European hardwood with walnut finish. **Sights:** None furnished. Grooved receiver for scope mounting or Anschutz micrometer rear sight. **Features:** Sliding safety, two-stage trigger. Adjustable buttplate; forend slide rail to accept Anschutz accessories. Imported from Germany by AcuSport Corp.
Price: $549.00

ANSCHUTZ 1451 TARGET RIFLE

Caliber: 22 LR. **Barrel:** 22". **Weight:** About 6.5 lbs. **Length:** 40". **Sights:** Optional. Receiver grooved for scope mounting. **Features:** Designed for the beginning junior shooter with adjustable length of pull from 13.25" to 14.25" via removable butt spacers. Two-stage trigger factory set at 2.6 lbs. Introduced 1999. Imported from Germany by Gunsmithing, Inc.
Price: $347.00
Price: #6834 Match Sight Set $227.10

ANSCHUTZ 1808D-RT SUPER RUNNING TARGET RIFLE

Caliber: 22 LR, single shot. **Barrel:** 32-1/2". **Weight:** 9 lbs. **Length:** 50" overall. **Stock:** European walnut. Heavy beavertail forend; adjustable cheekpiece and buttplate. Stippled grip and forend. **Sights:** None furnished. Grooved for scope mounting. **Features:** Designed for Running Target competition. Nine-way adjustable single-stage trigger, slide safety. Introduced 1991. Imported from Germany by Accuracy International, Gunsmithing, Inc.
Price: Right-hand $1,364.10

ANSCHUTZ 1903 MATCH RIFLE

Caliber: 22 LR, single shot. **Barrel:** 25.5", .75" diameter. **Weight:** 10.1 lbs. **Length:** 43.75" overall. **Stock:** Walnut-finished hardwood with adjustable cheekpiece; stippled grip and forend. **Sights:** None furnished. **Features:** Uses Anschutz Match 64 action and #5098 two-stage trigger. A medium weight rifle for intermediate and advanced Junior Match competition. Introduced 1987. Imported from Germany by Accuracy International, Gunsmithing, Inc.
Price: Right-hand $720.40
Price: Left-hand $757.90

ANSCHUTZ 64-MS R SILHOUETTE RIFLE

Caliber: 22 LR, 5-shot magazine. **Barrel:** 21-1/2", medium heavy; 7/8" diameter. **Weight:** 8 lbs. **Length:** 39.5" overall. **Stock:** Walnut-finished hardwood, silhouette-type. **Sights:** None furnished. **Features:** Uses Match 64 action. Designed for metallic silhouette competition. Stock has stippled checkering, contoured thumb groove with Wundhammer swell.

Two-stage #5098 trigger. Slide safety locks sear and bolt. Introduced 1980. Imported from Germany by AcuSport Corp., Accuracy International, Gunsmithing, Inc.
Price: 64-MS R $704.30

ANSCHUTZ 2013 BENCHREST RIFLE

Caliber: 22 LR, single shot. **Barrel:** 19.6". **Weight:** About 10.3 lbs. **Length:** 37.75" to 42.5" overall. **Stock:** Benchrest style of European hardwood. Stock length adjustable via spacers and buttplate. **Sights:** None furnished. Receiver grooved for mounts. **Features:** Uses the Anschutz 2013 target action, #5018 two-stage adjustable target trigger factory set at 3.9 oz. Introduced 1994. Imported from Germany by Accuracy International, Gunsmithing, Inc.
Price: $1,757.20

Anschutz 2007 Match Rifle

Uses same action as the Model 2013, but has a lighter barrel. European walnut stock in right-hand, true left-hand or extra-short models. Sights optional. Available with 19.6" barrel with extension tube, or 26", both in stainless or blue. Introduced 1998. Imported from Germany by Gunsmithing, Inc., Accuracy International.
Price: Right-hand, blue, no sights...................... $1,766.60
Price: Right-hand, blue, no sights, extra-short stock $1,756.60
Price: Left-hand, blue, no sights...................... $1,856.80

ANSCHUTZ 1827 BIATHLON RIFLE

Caliber: 22 LR, 5-shot magazine. **Barrel:** 21-1/2". **Weight:** 8-1/2 lbs. with sights. **Length:** 42-1/2" overall. **Stock:** European walnut with cheekpiece, stippled pistol grip and forend. **Sights:** Optional globe front specially designed for Biathlon shooting, micrometer rear with hinged snow cap. **Features:** Uses Super Match 54 action and nine-way adjustable trigger; adjustable wooden buttplate, Biathlon butthook, adjustable hand-stop rail. Introduced 1982. Imported from Germany by Accuracy International, Gunsmithing, Inc.
Price: Right-hand, with sights, about .... $1,500.50 to $1,555.00

Anschutz 1827BT Fortner Biathlon Rifle

Similar to the Anschutz 1827 Biathlon rifle except uses Anschutz/Fortner system straight-pull bolt action, blued or stainless steel barrel. Introduced 1982. Imported from Germany by Accuracy International, Gunsmithing, Inc.
Price: Right-hand, with sights................. $1,908.00 to $2,210.00
Price: Left-hand, with sights .... $2,099.20 to $2,395.00
Price: Right-hand, sights, stainless barrel (Gunsmithing, Inc.).. $2,045.20

RIFLES

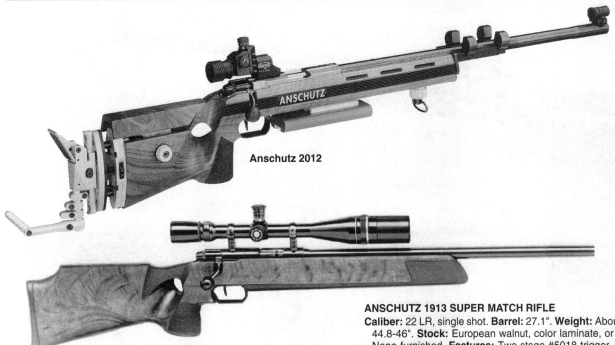

Anschutz 2012

Anschutz 54.18MS REP

ANSCHUTZ SUPER MATCH SPECIAL MODEL 2013 RIFLE

Caliber: 22 LR, single shot. **Barrel:** 25.9". **Weight:** 13 lbs. **Length:** 41.7-42.9". **Stock:** A thumbhole version made of European walnut, both the cheekpiece and buttplate are highly adjustable. **Sights:** None furnished. **Features:** Developed by Anschütz for women to shoot in the sport rifle category. Stainless or blue. This top of the line rifle was introduced in 1997.
Price: Right-hand, blue, no sights, walnut $2,219.30
Price: Right-hand, stainless, no sights, walnut $2,345.30
Price: Left-hand, blue, no sights, walnut $2,319.50

ANSCHUTZ 2012 SPORT RIFLE

Caliber: 22 LR, 5-shot magazine. **Barrel:** 22.4" match; detachable muzzle tube. **Weight:** 7.9 lbs. **Length:** 40.9" overall. **Stock:** European walnut, thumbhole design. **Sights:** None furnished. **Features:** Uses Anschutz 54.18 barreled action with two-stage match trigger. Introduced 1997. Imported from Germany by Accuracy International, AcuSport Corp.
Price: . . . . $1,425.00 to $2,219.95

ANSCHUTZ 1911 PRONE MATCH RIFLE

Caliber: 22 LR, single shot. **Barrel:** 27-1/4". **Weight:** 11 lbs. **Length:** 46" overall. **Stock:** Walnut-finished European hardwood; American prone-style with adjustable cheekpiece, textured pistol grip, forend with swivel rail and adjustable rubber buttplate. **Sights:** None furnished. Receiver grooved for Anschutz sights (extra). **Features:** Two-stage #5018 trigger adjustable from 2.1 to 8.6 oz. Extremely fast lock time. Stainless or blue barrel. Imported from Germany by Accuracy International, Gunsmithing, Inc.
Price: Right-hand, no sights $1,714.20

ANSCHUTZ 1912 SPORT RIFLE

Caliber: 22 LR, single shot. **Barrel:** 25.9". **Weight:** About 11.4 lbs. **Length:** 41.7-42.9". **Stock:** European walnut or aluminum. **Sights:** None furnished. **Features:** Light weight sport rifle version. Still uses the 54 match action like the 1913 but weighs 1.5 pounds less. Stainless or blue barrel. Introduced 1997.
Price: Right-hand, blue, no sights, walnut $1,789.50
Price: Right-hand, blue, no sights, aluminum $2,129.80
Price: Right-hand, stainless, no sights, walnut $1,910.30
Price: Left-hand, blue, no sights, walnut $1,879.00

ANSCHUTZ 1913 SUPER MATCH RIFLE

Caliber: 22 LR, single shot. **Barrel:** 27.1". **Weight:** About 14.3 lbs. **Length:** 44.8-46". **Stock:** European walnut, color laminate, or aluminum. **Sights:** None furnished. **Features:** Two-stage #5018 trigger. Extremely fast lock time. Stainless or blue barrel.
Price: Right-hand, blue, no sights, walnut stock $2,262.90
Price: Right-hand, blue, no sights, color laminate stock $2,275.10
Price: Right-hand, blue, no sights, aluminum stock $2,262.90
Price: Left-hand, blue, no sights, walnut stock $2,382.20

Anschutz 1913 Super Match Rifle

Same as the Model 1911 except European walnut International-type stock with adjustable cheekpiece, or color laminate, both available with straight or lowered forend, adjustable aluminum hook buttplate, adjustable hand stop, weighs 15.5 lbs., 46" overall. Stainless or blue barrel. Imported from Germany by Accuracy International, Gunsmithing, Inc.
Price: Right-hand, blue, no sights, walnut stock . . **$2,139.00 to $2,175.00**
Price: Right-hand, blue, no sights, color laminate stock **$2,199.40**
Price: Right-hand, blue, no sights, walnut, lowered forend **$2,181.80**
Price: Right-hand, blue, no sights, color laminate,
lowered forend **$2,242.20**
Price: Left-hand, blue, no sights, walnut stock . . . **$2,233.10 to $2,275.00**

Anschutz 54.18MS REP Deluxe Silhouette Rifle

Same basic action and trigger specifications as the Anschutz 1913 Super Match but with removable 5-shot clip magazine, 22.4" barrel extendable to 30" using optional extension and weight set. Weight is 8.1 lbs. Receiver drilled and tapped for scope mounting. Stock is thumbhole silhouette version or standard silhouette version, both are European walnut. Introduced 1990. Imported from Germany by Accuracy International, Gunsmithing, Inc.
Price: Thumbhole stock **$1,461.40**
Price: Standard stock **$1,212.10**

Anschutz 1907 Standard Match Rifle

Same action as Model 1913 but with 7/8" diameter 26" barrel (stainless or blue). Length is 44.5" overall, weighs 10.5 lbs. Choice of stock configurations. Vented forend. Designed for prone and position shooting ISU requirements; suitable for NRA matches. Also available with walnut flat-forend stock for benchrest shooting. Imported from Germany by Accuracy International, Gunsmithing, Inc.
Price: Right-hand, blue, no sights,
hardwood stock. . . . . **$1,253.40 to $1,299.00**
Price: Right-hand, blue, no sights, colored laminated
stock . . . . **$1,316.10 to $1,375.00**
Price: Right-hand, blue, no sights, walnut stock **$1,521.10**
Price: Left-hand, blue barrel, no sights, walnut stock **$1,584.60**

Anschutz 1907

Armalite
AR-10 (T)

Bushmaster XM15

ARMALITE AR-10 (T) RIFLE

Caliber: 308, 10-shot magazine. **Barrel:** 24" target-weight Rock 5R custom. **Weight:** 10.4 lbs. **Length:** 43.5" overall. **Stock:** Green or black compostion; N.M. fiberglass handguard tube. **Sights:** Detachable handle, front sight, or scope mount available. Comes with international-style flattop receiver with Picatinny rail. **Features:** National Match two-stage trigger. Forged upper receiver. Receivers hard-coat anodized. Introduced 1995. Made in U.S.A. by ArmaLite, Inc.

Price: Green **$2,075.00**
Price: Black **$2,090.00**
Price: AR-10 (T) Carbine, lighter 16" barrel, single stage trigger, weighs 8.8 lbs. Green **$1,970.00**
Price: Black **$1,985.00**

ARMALITE M15A4 (T) EAGLE EYE RIFLE

Caliber: 223, 7-shot magazine. **Barrel:** 24" heavy stainless; 1:8" twist. **Weight:** 9.2 lbs. **Length:** 42-3/8" overall. **Stock:** Green or black butt, N.M. fiberglass handguard tube. **Sights:** One-piece international-style flattop receiver with Weaver-type rail, including case deflector. **Features:** Detachable carry handle, front sight and scope mount (30mm or 1") avail-able. Upper and lower receivers have push-type pivot pin, hard coat anodized. Made in U.S.A. by ArmaLite, Inc.

Price: Green **$1,378.00**
Price: Black **$1,393.00**

ARMALITE M15A4 ACTION MASTER RIFLE

Caliber: 223, 7-shot magazine. **Barrel:** 20" heavy stainless; 1:9" twist. **Weight:** 9 lbs. **Length:** 40-1/2" overall. **Stock:** Green or black plastic; N.M. fiberglass handguard tube. **Sights:** One-piece international-style flattop receiver with Weaver-type rail. **Features:** Detachable carry handle, front sight and scope mount available. National Match two-stage trigger group; Picatinny rail; upper and lower receivers have push-type pivot pin; hard coat anodized finish. Made in U.S.A. by ArmaLite, Inc.

Price: **$1,175.00**

BLASER R93 LONG RANGE RIFLE

Caliber: 308 Win., 10-shot detachable box magazine. **Barrel:** 24". **Weight:** 10.4 lbs. **Length:** 44" overall. **Stock:** Aluminum with synthetic lining. **Sights:** None furnished; accepts detachable scope mount. **Features:** Straight-pull bolt action with adjustable trigger; fully adjustable stock; quick takedown; corrosion resistant finish. Introduced 1998. Imported from Germany by Sigarms.

Price: **$2,360.00**

BUSHMASTER XM15 E2S TARGET MODEL RIFLE

Caliber: 223. **Barrel:** 20", 24"; 1:9" twist; heavy. **Weight:** 8.3 lbs. **Length:** 38.25" overall (20" barrel). **Stock:** Black composition; A2 type. **Sights:** Adjustable post front, adjustable aperture rear. **Features:** Patterned after Colt M-16A2. Chrome-lined barrel with manganese phosphate exterior. Forged aluminum receivers with push-pin takedown. Available in stainless barrel and camo stock versions. Made in U.S.A. by Bushmaster Firearms Co.

Price: 20" match heavy barrel (A2 type) **$965.00**
Price: (A3 type) **$1,095.00**

BUSHMASTER DCM COMPETITION RIFLE

Similar to the XM15 E2S Target Model except has 20" extra-heavy (1" diameter) barrel with 1.8" twist for heavier competition bullets. Weighs about 12 lbs. with balance weights. Has special competition rear sight with interchangeable apertures, extra-fine 1/2- or 1/4-MOA windage and elevation adjustments; specially ground front sight post in choice of three widths. Full-length handguards over free-floater barrel tube. Introduced 1998. Made in U.S.A. by Bushmaster Firearms, Inc.

Price: **$1,495.00**

Bushmaster DCM

Bushmaster XM15 E2S V-Match Carbine

Colt Accurized

Colt Match Target HBAR

Colt Match Target HBAR II

BUSHMASTER XM15 E2S V-MATCH RIFLE

Caliber: 223. **Barrel:** 20", 24""; 1:9" twist; heavy. **Weight:** 8.1 lbs. **Length:** 38.25" overall (20" barrel). **Stock:** Black composition. A2 type. **Sights:** None furnished; upper receiver has integral scope mount base. **Features:** Chrome-lined .950" heavy barrel with counter-bored crown, manganese phosphate finish, free-floating aluminum handguard, forged aluminum receivers with push-pin takedown, hard anodized mil-spec finish. Competition trigger optional. Made in U.S.A. by Bushmaster Firearms, Inc.

Price: 20" Match heavy barrel. **$1,055.00**
Price: 24" Match heavy barrel. **$1,065.00**
Price: V-Match Carbine (16" barrel) **$1,045.00**

COLT MATCH TARGET MODEL RIFLE

Caliber: 223 Rem., 8-shot magazine. **Barrel:** 20". **Weight:** 7.5 lbs. **Length:** 39" overall. **Stock:** Composition stock, grip, forend. **Sights:** Post front, aperture rear adjustable for windage and elevation. **Features:** Five-round detachable box magazine, standard-weight barrel, sling swivels. Has forward bolt assist. Military matte black finish. Model introduced 1991.

Price: **$1,144.00**
Price: With compensator. **$1,150.00**

Colt Accurized Rifle

Similar to the Colt Match Target Model except has 24" stainless steel heavy barrel with 1.9" rifling, flattop receiver with scope mount and 1"

rings, weighs 9.25 lbs. Introduced 1998. Made in U.S.A. by Colt's Mfg. Co., Inc.

Price: **$1,424.00**

Colt Match Target HBAR Rifle

Similar to the Target Model except has heavy barrel, 800-meter rear sight adjustable for windage and elevation. Introduced 1991.

Price: **$1,194.00**

Colt Match Target Competition HBAR Rifle

Similar to the Sporter Target except has flat-top receiver with integral Weaver-type base for scope mounting. Counter-bored muzzle, 1:9" rifling twist. Introduced 1991.

Price: Model R6700 . . . . **$1,199.00**

Colt Match Target Competition HBAR II Rifle

Similar to the Match Target Competition HBAR except has 16:1" barrel, weighs 7.1 lbs., overall length 34.5"; 1:9" twist barrel. Introduced 1995.

Price: **$1,172.00**

COMPETITION RIFLES — CENTERFIRE & RIMFIRE

EAA/IZHMASH URAL 5.1

EAA/IZHMASH Biathlon

EAA/IZHMASH Biathlon Target

Ed Brown Model 702 Light Tactical

Ed Brown Model 702 Tactical

EAA/HW 660 MATCH RIFLE
Caliber: 22 LR. **Barrel:** 26". **Weight:** 10.7 lbs. **Length:** 45.3" overall. **Stock:** Match-type walnut with adjustable cheekpiece and buttplate. **Sights:** Globe front, match aperture rear. **Features:** Adjustable match trigger; stip-pled pistol grip and forend; forend accessory rail. Introduced 1991. Import-ed from Germany by European American Armory.
Price: About $999.00
Price: With laminate stock. $1,159.00

EAA/IZHMASH URAL 5.1 TARGET RIFLE
Caliber: 22 LR. **Barrel:** 26.5". **Weight:** 11.3 lbs. **Length:** 44.5". **Stock:** Wood, international style. **Sights:** Adjustable click rear, hooded front with inserts. **Features:** Forged barrel with rifling, adjustable trigger, aluminum rail for accessories, hooked adjustable butt plate. Adjustable comb, ad-justable large palm rest. Hand stippling on grip area.
Price: . . . . NA

EAA/Izhmash Biathlon Target Rifle
Similar to URAL with addition of snow covers for barrel and sights, stock holding extra mags, round trigger block. Unique bolt utilizes toggle action.

Designed to compete in 40 meter biathlon event. 22 LR, 19.5" bbl.
Price: $979.00

EAA/Izhmash Biathalon Basic Target Rifle
Same action as Biathlon but designed for plinking or fun. Beech stock, heavy barrel with Weaver rail for scope mount. 22 LR, 19.5" bbl.
Price: $339.00

ED BROWN MODEL 702 LIGHT TACTICAL
Caliber: 223, 308. **Barrel:** 21". **Weight:** 8.75 lbs. **Stock:** Fully glass-bed-ded fiberglass with recoil pad. Wide varmint-style forend. **Sights:** None furnished. Talley scope mounts utilizing heavy duty 8-40 screws. **Fea-tures:** Compact and super accurate, it is ideal for police, military and var-mint hunters.
Price: From $2,800.00

ED BROWN MODEL 702 TACTICAL
Caliber: 308, 300 Win. Mag. **Barrel:** 26". **Weight:** 11.25 lbs. **Stock:** Hand bedded McMillan A-3 fiberglass tactical stock with recoil pad. **Sights:** None furnished. Leupold Mark 4 30mm scope mounts utilizing heavy-duty 8-40 screws. **Features:** Custom short or long action, steel trigger guard, hinged floor plate, additional caliber available.
Price: From $2,900.00

Ed Brown 702

Harris Gunworks Long Range

Harris Gunworks M-86

ED BROWN MODEL 702, M40A2 MARINE SNIPER
Caliber: 308 Win., 30-06 Springfield. **Barrel:** Match-grade 24". **Weight:** 9.25 lbs. **Stock:** Hand bedded McMillan GP fiberglass tactical stock with recoil pad in special Woodland Camo molded-in colors. **Sights:** None furnished. Leupold Mark 4 30mm scope mounts with heavy-duty 8-40 screws. **Features:** Steel trigger guard, hinged floor plate, three position safety. Left-hand model available.
Price: From **$2,900.00**

HARRIS GUNWORKS NATIONAL MATCH RIFLE
Caliber: 7mm-08, 308, 5-shot magazine. **Barrel:** 24", stainless steel. **Weight:** About 11 lbs. (std. bbl.). **Length:** 43" overall. **Stock:** Fiberglass with adjustable buttplate. **Sights:** Barrel band and Tompkins front; no rear sight furnished. **Features:** Gunworks repeating action with clip slot, Canjar trigger. Match-grade barrel. Available in right-hand only. Fiberglass stock, sight installation, special machining and triggers optional. Introduced 1989. From Harris Gunworks, Inc.
Price: **$3,500.00**

HARRIS GUNWORKS LONG RANGE RIFLE
Caliber: 300 Win. Mag., 7mm Rem. Mag., 300 Phoenix, 338 Lapua, single shot. **Barrel:** 26", stainless steel, match-grade. **Weight:** 14 lbs. **Length:** 46-1/2" overall. **Stock:** Fiberglass with adjustable buttplate and cheekpiece. Adjustable for length of pull, drop, cant and cast-off. **Sights:** Barrel band and Tompkins front; no rear sight furnished. **Features:** Uses Gunworks solid bottom single shot action and Canjar trigger. Barrel twist 1:12". Introduced 1989. From Harris Gunworks, Inc.
Price: **$3,620.00**

HARRIS GUNWORKS M-86 SNIPER RIFLE
Caliber: 308, 30-06, 4-shot magazine; 300 Win. Mag., 3-shot magazine. **Barrel:** 24", Gunworks match-grade in heavy contour. **Weight:** 11-1/4 lbs. (308), 11-1/2 lbs. (30-06, 300). **Length:** 43-1/2" overall. **Stock:** Specially designed McHale fiberglass stock with textured grip and forend, recoil pad. **Sights:** None furnished. **Features:** Uses Gunworks repeating action. Comes with bipod. Matte black finish. Sling swivels. Introduced 1989. From Harris Gunworks, Inc.
Price: **$2,700.00**

HARRIS GUNWORKS M-89 SNIPER RIFLE
Caliber: 308 Win., 5-shot magazine. **Barrel:** 28" (with suppressor). **Weight:** 15 lbs., 4 oz. **Stock:** Fiberglass; adjustable for length; recoil pad. **Sights:** None furnished. Drilled and tapped for scope mounting. **Features:** Uses Gunworks repeating action. Comes with bipod. Introduced 1990. From Harris Gunworks, Inc.
Price: Standard (non-suppressed) **$3,200.00**

HARRIS GUNWORKS COMBO M-87 SERIES 50-CALIBER RIFLES
Caliber: 50 BMG, single shot. **Barrel:** 29, with muzzle brake. **Weight:** About 21-1/2 lbs. **Length:** 53" overall. **Stock:** Gunworks fiberglass. **Sights:** None furnished. **Features:** Right-handed Gunworks stainless steel receiver, chrome-moly barrel with 1:15" twist. Introduced 1987. From Harris Gunworks, Inc.
Price: **$3,885.00**
Price: M87R 5-shot repeater **$4,000.00**
Price: M-87 (5-shot repeater) "Combo". **$4,300.00**
Price: M-92 Bullpup (shortened M-87 single shot with bullpup stock) **$4,770.00**
Price: M-93 (10-shot repeater with folding stock, detachable magazine) **$4,150.00**

OLYMPIC ARMS PCR-SERVICEMATCH RIFLE
Caliber: 223, 10-shot magazine. **Barrel:** 20", broach-cut 416 stainless steel. **Weight:** About 10 lbs. **Length:** 39.5" overall. **Stock:** A2 stowaway grip and trapdoor buttstock. **Sights:** Post front, E2-NM fully adjustable aperture rear. **Features:** Based on the AR-15. Conforms to all DCM standards. Free-floating 1:8.5" or 1:10" barrel; crowned barrel; no bayonet lug. Introduced 1996. Made in U.S.A. by Olympic Arms, Inc.
Price: **$1,062.00**

OLYMPIC ARMS PCR-1 RIFLE
Caliber: 223, 10-shot magazine. **Barrel:** 20", 24"; 416 stainless steel. **Weight:** 10 lbs., 3 oz. **Length:** 38.25" overall with 20" barrel. **Stock:** A2 stowaway grip and trapdoor butt. **Sights:** None supplied; flattop upper receiver, cut-down front sight base. **Features:** Based on the AR-15 rifle. Broach-cut, free-floating barrel with 1:8.5" or 1:10" twist. No bayonet lug. Crowned barrel; fluting available. Introduced 1994. Made in U.S.A. by Olympic Arms, Inc.
Price: **$1,038.00**

COMPETITION RIFLES — CENTERFIRE & RIMFIRE

Remington 40-XB Rangemaster

Remington 40-XC KS

Springfield, Inc. M1A Super Match

Springfield, Inc.
M1A/M-21

Olympic Arms PCR-2, PCR-3 Rifles
Similar to the PCR-1 except has 16" barrel, weighs 8 lbs., 2 oz.; has post front sight, fully adjustable aperture rear. Model PCR-3 has flattop upper receiver, cut-down front sight base. Introduced 1994. Made in U.S.A. by Olympic Arms, Inc.
Price: **$958.00**

REMINGTON 40-XB RANGEMASTER TARGET CENTERFIRE
Caliber: 15 calibers from 220 Swift to 300 Win. Mag. **Barrel:** 27-1/4". **Weight:** 11-1/4 lbs. **Length:** 47" overall. **Stock:** American walnut, laminated thumbhole or Kevlar with high comb and beavertail forend stop. Rubber non-slip buttplate. **Sights:** None. Scope blocks installed. **Features:** Adjustable trigger. Stainless barrel and action. Receiver drilled and tapped for sights.
Price: Standard single shot. . . . .**$1,636.00** (right-hand)
. . . . **$1,761.00** (left-hand)
Price: Repeater. **$1,734.00**

REMINGTON 40-XBBR KS
Caliber: Five calibers from 22 BR to 308 Win. **Barrel:** 20" (light varmint class), 24" (heavy varmint class). **Weight:** 7-1/4 lbs. (light varmint class); 12 lbs. (heavy varmint class). **Length:** 38" (20" bbl.), 42" (24" bbl.). **Stock:** Aramid fiber. **Sights:** None. Supplied with scope blocks. **Features:** Unblued benchrest with stainless steel barrel, trigger adjustable from 1-1/2 lbs. to 3-1/2 lbs. Special 2-oz. trigger extra cost. Scope and mounts extra.
Price: Single shot **$1,876.00**

REMINGTON 40-XC KS TARGET RIFLE
Caliber: 7.62 NATO, 5-shot. **Barrel:** 24", stainless steel. **Weight:** 11 lbs. without sights. **Length:** 43-1/2" overall. **Stock:** Aramid fiber. **Sights:** None furnished. **Features:** Designed to meet the needs of competitive shooters. Stainless steel barrel and action.
Price: **$1,821.00**

REMINGTON 40-XR CUSTOM SPORTER
Caliber: 22 LR, 22 WM. **Features:** Model XR-40 Target rifle action with craftsmanship of Model 700 Custom. Many options available.
Price: Single shot **$3,383.00**

SAKO TRG-22 BOLT-ACTION RIFLE
Caliber: 308 Win., 10-shot magazine. **Barrel:** 26". **Weight:** 10-1/4 lbs. **Length:** 45-1/4" overall. **Stock:** Reinforced polyurethane with fully adjustable cheekpiece and buttplate. **Sights:** None furnished. Optional quick-detachable, one-piece scope mount base, 1" or 30mm rings. **Features:** Resistance-free bolt, free-floating heavy stainless barrel, 60-degree bolt lift. Two-stage trigger is adjustable for length, pull, horizontal or vertical pitch. Introduced 2000. Imported from Finland by Beretta USA.
Price: Green **$2,898.00**
Price: Model TRG-42, as above except in 338 Lapua Mag or 300
Win. Mag. **$2,829.00**
Price: Green (new) **$3,243.00**

SPRINGFIELD, INC. M1A SUPER MATCH
Caliber: 308 Win. **Barrel:** 22", heavy Douglas Premium. **Weight:** About 11 lbs. **Length:** 44.31" overall. **Stock:** Heavy walnut competition stock with longer pistol grip, contoured area behind the rear sight, thicker butt and forend, glass bedded. **Sights:** National Match front and rear. **Features:** Has figure-eight-style operating rod guide. Introduced 1987. From Springfield, Inc.
Price: About **$2,479.00**

Springfield, Inc. M1A/M-21 Tactical Model Rifle
Similar to M1A Super Match except special sniper stock with adjustable cheekpiece and rubber recoil pad. Weighs 11.6 lbs. From Springfield, Inc.
Price: **$2,975.00**

SPRINGFIELD, INC. M-1 GARAND AMERICAN COMBAT RIFLES
Caliber: 30-06, 308 Win., 8-shot. **Barrel:** 24". **Weight:** 9.5 lbs. **Length:** 43.6". **Stock:** American walnut. **Sights:** Military square post front, military aperture, MOA adjustable rear. **Features:** Limited production, certificate of authenticity, all new receiver, barrel and stock with remaining parts USGI mil-spec. 2-stage military trigger.
Price: About **$2,479.00**

RIFLES

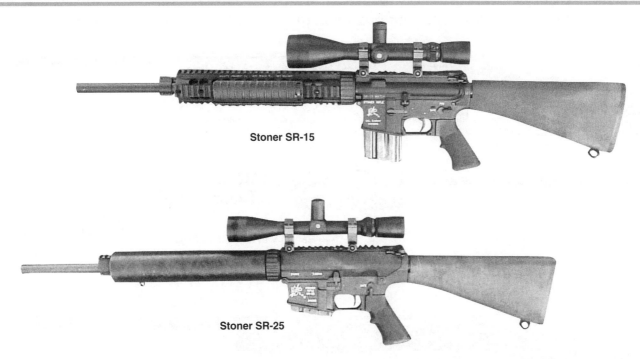

Stoner SR-15

Stoner SR-25

STONER SR-15 MATCH RIFLE
Caliber: 223. **Barrel:** 20". **Weight:** 7.9 lbs. **Length:** 38" overall. **Stock:** Black synthetic. **Sights:** None furnished; flat-top upper receiver for scope mounting. **Features:** Short Picatinny rail, two-stage match trigger. Introduced 1998. Made in U.S.A. by Knight's Mfg.Co.
Price: $1,650.00

CONSULT
SHOOTER'S
MARKETPLACE
Page 64, This Issue

STONER SR-25 MATCH RIFLE
Caliber: 7.62 NATO, 10-shot steel magazine, 5-shot optional. **Barrel:** 24" heavy match; 1:11.25" twist. **Weight:** 10.75 lbs. **Length:** 44" overall. **Stock:** Black synthetic AR-15A2 design. Full floating forend of Mil-spec synthetic attaches to upper receiver at a single point. **Sights:** None furnished. Has integral Weaver-style rail. Rings and iron sights optional. **Features:** Improved AR-15 trigger, AR-15-style seven-lug rotating bolt. Gas block rail mounts detachable front sight. Introduced 1993. Made in U.S.A. by Knight's Mfg. Co.
Price: $3,345.00
Price: SR-25 Lightweight Match (20" medium match target contour barrel, 9.5 lbs., 40" overall) $3,345.00

TIKKA TARGET RIFLE
Caliber: 223, 22-250, 308, detachable 5-shot magazine. **Barrel:** 23-1/2" heavy. **Weight:** 9 lbs. **Length:** 43-5/8" overall. **Stock:** European walnut with adjustable comb, adjustable buttplate; stippled grip and forend. **Sights:** None furnished; drilled and tapped for scope mounting. **Features:** Buttplate adjustable for distance, angle, height and pitch, adjustable trigger, free-floating barrel. Introduced 1998. Imported from Finland by Beretta USA.
Price: $950.00

Includes a wide variety of sporting guns and guns suitable for various competitions.

Benelli Legacy

Benelli M1 Field Camouflage

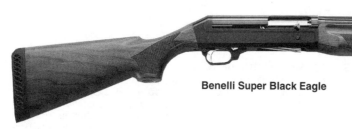

Benelli Super Black Eagle

BENELLI LEGACY SHOTGUN

Gauge: 12, 20, 2-3/4" and 3" chamber. **Barrel:** 24", 26", 28" (Full, Mod., Imp. Cyl., Imp. Mod., cylinder choke tubes). Mid-bead sight. **Weight:** 5.8 to 7.6 lbs. **Length:** 49-5/8" overall (28" barrel). **Stock:** Select European walnut with satin finish. **Features:** Uses the rotating bolt inertia recoil operating system with a two-piece steel/aluminum etched receiver (bright on lower, blue upper). Drop adjustment kit allows the stock to be custom fitted without modifying the stock. Introduced 1998. Imported from Italy by Benelli USA, Corp.
Price: **$1,400.00**

Benelli Sport II Shotgun

Similar to the Legacy model except has dual tone blue/silver receiver, two carbon fiber interchangeable ventilated ribs, adjustable butt pad, adjustable buttstock, and functions with ultra-light target loads. Walnut stock with satin finish. Introduced 1997. Imported from Italy by Benelli U.S.A.
Price: **$1,400.00**

BENELLI M1 FIELD SHOTGUN

Gauge: 12, 20 ga. **Barrel:** 21", 24", 26", 28". **Weight:** 7 lbs., 4 oz. **Stock:** High impact polymer; wood on 26", 28". **Sights:** Red bar. **Features:** Sporting version of the military & police gun. Uses the rotating Montefeltro bolt system. Ventilated rib; blue finish. Comes with set of five choke tubes. Imported from Italy by Benelli U.S.A.
Price: . . . (Synthetic) **$985.00**; (Wood) **$1,000.00**; (Timber HD) **$1,085.00**
Price: 24" rifled barrel . . . . . (Synthetic) **$1,060.00**; Timber HD **$1,165.00**
Price: Synthetic stock, left-hand version (24", 26", 28" brls.) . . . **$1,005.00**
Price: Timber HD camo left-hand, 21", 24" barrel. **$1,105.00**
Price: MI Field Steadygrip **$1,175.00**

Benelli Montefeltro Shotgun

Similar to the M1 Super except has checkered walnut stock with satin finish. Uses the Montefeltro rotating bolt system with a simple inertia recoil design. Full, Imp. Mod, Mod., Imp. Cyl. choke tubes, 12 and 20 ga. Weighs 6.8-7.1 lbs. Finish is blue. Introduced 1987.
Price: 24", 26", 28" **$1,005.00**
Price: Left-hand, 26", 28" **$1,020.00**

BENELLI SUPER BLACK EAGLE SHOTGUN

Gauge: 12, 3-1/2" chamber. **Barrel:** 24", 26", 28" (Cyl. Imp. Cyl., Mod., Imp. Mod., Full choke tubes). **Weight:** 7 lbs., 5 oz. **Length:** 49-5/8" overall (28" barrel). **Stock:** European walnut with satin finish, or polymer. Adjustable for drop. **Sights:** Red bar front. **Features:** Uses Montefeltro inertia recoil bolt system. Fires all 12 gauge shells from 2-3/4" to 3-1/2" magnums, vent rib. Introduced 1991. Imported from Italy by Benelli U.S.A.
Price: With 26" and 28" barrel, wood stock. **$1,300.00**
Price: Timber HD Camo 24", 26", 28" barrel. **$1,385.00**
Price: With 24", 26" and 28" barrel, polymer stock **$1,290.00**
Price: Left-hand, 24", 26", 28", polymer stock **$1,345.00**
Price: Left-hand, 24", 26", 28", camo stock **$1,435.00**
Price: Steadygrip Turkey Gun. **$1,465.00**

Benelli Super Black Eagle Slug Gun

Similar to the Benelli Super Black Eagle except has 24" rifled barrel with 2-3/4" and 3" chamber, drilled and tapped for scope. Uses the inertia recoil bolt system. Matte-finish receiver. Weight is 7.5 lbs., overall length 45.5". Wood or polymer stocks available. Introduced 1992. Imported from Italy by Benelli U.S.A.
Price: With wood stock **$1,345.00**
Price: With polymer stock **$1,335.00**
Price: 24" barrel, Timber HD Camo **$1,460.00**

Benelli Executive Series Shotgun

Similar to the Legacy except has grayed steel lower receiver, hand-engraved and gold inlaid (Grade III), and has highest grade of walnut stock with drop adjustment kit. Barrel lengths 26" or 28"; 2-3/4" and 3" chamber. Special order only. Introduced 1995. Imported from Italy by Benelli U.S.A.
Price: Grade I (engraved game scenes) **$5,465.00**
Price: Grade II (game scenes with scroll engraving) **$6,135.00**
Price: Grade III (full coverage, gold inlays) **$7,065.00**

BERETTA AL391 TEKNYS

Gauge: 12, 20 gauge; 3" chamber, semi-auto. **Barrel:** 26", 28". **Weight:** 5.9 lbs. (20 ga.), 7.3 lbs. (12 ga.). **Length:** N/A. **Stock:** X-tra wood (special process wood enhancement). **Features:** Flat 1/4 rib, TruGlo Tru-Bead sight, recoil reducer, stock spacers, overbored bbls., flush choke tubes. Comes with fitted, lined case.
Price: **$1,194.00**
Price: Teknys Gold (green enamel inlays, oil-finished walnut . . . **$1,515.00**
Price: Teknys Gold Sporting (blue inlays, select walnut) **$1,653.00**

Beretta AL391 Urika Gold Sporting

Beretta AL391 Urika Sporting

Beretta A391 Xtrema 3.5

Browning
Gold Deer Hunter

BERETTA AL391 URIKA AUTO SHOTGUNS

Gauge: 12, 20 gauge; 3" chamber. **Barrel:** 22", 24", 26", 28", 30"; five Mobilchoke choke tubes. **Weight:** 5.95 to 7.28 lbs. **Length:** Varies by model. **Stock:** Walnut, black or camo synthetic; shims, spacers and interchangeable recoil pads allow custom fit. **Features:** Self-compensating gas operation handles full range of loads; recoil reducer in receiver; enlarged trigger guard; reduced-weight receiver, barrel and forend; hard-chromed bore. Introduced 2000. Imported from Italy by Beretta USA.

Price: AL391 Urika (12 ga., 26", 28", 30" barrels) **$1,035.00**

Price: AL391 Urika (20 ga., 24", 26", 28" barrels) **$1,035.00**

Price: AL391 Urika Synthetic
(12 ga., 24", 26", 28", 30" barrels) **$1,035.00**

Price: AL391 Urika Camo. (12 ga., Realtree Hardwoods
or Max 4-HD) **$1,139.00**

Beretta AL391 Urika Gold and Gold Sporting Auto Shotguns

Similar to AL391 Urika except features deluxe wood, jeweled bolt and carrier, gold-inlaid receiver with black or silver finish. Introduced 2000. Imported from Italy by Beretta USA.

Price: AL391 Urika Gold Sporting
(12 or 20, black receiver, engraving) **$1,377.00**

Price: AL391 Urika Gold Sporting
(12 ga., silver receiver, engraving) **$1,377.00**

Beretta AL391 Urika Sporting Auto Shotguns

Similar to AL391 Urika except has competition sporting stock with rounded rubber recoil pad, wide ventilated rib with white front and mid-rib beads, satin-black receiver with silver markings. Available in 12 and 20 gauge. Introduced 2000. Imported from Italy by Beretta USA.

Price: AL391 Urika Sporting. **$1,101.00**

Beretta AL391 Urika Trap Auto Shotguns

Similar to AL391 Urika except in 12 ga. only, has wide ventilated rib with white front and mid-rib beads, Monte Carlo stock and special trap recoil pad. Gold Trap features highly figured walnut stock and forend, gold-filled Beretta logo and signature on receiver. Optima bore and Optima choke tubes. Introduced 2000. Imported from Italy by Beretta USA.

Price: AL391 Urika Trap **$1,101.00**

Beretta AL391 Urika Parallel Target RL and SL Auto Shotguns

Similar to AL391 Urika except has parallel-comb, Monte Carlo stock with tighter grip radius to reduce trigger reach and stepped ventilated rib. SL model has same features but with 13.5" length of pull stock. Introduced 2000. Imported from Italy by Beretta USA.

Price: AL391 Urika Parallel Target RL **$1,101.00**

Price: AL391 Urika Parallel Target SL **$1,101.00**

Beretta AL391 Urika Youth Shotgun

Similar to AL391 except has a 24" or 26" barrel with 13.5" stock for youth and smaller shooters. Introduced 2000. From Beretta USA.

Price: **$1,035.00**

BERETTA A391 XTREMA 3.5 AUTO SHOTGUNS

Gauge: 12 ga. 3-1/2" chamber. **Barrel:** 24", 26", 28". **Weight:** 7.8 lbs. **Stock:** Synthetic. **Features:** Semi-auto goes with two-lug rotating bolt and self-compensating gas valve, extended tang, cross bolt safety, self-cleaning, with case.

Price: Synthetic **$1,035.00**

Price: Realtree Hardwood HD Camo and Max 4-HD **$1,139.00**

BROWNING GOLD HUNTER AUTO SHOTGUN

Gauge: 12, 3" or 3-1/2" chamber; 20, 3" chamber. **Barrel:** 12 ga.-26", 28", 30", Invector Plus choke tubes; 20 ga.-26", 30", Invector choke tubes. **Weight:** 7 lbs., 9 oz. (12 ga.), 6 lbs., 12 oz. (20 ga.). **Length:** 46-1/4" overall (20 ga., 26" barrel). **Stock:** 14"x1-1/2"x2-1/3"; select walnut with gloss finish; palm swell grip. **Features:** Self-regulating, self-cleaning gas system shoots all loads; lightweight receiver with special non-glare deep black finish; large reversible safety button; large rounded trigger guard, gold trigger. The 20 gauge has slightly smaller dimensions; 12 gauge have back-bored barrels, Invector Plus tube system. Introduced 1994. Imported by Browning.

Price: 12 or 20 gauge, 3" chamber. **$894.00**

Price: 12 ga., 3-1/2" chamber. **$1,038.00**

Price: Extra barrels . . . . $336.00 to $415.00

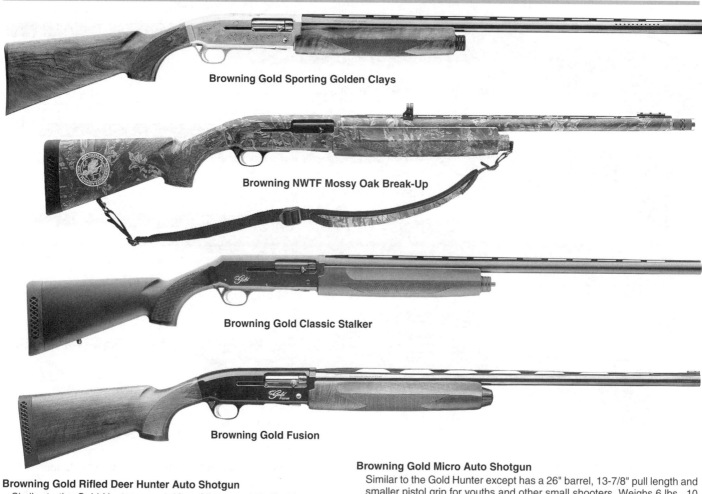

Browning Gold Sporting Golden Clays

Browning NWTF Mossy Oak Break-Up

Browning Gold Classic Stalker

Browning Gold Fusion

Browning Gold Rifled Deer Hunter Auto Shotgun

Similar to the Gold Hunter except 12 or 20 gauge, 22" rifled barrel with cantilever scope mount, walnut stock with extra-thick recoil pad. Weighs 7 lbs., 12 oz., overall length 42-1/2". Sling swivel studs fitted on the magazine cap and butt. Introduced 1997. Imported by Browning.

Price: 12 gauge **$887.00**
Price: With Mossy Oak Break-up camouflage **$1,046.00**
Price: 20 ga. (satin-finish walnut stock, 3" chamber) **$987.00**

Browning Gold Deer Stalker

Similar to the Gold Deer Hunter except has black composite stock and forend, fully rifled barrel, cantilever scope mount. Introduced 1999. Imported by Browning.

Price: 12 gauge **$967.00**

Browning Gold Sporting Clays Auto Shotgun

Similar to the Gold Hunter except 12 gauge only with 28" or 30" barrel; front Hi-Viz Pro-Comp and center bead on tapered ventilated rib; ported and back-bored Invector Plus barrel; 2-3/4" chamber; satin-finished stock with solid, radiused recoil pad with hard heel insert; non-glare black alloy receiver has "Sporting Clays" inscribed in gold. Introduced 1996. Imported from Japan by Browning.

Price: **$984.00**

Browning Gold Sporting Golden Clays

Similar to the Sporting Clays except has silvered receiver with gold engraving, high grade wood. Introduced 1999. Imported by Browning.

Price: **$1,457.00**

Browning Gold Ladies'/Youth Sporting Clays Auto

Similar to the Gold Sporting Clays except has stock dimensions of 14-1/4"x1-3/4"x2" for women and younger shooters. Introduced 1999. Imported by Browning.

Price: **$920.00**

Browning Gold Micro Auto Shotgun

Similar to the Gold Hunter except has a 26" barrel, 13-7/8" pull length and smaller pistol grip for youths and other small shooters. Weighs 6 lbs., 10 oz. Introduced 2001. From Browning.

Price: **$894.00**

Browning Gold Stalker Auto Shotgun

Similar to the Gold Hunter except has black composite stock and forend. Choice of 3" or 3-1/2" chamber.

Price: 12 ga. with 3" chamber **$856.00**
Price: With 3-1/2" chamber **$1,002.00**

Browning Gold Mossy Oak® Shadow Grass Shotgun

Similar to the Gold Hunter except 12 gauge only, completely covered with Mossy Oak® Shadow Grass camouflage. Choice of 3" or 3-1/2" chamber and 26" or 28" barrel. Introduced 1999. Imported by Browning.

Price: 12 ga. 3" chamber **$967.00**
Price: 12 ga., 3-1/2" chamber **$1,146.00**

Browning Gold Mossy Oak® Break-up Shotgun

Similar to the Gold Hunter except 12 gauge only, completely covered with Mossy Oak® Break-Up camouflage. Imported by Browning.

Price: 3" chamber **$1,069.00**
Price: 3-1/2" chamber **$1,282.00**
Price: NWTF model, 3" chamber, 24" bbl. with Hi-Viz sight **$998.00**
Price: NWTF model, 3-1/2" chamber, 24" bbl. with Hi-Viz sight . **$1,177.00**
Price: Gold Rifled Deer (22" rifled bbl., Cantilever scope mount) **$1,046.00**

Browning Gold Classic Hunter Auto Shotgun

Similar to the Gold Hunter 3" except has semi-hump back receiver, magazine cut-off, adjustable comb, and satin-finish wood. Introduced 1999. Imported by Browning.

Price: 12 or 20 gauge **$912.00**
Price: Classic High Grade (silvered, gold engraved receiver, high-grade wood) **$1,750.00**

Browning Gold Waterfowl

Browning Gold Light 10 Gauge

EAA/Baikal MP-153

Escort Model AS

Browning Gold Classic Stalker

Similar to the Gold Classic Hunter except has adjustable composite stock and forend. Introduced 1999. Imported by Browning.
Price: **$856.00**

Browning Gold Fusion™ Auto Shotgun

Similar to the Gold Hunter except is 1/2 lb. lighter, has a new-style vent rib, adjustable comb system, Hi-Viz Pro-Comp front sight and five choke tubes. Offered with 26", 28" or 30" barrel, 12 gauge, 3" chamber only. Includes hard case. Introduced 2001. Imported by Browning.
Price: **$1,055.00**

Browning Gold NWTF Turkey Series Camo Shotgun

Similar to the Gold Hunter except 10- or 12-gauge (3" or 3-1/2" chamber), 24" barrel with extra-full choke tube, Hi-Viz fiber-optic sights and complete gun coverage in Mossy Oak Break-Up camouflage with National Wild Turkey Federation logo on stock. Introduced 2001. From Browning.
Price: 10 gauge **$1,378.00**
Price: 12 gauge, 3-1/2" chamber Ultimate **$1,330.00**
Price: 12 gauge, 3" chamber **$1,101.00**

Browning Gold Upland Special Auto Shotgun

Similar to the Gold Classic Hunter except has straight-grip walnut stock, 12 or 20 gauge, 3" chamber. Introduced 2001. From Browning
Price: 12-gauge model (24" bbl., weighs 7 lbs.) **$958.00**
Price: 20-gauge model (26" bbl., weighs 6 lbs., 12 oz.) **$958.00**

Browning Gold Light 10 Gauge Auto Shotgun

Similar to the Browning Gold 10, except has an alloy receiver that is 1 lb. lighter than standard model. Offered in 26" or 28" bbls. With Mossy Oak Break-Up or Shadow Grass coverage; 5-shot magazine. Weighs 9 lbs., 10 oz. (28" bbl.). Introduced 2001. Imported by Browning.
Price: Camo model only **$1,297.00**

Browning Gold Evolve Shotgun

Similar to Browning Gold auto shotguns with new rib design, HiViz sights, three bbl. lengths (12 ga. only, 26", 28" or 30").
Price: **$1,118.00**

DIAMOND SEMI-AUTO SHOTGUNS

Gauge: 12 ga., 2-3/4" and 3" chambers. **Barrel:** 20"-30". **Stock:** Walnut, synthetic. **Features:** One-piece receiver, rotary butt, gas ejection, high strength steel. Gold, Silver Marine, Elite and Panther series with vented barrels and all but Silver have 3 chokes. Slug guns available, all but Panther with sights. Imported from Istanbul by Adco Sales, Inc.
Price: Gold, 28", walnut **$549.00**
Price: Gold, 28", synthetic **$499.00**
Price: Gold Slug, 24", w/sights, walnut **$549.00**
Price: Gold Slug, 24", w/sights, synthetic **$499.00**
Price: Silver Mariner, 22", synthetic **$499.00**
Price: Silver Mariner, 20" slug w/sights, synthetic **$479.00**
Price: Elite, 22" Slug, 24"-28", walnut . . . . **$429.00 to $449.00**
Price: Panther, 22" slug; 26", 28", vent rin w/3 chokes,
  synthetic . . . . **$379.00 to $399.00**
Price: Imperial 12, 20 ga., 24" slug w/sights, 26",
  28" vent rib w/3 chokes, walnut . . . . **$479.00 to $499.00**
Price: Imperial, 12 ga., 28" vent rib w/3 chokes,
  3.5" chamber, walnut **$499.00**

EAA/BAIKAL MP-153 AUTO SHOTGUN

Gauge: 12, 3-1/2" chamber. **Barrel:** 24", 26", 28"; imp., mod. and full choke tubes. **Weight:** 7.8 lbs. **Stock:** Walnut. **Features:** Gas-operated action with automatic gas-adjustment valve allows use of light and heavy loads interchangeably; 4-round magazine; rubber recoil pad. Introduced 2000. Imported by European American Armory.
Price: MP-153 (blued finish, walnut stock and forend) **$459.00**
Price: MP-153 (field grade, synthetic stock) **$349.00**

EAA/SAIGA AUTO SHOTGUN

Gauge: 12, 20, .410, 3" chamber. **Barrel:** 19", 21", 24". **Weight:** 6.6-7.6 lbs. **Length:** 40"-45". **Stock:** Synthetic. **Features:** Retains best features of the AK Rifle by Kalashnikov as the semi-auto shotgun. Magazine fed. Imported from Russia by EAA Corp.
Price: .410 ga. **$299.00**
Price: 20 ga. **$389.00**
Price: 12 ga. . . . . **$409.00 to $439.00**

SHOTGUNS — AUTOLOADERS

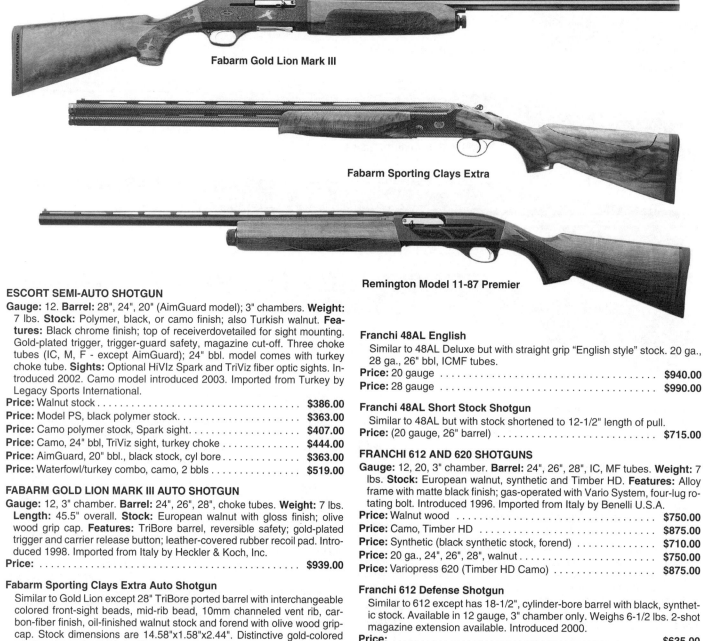

Fabarm Gold Lion Mark III

Fabarm Sporting Clays Extra

Remington Model 11-87 Premier

ESCORT SEMI-AUTO SHOTGUN

Gauge: 12. **Barrel:** 28", 24", 20" (AimGuard model); 3" chambers. **Weight:** 7 lbs. **Stock:** Polymer, black, or camo finish; also Turkish walnut. **Features:** Black chrome finish; top of receiverdovetailed for sight mounting. Gold-plated trigger, trigger-guard safety, magazine cut-off. Three choke tubes (IC, M, F - except AimGuard); 24" bbl. model comes with turkey choke tube. **Sights:** Optional HiVIz Spark and TriViz fiber optic sights. Introduced 2002. Camo model introduced 2003. Imported from Turkey by Legacy Sports International.

Price: Walnut stock **$386.00**
Price: Model PS, black polymer stock. **$363.00**
Price: Camo polymer stock, Spark sight. **$407.00**
Price: Camo, 24" bbl, TriViz sight, turkey choke **$444.00**
Price: AimGuard, 20" bbl., black stock, cyl bore **$363.00**
Price: Waterfowl/turkey combo, camo, 2 bbls **$519.00**

FABARM GOLD LION MARK III AUTO SHOTGUN

Gauge: 12, 3" chamber. **Barrel:** 24", 26", 28", choke tubes. **Weight:** 7 lbs. **Length:** 45.5" overall. **Stock:** European walnut with gloss finish; olive wood grip cap. **Features:** TriBore barrel, reversible safety; gold-plated trigger and carrier release button; leather-covered rubber recoil pad. Introduced 1998. Imported from Italy by Heckler & Koch, Inc.

Price: **$939.00**

Fabarm Sporting Clays Extra Auto Shotgun

Similar to Gold Lion except 28" TriBore ported barrel with interchangeable colored front-sight beads, mid-rib bead, 10mm channeled vent rib, carbon-fiber finish, oil-finished walnut stock and forend with olive wood grip-cap. Stock dimensions are 14.58"x1.58"x2.44". Distinctive gold-colored receiver logo. Available in 12 gauge only, 3" chamber. Introduced 1999. Imported from Italy by Heckler & Koch, Inc.

Price: **$1,249.00**

FRANCHI 48AL SHOTGUN

Gauge: 20 or 28, 2-3/4" chamber. **Barrel:** 24", 26", 28" (Full, cyl., mod., choke tubes). **Weight:** 5.5 lbs. (20 gauge). **Length:** 44"-48.". **Stock:** 14-1/4"x1-5/ 8"x2-1/2". Walnut with checkered grip and forend. **Features:** Long recoil-operated action. Chrome-lined bore; cross-bolt safety. Imported from Italy by Benelli U.S.A.

Price: 20 ga. **$715.00**
Price: 28 ga. **$825.00**

Franchi 48AL Deluxe Shotgun

Similar to 48AL but with select walnut stock and forend and high-polish blue finish with gold trigger. Introduced 2000.

Price: (20 gauge, 26" barrel) **$940.00**
Price: (28 gauge, 26" barrel) **$990.00**

Franchi 48AL English

Similar to 48AL Deluxe but with straight grip "English style" stock. 20 ga., 28 ga., 26" bbl, ICMF tubes.

Price: 20 gauge **$940.00**
Price: 28 gauge **$990.00**

Franchi 48AL Short Stock Shotgun

Similar to 48AL but with stock shortened to 12-1/2" length of pull.

Price: (20 gauge, 26" barrel) **$715.00**

FRANCHI 612 AND 620 SHOTGUNS

Gauge: 12, 20, 3" chamber. **Barrel:** 24", 26", 28", IC, MF tubes. **Weight:** 7 lbs. **Stock:** European walnut, synthetic and Timber HD. **Features:** Alloy frame with matte black finish; gas-operated with Vario System, four-lug rotating bolt. Introduced 1996. Imported from Italy by Benelli U.S.A.

Price: Walnut wood **$750.00**
Price: Camo, Timber HD **$875.00**
Price: Synthetic (black synthetic stock, forend) **$710.00**
Price: 20 ga., 24", 26", 28", walnut **$750.00**
Price: Variopress 620 (Timber HD Camo) **$875.00**

Franchi 612 Defense Shotgun

Similar to 612 except has 18-1/2", cylinder-bore barrel with black, synthetic stock. Available in 12 gauge, 3" chamber only. Weighs 6-1/2 lbs. 2-shot magazine extension available. Introduced 2000.

Price: **$635.00**

Franchi 612 Sporting Shotgun

Similar to 612 except has 30" ported barrel to reduce muzzle jump. Available in 12 gauge, 3" chamber only. Introduced 2000.

Price: **$1,275.00**

Franchi 620 Short Stock Shotgun

Similar to 620 but with stock shortened to 12-1/2" length of pull for smaller shooters. Introduced 2000.

Price: (20 gauge, 26" barrel) **$730.00**

FRANCHI MODEL 912

Gauge: 12. **Barrel:** 24", 26", 28", 30". **Weight:** 7.5 to 7.8lbs. **Length:** 46" to 52". **Stock:** Satin walnut; synthetic. **Sights:** White bead, front. **Features:** Chambered for 3-1/2" magnum shells with Dual-Recoil-Reduction-System, multi-lugged rotary bolt. Made in Italy and imported by Benelli USA.

Price: (Walnut) . . . . **$1,000.00**; (Synthetic) **$940.00**
Price: Timber HD Camo **$1,050.00**

SHOTGUNS

Remington Model 11-87 Dale Earnhardt Tribute

Remington Model 11-87 Special Purpose Magnum

Remington Model 11-87 SPS Camo

Remington Model 11-87 SPS-T Turkey Camo

Remington Model 11-87 SPS-T Synthetic Camo

REMINGTON MODEL 11-87 PREMIER SHOTGUN

Gauge: 12, 20, 3" chamber. **Barrel.** 20", 28", 30" Rem Choke tubes. Light Contour barrel. **Weight:** About 7-3/4 lbs. **Length:** 46" overall (26" bbl.). **Stock:** Walnut with satin or high-gloss finish; cut checkering; solid brown buttpad; no white spacers. **Sights:** Bradley-type white-faced front, metal bead middle. **Features:** Pressure compensating gas system allows shooting 2-3/4" or 3" loads interchangeably with no adjustments. Stainless magazine tube; redesigned feed latch, barrel support ring on operating bars; pinned forend. Introduced 1987.

Price: Light contour barrel $777.00
Price: Left-hand, 28" barrel. $831.00
Price: Premier cantilever deer barrel, fully-rifled, 21" sling, swivels, Monte Carlo stock. $859.00
Price: 3-1/2" Super Magnum, 28" barrel $865.00
Price: Dale Earnhardt Tribute, 12 ga., 28" barrel $972.00

Remington Model 11-87 Special Purpose Magnum

Similar to the 11-87 Premier except has dull stock finish, Parkerized exposed metal surfaces. Bolt and carrier have dull blackened coloring. Comes with 26" or 28" barrel with Rem Chokes, padded Cordura nylon sling and quick detachable swivels. Introduced 1987.

Price: With synthetic stock and forend (SPS) $791.00

Remington Model 11-87 SPS Special Purpose Synthetic Camo

Similar to the 11-87 Special Purpose Magnum except has synthetic stock and all metal (except bolt and trigger guard) and stock covered with Mossy Oak Break-Up camo finish. In 12 gauge only, 26", Rem Choke. Comes with camo sling, swivels. Introduced 1992.

Price: $925.00

Remington Model 11-87 SPS-T Turkey Camo

Similar to the 11-87 Special Purpose Magnum except with synthetic stock, 21" vent. rib barrel with Rem Choke tube. Completely covered with Mossy Oak Break-Up Brown camouflage. Bolt body, trigger guard and recoil pad are non-reflective black.

Price: $905.00
Price: Model 11-87 SPS-T Camo CL cantilever $907.00

Remington Model 11-87 SPS-T Super Magnum Synthetic Camo

Similar to the 11-87 SPS-T Turkey Camo except has 23" vent rib barrel with Turkey Super full choke tube, chambered for 12 ga., 3-1/2", TruGlo rifle sights. Version available without TruGlo sights. Introduced 2001.

Price: $963.00

Remington Model 11-87 SPS-Deer Shotgun

Similar to the 11-87 Special Purpose Camo except has fully-rifled 21" barrel with rifle sights, black non-reflective, synthetic stock and forend, black carrying sling. Introduced 1993.

Price: $824.00
Price: With wood stock (Model 11-87 SP Deer Gun) Rem choke, 21" barrel w/rifle sights $756.00

Remington Model 11-87 SPS-Deer

Remington Model 11-87 SPS Cantilever

Remington Model 11-87 SP

Remington Model 1100 Youth Turkey Camo

Remington 1100 LT-20 Deer

Remington Model 11-87 SPS Cantilever Shotgun

Similar to the 11-87 SPS except has fully rifled barrel; synthetic stock with Monte Carlo comb; cantilever scope mount deer barrel. Comes with sling and swivels. Introduced 1994.

Price: **$872.00**

Remington Model 11-87 SP and SPS Super Magnum Shotguns

Similar to Model 11-87 Special Purpose Magnum except has 3-1/2" chamber. Available in flat-finish American walnut or black synthetic stock, 26" or 28" black-matte finished barrel and receiver; imp. cyl., modified and full Rem Choke tubes. Overall length 45-3/4", weighs 8 lbs., 2 oz. Introduced 2000. From Remington Arms Co.

Price: 11-87 SP Super Magnum (walnut stock) **$865.00**
Price: 11-87 SPS Super Magnum (synthetic stock) **$879.00**
Price: 11-87 SPS Super Magnum, 28" (camo) **$963.00**

Remington Model 11-87 Upland Special Shotgun

Similar to 11-87 Premier except has 23" ventilated rib barrel with straight-grip, English-style walnut stock. Available in 12 or 20 gauge. Overall length 43-1/2", weighs 7-1/4 lbs. (6-1/2 lbs. in 20 ga.). Comes with imp. cyl., modified and full choke tubes. Introduced 2000.

Price: 12 or 20 gauge **$777.00**

REMINGTON MODEL 1100 SYNTHETIC LT-20 SHOTGUN

Gauge: 20. **Barrel:** 26" Rem Chokes. **Weight:** 6-3/4 lbs. **Stock:** 14"x1-1/2"x2-1/2". Black synthetic, checkered pistol grip and forend. **Fea-tures:** Matted receiver top with scroll work on both sides of receiver.

Price: **$549.00**
Price: Youth Gun LT-20 (21" Rem Choke) **$549.00**
Price: Remington Model 1100 Synthetic, 12 gauge, black synthetic stock; vent. rib 28" barrel, Mod. Rem Choke tube. Weighs about 7-1/2 lbs. Introduced 1996. . . . . **$549.00**

Remington Model 1100 Youth Synthetic Turkey Camo

Similar to the Model 1100 LT-20 except has 1" shorter stock, 21" vent rib barrel with Full Rem Choke tube; 3" chamber; synthetic stock and forend are covered with Skyline Excel camo, and barrel and receiver have non-reflective, black matte finish. Introduced 2003.

Price: **$612.00**

Remington Model 1100 LT-20 Synthetic Deer Shotgun

Similar to the Model 1100 LT-20 except has 21" fully rifled barrel with rifle sights, 2-3/4" chamber, and fiberglass-reinforced synthetic stock. Introduced 1997. Made in U.S. by Remington.

Price: **$583.00**

Remington Model 1100 Sporting 28

Remington Model 1100 Classic Trap

Remington Model 1100 Sporting 12

Remington Model SP-10

Remington Model SP-10 Camo

Remington Model 1100 Sporting 28

Similar to the 1100 LT-20 except in 28 gauge with 25" barrel; comes with Skeet, Imp. Cyl., Light Mod., Mod. Rem Choke tube. Semi-Fancy walnut with gloss finish, Sporting rubber butt pad. Made in U.S. by Remington. Introduced 1996.

Price: **$901.00**

Remington Model 1100 Sporting 20 Shotgun

Similar to Model 1100 LT-20 except tournament-grade American walnut stock with gloss finish and sporting-style recoil pad, 28" Rem choke barrel for Skeet, Imp. Cyl., Light Modified and Modified. Introduced 1998.

Price: **$868.00**

Remington Model 1100 Classic Trap Shotgun

Similar to Standard Model 1100 except 12 gauge with 30", low-profile barrel, semi-fancy American walnut stock, high-polish blued receiver with engraving and gold eagle inlay. Singles, mid handicap and long handicap choke tubes. Overall length 50-1/2", weighs 8 lbs., 4 oz. Introduced 2000. From Remington Arms Co.

Price: **$895.00**

Remington Model 1100 Sporting 12 Shotgun

Similar to Model 1100 Sporting 20 Shotgun except in 12 gauge, 28" ventilated barrel with semi-fancy American walnut stock, gold-plated trigger. Overall length 49", weighs 8 lbs. Introduced 2000. From Remington Arms Co.

Price: **$901.00**

Remington Model 1100 Synthetic Deer Shotgun

Similar to Model 1100 LT-20 except 12 gauge, 21" fully rifled barrel with cantilever scope mount and fiberglass-reinforced synthetic stock with Monte Carlo comb. Introduced 1997. Made in U.S. by Remington.

Price: **$629.00**

REMINGTON MODEL SP-10 MAGNUM SHOTGUN

Gauge: 10, 3-1/2" chamber, 2-shot magazine. **Barrel:** 26", 30" (full and mod. Rem chokes). **Weight:** 10-3/4 to 11 lbs. **Length:** 47-1/2" overall (26" barrel). **Stock:** Walnut with satin finish or black synthetic with 26" barrel. Checkered grip and forend. **Sights:** Twin bead. **Features:** Stainless steel gas system with moving cylinder; 3/8" ventilated rib. Receiver and barrel have matte finish. Brown recoil pad. Comes with padded Cordura nylon sling. Introduced 1989.

Price: **$1,317.00**

Remington Model SP-10 Magnum Camo Shotgun

Similar to SP-10 Magnum except buttstock, forend, receiver, barrel and magazine cap are covered with Mossy Oak Break-Up camo finish; bolt body and trigger guard have matte black finish. Rem choke tube, 26" vent. rib barrel with mid-rib bead and Bradley-style front sight, swivel studs and quick-detachable swivels, non-slip Cordura carrying sling in same camo pattern. Introduced 1993.

Price: **$1,453.00**

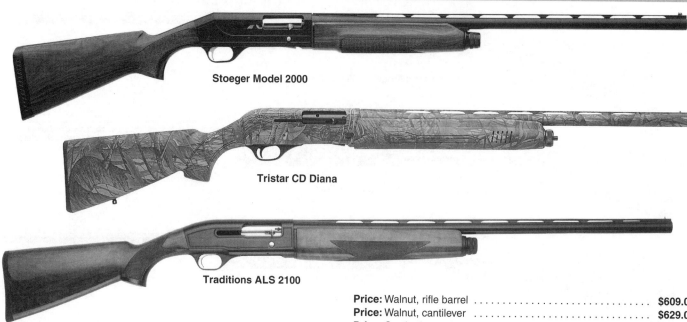

Stoeger Model 2000

Tristar CD Diana

Traditions ALS 2100

SARSILMAZ SEMI-AUTOMATIC SHOTGUN
Gauge: 12, 3" chamber. **Barrel:** 26" or 28"; fixed chokes. **Stock:** Walnut or synthetic. **Features:** Handles 2-3/4" or 3" magnum loads. Introduced 2000. Imported from Turkey by Armsport Inc.

Price: With walnut stock **$969.95**
Price: With synthetic stock **$919.95**

STOEGER MODEL 2000
Gauge: 12, 3" chamber, set of 5 choke tubes. **Barrel:** 24", 26", 28", 30". **Stock:** Walnut, deluxe, synthetic, and Timber HD. **Sights:** White bar. **Features:** Inertia-recoil for light target to turkey leads. Single trigger combo 26"/24" pack with optional 24" slug barrel.

Price: Walnut, 26", 28", 30" bbl. **$499.00**
Price: Synthetic, 24", 26", 28" bbl. **$480.00**
Price: Synthetic combo, 26"/24" bbl. **$560.00**
Price: Optional slug bbl., 26" **$105.00**
Price: Timber HD, 24", 26", 28" bbl. **$550.00**

TRADITIONS ALS 2100 SERIES SEMI-AUTOMATIC SHOTGUNS
Gauge: 12, 3" chamber; 20, 3" chamber. **Barrel:** 24", 26", 28" (imp. cyl., mod. and full choke tubes). **Weight:** 5 lbs., 10 oz. to 6 lbs., 5 oz. **Length:** 44" to 48" overall. **Stock:** Walnut or black composite. **Features:** Gas-operated; vent-rib barrel with Beretta-style threaded muzzle. Introduced 2001 by Traditions.

Price: (12 or 20 ga., 26" or 28" barrel, walnut stock) **$479.00**
Price: (12 or 20 ga., 24" barrel Youth Model, walnut stock) **$479.00**
Price: (12 or 20 ga., 26" or 28" barrel, composite stock) **$459.00**

Traditions ALS 2100 Turkey Semi-Automatic Shotgun
Similar to ALS 2100 Field Model except chambered in 12 gauge, 3" only with 26" barrel and Mossy Oak® Break Up™ camo finish. Weighs 6 lbs., 46" overall.

Price: **$519.00**

Traditions ALS 2100 Waterfowl Semi-Automatic Shotgun
Similar to ALS 2100 Field Model except chambered in 12 gauge, 3" only with 28" barrel and Advantage® Wetlands™ camo finish. Weighs 6.25 lbs.; 48" overall. Multi chokes.

Price: **$529.00**

Traditions ALS 2100 Hunter Combo
Similar to ALS 2100 Field Model except 2 barrels, 28" vent rib and 24" fully rifled deer. Weighs 6-6.5 lbs.; 48" overall. Choice TruGlo adj. sights or fixed cantilever mount on rifled barrel. Multi chokes.

Price: Walnut, rifle barrel **$609.00**
Price: Walnut, cantilever **$629.00**
Price: Synthetic **$579.00**

Traditions ALS 2100 Slug Hunter
Similar to ALS 2100 Field Model, 12 ga., 24" barrel, overall length 44", weighs 6.25 lbs. Designed specificaly for the deer hunter. Rifled barrel has 1 in 36" twist. Fully adjustable sights are fiber optic.

Price: Walnut, rifle barrel. **$529.00**
Price: Synthetic, rifle barrel. **$499.00**
Price: Walnut, cantilever **$549.00**
Price: Synthetic, cantilever **$529.00**

Traditions ALS 2100 Home Security
Similar to ALS 2100 Field Model, 12 ga., 20" barrel, overall length 40", weighs 6 lbs. Can be reloaded with one hand while shouldered and on-target. Swivel studs installed in stock.

Price: **$399.00**

TRISTAR CD DIANA AUTO SHOTGUNS
Gauge: 12, shoots 2-3/4" or 3" interchangeably. **Barrel:** 24", 26", 28" (Imp. Cyl., Mod., Full choke tubes). **Stock:** European walnut or black synthetic. **Features:** Gas-operated action; blued barrel; checkered pistol grip and forend; vent rib barrel. Available with synthetic and camo stock and in slug model. First introduced 1999 under the name "Tristar Phantom." Imported by Tristar Sporting Arms Ltd.

Price: . . . . **$399.00 to $576.00**

VERONA MODEL SX400 SEMI AUTO SHOTGUN
Gauge: 12. **Barrel:** 26", 30". **Weight:** 6-1/2 lbs. **Stock:** Walnut, black composite. **Sights:** Red dot. **Features:** Aluminum receivers, gas-operated, 2-3/4" or 3" Magnum shells without adj. or mod., 4 screw-in chokes and wrench included. Sling swivels, gold trigger. Blued barrel. Imported from Italy by B.C. Outdoors.

Price: 401S, 12 ga. **$398.40**
Price: 405SDS, 12 ga. **$610.00**
Price: 405L, 12 ga. **$331.20**

WEATHERBY SAS (SEMI-AUTOMATIC SHOTGUNS)
6 Models: SAS Field, SAS Sporting Clays, SAS Shadow Grass, SAS Break-Up, SAS Synthetic and a Slug Gun.
Gauge: 12 ga. **Barrel:** Vent ribbed, 24"-30". **Stock:** SAS Field and Sporting Clays, walnut. SAS Shadow Grass, Break-Up, Synthetic, composite. **Sights:** SAS Sporting Clays, frass front and mid-point back. SAS Shadow Grass and Break-Up, HiViz front and brass mid. Synthetic has brass front. **Features:** Easy to shoot, load, clean, lightweight, lessened recoil, IMC system includes 3 chrome moly screw-in choke tubes. Slug gun has 22" rifled barrel with matte blue finish and cantilever base for scope mounting.

Price: . . . . **$699.00 to 849.00**

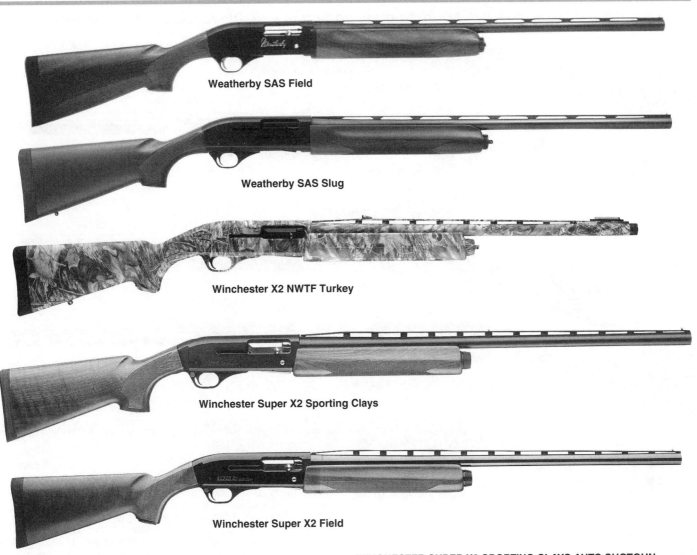

Weatherby SAS Field

Weatherby SAS Slug

Winchester X2 NWTF Turkey

Winchester Super X2 Sporting Clays

Winchester Super X2 Field

WINCHESTER SUPER X2 AUTO SHOTGUN

Gauge: 12, 3", 3-1/2" chamber. **Barrel:** Belgian, 24", 26", 28"; Invector Plus choke tubes. **Weight:** 7-1/4 to 7-1/2 lbs. **Stock:** 14-1/4"x1-3/4"x2". Walnut or black synthetic. **Features:** Gas-operated action shoots all loads without adjustment; vent. rib barrels; 4-shot magazine. Introduced 1999. Assembled in Portugal by U.S. Repeating Arms Co.

Price: Field, walnut or synthetic stock, 3" **$874.00**
Price: Magnum, 3-1/2", synthetic stock, 26" or 28" bbl. **$988.00**
Price: Camo Waterfowl, 3-1/2", Mossy Oak Shadow Grass **$1,139.00**
Price: NWTF Turkey, 3-1/2", Mossy Oak Break-Up camo. **$1,165.00**
Price: Universal Hunter Model **$1,139.00**

WINCHESTER SUPER X2 SPORTING CLAYS AUTO SHOTGUN

Similar to the Super X2 except has two gas pistons (one for target loads, one for heavy 3" loads), adjustable comb system and high-post rib. Back-bored barrel with Invector Plus choke tubes. Offered in 28" and 30" barrels. Introduced 2001. From U.S. Repeating Arms Co.

Price: Super X2 Sporting Clays **$959.00**
Price: Signature red stock **$976.00**

Winchester Super X2 Field 3" Auto Shotgun

Similar to the Super X2 except has a 3" chamber, walnut stock and fore-arm and high-profile rib. Back-bored barrel and Invector Plus choke tubes. Introduced 2001. From U.S. Repeating Arms Co.

Price: Super X2 Field 3", 26" or 28" bbl. **$874.00**

CONSULT
SHOOTER'S MARKETPLACE
Page 64, This Issue

Includes a wide variety of sporting guns and guns suitable for competitive shooting.

Armscor M-30F Field

Benelli Nova Pump

Benelli Nova Pump Slug

Browning BPS 10 gauge

Browning BPS 10 gauge Mossy Oak® Shadow Grass

ARMSCOR M-30F FIELD PUMP SHOTGUN

Gauge: 12, 3" chamber. **Barrel:** 28" fixed Mod., or with Mod. and Full choke tubes. **Weight:** 7.6 lbs. **Stock:** Walnut-finished hardwood. **Features:** Dou-ble action slide bars; blued steel receiver; damascened bolt. Introduced 1996. Imported from the Philippines by K.B.I., Inc.

Price: With fixed choke **$239.00**
Price: With choke tubes **$269.00**

BENELLI NOVA PUMP SHOTGUN

Gauge: 12, 20. **Barrel:** 24", 26", 28". **Stock:** Synthetic, X-tra Brown 12 ga., Timber HD 20 ga. **Sights:** Red bar. **Features:** 2-3/4", 3" chamber (3-2/1" 12 ga. only). Montefeltro rotating bolt design with dual action bars, magazine cut-off, synthetic trigger assembly, 4-shot magazine. Introduced 1999. Imported from Italy by Benelli USA.

Price: Synthetic **$335.00**
Price: Timber HD **$400.00**
Price: Youth model **$415.00**

Benelli Nova Pump Slug Gun

Similar to the Nova except has 18.5" barrel with adjustable rifle-type or ghost ring sights; weighs 7.2 lbs.; black synthetic stock. Introduced 1999. Imported from Italy by Benelli USA.

Price: With rifle sights **$355.00**
Price: With ghost-ring sights **$395.00**

Benelli Nova Pump Rifled Slug Gun

Similar to Nova Pump Slug Gun except has 24" barrel and rifled bore; open rifle sights; synthetic stock; weighs 8.1 pounds.

Price: . . . . (Synthetic) **$500.00**; Timber HD **$575.00**

BROWNING BPS PUMP SHOTGUN

Gauge: 10, 12, 3-1/2" chamber; 12 or 20, 3" chamber (2-3/4" in target guns), 28, 2-3/4" chamber, 5-shot magazine, .410, 3" chamber. **Barrel:** 10 ga.- 24" Buck Special, 28", 30", 32" Invector; 12, 20 ga.-22", 24", 26", 28", 30", 32" (Imp. Cyl., mod. or full). .410-26" barrel. (Imp. Cyl., mod. and full choke tubes.) Also available with Invector choke tubes, 12 or 20 ga.; Upland Special has 22" barrel with Invector tubes. BPS 3" and 3-1/2" have back-bored barrel. **Weight:** 7 lbs., 8 oz. (28" barrel). **Length:** 48-3/4" overall (28" barrel). **Stock:** 14-1/4"x1-1/2"x2-1/2". Select walnut, semi-beavertail forend, full pistol grip stock. **Features:** All 12 gauge 3" guns except Buck Special and game guns have back-bored barrels with Invector Plus choke tubes. Bottom feeding and ejection, receiver top safety, high post vent. rib. Double action bars eliminate binding. Vent. rib barrels only. All 12 and 20 gauge guns with 3" chamber available with fully engraved receiver flats at no extra cost. Each gauge has its own unique game scene. Introduced 1977. Imported from Japan by Browning.

Price: 12 ga., 3-1/2" Magnum Stalker (black syn. stock). **$562.00**
Price: 12, 20 ga., Hunter, Invector Plus **$494.00**
Price: 12 ga. Deer Hunter (22" rifled bbl., cantilever mount). **$606.00**
Price: 28 ga., Hunter, Invector **$528.00**
Price: .410, Hunter, Invector **$528.00**

Browning BPS 10 Gauge Shotguns

Chambered for the 10 gauge, 3-1/2" load. Offered in 24", 26" and 28" barrels. Offered with walnut, black composite (Stalker models) or camouflage stock and forend. Introduced 1999. Imported by Browning.

Price: Stalker (composite). **$562.00**
Price: Mossy Oak® Shadow Grass or Break-Up Camo **$668.00**

Browning BPS 10 Gauge Camo Pump Shotgun

Similar to the BPS 10 gauge Hunter except completely covered with Mossy Oak Shadow Grass camouflage. Available with 24", 26", 28" barrel. Introduced 1999. Imported by Browning.

Price: **$668.00**

SHOTGUNS

SHOTGUNS — SLIDE & LEVER ACTIONS

EAA/Baikal MP-133

Escort AimGuard

Escort FieldHunter

Fabarm Field Pump

Browning BPS Waterfowl Camo Pump Shotgun
Similar to the BPS Hunter except completely covered with Mossy Oak Shadow Grass camouflage. Available in 12 gauge, with 24", 26" or 28" barrel, 3" chamber. Introduced 1999. Imported by Browning.
Price: **$652.00**

Browning BPS Game Gun Deer Hunter
Similar to the standard BPS except has newly designed receiver/magazine tube/barrel mounting system to eliminate play, heavy 20.5" barrel with rifle-type sights with adjustable rear, solid receiver scope mount, "rifle" stock dimensions for scope or open sights, sling swivel studs. Gloss or matte finished wood with checkering, polished blue metal. Introduced 1992.
Price: **$568.00**

Browning BPS Game Gun Turkey Special
Similar to the standard BPS except has satin-finished walnut stock and dull-finished barrel and receiver. Receiver is drilled and tapped for scope mounting. Rifle-style stock dimensions and swivel studs. Has Extra-Full Turkey choke tube. Introduced 1992.
Price: **$500.00**

Browning BPS Stalker Pump Shotgun
Same gun as the standard BPS except all exposed metal parts have a matte blued finish and the stock has a durable black finish with a black recoil pad. Available in 10 ga. (3-1/2") and 12 ga. with 3" or 3-1/2" chamber, 22", 28", 30" barrel with Invector choke system. Introduced 1987.
Price: 12 ga., 3" chamber, Invector Plus..................... **$448.00**
Price: 10, 12 ga., 3-1/2" chamber.......................... **$537.00**

Browning BPS NWTF Turkey Series Pump Shotgun
Similar to the BPS Stalker except has full coverage Mossy Oak® Break-Up camo finish on synthetic stock, forearm and exposed metal parts. Offered in 10 and 12 gauge, 3" or 3-1/2" chamber; 24" bbl. has extra-full choke tube and Hi-Viz fiber optic sights. Introduced 2001. From Browning.
Price: 10 ga., 3-1/2" chamber.............................. **$637.00**
Price: 12 ga., 3-1/2" chamber.............................. **$637.00**
Price: 12 ga., 3" chamber.................................. **$549.00**

Browning BPS Micro Pump Shotgun
Same as BPS Upland Special except 20 ga. only, 22" Invector barrel, stock has pistol grip with recoil pad. Length of pull is 13-1/4"; weighs 6 lbs., 12 oz. Introduced 1986.
Price: **$482.00**

DIAMOND 12 GA. PUMP SHOTGUN
Gauge: 12, 2-3/4" and 3" chambers. **Barrel:** 18"-30". **Weight:** 7 lbs. **Stock:** Walnut, synthetic. **Features:** Aluminum one-piece receiver sculpted for lighter weight. Double locking on fixed bolt. Gold, Elite and Panther series with vented barrels and 3 chokes. All series slug guns available (Gold and Elite with sights). Imported from Istanbul by ADCO Sales.
Price: Gold, 28" vent rib w/3 chokes, walnut **$359.00**
Price: Gold, 28", synthetic **$329.00**
Price: Gold Slug, 24" w/sights, walnut or synthetic .. **$329.00 to $359.00**
Price: Silver Mariner 18.5" Slug, synthetic **$399.00**
Price: Silver Mariner 22" vent rib w/3 chokes **$419.00**
Price: Elite, 22" slug w/sights; 24", 28" ventib w/3 chokes, walnut .... **$329.00 to $349.00**
Price: Panther, 28", 30" vent rib w/3 chokes, synthetic......... **$279.00**
Price: Panther,18.5", 22" Slug, synthetic .... **$209.00 to $265.00**
Price: Imperial 12 ga., 28" vent rib w/3 chokes, 3.5" chamber, walnut **$399.00**

EAA/BAIKAL MP-133 PUMP SHOTGUN
Gauge: 12, 3-1/2" chamber. **Barrel:** 18-1/2", 20", 24", 26", 28"; imp., mod. and full choke tubes. **Weight:** NA. **Stock:** Walnut; checkered grip and grooved forearm. **Features:** Hammer-forged, chrome-lined barrel with ventilated rib; machined steel parts; dual action bars; trigger-block safety; 4-shot magazine tube; handles 2-3/4" through 3-1/2" shells. Introduced 2000. Imported by European American Armory.
Price: MP-133 (blued finish, walnut stock and forend) **$359.00**

ESCORT PUMP SHOTGUN
Gauge: 12, 3" chamber. **Barrel:** 20", fixed (AimGuard model); 24" and 28" (Field Hunter models), choke tubes (M, IC, F); turkey choke w/ 24" bbl. **Weight:** 6.4 to 7 lbs. **Stock:** Polymer, black chrome or camo finish. **Features:** Alloy receiver w/ dovetail for sight mounting. Two stock adjusting spacers included. Introduced 2003. From Legacy Sports International.
Price: Field Hunter, black stock **$224.00**
Price: Field Hunter, camo stock **$271.00**
Price: Camo, 24" bbl. **$444.00**
Price: AimGuard, 20" bbl., black stock **$199.00**

SHOTGUNS

Ithaca Model 37 Waterfowl

Ithaca Model 37 Deerslayer II

Mossberg Model 835
Mossy Oak Camo

FABARM FIELD PUMP SHOTGUN

Gauge: 12, 3" chamber. **Barrel:** 28" (24" rifled slug barrel available). **Weight:** 76.6 lbs. **Length:** 48.25" overall. **Stock:** Polymer. **Features:** Similar to Fabarm FP6 Pump Shotgun. Alloy receiver; twin action bars; available in black or Mossy Oak Break-Up™ camo finish. Includes cyl., mod. and full choke tubes. Introduced 2001. Imported from Italy by Heckler & Koch Inc.
Price: Matte black finish **$399.00**
Price: Mossy Oak Break-Up™ finish **$469.00**

ITHACA MODEL 37 DELUXE PUMP SHOTGUN

Gauge: 12, 16, 20, 3" chamber. **Barrel:** 26", 28", 30" (12 gauge) 26", 28" (16 and 20 gauge), choke tubes. **Weight:** 7 lbs. **Stock:** Walnut with cut-checkered grip and forend. **Features:** Steel receiver; bottom ejection; brushed blue finish, vent rib barrels. Reintroduced 1996. Made in U.S. by Ithaca Gun Co.
Price: **$633.00**
Price: With straight English-style stock **$803.00**
Price: Model 37 New Classic (ringtail forend, sunburst recoil pad, hand-finished walnut stock, 26" or 28" barrel) **$803.00**

ITHACA MODEL 37 WATERFOWL

Similar to Model 37 Deluxe except in 12 gauge only with 24", 26", or 30" barrel, special extended steel shot choke tube system. Complete coverage of Advantage Wetlands or Hardwoods camouflage. Introduced 1999. Made in U.S. by Ithaca Gun Co. Storm models have synthetic stock.
Price: . . . . **$499.00 to $549.00**

ITHACA MODEL 37 DEERSLAYER II PUMP SHOTGUN

Gauge: 12, 16, 20; 3" chamber. **Barrel:** 24", 26", fully rifled. **Weight:** 11 lbs. **Stock:** Cut-checkered American walnut with Monte Carlo comb. **Sights:** Rifle-type. **Features:** Integral barrel and receiver. Bottom ejection. Brushed blue finish. Reintroduced 1997. Made in U.S. by Ithaca Gun Co. Storm models have synthetic stock.
Price: **$633.00**
Price: Smooth Bore Deluxe **$582.00**
Price: Rifled Deluxe **$582.00**
Price: Storm **$399.00**

ITHACA MODEL 37 DEERSLAYER III PUMP SHOTGUN

Gauge: 12, 20, 2-3/4" and 3" chambers. **Barrel:** 26" free floated. **Weight:** 9 lbs. **Stock:** Monte Carlo laminate. **Sights:** Rifled. **Features:** Barrel length gives increased velocity. Trigger and sear set hand filed and stoned for creep free operation. Weaver-style scope base. Swivel studs. Matte blue.
Price: . . . . **Custom order only**

ITHACA MODEL 37 RUFFED GROUSE SPECIAL EDITION

Gauge: 20 ga. **Barrel:** 22", 24", interchangeable choke tubes. **Weight:** 5.25 lbs. **Stock:** American black walnut. **Features:** Laser engraved stock with line art drawing. Bottom eject. Vent rib and English style. Right- or left-hand thru simple safety change. Aluminum receiver. Made in U.S.A. by Ithaca Gun Co.
Price: **$840.00**

ITHACA TURKEYSLAYER STORM

Gauge: 12 or 20 ga., 3" chamber. **Barrel:** 24" ported. **Stock:** Composite. **Sights:** TruGlo front and rear. **Features:** Itha-Choke full turkey choke tube. Matte metal, Realtree Hardwoods pattern, swivel studs.
Price: Storm **$459.00**

ITHACA MODEL 37 ULTRALIGHT DELUXE

Gauge: 16 ga. 2-3/4" chamber. **Barrel:** 24", 26", 28". **Weight:** 5.25 lbs. **Stock:** Standard deluxe. **Sights:** Raybar. **Features:** Vent rib, drilled and tapped, interchangeable barrel. F, M, IC choke tubes.
Price: Deluxe **$649.00**
Price: Classic/English **$824.00**
Price: Classic/Pistol **$824.00**

MARLIN PARDNER PUMP

Gauge: 12 ga., 3". **Barrel:** 28" vent rib, screw-in modified choke tube. **Weight:** 7 1/2 pounds. **Length:** 48 1/2". **Stock:** American walnut, grooved forend, ventilated recoil pad. **Sights:** Bead front. **Features:** Machined steel receiver, double action bars, five-shot magazine.
Price: **$200.00**

MOSSBERG MODEL 835 ULTI-MAG PUMP

Gauge: 12, 3-1/2" chamber. **Barrel:** Ported 24" rifled bore, 24", 28", Accu-Mag choke tubes for steel or lead shot. **Weight:** 7-3/4 lbs. **Length:** 48-1/2" overall. **Stock:** 14"x1-1/2"x2-1/2". Dual Comb. Cut-checkered hardwood or camo synthetic; both have recoil pad. **Sights:** White bead front, brass mid-bead; Fiber Optic. **Features:** Shoots 2-3/4", 3" or 3-1/2" shells. Back-bored and ported barrel to reduce recoil, improve patterns. Ambidextrous thumb safety, twin extractors, dual slide bars. Mossberg Cablelock included. Introduced 1988.
Price: 28" vent. rib, hardwood stock **$394.00**
Price: Combos, 24" rifled or smooth bore, rifle sights, 24" vent. rib Accu-Mag Ulti-Full choke tube, Mossy Oak camo finish **$556.00**
Price: RealTree Camo Turkey, 24" vent. rib, Accu-Mag Extra-Full tube, synthetic stock **$460.00**
Price: Mossy Oak Camo, 28" vent. rib, Accu-Mag tubes, synthetic stock **$460.00**
Price: OFM Camo, 28" vent. rib, Accu-Mag Mod. tube, synthetic stock **$438.00**

Mossberg Model 500 Sporting

Mossberg Model 500 Bantam

Mossberg Model 500 Trophy Slugster

Remington 870 Wingmaster

Mossberg Model 835 Synthetic Stock

Similar to the Model 835, except with 28" ported barrel with Accu-Mag Mod. choke tube, Parkerized finish, black synthetic stock and forend. Introduced 1998. Made in U.S. by Mossberg.
Price: **$394.00**

MOSSBERG MODEL 500 SPORTING PUMP

Gauge: 12, 20, .410, 3" chamber. **Barrel:** 18-1/2" to 28" with fixed or Accu-Choke, plain or vent. rib. **Weight:** 6-1/4 lbs. (.410), 7-1/4 lbs. (12). **Length:** 48" overall (28" barrel). **Stock:** 14"x1-1/2"x2-1/2". Walnut-stained hardwood. Cut-checkered grip and forend. **Sights:** White bead front, brass mid-bead; Fiber Optic. **Features:** Ambidextrous thumb safety, twin extractors, disconnecting safety, dual action bars. Quiet Carry forend. Many barrels are ported. Mossberg Cablelock included. From Mossberg.
Price: From about **$316.00**
Price: Sporting Combos (field barrel and Slugster barrel), from .. **$381.00**

Mossberg Model 500 Bantam Pump

Same as the Model 500 Sporting Pump except 12 (new for 2001) or 20 gauge, 22" vent. rib Accu-Choke barrel with choke tube set; has 1" shorter stock, reduced length from pistol grip to trigger, reduced forend reach. Introduced 1992.
Price: **$316.00**
Price: With Realtree Hardwoods camouflage finish (20 ga. only). **$364.00**

Mossberg Model 500 Camo Pump

Same as the Model 500 Sporting Pump except 12 gauge only and entire gun is covered with Mossy Oak Advantage camouflage finish. Receiver drilled and tapped for scope mounting. Comes with quick detachable swivel studs, swivels, camouflage sling, Mossberg Cablelock.
Price: From about **$364.00**

MOSSBERG MODEL 500 PERSUADER/CRUISER SHOTGUN

Similar to Mossberg Model 500 except has 18-1/2" or 20" barrel with cylinder bore choke, synthetic stock and blue or Parkerized finish. Available in 12, 20 and .410 with bead or ghost ring sights, 6- or 8-shot mag-azines. From Mossberg.
Price: 12 gauge, 20" barrel, 8-shot, bead sight. **$391.00**
Price: 20 gauge or .410, 18-1/2" barrel, 6-shot, bead sight **$353.00**
Price: 12 gauge, parkerized finish, 6-shot, 18-1/2" barrel,
ghost ring sights **$468.00**
Price: Home Security 410 (.410, 18-1/2" barrel
with spreader choke) **$335.00**

Mossberg Model 590 Special Purpose Shotgun

Similar to Model 500 except has parkerized or Marinecote finish, 9-shot magazine and black synthetic stock (some models feature Speed Feed. Available in 12 gauge only with 20", cylinder bore barrel. Weighs 7-1/4 lbs. From Mossberg.
Price: Bead sight, heat shield over barrel **$417.00**
Price: Ghost ring sight, Speed Feed stock. **$586.00**

MOSSBERG MODEL 500 SLUGSTER

Gauge: 12, 20, 3" chamber. **Barrel:** 24", ported rifled bore. Integral scope mount. **Weight:** 7-1/4 lbs. **Length:** 44" overall. **Stock:** 14" pull, 1-3/8" drop at heel. Walnut; Dual Comb design for proper eye positioning with or without scoped barrels. Recoil pad and swivel studs. **Features:** Ambidextrous thumb safety, twin extractors, dual slide bars. Comes with scope mount. Mossberg Cablelock included. Introduced 1988.
Price: Rifled bore, integral scope mount, 12 or 20 ga. **$361.00**
Price: Fiber Optic, rifle sights **$361.00**
Price: Rifled bore, rifle sights **$338.00**
Price: 20 ga., Standard or Bantam, from **$338.00**

REMINGTON MODEL 870 WINGMASTER

Gauge: 12ga., 16 ga., 3" chamber. **Barrel:** 26", 28", 30" (Rem chokes). **Weight:** 7-1/4 lbs.. **Length:** 46", 48". **Stock:** Walnut, hardwood, synthetic. **Sights:** Single bead (Twin bead Wingmaster). **Features:** Balistically balanced performance, milder recoil. Light contour barrel. Double action bars, cross-bolt safety, blue finish.
Price: Wingmaster, walnut, blued, 26", 28", 30" **$584.00**
Price: 870 Wingmaster Super Magnum, 3-1/2" chamber, 28" ... **$665.00**

Remington Model 870 50th Anniversary Classic Trap

Remington Model 870 Marine Magnum

Remington Model 870 Wingmaster LW

Remington Model 870 Express Super Magnum

Remington Model 870 50th Anniversary Classic Trap Shotgun

Similar to Model 870 Wingmaster except has 30" ventilated rib, light contour barrel, singles, mid and long handicap choke tubes, semi-fancy American walnut stock, high-polish blued receiver with engraving. Chamber 2-1/2". From Remington Arms Co.

Price: **$792.00**

Remington Model 870 Marine Magnum

Similar to 870 Wingmaster except all metal plated with electroless nickel, black synthetic stock and forend. Has 18" plain barrel (cyl.), bead front sight, 7-shot magazine. Introduced 1992.

Price: **$573.00**

Remington Model 870 Wingmaster LW

Similar to Model 870 Wingmaster except in 20, 28 gauges and .410-bore only, 25" vent rib barrel with Rem choke tubes, high-gloss wood finish. 26" & 28" barrels-20 ga.

Price: 20 gauge **$584.00**
Price: .410-bore **$612.00**
Price: 28 gauge **$665.00**

Remington Model 870 Express

Similar to 870 Wingmaster except walnut-toned hardwood stock with solid, black recoil pad and pressed checkering on grip and forend. Outside metal surfaces have black oxide finish. Comes with 26" or 28" vent. rib barrel with mod. Rem choke tube.

Price: 12 ga., 20 ga., 16 ga. (28") **$332.00**
Price: Express Combo, 12 ga., 26" vent rib with mod. Rem choke and 20" fully rifled barrel with rifle sights, or Rem. choke.... **$443.00 to $476.00**
Price: Express L-H (left-hand), 12 ga., 28" vent rib with mod. Rem choke tube.. **$359.00**
Price: Express Synthetic, 12-ga., 26" or 28" **$332.00**
Price: Express Combo (20 ga.) with extra Deer rifled barrel, fully rifled or Rem. choke ....**$443.00 to $476.00**

Price: Express Small bore 28 ga., 25" **$359.00**
Price: Express Small bore .410, 25" **$359.00**

Remington Model 870 Express Super Magnum

Similar to 870 Express except 28" vent. rib barrel with 3-1/2" chamber, vented recoil pad. Introduced 1998.

Price: **$376.00**
Price: Super Magnum Synthetic, 26"...................... **$376.00**
Price: Super Magnum Turkey Camo (full-coverage RealTree Advantage camo), 23" **$500.00**
Price: Super Magnum Combo (26" with Mod. Rem Choke and 20" fully rifled deer barrel with 3" chamber and rifle sights; wood stock) . **$523.00**
Price: Super Magnum Synthetic Turkey, 23" (black) **$389.00**

Remington Model 870 Wingmaster Super Magnum Shotgun

Similar to Model 870 Express Super Magnum except high-polish blued finish, 28" ventilated barrel with imp. cyl., modified and full choke tubes, checkered high-gloss walnut stock. Overall length 48", weighs 7-1/2 lbs. Introduced 2000.

Price: 3-1/2" chamber **$665.00**

Remington Model 870 Express Youth Gun

Same as Model 870 Express except 13" length of pull, 21" barrel with mod. Rem choke tube. Weighs 6.25 lbs. Hardwood stock with low-luster finish. Introduced 1991.

Price: 20 ga. Express Youth (1" shorter stock), from. **$332.00**
Price: 20 ga. Youth Deer 20" FR/RS **$365.00**
Price: 16 ga. Youth Synthetic **$332.00**

Remington Model 870 Express Rifle-Sighted Deer Gun

Same as Model 870 Express except 20" barrel with fixed imp. cyl. choke, open iron sights, Monte Carlo stock. Introduced 1991.

Price: **$332.00**
Price: With fully rifled barrel **$365.00**
Price: Express Synthetic Deer (black synthetic stock, black matte metal) **$372.00**

SHOTGUNS

Remington Model 870 Express Deer Gun

Remington Model 870 Express Turkey

Remington Model 870 SPS Super Slug Deer Gun

Remington Model 870 SPS-T Camo

Remington Model 870 Express Turkey
Same as Model 870 Express except 3" chamber, 21" vent rib turkey barrel and extra-full Rem. choke turkey tube; 12 ga. only. Introduced 1991.
Price: **$345.00**
Price: Express Turkey Camo stock has Skyline Excel
camo, matte black metal **$399.00**
Price: Express Youth Turkey camo (as above with 1" shorter
length of pull), 20 ga., Skyline Excel camo **$399.00**

Remington Model 870 Express Synthetic 18"
Similar to 870 Express with 18" barrel except synthetic stock and forend; 7-shot. Introduced 1994.
Price: **$319.00**

Remington Model 870 SPS Super Slug Deer Gun
Similar to the Model 870 Express Synthetic except has 23" rifled, modified contour barrel with cantilever scope mount. Comes with black synthetic stock and forend with swivel studs, black Cordura nylon sling. Introduced 1999. Fully rifled centilever barrel.
Price: **$580.00**

Remington Model 870 SPS-T Synthetic Camo Shotgun
Chambered for 12 ga., 3" shells, has Mossy Oak Break-Up® synthetic stock and metal treatment, TruGlo fiber optic sights. Introduced 2001.
Price: 20" RS, Rem. choke **$595.00**
Price: Youth version **$595.00**
Price: Super Magnum Camo, 23", CL Rem. Choke **$609.00**
Price: Super Magnum Camo 23", VT Rem. Choke **$591.00**

Price: 20 ga., Truglo sights, Rem. Choke,
Mossy Oak Break-Up Camo **$595.00**

REMINGTON MODEL 870 SPS SUPER MAGNUM CAMO
Has synthetic stock and all metal (except bolt and trigger guard) and stock covered with Mossy Oak Break-Up camo finish. In 12 gauge 3-1/2", 26", 28" vent rib, Rem choke. Comes with camo sling, swivels.
Price: **$591.00**

SARSILMAZ PUMP SHOTGUN
Gauge: 12, 3" chamber. **Barrel:** 26" or 28". **Stocks:** Oil-finished hardwood. **Features:** Includes extra pistol-grip stock. Introduced 2000. Imported from Turkey by Armsport Inc.
Price: With pistol-grip stock **$299.95**
Price: With metal stock **$349.95**

TRISTAR MODEL 1887
Gauge: 12. **Barrel:** 22". **Weight:** 8.75 lbs. **Length:** 40-1/2". **Stocks:** Walnut. **Features:** Imp. cylinder choke, 5 shell, oil finish. Introduced 2002. Made in Australia. Available through AcuSport Corp.
Price: With pistol-grip stock **$299.95**

WINCHESTER MODEL 1300 WALNUT FIELD PUMP
Gauge: 12, 20, 3" chamber, 5-shot capacity. **Barrel:** 26", 28", vent. rib, with Full, Mod., Imp. Cyl. Winchoke tubes. **Weight:** 6-3/8 lbs. **Length:** 42-5/8" overall. **Stock:** American walnut, with deep cut checkering on pistol grip, traditional ribbed forend; high luster finish. **Sights:** Metal bead front. **Features:** Twin action slide bars; front-locking rotary bolt; roll-engraved receiver; blued, highly polished metal; cross-bolt safety with red indicator. Introduced 1984. From U.S. Repeating Arms Co., Inc.
Price: **$439.00**

Winchester 1300 Walnut Field Pump

Winchester 1300 Black Shadow Field Gun

Winchester 1300 Deer Black Shadow Gun

Winchester 1300 Ranger Compact

Winchester 9410

Winchester Model 1300 Upland Pump Shotgun

Similar to Model 1300 Walnut except straight-grip stock, 24" barrel. Introduced 1999. Made in U.S. by U.S. Repeating Arms Co.

Price: **$439.00**

Winchester Model 1300 Black Shadow Field Shotgun

Similar to Model 1300 Walnut except black composite stock and forend, matte black finish. Has vent rib 26" or 28" barrel, 3" chamber, mod. WinChoke tube. Introduced 1995. From U.S. Repeating Arms Co., Inc.

Price: 12 or 20 gauge **$353.00**

Winchester Model 1300 Deer Black Shadow Shotgun

Similar to Model 1300 Black Shadow Turkey Gun except ramp-type front sight, fully adjustable rear, drilled and tapped for scope mounting. Black composite stock and forend, matte black metal. Smoothbore 22" barrel with one imp. cyl. WinChoke tube; 12 gauge only, 3" chamber. Weighs 6-3/4 lbs. Introduced 1994. From U.S. Repeating Arms Co., Inc.

Price: With rifled barrel **$377.00**
Price: With cantilever scope mount **$422.00**
Price: Combo (22" rifled and 28" smoothbore bbls.) **$455.00**
Price: Wood stock (20 ga., 22" rifled barrel) **$377.00**

WINCHESTER MODEL 1300 RANGER PUMP SHOTGUN

Gauge: 12, 20, 3" chamber, 5-shot magazine. **Barrel:** 28" vent. rib with Full, Mod., Imp. Cyl. Winchoke tubes. **Weight:** 7 to 7-1/4 lbs. **Length:** 48-5/8"

to 50-5/8" overall. **Stock:** Walnut-finished hardwood with ribbed forend. **Sights:** Metal bead front. **Features:** Cross-bolt safety, black rubber recoil pad, twin action slide bars, front-locking rotating bolt. From U.S. Repeating Arms Co., Inc.

Price: Vent. rib barrel, Winchoke. **$367.00**
Price: Model 1300 Compact, 24" vent. rib **$367.00**
Price: Compact wood model, 20 ga. **$392.00**

Winchester Model 1300 Turkey, Universal Hunter Shotgun

Rotary bolt action. Durable Mossy oak break-up finish on 26" VR barrel extra full turkey improved cylinder, modified and full WinChoke tubes included. 3", 12 gauge chamber.

Price: Universal Hunter **$515.00**
Price: Buck and Tom **$554.00**
Price: Short Turkey **512.00**

WINCHESTER MODEL 9410 LEVER-ACTION SHOTGUN

Gauge: .410, 2-1/2" chamber. **Barrel:** 24" cyl. bore, also Invector choke system. **Weight:** 6-3/4 lbs. **Length:** 42-1/8" overall. **Stock:** Checkered walnut straight-grip; checkered walnut forearm. **Sights:** Adjustable "V" rear, TruGlo® front. **Features:** Model 94 rifle action (smoothbore) chambered for .410 shotgun. Angle Controlled Eject extractor/ejector; choke tubes; 9-shot tubular magazine; 13-1/2" length of pull. Introduced 2001. From U.S. Repeating Arms Co.

Price: 9410 fixed choke **$579.00**
Price: 9410 Packer w/chokes **$600.00**
Price: 9410 w/Invector, traditional model **$645.00**
Price: 9410 w/Invector, Packer model. **$667.00**
Price: 9410 w/Invector, semi-fancy traditional **$789.00**

Includes a variety of game guns and guns for competitive shooting.

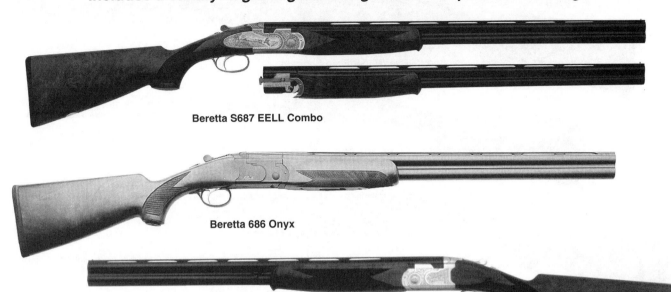

Beretta S687 EELL Combo

Beretta 686 Onyx

Beretta S686 Silver Pigeon

SHOTGUNS

BERETTA DT10 TRIDENT SHOTGUNS
Gauge: 12, 2-3/4", 3" chambers. **Barrel:** 28", 30", 32", 34"; competition-style vent rib; fixed or Optima Choke tubes. **Weight:** 7.9 to 9 lbs. **Stock:** High-grade walnut stock with oil finish; hand-checkered grip and forend, adjustable stocks available. **Features:** Detachable, adjustable trigger group, raised and thickened receiver, forend iron has replaceable nut to guarantee wood-to-metal fit, Optima Bore to improve shot pattern and reduce felt recoil. Introduced 2000. Imported from Italy by Beretta USA.
Price: DT10 Trident Trap (selective, lockable single trigger,
  adjustable stock). **$6,686.00**
Price: DT10 Trident Top Single **$6,686.00**
Price: DT10 Trident X Trap Combo
  (single and o/u barrels) . . . . **$9,005.00-$9,557.00**
Price: DT10 Trident Skeet (skeet stock with rounded recoil
  pad, tapered rib) **$6,866.00**
Price: DT10 Trident Sporting (sporting clays stock with
  rounded recoil pad) **$6,383.00**
Price: DT10L Sporting **$7,797.00**

BERETTA SERIES 682 GOLD E SKEET, TRAP, SPORTING OVER/UNDERS
Gauge: 12, 2-3/4" chambers. **Barrel:** Skeet-28"; trap-30" and 32", imp. mod. & full and Mobilchoke; trap mono shotguns-32" and 34" Mobilchoke, trap top single guns-32" and 34" full and Mobilchoke; trap combo sets-from 30" O/U, to 32" O/U, 34" top single. **Stock:** Close-grained walnut, hand checkered. **Sights:** White Bradley bead front sight and center bead. **Features:** Receiver has Greystone gunmetal gray finish with gold accents. Trap Monte Carlo stock has deluxe trap recoil pad. Various grades available; contact Beretta USA for details. Imported from Italy by Beretta USA.
Price: 682 Gold E Trap with adjustable stock **$3,933.00**
Price: 682 Gold E Trap Top Combo. . . . . **$3,485..00**
Price: 682 Gold E Sporting **$3,937.00**
Price: 682 Gold E Skeet, adjustable stock **$3,905.00**
Price: 682 Gold E Double Trap . . . . **NA**
Price: 687 EELL Diamond Pigeon Sporting **$6,207.00**

BERETTA 686 ONYX O/U SHOTGUN
Gauge: 12, 3" chambers. **Barrel:** 28", 30" (Mobilchoke tubes). **Weight:** 7.7 lbs. **Stock:** Checkered American walnut. **Features:** Intended for the beginning Sporting Clays shooter. Has wide, vented 12.5mm target rib, radiused recoil pad. Polished black finish on receiver and barrels. Introduced 1993. Imported from Italy by Beretta U.S.A.

Price: White Onyx. **$1,718.00**
Price: Onyx Pro **$1,856.00**
Price: Onyx Pro 3.5 . . . . **$1,929.00**

BERETTA 686 SILVER PIGEON O/U SHOTGUN
Gauge: 12, 20, 28, 3" chambers (2-3/4" 28 ga.). **Barrel:** 26", 28". **Weight:** 6.8 lbs. **Stock:** Checkered walnut. **Features:** Interchangeable barrels (20 and 28 ga.), single selective gold-plated trigger, boxlock action, auto safety, schnabel forend.
Price: Silver Pigeon S. **$1,994.00**
Price: Silver Pigeon S Combo **$2,757.00**

BERETTA ULTRALIGHT OVER/UNDER
Gauge: 12, 2-3/4" chambers. **Barrel:** 26", 28", Mobilchoke choke tubes. **Weight:** About 5 lbs., 13 oz. **Stock:** Select American walnut with checkered grip and forend. **Features:** Low-profile aluminum alloy receiver with titanium breech face insert. Electroless nickel receiver with game scene engraving. Single selective trigger; automatic safety. Introduced 1992. Imported from Italy by Beretta U.S.A.
Price: **$1,931.00**
Price: Silver Pigeon II **$2,270.00**
Price: Silver Pigeon II Combo. **$3,098.00**
Price: Silver Pigeon III **$2,408.00**
Price: Silver Pigeon IV **$2,684.00**
Price: Silver Pigeon V. **$3,171.00**

Beretta Over/Under Field Shotgun

Beretta SO9

**Browning Citori
White Lightning**

Beretta Ultralight Deluxe Over/Under Shotgun

Similar to the Ultralight except has matte electroless nickel finish receiver with gold game scene engraving; matte oil-finished, select walnut stock and forend. Imported from Italy by Beretta U.S.A.

Price: **$2,323.00**

BERETTA OVER/UNDER FIELD SHOTGUNS

Gauge: 12, 20, 28, and .410 bore, 2-3/4", 3" and 3-1/2" chambers. **Barrel:** 26" and 28" (Mobilchoke tubes). **Stock:** Close-grained walnut. **Features:** Highly-figured, American walnut stocks and forends, and a unique, weather-resistant finish on barrels. Silver designates standard 686, 687 models with silver receivers; 686 Silver Pigeon has enhanced engraving pattern, schnabel forend; 686 Silver Essential has matte chrome finish; Gold indicates higher grade 686EL, 687EL models with full sideplates; Diamond is for 687EELL models with highest grade wood, engraving. Case provided with Gold and Diamond grades. Imported from Italy by Beretta U.S.A.

Price: S686 Silver Pigeon two-bbl. set **$2,587.00**
Price: S686 Silver Pigeon **$1,817.00**
Price: S687 Silver Pigeon II Sporting **$2,196.00**
Price: Combo 29" and 30" **$3,151.00**
Price: S687EL Gold Pigeon (gold inlays, sideplates) **$4,099.00**
Price: S687EL Gold Pigeon, .410, 26"; 28 ga., 28". **$4,273.00**
Price: S687 EL Gold Pigeon II (deep relief engraving) **$4,513.00**
Price: S687 EL Gold Pigeon II Sporting (D.R. engraving). **$4,554.00**

BERETTA MODEL SO5, SO6, SO9 SHOTGUNS

Gauge: 12, 2-3/4" chambers. **Barrel:** To customer specs. **Stock:** To customer specs. **Features:** SO5-Trap, Skeet and Sporting Clays models SO5; SO6- SO6 and SO6 EELL are field models. SO6 has a case-hardened or silver receiver with contour hand engraving. SO6 EELL has hand-engraved receiver in a fine floral or "fine English" pattern or game scene, with bas-relief chisel work and gold inlays. SO6 and SO6 EELL are available with sidelocks removable by hand. Imported from Italy by Beretta U.S.A.

Price: SO5 Trap, Skeet, Sporting **$13,000.00**
Price: SO6 Trap, Skeet, Sporting **$17,500.00**
Price: SO6 EELL Field, custom specs **$28,000.00**
Price: SO9 (12, 20, 28, .410, 26", 28", 30", any choke) **$31,000.00**

Beretta S687EL Gold Pigeon Sporting O/U

Similar to S687 Silver Pigeon Sporting except sideplates with gold inlay game scene, vent side and top ribs, bright orange front sight. Stock and forend are high grade walnut with fine-line checkering. Available in 12

gauge only with 28" or 30" barrels and Mobilchoke tubes. Weighs 6 lbs., 13 oz. Imported from Italy by Beretta USA.
Price: **$4,971.00**
Price: Combo (28 and .410) **$5,520.00**

BRNO ZH 300 OVER/UNDER SHOTGUN

Gauge: 12, 2-3/4" chambers. **Barrel:** 26", 27-1/2", 29" (Skeet, Imp. Cyl., Mod., Full). **Weight:** 7 lbs. **Length:** 44.4" overall. **Stock:** European walnut. **Features:** Double triggers; automatic safety; polished blue finish engraved receiver. Announced 1998. Imported from the Czech Republic by Euro-Imports.

Price: ZH 301, field. **$594.00**
Price: ZH 302, skeet. **$608.00**
Price: ZH 303, 12 ga. trap. **$608.00**
Price: ZH 321, 16 ga. **$595.00**

BRNO 501.2 OVER/UNDER SHOTGUN

Gauge: 12, 2-3/4" chambers. **Barrel:** 27.5" (Full & Mod.). **Weight:** 7 lbs. **Length:** 44" overall. **Stock:** European walnut. **Features:** Boxlock action with double triggers, ejectors; automatic safety; hand-cut checkering. Announced 1998. Imported from The Czech Republic by Euro-Imports.
Price: **$850.00**

BROWNING CITORI O/U SHOTGUNS

Gauge: 12, 20, 28 and .410. **Barrel:** 26", 28" in 28 and .410. Offered with In-vector choke tubes. All 12 and 20 gauge models have back-bored barrels and Invector Plus choke system. **Weight:** 6 lbs., 8 oz. (26" .410) to 7 lbs., 13 oz. (30" 12 ga.). **Length:** 43" overall (26" bbl.). **Stock:** Dense walnut, hand checkered, full pistol grip, beavertail forend. Field-type recoil pad on 12 ga. field guns and trap and Skeet models. **Sights:** Medium raised beads, German nickel silver. **Features:** Barrel selector integral with safe-ty, automatic ejectors, three-piece takedown. Imported from Japan by Browning. Contact Browning for complete list of models and prices.

Price: Grade I, Hunter, Invector, 12 and 20 . . . . **$1,486.00**
Price: Grade I, Lightning, 28 and .410, Invector **$1,594.00**
Price: Grade III, Lightning, 28 and .410, Invector **$2,570.00**
Price: Grade VI, 28 and .410 Lightning, Invector **$3,780.00**
Price: Grade I, Lightning, Invector Plus, 12, 20 . . . . **$1,534.00**
Price: Grade I, Hunting, 28", 30" only, 3-1/2", Invector Plus **$1,489.00**
Price: Grade III, Lightning, Invector, 12, 20 . . . . **$2,300.00**
Price: Grade VI, Lightning, Invector, 12, 20 . . . . **$3,510.00**
Price: Gran Lightning, 26", 28", Invector, 12, 20. . . . . **$2,184.00**
Price: Gran Lightning, 28, .410. . . . . **$2,302.00**
Price: Micro Lightning, 20 ga., 24" bbl., 6 lbs., 4 oz. **$1,591.00**
Price: White Lightning (silver nitride receiver w/engraving, 12 or 20 ga., 26", 28") **$1,583.00**
Price: White Lightning, 28 or .410 gauge **$1,654.00**
Price: Citori Satin Hunter (12 ga., satin-finished wood, matte-finished barrels and receiver) 3-1/2" chambers. **$1,535.00**

SHOTGUNS

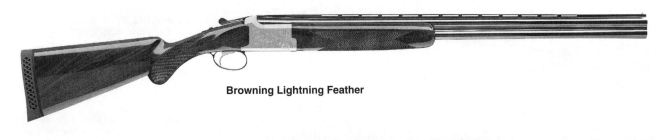

Browning Lightning Feather

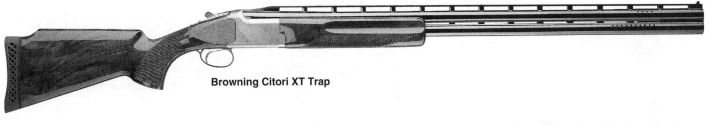

Browning Citori XT Trap

Browning Citori XS Special

BROWNING LIGHTNING FEATHER CITORI OVER/UNDER

Similar to the standard Citori except available in 12, 20, 28 or .410 with, 26" or 28" barrels choked Imp. Cyl., Mod. and Full. Has pistol grip stock, rounded forend. Lightning Feather 12 weighs 7 lbs., 15 oz. (26" barrels); Lightning Feather 20 weighs 6 lbs., 10 oz. (26" barrels). Introduced 2004.

Price: Lightning, 28 or .410 . . . . $1,659.00
Price: Lightning 12 or 20 . . . . $1,597.00
Price: White Lightning, 28 or .410 . . . . $1,738.00
Price: White Lightning, 12 or 20 . . . . $1,664.00
Price: Citori 525 Field, 28 or .410 . . . . $1,914.00
Price: Citori 525 Field, 12 or 20 . . . . $1,885.00
Price: Citori Superlight Feather, 12 or 20 . . . . $1,882.00
Price: Citori Lightning Feather, 12 or 20 . . . . $1,815.00
Price: Citori Lightning Feather Combo (20 & 28) $2,949.00

Browning Citori XT Trap Over/Under

Similar to the Citori Special Trap except has engraved silver nitride receiver with gold highlights, vented side barrel rib. Available In 12 gauge with 30" or 32" barrels, Invector-Plus choke tubes. Introduced 1999. Imported by Browning.

Price: $1,834.00
Price: With adjustable-comb stock $2,054.00

Browning Citori Lightning Feather O/U

Similar to the 12 gauge Citori Grade I except has 2-3/4" chambers, rounded pistol grip, lightning-style forend, and lightweight alloy receiver. Weighs 6 lbs. 15 oz. with 26" barrels (12 ga.); 6 lbs., 2 oz. (20 ga., 26" bbl.), sil-vered, engraved receiver. Introduced 1999. Imported by Browning.

Price: 12 or 20 ga., 26" or 28" barrels $1,693.00
Price: Lightning Feather Combo
(20 and 28 ga. bbls., 27" each) $2,751.00

Browning Citori XS Skeet

Similar to other Citori Ultra models except features a semi-beavertail forearm with deep finger grooves, ported barrels and triple system. Adjustable comb is optional. Introduced 2000.

Price: 12 ga., 28" or 30" barrel $2,363.00
Price: 20 ga., 28" or 30" barrel $2,363.00

Browning Citori XS Trap

Similar to other Citori Ultra models except offered in 12 ga. only with 30" or 32" ported barrel, high-post rib, ventilated side ribs, triple trigger system™ and silver nitride receiver. Includes full, modified and imp. cyl. choke tubes. From Browning.

Price: 30" or 32" barrel $2,209.00
Price: Adjustable-comb Model $2,475.00

Browning Citori XS Special

Similar to other Citori XS models except offered in 12 gauge ony, silver nitride receiver with new Special engraving, adjustable comb, low profile rib, right-hand palm swell, Triple Trigger™ system, HiViz® Pro-Comb sight with mid bead, Invector-Plus™ choke system with five Midas chokes. From Browning.

Price: $2,727.00

Browning Citori XS Sporting

Similar to other Citori XS models except offered in 12 and 20 gauge. silver nitride receiver, schnabel forearm, ventilated side rib. Imported by Browning.

Price: 12 or 20 ga. $2,400.00

Browning Citori Feather Shotgun

Similar to the standard Citori. Available in Lightning and Superlight models only. Introduced 2000.

Price: 28" or 30" barrel . . . . $2,266.00 To $2,338.00

Browning Citori High Grade Shotguns

Similar to standard Citori except has engraved hunting scenes and gold inlays, High-grade, Hand-oiled walnut stock and forearm. Introduced 2000. From Browning.

Price: Citori VI Lightning blue or gray (gold inlays of ducks and pheasants)
From $3,797.00
Price: Citori Grade III Superlight (bird scene engraving on grayed receiver, gold inlays) $2,464.00
Price: Citori 525 Golden Clays (engraving of game bird-clay bird transition, gold accents), 12 or 20 ga. $4,236.00

Browning Citori XS Sporting Clays

Similar to the Citori Grade I except has silver nitride receiver with gold accents, stock dimensions of 14-3/4"x1-1/2"x2-1/4" with satin finish, right-hand palm swell, schnabel forend. Comes with modified, imp. cyl. and skeet invector-plus choke tubes. Back-bored barrels; vented side ribs. Introduced 1999. Imported by Browning.

Price: 12, 20 ga. $2,400.00

Browning 525 Sporting Clays

Charles Daly Superior Trap

Charles Daly Field Hunter

Browning Lightning Sporting Clays

Similar to the Citori Lightning with rounded pistol grip and classic forend. Has high post tapered rib or lower hunting-style rib with 30" back-bored Invector Plus barrels, ported or non-ported, 3" chambers. Gloss stock finish, radiused recoil pad. Has "Lightning Sporting Clays Edition" engraved and gold filled on receiver. Introduced 1989.

Price: Low-rib, ported **$1,691.00**
Price: High-rib, ported. **$1,770.00**

BROWNING 525 SPORTING CLAYS

Gauge: 12, 20, 2-3/4" chambers. **Barrel:** 12 ga.-28", 30", 32" (Invector Plus tubes), back-bored; 20 ga.-28", 30" (Invector Plus tubes). **Weight:** 7 lbs., 13 oz. (12 ga., 28"). **Stock:** 14-13/16" (1/8")x1-7/16"x2-3/16" (12 ga.). Select walnut with gloss finish, cut checkering, schnabel forend. **Features:** Grayed receiver with engraving, blued barrels. Barrels are ported on 12 gauge guns. Has low 10mm wide vent rib. Comes with three interchangeable trigger shoes to adjust length of pull. Introduced in U.S. 1993. Imported by Browning.

Price: Grade I, 12, 20 ga., Invector Plus. **$2,645.00**
Price: Golden Clays, 12, 20 ga., Invector Plus **$4,236.00**

CHARLES DALY SUPERIOR TRAP AE MC

Gauge: 12, 2-3/4" chambers. **Barrel:** 30" choke tubes. **Weight:** About 7 lbs. **Stock:** Checkered walnut; pistol grip, semi-beavertail forend. **Features:** Silver engraved receiver, chrome moly steel barrels; gold single selective trigger; automatic safety, automatic ejectors; red bead front sight, metal bead center; recoil pad. Introduced 1997. Imported from Italy by K.B.I., Inc.
Price: **$1,339.00**

CHARLES DALY FIELD HUNTER OVER/UNDER SHOTGUN

Gauge: 12, 20, 28 and .410 bore (3" chambers, 28 ga. has 2-3/4"). **Barrel:** 28" Mod & Full, 26" Imp. Cyl. & Mod (.410 is Full & Full). **Weight:** About 7 lbs. **Length:** NA. **Stock:** Checkered walnut pistol grip and forend. **Features:** Blued engraved receiver, chrome moly steel barrels; gold single selective trigger; automatic safety; extractors; gold bead front sight. Introduced 1997. Imported from Italy by K.B.I., Inc.

Price: 12 or 20 ga. **$799.00**
Price: 28 ga. **$879.00**
Price: .410 bore **$919.00**

Charles Daly Field Hunter AE Shotgun

Similar to the Field Hunter except 28 gauge only; 26" (Imp. Cyl. & Mod., 28 gauge), 26" (Full & Full, .410); automatic; ejectors. Introduced 1997. Imported from Italy by K.B.I., Inc.
Price: 28 . . . . **$999.00**

Charles Daly Superior Hunter AE Shotgun

Similar to the Field Hunter AE except has silvered, engraved receiver. Introduced 1997. Imported from Italy by F.B.I., Inc.
Price: 28 ga. **$1,129.00**
Price: .410 bore **$1,129.00**

Charles Daly Field Hunter AE-MC

Similar to the Field Hunter except in 12 or 20 only, 26" or 28" barrels with five multichoke tubes; automatic ejectors. Introduced 1997. Imported from Italy by K.B.I., Inc.
Price: 12 or 20 . . . . **$979.95**

Charles Daly Superior Sporting O/U

Similar to the Field Hunter AE-MC except 28" or 30" barrels; silvered, engraved receiver; five choke tubes; ported barrels; red bead front sight. Introduced 1997. Imported from Italy by K.B.I., Inc.
Price: **$1,259.95**

CHARLES DALY DIAMOND REGENT GTX DL HUNTER O/U

Gauge: 12, 20, .410, 3" chambers, 28, 2-3/4" chambers. **Barrel:** 26", 28", 30" (choke tubes), 26" (Imp. Cyl. & Mod. in 28, 26" (Full & Full) in .410. **Weight:** About 7 lbs. **Stock:** Extra select fancy European walnut with 24" hand checkering, hand rubbed oil finish. **Features:** Boss-type action with internal side lumps. Deep cut hand-engraved scrollwork and game scene set in full sideplates. GTX detachable single selective trigger system with coil springs; chrome moly steel barrels; automatic safety; automatic ejectors, white bead front sight, metal bead center sight. Introduced 1997. Imported from Italy by K.B.I., Inc.

Price: 12 or 20 . . . . **Special order only**
Price: 28 . . . . **Special order only**
Price: .410 . . . . **Special order only**
Price: Diamond Regent GTX EDL Hunter (as above with engraved scroll and birds, 10 gold inlays), 12 or 20 . . . . **Special order only**
Price: As above, 28. . . . . **Special order only**
Price: As above, .410 . . . . **Special order only**

CHARLES DALY EMPIRE EDL HUNTER O/U

Gauge: 12, 20, .410, 3" chambers, 28 ga., 2-3/4". **Barrel:** 26", 28" (12, 20, choke tubes), 26" (Imp. Cyl. & Mod., 28 ga.), 26" (Full & Full, .410). **Weight:** About 7 lbs. **Stocks:** Checkered walnut pistol grip buttstock, semi-beaver-tail forend; recoil pad. **Features:** Silvered, engraved receiver; chrome moly barrels; gold single selective trigger; automatic safety; automatic ejectors; red bead front sight, metal bead middle sight. Introduced 1997. Imported from Italy by K.B.I., Inc.

Price: Empire EDL (dummy sideplates) 12 or 20 . . . . **$1,559.95**
Price: Empire EDL, 28 . . . . **$1,559.95**
Price: Empire EDL, .410. . . . . **$1,599.95**

SHOTGUNS

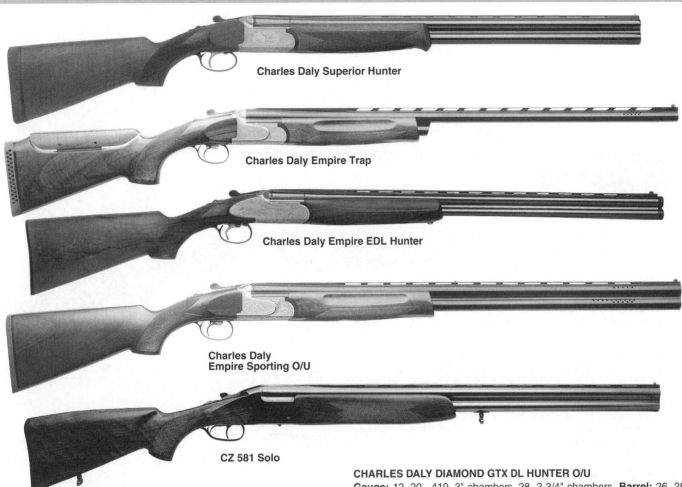

Charles Daly Superior Hunter

Charles Daly Empire Trap

Charles Daly Empire EDL Hunter

Charles Daly
Empire Sporting O/U

CZ 581 Solo

Charles Daly Empire Sporting O/U

Similar to the Empire EDL Hunter except 12 or 20 gauge only, 28", 30" barrels with choke tubes; ported barrels; special stock dimensions. Introduced 1997. Imported from Italy by K.B.I., Inc.
Price: **$1,499.95**

CHARLES DALY EMPIRE TRAP AE MC

Gauge: 12, 2-3/4" chambers. **Barrel:** 30" choke tubes. **Weight:** About 7 lbs. **Stock:** Checkered walnut; pistol grip, semi-beavertail forend. **Features:** Silvered, engraved, reinforced receiver; chrome moly steel barrels; gold single selective trigger; automatic safety, automatic ejector; red bead front sight, metal bead center; recoil pad. Imported from Italy by K.B.I., Inc.
Price: **$1,539.95**

CHARLES DALY DIAMOND GTX SPORTING O/U SHOTGUN

Gauge: 12, 20, 3" chambers. **Barrel:** 28", 30" with choke tubes. **Weight:** About 8.5 lbs. **Stock:** Checkered deluxe walnut; Sporting clays dimensions. Pistol grip; semi-beavertail forend; hand rubbed oil finish. **Features:** Chromed, hand-engraved receiver; chrome moly steel barrels; GTX de-ta-chable single selective trigger system with coil springs, automatic safety; automatic ejectors; red bead front sight; ported barrels. Introduced 1997. Imported from Italy by K.B.I., Inc.
Price: . . . . **Price on request**

CHARLES DALY DIAMOND GTX TRAP AE-MC O/U SHOTGUN

Gauge: 12, 2-3/4" chambers. **Barrel:** 30" (Full & Full). **Weight:** About 8.5 lbs. **Stock:** Checkered deluxe walnut; pistol grip; trap dimensions; semi-beaver-tail forend; hand-rubbed oil finish. **Features:** Silvered, hand-en-graved receiver; chrome moly steel barrels; GTX detachable single selec-tive trigger system with coil springs, automatic safety, automatic-ejectors; red bead front sight, metal bead middle; recoil pad. Imported from Italy by K.B.I., Inc.
Price: . . . . **Price on request**

CHARLES DALY DIAMOND GTX DL HUNTER O/U

Gauge: 12, 20, .410, 3" chambers, 28, 2-3/4" chambers. **Barrel:** 26, 28", choke tubes in 12 and 20 ga., 26" (Imp. Cyl. & Mod.), 26" (Full & Full) in .410-bore. **Weight:** About 8.5 lbs. **Stock:** Select fancy European walnut stock, with 24 lpi hand checkering; hand-rubbed oil finish. **Features:** Boss-type action with internal side lugs, hand-engraved scrollwork and game scene. GTX detachable single selective trigger system with coil springs; chrome moly steel barrels, automatic safety, automatic ejectors, red bead front sight, recoil pad. Introduced 1997. Imported from Italy by K.B.I., Inc.
Price: . . . . **Special order only**

CZ 581 SOLO OVER/UNDER SHOTGUN

Gauge: 12, 2-3/4" chambers. **Barrel:** 27.6" (Mod. & Full). **Weight:** 7.37 lbs. **Length:** 44.5" overall. **Stock:** Circassian walnut. **Features:** Automatic ejectors; double triggers; Kersten-style double lump locking system. Im-ported from the Czech Republic by CZ-USA.
Price: **$799.00**

EAA BAIKAL IZH27 OVER/UNDER SHOTGUN

Gauge: 12 (3" chambers), 16 (2-3/4" chambers), 20 (3" chambers), 28 (2-3/4" chambers), .410 (3"). **Barrel:** 26-1/2", 28-1/2" (imp., mod. and full choke tubes for 12 and 20 gauges; improved cylinder and modified for 16 and 28 gauges; improved modified and full for .410; 16 also offered in mod. and full). **Weight:** NA. **Stock:** Walnut, checkered forearm and grip. Imported by European American Armory.
Price: IZH-27 (12, 16 and 20 gauge) **$509.00**
Price: IZH-27 (28 gauge and .410). **$569.00**

EAA Baikal IZH27 Sporting O/U

Basic IZH-27 with barrel porting, wide vent rib with double sight beads, en-graved nickel receiver, checkered walnut stock and forend with palm swell and semi beavertail, 3 screw chokes, SS trigger, selectable ejectors, auto tang safety
Price: 12 ga., 29" bbl. **$589.00**

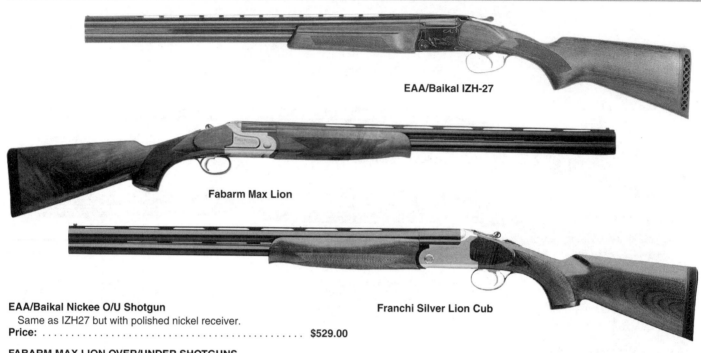

EAA/Baikal IZH-27

Fabarm Max Lion

Franchi Silver Lion Cub

EAA/Baikal Nickee O/U Shotgun
Same as IZH27 but with polished nickel receiver.
Price: **$529.00**

FABARM MAX LION OVER/UNDER SHOTGUNS
Gauge: 12, 3" chambers, 20, 3" chambers. **Barrel:** 26", 28", 30" (12 ga.); 26", 28" (20 ga.), choke tubes. **Weight:** 7.4 lbs. **Length:** 47.5" overall (26" barrel). **Stock:** European walnut; leather-covered recoil pad. **Features:** TriBore barrel, boxlock action with single selective trigger, manual safety, automatic ejectors; chrome-lined barrels; adjustable trigger. Silvered, engraved receiver. Comes with locking, fitted luggage case. Introduced 1998. Imported from Italy by Heckler & Koch, Inc.
Price: 12 or 20 .... **$1,799.00**

FABARM ULTRA CAMO MAG LION O/U SHOTGUN
Gauge: 12, 3-1/2" chambers. **Barrel:** 28" (cyl., imp. cyl., mod., imp. mod., full, SS-mod., SS-full choke tubes). **Weight:** 7.9 lbs. **Length:** 50" overall. **Stock:** Camo-colored walnut. **Features:** TriBore barrel, Wetlands Camo finished metal surfaces, single selective trigger, non-auto ejectors, leather-covered recoil pad. Locking hard plastic case. Introduced 1998. Imported from Italy by Heckler & Koch, Inc.
Price: **$1,229.00**

FABARM MAX LION PARADOX
Gauge: 12, 20, 3" chambers. **Barrel:** 24". **Weight:** 7.6 lbs. **Length:** 44.5" overall. **Stock:** Walnut with special enhancing finish. **Features:** TriBore upper barrel, both wood and receiver are enhanced with special finishes, color-case hardened type finish.
Price: 12 or 20 .... **$1,129.00**

FABARM SILVER LION OVER/UNDER SHOTGUNS
Gauge: 12, 3" chambers, 20, 3" chambers. **Barrel:** 26", 28", 30" (12 ga.); 26", 28" (20 ga.), choke tubes. **Weight:** 7.2 lbs. **Length:** 47.5" overall (26" barrels). **Stock:** Walnut; leather-covered recoil pad. **Features:** TriBore barrel, boxlock action with single selective trigger; silvered receiver with engraving; automatic ejectors. Comes with locking hard plastic case. Introduced 1998. Imported from Italy by Heckler & Koch, Inc.
Price: 12 or 20 .... **$1,229.00**

Fabarm Silver Lion Cub Model O/U
Similar to the Silver Lion except has 12.5" length of pull, is in 20 gauge only (3-1/2" chambers), and comes with 24" TriBore barrel system. Weight is 6 lbs. Introduced 1999. Imported from Italy by Heckler & Koch, Inc.
Price: **$1,229.00**

FABARM CAMO TURKEY MAG O/U SHOTGUN
Gauge: 12, 3-1/2" chambers. **Barrel:** 20" TriBore (Ultra-Full ported tubes). **Weight:** 7.5 lbs. **Length:** 46" overall. **Stock:** 14.5"x1.5"x2.29". Walnut.

Sights: Front bar, Picatinny rail scope base. **Features:** Completely covered with Xtra Brown camouflage finish. Unported barrels. Introduced 1999. Imported from Italy by Heckler & Koch, Inc.
Price: **$1,199.00**

FABARM SPORTING CLAYS COMPETITION EXTRA O/U
Gauge: 12, 20, 3" chambers. **Barrel:** 12 ga. has 30", 20 ga. has 28"; ported TriBore barrel system with five tubes. **Weight:** 7 to 7.8 lbs. **Length:** 49.6" overall (20 ga.). **Stock:** 14.50"x1.38"x2.17" (20 ga.); deluxe walnut; leather-covered recoil pad. **Features:** Single selective trigger, auto ejectors; 10mm channeled rib; carbon fiber finish. Introduced 1999. Imported from Italy by Heckler & Koch, Inc.
Price: **$1,749.00**

FRANCHI ALCIONE FIELD OVER/UNDER SHOTGUN
Gauge: 12, 20, 3" chambers. **Barrel:** 26", 28"; IC, M, F tubes. **Weight:** 7.5 lbs. **Length:** 43" overall with 26" barrels. **Stock:** European walnut. **Features:** Boxlock action with ejectors, barrel selector mounted on trigger; silvered, engraved receiver, vent center rib, automatic safety, interchangeable 20 ga. bbls., left-hand available. Imported from Italy by Benelli USA. Hard case included.
Price: **$1,275.00**
Price: (20 gauge barrel set) **$460.00**

Franchi Alcione SX O/U Shotgun
Similar to Alcione Field model with high grade walnut stock and forend. Gold engraved removeable sideplates, interchangeable barrels.
Price: $1,800.00
Price: (12 gauge barrel set) .... **$450.00 to $500.00**
Price: (20 gauge barrel set) **$450.00**

Franchi Alcione Sport SL O/U Shotgun
Similar to Alcione except 2-3/4" chambers, elongated forcing cones and porting for Sporting Clays shooting. 10mm vent rib, tightly curved pistol grip, manual safety, removeable sideplates. Imported from Italy by Benelli USA.
Price: **$1,650.00**

FRANCHI ALCIONE TITANIUM OVER/UNDER SHOTGUN
Gauge: 12, 20, 3" chambers. **Barrel:** 26", 28"; IC, M, F tubes. **Weight:** 6.8 lbs. **Length:** 43", 45". **Stock:** Select walnut. **Sights:** Front/mid. **Features:** Receiver (titanium inserts) made of aluminum alloy. 7mm vent rib. Fast locking triggers. Left-hand available.
Price: **$1,425.00**

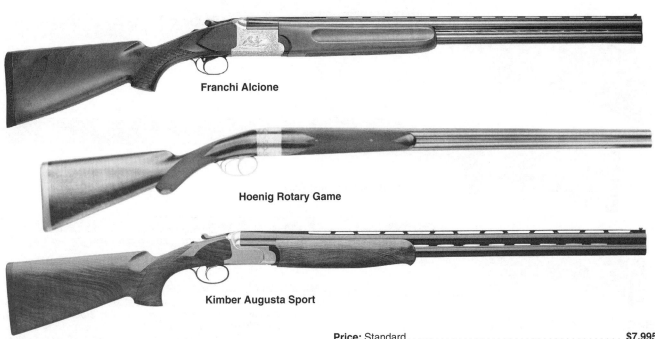

Franchi Alcione

Hoenig Rotary Game

Kimber Augusta Sport

FRANCHI 912 SHOTGUN
Gauge: 12 ga., 2-3/4", 3", 3-1/2"" chambers. **Barrel:** 24"-30". **Weight:** Appx. 7.6 lbs. **Length:** 46"-52". **Stock:** Walnut, synthetic, Timber HD. **Sights:** White bead front. **Features:** Based on 612 design, magazine cut-off, stepped vent rib, dual-recoil-reduction system.
Price: Satin walnut **$1,000.00**
Price: Synthetic **$940.00**
Price: Timber HD Camo **$1,050.00**

FRANCHI VELOCE OVER/UNDER SHOTGUN
Gauge: 20, 28. **Barrel:** 26", 28"; IC, M, F tubes. **Weight:** 5.5-5.8 lbs. **Length:** 43"-45". **Stock:** High grade walnut. **Features:** Aluminum receiver with steel reinforcement scaled to 20 gauge for light weight. Pistol grip stock with slip recoil pad. Imported by Benelli USA. Hard case included.
Price: **$1,425.00**
Price: 28 ga. **$1,500.00**

FRANCHI VELOCE ENGLISH OVER/UNDER SHOTGUN
Similar to Veloce standard model with straight grip English-style stock. Available with 26" barrels in 20 and 28 gauge. Hard case included.
Price: **$1,425.00**
Price: 28 ga. **$1,500.00**

HOENIG ROTARY ROUND ACTION GAME GUN
Gauge: 20, 28. **Barrel:** 26", 28", solid tapered rib. **Weight:** 6 lbs. and 6 1/4 lbs. **Stock:** English walnut to customer specifications. **Features:** Round action opens by rotating barrels, pulling forward. Inertia extraction system, rotary wing safety blocks strikers. Simple takedown without removing forend. Introduced 1997. Made in U.S.A. by George Hoenig.
Price: **$19,980.00**

Kimber Augusta Shotgun
Premium over/under, Boss type action. 12 ga. only. Tri-alloy barrel with choke tubes. Backbored 736. Long forcing cones. HiViz sight with center bead on vent ribl. Available with many features. Custom dimensions available. Imported from Italy by Kimber Mfg., Inc.
Price: **$6,000.00**

KOLAR SPORTING CLAYS O/U SHOTGUN
Gauge: 12, 2-3/4" chambers. **Barrel:** 30", 32", 34"; extended choke tubes. **Stock:** 14-5/8"x2-1/2"x1-7/8"x1-3/8". French walnut. Four stock versions available. **Features:** Single selective trigger, detachable, adjustable for length; overbored barrels with long forcing cones; flat tramline rib; matte blue finish. Made in U.S. by Kolar.

Price: Standard **$7,995.00**
Price: Elite **$10,990.00**
Price: Elite Gold **$12,990.00**
Price: Legend **$13,990.00**
Price: Select **$15,990.00**
Price: Custom . . . . **Price on request**

Kolar AAA Competition TRAP O/U Shotgun
Similar to the Sporting Clays gun except has 32" O/U /34" Unsingle or 30" O/U /34" Unsingle barrels as an over/under, unsingle, or combination set. Stock dimensions are 14-1/2"x2-1/2"x1-1/2"; American or French walnut; step parallel rib standard. Contact maker for full listings. Made in U.S. by Kolar.
Price: Over/under, choke tubes, Standard **$8,220.00**
Price: Unsingle, choke tubes, Standard **$8.600.00**
Price: Combo (30"/34", 32"/34"), Standard. **$10,995.00**

Kolar AAA Competition SKEET O/U Shotgun
Similar to the Sporting Clays gun except has 28" or 30" barrels with Kolarite AAA sub gauge tubes; stock of American or French walnut with matte finish; flat tramline rib; under barrel adjustable for point of impact. Many options available. Contact maker for complete listing. Made in U.S. by Kolar.
Price: Standard, choke tubes **$8,645.00**
Price: Standard, choke tubes, two-barrel set **$10,995.00**

KRIEGHOFF K-80 SPORTING CLAYS O/U
Gauge: 12. **Barrel:** 28", 30" or 32" with choke tubes. **Weight:** About 8 lbs. **Stock:** #3 Sporting stock designed for gun-down shooting. **Features:** Standard receiver with satin nickel finish and classic scroll engraving. Selective mechanical trigger adjustable for position. Choice of tapered flat or 8mm parallel flat barrel rib. Free-floating barrels. Aluminum case. Imported from Germany by Krieghoff International, Inc.
Price: Standard grade with five choke tubes, from **$8,150.00**

KRIEGHOFF K-80 SKEET SHOTGUN
Gauge: 12, 2-3/4" chambers. **Barrel:** 28", 30", (Skeet & Skeet), optional choke tubes). **Weight:** About 7-3/4 lbs. **Stock:** American Skeet or straight Skeet stocks, with palm-swell grips. Walnut. **Features:** Satin gray receiver finish. Selective mechanical trigger adjustable for position. Choice of ventilated 8mm parallel flat rib or ventilated 8-12mm tapered flat rib. Introduced 1980. Imported from Germany by Krieghoff International, Inc.
Price: Standard, Skeet chokes **$6,900.00**
Price: Skeet Special (28" or 30", tapered flat rib,
Skeet & Skeet choke tubes) **$7,575.00**

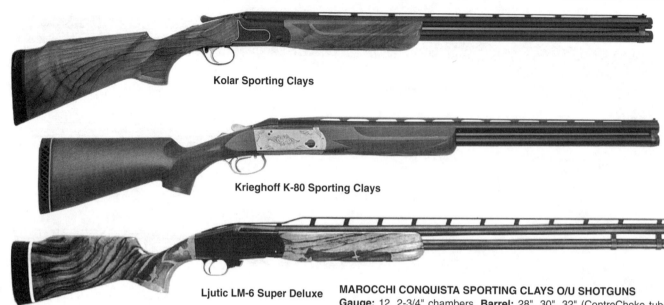

Kolar Sporting Clays

Krieghoff K-80 Sporting Clays

Ljutic LM-6 Super Deluxe

KRIEGHOFF K-80 O/U TRAP SHOTGUN

Gauge: 12, 2-3/4" chambers. **Barrel:** 30", 32" (Imp. Mod. & Full or choke tubes). **Weight:** About 8-1/2 lbs. **Stock:** Four stock dimensions or adjustable stock available; all have palm swell grips. Checkered European walnut. **Features:** Satin nickel receiver. Selective mechanical trigger, adjustable for position. Ventilated step rib. Introduced 1980. Imported from Germany by Krieghoff International, Inc.

Price: K-80 O/U (30", 32", Imp. Mod. & Full), from **$7,375.00**
Price: K-80 Unsingle (32", 34", Full), Standard, from **$7,950.00**
Price: K-80 Combo (two-barrel set), Standard, from **$10,475.00**

Krieghoff K-20 O/U Shotgun

Similar to the K-80 except built on a 20-gauge frame. Designed for skeet, sporting clays and field use. Offered in 20, 28 and .410, 28" and 30" barrels. Imported from Germany by Krieghoff International Inc.

Price: K-20, 20 gauge, from **$8,150.00**
Price: K-20, 28 gauge, from **$8,425.00**
Price: K-20, .410, from **$8,425.00**

LEBEAU - COURALLY BOSS-VEREES O/U

Gauge: 12, 20, 2-3/4" chambers. **Barrel:** 25" to 32". **Weight:** To customer specifications. **Stock:** Exhibition-quality French walnut. **Features:** Boss-type sidelock with automatic ejectors; single or double triggers; chopper lump barrels. A custom gun built to customer specifications. Imported from Belgium by Wm. Larkin Moore.

Price: From **$96,000.00**

LJUTIC LM-6 SUPER DELUXE O/U SHOTGUN

Gauge: 12. **Barrel:** 28" to 34", choked to customer specs for live birds, trap, International Trap. **Weight:** To customer specs. **Stock:** To customer specs. Oil finish, hand checkered. **Features:** Custom-made gun. Hollow-milled rib, pull or release trigger, pushbutton opener in front of trigger guard. From Ljutic Industries.

Price: Super Deluxe LM-6 O/U **$17,995.00**
Price: Over/Under Combo (interchangeable single barrel, two trigger guards, one for single trigger, one for doubles). **$24,995.00**
Price: Extra over/under barrel sets, 29"-32" **$5,995.00**

LUGER CLASSIC O/U SHOTGUNS

Gauge: 12, 3" and 3-1/2" chambers. **Barrel:** 26", 28", 30"; imp. cyl. mod. and full choke tubes. **Weight:** 7-1/2 lbs. **Length:** 45" overall (28" barrel) **Stock:** Select-grade European walnut, hand-checkered grip and forend. **Features:** Gold, single selective trigger; automatic ejectors. Introduced 2000.

Price: Classic (26", 28" or 30" barrel; 3-1/2" chambers) **$919.00**
Price: Classic Sporting (30" barrel; 3" chambers). **$964.00**

MAROCCHI CONQUISTA SPORTING CLAYS O/U SHOTGUNS

Gauge: 12, 2-3/4" chambers. **Barrel:** 28", 30", 32" (ContreChoke tubes); 10mm concave vent rib. **Weight:** About 8 lbs. **Stock:** 14-1/2"-14-7/8"x2-3/16"x1-7/16"; American walnut with checkered grip and forend; Sporting Clays butt pad. **Sights:** 16mm luminescent front. **Features:** Lower monoblock and frame profile. Fast lock time. Ergonomically-shaped trigger adjustable for pull length. Automatic selective ejectors. Coin-finished receiver, blued barrels. Five choke tubes, hard case. Available as true left-hand model-opening lever operates from left to right; stock has left-hand cast. Introduced 1994. Imported from Italy by Precision Sales International.

Price: Grade I, right-hand **$1,490.00**
Price: Grade I, left-hand **$1,615.00**
Price: Grade II, right-hand **$1,828.00**
Price: Grade II, left-hand **$2,180.00**
Price: Grade III, right-hand, from **$3,093.00**
Price: Grade III, left-hand, from **$3,093.00**

Marocchi Conquista TRAP O/U Shotgun

Similar to Conquista Sporting Clays model except 30" or 32" barrels choked Full & Full, stock dimensions of 14-1/2"-14-7/8"x1-11/16"x1-9/32"; weighs about 8-1/4 lbs. Introduced 1994. Imported from Italy by Precision Sales International.

Price: Grade I, right-hand **$1,490.00**
Price: Grade II, right-hand **$1,828.00**
Price: Grade III, right-hand, from **$3,093.00**

Marocchi Conquista Skeet O/U Shotgun

Similar to Conquista Sporting Clays except 28" (Skeet & Skeet) barrels, stock dimensions of 14-3/8"-14-3/4"x2-3/16"x1-1/2". Weighs about 7-3/4 lbs. Introduced 1994. Imported from Italy by Precision Sales International.

Price: Grade I, right-hand **$1,490.00**
Price: Grade II, right-hand **$1,828.00**
Price: Grade III, right-hand, from **$3,093.00**

MAROCCHI MODEL 99 SPORTING TRAP AND SKEET

Gauge: 12, 2-3/4", 3" chambers. **Barrel:** 28", 30", 32". **Stock:** French walnut. **Features:** Boss Locking system, screw-in chokes, low recoil, lightweight monoblock barrels and ribs. Imported from Italy by Precision Sales International.

Price: Grade I **$2,350.00**
Price: Grade II **$2,870.00**
Price: Grade II Gold **$3,025.00**
Price: Grade III **$3,275.00**
Price: Grade III Gold **$3,450.00**
Price: Blackgold **$4,150.00**
Price: Lodestar **$5,125.00**
Price: Brittania **$5,125.00**
Price: Diana **$6,350.00**

SHOTGUNS — OVER/UNDERS

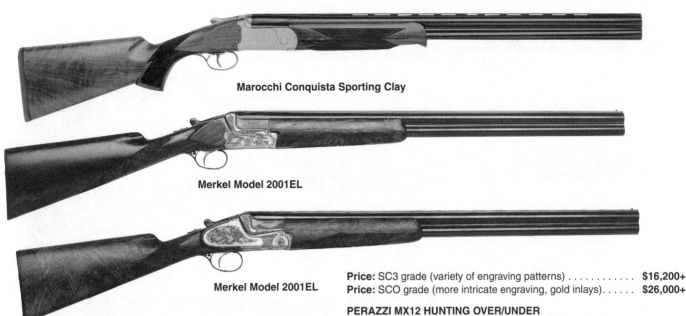

Marocchi Conquista Sporting Clay

Merkel Model 2001EL

Merkel Model 2001EL

**MAROCCHI CONQUISTA
USA MODEL 92 SPORTING CLAYS O/U SHOTGUN**
Gauge: 12, 3" chambers. **Barrel:** 30"; back-bored, ported (ContreChoke Plus tubes); 10 mm concave ventilated top rib, ventilated middle rib. **Weight:** 8 lbs. 2 oz. **Stock:** 14-1/4"-14-5/8"x 2-1/8"x1-3/8"; American walnut with checkered grip and forend; Sporting Clays butt pad. **Features:** Low profile frame; fast lock time; automatic selective ejectors; blued receiver and barrels. Comes with three choke tubes. Ergonomically shaped trigger adjustable for pull length without tools. Barrels are back-bored and ported. Introduced 1996. Imported from Italy by Precision Sales International.
Price: $1,490.00

MERKEL MODEL 2001EL O/U SHOTGUN
Gauge: 12, 20, 3" chambers, 28, 2-3/4" chambers. **Barrel:** 12-28"; 20, 28 ga.-26-3/4". **Weight:** About 7 lbs. (12 ga.). **Stock:** Oil-finished walnut; English or pistol grip. **Features:** Self-cocking Blitz boxlock action with cocking indicators; Kersten double cross-bolt lock; silver-grayed receiver with engraved hunting scenes; coil spring ejectors; single selective or double triggers. Imported from Germany by GSI, Inc.
Price: 12, 20 . . . . $7,295.00
Price: 28 ga. $7,295.00
Price: Model 2000EL (scroll engraving, 12, 20 or 28) $5,795.00

MERKEL MODEL 303EL O/U SHOTGUN
Similar to Model 2001 EL except Holland & Holland-style sidelock action with cocking indicators; English-style Arabesque engraving. Available in 12, 20, 28 gauge. Imported from Germany by GSI, Inc.
Price: $19,995.00

Merkel Model 2002 EL O/U Shotgun
Similar to Model 2001 EL except dummy sideplates, Arabesque engraving with hunting scenes; 12, 20, 28 gauge. Imported from Germany by GSI, Inc.
Price: $10,995.00

PERAZZI MX8 OVER/UNDER SHOTGUNS
Gauge: 12, 2-3/4" chambers. **Barrel:** 28-3/8" (Imp. Mod. & Extra Full), 29-1/2" (choke tubes). **Weight:** 7 lbs., 12 oz. **Stock:** Special specifications. **Features:** Has single selective trigger; flat 7/16" x 5/16" vent. rib. Many options available. Imported from Italy by Perazzi U.S.A., Inc.
Price: Sporting $10,800.00
Price: Trap Double Trap (removable trigger group) $9,560.00
Price: Skeet $9,560.00

Price: SC3 grade (variety of engraving patterns) . . . . $16,200+
Price: SCO grade (more intricate engraving, gold inlays) . . . . . $26,000+

PERAZZI MX12 HUNTING OVER/UNDER
Gauge: 12, 2-3/4" chambers. **Barrel:** 26-3/4", 27-1/2", 28-3/8", 29-1/2" (Mod. & Full); choke tubes available in 27-5/8", 29-1/2" only (MX12C). **Weight:** 7 lbs., 4 oz. **Stock:** To customer specs; Interchangeable. **Features:** Single selective trigger; coil springs used in action; schnabel forend tip. Imported from Italy by Perazzi U.S.A., Inc.
Price: From $10,841.00
Price: MX12C (with choke tubes), from $11,612.00

Perazzi MX20 Hunting Over/Under
Similar to the MX12 except 20 ga. frame size. Non-removable trigger group. Available in 20, 28, .410 with 2-3/4" or 3" chambers. 26" standard, and choked Mod. & Full. Weight is 6 lbs., 6 oz. Imported from Italy by Perazzi U.S.A., Inc.
Price: From $10,841.00
Price: MX20C (as above, 20 ga. only, choke tubes), from $11,612.00

PERAZZI MX8/MX8 SPECIAL TRAP, SKEET
Gauge: 12, 2-3/4" chambers. **Barrel:** Trap-29-1/2" (Imp. Mod. & Extra Full), 31-1/2" (Full & Extra Full). Choke tubes optional. Skeet-27-5/8" (Skeet & Skeet). **Weight:** About 8-1/2 lbs. (Trap); 7 lbs., 15 oz. (Skeet). **Stock:** Interchangeable and custom made to customer specs. **Features:** Has detachable and interchangeable trigger group with flat V springs. Flat 7/16" ventilated rib. Many options available. Imported from Italy by Perazzi U.S.A., Inc.
Price: From $10,841.00
Price: MX8 Special (adj. four-position trigger), from $11,476.00
Price: MX8 Special Combo (o/u and single barrel sets), from . $15,127.00

Perazzi MX8 Special Skeet O/U Shotgun
Similar to the MX8 Skeet except has adjustable four-position trigger, Skeet stock dimensions. Imported from Italy by Perazzi U.S.A., Inc.
Price: From $10,841.00

Perazzi MX8/20 Over/Under Shotgun
Similar to the MX8 except has smaller frame and has a removable trigger mechanism. Available in trap, Skeet, sporting or game models with fixed chokes or choke tubes. Stock is made to customer specifications. Introduced 1993. Imported from Italy by Perazzi U.S.A., Inc.
Price: From $10,841.00

PERAZZI MX10 OVER/UNDER SHOTGUN
Gauge: 12, 2-3/4" chambers. **Barrel:** 29.5", 31.5" (fixed chokes). **Weight:** NA. **Stock:** Walnut; cheekpiece adjustable for elevation and cast. **Features:** Adjustable rib; vent. side rib. Externally selective trigger. Available in single barrel, combo, over/under trap, Skeet, pigeon and sporting models. Introduced 1993. Imported from Italy by Perazzi U.S.A., Inc.
Price: MX200410 . . . . $13,608.00

Perazzi MX8

Perazzi MX28

Piotti Boss

Rizzini S790 Emel

PERAZZI MX28, MX410 GAME O/U SHOTGUNS
Gauge: 28, 2-3/4" chambers, .410, 3" chambers. **Barrel:** 26" (Imp. Cyl. & Full). **Weight:** NA. **Stock:** To customer specifications. **Features:** Made on scaled-down frames proportioned to the gauge. Introduced 1993. Imported from Italy by Perazzi U.S.A., Inc.
Price: From $19,120.00

PIOTTI BOSS OVER/UNDER SHOTGUN
Gauge: 12, 20. **Barrel:** 26" to 32", chokes as specified. **Weight:** 6.5 to 8 lbs. **Stock:** Dimensions to customer specs. Best quality figured walnut. **Features:** Essentially a custom-made gun with many options. Introduced 1993. Imported from Italy by Wm. Larkin Moore.
Price: From $48,000.00

REMINGTON MODEL 332 O/U SHOTGUN
Gauge: 12, 3" chambers. **Barrel:** 26", 28", 30". **Weight:** 7.75 lbs. **Length:** 42"-47" **Stock:** Satin-finished American walnut. **Sights:** Twin bead. **Features:** Light-contour, vent rib, Rem chock barrel, blued, traditional M-32 experience with M-300 Ideal performance, standard auto ejectors, set trigger. Proven boxlock action.
Price: $1,624.00

RIZZINI S790 EMEL OVER/UNDER SHOTGUN
Gauge: 20, 28, .410. **Barrel:** 26", 27.5" (Imp. Cyl. & Imp. Mod.). **Weight:** About 6 lbs. **Stock:** 14"x1-1/2"x2-1/8". Extra-fancy select walnut. **Features:** Boxlock action with profuse engraving; automatic ejectors; single selective trigger; silvered receiver. Comes with Nizzoli leather case. Introduced 1996. Imported from Italy by Wm. Larkin Moore & Co.
Price: From $9,725.00

RIZZINI S792 EMEL OVER/UNDER SHOTGUN
Similar to S790 EMEL except dummy sideplates with extensive engraving coverage. Nizzoli leather case. Introduced 1996. Imported from Italy by Wm. Larkin Moore & Co.
Price: From $9,075.00

RIZZINI UPLAND EL OVER/UNDER SHOTGUN
Gauge: 12, 16, 20, 28, .410. **Barrel:** 26", 27-1/2", Mod. & Full, Imp. Cyl. & Imp. Mod. choke tubes. **Weight:** About 6.6 lbs. **Stock:** 14-1/2"x1-1/2"x2-1/4". **Features:** Boxlock action; single selective trigger; ejectors; profuse engraving on silvered receiver. Comes with fitted case. Introduced 1996. Imported from Italy by Wm. Larkin Moore & Co.
Price: From $3,350.00

Rizzini Artemis Over/Under Shotgun
Same as Upland EL model except dummy sideplates with extensive game scene engraving. Fancy European walnut stock. Fitted case. Introduced 1996. Imported from Italy by Wm. Larkin Moore & Co.
Price: From $2,100.00

RIZZINI S782 EMEL OVER/UNDER SHOTGUN
Gauge: 12, 2-3/4" chambers. **Barrel:** 26", 27.5" (Imp. Cyl. & Imp. Mod.). **Weight:** About 6.75 lbs. **Stock:** 14-1/2"x1-1/2"x2-1/4". Extra fancy select walnut. **Features:** Boxlock action with dummy sideplates, extensive engraving with gold inlaid game birds, silvered receiver, automatic ejectors, single selective trigger. Nizzoli leather case. Introduced 1996. Imported from Italy by Wm. Larkin Moore & Co.
Price: From $11,450.00

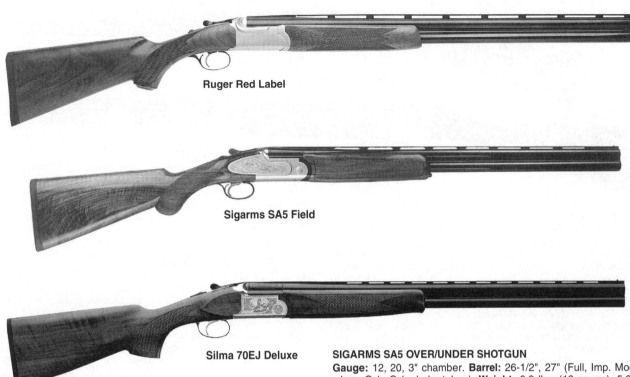

Ruger Red Label

Sigarms SA5 Field

Silma 70EJ Deluxe

RUGER RED LABEL O/U SHOTGUN

Gauge: 12, 20, 3" chambers; 28 2-3/4" chambers. **Barrel:** 26", 28" (Skeet [two], Imp. Cyl., Full, Mod. screw-in choke tubes). Proved for steel shot. **Weight:** About 7 lbs. (20 ga.); 7-1/2 lbs. (12 ga.). **Length:** 43" overall (26" barrels). **Stock:** 14"x1-1/2"x2-1/2". Straight grain American walnut or black synthetic. Checkered pistol grip and forend, rubber butt pad. **Features:** Stainless steel receiver. Single selective mechanical trigger, selective automatic ejectors; serrated free-floating vent. rib. Comes with two Skeet, one Imp. Cyl., one Mod., one Full choke tube and wrench. Made in U.S. by Sturm, Ruger & Co.

Price: Red Label with pistol grip stock **$1,489.00**
Price: English Field with straight-grip stock **$1,489.00**
Price: All-Weather Red Label with black
synthetic stock. . . . . **$1,489.00 to $1,545.00**
Price: Factory engraved All-Weather models . . . . **$1,650.00 to $1,725.00**

Ruger Engraved Red Label O/U Shotgun

Similar to Red Label except scroll engraved receiver with 24-carat gold game bird (pheasant in 12 gauge, grouse in 20 gauge, woodcock in 28 gauge, duck on All-Weather 12 gauge). Introduced 2000.
Price: Engraved Red Label (12 gauge, 30" barrel) **$1,725.00**
Price: Engraved Red Label (12, 20 and 28 gauge in 26"
and 28" barrels). **$1,650.00**
Price: Engraved Red Label, All-Weather (synthetic stock, 12 gauge only;
26" and 28" brls.) **$1,650.00**
Price: Engraved Red Label, All-Weather (synthetic stock, 12 gauge only,
30" barrel) **$1,650.00**

SARSILMAZ OVER/UNDER SHOTGUN

Gauge: 12, 3" chambers. **Barrel:** 26", 28"; fixed chokes or choke tubes. **Weight:** NA. **Length:** NA. **Stock:** Oil-finished hardwood. **Features:** Double or single selective trigger, wide ventilated rib, chrome-plated parts, blued finish. Introduced 2000. Imported from Turkey by Armsport Inc.

Price: Double triggers; mod. and full or imp. cyl. and mod. fixed
chokes. **$499.95**
Price: Single selective trigger; imp. cyl. and mod. or mod.
and full fixed chokes **$575.00**
Price: Single selective trigger; five choke tubes and wrench **$695.00**

SIGARMS SA5 OVER/UNDER SHOTGUN

Gauge: 12, 20, 3" chamber. **Barrel:** 26-1/2", 27" (Full, Imp. Mod., Mod., Imp. Cyl., Cyl. choke tubes). **Weight:** 6.9 lbs. (12 gauge), 5.9 lbs. (20 gauge). **Stock:** 14-1/2" x 1-1/2" x 2-1/2". Select grade walnut; checkered 20 l.p.i. at grip and forend. **Features:** Single selective trigger, automatic ejectors; hand-engraved detachable sideplated; matte nickel receiver, rest blued; tapered bolt lock-up. Introduced 1997. Imported by SIGARMS, Inc.

Price: Field, 12 gauge **$2,670.00**
Price: Sporting Clays **$2,800.00**
Price: Field 20 gauge **$2,670.00**

SILMA MODEL 70EJ DELUXE

Gauge: 12 (3-1/2" chambers), 20, .410 (3" chambers), 28 (2-3/4" chambers). **Barrel:** 28" (12 and 20 gauge, fixed and tubed, 28 and .410 fixed), 26" (12 and 20 fixed). **Weight:** 7.6 lbs 12 gauge, 6.9 lbs, 20, 28 and .410. **Stock:** Checkered select European walnut, pistol grip, solid rubber recoil pad. **Features:** Monobloc construction, chrome-moly blued steel barrels, raised vent rib, automatic safety and ejectors, single selective trigger, gold plated, bead front sight. Brushed, engraved receiver. Introduced 2002. Clays models introduced 2003. Imported from Italy by Legacy Sports International.

Price: 12 gauge **$1,020.00**
Price: 20 gauge **$945.00**
Price: 28, .410 . . . . **$1,060.00**

Silma Model 70 EJ Superlight

Similar to Silma 70EJ Deluxe except 12 gauge, 3" chambers, alloy receiver, weighs 5.6 lbs.
Price: 12, 20 multichokes (IC, M, F) **$1,105.00**

SHOTGUNS

SHOTGUNS — OVER/UNDERS

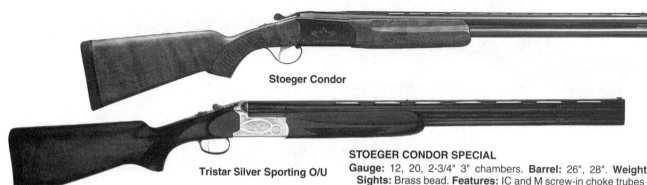

Stoeger Condor

Tristar Silver Sporting O/U

Silma Model 70 EJ Standard

Similar to Silma 70EJ Deluxe except 12 and 20 gauge only, standard walnut stock, light engraving, silver-plated trigger.

Price: 12 gauge **$940.00**
Price: 20 gauge **$865.00**
Price: Sporting Clays model **$1,305.00**

SKB MODEL 85TSS OVER/UNDER SHOTGUN

Gauge: 12, 20, .410 - 3"; 28, 2-3/4".**Barrel:** Chrome lined 26", 28", 30", 32" (w/choke tubes). **Weight:** 7 lbs., 7 oz. to 8 lbs, 14 oz. **Stock:** Hand-checkered American walnut with matte finish, schnabel or grooved forend. Target stocks available in various styles. **Sights:** Metal bead front or HiViz competition sights. **Features:** Low profile boxlock action with Greener-style cross bolt; single selective trigger; manual safety. Back-bored barrels with lengthened forcing cones. Introduced 2004. Imported from Japan by G.U. Inc.

Price: Sporting Clays, 12 or 20. . . . . **$1,949.00**
Price: Sporting Clays, 28 . . . . **$1,949.00**
Price: Sporting Clays set, 12 and 20 . . . . **$3,149.00**
Price: Skeet, 12 or 20 . . . . **$1,949.00**
Price: Skeet, 28 or .410 . . . . **$2,129.00 to $2,179.00**
Price: Skeet, three-barrel set, 20, 28, .410 . . . . **$4,679.00**
Price: Trap, standard or Monte Carlo **$1,499.00**
Price: Trap adjustable comb **$2,129.00**

SKB MODEL 585 OVER/UNDER SHOTGUN

Gauge: 12 or 20, 3"; 28, 2-3/4"; .410, 3". **Barrel:** 12 ga.-26", 28", 30", 32", 34" (Inter-Choke tubes); 20 ga.-26", 28" (Inter-Choke tube); 28-26", 28" (Inter-Choke tubes); .410-26", 28" (Inter-Choke tubes). Ventilated side ribs. **Weight:** 6.6 to 8.5 lbs. **Length:** 43" to 51-3/8" overall. **Stock:** 14-1/8"x1-1/2"x2-3/16". Hand checkered walnut with high-gloss finish. Target stocks available in standard and Monte Carlo. **Sights:** Metal bead front (field), target style on Skeet, trap, Sporting Clays. **Features:** Boxlock action; silver nitride finish with Field or Target pattern engraving; manual safety, automatic ejectors, single selective trigger. All 12 gauge barrels are back-bored, have lengthened forcing cones and longer choke tube system. Sporting Clays models in 12 gauge with 28" or 30" barrels available with optional 3/8" step-up target-style rib, matte finish, nickel center bead, white front bead. Introduced 1992. Imported from Japan by G.U., Inc.

Price: Field **$1,499.00**
Price: Two-barrel Field Set, 12 & 20 . . . . **$2,399.00**
Price: Two-barrel Field Set, 20 & 28 or 28 & .410 . . . . **$2,469.00**

SKB Model 585 Gold Package

Similar to Model 585 Field except gold-plated trigger, two gold-plated game inlays, schnabel forend. Silver or blue receiver. Introduced 1998. Imported from Japan by G.U. Inc.

Price: 12, 20 ga. **$1,689.00**
Price: 28, .410 . . . . **$1,749.00**

SKB Model 505 Shotguns

Similar to Model 585 except blued receiver, standard bore diameter, standard Inter-Choke system on 12, 20, 28, different receiver engraving. Imported from Japan by G.U. Inc.

Price: Field, 12 (26", 28"), 20 (26", 28") **$1,229.00**

STOEGER CONDOR SPECIAL

Gauge: 12, 20, 2-3/4" 3" chambers. **Barrel:** 26", 28". **Weight:** 7.7 lbs. **Sights:** Brass bead. **Features:** IC and M screw-in choke trubes with each gun. Oil finished hardwood with pistol grip and forend. Auto safety, single trigger, automatic extractors.

Price: **$390.00**
Price: Condor Special **$440.00**
Price: Supreme Deluxe w/SS and red bar sights **$500.00**

TRADITIONS CLASSIC SERIES O/U SHOTGUNS

Gauge: 12, 3"; 20, 3"; 16, 2-3/4"; 28, 2-3/4"; .410, 3". **Barrel:** 26" and 28". **Weight:** 6 lbs., 5 oz. to 7 lbs., 6 oz. **Length:** 43" to 45" overall. **Stock:** Walnut. **Features:** Single-selective trigger; chrome-lined barrels with screw-in choke tubes; extractors (Field Hunter and Field I models) or automatic ejectors (Field II and Field III models); rubber butt pad; top tang safety. Imported from Fausti of Italy by Traditions.

Price: (Field Hunter - blued receiver; 12 or 20 ga.; 26" bbl. has I.C. and mod. tubes, 28" has mod. and full tubes) **$669.00**
Price: (Field I - blued receiver; 12, 20, 28 ga. or .410; fixed chokes [26" has I.C. and mod., 28" has mod. and full]) **$619.00**
Price: (Field II - coin-finish receiver; 12, 16, 20, 28 ga. or .410; gold trigger; choke tubes) **$789.00**
Price: (Field III - coin-finish receiver; gold engraving and trigger; 12 ga.; 26" or 28" bbl.; choke tubes) **$999.00**
Price: (Upland II - blued receiver; 12 or 20 ga.; English-style straight walnut stock; choke tubes) **$839.00**
Price: (Upland III - blued receiver, gold engraving; 20 ga.; high-grade pistol grip walnut stock; choke tubes) **$1,059.00**
Price: (Upland III - blued, gold engraved receiver, 12 ga. Round pistol grip stock, choke tubes) **$1,059.00**
Price: (Sporting Clay II - silver receiver; 12 ga.; ported barrels with skeet, i.c., mod. and full extended tubes) **$959.00**
Price: (Sporting Clay III - engraved receivers, 12 and 20 ga., walnut stock, vent rib, extended choke tubes) **$1,189.00**

TRADITIONS MAG 350 SERIES O/U SHOTGUNS

Gauge: 12, 3-1/2". **Barrels:** 24", 26" and 28". **Weight:** 7 lbs. to 7 lbs., 4 oz. **Length:** 41" to 45" overall. **Stock:** Walnut or composite with Mossy Oak® Break-Up™ or Advantage® Wetlands ™ camouflage. **Features:** Black matte receiver, engraved receiver; vent rib; automatic ejectors; single-selective trigger; three screw-in choke tubes; rubber recoil pad; top tang safety. Imported from Fausti of Italy by Traditions.

Price: (Mag Hunter II - 28" black matte barrels, walnut stock, includes I.C., Mod. and Full tubes) **$799.00**
Price: (Turkey II - 24" or 26" camo barrels, Break-Up camo stock, includes Mod., Full and X-Full tubes) **$889.00**
Price: (Waterfowl II - 28" camo barrels, Advantage Wetlands camo stock, includes I.C., Mod. and Full tubes) **$899.00**

TRISTAR SILVER SPORTING O/U

Gauge: 12, 2-3/4" chambers, 20 3" chambers. **Barrel:** 28", 30" (Skeet, Imp. Cyl., Mod., Full choke tubes). **Weight:** 7-3/8 lbs. **Length:** 45-1/2" overall. **Stock:** 14-3/8"x1-1/2"x2-3/8". Figured walnut, cut checkering; Sporting Clays quick-mount buttpad. **Sights:** Target bead front. **Features:** Boxlock action with single selective trigger, automatic selective ejectors; special broadway channeled rib; vented barrel rib; chrome bores. Chrome-nickel finish on frame, with engraving. Introduced 1990. Imported from Italy by Tristar Sporting Arms Ltd.

Price: **$799.00**

Tristar Silver II

Tristar TR-SC "Emilio Rizzini"

Tristar TR Royal Emilio Rizzini

Tristar TR-L "Emilio Rizzini"

Tristar Silver II Shotgun

Similar to the Silver I except 26" barrel (Imp. Cyl., Mod., Full choke tubes, 12 and 20 ga.), 28" (Imp. Cyl., Mod., Full choke tubes, 12 ga. only), 26" (Imp. Cyl. & Mod. fixed chokes, 28 and .410), automatic selective ejectors. Weight is about 6 lbs., 15 oz. (12 ga., 26").
Price: **$669.00**

TRISTAR TR-SC "EMILIO RIZZINI" OVER/UNDER

Gauge: 12, 20, 3" chambers. **Barrel:** 28", 30" (Imp. Cyl., Mod., Full choke tubes). **Weight:** 7-1/2 lbs. **Length:** 46" overall (28" barrel). **Stock:** 1-1/2"x2-3/ 8"x14-3/8". Semi-fancy walnut; pistol grip with palm swell; semi-beavertail forend; black Sporting Clays recoil pad. **Features:** Silvered boxlock action with Four Locks locking system, auto ejectors, single selective (inertia) trigger, auto safety. Hard chrome bores. Vent. 10mm rib with target-style front and mid-rib beads. Introduced 1998. Imported from Italy by Tristar Sporting Arms, Ltd.
Price: Sporting Clay model **$1,047.00**
Price: 20 ga. **$1,127.00**

Tristar TR-Royal "Emilio Rizzini" O/U Shotgun

Similar to the TR-SC except has special parallel stock dimensions (1-1/2"x1-5/8"x14-3/8") to give low felt recoil; Rhino ported, extended choke tubes; solid barrel spacer; has "TR-Royal" gold engraved on the silvered receiver. Available in 12 gauge (28", 30") 20 and 28 gauge (28" only). Introduced 1999. Imported from Italy by Tristar Sporting Arms, Ltd.
Price: 12, 20, 28 ga. **$1,319.00**

Tristar TR-L "Emilio Rizzini" O/U Shotgun

Similar to the TR-SC except has stock dimensions designed for female shooters (1-1/2" x 3" x 13-1/2"). Standard grade walnut. Introduced 1998. Imported from Italy by Tristar Sporting Arms, Ltd.
Price: **$1,063.00**

TRISTAR TR-I, II "EMILIO RIZZINI" O/U SHOTGUN

Gauge: 12, 20, 3" chambers (TR-I); 12, 16, 20, 28, .410 3" chambers. **Barrel:** 12 ga., 26" (Imp. Cyl. & Mod.), 28" (Mod. & Full); 20 ga., 26" (Imp. Cyl. & Mod.), fixed chokes. **Weight:** 7-1/2 lbs. **Stock:** 1-1/2"x2-3/8"x14-3/8". Walnut with palm swell pistol grip, hand checkering, semi-beavertail forend, black recoil pad. **Features:** Boxlock action with blued finish, Four Locks locking system, gold single selective (inertia) trigger system, automatic safety, extractors. Introduced 1998. Imported from Italy by Tristar Sporting Arms, Ltd.
Price: TR-I **$779.00**
Price: TR-II (automatic ejectors, choke tubes) 12, 16 ga. **$919.00**
Price: 20, 28 ga., .410 . . . . **$969.00**

Tristar TR-Mag "Emilio Rizzini" O/U Shotgun

Similar to TR-I, 3-1/2" chambers; choke tubes; 24" or 28" barrels with three choke tubes; extractors; auto safety. Matte blue finish on all metal, non-reflective wood finish. Introduced 1998. Imported from Italy by Tristar Sporting Arms, Ltd.
Price: **$799.00**
Price: Mossy Oak® Break-Up camo **$969.00**
Price: Mossy Oak® Shadow Grass camo **$969.00**
Price: 10 ga., Mossy Oak® camo patterns **$1,132.10**

SHOTGUNS — OVER/UNDERS

Tristar TR-Mag "Emilio Rizzini"

**Tristar TR-Mag "Emilio Rizzini"
Mossy Oak Shadow Grass Camo**

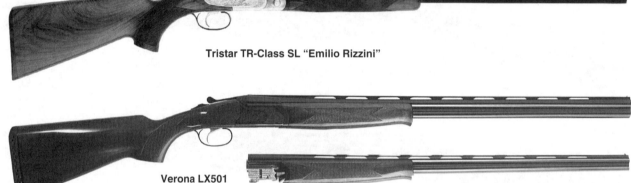

Tristar TR-Class SL "Emilio Rizzini"

**Verona LX501
Hunting Combo**

TRISTAR TR-CLASS SL EMILIO RIZZINI O/U
Gauge: 12, 2-3/4" chambers. **Barrel:** 28", 30". **Weight:** 7-3/4 lbs. **Stock:** Fancy walnut, hand checkering, semi-beavertail forend, black recoil pad, gloss finish. **Features:** Boxlock action with silvered, engraved sideplates; Four Lock locking system; automatic ejectors; hard chrome bores; vent tapered 7mm rib with target-style front bead. hand-fitted gun. Introduced 1999. Imported from Italy by Tristar Sporting Arms, Ltd.
Price: **$1,775.00**

TRISTAR WS/OU 12 SHOTGUN
Gauge: 12, 3-1/2" chambers. **Barrel:** 28" or 30" (imp. cyl., mod., full choke tubes). **Weight:** 6 lbs., 15 oz. **Length:** 46" overall. **Stock:** 14-1/8"x1-1/8"x2-3/8". European walnut with cut checkering, black vented recoil pad, matte finish. **Features:** Boxlock action with single selective trigger, automatic selective ejectors; chrome bores. Matte metal finish. Imported by Tristar Sporting Arms Ltd.
Price: **$645.00**

VERONA LX501 HUNTING O/U SHOTGUNS
Gauge: 12, 20, 28, .410 (2-3/4", 3" chambers). **Barrel:** 28"; 12, 20 ga. have Interchoke tubes, 28 ga. and .410 have fixed Full & Mod. **Weight:** 6-7 lbs. **Stock:** Matte-finished walnut with machine-cut checkering. **Features:** Gold-plated single-selective trigger; ejectors; engraved, blued receiver, non-automatic safety; coil spring-operated firing pins. Introduced 1999. Imported from Italy by B.C. Outdoors.
Price: 12 and 20 ga. **$878.08**
Price: 28 ga. and .410. . . . . **$926.72**
Price: .410 . . . . **$907.01**
Price: Combos 20/28, 28/.410 . . . . **$1,459.20**

Verona LX692 Gold Hunting O/U Shotgun
Similar to Verona LX501 except engraved, silvered receiver with false sideplates showing gold-inlaid bird hunting scenes on three sides; Schnabel forend tip; hand-cut checkering; black rubber butt pad. Available in 12 and 20 gauge only, five InterChoke tubes. Introduced 1999. Imported from Italy by B.C. Outdoors.
Price: **$1,295.00**
Price: LX692G Combo 28/.410. . . . . **$2,192.40**

Verona LX680 Sporting O/U Shotgun
Similar to Verona LX501 except engraved, silvered receiver; ventilated middle rib; beavertail forend; hand-cut checkering; available in 12 or 20 gauge only with 2-3/4" chambers. Introduced 1999. Imported from Italy by B.C. Outdoors.
Price: **$1,159.68**

Verona LX680 Skeet/Sporting/Trap O/U Shotgun
Similar to Verona LX501 except skeet or trap stock dimensions; beavertail forend, palm swell on pistol grip; ventilated center barrel rib. Introduced 1999. Imported from Italy by B.C. Outdoors.
Price: **$1,736.96**

Verona LX692 Gold Sporting O/U Shotgun
Similar to Verona LX680 except false sideplates have gold-inlaid bird hunting scenes on three sides; red high-visibility front sight. Introduced 1999. Imported from Italy by B.C. Outdoors.
Price: Skeet/Sporting **$1,765.12**
Price: Trap (32" barrel, 7-7/8 lbs.) **$1,594.80**

SHOTGUNS — OVER/UNDERS

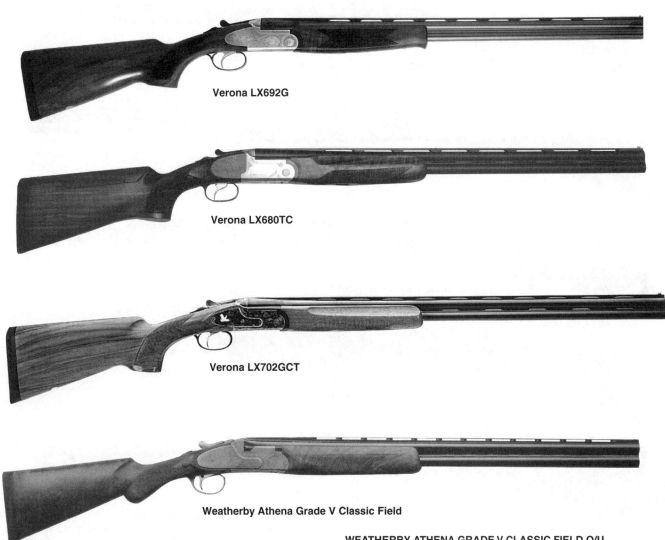

Verona LX692G

Verona LX680TC

Verona LX702GCT

Weatherby Athena Grade V Classic Field

SHOTGUNS

VERONA LX680 COMPETITION TRAP
Gauge: 12. **Barrel:** 30" O/U, 32" single bbl. **Weight:** 8-3/8 lbs. combo, 7 lbs. single. **Stock:** Walnut. **Sights:** White front, mid-rib bead. **Features:** Interchangeable barrels switch from O/U to single configurations. 5 Briley chokes in combo, 4 in single bbl. extended forcing cones, parted barrels 32" with raised rib. By B.C. Outdoors.
Price: Trap Single (LX680TGTSB) **$1,736.96**
Price: Trap Combo (LX680TC) **$2,553.60**

VERONA LX702 GOLD TRAP COMBO
Gauge: 20/28, 2-3/4"chamber. **Barrel:** 30". **Weight:** 7 lbs. **Stock:** Turkish walnut with beavertail forearm. **Sights:** White front bead. **Features:** 2-barrel competition gun. Color case-hardened side plates and receiver with gold inlaid pheasant. Ventilated rib between barrels. 5 interchokes. Imported from Italy by B.C. Outdoors.
Price: Combo **$2,467.84**
Price: 20 ga. **$1,829.12**

Verona LX702 Skeet/Trap O/U Shotgun
Similar to Verona LX702. Both are 12 gauge and 2-3/4" chamber. Skeet has 28" barrel and weighs 7-3/4 lbs. Trap has 32" barrel and weighs 7-7/8 lbs. By B.C. Outdoors.
Price: Skeet **$1,829.12**
Price: Trap. **$1,829.12**

WEATHERBY ATHENA GRADE V CLASSIC FIELD O/U
Gauge: 12, 20, 3" chambers. **Barrel:** 26", 28", IMC Multi-Choke tubes. **Weight:** 12 ga., 7-1/4-8 lbs.; 20 ga. 6-1/2-7-1/4 lbs. **Stock:** Oil-finished American Claro walnut with fine-line checkering, rounded pistol grip and slender forend. **Features:** Old English recoil pad. Sideplate receiver has rose and scroll engraving.
Price: **$3,037.00**

Weatherby Athena Grade III Classic Field O/U
Similar to Athena Grade V, has Grade III Claro walnut with oil finish, rounded pistol grip, slender forend; silver nitride/gray receiver has rose and scroll engraving with gold-overlay upland game scenes. Introduced 1999. Imported from Japan by Weatherby.
Price: 12, 20, 28 ga. **$2,173.00**

CONSULT SHOOTER'S MARKETPLACE
Page 64, This Issue

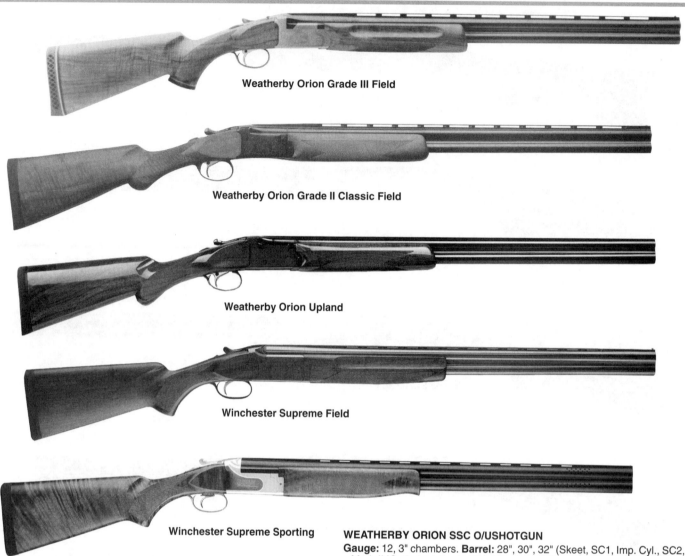

Weatherby Orion Grade III Field

Weatherby Orion Grade II Classic Field

Weatherby Orion Upland

Winchester Supreme Field

Winchester Supreme Sporting

WEATHERBY ORION GRADE III FIELD O/U SHOTGUNS

Gauge: 12, 20, 3" chambers. **Barrel:** 26", 28", IMC Multi-Choke tubes. **Weight:** 6-1/2 to 8 lbs. **Stock:** 14-1/4"x1-1/2"x2-1/2". American walnut, checkered grip and forend. Rubber recoil pad. **Features:** Selective automatic ejectors, single selective inertia trigger. Top tang safety, Greener cross bolt. Has silver-gray receiver with engraving and gold duck/pheasant. Imported from Japan by Weatherby.
Price: Orion III, Field, 12, IMC, 26", 28" **$1,955.00**
Price: Orion III, Field, 20, IMC, 26", 28" **$1,955.00**

Weatherby Orion Grade II Classic Field O/U

Similar to Orion III Classic Field except stock has high-gloss finish, and bird on receiver is not gold. Available in 12 gauge, 26", 28", 30" barrels, 20 gauge, 26" 28", 28 gauge, 26", 2-3/4" chambers. All have IMC choke tubes. Imported from Japan by Weatherby.
Price: **$1,622.00**

Weatherby Orion Upland O/U

Similar to Orion Grade I. Plain blued receiver, gold W on trigger guard; rounded pistol grip, slender forend of Claro walnut with high-gloss finish; black butt pad. Available in 12 and 20 gauge with 26" and 28" barrels. Introduced 1999. Imported from Japan by Weatherby.
Price: **$1,299.00**

WEATHERBY ORION SSC O/U SHOTGUN

Gauge: 12, 3" chambers. **Barrel:** 28", 30", 32" (Skeet, SC1, Imp. Cyl., SC2, Mod. IMC choke tubes). **Weight:** About 8 lbs. **Stock:** 14-3/4"x2-1/4"x1-1/2". Claro walnut with satin oil finish; schnabel forend tip; Sporter-style pistol grip; Pachmayr Decelerator recoil pad. **Features:** Designed for Sporting Clays competition. Has lengthened forcing cones and back-boring; ported barrels with 12mm grooved rib with mid-bead sight; mechanical trigger is adjustable for length of pull. Introduced 1998. Imported from Japan by Weatherby.
Price: SSC (Super Sporting Clays) **$2,059.00**

WINCHESTER SELECT O/U SHOTGUNS

Gauge: 12, 2-3/4", 3" chambers. **Barrel:** 28", 30", Invector Plus choke tubes. **Weight:** 7 lbs. 6 oz. to 7 lbs. 12. oz. **Length:** 45" overall (28" barrel). **Stock:** Checkered walnut stock. **Features:** Chrome-plated chambers; back-bored barrels; tang barrel selector/safety; deep-blued finish. Introduced 2000. From U.S. Repeating Arms. Co.
Price: Select Field (26" or 28" barrel, 6mm ventilated rib) **$1,438.00**
Price: Select Energy **$1,871.00**
Price: Select Eleganza **$2,227.00**
Price: Select Energy Trap **$1,871.00**
Price: Select Energy Trap adjustable **$2,030.00**
Price: Select Energy Sporting adjustable **$2,030.00**

Variety of models for utility and sporting use, including some competitive shooting.

Charles Daly Superior Hunter

Charles Daly Empire Hunter AE-MC

Charles Daly Diamond DL

Charles Daly Diamond Regent DL

ARRIETA SIDELOCK DOUBLE SHOTGUNS
Gauge: 12, 16, 20, 28, .410. **Barrel:** Length and chokes to customer specs. **Weight:** To customer specs. **Stock:** To customer specs. Straight English with checkered butt (standard), or pistol grip. Select European walnut with oil finish. **Features:** Essentially custom gun with myriad options. H&H pattern hand-detachable sidelocks, selective automatic ejectors, double triggers (hinged front) standard. Some have self-opening action. Finish and engraving to customer specs. Imported from Spain by Wingshooting Adventures.

Price: Model 557, auto ejectors, from	**$3,250.00**
Price: Model 570, auto ejectors, from	**$3,950.00**
Price: Model 578, auto ejectors, from	**$4,350.00**
Price: Model 600 Imperial, self-opening, from	**$6,050.00**
Price: Model 601 Imperial Tiro, self-opening, from	**$6,950.00**
Price: Model 801, from	**$9,135.00**
Price: Model 802, from	**$9,135.00**
Price: Model 803, from	**$6,930.00**
Price: Model 871, auto ejectors, from	**$5,060.00**
Price: Model 872, self-opening, from	**$12,375.00**
Price: Model 873, self-opening, from	**$8,200.00**
Price: Model 874, self-opening, from	**$9,250.00**
Price: Model 875, self-opening, from	**$14,900.00**

CHARLES DALY SUPERIOR HUNTER AND SUPERIOR MC DOUBLE SHOTGUN
Gauge: 12, 20, 3" chambers, 28, 2-3/4" chambers. **Barrel:** 28" (Mod. & Full) 26" (Imp. Cyl. & Mod.). **Weight:** About 7 lbs. **Stock:** Checkered walnut pis-tol grip buttstock, splinter forend. **Features:** Silvered, engraved receiver; chrome-lined barrels; gold single trigger; automatic safety; extractors; gold bead front sight. Introduced 1997. Imported from Italy by K.B.I., Inc.
Price: Superior Hunter, 28 gauge and .410 .... **$1,029.00**
Price: Superior Hunter MC 26"-28" **$1,059.00**

Charles Daly Empire Hunter AE-MC Double Shotgun
Similar to Superior Hunter except deluxe wood English-style stock, game scene engraving, automatic ejectors. Introduced 1997. Imported from Italy by K.B.I., Inc.
Price: 12 or 20 .... **$1,349.00**

CHARLES DALY DIAMOND DL DOUBLE SHOTGUN
Gauge: 12, 20, .410, 3" chambers, 28, 2-3/4" chambers. **Barrel:** 28" (Mod. & Full), 26" (Imp. Cyl. & Mod.), 26" (Full & Full, .410). **Weight:** About 5-7 lbs. **Stock:** Select fancy European walnut, English-style butt, beavertail forend; hand-checkered, hand-rubbed oil finish. **Features:** Drop-forged action with gas escape valves; demiblock barrels with concave rib; selective automatic ejectors; hand-detachable double safety sidelocks with hand-engraved rose and scrollwork. Hinged front trigger. Color case-hardened receiver. Introduced 1997. Imported from Spain by K.B.I., Inc.
Price: .... **Special order only**

CHARLES DALY DIAMOND REGENT DL DOUBLE SHOTGUN
Gauge: 12, 20, .410, 3" chambers, 28, 2-3/4" chambers. **Barrel:** 28" (Mod. & Full), 26" (Imp. Cyl. & Mod.), 26" (Full & Full, .410). **Weight:** About 5-7 lbs. **Stock:** Special select fancy European walnut, English-style butt, splinter forend; hand-checkered; hand-rubbed oil finish. **Features:** Drop-forged action with gas escape valves; demiblock barrels of chrome-nickel steel with concave rib; selective automatic-ejectors; hand-detachable, double-safety H&H sidelocks with demi-relief hand engraving; H&H pattern easy-opening feature; hinged trigger; coin finished action. Introduced 1997. Imported from Spain by K.B.I., Inc.
Price: Special Custom Order .... **NA**

CHARLES DALY FIELD II, AE-MC HUNTER DOUBLE SHOTGUN
Gauge: 12, 20, 28, .410 (3" chambers; 28 has 2-3/4"). **Barrel:** 32" (Mod. & Mod.), 28, 30" (Mod. & Full), 26" (Imp. Cyl. & Mod.) .410 (Full & Full). **Weight:** 6 lbs. to 11.4 lbs. **Stock:** Checkered walnut pistol grip and forend. **Features:** Silvered, engraved receiver; gold single selective trigger in 10-, 12, and 20 ga.; double triggers in 28 and .410; automatic safety; extractors; gold bead front sight. Introduced 1997. Imported from Spain by K.B.I., Inc.
Price: 28 ga., .410-bore **$729.00**
Price: 12 or 20 AE-MC **$799.00**

SHOTGUNS

Charles Daly Field Hunter

EAA/Baikal IZH-43 Bounty Hunter

EAA/Baikal MP-213

Fabarm Classic Lion

Fabarm Classic Lion Elite

DAKOTA PREMIER GRADE SHOTGUNS
Gauge: 12, 16, 20, 28, .410. **Barrel:** 27". **Weight:** NA. **Length:** NA. **Stock:** Exhibition-grade English walnut, hand-rubbed oil finish with straight grip and splinter forend. **Features:** French grey finish; 50 percent coverage engraving; double triggers; selective ejectors. Finished to customer specifications. Made in U.S. by Dakota Arms.
Price: 12, 16, 20 gauge $13,950.00
Price: 28 gauge and .410 . . . . $15,345.00

Dakota Legend Shotgun
Similar to Premier Grade except has special selection English walnut, full-coverage scroll engraving, oak and leather case. Made in U.S. by Dakota Arms.
Price: 12, 16, 20 gauge $18,000.00
Price: 28 gauge and .410 . . . . $19,800.00

EAA BAIKAL BOUNTY HUNTER IZH43K SHOTGUN
Gauge: 12, 3-inch chambers. **Barrel:** 18-1/2", 20", 24", 26", 28", three choke tubes. **Weight:** 7.28 lbs. Overall length: NA. **Stock:** Walnut, checkered forearm and grip. **Features:** Machined receiver; hammer-forged barrels with chrome-line bores; external hammers; double triggers (single, selective trigger available); rifle barrel inserts optional. Imported by European American Armory.
Price: . . . .$379.00 to 399.00

EAA BAIKAL IZH43 BOUNTY HUNTER SHOTGUN
Gauge: 12, 3-inch chambers.**Barrel:** 20", 24", 26", 28"; imp., mod. and full choke tubes. **Stock:** Hardwood or walnut; checkered forend and grip.

Features: Hammer forged barrel; internal hammers; extractors; engraved receiver; automatic tang safety; non-glare rib. Imported by European American Armory.
Price: IZH-43 Bounty Hunter (12 gauge, 2-3/4" chambers, 20" brl.,
dbl. triggers, hardwood stock) **$329.00**
Price: IZH-43 Bounty Hunter (20 gauge, 3" chambers,
20" bbl., dbl. triggers, walnut stock) **$359.00**

E.M.F. HARTFORD MODEL COWBOY SHOTGUN
Gauge: 12. **Barrel:** 20". **Weight:** NA. **Length:** NA. **Stock:** Checkered walnut. **Sights:** Center bead. **Features:** Exposed hammers; color-case hardened receiver; blued barrel. Introduced 2001. Imported from Spain by E.M.F. Co. Inc.
Price: **$625.00**

FABARM CLASSIC LION DOUBLE SHOTGUN
Gauge: 12, 3" chambers. **Barrel:** 26", 28", 30" (Cyl., Imp. Cyl., Mod., Imp. Mod., Full choke tubes). **Weight:** 7.2 lbs. **Length:** 44.5"-48.5. **Stock:** English-style or pistol grip oil-finished European walnut. **Features:** Boxlock action with double triggers, automatic ejectors, automatic safety. Introduced 1998. Imported from Italy by Heckler & Koch, Inc.
Price: Grade I $1,499.00
Price: Grade II $2,099.00
Price: Elite (color-case hardened type finish, 44.5") $1,689.00

A.H. Fox DE Grade

Garbi Model 100

Bill Hanus Birdgun

FOX, A.H., SIDE-BY-SIDE SHOTGUNS

Gauge: 16, 20, 28, .410. **Barrel:** Length and chokes to customer specifica-tions. Rust-blued Chromox or Krupp steel. **Weight:** 5-1/2 to 6-3/4 lbs. **Stock:** Dimensions to customer specifications. Hand-checkered Turkish Circassian walnut with hand-rubbed oil finish. Straight, semi or full pistol grip; splinter, schnabel or beavertail forend; traditional pad, hard rubber buttplate or skeleton butt. **Features:** Boxlock action with automatic ejec-tors; double or Fox single selective trigger. Scalloped, rebated and color case-hardened receiver; hand finished and hand-engraved. Grades differ in engraving, inlays, grade of wood, amount of hand finishing. Add $1,500 for 28 or .410-bore. Introduced 1993. Made in U.S. by Connecticut Shot-gun Mfg.

Price: CE Grade	**$11,000.00**
Price: XE Grade	**$12,500.00**
Price: DE Grade	**$15,000.00**
Price: FE Grade	**$20,000.00**
Price: Exhibition Grade	**$30,000.00**
Price: 28/.410 CE Grade	**$12,500.00**
Price: 28/.410 XE Grade	**$14,000.00**
Price: 28/.410 DE Grade	**$16,500.00**
Price: 28/.410 FE Grade	**$21,500.00**
Price: 28/.410 Exhibition Grade	**$30,000.00**

GARBI MODEL 100 DOUBLE

Gauge: 12, 16, 20, 28. **Barrel:** 26", 28", choked to customer specs. **Weight:** 5-1/2 to 7-1/2 lbs. **Stock:** 14-1/2"x2-1/4"x1-1/2". European walnut. Straight grip, checkered butt, classic forend. **Features:** Sidelock action, automatic ejectors, double triggers standard. Color case-hardened action, coin finish optional. Single trigger; beavertail forend, etc. optional. Five other models are available. Imported from Spain by Wm. Larkin Moore.
Price: From **$4,850.00**

Garbi Model 200 Side-by-Side

Similar to the Garbi Model 100 except has heavy-duty locks, magnum proofed. Very fine Continental-style floral and scroll engraving, well fig-ured walnut stock. Other mechanical features remain the same. Imported from Spain by Wm. Larkin Moore.
Price: **$11,200.00**

Garbi Model 101 Side-by-Side

Similar to the Garbi Model 100 except is hand engraved with scroll en-graving, select walnut stock. Better overall quality than the Model 100. Im-ported from Spain by Wm. Larkin Moore.
Price: From **$6,250.00**

Garbi Model 103 A & B Side-by-Side

Similar to the Garbi Model 100 except has Purdey-type fine scroll and ro-sette engraving. Better overall quality than the Model 101. Model 103B has nickel-chrome steel barrels, H&H-type easy opening mechanism; oth-er mechanical details remain the same. Imported from Spain by Wm. Lar-kin Moore.
Price: Model 103A, from **$8,000.00**
Price: Model 103B, from **11,800.00**

HANUS BIRDGUN

Gauge: 16, 20, 28. **Barrel:** 27", 20 and 28 ga.; 28", 16 ga. (Skeet 1 & Skeet 2). **Weight:** 5 lbs., 4 oz. to 6 lbs., 4 oz. **Stock:** 14-3/8"x1-1/2"x2-3/8", with 1/4" cast-off. Select walnut. **Features:** Boxlock action with ejectors; splin-ter forend, straight English grip; checkered butt; English leather-covered handguard and AyA snap caps included. Made by AyA. Introduced 1998. Imported from Spain by Bill Hanus Birdguns.
Price: **$2,495.00**

ITHACA CLASSIC DOUBLES SKEET GRADE SxS

Gauge: 20, 28, 2-3/4" chambers, .410, 3". **Barrel:** 26", 28", 30", fixed chokes. **Weight:** 5 lbs., 14 oz. (20 gauge). **Stock:** 14-1/2"x2-1/4"x1-3/8". High-grade American black walnut, hand-rubbed oil finish; splinter or bea-vertail forend, straight or pistol grip. **Features:** Double triggers, ejectors; color case-hardened, engraved action body with matted top surfaces. In-troduced 1999. Made in U.S. by Ithaca Classic Doubles.
Price: From **$5,999.00**

Ithaca Classic Doubles Grade 4E Classic SxS Shotgun

Gold-plated triggers, jeweled barrel flats and hand-turned locks. Feather crotch and flame-grained black walnut hand-checkered 28 lpi with fleur de lis pattern. Action body engraved with three game scenes and bank note scroll, color case-hardened. Introduced 1999. Made in U.S. by Ithaca Classic Doubles.
Price: From **$7,500.00**

Ithaca Classic Doubles Grade 7E Classic SxS Shotgun

Engraved with bank note scroll and flat 24k gold game scenes: gold setter and gold pointer on opposite action sides, American bald eagle inlaid on bottom plate. Hand-timed, polished, jeweled ejectors and locks. Exhibi-tion grade American black walnut stock and forend with eight-panel fleur de lis borders. Introduced 1999. Made in U.S. by Ithaca Classic Doubles.
Price: From **$11,000.00**

Ithaca Classic Doubles Grade 5E SxS Shotgun

Completely hand-made, it is based on the early Ithaca engraving patterns of master engraver William McGraw. The hand engraving is at 90% cov-erage in deep chiseled floral scroll with game scenes in 24kt gold inlays. Stocks are of high-grade Turkish and American walnut and are hand-checkered. Available in 12, 16, 20, 28 gauges and .410 bore including two barrel combination sets in 16/20 ga. and 28/.410 bore. Introduced 2003. Made in U.S.A. by Ithaca Classic Doubles.
Price: From **$8,500.00**

Merkel Model 47E

Merkel Model 47SL

Merkel Model 280EL/360EL
Two-Barrel Set

Ithaca Classic Doubles Grade 6e Side-by-Side Shotgun

Features hand engraving of fine English scroll coupled with game scenes and 24kt gold inlays. Stockare hand-made of best quality American, Turkish or English walnut with hand checkering. All metal work is finished in traditional bone and charcoal color case hardening and deep rust blue. Available in 12, 16, 20, 28 gauges and .410 bore. Introduced 2003. Made in U.S.A. by Ithaca Classic Doubles.
Price: From **$9,999.00**

Ithaca Classic Doubles Sousa Grade Side-by-Side Shotgun

Presentation grade American black walnut, hand-carved and checkered; hand-engraving with 24-karat gold inlays; tuned action and hand-applied finishes. Made in U.S. by Ithaca Classic Doubles.
Price: From **$18,000.00**

LEBEAU - COURALLY BOXLOCK SIDE-BY-SIDE SHOTGUN

Gauge: 12, 16, 20, 28, .410-bore. **Barrel:** 25" to 32". **Weight:** To customer specifications. **Stock:** French walnut. **Features:** Anson & Deely-type action with automatic ejectors; single or double triggers. Essentially a custom gun built to customer specifications. Imported from Belgium by Wm. Larkin Moore.
Price: From **$25,500.00**

LEBEAU - COURALLY SIDELOCK SIDE-BY-SIDE SHOTGUN

Gauge: 12, 16, 20, 28, .410-bore. **Barrel:** 25" to 32". **Weight:** To customer specifications. **Stock:** Fancy French walnut. **Features:** Holland & Holland-type action with automatic ejectors; single or double triggers. Essentially a custom gun built to customer specifications. Imported from Belgium by Wm. Larkin Moore.
Price: From **$56,000.00**

MERKEL MODEL 47E, 147E SIDE-BY-SIDE SHOTGUNS

Gauge: 12, 3" chambers, 16, 2-3/4" chambers, 20, 3" chambers. **Barrel:** 12, 16 ga.-28"; 20 ga.-26-3/4" (Imp. Cyl. & Mod., Mod. & Full). **Weight:** About 6-3/4 lbs. (12 ga.). **Stock:** Oil-finished walnut; straight English or pistol grip. **Features:** Anson and Deely-type boxlock action with single selective or double triggers, automatic safety, cocking indicators. Color case-hardened receiver with standard Arabesque engraving. Imported from Germany by GSI.
Price: Model 47E (H&H ejectors) **$3,295.00**
Price: Model 147E (as above with ejectors) **$3,995.00**

Merkel Model 47SL, 147SL Side-by-Side Shotguns

Similar to Model 122 except H&H style sidelock action with cocking indicators, ejectors. Silver-grayed receiver and sideplates have Arabesque engraving, engraved border and screws (Model 47S), or fine hunting scene engraving (Model 147S). Imported from Germany by GSI.
Price: Model 47SL **$5,995.00**
Price: Model 147SL **$7,995.00**
Price: Model 247SL (English-style engraving, large scrolls). . . . **$7,995.00**
Price: Model 447SL (English-style engraving, small scrolls) . . . **$9,995.00**

Merkel Model 280EL, 360EL Shotguns

Similar to Model 47E except smaller frame. Greener cross bolt with double under-barrel locking lugs, fine engraved hunting scenes on silver-grayed receiver, luxury-grade wood, Anson and Deely box-lock action. H&H ejectors, single-selective or double triggers. Introduced 2000. From Merkel.
Price: Model 280EL (28 gauge, 28" barrel, imp. cyl. and
mod. chokes) 4 mod. chokes) **$5,795.00**
Price: Model 360EL (.410, 28" barrel, mod. and
full chokes). **$5,795.00**
Price: Model 280/360EL two-barrel set (28 and .410 gauge
as above) **$8,295.00**

Merkel Model 280SL and 360SL Shotguns

Similar to Model 280EL and 360EL except has sidelock action, double triggers, English-style Arabesque engraving. Introduced 2000. From Merkel.
Price: Model 280SL (28 gauge, 28" barrel, imp. cyl. and
mod. chokes) **$8,495.00**
Price: Model 360SL (.410, 28" barrel, mod. and
full chokes) **$8,495.00**
Price: Model 280/360SL two-barrel set **$11,995.00**

PIOTTI KING NO. 1 SIDE-BY-SIDE

Gauge: 12, 16, 20, 28, .410. **Barrel:** 25" to 30" (12 ga.), 25" to 28" (16, 20, 28, .410). To customer specs. Chokes as specified. **Weight:** 6-1/2 lbs. to 8 lbs. (12 ga. to customer specs.). **Stock:** Dimensions to customer specs. Finely figured walnut; straight grip with checkered butt with classic splinter forend and hand-rubbed oil finish standard. Pistol grip, beavertail forend. **Features:** Holland & Holland pattern sidelock action, automatic ejectors. Double trigger; non-selective single trigger optional. Coin finish standard; color case-hardened optional. Top rib; level, file-cut; concave, ventilated optional. Very fine, full coverage scroll engraving with small floral bouquets. Imported from Italy by Wm. Larkin Moore.
Price: From **$29,600.00**

SHOTGUNS

SHOTGUNS — SIDE-BY-SIDES

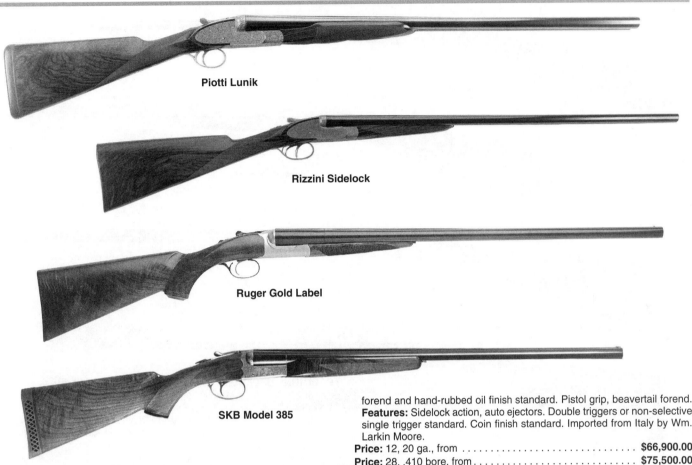

Piotti Lunik

Rizzini Sidelock

Ruger Gold Label

SKB Model 385

Piotti King Extra Side-by-Side
Similar to the Piotti King No. 1 except with upgraded engraving. Choice of any type of engraving, including bulino game scene engraving and game scene engraving with gold inlays. Engraved and signed by a master engraver. Other mechanical specifications remain the same. Imported from Italy by Wm. Larkin Moore.
Price: From **$35,000.00**

Piotti Lunik Side-by-Side
Similar to the Piotti King No. 1 in overall quality. Has Renaissance-style large scroll engraving in relief. Best quality Holland & Holland-pattern sidelock ejector double with chopper lump (demi-bloc) barrels. Other mechanical specifications remain the same. Imported from Italy by Wm. Larkin Moore.
Price: From **$30,900.00**

PIOTTI PIUMA SIDE-BY-SIDE
Gauge: 12, 16, 20, 28, .410. **Barrel:** 25" to 30" (12 ga.), 25" to 28" (16, 20, 28, .410). **Weight:** 5-1/2 to 6-1/4 lbs. (20 ga.). **Stock:** Dimensions to customer specs. Straight grip stock with walnut checkered butt, classic splinter forend, hand-rubbed oil finish are standard; pistol grip, beavertail forend, satin luster finish optional. **Features:** Anson & Deeley boxlock ejector double with chopper lump barrels. Level, file-cut rib, light scroll and rosette engraving, scalloped frame. Double triggers; single non-selective optional. Coin finish standard, color case-hardened optional. Imported from Italy by Wm. Larkin Moore.
Price: From **$14,800.00**

RIZZINI SIDELOCK SIDE-BY-SIDE
Gauge: 12, 16, 20, 28, .410. **Barrel:** 25" to 30" (12, 16, 20 ga.), 25" to 28" (28, .410). To customer specs. Chokes as specified. **Weight:** 6-1/2 lbs. to 8 lbs. (12 ga. to customer specs). **Stock:** Dimensions to customer specs. Finely figured walnut; straight grip with checkered butt with classic splinter

forend and hand-rubbed oil finish standard. Pistol grip, beavertail forend. **Features:** Sidelock action, auto ejectors. Double triggers or non-selective single trigger standard. Coin finish standard. Imported from Italy by Wm. Larkin Moore.
Price: 12, 20 ga., from **$66,900.00**
Price: 28, .410 bore, from **$75,500.00**

RUGER GOLD LABEL SIDE-BY-SIDE SHOTGUN
Gauge: 12, 3" chambers. **Barrel:** 28" with skeet tubes. **Weight:** 6-1/2 lbs. **Length:** 45". **Stock:** American walnut straight or pistol grip. **Sights:** Gold bead front, full length rib, serrated top. **Features:** Spring-assisted break-open, SS trigger, auto eject. 5 interchangeable screw-in choke tubes, combination safety/barrel selector with auto safety reset.
Price: **$1,950.00**

SKB MODEL 385 SIDE-BY-SIDE
Gauge: 12, 20, 3" chambers; 28, 2-3/4" chambers. **Barrel:** 26" (Imp. Cyl., Mod., Skeet choke tubes). **Weight:** 6-3/4 lbs. **Length:** 42-1/2" overall. **Stock:** 14-1/8"x1-1/2"x2-1/2" American walnut with straight or pistol grip stock, semi-beavertail forend. **Features:** Boxlock action. Silver nitrided receiver with engraving; solid barrel rib; single selective trigger, selective automatic ejectors, automatic safety. Introduced 1996. Imported from Japan by G.U. Inc.
Price: **$2,159.00**
Price: Field Set, 20, 28 ga., 26" or 28", English or pistol grip. . . **$3,059.00**

SKB Model 385 Sporting Clays
Similar to the Field Model 385 except 12 gauge only; 28" barrel with choke tubes; raised ventilated rib with metal middle bead and white front. Stock dimensions 14-1/4"x1-7/16"x1-7/8". Introduced 1998. Imported from Japan by G.U. Inc.
Price: **$2,159.00**
Price: Sporting Clays set, 20, 28 ga. **$3,059.00**

SKB Model 485 Side-by-Side
Similar to the Model 385 except has dummy sideplates, raised ventilated rib with metal middle bead and white front, extensive upland game scene engraving, semi-fancy American walnut English or pistol grip stock. Imported from Japan by G.U. Inc.
Price: **$2,769.00**
Price: Field set, 20, 28 ga., 26". **$2,769.00**

SHOTGUNS — SIDE-BY-SIDES

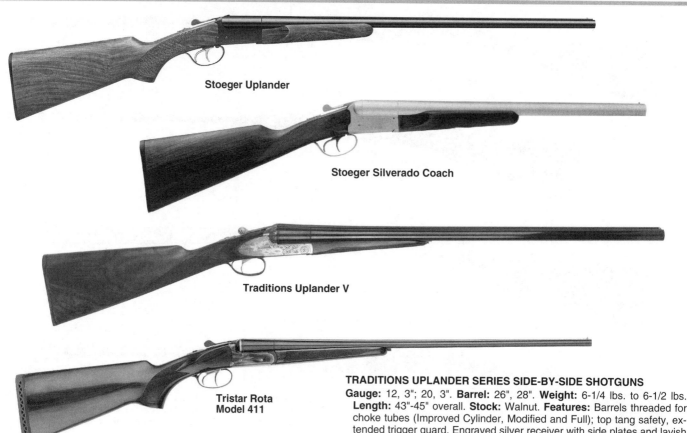

Stoeger Uplander

Stoeger Silverado Coach

Traditions Uplander V

Tristar Rota Model 411

STOEGER UPLANDER SIDE-BY-SIDE SHOTGUN

Gauge: 16, 28, 2-3/4 chambers. 12, 20, .410, 3" chambers. **Barrel:** 26", 28". **Weight:** 7.3 lbs. **Sights:** Brass bead. **Features:** Double trigger, IC, M fixed choke tubes with gun.
Price: . . . . . (With fixed chokes) **$335.00**; (With screw-in chokes) **$350.00**
Price: With English stock . . . . **$335.00 to $350.00**
Price: Upland Special **$375.00**
Price: Upland Supreme with SST, red bar sights **$445.00**
Price: Upland Short Stock (Youth) **$335.00**

STOEGER COACH GUN SIDE-BY-SIDE SHOTGUN

Gauge: 12, 20, .410, 2-3/4", 3" chambers. **Barrel:** 20". **Weight:** 6-1/2 lbs. **Stock:** Brown hardwood, classic beavertail forend. **Sights:** Brass bead. **Features:** IC & M fixed chokes, tang auto safety, auto extractors, black plastic butt plate. 12 ga. and 20 ga. also with English style stock.
Price: . . . . **$320.00**; (Nickel) **$375.00**
Price: Silverado . . . . **$375.00**; (With English stock) **$375.00**

TRADITIONS ELITE SERIES SIDE-BY-SIDE SHOTGUNS

Gauge: 12, 3"; 20, 3"; 28, 2-3/4"; .410, 3". **Barrel:** 26". **Weight:** 5 lbs., 12 oz. to 6-1/2 lbs. **Length:** 43" overall. **Stock:** Walnut. **Features:** Chrome-lined barrels; fixed chokes (Elite Field III ST, Field I DT and Field I ST) or choke tubes (Elite Hunter ST); extractors (Hunter ST and Field I models) or au-tomatic ejectors (Field III ST); top tang safety. Imported from Fausti of Italy by Traditions.
Price: (Elite Field I DT - 12, 20, 28 ga. or .410; I.C. and Mod. fixed chokes [F and F on .410]; double triggers) . . . . **$789.00 to $969.00**
Price: (Elite Field I ST - 12, 20, 28 ga. or .410; same as DT but with single trigger) . . . . **$969.00 to $1,169.00**
Price: (Elite Field III ST - 28 ga. or .410; gold-engraved receiver; high-grade walnut stock) **$2,099.00**
Price: (Elite Hunter ST - 12 or 20 ga.; blued receiver; I.C. and Mod. choke tubes) **$999.00**

TRADITIONS UPLANDER SERIES SIDE-BY-SIDE SHOTGUNS

Gauge: 12, 3"; 20, 3". **Barrel:** 26", 28". **Weight:** 6-1/4 lbs. to 6-1/2 lbs. **Length:** 43"-45" overall. **Stock:** Walnut. **Features:** Barrels threaded for choke tubes (Improved Cylinder, Modified and Full); top tang safety, extended trigger guard. Engraved silver receiver with side plates and lavish gold inlays. From Traditions.
Price: Uplander III Silver 12, 20 ga. **$2,699.00**
Price: Uplander V Silver 12, 20 ga. **$3,199.00**

TRISTAR ROTA MODEL 411 SIDE-BY-SIDE

Gauge: 12, 16, 20, .410, 3" chambers; 28, 2-3/4". **Barrel:** 12 ga., 26", 28"; 16, 20, 28 ga., .410-bore, 26"; 12 and 20 ga. have three choke tubes, 16, 28 (Imp. Cyl. & Mod.), .410 (Mod. & Full) fixed chokes. **Weight:** 6-1/2 to 7-1/4 lbs. **Stock:** 14-3/8" l.o.p. Standard walnut with pistol-style forend; hand checkered. **Features:** Engraved, color case-hardened box-lock action; double triggers, extractors; solid barrel rib. Introduced 1998. Imported from Italy by Tristar Sporting Arms, Ltd.
Price: **$849.00**

Tristar Rota Model 411D Side-by-Side

Similar to Model 411 except automatic ejectors, straight English-style stock, single trigger. Solid barrel rib with matted surface; chrome bores; color case-hardened frame; splinter forend. Introduced 1999. Imported from Italy by Tristar Sporting Arms, Ltd.
Price: **$1,110.00**

Tristar Rota Model 411R Coach Gun Side-by-Side

Similar to Model 411 except in 12 or 20 gauge only with 20" barrels and fixed chokes (Cyl. & Cyl.). Double triggers, extractors, choke tubes. Introduced 1999. Imported from Italy by Tristar Sporting Arms, Ltd.
Price: **$745.00**

Tristar Rota Model 411F Side-by-Side

Similar to Model 411 except silver, engraved receiver, ejectors, IC, M and F choke tubes, English-style stock, single gold trigger, cut checkering. Imported from Italy by Tristar Sporting Arms Ltd.
Price: **$1,608.00**

TRISTAR DERBY CLASSIC SIDE-BY-SIDE

Gauge: 12. **Barrel:** 28" Mod. & Full fixed chokes. **Features:** Sidelock action, engraved, double trigger, auto ejectors, English straight stock. Made in Europe for Tristar Sporting Arms Ltd.
Price: **$1,059.00**

Variety of designs for utility and sporting purposes, as well as for competitive shooting.

Browning BT-99 Trap

EAA/Baikal IZH-18

EAA/Baikal IZH-18Max

H&R 928 Ultra Slug Hunter Deluxe

BERETTA DT10 TRIDENT TRAP TOP SINGLE SHOTGUN
Gauge: 12, 3" chamber. **Barrel:** 34"; five Optima Choke tubes (full, full, imp. modified, mod. and imp. cyl.). **Weight:** 8.8 lbs. **Stock:** High-grade walnut; adjustable. **Features:** Detachable, adjustable trigger group; Optima Bore for improved shot pattern and reduced recoil; slim Optima Choke tubes; raised and thickened receiver for long life. Introduced 2000. Imported from Italy by Beretta USA.
Price: **$8,500.00**

BRNO ZBK 100 SINGLE BARREL SHOTGUN
Gauge: 12 or 20. **Barrel:** 27.5". **Weight:** 5.5 lbs. **Length:** 44" overall. **Stock:** Beech. **Features:** Polished blue finish; sling swivels. Announced 1998. Imported from The Czech Republic by Euro-Imports.
Price: **$185.00**

BROWNING BT-99 TRAP SHOTGUN
Gauge: 12, 2-3/4" chamber. **Barrel:** 32" or 34"; Invector choke system (full choke tube only included); High Post Rib; back-bored. **Weight:** 8 lbs., 10 oz. (34" bbl.). **Length:** 50-1/2" overall (34" bbl.). **Stock:** Conventional or adjustable-comb. **Features:** Re-introduction of the BT-99 Trap Shotgun. Full beavertail forearm; checkered walnut stock; ejector; rubber butt pad. Re-introduced 2001. Imported by Browning.
Price: Conventional stock, 32" or 34" barrel **$1,290.00**
Price: Adj.-comb stock, 32" or 34" barrel **$1,558.00**
Price: Micro (for small-framed shooters). **$1,290.00**

BROWNING GOLDEN CLAYS SHOTGUN
Gauge: 12, 3" chamber. **Barrel:** 32", 34" with Full, Improved Modified, Modified tubes. **Weight:** 8 lbs. 14 oz. to 9 lbs. **Length:** 49" to 51" overall. **Stock:** Adjustable comb; Walnut with high gloss finish; cut checkering. GraCoil recoil reduction system. Imported from Japan by Browning.
Price: 34" bbl. **$3,407.00**
Price: 32" bbl. **$3,407.00**

CHIPMUNK 410 YOUTH SHOTGUN
Gauge: .410. **Barrel:** 18-1/4" tapered, blue. **Weight:** 3.25 lbs. **Length:** 33". **Stock:** Walnut. **Features:** Manually cocking single shot bolt, blued receiver.
Price: **$225.95**

EAA BAIKAL IZH-18 SINGLE BARREL SHOTGUN
Gauge: 12 (2-3/4" and 3" chambers), 20 (2-3/4" and 3"), 16 (2-3/4"), .410 (3"). **Barrel:** 26-1/2", 28-1/2"; modified or full choke (12 and 20 gauge); full only (16 gauge), improved cylinder (20 gauge) and full or improved modified (.410). **Stock:** Walnut-stained hardwood; rubber recoil pad. **Features:** Hammer-forged steel barrel; machined receiver; cross-block safety; cocking lever with external cocking indicator; optional automatic ejector, screw- in chokes and rifle barrel. Imported by European American Armory.
Price: IZH-18 (12, 16, 20 or .410). **$109.00**
Price: IZH-18 (20 gauge w/imp. cyl. or .410 w/imp. mod.). **$109.00**

EAA BAIKAL IZH-18MAX SINGLE BARREL SHOTGUN
Gauge: 12, 3"; 20, 3"; 410, 3". **Barrel:** 24" (.410), 26" (.410 or 20 ga.) or 28" (12 ga.). **Weight:** 6.4 to 6.6 lbs. **Stock:** Walnut. **Features:** Polished nickel receiver; ventilated rib; I.C., Mod. and Full choke tubes; titanium-coated trigger; internal hammer; selectable ejector/extractor; rubber butt pad; decocking system. Imported by European American Armory.
Price: (12 or 20 ga., choke tubes). **$229.00**
Price: (.410, full choke only) **$239.00**
Price: Sporting, 12 ga., ported, Monte Carlo stock **$219.00**

HARRINGTON & RICHARDSON SB2-980 ULTRA SLUG
Gauge: 12, 20, 3" chamber. **Barrel:** 22" (20 ga. Youth) 24", fully rifled. **Weight:** 9 lbs. **Length:** NA. **Stock:** Walnut-stained hardwood. **Sights:** None furnished; comes with scope mount. **Features:** Uses the H&R 10 gauge action with heavy-wall barrel. Monte Carlo stock has sling swivels; comes with black nylon sling. Introduced 1995. Made in U.S. by H&R 1871, LLC.
Price: **$259.00**

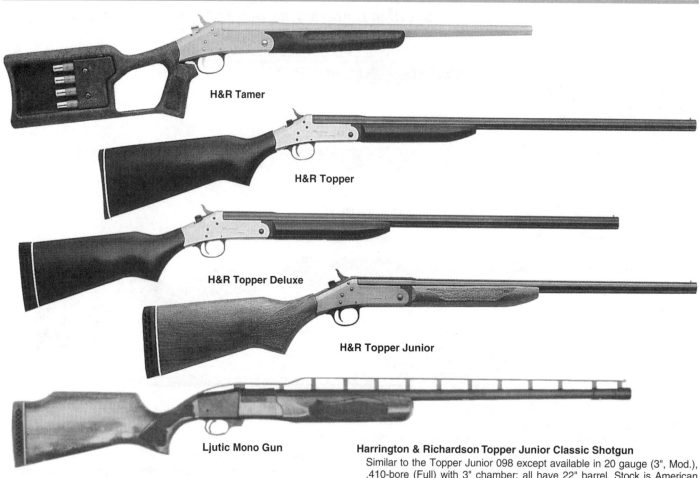

H&R Tamer

H&R Topper

H&R Topper Deluxe

H&R Topper Junior

Ljutic Mono Gun

Harrington & Richardson Topper Junior Classic Shotgun

Harrington & Richardson Model 928 Ultra Slug Hunter Deluxe

Similar to the SB2-980 Ultra Slug except uses 12 gauge action and 12 gauge barrel blank bored to 20 gauge, then fully rifled with 1:28" twist. Has hand-checkered camo laminate Monte Carlo stock and forend. Comes with Weaver-style scope base, offset hammer extension, ventilat-ed recoil pad, sling swivels and nylon sling. Introduced 1997. Made in U.S. by H&R 1871 LLC.

Price: **$315.00**

HARRINGTON & RICHARDSON TAMER SHOTGUN

Gauge: .410, 3" chamber. **Barrel:** 20" (Full). **Weight:** 5-6 lbs. **Length:** 33" overall. **Stock:** Thumbhole grip of high density black polymer. **Features:** Uses H&R Topper action with matte electroless nickel finish. Stock holds four spare shotshells. Introduced 1994. From H&R 1871, LLC.

Price: **$164.00**

HARRINGTON & RICHARDSON TOPPER MODEL 098

Gauge: 12, 16, 20, 28 (2-3/4"), .410, 3" chamber. **Barrel:** 12 ga.-28" (Mod.); 16 ga.- 28" (Full.); 20 ga.-26" (Mod.); 28 ga.-26" (Mod.); .410 bore- 26" (Full). **Weight:** 5-6 lbs. **Stock:** Black-finish hardwood with full pistol grip; semi-beavertail forend. **Sights:** Gold bead front. **Features:** Break-open action with side-lever release, automatic ejector. Satin nickel frame, blued barrel. Reintroduced 1992. From H&R 1871, LLC.

Price: **$145.00**
Price: Topper Junior 098 (as above except 22" barrel, 20 ga. (Mod.), .410-bore (Full), 12-1/2" length of pull) **$152.00**

Harrington & Richardson Topper Deluxe Model 098

Similar to the standard Topper 098 except 12 gauge only with 3-1/2" chamber, 28" barrel with choke tube (comes with Mod. tube, others optional). Satin nickel frame, blued barrel, black-finished wood. Introduced 1992. From H&R 1871, LLC.

Price: **$169.00**

Harrington & Richardson Topper Junior Classic Shotgun

Similar to the Topper Junior 098 except available in 20 gauge (3", Mod.), .410-bore (Full) with 3" chamber; all have 22" barrel. Stock is American black walnut with cut-checkered pistol grip and forend. Ventilated rubber recoil pad. Blued barrel, blued frame. Introduced 1992. From H&R 1871, LLC.

Price: **$184.00**

Ithaca Classic Doubles Knickerbocker Trap Gun

A reissue of the famous Ithaca Knickerbocker Trap Gun. Built on a custom basis only. Introduced 2003. Made in U.S.A. by Ithaca Classic Doubles.

Price: From **$9,000.00**

KRIEGHOFF K-80 SINGLE BARREL TRAP GUN

Gauge: 12, 2-3/4" chamber. **Barrel:** 32" or 34" Unsingle. Fixed Full or choke tubes. **Weight:** About 8-3/4 lbs. **Stock:** Four stock dimensions or adjustable stock available. All hand-checkered European walnut. **Features:** Satin nickel finish. Selective mechanical trigger adjustable for finger position. Tapered step vent. rib. Adjustable point of impact.

Price: Standard grade full Unsingle, from **$7,950.00**

KRIEGHOFF KX-5 TRAP GUN

Gauge: 12, 2-3/4" chamber. **Barrel:** 34"; choke tubes. **Weight:** About 8-1/2 lbs. **Stock:** Factory adjustable stock. European walnut. **Features:** Ventilated tapered step rib. Adjustable position trigger, optional release trigger. Fully adjustable rib. Satin gray electroless nickel receiver. Fitted aluminum case. Imported from Germany by Krieghoff International, Inc.

Price: **$4,200.00**

LJUTIC MONO GUN SINGLE BARREL

Gauge: 12 only. **Barrel:** 34", choked to customer specs; hollow-milled rib, 35-1/2" sight plane. **Weight:** Approx. 9 lbs. **Stock:** To customer specs. Oil finish, hand checkered. **Features:** Totally custom made. Pull or release trigger; removable trigger guard contains trigger and hammer mechanism; Ljutic pushbutton opener on front of trigger guard. From Ljutic Industries.

Price: Std., med. or Olympic rib, custom bbls., fixed choke..... **$5,795.00**
Price: As above with screw-in choke barrel **$6,095.00**
Price: Stainless steel mono gun **$6,795.00**

Mossberg SSi One

New England Firearms Camo Turkey

New England Firearms Tracker II

New England Firearms Special Purpose

Ljutic LTX Pro 3 Deluxe Mono Gun
Deluxe, lightweight version of the Mono Gun with high quality wood, up-grade checkering, special rib height, screw-in chokes, ported and cased.
Price: $8,995.00
Price: Stainless steel model **$9,995.00**

MOSSBERG SSi-ONE 12 GAUGE SLUG SHOTGUN
Gauge: 12, 3" chamber. **Barrel:** 24", fully rifled. **Weight:** 8 pounds. **Length:** 40" overall. **Stock:** Walnut, fluted and cut checkered; sling-swivel studs; drilled and tapped for scope base. **Sights:** None (scope base supplied). **Features:** Frame accepts interchangeable rifle barrels (see Mossberg SSi-One rifle listing); lever-opening, break-action design; ambidextrous, top-tang safety; internal eject/extract selector. Introduced 2000. From Mossberg.
Price: **$480.00**

Mossberg SSi-One Turkey Shotgun
Similar to SSi-One 12 gauge Slug Shotgun, but chambered for 12 ga., 3-1/2" loads. Includes Accu-Mag Turkey Tube. Introduced 2001. From Mossberg.
Price: **$459.00**

NEW ENGLAND FIREARMS CAMO TURKEY SHOTGUNS
Gauge: 10, 3-1/2"; 12, 20, 3" chamber. **Barrel:** 24"; extra-full, screw-in choke tube (10 ga.); fixed full choke (12, 20). **Weight:** NA. **Stock:** American hardwood, green and black camouflage finish with sling swivels and ventilated recoil pad. **Sights:** Bead front. **Features:** Matte metal finish; stock counterweight to reduce recoil; patented transfer bar system for hammer-down safety; includes camo sling and trigger lock. Accepts other factory-fitted barrels. Introduced 2000. From New England Firearms.
Price: . . . . 10 ga. **$278.00**; 12 ga., **$189.00**
Price: 20 ga. youth model (22" bbl.) **$189.00**

NEW ENGLAND FIREARMS TRACKER II SLUG GUN
Gauge: 12, 20, 3" chamber. **Barrel:** 24" (Cyl.), rifle bore. **Weight:** 5-1/4 lbs. **Length:** 40" overall. **Stock:** Walnut-finished hardwood with full pistol grip, recoil pad. **Sights:** Blade front, fully adjustable rifle-type rear. **Features:** Break-open action with side-lever release; blued barrel, color case-hardened frame. Introduced 1992. From New England Firearms.
Price: Tracker II **$187.00**

NEW ENGLAND FIREARMS SPECIAL PURPOSE SHOTGUNS
Gauge: 10, 3-1/2" chamber. **Barrel:** 28" (Full), 32" (Mod.). **Weight:** 9.5 lbs. **Length:** 44" overall (28" barrel). **Stock:** American hardwood with walnut or matte camo finish; ventilated rubber recoil pad. **Sights:** Bead front. **Features:** Break-open action with side-lever release; ejector. Matte finish on metal. Introduced 1992. From New England Firearms.
Price: Walnut-finish wood sling and swivels **$215.00**
Price: Camo finish, sling and swivels **$278.00**
Price: Camo finish, 32", sling and swivels **$272.00**
Price: Black matte finish, 24", Turkey Full choke tube,
sling and swivels **$251.00**

NEW ENGLAND FIREARMS SURVIVOR
Gauge: .410/45 Colt, 3" chamber. **Barrel:** 22" (Mod.); 20" (.410/45 Colt, rifled barrel, choke tube). **Weight:** 6 lbs. **Length:** 36 overall. **Stock:** Black polymer with thumbhole/pistol grip, sling swivels; beavertail forend. **Sights:** Bead front. **Features:** Buttplate removes to expose storage for extra ammunition; forend also holds extra ammunition. Black or nickel finish. Introduced 1993. From New England Firearms.
Price: .410/45 Colt, black **$203.00**
Price: .410/45 Colt, nickel **$221.00**

SHOTGUNS

New England Firearms Survivor

New England Firearms Standard Pardner

Rossi Single-Shot

Rossi Matched Pair

Ruger KTS-1234-BRE

NEW ENGLAND FIREARMS STANDARD PARDNER

Gauge: 12, 20, .410, 3" chamber; 16, 28, 2-3/4" chamber. **Barrel:** 12 ga.-28" (Full, Mod.), 32" (Full); 16 ga.-28" (Full), 32" (Full); 20 ga.-26" (Full, Mod.); 28 ga.-26" (Mod.); .410-bore-26" (Full). **Weight:** 5-6 lbs. **Length:** 43" overall (28" barrel). **Stock:** Walnut-finished hardwood with full pistol grip. **Sights:** Bead front. **Features:** Transfer bar ignition; break-open action with side-lever release. Introduced 1987. From New England Firearms.
Price: **$132.00**
Price: Youth model (12, 20, 28 ga., .410, 22" barrel, recoil pad). . **$141.00**

CONSULT

SHOOTER'S MARKETPLACE

Page 64, This Issue

ROSSI SINGLE-SHOT SHOTGUN

Gauge: 12, 20, 2-3/4" chamber; .410, 3" chamber. **Barrel:** 28" full, 22" Youth. **Weight:** 5 lbs. **Stock:** Stained hardwood. **Sights:** Bead. **Features:** Break-open, positive ejection, internal transfer bar, trigger block.
Price: **$101.00**

ROSSI MATCHED PAIR SINGLE-SHOT SHOTGUN/RIFLE

Gauge: .410, 20 or 12. **Barrel:** 22" (18.5" Youth), 28" (23"full). **Weight:** 4-6 lbs **Stock:** Hardwood (brown or black finish). **Sights:** Bead front. **Features:** Break-open internal transfer bar manual external safety; blued or stainless steel finish; sling-swivel studs; includes matched 22 LR or 22 Mag. barrel with fully adjustable front and rear sight. Trigger block system. Introduced 2001. Imported by BrazTech/Taurus.
Price: Blue **$139.95**
Price: Stainless steel **$169.95**

RUGER KTS-1234-BRE TRAP MODEL SINGLE-BARREL SHOTGUN

Gauge: 12, 2-3/4" chamber. **Barrel:** 34". **Weight:** 9 lbs. **Length:** 50-1/2" overall. **Stock:** Select walnut checkered; adjustable pull length 13"-15". **Features:** Fully adjustable rib for pattern position; adjustable stock comb cast for right- or left-handed shooters; straight grooves the length of barrel to keep wad from rotating for pattern improvement. Full and modified choke tubes supplied. Gold inlaid eagle and Ruger name on receiver. Introduced 2000. From Sturm Ruger & Co.
Price: **$2,850.00**

Savage 210F Master Shot Slug Warrior

Stoeger Single-Shot

Tar-Hunt RSG-20 Mountaineer

Thompson/Center Encore Rifled Slug

Thompson/Center Encore Turkey

SAVAGE MODEL 210F SLUG WARRIOR

Gauge: 12, 3" chamber; 2-shot magazine. **Barrel:** 24" 1:35" rifling twist. **Weight:** 7-1/2 lbs. **Length:** 43.5" overall. **Stock:** Glass-filled polymer with positive checkering. **Features:** Based on the Savage Model 110 action; 60 bolt lift; controlled round feed; comes with scope mount. Introduced 1996. Made in U.S. by Savage Arms.

Price: **$458.00**
Price: (Camo) **$495.00**

STOEGER SINGLE-SHOT SHOTGUN

Gauge: 12, 20, .410, 2-3/4", 3" chambers. **Barrel:** 26", 28". **Weight:** 5.4 lbs. **gth:** 40-1/2" to 42-1/2" overall. **Sights:** Brass bead. **Features:** .410, full fixed choke tubes, rest M, screw-in. .410 12 ga. hardwood pistol-grip stock and forend. 20 ga. 26" bbl., hardwood forend.

Price: Blue; Youth **$109.00**
Price: Youth with English stock **$119.00**

TAR-HUNT RSG-12 PROFESSIONAL RIFLED SLUG GUN

Gauge: 12, 16 & 20, 2-3/4" or 3" chamber, 1-shot magazine. **Barrel:** 23", fully rifled with muzzle brake. **Weight:** 7-3/4 lbs. **Length:** 41-1/2" overall. **Stock:** Matte black McMillan fiberglass with Pachmayr Decelera-tor pad. **Sights:** None furnished; comes with Leupold windage or Weaver bases. **Features:** Uses rifle-style action with two locking lugs; two-position safety; Shaw barrel; single-stage, trigger; muzzle brake. Many options available. Right- and left-hand models at same prices. Introduced 1991. Made in U.S. by Tar-Hunt Custom Rifles, Inc.

Price: 12 ga. Professional model, right- or left-hand;
Elite 16 ga. **$2,395.00**
Price: Millennium/10th Anniversary models (limited to 25 guns):
NP-3 nickel/Teflon metal finish, black McMillan
Fibergrain stock, Jewell adj. trigger. **$2,300.00**

Tar-Hunt RSG-20 Mountaineer Slug Gun

Similar to the RSG-12 Professional except chambered for 20 gauge (3" shells); 23" Shaw rifled barrel, with muzzle brake; two-lug bolt; one- shot blind magazine; matte black finish; McMillan fiberglass stock with Pach-mayr Decelerator pad; receiver drilled and tapped for Rem. 700 bases. Weighs 6-1/2 lbs. Introduced 1997. Made in U.S. by Tar-Hunt Cus-tom Ri-fles, Inc.

Price: **$2,395.00**

THOMPSON/CENTER ENCORE RIFLED SLUG GUN

Gauge: 20, 3" chamber. **Barrel:** 26", fully rifled. **Weight:** About 7 pounds. **Length:** 40-1/2" overall. **Stock:** Walnut with walnut forearm. **Sights:** Steel, click-adjustable rear and ramp-style front, both with fiber optics. **Features:** Encore system features a variety of rifle, shotgun and muzzle-loading rifle barrels interchangeable with the same frame. Break-open de-sign operates by pulling up and back on trigger guard spur. Composite stock and forearm available. Introduced 2000.

Price: **$665.00**

THOMPSON/CENTER ENCORE TURKEY GUN

Gauge: 12 ga. **Barrel:** 24". **Features:** All-camo finish, high definition Real-tree Hardwoods HD camo.

Price: **$740.00**

Designs for utility, suitable for and adaptable to competitions and other sporting purposes.

Benelli M3 Convertible

Benelli M1 Tactical

Benelli M1 Practical

Fabarm Tactical

BENELLI M3 CONVERTIBLE SHOTGUN

Gauge: 12, 2-3/4", 3" chambers, 5-shot magazine. **Barrel:** 19-3/4" (Cyl.). **Weight:** 7 lbs., 4oz. **Length:** 41" overall. **Stock:** High-impact polymer with sling loop in side of butt; rubberized pistol grip on stock. **Sights:** Open rifle, fully adjustable. Ghost ring and rifle type. **Features:** Combination pump/auto action. Alloy receiver with inertia recoil rotating locking lug bolt; matte finish; automatic shell release lever. Introduced 1989. Imported by Benelli USA. Price with pistol grip, open rifle sights.

Price: With standard stock, open rifle sights **$1,135.00**
Price: With ghost ring sight system, standard stock **$1,185.00**
Price: With ghost ring sights, pistol grip stock. **$1,200.00**

BENELLI M1 TACTICAL SHOTGUN

Gauge: 12, 2-3/4", 3" chambers, 5-shot magazine. **Barrel:** 18.5" IC, M, F choke tubes. **Weight:** 6.7 lbs. **Length:** 39.75" overall. **Stock:** Black polymer. **Sights:** Rifle type with ghost ring system, tritium night sights optional. **Features:** Semi-auto intertia recoil action. Cross-bolt safety; bolt release button; matte-finish metal. Introduced 1993. Imported from Italy by Benelli USA.

Price: With rifle sights, standard stock **$945.00**
Price: With ghost ring rifle sights, standard stock **$1,015.00**
Price: With ghost ring sights, pistol grip stock. **$1,030.00**
Price: With rifle sights, pistol grip stock. **$960.00**
Price: MI Entry, 14" barrel (law enforcement only) . . **$980.00 to $1,060.00**

Benelli M1 Practical

Similar to M1 Field Shotgun, Picatinny receiver rail for scope mounting, nine-round magazine, 26" compensated barrel and ghost ring sights. Designed for IPSC competition.

Price: **$1,265.00**

CROSSFIRE SHOTGUN/RIFLE

Gauge/Caliber: 12, 2-3/4" Chamber: 4-shot/223 Rem. (5-shot). **Barrel:** 20" (shotgun), 18" (rifle). **Weight:** About 8.6 lbs. **Length:** 40" overall. **Stock:** Composite. **Sights:** Meprolight night sights. Integral Weaver-style scope rail. **Features:** Combination pump-action shotgun, rifle; single selector, single trigger; dual action bars for both upper and lower actions; ambidextrous selector and safety. Introduced 1997. Made in U.S. From Hesco.

Price: About **$1,895.00**
Price: With camo finish **$1,995.00**

FABARM TACTICAL SEMI-AUTOMATIC SHOTGUN

Gauge: 12, 3" chamber. **Barrel:** 20". **Weight:** 6.6 lbs. **Length:** 41.2" overall. **Stock:** Polymer or folding. **Sights:** Ghost ring (tritium night sights optional). **Features:** Gas operated; matte receiver; twin forged action bars; over-sized bolt handle and safety button; Picatinny rail; includes cylinder bore choke tube. New features include polymer pistol grip stock. Introduced 2001. Imported from Italy by Heckler & Koch Inc.

Price: **$999.00**

Fabarm FP6

Mossberg Model 500 Persuader

Mossberg Model 500 Persuader

Mossberg Ghost Ring

Mossberg Model HS410

FABARM FP6 PUMP SHOTGUN

Gauge: 12, 3" chamber. **Barrel:** 20" (Cyl.); accepts choke tubes. **Weight:** 6.6 lbs. **Length:** 41.25" overall. **Stock:** Black polymer with textured grip, grooved slide handle. **Sights:** Blade front. **Features:** Twin action bars; anodized finish; free carrier for smooth reloading. Introduced 1998. New features include ghost-ring sighting system, low profile Picatinny rail, and pistol grip stock. Imported from Italy by Heckler & Koch, Inc.
Price: (Carbon fiber finish) **$499.00**
Price: With flip-up front sight, Picatinny rail with rear sight, oversize safety button **$499.00**

MOSSBERG MODEL 500 PERSUADER SECURITY SHOTGUNS

Gauge: 12, 20, .410, 3" chamber. **Barrel:** 18-1/2", 20" (Cyl.). **Weight:** 7 lbs. **Stock:** Walnut-finished hardwood or black synthetic. **Sights:** Metal bead front. **Features:** Available in 6- or 8-shot models. Top-mounted safety, double action slide bars, swivel studs, rubber recoil pad. Blue, Parkerized, Marinecote finishes. Mossberg Cablelock included. From Mossberg.
Price: 12 ga., 18-1/2", blue, wood or synthetic stock, 6-shot **$353.00**
Price: Cruiser, 12 ga., 18-1/2", blue, pistol grip, heat shield. **$357.00**
Price: As above, 20 ga. or .410 bore. **$345.00**

Mossberg Model 500, 590 Mariner Pump

Similar to the Model 500 or 590 Security except all metal parts finished with Marinecote metal finish to resist rust and corrosion. Synthetic field stock; pistol grip kit included. Mossberg Cablelock included.
Price: 6-shot, 18-1/2" barrel **$497.00**
Price: 9-shot, 20" barrel **$513.00**

Mossberg Model 500, 590 Ghost-Ring Shotguns

Similar to the Model 500 Security except has adjustable blade front, adjustable Ghost-Ring rear sight with protective "ears." Model 500 has 18.5" (Cyl.) barrel, 6-shot capacity; Model 590 has 20" (Cyl.) barrel, 9-shot capacity. Both have synthetic field stock. Mossberg Cablelock included. Introduced 1990. From Mossberg.
Price: 500 parkerized **$468.00**
Price: 590 parkerized **$543.00**
Price: 590 parkerized Speedfeed stock **$586.00**

Mossberg Model HS410 Shotgun

Similar to the Model 500 Security pump except chambered for 20 gauge or .410 with 3" chamber; has pistol grip forend, thick recoil pad, muzzle brake and has special spreader choke on the 18.5" barrel. Overall length is 37.5", weight is 6.25 lbs. Blue finish; synthetic field stock. Mossberg Cablelock and video included. Introduced 1990.
Price: HS 410 . . . . **$355.00**

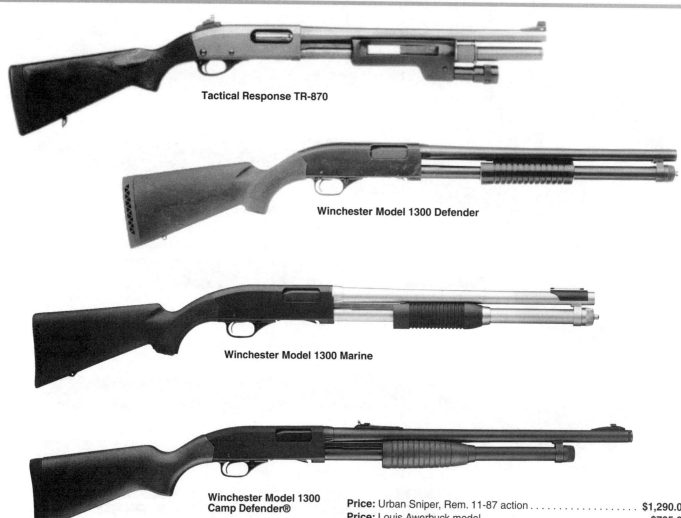

Tactical Response TR-870

Winchester Model 1300 Defender

Winchester Model 1300 Marine

Winchester Model 1300 Camp Defender®

MOSSBERG MODEL 590 SHOTGUN

Gauge: 12, 3" chamber. **Barrel:** 20" (Cyl.). **Weight:** 7-1/4 lbs. **Stock:** Synthetic field or Speedfeed. **Sights:** Metal bead front. **Features:** Top-mounted safety, double slide action bars. Comes with heat shield, bayonet lug, swivel studs, rubber recoil pad. Blue, Parkerized or Marinecote finish. Mossberg Cablelock included. From Mossberg.

Price: Blue, synthetic stock **$417.00**
Price: Parkerized, synthetic stock **$476.00**
Price: Parkerized, Speedfeed stock **$519.00**

TACTICAL RESPONSE TR-870 STANDARD MODEL SHOTGUN

Gauge: 12, 3" chamber, 7-shot magazine. **Barrel:** 18" (Cyl.). **Weight:** 9 lbs. **Length:** 38" overall. **Stock:** Fiberglass-filled polypropolene with non-snag recoil absorbing butt pad. Nylon tactical forend houses flashlight. **Sights:** Trak-Lock ghost ring sight system. Front sight has tritium insert. **Features:** Highly modified Remington 870P with Parkerized finish. Comes with nylon three-way adjustable sling, high visibility non-binding follower, high performance magazine spring, Jumbo Head safety, and Side Saddle extended 6-shot shell carrier on left side of receiver. Introduced 1991. From Scattergun Technologies, Inc.

Price: Standard model **$815.00**
Price: FBI model **$770.00**
Price: Patrol model **$595.00**
Price: Border Patrol model **$605.00**
Price: K-9 model (Rem. 11-87 action) **$995.00**

Price: Urban Sniper, Rem. 11-87 action **$1,290.00**
Price: Louis Awerbuck model **$705.00**
Price: Practical Turkey model **$725.00**
Price: Expert model **$1,350.00**
Price: Professional model **$815.00**
Price: Entry model **$840.00**
Price: Compact model **$635.00**
Price: SWAT model **$1,195.00**

WINCHESTER MODEL 1300 DEFENDER PUMP GUN

Gauge: 12, 20, 3" chamber, 5- or 8-shot capacity. **Barrel:** 18" (Cyl.). **Weight:** 6-3/4 lbs. **Length:** 38-5/8" overall. **Stock:** Walnut-finished hardwood stock and ribbed forend, synthetic or pistol grip. **Sights:** Metal bead front or TRUGLO® fiber-optic. **Features:** Cross-bolt safety, front-locking rotary bolt, twin action slide bars. Black rubber butt pad. From U.S. Repeating Arms Co.

Price: 8-Shot (black synthetic stock, TRUGLO® sight). **$343.00**
Price: 8-Shot Pistol Grip (pistol grip synthetic stock) **$343.00**

Winchester Model 1300 Coastal Pump Gun

Same as the Defender 8-Shot except has bright chrome finish, nickel-plated barrel, bead front sight. Phosphate coated receiver for corrosion resistance.

Price: **$576.00**

Winchester Model 1300 Camp Defender®

Same as the Defender 8-Shot except has hardwood stock and forearm, fully adjustable open sights and 22" barrel with WinChoke® choke tube system (cylinder choke tube included). Weighs 6-7/8 lbs. Introduced 2001. From U.S. Repeating Arms Co.

Price: Camp Defender® **$392.00**

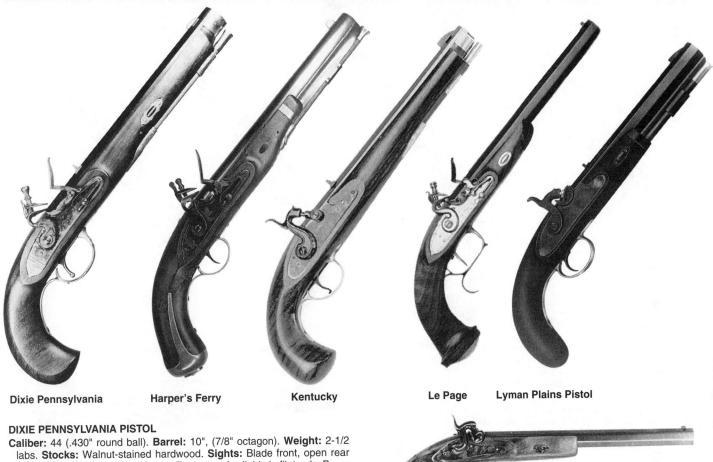

Dixie Pennsylvania   Harper's Ferry   Kentucky   Le Page   Lyman Plains Pistol

Pedersoli Mang

DIXIE PENNSYLVANIA PISTOL
Caliber: 44 (.430" round ball). **Barrel:** 10", (7/8" octagon). **Weight:** 2-1/2 labs. **Stocks:** Walnut-stained hardwood. **Sights:** Blade front, open rear drift-adjustable for windage; brass. **Features:** Available in flint only. Brass trigger guard, thimbles, instep, wedge plates; high-luster blue barrel. Imported from Italy by Dixie Gun Works.
Price: Finished $215.00
Price: Kit $195.00

FRENCH-STYLE DUELING PISTOL
Caliber: 44. **Barrel:** 10". **Weight:** 35 oz. **Length:** 15-3/4" overall. **Stocks:** Carved walnut. **Sights:** Fixed. **Features:** Comes with velvet-lined case and accessories. Imported by Mandall Shooting Supplies.
Price: $295.00

HARPER'S FERRY 1806 PISTOL
Caliber: 58 (.570" round ball). **Barrel:** 10". **Weight:** 40 oz. **Length:** 16" overall. **Stocks:** Walnut. **Sights:** Fixed. **Features:** Case-hardened lock, brass-mounted browned barrel. Replica of the first U.S. Gov't.-made flint-lock pistol. Imported by Navy Arms, Dixie Gun Works.
Price: .... $275.00 to $405.00
Price: Kit (Dixie) $250.00

KENTUCKY FLINTLOCK PISTOL
Caliber: 44, 45. **Barrel:** 10-1/8". **Weight:** 32 oz. **Length:** 15-1/2" overall. **Stocks:** Walnut. **Sights:** Fixed. **Features:** Specifications, including caliber, weight and length may vary with importer. Case-hardened lock, blued barrel; available also as brass barrel flint Model 1821. Imported by Navy Arms, The Armoury, Dixie Gun Works.
Price: $300.00
Price: In kit form, from. .... $90.00 to $112.00
Price: Single cased set (Navy Arms) $360.00
Price: Double cased set (Navy Arms). $590.00

Kentucky Percussion Pistol
Similar to flint version but percussion lock. Imported by The Armoury, Navy Arms, CVA (50-cal.).
Price: .... $129.95 to $225.00

Price: Steel barrel (Armoury) $179.00
Price: Single cased set (Navy Arms) $355.00
Price: Double cased set (Navy Arms). $600.00

LE PAGE PERCUSSION DUELING PISTOL
Caliber: 44. **Barrel:** 10", rifled. **Weight:** 40 oz. **Length:** 16" overall. **Stocks:** Walnut, fluted butt. **Sights:** Blade front, notch rear. **Features:** Double-set triggers. Blued barrel; trigger guard and buttcap are polished silver. Imported by Dixie Gun Works.
Price: $545.00

LYMAN PLAINS PISTOL
Caliber: 50 or 54. **Barrel:** 8"; 1:30" twist, both calibers. **Weight:** 50 oz. **Length:** 15" overall. **Stocks:** Walnut half-stock. **Sights:** Blade front, square notch rear adjustable for windage. **Features:** Polished brass trigger guard and ramrod tip, color case-hardened coil spring lock, spring-loaded trigger, stainless steel nipple, blackened iron furniture. Hooked patent breech, detachable belt hook. Introduced 1981. From Lyman Products.
Price: Finished $244.95
Price: Kit $189.95

PEDERSOLI MANG TARGET PISTOL
Caliber: 38. **Barrel:** 10.5", octagonal; 1:15" twist, **Weight:** 2.5 lbs. **Length:** 17.25" overall. **Stocks:** Walnut with fluted grip. **Sights:** Blade front, open rear adjustable for windage. **Features:** Browned barrel, polished breech plug, rest color case-hardened. Imported from Italy by Dixie Gun Works.
Price: $925.00

BLACKPOWDER

Queen Anne   Thompson/Center Encore   Traditions Pioneer   Traditions William Parker

Traditions Buckhunter Pro

QUEEN ANNE FLINTLOCK PISTOL
Caliber: 50 (.490" round ball). **Barrel:** 7-1/2", smoothbore. **Stocks:** Walnut.
Sights: None. **Features:** Browned steel barrel, fluted brass trigger guard,
brass mask on butt. Lockplate left in the white. Made by Pedersoli in Italy.
Introduced 1983. Imported by Dixie Gun Works.
Price: $275.00
Price: Kit $195.00

THOMPSON/CENTER ENCORE 209x50 MAGNUM PISTOL
Caliber: 50. **Barrel:** 15"; 1:20" twist. **Weight:** About 4 lbs. **Grips:** American
walnut grip and forend. **Sights:** Click-adjustable, steel rear, ramp front.
Features: Uses 209 shotgun primer for closed-breech ignition; accepts
charges up to 110 grains of FFg black powder or two, 50-grain Pyrodex
pellets. Introduced 2000.
Price: $611.00
Price: (barrel only) $325.00

TRADITIONS BUCKHUNTER PRO IN-LINE PISTOL
Caliber: 50. **Barrel:** 9-1/2", round. **Weight:** 48 oz. **Length:** 14" overall.
Stocks: Smooth walnut or black epoxy-coated hardwood grip and forend.
Sights: Beaded blade front, folding adjustable rear. **Features:** Thumb
safety; removable stainless steel breech plug; adjustable trigger, barrel
drilled and tapped for scope mounting. From Traditions.
Price: With walnut grip $229.00
Price: Nickel with black grip $239.00
Price: With walnut grip and 12-1/2" barrel $239.00
Price: Nickel with black grip, muzzle brake and 14-3/4"
fluted barrel. $289.00
Price: 45 cal. nickel w/bl. grip, muzzlebrake and 14-3/4" fluted bbl.
. . . . $289.00

TRADITIONS KENTUCKY PISTOL
Caliber: 50. **Barrel:** 10"; octagon with 7/8" flats; 1:20" twist. **Weight:** 40 oz.
Length: 15" overall. **Stocks:** Stained beech. **Sights:** Blade front, fixed
rear. **Features:** Birds-head grip; brass thimbles; color case-hardened
lock. Percussion only. Introduced 1995. From Traditions.
Price: Finished $139.00
Price: Kit $109.00

TRADITIONS PIONEER PISTOL
Caliber: 45. **Barrel:** 9-5/8"; 13/16" flats, 1:16" twist. **Weight:** 31 oz. **Length:**
15" overall. **Stocks:** Beech. **Sights:** Blade front, fixed rear. **Features:** V-

type mainspring. Single trigger. German silver furniture, blackened hard-
ware. From Traditions.
Price: $139.00
Price: Kit. $119.00

TRADITIONS TRAPPER PISTOL
Caliber: 50. **Barrel:** 9-3/4"; 7/8" flats; 1:20" twist. **Weight:** 2-3/4 lbs.
Length: 16" overall. **Stocks:** Beech. **Sights:** Blade front, adjustable rear.
Features: Double-set triggers; brass buttcap, trigger guard, wedge plate,
forend tip, thimble. From Traditions.
Price: Percussion $189.00
Price: Flintlock $209.00
Price: Kit $149.00

TRADITIONS VEST-POCKET DERRINGER
Caliber: 31. **Barrel:** 2-1/4"; brass. **Weight:** 8 oz. **Length:** 4-3/4" overall.
Stocks: Simulated ivory. **Sights:** Beed front. **Features:** Replica of river-
boat gamblers' derringer; authentic spur trigger. From Traditions.
Price: $109.00

TRADITIONS WILLIAM PARKER PISTOL
Caliber: 50. **Barrel:** 10-3/8"; 15/16" flats; polished steel. **Weight:** 37 oz.
Length: 17-1/2" overall. **Stocks:** Walnut with checkered grip. **Sights:**
Brass blade front, fixed rear. **Features:** Replica dueling pistol with 1:20"
twist, hooked breech. Brass wedge plate, trigger guard, cap guard; sepa-
rate ramrod. Double-set triggers. Polished steel barrel, lock. Imported by
Traditions.
Price: $269.00

BLACKPOWDER REVOLVERS

Army 1860

Baby Dragoon 1848

Dixie Wyatt Earp

Le Mat Revolver

Navy Arms 1836 Paterson

ARMY 1860 PERCUSSION REVOLVER

Caliber: 44, 6-shot. **Barrel:** 8". **Weight:** 40 oz. **Length:** 13-5/8" overall. **Stocks:** Walnut. **Sights:** Fixed. **Features:** Engraved Navy scene on cylinder; brass trigger guard; case-hardened frame, loading lever and hammer. Some importers supply pistol cut for detachable shoulder stock, have accessory stock available. Imported by Cabela's (1860 Lawman), E.M.F., Navy Arms, The Armoury, Cimarron, Dixie Gun Works (half-fluted cylinder, not roll engraved), Euroarms of America (brass or steel model), Armsport, Traditions (brass or steel), Uberti U.S.A. Inc., United States Patent Fire-Arms.

Price: About $195.00
Price: Hartford model, steel frame, German silver trim, cartouches (E.M.F.) $215.00
Price: Single cased set (Navy Arms) $300.00
Price: Double cased set (Navy Arms) $490.00
Price: 1861 Navy: Same as Army except 36-cal., 7-1/2" bbl., weighs 41 oz., cut for shoulder stock; round cylinder (fluted available), from Cabela's, CVA (brass frame, 44-cal.), United States Patent Fire-Arms . . . . $99.95 to $385.00
Price: Steel frame kit (E.M.F., Euroarms) . . . . $125.00 to $216.25
Price: Colt Army Police, fluted cyl., 5-1/2", 36-cal. (Cabela's). . . . $124.95
Price: With nickeled frame, barrel and backstrap, gold-tone fluted cylinder, trigger and hammer, simulated ivory grips (Traditions) $199.00

BABY DRAGOON 1848, 1849 POCKET, WELLS FARGO

Caliber: 31. **Barrel:** 3", 4", 5", 6"; seven-groove; RH twist. **Weight:** About 21 oz. **Stocks:** Varnished walnut. **Sights:** Brass pin front, hammer notch rear. **Features:** No loading lever on Baby Dragoon or Wells Fargo models. Unfluted cylinder with stagecoach holdup scene; cupped cylinder pin; no grease grooves; one safety pin on cylinder and slot in hammer face; straight (flat) mainspring. From Armsport, Cimarron F.A. Co., Dixie Gun Works, Uberti U.S.A. Inc.

Price: 6" barrel, with loading lever (Dixie Gun Works) $275.00
Price: 4" (Uberti USA Inc.) $335.00

CABELA'S 1860 ARMY SNUBNOSE REVOLVER

Caliber: .44. **Barrel:** 3". **Weight:** 2 lbs., 3 oz. **Length:** 9" overall. **Grips:** Hardwood. **Sights:** Blade front, hammer notch near. **Features:** Shortened barrels w/o loading lever. Separate brass loading tool included.

Price: Revolver only $189.99
Price: W/starter kit $289.99

CABELA'S 1862 POLICE SNUBNOSE REVOLVER

Caliber: .36. **Barrel:** 3". **Weight:** 2 lbs., 3 oz. **Length:** 8.5" overall. **Grips:** Hardwood. **Sights:** Blade front, hammer notch rear. **Features:** Shortened barrel, removed loading lever. Separate brass loading tool included.

Price: . . . . $169.99 (revolver only); $209.99 (with starter kit).

DIXIE WYATT EARP REVOLVER

Caliber: 44. **Barrel:** 12", octagon. **Weight:** 46 oz. **Length:** 18" overall. **Stocks:** Two-piece walnut. **Sights:** Fixed. **Features:** Highly polished brass frame, backstrap and trigger guard; blued barrel and cylinder; case-hardened hammer, trigger and loading lever. Navy-size shoulder stock ($45) will fit with minor fitting. From Dixie Gun Works.

Price: $160.00

LE MAT REVOLVER

Caliber: 44/65. **Barrel:** 6-3/4" (revolver); 4-7/8" (single shot). **Weight:** 3 lbs., 7 oz. **Stocks:** Hand-checkered walnut. **Sights:** Post front, hammer notch rear. **Features:** Exact reproduction with all-steel construction; 44-cal. 9-shot cylinder, 65-cal. single barrel; color case-hardened hammer with selector; spur trigger guard; ring at butt; lever-type barrel release. From Navy Arms.

Price: Cavalry model (lanyard ring, spur trigger guard) $595.00
Price: Army model (round trigger guard, pin-type barrel release) $595.00
Price: Naval-style (thumb selector on hammer) $595.00

NAVY ARMS NEW MODEL POCKET REVOLVER

Caliber: 31, 5-shot. **Barrel:** 3-1/2", octagon. **Weight:** 15 oz. **Length:** 7-3/4". **Stocks:** Two-piece walnut. **Sights:** Fixed. **Features:** Replica of the Remington New Model Pocket. Available with polisehd brass frame or nickel plated finish. Introduced 2000. Imported by Navy Arms.

Price: $300.00

NAVY ARMS 1836 PATERSON REVOLVER

Features: Hidden trigger, 36 cal., blued barrel, replica of 5-shooter, roll-engraved with stagecoach hold-up.

Price: . . . . $340.00 to $499.00

BLACKPOWDER REVOLVERS

North American Companion

Navy Arms
1858 Army Percussion

Pocket Police 1862

Rogers & Spencer

Ruger Old Army

NAVY MODEL 1851 PERCUSSION REVOLVER

Caliber: 36, 44, 6-shot. **Barrel:** 7-1/2". **Weight:** 44 oz. **Length:** 13" overall. **Stocks:** Walnut finish. **Sights:** Post front, hammer notch rear. **Features:** Brass backstrap and trigger guard; some have 1st Model squareback trigger guard, engraved cylinder with navy battle scene; case-hardened frame, hammer, loading lever. Imported by The Armoury, Cabela's, Cimarron F.A. Co., Navy Arms, E.M.F., Dixie Gun Works, Euroarms of America, Armsport, CVA (44-cal. only), Traditions (44 only), Uberti U.S.A. Inc., United States Patent Fire-Arms.

Price: Brass frame . . . . $99.95 to $385.00
Price: Steel frame . . . . $130.00 to $285.00
Price: Kit form . . . . $110.00 to $123.95
Price: Engraved model (Dixie Gun Works) $182.50
Price: Single cased set, steel frame (Navy Arms) $280.00
Price: Double cased set, steel frame (Navy Arms) $455.00
Price: Confederate Navy (Cabela's) $89.99
Price: Hartford model, steel frame, German silver trim,
cartouche (E.M.F.) $190.00

NEW MODEL 1858 ARMY PERCUSSION REVOLVER

Caliber: 36 or 44, 6-shot. **Barrel:** 6-1/2" or 8". **Weight:** 38 oz. **Length:** 13-1/2" overall. **Stocks:** Walnut. **Sights:** Blade front, groove-in-frame rear. **Features:** Replica of Remington Model 1858. Also available from some importers as Army Model Belt Revolver in 36-cal., a shortened and light-ened version of the 44. Target Model (Uberti U.S.A. Inc., Navy Arms) has fully adjustable target rear sight, target front, 36 or 44. Imported by Cabe-la's, Cimarron F.A. Co., CVA (as 1858 Army, brass frame, 44 only), Dixie Gun Works, Navy Arms, The Armoury, E.M.F., Euroarms of America (engraved, stainless and plain), Armsport, Traditions (44 only), Uberti U.S.A. Inc.

Price: Steel frame, about . . . . $99.95 to $280.00
Price: Steel frame kit (Euroarms, Navy Arms) . . . . . . $115.95 to $150.00
Price: Single cased set (Navy Arms) $290.00
Price: Double cased set (Navy Arms) $480.00
Price: Stainless steel Model 1858 (Euroarms, Uberti U.S.A. Inc., Cabela's, Navy Arms, Armsport, Traditions) . . . . $169.95 to $380.00
Price: Target Model, adjustable rear sight (Cabela's, Euroarms, Uberti U.S.A. Inc., Stone Mountain Arms) . . . . $95.95 to $399.00
Price: Brass frame (CVA, Cabela's, Traditions, Navy Arms) . . . . $79.95 to $159.95
Price: As above, kit (Dixie Gun Works, Navy Arms) . . $145.00 to $188.95
Price: Buffalo model, 44-cal. (Cabela's) $119.99
Price: Hartford model, steel frame, German silver trim,
cartouche (E.M.F.) $215.00

NORTH AMERICAN COMPANION PERCUSSION REVOLVER

Caliber: 22. **Barrel:** 1-1/8". **Weight:** 5.1 oz. **Length:** 4-5/10" overall. **Stocks:** Laminated wood. **Sights:** Blade front, notch fixed rear. **Features:**

All stainless steel construction. Uses standard #11 percussion caps. Comes with bullets, powder measure, bullet seater, leather clip holster, gun rug. Long Rifle or Magnum frame size. Introduced 1996. Made in U.S. by North American Arms.

Price: Long Rifle frame $156.00

North American Magnum Companion Percussion Revolver

Similar to the Companion except has larger frame. Weighs 7.2 oz., has 1-5/8" barrel, measures 5-7/16" overall. Comes with bullets, powder measure, bullet seater, leather clip holster, gun rag. Introduced 1996. Made in U.S. by North American Arms.

Price: $215.00

POCKET POLICE 1862 PERCUSSION REVOLVER

Caliber: 36, 5-shot. **Barrel:** 4-1/2", 5-1/2", 6-1/2", 7-1/2". **Weight:** 26 oz. **Length:** 12" overall (6-1/2" bbl.). **Stocks:** Walnut. **Sights:** Fixed. **Features:** Round tapered barrel; half-fluted and rebated cylinder; case-hardened frame, loading lever and hammer; silver or brass trigger guard and backstrap. Imported by Dixie Gun Works, Navy Arms (5-1/2" only), Uberti U.S.A. Inc. (5-1/2", 6-1/2" only), United States Patent Fire-Arms and Cimarron F.A. Co.

Price: About . . . . $139.95 to $335.00
Price: Single cased set with accessories (Navy Arms) $365.00
Price: Hartford model, steel frame, German silver trim,
cartouche (E.M.F.) $215.00

ROGERS & SPENCER PERCUSSION REVOLVER

Caliber: 44. **Barrel:** 7-1/2". **Weight:** 47 oz. **Length:** 13-3/4" overall. **Stocks:** Walnut. **Sights:** Cone front, integral groove in frame for rear. **Features:** Accurate reproduction of a Civil War design. Solid frame; extra large nipple cut-out on rear of cylinder; loading lever and cylinder easily removed for cleaning. From Dixie Gun Works, Euroarms of America (standard blue, engraved, burnished, target models), Navy Arms.

Price: . . . . $160.00 to $299.95
Price: Nickel-plated $215.00
Price: Engraved (Euroarms) $287.00
Price: Kit version . . . . $245.00 to $252.00
Price: Target version (Euroarms) . . . . $239.00 to $270.00
Price: Burnished London Gray (Euroarms) . . . . $245.00 to $270.00

BLACKPOWDER REVOLVERS

Spiller & Burr

Texas Paterson

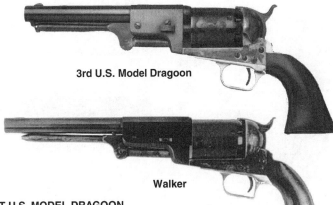

3rd U.S. Model Dragoon

Walker

RUGER OLD ARMY PERCUSSION REVOLVER
Caliber: 45, 6-shot. Uses .457" dia. lead bullets or 454 conical. **Barrel:** 7-1/2" (6-groove; 1:16" twist). **Weight:** 2-7/8 lbs. **Length:** 13-1/2" overall. **Stocks:** Rosewood. **Sights:** Ramp front, rear adjustable for windage and elevation; or fixed (groove). **Features:** Stainless steel; standard size nipples, chrome-moly steel cylinder and frame, same lockwork as original Super Blackhawk. Also stainless steel. Includes hard case and lock. Made in USA. From Sturm, Ruger & Co.
Price: Blued steel, fixed sight (Model BP-5F) $499.00
Price: Stainless steel, fixed sight (Model KBP-5F-I) $576.00
Price: Stainless steel (Model KBP-7) $535.00
Price: Blued steel (Model BP-7) $499.00
Price: Blued steel, fixed sight (BP-7F) $499.00
Price: Stainless steel, fixed sight (KBP-7F) $535.00

SHERIFF MODEL 1851 PERCUSSION REVOLVER
Caliber: 36, 44, 6-shot. **Barrel:** 5". **Weight:** 40 oz. **Length:** 10-1/2" overall. **Stocks:** Walnut. **Sights:** Fixed. **Features:** Brass backstrap and trigger guard; engraved navy scene; case-hardened frame, hammer, loading lever. Imported by E.M.F.
Price: Steel frame $169.95
Price: Brass frame $140.00

SPILLER & BURR REVOLVER
Caliber: 36 (.375" round ball). **Barrel:** 7", octagon. **Weight:** 2-1/2 lbs. **Length:** 12-1/2" overall. **Stocks:** Two-piece walnut. **Sights:** Fixed. **Features:** Reproduction of the C.S.A. revolver. Brass frame and trigger guard. Also available as a kit. From Dixie Gun Works, Navy Arms.
Price: $150.00
Price: Kit form (Dixie) $125.00
Price: Single cased set (Navy Arms) $270.00
Price: Double cased set (Navy Arms). $430.00

TEXAS PATERSON 1836 REVOLVER
Caliber: 36 (.375" round ball). **Barrel:** 7-1/2". **Weight:** 42 oz. **Stocks:** One-piece walnut. **Sights:** Fixed. **Features:** Copy of Sam Colt's first commercially-made revolving pistol. Has no loading lever but comes with loading tool. From Cimarron F.A. Co., Dixie Gun Works, Navy Arms, Uber-ti U.S.A. Inc.
Price: About $495.00
Price: With loading lever (Uberti U.S.A. Inc.) $450.00
Price: Engraved (Navy Arms) $485.00

UBERTI 1861 NAVY PERCUSSION REVOLVER
Caliber: 36. **Barrel:** 7-1/2", round. **Weight:** 40-1/2 oz. **Stocks:** One-piece oiled American walnut. **Sights:** Brass pin front, hammer notch rear. **Features:** Rounded trigger guard, German silver blade front sight, "creeping" loading lever. Available with fluted or round cylinder. Imported by Uberti U.S.A. Inc.
Price: Steel backstrap, trigger guard, cut for stock $265.00

1ST U.S. MODEL DRAGOON
Caliber: 44. **Barrel:** 7-1/2", part round, part octagon. **Weight:** 64 oz. **Stocks:** One-piece walnut. **Sights:** German silver blade front, hammer notch rear. **Features:** First model has oval bolt cuts in cylinder, square- back flared trigger guard, V-type mainspring, short trigger. Ranger and Indian scene roll-engraved on cylinder. Color case-hardened frame, loading lever, plunger and hammer; blue barrel, cylinder, trigger and wedge. Available with old-time charcoal blue or standard blue-black finish. Polished brass backstrap and trigger guard. From Cimarron F.A. Co., Dixie Gun Works, Uberti U.S.A. Inc., Navy Arms.
Price: . . . . **$295.00 to $435.00**

2nd U.S. Model Dragoon Revolver
Similar to the 1st Model except distinguished by rectangular bolt cuts in the cylinder. From Cimarron F.A. Co., Uberti U.S.A. Inc., United States Patent Fire-Arms, Navy Arms, Dixie Gunworks.
Price: . . . . **$295.00 to $435.00**

3rd U.S. Model Dragoon Revolver
Similar to the 2nd Model except for oval trigger guard, long trigger, modifications to the loading lever and latch. Imported by Cimarron F.A. Co., Uberti U.S.A. Inc., United States Patent Fire-Arms, Dixie Gunworks.
Price: Military model (frame cut for shoulder stock, steel backstrap) . . . . **$295.00 to $435.00**
Price: Civilian (brass backstrap, trigger guard) . . . . . . **$295.00 to $325.00**

1862 POCKET NAVY PERCUSSION REVOLVER
Caliber: 36, 5-shot. **Barrel:** 5-1/2", 6-1/2", octagonal, 7-groove, LH twist. **Weight:** 27 oz. (5-1/2" barrel). **Length:** 10-1/2" overall (5-1/2" bbl.). **Stocks:** One-piece varnished walnut. **Sights:** Brass pin front, hammer notch rear. **Features:** Rebated cylinder, hinged loading lever, brass or silver-plated backstrap and trigger guard, color-cased frame, hammer, loading lever, plunger and latch, rest blued. Has original-type markings. From Cimarron F.A. Co., Uberti U.S.A. Inc., Dixie Gunworks.
Price: With brass backstrap, trigger guard . . . . **$260.00 to $310.00**

1861 Navy Percussion Revolver
Similar to Colt 1851 Navy except has round 7-1/2" barrel, rounded trigger guard, German silver blade front sight, "creeping" loading lever. Fluted or round cylinder. Imported by Cimarron F.A. Co., Uberti U.S.A. Inc., Dixie Gunworks.
Price: Steel backstrap, trigger guard, cut for stock . . . **$255.00 to $300.00**

WALKER 1847 PERCUSSION REVOLVER
Caliber: 44, 6-shot. **Barrel:** 9". **Weight:** 84 oz. **Length:** 15-1/2" overall. **Stocks:** Walnut. **Sights:** Fixed. **Features:** Case-hardened frame, loading lever and hammer; iron backstrap; brass trigger guard; engraved cylinder. Imported by Cabela's, Cimarron F.A. Co., Navy Arms, Dixie Gun Works, Uberti U.S.A. Inc., E.M.F., Cimarron, Traditions, United States Patent Fire-Arms.
Price: About . . . . **$225.00 to $445.00**
Price: Single cased set (Navy Arms) $405.00
Price: Deluxe Walker with French fitted case (Navy Arms) $540.00
Price: Hartford model, steel frame, German silver trim, cartouche (E.M.F.) $295.00

Austin & Halleck 420 LR In-Line

Austin & Halleck 320 LR In-Line

Austin & Halleck Mountain

Cabela's Blue Ridge

Cabela's Traditional Hawken

ARMOURY R140 HAWKEN RIFLE

Caliber: 45, 50 or 54. **Barrel:** 29". **Weight:** 8-3/4 to 9 lbs. **Length:** 45-3/4" overall. **Stock:** Walnut, with cheekpiece. **Sights:** Dovetail front, fully adjustable rear. **Features:** Octagon barrel, removable breech plug; double set triggers; blued barrel, brass stock fittings, color case-hardened percussion lock. From Armsport, The Armoury.
Price: .... $225.00 to $245.00

AUSTIN & HALLECK MODEL 420 LR IN-LINE RIFLE

Caliber: 50. **Barrel:** 26", 1" octagon to 3/4" round; 1:28" twist. **Weight:** 7-7/8 lbs. **Length:** 47-1/2" overall. **Stock:** Lightly figured maple in Classic or Monte Carlo style. **Sights:** Ramp front, fully adjustable rear. **Features:** Blue or electroless nickel finish; in-line percussion action with removable weather shroud; Timney adjustable target trigger with sear block safety. Introduced 1998. Made in U.S. by Austin & Halleck.
Price: Blue $549.00
Price: Stainless steel $549.00
Price: Blue, hand-select highly figured stock $709.00
Price: Stainless steel, select stock $739.00

Austin & Halleck Model 320 LR In-Line Rifle

Similar to the Model 420 LR except has black resin synthetic stock with checkered grip and forend. Introduced 1998. Made in U.S. by Austin & Halleck.
Price: Blue $419.00
Price: Stainless steel $449.00

AUSTIN & HALLECK MOUNTAIN RIFLE

Caliber: 50. **Barrel:** 32"; 1:28" or 1:66" twist; 1" flats. **Weight:** 7-1/2 lbs. **Length:** 49" overall. **Stock:** Curly maple. **Sights:** Silver blade front, buckhorn rear. **Features:** Available in percussion or flintlock; double throw adjustable set triggers; rust brown finish. Made in U.S. by Austin & Halleck.
Price: Flintlock, fancy wood $589.00
Price: Flintlock, select wood $769.00
Price: Percussion, fancy wood $539.00
Price: Percussion, select wood $719.00

BOSTONIAN PERCUSSION RIFLE

Caliber: 45. **Barrel:** 30", octagonal. **Weight:** 7-1/4 lbs. **Length:** 46" overall. **Stock:** Walnut. **Sights:** Blade front, fixed notch rear. **Features:** Color case-hardened lock, brass trigger guard, buttplate, patchbox. Imported from Italy by E.M.F.
Price: $285.00

CABELA'S BLUE RIDGE RIFLE

Caliber: 32, 36, 45, 50, .54. **Barrel:** 39", octagonal. **Weight:** About 7-3/4 lbs. **Length:** 55" overall. **Stock:** American black walnut. **Sights:** Blade front, rear drift adjustable for windage. **Features:** Color case-hardened lockplate and cock/hammer, brass trigger guard and buttplate, double set, double-phased triggers. From Cabela's.
Price: Percussion $409.99
Price: Flintlock $519.99

CABELA'S TRADITIONAL HAWKEN

Caliber: 50, 54. **Barrel:** 29". **Weight:** About 9 lbs. **Stock:** Walnut. **Sights:** Blade front, open adjustable rear. **Features:** Flintlock or percussion. Adjustable double-set triggers. Polished brass furniture, color case-hardened lock. Imported by Cabela's.
Price: Percussion, right-hand $269.99
Price: Percussion, left-hand $269.99
Price: Flintlock, right-hand $299.99

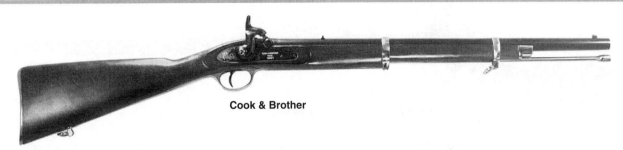

Cook & Brother

Cabela's Sporterized Hawken Hunter Rifle
Similar to the Traditional Hawken except has more modern stock style with rubber recoil pad, blued furniture, sling swivels. Percussion only, in 50- or 54-caliber.
Price: Carbine or rifle, right-hand **$329.99**

CABELA'S KODIAK EXPRESS DOUBLE RIFLE
Caliber: 50, 54, 58, 72. **Barrel:** Length n/a; 1:48" twist. **Weight:** 9.3 lbs. **Length:** 45-1/4" overall. **Stock:** European walnut, oil finish. **Sights:** Fully adjustable double folding-leaf rear, ramp front. **Features:** Percussion. Barrels regulated to point of aim at 75 yards; polished and engraved lock, top tartg and trigger guard. From Cabela's.
Price: 50, 54, 58 calibers **$899.99**
Price: 72 caliber **$929.99**

COOK & BROTHER CONFEDERATE CARBINE
Caliber: 58. **Barrel:** 24". **Weight:** 7-1/2 lbs. **Length:** 40-1/2" overall. **Stock:** Select walnut. **Features:** Recreation of the 1861 New Orleans-made artillery carbine. Color case-hardened lock, browned barrel. Buttplate, trigger guard, barrel bands, sling swivels and nosecap of polished brass. From Euroarms of America.
Price: **$513.00**
Price: Cook & Brother rifle (33" barrel) **$552.00**

KODIAK MAGNUM RIFLE
Caliber: 45, 50. No. 209 primer ignition. **Barrel:** 28"; 1:28" twist. **Stock:** Ambidextrous black or Mossy Oak camo. **Sights:** Fiber optic. **Features:** Blue or nickel finish, recoil pa, lifetime warranty. From CVA.
Price: Mossy Oak camo; nickel barrel. **$329.95**
Price: Mossy Oak camo; blued barrel. **$309.95**
Price: Black stock; nickel barrel **$289.95**
Price: Black stock; blued barrel **$259.95**

CVA BOBCAT RIFLE
Caliber: 50 percussion. **Barrel:** 26"; 1:48" twist, octagonal. **Weight:** 6 lbs. **Length:** 42" overall. **Stock:** Dura-Grip synthetic or wood. **Sights:** Blade front, open rear. **Features:** Oversize trigger guard; wood ramrod; matte black finish. From CVA.
Price: (Wood stock) **$99.95**
Price: (Black synthetic stock) **$69.95**

CVA MOUNTAIN RIFLE
Caliber: 50. **Barrel:** 32"; 1:48" rifling. **Weight:** 8-1/2 lbs. **Length:** NA. **Sights:** Blade front, buckhorn rear. **Features:** Browned steel furniture, patchbox. Made in U.S. From CVA.
Price: **$259.95**

CVA ST. LOUIS HAWKEN RIFLE
Caliber: 50, 54. **Barrel:** 28", octagon; 15/16" across flats; 1:48" twist. **Weight:** 8 lbs. **Length:** 44" overall. **Stock:** Select hardwood. **Sights:** Beaded blade front, fully adjustable open rear. **Features:** Fully adjustable double-set triggers; synthetic ramrod (kits have wood); brass patchbox, wedge plates, nosecap, thimbles, trigger guard and buttplate; blued barrel; color case-hardened, engraved lockplate. V-type mainspring. Button breech. Introduced 1981. From CVA.
Price: St. Louis Hawken, finished (50- , 54-cal.) **$229.95**

CVA FIREBOLT MUSKETMAG BOLT-ACTION IN-LINE RIFLES
Caliber: 45 or 50. **Barrel:** 26". **Weight:** 7 lbs. **Length:** 44". **Stock:** Rubber-coated black or Mossy Oak® Break-Up™ camo synthetic. **Sights:** CVA Il-luminator Fiber Optic Sight System. **Features:** Bolt-action, inline ignition

system handles up to 150 grains blackpowder or Pyrodex; Nickel or matte blue barrel; removable breech plug; trigger-block safety. Three-way ignition system. From CVA.
Price: FiberGrip/nickel, 50 cal. **$294.95**
Price: Breakup/nickel, 50 cal. **$259.95**
Price: FiberGrip/nickel, 45 cal. **$294.95**
Price: Breakup/nickel, 45 cal. **$259.95**
Price: FiberGrip/blue, 50 cal. **$199.95**
Price: Breakup/blue, 50 cal. **$239.95**
Price: FiberGrip/blue, 45 cal. **$199.95**
Price: Breakup/blue, 45 cal. **$239.95**

CVA Hunterbolt209 Magnum Rifle
Similar to the Firebolt except has 26" barrel and black or Mossy Oak® Break-Up™ synthetic stock. Three-way ignition system. Weighs 6 lbs. From CVA.
Price: 45 or 50 cal. . . . . **$179.95 to $234.95**

CVA OPTIMA PRO BREAK-ACTION RIFLE
Caliber: 45, 50. **Barrel:** 29" fluted, blue or nickel. **Weight:** 8.8 lbs. **Stock:** Ambidextrous Mossy Oak camo or black Fiber-Grip. **Sights:** Adj. Fiber Optic. **Features:** Break-action, stainless No. 209 breech plug, aluminum loading rod, cocking spur, lifetime warranty.
Price: Mossy Oak Camo/nickel. **$364.95**
Price: Mossy Oak Camo/blued **$329.95**
Price: Black/nickel. **$309.95**
Price: Black/blued. **$279.95**
Price: Blued fluted bbl. **$94.95**
Price: Nickel fluted bbl. **$109.95**

CVA Optima Magnum Break-Action Rifle
Similar to Optima Pro but with 26" bbl., nickel or blue finish
Price: Mossy Oak Camo/nickel. **$299.95**
Price: Mossy Oak Camo/blue **$279.95**
Price: Black/nickel. **$254.95**
Price: Black/blued. **$224.95**

DIXIE EARLY AMERICAN JAEGER RIFLE
Caliber: 54. **Barrel:** 27-1/2" octagonal; 1.24" twist. **Weight:** 8-1/4 lbs. **Length:** 43-1/2" overall. **Stock:** American walnut; sliding wooden patchbox on on butt. **Sights:** Notch rear, blade front. **Features:** Flintlock or percussion. Browned steel furniture. Imported from Italy by Dixie Gun Works.
Price: Flintlock or percussion **$795.00**

DIXIE DELUXE CUB RIFLE
Caliber: 40. **Barrel:** 28". **Weight:** 6-1/2 lbs. **Stock:** Walnut. **Sights:** Fixed.**Features:** Short rifle for small game and beginning shooters. Brass patchbox and furniture. Flint or percussion. From Dixie Gun Works.
Price: Finished **$450.00**
Price: Kit **$390.00**
Price: Super Cub (50-caliber) **$485.00**

DIXIE 1863 SPRINGFIELD MUSKET
Caliber: 58 (.570" patched ball or .575" Minie). **Barrel:** 50", rifled. **Stock:** Walnut stained. **Sights:** Blade front, adjustable ladder-type rear. **Features:** Bright-finish lock, barrel, furniture. Reproduction of the last of the regulation muzzleloaders. Imported from Japan by Dixie Gun Works.
Price: Finished **$625.00**
Price: Kit **$550.00**

BLACKPOWDER

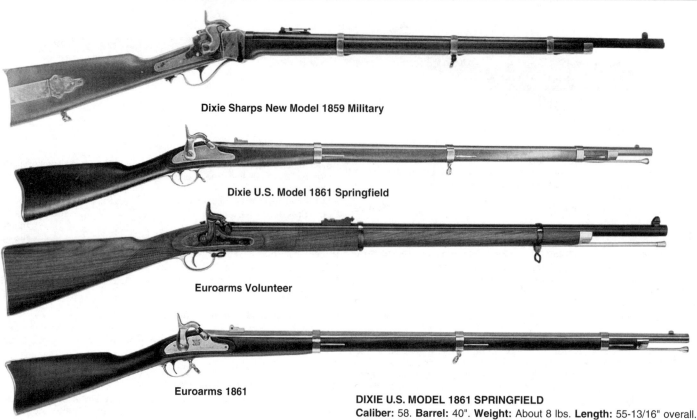

Dixie Sharps New Model 1859 Military

Dixie U.S. Model 1861 Springfield

Euroarms Volunteer

Euroarms 1861

DIXIE INLINE CARBINE
Caliber: 50, 54. **Barrel:** 24"; 1:32" twist. **Weight:** 6.5 lbs. **Length:** 41" overall. **Stock:** Walnut-finished hardwood with Monte Carlo comb. **Sights:** Ramp front with red insert, open fully adjustable rear. **Features:** Sliding "bolt" fully encloses cap and nipple. Fully adjustable trigger, automatic safety. Aluminum ramrod. Imported from Italy by Dixie Gun Works.
Price: **$375.00**

DIXIE PEDERSOLI 1857 MAUSER RIFLE
Caliber: 54. **Barrel:** 39-3/8". **Weight:** N/A. **Length:** 52" overall. **Stock:** European walnut with oil finish, sling swivels. **Sights:** Fully adjustable rear, lug front. **Features:** Percussion (musket caps). Armory bright finish with color case-hardened lock and barrel tang, engraved lockplate, steel ramrod. Introduced 2000. Imported from Italy by Dixie Gun Works.
Price: **$950.00**

DIXIE PEDERSOLI 1766 CHARLEVILLE MUSKET
Caliber: 69. **Barrel:** 44-3/4". **Weight:** 10-1/2 lbs. **Length:** 57-1/2" overall. **Stock:** European walnut with oil finish. **Sights:** Fixed rear, lug front. **Features:** Smoothbore flintlock. Armory bright finish with steel furniture and ramrod. Introduced 2000. Imported from Italy by Dixie Gun Works.
Price: **$895.00**

DIXIE SHARPS NEW MODEL 1859 MILITARY RIFLE
Caliber: 54. **Barrel:** 30", 6-groove; 1:48" twist. **Weight:** 9 lbs. **Length:** 45-1/2" overall. **Stock:** Oiled walnut. **Sights:** Blade front, ladder-style rear. **Features:** Blued barrel, color case-hardened barrel bands, receiver, hammer, nosecap, lever, patchbox cover and buttplate. Introduced 1995. Imported from Italy by Dixie Gun Works.
Price: **$995.00**

DIXIE U.S. MODEL 1816 FLINTLOCK MUSKET
Caliber: 69. **Barrel:** 42", smoothbore. **Weight:** 9.75 lbs. **Length:** 56.5" overall. **Stock:** Walnut with oil finish. **Sights:** Blade front. **Features:** All metal finished "National Armory Bright"; three barrel bands with springs; steel ramrod with button-shaped head. Imported by Dixie Gun Works.
Price: **$875.00**

DIXIE U.S. MODEL 1861 SPRINGFIELD
Caliber: 58. **Barrel:** 40". **Weight:** About 8 lbs. **Length:** 55-13/16" overall. **Stock:** Oil-finished walnut. **Sights:** Blade front, step adjustable rear. **Features:** Exact recreation of original rifle. Sling swivels attached to trigger guard bow and middle barrel band. Lockplate marked "1861" with eagle motif and "U.S. Springfield" in front of hammer; "U.S." stamped on top of buttplate. From Dixie Gun Works.
Price: Kit **$550.00**

E.M.F. 1863 SHARPS MILITARY CARBINE
Caliber: 54. **Barrel:** 22", round. **Weight:** 8 lbs. **Length:** 39" overall. **Stock:** Oiled walnut. **Sights:** Blade front, military ladder-type rear. **Features:** Color case-hardened lock, rest blued. Imported by E.M.F.
Price: **$600.00**

EUROARMS VOLUNTEER TARGET RIFLE
Caliber: .451. **Barrel:** 33" (two-band), 36" (three-band). **Weight:** 11 lbs. (two-band). **Length:** 48.75" overall (two-band). **Stock:** European walnut with checkered wrist and forend. **Sights:** Hooded bead front, adjustable rear with interchangeable leaves. **Features:** Alexander Henry-type rifling with 1:20" twist. Color case-hardened hammer and lockplate, brass trigger guard and nosecap, rest blued. Imported by Euroarms of America, Dixie Gun Works.
Price: Two-band **$795.00**
Price: (Three-band) **$845.00**

EUROARMS 1861 SPRINGFIELD RIFLE
Caliber: 58. **Barrel:** 40". **Weight:** About 10 lbs. **Length:** 55.5" overall. **Stock:** European walnut. **Sights:** Blade front, three-leaf military rear. **Features:** Reproduction of the original three-band rifle. Lockplate marked "1861" with eagle and "U.S. Springfield." Metal left in the white. Imported by Euroarms of America.
Price: **$530.00**

EUROARMS ZOUAVE RIFLE
Caliber: 58 percussion. **Barrel:** 33 inches. **Overall length:** 49 inches.
Price: **$469.00**

EUROARMS HARPERS FERRY RIFLE
Caliber: 54 flintlock. **Barrel:** 35 inches. **Overall length:** 50 1/2 inches.
Price: **$735.00**

BLACKPOWDER

BLACKPOWDER MUSKETS & RIFLES

Gonic Model 93 Thumbhole

Harper's Ferry 1803

J.P. Murray

EUROARMS RICHMOND RIFLE
Caliber: 58 percussion. **Barrel:** 40 inches. **Overall length:** 49 inches.
Price: **$579.00**

GONIC MODEL 93 M/L RIFLE
Caliber: 45, 50. **Barrel:** 26"; 1:24" twist. **Weight:** 6-1/2 to 7 lbs. **Length:** 43" overall. **Stock:** American hardwood with black finish. **Sights:** Adjustable or aperture rear, hooded post front. **Features:** Adjustable trigger with side safety; unbreakable ram rod; comes with A. Z. scope bases installed. Introduced 1993. Made in U.S. by Gonic Arms, Inc.
Price: Model 93 Standard (blued barrel). **$720.00**
Price: Model 93 Standard (stainless brl., 50 cal. only) **$782.00**

Gonic Model 93 Deluxe M/L Rifle
Similar to the Model 93 except has classic-style walnut or gray laminated wood stock. Introduced 1998. Made in U.S. by Gonic Arms, Inc.
Price: Blue barrel, sights, scope base, choice of stock. **$902.00**
Price: Stainless barrel, sights, scope base, choice of stock
(50 cal. only) **$964.00**

Gonic Model 93 Mountain Thumbhole M/L Rifles
Similar to the Model 93 except has high-grade walnut or gray laminate stock with extensive hand-checkered panels, Monte Carlo cheekpiece and beavertail forend; integral muzzle brake. Introduced 1998. Made in U.S. by Gonic Arms, Inc.
Price: Blued or stainless. **$2,700.00**

H&R SIDEKICK
Caliber: 50, 209 primer ignition. **Barrel:** 24 or 26 (magnum). **Weight:** 6 1/2 lbs. **Length:** 39-1/4 to 41-1/4. **Stock:** Black matte polymer or hardwood. **Sights:** Adjustable fiber optic open, tapped for scope mounts. **Features:** Break-action single-shot. Uses No. 209 shotgun primer held in place by special primer carrier. Telescoping brass ramrod. Introduced 2004.
Price: (Wood stock, blued finish, case-hardened frame) . . . . **N/A**
Price: (Stainless, polymer stock) . . . . **N/A**

H&R HUNTSMAN
Caliber: 50, 209 primer ignition. **Barrel:** 24". **Weight:** 6 1/2 lbs. **Length:** 40". **Stock:** Black matte polymer or hardwood. **Sights:** Fiber optic open sights, tapped for scope mounts. **Features:** Break-open action, transfer-bar safety system, breech plug removable for cleaning. Introduced 2004.
Price: Stainless model . . . . **N/A**
Price: Blued finish. . . . . **N/A**
Price: Combo model (12 ga., .50 cal. muzzleloader, .243 Win). . . . . **N/A**

HARPER'S FERRY 1803 FLINTLOCK RIFLE
Caliber: 54 or 58. **Barrel:** 35". **Weight:** 9 lbs. **Length:** 59-1/2" overall. **Stock:** Walnut with cheekpiece. **Sights:** Brass blade front, fixed steel rear. **Features:** Brass trigger guard, sideplate, buttplate; steel patchbox. Imported by Euroarms of America, Navy Arms (54-cal. only), Cabela's, and Dixie Gun Works.
Price: . . . . **$495.95 to $729.00**
Price: 54-cal. (Navy Arms) **$625.00**
Price: 54-caliber (Cabela's) **$599.99**
Price: 54-caliber (Dixie Gun Works) **$795.00**
Price: 54 and 58 caliber (Euroarms). **$575.00**

HAWKEN RIFLE
Caliber: 45, 50, 54 or 58. **Barrel:** 28", blued, 6-groove rifling. **Weight:** 8-3/4 lbs. **Length:** 44" overall. **Stock:** Walnut with cheekpiece. **Sights:** Blade front, fully adjustable rear. **Features:** Coil mainspring, double-set triggers, polished brass furniture. From Armsport and E.M.F.
Price: . . . . **$220.00 to $345.00**

J.P. MURRAY 1862-1864 CAVALRY CARBINE
Caliber: 58 (.577" Minie). **Barrel:** 23". **Weight:** 7 lbs., 9 oz. **Length:** 39" overall. **Stock:** Walnut. **Sights:** Blade front, rear drift adjustable for windage. **Features:** Browned barrel, color case-hardened lock, blued swivel and band springs, polished brass buttplate, trigger guard, barrel bands. From Euroarms of America.
Price: . . . . **$405.00 to $453.00**

J.P. HENRY TRADE RIFLE
Caliber: 54. **Barrel:** 34"; 1" flats. **Weight:** 8-1/2 lbs. **Length:** 45" overall. **Stock:** Premium curly maple. **Sights:** Silver blade front, fixed buckhorn rear. **Features:** Brass buttplate, side plate, trigger guard and nosecap; browned barrel and lock; L&R Large English percussion lock; single trigger. Made in U.S. by J.P. Gunstocks, Inc.
Price: **$965.50**

KENTUCKIAN RIFLE
Caliber: 44. **Barrel:** 35". **Weight:** 7 lbs. (Rifle), 5-1/2 lbs. (Carbine). **Length:** 51" overall (Rifle), 43" (Carbine). **Stock:** Walnut stain. **Sights:** Brass blade front, steel V-ramp rear. **Features:** Octagon barrel, case-hardened and engraved lockplates. Brass furniture. Imported by Dixie Gun Works.
Price: Flintlock or Percussion **$395.00**

KENTUCKY FLINTLOCK RIFLE
Caliber: 44, 45, or 50. **Barrel:** 35". **Weight:** 7 lbs. **Length:** 50" overall. **Stock:** Walnut stained, brass fittings. **Sights:** Fixed. **Features:** Available in carbine model also, 28" bbl. Some variations in detail, finish. Kits also available from some importers. Imported by The Armoury.
Price: About . . . . **$217.95 to $345.00**

BLACKPOWDER MUSKETS & RIFLES

Kentucky Flintlock

Knight 50 Caliber Disc In-Line

Knight Master Hunter Disc Extreme

London Armory 1861

Kentucky Percussion Rifle
Similar to flintlock except percussion lock. Finish and features vary with importer. Imported by The Armoury and CVA.
Price: About $259.95
Price: 45 or 50 cal. (Navy Arms) $425.00
Price: Kit, 50 cal. (CVA) $189.95

KNIGHT 50 CALIBER DISC IN-LINE RIFLE
Caliber: 50. **Barrel:** 24", 26". **Weight:** 7 lbs., 14 oz. **Length:** 43" overall (24" barrel). **Stock:** Checkered synthetic with palm swell grip, rubber recoil pad, swivel studs; black, Advantage or Mossy Oak Break-Up camouflage. **Sights:** Bead on ramp front, fully adjustable open rear. **Features:** Bolt-action in-line system uses #209 shotshell primer for ignition; primer is held in plastic drop-in Primer Disc. Available in blued or stainless steel. Made in U.S. by Knight Rifles (Modern Muzzleloading).
Price: . . . . $439.95 to $632.45

Knight Master Hunter II DISC In-Line Rifle
Similar to Knight 50 caliber DISC rifle except features premier, wood laminated two-tone stock, gold-plated trigger and engraved trigger guard, jeweled bolt and fluted, air-gauged Green Mountain 26" barrel. Length 45" overall, weighs 7 lbs., 7 oz. Includes black composite thumbhole stock. Introduced 2000. Made in U.S. by Knight Rifles (Modern Muzzleloading).
Price: $1,099.95

KNIGHT MUZZLELOADER DISC EXTREME
Caliber: 45 fluted, 50. **Barrel:** 26". **Stock:** Stainless steel laminate, blued walnut, black composite thumbhole with blued or SS. **Sights:** Fully adjustable metallic. **Features:** New full plastic jacket ignition system.
Price: 50 SS laminate $703.95
Price: 45 SS laminate $769.95
Price: 50 blue walnut $626.95

Price: 45 blue walnut $703.95
Price: 50 blue composite $549.95
Price: 45 blue composite $632.45
Price: 50 SS composite $632.45
Price: 45 SS composite $703.95

Knight Master Hunter DISC Extreme
Similar to DISC Extreme except fluted barrel, two-tone laminated thumbhole Monte Carlo-style stock, black composite thumbhole field stock included. Jeweled bolt, adjustable premium trigger.
Price: 50 . . . . $1,044.95

KNIGHT AMERICAN KNIGHT M/L RIFLE
Caliber: 50. **Barrel:** 22"; 1:28" twist. **Weight:** 6 lbs. **Length:** 41" overall. **Stock:** Black composite. **Sights:** Bead on ramp front, open fully adjustable rear. **Features:** Double safety system; one-piece removable hammer assembly; drilled and tapped for scope mounting. Introduced 1998. Made in U.S. by Knight Rifles.
Price: blued, black comp. $197.95
Price: blued, black comp VP $225.45

KNIGHT WOLVERINE 209
Caliber: 50. **Barrel:** 22". **Stock:** HD stock with SS barrel, break-up stock blued, black composite thumbhole with stainless steel, standard black composite with blued or SS. **Sights:** Metallic with fiber optic. **Features:** Double safety system, adjustable match grade trigger, left-hand model available. Full plastic jacket ignition system.
Price: Starting at $302.45

KNIGHT REVOLUTION
Caliber: 50, 209 primer ignition. **Barrel:** Stainless, 27". **Weight:** 7 lbs., 14 oz. **Stock:** Walnut, laminated, black composite, Mossy Oak Breakup or Hardwoods Green finish. **Features:** Blued or stainless finish, adjustable trigger and sights.
Price: . . . . N/A

Lyman Trade

Lyman Deerstalker

Lyman Great Plains

Markesbery KM Colorado

LONDON ARMORY 2-BAND 1858 ENFIELD
Caliber: .577" Minie, .575" round ball. **Barrel:** 33". **Weight:** 10 lbs. **Length:** 49" overall. **Stock:** Walnut. **Sights:** Folding leaf rear adjustable for elevation. **Features:** Blued barrel, color case-hardened lock and hammer, polished brass buttplate, trigger guard, nosecap. From Navy Arms, Euroarms of America, Dixie Gun Works.
Price: . . . . $385.00 to $600.00

LONDON ARMORY 1861 ENFIELD MUSKETOON
Caliber: 58, Minie ball. **Barrel:** 24", round. **Weight:** 7 - 7-1/2 lbs. **Length:** 40-1/2" overall. **Stock:** Walnut, with sling swivels. **Sights:** Blade front, graduated military-leaf rear. **Features:** Brass trigger guard, nosecap, buttplate; blued barrel, bands, lockplate, swivels. Imported by Euroarms of America, Navy Arms.
Price: . . . . $300.00 to $515.00
Price: Kit . . . . $365.00 to $373.00

LONDON ARMORY 3-BAND 1853 ENFIELD
Caliber: 58 (.577" Minie, .575" round ball, .580" maxi ball). **Barrel:** 39". **Weight:** 9 1/2 lbs. **Length:** 54" overall. **Stock:** European walnut. **Sights:** Inverted "V" front, traditional Enfield folding ladder rear. **Features:** Recreation of the famed London Armory Company Pattern 1853 Enfield Musket. One- piece walnut stock, brass buttplate, trigger guard and nosecap. Lock-plate marked "London Armoury Co." and with a British crown. Blued Badde-ley barrel bands. From Dixie Gun Works, Euroarms of America, Navy Arms.
Price: About . . . . $350.00 to $645.00
Price: Assembled kit (Dixie, Euroarms of America) $495.00

LYMAN TRADE RIFLE
Caliber: 50, 54. **Barrel:** 28" octagon;1:48" twist. **Weight:** 8-3/4 lbs. **Length:** 45" overall. **Stock:** European walnut. **Sights:** Blade front, open rear adjustable for windage or optional fixed sights. **Features:** Fast twist rifling for conical bullets. Polished brass furniture with blue steel parts, stainless steel nipple. Hook breech, single trigger, coil spring percussion lock. Steel barrel rib and ramrod ferrules. Introduced 1980. From Lyman.
Price: 50 cal. Percussion $581.80
Price: 50 cal. Flintlock. $652.80
Price: 54 cal. Percussion $581.80
Price: 54 cal. Flintlock. $652.80

LYMAN DEERSTALKER RIFLE
Caliber: 50, 54. **Barrel:** 24", octagonal; 1:48" rifling. **Weight:** 7-1/2 lbs. **Stock:** Walnut with black rubber buttpad. **Sights:** Lyman #37MA beaded front, fully adjustable fold-down Lyman #16A rear. **Features:** Stock has less drop for quick sighting. All metal parts are blackened, with color case-hardened lock; single trigger. Comes with sling and swivels. Available in flint or percussion. Introduced 1990. From Lyman.
Price: 50 cal. flintlock $652.80
Price: 50- or 54-cal., percussion, left-hand, carbine $695.40
Price: 50- or 54-cal., flintlock, left-hand $645.00
Price: 54 cal. flintlock $780.50
Price: 54 cal. percussion. $821.80
Price: Stainless steel $959.80

LYMAN GREAT PLAINS RIFLE
Caliber: 50- or 54-cal. **Barrel:** 32"; 1:60" twist. **Weight:** 9 lbs. **Stock:** Walnut. **Sights:** Steel blade front, buckhorn rear adjustable for windage and elevation and fixed notch primitive sight included. **Features:** Blued steel furniture. Stainless steel nipple. Coil spring lock, Hawken-style trigger guard and double-set triggers. Round thimbles recessed and sweated into rib. Steel wedge plates and toe plate. Introduced 1979. From Lyman.
Price: Percussion $469.95
Price: Flintlock $494.95
Price: Percussion kit $359.95
Price: Flintlock kit $384.95
Price: Left-hand percussion $474.95
Price: Left-hand flintlock $499.95

Lyman Great Plains Hunter Model
Similar to Great Plains model except 1:32" twist shallow-groove barrel and comes drilled and tapped for Lyman 57GPR peep sight.
Price: $959.80

BLACKPOWDER MUSKETS & RIFLES

Mississippi 1841

Navy Arms Charleville

Navy Arms 1859 Sharps

MARKESBERY KM BLACK BEAR M/L RIFLE

Caliber: 36, 45, 50, 54. **Barrel:** 24"; 1:26" twist. **Weight:** 6-1/2 lbs. **Length:** 38-1/2" overall. **Stock:** Two-piece American hardwood, walnut, black laminate, green laminate, black composition, X-Tra or Mossy Oak Break-Up camouflage. **Sights:** Bead front, open fully adjustable rear. **Features:** Interchangeable barrels; exposed hammer; Outer-Line Magnum ignition system uses small rifle primer or standard No. 11 cap and nipple. Blue, black matte, or stainless. Made in U.S. by Markesbery Muzzle Loaders.

Price: American hardwood walnut, blue finish $536.63
Price: American hardwood walnut, stainless $553.09
Price: Black laminate, blue finish $539.67
Price: Black laminate, stainless $556.27
Price: Camouflage stock, blue finish $556.46
Price: Camouflage stock, stainless $573.73
Price: Black composite, blue finish $532.65
Price: Black composite, stainless $549.93
Price: Green laminate, blue finish $539.00
Price: Green laminate, stainless $556.27

MARKESBERY KM COLORADO ROCKY MOUNTAIN RIFLE

Caliber: 36, 45, 50, 54. **Barrel:** 24"; 1:26" twist. **Weight:** 6-1/2 lbs. **Length:** 38-1/2" overall. **Stock:** American hardwood walnut, green or black laminate. **Sights:** Firesight bead on ramp front, fully adjustable open rear. **Features:** Replicates Reed/Watson rifle of 1851. Straight grip stock with or without two barrel bands, rubber recoil pad, large-spur hammer. Made in U.S. by Markesbery Muzzle Loaders, Inc.

Price: American hardwood walnut, blue finish $545.92
Price: Black or green laminate, blue finish $548.30
Price: American hardwood walnut, stainless $563.17
Price: Black or green laminate, stainless $566.34

Markesberry KM Brown Bear Rifle

Similar to KM Black Bear except one-piece thumbhole stock with Monte Carlo comb. Stock in Crotch Walnut composite, green or black laminate, black composite or X-Tra or Mossy Oak Break-Up camouflage. Contact maker for complete price listing. Made in U.S. by Markesbery Muzzle Loaders, Inc.

Price: Black composite, blue finish $658.83
Price: Crotch Walnut, blue finish $658.83
Price: Camo composite, blue finish $682.64
Price: Walnut wood $662.81
Price: Black wood $662.81
Price: Black laminated wood $662.81
Price: Green laminated wood $662.81

Price: Camo wood $684.69
Price: Black composite, stainless $676.11
Price: Crotch Walnut composite, stainless $676.11
Price: Camo composite, stainless $697.69
Price: Walnut wood, stainless $680.07
Price: Black wood, stainless $680.07
Price: Black laminated wood, stainless $680.07
Price: Green laminate, stainless $680.07
Price: Camo wood, stainless $702.76

Markesberry KM Grizzly Bear Rifle

Similar to KM Black Bear except thumbhole buttstock with Monte Carlo comb. Stock in Crotch Walnut composite, green or black laminate, black composite or X-Tra or Mossy Oak Break-Up camouflage. Contact maker for complete price listing. Made in U.S. by Markesbery Muzzle Loaders, Inc.

Price: Black composite, blue finish $642.96
Price: Crotch Walnut, blue finish $642.96
Price: Camo composite, blue finish $666.67
Price: Walnut wood $646.93
Price: Black wood $646.93
Price: Black laminate wood $646.93
Price: Green laminate wood $646.93
Price: Camo wood $670.74
Price: Black composite, stainless $660.98
Price: Crotch Walnut composite, stainless $660.98
Price: Black laminate wood, stainless $664.20
Price: Green laminate, stainless $664.20
Price: Camo wood, stainless $685.74
Price: Camo composite, stainless $684.04
Price: Walnut wood, stainless $664.20
Price: Black wood, stainless $664.20

Markesberry KM Polar Bear Rifle

Similar to KM Black Bear except one-piece stock with Monte Carlo comb. Stock in American Hardwood walnut, green or black laminate, black composite, or X-Tra or Mossy Oak Break-Up camouflage. Interchangeable barrel system, Outer-Line ignition system, cross-bolt double safety. Available in 36, 45, 50, 54 caliber. Contact maker for full price listing. Made in U.S. by Markesbery Muzzle Loaders, Inc.

Price: American Hardwood walnut , blue finish $539.01
Price: Black composite, blue finish $536.63
Price: Black laminate, blue finish $541.17
Price: Green laminate, blue finish $541.17
Price: Camo, blue finish $560.43
Price: American Hardwood walnut, stainless $556.27
Price: Black composite, stainless $556.04
Price: Black laminate, stainless $570.56
Price: Green laminate, stainless $570.56
Price: Camo, stainless $573.94

BLACKPOWDER MUSKETS & RIFLES

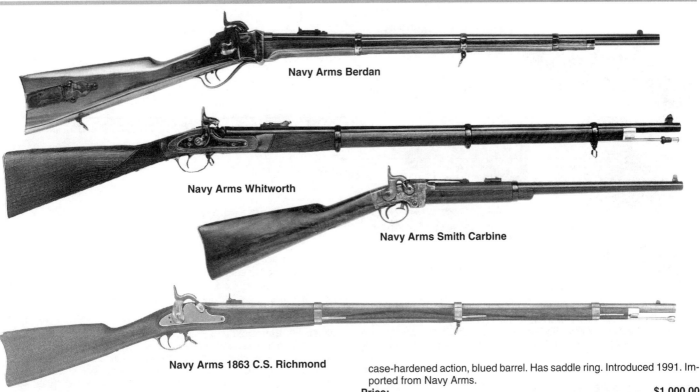

Navy Arms Berdan

Navy Arms Whitworth

Navy Arms Smith Carbine

Navy Arms 1863 C.S. Richmond

MDM BUCKWACKA IN-LINE RIFLES

Caliber: 45, 50. **Barrel:** 23", 25". **Weight:** 7 to 7-3/4 lbs. **Stock:** Black, walnut, laminated and camouflage finishes. **Sights:** Williams Fire Sight blade front, Williams fully adjustable rear with ghost-ring peep aperture. **Features:** Break-open action; Incinerating Ignition System incorporates 209 shotshell primer directly into breech plug; 50-caliber models handle up to 150 grains of Pyrodex; synthetic ramrod; transfer bar safety; stainless or blued finish. Made in U.S. by Millennium Designed Muzzleloaders Ltd.
Price: 50 cal., blued finish. **$309.95**
Price: 50 cal., stainless. **$339.95**
Price: Camouflage stock. . . . . **$359.95 to $389.95**

MDM M2K In-Line Rifle

Similar to Buckwacka except adjustable trigger and double-safety mechanism designed to prevent misfires. Made in U.S. by Millennium Designed Muzzleloaders Ltd.
Price: . . . . **$529.00 to $549.00**

Mississippi 1841 Percussion Rifle

Similar to Zouave rifle but patterned after U.S. Model 1841. Caliber: 54, 58. Imported by Dixie Gun Works, Euroarms of America, Navy Arms.
Price: About **$595.00**

NAVY ARMS 1763 CHARLEVILLE

Caliber: 69. **Barrel:** 44-5/8". **Weight:** 8 lbs., 12 oz. **Length:** 59-3/8" overall. **Stock:** Walnut. **Sights:** Brass blade front. **Features:** Replica of French musket used by American troops during the Revolution. Imported by Navy Arms.
Price: **$1,020.00**

NAVY ARMS PARKER-HALE VOLUNTEER RIFLE

Caliber: .451. **Barrel:** 32". **Weight:** 9-1/2 lbs. **Length:** 49" overall. **Stock:** Walnut, checkered wrist and forend. **Sights:** Globe front, adjustable ladder-type rear. **Features:** Recreation of the type of gun issued to volunteer regiments during the 1860s. Rigby-pattern rifling, patent breech, detented lock. Stock is glass bedded for accuracy. Imported by Navy Arms.
Price: **$905.00**

NAVY ARMS 1859 SHARPS CAVALRY CARBINE

Caliber: 54. **Barrel:** 22". **Weight:** 7-3/4 lbs. **Length:** 39" overall. **Stock:** Walnut. **Sights:** Blade front, military ladder-type rear. **Features:** Color

case-hardened action, blued barrel. Has saddle ring. Introduced 1991. Imported from Navy Arms.
Price: **$1,000.00**

NAVY ARMS BERDAN 1859 SHARPS RIFLE

Caliber: 54. **Barrel:** 30". **Weight:** 8 lbs., 8 oz. **Length:** 46-3/4" overall. **Stock:** Walnut. **Sights:** Blade front, folding military ladder-type rear. **Features:** Replica of the Union sniper rifle used by Berdan's 1st and 2nd Sharpshooter regiments. Color case-hardened receiver, patchbox, furniture. Double-set triggers. Imported by Navy Arms.
Price: **$1,165.00**
Price: 1859 Sharps Infantry Rifle (three-band) **$1,100.00**

NAVY ARMS PARKER-HALE WHITWORTH MILITARY TARGET RIFLE

Caliber: 45. **Barrel:** 36". **Weight:** 9-1/4 lbs. **Length:** 52-1/2" overall. **Stock:** Walnut. Checkered at wrist and forend. **Sights:** Hooded post front, open step-adjustable rear. **Features:** Faithful reproduction of Whitworth rifle, only bored for 45-cal. Trigger has detented lock, capable of being adjusted very finely without risk of the sear nose catching on the half-cock bent and damaging both parts. Introduced 1978. Imported by Navy Arms.
Price: **$930.00**

NAVY ARMS SMITH CARBINE

Caliber: 50. **Barrel:** 21-1/2". **Weight:** 7-3/4 lbs. **Length:** 39" overall. **Stock:** American walnut. **Sights:** Brass blade front, folding ladder-type rear. **Features:** Replica of breech-loading Civil War carbine. Color case-hardened receiver, rest blued. Cavalry model has saddle ring and bar, Artillery model has sling swivels. Imported by Navy Arms.
Price: Cavalry model. **$645.00**
Price: Artillery model **$645.00**

NAVY ARMS 1863 C.S. RICHMOND RIFLE

Caliber: 58. **Barrel:** 40". **Weight:** 10 lbs. **Length:** NA. **Stocks:** Walnut. **Sights:** Blade front, adjustable rear. **Features:** Copy of three-band rifle musket made at Richmond Armory for the Confederacy. All steel polished bright. Imported by Navy Arms.
Price: **$590.00**

NAVY ARMS 1861 SPRINGFIELD RIFLE

Caliber: 58. **Barrel:** 40" **Weight:** 10 lbs., 4 oz. **Length:** 56" overall. **Stock:** Walnut. **Sights:** Blade front, military leaf rear. **Features:** Steel barrel, lock and all furniture have polished bright finish. Has 1855-style hammer. Imported by Navy Arms.
Price: **$590.00**

BLACKPOWDER

BLACKPOWDER MUSKETS & RIFLES

New England Firearms Huntsman

Peifer TS-93

Remington Model 700 ML

NAVY ARMS 1863 SPRINGFIELD

Caliber: 58, uses .575 Minie. **Barrel:** 40", rifled. **Weight:** 9-1/2 lbs. **Length:** 56" overall. **Stock:** Walnut. **Sights:** Open rear adjustable for elevation. **Features:** Full-size, three-band musket. Polished bright metal, including lock. From Navy Arms.
Price: Finished rifle $590.00

NEW ENGLAND FIREARMS HUNTSMAN

Caliber: 50. **Barrel:** 24". **Weight:** 6-1/2 lbs. **Length:** 40". **Stock:** Walnut-finished American hardwood with pistol grip. **Sights:** Adjustable fiber optics open sights, tapped for scope base. **Features:** Break-open action, color case-hardened frame, black oxide barrel. Made in U.S.A. by New England Firearms.
Price: $188.00

New England Firearms Stainless Huntsman

Similar to Huntsman, but with matte nickel finish receiver and stainless bbl. Introduced 2003. From New England Firearms.
Price: 81.00

PACIFIC RIFLE MODEL 1837 ZEPHYR

Caliber: 62. **Barrel:** 30", tapered octagon. **Weight:** 7-3/4 lbs. **Length:** NA. **Stock:** Oil-finished fancy walnut. **Sights:** German silver blade front, semi-buckhorn rear. Options available. **Features:** Improved underhammer action. First production rifle to offer Forsyth rifle, with narrow lands and shallow rifling with 1:144" pitch for high-velocity round balls. Metal finish is slow rust brown with nitre blue accents. Optional sights, finishes and integral muzzle brake available. Introduced 1995. Made in U.S. by Pacific Rifle Co.
Price: From $995.00

Pacific Rifle Big Bore African Rifles

Similar to the 1837 Zephyr except in 72-caliber and 8-bore. The 72-caliber is available in standard form with 28" barrel, or as the African with flat buttplate, checkered upgraded wood; weight is 9 lbs. The 8-bore African has dual-cap ignition, 24" barrel, weighs 12 lbs., checkered English walnut, engraving, gold inlays. Introduced 1998. Made in U.S. by Pacific Rifle Co.
Price: 72-caliber, from $1,150.00
Price: 8-bore from $2,500.00

PEIFER MODEL TS-93 RIFLE

Caliber: 45, 50. **Barrel:** 24" Douglas premium; 1:20" twist in 45; 1:28" in 50. **Weight:** 7 lbs. **Length:** 43-1/4" overall. **Stock:** Bell & Carlson solid composite, with recoil pad, swivel studs. **Sights:** Williams bead front on ramp, fully adjustable open rear. Drilled and tapped for Weaver scope mounts with dovetail for rear peep. **Features:** In-line ignition uses #209 shotshell primer; extremely fast lock time; fully enclosed breech; adjustable trigger; automatic safety; removable primer holder. Blue or stainless. Made in U.S. by Peifer Rifle Co. Introduced 1996.

Price: Blue, black stock. $730.00
Price: Blue, wood or camouflage composite stock, or stainless with black composite stock $803.00
Price: Stainless, wood or camouflage composite stock $876.00

PRAIRIE RIVER ARMS PRA BULLPUP RIFLE

Caliber: 50. **Barrel:** 28"; 1:28" twist. **Weight:** 7-1/2 lbs. **Length:** 31-1/2" overall. **Stock:** Hardwood or black all-weather. **Sights:** Blade front, open adjustable rear. **Features:** Bullpup design thumbhole stock. Patented internal percussion ignition system. Left-hand model available. Dovetailed for scope mount. Introduced 1995. Made in U.S. by Prairie River Arms, Ltd.
Price: 4140 alloy barrel, hardwood stock $199.00
Price: All Weather stock, alloy barrel $205.00

REMINGTON MODEL 700 ML, MLS RIFLES

Caliber: 50, new 45 (MLS Magnum).**Barrel:** 24"; 1:28" twist, 26" (Magnum). **Weight:** 7-3/4 lbs. **Length:** 42"-44-1/2" overall. **Stock:** Black fiberglass-reinforced synthetic with checkered grip and forend; magnum-style buttpad. **Sights:** Ramped bead front, open fully adjustable rear. Drilled and tapped for scope mounts. **Features:** Uses the Remington 700 bolt action, stock design, safety and trigger mechanisms; removable stainelss steel breech plug, No. 11 nipple; solid aluminum ramrod. Comes with cleaning tools and accessories; 3-way ignition.
Price: ML, blued, 50-caliber only $415.00
Price: MLS, stainless, 45 Magnum, 50-caliber $533.00
Price: MLS, stainless, Mossy Oak Break-Up camo stock. $569.00

RICHMOND, C.S., 1863 MUSKET

Caliber: 58. **Barrel:** 40". **Weight:** 11 lbs. **Length:** 56-1/4" overall. **Stock:** European walnut with oil finish. **Sights:** Blade front, adjustable folding leaf rear. **Features:** Reproduction of the three-band Civil War musket. Sling swivels attached to trigger guard and middle barrel band. Lockplate marked "1863" and "C.S. Richmond." All metal left in white. Brass buttplate and forend cap. Imported by Euroarms of America, Navy Arms, and Dixie Gun Works.
Price: Euroarms $530.00
Price: Dixie Gun Works $675.00

RUGER 77/50 IN-LINE PERCUSSION RIFLE

Caliber: 50. **Barrel:** 22"; 1:28" twist. **Weight:** 6-1/2 lbs. **Length:** 41-1/2" overall. **Stock:** Birch with rubber buttpad and swivel studs. **Sights:** Gold bead front, folding leaf rear. Comes with Ruger scope mounts. **Features:** Shares design features with Ruger 77/22 rifle. Stainless steel bolt and nipple/breech plug; uses #11 caps, three-position safety, blued steel ramrod. Introduced 1997. Made in U.S. by Sturm, Ruger & Co.
Price: 77/50RS $434.00
Price: 77/50RSO Officer's
(straight-grip checkered walnut stock, blued) $555.00
Price: K77/50RSBBZ (stainless steel, black laminated stock) . . . $601.00
Price: K77/50RSP All-Weather (stainless steel, synthetic stock) . $580.00
Price: 77/50 RSP (blued, synthetic stock) $434.00

BLACKPOWDER

BLACKPOWDER MUSKETS & RIFLES

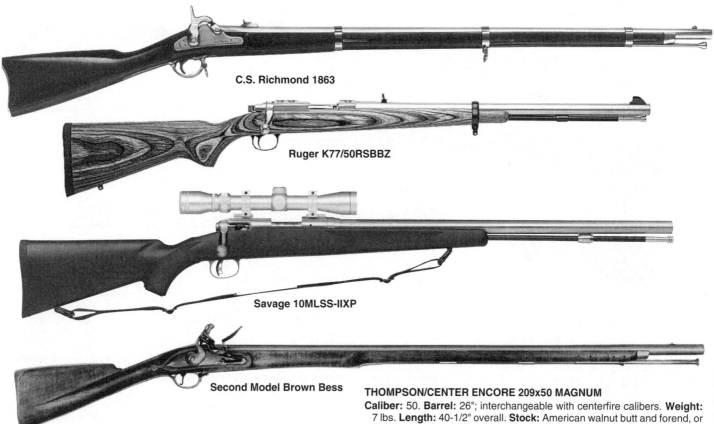

C.S. Richmond 1863

Ruger K77/50RSBBZ

Savage 10MLSS-IIXP

Second Model Brown Bess

SAVAGE MODEL 10ML MUZZLELOADER RIFLE SERIES
Caliber: 50. **Barrel:** 24", 1:24 twist, blue or stainless. **Weight:** 7.75 lbs. **Stock:** Black synthetic, Realtree Hardwood JD Camo, brown laminate. **Sights:** Green adjustable rear, Red FiberOptic front. **Features:** XP Models scoped, no sights, smokeless powder, "easy to prime", #209 primer ignition. Removeable breech plut and vent liner.
Price: Model 10ML-II $512.00
Price: Model 10ML-II Camo $549.00
Price: Model 10MLSS-II Camo $607.00
Price: Model 10MLBSS-II $645.00
Price: Model 10ML-IIXP $549.00
Price: Model 10MLSS-IIXP $607.00

SECOND MODEL BROWN BESS MUSKET
Caliber: 75, uses .735" round ball. **Barrel:** 42", smoothbore. **Weight:** 9-1/2 lbs. **Length:** 59" overall. **Stock:** Walnut (Navy); walnut-stained hardwood (Dixie). **Sights:** Fixed. **Features:** Polished barrel and lock with brass trigger guard and buttplate. Bayonet and scabbard available. From Navy Arms, Dixie Gun Works, Cabela's.
Price: Finished . . . . $475.00 to $850.00
Price: Kit (Dixie Gun Works, Navy Arms) . . . . $575.00 to $625.00
Price: Carbine (Navy Arms) $835.00
Price: Dixie Gun Works $765.00

THOMPSON/CENTER FIRE STORM RIFLE
Caliber: 50. **Barrel:** 26"; 1:28" twist. **Weight:** 7 lbs. **Length:** 41-3/4" overall. **Stock:** Black synthetic with rubber recoil pad, swivel studs. **Sights:** Click-adjustable steel rear and ramp-style front, both with fiber optic inserts. **Features:** Side hammer lock is the first designed for up to three 50-grain Pyrodex pellets; patented Pyrodex Pyramid breech directs ignition fire 360 degrees around base of pellet. Quick Load Accurizor Muzzle System; aluminum ramrod. Flintlock only. Introduced 2000. Made in U.S. by Thomson/Center Arms.
Price: Blue finish, flintlock model with 1:48" twist for round balls, conicals $423.00
Price: SST, flintlock $473.00

THOMPSON/CENTER ENCORE 209x50 MAGNUM
Caliber: 50. **Barrel:** 26"; interchangeable with centerfire calibers. **Weight:** 7 lbs. **Length:** 40-1/2" overall. **Stock:** American walnut butt and forend, or black composite. **Sights:** Tru-Glo Fiber Optic front, Tru-Glo Fiber Optic rear. **Features:** Blue or stainless steel. Uses the stock, frame and forend of the Encore centerfire pistol; break-open design using trigger guard spur; stainless steel universal breech plug; uses #209 shotshell primers. Introduced 1998. Made in U.S. by Thompson/Center Arms.
Price: Stainless wtih camo stock $765.00
Price: Blue, walnut stock and forend $665.00
Price: Blue, composite stock and forend 634.00
Price: Stainless, composite stock and forend $706.00
Price: All camo Realtree Hardwoods $723.00

THOMPSON/CENTER BLACK DIAMOND RIFLE XR
Caliber: 50. **Barrel:** 26" with QLA; 1:28" twist. **Weight:** 6 lbs., 9 oz. **Length:** 41-1/2" overall. **Stock:** Black Rynite with moulded-in checkering and grip cap, or walnut. **Sights:** Tru-Glo Fiber Optic ramp-style front, Tru-Glo Fiber Optic open rear. **Features:** In-line ignition system for musket cap, No. 11 cap, or 209 shotshell primer; removable universal breech plug; stain-less steel construction. Selected models available in .45 cal. Made in U.S. by Thompson/Center Arms.
Price: With composite stock, blued $337.00
Price: With walnut stock $412.00

THOMPSON/CENTER HAWKEN RIFLE
Caliber: 50. **Barrel:** 28" octagon, hooked breech. **Stock:** Ameri-can walnut. **Sights:** Blade front, rear adjustable for windage and elevation. **Features:** Solid brass furniture, double-set triggers, button rifled barrel, coil-type mainspring. From Thompson/Center Arms.
Price: Percussion model $545.00
Price: Flintlock model $570.00

TRADITIONS BUCKSKINNER CARBINE
Caliber: 50. **Barrel:** 21"; 15/16" flats, half octagon, half round; 1:20" or 1:66" twist. **Weight:** 6 lbs. **Length:** 37" overall. **Stock:** Beech or black laminated. **Sights:** Beaded blade front, fiber optic open rear click adjustable for windage and elevation or fiber optics. **Features:** Uses V-type mainspring, single trigger. Non-glare hardware; sling swivels. From Traditions.
Price: Flintlock $249.00
Price: Flintlock, laminated stock $303.00

BLACKPOWDER MUSKETS & RIFLES

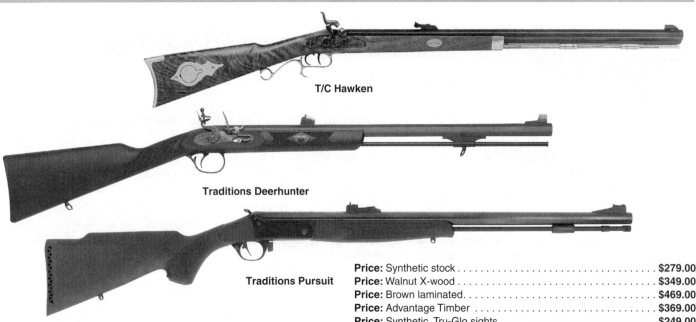

T/C Hawken

Traditions Deerhunter

Traditions Pursuit

TRADITIONS DEERHUNTER RIFLE SERIES

Caliber: 32, 50 or 54. **Barrel:** 24", octagonal; 15/16" flats; 1:48" or 1:66" twist. **Weight:** 6 lbs. **Length:** 40" overall. **Stock:** Stained hardwood or All-Weather composite with rubber buttpad, sling swivels. **Sights:** Lite Optic blade front, adjustable rear fiber optics. **Features:** Flint or percussion with color case-hardened lock. Hooked breech, oversized trigger guard, blackened furniture, PVC ramrod. All-Weather has composite stock and C-Nickel barrel. Drilled and tapped for scope mounting. Imported by Traditions, Inc.
Price: Percussion, 50; blued barrel; 1:48" twist $189.00
Price: Percussion, 54 . . . . $169.00
Price: Flintlock, 50 caliber only; 1:48" twist $179.00
Price: Flintlock, All-Weather, 50-cal. $239.00
Price: Redi-Pak, 50 cal. flintlock $219.00
Price: Flintlock, left-handed hardwood, 50 cal. $209.00
Price: Percussion, All-Weather, 50 or 54 cal. $179.00
Price: Percussion, 32 cal. $199.00

Traditions Panther Sidelock Rifle

Similar to Deerhunter rifle, but has blade front and windage-adjustable-only rear sight, black composite stock.
Price: $129.00

TRADITIONS PURSUIT BREAK-OPEN MUZZLELOADER

Caliber: 45, 54 and 12 gauge. **Barrel:** 28", tapered, fluted; blued, stainless or Hardwoods Green camo. **Stock:** Synthetic black or Hardwoods Green. **Sights:** Steel fiber optic rear, bead front. **Weight:** 8 1/4 lbs. **Overall length:** 44". Introduced 2004 by Traditions, Inc.
Price: Steel, blued, 45 or 50 cal., synthetic stock $279.00
Price: Steel, nickel, 45 or 50 cal., synthetic stock $309.00
Price: Steel, nickel w/Hardwoods Green stock $359.00
Price: Matte blued; 12 ga., synthetic stock $369.00
Price: Matte blued; 12 ga. w/Hardwoods Green stock $439.00
Price: Lightweight model, blued, synthetic stock $199.00
Price: Lightweight model, blued, Mossy Oak
Breakup Camo stock. $239.00
Price: Lightweight model, nickel, Mossy Oak
Breakup Camo stock. $279.00

TRADITIONS EVOLUTION BOLT-ACTION BLACKPOWDER RIFLE

Caliber: 50 percussion. **Barrel:** 26", fluted with porting. **Sights:** Steel fiber optic. **Weight:** 7 lbs. to 7 1/4 lbs. **Overall length:** 45". **Features:** Bolt-action, cocking indicator, thumb safety, aluminum ramrod, sling studs. Wide variety of stocks and metal finishes. Introduced 2004 by Traditions, Inc.

Price: Synthetic stock $279.00
Price: Walnut X-wood $349.00
Price: Brown laminated. $469.00
Price: Advantage Timber $369.00
Price: Synthetic, Tru-Glo sights. $249.00
Price: Mossy Oak Breakup. $279.00
Price: Nickel finish $309.00
Price: Beech/nickel, Advantage/nickel, Advantage 54 cal. $289.00

TRADITIONS PA PELLET FLINTLOCK

Caliber: 50. **Barrel:** 26", blued, nickel. **Weight:** 7 lbs. **Stock:** Hardwood, synthetic and synthetic break-up. **Sights:** FO. **Features:** Removeable breech plug, left-hand model with hardwood stock. 1:48" twist.
Price: Hardwood, blued $259.00
Price: Hardwood left, blued. $269.00

TRADITIONS HAWKEN WOODSMAN RIFLE

Caliber: 50 and 54. **Barrel:** 28"; 15/16" flats. **Weight:** 7 lbs., 11 oz. **Length:** 44-1/2" overall. **Stock:** Walnut-stained hardwood. **Sights:** Beaded blade front, hunting-style open rear adjustable for windage and elevation. **Features:** Percussion only. Brass patchbox and furniture. Double triggers. From Traditions.
Price: 50 or 54 . . . . $299.00
Price: 50-cal., left-hand. $279.00
Price: 50-caliber, flintlock $299.00

TRADITIONS KENTUCKY RIFLE

Caliber: 50. **Barrel:** 33-1/2"; 7/8" flats; 1:66" twist. **Weight:** 7 lbs. **Length:** 49" overall. **Stock:** Beech; inletted toe plate. **Sights:** Blade front, fixed rear. **Features:** Full-length, two-piece stock; brass furniture; color case-hardened lock. From Traditions.
Price: $279.00

TRADITIONS PENNSYLVANIA RIFLE

Caliber: 50. **Barrel:** 40-1/4"; 7/8" flats; 1:66" twist, octagon. **Weight:** 9 lbs. **Length:** 57-1/2" overall. **Stock:** Walnut. **Sights:** Blade front, adjustable rear. **Features:** Brass patchbox and ornamentation. Double-set triggers. From Traditions.
Price: Flintlock $529.00
Price: Percussion $519.00

TRADITIONS SHENANDOAH RIFLE

Caliber: 36, 50. **Barrel:** 33-1/2" octagon; 1:66" twist. **Weight:** 7 lbs., 3 oz. **Length:** 49-1/2" overall. **Stock:** Walnut. **Sights:** Blade front, buckhorn rear. **Features:** V-type mainspring; double-set trigger; solid brass buttplate, patchbox, nosecap, thimbles, trigger guard. Introduced 1996. From Traditions.
Price: Flintlock $419.00
Price: Percussion $399.00
Price: 36 cal. Flintlock, 1:48"twist $419.00
Price: 36 cal. Percussion, 1:48"twist $449.00

BLACKPOWDER

BLACKPOWDER MUSKETS & RIFLES

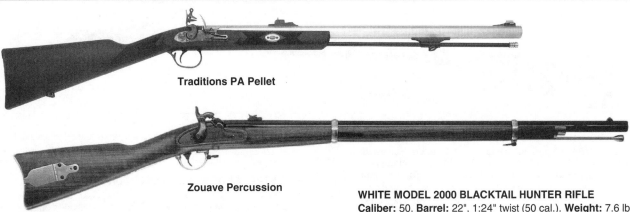

Traditions PA Pellet

Zouave Percussion

TRADITIONS TENNESSEE RIFLE

Caliber: 50. **Barrel:** 24", octagon; 15/16" flats; 1:66" twist. **Weight:** 6 lbs. **Length:** 40-1/2" overall. **Stock:** Stained beech. **Sights:** Blade front, fixed rear. **Features:** One-piece stock has inletted brass furniture, cheekpiece; double-set trigger; V-type mainspring. Flint or percussion. From Traditions.
Price: Flintlock **$339.00**
Price: Percussion **$329.00**

TRADITIONS TRACKER 209 IN-LINE RIFLES

Caliber: 45, 50. **Barrel:** 22" blued or C-Nickel finish; 1:28" twist, 50 cal. 1:20" 45 cal. **Weight:** 6 lbs., 4 oz. **Length:** 41" overall. **Stock:** Black, Advantage Timber® composite, synthetic. **Sights:** Lite Optic blade front, adjustable rear. **Features:** Thumb safety; adjustable trigger; rubber butt pad and sling swivel studs; takes 150 grains of Pyrodex pellets; one-piece breech system takes 209 shotshell primers. Drilled and tapped for scope. From Traditions.
Price: (Black composite or synthetic stock, 22" blued barrel). . . . **$129.00**
Price: (Black composite or synthetic stock, 22" C-Nickel barrel) . **$139.00**
Price: (Advantage Timber® stock, 22" C-Nickel barrel) **$189.00**
Price: (Redi-Pak, black stock and blued barrel, powder flask,
capper, ball starter, other accessories). **$179.00**
Price: (Redi-Pak, synthetic stock and blued barrel, with scope). . **$229.00**

WHITE MODEL 97 WHITETAIL HUNTER RIFLE

Caliber: 45, 50. **Barrel:** 22", 1:20 twist (45 cal.); 1:24 twist (50 cal.). **Weight:** 7.7 lbs. **Length:** 40" overall. **Stock:** Black laminated or black composite. **Sights:** Marble TruGlo fully adjustable, steel rear with white di-amond, red bead front with high-visibility inserts. **Features:** In-line ignition with FlashFire one-piece nipple and breech plug that uses standard or magnum No. 11 caps, fully adjustable trigger, double safety system, alu-minum ramrod; drilled and tapped for scope. Hard gun case. Made in U.S.A. by Split Fire Sporting Goods.
Price: Whitetail w/laminated or composite stock. **$499.95**
Price: Adventurer w/26" stainless barrel & thumbhole stock) . . . **$699.95**
Price: Odyssey w/24" carbon fiber wrapped
barrel & thumbhole stock **$1,299.95**

WHITE MODEL 98 ELITE HUNTER RIFLE

Caliber: 45, 50. **Barrel:** 24", 1:24" twist (50 cal). **Weight:** 8.6 lbs. **Length:** 43-1/2" overall. **Stock:** Black laminate wtih swivel studs. **Sights:** TruGlo fully adjustable, steel rear with white diamond, red bead front with high-visibility inserts. **Features:** In-line ignition with FlashFire one-piece nipple and breech plug that uses standard or magnum No. 11 caps, fully adjustable trigger, double safety system, aluminum ramrod, drilled and taped for scope, hard gun case. Made in U.S.A. by Split Fire Sporting Goods.
Price: Composite or laminate wood stock. **$499.95**

White Thunderbolt Rifle

Similar to the Elite Hunter but is designed to handle 209 shotgun primers only. Has 26" stainless steel barrel, weighs 9.3 lbs. and is 45-1/2" long. Composite or laminate stock.
Price: **$599.95**

WHITE MODEL 2000 BLACKTAIL HUNTER RIFLE

Caliber: 50. **Barrel:** 22", 1:24" twist (50 cal.). **Weight:** 7.6 lbs. **Length:** 39-7/8" overall. **Stock:** Black laminated with swivel studs with laser engraved deer or elk scene. **Sights:** TruGlo fully adjustable, steel rear with white di-amond, red bead front with high-visibility inserts. **Features:** Teflon finished barrel, in-line ignition with FlashFire one-piece nipple and breech plug that uses standard or magnum No. 11 caps, fully adjustable trigger, double safety system, aluminum ramrod, drilled and tapped for scope. Hard gun case. Made in U.S.A. by Split Fire Sporting Goods.
Price: Laminate wood stock, w/laser engraved game scene **$599.95**

WHITE LIGHTNING II RIFLE

Caliber: 45 and 50 percussion. **Barrel:** 24", 1:32 twist. **Sights:** Adj. rear. **Stock:** Black polymer. **Weight:** 6 lbs. **Features:** In-line, 209 primer ignition system, blued or nickel-plated bbl., adj. trigger, Delrin ramrod, sling studs, recoil pad.
Price: **$299.95**

WHITE ALPHA RIFLE

Caliber: 45, 50 percussion. **Barrel:** 27" tapered, stainless. **Sights:** Marble TruGlo rear, fiber optic front. **Stock:** Laminated. **Features:** Lever action rotating block, hammerless; adj. trigger, positive safety. All stainless metal, including trigger.
Price: **$449.95**

WINCHESTER APEX SWING-ACTION MAGNUM RIFLE

Caliber: 45, 50. **Barrel:** 28". **Stock:** Mossy Oak Camo, Black Fleck. **Sights:** Adj. Fiber Optic. **Weight:** 7 lbs., 12 oz. **Overall length:** 42". **Features:** Monte Carlo cheekpiece, swing-action design, external hammer.
Price: Mossy Oak/stainless **$489.95**
Price: Black Fleck/stainless **$449.95**
Price: Full Mossy Oak. **$469.95**
Price: Black Fleck/blued **$364.95**

WINCHESTER X-150 BOLT-ACTION MAGNUM RIFLE

Caliber: 45, 50. **Barrel:** 26". **Stock:** Hardwoods or Timber HD, Black Fleck, Breakup. **Weight:** 8 lbs., 3 oz. **Sights:** Ajd. Fiber Optic. **Features:** No. 209 shotgun primer ignition, stainless steel bolt, stainless fluted bbl.
Price: Mossy Oak, Timber, Hardwoods/stainless **$349.95**
Price: Black Fleck/stainless **$299.95**
Price: Mossy Oak, Timber, Hardwoods/blued. **$279.95**
Price: Black Fleck/blued **$229.95**

ZOUAVE PERCUSSION RIFLE

Caliber: 58, 59. **Barrel:** 32-1/2". **Weight:** 9-1/2 lbs. **Length:** 48-1/2" overall. **Stock:** Walnut finish, brass patchbox and buttplate. **Sights:** Fixed front, rear adjustable for elevation. **Features:** Color case-hardened lockplate, blued barrel. From Navy Arms, Dixie Gun Works, E.M.F., Cabela's, Euroarms of America.
Price: . . . . **$415.00 to $515.00**

BLACKPOWDER SHOTGUNS

Knight TK2000

CABELA'S BLACKPOWDER SHOTGUNS

Gauge: 10, 12, 20. **Barrel:** 10-ga., 30"; 12-ga., 28-1/2" (Extra-Full, Mod., Imp. Cyl. choke tubes); 20-ga., 27-1/2" (Imp. Cyl. & Mod. fixed chokes). **Weight:** 6-1/2 to 7 lbs. **Length:** 45" overall (28-1/2" barrel). **Stock:** American walnut with checkered grip; 12- and 20-gauge have straight stock, 10-gauge has pistol grip. **Features:** Blued barrels, engraved, color case-hardened locks and hammers, brass ramrod tip. From Cabela's.

Price: 10-gauge **$799.99**
Price: 12-gauge **$649.99**
Price: 20-gauge **$659.99**

DIXIE MAGNUM PERCUSSION SHOTGUN

Gauge: 10, 12, 20. **Barrel:** 30" (Imp. Cyl. & Mod.) in 10-gauge; 28" in 12-gauge. **Weight:** 6-1/4 lbs. **Length:** 45" overall. **Stock:** Hand-checkered walnut, 14" pull. **Features:** Double triggers; light hand engraving; case-hardened locks in 12-gauge, polished steel in 10-gauge; sling swivels. From Dixie Gun Works.

Price: Upland **$650.00**
Price: 12-ga. kit. **$445.00**
Price: 20-ga. **$525.00**
Price: 10-ga. **$575.00**
Price: 10-ga. kit. **$445.00**

KNIGHT TK2000 MUZZLELOADING SHOTGUN (209)

Gauge: 12. **Barrel:** 26", extra-full choke tube. **Weight:** 7 lbs., 9 oz. **Length:** 45" overall. **Stock:** Synthetic black or Advantage Timber HD; recoil pad; swivel studs. **Sights:** Fully adjustable rear, blade front with fiber optics. **Features:** Receiver drilled and tapped for scope mount; in-line ignition; adjustable trigger; removable breech plug; double safety system; imp. cyl. choke tube available. Made in U.S. by Knight Rifles.

Price: . . . . **$349.95 to $399.95**

KNIGHT VERSATILE TK2002

Gauge: 12. **Stock:** Black composite, blued, Advantage Timber HD finish. Both with sling swivel studs installed. **Sights:** Adjustable metallic TruGol fiber optic. **Features:** Full plastic jacket ignition system, screw-on choke tubes, load without removing choke tubes, incredible shot density with jug-chocked barrel design. Improved cylinder and modified choke tubes available.

Price: . . . . **$349.95 to $399.95**

NAVY ARMS STEEL SHOT MAGNUM SHOTGUN

Gauge: 10. **Barrel:** 28" (Cyl. & Cyl.). **Weight:** 7 lbs., 9 oz. **Length:** 45-1/2" overall. **Stock:** Walnut, with cheekpiece. **Features:** Designed specifically for steel shot. Engraved, polished locks; sling swivels; blued barrels. Imported by Navy Arms.

Price: **$605.00**

NAVY ARMS T&T SHOTGUN

Gauge: 12. **Barrel:** 28" (Full & Full). **Weight:** 7-1/2 lbs. **Stock:** Walnut. **Sights:** Bead front. **Features:** Color case-hardened locks, double triggers, blued steel furniture. From Navy Arms.

Price: **$580.00**

WHITE TOMINATOR SHOTGUN

Caliber: 12. **Barrel:** 25" blue, straight, tapered stainless steel. **Weight:** NA. **Length:** NA. **Stock:** Black laminated or black wood. **Sights:** Drilled and tapped for easy scope mounting. **Features:** Interchangeable choke tubes. Custom vent-rib with high visibility front bead. Double safeties. Fully adjustable custom trigger. Recoil pad and sling swivel studs.

Price: **$349.95**

CONSULT

SHOOTER'S
MARKETPLACE

Page 64, This Issue

Gamo PT-80

Daisy 662X

BEEMAN/FWB P34 MATCH AIR PISTOL
Caliber: 177, single shot. **Barrel:** 10-5/16", with muzzlebrake. **Weight:** 2.4 lbs. **Length:** 16.5" overall. **Power:** Pre-charged pneumatic. **Stocks:** Stippled walnut; adjustable match type. **Sights:** Undercut blade front, fully adjustable match rear. **Features:** Velocity to 525 fps; up to 200 shots per CO2 cartridge. Fully adjustable trigger; built-in muzzlebrake. Imported from Germany by Beeman.
Price: Right-hand **$1,395.00**
Price: Left-hand **$1,440.00**

BEEMAN HW70A AIR PISTOL
Caliber: 177, single shot. **Barrel:** 6-1/4", rifled. **Weight:** 38 oz. **Length:** 12-3/4" overall. **Power:** Spring, barrel cocking. **Stocks:** Plastic, with thumbrest. **Sights:** Hooded post front, square notch rear adjustable for windage and elevation. Comes with scope base. **Features:** Adjustable trigger, 31-lb. cocking effort, 440 fps MV; automatic barrel safety. Imported by Beeman.
Price: **$190.00**

BEEMAN/WEBLEY TEMPEST AIR PISTOL
Caliber: 177, 22, single shot. **Barrel:** 6-7/8". **Weight:** 32 oz. **Length:** 8.9" overall. **Power:** Spring-piston, break barrel. **Stocks:** Checkered black plastic with thumbrest. **Sights:** Blade front, adjustable rear. **Features:** Velocity to 500 fps (177), 400 fps (22). Aluminum frame; black epoxy finish; manual safety. Imported from England by Beeman.
Price: **$205.00**

Beeman/Webley Hurricane Air Pistol
Similar to the Tempest except has extended frame in the rear for a click-adjustable rear sight; hooded front sight; comes with scope mount. Imported from England by Beeman.
Price: **$255.00**

BENJAMIN SHERIDAN CO2 PELLET PISTOLS
Caliber: 177, 20, 22, single shot. **Barrel:** 6-3/8", rifled brass. **Weight:** 29 oz. **Length:** 9.8" overall. **Power:** 12-gram CO2 cylinder. **Stocks:** Walnut. **Sights:** High ramp front, fully adjustable notch rear. **Features:** Velocity to 500 fps. Turnbolt action with cross-bolt safety. Gives about 40 shots per CO2 cylinder. Black or nickel finish. Made in U.S. by Benjamin Sheridan Co.
Price: Black finish, EB17 (177), EB20 (20), ... **$190.00**

BENJAMIN SHERIDAN PNEUMATIC PELLET PISTOLS
Caliber: 177, 20, 22, single shot. **Barrel:** 9-3/8", rifled brass. **Weight:** 38 oz. **Length:** 13-1/8" overall. **Power:** Underlever pnuematic, hand pumped. **Stocks:** Walnut stocks and pump handle. **Sights:** High ramp front, fully adjustable notch rear. **Features:** Velocity to 525 fps (variable). Bolt action with cross-bolt safety. Choice of black or nickel finish. Made in U.S. by Benjamin Sheridan Co.
Price: Black finish, HB17 (177), HB20 (20) **$190.00**
Price: HB22 (22) **$199.00**

BRNO TAU-7 CO2 MATCH PISTOL
Caliber: 177. **Barrel:** 10.24". **Weight:** 37 oz. **Length:** 15.75" overall. **Power:** 12.5-gram CO2 cartridge. **Stocks:** Stippled hardwood with adjustable palm rest. **Sights:** Blade front, open fully adjustable rear. **Features:** Comes with extra seals and counterweight. Blue finish. Imported by Great Lakes Airguns.
Price: **$299.50**

CROSMAN BLACK VENOM PISTOL
Caliber: 177 pellets, BB, 17-shot magazine; darts, single shot. **Barrel:** 4.75" smooth-bore. **Weight:** 16 oz. **Length:** 10.8" overall. **Power:** Spring. **Sights:** Blade front, adjustable rear. **Features:** Velocity to 270 fps (BBs), 250 fps (pellets). Spring-fed magazine; cross-bolt safety. Made in U.S.A. by Crosman Corp.
Price: **$60.00**

CROSMAN MODEL 1377 AIR PISTOLS
Caliber: 177, single shot. **Barrel:** 8", rifled steel. **Weight:** 39 oz. **Length:** 13-5/8". **Power:** Hand pumped. **Sights:** Blade front, rear adjustable for windage and elevation. **Features:** Bolt action moulded plastic grip, hand size pump forearm. Cross-bolt safety. From Crosman.
Price: **$60.00**

AIR FORCE CONDOR
Caliber: 177, 22. **Barrel:** 24" rifled. **Weight:** 6.5 lbs. **Overall length:** 38.75". **Sights:** None, integral mount supplied. **Features:** 600-1,300 fps. 3,000 psi fill pressure. Automatic safety. Air tank volume: 490cc.
Price: 22 w/refill clamp and open sights **$649.95**
Price: 177 w/refill clamp and open sights **$599.95**
Price: Gun only (22 or 177) **$549.95**

AIR FORCE TALON SS
Caliber: 177, 22. **Barrel:** 12". **Weight:** 5.25 lbs. **Overall length:** 32.75". **Sights:** None, integral mount supplied. **Features:** 400-1000 fps. Fill pressure: 3000 psi. Air tank volume: 490cc.
Price: 22 w/refill clamp, open sights **$559.95**
Price: 177 w/refill clamp, open sights **$559.95**
Price: Gun only (22 or 177) **$459.95**

AIR FORCE TALON
Same as Talon SS but 32.6" long, weight: 5.5 lbs.
Price: 22 w/refill clamp, open sights **$539.95**
Price: 177 w/refill clamp, open sights **$539.95**
Price: Gun only **$439.95**

ARS HUNTING MASTER AR6 PISTOL
Caliber: 22 (177 +20 special order). **Barrel:** 12" rifled. **Weight:** 3 lbs. **Length:** 18.25 overall. **Stock:** Indonesian walnut with checkered grip. **Sights:** Adjustable rear, blade front. **Features:** 6 shot repeater with rotary magazine, single or double action, receiver grooved for scope, hammer block and trigger block safeties.
Price: . . . . **NA**

BEEMAN P1 MAGNUM AIR PISTOL
Caliber: 177, 5mm, single shot. **Barrel:** 8.4". **Weight:** 2.5 lbs. **Length:** 11" overall. **Power:** Top lever cocking; spring-piston. **Stocks:** Checkered walnut. **Sights:** Blade front, square notch rear with click micrometer adjustments for windage and elevation. Grooved for scope mounting. **Features:** Dual power for 177 and 20-cal.: low setting gives 350-400 fps; high setting 500-600 fps. Rearward expanding mainspring simulates firearm recoil. All Colt 45 auto grips fit gun. Dry firing feature for practice. Optional wooden shoulder stock. Imported by Beeman.
Price: 177, 5mm **$440.00**

BEEMAN P3 AIR PISTOL
Caliber: 177 pellet, single shot. **Barrel:** N/A. **Weight:** 1.7 lbs. **Length:** 9.6" overall. **Power:** Single-stroke pneumatic; overlever barrel cocking. **Grips:** Reinforced polymer. **Sights:** Adjustable rear, blade front. **Features:** Velocity 410 fps. Polymer frame; automatic safety; two-stage trigger; built-in muzzle brake.
Price: **$180.00**
Price: Combo **$285.00**

BEEMAN/FEINWERKBAU 103 PISTOL
Caliber: 177, single shot. **Barrel:** 10.1", 12-groove rifling. **Weight:** 2.5 lbs. **Length:** 16.5" overall. **Power:** Single-stroke pneumatic, underlever cocking. **Stocks:** Stippled walnut with adjustable palm shelf. **Sights:** Blade front, open rear adjustable for windage and elevation. Notch size adjustable for width. Interchangeable front blades. **Features:** Velocity 510 fps. Fully adjustable trigger. Cocking effort of 2 lbs. Imported by Beeman.
Price: Right-hand **$1,236.00**
Price: Left-hand **$1,275.00**

CROSMAN AUTO AIR II PISTOL
Caliber: BB, 17-shot magazine, 177 pellet, single shot. **Barrel:** 8-5/8" steel, smooth-bore. **Weight:** 13 oz. **Length:** 10-3/4" overall. **Power:** CO2 Powerlet. **Sights:** Blade front, adjustable rear; highlighted system. **Features:** Velocity to 480 fps (BBs), 430 fps (pellets). Semi-automatic action with BBs, single shot with pellets. Black. From Crosman.
Price: AAIIB **$38.00**
Price: AAIIBRD . . . . **NA**

CROSMAN MODEL 1008 REPEAT AIR
Caliber: 177, 8-shot pellet clip. **Barrel:** 4.25", rifled steel. **Weight:** 17 oz. **Length:** 8.625" overall. **Power:** CO2 Powerlet. **Stocks:** Checkered black plastic. **Sights:** Post front, adjustable rear. **Features:** Velocity about 430 fps. Break-open barrel for easy loading; single or double semi-automatic action; two 8-shot clips included. Optional carrying case available. From Crosman.
Price: **$60.00**
Price: Model 1008SB (silver and black finish), about **$60.00**

CROSMAN SEMI AUTO AIR PISTOL
Caliber: 177, pellets. **Barrel:** Rifled steel. **Weight:** 40 oz. **Length:** 8.63". **Power:** CO2. **Sights:** Blade front, rear adjustable. **Features:** Velocity up to 430 fps. Synthetic grips, zinc alloy frame. From Crosman.
Price: C40 . . . . **NA**

CROSMAN MAGNUM AIR PISTOLS
Caliber: 177, pellets. **Barrel:** Rifled steel. **Weight:** 27 oz. **Length:** 9.38". **Power:** CO2. **Sights:** Blade front, rear adjustable. **Features:** Single/double action accepts sights and scopes with standard 3/8" dovetail mount. Model 3576W features 6" barrel for increased accuracy. From Crosman.
Price: 3574W . . . . **NA**
Price: 3576W . . . . **NA**

DAISY/POWERLINE MODEL 15XT AIR PISTOL
Caliber: 177 BB, 15-shot built-in magazine. **Barrel:** NA. **Weight:** NA. **Length:** 7.21". **Power:** CO2. **Stocks:** NA. **Sights:** NA. **Features:** Velocity 425 fps. Made in the U.S.A. by Daisy Mfg. Co.
Price: **$36.95**
New! Price: 15XK Shooting Kit **$59.95**

DAISY/POWERLINE 717 PELLET PISTOL
Caliber: 177, single shot. **Barrel:** 9.61". **Weight:** 2.25 lbs. **Length:** 13-1/2" overall. **Stocks:** Moulded wood-grain plastic, with thumbrest. **Sights:** Blade and ramp front, micro-adjustable notch rear. **Features:** Single pump pneumatic pistol. Rifled steel barrel. Cross-bolt trigger block. Muzzle velocity 385 fps. From Daisy Mfg. Co.
Price: **$71.95**

DAISY/POWERLINE 1270 CO2 AIR PISTOL
Caliber: BB, 60-shot magazine. **Barrel:** Smoothbore steel. **Weight:** 17 oz. **Length:** 11.1" overall. **Power:** CO2 pump action. **Stocks:** Moulded black polymer. **Sights:** Blade on ramp front, adjustable rear. **Features:** Velocity to 420 fps. Crossbolt trigger block safety; plated finish. Made in U.S. by Daisy Mfg. Co.
Price: **$39.95**

DAISY/POWERLINE 93 AIR PISTOL
Caliber: BB, 15-shot magazine. **Barrel:** Smoothbore steel. **Weight:** 1.1 lbs. **Length:** 7.9" overall. **Power:** CO2 powered semi-auto. **Stocks:** Moulded brown checkered. **Sights:** Blade on ramp front, fixed open rear. **Features:** Velocity to 400 fps. Manual trigger block. Made in U.S.A. by Daisy Mfg. Co.
Price: **$48.95**

Daisy/Powerline 693 Air Pistol
Similar to Model 93 except has velocity to 235 fps.
Price: **$52.95**

DAISY/POWERLINE 622X PELLET PISTOL
Caliber: 22 (5.5mm), 6-shot. **Barrel:** Rifled steel. **Weight:** 1.3 lbs. **Length:** 8.5". **Power:** CO2. **Grips:** Molded black checkered. **Sights:** Fiber optic front, fixed open rear. **Features:** Velocity 225 fps. Rotary hammer block. Made by Daisy Mfg. Co.
Price: **$69.95**

DAISY/POWERLINE 45 AIR PISTOL
Caliber: BB, 13-shot magazine. **Barrel:** Rifled steel. **Weight:** 1.25 lbs. **Length:** 8.5" overall. **Power:** CO2 powered semi-auto. **Stocks:** Moulded black checkered. **Sights:** TRUGLO® fiber optic front, fixed open rear. **Features:** Velocity to 224 fps. Manual trigger block. Made in U.S.A. by Daisy Mfg. Co.

EAA MP651K

Price: **$54.95**

Daisy/Powerline 645 Air Pistol
Similar to Model 93 except has distinctive black and nickel-finish.
Price: **$59.95**

EAA/BAIKAL IZH-M46 TARGET AIR PISTOL
Caliber: 177, single shot. **Barrel:** 10". **Weight:** 2.4 lbs. **Length:** 16.8" overall. **Power:** Underlever single-stroke pneumatic. **Grips:** Adjustable wooden target. **Sights:** Micrometer fully adjustable rear, blade front. **Features:** Velocity about 420 fps. Hammer-forged, rifled barrel. Imported from Russia by European American Armory.
Price: **$349.00**

GAMO AUTO 45
Caliber: .177 (12-shot). **Barrel:** 4.25". **Weight:** 1.10 lbs. **Length:** 7.50". **Power:** CO2 cartridge, semi-automatic, 410 fps. **Stock:** Plastic. **Sights:** Rear sights adjusts for windage. **Features:** Looking very much like a Glock cartridge pistol, it fires in the double-action model and has a manual safety. Imported from Spain by Gamo.
Price: **$99.95**

GAMO COMPACT TARGET PISTOL
Caliber: .177, single shot. **Barrel:** 8.26". **Weight:** 1.95 lbs. **Length:** 12.60. **Power:** Spring-piston, 400 fps. **Stock:** Walnut. **Sights:** Micro-adjustable. **Features:** Rifle steel barrel, adjustable match trigger, recoil and vibration-free. Imported from Spain by Gamo.
Price: **$229.95**

GAMO P-23, P-23 LASER PISTOL
Caliber: .177 (12-shot). **Barrel:** 4.25". **Weight:** 1 lb. **Length:** 7.5". **Power:** CO2 cartridge, semi-automatic, 410 fps. **Stock:** Plastic. **Sights:** NA. **Features:** Style somewhat like a Walther PPK cartridge pistol, an optional laser allows fast sight acquisition. Imported from Spain by Gamo.
Price: . . . . **$89.95**, (with laser) **$129.95**

GAMO PT-80, PT-80 LASER PISTOL
Caliber: .177 (8-shot). **Barrel:** 4.25". **Weight:** 1.2 lbs. **Length:** 7.2". **Power:** CO2 cartridge, semi-automatic, 410 fps. **Stock:** Plastic. **Sights:** 3-dot. **Features:** Available with optional laser sight and with optional walnut grips. Imported from Spain by Gamo.
Price: . . . . **$108.95**, (with laser) **$129.95**, (with walnut grip) **$119.95**

"GAT" AIR PISTOL
Caliber: 177, single shot. **Barrel:** 7-1/2" cocked, 9-1/2" extended. **Weight:** 22 oz. **Power:** Spring-piston. **Stocks:** Cast checkered metal. **Sights:** Fixed. **Features:** Shoots pellets, corks or darts. Matte black finish. Imported from England by Stone Enterprises, Inc.
Price: **$24.95**

HAMMERLI AP40 AIR PISTOL
Caliber: 177. **Barrel:** 10". **Stocks:** Adjustable orthopaedic. **Sights:** Fully adjustable micrometer. **Features:** Sleek, light, well balanced and accurate. Imported from Switzerland by Nygord Precision Products.
Price: **$1,195.00**

MARKSMAN 2000 REPEATER PISTOL
Caliber: 177, 18-shot BB repeater. **Barrel:** 2-1/2", smoothbore. **Weight:** 24 oz. **Length:** 8-1/4" overall. **Power:** Spring. **Features:** Velocity to 200 fps. Thumb safety. Uses BBs, darts, bolts or pellets. Repeats with BBs only. From Marksman Products.
Price: **$27.00**

MARKSMAN 2005 LASERHAWK SPECIAL EDITION AIR PISTOL

Caliber: 177, 24-shot magazine. **Barrel:** 3.8", smoothbore. **Weight:** 22 oz. **Length:** 10.3" overall. **Power:** Spring-air. **Stocks:** Checkered. **Sights:** Fixed fiber optic front sight. **Features:** Velocity to 300 fps with Hyper-Velocity pellets. Square trigger guard with skeletonized trigger; extended barrel for greater velocity and accuracy. Shoots BBs, pellets, darts or bolts. Made in the U.S. From Marksman Products.
Price: **$32.00**

MORINI 162E MATCH AIR PISTOL

Caliber: 177, single shot. **Barrel:** 9.4". **Weight:** 32 oz. **Length:** 16.1" overall. **Power:** Scuba air. **Stocks:** Adjustable match type. **Sights:** Interchangeable blade front, fully adjustable match-type rear. **Features:** Power mechanism shuts down when pressure drops to a preset level. Adjustable electronic trigger. Imported from Switzerland by Nygord Precision Products.
Price: **$825.00**
Price: 162 EI **$1,075.00**

MORINI SAM K-11 AIR PISTOL

Caliber: 177. **Barrel:** 10". **Weight:** 38 oz. **Stocks:** Fully adjustable. **Sights:** Fully adjustable. **Features:** Improved trigger, more angle adjustment on grip. Sophisticated counter balance system. Deluxe aluminum case, two cylinders and manometer. Imported from Switzerland by Nygord Precision Products.
Price: **$975.00**

PARDINI K58 MATCH AIR PISTOL

Caliber: 177, single shot. **Barrel:** 9". **Weight:** 37.7 oz. **Length:** 15.5" overall. **Power:** Precharged compressed air; single-stroke cocking. **Stocks:** Adjustable match type; stippled walnut. **Sights:** Interchangeable post front, fully adjustable match rear. **Features:** Fully adjustable trigger. Short version K-2 available. Imported from Italy by Nygord Precision Products.
Price: **$795.00**
Price: K2S model, precharged air pistol, introduced in 1998 . . . . **$945.00**

RWS 9B/9N AIR PISTOLS

Caliber: 177, single shot. **Grips:** Plastic with thumbrest. **Sights:** Adjustable. **Features:** Spring-piston powered; 550 fps. Black or nickel finish. Imported from Spain by Dynamit Nobel-RWS.
Price: 9B **$169.00**
Price: 9N **$185.00**

STEYR LP 5CP MATCH AIR PISTOL

Caliber: 177, 5-shot magazine. **Weight:** 40.7 oz. **Length:** 15.2" overall. **Power:** Precharged air cylinder. **Stocks:** Adjustable match type. **Sights:** Interchangeable blade front, fully adjustable match rear. **Features:** Adjustable sight radius; fully adjustable trigger. Barrel compensator. One-shot magazine available. Imported from Austria by Nygord Precision Products.
Price: **$1,100.00**

STEYR LP10P MATCH PISTOL

Caliber: 177, single shot. **Barrel:** 9". **Weight:** 38.7 oz. **Length:** 15.3" overall. **Power:** Scuba air. **Stocks:** Fully adjustable Morini match, palm shelf, stippled walnut. **Sights:** Interchangeable blade in 4mm, 4.5mm or 5mm widths, fully adjustable open rear, interchangeable 3.5mm or 4mm leaves. **Features:** Velocity about 500 fps. Adjustable trigger, adjustable sight radius from 12.4" to 13.2". With compensator. New "absorber" eliminates recoil. Imported from Austria by Nygord Precision Products.
Price: **$1,175.00**

TECH FORCE SS2 OLYMPIC COMPETITION AIR PISTOL

Caliber: 177 pellet, single shot. **Barrel:** 7.4". **Weight:** 2.8 lbs. **Length:** 16.5" overall. **Power:** Spring piston, sidelever. **Grips:** Hardwood. **Sights:** Extended adjustable rear, blade front accepts inserts. **Features:** Velocity 520 fps. Recoilless design; adjustments allow duplication of a firearm's feel. Match-grade, adjustable trigger; includes carrying case. Imported from China by Compasseco Inc.
Price: **$295.00**

TECH FORCE 35 AIR PISTOL

Caliber: 177 pellet, single shot. **Weight:** 2.86 lbs. **Length:** 14.9" overall. **Power:** Spring piston, underlever. **Grips:** Hardwood. **Sights:** Micrometer adjustable rear, blade front. **Features:** Velocity 400 fps. Grooved for scope mount; trigger safety. Imported from China by Compasseco Inc.
Price: **$39.95**

Tech Force 8 Air Pistol

Similar to Tech Force 35, but with break-barrel action, ambidextrous polymer grips.
Price: **$59.95**

Tech Force S2-1 Air Pistol

Similar to Tech Force 8, more basic grips and sights for plinking.
Price: **$29.95**

WALTHER LP300 MATCH PISTOL

Caliber: 177. **Barrel:** 236mm. **Weight:** 1.018g. **Length:** NA. **Power:** NA. **Stocks:** NA. **Sights:** Integrated front with three different widths, adjustable rear. **Features:** Adjustable grip and trigger. Imported from Germany by Nygord Precision Products.
Price: **$1,095.00**

AIRGUNS

Crosman 2289G

Daisy 7840 Buckmaster

AIR FORCE TALON AIR RIFLE
Caliber: .177, .22, single-shot. **Barrel:** 18". **Weight:** 5.5 lbs. **Length:** 32.6". **Power:** Precharged pneumatic. **Sights:** Intended for scope use, fiber optic open sights optional. **Features:** Lothar Walther match barrel, adjustable power levels from 400-1000 FPS, operates on high pressure air from scuba tank or hand pump. Wide variety of accessories easily attach to multiple dovetail mounting rails. Manufactured in the U.S.A. by AirForce Airguns.
Price: **$439.95**

AIR FORCE TALON SS AIR RIFLE
Caliber: 177, 22, single-shot. **Barrel:** 12". **Weight:** 5.25 lbs. **Length:** 32.75". **Power:** Precharged pneumatic. **Sights:** Intended for scope use, fiber optic open sights optional. **Features:** Lothar Walther match barrel, adjustable power levels from 400-1000 FPS. Chamber in front of barrel strips away air turbulence, protects muzzle and reduces firing report. Operates on high pressure air from scuba tank or hand pump. Wide variety of accessories easily attach to multiple dovetail mounting rails. Manufactured in the U.S.A. by AirForce Airguns.
Price: **$439.95**

AIRROW MODEL A-8SRB STEALTH AIR GUN
Caliber: 177, 22, 25, 9-shot. **Barrel:** 20"; rifled. **Weight:** 6 lbs. **Length:** 34" overall. **Power:** CO2 or compressed air; variable power. **Stock:** Telescoping CAR-15-type. **Sights:** Variable 3.5-10x scope. **Features:** Velocity 1100 fps in all calibers. Pneumatic air trigger. All aircraft aluminum and stainless steel construction. Mil-spec materials and finishes. From Swivel Machine Works, Inc.
Price: About **$2,299.00**

AIRROW MODEL A-8S1P STEALTH AIR GUN
Caliber: #2512 16" arrow. **Barrel:** 16". **Weight:** 4.4 lbs. **Length:** 30.1" overall. **Power:** CO2 or compressed air; variable power. **Stock:** Telescoping CAR-15-type. **Sights:** Scope rings only. 7 oz. rechargeable cylinder and valve. **Features:** Velocity to 650 fps with 260-grain arrow. Pneumatic air trigger. Broadhead guard. All aircraft aluminum and stainless steel construction. Mil-spec materials and finishes. A-8S Models perform to 2,000 PSIG above or below water levels. Waterproof case. From Swivel Machine Works, Inc.
Price: **$1,699.00**

ARS HUNTING MASTER AR6 AIR RIFLE
Caliber: 22, 6-shot repeater. **Barrel:** 25-1/2". **Weight:** 7 lbs. **Length:** 41-1/4" overall. **Power:** Pre-compressed air from 3000 psi diving tank. **Stock:** Indonesian walnut with checkered grip; rubber buttpad. **Sights:** Blade front, adjustable peep rear. **Features:** Velocity over 1000 fps with 32-grain pellet. Receiver grooved for scope mounting. Has 6-shot rotary magazine. Imported by Air Rifle Specialists.
Price: **$580.00**

ARS/CAREER 707 AIR RIFLE
Caliber: 22, 6-shot repeater. **Barrel:** 23". **Weight:** 7.75 lbs. **Length:** 40.5" overall. **Power:** Pre-compressed air; variable power. **Stock:** Indonesian walnut with checkered grip, gloss finish. **Sights:** Hooded post front with interchangeable inserts, fully adjustable diopter rear. **Features:** Velocity to 1000 fps. Lever-action with straight feed magazine; pressure gauge in lower front air reservoir; scope mounting rail included. Imported from the Philippines by Air Rifle Specialists.
Price: **$580.00**

ANSCHUTZ 2002 MATCH AIR RIFLE
Caliber: 177, single shot. **Barrel:** 25.2". **Weight:** 10.4 lbs. **Length:** 44.5" overall. **Stock:** European walnut, blonde hardwood or colored laminated hardwood; stippled grip and forend. Also available with flat-forend walnut stock for benchrest shooting and aluminum. **Sights:** Optional sight set #6834. **Features:** Muzzle velocity 575 fps. Balance, weight match the 1907 ISU smallbore rifle. Uses #5021 match trigger. Recoil and vibration free. Fully adjustable cheekpiece and buttplate; accessory rail under forend. Available in Pneumatic and Compressed Air versions. Imported from Germany by Gunsmithing, Inc., Accuracy International, Champion's Choice.
Price: Right-hand, blonde hardwood stock, with sights **$1,275.00**
Price: Right-hand, walnut stock **$1,275.00**
Price: Right-hand, color laminate stock **$1,300.00**
Price: Right-hand, aluminum stock, butt plate **$1,495.00**
Price: Left-hand, color laminate stock **$1,595.00**
Price: Model 2002D-RT Running Target, right-hand, no sights . **$1,248.90**
Price: #6834 Sight Set **$227.10**

BEEMAN CROW MAGNUM AIR RIFLE
Caliber: 20, 22, 25, single shot. **Barrel:** 16"; 10-groove rifling. **Weight:** 8.5 lbs. **Length:** 46" overall. **Power:** Gas-spring; adjustable power to 32 foot pounds muzzle energy. Barrel-cocking. **Stock:** Classic-style hardwood; hand checkered. **Sights:** For scope use only; built-in base and 1" rings included. **Features:** Adjustable two-stage trigger. Automatic safety. Available in 22-caliber on special order. Imported by Beeman.
Price: **$1,290.00**

BEEMAN KODIAK AIR RIFLE
Caliber: 25, single shot. **Barrel:** 17.6". **Weight:** 9 lbs. **Length:** 45.6" overall. **Power:** Spring-piston, barrel cocking. **Stock:** Stained hardwood. **Sights:** Blade front, open fully adjustable rear. **Features:** Velocity to 820 fps. Up to 30 foot pounds muzzle energy. Imported by Beeman.
Price: **$670.00**

BEEMAN MAKO MKII AIR RIFLE
Caliber: 177, 22 single shot. **Barrel:** 20", with compensator. **Weight:** 5.5 to 7.8 lbs. **Length:** 39" overall. **Power:** Pre-charged pneumatic. **Stock:** Stained beech; Monte Carlo cheekpiece; checkered grip. **Sights:** None furnished. **Features:** Velocity to 930 fps. Gives over 50 shots per charge. Manual safety; brass trigger blade; vented rubber butt pad. Requires scuba tank for air. Imported from England by Beeman.
Price: **$999.00**

BEEMAN R1 AIR RIFLE
Caliber: 177, 20 or 22, single shot. **Barrel:** 19.6", 12-groove rifling. **Weight:** 8.5 lbs. **Length:** 45.2" overall. **Power:** Spring-piston, barrel cocking. **Stock:** Walnut-stained beech; cut-checkered pistol grip; Monte Carlo comb and cheekpiece; rubber buttpad. **Sights:** Tunnel front with interchangeable inserts, open rear click-adjustable for windage and elevation. Grooved for scope mounting. **Features:** Velocity of 940-1000 fps (177), 860 fps (20), 800 fps (22). Non-drying nylon piston and breech seals. Adjustable metal trigger. Milled steel safety. Right- or left-hand stock. Adjustable cheekpiece and buttplate at extra cost. Custom and Super Laser versions available. Imported by Beeman.
Price: Right-hand, 177, 20, 22 . . . . **$605.00**
Price: Left-hand, 177, 20, 22 . . . . **$680.00**

BEEMAN R7 AIR RIFLE
Caliber: 177, 20, single shot. **Barrel:** 17". **Weight:** 6.1 lbs. **Length:** 40.2" overall. **Power:** Spring piston. **Stock:** Stained beech. **Sights:** Hooded front, fully adjustable micrometer click open rear. **Features:** Velocity to 700 fps (177), 620 fps (20). Receiver grooved for scope mounting; double-jointed cocking lever; fully adjustable trigger; checkered grip. Imported by Beeman.
Price: **$330.00**

BEEMAN R9 AIR RIFLE

Caliber: 177, 20, single shot. **Barrel:** NA. **Weight:** 7.3 lbs. **Length:** 43" overall. **Power:** Spring-piston, barrel cocking. **Stock:** Stained hardwood. **Sights:** Tunnel post front, fully adjustable open rear. **Features:** Velocity to 1000 fps (177), 800 fps (20). Adjustable Rekord trigger; automatic safety; receiver dovetailed for scope mounting. Imported from Germany by Beeman Precision Airguns.
Price: **$360.00**

Beeman R9 Deluxe Air Rifle

Same as R9 except has extended forend stock, checkered pistol grip, grip cap, carved Monte Carlo cheekpiece. Globe front sight with inserts. Imported by Beeman.
Price: **$440.00**

BEEMAN R11 MKII AIR RIFLE

Caliber: 177, single shot. **Barrel:** 19.6". **Weight:** 8.6 lbs. **Length:** 43.5" overall. **Power:** Spring-piston, barrel cocking. **Stock:** Walnut-stained beech; adjustable buttplate and cheekpiece. **Sights:** None furnished. Has dovetail for scope mounting. **Features:** Velocity 910-940 fps. All-steel barrel sleeve. Imported by Beeman.
Price: **$620.00**

BEEMAN SUPER 12 AIR RIFLE

Caliber: 22, 25, 12-shot magazine. **Barrel:** 19", 12-groove rifling. **Weight:** 7.8 lbs. **Length:** 41.7" overall. **Power:** Pre-charged pneumatic; external air reservoir. **Stock:** European walnut. **Sights:** None furnished; drilled and tapped for scope mounting; scope mount included. **Features:** Velocity to 850 fps (25-caliber). Adjustable power setting gives 30-70 shots per 400 cc air bottle. Requires scuba tank for air. Imported by Beeman.
Price: **$1,940.00**

BEEMAN RX-2 GAS-SPRING MAGNUM AIR RIFLE

Caliber: 177, 20, 22, 25, single shot. **Barrel:** 19.6", 12-groove rifling. **Weight:** 8.8 lbs. **Power:** Gas-spring piston air; single stroke barrel cocking. **Stock:** Walnut-finished hardwood, hand checkered, with cheekpiece. Adjustable cheekpiece and buttplate. **Sights:** Tunnel front, click-adjustable rear. **Features:** Velocity adjustable to about 1200 fps. Uses special sealed chamber of air as a mainspring. Gas-spring cannot take a set. Imported by Beeman.
Price: 177, 20, 22 or 25 regular, right-hand **$670.00**
Price: 177, 20, 22, 25, left-hand **$670.00**

BEEMAN R1 CARBINE

Caliber: 177, 20, 22, 25, single shot. **Barrel:** 16.1". **Weight:** 8.6 lbs. **Length:** 41.7" overall. **Power:** Spring-piston, barrel cocking. **Stock:** Stained beech; Monte Carlo comb and checkpiece; cut checkered pistol grip; rubber buttpad. **Sights:** Tunnel front with interchangeable inserts, open adjustable rear; receiver grooved for scope mounting. **Features:** Velocity up to 1000 fps (177). Non-drying nylon piston and breech seals. Adjustable metal trigger. Machined steel receiver end cap and safety. Right- or left-hand stock. Imported by Beeman.
Price: 177, 20, 22, 25, right hand **$605.00**
Price: As above, left-hand. **$680.00**

BEEMAN/FEINWERKBAU 603 AIR RIFLE

Caliber: 177, single shot. **Barrel:** 16.6". **Weight:** 10.8 lbs. **Length:** 43" overall. **Power:** Single stroke pneumatic. **Stock:** Special laminated hardwoods and hard rubber for stability. Multi-colored stock also available. **Sights:** Tunnel front with interchangeable inserts, click micrometer match aperture rear. **Features:** Velocity to 570 fps. Recoilless action; double supported barrel; special, short rifled area frees pellet form barrel faster so shooter's motion has minimum effect on accuracy. Fully adjustable match trigger with separately adjustable trigger and trigger slack weight. Trigger and sights blocked when loading latch is open. Imported by Beeman.
Price: Right-hand **$1,625.00**
Price: Left-hand **$1,775.00**
Price: Junior **$1,500.00**

BEEMAN/FEINWERKBAU 300-S AND 300 JUNIOR MINI-MATCH

Caliber: 177, single shot. **Barrel:** 17-1/8". **Weight:** 8.8 lbs. **Length:** 40" overall. **Power:** Spring-piston, single stroke sidelever cocking. **Stock:** Walnut. Stippled grip, adjustable buttplate. Scaled-down for youthful or slightly built shooters. **Sights:** Globe front with interchangeable inserts, micro. adjustable rear. Front and rear sights move as a single unit. **Features:** Recoilless, vibration free. Grooved for scope mounts. Steel piston ring. Cocking effort about 9-1/2 lbs. Barrel sleeve optional. Left-hand model available. Imported by Beeman.
Price: Right-hand **$1,680.00**
Price: Left-hand **$1,825.00**

BEEMAN/FEINWERKBAU P70 AND P70 JUNIOR AIR RIFLE

Caliber: 177, single shot. **Barrel:** 16.6". **Weight:** 10.6 lbs. **Length:** 42.6" overall. **Power:** Precharged pneumatic. **Stock:** Laminated hardwoods and hard rubber for stability. Multi-colored stock also available. **Sights:** Tunnel front with interchangeable inserts, click micrometer match aperture rear. **Features:** Velocity to 570 fps. Recoilless action; double supported barrel; special short rifled area frees pellet from barrel faster so shooter's motion has minimum effect on accuracy. Fully adjustable match trigger with separately adjustable trigger and trigger slack weight. Trigger and sights blocked when loading latch is open. Imported by Beeman.
Price: P70, pre-charged, right-hand **$1,600.00**
Price: P70, pre-charged, left-hand **$1,690.00**
Price: P70, pre-charged, Junior **$1,600.00**
Price: P70, pre-charged, right-hand, multi **$1,465.00**

BEEMAN/HW 97 AIR RIFLE

Caliber: 177, 20, single shot. **Barrel:** 17.75". **Weight:** 9.2 lbs. **Length:** 44.1" overall. **Power:** Spring-piston, underlever cocking. **Stock:** Walnut-stained beech; rubber buttpad. **Sights:** None. Receiver grooved for scope mounting. **Features:** Velocity 830 fps (177). Fixed barrel with fully opening, direct loading breech. Adjustable trigger. Imported by Beeman Precision Airguns.
Price: Right-hand only **$605.00**

BENJAMIN SHERIDAN PNEUMATIC (PUMP-UP) AIR RIFLES

Caliber: 177 or 22, single shot. **Barrel:** 19-3/8", rifled brass. **Weight:** 5-1/2 lbs. **Length:** 36-1/4" overall. **Power:** Underlever pneumatic, hand pumped. **Stock:** American walnut stock and forend. **Sights:** High ramp front, fully adjustable notch rear. **Features:** Variable velocity to 800 fps. Bolt action with ambidextrous push-pull safety. Black or nickel finish. Made in the U.S. by Benjamin Sheridan Co.
Price: Black finish, Model 397 (177), Model 392 (22) **$224.00**
Price: Nickel finish, Model S397 (177), Model S392 (22) **$245.00**

BRNO TAU-200 AIR RIFLE

Caliber: 177, single shot. **Barrel:** 19", rifled. **Weight:** 7-1/2 lbs. **Length:** 42" overall. **Power:** 6-oz. CO2 cartridge. **Stock:** Wood match style with adjustable comb and buttplate. **Sights:** Globe front with interchangeable inserts, fully adjustable open rear. **Features:** Adjustable trigger. Comes with extra seals, large CO2 bottle, counterweight. Imported by Great Lakes Airguns. Available in Standard Universal, Deluxe Universal, International and Target Sporter versions.
Price: Standard Universal (ambidex. stock with buttstock extender, adj. cheekpiece).. . . . . **$349.50**
Price: Deluxe Universal (as above but with micro-adj. aperture sight) **$449.50**
Price: International (like Deluxe Universal but with right- or left-hand stock) **$454.50**
Price: Target Sporter (like Std. Universal but with 4X scope, no sights) **$412.50**

BSA MAGNUM SUPERSTAR™ MK2 MAGNUM AIR RIFLE, CARBINE

Caliber: 177, 22, 25, single shot. **Barrel:** 18-1/2". **Weight:** 8 lbs., 8 oz. **Length:** 43" overall. **Power:** Spring-air, underlever cocking. **Stock:** Oil-finished hardwood; Monte Carlo with cheekpiece, checkered at grip; recoil pad. **Sights:** Ramp front, micrometer adjustable rear. Maxi-Grip scope rail. **Features:** Velocity 950 fps (177), 750 fps (22), 600 fps (25). Patented rotating breech design. Maxi-Grip scope rail protects optics from recoil; automatic anti-beartrap plus manual safety. Imported from U.K. by Precision Sales International, Inc.
Price: **$349.95**
Price: MKII Carbine (14" barrel, 39-1/2" overall). **$349.95**

AIRGUNS

AIRGUNS—LONG GUNS

BSA MAGNUM SUPERSPORT™ AIR RIFLE
Caliber: 177, 22, 25, single shot. **Barrel:** 18-1/2". **Weight:** 6 lbs., 8 oz. **Length:** 41" overall. **Power:** Spring-air, barrel cocking. **Stock:** Oil-finished hardwood; Monte Carlo with cheekpiece, recoil pad. **Sights:** Ramp front, micrometer adjustable rear. **Features:** Velocity 950 fps (177), 750 fps (22), 600 fps (25). Patented Maxi-Grip scope rail protects optics from recoil; automatic anti-beartrap plus manual tang safety. Muzzle brake standard. Imported for U.K. by Precision Sales International, Inc.
Price: $194.95
Price: Carbine, 14" barrel, muzzle brake $214.95

BSA MAGNUM GOLDSTAR MAGNUM AIR RIFLE
Caliber: 177, 22, 10-shot repeater. **Barrel:** 17-1/2". **Weight:** 8 lbs., 8 oz. **Length:** 42.5" overall. **Power:** Spring-air, underlever cocking. **Stock:** Oil-finished hardwood; Monte Carlo with cheekpiece, checkered at grip; recoil pad. **Sights:** Ramp front, micrometer adjustable rear; comes with Maxi-Grip scope rail. **Features:** Velocity 950 fps (177), 750 fps (22). Patented 10-shot indexing magazine; Maxi-Grip scope rail protects optics from recoil; automatic anti-beartrap plus manual safety; muzzlebrake standard. Imported from U.K. by Precision Sales International, Inc.
Price: $499.95

BSA MAGNUM SUPERTEN AIR RIFLE
Caliber: 177, 22 10-shot repeater. **Barrel:** 17-1/2". **Weight:** 7 lbs., 8 oz. **Length:** 37" overall. **Power:** Precharged pneumatic via buddy bottle. **Stock:** Oil-finished hardwood; Monte Carlo with cheekpiece, cut checkering at grip; adjustable recoil pad. **Sights:** No sights; intended for scope use. **Features:** Velocity 1000+ fps (177), 1000+ fps (22). Patented 10-shot indexing magazine, bolt-action loading. Left-hand version also available. Imported from U.K. by Precision Sales International, Inc.
Price: $599.95

BSA METEOR MK6 AIR RIFLE
Caliber: 177, 22, single shot. **Barrel:** 18-1/2". **Weight:** 6 lbs. **Length:** 41" overall. **Power:** Spring-air, barrel cocking. **Stock:** Oil-finished hardwood. **Sights:** Ramp front, micrometer adjustable rear. **Features:** Velocity 650 fps (177), 500 fps (22). Automatic anti-beartrap; manual tang safety. Receiver grooved for scope mounting. Imported from U.K. by Precision Sales International, Inc.
Price: Rifle $144.95
Price: Carbine $164.95

CROSMAN MODEL 66 POWERMASTER
Caliber: 177 (single shot pellet) or BB, 200-shot reservoir. **Barrel:** 20", rifled steel. **Weight:** 3 lbs. **Length:** 38-1/2" overall. **Power:** Pneumatic; hand pumped. **Stock:** Wood-grained ABS plastic; checkered pistol grip and forend. **Sights:** Fiber optic front, fully adjustable open rear. **Features:** Velocity about 645 fps. Bolt action, cross-bolt safety. From Crosman.
Price: Model 66BX $60.00
Price: Model 664X (as above, with 4x scope). $70.00
Price: Model 664SB (as above with silver and black finish), about . . . $75.00

CROSMAN REMINGTON GENESIS AIR RIFLE
Caliber: 177 **Barrel:** Break-action. **Sights:** Fiber optic front, adj. rear. Dovetailed for scope. **Stock:** Synthetic, thumbhole pistol grip. **Weight:** 6.5 lbs. **Overall length:** 43".
Price: $249.99
Price: W 3-9x40 scope $279.99

CROSMAN MODEL 760 PUMPMASTER
Caliber: 177 pellets (single shot) or BB (200-shot reservoir). **Barrel:** 19-1/2", rifled steel. **Weight:** 2 lbs., 12 oz. **Length:** 33.5" overall. **Power:** Pneumatic, hand pumped. **Stock:** Walnut-finished ABS plastic stock and forend. **Features:** Velocity to 590 fps (BBs, 10 pumps). Short stroke, power determined by number of strokes. Fiber optic front sight and adjustable rear sight. Cross-bolt safety. From Crosman.
Price: Model 760B $40.00
Price: Model 764SB (silver and black finish), about $55.00
Price: Model 760SK . . . . NA
Price: Model 760BRO . . . . NA

CROSMAN MODEL 1077 REPEAT AIR RIFLE
Caliber: 177 pellets, 12-shot clip. **Barrel:** 20.3", rifled steel. **Weight:** 3 lbs., 11 oz. **Length:** 38.8" overall. **Power:** CO2 Powerlet. **Stock:** Textured synthetic or hardwood. **Sights:** Blade front, fully adjustable rear. **Features:**
Velocity 590 fps. Removable 12-shot clip. True semi-automatic action. From Crosman.
Price: $75.00
Price: 1077W (walnut stock) $110.00

CROSMAN 2260 AIR RIFLE
Caliber: 22, single shot. **Barrel:** 24". **Weight:** 4 lbs., 12 oz. **Length:** 39.75" overall. **Power:** CO2 Powerlet. **Stock:** Hardwood. **Sights:** Blade front, adjustable rear open or peep. **Features:** About 600 fps. Made in U.S. by Crosman Corp.
Price: . . . . NA

CROSMAN MODEL 2100 CLASSIC AIR RIFLE
Caliber: 177 pellets (single shot), or BB (200-shot BB reservoir). **Barrel:** 21", rifled. **Weight:** 4 lbs., 13 oz. **Length:** 39-3/4" overall. **Power:** Pump-up, pneumatic. **Stock:** Wood-grained checkered ABS plastic. **Features:** Three pumps give about 450 fps, 10 pumps about 755 fps (BBs). Cross-bolt safety; concealed reservoir holds over 200 BBs. From Crosman.
Price: Model 2100B $75.00

CROSMAN MODEL 2200 MAGNUM AIR RIFLE
Caliber: 22, single shot. **Barrel:** 19", rifled steel. **Weight:** 4 lbs., 12 oz. **Length:** 39" overall. **Stock:** Full-size, wood-grained ABS plastic with checkered grip and forend or American walnut. **Sights:** Ramp front, open step-adjustable rear. **Features:** Variable pump power; three pumps give 395 fps, six pumps 530 fps, 10 pumps 595 fps (average). Full-size adult air rifle. Has white line spacers at pistol grip and buttplate. From Crosman.
Price: $75.00

DAISY 1938 RED RYDER 60th ANNIVERSARY CLASSIC
Caliber: BB, 650-shot repeating action. **Barrel:** Smoothbore steel with shroud. **Weight:** 2.2 lbs. **Length:** 35.4" overall. **Stock:** Walnut stock burned with Red Ryder lariat signature. **Sights:** Post front, adjustable V-slot rear. **Features:** Walnut forend. Saddle ring with leather thong. Lever cocking. Gravity feed. Controlled velocity. One of Daisy's most popular guns. From Daisy Mfg. Co.
Price: $39.95

DAISY MODEL 840 GRIZZLY
Caliber: 177 pellet single shot; or BB 350-shot. **Barrel:** 19", smoothbore, steel. **Weight:** 2.25 lbs. **Length:** 36.8" overall. **Power:** Pneumatic, single pump. **Stock:** Moulded wood-grain stock and forend. **Sights:** Ramp front, open, adjustable rear. **Features:** Muzzle velocity 320 fps (BB), 300 fps (pellet). Steel buttplate; straight pull bolt action; cross-bolt safety. Forend forms pump lever. From Daisy Mfg. Co.
Price: $32.95
Price: 840C Mossy Oak® Break Up™ camo $49.95

DAISY MODEL 7840 BUCKMASTER
Caliber: 177 pellets, or BB. **Barrel:** Smoothbore steel. **Weight:** 2.25 lbs. **Length:** 36.8" overall. **Power:** Single-pump pneumatic. **Stock:** Moulded with checkering and woodgrain. **Sights:** Ramp and blade front, adjustable open rear plus Electronic Point Sight. **Features:** Velocity to 320 fps (BB), 300fps (pellet). Cross-bolt trigger block safety. From Daisy Mfg. Co.
Price: $54.95

DAISY MODEL 105 BUCK
Caliber: 177 or BB. **Barrel:** Smoothbore steel. **Weight:** 1.6 lbs. **Length:** 29.8" overall. **Power:** Lever cocking, spring air. **Stock:** Stained solid wood. **Sights:** TRUGLO® Fiber Optic, open fixed rear. **Features:** Velocity to 275. Cross-bolt trigger block safety. From Daisy Mfg. Co.
Price: . . . . NA

Daisy Model 95 Timberwolf
Similar to the 105 Buck except velocity to 325 fps. Weighs 2.4 lbs, overall length 35.2".
Price: $38.95

DAISY/POWERLINE 853
Caliber: 177 pellets, single shot. **Barrel:** 20.9"; 12-groove rifling, high-grade solid steel by Lothar Waltherô, precision crowned; bore size for precision match pellets. **Weight:** 5.08 lbs. **Length:** 38.9" overall. **Power:** Single-pump pneumatic. **Stock:** Full-length select American hardwood, stained and finished; black buttplate with white spacers. **Sights:** Globe front with four aperture inserts; precision micrometer adjustable rear peep sight mounted on a standard 3/8" dovetail receiver mount.
Price: $225.00

AIRGUNS—LONG GUNS

DAISY/POWERLINE 856 PUMP-UP AIRGUN

Caliber: 177 pellets (single shot) or BB (100-shot reservoir). **Barrel:** Rifled steel with shroud. **Weight:** 2.7 lbs. **Length:** 37.4" overall. **Power:** Pneumatic pump-up. **Stock:** Moulded wood-grain with Monte Carlo cheekpiece. **Sights:** Ramp and blade front, open rear adjustable for elevation. **Features:** Velocity from 315 fps (two pumps) to 650 fps (10 pumps). Shoots BBs or pellets. Heavy die-cast metal receiver. Cross-bolt trigger-block safety. From Daisy Mfg. Co.

Price: **$39.95**
Price: 856C **$59.95**

DAISY/POWERLINE 1170 PELLET RIFLE

Caliber: 177, single shot. **Barrel:** Rifled steel. **Weight:** 5.5 lbs. **Length:** 42.5" overall. **Power:** Spring-air, barrel cocking. **Stock:** Hardwood. **Sights:** Hooded post front, micrometer adjustable open rear. **Features:** Velocity to 800 fps. Monte Carlo comb. From Daisy Mfg. Co.

Price: **$129.95**
Price: Model 131 (velocity to 600 fps) **$117.95**
Price: Model 1150 (black copolymer stock, velocity to 600 fps) ... **$77.95**

DAISY/POWERLINE EAGLE 7856 PUMP-UP AIRGUN

Caliber: 177 (pellets), BB, 100-shot BB magazine. **Barrel:** Rifled steel with shroud. **Weight:** 3.3 lbs. **Length:** 37.4" overall. **Power:** Pneumatic pump-up. **Stock:** Moulded wood-grain plastic. **Sights:** Ramp and blade front, open rear adjustable for elevation. **Features:** Velocity from 315 fps (two pumps) to 650 fps (10 pumps). Finger grooved forend. Cross-bolt trigger-block safety. From Daisy Mfg. Co.

Price: With 4x scope, about **$49.95**

DAISY/POWERLINE 880

Caliber: 177 pellet or BB, 50-shot BB magazine, single shot for pellets. **Barrel:** Rifled steel. **Weight:** 3.7 lbs. **Length:** 37.6" overall. **Power:** Multi-pump pneumatic. **Stock:** Moulded wood grain; Monte Carlo comb. **Sights:** Hooded front, adjustable rear. **Features:** Velocity to 685 fps. (BB). Variable power (velocity, range) increase with pump strokes; resin receiver with dovetail scope mount. Made in U.S.A. by Daisy Mfg. Co.

Price: **$50.95**

DAISY/POWERLINE 1000 AIR RIFLE

Caliber: 177, single shot. **Barrel:** NA. **Weight:** 6.15 lbs. **Length:** 43" overall. **Power:** Spring-air, barrel cocking. **Stock:** Stained hardwood. **Sights:** Hooded blade front on ramp, fully adjustable micrometer rear. **Features:** Velocity to 1000 fps. Blued finish; trigger block safety. From Daisy Mfg. Co.

Price: **$208.95**

DAISY/YOUTHLINE MODEL 105 AIR RIFLE

Caliber: BB, 400-shot magazine. **Barrel:** 13-1/2". **Weight:** 1.6 lbs. **Length:** 29.8" overall. **Power:** Spring. **Stock:** Moulded woodgrain. **Sights:** Blade on ramp front, fixed rear. **Features:** Velocity to 275 fps. Blue finish. Cross-bolt trigger block safety. Made in U.S. by Daisy Mfg. Co.

Price: **$28.95**

DAISY/YOUTHLINE MODEL 95 AIR RIFLE

Caliber: DD, 700-shot magazine. **Barrel:** 18". **Weight:** 2.4 lbs. **Length:** 35.2" overall. **Power:** Spring. **Stock:** Stained hardwood. **Sights:** Blade on ramp front, open adjustable rear. **Features:** Velocity to 325 fps. Cross-bolt trigger block safety. Made in U.S. by Daisy Mfg. Co.

Price: **$38.95**

EAA/BAIKAL MP-512 AIR RIFLE

Caliber: 177, single shot. **Barrel:** 17.7". **Weight:** 6.2 lbs. **Length:** 41.3" overall. **Power:** Spring-piston, single stroke. **Stock:** Black synthetic. **Sights:** Adjustable rear, hooded front. **Features:** Velocity 490 fps. Hammer-forged, rifled barrel; automatic safety; scope mount rail. Imported from Russia by European American Armory.

Price: 177 caliber **$49.00**
Price: 512M (590 fps) **$65.00**

EAA/BAIKAL IZH-61 AIR RIFLE

Caliber: 177 pellet, 5-shot magazine. **Barrel:** 17.8". **Weight:** 6.4 lbs. **Length:** 31" overall. **Power:** Spring piston, side-cocking lever. **Stock:** Black plastic. **Sights:** Adjustable rear, fully hooded front. **Features:** Velocity 490 fps. Futuristic design with adjustable stock. Imported from Russia by European American Armory.

Price: **$99.00**

EAA/BAIKAL IZHMP-532 AIR RIFLE

Caliber: 177 pellet, single shot. **Barrel:** 15.8". **Weight:** 9.3 lbs. **Length:** 46.1" overall. **Power:** Single-stroke pneumatic. **Stock:** One- or two-piece competition-style stock with adjustable butt pad, pistol grip. **Sights:** Fully adjustable rear, hooded front. **Features:** Velocity 460 fps. Five-way adjustable trigger. Imported from Russia by European American Armory.

Price: **$599.00**

GAMO DELTA AIR RIFLE

Caliber: 177. **Barrel:** 15.7". **Weight:** 4.2 lbs. **Length:** 37.8". **Power:** Single-stroke pneumatic, 525 fps. **Stock:** Synthetic. **Sights:** Truglo fiber optic.

Price: **$89.95**

GAMO YOUNG HUNTER AIR RIFLE

Caliber: 177. **Barrel:** 17.7". **Weight:** 5.5 lbs. **Length:** 41". **Power:** Single-stroke pneumatic, 640 fps. **Stock:** Wood. **Sights:** Truglo fiber optic adjustable. **Features:** Excellent for young adults, it has a rifled steel barrel, hooded front sight, grooved receiver for scope. Imported from Spain by Gamo.

Price: **$129.95**
Price: Combo packed with BSA 4x32 scope and rings **$169.95**

GAMO SPORTER AIR RIFLE

Caliber: 177. **Barrel:** NA **Weight:** 5.5 lbs. **Length:** 42.5". **Power:** Single-stroke pneumatic, 760 fps. **Stock:** Wood. **Sights:** Adjustable Truglo fiber optic. **Features:** Intended to bridge the gap between Gamo's Young Hunter model and the adult-sized Hunter 440. Imported from Spain by Gamo.

Price: **$159.95**

GAMO HUNTER 440 AIR RIFLE

Caliber: 177, 22. **Barrel:** NA. **Weight:** 6.6 lbs. **Length:** 43.3". **Power:** Single-stroke pneumatifc, 1,000 fps (177), 750 fps (22). **Stock:** Wood. **Sights:** Adjustable Truglo fiber optic. **Features:** Adjustable two-stage trigger, rifled barrel, raised scope ramp on receiver. Realtree camo model available.

Price: **$229.95**
Price: Hunter 440 Combo with BSA 4x32mm scope **$259.95**

HAMMERLI AR 50 AIR RIFLE

Caliber: 177. **Barrel:** 19.8". **Weight:** 10 lbs. **Length:** 43.2" overall. **Power:** Compressed air. **Stock:** Anatomically-shaped universal and right-hand; match style; multi-colored laminated wood. **Sights:** Interchangeable element tunnel front, fully adjustable Hammerli peep rear. **Features:** Vibration-free firing release; fully adjustable match trigger and trigger stop; stainless air tank, built-in pressure gauge. Gives 270 shots per filling. Imported from Switzerland by Sigarms, Inc.

Price: **$1,653.00**

HAMMERLI MODEL 450 MATCH AIR RIFLE

Caliber: 177, single shot. **Barrel:** 19.5". **Weight:** 9.8 lbs. **Length:** 43.3" overall. **Power:** Pneumatic. **Stock:** Match style with stippled grip, rubber buttpad. Beach or walnut. **Sights:** Match tunnel front, Hammerli diopter rear. **Features:** Velocity about 560 fps. Removable sights; forend sling rail; adjustable trigger; adjustable comb. Imported from Switzerland by Sigarms, Inc.

Price: Beech stock **$1,355.00**
Price: Walnut stock **$1,395.00**

MARKSMAN BB BUDDY AIR RIFLE

Caliber: 177, 20-shot magazine. **Barrel:** 10.5" smoothbore. **Weight:** 1.6 lbs. **Length:** 33" overall. **Power:** Spring-air. **Stock:** Moulded composition. **Sights:** Blade on ramp front, adjustable V-slot rear. **Features:** Velocity 275 fps. Positive feed; automatic safety. Youth-sized lightweight design. Made in U.S. From Marksman Products.

Price: **$27.95**

MARKSMAN 2015 LASERHAWK™ BB REPEATER AIR RIFLE

Caliber: 177 BB, 20-shot magazine. **Barrel:** 10.5" smoothbore. **Weight:** 1.6 lbs. **Length:** Adjustable to 33", 34" or 35" overall. **Power:** Spring-air. **Stock:** Moulded composition. **Sights:** Fixed fiber optic front sight, adjustable elevation V-slot rear. **Features:** Velocity about 275 fps. Positive feed; automatic safety. Adjustable stock. Made in the U.S. From Marksman Products.

Price: **$33.00**

RWS/DIANA MODEL 24 AIR RIFLE

Caliber: 177, 22, single shot. **Barrel:** 17", rifled. **Weight:** 6 lbs. **Length:** 42" overall. **Power:** Spring-air, barrel cocking. **Stock:** Beech. **Sights:** Hooded front, adjustable rear. **Features:** Velocity of 700 fps (177). Easy cocking effort; blue finish. Imported from Germany by Dynamit Nobel-RWS, Inc.
Price: 24, 24C **$215.00**

RWS/Diana Model 34 Air Rifle

Similar to the Model 24 except has 19" barrel, weighs 7.5 lbs. Gives velocity of 1000 fps (177), 800 fps (22). Adjustable trigger, synthetic seals. Comes with scope rail.
Price: 177 or 22 . . . . **$290.00**
Price: Model 34N (nickel-plated metal, black epoxy-coated wood stock) **$350.00**
Price: Model 34BC (matte black metal, black stock, 4x32 scope, mounts) **$510.00**

RWS/DIANA MODEL 36 AIR RIFLE

Caliber: 177, 22, single shot. **Barrel:** 19", rifled. **Weight:** 8 lbs. overall. **Power:** Spring-air, barrel cocking. **Stock:** Beech. **Sights:** Hooded front (interchangeable inserts available), adjustable rear. **Features:** Velocity of 1000 fps (177-cal.). Comes with scope mount; two-stage adjustable trigger. Imported from Germany by Dynamit Nobel-RWS, Inc.
Price: 36, 36C **$435.00**

RWS/DIANA MODEL 52 AIR RIFLE

Caliber: 177, 22, 25, single shot. **Barrel:** 17", rifled. **Weight:** 8-1/2 lbs. **Length:** 43" overall. **Power:** Spring-air, sidelever cocking. **Stock:** Beech, with Monte Carlo, cheekpiece, checkered grip and forend. **Sights:** Ramp front, adjustable rear. **Features:** Velocity of 1100 fps (177). Blue finish. Solid rubber buttpad. Imported from Germany by Dynamit Nobel-RWS, Inc.
Price: 177, 22 . . . . **$565.00**
Price: 25 . . . . **$605.00**
Price: Model 52 Deluxe (177) **$810.00**
Price: Model 48B (as above except matte black metal, black stock) **$535.00**
Price: Model 48 (same as Model 52 except no Monte Carlo, cheekpiece or checkering) **$520.00**

RWS/DIANA MODEL 45 AIR RIFLE

Caliber: 177, single shot. **Weight:** 8 lbs. **Length:** 45" overall. **Power:** Spring-air, barrel cocking. **Stock:** Walnut-finished hardwood with rubber recoil pad. **Sights:** Globe front with interchangeable inserts, micro. click open rear with four-way blade. **Features:** Velocity of 820 fps. Dovetail base for either micrometer peep sight or scope mounting. Automatic safety. Imported from Germany by Dynamit Nobel-RWS, Inc.
Price: **$350.00**

RWS/DIANA MODEL 46 AIR RIFLE

Caliber: 177, 22, single shot. **Barrel:** 18". **Weight:** 8.2 lbs. **Length:** 45" overall. **Stock:** Hardwood Monte Carlo. **Sights:** Blade front, adjustable rear. **Features:** Underlever cocking spring-air (950 fps in 177, 780 fps in 22); extended scope rail, automatic safety, rubber buttpad, adjustable trigger. Imported from Germany by Dynamit Nobel-RWS Inc.
Price: **$470.00**
Price: Model 46E (as above except matte black metal, black stock) **$430.00**

RWS/DIANA MODEL 54 AIR RIFLE

Caliber: 177, 22, single shot. **Barrel:** 17". **Weight:** 9 lbs. **Length:** 43" overall. **Power:** Spring-air, sidelever cocking. **Stock:** Walnut with Monte Carlo cheekpiece, checkered grip and forend. **Sights:** Ramp front, fully adjustable rear. **Features:** Velocity to 1000 fps (177), 900 fps (22). Totally recoilless system; floating action absorbs recoil. Imported from Germany by Dynamit Nobel-RWS, Inc.
Price: **$785.00**

RWS/DIANA MODEL 92/93/94 AIR RIFLES

Caliber: 177, 22, single shot. **Barrel:** N/A. **Weight:** N/A. **Length:** N/A. **Stock:** Beechwood; Monte Carlo. **Sights:** Hooded front, fully adjustable rear. **Features:** Break-barrel, spring-air; receiver grooved for scope; adjustable trigger; lifetime warranty. Imported from Spain by Dynamit Nobel-RWS Inc.
Price: Model 92 (auto safety, 700 fps in 177) . . . . **NA**
Price: Model 93 (manual safety, 850 fps in 177) . . . . **NA**
Price: Model 94 (auto safety, 1,000 fps in 177) . . . . **NA**

RWS/DIANA MODEL 350 MAGNUM AIR RIFLE

Caliber: 177, 22, single shot. **Barrel:** 19-1/2". **Weight:** 8 lbs. **Length:** 48". **Stock:** Beechwood; Monte Carlo. **Sights:** Hooded front, fully adjustable rear. **Features:** Break-barrel, spring-air; 1,250 fps. Imported from Germany by Dynamit Nobel-RWS Inc.
Price: Model 350. . . . . **NA**

TECH FORCE BS4 OLYMPIC COMPETITION AIR RIFLE

Caliber: 177 pellet, single shot. **Barrel:** N/A. **Weight:** 10.8 lbs. **Length:** 43.3" overall. **Power:** Spring piston, sidelever action. **Stock:** Wood with semi-pistol grip, adjustable butt plate. **Sights:** Micro-adjustable competition rear, hooded front. **Features:** Velocity 640 fps. Recoilless action; adjustable trigger. Includes carrying case. Imported from China by Compasseco Inc.
Price: **$595.00**
Price: Optional diopter rear sight **$79.95**

TECH FORCE 6 AIR RIFLE

Caliber: 177 pellet, single shot. **Barrel:** 14". **Weight:** 6 lbs. **Length:** 35.5" overall. **Power:** Spring piston, sidelever action. **Stock:** Paratrooper-style folding, full pistol grip. **Sights:** Adjustable rear, hooded front. **Features:** Velocity 800 fps. All-metal construction; grooved for scope mounting. Imported from China by Compasseco Inc.
Price: **$69.95**

Tech Force 51 Air Rifle

Similar to Tech Force 6, but with break-barrel cocking mechanism and folding stock fitted with recoil pad. Overall length, 36". Weighs 6 lbs. From Compasseco Inc.
Price: **$69.95**

TECH FORCE 25 AIR RIFLE

Caliber: 177, 22 pellet; single shot. **Barrel:** N/A. **Weight:** 7.5 lbs. **Length:** 46.2" overall. **Power:** Spring piston, break-action barrel. **Stock:** Oil-finished wood; Monte Carlo stock with recoil pad. **Sights:** Adjustable rear, hooded front with insert. **Features:** Velocity 1,000 fps (177); grooved receiver and scope stop for scope mounting; adjustable trigger; trigger safety. Imported from China by Compasseco Inc.
Price: 177 or 22 caliber **$125.00**
Price: Includes rifle and Tech Force 96 red dot point sight **$164.95**

TECH FORCE 36 AIR RIFLE

Caliber: 177 pellet, single shot. **Barrel:** N/A. **Weight:** 7.4 lbs. **Length:** 43" overall. **Power:** Spring piston, underlever cocking. **Stock:** Monte Carlo hardwood stock; recoil pad. **Sights:** Adjustable rear, hooded front. **Features:** Velocity 900 fps; grooved receiver and scope stop for scope mounting; auto-reset safety. Imported from China by Compasseco Inc.
Price: **$89.95**

WHISCOMBE JW SERIES AIR RIFLES

Caliber: 177, 20, 22, 25, single shot. **Barrel:** 15", Lothar Walther. Polygonal rifling. **Weight:** 9 lbs., 8 oz. **Length:** 39" overall. **Power:** Dual spring-piston, multi-stroke; underlever cocking. **Stock:** Walnut with adjustable buttplate and cheekpiece. **Sights:** None furnished; grooved scope rail. **Features:** Velocity 660-1000 (JW80) fps (22-caliber, fixed barrel) depending upon model. Interchangeable barrels; automatic safety; muzzle weight; semi-floating action; twin opposed pistons with counter-wound springs; adjustable trigger. All models include H.O.T. System (Harmonic Optimization Tunable System). Imported from England by Pelaire Products.
Price: JW50, MKII fixed barrel only. **$2,085.00**
Price: JW65, MKII. **$2,085.00**
Price: JW80, MKII. **$2,195.00**

AIRGUNS

COMPENDIUM OF STATE LAWS GOVERNING FIREARMS

The following chart lists the main provisions of state firearms laws as of the date of publication (9-2003). In addition to the state provisions, the purchase, sale, and, in certain circumstances, the possession and interstate transportation of firearms are regulated by the Federal Gun Control Act of 1968 as amended by the Firearms Owners' Protection Act of 1986. Also, cities and localities may have their own gun ordinances in addition to federal and state restrictions. Details may be obtained by contacting local law enforcement authorities or by consulting your state's firearms law digest compiled by the NRA Institute for Legislative Action.

STATE	GUN BAN	EXEMPTIONS TO NICS[2]	STATE WAITING PERIOD - NUMBER OF DAYS		LICENSE OR PERMIT TO PURCHASE or other prerequesite		REGISTRATION		RECORD OF SALE REPORTED TO STATE OR LOCAL GOVT.
			HANDGUNS	LONG GUNS	HANDGUNS	LONG GUNS	HANDGUNS	LONG GUNS	
Alabama	—	—	—	—	—	—	—	—	—
Alaska	—	RTC	—	—	—	—	—	—	—
Arizona	—	RTC	—	—	—	—	—	—	—
Arkansas	—	RTC[3]	—	—	—	—	—	—	—
California	X_{20}	—	10_{14}	$10_{14,15}$	8, 23	—	X	24	X
Colorado	—	—	—	—	—	—	—	—	—
Connecticut	X_{20}	—	$14_{14,15}$	$14_{14,15}$	$X_{16,23}$	—	—	24	X
Delaware	—	—	—	—	—	—	—	—	—
Florida	—	GRTC	$3_{14,15}$	—	—	—	—	—	—
Georgia	—	RTC	—	—	—	—	—	—	—
Hawaii	X_{20}	L, RTC	—	—	$X_{16,23}$	X_{16}	X_{12}	X_{12}	X
Idaho	—	RTC	—	—	—	—	—	—	—
Illinois	20	—	3	2	X_{16}	X_{16}	4	4	X
Indiana	—	RTC, O_3	—	—	—	—	—	—	X
Iowa	—	L, RTC	—	—	X_{16}	—	—	—	—
Kansas	—	—	1	—	1	—	1	—	1
Kentucky	—	RTC[3]	—	—	—	—	—	—	—
Louisiana	—	GRTC	—	—	—	—	—	—	—
Maine	—	—	—	—	—	—	—	—	—
Maryland	X_{20}	O_3	7_{14}	$7_{9,14}$	8, 23	—	—	—	X
Massachusetts	X_{20}	GRTC	—	—	X_{16}	X_{16}	X	—	X
Michigan	—	O_3	—	—	$X_{16,23}$	—	X	—	X
Minnesota	—	—	7_{16}	16	X_{16}	X_{16}	—	—	—
Mississippi	—	RTC[3]	—	—	—	—	—	—	—
Missouri	—	—	—	—	X_{16}	—	—	—	X
Montana	—	RTC	—	—	—	—	—	—	—
Nebraska	—	L	—	—	X	—	—	—	—
Nevada	—	RTC	1	—	—	—	1	—	—
New Hampshire	—	—	—	—	—	—	—	—	—
New Jersey	X_{20}	—	—	—	X_{16}	X_{16}	—	24	X
New Mexico	—	—	—	—	—	—	—	—	—
New York	X_{20}	L, RTC	—	—	$X_{16,23}$	16	X	7	X
North Carolina	—	L, RTC	—	—	X_{16}	—	—	—	X
North Dakota	—	RTC	—	—	—	—	—	—	—
Ohio	20	—	1	—	16	—	1	—	1
Oklahoma	—	—	—	—	—	—	—	—	—
Oregon	—	GRTC	—	—	—	—	—	—	X
Pennsylvania	—	—	—	—	—	—	—	—	X
Rhode Island	—	—	7	7	23	—	—	—	X
South Carolina	—	RTC	8	—	8	—	—	—	X
South Dakota	—	GRTC	2	—	—	—	—	—	X
Tennessee	—	—	—	—	—	—	—	—	—
Texas	—	RTC[3]	—	—	—	—	—	—	—
Utah	—	RTC	—	—	—	—	—	—	—
Vermont	—	—	—	—	—	—	—	—	—
Virginia	X_{20}	—	1,8	—	1,8	—	—	—	1
Washington	—	O_3	5_{10}	—	—	—	—	—	X
West Virginia	—	—	—	—	—	—	—	—	X
Wisconsin	—	—	2	—	—	—	—	—	—
Wyoming	—	RTC	—	—	—	—	—	—	—
District of Columbia	X_{20}	L	—	—	X_{16}	X_{16}	X_{16}	X	X

COMPENDIUM OF STATE LAWS GOVERNING FIREARMS

**Since state laws are subject to frequent change, this chart is
not to be considered legal advice or a restatement of the law.**

All fifty states have sportsmen's protections laws to halt harrassment.

STATE	STATE PROVISION FOR RIGHT-TO-CARRY CONCEALED	CARRYING OPENLY PROHIBITED	OWNER ID CARDS OR LICENSING	FIREARM RIGHTS CONSTITU-TIONAL PROVISION	STATE FIREARMS PREEMPTION LAWS	RANGE PROTECTION LAW
Alabama	R	X_{11}	—	X	X	X
Alaska	R_{19}	—	—	X	—	X
Arizona	R	—	—	X	X	X
Arkansas	R	X_5	—	X	X	X
California	L	X_6	—	—	X	X
Colorado	R	25	—	X	X_{25}	X
Connecticut	R	X	—	X	X_{17}	X
Delaware	L	—	—	X	X	—
Florida	R	X	—	X	X	X
Georgia	R	X	—	X	X	X
Hawaii	L	X	X	X	—	—
Idaho	R	—	—	X	X	—
Illinois	D	X	X	X	—	X
Indiana	R	X	—	X	X_{18}	X
Iowa	L	X	—	—	X	X
Kansas	D	1	—	X	—	X
Kentucky	R	—	—	X	X	X
Louisiana	R	—	—	X	X	X
Maine	R	—	—	X	X	X
Maryland	L	X	—	—	X	X
Massachusetts	L	X	X	X	X_{17}	X
Michigan	R	X_{11}	—	X	X	X
Minnesota	R	X	—	—	X	—
Mississippi	R	—	—	X	X	X
Missouri	R	—	—	X	X	X
Montana	R	—	—	X	X	X
Nebraska	D	—	—	X	—	—
Nevada	R	—	—	X	X	X
New Hampshire	R	—	—	X	X	X
New Jersey	L	X	X	—	X_{17}	X
New Mexico	R	—	—	X	X	X
New York	L	X	X	—	X_{22}	X
North Carolina	R	—	—	X	X	X
North Dakota	R	X_6	—	X	X	X
Ohio	D	1	16	X	—	X
Oklahoma	R	X_6	—	X	X	X
Oregon	R	—	—	X	X	X
Pennsylvania	R	X_{11}	—	X	X	X
Rhode Island	L	X	—	X	X	X
South Carolina	R	X	—	X	X	X
South Dakota	R	—	—	X	X	X
Tennessee	R	X_5	—	X	X	X
Texas	R	X	—	X	X	X
Utah	R	X_6	—	X	X	X
Vermont	R_{19}	X_5	—	X	X	X
Virginia	R	—	—	X	X	X
Washington	R	X_{21}	—	X	X	—
West Virginia	R	—	—	X	X	X
Wisconsin	D	—	—	X	X	X
Wyoming	R	—	—	X	X	X
District of Columbia	D	X	X	NA	—	—

> With over 20,000 "gun control" laws on the books in America, there are two challenges facing every gun owner. First, you owe it to yourself to become familiar with the federal laws on gun ownership. Only by knowing the laws can you avoid innocently breaking one.
>
> Second, while federal legislation receives much more media attention, state legislatures and city councils make many more decisions regarding your right to own and carry firearms. NRA members and all gun owners must take extra care to be aware of anti-gun laws and ordinances at the state and local levels.

Notes:

1. In certain cities or counties.

2. **National Instant Check System (NICS) exemption codes:**
   RTC-Carry Permit Holders Exempt From NICS
   GRTC-Holders of RTC Permits issued before November 30, 1998 exempt from NICS. Holders of more recent permits are not exempt.
   L-Holders of state licenses to possess or purchase or firearms ID cards exempt from NICS.
   O-Other, See Note 3.

3. **NICS exemption notes: Arkansas:** RTC permits issued prior to 11/30/98 and those issued on and after 4/1/99 qualify. Those issued between 11/1/98 and 3/31/99 do not qualify. **Indiana:** Personal protection, hunting and target permits all qualify for exemptions. **Kentucky:** RTC permits issued after July 15, 1998 and prior to November 30, 1998 are exempt. **Maryland:** There are no exemptions for handgun purchases. For long gun purchases, those holding RTC permits issued before November 30, 1998 are exempt. **Michigan:** No exemptions for handguns, license for long guns. **Mississippi:** Permits issued to security guards do not qualify. **Texas:** Texas Peace Officer License, TCLEOSE Card, is valid only if issued prior to November 30, 1998. **Washington:** RTC permits issued after July 1, 1996 and prior to November 30, 1998 are exempt.

4. Chicago only. No handgun not already registered may be possessed.

5. **Arkansas** prohibits carrying a firearm "with a purpose to employ it as a weapon against a person." **Tennessee** prohibits carrying "with the intent to go armed." **Vermont** prohibits carrying a firearm "with the intent or purpose of injuring another."

6. Loaded.

7. New York City only.

8. A permit is required to acquire another handgun before 30 days have elapsed following the acquisition of a handgun.

9. **Maryland** subjects purchases of "assault weapons" to a 7-day waiting period.

10. May be extended by police to 30 days in some circumstances. An individual not holding a driver's license must wait 90 days.

11. Carrying a handgun openly in a motor vehicle requires a license.

12. Every person arriving in **Hawaii** is required to register any firearm(s) brought into the State within 3 days of arrival of the person or firearm(s), whichever occurs later. Handguns purchased from licensed dealers must be registered within 5 days.

13. Concealed carry laws vary significantly between the states. Ratings reflect the real effect a state's particular laws have on the ability of citizens to carry firearms for self-defense.

14. Purchases from dealers only. **Maryland:** 7 business days. Purchasers of regulated firearms must undergo background checks performed by the State Police, either through a dealer or directly through the State Police.

15. The waiting period does not apply to a person holding a valid permit or license to carry a firearm. In **Connecticut**, a hunting license also exempts the holder for long gun purchasers. **California:** transfers of a long gun to a person's parent, child or grandparent are exempt from the waiting period.

16. **Connecticut:** A certificate of eligibility or a carry permit is required to obtain a handgun and a carry permit is required to transport a handgun outside your home. **District of Columbia:** No handgun may be possessed unless it was registered prior to Sept. 23, 1976 and re-registered by Feb. 5, 1977. A permit to purchase is required for a rifle or shotgun. **Hawaii:** Purchase permits, required for all firearms, may not be issued until 14 days after application. A handgun purchase permit is valid for 10 days, for one handgun; a long gun permit is valid for one year, for multiple long guns. **Illinois:** A Firearm Owner's Identification Card (FOI) is required to possess or purchase a firearm, must be issued to qualified applicants within 30 days, and is valid for 5 years. **Iowa:** A purchase permit is required for handguns, and is valid for one year, beginning three days after issuance. **Massachusetts:** Firearms and feeding devices for firearms are divided into classes. Depending on the class, a firearm identification card (FID) or class A license or class B license is required to possess, purchase, or carry a firearm, ammunition thereof, or firearm feeding device, or "large capacity feeding device." **Michigan:** A handgun purchaser must obtain a license to purchase from local law enforcement, and within 10 days present the license and handgun to obtain a certificate of inspection. **Minnesota:** A handgun transfer or carrying permit, or a 7-day waiting period and handgun transfer report, is required to purchase handguns or "assault weapons" from a dealer. A permit or transfer report must be issued to qualified applicants within 7 days. A permit is valid for one year, a transfer report for

30 days. **Missouri:** A purchase permit is required for a handgun, must be issued to qualified applicants within 7 days, and is valid for 30 days. **New Jersey:** Firearm owners must possess a FID, which must be issued to qualified applicants within 30 days. To purchase a handgun, a purchase permit, which must be issued within 30 days to qualified applicants and is valid for 90 days, is required. An FID is required to purchase long guns. **New York:** Purchase, possession and/or carrying of a handgun require a single license, which includes any restrictions made upon the bearer. New York City also requires a license for long guns. **North Carolina:** To purchase a handgun, a license or permit is required, which must be issued to qualified applicants within 30 days. **Ohio:** Some cities require a permit-to-purchase or firearm owner ID card.

17. Preemption through judicial ruling. Local regulation may be instituted in **Massachusetts** if ratified by the legislature.

18. Except Gary and East Chicago and local laws enacted before January, 1994.

19. **Vermont and Alaska** law respect your right to carry without a permit. Alaska also has a permit to carry system to establish reciprocity with other states.

20. "Assault weapons" are prohibited in **California, Connecticut, New Jersey** and **New York**. Some local jurisdictions in **Ohio** also ban "assault weapons." **Hawaii** prohibits "assault pistols." **California** bans "unsafe handguns." **Illinois:** Chicago, Evanston, Oak Park, Morton Grove, Winnetka, Wilmette, and Highland Park prohibit handguns; some cities prohibit other kinds of firearms. **Maryland** prohibits "assault pistols" and the sale or manufacture of any handgun manufactured after Jan. 1, 1985, that appears on the Handgun Roster. **Massachusetts:** It is unlawful to sell, transfer or possess "any assault weapon or large capacity feeding device" [more than 10 rounds] that was not legally possessed on September 13, 1994. **Ohio:** some cities prohibit handguns of certain magazine capacities." **Virginia** prohibits "Street Sweeper" shotguns. The **District of Columbia** prohibits new acquisition of handguns and any semi-automatic firearm capable of using a detachable ammunition magazine of more than 12 rounds capacity. (With respect to some of these laws and ordinances, individuals may retain prohibited firearms owned previously, with certain restrictions.)

21. Local jurisdictions may opt out of prohibition.

22. Preemption only applies to handguns.

23. Requires proof of safety training for purchase. **California:** Must have Handgun Safety Certificate receipt which is valid for five years. **Connecticut:** To receive certificate of eligibility, must complete a handgun safety course approved by the Commissioner of Public Safety. **Hawaii:** Must have completed an approved handgun safety course. **Maryland:** Must complete an approved handgun safety course. **Michigan:** A person must correctly answer 70% of the questions on a basic safety review questionnaire in order to obtain a license to purchase. **New York:** Some counties require a handgun safety training course to receive a license. **Rhode Island:** Must receive a state-issued handgun safety card.

24. "Assault weapon" registration. **California** had two dates by which assault weapons had to be registered or possession after such date would be considered a felony: March 31, 1992 for the named make and model firearms banned in the 1989 legislation and December 31, 2000 for the firearms meeting the definition of the "assault weapons in the 1999 legislation. In **Connecticut**, those firearms banned by specific make and model in the 1993 law had to be registered by October 1, 1994 or possession would be considered a felony. A recent law requires registration of additional guns by October 1, 2003. In **New Jersey**, any "assault weapon" not registered, licensed, or rendered inoperable pursuant to a state police certificate by May 1, 1991, is considered contraband.

25. Local governments cannot enact ordinances that prohibit the sale, purchase, or possession of a firearm. Municipalities cannot restrict a person's ability to travel into, through, or within their jurisdiction for hunting or personal protection. Local governments, including law enforcement agencies, cannot maintain a database of guns or gun owners. Municipalities may prohibit open carry in government buildings if such prohibition is clearly posted.

Concealed carry codes:

R: Right-to-Carry "Shall issue" or less restrictive discretionary permit system (Ala., Conn.) (See also note #21.)

L: Right-to-Carry Limited by local authority's discretion over permit issuance.

D: Right-to-Carry Denied, no permit system exists; concealed carry is prohibited.

NL 00930

Rev. 9/2003 10m

DIRECTORY

Manufacturer's Directory

A

A Zone Bullets, 2039 Walter Rd., Billings, MT 59105 / 800-252-3111; FAX: 406-248-1961
A&B Industries, Inc (See Top-Line USA Inc.)
A&W Repair, 2930 Schneider Dr., Arnold, MO 63010 / 617-287-3725
A.A. Arms, Inc., 4811 Persimmont Ct., Monroe, NC 28110 / 704-289-5356; or 800-935-1119; FAX: 704-289-5859
A.B.S. III, 9238 St. Morritz Dr., Fern Creek, KY 40291
A.G. Russell Knives, Inc., 1920 North 26th Street, Springdale, AR 72764 / 479-751-7341; FAX: 479-751-4520 ag@agrussell.com agrussell.com
A.R.M.S., Inc., 230 W. Center St., West Bridgewater, MA 02379-1620 / 508-584-7816; FAX: 508-588-8045
A.W. Peterson Gun Shop, Inc., 4255 W. Old U.S. 441, Mt. Dora, FL 32757-3299 / 352-383-4258; FAX: 352-735-1001
AC Dyna-tite Corp., 155 Kelly St., P.O. Box 0984, Elk Grove Village, IL 60007 / 847-593-5566; FAX: 847-593-1304
Acadian Ballistic Specialties, P.O. Box 787, Folsom, LA 70437 / 504-796-0078 gunsmith@neasolft.com
Accuracy International, Foster, PO Box 111, Wilsall, MT 59086 / 406-587-7922; FAX: 406-585-9434
Accuracy Internationl Precision Rifles (See U.S.)
Accuracy Int'l. North America, Inc., PO Box 5267, Oak Ridge, TN 37831 / 423-482-0330; FAX: 423-482-0336
Accuracy Unlimited, 16036 N. 49 Ave., Glendale, AZ 85306 / 602-978-9089; FAX: 602-978-9089 fglenn@cox.net www.glenncustom.com
Accuracy Unlimited, 7479 S. DePew St., Littleton, CO 80123
Accura-Site (See All's, The Jim Tembelis Co., Inc.)
Accurate Arms Co., Inc., 5891 Hwy. 230 West, McEwen, TN 37101 / 931-729-4207; FAX: 931-729-4211 burrensburg@aac-ca.com www.accuratepowder.com
Accu-Tek, 4510 Carter Ct., Chino, CA 91710
Ace Custom 45's, Inc., 1880 1/2 Upper Turtle Creek Rd., Kerrville, TX 78028 / 830-257-4290; FAX: 830-257-5724 www.acecustom45.com
Ackerman & Co., Box 133 US Highway Rt. 7, Pownal, VT 05261 / 802-823-9874 muskets@togsther.net
Ackerman, Bill (See Optical Services Co.)
Acra-Bond Laminates, 134 Zimmerman Rd., Kalispell, MT 59901 / 406-257-9003; FAX: 406-257-9003 merlins@digisys.net www.acrabondlaminates.com
Action Bullets & Alloy Inc., RR 1, P.O. Box 189, Quinter, KS 67752 / 785-754-3609; FAX: 785-754-3629 bullets@ruraltel.net
Action Direct, Inc., P.O. Box 770400, Miami, FL 33177 / 305-969-0056; FAX: 305-256-3541 www.action-direct.com
Action Products, Inc., 22 N. Mulberry St., Hagerstown, MD 21740 / 301-797-1414; FAX: 301-733-2073
Action Target, Inc., PO Box 636, Provo, UT 84603 / 801-377-8033; FAX: 801-377-8096
Actions by "T" Teddy Jacobson, 16315 Redwood Forest Ct., Sugar Land, TX 77478 / 281-277-4008; FAX: 281-277-9112 tjacobson@houston.rr.com www.actionsbyt.us
AcuSport Corporation, 1 Hunter Place, Bellefontaine, OH 43311-3001 / 513-593-7010; FAX: 513-592-5625
Ad Hominem, 3130 Gun Club Lane, RR #3, Orillia, ON L3V 6H3 CANADA / 705-689-5303; FAX: 705-689-5303
Adair Custom Shop, Bill, 2886 Westridge, Carrollton, TX 75006
ADCO Sales, Inc., 4 Draper St. #A, Woburn, MA 01801 / 781-935-1799; FAX: 781-935-1011
Adkins, Luther, 1292 E. McKay Rd., Shelbyville, IN 46176-8706 / 317-392-3795
Advance Car Mover Co., Rowell Div., P.O. Box 1, 240 N. Depot St., Juneau, WI 53039 / 414-386-4464; FAX: 414-386-4416
Advantage Arms, Inc., 25163 W. Ave. Stanford, Valencia, CA 91355 / 661-257-2290
Adventure 16, Inc., 4620 Alvarado Canyon Rd., San Diego, CA 92120 / 619-283-6314
Aero Peltor, 90 Mechanic St., Southbridge, MA 01550 / 508-764-5500; FAX: 508-764-0188
African Import Co., 22 Goodwin Rd, Plymouth, MA 02360 / 508-746-8552; FAX: 508-746-0404 africanimport@aol.com
AFSCO Ammunition, 731 W. Third St., P.O. Box L, Owen, WI 54460 / 715-229-2516 sailers@webtv.net
Ahlman Guns, 9525 W. 230th St., Morristown, MN 55052 / 507-685-4243; FAX: 507-685-4280 www.ahlmans.com
Ahrends, Kim (See Custom Firearms, Inc), Box 203, Clarion, IA 50525 / 515-532-3449; FAX: 515-532-3926
Aimtech Mount Systems, P.O. Box 223, Thomasville, GA 31799 / 229-226-4313; FAX: 229-227-0222 mail@aimtech-mounts.com www.aimtech-mounts.com
Air Arms, Hailsham Industrial Park, Diplocks Way, Hailsham, E. Sussex, BN27 3JF ENGLAND / 011-0323-845853
Air Rifle Specialists, P.O. Box 138, 130 Holden Rd., Pine City, NY 14871-0138 / 607-734-7340; FAX: 607-733-3261 ars@stny.rr.com www.air-rifles.com
Air Venture Airguns, 9752 E. Flower St., Bellflower, CA 90706 / 562-867-6355
AirForce Airguns, P.O. Box 2478, Fort Worth, TX 76113 / 817-451-8966; FAX: 817-451-1613 www.airforceairguns.com
Airrow, 11 Monitor Hill Rd., Newtown, CT 06470 / 203-270-6343
Aitor-Cuchilleria Del Norte S.A., Izelaieta, 17, 48260, Ermua, S SPAIN / 43-17-08-50 info@aitor.com www.ailor.com
Ajax Custom Grips, Inc., 9130 Viscount Row, Dallas, TX 75247 / 214-630-8893; FAX: 214-630-4942
Aker International, Inc., 2248 Main St., Suite 6, Chula Vista, CA 91911 / 619-423-5182; FAX: 619-423-1363 aker@akerleather.com www.akerleather.com
AKJ Concealco, P.O. Box 871596, Vancouver, WA 98687-1596 / 360-891-8222; FAX: 360-891-8221 Concealco@aol.com www.greatholsters.com
Alana Cupp Custom Engraver, P.O. Box 207, Annabella, UT 84711 / 801-896-4834
Alaska Bullet Works, Inc., 9978 Crazy Horse Drive, Juneau, AK 99801 / 907-789-3834; FAX: 907-789-3433
Alaskan Silversmith, The, 2145 Wagner Hollow Rd., Fort Plain, NY 13339 / 518-993-3983 sidbell@capital.net www.sidbell.cizland.com
Aldis Gunsmithing & Shooting Supply, 502 S. Montezuma St., Prescott, AZ 86303 / 602-445-6723; FAX: 602-445-6763
Alessi Holsters, Inc., 2465 Niagara Falls Blvd., Amherst, NY 14228-3527 / 716-691-5615
Alex, Inc., 3420 Cameron Bridge Rd., Manhattan, MT 59741-8523 / 406-282-7396; FAX: 406-282-7396
Alfano, Sam, 36180 Henry Gaines Rd., Pearl River, LA 70452 / 504-863-3364; FAX: 504-863-7715
All American Lead Shot Corp., P.O. Box 224566, Dallas, TX 75062
All Rite Products, Inc., 9554 Wells Circle, Suite D, West Jordan, UT 84088-6226 / 800-771-8471; FAX: 801-280-8302 info@allriteproducts.com www.allriteproducts.com
Allard, Gary/Creek Side Metal & Woodcrafters, Fishers Hill, VA 22626 / 703-465-3903
Allen Co., Inc., 525 Burbank St., Broomfield, CO 80020 / 303-469-1857; or 800-876-8600; FAX: 303-466-7437
Allen Firearm Engraving, P.O. Box 155, Camp Verde, AZ 86322 / 928-567-6711 rosebudmukco@netzero.com
Allen Mfg., 6449 Hodgson Rd., Circle Pines, MN 55014 / 612-429-8231
Alley Supply Co., PO Box 848, Gardnerville, NV 89410 / 775-782-3800; FAX: 775-782-3827 jetalley@aol.com www.alleysupplyco.com
Alliant Techsystems Smokeless Powder Group, P.O. Box 6, Rt. 114, Bldg. 229, Radford, VA 24141-0096 www.alliantpowder.com
Allred Bullet Co., 932 Evergreen Drive, Logan, UT 84321 / 435-752-6983; FAX: 435-752-6983
All's, The Jim J. Tembelis Co., Inc., 216 Loper Ct., Neenah, WI 54956 / 920-725-5251; FAX: 920-725-5251
Alpec Team, Inc., 201 Ricken Backer Cir., Livermore, CA 94550 / 510-606-8245; FAX: 510-606-4279
Alpha 1 Drop Zone, 2121 N. Tyler, Wichita, KS 67212 / 316-729-0800; FAX: 316-729-4262 www.alpha1dropzone.com
Alpha LaFranck Enterprises, P.O. Box 81072, Lincoln, NE 68501 / 402-466-3193
Alpha Precision, Inc., 3238 Della Slaton Rd., Comer, GA 30629-2212 / 706-783-2131 jim@alphaprecisioninc.com www.alphaprecisioninc.com
Alpine Indoor Shooting Range, 2401 Government Way, Coeur d'Alene, ID 83814 / 208-676-8824; FAX: 208-676-8824
Altamont Co., 901 N. Church St., P.O. Box 309, Thomasboro, IL 61878 / 217-643-3125; or 800-626-5774; FAX: 217-643-7973
Alumna Sport by Dee Zee, 1572 NE 58th Ave., P.O. Box 3090, Des Moines, IA 50316 / 800-798-9899
Amadeo Rossi S.A., Rua: Amadeo Rossi, 143, Sao Leopoldo, RS 93030-220 BRAZIL / 051-592-5566
AmBr Software Group Ltd., P.O. Box 301, Reistertown, MD 21136-0301 / 800-888-1917; FAX: 410-526-7212
American Ammunition, 3545 NW 71st St., Miami, FL 33147 / 305-835-7400; FAX: 305-694-0037
American Derringer Corp., 127 N. Lacy Dr., Waco, TX 76705 / 800-642-7817; or 254-799-9111; FAX: 254-799-7935
American Display Co., 55 Cromwell St., Providence, RI 02907 / 401-331-2464; FAX: 401-421-1264
American Gas & Chemical Co., Ltd, 220 Pegasus Ave, Northvale, NJ 07647 / 201-767-7300
American Gripcraft, 3230 S Dodge 2, Tucson, AZ 85713 / 602-790-1222
American Gunsmithing Institute, 1325 Imola Ave #504, Napa, CA 94559 / 707-253-0462; FAX: 707-253-7149
American Handgunner Magazine, 591 Camino de la Reina, Ste. 200, San Diego, CA 92108 / 619-297-5350; FAX: 619-297-5353
American Pioneer Video, PO Box 50049, Bowling Green, KY 42102-2649 / 800-743-4675
American Products, Inc., 14729 Spring Valley Road, Morrison, IL 61270 / 815-772-3336; FAX: 815-772-8046
American Safe Arms, Inc., 1240 Riverview Dr., Garland, UT 84312 / 801-257-7472; FAX: 801-785-8156
American Security Products Co., 11925 Pacific Ave., Fontana, CA 92337 / 909-685-9680; or 800-421-6142; FAX: 909-685-9685
American Small Arms Academy, P.O. Box 12111, Prescott, AZ 86304 / 602-778-5623
American Target, 1328 S. Jason St., Denver, CO 80223 / 303-733-0433; FAX: 303-777-0311
American Target Knives, 1030 Brownwood NW, Grand Rapids, MI 49504 / 616-453-1998
Americase, P.O. Box 271, 1610 E. Main, Waxahachie, TX 75165 / 800-880-3629; FAX: 214-937-8373
Ames Metal Products, 4323 S. Western Blvd., Chicago, IL 60609 / 773-523-3230; or 800-255-6937; FAX: 773-523-3854
Amherst Arms, P.O. Box 1457, Englewood, FL 34295 / 941-475-2020; FAX: 941-473-1212
Ammo Load, Inc., 1560 E. Edinger, Suite G, Santa Ana, CA 92705 / 714-558-8858; FAX: 714-569-0319
Amrine's Gun Shop, 937 La Luna, Ojai, CA 93023 / 805-646-2376
Amsec, 11925 Pacific Ave., Fontana, CA 92337
Analog Devices, Box 9106, Norwood, MA 02062
Andela Tool & Machine, Inc., RD3, Box 246, Richfield Springs, NY 13439
Anderson Manufacturing Co., Inc., 22602 53rd Ave. SE, Bothell, WA 98021 / 206-481-1858; FAX: 206-481-7839
Andres & Dworsky KG, Bergstrasse 18, A-3822 Karlstein, Thaya, AUSTRIA / 0 28 44-285; FAX: 02844 28619 andres.dnorsky@wvnet.as
Angelo & Little Custom Gun Stock Blanks, P.O. Box 240046, Dell, MT 59724-0046
Answer Products Co., 1519 Westbury Drive, Davison, MI 48423 / 810-653-2911
Antique American Firearms, P.O. Box 71035, Dept. GD, Des Moines, IA 50325 / 515-224-6552
Antique Arms Co., 1110 Cleveland Ave., Monett, MO 65708 / 417-235-6501
AO Sight Systems, 2401 Ludelle St., Fort Worth, TX 76105 / 888-744-4880; or 817-536-0136; FAX: 817-536-3517
Apel GmbH, Ernst, Am Kirschberg 3, D-97218, Gerbrunn, GERMANY / 0 (931) 707192 info@eaw.de www.eaw.de
Aplan Antiques & Art, James O., James O., HC 80, Box 793-25, Piedmont, SD 57769 / 605-347-5016
AR-7 Industries, LLC, 998 N. Colony Rd., Meriden, CT 06450 / 203-630-3536; FAX: 203-630-3637
Arizona Ammunition, Inc., 21421 No. 14th Ave., Suite E, Phoenix, AZ 85027 / 623-516-9004; FAX: 623-516-9012 www.azammo.com
ArmaLite, Inc., P.O. Box 299, Geneseo, IL 61254 / 800-336-0184; or 309-944-6939; FAX: 309-944-6949
Armament Gunsmithing Co., Inc., 525 Rt. 22, Hillside, NJ 07205 / 908-686-0960; FAX: 718-738-5019 armamentgunsmithing@worldnet.att.net
Armas Garbi, S.A., 12-14 20.600 Urki, 12, Eibar (Guipuzcoa), SPAIN / 943203873; FAX: 943203873 armosgarbi@euskalnet.n
Armas Kemen S. A. (See U.S. Importers)
Armfield Custom Bullets, 10584 County Road 100, Carthage, MO 64836 / 417-359-8480; FAX: 417-359-8497
Armi Perazzi S.P.A., Via Fontanelle 1/3, 1-25080, Botticino Mattina, ITALY / 030-2692591; FAX: 030 2692594
Armi San Marco (See U.S. Importers-Taylor's & Co.)
Armi San Paolo, 172-A, I-25062, via Europa, ITALY / 030-2751725
Armi Sport (See U.S. Importers-Cape Outfitters)
Armite Laboratories, 1560 Superior Ave., Costa Mesa, CA 92627 / 213-587-7768; FAX: 213-587-5075
Armoloy Co. of Ft. Worth, 204 E. Daggett St., Fort Worth, TX 76104 / 817-332-5604; FAX: 817-335-6517
Armor (See Buck Stop Lure Co., Inc.)
Armor Metal Products, P.O. Box 4609, Helena, MT 59604 / 406-442-5560; FAX: 406-442-5650
Armory Publications, 2120 S. Reserve St., PMB 253, Missoula, MT 59801 / 406-549-7670; FAX: 406-728-0597 armorypub@aol.com www.armorypub.com
Armoury, Inc., The, Rt. 202, Box 2340, New Preston, CT 06777 / 860-868-0001; FAX: 860-868-2919
Arms & Armour Press, Wellington House, 125 Strand, London, WC2R 0BB ENGLAND / 0171-420-5555; FAX: 0171-240-7265
Arms Corporation of the Philippines, Bo. Parang Marikina, Metro Manila, PHILIPPINES / 632-941-6243; or 632-941-6244; FAX: 632-942-0682
Arms Craft Gunsmithing, 1106 Linda Dr., Arroyo Grande, CA 93420 / 805-481-2830
Arms Software, 4851 SW Madrona St., Lake Oswego, OR 97035 / 800-366-5559; or 503-697-0533; FAX: 503-697-3337
Arms, Programming Solutions (See Arms Software)
Armscor Precision, 5740 S. Arville St. #219, Las Vegas, NV 89118 / 702-362-7750
Armscorp USA, Inc., 4424 John Ave., Baltimore, MD 21227 / 410-247-6200; FAX: 410-247-6205 info@armscorpusa.com www.armscorpusa.com
Arratoonian, Andy (See Horseshoe Leather Products)
Arrieta S.L., Morkaiko 5, 20870, Elgoibar, SPAIN / 34-43-743150; FAX: 34-43-743154
Art Jewel Enterprises Ltd., Eagle Business Ctr., 460 Randy Rd., Carol Stream, IL 60188 / 708-260-0400
Artistry in Wood, 134 Zimmerman Rd., Kalispell, MT 59901 / 406-257-9003; FAX: 406-257-9167 merlins@digisys.net www.acrabondlaminates.com
Art's Gun & Sport Shop, Inc., 6008 Hwy. Y, Hillsboro, MO 63050
Arundel Arms & Ammunition, Inc., A., 24A Defense St., Annapolis, MD 21401 / 410-224-8683
Ashley Outdoors, Inc., 2401 Ludelle St., Fort Worth, TX 76105 / 888-744-4880; FAX: 800-734-7939
Aspen Outfitting Co., Jon Hollinger, 9 Dean St., Aspen, CO 81611 / 970-925-3406
A-Square Co., 205 Fairfield Ave., Jeffersonville, IN 47130 / 812-283-0577; FAX: 812-283-0375
Astra Sport, S.A., Apartado 3, 48300 Guernica, Espagne, SPAIN / 34-4-6250100; FAX: 34-4-6255186
Atamec-Bretton, 19 rue Victor Grignard, F-42026, St.-Etienne (Cedex 1, FRANCE / 77-93-54-69; FAX: 33-77-93-57-98
Atlanta Cutlery Corp., 2143 Gees Mill Rd., Box 839 CIS, Conyers, GA 30207 / 800-883-0300; FAX: 404-388-0246
Atlantic Mills, Inc., 1295 Towbin Ave., Lakewood, NJ 08701-5934 / 800-242-7374
Atlantic Rose, Inc., P.O. Box 10717, Bradenton, FL 34282-0717
Atsko/Sno-Seal, Inc., 2664 Russell St., Orangeburg, SC 29115 / 803-531-1820; FAX: 803-531-2139 info@atsko.com www.atsko.com

MANUFACTURER'S DIRECTORY

Auguste Francotte & Cie S.A., rue du Trois Juin 109, 4400 Herstal-Liege, BELGIUM / 32-4-248-13-18; FAX: 32-4-948-11-79

Austin & Halleck, Inc., 2150 South 950 East, Provo, UT 84606-6285 / 877-543-3256; or 801-374-9990; FAX: 801-374-9998 www.austinhallek.com

Austin Sheridan USA, Inc., P.O. Box 577, 36 Haddam Quarter Rd., Durham, CT 06422 / 860-349-1772; FAX: 860-349-1771 swalzer@palm.net

Autauga Arms, Inc., Pratt Plaza Mall No. 13, Prattville, AL 36067 / 800-262-9563; FAX: 334-361-2961

Auto Arms, 738 Clearview, San Antonio, TX 78228 / 512-434-5450

Auto-Ordnance Corp., PO Box 220, Blauvelt, NY 10913 / 914-353-7770

Autumn Sales, Inc. (Blaser), 1320 Lake St., Fort Worth, TX 76102 / 817-335-1634; FAX: 817-338-0119

Avnda Otaola Norica, 16 Apartado 68, 20600, Eibar, SPAIN

AWC Systems Technology, P.O. Box 41938, Phoenix, AZ 85080-1938 / 623-780-1050; FAX: 623-780-2967 awc@awcsystech.com www.awcsystech.com

Axtell Rifle Co., 353 Mill Creek Road, Sheridan, MT 59749 / 406-842-5814

AYA (See U.S. Importer-New England Custom Gun Serv

B

B&D Trading Co., Inc., 3935 Fair Hill Rd., Fair Oaks, CA 95628 / 800-334-3790; or 916-967-9366; FAX: 916-967-4873

B&P America, 12321 Brittany Cir., Dallas, TX 75230 / 972-726-9069

B.A.C., 17101 Los Modelos St., Fountain Valley, CA 92708 / 435-586-3286

B.B. Walker Co., PO Box 1167, 414 E Dixie Dr, Asheboro, NC 27204 / 910-625-1380; FAX: 910-625-8125

B.C. Outdoors, Larry McGhee, PO Box 61497, Boulder City, NV 89006 / 702-294-3056; FAX: 702-294-0413 jdalton@pmcammo.com www.pmcammo.com

B.M.F. Activator, Inc., 12145 Mill Creek Run, Plantersville, TX 77363 / 936-894-2397; FAX: 936-894-2397 bmf25years@aol.com

Badger Creek Studio, 1629 Via Monserate, Fallbrook, CA 92028 / 760-723-9279; or 619-728-2663

Badger Shooters Supply, Inc., P.O. Box 397, Owen, WI 54460 / 800-424-9069; FAX: 715-229-2332

Baekgaard Ltd., 1855 Janke Dr., Northbrook, IL 60062 / 708-498-3040; FAX: 708-493-3106

Baelder, Harry, Alte Goennebeker Strasse 5, 24635, Rickling, GERMANY / 04328-722732; FAX: 04328-722733

Baer's Hollows, P.O. Box 284, Eads, CO 81036 / 719-438-5718

Bagmaster Mfg., Inc., 2731 Sutton Ave., St. Louis, MO 63143 / 314-781-8002; FAX: 314-781-3363 sales@bagmaster.com www.bagmaster.com

Bain & Davis, Inc., 307 E. Valley Blvd., San Gabriel, CA 91776-3522 / 626-573-4241 baindavis@aol.com

Baker, Stan. See: STAN BAKER SPORTS

Baker's Leather Goods, Roy, PO Box 893, Magnolia, AR 71754 / 870-234-0344 pholsters@ipa.net

Bald Eagle Precision Machine Co., 101-A Allison St., Lock Haven, PA 17745 / 570-748-6772; FAX: 570-748-4443

Balickie, Joe, 408 Trelawney Lane, Apex, NC 27502 / 919-362-5185

Ballard, Donald. See: BALLARD INDUSTRIES

Ballard Industries, Donald Ballard Sr., PO Box 2035, Arnold, CA 95223 / 408-996-0957; FAX: 408-257-6828

Ballard Rifle & Cartridge Co., LLC, 113 W. Yellowstone Ave., Cody, WY 82414 / 307-587-4914; FAX: 307-527-6097 ballard@wyoming.com www.ballardrifles.com

Ballistic Products, Inc., 20015 75th Ave. North, Corcoran, MN 55340-9456 / 763-494-9237; FAX: 763-494-9236 info@ballisticproducts.com www.ballisticproducts.com

Ballistic Research, 1108 W. May Ave., McHenry, IL 60050 / 815-385-0037

Ballisti-Cast, Inc., P.O. Box 1057, Minot, ND 58702-1057 / 701-497-3333; FAX: 701-497-3335

Bandcor Industries, Div. of Man-Sew Corp., 6108 Sherwin Dr., Port Richey, FL 34668 / 813-848-0432

Bang-Bang Boutique (See Holster Shop, The)

Bansner's Ultimate Rifles, LLC, P.O. Box 839, 261 E. Main St., Adamstown, PA 19501 / 717-484-2370; FAX: 717-484-0523 bansner@aol.com www.bansnersrifle.com

Barbour, Inc., 55 Meadowbrook Dr., Milford, NH 03055 / 603-673-1313; FAX: 603-673-6510

Barnes, 4347 Tweed Dr., Eau Claire, WI 54703-6302

Barnes Bullets, Inc., P.O. Box 215, American Fork, UT 84003 / 801-756-4222; or 800-574-9200; FAX: 801-756-2465 email@barnesbullets.com www.barnesbullets.com

Baron Technology, 62 Spring Hill Rd., Trumbull, CT 06611 / 203-452-0515; FAX: 203-452-0663 dbaron@baronengraving.com www.baronengraving.com

Barraclough, John K., 55 Merit Park Dr., Gardena, CA 90247 / 310-324-2574 johnbar120@aol.com

Barramundi Corp., P.O. Drawer 4259, Homosassa Springs, FL 32687 / 904-628-0200

Barrel & Gunworks, 2601 Lake Valley Rd., Prescott Valley, AZ 86314 / 928-772-4060 www.cutrifle.com

Barrett Firearms Manufacturer, Inc., P.O. Box 1077, Murfreesboro, TN 37133 / 615-896-2938; FAX: 615-896-7313

Bar-Sto Precision Machine, 73377 Sullivan Rd., PO Box 1838, Twentynine Palms, CA 92277 / 760-367-2747; FAX: 760-367-2407 barsto@eee.org www.barsto.com

Barta's Gunsmithing, 10231 US Hwy. 10, Cato, WI 54230 / 920-732-4472

Barteaux Machete, 1916 SE 50th Ave., Portland, OR 97215-3238 / 503-233-5880

Bartlett Engineering, 40 South 200 East, Smithfield, UT 84335-1645 / 801-563-5910

Bates Engraving, Billy, 2302 Winthrop Dr. SW, Decatur, AL 35603 / 256-355-3690 bbrn@aol.com

Battenfeld Technologies Inc., 5885 W. Van Horn Tavern Rd., Columbia, MO 65203 / 573-445-9200; FAX: 573-447-4158 battenfeldtechnologies.com

Bauer, Eddie, 15010 NE 36th St., Redmond, WA 98052

Baumgartner Bullets, 3011 S. Alane St., W. Valley City, UT 84120

Bauska Barrels, 105 9th Ave. W., Kalispell, MT 59901 / 406-752-7706

Bear Archery, RR 4, 4600 Southwest 41st Blvd., Gainesville, FL 32601 / 904-376-2327

Bear Arms, 374-A Carson Road, St. Mathews, SC 29135

Bear Mountain Gun & Tool, 120 N. Plymouth, New Plymouth, ID 83655 / 208-278-5221; FAX: 208-278-5221

Beartooth Bullets, PO Box 491, Dept. HLD, Dover, ID 83825-0491 / 208-448-1865 bullets@beartoothbullets.com beartoothbullets.com

Beaver Park Product, Inc., 840 J St., Penrose, CO 81240 / 719-372-6744

BEC, Inc., 1227 W. Valley Blvd., Suite 204, Alhambra, CA 91803 / 626-281-5751; FAX: 626-293-7073

Beeks, Mike. See: GRAYBACK WILDCATS

Beeman Precision Airguns, 5454 Argosy Dr., Huntington Beach, CA 92649 / 714-890-4808; FAX: 714-890-4808

Behlert Precision, Inc., P.O. Box 288, 7067 Easton Rd., Pipersville, PA 18947 / 215-766-8681; or 215-766-7301; FAX: 215-766-8681

Beitzinger, George, 116-20 Atlantic Ave., Richmond Hill, NY 11419 / 718-847-7661

Belding's Custom Gun Shop, 10691 Sayers Rd., Munith, MI 49259 / 517-596-2388

Bell & Carlson, Inc., Dodge City Industrial Park, 101 Allen Rd., Dodge City, KS 67801 / 800-634-8586; or 620-225-6688; FAX: 620-225-6688 email@bellandcarlson.com www.bellandcarlson.com

Bell Reloading, Inc., 1725 Harlin Lane Rd., Villa Rica, GA 30180

Bell's Gun & Sport Shop, 3309-19 Mannheim Rd, Franklin Park, IL 60131

Bell's Legendary Country Wear, 22 Circle Dr., Bellmore, NY 11710 / 516-679-1158

Benchmark Knives (See Gerber Legendary Blades)

Benelli Armi S.P.A., Via della Stazione, 61029, Urbino, ITALY / 39-722-307-1; FAX: 39-722-327427

Benelli USA Corp, 17603 Indian Head Hwy, Accokeek, MD 20607 / 301-283-6981; FAX: 301-283-6988 benelliusa.com

Bengtson Arms Co., L., 6345-B E. Akron St., Mesa, AZ 85205 / 602-981-6375

Benjamin/Sheridan Co., Crosman, Rts. 5 and 20, E. Bloomfield, NY 14443 / 716-657-6161; FAX: 716-657-5405 www.crosman.com

Bentley, John, 128-D Watson Dr., Turtle Creek, PA 15145

Beretta S.P.A., Pietro, Via Beretta, 18, 25063, Gardone Vae Trompia, ITALY / 39-30-8341-1 info@benetta.com www.benetta.com

Beretta U.S.A. Corp., 17601 Beretta Drive, Accokeek, MD 20607 / 301-283-2191; FAX: 301-283-0435

Berger Bullets Ltd., 5443 W. Westwind Dr., Glendale, AZ 85310 / 602-842-4001; FAX: 602-934-9083

Bernardelli, Vincenzo, P.O. Box 460243, Houston, TX 77056-8243 www.bernardelli.com

Bernardelli, Vincenzo, Via Grande, 10, Sede Legale Torbole Casaglia, Brescia, ITALY / 39-30-8912851-2-3; FAX: 39-030-2150963 bernardelli@bernardelli.com www.bernardelli.com

Berry's Mfg., Inc., 401 North 3050 East St., St. George, UT 84770 / 435-634-1682; FAX: 435-634-1683 sales@berrysmfg.com www.berrysmfg.com

Bersa S.A., Benso Bonadimani, Magallanes 775 B1704 FLC, Ramos Mejia, ARGENTINA / 011-4656-2377; FAX: 011-4656-2093+ info@bersa-sa.com.dr www.bersa-sa.com.ar

Bort Johanssons Vapentillbehor, S-430 20 Veddige, SWEDEN,

Bertuzzi (See U.S. Importer-New England Arms Co)

Better Concepts Co., 663 New Castle Rd., Butler, PA 16001 / 412-285-9000

Beverly, Mary, 3201 Horseshoe Trail, Tallahassee, FL 32312

Bianchi International, Inc., 100 Calle Cortez, Temecula, CA 92590 / 909-676-5621; FAX: 909-676-6777

Big Bear Arms & Sporting Goods, Inc., 1112 Milam Way, Carrollton, TX 75006 / 972-416-8051; or 800-400-BEAR; FAX: 972-416-0771

Big Bore Bullets of Alaska, PO Box 521455, Big Lake, AK 99652 / 907-373-2673; FAX: 907-373-2673 doug@mtaonline.net ww.awloo.com/bbb/index.

Big Bore Express, 16345 Midway Rd., Nampa, ID 83651 / 208-466-9975; FAX: 208-466-6927 bigbore.com

Big Spring Enterprises "Bore Stores", P.O. Box 1115, Big Spring Rd., Yellville, AR 72687 / 870-449-5297; FAX: 870-449-4446

Bilal, Mustafa. See: TURK'S HEAD PRODUCTIONS

Bilinski, Bryan. See: FIELDSPORT LTD.

Bill Adair Custom Shop, 2886 Westridge, Carrollton, TX 75006 / 972-418-0950

Bill Austin's Calls, Box 284, Kaycee, WY 82639 / 307-738-2552

Bill Hanus Birdguns, P.O. Box 533, Newport, OR 97365 / 541-265-7433; FAX: 541-265-7400 www.billhanusbirdguns.com

Bill Russ Trading Post, William A. Russ, 25 William St., Addison, NY 14801-1326 / 607-359-3896

Bill Wiseman and Co., P.O. Box 3427, Bryan, TX 77805 / 409-690-3456; FAX: 409-690-0156

Billeb, Stepehn. See: QUALITY CUSTOM FIREARMS

Billings Gunsmiths, 1841 Grand Ave., Billings, MT 59102 / 406-256-8390; FAX: 406-256-6530 blgsgunsmiths@msn.com www.billingsgunsmiths.net

Billingsley & Brownell, P.O. Box 25, Dayton, WY 82836 / 307-655-9344

Bill's Gun Repair, 1007 Burlington St., Mendota, IL 61342 / 815-539-5786

Billy Bates Engraving, 2302 Winthrop Dr. SW, Decatur, AL 35603 / 256-355-3690 bbrn@aol.com

Birchwood Casey, 7900 Fuller Rd., Eden Prairie, MN 55344 / 800-328-6156; or 612-937-7933; FAX: 612-937-7979

Birdsong & Assoc., W. E., 1435 Monterey Rd, Florence, MS 39073-9748 / 601-366-8270

Bismuth Cartridge Co., 3500 Maple Ave., Suite 1650, Dallas, TX 75219 / 214-521-5880; FAX: 214-521-9035

Bison Studios, 1409 South Commerce St., Las Vegas, NV 89102 / 702-388-2891; FAX: 702-383-9967

Bitterroot Bullet Co., 2001 Cedar Ave., Lewiston, ID 83501-0412 / 208-743-5635 brootbil@lewiston.com

BKL Technologies, PO Box 5237, Brownsville, TX 78523

Black Belt Bullets (See Big Bore Express)

Black Hills Ammunition, Inc., P.O. Box 3090, Rapid City, SD 57709-3090 / 605-348-5150; FAX: 605-348-9827

Black Hills Shooters Supply, P.O. Box 4220, Rapid City, SD 57709 / 800-289-2506

Black Powder Products, 67 Township Rd. 1411, Chesapeake, OH 45619 / 614-867-8047

Black Sheep Brand, 3220 W. Gentry Parkway, Tyler, TX 75702 / 903-592-3853; FAX: 903-592-0527

Blacksmith Corp., P.O. Box 280, North Hampton, OH 45349 / 937-969-8389; FAX: 937-969-8399 sales@blacksmithcorp.com www.blacksmithcorp.com

BlackStar AccuMax Barrels, 11501 Brittmoore Park Drive, Houston, TX 77041 / 281-721-6040; FAX: 281-721-6041

BlackStar Barrel Accurizing (See BlackStar AccuMax)

Blacktail Mountain Books, 42 First Ave. W., Kalispell, MT 59901 / 406-257-5573

Blammo Ammo, P.O. Box 1677, Seneca, SC 29679 / 803-882-1768

Blaser Jagdwaffen GmbH, D-88316, Isny Im Allgau, GERMANY

Blount, Inc., Sporting Equipment Div., 2299 Snake River Ave., P.O. Box 856, Lewiston, ID 83501 / 800-627-3640; or 208-746-2351; FAX: 208-799-3904

Blount/Outers ATK, P.O. Box 39, Onalaska, WI 54650 / 608-781-5800; FAX: 608-781-0368

Blue and Gray Products Inc. (See Ox-Yoke Originals)

Blue Book Publications, Inc., 8009 34th Ave. S., Ste. 175, Minneapolis, MN 55425 / 952-854-5229; FAX: 952-853-1486 bluebook@bluebookinc.com www.bluebookinc.com

Blue Mountain Bullets, 64146 Quail Ln., Box 231, John Day, OR 97845 / 541-820-4594; FAX: 541-820-4594

Blue Ridge Machinery & Tools, Inc., P.O. Box 536-GD, Hurricane, WV 25526 / 800-872-6500; FAX: 304-562-5311 blueridgemachine@worldnet.att.net www.blueridgemachinery.com

BMC Supply, Inc., 26051 - 179th Ave. S.E., Kent, WA 98042

Bob Allen Co., P.O. Box 477, 214 SW Jackson, Des Moines, IA 50315 / 800-685-7020; FAX: 515-283-0779

Bob Allen Sportswear, 220 S. Main St., Osceola, IA 50213 / 210-344-8531; FAX: 210-342-2703 sales@bob-allen.com www.bob-allen.com

Bob Rogers Gunsmithing, P.O. Box 305, 344 S. Walnut St., Franklin Grove, IL 61031 / 815-456-2685; FAX: 815-456-2685

Bob's Gun Shop, P.O. Box 200, Royal, AR 71968 / 501-767-1970; FAX: 501-767-1970 gunparts@hsnp.com www.gun-parts.com

Bob's Tactical Indoor Shooting Range & Gun Shop, 90 Lafayette Rd., Salisbury, MA 01952 / 508-465-5561

Boessler, Erich, Am Vogeltal 3, 97702, Munnerstadt, GERMANY

Boker USA, Inc., 1550 Balsam Street, Lakewood, CO 80214 / 303-462-0662; FAX: 303-462-0668 sales@bokerusa.com bokerusa.com

Boltin, John M., P.O. Box 644, Estill, SC 29918 / 803-625-2185

Bo-Mar Tool & Mfg. Co., 6136 State Hwy. 300, Longview, TX 75604 / 903-759-4784; FAX: 903-759-9141 marykor@earthlink.net bo-mar.com

Bonadimani, Benso. See: BERSA S.A.

Bonanza (See Forster Products), 310 E. Lanark Ave., Lanark, IL 61046 / 815-493-6360; FAX: 815-493-2371

Bond Arms, Inc., P.O. Box 1296, Granbury, TX 76048 / 817-573-4445; FAX: 817-573-5636

Bond Custom Firearms, 8954 N. Lewis Ln., Bloomington, IN 47408 / 812-332-4519

Bonham's & Butterfields, 220 San Bruno Ave., San Francisco, CA 94103 / 415-861-7500; FAX: 415-861-0183 arms@butterfields.com www.butterfields.com

Boone Trading Co., Inc., PO Box 669, Brinnon, WA 98320 / 800-423-1945; or 360-796-4330; FAX: 360-796-4511 sales@boonetrading.com boonetrading.com

Boone's Custom Ivory Grips, Inc., 562 Coyote Rd., Brinnon, WA 98320 / 206-796-4330

Boonie Packer Products, P.O. Box 12517, Salem, OR 97309-0517 / 800-477-3244; or 503-581-3244; FAX: 503-581-3191 booniepacker@aol.com www.booniepacker.com

Borden Ridges Rimrock Stocks, RR 1 Box 250 BC, Springville, PA 18844 / 570-965-2505; FAX: 570-965-2328

Borden Rifles Inc., RD 1, Box 250BC, Springville, PA 18844 / 717-965-2505; FAX: 717-965-2328

Border Barrels Ltd., Riccarton Farm, Newcastleton, SCOTLAND UK

Borovnik KG, Ludwig, 9170 Ferlach, Bahnhofstrasse 7, AUSTRIA / 042 27 24 42; FAX: 042 26 43 49

MANUFACTURER'S DIRECTORY

Bosis (See U.S. Importer-New England Arms Co.)
Boss Manufacturing Co., 221 W. First St., Kewanee, IL 61443 / 309-852-2131; or 800-447-4581; FAX: 309-852-0848
Bostick Wildlife Calls, Inc., P.O. Box 728, Estill, SC 29918 / 803-625-2210; or 803-625-4512
Bowen Classic Arms Corp., P.O. Box 67, Louisville, TN 37777 / 865-984-3583 www.bowenclassicarms.com
Bowen Knife Co., Inc., P.O. Box 590, Blackshear, GA 31516 / 912-449-4794
Bowerly, Kent, 710 Golden Pheasant Dr., Redmond, OR 97756 / 541-923-3501 jkbowerly@aol.com
Boyds' Gunstock Industries, Inc., 25376 403 Rd. Ave., Mitchell, SD 57301 / 605-996-5011; FAX: 605-996-9878
Brace, Larry D., 771 Blackfoot Ave., Eugene, OR 97404 / 541-688-1278; FAX: 541-607-5833
Brass Eagle, Inc., 7050A Bramalea Rd., Unit 19, Mississauga,, ON L4Z 1C7 CANADA / 416-848-4844
Brauer Bros., 1520 Washington Avenue., St. Louis, MO 63103 / 314-231-2864; FAX: 314-249-4952 www.brauerbros.com
Break-Free, Inc., 13386 International Parkway, Jacksonville, FL 32218 / 800-428-0588; FAX: 904-741-5407 contactus@armorholdings.com www.break-free.com
Brenneke GmbH, P.O. Box 1646, 30837 Langenhagen, Langenhagen, GERMANY / +49-511-97262-0; FAX: +49-511-97262-62 info@brenneke.de brenneke.com
Bridgeman Products, Harry Jaffin, 153 B Cross Slope Court, Englishtown, NJ 07726 / 732-536-3604; FAX: 732-972-1004
Bridgers Best, P.O. Box 1410, Berthoud, CO 80513
Briese Bullet Co., Inc., 3442 42nd Ave. SE, Tappen, ND 58487 / 701-327-4578; FAX: 701-327-4579
Brigade Quartermasters, 1025 Cobb International Blvd., Dept. VH, Kennesaw, GA 30144-4300 / 404-428-1248; or 800-241-3125; FAX: 404-426-7726
Briganti, A.J., 512 Rt. 32, Highland Mills, NY 10930 / 914-928-9573
Briley Mfg. Inc., 1230 Lumpkin, Houston, TX 77043 / 800-331-5718; or 713-932-6995; FAX: 713-932-1043
Brill, R. See: ROYAL ARMS INTERNATIONAL
British Sporting Arms, RR1, Box 130, Millbrook, NY 12545 / 914-677-8303
Broad Creek Rifle Works, Ltd., 120 Horsey Ave., Laurel, DE 19956 / 302-875-5446; FAX: 302-875-1448 bcrw4guns@aol.com
Brockman's Custom Gunsmithing, P.O. Box 357, Gooding, ID 83330 / 208-934-5050
Brocock Ltd., 43 River Street, Digbeth, Birmingham, B5 5SA ENGLAND / 011-021-773-1200; FAX: 011-021-773-1211 sales@brocock.co.un www.brocock.co.uk
Broken Gun Ranch, 10739 126 Rd., Spearville, KS 67876 / 316-385-2587; FAX: 316-385-2597 nbowlin@ucom.net www.brokengunranch
Brooker, Dennis, Rt. 1, Box 12A, Derby, IA 50068 / 515-533-2103
Brooks Tactical Systems-Agrip, 279-C Shorewood Ct., Fox Island, WA 98333 / 253-549-2866 FAX: 253-549-2703 brooks@brookstactical.com www.brookstactical.com
Brown Co., E. Arthur, 3404 Pawnee Dr., Alexandria, MN 56308 / 320-762-8847
Brown Dog Ent., 2200 Calle Camelia, 1000 Oaks, CA 91360 / 805-497-2318; FAX: 805-497-1618
Brown Precision, Inc., 7786 Molinos Ave., Los Molinos, CA 96055 / 530-384-2506; FAX: 916-384-1638 www.brownprecision.com
Brown Products, Inc., Ed, 43825 Muldrow Trail, Perry, MO 63462 / 573-565-3261; FAX: 573-565-2791 edbrown@edbrown.com www.edbrown.com
Brownells, Inc., 200 S. Front St., Montezuma, IA 50171 / 800-741-0015; FAX: 800-264-3068 orderdesk@brownells.com www.brownells.com
Browning Arms Co., One Browning Place, Morgan, UT 84050 / 801-876-2711; FAX: 801-876-3331 www.browning.com
Browning Arms Co. (Parts & Service), 3005 Arnold Tenbrook Rd., Arnold, MO 63010 / 617-287-6800; FAX: 617-287-9751
BRP, Inc. High Performance Cast Bullets, 1210 Alexander Rd., Colorado Springs, CO 80909 / 719-633-0658
Brunton U.S.A., 620 E. Monroe Ave., Riverton, WY 82501 / 307-856-6559; FAX: 307-857-4702 info@brunton.com www.brunton.com
Bryan & Assoc., R D Sauls, PO Box 5772, Anderson, SC 29623-5772 / 864-261-6810 bryanandac@aol.com www.huntersweb.com/bryanandac
Brynin, Milton, P.O. Box 383, Yonkers, NY 10710 / 914-779-4333
BSA Guns Ltd., Armoury Rd. Small Heath, Birmingham B11 2PP, ENGLAND / 011-021-772-8543; FAX: 011-021-773-0845 sales@bsagun.com www.bsagun.com
BSA Optics, 3911 SW 47th Ave., Ste. 914, Ft. Lauderdale, FL 33314 / 954-581-2144; FAX: 954-581-3165 4info@basaoptics.com www.bsaoptics.com
B-Square Company, Inc., P.O. Box 11281, 2708 St. Louis Ave., Ft. Worth, TX 76110 / 817-923-0964 or 800-433-2909; FAX: 817-926-7012
Buchsenmachermeister, Peter Hofer Jagdwaffen, Buchsenmachermeister, Kirchgasse 24 A-9170, Ferlach, AUSTRIA / 43 4227 3683; FAX: 43 4227 368330 peterhofer@hoferwaffen.com www.hoferwaffen.com
Buck Knives, Inc., 1900 Weld Blvd., P.O. Box 1267, El Cajon, CA 92020 / 619-449-1100; or 800-326-2825; FAX: 619-562-5774
Buck Stix-SOS Products Co., Box 3, Neenah, WI 54956
Buck Stop Lure Co., Inc., 3600 Grow Rd. NW, P.O. Box 636, Stanton, MI 48888 / 989-762-5091; FAX: 989-762-5124 buckstop@nethawk.com www.buckstopscents.com
Buckeye Custom Bullets, 6490 Stewart Rd., Elida, OH 45807 / 419-641-4463
Buckhorn Gun Works, 8109 Woodland Dr., Black Hawk, SD 57718 / 605-787-6472
Buckskin Bullet Co., P.O. Box 1893, Cedar City, UT 84721 / 435-586-3286
Budin, Dave, 817 Main St., P.O. Box 685, Margaretville, NY 12455 / 914-568-4103; FAX: 914-586-4105
Budin, Dave. See: DEL-SPORTS, INC.
Buenger Enterprises/Goldenrod Dehumidifier, 3600 S. Harbor Blvd., Oxnard, CA 93035 / 800-451-6797; or 805-985-5828; FAX: 805-985-1534
Buffalo Arms Co., 660 Vermeer Ct., Ponderay, ID 83852 / 208-263-6953; FAX: 208-265-2096 www.buffaloarms.com
Buffalo Bullet Co., Inc., 12637 Los Nietos Rd., Unit A, Santa Fe Springs, CA 90670 / 800-423-8069; FAX: 562-944-5054
Buffalo Gun Center, 3385 Harlem Rd., Buffalo, NY 14225 / 716-833-2581; FAX: 716-833-2265 www.buffaloguncenter.com
Buffalo Rock Shooters Supply, R.R. 1, Ottawa, IL 61350 / 815-433-2471
Buffer Technologies, P.O. Box 104930, Jefferson City, MO 65110 / 573-634-8529; FAX: 573-634-8522
Bull Mountain Rifle Co., 6327 Golden West Terrace, Billings, MT 59106 / 406-656-0778
Bullberry Barrel Works, Ltd., 2430 W. Bullberry Ln., Hurricane, UT 84737 / 435-635-9866; FAX: 435-635-0348 fred@bullberry.com www.bullberry.com
Bullet Metals, Bill Ferguson, P.O. Box 1238, Sierra Vista, AZ 85636 / 520-458-5321; FAX: 520-458-1421 info@theantimonyman.com www.bullet-metals.com
Bullet N Press, 1210 Jones St., Gastonia, NC 28052 / 704-853-0265 bnpress@quik.com www.clt.quik.com/bnpress
Bullet Swaging Supply, Inc., P.O. Box 1056, 303 McMillan Rd., West Monroe, LA 71291 / 318-387-3266; FAX: 318-387-7779 leblackmon@colla.com
Bull-X, Inc., 411 E. Water St., Farmer City, IL 61842-1556 / 309-928-2574 or 800-248-3845; FAX: 309-928-2130
Burkhart Gunsmithing, Don, P.O. Box 852, Rawlins, WY 82301 / 307-324-6007
Burnham Bros., P.O. Box 1148, Menard, TX 78659 / 915-396-4572; FAX: 915-396-4574
Burris Co., Inc., PO Box 1747, 331 E. 8th St., Greeley, CO 80631 / 970-356-1670; FAX: 970-356-8702
Bushmaster Firearms, Inc., 999 Roosevelt Trail, Windham, ME 04062 / 800-998-7928; FAX: 207-892-8068 info@bushmaster.com www.bushmaster.com
Bushmaster Hunting & Fishing, 451 Alliance Ave., Toronto, ON M6N 2J1 CANADA / 416-763-4040; FAX: 416-763-0623
Bushnell Sports Optics Worldwide, 9200 Cody, Overland Park, KS 66214 / 913-752-3400 or 800-423-3537; FAX: 913-752-3550
Buster's Custom Knives, P.O. Box 214, Richfield, UT 84701 / 435-896-5319; FAX: 435-896-8333 www.warenskiknives.com
Butler Creek Corp., 2100 S. Silverstone Way, Meridian, ID 83642-8151 / 800-423-8327 or 406-388-1356; FAX: 406-388-7204
Butler Enterprises, 834 Oberting Rd., Lawrenceburg, IN 47025 / 812-537-3584
Buzz Fletcher Custom Stockmaker, 117 Silver Road, P.O. Box 189, Taos, NM 87571 / 505-758-3486

C

C&D Special Products (See Claybuster Wads & Harvester Bullets)
C&H Research, 115 Sunnyside Dr., Box 351, Lewis, KS 67552 / 316-324-5445; or 888-324-5445; FAX: 620-324-5984 info@mercuryrecoil.com www.mercuryrecoil.com
C. Palmer Manufacturing Co., Inc., P.O. Box 220, West Newton, PA 15089 / 412-872-8200; FAX: 412-872-8302
C. Sharps Arms Co. Inc./Montana Armory, 100 Centennial Dr., PO Box 885, Big Timber, MT 59011 / 406-932-4353; FAX: 406-932-4443
C.S. Van Gorden & Son, Inc., 1815 Main St., Bloomer, WI 54724 / 715-568-2612 vangorden@bloomer.net
C.W. Erickson's L.L.C., 530 Garrison Ave. NE, PO Box 522, Buffalo, MN 55313 / 763-682-3665; FAX: 763-682-4328 www.archerhunter.com
Cabanas (See U.S. Importer-Mandall Shooting Supply
Cabela's, One Cabela Drive, Sidney, NE 69160 / 308-254-5505; FAX: 308-254-8420
Cabinet Mtn. Outfitters Scents & Lures, P.O. Box 766, Plains, MT 59859 / 406-826-3970
Cache La Poudre Rifleworks, 140 N. College, Ft. Collins, CO 80524 / 920-482-6913
Calhoon Mfg., 4343 U.S. Highway 87, Havre, MT 59501 / 406-395-4079 www.jamescalhoon.com
Cali'co Hardwoods, Inc., 3580 Westwind Blvd., Santa Rosa, CA 95403 / 707-546-4045; FAX: 707-546-4027 calicohardwoods@msn.com
Calico Light Weapon Systems, 1489 Greg St., Sparks, NV 89431
California Sights (See Fautheree, Andy)
Cambos Outdoorsman, 532 E. Idaho Ave., Ontario, OR 97914 / 541-889-3135; FAX: 541-889-2633
Cambos Outdoorsman, Fritz Hallberg, 532 E. Idaho Ave, Ontario, OR 97914 / 541-889-3135; FAX: 541-889-2633
Camdex, Inc., 2330 Alger, Troy, MI 48083 / 810-528-2300; FAX: 810-528-0989
Cameron's, 16690 W. 11th Ave., Golden, CO 80401 / 303-279-7365; FAX: 303-628-5413 ncnoremac@aol.com
Camillus Cutlery Co., 54 Main St., Camillus, NY 13031 / 315-672-8111; FAX: 315-672-8832
Campbell, Dick, 20000 Silver Ranch Rd., Conifer, CO 80433 / 303-697-0150; FAX: 303-697-0150 dicksknives@aol.com
Camp-Cap Products, P.O. Box 3805, Chesterfield, MO 63006 / 314-532-4340; FAX: 314-532-4340
Cannon Safe, Inc., 216 S. 2nd Ave. #BLD-932, San Bernardino, CA 92400 / 310-692-0636; or 800-242-1055; FAX: 310-692-7252
Canons Delcour, Rue J.B. Cools, B-4040, Herstal, BELGIUM / 32.(0)42.40.61.40; FAX: 32(0)42.40.22.88
Canyon Cartridge Corp., P.O. Box 152, Albertson, NY 11507 FAX: 516-294-8946
Cape Outfitters, 599 County Rd. 206, Cape Girardeau, MO 63701 / 573-335-4103; FAX: 573-335-1555
Caraville Manufacturing, P.O. Box 4545, Thousand Oaks, CA 91359 / 805-499-1234
Carbide Checkering Tools (See J&R Engineering)
Carhartt, Inc., P.O. Box 600, 3 Parklane Blvd., Dearborn, MI 48121 / 800-358-3825; or 313-271-8460; FAX: 313-271-3455
Carl Walther GmbH, B.P. 4325, D-89033, Ulm, GERMANY
Carl Zeiss Inc., 13005 N. Kingston Ave., Chester, VA 23836 / 800-441-3005; FAX: 804-530-8481
Carlson, Douglas R, Antique American Firearms, P.O. Box 71035, Dept GD, Des Moines, IA 50325 / 515-224-6552
Carolina Precision Rifles, 1200 Old Jackson Hwy., Jackson, SC 29831 / 803-827-2069
Carrell, William. See: CARRELL'S PRECISION FIREARMS
Carrell's Precision Firearms, William Carrell, 1952 W.Silver Falls Ct., Meridian, ID 83642-3837
Carry-Lite, Inc., P.O. Box 1587, Fort Smith, AR 72902 / 479-782-8971; FAX: 479-783-0234
Carter's Gun Shop, 225 G St., Penrose, CO 81240 / 719-372-6240
Cascade Bullet Co., Inc., 2355 South 6th St., Klamath Falls, OR 97601 / 503-884-9316
Cascade Shooters, 2155 N.W. 12th St., Redwood, OR 97756
Case & Sons Cutlery Co., W R, Owens Way, Bradford, PA 16701 / 814-368-4123; or 800-523-6350; FAX: 814-768-5369
Case Sorting System, 12695 Cobblestone Creek Rd., Poway, CA 92064 / 619-486-9340
Cash Mfg. Co., Inc., P.O. Box 130, 201 S. Klein Dr., Waunakee, WI 53597-0130 / 608-849-5664; FAX: 608-849-5664
Caspian Arms, Ltd., 14 North Main St., Hardwick, VT 05843 / 802-472-6454; FAX: 802-472-6709
Cast Performance Bullet Company, P.O. Box 153, Riverton, WY 82501 / 307-857-2940; FAX: 307-857-3132 castperform@wyoming.com castperformance.com
Casull Arms Corp., P.O. Box 1629, Afton, WY 83110 / 307-886-0200
Caswell International, 720 Industrial Dr. No. 112, Cary, IL 60013 / 847-639-7666; FAX: 847-639-7694 www.caswellintl.com
Cathey Enterprises, Inc., P.O. Box 2202, Brownwood, TX 76804 / 915-643-2553; FAX: 915-643-3653
Cation, 2341 Alger St., Troy, MI 48083 / 810-689-0658; FAX: 810-689-7558
Caywood, Shane J., P.O. Box 321, Minocqua, WI 54548 / 715-277-3866
Caywood Gunmakers, 18 Kings Hill Estates, Berryville, AR 72616 / 870-423-4741 www.caywoodguns.com
CBC, Avenida Humberto de Campos 3220, 09400-000, Ribeirao Pires, SP, BRAZIL / 55 11 4822 8378; FAX: 55 11 4822 8323 export@cbc.com.bc www.cbc.com.bc
CBC-BRAZIL, 3 Cuckoo Lane, Honley, Yorkshire HD7 2BR, ENGLAND / 44-1484-661062; FAX: 44-1484-663709
CCG Enterprises, 5217 E. Belknap St., Halton City, TX 76117 / 800-819-7464
CCI/Speer Div of ATK, P.O. Box 856, 2299 Snake River Ave., Lewiston, ID 83501 / 800-627-3640 or 208-746-2351
CCL Security Products, 199 Whiting St, New Britain, CT 06051 / 800-733-8588
Cedar Hill Game Calls, Inc., 238 Vic Allen Rd, Downsville, LA 71234 / 318-982-5632; FAX: 318-368-2245
Centaur Systems, Inc., 1602 Foothill Rd., Kalispell, MT 59901 / 406-755-8609; FAX: 406-755-8609
Center Lock Scope Rings, 9901 France Ct., Lakeville, MN 55044 / 952-461-2114; FAX: 952-461-2194 marklee55044@usfamily.net
Central Specialties Ltd (See Trigger Lock Division
Century Gun Dist. Inc., 1467 Jason Rd., Greenfield, IN 46140 / 317-462-4524
Century International Arms, Inc., 1161 Holland Dr, Boca Raton, FL 33487 / 800-527-1252; FAX: 561-998-1993 support@centuryarms.com www.centuryarms.com
CFVentures, 509 Harvey Dr., Bloomington, IN 47403-1715 paladinwilltravel@yahoo.com www.caversam16.freeserve.co.uk
CH Tool & Die Co. (See 4-D Custom Die Co.), 711 N Sandusky St., P.O. Box 889, Mt. Vernon, OH 43050-0889 / 740-397-7214; FAX: 740-397-6600
Chace Leather Products, 507 Alden St., Fall River, MA 02722 / 508-678-7556; FAX: 508-675-9666 chacelea@aol.com www.chaceleather.com
Chadick's Ltd., P.O. Box 100, Terrell, TX 75160 / 214-563-7577
Chambers Flintlocks Ltd., Jim, 116 Sams Branch Rd., Candler, NC 28715 / 828-667-8361; FAX: 828-665-0852 www.flintlocks.com
Champion Shooters' Supply, P.O. Box 303, New Albany, OH 43054 / 614-855-1603; FAX: 614-855-1209
Champion Target Co., 232 Industrial Parkway, Richmond, IN 47374 / 800-441-4971
Champion's Choice, Inc., 201 International Blvd., LaVergne, TN 37086 / 615-793-4066; FAX: 615-793-4070 champ.choice@earthlink.net www.champchoice.com

MANUFACTURER'S DIRECTORY

Champlin Firearms, Inc., P.O. Box 3191, Woodring Airport, Enid, OK 73701 / 580-237-7388; FAX: 580-242-6922 info@champlinarms.com www.champlinarms.com
Chapman Academy of Practical Shooting, 4350 Academy Rd., Hallsville, MO 65255 / 573-696-5544; FAX: 573-696-2266 ha@chapmanacademy.com
Chapman, J Ken. See: OLD WEST BULLET MOULDS
Chapman Manufacturing Co., 471 New Haven Rd., P.O. Box 250, Durham, CT 06422 / 860-349-9228; FAX: 860-349-0084 sales@chapmanmfg.com www.chapmanmfg.com
Chapuis Armes, 21 La Gravoux, BP15, 42380, St. Bonnet-le-Chatea, FRANCE / (33)77.50.06.96
Chapuis USA, 416 Business Park, Bedford, KY 40006
Charter 2000, 273 Canal St, Shelton, CT 06484 / 203-922-1652
Checkmate Refinishing, 370 Champion Dr., Brooksville, FL 34601 / 352-799-5774; FAX: 352-799-2986 checkmatecustom.com
Cheddite, France S.A., 99 Route de Lyon, F-26501, Bourg-les-Valence, FRANCE / 33-75-56-4545; FAX: 33-75-56-3587 export@cheddite.com
Chelsea Gun Club of New York City Inc., 237 Ovington Ave., Apt. D53, Brooklyn, NY 11209 / 718-836-9422; or 718-833-2704
Cherry Creek State Park Shooting Center, 12500 E. Belleview Ave., Englewood, CO 80111 / 303-693-1765
CheVron Bullets, RR1, Ottawa, IL 61350 / 815-433-2471
Cheyenne Pioneer Products, PO Box 28425, Kansas City, MO 64188 / 816-413-9196; FAX: 816-455-2859 cheyennepp@aol.com www.cartridgeboxes.com
Chicago Cutlery Co., 1536 Beech St., Terre Haute, IN 47804 / 800-457-2665
Chicasaw Gun Works, 4 Mi. Mkr., Pluto Rd., Box 868, Shady Spring, WV 25918-0868 / 304-763-2848; FAX: 304-763-3725
Chip McCormick Corp., P.O. Box 1560, Manchaca, TX 78652 / 800-328-2447; FAX: 512-280-4282 www.chipmccormick.com
Chipmunk (See Oregon Arms, Inc.)
Choate Machine & Tool Co., Inc., P.O. Box 218, 116 Lovers Ln., Bald Knob, AR 72010 / 501-724-6193; or 800-972-6390; FAX: 501-724-5873
Christensen Arms, 192 East 100 North, Fayette, UT 84630 / 435-528-7999; FAX: 435-528-7494 www.christensenarms.com
Christie's East, 20 Rockefeller Plz., New York, NY 10020-1902 / 212-606-0406 christics.com
Chu Tani Ind., Inc., P.O. Box 2064, Cody, WY 82414-2064
Chuck's Gun Shop, P.O. Box 597, Waldo, FL 32694 / 904-468-2264
Chuilli, Stephen, 8895 N. Military Trl. Ste., Ste. 201E, Palm Beach Gardens, FL 33410
Churchill (See U.S. Importer-Ellett Bros.)
Churchill, Winston G., 2838 20 Mile Stream Rd., Proctorville, VT 05153 / 802-226-7772
Churchill Glove Co., James, PO Box 298, Centralia, WA 98531 / 360-736-2816; FAX: 360-330-0151
CIDCO, 21480 Pacific Blvd., Sterling, VA 22170 / 703-444-5353
Cimarron F.A. Co., P.O. Box 906, Fredericksburg, TX 78624-0906 / 830-997-9090; FAX: 830-997-0802 cimgraph@koc.com www.cimarron-firearms.com
Cincinnati Swaging, 2605 Marlington Ave., Cincinnati, OH 45208
Clark Custom Guns, Inc., 336 Shootout Lane, Princeton, LA 71067 / 318-949-9884; FAX: 318-949-9829
Clark Firearms Engraving, P.O. Box 80746, San Marino, CA 91118 / 818-287-1652
Clarkfield Enterprises, Inc., 1032 10th Ave., Clarkfield, MN 56223 / 612-669-7140
Claro Walnut Gunstock Co., 1235 Stanley Ave., Chico, CA 95928 / 530-342-5188; FAX: 530-342-5199 wally@clarowalnutgunstocks.com www.clarowalnutgunstocks.com
Classic Arms Company, Rt 1 Box 120F, Burnet, TX 78611 / 512-756-4001
Classic Arms Corp., P.O. Box 106, Dunsmuir, CA 96025-0106 / 530-235-2000
Classic Old West Styles, 1060 Doniphan Park Circle C, El Paso, TX 79936 / 915-587-0684
Claybuster Wads & Harvester Bullets, 309 Sequoya Dr., Hopkinsville, KY 42240 / 800-922-6287; or 800-284-1746; FAX: 502-885-8088
Clean Shot Technologies, 21218 St. Andrews Blvd. Ste 504, Boca Raton, FL 33433 / 888-866-2532
Clearview Mfg. Co., Inc., 413 S. Oakley St., Fordyce, AR 71742 / 501-352-8557; FAX: 501-352-7120
Clearview Products, 3021 N. Portland, Oklahoma City, OK 73107
Cleland's Outdoor World, Inc, 10306 Airport Hwy., Swanton, OH 43558 / 419-865-4713; FAX: 419-865-5865
Clements' Custom Leathercraft, Chas, 1741 Dallas St., Aurora, CO 80010-2018 / 303-364-0403; FAX: 303-739-9824 gryphons@home.com kuntaoslcat.com
Clenzoil Worldwide Corp, Jack Fitzgerald, 25670 1st St., Westlake, OH 44145-1430 / 440-899-0482; FAX: 440-899-0483
Clift Mfg., L. R., 3821 Hammonton Rd., Marysville, CA 95901 / 916-755-3390; FAX: 916-755-3393
Clymer Mfg. Co., 1645 W. Hamlin Rd., Rochester Hills, MI 48309-3312 / 248-853-5555; FAX: 248-853-1530
C-More Systems, P.O. Box 1750, 7553 Gary Rd., Manassas, VA 20108 / 703-361-2663; FAX: 703-361-5881
Cobra Enterprises, Inc., 1960 S. Milestone Drive, Suite F, Salt Lake City, UT 84104 FAX: 801-908-8301 www.cobrapistols@networld.com
Cobra Sport S.R.I., Via Caduti Nei Lager No. 1, 56020 San Romano, Montopoli v/Arno (Pi, ITALY / 0039-571-450490; FAX: 0039-571-450492
Coffin, Charles H., 3719 Scarlet Ave., Odessa, TX 79762 / 915-366-4729; FAX: 915-366-4729
Coffin, Jim (See Working Guns)
Coffin, Jim. See: WORKING GUNS
Cogar's Gunsmithing, 206 Redwine Dr., Houghton Lake, MI 48629 / 517-422-4591
Coghlan's Ltd., 121 Irene St., Winnipeg, MB R3T 4C7 CANADA / 204-284-9550; FAX: 204-475-4127
Cold Steel Inc., 3036 Seaborg Ave. Ste. A, Ventura, CA 93003 / 800-255-4716; or 800-624-2363; FAX: 805-642-9727
Cole-Grip, 16135 Cohasset St., Van Nuys, CA 91406 / 818-782-4424
Coleman Co., Inc., 3600 N. Hydraulic, Wichita, KS 67219 / 1-800-835-3278; www.coleman.com
Cole's Gun Works, Old Bank Building, Rt. 4 Box 250, Moyock, NC 27958 / 919-435-2345
Collector's Armoury, Ltd., Tom Nelson, 9404 Gunston Cove Rd., Lorton, VA 22079 / 703-493-9120; FAX: 703-493-9424 www.collectorsarmoury.com
Collings, Ronald, 1006 Cielta Linda, Vista, CA 92083
Colonial Arms, Inc., P.O. Box 636, Selma, AL 36702-0636 / 334-872-9455; FAX: 334-872-9540 colonialarms@mindspring.com www.colonialarms.com
Colonial Repair, 47 Navarre St., Roslindale, MA 02131-4725 / 617-469-4951
Colorado Gunsmithing Academy, RR 3 Box 79B, El Campo, TX 77437 / 719-336-4099; or 800-754-2046; FAX: 719-336-9642
Colorado School of Trades, 1575 Hoyt St., Lakewood, CO 80215 / 800-234-4594; FAX: 303-233-4723
Colt Blackpowder Arms Co., 110 8th Street, Brooklyn, NY 11215 / 718-499-4678; FAX: 718-768-8056
Colt's Mfg. Co., Inc., PO Box 1868, Hartford, CT 06144-1868 / 800-962-COLT; or 860-236-6311; FAX: 860-244-1449
Compass Industries, Inc., 104 East 25th St., New York, NY 10010 / 212-473-2614 or 800-221-9904; FAX: 212-353-0826
Compasseco, Ltd., 151 Atkinson Hill Ave., Bardtown, KY 40004 / 502-349-0910
Competition Electronics, Inc., 3469 Precision Dr., Rockford, IL 61109 / 815-874-8001; FAX: 815-874-8181
Competitor Corp., Inc., 26 Knight St. Unit 3, Jaffrey, NH 03452 / 603-532-9483; FAX: 603-532-8209 competitorcorp@aol.com competitor-pistol.com
Component Concepts, Inc., 530 S. Springbrook Road, Newberg, OR 97132 / 503-554-8095; FAX: 503-554-9370 cci@cybcon.com www.phantomonline.com
Concept Development Corp., 16610 E. Laser Drive, Suite 5, Fountain Hills, AZ 85268-6644
Conetrol Scope Mounts, 10225 Hwy. 123 S., Seguin, TX 78155 / 830-379-3030; or 800-CONETROL; FAX: 830-379-3030 email@conetrol.com www.conetrol.com
Connecticut Shotgun Mfg. Co., P.O. Box 1692, 35 Woodland St., New Britain, CT 06051 / 860-225-6581; FAX: 860-832-8707
Connecticut Valley Classics (See CVC, BPI)
Conrad, C. A., 3964 Ebert St., Winston-Salem, NC 27127 / 919-788-5469
Cook Engineering Service, 891 Highbury Rd., Vict, 3133 AUSTRALIA
Cooper Arms, P.O. Box 114, Stevensville, MT 59870 / 406-777-0373; FAX: 406-777-5228
Cooper-Woodward Perfect Lube, 4120 Oesterle Rd., Helena, MT 59602 / 406-459-2287 cwperfectlube@mt.net cwperfectlube.com
Corbin Mfg. & Supply, Inc., 600 Industrial Circle, P.O. Box 2659, White City, OR 97503 / 541-826-5211; FAX: 541-826-8669 sales@corbins.com www.corbins.com
Cor-Bon Inc./Glaser LLC, P.O. Box 173, 1311 Industry Rd., Sturgis, SD 57785 / 605-347-4544; or 800-221-3489; FAX: 605-347-5055 email@corbon.com www.corbon.com
Corkys Gun Clinic, 4401 Hot Springs Dr., Greeley, CO 80634-9226 / 970-330-0516
Corry, John, 861 Princeton Ct., Neshanic Station, NJ 08853 / 908-369-8019
Cosmi Americo & Figlio S.N.C., Via Flaminia 307, Ancona, ITALY / 071-888208; FAX: 39-071-887008
Coulston Products, Inc., P.O. Box 30, 201 Ferry St. Suite 212, Easton, PA 18044-0030 / 215-253-0167; or 800-445-9927; FAX: 215-252-1511
Counter Assault, 120 Industrial Court, Kalispell, MT 59901 / 406-257-4740; FAX: 406-257-6674
Cousin Bob's Mountain Products, 7119 Ohio River Blvd., Ben Avon, PA 15202 / 412-766-5114; FAX: 412-766-5114
CP Bullets, 1310 Industrial Hwy #5-6, South Hampton, PA 18966 / 215-953-7264; FAX: 215-953-7275
CQB Training, P.O. Box 1739, Manchester, MO 63011
Craftguard, 3624 Logan Ave., Waterloo, IA 50703 / 319-232-2959; FAX: 319-234-0804
Crandall Tool & Machine Co., 19163 21 Mile Rd., Tustin, MI 49688 / 616-829-4430
Creedmoor Sports, Inc., P.O. Box 1040, Oceanside, CA 92051 / 767-757-5529; FAX: 760-757-5558 shoot@creedmoorsports.com www.creedmoorsports.com
Creek Side Metal & Woodcrafters, Fishers Hill, VA 22626 / 703-465-3903
Creighton Audette, 19 Highland Circle, Springfield, VT 05156 / 802-885-2331
Crimson Trace Lasers, 8090 SW Cirrus Dr., Beverton, OR 97008 / 800-442-2406; FAX: 503-627-0166 www.crimsontrace.com
Crit'R Call (See Rocky Mountain Wildlife Products)
Crosman Airguns, Rts. 5 and 20, E. Bloomfield, NY 14443 / 716-657-6161; FAX: 716-657-5405
Crosman Blades (See Coleman Co., Inc.)
Crouse's Country Cover, P.O. Box 160, Storrs, CT 06268 / 860-423-8736
CRR, Inc./Marble's Inc., 420 Industrial Park, P.O. Box 111, Gladstone, MI 49837 / 906-428-3710; FAX: 906-428-3711
Crucelegui, Hermanos (See U.S. Importer-Mandall)
Cubic Shot Shell Co., Inc., 98 Fatima Dr., Campbell, OH 44405 / 330-755-0349
Cullity Restoration, 209 Old Country Rd., East Sandwich, MA 02537 / 508-888-1147
Cumberland Arms, 514 Shafer Road, Manchester, TN 37355 / 800-797-8414
Cumberland Mountain Arms, P.O. Box 710, Winchester, TN 37398 / 615-967-8414; FAX: 615-967-9199
Cummings Bullets, 1417 Esperanza Way, Escondido, CA 92027
Cupp, Alana, Custom Engraver, P.O. Box 207, Annabella, UT 84711 / 801-896-4834
Curly Maple Stock Blanks (See Tiger-Hunt)
Curtis Cast Bullets, 527 W. Babcock St., Bozeman, MT 59715 / 406-587-8117; FAX: 406-587-8117
Curtis Gun Shop (See Curtis Cast Bullets)
Custom Bullets by Hoffman, 2604 Peconic Ave., Seaford, NY 11783
Custom Calls, 607 N. 5th St., Burlington, IA 52601 / 319-752-4465
Custom Checkering Service, Kathy Forster, 2124 S.E. Yamhill St., Portland, OR 97214 / 503-236-5874
Custom Chronograph, Inc., 5305 Reese Hill Rd., Sumas, WA 98295 / 360-988-7801
Custom Firearms (See Ahrends, Kim)
Custom Products (See Jones Custom Products)
Custom Quality Products, Inc., 345 W. Girard Ave., P.O. Box 71129, Madison Heights, MI 48071 / 810-585-1616; FAX: 810-585-0644
Custom Riflestocks, Inc., Michael M. Kokolus, 7005 Herber Rd., New Tripoli, PA 18066 / 610-298-3013; FAX: 610-298-2431 mkokolus@prodigy.net
Custom Single Shot Rifles, 9651 Meadows Lane, Guthrie, OK 73044 / 405-282-3634
Custom Tackle and Ammo, P.O. Box 1886, Farmington, NM 87499 / 505-632-3539
Cutco Cutlery, P.O. Box 810, Olean, NY 14760 / 716-372-3111
CVA, 5988 Peachtree Corners East, Norcross, GA 30071 / 770-449-4687; FAX: 770-242-8546 info@cva.com www.cva.com
Cylinder & Slide, Inc., William R. Laughridge, 245 E. 4th St., Fremont, NE 68025 / 402-721-4277; FAX: 402-721-0263 bill@cylinder-slide.com www.clinder-slide.com
CZ USA, PO Box 171073, Kansas City, KS 66117 / 913-321-1811; FAX: 913-321-4901

D

D&D Gunsmiths, Ltd., 363 E. Elmwood, Troy, MI 48083 / 810-583-1512; FAX: 810-583-1524
D&G Precision Duplicators (See Greene Precision)
D&H Precision Tooling, 7522 Barnard Mill Rd., Ringwood, IL 60072 / 815-653-4011
D&L Industries (See D.J. Marketing)
D&L Sports, P.O. Box 651, Gillette, WY 82717 / 307-686-4008
D.C.C. Enterprises, 259 Wynburn Ave., Athens, GA 30601
D.J. Marketing, 10602 Horton Ave., Downey, CA 90241 / 310-806-0891; FAX: 310-806-6231
D.L. Unmussig Bullets, 7862 Brentford Dr., Richmond, VA 23225 / 804-320-1165; FAX: 804-320-4587
Dade Screw Machine Products, 2319 NW 7th Ave., Miami, FL 33127 / 305-573-5050
Daisy Outdoor Products, P.O. Box 220, Rogers, AR 72757 / 479-636-1200; FAX: 479-636-0573 www.daisy.com
Dakota (See U.S. Importer-EMF Co., Inc.)
Dakota Arms, Inc., 130 Industry Road, Sturgis, SD 57785 / 605-347-4686; FAX: 605-347-4459 info@dakotaarms.com www.dakotaarms.com
Dakota Corp., 77 Wales St., P.O. Box 543, Rutland, VT 05701 / 802-775-6062, or 800-451-4167, FAX: 802-773-3919
Daly, Charles/KBI, P.O. Box 6625, Harrisburg, PA 17112 / 866-DALY GUN
Da-Mar Gunsmith's, Inc., 102 1st St., Solvay, NY 13209
damascususa@inteliport.com, 149 Deans Farm Rd., Tyner, NC 27980 / 252-221-2010; FAX: 252-221-2010 damascususa@inteliport.com
Dan Wesson Firearms, 5169 Rt. 12 South, Norwich, NY 13815 / 607-336-1174; FAX: 607-336-2730 danwessonfirearms@citlink.net danwessonfirearms.com
Danforth, Mikael. See: VEKTOR USA
Dangler, Homer L., 2870 Lee Marie Dr., Adrian, MI 49221 / 517-266-1997
Danner Shoe Mfg. Co., 12722 NE Airport Way, Portland, OR 97230 / 503-251-1100; or 800-345-0430; FAX: 503-251-1119
Dan's Whetstone Co., Inc., 130 Timbs Place, Hot Springs, AR 71913 / 501-767-1616; FAX: 501-767-9598 questions@danswhetstone.com www.danswhetstone.com
Danuser Machine Co., 550 E. Third St., P.O. Box 368, Fulton, MO 65251 / 573-642-2246; FAX: 573-642-2240 sales@danuser.com www.danuser.com
Dara-Nes, Inc. (See Nesci Enterprises, Inc.)
D'Arcy Echols & Co., P.O. Box 421, Millville, UT 84326 / 435-755-6842
Darlington Gun Works, Inc., P.O. Box 698, 516 S. 52 Bypass, Darlington, SC 29532 / 803-393-3931
Dart Bell/Brass (See MAST Technology)
Darwin Hensley Gunmaker, P.O. Box 329, Brightwood, OR 97011 / 503-622-5411

MANUFACTURER'S DIRECTORY

Data Tech Software Systems, 19312 East Eldorado Drive, Aurora, CO 80013
Dave Norin Schrank's Smoke & Gun, 2010 Washington St., Waukegan, IL 60085 / 708-662-4034
Dave's Gun Shop, P.O. Box 2824, Casper, WY 82602-2824 / 307-754-9724
David Clark Co., Inc., P.O. Box 15054, Worcester, MA 01615 / 508-756-6216; FAX: 508-753-5827 sales@davidclark.com www.davidclark.com
David Condon, Inc., 109 E. Washington St., Middleburg, VA 22117 / 703-687-5642
David Miller Co., 3131 E. Greenlee Rd., Tucson, AZ 85716 / 520-326-3117
David R. Chicoine, 1210 Jones Street, Gastonia, NC 28052 / 704-853-0265 bnpress@quik.com www.icxquik.com/bnpress
David W. Schwartz Custom Guns, 2505 Waller St., Eau Claire, WI 54703 / 715-832-1735
Davide Pedersoli and Co., Via Artigiani 57, Gardone VT, Brescia 25063, ITALY / 030-8915000; FAX: 030-8911019 info@davidepedersoli.com www.davide_pedersoli.com
Davis, Don, 1619 Heights, Katy, TX 77493 / 713-391-3090
Davis Industries (See Cobra Enterprises, Inc.)
Davis Products, Mike, 643 Loop Dr., Moses Lake, WA 98837 / 509-765-6178; or 509-766-7281
Daystate Ltd., Birch House Lanee, Cotes Heath Staffs, ST15.022, ENGLAND / 01782-791755; FAX: 01782-791617
Dayton Traister, 4778 N. Monkey Hill Rd., P.O. Box 593, Oak Harbor, WA 98277 / 360-679-4657; FAX: 360-675-1114
DBI Books Division of Krause Publications, 700 E. State St., Iola, WI 54990-0001 / 715-445-2214
D-Boone Ent., Inc., 5900 Colwyn Dr., Harrisburg, PA 17109
Dead Eye's Sport Center, 76 Baer Rd., Shickshinny, PA 18655 / 570-256-7432 deadeyeprizz@aol.com
Deepeeka Exports Pvt. Ltd., D-78, Saket, Meerut-250-006, INDIA / 011-91-121-640363 or ; FAX: 011-91-121-640988 deepeeka@poboxes.com www.deepeeka.com
Defense Training International, Inc., 749 S. Lemay, Ste. A3-337, Ft. Collins, CO 80524 / 303-482-2520; FAX: 303-482-0548
Degen Inc. (See Aristocrat Knives)
deHaas Barrels, 20049 W. State Hwy. Z, Ridgeway, MO 64481 / 660-872-6308
Del Rey Products, P.O. Box 5134, Playa Del Rey, CA 90296-5134 / 213-823-0494
Delhi Gun House, 1374 Kashmere Gate, New Delhi 110 006, INDIA / 2940974; or 394-0974; FAX: 2917344 dgh@vsnl.com
Delorge, Ed, 6734 W. Main, Houma, LA 70360 / 985-223-0206 delorge@triparish.net www.eddelorge.com
Del-Sports, Inc., Dave Budin, Box 685, 817 Main St., Margaretville, NY 12455 / 845-586-4103; FAX: 845-586-4105
Delta Arms Ltd., P.O. Box 1000, Delta, VT 84624-1000
Delta Enterprises, 284 Hagemann Drive, Livermore, CA 94550
Delta Frangible Ammunition LLC, P.O. Box 2350, Stafford, VA 22555-2350 / 540-720-5778; or 800-339-1933; FAX: 540-720-5667 dfa@dfanet.com www.dfanet.com
Dem-Bart Checkering Tools, Inc., 1825 Bickford Ave., Snohomish, WA 98290 / 360-568-7356 walt@dembartco.com www.dembartco.com
Denver Instrument Co., 6542 Fig St., Arvada, CO 80004 / 800-321-1135; or 303-431-7255; FAX: 303-423-4831
DeSantis Holster & Leather Goods, Inc., P.O. Box 2039, 149 Denton Ave., New Hyde Park, NY 11040-0701 / 516-354-8000; FAX: 516-354-7501
Desert Mountain Mfg., P.O. Box 130184, Coram, MT 59913 / 800-477-0762; or 406-387-5361; FAX: 406-387-5361
Detonics USA, 53 Perimeter Center East #200, Atlanta, GA 30346 / 866-759-1169
DGR Custom Rifles, 4191 37th Ave. SE, Tappen, ND 58487 / 701-327-8135
DGS, Inc., Dale A. Storey, 1117 E. 12th, Casper, WY 82601 / 307-237-2414; FAX: 307-237-2414 dalest@trib.com www.dgsrifle.com
DHB Products, 336 River View Dr., Verona, VA 24482-2547 / 703-836-2648
Diamond Machining Technology, Inc. (See DMT)
Diamond Mfg. Co., P.O. Box 174, Wyoming, PA 18644 / 800-233-9601
Dibble, Derek A., 555 John Downey Dr., New Britain, CT 06051 / 203-224-2630
Dietz Gun Shop & Range, Inc., 421 Range Rd., New Braunfels, TX 78132 / 210-885-4662
Dilliott Gunsmithing, Inc., 657 Scarlett Rd., Dandridge, TN 37725 / 865-397-9204 gunsmithd@aol.com dilliottgunsmithing.com
Dillon Precision Products, Inc., 8009 East Dillon's Way, Scottsdale, AZ 85260 / 480-948-8009; or 800-762-3845; FAX: 480-998-2786 sales@dillonprecision.com www.dillonprecision.com
Dina Arms Corporation, P.O. Box 46, Royersford, PA 19468 / 610-287-0266; FAX: 610-287-0266
Dixie Gun Works, P.O. Box 130, Union City, TN 38281 / 731-885-0700; FAX: 731-885-0440 info@dixiegunworks.com www.dixiegunworks.com
Dixon Muzzleloading Shop, Inc., 9952 Kunkels Mill Rd., Kempton, PA 19529 / 610-756-6271 dixonmuzzleloading.com
DKT, Inc., 14623 Vera Drive, Union, MI 49130-9744 / 800-741-7083 orders; FAX: 616-641-2015
DLO Mfg., 10807 SE Foster Ave., Arcadia, FL 33821-7304
DMT--Diamond Machining Technology Inc., 85 Hayes Memorial Dr., Marlborough, MA 01752 FAX: 508-485-3924
Dohring Bullets, 100 W. 8 Mile Rd., Ferndale, MI 48220
Dolbare, Elizabeth, P.O. Box 502, Dubois, WY 82513-0502 / 307-450-7500 edolbare@hotmail.com www.scrimshaw-engraving.com
Domino, P.O. Box 108, 20019 Settimo Milanese, Milano, ITALY / 1-39-2-33512040; FAX: 1-39-2-33511587
Don Klein Custom Guns, 433 Murray Park Dr., Ripon, WI 54971 / 920-748-2931 daklein@charter.net www.donkleincustomguns.com
Donnelly, C. P., 405 Kubli Rd., Grants Pass, OR 97527 / 541-846-6604
Doskocil Mfg. Co., Inc., P.O. Box 1246, 4209 Barnett, Arlington, TX 76017 / 817-467-5116; FAX: 817-472-9810
Douglas Barrels, Inc., 5504 Big Tyler Rd., Charleston, WV 25313-1398 / 304-776-1341; FAX: 304-776-8560 www.benchrest.com/douglas
Downsizer Corp., P.O. Box 710316, Santee, CA 92072-0316 / 619-448-5510 www.downsizer.com
DPMS (Defense Procurement Manufacturing Services, Inc.), 13983 Industry Avenue, Becker, MN 55308 / 800-578-DPMS; or 763-261-5600; FAX: 763-261-5599
Dr. O's Products Ltd., P.O. Box 111, Niverville, NY 12130 / 518-784-3333; FAX: 518-784-2800
Drain, Mark, SE 3211 Kamilche Point Rd., Shelton, WA 98584 / 206-426-5452
Dremel Mfg. Co., 4915-21st St., Racine, WI 53406
Dri-Slide, Inc., 411 N. Darling, Fremont, MI 49412 / 616-924-3950
Dropkick, 1460 Washington Blvd., Williamsport, PA 17701 / 717-326-6561; FAX: 717-326-4950
DS Arms, Inc., P.O. Box 370, 27 West 990 Industrial Ave., Barrington, IL 60010 / 847-277-7258; FAX: 847-277-7259 www.dsarms.com
DTM International, Inc., 40 Joslyn Rd., P.O. Box 5, Lake Orion, MI 48362 / 313-693-6670
Duane A. Hobbie Gunsmithing, 2412 Pattie Ave., Wichita, KS 67216 / 316-264-8266
Duane's Gun Repair (See DGR Custom Rifles)
Dubber, Michael W., P.O. Box 312, Evansville, IN 47702 / 812-424-9000; FAX: 812-424-6551
Duck Call Specialists, P.O. Box 124, Jerseyville, IL 62052 / 618-498-9855
Duffy, Charles E. (See Guns Antique & Modern DBA), Williams Lane, P.O. Box 2, West Hurley, NY 12491 / 914-679-2997
Du-Lite Corp., 171 River Rd., Middletown, CT 06457 / 203-347-2505; FAX: 203-347-9404
Dumoulin, Ernest, Rue Florent Boclinville 8-10, 13-4041, Votten, BELGIUM / 41 27 78 92
Duncan's Gun Works, Inc., 1619 Grand Ave., San Marcos, CA 92069 / 760-727-0515
DunLyon R&D, Inc., 52151 E. US Hwy. 60, Miami, AZ 85539 / 928-473-9027
Duofold, Inc., RD 3 Rt. 309, Valley Square Mall, Tamaqua, PA 18252 / 717-386-2666; FAX: 717-386-3652
Dutchman's Firearms, Inc., 4143 Taylor Blvd., Louisville, KY 40215 / 502-366-0555
Dybala Gun Shop, P.O. Box 1024, FM 3156, Bay City, TX 77414 / 409-245-0866
Dykstra, Doug, 411 N. Darling, Fremont, MI 49412 / 616-924-3950
Dynalite Products, Inc., 215 S. Washington St., Greenfield, OH 45123 / 513-981-2124
Dynamit Nobel-RWS, Inc., 81 Ruckman Rd., Closter, NJ 07624 / 201-767-7971; FAX: 201-767-1589

E

E&L Mfg., Inc., 4177 Riddle Bypass Rd., Riddle, OR 97469 / 541-874-2137; FAX: 541-874-3107
E. Arthur Brown Co., 3404 Pawnee Dr., Alexandria, MN 56308 / 320-762-8847
E.A.A. Corp., P.O. Box 1299, Sharpes, FL 32959 / 407-639-4842; or 800-536-4442; FAX: 407-639-7006
Eagan, Donald V., P.O. Box 196, Benton, PA 17814 / 717-925-6134
Eagle Arms, Inc. (See ArmaLite, Inc.)
Eagle Grips, Eagle Business Center, 460 Randy Rd., Carol Stream, IL 60188 / 800-323-6144; or 708-260-0400; FAX: 708-260-0486
Eagle Imports, Inc., 1750 Brielle Ave., Unit B1, Wanamassa, NJ 07712 / 732-493-0333; FAX: 732-493-0301 gsodini@aol.com www.bersa-11ama.com
E-A-R, Inc., Div. of Cabot Safety Corp., 5457 W. 79th St., Indianapolis, IN 46268 / 800-327-3431; FAX: 800-488-8007
EAW (See U.S. Importer-New England Custom Gun Serv
Eckelman Gunsmithing, 3125 133rd St. SW, Fort Ripley, MN 56449 / 218-829-3176
Eclectic Technologies, Inc., 45 Grandview Dr., Suite A, Farmington, CT 06034
Ed Brown Products, Inc., P.O. Box 492, Perry, MO 63462 / 573-565-3261; FAX: 573-565-2791 edbrown@edbrown.com www.edbrown.com
Edenpine, Inc. c/o Six Enterprises, Inc., 320 D Turtle Creek Ct., San Jose, CA 95125 / 408-999-0201; FAX: 408-999-0216
EdgeCraft Corp., S. Weiner, 825 Southwood Road, Avondale, PA 19311 / 610-268-0500; or 800-342-3255; FAX: 610-268-3545 www.edgecraft.com
Edmisten Co., P.O. Box 1293, Boone, NC 28607
Edmund Scientific Co., 101 E. Gloucester Pike, Barrington, NJ 08033 / 609-543-6250
Ednar, Inc., 2-4-8 Kayabacho, Nihonbashi Chuo-ku, Tokyo, JAPAN / 81-3-3667-1651; FAX: 81-3-3661-8113
Ed's Gun House, Ed Kukowski, P.O. Box 62, Minnesota City, MN 55959 / 507-689-2925
Effebi SNC-Dr. Franco Beretta, via Rossa, 4, 25062, ITALY / 030-2751955; FAX: 030-2180414
Eggleston, Jere D., 400 Saluda Ave., Columbia, SC 29205 / 803-799-3402
Eichelberger Bullets, Wm., 158 Crossfield Rd., King Of Prussia, PA 19406
Ekol Leather Care, P.O. Box 2652, West Lafayette, IN 47906 / 317-463-2250; FAX: 317-463-7004
El Paso Saddlery Co., P.O. Box 27194, El Paso, TX 79926 / 915-544-2233; FAX: 915-544-2535 epsaddlery.com www.epsaddlery.com
Electro Prismatic Collimators, Inc., 1441 Manatt St., Lincoln, NE 68521
Electronic Shooters Protection, Inc., 15290 Gadsden Ct., Brighton, CO 80603 / 800-797-7791; FAX: 303-659-8668 esp@usa.net espamerican.com
Electronic Trigger Systems, Inc., P.O. Box 645, Park Rapids, MN 56470 / 218-732-5333
Eley Ltd., P.O. Box 705, Witton, Birmingham, B6 7UT ENGLAND / 021-356-8899; FAX: 021-331-4173
Elite Ammunition, P.O. Box 3251, Oakbrook, IL 60522 / 708-366-9006
Ellett Bros., 267 Columbia Ave., P.O. Box 128, Chapin, SC 29036 / 803-345-3751; or 800-845-3711; FAX: 803-345-1820
Ellicott Arms, Inc. / Woods Pistolsmithing, 8390 Sunset Dr., Ellicott City, MD 21043 / 410-465-7979
Elliott, Inc., G. W., 514 Burnside Ave, East Hartford, CT 06108 / 203-289-5741; FAX: 203-289-3137
EMAP USA, 6420 Wilshire Blvd., Los Angeles, CA 90048 / 213-782-2000; FAX: 213-782-2867
Emerging Technologies, Inc. (See Laseraim Technologies, Inc.)
EMF Co., Inc., 1900 E. Warner Ave., Suite 1-D, Santa Ana, CA 92705 / 949-261-6611; FAX: 949-756-0133
Empire Cutlery Corp., 12 Kruger Ct., Clifton, NJ 07013 / 201-472-5155; FAX: 201-779-0759
English, Inc., A.G., 708 S. 12th St., Broken Arrow, OK 74012 / 918-251-3399 agenglish@wedzone.net www.agenglish.com
Engraving Artistry, 36 Alto Rd., Burlington, CT 06013 / 860-673-6837 bobburt44@hotmail.com
Engraving Only, Box 55 Rabbit Gulch, Hill City, SD 57745 / 605-574-2239
Enguix Import-Export, Alpujarras 58, Alzira, Valencia, SPAIN / (96) 241 43 95; FAX: (96) 241 43 95
Enhanced Presentations, Inc., 5929 Market St., Wilmington, NC 28405 / 910-799-1622; FAX: 910-799-5004
Enlow, Charles, 895 Box, Beaver, OK 73932 / 405-625-4487
Entre`prise Arms, Inc., 15861 Business Center Dr., Irwindale, CA 91706
EPC, 1441 Manatt St., Lincoln, NE 68521 / 402-476-3946
Erhardt, Dennis, 4508 N. Montana Ave., Helena, MT 59602 / 406-442-4533
Essex Arms, P.O. Box 363, Island Pond, VT 05846 / 802-723-6203; FAX: 802-723-6203
Estate Cartridge, Inc., 900 Bob Ehlen Dr., Anoka, MN 55303-7502 / 409-856-7277; FAX: 409-856-5486
Euber Bullets, No. Orwell Rd., Orwell, VT 05760 / 802-948-2621
Euroarms of America, Inc., P.O. Box 3277, Winchester, VA 22604 / 540-662-1863; FAX: 540-662-4464 www.euroarms.net
Euro-Imports, 2221 Upland Ave. S., Pahrump, NV 89048 / 775-751-6671; FAX: 775-751-6671
European American Armory Corp. (See E.A.A. Corp.)
Eversull Co., Inc., 1 Tracemont, Boyce, LA 71409 / 318-793-8728; FAX: 318-793-5483 bestguns@aol.com
Evolution Gun Works, Inc., 4050 B-8 Skyron Dr., Doylestown, PA 18901 / 215-348-9892; FAX: 215-348-1056 egw@pil.net www.egw-guns.com
Excalibur Electro Optics, Inc., P.O. Box 400, Fogelsville, PA 18051-0400 / 610-391-9105; FAX: 610-391-9220
Excalibur Publications, P.O. Box 89667, Tucson, AZ 85752 / 520-575-9057 excalibureditor@earthlink.net
Excel Industries, Inc., 4510 Carter Ct., Chino, CA 91710 / 909-627-2404; FAX: 909-627-7817
Executive Protection Institute, P.O. Box 802, Berryville, VA 22611 / 540-554-2540; FAX: 540-554-2558 ruk@crosslink.net www.personalprotecion.com
Eze-Lap Diamond Prods., P.O. Box 2229, 15164 West State St., Westminster, CA 92683 / 714-847-1555; FAX: 714-897-0280
E-Z-Way Systems, P.O. Box 4310, Newark, OH 43058-4310 / 614-345-6645; or 800-848-2072; FAX: 614-345-6600

F

F.A.I.R., Via Gitti, 41, 25060 Marcheno Bresc, ITALY / 030/861162-8610344; FAX: 030/8610179 info@fair.it www.fair.it
Fabarm S.p.A., Via Averolda 31, 25039 Travagliato, Brescia, ITALY / 030-6863629; FAX: 030-6863684 info@fabarm.com www.fabarm.com
Fagan Arms, 22952 15 Mile Rd, Clinton Township, MI 48035 / 810-465-4637; FAX: 810-792-6996
Faith Associates, P.O. Box 549, Flat Rock, NC 28731-0549 FAX: 828-697-6827
Falcon Industries, Inc., P.O. Box 1060, Tijeras, NM 87059 / 505-281-3783; FAX: 505-281-3991 shines@ergogrips.net www.ergogrips.net
Far North Outfitters, Box 1252, Bethel, AK 99559
Farm Form Decoys, Inc., 1602 Biovu, P.O. Box 748, Galveston, TX 77553 / 409-744-0762; or 409-765-6361; FAX: 409-765-8513

MANUFACTURER'S DIRECTORY

Farr Studio, Inc., 183 Hunters Rd., Washington, VA 22747-2001 / 615-638-8825

Farrar Tool Co., Inc., 11855 Cog Hill Dr., Whittier, CA 90601-1902 / 310-863-4367; FAX: 310-863-5123

Faulhaber Wildlocker, Dipl.-Ing. Norbert Wittasek, Seilergasse 2, A-1010 Wien, AUSTRIA / 43-1-5137001; FAX: 43-1-5137001 faulhaber1@utanet.at

Faulk's Game Call Co., Inc., 616 18th St., Lake Charles, LA 70601 / 337-436-9726; FAX: 337-494-7205

Faust Inc., T. G., 544 Minor St, Reading, PA 19602 / 610-375-8549; FAX: 610-375-4488

Fautheree, Andy, P.O. Box 4607, Pagosa Springs, CO 81157 / 970-731-5003; FAX: 970-731-5009

Feather, Flex Decoys, 4500 Doniphan Dr., Neosho, MO 64850 / 318-746-8596; FAX: 318-742-4815

Federal Arms Corp. of America, 7928 University Ave., Fridley, MN 55432 / 612-780-8780; FAX: 612-780-8780

Federal Cartridge Co., 900 Ehlen Dr., Anoka, MN 55303 / 612-323-2300; FAX: 612-323-2506

Federal Champion Target Co., 232 Industrial Parkway, Richmond, IN 47374 / 800-441-4971; FAX: 317-966-7747

Federated-Fry (See Fry Metals)

FEG, Budapest, Soroksariut 158, H-1095, HUNGARY

Feinwerkbau Westinger & Altenburger, Neckarstrasse 43, 78727, Oberndorf a. N., GERMANY / 07423-814-00; FAX: 07423-814-200 info@feinwerkbau.de www.feinwerkbau.de

Feken, Dennis, Rt. 2, Box 124, Perry, OK 73077 / 405-336-5611

Felk Pistols, Inc., 2121 Castlebridge Rd., Midlothian, VA 23113 / 804-794-3744; FAX: 208-988-4834

Ferguson, Bill, P.O. Box 1238, Sierra Vista, AZ 85636 / 520-458-5321; FAX: 520-458-9125

Ferguson, Bill. See: BULLET METALS

FERLIB, Via Parte 33 Marcheno/BS, Marcheno/BS, ITALY / 00390308610191; FAX: 00390308966882 info@ferlib.com www.ferlib.com

Ferris Firearms, 7110 F.M. 1863, Bulverde, TX 78163 / 210-980-4424

Fibron Products, Inc., P.O. Box 430, Buffalo, NY 14209-0430 / 716-886-2378; FAX: 716-886-2394

Fieldsport Ltd., Bryan Bilinski, 3313 W. South Airport Rd., Traverse City, MI 49684 / 616-933-0767

Fiocchi Munizioni S.P.A. (See U.S. Importer-Fiocch

Fiocchi of America, Inc., 5030 Fremont Rd., Ozark, MO 65721 / 417-725-4118; or 800-721-2666; FAX: 417-725-1039

Firearms Co. Ltd. / Alpine (See U.S. Importer-Mandall

Firearms Engraver's Guild of America, 332 Vine St., Oregon City, OR 97045 / 503-656-5693

Firearms International, 5709 Hartsdale, Houston, TX 77036 / 713-460-2447

Fisher, Jerry A., 631 Crane Mt. Rd., Big Fork, MT 59911 / 406-837-2722

Fisher Custom Firearms, 2199 S. Kittredge Way, Aurora, CO 80013 / 303-755-3710

Fitzgerald, Jack. See: CLENZOIL WORLDWIDE CORP

Flambeau, Inc., 15981 Valplast Rd., Middlefield, OH 44062 / 216-632-1631; FAX: 216-632-1581 www.flambeau.com

Flayderman & Co., Inc., P.O. Box 2446, Ft. Lauderdale, FL 33303 / 954-761-8855

Fleming Firearms, 7720 E. 126th St. N., Collinsville, OK 74021-7016 / 918-665-3624

Fletcher-Bidwell, LLC., 305 E. Terhune St., Viroqua, WI 54665-1631 / 866-637-1860 fbguns@netscape.net

Flintlocks, Etc., 160 Rossiter Rd., P.O. Box 181, Richmond, MA 01254 / 413-698-3822; FAX: 413-698-3866 flintetc@berkshire.rr.com

Flitz International Ltd., 821 Mohr Ave., Waterford, WI 53185 / 414-534-5898; FAX: 414-534-2991

Fluoramics, Inc., 18 Industrial Ave., Mahwah, NJ 07430 / 800-922-0075; FAX: 201-825-7035

Flynn's Custom Guns, P.O. Box 7461, Alexandria, LA 71306 / 318-455-7130

FN Manufacturing, P.O. Box 24257, Columbia, SC 29224 / 803-736-0522

Folks, Donald E., 205 W. Lincoln St., Pontiac, IL 61764 / 815-844-7901

Foothills Video Productions, Inc., P.O. Box 651, Spartanburg, SC 29304 / 803-573-7023; or 800-782-5358

Foredom Electric Co., Rt. 6, 16 Stony Hill Rd., Bethel, CT 06801 / 203-792-8622

Forgett, Valmore. See: NAVY ARMS COMPANY

Forgreens Tool & Mfg., Inc., P.O. Box 955, Robert Lee, TX 76945 / 915-453-2800; FAX: 915-453-2460

Forkin Custom Classics, 205 10th Avenue S.W., White Sulphur Spring, MT 59645 / 406-547-2344

Forrest Tool Co., P.O. Box 768, 44380 Gordon Lane, Mendocino, CA 95460 / 707-937-2141; FAX: 717-937-1817

Forster, Kathy (See Custom Checkering)

Forster, Larry L., Box 212, 216 Highway 13 E., Gwinner, ND 58040-0212 / 701-678-2475

Forster Products, 310 E. Lanark Ave., Lanark, IL 61046 / 815-493-6360; FAX: 815-493-2371

Fort Hill Gunstocks, 12807 Fort Hill Rd., Hillsboro, OH 45133 / 513-466-2763

Fort Knox Security Products, 1051 N. Industrial Park Rd., Orem, UT 84057 / 801-224-7233; or 800-821-5216; FAX: 801-226-5493

Forthofer's Gunsmithing & Knifemaking, 5535 U.S. Hwy. 93S, Whitefish, MT 59937-8411 / 406-862-2674

Fortune Products, Inc., 205 Hickory Creek Rd., Marble Falls, TX 78654 / 210-693-6111; FAX: 210-693-6394 randy@accusharp.com

Forty-Five Ranch Enterprises, Box 1080, Miami, OK 74355-1080 / 918-542-5875

Foster, See: ACCURACY INTERNATIONAL

Fountain Products, 492 Prospect Ave., West Springfield, MA 01089 / 413-781-4651; FAX: 413-733-8217

4-D Custom Die Co., 711 N. Sandusky St., PO Box 889, Mt. Vernon, OH 43050-0889 / 740-397-7214; FAX: 740-397-6600 info@ch4d.com ch4d.com

Fowler Bullets, 806 Dogwood Dr., Gastonia, NC 28054 / 704-867-3259

Fowler, Bob (See Black Powder Products)

Fox River Mills, Inc., P.O. Box 298, 227 Poplar St., Osage, IA 50461 / 515-732-3798; FAX: 515-732-5128

Francotte & Cie S.A. Auguste, rue de Trois Juin 109, 4400 Herstal-Liege, BELGIUM / 32-4-248-13-18; FAX: 32-4-248-11-79

Frank Knives, 13868 NW Keleka Pl., Seal Rock, OR 97376 / 541-563-3041; FAX: 541-563-3041

Frank Mittermeier, Inc., P.O. Box 1, Bronx, NY 10465

Franzen International, Inc. (See U.S. Importer for)

Fred F. Wells/Wells Sport Store, 110 N Summit St., Prescott, AZ 86301 / 928-445-3655 www.wellssportstore@cableone-net

Freedom Arms, Inc., P.O. Box 150, Freedom, WY 83120 / 307-883-2468; FAX: 307-883-2005

Fremont Tool Works, 1214 Prairie, Ford, KS 67842 / 316-369-2327

Front Sight Firearms Training Institute, P.O. Box 2619, Aptos, CA 95001 / 800-987-7719; FAX: 408-684-2137

Frontier, 2910 San Bernardo, Laredo, TX 78040 / 956-723-5409; FAX: 956-723-1774

Frontier Arms Co., Inc., 401 W. Rio Santa Cruz, Green Valley, AZ 85614-3932

Frontier Products Co., 2401 Walker Rd., Roswell, NM 88201-8950 / 614-262-9357

Frontier Safe Co., 3201 S. Clinton St., Fort Wayne, IN 46806 / 219-744-7233; FAX: 219-744-6678

Frost Cutlery Co., P.O. Box 22636, Chattanooga, TN 37422 / 615-894-6079; FAX: 615-894-9576

Fry Metals, 4100 6th Ave., Altoona, PA 16602 / 814-946-1611

Fujinon, Inc., 10 High Point Dr., Wayne, NJ 07470 / 201-633-5600; FAX: 201-633-5216

Fullmer, Geo. M., 2499 Mavis St., Oakland, CA 94601 / 510-533-4193

Fulton Armory, 8725 Bollman Place No. 1, Savage, MD 20763 / 301-490-9485; FAX: 301-490-9547 www.fulton.armory.com

Furr Arms, 91 N. 970 W., Orem, UT 84057 / 801-226-3877; FAX: 801-226-3877

G

G&H Decoys, Inc., P.O. Box 1208, Hwy. 75 North, Henryetta, OK 74437 / 918-652-3314; FAX: 918-652-3400

G.C. Bullet Co., Inc., 40 Mokelumne River Dr., Lodi, CA 95240

G.G. & G., 3602 E. 42nd Stravenue, Tucson, AZ 85713 / 520-748-7167; FAX: 520-748-7583 ggg&3@aol.com www.ggg&3.com

G.H. Enterprises Ltd., Bag 10, Okotoks, AB T0L 1T0 CANADA / 403-938-6070

G.U., Inc. (See U.S. Importer for New SKB Arms Co.)

G.W. Elliott, Inc., 514 Burnside Ave., East Hartford, CT 06108 / 203-289-5741; FAX: 203-289-3137

G96 Products Co., Inc., 85 5th Ave., Bldg. #6, Paterson, NJ 07544 / 973-684-4050; FAX: 973-684-3848 g96prod@aol

Gage Manufacturing, 663 W. 7th St., A, San Pedro, CA 90731 / 310-832-3546

Gaillard Barrels, P.O. Box 21, Pathlow, SK S0K 3B0 CANADA / 306-752-3769; FAX: 306-752-5969

Gain Twist Barrel Co., Rifle Works and Armory, 707 12th St., Cody, WY 82414 / 307-587-4919; FAX: 307-527-6097

Galati International, P.O. Box 10, 616 Burley Ridge Rd., Wesco, MO 65586 / 636-584-0785; FAX: 573-775-4308 support@galatiinternational.com www.galatiinternational.com

Galaxy Imports Ltd., Inc., P.O. Box 3361, Victoria, TX 77903 / 361-573-4867; FAX: 361-576-9622 galaxy@cox-internet.com

GALCO International Ltd., 2019 W. Quail Ave., Phoenix, AZ 85027 / 623-474-7070; FAX: 623-582-6854 customerservice@usgalco.com www.usgalco.com

Galena Industries AMT, 5463 Diaz St., Irwindale, CA 91706 / 626-856-8883; FAX: 626-856-8878

Gamba S.p.A. Societa Armi Bresciane Srl, Renato, Via Artigiani 93, ITALY / 30-8911640; FAX: 30-8911648

Gamba, USA, P.O. Box 60452, Colorado Springs, CO 80960 / 719-578-1145; FAX: 719-444-0731

Game Haven Gunstocks, 13750 Shire Rd., Wolverine, MI 49799 / 616-525-8257

Gamebore Division, Polywad, Inc., P.O. Box 7916, Macon, GA 31209 / 478-477-0669; or 800-998-0669

Gamo (See U.S. Importers-Arms United Corp, Daisy M

Gamo USA, Inc., 3911 SW 47th Ave., Suite 914, Ft. Lauderdale, FL 33314 / 954-581-5822; FAX: 954-581-3165 gamousa@gate.net www.gamo.com

Gander Mountain, Inc., 12400 Fox River Rd., Wilmont, WI 53192 / 414-862-6848

GAR, 590 McBride Ave., West Paterson, NJ 07424 / 973-754-1114; FAX: 973-754-1114 garreloading@aol.com www.garreloading.com

Garcia National Gun Traders, Inc., 225 SW 22nd Ave., Miami, FL 33135 / 305-642-2355

Garrett Cartridges, Inc., P.O. Box 178, Chehalis, WA 98532 / 360-736-0702 www.garrettcartridges.com

Garthwaite Pistolsmith, Inc., Jim, 12130 State Route 405, Watsontown, PA 17777 / 570-538-1566; FAX: 570-538-2965 www.garthwaite.com

Gary Goudy Classic Stocks, 1512 S. 5th St., Dayton, WA 99328 / 509-382-2726 goudy@innw.net

Gary Reeder Custom Guns, 2601 7th Avenue East, Flagstaff, AZ 86004 / 928-526-3313; FAX: 928-527-0840 gary@reedercustomguns.com www.reedercustomguns.com

Gator Guns & Repair, 7952 Kenai Spur Hwy., Kenai, AK 99611-8311

Gaucher Armes, S.A., 46 rue Desjoyaux, 42000, Saint-Etienne, FRANCE / 04-77-33-38-92; FAX: 04-77-61-95-72

GDL Enterprises, 409 Le Gardeur, Slidell, LA 70460 / 504-649-0693

Gehmann, Walter (See Huntington Die Specialties)

Genco, P.O. Box 5704, Asheville, NC 28803

Genecco Gun Works, 10512 Lower Sacramento Rd., Stockton, CA 95210 / 209-951-0706; FAX: 209-931-3872

Gene's Custom Guns, P.O. Box 10534, White Bear Lake, MN 55110 / 651-429-5105; FAX: 651-429-7365

Gentex Corp., 5 Tinkham Ave., Derry, NH 03038 / 603-434-0311; FAX: 603-434-3002 sales@derry.gentexcorp.com www.derry.gentexcorp.com

Gentner Bullets, 109 Woodlawn Ave., Upper Darby, PA 19082 / 610-352-9396

Gentry Custom LLC, 314 N. Hoffman, Belgrade, MT 59714 / 406-388-GUNS davidgent@mcn.net www.gentrycustom.com

George & Roy's, P.O. Box 2125, Sisters, OR 97759-2125 / 503-228-5424; or 800-553-3022; FAX: 503-225-9409

George Hoenig, Inc., 6521 Morton Dr., Boise, ID 83704 / 208-375-1116; FAX: 208-375-1116

George Ibberson (Sheffield) Ltd., 25-31 Allen St., Sheffield, S3 7AW ENGLAND / 0114-2766123; FAX: 0114-2738465 sales@eggintongroupco.uk www.eggintongroup.co.uk

George Madis Winchester Consultants, George Madis, P.O. Box 545, Brownsboro, TX 75756 / 903-852-6480; FAX: 903-852-3045 gmadis@earthlink.com www.georgemadis.com

Gerber Legendary Blades, 14200 SW 72nd Ave., Portland, OR 97223 / 503-639-6161; or 800-950-6161; FAX: 503-684-7008

Gervais, Mike, 3804 S. Cruise Dr., Salt Lake City, UT 84109 / 801-277-7729

Getz Barrel Company, P.O. Box 88, 426 E. Market St., Beavertown, PA 17813 / 570-658-7263; FAX: 570-658-4110 www.getzbrl.com

Giacomo Sporting USA, 6234 Stokes Lee Center Rd., Lee Center, NY 13363

Gibbs Rifle Co., Inc., 219 Lawn St., Martinsburg, WV 25401 / 304-262-1651; FAX: 304-262-1658 support@gibbsrifle.com www.gibbsrifle.com

Gil Hebard Guns, Inc., 125 Public Square, Knoxville, IL 61448 / 309-289-2700; FAX: 309-289-2233

Gilbert Equipment Co., Inc., 960 Downtowner Rd., Mobile, AL 36609 / 205-344-3322

Gillmann, Edwin, 33 Valley View Dr., Hanover, PA 17331 / 717-632-1662 gillmaned@super-pa.net

Gilmore Sports Concepts, Inc., 5949 S. Garnett Rd., Tulsa, OK 74146 / 918-250-3810; FAX: 918-250-3845 info@gilmoresports.com www.gilmoresports.com

Giron, Robert E., 12671 Cousins Rd., Peosta, IA 52068 / 412-731-6041

Glacier Glove, 4890 Aircenter Circle, Suite 210, Reno, NV 89502 / 702-825-8225; FAX: 702-825-6544

Glaser LLC, P.O. Box 173, Sturgis, SD 57785 / 605-347-4544; or 800-221-3489; FAX: 605-347-5055 email@corbon.com www.safetyslug.com

Glaser Safety Slug, Inc., P.O. Box 8223, Foster City, CA 94404 / 800-221-3489; FAX: 510-785-6685 safetyslug.com

Glass, Herb, P.O. Box 25, Bullville, NY 10915 / 914-361-3021

Glimm, Jerome. See: GLIMM'S CUSTOM GUN ENGRAVING

Glimm's Custom Gun Engraving, Jerome C. Glimm, 19 S. Maryland, Conrad, MT 59425 / 406-278-3574 jandlglimm@mcn.net

Glock GmbH, P.O. Box 50, A-2232, Deutsch Wagram, AUSTRIA

Glock, Inc., P.O. Box 369, Smyrna, GA 30081 / 770-432-1202; FAX: 770-433-8719

Glynn Scobey Duck & Goose Calls, Rt. 3, Box 37, Newbern, TN 38059 / 731-643-6128

GML Products, Inc., 394 Laredo Dr., Birmingham, AL 35226 / 205-979-4867

Gner's Hard Cast Bullets, 1107 11th St., LaGrande, OR 97850 / 503-963-8796

Goens, Dale W., P.O. Box 224, Cedar Crest, NM 87008 / 505-281-5419

Goergen's Gun Shop, Inc., 17985 538th Ave., Austin, MN 55912 / 507-433-9280

GOEX, Inc., P.O. Box 659, Doyline, LA 71023-0659 / 318-382-9300; FAX: 318-382-9303 mfahringer@goexpowder.com www.goexpowder.com

Golden Age Arms Co., 115 E. High St., Ashley, OH 43003 / 614-747-2488

Golden Bear Bullets, 3065 Fairfax Ave., San Jose, CA 95148 / 408-238-9515

Gonic Arms/North American Arms, Inc., 134 Flagg Rd., Gonic, NH 03839 / 603-332-8456; or 603-332-8457

Goodling's Gunsmithing, 1950 Stoverstown Rd., Spring Grove, PA 17362 / 717-225-3350

Goodwin, Fred. See: GOODWIN'S PAWN SHOP

Goodwin's Pawn Shop, Fred Goodwin, Silver Ridge, ME 04776 / 207-365-4451

Gotz Bullets, 11426 Edgemere Ter., Roscoe, IL 61073-8232

Gould & Goodrich, 709 E. McNeil, Lillington, NC 27546 / 910-893-2071; FAX: 910-893-4742

MANUFACTURER'S DIRECTORY

Gournet Artistic Engraving, Geoffroy Gournet, 820 Paxinosa Ave., Easton, PA 18042 / 610-559-0710 www.geoffroygournet.com
Gournet, Geoffroy. See: GOURNET ARTISTIC ENGRAVING
Grace, Charles E., 718 E. 2nd, Trinidad, CO 81082 / 719-846-9435 chuckgrace@sensonics.org
Grace Metal Products, P.O. Box 67, Elk Rapids, MI 49629 / 616-264-8133
Graf & Sons, 4050 S. Clark St., Mexico, MO 65265 / 573-581-2266; FAX: 573-581-2875 customerservice@grafs.com www.grafs.com
Grand Slam Hunting Products, Box 121, 25454 Military Rd., Cascade, MD 21719 / 301-241-4900; FAX: 301-241-4900 rlj6call@aol.com
Granite Mountain Arms, Inc., 3145 W. Hidden Acres Trail, Prescott, AZ 86305 / 520-541-9758; FAX: 520-445-6826
Grant, Howard V., Hiawatha 15, Woodruff, WI 54568 / 715-356-7146
Graphics Direct, P.O. Box 372421, Reseda, CA 91337-2421 / 818-344-9002
Graves Co., 1800 Andrews Ave., Pompano Beach, FL 33069 / 800-327-9103; FAX: 305-960-0301
Grayback Wildcats, Mike Beeks, 5306 Bryant Ave., Klamath Falls, OR 97603 / 541-884-1072; FAX: 541-884-1072 graybackwildcats@aol.com
Graybill's Gun Shop, 1035 Ironville Pike, Columbia, PA 17512 / 717-684-2739
Great American Gunstock Co., 3420 Industrial Drive, Yuba City, CA 95993 / 800-784-4867; FAX: 530-671-3906 gunstox@hotmail.com www.gunstocks.com
Great Lakes Airguns, 6175 S. Park Ave., Hamburg, NY 14075 / 716-648-6666; FAX: 716-648-6666 www.greatlakesairguns.com
Green, Arthur S., 485 S. Robertson Blvd., Beverly Hills, CA 90211 / 310-274-1283
Green, Roger M., P.O. Box 984, 435 E. Birch, Glenrock, WY 82637 / 307-436-9804
Green Head Game Call Co., RR 1, Box 33, Lacon, IL 61540 / 309-246-2155
Green Mountain Rifle Barrel Co., Inc., P.O. Box 2670, 153 West Main St., Conway, NH 03818 / 603-447-1095; FAX: 603-447-1099 www.gmriflebarrel.com
Greenwood Precision, P.O. Box 407, Rogersville, MO 65742 / 417-725-2330
Greg Gunsmithing Repair, 3732 26th Ave. North, Robbinsdale, MN 55422 / 612-529-8103
Greg's Superior Products, P.O. Box 46219, Seattle, WA 98146
Greider Precision, 431 Santa Marina Ct., Escondido, CA 92029 / 760-480-8892; FAX: 760-480-9800 greider@msn.com
Gre-Tan Rifles, 29742 W.C.R. 50, Kersey, CO 80644 / 970-353-6176; FAX: 970-356-5940 www.gtrtooling.com
Grier's Hard Cast Bullets, 1107 11th St., LaGrande, OR 97850 / 503-963-8796
Griffin & Howe, Inc., 36 W. 44th St., Suite 1011, New York, NY 10036 / 212-921-0980 info@griffinhowe.com www.griffinhowe.com
Griffin & Howe, Inc., 340 W. Putnam Ave., Greenwich, CT 06830 / 203-618-0270 info@griffinhowe.com www.griffinhowe.com
Griffin & Howe, Inc., 33 Claremont Rd., Bernardsville, NJ 07924 / 908-766-2287; FAX: 908-766-1068 info@griffinhowe.com www.griffinhowe.com
Grifon, Inc., 58 Guinam St., Waltham, MS 02154
Groenewold, John, P.O. Box 830, Mundelein, IL 60060 / 847-566-2365; FAX: 847-566-4065 jgairguns@direcway.com http://jgairguns.tripod.com/airgun
GRS / Glendo Corp., P.O. Box 1153, 900 Overlander St., Emporia, KS 66801 / 620-343-1084; or 800-836-3519; FAX: 620-343-9640 glendo@glendo.com www.glendo.com
Grulla Armes, Apartado 453, Avda Otaloa 12, Eiber, SPAIN
Gruning Precision, Inc., 7101 Jurupa Ave., No. 12, Riverside, CA 92504 / 909-289-4371; FAX: 909-689-7791 gruningprecision@earthlink.net www.gruningprecision.com
GSI, Inc., 7661 Commerce Ln., Trussville, AL 35173 / 205-655-8299
GTB-Custom Bullets, 482 Comerwood Court, S. San Francisco, CA 94080 / 650-583-1550
Guarasi, Robert. See: WILCOX INDUSTRIES CORP.
Guardsman Products, 411 N. Darling, Fremont, MI 49412 / 616-924-3950
Gun City, 212 W. Main Ave., Bismarck, ND 58501 / 701-223-2304
Gun Hunter Books (See Gun Hunter Trading Co.), 5075 Heisig St., Beaumont, TX 77705 / 409-835-3006; FAX: 409-838-2266 gunhuntertrading@hotmail.com
Gun Hunter Trading Co., 5075 Heisig St., Beaumont, TX 77705 / 409-835-3006; FAX: 409-838-2266 gunhuntertrading@hotmail.com
Gun Leather Limited, 116 Lipscomb, Ft. Worth, TX 76104 / 817-334-0225; FAX: 800-247-0609
Gun List (See Krause Publications), 700 E State St., Iola, WI 54990 / 715-445-2214; FAX: 715-445-4087
Gun South, Inc. (See GSI, Inc.)
Gun Vault, 7339 E. Acoma Dr., Ste. 7, Scottsdale, AZ 85260 / 602-951-6855
Gun-Alert, 1010 N. Maclay Ave., San Fernando, CA 91340 / 818-365-0864; FAX: 818-365-1308
Guncraft Books (See Guncraft Sports, Inc.), 10737 Dutchtown Rd., Knoxville, TN 37932 / 865-966-4545; FAX: 865-966-4500 findit@guncraft.com www.guncraft.com
Guncraft Sports, Inc., 10737 Dutchtown Rd., Knoxville, TN 37932 / 865-966-4545; FAX: 865-966-4500 findit@guncraft.com www.usit.net/guncraft
Guncraft Sports, Inc., Marie C. Wiest, 10737 Dutchtown Rd., Knoxville, TN 37932 / 865-966-4545; FAX: 865-966-4500 findit@guncraft.com www.guncraft.com
Guncrafter Industries, 171 Madison 1510, Huntsville, AR 72740 / 479-665-2466 www.guncrafterindustries.com
Gun-Ho Sports Cases, 110 E. 10th St., St. Paul, MN 55101 / 612-224-9491
Gunline Tools, 2950 Saturn St., "O", Brea, CA 92821 / 714-993-5100; FAX: 714-572-4128
Gunnerman Books, P.O. Box 81697, Rochester Hills, MI 48308 / 248-608-2856
Guns Antique & Modern DBA / Charles E. Duffy, Williams Lane, West Hurley, NY 12491 / 914-679-2997
Guns Div. of D.C. Engineering, Inc., 8633 Southfield Fwy., Detroit, MI 48228 / 313-271-7111; or 800-886-7623; FAX: 313-271-7112 guns@rifletech.com www.rifletech.com
GUNS Magazine, 591 Camino de la Reina, Suite 200, San Diego, CA 92108 / 619-297-5350; FAX: 619-297-5353
Gunsite Training Center, P.O. Box 700, Paulden, AZ 86334 / 520-636-4565; FAX: 520-636-1236
Gunsmithing Ltd., 57 Unquowa Rd., Fairfield, CT 06824 / 203-254-0436; FAX: 203-254-1535
Gunsmithing, Inc., 30 West Buchanan St., Colorado Springs, CO 80907 / 719-632-3795; FAX: 719-632-3493
Gurney, F. R., Box 13, Sooke, BC V0S 1N0 CANADA / 604-642-5282; FAX: 604-642-7859

H

H&B Forge Co., Rt. 2, Geisinger Rd., Shiloh, OH 44878 / 419-895-1856
H&P Publishing, 7174 Hoffman Rd., San Angelo, TX 76905 / 915-655-5953
H&R 1871.LLC, 60 Industrial Rowe, Gardner, MA 01440 / 508-632-9393; FAX: 508-632-2300 hr1871@hr1871.com www.hr1871.com
H. Krieghoff Gun Co., Boschstrasse 22, D-89079, Ulm, GERMANY / 731-401820; FAX: 731-4018270
H.K.S. Products, 7841 Founion Dr., Florence, KY 41042 / 606-342-7841; or 800-354-9814; FAX: 606-342-5865
H.P. White Laboratory, Inc., 3114 Scarboro Rd., Street, MD 21154 / 410-838-6550; FAX: 410-838-2802
Hafner World Wide, Inc., P.O. Box 1987, Lake City, FL 32055 / 904-755-6481; FAX: 904-755-6595 hafner@isgroupe.net
Hakko Co. Ltd., 1-13-12, Narimasu, Itabashiku Tokyo, JAPAN / 03 5997 7870/2; FAX: 01-3-5997-7840
Half Moon Rifle Shop, 490 Halfmoon Rd., Columbia Falls, MT 59912 / 406-892-4409 halfmoonrs@centurytel.net
Hall Manufacturing, 142 CR 406, Clanton, AL 35045 / 205-755-4094
Hall Plastics, Inc., John, P.O. Box 1526, Alvin, TX 77512 / 713-489-8709
Hallberg, Fritz. See: CAMBOS OUTDOORSMAN
Hallowell & Co., P.O. Box 1445, Livingston, MT 59047 / 406-222-4770; FAX: 406-222-4792 morris@hallowellco.com www.hallowellco.com
Hally Caller, 443 Wells Rd., Doylestown, PA 18901 / 215-345-6354; FAX: 215-345-8892 info@hallycaller.com www.hallycaller.com
Hamilton, Alex B. (See Ten-Ring Precision, Inc.)
Hammans, Charles E., P.O. Box 788, 2022 McCracken, Stuttgart, AR 72160-0788 / 870-673-1388
Hammerli Ltd., Seonerstrasse 37, CH-5600, SWITZERLAND / 064-50 11 44; FAX: 064-51 38 27
Hammerli Service-Precision Mac, Rudolf Marent, 9711 Tiltree St., Houston, TX 77075 / 713-946-7028 rmarent@webtv.net
Hammerli USA, 19296 Oak Grove Circle, Groveland, CA 95321 FAX: 209-962-5311
Hammond Custom Guns Ltd., 619 S. Pandora, Gilbert, AZ 85234 / 602-892-3437
HandCrafts Unltd. (See Clements' Custom Leather), 1741 Dallas St., Aurora, CO 80010-2018 / 303-364-0403; FAX: 303-739-9824 gryphons@home.com kuntaoslcat.com
Handgun Press, P.O. Box 406, Glenview, IL 60025 / 847-657-6500; FAX: 847-724-8831 handgunpress@earthlink.net
Hank's Gun Shop, Box 370, 50 West 100 South, Monroe, UT 84754 / 801-527-4456
Hanned Precision (See The Hanned Line)
Hansen & Co., 244-246 Old Post Rd., Southport, CT 06490 / 203-259-6222; FAX: 203-254-3832
Hanson's Gun Center, Dick, 233 Everett Dr., Colorado Springs, CO 80911
Harford (See U.S. Importer-EMF Co. Inc.)
Harper's Custom Stocks, 928 Lombrano St., San Antonio, TX 78207 / 210-732-7174
Harrell's Precision, 5756 Hickory Dr., Salem, VA 24153 / 540-380-2683
Harrington & Richardson (See H&R 1871, Inc.)
Harris Engineering Inc., Dept GD54, Barlow, KY 42024 / 502-334-3633; FAX: 502-334-3000
Harris Enterprises, P.O. Box 105, Bly, OR 97622 / 503-353-2625
Harris Hand Engraving, Paul A., 113 Rusty Ln., Boerne, TX 78006-5746 / 512-391-5121
Harris Publications, 1115 Broadway, New York, NY 10010 / 212-807-7100; FAX: 212-627-4678
Harrison Bullets, 6437 E. Hobart St., Mesa, AZ 85205
Harry Lawson Co., 3328 N. Richey Blvd., Tucson, AZ 85716 / 520-326-1117; FAX: 520-326-1117
Hart & Son, Inc., Robert W., 401 Montgomery St., Nescopeck, PA 18635 / 717-752-3655; FAX: 717-752-1088
Hart Rifle Barrels, Inc., P.O. Box 182, 1690 Apulia Rd., Lafayette, NY 13084 / 315-677-9841; FAX: 315-677-9610 hartrb@aol.com hartbarrels.com
Hartford (See U.S. Importer-EMF Co. Inc.)
Hartmann & Weiss GmbH, Rahlstedter Bahnhofstr. 47, 22143, Hamburg, GERMANY / (40) 677 55 85; FAX: (40) 677 55 92 hartmannundweisst-online.de
Harvey, Frank, 218 Nightfall, Terrace, NV 89015 / 702-558-6998
Harwood, Jack O., 1191 S. Pendlebury Lane, Blackfoot, ID 83221 / 208-785-5368
Hastings, P.O. Box 224, Clay Center, KS 67432 / 785-632-3169; FAX: 785-632-6554
Hatfield Gun, 224 N. 4th St., St. Joseph, MO 64501
Hawk Laboratories, Inc. (See Hawk, Inc.), 849 Hawks Bridge Rd., Salem, NJ 08079 / 609-299-2700; FAX: 609-299-2800
Hawk, Inc., 849 Hawks Bridge Rd., Salem, NJ 08079 / 609-299-2700; FAX: 609-299-2800 info@hawkbullets.com www.hawkbullets.com
Hawken Shop, The (See Dayton Traister)
Haydel's Game Calls, Inc., 5018 Hazel Jones Rd., Bossier City, LA 71111 / 318-746-3586; FAX: 318-746-3711
Heatbath Corp., P.O. Box 2978, Springfield, MA 01101 / 413-543-3381
Hecht, Hubert J., Waffen-Hecht, P.O. Box 2635, Fair Oaks, CA 95628 / 916-966-1020
Heckler & Koch GmbH, PO Box 1329, 78722 Oberndorf, Neckar, GERMANY / 49-7423179-0; FAX: 49-7423179-2406
Heckler & Koch, Inc., 21480 Pacific Blvd., Sterling, VA 20166-8900 / 703-450-1900; FAX: 703-450-8160 www.hecklerkoch-usa.com
Hege Jagd-u. Sporthandels GmbH, P.O. Box 101461, W-7770, Ueberlingen a. Boden, GERMANY
Heidenstrom Bullets, Dalghte 86-3660 Rjukan, 35091818, NORWAY, olau.joh@online.tuo
Heilmann, Stephen, P.O. Box 657, Grass Valley, CA 95945 / 530-272-8758; FAX: 530-274-0285 sheilmann@jps.net www.metalwood.com
Heinie Specialty Products, 301 Oak St., Quincy, IL 62301-2500 / 217-228-9500; FAX: 217-228-9502 rheinie@heinie.com www.heinie.com
Helwan (See U.S. Importer-Interarms)
Henigson & Associates, Steve, PO Box 2726, Culver City, CA 90231 / 310-305-8288; FAX: 310-305-1905
Henriksen Tool Co., Inc., 8515 Wagner Creek Rd., Talent, OR 97540 / 541-535-2309; FAX: 541-535-2309
Henry Repeating Arms Co., 110 8th St., Brooklyn, NY 11215 / 718-499-5600; FAX: 718-768-8056 info@henryrepeating.com www.henryrepeating.com
Hensley, Gunmaker, Darwin, PO Box 329, Brightwood, OR 97011 / 503-622-5411
Heppler, Keith. See: KEITH'S CUSTOM GUNSTOCKS
Hercules, Inc. (See Alliant Techsystems, Smokeless)
Heritage Firearms (See Heritage Mfg., Inc.)
Heritage Manufacturing, Inc., 4600 NW 135th St., Opa Locka, FL 33054 / 305-685-5966; FAX: 305-687-6721 infohmi@heritagemfg.com www.heritagemfg.com
Heritage/VSP Gun Books, P.O. Box 887, McCall, ID 83638 / 208-634-4104; FAX: 208-634-3101 heritage@gunbooks.com www.gunbooks.com
Herrett's Stocks, Inc., P.O. Box 741, Twin Falls, ID 83303 / 208-733-1498
Herter's Manufacturing Inc., 111 E. Burnett St., P.O. Box 518, Beaver Dam, WI 53916-1811 / 414-887-1765; FAX: 414-887-8444
Hesco-Meprolight, 2139 Greenville Rd., LaGrange, GA 30241 / 706-884-7967; FAX: 706-882-4683
Hesse Arms, Robert Hesse, 1126 70th Street E., Inver Grove Heights, MN 55077-2416 / 651-455-5760; FAX: 612-455-5760
Hesse, Robert. See: HESSE ARMS
Heydenberk, Warren R., 1059 W. Sawmill Rd., Quakertown, PA 18951 / 215-538-2682
Hickman, Jaclyn, Box 1900, Glenrock, WY 82637
Hidalgo, Tony, 12701 SW 9th Pl., Davie, FL 33325 / 954-476-7645
High Bridge Arms, Inc., 3185 Mission St., San Francisco, CA 94110 / 415-282-8358
High North Products, Inc., P.O. Box 2, Antigo, WI 54409 / 715-627-2331; FAX: 715-623-5451
High Performance International, 5734 W. Florist Ave., Milwaukee, WI 53218 / 414-466-9040
High Precision, Bud Welsh, 80 New Road, E. Amherst, NY 14051 / 716-688-6344; FAX: 716-688-0425 welsh5168@aol.com www.high-precision.com
High Standard Mfg. Co./F.I., Inc., 5200 Mitchelldale St., Ste. E17, Houston, TX 77092-7222 / 713-462-4200; or 800-272-7816; FAX: 713-681-5665 info@highstandard.com www.highstandard.com
High Tech Specialties, Inc., P.O. Box 839, 293 E Main St., Rear, Adamstown, PA 19501 / 717-484-0405; FAX: 717-484-0523 bansner@aol.com www.bansmersrifle.com/hightech
Highline Machine Co., Randall Thompson, Randall Thompson, 654 Lela Place, Grand Junction, CO 81504 / 970-434-4971
Highwood Special Products, 1531 E. Highwood, Pontiac, MI 48340
Hi-Grade Imports, 8655 Monterey Rd., Gilroy, CA 95021 / 408-842-9301; FAX: 408-842-2374
Hill, Loring F., 304 Cedar Rd., Elkins Park, PA 19027
Hill Speed Leather, Ernie, 4507 N 195th Ave., Litchfield Park, AZ 85340 / 602-853-9222; FAX: 602-853-9235
Hinman Outfitters, Bob, 107 N Sanderson Ave., Bartonville, IL 61607-1839 / 309-691-8132
Hi-Performance Ammunition Company, 484 State Route 366, Apollo, PA 15613 / 412-327-8100
HIP-GRIP Barami Corp., P.O. Box 252224, West Bloomfield, MI 48325-2224 / 248-738-0462; FAX: 248-738-2542 hipgripja@aol.com www.hipgrip.com

Hi-Point Firearms/MKS Supply, 8611-A North Dixie Dr., Dayton, OH 45414 / 877-425-4867; FAX: 937-454-0503 www.hi-pointfirearms.com

Hiptmayer, Armurier, RR 112 750, P.O. Box 136, Eastman, PQ J0E 1P0 CANADA / 514-297-2492

Hiptmayer, Heidemarie, RR 112 750, P.O. Box 136, Eastman, PQ J0E 1P0 CANADA / 514-297-2492

Hiptmayer, Klaus, RR 112 750, P.O. Box 136, Eastman, PQ J0E 1P0 CANADA / 514-297-2492

Hirtenberger AG, Leobersdorferstrasse 31, A-2552, Hirtenberg, AUSTRIA / 43(0)2256 81184; FAX: 43(0)2256 81808 www.hirtenberger.ot

HJS Arms, Inc., P.O. Box 3711, Brownsville, TX 78523-3711 / 956-542-2767; FAX: 956-542-2767

Hoag, James W., 8523 Canoga Ave., Suite C, Canoga Park, CA 91304 / 818-998-1510

Hobson Precision Mfg. Co., 210 Big Oak Ln., Brent, AL 35034 / 205-926-4662; FAX: 205-926-3193 cahobbob@dbtech.net

Hodgdon Powder Co., 6231 Robinson, Shawnee Mission, KS 66202 / 913-362-9455; FAX: 913-362-1307

Hodgman, Inc., 1750 Orchard Rd., Montgomery, IL 60538 / 708-897-7555; FAX: 708-897-7558

Hodgson, Richard, 9081 Tahoe Lane, Boulder, CO 80301

Hoehn Sales, Inc., 2045 Kohn Road, Wright City, MO 63390 / 636-745-8144; FAX: 636-745-7868 hoehnsal@usmo.com

Hofer Jagdwaffen, P., Buchsenmachermeister, Kirchgasse 24, A-9170 Ferlach, AUSTRIA / 43 4227 3683; FAX: 43 4227 368330 peterhofer@hoferwaffen.com www.hoferwaffen.com

Hoffman New Ideas, 821 Northmoor Rd., Lake Forest, IL 60045 / 312-234-4075

Hogue Grips, P.O. Box 1138, Paso Robles, CA 93447 / 800-438-4747 or 805-239-1440; FAX: 805-239-2553

Holland & Holland Ltd., 33 Bruton St., London, ENGLAND / 44-171-499-4411; FAX: 44-171-408-7962

Holland's Gunsmithing, P.O. Box 69, Powers, OR 97466 / 541-439-5155; FAX: 541-439-5155

Hollinger, Jon. See: ASPEN OUTFITTING CO.

Hollywood Engineering, 10642 Arminta St., Sun Valley, CA 91352 / 818-842-8376; FAX: 818-504-4168 cadqueenel1@aol.com

Homak, 5151 W. 73rd St., Chicago, IL 60638-6613 / 312-523-3100; FAX: 312-523-9455

Home Shop Machinist, The Village Press Publications, P.O. Box 1810, Traverse City, MI 49685 / 800-447-7367; FAX: 616-946-3289

Hondo Ind., 510 S. 52nd St., I04, Tempe, AZ 85281

Hoppe's Div. Penguin Industries, Inc., P.O. Box 1690, Oregon City, OR 97045-0690 / 610-384-6000

Horizons Unlimited, P.O. Box 426, Warm Springs, GA 31830 / 706-655-3603; FAX: 706-655-3603

Hornady Mfg. Co., P.O. Box 1848, Grand Island, NE 68802 / 800-338-3220 or 308-382-1390; FAX: 308-382-5761

Horseshoe Leather Products, Andy Arratoonian, The Cottage Sharow, Ripon U.K., ENGLAND U.K. / 44-1765-605858 andy@horseshoe.co.uk www.holsters.org

House of Muskets, Inc., The, PO Box 4640, Pagosa Springs, CO 81157 / 970-731-2295

Houtz & Barwick, P.O. Box 435, W. Church St., Elizabeth City, NC 27909 / 800-775-0337; or 919-335-4191; FAX: 919-335-1152

Howa Machinery, Ltd., Sukaguchi, Shinkawa-cho Nishikasugai-gun, Aichi 452-8601, JAPAN / 81-52-408-1231; FAX: 81-52-401-4999 howa@howa.co.jp http://www.howa.cojpl

Howell Machine, 815 1/2 D St., Lewiston, ID 83501 / 208-743-7418

H-S Precision, Inc., 1301 Turbine Dr., Rapid City, SD 57701 / 605-341-3006; FAX: 605-342-8964

HT Bullets, 244 Belleville Rd., New Bedford, MA 02745 / 508-999-3338

Hubert J. Hecht Waffen-Hecht, P.O. Box 2635, Fair Oaks, CA 95628 / 916-966-1020

Huebner, Corey O., P.O. Box 564, Frenchtown, MT 59834 / 406-721-7168 bugsboys@hotmail.com

Huey Gun Cases, 820 Indiana St., Lawrence, KS 66044-2645 / 816-444-1637; FAX: 816-444-1637 hueycases@aol.com www.hueycases.com

Hume, Don, P.O. Box 351, Miami, OK 74355 / 800-331-2686; FAX: 918-542-4340 info@donhume.com www.donhume.com

Hunkeler, A. (See Buckskin Machine Works), 3235 S 358th St., Auburn, WA 98001 / 206-927-5412

Hunter Co., Inc., 3300 W. 71st Ave., Westminster, CO 80030 / 303-427-4626; FAX: 303-428-3980 debbiet@huntercompany.com www.huntercompany.com

Hunterjohn, PO Box 771457, St. Louis, MO 63177 / 314-531-7250 www.hunterjohn.com

Hunter's Specialties Inc., 6000 Huntington Ct. NE, Cedar Rapids, IA 52402-1268 / 319-395-0321; FAX: 319-395-0326

Hunters Supply, Inc., P.O. Box 313, Tioga, TX 76271 / 940-437-2458; FAX: 940-437-2228 hunterssupply@hotmail.com www.hunterssupply.net

Huntington Die Specialties, 601 Oro Dam Blvd., Oroville, CA 95965 / 530-534-1210; FAX: 530-534-1212 buy@huntingtons.com www.huntingtons.com

Hutton Rifle Ranch, P.O. Box 170317, Boise, ID 83717 / 208-345-8781 www.martinbrevik@aol.com

Hydrosorbent Products, PO Box 437, Ashley Falls, MA 01222 / 800-448-7903; FAX: 413-229-8743 orders@dehumidify.com www.dehumidify.com

I

I.A.B. (See U.S. Importer-Taylor's & Co. Inc.)

I.D.S.A. Books, 1324 Stratford Drive, Piqua, OH 45356 / 937-773-4203; FAX: 937-778-1922

I.N.C. Inc. (See Kickeez I.N.C., Inc.)

I.S.S., P.O. Box 185234, Ft. Worth, TX 76181 / 817-595-2090; FAX: 817-595-2090 iss@concentric.net

I.S.W., 106 E. Cairo Dr., Tempe, AZ 85282

IAR Inc., 33171 Camino Capistrano, San Juan Capistrano, CA 92675 / 949-443-3642; FAX: 949-443-3647 sales@iar-arms.com iar-arms.com

Ide, Ken. See: STURGEON VALLEY SPORTERS

IGA (See U.S. Importer-Stoeger Industries)

Image Ind. Inc., 382 Balm Court, Wood Dale, IL 60191 / 630-766-2402; FAX: 630-766-7373

Impact Case & Container, Inc., P.O. Box 1129, Rathdrum, ID 83858 / 877-687-2452; FAX: 208-687-0632 bradk@icc-case.com www.icc-case.com

Imperial (See E-Z-Way Systems), P.O. Box 4310, Newark, OH 43058-4310 / 614-345-6645; FAX: 614-345-6600 ezway@infinet.com www.jcunald.com

Imperial Magnum Corp., P.O. Box 249, Oroville, WA 98844 / 604-495-3131; FAX: 604-495-2816

Imperial Miniature Armory, 10547 S. Post Oak Road, Houston, TX 77035-3305 / 713-729-8428; FAX: 713-729-2274 miniguns@aol.com www.1800miniature.com

Imperial Schrade Corp., 7 Schrade Ct., Box 7000, Ellenville, NY 12428 / 914-647-7601; FAX: 914-647-8701 csc@schradeknives.com www.schradeknives.com

Import Sports Inc., 1750 Brielle Ave., Unit B1, Wanamassa, NJ 07712 / 732-493-0302; FAX: 732-493-0301 gsodini@aol.com www.bersa-11ama.com

IMR Powder Co., 1080 Military Turnpike, Suite 2, Plattsburgh, NY 12901 / 518-563-2253; FAX: 518-563-6916

Info-Arm, P.O. Box 1262, Champlain, NY 12919 / 514-955-0355; FAX: 514-955-0357 infoarm@qc.aira.com

Ingle, Ralph W., Engraver, 112 Manchester Ct., Centerville, GA 31028 / 478-953-5824 riengraver@aol.com www.fega.com

Innovative Weaponry Inc., 2513 E. Loop 820 N., Fort Worth, TX 76118 / 817-284-0099 or 800-334-3573

INTEC International, Inc., P.O. Box 5708, Scottsdale, AZ 85261 / 602-483-1708

Inter Ordnance of America LP, 3305 Westwood Industrial Dr., Monroe, NC 28110-5204 / 704-821-8337; FAX: 704-821-8523

Intercontinental Distributors, Ltd., PO Box 815, Beulah, ND 58523

Intrac Arms International, 5005 Chapman Hwy., Knoxville, TN 37920

Ion Industries, Inc., 3508 E Allerton Ave., Cudahy, WI 53110 / 414-486-2007; FAX: 414-486-2017

Iosso Products, 1485 Lively Blvd., Elk Grove Village, IL 60007 / 847-437-8400; FAX: 847-437-8478

Iron Bench, 12619 Bailey Rd., Redding, CA 96003 / 916-241-4623

Ironside International Publishers, Inc., P.O. Box 1050, Lorton, VA 22199

Ironsighter Co., P.O. Box 85070, Westland, MI 48185 / 734-326-8731; FAX: 734-326-3378 www.ironsighter.com

Irwin, Campbell H., 140 Hartland Blvd., East Hartland, CT 06027 / 203-653-3901

Island Pond Gun Shop, Cross St., Island Pond, VT 05846 / 802-723-4546

Israel Arms Inc., 5625 Star Ln. #B, Houston, TX 77057 / 713-789-0745; FAX: 713-914-9515 www.israelarms.com

Ithaca Classic Doubles, Stephen Lamboy, No. 5 Railroad St., Victor, NY 14564 / 716-924-2710; FAX: 716-924-2737 ithacadoubles.com

Ithaca Gun Company LLC, 901 Rt. 34 B, King Ferry, NY 13081 / 315-364-7171; FAX: 315-364-5134 info@ithacagun.com

Ivanoff, Thomas G. (See Tom's Gun Repair)

J

J J Roberts Firearm Engraver, 7808 Lake Dr, Manassas, VA 20111 / 703-330-0448; FAX: 703-264-8600 james..roberts@angelfire.com www.angelfire.com/va2/engraver

J&D Components, 75 East 350 North, Orem, UT 84057-4719 / 801-225-7007 www.jdcomponents.com

J&J Products, Inc., 9240 Whitmore, El Monte, CA 91731 / 818-571-5228; FAX: 800-927-8361

J&J Sales, 1501 21st Ave. S., Great Falls, MT 59405 / 406-727-9789 mtshootingbench@yahoo.com www.j&jsales.us

J&L Superior Bullets (See Huntington Die Special)

J&R Engineering, P.O. Box 77, 200 Lyons Hill Rd., Athol, MA 01331 / 508-249-9241

J&R Enterprises, 4550 Scotts Valley Rd., Lakeport, CA 95453

J&S Heat Treat, 803 S. 16th St., Blue Springs, MO 64015 / 816-229-2149; FAX: 816-228-1135

J. Dewey Mfg. Co., Inc., P.O. Box 2014, Southbury, CT 06488 / 203-264-3064; FAX: 203-262-6907 deweyrods@worldnet.att.net www.deweyrods.com

J. Korzinek Riflesmith, RD 2, Box 73D, Canton, PA 17724 / 717-673-8512

J.A. Blades, Inc. (See Christopher Firearms Co.)

J.A. Henckels Zwillingswerk Inc., 9 Skyline Dr., Hawthorne, NY 10532 / 914-592-7370

J.G. Anschutz GmbH & Co. KG, Daimlerstr. 12, D-89079 Ulm, Ulm, GERMANY / 49 731 40120; FAX: 49 731 4012700 JGA-info@anschuetz-sport.com www.anschuetz-sport.com

J.G. Dapkus Co., Inc., Commerce Circle, P.O. Box 293, Durham, CT 06422 www.explodingtargets.com

J.I.T. Ltd., P.O. Box 230, Freedom, WY 83120 / 708-494-0937

J.J. Roberts / Engraver, 7808 Lake Dr., Manassas, VA 20111 / 703-330-0448 jjrengraver@aol.com www.angelfire.com/va2/engraver

J.P. Enterprises Inc., P.O. Box 378, Hugo, MN 55110 / 612-486-9064; FAX: 612-482-0970

J.R. Williams Bullet Co., 2008 Tucker Rd., Perry, GA 31069 / 912-987-0274

J.W. Morrison Custom Rifles, 4015 W. Sharon, Phoenix, AZ 85029 / 602-978-3754

J/B Adventures & Safaris Inc., 2275 E. Arapahoe Rd., Ste. 109, Littleton, CO 80122-1521 / 303-771-0977

Jack A. Rosenberg & Sons, 12229 Cox Ln., Dallas, TX 75234 / 214-241-6302

Jack Dever Co., 8520 NW 90th St., Oklahoma City, OK 73132 / 405-721-6393 jbdever1@home.com

Jack First, Inc., 1201 Turbine Dr., Rapid City, SD 57703 / 605-343-8481; FAX: 605-343-9420

Jack Jonas Appraisals & Taki, 13952 E. Marina Dr., #604, Aurora, CO 80014

Jackalope Gun Shop, 1048 S. 5th St., Douglas, WY 82633 / 307-358-3441

Jaffin, Harry. See: BRIDGEMAN PRODUCTS

Jagdwaffen, Peter. See: BUCHSENMACHERMEISTER

James Churchill Glove Co., PO Box 298, Centralia, WA 98531 / 360-736-2816; FAX: 360-330-0151 churchillglove@localaccess.com

James Wayne Firearms for Collectors and Investors, 2608 N. Laurent, Victoria, TX 77901 / 361-578-1258; FAX: 361-578-3559

Jamison International, Marc Jamison, 3551 Mayer Ave., Sturgis, SD 57785 / 605-347-5090; FAX: 605-347-4704 jbell2@masttechnology.com

Jamison, Marc. See: JAMISON INTERNATIONAL

Jamison's Forge Works, 4527 Rd. 6.5 NE, Moses Lake, WA 98837 / 509-762-2659

Jantz Supply, 309 West Main Dept HD, Davis, OK 73030-0584 / 580-369-2316; FAX: 580-369-3082 jantz@brightok.net www.knifemaking.com

Jarrett Rifles, Inc., 383 Brown Rd., Jackson, SC 29831 / 803-471-3616 www.jarrettrifles.com

Jarvis, Inc., 1123 Cherry Orchard Lane, Hamilton, MT 59840 / 406-961-4392

Javelina Lube Products, P.O. Box 337, San Bernardino, CA 92402 / 909-350-9556; FAX: 909-429-1211

Jay McCament Custom Gunmaker, Jay McCament, 1730-134th St. Ct. S., Tacoma, WA 98444 / 253-531-8832

JB Custom, P.O. Box 6912, Leawood, KS 66206 / 913-381-2329

Jeff Flannery Engraving, 11034 Riddles Run Rd., Union, KY 41091 / 859-384-3127; FAX: 859-384-2222 engraving@fuse.net http://home.fuse.net/engraving/

Jeffredo Gunsight, P.O. Box 669, San Marcos, CA 92079 / 760-728-2695

Jena Eur, PO Box 319, Dunmore, PA 18512

Jenco Sales, Inc., P.O. Box 1000, Manchaca, TX 78652 / 800-531-5301; FAX: 800-266-2373 jencosales@sbcglobal.net

Jenkins Recoil Pads, 5438 E. Frontage Ln., Olney, IL 62450 / 618-395-3416

Jensen Bullets, RR 1 Box 187, Arco, ID 83213 / 208-785-5590

Jensen's Custom Ammunition, 5146 E. Pima, Tucson, AZ 85712 / 602-325-3346; FAX: 602-322-5704

Jensen's Firearms Academy, 1280 W. Prince, Tucson, AZ 85705 / 602-293-8516

Jericho Tool & Die Co., Inc., 2917 St. Hwy. 7, Bainbridge, NY 13733 / 607-563-8222; FAX: 607-563-8560 jerichotool.com www.jerichotool.com

Jerry Phillips Optics, P.O. Box L632, Langhorne, PA 19047 / 215-757-5037; FAX: 215-757-7097

Jesse W. Smith Saddlery, 0499 County Road J, Pritchett, CO 81064 / 509-325-0622

Jester Bullets, Rt. 1 Box 27, Orienta, OK 73737

Jewell Triggers, Inc., 3620 Hwy. 123, San Marcos, TX 78666 / 512-353-2999; FAX: 512-392-0543

JGS Precision Tool Mfg., LLC, 60819 Selander Rd., Coos Bay, OR 97420 / 541-267-4331; FAX: 541-267-5996 jgstools@harborside.com www.jgstools.com

Jim Blair Engraving, P.O. Box 64, Glenrock, WY 82637 / 307-436-8115 jblairengrav@msn.com

Jim Noble Co., 1305 Columbia St., Vancouver, WA 98660 / 360-695-1309; FAX: 360-695-6835 jnobleco@aol.com

Jim Norman Custom Gunstocks, 14281 Cane Rd., Valley Center, CA 92082 / 619-749-6252

Jim's Precision, Jim Ketchum, 1725 Moclips Dr., Petaluma, CA 94952 / 707-762-3014

JLK Bullets, 414 Turner Rd., Dover, AR 72837 / 501-331-4194

Johanssons Vapentillbehor, Bert, S-430 20, Veddige, SWEDEN

John Hall Plastics, Inc., P.O. Box 1526, Alvin, TX 77512 / 713-489-8709

John J. Adams & Son Engravers, 7040 VT Rt 113, Vershire, VT 05079 / 802-685-0019

John Masen Co. Inc., 1305 Jelmak, Grand Prairie, TX 75050 / 817-430-8732; FAX: 817-430-1715

John Partridge Sales Ltd., Trent Meadows Rugeley, Staffordshire, WS15 2HS ENGLAND

John Rigby & Co., 500 Linne Rd. Ste. D, Paso Robles, CA 93446 / 805-227-4236; FAX: 805-227-4723 jribgy@calinet www.johnrigbyandco.com

John's Custom Leather, 523 S. Liberty St., Blairsville, PA 15717 / 724-459-6802; FAX: 724-459-5996

Johnson Wood Products, 34897 Crystal Road, Strawberry Point, IA 52076 / 563-933-6504 johnsonwoodproducts@yahoo.com
Johnston Bros. (See C&T Corp. TA Johnson Brothers)
Jonad Corp., 2091 Lakeland Ave., Lakewood, OH 44107 / 216-226-3161
Jonathan Arthur Ciener, Inc., 8700 Commerce St., Cape Canaveral, FL 32920 / 321-868-2200; FAX: 321-868-2201 www.22lrconversions.com
Jones Co., Dale, 680 Hoffman Draw, Kila, MT 59920 / 406-755-4684
Jones Custom Products, Neil A., 17217 Brookhouser Rd., Saegertown, PA 16433 / 814-763-2769; FAX: 814-763-4228
Jones, J. See: SSK INDUSTRIES
Jones Moulds, Paul, 4901 Telegraph Rd., Los Angeles, CA 90022 / 213-262-1510
JP Sales, Box 307, Anderson, TX 77830
JRP Custom Bullets, RR2 2233 Carlton Rd., Whitehall, NY 12887 / 518-282-0084 or 802-438-5548
JSL Ltd. (See U.S. Importer-Specialty Shooters)
Juenke, Vern, 25 Bitterbush Rd., Reno, NV 89523 / 702-345-0225
Jungkind, Reeves C., 509 E. Granite St., Llano, TX 78643-3055 / 325-247-1151
Jurras, L. See: L. E. JURRAS & ASSOC.
Justin Phillippi Custom Bullets, P.O. Box 773, Ligonier, PA 15658 / 412-238-9671

K

K&M Industries, Inc., Box 66, 510 S. Main, Troy, ID 83871 / 208-835-2281; FAX: 208-835-5211
K&M Services, 5430 Salmon Run Rd., Dover, PA 17315 / 717-292-3175; FAX: 717-292-3175
K. Eversull Co., Inc., 1 Tracemont, Boyce, LA 71409 / 318-793-8728; FAX: 318-793-5483 bestguns@aol.com
K.B.I. Inc., P.O. Box 6625, Harrisburg, PA 17112 / 717-540-8518; FAX: 717-540-8567
K.L. Null Holsters Ltd., 161 School St. NW, Hill City Station, Resaca, GA 30735 / 706-625-5643; FAX: 706-625-9392 ken@klnullholsters.com www.klnullholsters.com
Ka Pu Kapili, P.O. Box 745, Honokaa, HI 96727 / 808-776-1644; FAX: 808-776-1731
KA-BAR Knives, 200 Homer St., Olean, NY 14760 / 800-282-0130; FAX: 716-790-7188 info@ka-bar.com www.ka-bar.com
Kahles A. Swarovski Company, 2 Slater Rd., Cranston, RI 02920 / 401-946-2220; FAX: 401-946-2587
Kahr Arms, PO Box 220, 630 Route 303, Blauvelt, NY 10913 / 845-353-7770; FAX: 845-353-7833 www.kahr.com
Kailua Custom Guns Inc., 51 N. Dean Street, Coquille, OR 97423 / 541-396-5413 kailuacustom@aol.com www.kailuacustom.com
Kalispel Case Line, P.O. Box 267, Cusick, WA 99119 / 509-445-1121
Kamik Outdoor Footwear, 554 Montee de Liesse, Montreal, PQ H4T 1P1 CANADA / 514-341-3950; FAX: 514-341-1861
Kane, Edward, P.O. Box 385, Ukiah, CA 95482 / 707-462-2937
Kapro Mfg. Co. Inc. (See R.E.I.)
Kasenit Co., Inc., 39 Park Ave., Highland Mills, NY 10930 / 845-928-9595; FAX: 845-986-8038
Kaswer Custom, Inc., 13 Surrey Drive, Brookfield, CT 06804 / 203-775-0564; FAX: 203-775-6872
KDF, Inc., 2485 Hwy. 46 N., Seguin, TX 78155 / 830-379-8141; FAX: 830-379-5420
KeeCo Impressions, Inc., 346 Wood Ave., North Brunswick, NJ 08902 / 800-468-0546
Kehr, Roger, 2131 Agate Ct. SE, Lacy, WA 98503 / 360-491-0691
Keith's Bullets, 942 Twisted Oak, Algonquin, IL 60102 / 708-658-3520
Keith's Custom Gunstocks, Keith M. Heppler, 540 Banyan Circle, Walnut Creek, CA 94598 / 925-934-3509; FAX: 925-934-3143 kmheppler@hotmail.com
Kelbly, Inc., 7222 Dalton Fox Lake Rd., North Lawrence, OH 44666 / 216-683-4674; FAX: 216-683-7349
Kelley's, P.O. Box 125, Woburn, MA 01801-0125 / 800-879-7273; FAX: 781-272-7077 kels@star.net www.kelsmilitary.com
Kellogg's Professional Products, 325 Pearl St., Sandusky, OH 44870 / 419-625-6551; FAX: 419-625-6167 skwigton@aol.com
Kelly, Lance, 1723 Willow Oak Dr., Edgewater, FL 32132 / 904-423-4933
Kel-Tec CNC Industries, Inc., PO Box 236009, Cocoa, FL 32923 / 407-631-0068; FAX: 407-631-1169
Kemen America, 2550 Hwy. 23, Wrenshall, MN 55797 / 218-384-3670 patrickl@midwestshootingschool.com midwestshootingschool.com
Ken Eyster Heritage Gunsmiths, Inc., 6441 Bisop Rd., Centerburg, OH 43011 / 740-625-6131; FAX: 740-625-7811
Ken Starnes Gunmaker, 15940 SW Holly Hill Rd., Hillsboro, OR 97123-9033 / 503-628-0705; FAX: 503-443-2096 kstarnes@kdsa.com
Keng's Firearms Specialty, Inc./US Tactical Systems, 875 Wharton Dr., P.O. Box 44405, Atlanta, GA 30336-1405 / 404-691-7611; FAX: 404-505-8445
Kennebec Journal, 274 Western Ave., Augusta, ME 04330 / 207-622-6288
Kennedy Firearms, 10 N. Market St., Muncy, PA 17756 / 717-546-6695
Kenneth W. Warren Engraver, P.O. Box 2842, Wenatchee, WA 98807 / 509-663-6123; FAX: 509-665-6123
Ken's Kustom Kartridges, 331 Jacobs Rd., Hubbard, OH 44425 / 216-534-4595
Kent Cartridge America, Inc., PO Box 849, 1000 Zigor Rd., Kearneysville, WV 25430
Keowee Game Calls, 608 Hwy. 25 North, Travelers Rest, SC 29690 / 864-834-7204; FAX: 864-834-7831
Kershaw Knives, 25300 SW Parkway Ave., Wilsonville, OR 97070 / 503-682-1966; or 800-325-2891; FAX: 503-682-7168
Kesselring Gun Shop, 4024 Old Hwy. 99N, Burlington, WA 98233 / 360-724-3113; FAX: 360-724-7003 info@kesselrings.com www.kesselrings.com
Ketchum, Jim (See Jim's Precision)
Keystone Sporting Arms, Inc. (Crickett Rifles), 8920 State Route 405, Milton, PA 17847 / 800-742-2777; FAX: 570-742-1455
Kickeez I.N.C., Inc., 301 Industrial Dr., Carl Junction, MO 64834-8806 / 419-649-2100; FAX: 417-649-2200 kickey@ipa.net
Kilham & Co., Main St., P.O. Box 37, Lyme, NH 03768 / 603-795-4112
Kim Ahrends Custom Firearms, Inc., Box 203, Clarion, IA 50525 / 515-532-3449; FAX: 515-532-3926
Kimar (See U.S. Importer-IAR,Inc)
Kimber of America, Inc., 1 Lawton St., Yonkers, NY 10705 / 800-880-2418; FAX: 914-964-9340
King & Co., P.O. Box 1242, Bloomington, IL 61702 / 309-473-3964; FAX: 309-473-2161
King's Gun Works, 1837 W. Glenoaks Blvd., Glendale, CA 91201 / 818-956-6010; FAX: 818-548-8606
Kirkpatrick Leather Co., PO Box 677, Laredo, TX 78040 / 956-723-6631; FAX: 956-725-0672 mike@kirkpatrickleather.com www.kirkpatrickleather.com
KK Air International (See Impact Case & Container Co.)
Kleen-Bore, Inc., 16 Industrial Pkwy., Easthampton, MA 01027 / 413-527-0300; FAX: 413-527-2522 info@kleen-bore.com www.kleen-bore.com
Kleinendorst, K. W., RR 1, Box 1500, Hop Bottom, PA 18824 / 717-289-4687
Klingler Woodcarving, P.O. Box 141, Thistle Hill, Cabot, VT 05647 / 802-426-3811
Knifeware, Inc., P.O. Box 3, Greenville, WV 24945 / 304-832-6878
Knight Rifles, 21852 Hwy. J46, P.O. Box 130, Centerville, IA 52544 / 515-856-2626; FAX: 515-856-2628 www.knightrifles.com
Knight Rifles (See Modern Muzzle Loading, Inc.)
Knight's Mfg. Co., 7750 Ninth St. SW, Vero Beach, FL 32968 / 561-562-5697; FAX: 561-569-2955 civiliansales@knightarmco.com
Knock on Wood Antiques, 355 Post Rd., Darien, CT 06820 / 203-655-9031
Knoell, Doug, 9737 McCardle Way, Santee, CA 92071 / 619-449-5189
Knopp, Gary. See: SUPER 6 LLC
KOGOT, 410 College, Trinidad, CO 81082 / 719-846-9406; FAX: 719-846-9406
Kolar, 1925 Roosevelt Ave., Racine, WI 53406 / 414-554-0800; FAX: 414-554-9093
Kolpin Outdoors, Inc., P.O. Box 107, 205 Depot St., Fox Lake, WI 53933 / 414-928-3118; FAX: 414-928-3687 cdutton@kolpin.com www.kolpin.com
Korth Germany GmbH, Robert Bosch Strasse, 11, D-23909, 23909 Ratzeburg, GERMANY / 4541-840363; FAX: 4541-84 05 35 info@korthwaffen.de www.korthwaffen.com
Korth USA, 437R Chandler St., Tewksbury, MA 01876 / 978-851-8656; FAX: 978-851-9462 info@kortusa.com www.korthusa.com
Korzinek Riflesmith, J., RD 2 Box 73D, Canton, PA 17724 / 717-673-8512
Koval Knives, 5819 Zarley St., Suite A, New Albany, OH 43054 / 614-855-0777; FAX: 614-855-0945 koval@kovalknives.com www.kovalknives.com
Kowa Optimed, Inc., 20001 S. Vermont Ave., Torrance, CA 90502 / 310-327-1913; FAX: 310-327-4177 scopekowa@kowa.com www.kowascope.com
Kramer Designs, P.O. Box 129, Clancy, MT 59634 / 406-933-8658; FAX: 406-933-8658
Kramer Handgun Leather, P.O. Box 112154, Tacoma, WA 98411 / 800-510-2666; FAX: 253-564-1214 www.kramerleather.com
Krause Publications, Inc., 700 E. State St., Iola, WI 54990 / 715-445-2214; FAX: 715-445-4087
Krico Deutschland GmbH, Nurnbergerstrasse 6, D-90602, Pyrbaum, GERMANY / 09180-2780; FAX: 09180-2661
Krieger Barrels, Inc., 2024 Mayfield Rd, Richfield, WI 53076 / 262-628-8558; FAX: 262-628-8748
Krieghoff Gun Co., H., Boschstrasse 22, D-89079 Elm, GERMANY / 731-4018270
Krieghoff International,Inc., 7528 Easton Rd., Ottsville, PA 18942 / 610-847-5173; FAX: 610-847-8691
Kukowski, Ed. See: ED'S GUN HOUSE
Kulis Freeze Dry Taxidermy, 725 Broadway Ave., Bedford, OH 44146 / 216-232-8352; FAX: 216-232-7305 jkulis@kastaway.com kastaway.com
KVH Industries, Inc., 110 Enterprise Center, Middletown, RI 02842 / 401-847-3327; FAX: 401-849-0045
Kwik-Site Co., 5555 Treadwell St., Wayne, MI 48184 / 734-326-1500; FAX: 734-326-4120 kwiksiteco@aol.com

L

L&R Lock Co., 1137 Pocalla Rd., Sumter, SC 29150 / 803-775-6127; FAX: 803-775-5171
L&S Technologies Inc. (See Aimtech Mount Systems)
L. Bengtson Arms Co., 6345-B E. Akron St., Mesa, AZ 85205 / 602-981-6375
L. E. Jurras & Assoc., L. E. Jurras, P.O. Box 680, Washington, IN 47501 / 812-254-6170; FAX: 812-254-6170 jurasgun@rtcc.net
L.A.R. Mfg., Inc., 4133 W. Farm Rd., West Jordan, UT 84088 / 801-280-3505; FAX: 801-280-1972
L.B.T., Judy Smith, HCR 62, Box 145, Moyie Springs, ID 83845 / 208-267-3588
L.E. Wilson, Inc., Box 324, 404 Pioneer Ave., Cashmere, WA 98815 / 509-782-1328; FAX: 509-782-7200
L.L. Bean, Inc., Freeport, ME 04032 / 207-865-4761; FAX: 207-552-2802
L.P.A. Inc., Via Alfieri 26, Gardone V.T., Brescia, ITALY / 30-891-14-81; FAX: 30-891-09-51
L.R. Clift Mfg., 3821 Hammonton Rd., Marysville, CA 95901 / 916-755-3390; FAX: 916-755-3393
L.W. Seecamp Co., Inc., PO Box 255, New Haven, CT 06502 / 203-877-3429; FAX: 203-877-3429 seecamp@optonline.net
La Clinique du .45, 1432 Rougemont, Chambly, PQ J3L 2L8 CANADA / 514-658-1144
Labanu, Inc., 2201-F Fifth Ave., Ronkonkoma, NY 11779 / 516-467-6197; FAX: 516-981-4112
LaBoone, Pat. See: THE MIDWEST SHOOTING SCHOOL
LaBounty Precision Reboring, Inc, 7968 Silver Lake Rd., PO Box 186, Maple Falls, WA 98266 / 360-599-2047; FAX: 360-599-3018
LaCrosse Footwear, Inc., 18550 NE Riverside Parkway, Portland, OR 97230 / 503-766-1010; or 800-323-2668; FAX: 503-766-1015
LaFrance Specialties, P.O. Box 87933, San Diego, CA 92138 / 619-293-3373; FAX: 619-293-0819 timlafrance@att.net lafrancespecialties.com
Lake Center Marina, PO Box 670, St. Charles, MO 63302 / 314-946-7500
Lakefield Arms Ltd. (See Savage Arms, Inc.)
Lakewood Products LLC, 275 June St., Berlin, WI 54923 / 800-872-8458; FAX: 920-361-7719 lakewood@centurytel.net www.lakewoodproducts.com
Lamboy, Stephen. See: ITHACA CLASSIC DOUBLES
Lampert, Ron, Rt. 1, 44857 Schoolcraft Trl., Guthrie, MN 56461 / 218-854-7345
Lamson & Goodnow Mfg. Co., 45 Conway St., Shelburne Falls, MA 03170 / 413-625-6564; or 800-872-6564; FAX: 413-625-9816 www.lamsonsharp.com
Lansky Levine, Arthur. See: LANSKY SHARPENERS
Lansky Sharpeners, Arthur Lansky Levine, PO Box 50830, Las Vegas, NV 89016 / 702-361-7511; FAX: 702-896-9511
LaPrade, PO Box 250, Ewing, VA 24248 / 423-733-2615
Lapua Ltd., P.O. Box 5, Lapua, FINLAND / 6-310111; FAX: 6-4388991
LaRocca Gun Works, 51 Union Place, Worcester, MA 01608 / 508-754-2887; FAX: 508-754-2887 www.laroccagunworks.com
Larry Lyons Gunworks, 110 Hamilton St., Dowagiac, MI 49047 / 616-782-9478
Laser Devices, Inc., 2 Harris Ct. A-4, Monterey, CA 93940 / 831-373-0701; FAX: 831-373-0903 sales@laserdevices.com www.laserdevices.com
Laseraim Technologies, Inc., P.O. Box 3548, Little Rock, AR 72203 / 501-375-2227
Laserlyte, 2201 Amapola Ct., Torrance, CA 90501
LaserMax, Inc., 3495 Winton Place, Bldg. B, Rochester, NY 14623-2807 / 800-527-3703; FAX: 716-272-5427 customerservice@lasermax-inc.com www.lasermax-inc.com
Lassen Community College, Gunsmithing Dept., P.O. Box 3000, Hwy. 139, Susanville, CA 96130 / 916-251-8800; FAX: 916-251-8838
Lathrop's, Inc., 5146 E. Pima, Tucson, AZ 85712 / 520-881-0266; or 800-875-4867; FAX: 520-322-5704
Laughridge, William R. (See Cylinder & Slide Inc.)
Laurel Mountain Forge, P.O. Box 52, Crown Point, IN 46308 / 219-548-2950; FAX: 219-548-2950
Laurona Armas Eibar, S.A.L., Avenida de Otaola 25, P.O. Box 260, Eibar 20600, SPAIN / 34-43-700600; FAX: 34-43-700616
Lawrence Brand Shot (See Precision Reloading)
Lawrence Leather Co., P.O. Box 1479, Lillington, NC 27546 / 910-893-2071; FAX: 910-893-4742
Lawson Co., Harry, 3328 N Richey Blvd., Tucson, AZ 85716 / 520-326-1117; FAX: 520-326-1117
Lawson, John. See: THE SIGHT SHOP
Lawson, John G. (See Sight Shop, The)
Lazzeroni Arms Co., PO Box 26696, Tucson, AZ 85726 / 888-492-7247; FAX: 520-624-4250
Le Clear Industries (See E-Z-Way Systems), P.O. Box 4310, Newark, OH 43058-4310 / 614-345-6645; FAX: 614-345-6600
Leapers, Inc., 7675 Five Mile Rd., Northville, MI 48167 / 248-486-1231; FAX: 248-486-1430
Leatherman Tool Group, Inc., 12106 NE Ainsworth Cir., P.O. Box 20595, Portland, OR 97294 / 503-253-7826; FAX: 503-253-7830
Lebeau-Courally, Rue St. Gilles, 386 4000, Liege, BELGIUM / 042-52-48-43; FAX: 32-4-252-2008 info@lebeau-courally.com www.lebeau-courally.com
Leckie Professional Gunsmithing, 546 Quarry Rd., Ottsville, PA 18942 / 215-847-8594
Ledbetter Airguns, Riley, 1804 E Sprague St, Winston Salem, NC 27107-3521 / 919-784-0676
Lee Precision, Inc., 4275 Hwy. U, Hartford, WI 53027 / 262-673-3075; FAX: 262-673-9273 info@leeprecision.com www.leeprecision.com
Lee Supplies, Mark, 9901 France Ct., Lakeville, MN 55044 / 612-461-2114
LeFever Arms Co., Inc., 6234 Stokes, Lee Center Rd., Lee Center, NY 13363 / 315-337-6722; FAX: 315-337-1543
Legacy Sports International, 206 S. Union St., Alexandria, VA 22314 / 703-548-4837 www.legacysports.com
Leibowitz, Leonard, 1205 Murrayhill Ave., Pittsburgh, PA 15217 / 412-361-5455

MANUFACTURER'S DIRECTORY

Leica USA, Inc., 156 Ludlow Ave., Northvale, NJ 07647 / 201-767-7500; FAX: 201-767-8666
LEM Gun Specialties, Inc. The Lewis Lead Remover, P.O. Box 2855, Peachtree City, GA 30269-2024 / 770-487-0556
Leonard Day, 6 Linseed Rd Box 1, West Hatfield, MA 01088-7505 / 413-337-8369
Les Baer Custom, Inc., 29601 34th Ave., Hillsdale, IL 61257 / 309-658-2716; FAX: 309-658-2610 www.lesbaer.com
LesMerises, Felix. See: ROCKY MOUNTAIN ARMOURY
Lethal Force Institute (See Police Bookshelf), PO Box 122, Concord, NH 03301 / 603-224-6814; FAX: 603-226-3554
Lett Custom Grips, 672 Currier Rd., Hopkinton, NH 03229-2652 / 800-421-5388; FAX: 603-226-4580 info@lettgrips.com www.lettgrips.com
Leupold & Stevens, Inc., 14400 NW Greenbrier Pky., Beaverton, OR 97006 / 503-646-9171; FAX: 503-526-1455
Lever Arms Service Ltd., 2131 Burrard St., Vancouver, BC V6J 3H7 CANADA / 604-736-2711; FAX: 604-738-3503 leverarms@leverarms.com www.leverarms.com
Lew Horton Dist. Co., Inc., 15 Walkup Dr., Westboro, MA 01581 / 508-366-7400; FAX: 508-366-5332
Liberty Metals, 2233 East 16th St., Los Angeles, CA 90021 / 213-581-9171; FAX: 213-581-9351 libertymfgsolder@hotmail.com
Liberty Safe, 999 W. Utah Ave., Payson, UT 84651-1744 / 800-247-5625; FAX: 801-489-6409
Liberty Shooting Supplies, P.O. Box 357, Hillsboro, OR 97123 / 503-640-5518; FAX: 503-640-5518 info@libertyshootingsupplies.com www.libertyshootingsupplies.com
Lightning Performance Innovations, Inc., RD1 Box 555, Mohawk, NY 13407 / 315-866-8819; FAX: 315-867-5701
Lilja Precision Rifle Barrels, P.O. Box 372, Plains, MT 59859 / 406-826-3084; FAX: 406-826-3083 lilja@riflebarrels.com www.riflebarrels.com
Lincoln, Dean, Box 1886, Farmington, NM 87401
Linder Solingen Knives, 4401 Sentry Dr. #B, Tucker, GA 30084 / 770-939-6915; FAX: 770-939-6738
Lindsay Engraving & Tools, Steve Lindsay, 3714 W. Cedar Hills, Kearney, NE 68845 / 308-236-7885 steve@lindsayengraving.com www.handgravers.com
Lindsay, Steve. See: LINDSAY ENGRAVING & TOOLS
Lindsley Arms Cartridge Co., P.O. Box 757, 20 College Hill Rd., Henniker, NH 03242 / 603-428-3127
Linebaugh Custom Sixguns, P.O. Box 455, Cody, WY 82414 / 307-645-3332 www.sixgunner.com
Lion Country Supply, P.O. Box 480, Port Matilda, PA 16870
List Precision Engineering, Unit 1 Ingley Works, 13 River Road, Barking, ENGLAND / 011-081-594-1686
Lithi Bee Bullet Lube, 1728 Carr Rd., Muskegon, MI 49442 / 616-788-4479 lithibee@att.net
"Little John's" Antique Arms, 1740 W. Laveta, Orange, CA 92668
Little Trees Ramble (See Scott Pilkington)
Littler Sales Co., 20815 W. Chicago, Detroit, MI 48228 / 313-273-6888; FAX: 313-273-1099 littlerptg@aol.com
Littleton, J. F., 275 Pinedale Ave., Oroville, CA 95966 / 916-533-6084
Ljutic Industries, Inc., 732 N. 16th Ave., Suite 22, Yakima, WA 98902 / 509-248-0476; FAX: 509-576-8233 ljuticgun@earthlink.net www.ljuticgun.com
Llama Gabilondo Y Cia, Apartado 290, E-01080, Victoria, SPAIN
Loch Leven Industries/Convert-A-Pell, P.O. Box 2751, Santa Rosa, CA 95405 / 707-573-8735; FAX: 707-573-0369
Lock's Philadelphia Gun Exchange, 6700 Rowland Ave., Philadelphia, PA 19149 / 215-332-6225; FAX: 215-332-4800 locks.gunshop@verizon.net
Lodewick, Walter H., 2816 NE Halsey St., Portland, OR 97232 / 503-284-2554 wlodewick@aol.com
Lodgewood Mfg., P.O. Box 611, Whitewater, WI 53190 / 262-473-5444; FAX: 262-473-6448 lodgewd@idcnet.com lodgewood.com
Log Cabin Sport Shop, 8010 Lafayette Rd., Lodi, OH 44254 / 330-948-1082; FAX: 330-948-4307 logcabin@logcabinshop.com www.logcabinshop.com
Logan, Harry M., Box 745, Honokaa, HI 96727 / 808-776-1644
Logdewood Mfg., P.O. Box 611, Whitewater, WI 53190 / 262-473-5444; FAX: 262-473-6448 lodgewd@idcnet.com www.lodgewood.com
Lohman Mfg. Co., Inc., 4500 Doniphan Dr., P.O. Box 220, Neosho, MO 64850 / 417-451-4438; FAX: 417-451-2576
Lomont Precision Bullets, 278 Sandy Creek Rd., Salmon, ID 83467 / 208-756-6819; FAX: 208-756-6824 www.klomont.com
London Guns Ltd., Box 3750, Santa Barbara, CA 93130 / 805-683-4141; FAX: 805-683-1712
Lone Star Gunleather, 1301 Brushy Bend Dr., Round Rock, TX 78681 / 512-255-1805
Lone Star Rifle Company, 11231 Rose Road, Conroe, TX 77303 / 936-856-3363; FAX: 936-856-3363 dave@lonestar.com
Long, George F., 1500 Rogue River Hwy., Ste. F, Grants Pass, OR 97527 / 541-476-7552
Lortone Inc., 2856 NW Market St., Seattle, WA 98107
Lothar Walther Precision Tool Inc., 3425 Hutchinson Rd., Cumming, GA 30040 / 770-889-9998; FAX: 770-889-4919 lotharwalther@mindspring.com www.lothar-walther.com
LPS Laboratories, Inc., 4647 Hugh Howell Rd., P.O. Box 3050, Tucker, GA 30084 / 404-934-7800
Lucas, Edward E, 32 Garfield Ave., East Brunswick, NJ 08816 / 201-251-5526
Lupton, Keith. See: PAWLING MOUNTAIN CLUB
Lyman Instant Targets, Inc. (See Lyman Products)
Lyman Products Corp., 475 Smith Street, Middletown, CT 06457-1541 / 800-423-9704; FAX: 860-632-1699 lymansales@cshore.com www.lymanproducts.com

M

M.H. Canjar Co., 6510 Raleigh St., Arvada, CO 80003 / 303-295-2638; FAX: 303-295-2638
MA Systems, Inc., P.O. Box 894, Pryor, OK 74362-0894 / 918-824-3705; FAX: 918-824-3710
Mac-1 Airgun Distributors, 13974 Van Ness Ave., Gardena, CA 90249-2900 / 310-327-3581; FAX: 310-327-0238 mac1@maclairgun.com www.mac1airgun.com
Madis Books, 2453 West Five Mile Pkwy., Dallas, TX 75233 / 214-330-7168
Madis, George. See: GEORGE MADIS WINCHESTER CONSULTANTS
MAG Instrument, Inc., 1635 S. Sacramento Ave., Ontario, CA 91761 / 909-947-1006; FAX: 909-947-3116
Magma Engineering Co., P.O. Box 161, 20955 E. Ocotillo Rd., Queen Creek, AZ 85242 / 602-987-9008; FAX: 602-987-0148
Mag-Na-Port International, Inc., 41302 Executive Dr., Harrison Twp., MI 48045-1306 / 586-469-6727; FAX: 586-469-0425 email@magnaport.com www.magnaport.com
Magnolia Sports, Inc., 211 W. Main, Magnolia, AR 71753 / 501-234-8410; or 800-530-7816; FAX: 501-234-8117
Magnum Power Products, Inc., P.O. Box 17768, Fountain Hills, AZ 85268
Magnum Research, Inc., 7110 University Ave. NE, Minneapolis, MN 55432 / 800-772-6168 or 763-574-1868; FAX: 763-574-0109 info@magnumresearch.com
Magnus Bullets, P.O. Box 239, Toney, AL 35773 / 256-420-8359; FAX: 256-420-8360
Mag-Pack Corp., P.O. Box 846, Chesterland, OH 44026 / 440-285-9480 magpack@hotmail.com
MagSafe Ammo Co., 4700 S US Highway 17/92, Casselberry, FL 32707-3814 / 407-834-9966; FAX: 407-834-8185 www.magsafeonline.com
Magtech Ammunition Co. Inc., 6845 20th Ave. S., Ste. 120, Centerville, MN 55038
Mahony, Philip Bruce, 67 White Hollow Rd., Lime Rock, CT 06039-2418 / 203-435-9341 filbalony-redbeard@snet.net
Mahovsky's Metalife, R.D. 1, Box 149a Eureka Road, Grand Valley, PA 16420 / 814-436-7747
Maine Custom Bullets, RFD 1, Box 1755, Brooks, ME 04921
Makinson, Nicholas, RR 3, Komoka, ON N0L 1R0 CANADA / 519-471-5462
Mallardtone Game Calls, 10406 96th St., Court West, Taylor Ridge, IL 61284 / 309-798-2481; FAX: 309-798-2501
Mandall Shooting Supplies Inc., 3616 N. Scottsdale Rd., Scottsdale, AZ 85251 / 480-945-2553; FAX: 480-949-0734
Marble Arms (See CRR, Inc./Marble's Inc.)
Marchmon Bullets, 6502 Riverdale Rd., Whitmore Lake, MI 48189
Marent, Rudolf. See: HAMMERLI SERVICE-PRECISION MAC
Mark Lee Supplies, 9901 France Ct., Lakeville, MN 55044 / 952-461-2114; FAX: 952-461-2194 marklee55044@usfamily.net
Markell, Inc., 422 Larkfield Center 235, Santa Rosa, CA 95403 / 707-573-0792; FAX: 707-573-9867
Markesbery Muzzle Loaders, Inc., 7785 Foundation Dr., Ste. 6, Florence, KY 41042 / 606-342-5553 or 606-342-2380
Marksman Products, 5482 Argosy Dr., Huntington Beach, CA 92649 / 714-898-7535; or 800-822-8005; FAX: 714-891-0782
Marlin Firearms Co., 100 Kenna Dr., North Haven, CT 06473 / 203-239-5621; FAX: 203-234-7991 www.marlinfirearms.com
MarMik, Inc., 2116 S. Woodland Ave., Michigan City, IN 46360 / 219-872-7231; FAX: 219-872-7231
Marocchi F.lli S.p.A, Via Galileo Galilei 8, I-25068 Zanano, ITALY
Marquart Precision Co., P.O. Box 1740, Prescott, AZ 86302 / 520-445-5646
Marsh, Mike, Croft Cottage, Main St., Derbyshire, DE4 2BY ENGLAND / 01629 650 669
Marshall Enterprises, 792 Canyon Rd., Redwood City, CA 94062
Marshall Fish Mfg. Gunsmith Sptg. Co., Rd. Box 2439, Westport, NY 12993 / 518-962-4897; FAX: 518-962-4897
Martin B. Retting Inc., 11029 Washington, Culver City, CA 90232 / 213-837-2412
Martini & Hagn, 1264 Jimsmith Lake Rd, Cranbrook, BC V1C 6V6 CANADA / 250-417-2926; FAX: 250-417-2928
Martin's Gun Shop, 937 S. Sheridan Blvd., Lakewood, CO 80226 / 303-922-2184
Martz, John V., 8060 Lakeview Lane, Lincoln, CA 95648 FAX: 916-645-3815
Marvel, Alan, 3922 Madonna Rd., Jarretsville, MD 21084 / 301-557-6545
Marx, Harry (See U.S. Importer for FERLIB)
Maryland Paintball Supply, 8507 Harford Rd., Parkville, MD 21234 / 410-882-5607
MAST Technology, Inc., 14555 US Hwy. 95 S., P.O. Box 60969, Boulder City, NV 89006 / 702-293-6969; FAX: 702-293-7255 info@masttechnology.com www.bellammo.com
Master Lock Co., 2600 N. 32nd St., Milwaukee, WI 53245 / 414-444-2800
Match Prep-Doyle Gracey, P.O. Box 155, Tehachapi, CA 93581 / 661-822-5383; FAX: 661-823-8680
Mathews Gun Shop & Gunsmithing, Inc., 10224 S. Paramount Blvd., Downey, CA 90241 / 562-928-2129; FAX: 562-928-8629
Matthews Cutlery, 4401 Sentry Dr. #B, Tucker, GA 30084 / 770-939-6915
Mauser Werke Oberndorf Waffensysteme GmbH, Postfach 1349, 78722, Oberndorf/N., GERMANY
Maverick Arms, Inc., 7 Grasso Ave., P.O. Box 497, North Haven, CT 06473 / 203-230-5300; FAX: 203-230-5420
Maxi-Mount Inc., P.O. Box 291, Willoughby Hills, OH 44096-0291 / 440-944-9456; FAX: 440-944-9456 maximount454@yahoo.com
Mayville Engineering Co. (See MEC, Inc.)
Mazur Restoration, Pete, 13083 Drummer Way, Grass Valley, CA 95949 / 530-268-2412
McBros Rifle Co., P.O. Box 86549, Phoenix, AZ 85080 / 602-582-3713; FAX: 602-581-3825
McCament, Jay. See: JAY MCCAMENT CUSTOM GUNMAKER
McCann, Tom, 14 Walton Dr., New Hope, PA 18938 / 215-862-2728
McCann Industries, P.O. Box 641, Spanaway, WA 98387 / 253-537-6919; FAX: 253-537-6919 mccann.machine@worldnet.att.net www.mccannindustries.com
McCluskey Precision Rifles, 10502 14th Ave. NW, Seattle, WA 98177 / 206-781-2776
McCombs, Leo, 1862 White Cemetery Rd., Patriot, OH 45658 / 740-256-1714
McDonald, Dennis, 8359 Brady St., Peosta, IA 52068 / 319-556-7940
McFarland, Stan, 2221 Idella Ct., Grand Junction, CO 81505 / 970-243-4704
McGhee, Larry. See: B.C. OUTDOORS
McGowen Rifle Barrels, 5961 Spruce Lane, St. Anne, IL 60964 / 815-937-9816; FAX: 815-937-4024
Mchalik, Gary. See: ROSSI FIREARMS
McKenzie, Lynton, 6940 N. Alvernon Way, Tucson, AZ 85718 / 520-299-5090
McMillan Fiberglass Stocks, Inc., 1638 W. Knudsen Dr. #102, Phoenix, AZ 85027 / 623-582-9635; FAX: 623-581-3825 mfsinc@mcmfamily.com www.mcmfamily.com
McMillan Optical Gunsight Co., 28638 N. 42nd St., Cave Creek, AZ 85331 / 602-585-7868; FAX: 602-585-7872
McMillan Rifle Barrels, P.O. Box 3427, Bryan, TX 77805 / 409-690-3456; FAX: 409-690-0156
McMurdo, Lynn (See Specialty Gunsmithing), PO Box 404, Afton, WY 83110 / 307-886-5535
MCS, Inc., 166 Pocono Rd., Brookfield, CT 06804-2023 / 203-775-1013; FAX: 203-775-9462
McWelco Products, 6730 Santa Fe Ave., Hesperia, CA 92345 / 619-244-8876; FAX: 619-244-9398 products@mcwelco.com www.mawelco.com
MDS, P.O. Box 1441, Brandon, FL 33509-1441 / 813-653-1180; FAX: 813-684-5953
Measurement Group Inc., Box 27777, Raleigh, NC 27611
Measures, Leon. See: SHOOT WHERE YOU LOOK
MEC, Inc., 715 South St., Mayville, WI 53050 / 414-387-4500; FAX: 414-387-5802 reloaders@mayul.com www.mayvl.com
MEC-Gar S.R.L., Via Madonnina 64, Gardone V.T. Brescia, ITALY / 39-30-8912687; FAX: 39-30-8910065
MEC-Gar U.S.A., Inc., Hurley Farms Industr. Park, 115, Hurley Road 6G, Oxford, CT 06478 / 203-262-1525; FAX: 203-262-1719 mecgar@aol.com www.mec-gar.com
Mech-Tech Systems, Inc., 1602 Foothill Rd., Kalispell, MT 59901 / 406-755-8055
Meister Bullets (See Gander Mountain)
Mele, Frank, 201 S. Wellow Ave., Cookeville, TN 38501 / 615-526-4860
Menck, Gunsmith Inc., T.W., 5703 S 77th St., Ralston, NE 68127
Mendez, John A., P.O. Box 620984, Orlando, FL 32862 / 407-344-2791
Men-Metallwerk Elisenhuette GmbH, P.O. Box 1263, Nassau/Lahn, D-56372 GERMANY / 2604-7819
Meprolight (See Hesco-Meprolight)
Mercer Custom Guns, 216 S. Whitewater Ave., Jefferson, WI 53549 / 920-674-3839
Merit Corp., PO Box 9044, Schenectady, NY 12309 / 518-346-1420 sales@meritcorporation.com www.meritcorporation.com
Merkel, Schutzenstrasse 26, D-98527 Suhl, Suhl, GERMANY FAX: 011-49-3681-854-203 www.merkel-waffen.de
Merkuria Ltd., Argentinska 38, 17005, Praha 7, CZECH REPUBLIC / 422-875117; FAX: 422-809152
Metal Merchants, PO Box 186, Walled Lake, MI 48390-0186
Metalife Industries (See Mahovsky's Metalife)
Michael's Antiques, Box 591, Waldoboro, ME 04572
Michaels Of Oregon, Co., P.O. Box 1690, Oregon City, OR 97045 www.michaels-oregon.com
Micro Sight Co., 242 Harbor Blvd., Belmont, CA 94002 / 415-591-0769; FAX: 415-591-7531
Microfusion Alfa S.A., Paseo San Andres N8, P.O. Box 271, Eibar, 20600 SPAIN / 34-43-11-89-16; FAX: 34-43-11-40-38
Mid-America Recreation, Inc., 1328 5th Ave., Moline, IL 61265 / 309-764-5089; FAX: 309-764-5089 fmilcusguns@aol.com www.midamericarecreation.com
Middlebrooks Custom Shop, 7366 Colonial Trail East, Surry, VA 23883 / 757-357-0881; FAX: 757-365-0442
Midway Arms, Inc., 5875 W. Van Horn Tavern Rd., Columbia, MO 65203 / 800-243-3220; or 573-445-6363; FAX: 573-446-1018
Midwest Gun Sport, 1108 Herbert Dr., Zebulon, NC 27597 / 919-269-5570
Midwest Sport Distributors, Box 129, Fayette, MO 65248
Mike Davis Products, 643 Loop Dr., Moses Lake, WA 98837 / 509-765-6178; or 509-766-7281
Mike Yee Custom Stocking, 29927 56 Pl. S., Auburn, WA 98001 / 253-839-3991
Military Armament Corp., P.O. Box 120, Mt. Zion Rd., Lingleville, TX 76461 / 817-965-3253

DIRECTORY

Manufacturer's Directory

Millennium Designed Muzzleloaders, PO Box 536, Routes 11 & 25, Limington, ME 04049 / 207-637-2316
Miller Arms, Inc., P.O. Box 260 Purl St., St. Onge, SD 57779 / 605-642-5160; FAX: 605-642-5160
Miller Custom, 210 E. Julia, Clinton, IL 61727 / 217-935-9362
Miller Single Trigger Mfg. Co., 6680 Rt. 5-20, P.O. Box 471, Bloomfield, NY 14469 / 585-657-6338
Millett Sights, 7275 Murdy Circle, Adm. Office, Huntington Beach, CA 92647 / 714-842-5575 or 800-645-5388; FAX: 714-843-5707
Mills Jr., Hugh B., 3615 Canterbury Rd., New Bern, NC 28560 / 919-637-4631
Milstor Corp., 80-975 Indio Blvd. C-7, Indio, CA 92201 / 760-775-9998; FAX: 760-775-5229 milstor@webtv.net
Minute Man High Tech Industries, 10611 Canyon Rd. E., Suite 151, Puyallup, WA 98373 / 800-233-2734
Mirador Optical Corp., P.O. Box 11614, Marina Del Rey, CA 90295-7614 / 310-821-5587; FAX: 310-305-0386
Mitchell, Jack, c/o Geoff Gaebe, Addieville East Farm, 200 Pheasant Dr., Mapleville, RI 02839 / 401-568-3185
Mitchell Bullets, R.F., 430 Walnut St., Westernport, MD 21562
Mitchell Mfg. Corp., P.O. Box 9295, Fountain Valley, CA 92728 / 714-444-2220
Mitchell Optics, Inc., 2072 CR 1100 N, Sidney, IL 61877 / 217-688-2219; or 217-621-3018; FAX: 217-688-2505 mitche1@attglobal.net
Mitchell's Accuracy Shop, 68 Greenridge Dr., Stafford, VA 22554 / 703-659-0165
Mitchell's Mauser, P.O. Box 9295, Fountain Valley, CA 92728 / 714-979-7663; FAX: 714-899-3660
MI-TE Bullets, 1396 Ave. K, Ellsworth, KS 67439 / 785-472-4575; FAX: 785-472-5579
Mittleman, William, P.O. Box 65, Etna, CA 96027
Mixson Corp., 7635 W. 28th Ave., Hialeah, FL 33016 / 305-821-5190; or 800-327-0078; FAX: 305-558-9318
MJK Gunsmithing, Inc., 417 N. Huber Ct., E. Wenatchee, WA 98802 / 509-884-7683
MKS Supply, Inc. (See Hi-Point Firearms)
MMC, 5050 E. Belknap St., Haltom City, TX 76117 / 817-831-9557; FAX: 817-834-5508
MOA Corporation, 2451 Old Camden Pike, Eaton, OH 45320 / 937-456-3669 www.moaguns
Modern Gun Repair School, PO Box 846, Saint Albans, VT 05478 / 802-524-2223; FAX: 802-524-2053 jfwp@dlilearn.com www.mgsinfoadlifearn.com
Modern Muzzleloading, Inc., P.O. Box 130, Centerville, IA 52544 / 515-856-2626
Moeller, Steve, 1213 4th St., Fulton, IL 61252 / 815-589-2300
Mogul Co./Life Jacket, 500 N. Kimball Rd., Ste. 109, South Lake, TX 76092
Molin Industries, Tru-Nord Division, P.O. Box 365, 204 North 9th St., Brainerd, MN 56401 / 218-829-2870
Monell Custom Guns, 228 Red Mills Rd., Pine Bush, NY 12566 / 914-744-3021
Moneymaker Guncraft Corp., 1420 Military Ave., Omaha, NE 68131 / 402-556-0226
Montana Armory, Inc. (See C. Sharps Arms Co. Inc.), 100 Centennial Dr., P.O. Box 885, Big Timber, MT 59011 / 406-932-4353; FAX: 406-932-4443
Montana Outfitters, Lewis E. Yearout, 308 Riverview Dr. E., Great Falls, MT 59404 / 406-761-0859; or 406-727-4560
Montana Precision Swaging, P.O. Box 4746, Butte, MT 59702 / 406-494-0600; FAX: 406-494-0600
Montana Rifleman, Inc., 2593A Hwy. 2 East, Kalispell, MT 59901 / 406-755-4867
Montana Vintage Arms, 2354 Bear Canyon Rd., Bozeman, MT 59715
Morini (See U.S. Importers-Mandall Shooting Supply)
Morrison Custom Rifles, J. W., 4015 W Sharon, Phoenix, AZ 85029 / 602-978-3754
Morrison Precision, 6719 Calle Mango, Hereford, AZ 85615 / 520-378-6207 morprec@c2i2.com
Morrow, Bud, 11 Hillside Lane, Sheridan, WY 82801-9729 / 307-674-8360
Morton Booth Co., P.O. Box 123, Joplin, MO 64802 / 417-673-1962; FAX: 417-673-3642
Mo's Competitor Supplies (See MCS, Inc.)
Moss Double Tone, Inc., P.O. Box 1112, 2101 S. Kentucky, Sedalia, MO 65301 / 816-827-0827
Mountain Plains Industries, 3720 Otter Place, Lynchburg, VA 24503 / 800-687-3000; FAX: 434-845-6594 mpitargets@cstone.net
Mountain State Muzzleloading Supplies, Inc., Box 154-1, Rt. 2, Williamstown, WV 26187 / 304-375-7842; FAX: 304-375-3737
Mowrey Gun Works, P.O. Box 246, Waldron, IN 46182 / 317-525-6181; FAX: 317-525-9595
Mowrey's Guns & Gunsmithing, 119 Fredericks St., Canajoharie, NY 13317 / 518-673-3483
MPC, P.O. Box 450, McMinnville, TN 37110-0450 / 615-473-5513; FAX: 615-473-5516 thebox@blomand.net www.mpc-thebox.com
MPI Stocks, PO Box 83266, Portland, OR 97283 / 503-226-1215; FAX: 503-226-2661
MSR Targets, P.O. Box 1042, West Covina, CA 91793 / 818-331-7840
MTM Molded Products Co., Inc., 3370 Obco Ct., Dayton, OH 45414 / 937-890-7461; FAX: 937-890-1747
Mulberry House Publishing, P.O. Box 2180, Apache Junction, AZ 85217 / 888-738-1567; FAX: 480-671-1015
Mulhern, Rick, Rt. 5, Box 152, Rayville, LA 71269 / 318-728-2688
Mullins Ammunition, Rt. 2 Box 304N, Clintwood, VA 24228 / 276-926-6772; FAX: 276-926-6092 mammo@extremeshockusa.com www.extremeshockusa
Mullis Guncraft, 3523 Lawyers Road E., Monroe, NC 28110 / 704-283-6683
Multiplex International, 26 S. Main St., Concord, NH 03301 FAX: 603-796-2223
Multipropulseurs, La Bertrandiere, 42580, FRANCE / 77 74 01 30; FAX: 77 93 19 34
Mundy, Thomas A., 69 Robbins Road, Somerville, NJ 08876 / 201-722-2199
Murmur Corp., 2823 N. Westmoreland Ave., Dallas, TX 75222 / 214-630-5400
Murphy, R.R. Murphy Co., Inc. See: MURPHY, R.R. CO., INC.
Murphy, R.R. Co., Inc., R.R. Murphy Co., Inc. Murphy, P.O. Box 102, Ripley, TN 38063 / 901-635-4003; FAX: 901-635-2320
Murray State College, 1 Murray Campus St., Tishomingo, OK 73460 / 508-371-2371 darnold@mscok.edu
Muscle Products Corp., 112 Fennell Dr., Butler, PA 16002 / 800-227-7049; or 724-283-0567; FAX: 724-283-8310 mpc@mpc_home.com www.mpc_home.com
Muzzleloaders Etcetera, Inc., 9901 Lyndale Ave. S., Bloomington, MN 55420 / 952-884-1161 www.muzzleloaders-etcetera.com
MWG Co., P.O. Box 971202, Miami, FL 33197 / 800-428-9394; or 305-253-8393; FAX: 305-232-1247

N

N.B.B., Inc., 24 Elliot Rd., Sterling, MA 01564 / 508-422-7538; or 800-942-9444
N.C. Ordnance Co., P.O. Box 3254, Wilson, NC 27895 / 919-237-2440; FAX: 919-243-9845
Nagel's Custom Bullets, 100 Scott St., Baytown, TX 77520-2849
Nalpak, 1937-C Friendship Drive, El Cajon, CA 92020 / 619-258-1200
Nastoff, Steve. See: NASTOFFS 45 SHOP, INC.
Nastoffs 45 Shop, Inc., Steve Nastoff, 1057 Laverne Dr., Youngstown, OH 44511
National Bullet Co., 1585 E. 361 St., Eastlake, OH 44095 / 216-951-1854; FAX: 216-951-7761
National Target Co., 4690 Wyaconda Rd., Rockville, MD 20852 / 800-827-7060 or 301-770-7060; FAX: 301-770-7892
Nationwide Airgun Repair, 2310 Windsor Forest Dr., Louisville, KY 40272 / 502-937-2614; FAX: 812-637-1463 shortshoestring@insightbb.com
Naval Ordnance Works, Rt. 2, Box 919, Sheperdstown, WV 25443 / 304-876-0998
Navy Arms Co., 219 Lawn St., Martinsburg, WV 25401 / 304-262-9870; FAX: 304-262-1658
Navy Arms Company, Valmore J. Forgett Jr., 815 22nd Street, Union City, NJ 07087 / 201-863-7100; FAX: 201-863-8770 info@navyarms.com www.navyarms.com
NCP Products, Inc., 3500 12th St. N.W., Canton, OH 44708 / 330-456-5130; FAX: 330-456-5234
Necessary Concepts, Inc., P.O. Box 571, Deer Park, NY 11729 / 516-667-8509; FAX: 516-667-8588
NEI Handtools, Inc., 10960 Gary Player Dr., El Paso, TX 79935
Neil A. Jones Custom Products, 17217 Brookhouser Road, Saegertown, PA 16433 / 814-763-2769; FAX: 814-763-4228
Nelson, Gary K., 975 Terrace Dr., Oakdale, CA 95361 / 209-847-4590
Nelson, Stephen. See: NELSON'S CUSTOM GUNS, INC.
Nelson's Custom Guns, Inc., Stephen Nelson, 7430 Valley View Dr. N.W., Corvallis, OR 97330 / 541-745-5232 nelsons-custom@attbi.com
Nesci Enterprises Inc., P.O. Box 119, Summit St., East Hampton, CT 06424 / 203-267-2588
Nesika Bay Precision, 22239 Big Valley Rd., Poulsbo, WA 98370 / 206-697-3830
Nettestad Gun Works, 38962 160th Avenue, Pelican Rapids, MN 56572 / 218-863-4301
Neumann GmbH, Am Galgenberg 6, 90575, GERMANY / 09101/8258; FAX: 09101/6356
Nevada Pistol Academy, Inc., 4610 Blue Diamond Rd., Las Vegas, NV 89139 / 702-897-1100
New England Ammunition Co., 1771 Post Rd. East, Suite 223, Westport, CT 06880 / 203-254-8048
New England Arms Co., Box 278, Lawrence Lane, Kittery Point, ME 03905 / 207-439-0593; FAX: 207-439-0525 info@newenglandarms.com www.newenglandarms.com
New England Custom Gun Service, 438 Willow Brook Rd., Plainfield, NH 03781 / 603-469-3450; FAX: 603-469-3471 bestguns@cyborportal.net www.newenglandcustom.com
New Orleans Jewelers Supply Co., 206 Charters St., New Orleans, LA 70130 / 504-523-3839; FAX: 504-523-3836
New SKB Arms Co., C.P.O. Box 1401, Tokyo, JAPAN / 81-3-3943-9550; FAX: 81-3-3943-0695
New Ultra Light Arms, LLC, P.O. Box 340, Granville, WV 26534
Newark Electronics, 4801 N. Ravenswood Ave., Chicago, IL 60640
Newell, Robert H., 55 Coyote, Los Alamos, NM 87544 / 505-662-7135
Newman Gunshop, 2035 Chester Ave. #411, Ottumwa, IA 52501-3715 / 515-937-5775
Nicholson Custom, 17285 Thornlay Road, Hughesville, MO 65334 / 816-826-8746
Nickels, Paul R., 4328 Seville St., Las Vegas, NV 89121 / 702-435-5318
Nicklas, Ted, 5504 Hegel Rd., Goodrich, MI 48438 / 810-797-4493
Niemi Engineering, W. B., Box 126 Center Rd., Greensboro, VT 05841 / 802-533-7180; FAX: 802-533-7141
Nikon, Inc., 1300 Walt Whitman Rd., Melville, NY 11747 / 516-547-8623; FAX: 516-547-0309
Nitex Gun Shop, P.O. Box 1706, Uvalde, TX 78801 / 830-278-8843
Noreen, Peter H., 5075 Buena Vista Dr., Belgrade, MT 59714 / 406-586-7383
Norica, Avnda Otaola, 16 Apartado 68, Eibar, SPAIN
Norinco, 7A Yun Tan N, Beijing, CHINA
Norincoptics (See BEC, Inc.)
Norma Precision AB (See U.S. Importers-Dynamit)
Normark Corp., 10395 Yellow Circle Dr., Minnetonka, MN 55343-9101 / 612-933-7060; FAX: 612-933-0046
North American Arms, Inc., 2150 South 950 East, Provo, UT 84606-6285 / 800-821-5783; or 801-374-9990; FAX: 801-374-9998
North American Correspondence Schools The Gun Pro, Oak & Pawney St., Scranton, PA 18515 / 717-342-7701
North American Shooting Systems, P.O. Box 306, Osoyoos, BC V0H 1V0 CANADA / 250-495-3131; FAX: 250-495-3131 rifle@cablerocket.com
North Devon Firearms Services, 3 North St., Braunton, EX33 1AJ ENGLAND / 01271 813624; FAX: 01271 813624
North Mountain Pine Training Center (See Executive
North Star West, P.O. Box 488, Glencoe, CA 95232 / 209-293-7010 northstarwest.com
Northern Precision, 329 S. James St., Carthage, NY 13619 / 315-493-1711
Northlake Outdoor Footwear, P.O. Box 10, Franklin, TN 37065-0010 / 615-794-1556; FAX: 615-790-8005
Northside Gun Shop, 2725 NW 109th, Oklahoma City, OK 73120 / 405-840-2353
Northwest Arms, 26884 Pearl Rd., Parma, ID 83660 / 208-722-6771; FAX: 208-722-1062
No-Sho Mfg. Co., 10727 Glenfield Ct., Houston, TX 77096 / 713-723-5332
Nosler, Inc., P.O. Box 671, Bend, OR 97709 / 800-285-3701; or 541-382-3921; FAX: 541-388-4667 www.nosler.com
Novak's, Inc., 1206 1/2 30th St., P.O. Box 4045, Parkersburg, WV 26101 / 304-485-9295; FAX: 304-428-6722
Nowlin Mfg. Co., 20622 S 4092 Rd., Claremore, OK 74017 / 918-342-0689; FAX: 918-342-0624 nowlinguns@msn.com nowlinguns.com
NRI Gunsmith School, P.O. Box 182968, Columbus, OH 43218-2968
Nu-Line Guns,Inc., 1053 Caulks Hill Rd., Harvester, MO 63304 / 314-441-4500; or 314-447-4501; FAX: 314-447-5018
Null Holsters Ltd. K.L., 161 School St NW, Resaca, GA 30735 / 706-625-5643; FAX: 706-625-9392
Numrich Gun Parts Corporation, 226 Williams Lane, P.O. Box 299, West Hurley, NY 12491 / 866-686-7424; FAX: 877-GUNPART info@gunpartscorp.com www.@-gunparts.com
Nygord Precision Products, Inc., P.O. Box 12578, Prescott, AZ 86304 / 928-717-2315; FAX: 928-717-2198 nygords@northlink.com www.nygordprecision.com

O

O.F. Mossberg & Sons, Inc., 7 Grasso Ave., North Haven, CT 06473 / 203-230-5300; FAX: 203-230-5420
Oakman Turkey Calls, RD 1, Box 825, Harrisonville, PA 17228 / 717-485-4620
Obermeyer Rifled Barrels, 23122 60th St., Bristol, WI 53104 / 262-843-3537; FAX: 262-843-2129
October Country Muzzleloading, P.O. Box 969, Dept. GD, Hayden, ID 83835 / 208-772-2068; FAX: 208-772-9230 ocinfo@octobercountry.com www.octobercountry.com
Oehler Research, Inc., P.O. Box 9135, Austin, TX 78766 / 512-327-6900; or 800-531-5125; FAX: 512-327-6903 www.oehler-research.com
Oil Rod and Gun Shop, 69 Oak St., East Douglas, MA 01516 / 508-476-3687
OK Weber, Inc., P.O. Box 7485, Eugene, OR 97401 / 541-747-0458; FAX: 541-747-5927 okweber@pacinfo www.okweber.com
Oker's Engraving, P.O. Box 126, Shawnee, CO 80475 / 303-838-6042
Oklahoma Ammunition Co., 3701A S. Harvard Ave., No. 367, Tulsa, OK 74135-2265 / 918-396-3187; FAX: 918-396-4270
Oklahoma Leather Products, Inc., 500 26th NW, Miami, OK 74354 / 918-542-6651; FAX: 918-542-6653
Olathe Gun Shop, 716-A South Rogers Road, Olathe, KS 66062 / 913-782-6900; FAX: 913-782-6902 info@olathegunshop.com www.olathegunshop.com
Old Wagon Bullets, 32 Old Wagon Rd., Wilton, CT 06897
Old West Bullet Moulds, J Ken Chapman, P.O. Box 519, Flora Vista, NM 87415 / 505-334-6970
Old West Reproductions, Inc. R.M. Bachman, 446 Florence S. Loop, Florence, MT 59833 / 406-273-2615; FAX: 406-273-2615 rick@oldwestreproductions.com www.oldwestreproductions.com
Old Western Scrounger Ammunition Inc., 50 Industrial Parkway, Carson City, NV 89706 / 775-246-2091; FAX: 775-246-2095 www.ows-ammunition.com
Old World Gunsmithing, 2901 SE 122nd St., Portland, OR 97236 / 503-760-7681
Old World Oil Products, 3827 Queen Ave. N., Minneapolis, MN 55412 / 612-522-5037
Ole Frontier Gunsmith Shop, 2617 Hwy. 29 S., Cantonment, FL 32533 / 904-477-8074
Olson, Myron, 989 W. Kemp, Watertown, SD 57201 / 605-886-9787
Olson, Vic, 5002 Countryside Dr., Imperial, MO 63052 / 314-296-8086
Olympic Arms Inc., 620-626 Old Pacific Hwy. SE, Olympia, WA 98513 / 360-456-3471; FAX: 360-491-3447 info@olyarms.com www.olyarms.com

MANUFACTURER'S DIRECTORY

Olympic Optical Co., P.O. Box 752377, Memphis, TN 38175-2377 / 901-794-3890; or 800-238-7120; FAX: 901-794-0676 80
Omega Sales, P.O. Box 1066, Mt. Clemens, MI 48043 / 810-469-7323; FAX: 810-469-0425
100 Straight Products, Inc., P.O. Box 6148, Omaha, NE 68106 / 402-556-1055; FAX: 402-556-1055
One Of A Kind, 15610 Purple Sage, San Antonio, TX 78255 / 512-695-3364
One Ragged Hole, P.O. Box 13624, Tallahassee, FL 32317-3624
Op-Tec, P.O. Box L632, Langhorn, PA 19047 / 215-757-5037; FAX: 215-757-7097
Optical Services Co., P.O. Box 1174, Santa Teresa, NM 88008-1174 / 505-589-3833
Orchard Park Enterprise, P.O. Box 563, Orchard Park, NY 14127 / 616-656-0356
Oregon Arms, Inc. (See Rogue Rifle Co., Inc.)
Oregon Trail Bullet Company, PO Box 529, Dept. P, Baker City, OR 97814 / 800-811-0548; FAX: 514-523-1803
Original Box, Inc., 700 Linden Ave., York, PA 17404 / 717-854-2897; FAX: 717-845-4276
Original Deer Formula Co., The, P.O. Box 1705, Dickson, TN 37056 / 800-874-6965; FAX: 615-446-0646 deerformula1@aol.com www.deerformula
Orion Rifle Barrel Co., RR2, 137 Cobler Village, Kalispell, MT 59901 / 406-257-5649
Otis Technology, Inc., RR 1 Box 84, Boonville, NY 13309 / 315-942-3320
Ottmar, Maurice, Box 657, 113 E. Fir, Coulee City, WA 99115 / 509-632-5717
Outa-Site Gun Carriers, 219 Market St., Laredo, TX 78040 / 210-722-4678; or 800-880-9715; FAX: 210-726-4858
Outdoor Edge Cutlery Corp., 4699 Nautilus Ct. S. Ste. 503, Boulder, CO 80301-5310 / 303-652-8212; FAX: 303-652-8238
Outdoor Enthusiast, 3784 W. Woodland, Springfield, MO 65807 / 417-883-9841
Outdoor Sports Headquarters, Inc., 967 Watertower Ln., West Carrollton, OH 45449 / 513-865-5855; FAX: 513-865-5962
Outers Laboratories Div. of ATK, Route 2, P.O. Box 39, Onalaska, WI 54650 / 608-781-5800; FAX: 608-781-0368
Ox-Yoke Originals, Inc., 34 Main St., Milo, ME 04463 / 800-231-8313; or 207-943-7351; FAX: 207-943-2416
Ozark Gun Works, 11830 Cemetery Rd., Rogers, AR 72756 / 479-631-1024; FAX: 479-631-1024 ogw@hotmail.com www.eocities.com/ocarkgunworks

P

P&M Sales & Services, LLC, 4697 Tote Rd. Bldg. H-B, Comins, MI 48619 / 989-848-8364; FAX: 989-848-8364 info@pmsales-online.com
P.A.C.T., Inc., P.O. Box 531525, Grand Prairie, TX 75053 / 214-641-0049
P.S.M.G. Gun Co., 10 Park Ave., Arlington, MA 02174 / 781-646-1699; FAX: 781-643-7212 psmg2@aol.com
Pachmayr Div. Lyman Products, 475 Smith St., Middletown, CT 06457 / 860-632-2020; or 800-225-9626; FAX: 860-632-1699 lymansales@cshore.com www.pachmayr.com
Pacific Armament Corp, 4813 Enterprise Way, Unit K, Modesto, CA 95356 / 209-545-2800 gunsparts@att.net
Pacific Rifle Co., P.O. Box 841, Carlton, OR 97111 / 503-852-6276 pacificrifle@aol.com
PAC-NOR Barreling, 99299 Overlook Rd., P.O. Box 6188, Brookings, OR 97415 / 503-469-7330; FAX: 503-469-7331 info@pac-nor.com www.pac-nor.com
Paco's (See Small Custom Mould & Bullet Co.)
Page Custom Bullets, P.O. Box 25, Port Moresby, NEW GUINEA
Pagel Gun Works, Inc., 2 SE 1st St., Grand Rapids, MN 55744
Pager Pal, 200 W Pleasantview, Hurst, TX 76054 / 800-561-1603; FAX: 817-285-8769 www.pagerpal.com
Paintball Games International Magazine Aceville, Castle House 97 High St., Essex, ENGLAND / 011-44-206-564840
Palsa Outdoor Products, P.O. Box 81336, Lincoln, NE 68501 / 402-488-5288; FAX: 402-488-2321
Pansch, Robert F, 1004 Main St. #10, Neenah, WI 54956 / 920-725-8175
Paragon Sales & Services, Inc., 2501 Theodore St., Crest Hill, IL 60435-1613 / 815-725-9212; FAX: 815-725-8974
Para-Ordnance Mfg., Inc., 980 Tapscott Rd., Scarborough, ON M1X 1E7 CANADA / 416-297-7855; FAX: 416-297-1289
Para-Ordnance, Inc., 1919 NE 45th St., Ste 215, Ft. Lauderdale, FL 33308 info@paraord.com www.paraord.com
Pardini Armi Srl, Via Italica 154, 55043, Lido Di Camaiore Lu, ITALY / 584-90121; FAX: 584-90122
Paris, Frank J., 17417 Pershing St., Livonia, MI 48152-3822
Parker & Sons Shooting Supply, 9337 Smoky Row Road, Strawberry Plains, TN 37871 / 865-933-3286; FAX: 865-932-8586
Parker Gun Finishes, 9337 Smokey Row Rd., Strawberry Plains, TN 37871 / 865-933-3286; FAX: 865-932-8586
Parsons Optical Mfg. Co., PO Box 192, Ross, OH 45061 / 513-867-0820; FAX: 513-867-8380 psscopes@concentric.net
Partridge Sales Ltd., John, Trent Meadows, Rugeley, ENGLAND
Pasadena Gun Center, 206 E. Shaw, Pasadena, TX 77506 / 713-472-0417; FAX: 713-472-1322
Passive Bullet Traps, Inc. (See Savage Range Systems, Inc.)
Paterson Gunsmithing, 438 Main St., Paterson, NJ 07502 / 201-345-4100
Pathfinder Sports Leather, 2920 E. Chambers St., Phoenix, AZ 85040 / 602-276-0016
Patrick W. Price Bullets, 16520 Worthley Drive, San Lorenzo, CA 94580 / 510-278-1547
Pattern Control, 114 N. Third St., P.O. Box 462105, Garland, TX 75046 / 214-494-3551; FAX: 214-272-8447
Paul A. Harris Hand Engraving, 113 Rusty Lane, Boerne, TX 78006-5746 / 512-391-5121
Paul and Sharon Dressel, 209 N. 92nd Ave., Yakima, WA 98908 / 509-966-9233; FAX: 509-966-3365 dressels@nwinfo.net www.dressels.com
Paul D. Hillmer Custom Gunstocks, 7251 Hudson Heights, Hudson, IA 50643 / 319-988-3941
Paul Jones Moulds, 4901 Telegraph Rd., Los Angeles, CA 90022 / 213-262-1510
Paulsen Gunstocks, Rt. 71, Box 11, Chinook, MT 59523 / 406-357-3403
Pawling Mountain Club, Keith Lupton, PO Box 573, Pawling, NY 12564 / 914-855-3825
Paxton Quigley's Personal Protection Strategies, 9903 Santa Monica Blvd., 300, Beverly Hills, CA 90212 / 310-281-1762 www.defend-net.com/paxton
Payne Photography, Robert, Robert, P.O. Box 141471, Austin, TX 78714 / 512-272-4554
Peacemaker Specialists, P.O. Box 157, Whitmore, CA 96096 / 530-472-3438 www.peacemakerspecialists.com
Pearce Grip, Inc., P.O. Box 40367, Fort Worth, TX 76140 / 817-568-9704; FAX: 817-568-9707 info@pearcegrip.com www.pearcegrip.com
Pease Accuracy, Bob, P.O. Box 310787, New Braunfels, TX 78131 / 210-625-1342
PECAR Herbert Schwarz GmbH, Kreuzbergstrasse 6, 10965, Berlin, GERMANY / 004930-785-7383; FAX: 004930-785-1934 michael.schwart@pecar-berlin.de www.pecar-berlin.de
Pecatonica River Longrifle, 5205 Nottingham Dr., Rockford, IL 61111 / 815-968-1995; FAX: 815-968-1996
Pedersen, C. R., 2717 S. Pere Marquette Hwy., Ludington, MI 49431 / 231-843-2061; FAX: 231-845-7695 fega@fega.com
Pedersen, Rex C., 2717 S. Pere Marquette Hwy., Ludington, MI 49431 / 231-843-2061; FAX: 231-845-7695 fega@fega.com
Peifer Rifle Co., P.O. Box 220, Nokomis, IL 62075
Pejsa Ballistics, 1314 Marquette Ave., Apt 906, Minneapolis, MN 55403 / 612-332-5073; FAX: 612-332-5204 pejsa@sprintmail.com pejsa.com
Pelaire Products, 5346 Bonky Ct., W. Palm Beach, FL 33415 / 561-439-0691; FAX: 561-967-0052
Peltor, Inc. (See Aero Peltor)
PEM's Mfg. Co., 5063 Waterloo Rd., Atwater, OH 44201 / 216-947-3721
Pence Precision Barrels, 7567 E. 900 S., S. Whitley, IN 46787 / 219-839-4745
Pendleton Royal, c/o Swingler Buckland Ltd., 4/7 Highgate St., Birmingham, ENGLAND / 44 121 440 3060; or 44 121 446 5898; FAX: 44 121 446 4165
Pendleton Woolen Mills, P.O. Box 3030, 220 N.W. Broadway, Portland, OR 97208 / 503-226-4801
Penn Bullets, P.O. Box 756, Indianola, PA 15051
Pennsylvania Gun Parts Inc., RR 7 Box 150, Mount Pleasant, PA 15666
Pennsylvania Gunsmith School, 812 Ohio River Blvd., Avalon, Pittsburgh, PA 15202 / 412-766-1812; FAX: 412-766-0855 pgs@pagunsmith.com www.pagunsmith.com
Penrod Precision, 312 College Ave., P.O. Box 307, N. Manchester, IN 46962 / 260-982-8385; FAX: 260-982-1819
Pentax Corp., 35 Inverness Dr. E., Englewood, CO 80112 / 303-799-8000; FAX: 303-790-1131
Pentheny de Pentheny, c/o H.P. Okelly, 321 S. Main St., Sebastopol, CA 95472 / 707-824-1637; FAX: 707-824-1637
Perazone-Gunsmith, Brian, Cold Spring Rd., Roxbury, NY 12474 / 607-326-4088; FAX: 607-326-3140 bpgunsmith@catskill.net www.bpgunsmith@catskill.net
Perazzi U.S.A. Inc., 1010 West Tenth, Azusa, CA 91702 / 626-334-1234; FAX: 626-334-0344 perazziusa@aol.com
Performance Specialists, 308 Eanes School Rd., Austin, TX 78746 / 512-327-0119
Perugini Visini & Co. S.r.l., Via Camprelle, 126, 25080 Nuvolera, ITALY / 30-6897535; FAX: 30-6897821 peruvisi@virgilia.it
Pete de Coux Auction House, HC 30 Box 932 G, Prescott, AZ 86305-7447 / 928-776-8285; FAX: 928-776-8276 pdbullets@commspeed.net
Pete Mazur Restoration, 13083 Drummer Way, Grass Valley, CA 95949 / 530-268-2412; FAX: 530-268-2412
Pete Rickard, Inc., 115 Roy Walsh Rd, Cobleskill, NY 12043 / 518-234-2731; FAX: 518-234-2454 rickard@telenet.net www.peterickard.com
Peter Dyson & Son Ltd., 3 Cuckoo Lane, Honley, Holmfirth, Yorkshire, HD9 6AS ENGLAND / 44-1484-661062; FAX: 44-1484-663709 peter@peterdyson.co.uk www.peterdyson.co.uk
Peter Hale/Engraver, 800 E. Canyon Rd., Spanish Fork, UT 84660 / 801-798-8215
Peters Stahl GmbH, Stettiner Strasse 42, D-33106, Paderborn, GERMANY / 05251-750025; FAX: 05251-75611
Peterson Gun Shop, Inc., A.W., 4255 W. Old U.S. 441, Mt. Dora, FL 32757-3299 / 352-383-4258; FAX: 352-735-1001
Petro-Explo Inc., 7650 U.S. Hwy. 287, Suite 100, Arlington, TX 76017 / 817-478-8888
Pettinger Books, Gerald, 47827 300th Ave., Russell, IA 50238 / 641-535-2239 gpettinger@lisco.com
Pflumm Mfg. Co., 10662 Widmer Rd., Lenexa, KS 66215 / 800-888-4867; FAX: 913-451-7857
PFRB Co., P.O. Box 1242, Bloomington, IL 61702 / 309-473-3964; or 800-914-5464; FAX: 309-473-2161
Philip S. Olt Co., P.O. Box 550, 12662 Fifth St., Pekin, IL 61554 / 309-348-3633; FAX: 309-348-3300
Phillippi Custom Bullets, Justin, P.O. Box 773, Ligonier, PA 15658 / 724-238-2962; FAX: 724-238-9671 jrp@wpa.net http://www.wpa.net~jrphil
Phillips & Rogers, Inc., 100 Hilbig #C, Conroe, TX 77301 / 409-435-0011
Phoenix Arms, 4231 Brickell St., Ontario, CA 91761 / 909-937-6900; FAX: 909-937-0060
Photronic Systems Engineering Company, 6731 Via De La Reina, Bonsall, CA 92003 / 619-758-8000
Piedmont Community College, P.O. Box 1197, Roxboro, NC 27573 / 336-599-1181; FAX: 336-597-3817 www.piedmont.cc.nc.us
Pierce Pistols, 55 Sorrellwood Lane, Sharpsburg, GA 30277-9523 / 404-253-8192
Pietta (See U.S. Importers-Navy Arms Co, Taylor's
Pilgrim Pewter, Inc. (See Bell Originals Inc. Sid)
Pilkington, Scott (See Little Trees Ramble)
Pine Technical College, 1100 4th St., Pine City, MN 55063 / 800-521-7463; FAX: 612-629-6766
Pinetree Bullets, 133 Skeena St., Kitimat, BC V8C 1Z1 CANADA / 604-632-3768; FAX: 604-632-3768
Pioneer Arms Co., 355 Lawrence Rd., Broomall, PA 19008 / 215-356-5203
Piotti (See U.S. Importer-Moore & Co., Wm. Larkin)
Piquette, Paul. See: PIQUETTE'S CUSTOM ENGRAVING
Piquette's Custom Engraving, Paul R. Piquette, 80 Bradford Dr., Feeding Hills, MA 01030 / 413-789-4582; FAX: 413-786-8118 ppiquette@aol.com www.pistoldynamics.com
Plaza Cutlery, Inc., 3333 Bristol, 161 South Coast Plaza, Costa Mesa, CA 92626 / 714-549-3932
Plum City Ballistic Range, N2162 80th St., Plum City, WI 54761 / 715-647-2539
PlumFire Press, Inc., 30-A Grove Ave., Patchogue, NY 11772-4112 / 800-695-7246; FAX: 516-758-4071
PMC/Eldorado Cartridge Corp., P.O. Box 62508, 12801 U.S. Hwy. 95 S., Boulder City, NV 89005 / 702-294-0025; FAX: 702-294-0121 kbauer@pmcammo.com www.pmcammo.com
Poburka, Philip (See Bison Studios)
Pointing Dog Journal, Village Press Publications, P.O. Box 968, Dept. PGD, Traverse City, MI 49685 / 800-272-3246; FAX: 616-946-3289
Police Bookshelf, PO Box 122, Concord, NH 03301 / 603-224-6814; FAX: 603-226-3554
Polywad, Inc., P.O. Box 7916, Macon, GA 31209 / 478-477-0669; or 800-998-0669 FAX: 478-477-0666 polywadmpb@aol.com www.polywad.com
Ponsness/Warren, 768 Ohio St., Rathdrum, ID 83858 / 800-732-0706; FAX: 208-687-2233
Pony Express Reloaders, 608 E. Co. Rd. D, Suite 3, St. Paul, MN 55117 / 612-483-9406; FAX: 612-483-9884
Pony Express Sport Shop, 23404 Lyons Ave., PMB 448, Newhall, CA 91321-2511 / 818-895-1231
Potts, Wayne E., 912 Poplar St., Denver, CO 80220 / 303-355-5462
Powder Horn Ltd., PO Box 565, Glenview, IL 60025 / 305-565-6060
Powell & Son (Gunmakers) Ltd., William, 35-37 Carrs Lane, Birmingham, B4 7SX ENGLAND / 121-643-0689; FAX: 121-631-3504 sales@william-powell.co.uk www.william-powell.co.uk
Powell Agency, William, 22 Circle Dr., Bellmore, NY 11710 / 516-679-1158
Power Custom, Inc., 29739 Hwy. J, Gravois Mills, MO 65037 / 573-372-5684; FAX: 573-372-5799 rwpowers@laurie.net www.powercustom.com
Power Plus Enterprises, Inc., PO Box 38, Warm Springs, GA 31830 / 706-655-2132
Powley Computer (See Hutton Rifle Ranch)
Practical Tools, Inc., 7067 Easton Rd., P.O. Box 133, Pipersville, PA 18947 / 215-766-7301, FAX. 215-766-8681
Prairie Gun Works, 1-761 Marion St., Winnipeg, MB R2J 0K6 CANADA / 204-231-2976; FAX: 204-231-8566
Prairie River Arms, 1220 N. Sixth St., Princeton, IL 61356 / 815-875-1616; or 800-445-1541; FAX: 815-875-1402
Pranger, Ed G., 1414 7th St., Anacortes, WA 98221 / 206-293-3488
Precision Airgun Sales, Inc., 5247 Warrensville Ctr Rd., Maple Hts., OH 44137 / 216-587-5005; FAX: 216-587-5005
Precision Cast Bullets, 101 Mud Creek Lane, Ronan, MT 59864 / 406-676-5135
Precision Delta Corp., PO Box 128, Ruleville, MS 38771 / 662-756-2810; FAX: 662-756-2590
Precision Firearm Finishing, 25 N.W. 44th Avenue, Des Moines, IA 50313 / 515-288-8680; FAX: 515-244-3925
Precision Gun Works, 104 Sierra Rd., Dept. GD, Kerrville, TX 78028 / 830-367-4587
Precision Reloading, Inc., P.O. Box 122, Stafford Springs, CT 06076 / 860-684-7979; FAX: 860-684-6788 info@precisionreloading.com www.precisionreloading.com
Precision Sales International, Inc., PO Box 1776, Westfield, MA 01086 / 413-562-5055; FAX: 413-562-5056 precision-sales.com
Precision Shooting, Inc., 222 McKee St., Manchester, CT 06040 / 860-645-8776; FAX: 860-643-8215 www.theaccuraterifle.com
Precision Small Arms Inc., 9272 Jeronimo Rd, Ste 121, Irvine, CA 92618 / 800-554-5515; or 949-768-3530; FAX: 949-768-4808 www.tcbebe.com
Precision Specialties, 131 Hendom Dr., Feeding Hills, MA 01030 / 413-786-3365; FAX: 413-786-3365

DIRECTORY

MANUFACTURER'S DIRECTORY

Precision Sport Optics, 15571 Producer Lane, Unit G, Huntington Beach, CA 92649 / 714-891-1309; FAX: 714-892-6920
Premier Reticles, 920 Breckinridge Lane, Winchester, VA 22601-6707 / 540-722-0601; FAX: 540-722-3522
Prescott Projectile Co., 1808 Meadowbrook Road, Prescott, AZ 86303
Preslik's Gunstocks, 4245 Keith Ln., Chico, CA 95926 / 916-891-8236
Price Bullets, Patrick W., 16520 Worthley Dr., San Lorenzo, CA 94580 / 510-278-1547
Prime Reloading, 30 Chiswick End, Meldreth, ROYSTON UK / 0763-260636
Primedia Publishing Co., 6420 Wilshire Blvd., Los Angeles, CA 90048 / 213-782-2000; FAX: 213-782-2867
Primos Hunting Calls, 4436 North State St., Ste. A-7, Jackson, MS 39206 / 601-366-1288; FAX: 601-362-3274 www.primos.com
PRL Bullets, c/o Blackburn Enterprises, 114 Stuart Rd., Ste. 110, Cleveland, TN 37312 / 423-559-0340
Pro Load Ammunition, Inc., 5180 E. Seltice Way, Post Falls, ID 83854 / 208-773-9444; FAX: 208-773-9441
Professional Gunsmiths of America, Rt 1 Box 224, Lexington, MO 64067 / 660-259-2636
Professional Hunter Supplies (See Star Custom Bullets), P.O. Box 608, 468 Main St., Ferndale, CA 95536 / 707-786-9140; FAX: 707-786-9117 wmebride@humboldt.com
PrOlixr Lubricants, P.O. Box 1348, Victorville, CA 92393 / 760-243-3129; FAX: 760-241-0148 prolix@accex.net www.prolixlubricant.com
Pro-Mark Div. of Wells Lamont, 6640 W. Touhy, Chicago, IL 60648 / 312-647-8200
Proofmark Corp., P.O. Box 357, Burgess, VA 22432 / 804-453-4337; FAX: 804-453-4337 proofmark@rivnet.net www.proofmarkbullets.com
Pro-Port Ltd., 41302 Executive Dr., Harrison Twp., MI 48045-1306 / 586-469-6727; FAX: 586-469-0425 e-mail@magnaport.com www.magnaport.com
Pro-Shot Products, Inc., P.O. Box 763, Taylorville, IL 62568 / 217-824-9133; FAX: 217-824-8861 www.proshotproducts.com
Protektor Model, 1-11 Bridge St., Galeton, PA 16922 / 814-435-2442 mail@protektormodel.com www.protektormodel.com
Prototech Industries, Inc., 10532 E Road, Delia, KS 66418 / 785-771-3571 prototec@grapevine.net
ProWare, Inc., 15847 NE Hancock St., Portland, OR 97230 / 503-239-0159
PWL Gunleather, P.O. Box 450432, Atlanta, GA 31145 / 800-960-4072; FAX: 770-822-1704 covert@pwlusa.com www.pwlusa.com
PWM Sales Ltd., N.D.F.S., Gowdall Lane, Pollington DN14 0AU, ENGLAND / 01405862688; FAX: 01405862622 Paulwelburn9@aol.com
Pyramyd Stone Inter. Corp., 2447 Suffolk Lane, Pepper Pike, OH 44124-4540

Q

Quack Decoy & Sporting Clays, 4 Ann & Hope Way, P.O. Box 98, Cumberland, RI 02864 / 401-723-8202; FAX: 401-722-5910
Quaker Boy, Inc., 5455 Webster Rd., Orchard Parks, NY 14127 / 716-662-3979; FAX: 716-662-9426
Quality Arms, Inc., Box 19477, Dept. GD, Houston, TX 77224 / 281-870-8377 arrieta2@excite.com www.gunshop.com
Quality Cartridge, P.O. Box 445, Hollywood, MD 20636 / 301-373-3719 www.qual-cart.com
Quality Custom Firearms, Stepehn Billeb, 22 Vista View Drive, Cody, WY 82414 / 307-587-4278; FAX: 307-587-4297 stevebilleb@wyoming.com
Quarton Beamshot, 4538 Centerview Dr., Ste. 149, San Antonio, TX 78228 / 800-520-8435; FAX: 210-735-1326 www.beamshot.com
Que Industries, Inc., PO Box 2471, Everett, WA 98203 / 425-303-9088; FAX: 206-514-3266 queinfo@queindustries.com
Queen Cutlery Co., PO Box 500, Franklinville, NY 14737 / 800-222-5233; FAX: 800-299-2618

R

R&C Knives & Such, 2136 CANDY CANE WALK, Manteca, CA 95336-9501 / 209-239-3722; FAX: 209-825-6947
R&D Gun Repair, Kenny Howell, RR1 Box 283, Beloit, WI 53511
R&J Gun Shop, 337 S. Humbolt St., Canyon City, OR 97820 / 541-575-2130 rjgunshop@highdestertnet.com
R&S Industries Corp., 8255 Brentwood Industrial Dr., St. Louis, MO 63144 / 314-781-5169 ron@miraclepolishingcloth.com www.miraclepolishingcloth.com
R. Murphy Co., Inc., 13 Groton-Harvard Rd., P.O. Box 376, Ayer, MA 01432 / 617-772-3481 www.r.murphyknives.com
R.A. Wells Custom Gunsmith, 3452 1st Ave., Racine, WI 53402 / 414-639-5223
R.E. Seebeck Assoc., P.O. Box 59752, Dallas, TX 75229
R.E.I., P.O. Box 88, Tallevast, FL 34270 / 813-755-0085
R.E.T. Enterprises, 2608 S. Chestnut, Broken Arrow, OK 74012 / 918-251-GUNS; FAX: 918-251-0587
R.F. Mitchell Bullets, 430 Walnut St., Westernport, MD 21562
R.I.S. Co., Inc., 718 Timberlake Circle, Richardson, TX 75080 / 214-235-0933
R.T. Eastman Products, P.O. Box 1531, Jackson, WY 83001 / 307-733-3217; or 800-624-4311
Rabeno, Martin, 530 The Eagle Pass, Durango, CO 81301 / 970-382-0353 fancygun@aol.com
Radack Photography, Lauren, 21140 Jib Court L-12, Aventura, FL 33180 / 305-931-3110
Radiator Specialty Co., 1900 Wilkinson Blvd., P.O. Box 34689, Charlotte, NC 28234 / 800-438-6947; FAX: 800-421-9525
Radical Concepts, P.O. Box 1473, Lake Grove, OR 97035 / 503-538-7437
Rainier Ballistics, 4500 15th St. East, Tacoma, WA 98424 / 800-638-8722; FAX: 253-922-7854 sales@rainierballistics.com www.rainierballistics.com
Ralph Bone Engraving, 718 N. Atlanta St., Owasso, OK 74055 / 918-272-9745
Ram-Line ATK, P.O. Box 39, Onalaska, WI 54650
Ramon B. Gonzalez Guns, P.O. Box 370, Monticello, NY 12701 / 914-794-4515; FAX: 914-794-4515
Rampart International, 2781 W. MacArthur Blvd., B-283, Santa Ana, CA 92704 / 800-976-7240 or 714-557-6405
Ranch Products, P.O. Box 145, Malinta, OH 43535 / 313-277-3118; FAX: 313-565-8536
Randall-Made Knives, P.O. Box 1988, Orlando, FL 32802 / 407-855-8075
Randco UK, 286 Gipsy Rd., Welling, DA16 1JJ ENGLAND / 44 81 303 4118
Randolph Engineering, Inc., Ranger Shooting Glasses, 26 Thomas Patten Dr., Randolph, MA 02368 / 800-541-1405; FAX: 781-986-0337 sales@randolphusa.com www.randolphusa.com
Randy Duane Custom Stocks, 7822 Church St., Middletown, VA 22645-9521
Range Brass Products Company, P.O. Box 218, Rockport, TX 78381
Ransom International Corp., 1027 Spire Dr, Prescott, AZ 86302 / 520-778-7899; FAX: 520-778-7993 ransom@primenet.com www.ransom-intl.com
Rapine Bullet Mould Mfg. Co., 9503 Landis Lane, East Greenville, PA 18041 / 215-679-5413; FAX: 215-679-9795
Ravell Ltd., 289 Diputacion St., 08009, Barcelona, SPAIN / 34(3) 4874486; FAX: 34(3) 4881394
Ray Riling Arms Books Co., 6844 Gorsten St., Philadelphia, PA 19119 / 215-438-2456; FAX: 215-438-5395 sales@rayrilingarmsbooks.com www.rayrilingarmsbooks.com
Ray's Gunsmith Shop, 3199 Elm Ave., Grand Junction, CO 81504 / 970-434-6162; FAX: 970-434-6162
Raytech Div. of Lyman Products Corp., 475 Smith Street, Middletown, CT 06457-1541 / 860-632-2020 or 800-225-9626; FAX: 860-632-1699 raysales@cshore.com www.raytech-ind.com
RCBS Operations/ATK, 605 Oro Dam Blvd., Oroville, CA 95965 / 530-533-5191 or 800-533-5000; FAX: 530-533-1647 www.rcbs.com
Reardon Products, P.O. Box 126, Morrison, IL 61270 / 815-772-3155
Red Diamond Dist. Co., 1304 Snowdon Dr., Knoxville, TN 37912
Redding Reloading Equipment, 1089 Starr Rd., Cortland, NY 13045 / 607-753-3331; FAX: 607-756-8445 techline@redding-reloading.com www.redding-reloading.com
Redfield Media Resource Center, 4607 N.E. Cedar Creek Rd., Woodland, WA 98674 / 360-225-5000; FAX: 360-225-7616
Redman's Rifling & Reboring, 189 Nichols Rd., Omak, WA 98841 / 509-826-5512
Redwood Bullet Works, 3559 Bay Rd., Redwood City, CA 94063 / 415-367-6741
Reed, Dave, Rt. 1, Box 374, Minnesota City, MN 55959 / 507-689-2944
Reimer Johannsen, Inc., 438 Willow Brook Rd., Plainfield, NH 03781 / 603-469-3450; FAX: 603-469-3471
Reloaders Equipment Co., 4680 High St., Ecorse, MI 48229
Reloading Specialties, Inc., Box 1130, Pine Island, MN 55463 / 507-356-8500; FAX: 507-356-8800
Remington Arms Co., Inc., 870 Remington Drive, P.O. Box 700, Madison, NC 27025-0700 / 800-243-9700; FAX: 910-548-8700
Remington Double Shotguns, 7885 Cyd Dr., Denver, CO 80221 / 303-429-6947
Renato Gamba S.p.A.-Societa Armi Bresciane Srl., Via Artigiani 93, 25063 Gardone, Val Trompia (BS), ITALY / 30-8911640; FAX: 30-8911648
Renegade, P.O. Box 31546, Phoenix, AZ 85046 / 602-482-6777; FAX: 602-482-1952
Renfrew Guns & Supplies, R.R. 4, Renfrew, ON K7V 3Z7 CANADA / 613-432-7080
Reno, Wayne, 2808 Stagestop Road, Jefferson, CO 80456
Republic Arms, Inc. (See Cobra Enterprises, Inc.)
Retting, Inc., Martin B., 11029 Washington, Culver City, CA 90232 / 213-837-2412
RG-G, Inc., P.O. Box 935, Trinidad, CO 81082 / 719-845-1436
RH Machine & Consulting Inc., P.O. Box 394, Pacific, MO 63069 / 314-271-8465
Rhino, P.O. Box 787, Locust, NC 28097 / 704-753-2198
Rhodeside, Inc., 1704 Commerce Dr., Piqua, OH 45356 / 513-773-5781
Rice, Keith (See White Rock Tool & Die)
Richards Micro-Fit Stocks, 8331 N. San Fernando Ave., Sun Valley, CA 91352 / 818-767-6097; FAX: 818-767-7121
Ridgeline, Inc., Bruce Sheldon, P.O. Box 930, Dewey, AZ 86327-0930 / 800-632-5900; FAX: 520-632-5900
Ridgetop Sporting Goods, P.O. Box 306, 42907 Hilligoss Ln. East, Eatonville, WA 98328 / 360-832-6422; FAX: 360-832-6422
Ries, Chuck, 415 Ridgecrest Dr., Grants Pass, OR 97527 / 503-476-5623
Rifles, Inc., 3580 Leal Rd., Pleasanton, TX 78064 / 830-569-2055; FAX: 830-569-2297
Riggs, Jim, 206 Azalea, Boerne, TX 78006 / 210-249-8567
Riley Ledbetter Airguns, 1804 E. Sprague St., Winston Salem, NC 27107-3521 / 919-784-0676
Rim Pac Sports, Inc., 1034 N. Soldano Ave., Azusa, CA 91702-2135
Ringler Custom Leather Co., 31 Shining Mtn. Rd., Powell, WY 82435 / 307-645-3255
Ripley Rifles, 42 Fletcher Street, Ripley, Derbyshire, DE5 3LP ENGLAND / 011-0773-748353
Rizzini F.lli (See U.S. Importers-Moore & C England)
Rizzini SNC, Via 2 Giugno, 7/7Bis-25060, Marcheno (Brescia), ITALY
RLCM Enterprises, 110 Hill Crest Drive, Burleson, TX 76028
RMS Custom Gunsmithing, 4120 N. Bitterwell, Prescott Valley, AZ 86314 / 520-772-7626
Robert Evans Engraving, 332 Vine St., Oregon City, OR 97045 / 503-656-5693
Robert Valade Engraving, 931 3rd Ave., Seaside, OR 97138 / 503-738-7672
Robinett, R. G., P.O. Box 72, Madrid, IA 50156 / 515-795-2906
Robinson, Don, Pennsylvania Hse, 36 Fairfax Crescent, W Yorkshire, ENGLAND / 0422-364458 donrobinsonuk@yahoo.co.uk www.guns4u2.co.uk
Robinson Armament Co., PO Box 16776, Salt Lake City, UT 84116 / 801-355-0401; FAX: 801-355-0402 zdf@robarm.com www.robarm.com
Robinson Firearms Mfg. Ltd., 1699 Blondeaux Crescent, Kelowna, BC V1Y 4J8 CANADA / 604-868-9596
Robinson H.V. Bullets, 3145 Church St., Zachary, LA 70791 / 504-654-4029
Rochester Lead Works, 76 Anderson Ave., Rochester, NY 14607 / 716-442-8500; FAX: 716-442-4712
Rock River Arms, 101 Noble St., Cleveland, IL 61241
Rockwood Corp., Speedwell Division, 136 Lincoln Blvd., Middlesex, NJ 08846 / 800-243-8274; FAX: 980-560-7475
Rocky Mountain Armoury, Mr. Felix LesMerises, 610 Main Street, P.O. Box 691, Frisco, CO 80443-0691 / 970-668-0136; FAX: 970-668-4484 felix@rockymountainarmoury.com
Rocky Mountain Arms, Inc., 1813 Sunset Pl, Unit D, Longmont, CO 80501 / 800-375-0846; FAX: 303-678-8766
Rocky Mountain Target Co., 3 Aloe Way, Leesburg, FL 34788 / 352-365-9598
Rocky Mountain Wildlife Products, P.O. Box 999, La Porte, CO 80535 / 970-484-2768; FAX: 970-484-0807 critrcall@earthlink.net www.critrcall.com
Rocky Shoes & Boots, 294 Harper St., Nelsonville, OH 45764 / 800-848-9452; or 614-753-1951; FAX: 614-753-4024
Rogue Rifle Co., Inc., 1140 36th St. N., Ste. B, Lewiston, ID 83501 / 208-743-4355; FAX: 208-743-4163
Rogue River Rifleworks, 500 Linne Road #D, Paso Robles, CA 93446 / 805-227-4706; FAX: 805-227-4723 rrrifles@calinet.com
Rohner, Hans, 1148 Twin Sisters Ranch Rd., Nederland, CO 80466-9600
Rohner, John, 186 Virginia Ave, Asheville, NC 28806 / 303-444-3841
Rohrbaugh, P.O. Box 785, Bayport, NY 11705 / 631-363-2843; FAX: 631-363-2681 API380@aol.com
Romain's Custom Guns, Inc., RD 1, Whetstone Rd., Brockport, PA 15823 / 814-265-1948 romwhetstone@penn.com
Ron Frank Custom Classic Arms, 7131 Richland Rd., Ft. Worth, TX 76118 / 817-284-9300; FAX: 817-284-9300 rfrank3974@aol.com
Rooster Laboratories, P.O. Box 414605, Kansas City, MO 64141 / 816-474-1622; FAX: 816-474-7622
Rorschach Precision Products, 417 Keats Cir., Irving, TX 75061 / 214-790-3487
Rosenberg & Son, Jack A., 12229 Cox Ln., Dallas, TX 75234 / 214-241-6302
Ross, Don, 12813 West 83 Terrace, Lenexa, KS 66215 / 913-492-6982
Rosser, Bob, 2809 Crescent Ave., Suite 20, Homewood, AL 35209 / 205-870-4422; FAX: 205-870-4421 www.hand-engravers.com
Rossi Firearms, Gary Mchalik, 16175 NW 49th Ave., Miami, FL 33014-6314 / 305-474-0401; FAX: 305-623-7506
Rottweil Compe, 1330 Glassell, Orange, CA 92667
Roy Baker's Leather Goods, PO Box 893, Magnolia, AR 71754 / 870-234-0344
Royal Arms Gunstocks, 919 8th Ave. NW, Great Falls, MT 59404 / 406-453-1149 royalarms@lmt.net www.lmt.net/~royalarms
Royal Arms International, R J Brill, P.O. Box 6083, Woodland Hills, CA 91365 / 818-704-5110; FAX: 818-887-2059 royalarms.com
Roy's Custom Grips, 793 Mt. Olivet Church Rd., Lynchburg, VA 24504 / 434-993-3470
RPM, 15481 N. Twin Lakes Dr., Tucson, AZ 85739 / 520-825-1233; FAX: 520-825-3333
Rubright Bullets, 1008 S. Quince Rd., Walnutport, PA 18088 / 215-767-1339
Rucker Dist. Inc., P.O. Box 479, Terrell, TX 75160 / 214-563-2094
Ruger (See Sturm, Ruger & Co., Inc.)
Ruger, Chris. See: RUGER'S CUSTOM GUNS
Ruger's Custom Guns, Chris Ruger, 1050 Morton Blvd., Kingston, NY 12401 / 845-336-7106; FAX: 845-336-7106 rugerscustom@outdrs.net rugergunsmith.com
Rundell's Gun Shop, 6198 Frances Rd., Clio, MI 48420 / 313-687-0559
Rupert's Gun Shop, 2202 Dick Rd., Suite B, Fenwick, MI 48834 / 517-248-3252 17rupert@pathwaynet.com
Russ Haydon's Shooters' Supply, 15018 Goodrich Dr. NW, Gig Harbor, WA 98329 / 877-663-6249; FAX: 253-857-7884 www.shooters-supply.com
Russ, William. See: BILL RUSS TRADING POST

DIRECTORY

MANUFACTURER'S DIRECTORY

Rusteprufe Laboratories, 1319 Jefferson Ave., Sparta, WI 54656 / 608-269-4144; FAX: 608-366-1972 rusteprufe@centurytel.net www.rusteprufe.com
Rusty Duck Premium Gun Care Products, 7785 Foundation Dr., Suite 6, Florence, KY 41042 / 606-342-5553; FAX: 606-342-5556
Rutgers Book Center, 127 Raritan Ave., Highland Park, NJ 08904 / 732-545-4344; FAX: 732-545-6686 gunbooks@rutgersgunbooks.com www.rutgersgunbooks.com
Rutten (See U.S. Importer-Labanu Inc)
RWS (See U.S. Importer-Dynamit Nobel-RWS, Inc.), 81 Ruckman Rd., Closter, NJ 07624 / 201-767-7971; FAX: 201-767-1589

S

S&K Scope Mounts, RD 2 Box 72E, Sugar Grove, PA 16350 / 814-489-3091; or 800-578-9862; FAX: 814-489-5466 comments@scopemounts.com www.scopemounts.com
S&S Firearms, 74-11 Myrtle Ave., Glendale, NY 11385 / 718-497-1100; FAX: 718-497-1105 info@ssfirearms.com ssfirearms.com
S.A.R.L. G. Granger, 66 cours Fauriel, 42100, Saint Etienne, FRANCE / 04 77 25 14 73; FAX: 04 77 38 66 99
S.C.R.C., P.O. Box 660, Katy, TX 77492-0660 FAX: 281-492-6332
S.D. Meacham, 1070 Angel Ridge, Peck, ID 83545
S.I.A.C.E. (See U.S. Importer-IAR Inc)
Sabatti SPA, Via A Volta 90, 25063 Gandome V.T.(BS), Brescia, ITALY / 030-8912207-831312; FAX: 030-8912059 info@sabatti.it www.sabatti.com
SAECO (See Redding Reloading Equipment)
Safari Arms/Schuetzen Pistol Works, 620-626 Old Pacific Hwy. SE, Olympia, WA 98513 / 360-459-3471; FAX: 360-491-3447 info@yarms.com www.olyarms.com
Safari Press, Inc., 15621 Chemical Lane B, Huntington Beach, CA 92649 / 714-894-9080; FAX: 714-894-4949 info@safaripress.com www.safaripress.com
Safariland Ltd., Inc., 3120 E. Mission Blvd., P.O. Box 51478, Ontario, CA 91761 / 909-923-7300; FAX: 909-923-7400
SAFE, PO Box 864, Post Falls, ID 83877 / 208-773-3624; FAX: 208-773-6819 staysafe@safe-llc.com www.safe-llc.com
Safety Speed Holster, Inc., 910 S. Vail Ave., Montebello, CA 90640 / 323-723-4140; FAX: 323-726-6973 e-mail@safetyspeedholster.com www.safetyspeedholster.com
Sako Ltd (See U.S. Importer-Stoeger Industries)
Sam Welch Gun Engraving, Sam Welch, HC 64 Box 2110, Moab, UT 84532 / 435-259-8131
Samco Global Arms, Inc., 6995 NW 43rd St., Miami, FL 33166 / 305-593-9782; FAX: 305-593-1014 samco@samcoglobal.com www.samcoglobal.com
Sampson, Roger, 2316 Mahogany St., Mora, MN 55051 / 612-679-4868
San Marco (See U.S. Importers-Cape Outfitters-EMF
Sandia Die & Cartridge Co., 37 Atancacio Rd. NE, Albuquerque, NM 87123 / 505-298-5729
Sarco, Inc., 323 Union St., Stirling, NJ 07980 / 908-647-3800; FAX: 908-647-9413
Sarsilmaz Shotguns - Turkey (see B.C. Outdoors)
Sauer (See U.S. Importers-Paul Co., The, Sigarms I
Sauls, R. See: BRYAN & ASSOC.
Saunders Gun & Machine Shop, 145 Delhi Rd, Manchester, IA 52057 / 563-927-4026
Savage Arms (Canada), Inc., 248 Water St., P.O. Box 1240, Lakefield, ON K0L 2H0 CANADA / 705-652-8000; FAX: 705-652-8431 www.savagearms.com
Savage Arms, Inc., 100 Springdale Rd., Westfield, MA 01085 / 413-568-7001; FAX: 413-562-7764
Savage Range Systems, Inc., 100 Springdale Rd., Westfield, MA 01085 / 413-568-7001; FAX: 413-562-1152 snailtraps@savagearms.com www.snailtraps.com
Saville Iron Co. (See Greenwood Precision)
Savino, Barbara J., P.O. Box 51, West Burke, VT 05871-0051
Scansport, Inc., P.O. Box 700, Enfield, NH 03748 / 603-632-7654
Sceery Game Calls, P.O. Box 6520, Sante Fe, NM 87502 / 505-471-9110; FAX: 505-471-3476
Schaefer Shooting Sports, P.O. Box 1515, Melville, NY 11747-0515 / 516-643-5466; FAX: 516-643-2426 robert@robertschaefer.com www.schaefershooting.com
Scharch Mfg., Inc.-Top Brass, 10325 Co. Rd. 120, Salida, CO 81201 / 719-539-7242; or 800-836-4683; FAX: 719-539-3021 scharch@chaffee.net www.topbraass.tv
Scherer, Liz. See: SCHERER SUPPLIES
Scherer Supplies, Liz Scherer, Box 250, Ewing, VA 24248 FAX: 423-733-2073
Schiffman, Curt, 2938 S. Greenwood, Mesa, AZ 85212
Schiffman, Mike, 8233 S. Crystal Springs, McCammon, ID 83250 / 208-254-9114
Schmidt & Bender, Inc., P.O. Box 134, Meriden, NH 03770 / 603-469-3565; FAX: 603-469-3471 scopes@cyberportal.net www.schmidtbender.com
Schmidtke Group, 17050 W. Salentine Dr., New Berlin, WI 53151-7349
Schneider Bullets, 3655 West 214th St., Fairview Park, OH 44126
Schneider Rifle Barrels, Inc., 1403 W Red Baron Rd., Payson, AZ 85541 / 602-948-2525
Schroeder Bullets, 1421 Thermal Ave., San Diego, CA 92154 / 619-423-3523; FAX: 619-423-8124
Schulz Industries, 16247 Minnesota Ave., Paramount, CA 90723 / 213-439-5903
Schumakers Gun Shop, 512 Prouty Corner Lp. A, Colville, WA 99114 / 509-684-4848
Scope Control, Inc., 5775 Co. Rd. 23 SE, Alexandria, MN 56308 / 612-762-7295
Score High Gunsmithing, 9812-A, Cochiti SE, Albuquerque, NM 087123 / 800-326-5632 or 505-292-5532; FAX: 505-292-2592
Scot Powder, Rt.1 Box 167, McEwen, TN 37101 / 800-416-3006; FAX: 615-729-4211
Scott Fine Guns Inc., Thad, P.O. Box 412, Indianola, MS 38751 / 601-887-5929
Searcy Enterprises, P.O. Box 584, Boron, CA 93596 / 760-762-6771; FAX: 760-762-0191
Second Chance Body Armor, P.O. Box 578, Central Lake, MI 49622 / 616-544-5721; FAX: 616-544-9824
Seebeck Assoc., R.E., P. O. Box 59752, Dallas, TX 75229
Seecamp Co. Inc., L. W., PO Box 255, New Haven, CT 06502 / 203-877-3429; FAX: 203-877-3429
Segway Industries, P.O. Box 783, Suffern, NY 10901-0783 / 914-357-5510
Seligman Shooting Products, Box 133, Seligman, AZ 86337 / 602-422-3607 shootssp@yahoo.com
Sellier & Bellot, USA, Inc., P.O. Box 27006, Shawnee Mission, KS 66225 / 913-685-0916; FAX: 913-685-0917
Selsi Co., Inc., P.O. Box 10, Midland Park, NJ 07432-0010 / 201-935-0388; FAX: 201-935-5851
Semmer, Charles (See Remington Double Shotguns), 7885 Cyd Dr, Denver, CO 80221 / 303-429-6947
Sentinel Arms, P.O. Box 57, Detroit, MI 48231 / 313-331-1951; FAX: 313-331-1456
Servus Footwear Co., 1136 2nd St., Rock Island, IL 61204 / 309-786-7741; FAX: 309-786-9808
Shappy Bullets, 76 Milldale Ave., Plantsville, CT 06479 / 203-621-3704
Sharp Shooter Supply, 4970 Lehman Road, Delphos, OH 45833 / 419-695-3179
Sharps Arms Co., Inc., C., 100 Centennial, Box 885, Big Timber, MT 59011 / 406-932-4353
Shaw, Inc., E. R. (See Small Arms Mfg. Co.)
Shay's Gunsmithing, 931 Marvin Ave., Lebanon, PA 17042
Sheffield Knifemakers Supply, Inc., P.O. Box 741107, Orange City, FL 32774-1107 / 386-775-6453; FAX: 386-774-5754
Sheldon, Bruce. See: RIDGELINE, INC.
Shepherd Enterprises, Inc., Box 189, Waterloo, NE 68069 / 402-779-2424; FAX: 402-779-4010 sshepherd@shepherdscopes.com www.shepherdscopes.com
Sherwood, George, 46 N. River Dr., Roseburg, OR 97470 / 541-672-3159
Shilen, Inc., 205 Metro Park Blvd., Ennis, TX 75119 / 972-875-5318; FAX: 972-875-5402
Shiloh Rifle Mfg., P.O. Box 279, Big Timber, MT 59011
Shockley, Harold H., 204 E. Farmington Rd., Hanna City, IL 61536 / 309-565-4524
Shoot Where You Look, Leon Measures, Dept GD, 408 Fair, Livingston, TX 77351
Shooters Arms Manufacturing, Inc., Rivergate Mall, Gen. Maxilom Ave., Cebu City 6000, PHILIPPINES / 6332-254-8478 www.shootersarms.com.ph
Shooter's Choice Gun Care, 15050 Berkshire Ind. Pky., Middlefield, OH 44062 / 440-834-8888; FAX: 440-834-3388 www.shooterschoice.com
Shooter's Edge Inc., 3313 Creekstone Dr., Fort Collins, CO 80525
Shooters Supply, 1120 Tieton Dr., Yakima, WA 98902 / 509-452-1181
Shooter's World, 3828 N. 28th Ave., Phoenix, AZ 85017 / 602-266-0170
Shooters, Inc., 5139 Stanart St., Norfolk, VA 23502 / 757-461-9152; FAX: 757-461-9155 gflocker@aol.com
Shootin' Shack, 357 Cypress Drive, No. 10, Tequesta, FL 33469 / 561-842-0990; FAX: 561-545-4861
Shooting Specialties (See Titus, Daniel)
Shooting Star, 1715 FM 1626 Ste 105, Manchaca, TX 78652 / 512-462-0009
Shoot-N-C Targets (See Birchwood Casey)
Shotgun Sports, P.O. Box 6810, Auburn, CA 95604 / 530-889-2220; FAX: 530-889-9106 custsrv@shotgunsportsmagazine.com shotgunsportsmagazine.com
Shotgun Sports Magazine, dba Shootin' Accessories Ltd., P.O. Box 6810, Auburn, CA 95604 / 916-889-2220 custsrv@shotgunsportsmagazine.com shotgunspotsmagazine.com
Shotguns Unlimited, 2307 Fon Du Lac Rd., Richmond, VA 23229 / 804-752-7115
Siegrist Gun Shop, 8752 Turtle Road, Whittemore, MI 48770 / 989-873-3929
Sierra Bullets, 1400 W. Henry St., Sedalia, MO 65301 / 816-827-6300; FAX: 816-827-6300
Sierra Specialty Prod. Co., 1344 Oakhurst Ave., Los Altos, CA 94024 FAX: 415-965-1536
SIG, CH-8212 Neuhausen, SWITZERLAND
Sigarms, Inc., 18 Industrial Dr., Exeter, NH 03833 / 603-772-2302; FAX: 603-772-9082 www.sigarms.com
Sightron, Inc., 1672B Hwy. 96, Franklinton, NC 27525 / 919-528-8783; FAX: 919-528-0995 info@sightron.com www.sightron.com
SIG-Sauer (See U.S. Importer-Sigarms Inc.)
Silencio/Safety Direct, 56 Coney Island Dr., Sparks, NV 89431 / 800-648-1812 or 702-354-4451; FAX: 702-359-1074
Silent Hunter, 1100 Newton Ave., W. Collingswood, NJ 08107 / 609-854-3276
Silhouette Leathers, P.O. Box 1161, Gunnison, CO 81230 / 970-641-6630 oldshooter@yahoo.com
Silver Eagle Machining, 18007 N. 69th Ave., Glendale, AZ 85308
Silver Ridge Gun Shop (See Goodwin, Fred)
Simmons, Jerry, 715 Middlebury St., Goshen, IN 46528-2717 / 574-533-8546
Simmons Gun Repair, Inc., 700 S. Rogers Rd., Olathe, KS 66062 / 913-782-3131; FAX: 913-782-4189
Simmons Outdoor Corp., 6001 Oak Canyon, Irvine, CA 92618 / 949-451-1450; FAX: 949-451-1460 www.meade.com
Sinclair International, Inc., 2330 Wayne Haven St., Fort Wayne, IN 46803 / 260-493-1858; FAX: 260-493-2530 sales@sinclairintl.com www.sinclairintl.com
Singletary, Kent, 4538 W Carol Ave., Glendale, AZ 85302 / 602-526-6836 kent@kscustom www.kscustom.com
Siskiyou Gun Works (See Donnelly, C. P.)
Six Enterprises, 320-D Turtle Creek Ct., San Jose, CA 95125 / 408-999-0201; FAX: 408-999-0216
SKB Shotguns, 4325 S. 120th St., Omaha, NE 68137 / 800-752-2767; FAX: 402-330-8040 skb@skbshotguns.com www.skbshotguns.com
Skeoch, Brian R., P.O. Box 279, Glenrock, WY 82637 / 307-436-9655 brianskeoch@aol.com
Skip's Machine, 364 29 Road, Grand Junction, CO 81501 / 303-245-5417
Sklany's Machine Shop, 566 Birch Grove Dr., Kalispell, MT 59901 / 406-755-4257
Slezak, Jerome F., 1290 Marlowe, Lakewood (Cleveland), OH 44107 / 216-221-1668
Slug Site, Ozark Wilds, 21300 Hwy. 5, Versailles, MO 65084 / 573-378-6430 john@ebeling.com john.ebeling.com
Small Arms Mfg. Co., 5312 Thoms Run Rd., Bridgeville, PA 15017 / 412-221-4343; FAX: 412-221-4303
Small Arms Specialists, 443 Firchburg Rd., Mason, NH 03048 / 603-878-0427; FAX: 603-878-3905 miniguns@empire.net miniguns.com
Small Custom Mould & Bullet Co., Box 17211, Tucson, AZ 85731
Smart Parts, 1203 Spring St., Latrobe, PA 15650 / 412-539-2660; FAX: 412-539-2298
Smires, C. L., 5222 Windmill Lane, Columbia, MD 21044-1328
Smith & Wesson, 2100 Roosevelt Ave., Springfield, MA 01104 / 413-781-8300; FAX: 413-731-8980
Smith, Art, P.O. Box 645, Park Rapids, MN 56470 / 218-732-5333;
Smith, Mark A., P.O. Box 182, Sinclair, WY 82334 / 307-324-7929
Smith, Michael, 2612 Ashmore Ave., Red Bank, TN 37415 / 615-267-8341
Smith, Ron, 5869 Straley, Ft. Worth, TX 76114 / 817-732-6768
Smith, Sharmon, 4545 Speas Rd., Fruitland, ID 83619 / 208-452-6329 sharmon@fmtc.com
Smith Abrasives, Inc., 1700 Sleepy Valley Rd., P.O. Box 5095, Hot Springs, AR 71902-5095 / 501-321-2244; FAX: 501-321-9232
Smith, Judy. See: L.B.T.
Smith Saddlery, Jesse W., 0499 County Road J, Pritchett, CO 81064 / 509-325-0622
Smokey Valley Rifles, E1976 Smokey Valley Rd., Scandinavia, WI 54977 / 715-467-2674
Snapp's Gunshop, 6911 E. Washington Rd., Clare, MI 48617 / 989-386-9226 snapp@glccomputers.com
Sno-Seal, Inc. (See Atsko/Sno-Seal, Inc.)
Societa Armi Bresciane Srl (See U.S. Importer-Cape
SOS Products Co. (See Buck Stix-SOS Products Co.), Box 3, Neenah, WI 54956
Sotheby's, 1334 York Ave. at 72nd St., New York, NY 10021 / 212-606-7260
Sound Tech Silencers, Box 391, Pelham, AL 35124 / 205-664-5860 silenceio@wmconnect.com www.soundtechsilencers.com
South Bend Replicas, Inc., 61650 Oak Rd., South Bend, IN 46614 / 219-289-4500
Southeastern Community College, 1015 S. Gear Ave., West Burlington, IA 52655 / 319-752-2731
Southern Ammunition Co., Inc., 4232 Meadow St., Loris, SC 29569-3124 / 803-756-3262; FAX: 803-756-3583
Southern Bloomer Mfg. Co., P.O. Box 1621, Bristol, TN 37620 / 615-878-6660; FAX: 615-878-8761
Southern Security, 1700 Oak Hills Dr., Kingston, TN 37763 / 423-376-6297; FAX: 800-251-9992
Sparks, Milt, 605 E. 44th St. No. 2, Boise, ID 83714-4800
Spartan-Realtree Products, Inc., 1390 Box Circle, Columbus, GA 31907 / 706-569-9101; FAX: 706-569-0042
Specialty Gunsmithing, Lynn McMurdo, P.O. Box 404, Afton, WY 83110 / 307-886-5535
Specialty Shooters Supply, Inc., 3325 Griffin Rd., Suite 9mm, Fort Lauderdale, FL 33317
Speer Bullets, P.O. Box 856, Lewiston, ID 83501 / 208-746-2351; www.speer-bullets.com
Spegel, Craig, P.O. Box 387, Nehalem, OR 97131 / 503-368-5653
Speiser, Fred D., 2229 Dearborn, Missoula, MT 59801 / 406-549-8133
Spencer Reblue Service, 1820 Tupelo Trail, Holt, MI 48842 / 517-694-7474
Spencer's Rifle Barrels, Inc., 4107 Jacobs Creek Dr., Scottsville, VA 24590 / 804-293-6836; FAX: 804-293-6836 www.spencerriflebarrels.com
SPG LLC, P.O. Box 1625, Cody, WY 82414 / 307-587-7621; FAX: 307-587-7695 spg@cody.wtp.net www.blackpowderspg.com

Manufacturer's Directory

Sphinx Systems Ltd., Gesteigtstrasse 12, CH-3800, Matten, BRNE, SWITZERLAND
Splitfire Sporting Goods, L.L.C., P.O. Box 1044, Orem, UT 84059-1044 / 801-932-7950; FAX: 801-932-7959 www.splitfireguns.com
Spolar Power Load, Inc., 17376 Filbert, Fontana, CA 92335 / 800-227-9667
Sport Flite Manufacturing Co., P.O. Box 1082, Bloomfield Hills, MI 48303 / 248-647-3747
Sporting Clays Of America, 9257 Bluckeye Rd, Sugar Grove, OH 43155-9632 / 740-746-8334; FAX: 740-746-8605
Sports Afield Magazine, 15621 Chemical Lane B, Huntington Beach, CA 92649 / 714-894-9080; FAX: 714-894-4949 info@sportsafield.com www.sportsafield.com
Sports Innovations, Inc., P.O. Box 5181, 8505 Jacksboro Hwy., Wichita Falls, TX 76307 / 817-723-6015
Sportsman Safe Mfg. Co., 6309-6311 Paramount Blvd., Long Beach, CA 90805 / 800-266-7150; or 310-984-5445
Sportsman's Communicators, 588 Radcliffe Ave., Pacific Palisades, CA 90272 / 800-538-3752
Sportsmatch U.K. Ltd., 16 Summer St. Leighton,, Buzzard Beds, Bedfordshire, LU7 8HT ENGLAND / 4401525-381638; FAX: 4401525-851236 info@sportsmatch-uk.com www.sportsmatch-uk.com
Sportsmen's Exchange & Western Gun Traders, Inc., 560 S. C St., Oxnard, CA 93030 / 805-483-1917
Spradlin's, 457 Shannon Rd., Texas CreekCotopaxi, CO 81223 / 719-275-7105; FAX: 719-275-3852 spradlins@prodigy.net www.spradlins.net
Springfield Armory, 420 W. Main St, Geneseo, IL 61254 / 309-944-5631; FAX: 309-944-3676 sales@springfield-armory.com www.springfieldarmory.com
Springfield Sporters, Inc., RD 1, Penn Run, PA 15765 / 412-254-2626; FAX: 412-254-9173
Springfield, Inc., 420 W. Main St., Geneseo, IL 61254 / 309-944-5631; FAX: 309-944-3676
Spyderco, Inc., 820 Spyderco Way, Golden, CO 80403 / 800-525-7770; or 800-525-7770; FAX: 303-278-2229 sales@spyderco.com www.spyderco.com
SSK Industries, J. D. Jones, 590 Woodvue Lane, Wintersville, OH 43953 / 740-264-0176; FAX: 740-264-2257 www.sskindustries.com
Stackpole Books, 5067 Ritter Rd., Mechanicsburg, PA 17055-6921 / 717-796-0411; or 800-732-3669; FAX: 717-796-0412 tmanney@stackpolebooks.com www.stackpolebooks.com
Stalker, Inc., P.O. Box 21, Fishermans Wharf Rd., Malakoff, TX 75148 / 903-489-1010
Stalwart Corporation, P.O. Box 46, Evanston, WY 82931 / 307-789-7687; FAX: 307-789-7688
Stan Baker Sports, Stan Baker, 10000 Lake City Way, Seattle, WA 98125 / 206-522-4575
Stan De Treville & Co., 4129 Normal St., San Diego, CA 92103 / 619-298-3393
Stanley Bullets, 2085 Heatheridge Ln., Reno, NV 89509
Star Ammunition, Inc., 5520 Rock Hampton Ct., Indianapolis, IN 46268 / 800-221-5927; FAX: 317-872-5847
Star Custom Bullets, P.O. Box 608, 468 Main St., Ferndale, CA 95536 / 707-786-9140; FAX: 707-786-9117 wmebridge@humboldt.com
Star Machine Works, P.O. Box 1872, Pioneer, CA 95666 / 209-295-5000
Starke Bullet Company, P.O. Box 400, 605 6th St. NW, Cooperstown, ND 58425 / 888-797-3431
Starkey Labs, 6700 Washington Ave. S., Eden Prairie, MN 55344
Starkey's Gun Shop, 9430 McCombs, El Paso, TX 79924 / 915-751-3030
Starlight Training Center, Inc., Rt. 1, P.O. Box 88, Bronaugh, MO 64728 / 417-843-3555
Starline, Inc., 1300 W. Henry St., Sedalia, MO 65301 / 660-827-6640; FAX: 660-827-6650 info@starlinebrass.com http://www.starlinebrass.com
Starr Trading Co., Jedediah, P.O. Box 2007, Farmington Hills, MI 48333 / 810-683-4343; FAX: 810-683-3282
Starrett Co., L. S., 121 Crescent St., Athol, MA 01331 / 978-249-3551; FAX: 978-249-8495
Steelman's Gun Shop, 10465 Beers Rd., Swartz Creek, MI 48473 / 810-735-4884
Steffens, Ron, 18396 Mariposa Creek Rd., Willits, CA 95490 / 707-485-0873
Stegall, James B., 26 Forest Rd., Wallkill, NY 12589
Steve Henigson & Associates, P.O. Box 2726, Culver City, CA 90231 / 310-305-8288; FAX: 310-305-1905
Steve Kamyk Engraver, 9 Grandview Dr., Westfield, MA 01085-1810 / 413-568-0457 stevek201@attbi
Steven Dodd Hughes, P.O. Box 545, Livingston, MT 59047 / 406-222-9377; FAX: 406-222-9377
Steves House of Guns, Rt. 1, Minnesota City, MN 55959 / 507-689-2573
Stewart Game Calls, Inc., Johnny, P.O. Box 7954, 5100 Fort Ave., Waco, TX 76714 / 817-772-3261; FAX: 817-772-3670
Stewart's Gunsmithing, P.O. Box 5854, Pietersburg North 0750, Transvaal, SOUTH AFRICA / 01521-89401
Steyr Mannlicher GmbH & Co KG, Mannlicherstrasse 1, 4400 Steyr, Steyr, AUSTRIA / 0043-7252-896-0; FAX: 0043-7252-78620 office@steyr-mannlicher.com www.steyr-mannlicher.com
STI International, 114 Halmar Cove, Georgetown, TX 78628 / 800-959-8201; FAX: 512-819-0465 www.stiguns.com
Stiles Custom Guns, 76 Cherry Run Rd., Box 1605, Homer City, PA 15748 / 712-479-9945
Stillwell, Robert, 421 Judith Ann Dr., Schertz, TX 78154
Stoeger Industries, 17603 Indian Head Hwy., Suite 200, Accokeek, MD 20607-2501 / 301-283-6300; FAX: 301-283-6986 www.stoegerindustries.com
Stoeger Publishing Co. (See Stoeger Industries)
Stone Enterprises Ltd., 426 Harveys Neck Rd., P.O. Box 335, Wicomico Church, VA 22579 / 804-580-5114; FAX: 804-580-8421
Stone Mountain Arms, 5988 Peachtree Corners E., Norcross, GA 30071 / 800-251-9412
Stoney Point Products, Inc., P.O. Box 234, 1822 N Minnesota St., New Ulm, MN 56073-0234 / 507-354-3360; FAX: 507-354-7236 stoney@newulmtel.net www.stoneypoint.com
Storm, Gary, P.O. Box 5211, Richardson, TX 75083 / 214-385-0862
Stott's Creek Armory, Inc., 2526 S. 475W, Morgantown, IN 46160 / 317-878-5489; FAX: 317-878-9489 sccalendar@aol.com www.Sccalendar.aol.com
Stratco, Inc., P.O. Box 2270, Kalispell, MT 59901 / 406-755-1221; FAX: 406-755-1226
Strayer, Sandy. See: STRAYER-VOIGT, INC.
Strayer-Voigt, Inc., Sandy Strayer, 3435 Ray Orr Blvd, Grand Prairie, TX 75050 / 972-513-0575
Strong Holster Co., 39 Grove St., Gloucester, MA 01930 / 508-281-3300; FAX: 508-281-6321
Strutz Rifle Barrels, Inc., W. C., P.O. Box 611, Eagle River, WI 54521 / 715-479-4766
Stuart, V. Pat, Rt.1, Box 447-S, Greenville, VA 24440 / 804-556-3845
Sturgeon Valley Sporters, Ken Ide, P.O. Box 283, Vanderbilt, MI 49795 / 517-983-4338 k.ide@mail.com
Sturm Ruger & Co. Inc., 200 Ruger Rd., Prescott, AZ 86301 / 928-541-8820; FAX: 520-541-8850 www.ruger.com
"Su-Press-On", Inc., P.O. Box 09161, Detroit, MI 48209 / 313-842-4222
Sullivan, David S. (See Westwind Rifles, Inc.)
Sun Welding Safe Co., 290 Easy St. No.3, Simi Valley, CA 93065 / 805-584-6678; or 800-729-SAFE; FAX: 805-584-6169 sunwelding.com
Sunny Hill Enterprises, Inc., W1790 Cty. HHH, Malone, WI 53049 / 920-795-4722; FAX: 920-795-4822
Super 6 LLC, Gary Knopp, 3806 W. Lisbon Ave., Milwaukee, WI 53208 / 414-344-3343; FAX: 414-344-0304
Sure-Shot Game Calls, Inc., P.O. Box 816, 6835 Capitol, Groves, TX 77619 / 409-962-1636; FAX: 409-962-5465
Svon Corp., 2107 W. Blue Heron Blvd., Riviera Beach, FL 33404 / 508-881-8852
Swann, D. J., 5 Orsova Close, Eltham North Vic., 3095 AUSTRALIA / 03-431-0323
Swanndri New Zealand, 152 Elm Ave., Burlingame, CA 94010 / 415-347-6158
Swanson, Mark, 975 Heap Avenue, Prescott, AZ 86301 / 928-778-4423
Swarovski Optik North America Ltd., 2 Slater Rd., Cranston, RI 02920 / 401-946-2220; or 800-426-3089; FAX: 401-946-2587
Sweet Home, Inc., P.O. Box 900, Orrville, OH 44667-0900
Swenson's 45 Shop, A. D., 3839 Ladera Vista Rd, Fallbrook, CA 92028-9431
Swift Bullet Co., P.O. Box 27, 201 Main St., Quinter, KS 67752 / 913-754-3959; FAX: 913-754-2359
Swift Instruments, Inc., 952 Dorchester Ave., Boston, MA 02125 / 617-436-2960; FAX: 617-436-3232
Swift River Gunworks, 450 State St., Belchertown, MA 01007 / 413-323-4052
Szweda, Robert (See RMS Custom Gunsmithing)

T

T&S Industries, Inc., 1027 Skyview Dr., W. Carrollton, OH 45449 / 513-859-8414
T.F.C. S.p.A., Via G. Marconi 118, B, Villa Carcina 25069, ITALY / 030-881271; FAX: 030-881826
T.G. Faust, Inc., 544 Minor St., Reading, PA 19602 / 610-375-8549; FAX: 610-375-4488
T.K. Lee Co., 1282 Branchwater Ln., Birmingham, AL 35216 / 205-913-5222 odonmich@aol.com www.scopedot.com
T.W. Menck Gunsmith, Inc., 5703 S. 77th St., Ralston, NE 68127 guntools@cox.net http://llwww.members.cox.net/guntools
Tabler Marketing, 2554 Lincoln Blvd., Suite 555, Marina Del Rey, CA 90291 / 818-755-4565; FAX: 818-755-0972
Taconic Firearms Ltd., Perry Lane, P.O. Box 553, Cambridge, NY 12816 / 518-677-2704; FAX: 518-677-5974
Tactical Defense Institute, 2174 Bethany Ridges, West Union, OH 45693 / 937-544-7228; FAX: 937-544-2887 tdiohio@dragonbbs.com www.tdiohio.com
Talley, Dave, P.O. Box 821, Glenrock, WY 82637 / 307-436-8724; or 307-436-9315
Talon Industries Inc. (See Cobra Enterprises, Inc.)
Tamarack Products, Inc., P.O. Box 625, Wauconda, IL 60084 / 708-526-9333; FAX: 708-526-9353
Tanfoglio Fratelli S.r.l., via Valtrompia 39, 41, Brescia, ITALY / 30-8910361; FAX: 30-8910183
Tanglefree Industries, 1261 Heavenly Dr., Martinez, CA 94553 / 800-982-4868; FAX: 510-825-3874
Tank's Rifle Shop, P.O. Box 474, Fremont, NE 68026-0474 / 402-727-1317 jtank@tanksrifleshop.com www.tanksrifleshop.com
Tanner (See U.S. Importer-Mandall Shooting Supply)
Taracorp Industries, Inc., 1200 Sixteenth St., Granite City, IL 62040 / 618-451-4400
Target Shooting, Inc., P.O. Box 773, Watertown, SD 57201 / 605-882-6955; FAX: 605-882-8840
Tar-Hunt Custom Rifles, Inc., 101 Dogtown Rd., Bloomsburg, PA 17815 / 570-784-6368; FAX: 570-389-9150 www.tar-hunt.com
Tarnhelm Supply Co., Inc., 431 High St., Boscawen, NH 03303 / 603-796-2551; FAX: 603-796-2918 info@tarnhelm.com www.tarnhelm.com
Tasco Sales, Inc., 2889 Commerce Pky., Miramar, FL 33025
Taurus Firearms, Inc., 16175 NW 49th Ave., Miami, FL 33014 / 305-624-1115; FAX: 305-623-7506
Taurus International Firearms (See U.S. Importer)
Taurus S.A. Forjas, Avenida Do Forte 511, Porto Alegre, RS BRAZIL 91360 / 55-51-347-4050; FAX: 55-51-347-3065
Taylor & Robbins, P.O. Box 164, Rixford, PA 16745 / 814-966-3233
Taylor's & Co., Inc., 304 Lenoir Dr., Winchester, VA 22603 / 540-722-2017; FAX: 540-722-2018
TCCI, P.O. Box 302, Phoenix, AZ 85001 / 602-237-3823; FAX: 602-237-3858
TCSR, 3998 Hoffman Rd., White Bear Lake, MN 55110-4626 / 800-328-5323; FAX: 612-429-0526
TDP Industries, Inc., P.O. Box 249, Ottsville, PA 18942-0249 / 215-345-8687; FAX: 215-345-6057
Techno Arms (See U.S. Importer- Auto-Ordnance Corp
Tecnolegno S.p.A., Via A. Locatelli, 6 10, 24019 Zogno, I ITALY / 0345-55111; FAX: 0345-55155
Ted Blocker Holsters, Inc., 9396 S.W. Tigard St., Tigard, OR 97223 / 800-650-9742; FAX: 503-670-9692 www.tedblocker.com
Tele-Optics, 630 E. Rockland Rd., P.O. Box 6313, Libertyville, IL 60048 / 847-362-7757; FAX: 847-362-7757
Tennessee Valley Mfg., 14 County Road 521, Corinth, MS 38834 / 601-286-5014 tvm@avsia.com www.avsia.com/tvm
Ten-Ring Precision, Inc., Alex B. Hamilton, 1449 Blue Crest Lane, San Antonio, TX 78232 / 210-494-3063; FAX: 210-494-3066
TEN-X Products Group, 1905 N Main St, Suite 133, Cleburne, TX 76031-1305 / 972-243-4016; or 800-433-2225; FAX: 972-243-4112
Tepeco, P.O. Box 342, Friendswood, TX 77546 / 713-482-2702
Terry K. Kopp Professional Gunsmithing, Rt 1 Box 224, Lexington, MO 64067 / 816-259-2636
Testing Systems, Inc., 220 Pegasus Ave., Northvale, NJ 07647
Tetra Gun Care, 8 Vreeland Rd., Florham Park, NJ 07932 / 973-443-0004; FAX: 973-443-0263
Tex Shoemaker & Sons, Inc., 714 W. Cienega Ave., San Dimas, CA 91773 / 909-592-2071; FAX: 909-592-2378 texshoemaker@texshoemaker.com www.texshoemaker.com
Texas Armory (See Bond Arms, Inc.)
Texas Platers Supply Co., 2453 W. Five Mile Parkway, Dallas, TX 75233 / 214-330-7168
Thad Rybka Custom Leather Equipment, 2050 Canoe Creek Rd., Springvale, AL 35146-6709
Thad Scott Fine Guns, Inc., P.O. Box 412, Indianola, MS 38751 / 601-887-5929
The A.W. Peterson Gun Shop, Inc., 4255 West Old U.S. 441, Mount Dora, FL 32757-3299 / 352-383-4258
The Accuracy Den, 25 Bitterbrush Rd., Reno, NV 89523 / 702-345-0225
The Ballistic Program Co., Inc., 2417 N. Patterson St., Thomasville, GA 31792 / 912-228-5739 or 800-368-0835
The BulletMakers Workshop, RFD 1 Box 1755, Brooks, ME 04921
The Competitive Pistol Shop, 5233 Palmer Dr., Ft. Worth, TX 76117-2433 / 817-834-8479
The Concealment Shop, Inc., 3550 E. Hwy. 80, Mesquite, TX 75149 / 972-289-8997; or 800-444-7090; FAX: 972-289-4410 info@theconcealmentshop.com www.theconcealmentshop.com
The Country Armourer, P.O. Box 308, Ashby, MA 01431-0308 / 508-827-6797; FAX: 508-827-4845
The Creative Craftsman, Inc., 95 Highway 29 North, P.O. Box 331, Lawrenceville, GA 30246 / 404-963-2112; FAX: 404-513-9488
The Custom Shop, 890 Cochrane Crescent, Peterborough, ON K9H 5N3 CANADA / 705-742-6693
The Ensign-Bickford Co., 660 Hopmeadow St., Simsbury, CT 06070
The Firearm Training Center, 9555 Blandville Rd., West Paducah, KY 42086 / 502-554-5886
The Fouling Shot, 6465 Parfet St., Arvada, CO 80004
The Gun Doctor, 435 East Maple, Roselle, IL 60172 / 708-894-0668
The Gun Room, 1121 Burlington, Muncie, IN 47302 / 765-282-9073; FAX: 765-282-5270 bshstleguns@aol.com
The Gun Room Press, 127 Raritan Ave., Highland Park, NJ 08904 / 732-545-4344; FAX: 732-545-6686 gunbooks@rutgersgunbooks.com www.rutgersgunbooks.com
The Gun Shop, 62778 Spring Creek Rd., Montrose, CO 81401
The Gun Shop, 5550 S. 900 East, Salt Lake City, UT 84117 / 801-263-3633
The Gun Works, 247 S. 2nd St., Springfield, OR 97477 / 541-741-4118; FAX: 541-988-1097 gunworks@worldnet.att.net www.thegunworks.com
The Gunsight, 1712 North Placentia Ave., Fullerton, CA 92631
The Hanned Line, 4463 Madoc Way, San Jose, CA 95130 smith@hanned.com www.hanned.com
The Hawken Shop, P.O. Box 593, Oak Harbor, WA 98277 / 206-679-4657; FAX: 206-675-1114
The Keller Co., P.O. Box 4057, Port Angeles, WA 98363-0997 / 214-770-8585
The Lewis Lead Remover (See LEM Gun Specialties)
The Midwest Shooting School, Pat LaBoone, 2550 Hwy. 23, Wrenshall, MN 55797 / 218-384-3670 shootingschool@starband.net
The NgraveR Co., 67 Wawecus Hill Rd., Bozrah, CT 06334 / 860-823-1533; FAX: 860-887-6252 ngraver98@aol.com www.ngraver.com

Manufacturer's Directory

The Ordnance Works, 2969 Pidgeon Point Road, Eureka, CA 95501 / 707-443-3252
The Orvis Co., Rt. 7, Manchester, VT 05254 / 802-362-3622; FAX: 802-362-3525
The Outdoor Connection, Inc., 7901 Panther Way, Waco, TX 76712-6556 / 800-533-6076 or 254-772-5575; FAX: 254-776-3553 floyd@outdoorconnection.com www.outdoorconnection.com
The Park Rifle Co., Ltd., Unit 6a Dartford Trade Park, Power Mill Lane, Dartford DA7 7NX, ENGLAND / 011-0322-222512
The Paul Co., 27385 Pressonville Rd., Wellsville, KS 66092 / 785-883-4444; FAX: 785-883-2525
The Protector Mfg. Co., Inc., 443 Ashwood Place, Boca Raton, FL 33431 / 407-394-6011
The Robar Co., Inc., 21438 N. 7th Ave., Suite B, Phoenix, AZ 85027 / 623-581-2648; FAX: 623-582-0059 info@robarguns.com www.robarguns.com
The School of Gunsmithing, 6065 Roswell Rd., Atlanta, GA 30328 / 800-223-4542
The Shooting Gallery, 8070 Southern Blvd., Boardman, OH 44512 / 216-726-7788
The Sight Shop, John G. Lawson, 1802 E. Columbia Ave., Tacoma, WA 98404 / 253-474-5465 parahellum9@aol.com www.thesightshop.org
The Southern Armory, 25 Millstone Road, Woodlawn, VA 24381 / 703-238-1343; FAX: 703-238-1453
The Surecase Co., 233 Wilshire Blvd., Ste. 900, Santa Monica, CA 90401 / 800-92ARMLOC
The Swampfire Shop (See Peterson Gun Shop, Inc.)
The Wilson Arms Co., 63 Leetes Island Rd., Branford, CT 06405 / 203-488-7297; FAX: 203-488-0135
Theis, Terry, 21452 FM 2093, Harper, TX 78631 / 830-864-4438
Thiewes, George W., 14329 W. Parada Dr., Sun City West, AZ 85375
Things Unlimited, 235 N. Kimbau, Casper, WY 82601 / 307-234-5277
Thirion Gun Engraving, Denise, PO Box 408, Graton, CA 95444 / 707-829-1876
Thomas, Charles C., 2600 S. First St., Springfield, IL 62704 / 217-789-8980; FAX: 217-789-9130 books@ccthomas.com ccthomas.com
Thompson Bullet Lube Co., P.O. Box 409, Wills Point, TX 75169 / 866-476-1500; FAX: 866-476-1500 thompsonbulletlube.com www.thompsonbulletlube.com
Thompson Precision, 110 Mary St., P.O. Box 251, Warren, IL 61087 / 815-745-3625
Thompson, Randall. See: HIGHLINE MACHINE CO.
Thompson Target Technology, 4804 Sherman Church Ave. S.W., Canton, OH 44710 / 330-484-6480; FAX: 330-491-1087 www.thompsontarget.com
Thompson Tool Mount, 1550 Solomon Rd., Santa Maria, CA 93455 / 805-934-1281 ttm@pronet.net www.thompsontoolmount.com
Thompson/Center Arms, P.O. Box 5002, Rochester, NH 03866 / 603-332-2394; FAX: 603-332-5133 tech@tcarms.com www.tcarms.com
3-Ten Corp., P.O. Box 269, Feeding Hills, MA 01030 / 413-789-2086; FAX: 413-789-1549
Thunden Ranch, HCR 1, Box 53, Mt. Home, TX 78058 / 830-640-3138
Thurston Sports, Inc., RD 3 Donovan Rd., Auburn, NY 13021 / 315-253-0966
Tiger-Hunt Gunstocks, Box 379, Beaverdale, PA 15921 / 814-472-5161 tigerhunt4@aol.com www.gunstockwood.com
Tikka (See U.S. Importer-Stoeger Industries)
Time Precision, 4 Nicholas Sq., New Milford, CT 06776-3506 / 203-775-8343
Tinks & Ben Lee Hunting Products (See Wellington)
Tink's Safariland Hunting Corp., P.O. Box 244, 1140 Monticello Rd., Madison, GA 30650 / 706-342-4915; FAX: 706-342-7568
Tioga Engineering Co., Inc., P.O. Box 913, 13 Cone St., Wellsboro, PA 16901 / 570-724-3533; FAX: 570-724-3895 tiogaeng@epix.net
Tippman Pneumatics, Inc., 2955 Adams Center Rd., Fort Wayne, IN 46803
Tirelli, Snc Di Tirelli Primo E.C., Via Matteotti No. 359, Gardone V.T. Brescia, I ITALY / 030-8912819; FAX: 030-832240
TM Stockworks, 6355 Maplecrest Rd., Fort Wayne, IN 46835 / 219-485-5389
TMI Products (See Haselbauer Products, Jerry)
Tom Forrest, Inc., P.O. Box 326, Lakeside, CA 92040 / 619-561-5800; FAX: 888-GUN-CLIP info@gunmag.com www.gunmags.com
Tombstone Smoke`n' Deals, PO Box 31298, Phoenix, AZ 85046 / 602-905-7013; FAX: 602-443-1998
Tom's Gun Repair, Thomas G. Ivanoff, 76-6 Rt. Southfork Rd., Cody, WY 82414 / 307-587-6949
Tom's Gunshop, 3601 Central Ave., Hot Springs, AR 71913 / 501-624-3856
Tonoloway Tack Drives, HCR 81, Box 100, Needmore, PA 17238
Torel, Inc., 1708 N. South St., P.O. Box 592, Yoakum, TX 77995 / 512-293-2341; FAX: 512-293-3413
TOZ (See U.S. Importer-Nygord Precision Products)
Track of the Wolf, Inc., 18308 Joplin St. NW, Elk River, MN 55330-1773 / 763-633-2500; FAX: 763-633-2550
Traditions Performance Firearms, P.O. Box 776, 1375 Boston Post Rd., Old Saybrook, CT 06475 / 860-388-4656; FAX: 860-388-4657 info@traditionsfirearms.com www.traditionsfirearms.com
Trafalgar Square, P.O. Box 257, N. Pomfret, VT 05053 / 802-457-1911
Trail Visions, 5800 N. Ames Terrace, Glendale, WI 53209 / 414-228-1328
Trax America, Inc., PO Box 898, 1150 Eldridge, Forrest City, AR 72335 / 870-633-0410; or 800-232-2327; FAX: 870-633-4788 trax@ipa.net www.traxamerica.com
Treadlok Gun Safe, Inc., 1764 Granby St. NE, Roanoke, VA 24012 / 800-729-8732; or 703-982-6881; FAX: 703-982-1059
Treemaster, P.O. Box 247, Guntersville, AL 35976 / 205-878-3597
Trevallion Gunstocks, 9 Old Mountain Rd., Cape Neddick, ME 03902 / 207-361-1130
Trico Plastics, 28061 Diaz Rd., Temecula, CA 92590 / 909-676-7714; FAX: 909-676-0267 ustinfo@ustplastics.com www.tricoplastics.com
Trigger Lock Division / Central Specialties Ltd., 220-D Exchange Dr., Crystal Lake, IL 60014 / 847-639-3900; FAX: 847-639-3972
Trijicon, Inc., 49385 Shafer Ave., P.O. Box 930059, Wixom, MI 48393-0059 / 248-960-7700 or 800-338-0563
Trilby Sport Shop, 1623 Hagley Rd., Toledo, OH 43612-2024 / 419-472-6222
Trilux, Inc., P.O. Box 24608, Winston-Salem, NC 27114 / 910-659-9438; FAX: 910-768-7720
Trinidad St. Jr. Col. Gunsmith Dept., 600 Prospect St., Trinidad, CO 81082 / 719-846-5631; FAX: 719-846-5667
Triple-K Mfg. Co., Inc., 2222 Commercial St., San Diego, CA 92113 / 619-232-2066; FAX: 619-232-7675 sales@triplek.com www.triplek.com
Tristar Sporting Arms, Ltd., 1814 Linn St. #16, N. Kansas City, MO 64116-3627 / 816-421-1400; FAX: 816-421-4182 tristar@blitz-it.net www.tristarsportingarms
Trius Traps, Inc., P.O. Box 25, 221 S. Miami Ave., Cleves, OH 45002 / 513-941-5682; FAX: 513-941-7970 triustraps@fuse.net www.triustraps.com
Trooper Walsh, 2393 N. Edgewood St., Arlington, VA 22207
Trotman, Ken, 135 Ditton Walk, Unit 11, Cambridge, CB5 8PY ENGLAND / 01223-211030; FAX: 01223-212317 www.kentrolman.com
Tru-Balance Knife Co., P.O. Box 140555, Grand Rapids, MI 49514 / 616-647-1215
True Flight Bullet Co., 5581 Roosevelt St., Whitehall, PA 18052 / 610-262-7630; FAX: 610-262-7806
Truglo, Inc., P.O. Box 1612, McKinna, TX 75070 / 972-774-0300; FAX: 972-774-0323 www.truglosights.com
Trulock Tool, P.O. Box 530, Whigham, GA 31797 / 229-762-4678; FAX: 229-762-4050 trulockchokes@hotmail.com trulockchokes.com
Tru-Square Metal Products, Inc., 640 First St. SW, P.O. Box 585, Auburn, WA 98071 / 253-833-2310; or 800-225-1017; FAX: 253-833-2349 t-tumbler@qwest.net
Tucker, James C., P.O. Box 366, Medford, OR 97501 / 541-245-3887 jctstocker@yahoo.com
Tucson Mold, Inc., 930 S. Plumer Ave., Tucson, AZ 85719 / 520-792-1075; FAX: 520-792-1075
Turk's Head Productions, Mustafa Bilal, 908 NW 50th St., Seattle, WA 98107-3634 / 206-782-4164; FAX: 206-783-5677 info@turkshead.com www.turkshead.com
Turnbull Restoration, Doug, 6680 Rt. 5 & 20, P.O. Box 471, Bloomfield, NY 14469 / 585-657-6338; FAX: 585-657-6338 turnbullrest@mindspring.com www.turnbullrestoration.com
Tuttle, Dale, 4046 Russell Rd., Muskegon, MI 49445 / 616-766-2250
Tyler Manufacturing & Distributing, 3804 S. Eastern, Oklahoma City, OK 73129 / 405-677-1487; or 800-654-8415

U

U.S. Fire Arms Mfg. Co., Inc., 55 Van Dyke Ave., Hartford, CT 06106 / 877-227-6901; FAX: 800-644-7265 usfirearms.com
U.S. Importer-Wm. Larkin Moore, 8430 E. Raintree Ste. B-7, Scottsdale, AZ 85260
U.S. Optics, A Division of Zeitz Optics U.S.A., 5900 Dale St., Buena Park, CA 90621 / 714-994-4901; FAX: 714-994-4904 www.usoptics.com
U.S. Repeating Arms Co., Inc., 275 Winchester Ave., Morgan, UT 84050-9333 / 801-876-3440; FAX: 801-876-3737 www.winchester-guns.com
U.S. Tactical Systems (See Keng's Firearms Specialty)
Ugartechea S. A., Ignacio, Chonta 26, Eibar, SPAIN / 43-121257; FAX: 43-121669
Ultra Dot Distribution, P.O. Box 362, 6304 Riverside Dr., Yankeetown, FL 34498 / 352-447-2255; FAX: 352-447-2266
Ultralux (See U.S. Importer-Keng's Firearms)
UltraSport Arms, Inc., 1955 Norwood Ct., Racine, WI 53403 / 414-554-3237; FAX: 414-554-9731
Uncle Bud's, HCR 81, Box 100, Needmore, PA 17238 / 717-294-6000; FAX: 717-294-6005
Uncle Mike's (See Michaels of Oregon Co.)
Unertl Optical Co., Inc., 103 Grand Avenue, P.O. Box 895, Mars, PA 16046-0895 / 724-625-3810; FAX: 724-625-3819 unertl@nauticom.net www.unertloptics.net
Unique/M.A.P.F., 10 Les Allees, 64700, Hendaye, FRANCE / 33-59 20 71 93
UniTec, 1250 Bedford SW, Canton, OH 44710 / 216-452-4017
United Binocular Co., 9043 S. Western Ave., Chicago, IL 60620
United Cutlery Corp., 1425 United Blvd., Sevierville, TN 37876 / 865-428-2532; or 800-548-0835; FAX: 865-428-2267
United States Products Co., 518 Melwood Ave., Pittsburgh, PA 15213-1136 / 412-621-2130; FAX: 412-621-8740 sales@us-products.com www.us-products.com
Universal Sports, P.O. Box 532, Vincennes, IN 47591 / 812-882-8680; FAX: 812-882-8680
Upper Missouri Trading Co., P.O. Box 100, 304 Harold St., Crofton, NE 68730-0100 / 402-388-4844
USAC, 4500-15th St. East, Tacoma, WA 98424 / 206-922-7589
Uselton/Arms, Inc., 842 Conference Dr., Goodlettsville, TN 37072 / 615-851-4919
Utica Cutlery Co., 820 Noyes St., Utica, NY 13503 / 315-733-4663; FAX: 315-733-6602

V

V.H. Blackinton & Co., Inc., 221 John L. Dietsch, Attleboro Falls, MA 02763-0300 / 508-699-4436; FAX: 508-695-5349
Valdada Enterprises, P.O. Box 773122, 31733 County Road 35, Steamboat Springs, CO 80477 / 970-879-2983; FAX: 970-879-0851 www.valdada.com
Valtro USA, Inc., 1281 Andersen Dr., San Rafael, CA 94901 / 415-256-2575; FAX: 415-256-2576
VAM Distribution Co. LLC, 1141-B Mechanicsburg Rd., Wooster, OH 44691 www.rex10.com
Van Gorden & Son Inc., C. S., 1815 Main St., Bloomer, WI 54724 / 715-568-2612
Van Horn, Gil, P.O. Box 207, Llano, CA 93544
Van Patten, J. W., P.O. Box 145, Foster Hill, Milford, PA 18337 / 717-296-7069
Vann Custom Bullets, 2766 N. Willowside Way, Meridian, ID 83642
Van's Gunsmith Service, 224 Route 69-A, Parish, NY 13131 / 315-625-7251
Varmint Masters, LLC, Rick Vecqueray, P.O. Box 6724, Bend, OR 97708 / 541-318-7306; FAX: 541-318-7306 varmintmasters@bendcable.com www.varmintmasters.net
Vecqueray, Rick. See: VARMINT MASTERS, LLC
Vega Tool Co., c/o T.R. Ross, 4865 Tanglewood Ct., Boulder, CO 80301 / 303-530-0174 clanlaird@aol.com www.vegatool.com
Vektor USA, Mikael Danforth, 5139 Stanart St, Norfolk, VA 23502 / 888-740-0837; or 757-455-8895; FAX: 757-461-9155
Venco Industries, Inc. (See Shooter's Choice Gun Care)
Venus Industries, P.O. Box 246, Sialkot-1, PAKISTAN FAX: 92 432 85579
Verney-Carron, BP 72-54 Boulevard Thiers, 42002 St Etienne Cedex 1, St Etienne Cedex 1, FRANCE / 33-477791500; FAX: 33-477790702 email@verney-carron.com www.verney-carron.com
Vest, John, 1923 NE 7th St., Redmond, OR 97756 / 541-923-8898
VibraShine, Inc., P.O. Box 577, Taylorsville, MS 39168 / 601-785-9854; FAX: 601-785-9874 rdbekevibrashine.com www.vibrashine.com
Vibra-Tek Co., 1844 Arroya Rd., Colorado Springs, CO 80906 / 719-634-8611; FAX: 719-634-6886
Vic's Gun Refinishing, 6 Pineview Dr., Dover, NH 03820-6422 / 603-742-0013
Victory Ammunition, P.O. Box 1022, Milford, PA 18337 / 717-296-5768; FAX: 717-296-9298
Victory USA, P.O. Box 1021, Pine Bush, NY 12566 / 914-744-2060; FAX: 914-744-5181
Vihtavuori Oy, FIN-41330 Vihtavuori, FINLAND, / 358-41-3779211; FAX: 358-41-3771643
Vihtavuori Oy/Kaltron-Pettibone, 1241 Ellis St., Bensenville, IL 60106 / 708-350-1116; FAX: 708-350-1606
Viking Video Productions, P.O. Box 251, Roseburg, OR 97470
Village Restorations & Consulting, Inc., P.O. Box 569, Claysburg, PA 16625 / 814-239-8200; FAX: 814-239-2165 www.villagerestoration@yahoo.com
Vincent's Shop, 210 Antoinette, Fairbanks, AK 99701
Vintage Industries, Inc., 2772 Depot St., Sanford, FL 32773
Viper Bullet and Brass Works, 11 Brock St., Box 582, Norwich, ON N0J 1P0 CANADA
Viramontez Engraving, Ray Viramontez, 601 Springfield Dr., Albany, GA 31721 / 229-432-9683 sgtvira@aol.com
Viramontez, Ray. See: VIRAMONTEZ ENGRAVING
Virgin Valley Custom Guns, 450 E 800 N #20, Hurricane, UT 84737 / 435-635-8941; FAX: 435-635-8943 vvcguns@infowest.com www.virginvalleyguns.com
Visible Impact Targets, Rts. 5 & 20, E. Bloomfield, NY 14443 / 716-657-6161; FAX: 716-657-5405
Vitt/Boos, 1195 Buck Hill Rd., Townshend, VT 05353 / 802-365-9232
Voere-KGH GmbH, Untere Sparchen 56, A-6330 Kufstein, Tirol, AUSTRIA / 0043-5372-62547; FAX: 0043-5372-65752 voere@aon.com www.voere.com
Volquartsen Custom Ltd., 24276 240th Street, PO Box 397, Carroll, IA 51401 / 712-792-4238; FAX: 712-792-2542 vcl@netins.net www.volquartsen.com
Vorhes, David, 3042 Beecham St., Napa, CA 94558 / 707-226-9116; FAX: 707-253-7334
VSP Publishers (See Heritage/VSP Gun Books), P.O. Box 887, McCall, ID 83638 / 208-634-4104; FAX: 208-634-3101 heritage@gunbooks.com www.gunbooks.com
VTI Gun Parts, P.O. Box 509, Lakeville, CT 06039 / 860-435-8068; FAX: 860-435-8146 mail@vtigunparts.com www.vtigunparts.com
Vulpes Ventures, Inc., Fox Cartridge Division, P.O. Box 1363, Bolingbrook, IL 60440-7363 / 630-759-1229

W

W. Square Enterprises, 9826 Sagedale Dr., Houston, TX 77089 / 281-484-0935; FAX: 281-464-9940 lfdw@pdq.net www.loadammo.com
W. Waller & Son, Inc., 2221 Stoney Brook Rd., Grantham, NH 03753-7706 / 603-863-4177 www.wallerandson.com

MANUFACTURER'S DIRECTORY

W.B. Niemi Engineering, Box 126 Center Road, Greensboro, VT 05841 / 802-533-7180 or 802-533-7141
W.C. Wolff Co., P.O. Box 458, Newtown Square, PA 19073 / 610-359-9600; or 800-545-0077; mail@gunsprings.com www.gunsprings.com
W.E. Birdsong & Assoc., 1435 Monterey Rd., Florence, MS 39073-9748 / 601-366-8270
W.E. Brownell Checkering Tools, 9390 Twin Mountain Cir., San Diego, CA 92126 / 858-695-2479; FAX: 858-695-2479
W.J. Riebe Co., 3434 Tucker Rd., Boise, ID 83703
W.R. Case & Sons Cutlery Co., Owens Way, Bradford, PA 16701 / 814-368-4123; or 800-523-6350; FAX: 814-368-1736 jsullivan@wrcase.com www.wrcase.com
Wagoner, Vernon G., 2325 E. Encanto St., Mesa, AZ 85213-5917 / 480-835-1307
Wakina by Pic, 24813 Alderbrook Dr., Santa Clarita, CA 91321 / 800-295-8194
Waldron, Herman, Box 475, 80 N. 17th St., Pomeroy, WA 99347 / 509-843-1404
Walker Arms Co., Inc., 499 County Rd. 820, Selma, AL 36701 / 334-872-6231; FAX: 334-872-6262
Wallace, Terry, 385 San Marino, Vallejo, CA 94589 / 707-642-7041
Walls Industries, Inc., P.O. Box 98, 1905 N. Main, Cleburne, TX 76033 / 817-645-4366; FAX: 817-645-7946 www.wallsoutdoors.com
Walters Industries, 6226 Park Lane, Dallas, TX 75225 / 214-691-6973
Walters, John. See: WALTERS WADS
Walters Wads, John Walters, 500 N. Avery Dr., Moore, OK 73160 / 405-799-0376; FAX: 405-799-7727 www.tinwadman@cs.com
Walther America, P.O. Box 22, Springfield, MA 01102 / 413-747-3443 www.walther-usa.com
Walther GmbH, Carl, B.P. 4325, D-89033 Ulm, GERMANY
Walt's Custom Leather, Walt Whinney, 1947 Meadow Creek Dr., Louisville, KY 40218 / 502-458-4361
WAMCO-New Mexico, P.O. Box 205, Peralta, NM 87042-0205 / 505-869-0826
Ward & Van Valkenburg, 114 32nd Ave. N., Fargo, ND 58102 / 701-232-2351
Ward Machine, 5620 Lexington Rd., Corpus Christi, TX 78412 / 512-992-1221
Wardell Precision Handguns Ltd., 48851 N. Fig Springs Rd., New River, AZ 85027-8513 / 602-465-7995
Warenski Engraving, Julie Warenski, 590 E. 500 N., Richfield, UT 84701 / 435-896-5319; FAX: 435-896-8333 julie@warenskiknives.com
Warenski, Julie. See: WARENSKI ENGRAVING
Warne Manufacturing Co., 9057 SE Jannsen Rd., Clackamas, OR 97015 / 503-657-5590 or 800-683-5590; FAX: 503-657-5695 info@warnescopemounts.com www.warnescopemounts.com
Warren Muzzleloading Co., Inc., Hwy. 21 North, P.O. Box 100, Ozone, AR 72854 / 501-292-3268
Washita Mountain Whetstone Co., P.O. Box 378, Lake Hamilton, AR 71951 / 501-525-3914
Wasmundt, Jim, P.O. Box 511, Fossil, OR 97830
Watson Bros., 39 Redcross Way, SE1 1H6, London, ENGLAND FAX: 44-171-403-336
Watson Bullets, 231 Allies Pass, Frostproof, FL 33843 / 863-635-7948 cbestbullet@aol.com
Wayne E. Schwartz Custom Guns, 970 E. Britton Rd., Morrice, MI 48857 / 517-625-4079
Wayne Firearms For Collectors & Investors
Wayne Specialty Services, 260 Waterford Drive, Florissant, MO 63033 / 413-831-7083
WD-40 Co., 1061 Cudahy Pl., San Diego, CA 92110 / 619-275-1400; FAX: 619-275-5823
Weatherby, Inc., 3100 El Camino Real, Atascadero, CA 93422 / 805-466-1767; FAX: 805-466-2527 www.weatherby.com
Weaver Products ATK, P.O. Box 39, Onalaska, WI 54650 / 800-648-9624 or 608-781-5800; FAX: 608-781-0368
Weaver Scope Repair Service, 1121 Larry Mahan Dr., Suite B, El Paso, TX 79925 / 915-593-1005
Webb, Bill, 6504 North Bellefontaine, Kansas City, MO 64119 / 816-453-7431
Weber & Markin Custom Gunsmiths, 4-1691 Powick Rd., Kelowna, BC V1X 4L1 CANADA / 250-762-7575; FAX: 250-861-3655 www.weberandmarkinguns.com
Webley and Scott Ltd., Frankley Industrial Park, Tay Rd., Birmingham, B45 0PA ENGLAND / 011-021-453-1864; FAX: 0121-457-7846 guns@webley.co.uk www.webley.co.uk
Webster Scale Mfg. Co., P.O. Box 188, Sebring, FL 33870 / 813-385-6362
Weems, Cecil, 510 W Hubbard St., Mineral Wells, TX 76067-4847 / 817-325-1462
Weigand Combat Handguns, Inc., 1057 South Main Rd., Mountain Top, PA 18707 / 570-868-8358; FAX: 570-868-5218 sales@jackweigand.com www.jackweigand.com
Weihrauch KG, Hermann, Industriestrasse 11, 8744 Mellrichstadt, Mellrichstadt, GERMANY
Welch, Sam. See: SAM WELCH GUN ENGRAVING
Wellington Outdoors, P.O. Box 244, 1140 Monticello Rd., Madison, GA 30650 / 706-342-4915; FAX: 706-342-7568
Wells, Rachel, 110 N. Summit St., Prescott, AZ 86301 / 928-445-3655 wellssportstore@cableone.net wellssportstore@cableone-net
Wells Creek Knife & Gun Works, 32956 State Hwy. 38, Scottsburg, OR 97473 / 541-587-4202; FAX: 541-587-4223
Welsh, Bud. See: HIGH PRECISION
Wenger North America/Precise Int'l., 15 Corporate Dr., Orangeburg, NY 10962 / 800-431-2996; FAX: 914-425-4700

Wenig Custom Gunstocks, 103 N. Market St., P.O. Box 249, Lincoln, MO 65338 / 660-547-3334; FAX: 660-547-2881 gustock@wenig.com www.wenig.com
Werth, T. W., 1203 Woodlawn Rd., Lincoln, IL 62656 / 217-732-1300
Wescombe, Bill (See North Star West)
Wessinger Custom Guns & Engraving, 268 Limestone Rd., Chapin, SC 29036 / 803-345-5677
West, Jack L., 1220 W. Fifth, P.O. Box 427, Arlington, OR 97812
Western Cutlery (See Camillus Cutlery Co.)
Western Design (See Alpha Gunsmith Division)
Western Mfg. Co., 550 Valencia School Rd., Aptos, CA 95003 / 831-688-5884 lotsabears@eathlink.net
Western Missouri Shooters Alliance, P.O. Box 11144, Kansas City, MO 64119 / 816-597-3950; FAX: 816-229-7350
Western Nevada West Coast Bullets, P.O. BOX 2270, DAYTON, NV 89403-2270 / 702-246-3941; FAX: 702-246-0836
Westley Richards & Co. Ltd., 40 Grange Rd., Birmingham, ENGLAND / 010-214722953; FAX: 010-214141138 sales@westleyrichards.com www.westleyrichards.com
Westley Richards Agency USA (See U.S. Importer for Westwind Rifles, Inc., David S. Sullivan, P.O. Box 261, 640 Briggs St., Erie, CO 80516 / 303-828-3823
Weyer International, 2740 Nebraska Ave., Toledo, OH 43607 / 419-534-2020; FAX: 419-534-2697
Whildin & Sons Ltd, E.H., RR 2 Box 119, Tamaqua, PA 18252 / 717-668-6743; FAX: 717-668-6745
Whinnery, Walt (See Walt's Custom Leather)
Whiscombe (See U.S. Importer-Pelaire Products)
White Barn Wor, 431 County Road, Broadlands, IL 61816
White Pine Photographic Services, Hwy. 60, General Delivery, Wilno, ON K0J 2N0 CANADA / 613-756-3452
White Rifles, Inc., 234 S.1250 W., Linden, UT 84042 / 801-932-7950 www.whiterifles.com
White Rock Tool & Die, 6400 N. Brighton Ave., Kansas City, MO 64119 / 816-454-0478
Whitestone Lumber Corp., 148-02 14th Ave., Whitestone, NY 11357 / 718-746-4400; FAX: 718-767-1748 whstco@aol.com
Wichita Arms, Inc., 923 E. Gilbert, P.O. Box 11371, Wichita, KS 67211 / 316-265-0661; FAX: 316-265-0760 sales@wichitaarms.com www.wichitaarms.com
Wick, David E., 1504 Michigan Ave., Columbus, IN 47201 / 812-376-6960
Widener's Reloading & Shooting Supply, Inc., P.O. Box 3009 CRS, Johnson City, TN 37602 / 615-282-6786; FAX: 615-282-6651
Wideview Scope Mount Corp., 13535 S. Hwy. 16, Rapid City, SD 57702 / 605-341-3220; FAX: 605-341-9142 wvdon@rapidnet.com www.jii.to
Wiebe, Duane, 5300 Merchant Cir. #2, Placerville, CA 95667 / 530-344-1357; FAX: 530-344-1357 wiebe@d-wdb.com
Wiest, Marie. See: GUNCRAFT SPORTS, INC.
Wilcox All-Pro Tools & Supply, 4880 147th St., Montezuma, IA 50171 / 515-623-3138; FAX: 515-623-3104
Wilcox Industries Corp., Robert F Guarasi, 53 Durham St., Portsmouth, NH 03801 / 603-431-1331; FAX: 603-431-1221
Wild Bill's Originals, P.O. Box 13037, Burton, WA 98013 / 206-463-5738; FAX: 206-465-5975 wildbill@halcyon.com
Wild West Guns, 7521 Old Seward Hwy., Unit A, Anchorage, AK 99518 / 800-992-4570 or 907-344-4500; FAX: 907-344-4005 wwguns@ak.net www.wildwestguns.com
Wilderness Sound Products Ltd., 4015 Main St. A, Springfield, OR 97478 / 800-47-0006; FAX: 541-741-0263
Wildey, Inc., 45 Angevine Rd, Warren, CT 06754-1818 / 203-355-9000; FAX: 203-354-7759
Wildlife Research Center, Inc., 1050 McKinley St., Anoka, MN 55303 / 763-427-3350; or 800-USE-LURE; FAX: 763-427-8354
Will-Burt Co., 169 S. Main, Orrville, OH 44667
William E. Phillips Firearms, 38 Avondale Rd., Wigston, Leicester, ENGLAND / 0116 2886334; FAX: 0116 2810644 wephillips@aol.com
William Powell Agency, 22 Circle Dr., Bellmore, NY 11710 / 516-679-1158
Williams Gun Sight Co., 7389 Lapeer Rd., Box 329, Davison, MI 48423 / 810-653-2131 or 800-530-9028; FAX: 810-658-2140 williamsgunsight.com
Williams Mfg. of Oregon, 110 East B St., Drain, OR 97435 / 503-836-7461; FAX: 503-836-7245
Williams Shootin' Iron Service, The Lynx-Line, Rt. 2 Box 223A, Mountain Grove, MO 65711 / 417-948-0902; FAX: 417-948-0902
Williamson Precision Gunsmithing, 117 W. Pipeline, Hurst, TX 76053 / 817-285-0064; FAX: 817-280-0044
Willow Bend, P.O. Box 203, Chelmsford, MA 01824 / 978-256-8508; FAX: 978-256-8508
Wilsom Combat, 2234 CR 719, Berryville, AR 72616-4573 / 800-955-4856; FAX: 870-545-3310
Wilson Case, Inc., P.O. Box 1106, Hastings, NE 68902-1106 / 800-322-5493; FAX: 402-463-5276 sales@wilsoncase.com www.wilsoncase.com
Wilson Combat, 2234 CR 719, Berryville, AR 72616-4573 / 800-955-4856
Winchester Div. Olin Corp., 427 N. Shamrock, E. Alton, IL 62024 / 618-258-3566; FAX: 618-258-3599
Winchester Sutler, Inc., The, 270 Shadow Brook Lane, Winchester, VA 22603 / 540-888-3595; FAX: 540-888-4632
Windish, Jim, 2510 Dawn Dr., Alexandria, VA 22306 / 703-765-1994
Wingshooting Adventures, 0-1845 W. Leonard, Grand Rapids, MI 49544 / 616-677-1980; FAX: 616-677-1986
Winkle Bullets, R.R. 1, Box 316, Heyworth, IL 61745

Winter, Robert M., P.O. Box 484, 42975-287th St., Menno, SD 57045 / 605-387-5322
Wise Custom Guns, 1402 Blanco Rd., San Antonio, TX 78212-2716 / 210-828-3388
Wise Guns, Dale, 1402 Blanco Rd., San Antonio, TX 78212 / 210-734-9999
Wiseman and Co., Bill, P.O. Box 3427, Bryan, TX 77805 / 409-690-3456; FAX: 409-690-0156
Wisners, Inc., P.O. Box 58, Adna, WA 98522 / 360-748-4590; FAX: 360-748-6028 parts@gunpartsspecialist.com www.wisnersinc.com
Wolf (See J.R. Distributing)
Wolf Performance Ammunition, 2201 E. Winston Rd., Ste. K, Anaheim, CA 92806-5537 / 702-837-8506; FAX: 702-837-9250
Wolfe Publishing Co., 2625 Stearman Rd., Ste. A, Prescott, AZ 86301 / 928-445-7810; or 800-899-7810; FAX: 928-778-5124
Wolf's Western Traders, 1250 Santa Cora Ave. #613, Chula Vista, CA 91913 / 619-482-1701 patwolf4570book@aol.com
Wolverine Footwear Group, 9341 Courtland Dr. NE, Rockford, MI 49351 / 616-866-5500; FAX: 616-866-5658
Wood, Frank (See Classic Guns, Inc.), 5305 Peachtree Ind. Blvd., Norcross, GA 30092 / 404-242-7944
Woodleigh (See Huntington Die Specialties)
Woods Wise Products, P.O. Box 681552, Franklin, TN 37068 / 800-735-8182; FAX: 615-726-2637
Woodstream, P.O. Box 327, Lititz, PA 17543 / 717-626-2125; FAX: 717-626-1912
Woodworker's Supply, 1108 North Glenn Rd., Casper, WY 82601 / 307-237-5354
Woolrich, Inc., Mill St., Woolrich, PA 17701 / 800-995-1299; FAX: 717-769-6234/6259
Working Guns, Jim Coffin, 1224 NW Fernwood Cir., Corvallis, OR 97330-2909 / 541-928-4391
World of Targets (See Birchwood Casey)
World Trek, Inc., 7170 Turkey Creek Rd., Pueblo, CO 81007-1046 / 719-546-2121; FAX: 719-543-6886
Worthy Products, Inc., RR 1, P.O. Box 213, Martville, NY 13111 / 315-324-5298
Wostenholm (See Ibberson [Sheffield] Ltd., George)
Wright's Gunstock Blanks, 8540 SE Kane Rd., Gresham, OR 97080 / 503-666-1705 doyal@wrightsguns.com www.wrightsguns.com
WTA Manufacturing, P.O. Box 164, Kit Carson, CO 80825 / 800-700-3054; FAX: 719-962-3570 wta@rebeltec.net http://www.members.aol.com/ductman249/wta.html
Wyant Bullets, Gen. Del., Swan Lake, MT 59911
Wyant's Outdoor Products, Inc., P.O. Box 9, Broadway, VA 22815
Wyoming Custom Bullets, 1626 21st St., Cody, WY 82414
Wyoming Knife Corp., 101 Commerce Dr., Ft. Collins, CO 80524 / 303-224-3454

X

X-Spand Target Systems, 26-10th St. SE, Medicine Hat, AB T1A 1P7 CANADA / 403-526-7997; FAX: 403-528-2362

Y

Yankee Gunsmith "Just Glocks", 2901 Deer Flat Dr., Copperas Cove, TX 76522 / 817-547-8433; FAX: 254-547-8887 ed@justglocks.com www.justglocks.com
Yavapai College, 1100 E. Sheldon St., Prescott, AZ 86301 / 520-776-2353; FAX: 520-776-2355
Yavapai Firearms Academy Ltd., P.O. Box 27290, Prescott Valley, AZ 86312 / 928-772-8262; FAX: 928-772-0062 info@yfainc.corn www.yfainc.com
Yearout, Lewis E. (See Montana Outfitters), 308 Riverview Dr. E., Great Falls, MT 59404 / 406-761-0859; or 406-727-4569
Yellowstone Wilderness Supply, P.O. Box 129, W. Yellowstone, MT 59758 / 406-646-7613
Yesteryear Armory & Supply, P.O. Box 408, Carthage, TN 37030
York M-1 Conversion, 12145 Mill Creek Run, Plantersville, TX 77363 / 936-894-2397; FAX: 936-894-2397 bmf25years@aol.com
Young Country Arms, William, 1409 Kuehner Dr. #13, Simi Valley, CA 93063-4478

Z

Zabala Hermanos S.A., P.O. Box 97, 20600 Elbar, Elgueta, Guipuzcoa, 20600 SPAIN / 943-768076; FAX: 943-768201 imanol@zabalahermanos.com www.zabalahermanos.com
Zander's Sporting Goods, 7525 Hwy 154 West, Baldwin, IL 62217-9706 / 800-851-4373; FAX: 618-785-2320
Zanotti Armor, Inc., 123 W. Lone Tree Rd., Cedar Falls, IA 50613 / 319-232-9650 www.zanottiarmor.com
Zeeryp, Russ, 1601 Foard Dr., Lynn Ross Manor, Morristown, TN 37814 / 615-586-2357
Zero Ammunition Co., Inc., 1601 22nd St. SE, P.O. Box 1188, Cullman, AL 35056-1188 / 800-545-9376; FAX: 205-739-4683
Ziegel Engineering, 1390 E. Bunnett St. "F", Signal Hill, CA 90755 / 562-596-9481; FAX: 562-598-4734 ziegel@aol.com www.ziegeleng.com
Zim's, Inc., 4370 S. 3rd West, Salt Lake City, UT 84107 / 801-268-2505
Z-M Weapons, 203 South St., Bernardston, MA 01337 / 413-648-9501; FAX: 413-648-0219
Zufall, Joseph F., P.O. Box 304, Golden, CO 80402-0304